THE AFRICAN ORIGINS

OF
CIVILIZATION, RELIGION, YOGA MYSTICAL SPIRITUALITY,
ETHICS PHILOSOPHY
AND
A HISTORY OF EGYPTIAN YOGA

Dr. Muata Abhaya Ashby
Edited by Dr. Karen Vijaya Ashby

About
The African Origins
of
Civilization, Religion, Yoga Mystical Spirituality and Ethics Philosophy

"The work of Muata Ashby confronts the intellectual and spiritual problems in contemporary society by stressing the need to return to the African source. I found his writing to be inspirational, informative and scholarly."

-MOLEFI ASANTE, July 31, 2002

Plates

Color Plate 1: Below left – late 20th century Nubian man. Below right-Nubian Prisoners of Rameses II - Image at the Abu Simbel Temple

Color Plate 2: Bottom left-Ancient Egyptians (musicians) and Nubians (dancers) depicted in the Tombs of the Nobles with the same hue and features. Bottom right- Nubian King Taharka and the Queen offering to Amun (blue) and Mut (yellow) depicted as a red Egyptians. 7th cent BCE

Color Plate 3: Below-left, Egyptian man and woman-(tomb of Payry) 18th Dynasty displaying the naturalistic style (as people really appeared in ancient times). Below right- Egyptian man and woman- Theban tomb – displaying the colors red and yellow.

Color Plate 4: Below-left, Stele of Niptah - end of Middle Kingdom (man in red, woman in white with breasts exposed). Below right- Minoan man in red and Minoan woman in white with breasts exposed. (1400 B.C.E.).

AFRICAN ORIGINS Of Civilization, Religion, Yoga Mystical Spirituality And Ethics Philosophy

Color Plate 5: Nubians (three figures prostrating) and Egyptians (standing figures) are depicted with the same colors of their skin of alternating black and brown -Tomb of Huy

Color Plate 6: Black and Red Pottery, Below left (A)- Painted Pottery from Mohenjodaro –Indus Valley, India[1]: Below right (B & C)- Painted Pottery from the Pre-Dynastic Period – Egypt Africa.[2]

(A) (B) (C)

Color Plate 7: Below left- Pottery Black and Red - from north and south India- c. 500 B.C.E. tomb at Manla Ali, Hyderabad (British Museum) – Below right- Black and Red pottery from Pre-Dynastic Egyptian burial now at Metropolitan Museum New York.
Photos by M. Ashby.

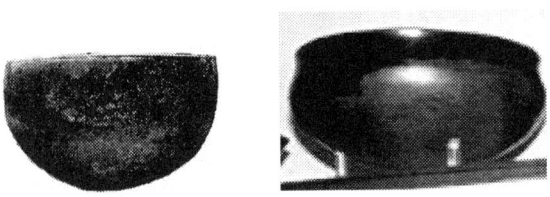

Color Plate 8 above right - Nubian depictions from Akhnaton period (1352 B.C.E-1347 B.C.E)

AFRICAN ORIGINS Of Civilization, Religion, Yoga Mystical Spirituality And Ethics Philosophy

Color Plate 9: Ancient Egyptians and Nubians depicted in the Tomb of Rameses III

The Tomb of Seti I (1306-1290 B.C.E.-below) which comes earlier than that of Rameses III (above) shows a different depiction. Note that the same labels are used to describe the Egyptians and Nubians in the pictures of both tombs.

Color Plate 10: Ancient Egyptians and Nubians depicted in the Tomb of Seti I

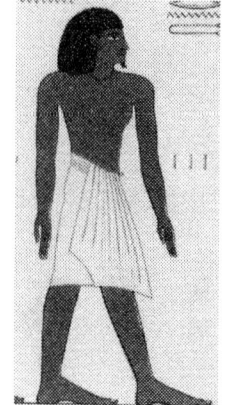 

Rtji Ancient Egyptian   *Ahsu* Ancient Nubian

Philip Arrhidaeus, successor of Alexander, a Greek, in depicted in Red (From the Napoleonic Expedition)

Cruzian Mystic Books / Sema Institute of Yoga

P. O. Box 570459
Miami, Florida, 33257
(305) 378-6253 Fax: (305) 378-6253

© 2002-2005 By Sema Institute of Yoga and Reginald Muata Ashby
    Second Edition -2005

All rights reserved. No part of this book may be used or reproduced in any manner whatsoever without written permission (address above) except in the case of brief quotations embodied in critical articles and reviews. All inquiries may be addressed to the address above.

The author is available for group lectures. For further information contact the publisher.

Publisher's Cataloging-in-Publication

Publisher's Cataloging-in-Publication
(Provided by Quality Books, Inc.)

Ashby, Muata.
   The African origins of civilization, religion, yoga mystical spirituality, ethics philosophy and a history of Egyptian yoga / Muata Abhaya Ashby; edited by Karen Vijaya Ashby. -- 1 st ed.
p. cm.
Includes bibliographical references and index.
ISBN 1-884564-50-X

1. Civilization, Western--African influences.
2. Civilization, Western--Egyptian influences.
3. Spirituality--Africa. 4. Yoga. 5. Egypt--Religion.
6. Mysticism--History. 7. Ethics--History. I. Ashby, Karen Vijaya. II. Title. III. Title: African origins of civilization, religion, yoga mystical spirituality and ethics philosophy, 36,000 B.C.E.-2,000 A.C.E. Volume 1 & 2 IV. Title: African origins of civilization, religion, yoga mysticism and ethics philosophy, 36,000 B.C.E.-2,000 A.C.E. Volume 1 & 3

CB245.A74 2002   909'.09821
                                QB133-673

Website   www.Egyptianyoga.com

AFRICAN ORIGINS Of Civilization, Religion, Yoga Mystical Spirituality And Ethics Philosophy

The Book

AFRICAN ORIGINS
OF CIVILIZATION, RELIGION AND YOGA SPIRITUALITY

is inspired by the Original Research Which Was presented in the Book

Egyptian Yoga Vol.1: The Philosophy of Enlightenment
By
Dr. Muata Ashby

1st Edition Published in 1995

AFRICAN ORIGINS Of Civilization, Religion, Yoga Mystical Spirituality And Ethics Philosophy

With gratitude

To

Cheikh Anta Diop

An African Genius

"Today, what interests me most is to see the formation of teams, not of passive readers, but of honest, bold search workers, allergic to complacency and busy substantiating a exploring ideas expressed in our work, such as…"

"Ancient Egypt was a Negro civilization. The history of Black Africa will remain suspended in air and cannot be written correct until African historians dare to connect it with the history of Egypt In particular, the study of languages, institutions, and so forth, cannot be treated properly; in a word, it will be impossible to build African humanities, a body of African human sciences, so long as that relationship does not appear legitimate. The African historian who evades the problem of Egypt is neither modest nor objective, nor unruffled; he is ignorant, cowardly, and neurotic. Imagine, if you can, the uncomfortable position of a western historian who was to write the history of Europe without referring to Greco-Latin Antiquity and try to pass that off as a scientific approach."

"I should like to conclude by urging young American scholars of good will, both Blacks and Whites, to form university teams and to become involved, like Professor Lawrence, in the effort to confirm various ideas that I have advanced, instead of limiting themselves to a negative, sterile skepticism. They would soon be dazzled, if not blinded, by the bright light of their future discoveries. In fact, our conception of African history, as exposed here, has practically triumphed, and those who write on African history now, whether willingly or not, base themselves upon it. But the American contribution to this final phase could be decisive."

"It is evident that if starting from Nubia and Egypt, we had followed a continental geographical direction, such as Nubia-Gulf of Benin, Nubia-Congo, Nubia-Mozambique, the course of African history would still have appeared to be uninterrupted.

This is the perspective in which the African past should be viewed. So long as it is avoided, the most learned speculations will be headed for lamentable failure, for there are no fruitful speculations outside of reality. Inversely, Egyptology will stand on solid ground only when it unequivocally officially recognizes its Negro-African foundation. On the strength of the above facts and those which are to follow, we can affirm with assurance that so long as Egyptology avoids that Negro foundation, so long as it is content merely to flirt with it, as if to prove its own honesty, so long will the stability of its foundations be comparable to that of a pyramid resting on its summit; at the end of those scholarly speculations, it will still be headed down a blind alley."

-Cheikh Anta Diop July 1973
African Origins of Civilization: Myth or Reality
(Edited by Mercer Cook)

AFRICAN ORIGINS Of Civilization, Religion, Yoga Mystical Spirituality And Ethics Philosophy

DEDICATION

To the *Shepsu* (departed venerated ancestors) and opener of the road upon which this work treads.

Chancellor Williams,
Cheikh Anta Diop,
John Henrik Clarke,
Joseph Campbell
Swami Sivananda Radha,

This book is also dedicated to all who have assisted me in the journey of life to disseminate the wisdom of the past which is so desperately needed in our times. While the list is too numerous to place here in its entirety, the following deserve special mention.

My Parents Reginald Ashby Sr. and Carmen Nieves Ashby

To my students, and all the practitioners and teachers of Indian and Kamitan Yoga around the world.

To my spiritual partner and editor as well as colleague and best friend, Dja (Karen Vijaya Ashby) without whom this project would not have reached the height of quality and concordance. She is a proficient editor but even more valuable than her editorial qualities are her sagely wisdom and knowledge of the teachings, which allow her to fill a position that no one else can. She understands and can therefore facilitate my words and thus this work has truly been a collaborative effort not unlike the creation of a new life. Such works produced by such partnerships are few in history and are therefore special and precious. May God bless her with the glory of long life with health and unobstructed happiness.

May you find this book enlightening and may it strengthen your ability to teach the wisdom of the ancients and the glorious path of life!

Table of Contents

Color Plates 3
DEDICATION 11
Table of Color Plates 17
Table of Figures 18
Table of Plates 24
List of Tables 26
    About the Author 27
Preface 29
    The Impetus For This Work 29
Foreword 31
Introduction to The Study of African Origins of Civilization And Religion and Comparative Cultural and Mythological Studies 32
    The Basis for the Study of Comparative Religions and Mythologies 33
        The Origins of Civilization and the Classifications of Human Social Evolution 33
    Principles of Cultural Expression 35
        What is Culture? 35
        Definitions of the Categories of Cultural Expression and Factors of Cultural Expression system of Cultural Anthropology 39
        The Universal Vision of Comparative Mythology 44
        Myth in Orthodox Religion 50
    Cultural Interactions, Their Effect on the Emergence of New Religions and The Adoption of Myths, Symbols and Traditions from one Culture to Another 52
        What is Civilization, What is the Difference Between Civilization and Culture and What Causes the Rise and Fall of Civilizations? 54
        The Rediscovery of Ancient Egyptian Culture, Philosophy and Religion 57
    Cultural Category - Factor Correlation System Application 60
        Methodology for the Comparisons Between Cultures in Order to Determine the Correlations Between Cultures 63
        The Possible Standards for Use in Determining the Correlations Between Cultures 64
        Refutation of Conclusions arrived at through the Scientific Method 64
        Examples of Cultural Interactions Throughout History 79

Part I: The African Origins of African Civilization, Religion, Yoga Mysticism and Ethics Philosophy 88
    Chapter 1: The People and History of Ancient Egypt and Nubia 89
        Chapter 1-Section 1: Introduction 90
            Who Were the Ancient Egyptians and why Should we Learn About Them? 90
            Where is Egypt? 91
            The Controversy Over the "Race" of the Ancient Egyptians (Kamitans) in European Scholarship and the Move to Refute the Testimony of the Seventeenth- and Eighteenth-century European Travelers to Egypt 108
            References to the Nubian Genealogy of Kamitans in Kamitan Texts and Monuments 115
        Chapter 1 Section 2: The Nubian Origins of Ancient Egypt 120
            Images From The Early European Explorers of the Nile Valley 122
            The Term Kamit (Qamit, Kamit, Kamit) and Its Relation to Nubia and the term "Black" 123
            The Ancient History of Nubia 125
            The Nubian Gods and Goddesses in the Kamitan Paut 128
        Chapter 1 Section 3: History of Predynastic and Dynastic Egypt 138
            The Connections between the Pre-Dynastic and Dynastic culture of Ancient Egypt 148
        History of Dynastic Ancient Egypt 151
            Old Kingdom Period 5,500-3,800 B.C.E. 153
            Middle Kingdom Period 3,500-1,730 B.C.E. 154

AFRICAN ORIGINS Of Civilization, Religion, Yoga Mystical Spirituality And Ethics Philosophy

- New Kingdom Period 1,580 B.C.E 156
  - Late Period 160
- The Revised Chronology of Ancient Egypt Based On New Archeological Evidence and the Omitted Records 163
  - The Stellar Symbolism related to the Pole Star and the Opening of the mouth and Eyes Ceremony in Ancient Egypt 170

Chapter 2: Religion and Culture in Ancient Egypt and Other African Nations 185
- Overview of African Religions\\\\ 185
  - The Common Fundamental Principles of African Religion 190
  - The Stages of African Religion 191
  - The African Definition for the Word "Religion" 191
  - The Concept of The Supreme Being and the Gods and Goddesses in African Religion 192
  - Changes in the Way Lesser Beings (Spirits) are Viewed in African Religion Over Time 195
  - Manifestations of African Religious Expression and Transmission to the Next Generation 196
  - Rites of Passage 196
  - Religion and Dance 198
  - Evil, Suffering, Sin, and the Devil in African Religion 198
- MAAT-UBUNTU: Maat Philosophy of Ancient Africa and Humanism in Present Day African Religious Practice 203
- The Fundamental Principles of Neterian Religion 209
  - Neterian Great Truths 209
  - Summary of The Great Truths and the Shedy Paths to their Realization 211
  - The Spiritual Culture and the Purpose of Life: Shetaut Neter 212
- Shetaut Neter 212
- Who is Neter in Kamitan Religion? 213
  - Sacred Scriptures of Shetaut Neter 213
- Neter and the Neteru 214
- The Neteru 214
  - The Neteru and Their Temples 215
  - The Neteru and Their Interrelationships 216
  - Listening to the Teachings 217
  - The Anunian Tradition 218
  - The Theban Tradition 220
  - The Theban Tradition 220
  - The Goddess Tradition 221
  - The Aton Tradition 223
  - Akhnaton, Nefertiti and Daughters 223
- The General Principles of Shetaut Neter 224
  - The Forces of Entropy 225
  - The Great Awakening of Neterian Religion 226
  - Kamitan Religion as a Development of African Spirituality and the Influence of Kamitan Culture and Spirituality on African Cultures and World Cultures Over Time. 227
- Ancient Egypt and Its Influence on Other African Religions 231
  - Evidence of Contact Between Ancient Egypt and other African Nations 235
  - Interactions Between the Ancient Egyptians and the Yoruba Nation 237
  - Other Correlations Between Kamitan and Yoruba Religion 244
  - Interactions Between the Ancient Egyptians and Cultures in the Americas 246
  - Parapsychology and the Proofs of Ancient African Mysticism and Religion 247
- Conclusion 251

Part II: The African Origins of Western Civilization, Religion, and Ethics Philosophy 254

Chapter 3: Atlantis, Mesopotamia, Ancient Egypt and The Origins of Civilization 255
- Ancient Egypt and Atlantis 256
- Overview of Ancient Greek History 256
- The Ancient Egyptian Origins Of Greek Gods and Goddesses 263
- Ancient Egypt and the Origins of Mesopotamian Religion and Civilization 268
  - Colchis, Mesopotamia and Ancient Egypt in the First Millennium B.C.E. 270
  - The Ibex Period 271

AFRICAN ORIGINS Of Civilization, Religion, Yoga Mystical Spirituality And Ethics Philosophy

Chapter 4: The Ancient Egyptian Origins of Western Religions: Judaism, Christianity and Islam and The Arabian Religions 279
- What is Religion? 279
  - Selected Spiritual Categories Compared 283
- The Gods and Goddesses From Ancient Egypt in Pre-Judaic/Christian/Islamic Canaan and Arabia . 285
  - Lilith, Sumerian Religion, Judaism and the Ancient Egyptian Connection 291
- The Ancient Egyptian Ancestry of 296
- The early Hebrews and Arabs 296
  - Canaan, Palestine and Israel in Ancient and Modern Times 306
  - Who were the Jewish People? 306
  - The Effect of Zoroastrianism on Western Religions 308
  - Ethiopia and the History of Judaism 310
  - Rastafarianism and the Judeo-Christian Religion 312
  - Kabbalism, Ancient Egypt and the Mysticism of the Tree of Life 315
- The Ancient Egyptian Origins of Christian Philosophy According to the Bible 323
  - The Personality of Jesus and the Mystical Christ 323
  - Savior from 327
  - Ancient Egypt 327
  - Savior from Judaic/Christian Arabia 327
  - Savior from Indian Hinduism 327
  - Heru 327
  - Jesus 327
  - Krishna 327
  - The Christian Crosses and the Mystical Ankh Cross 328
  - Early Christian, Roman Christian Conquest Periods and the Closing of Egyptian Temples 333
  - Overview of the Judeo-Christian Manifest Destiny Philosophy 337
  - A Short History of Ancient and Modern Jewish Zionism 341
  - Overview of Christianity in Africa and The Missionary Movements 343
  - The Methodist and African Methodist Episcopal Churches 346
- The Ancient Egyptian Origins of Islam 349
  - Overview of Islam 349
  - Out of Egypt: "The Arabian People" 350
  - Islam and Christianity 353
  - Islamic Imperialism, The Fall of Rome and the Breakup of the Christian Church 355
  - Arab and Muslim Conquest of Egypt and the Schism between Judaism and Christianity and Between Judaism, Christianity and Islam 357
  - Akhnaton, Moses and the Concept of One God (Monotheism) in Ancient Egyptian Mythology and its effect on Judaism and Islam 362
  - The Origins of Esoteric (Mystical) Islam: Sufism (c. 700 A.C.E) 377
  - Babism and Bahaism and Their Relation to Islam and African Religion 378
  - Slavery in Ancient Egypt, among the Hebrews, Greeks, and Muslims 380
  - The Sikh Religion 382
  - Conclusion 383

Part III: The African Origins of Eastern Civilization, Religion, Yoga Mysticism and Ethics Philosophy ... **386**

Chapter 5: The Ancient Egyptian Origins of the Indus Valley Civilization of Ancient India, Hinduism and Indian Yoga 387
- Where was the Indus Valley and the Indus Valley Civilization? 388
  - Indology and Egyptology, Eurocentrism, Indocentrism, Africentrism, Racism, and the Origins of the Indus Valley Culture and Yoga 390
  - The Aryan Culture, the Indus Culture and the Origins of Civilization 400
- Evidence of Contact Between Ancient Egypt and India 419
  - Item for Comparison 1: Evidence of Contact-Eye Witness Accounts, Anthropology, Linguistics, Mythology 420
  - Item for Comparison 2: The Gods Murungu and Muntju of Africa and the Gods Murugan, Subrahmania and Karttikeya of India 432
  - Item for Comparison 3: Body art and the use of Henna in Ancient Egypt and India 437
  - Item for Comparison 4: Black and Red Pottery 438

Chapter 6: Kamitan (Ancient Egyptian) Origins of Yoga Philosophy, Yoga Disciplines And Yoga Mystic Spirituality 444

    Indologists on the Origins of Yoga 447
    The Kamitan (Ancient Egyptian) and Universal Origins of Yoga 448
    The Debate On The Question Of The Origins Of Yoga... 448
    Item for Comparison 5: The Disciplines of Yoga Practiced in India and Ancient Egypt........... 457
    Item for Comparison 6: The Yoga of Wisdom.. 460
    Item for Comparison 7: The Yoga of Righteous Action 462
    Item for Comparison 9: The Discipline of Meditation 464
    Item for Comparison 10: The Physical Yoga Postures.. 467
    The Yogic Postures in Ancient Egypt and India 475
    Item for Comparison 12: Tantric Philosophy... 480
    Item for Comparison 12: Tantric Philosophy... 480
    Item for Comparison 13: The Serpent Power Philosophy and Iconography in Ancient Egypt and India 485
    History of the Serpent Power in Ancient Egypt 485

Chapter 7: Comparison of Ancient Egyptian and Indian Religious Iconographical, Symbolic, and Metaphorical Cultural Factors... 495

    Item for Comparison 14: Exact Ancient Egyptian and Dravidian-Hindu and Bengali Terms and Names and Philosophical Correlations.. 496
    Item for Comparison 15: Kamitan and Dravidian-Hindu Motifs, Symbols and Metaphysics Correlations 499
    Item for Comparison 16: The Creation Myth of The Kamitan God Khepri and the Hindu God Vishnu 501
    Item for Comparison 17: The Soul House... 502
    Item for Comparison 18: Mysticism of Pointing to the Mouth and Name in Ancient Egypt 503
    Item for Comparison 19: The Gods Brahma (Prajapati, Krishna) of India and Nefertem (Heru) 504
    Item for Comparison 20: The Lotus Symbol of Ancient Egypt and Indian Hinduism.................. 505
    Item for Comparison 21: The Spiritual Eyes... 506
    Item for Comparison 22: The God Ra and the God Shiva and the Solar Serpentine Symbolism 507
    Item for Comparison 23: The Lioness Goddess and Her Destructive Aspect 508
    Item for Comparison 24: The Sacred Cow of Ancient Egypt and India................................... 510
    Item for Comparison 25: Amun and Krishna 511
    Item for Comparison 26: Heru and Krishna fighting Against the Forces of Evil...................... 512
    Item for Comparison 27: The Mythology of Heru of Ancient Egypt and Krishna of India 513
    Item for Comparison 28: The Goddess of Wisdom- Aset (Isis) of Kamit and Saraswati of India and the Avian Principle 516
    Item for Comparison 29: The Ancient Egyptian Hetep (Offering) Slab and the Hindu Lingam Yoni 517
    Item for Comparison 30: The Lotus Feet of Vishnu and Asar 518
    Item for Comparison 31: The Crescent Moon... 519
    Item for Comparison 32: Worship of the Tree Goddess in Ancient Egypt and India 520
    Item for Comparison 33: The Multi-armed Divinity in Ancient Egypt and India..................... 521
    Item for Comparison 34: Asar of Kamit, Vishnu of India and the Sacred Cows 522
    Item for Comparison 35: The Gods Asar of Kamit and Shiva of India and their Symbols........ 523
    Item for Comparison 36: The Primordial Mother of Creation in Ancient Egypt and India 524
    Item for Comparison 37: The Divine Egg in Ancient Egypt and India.................................... 525
    Item for Comparison 38: The Philosophy of the Primeval Ocean in Ancient Egypt and India.... 527
    Item for Comparison 38: The Philosophy of the Primeval Ocean in Ancient Egypt and India.... 527
    Item for Comparison 39: The Trinity Systems of Ancient Kamit (Egypt) and India 528
    Item for Comparison 40: The Number Nine and The Indian Yantra and the Kamitan Sundisk .. 529

Chapter 8: Comparison of Ancient Egyptian and Indian Yoga Philosophy 531

    Item for Comparison 41: Ancient Egyptian Memphite Theology and Indian Vaishnavism 548
    Item for Comparison 42: The Mystical Philosophy behind the Trinity of Enlightened Human Consciousness in Ancient Egypt and India 557
    Item for Comparison 43: The Indian Philosophy of the Veil of Maya and The Kamitan Philosophy of the Veil of Aset... 560

Item for Comparison 44: The terms "Hari" and "Om" in Ancient Egypt and India 562
Item for Comparison 45: The Kingship of the Southern Land and the Northern Land 563
Item for Comparison 46: The Philosophy of Righteous Action, Social Order and Spiritual Upliftment of Humanity in Ancient Egypt and India 565
Item for Comparison 47: The Philosophy of Reincarnation in Ancient Egypt and India............. 572
Goddess Meskhent 573
Item for Comparison 48: The Philosophy of the Three States of Consciousness in Ancient Egypt and India 575
Item for Comparison 48: The Philosophy of the Three States of Consciousness in Ancient Egypt and India 575
Item for Comparison 49: The Divine Mother and Child (below- left to right) of Ancient Egypt and India and the Metaphor of Blackness 576
Item for Comparison 50: Comparing The Indian and Kamitan Fundamental Principles 578
Item for Comparison 51: Vegetarianism, Asceticism and the control and Sublimation of Sexual Energy in Ancient Egypt and India 580
Item for Comparison 52: The Origins of the Philosophy of the Absolute in India and Egypt 585
Item for Comparison 53: The Teaching of Non-Duality in Ancient Egypt and India 587
Item for Comparison 54: The Philosophy of Pantheism in Ancient Egypt and India 590
Item for Comparison 55: Mantra, Hekau and The Importance Of The "I Am" Formula in Ancient Egypt and India 592

Chapter 9: The Neterian Religion Origins of Indian Buddhism 599
The Early History of Buddhism 599
The Concept of The Trinity in Christianity 600
The Concept Trinity According to Ancient Egyptian Religion and Mystical Philosophy 600
Evidence of Contact Between Early Buddhists and Ancient Egyptians 602
Introduction to Buddhist Philosophy 607
The Buddhist Wheel of Life 608
The Teaching of Enlightenment in India and Ancient Egypt 608
Buddhism and Neterianism – the divinity Buddha and the god Asar 619
The Ankh Symbol in Ancient Egypt and India (Hinduism and Buddhism) 620
The Philosophy of The Witnessing Inner Self in Ancient Egypt and Indian Buddhism 624
Changes in Indian religion from Ancient to Modern Times, Contrasts With Ancient Egyptian Religion 629
Basic Differences and Similarities Between Kamitan and Ancient Indian Cultural Factors........ 629
Summary of the Main Tenets of Hinduism and Buddhism were not Present in Vedic Culture (1500 B.C.E.) but emerged in Hindu Culture 500 years later. ✽ 629
Conclusion... 634
EPILOG: What Is The Meaning Of The Correlation Between Cultures. How Should They Be Used? 637

Appendix A: Timeline of the Ancient World 640
Pre-history and Dynasties of Ancient Egypt 640

Appendix B: Defining Civilization 645

Appendix C: Ancient Egyptian Colonization of the Ancient World 647

Appendix D: Origins of Monasticism and Christian Monasticism in Ancient Egypt 648

General Index 649

Bibliography 669

Bibliography 669

Syllabus for Course Title: 675
Course Texts: 675

Books by Sebai Muata Ashby 678

Music Based on the Prt M Hru and other Kamitan Texts 685

AFRICAN ORIGINS Of Civilization, Religion, Yoga Mystical Spirituality And Ethics Philosophy

Table of Color Plates

Color Plate 1: Below left – late 20th century Nubian man. Below right-Nubian Prisoners of Rameses II -Image at the Abu Simbel Temple 4

Color Plate 2: Bottom left-Ancient Egyptians (musicians) and Nubians (dancers) depicted in the Tombs of the Nobles with the same hue and features. Bottom right- Nubian King Taharka and the Queen offering to Amun (blue) and Mut (yellow) depicted as a red Egyptians. 7th cent BCE 4

Color Plate 3: Below-left, Egyptian man and woman-(tomb of Payry) 18th Dynasty displaying the naturalistic style (as people really appeared in ancient times). Below right- Egyptian man and woman-Theban tomb – displaying the colors red and yellow. 5

Color Plate 4: Below-left, Stele of Niptah - end of Middle Kingdom (man in red, woman in white with breasts exposed). Below right- Minoan man in red and Minoan woman in white with breasts exposed. (1400 B.C.E.). 5

Color Plate 5: Nubians (three figures prostrating) and Egyptians (standing figures) are depicted with the same colors of their skin of alternating black and brown -Tomb of Huy 6

Color Plate 6: Black and Red Pottery, Below left (A)- Painted Pottery from Mohenjodaro –Indus Valley, India: Below right (B & C)- Painted Pottery from the Pre-Dynastic Period – Egypt Africa. 6

Color Plate 7: Below left- Pottery Black and Red - from north and south India- c. 500 B.C.E. tomb at Manla Ali, Hyderabad (British Museum) – Below right- Black and Red pottery from Pre-Dynastic Egyptian burial now at Metropolitan Museum New York. Photos by M. Ashby. 6

Color Plate 8 above right - Nubian depictions from Akhnaton period (1352 B.C.E-1347 B.C.E) 6

Color Plate 9: Ancient Egyptians and Nubians depicted in the Tomb of Rameses III 7

Color Plate 10: Ancient Egyptians and Nubians depicted in the Tomb of Seti I 7

AFRICAN ORIGINS Of Civilization, Religion, Yoga Mystical Spirituality And Ethics Philosophy

Table of Figures

Figure 1: Below: The Culture-Myth Model, showing how the folk expression of religion is based on culture and local traditions. 36
Figure 2: Below: The Culture-Myth Models of two world spiritual systems, showing how the folk expression of each religion is based on culture and local traditions. 37
Figure 3: The African Family Tree of Cultural Interactions 58
Figure 4: The Pharaoh Amenhotep III 83
Figure 5: The Colossi of Memnon- built under Amenhotep III, 1,417 B.C.E. -1,379 B.C.E. 59 feet tall ... 83
Figure 6: Egypt is located in the north-eastern corner of the African Continent. 91
Figure 7: Below left: A map of North East Africa showing the location of the land of *Ta-Meri* or *Kamit*, also known as Ancient Egypt and South of it is located the land which in modern times is called Sudan. 92
Figure 8: Above right- The Land of Ancient Egypt-Nile Valley 92
Figure 9: Below- the Ancient Egyptian Hor-m-Akhet (Sphinx). 94
Figure 10: Pictorial Evidence of the African Origins of Ancient Egyptian Culture and Civilization. 101
Figure 11: Ancient Egyptians and Nubians depicted in the Tomb of Rameses III 104
Figure 12: Ancient Egyptians and Nubians depicted in the Tomb of Seti I. 104
Figure 13: Below left – late 20th century Nubian man. Below right-Nubian Prisoners of Rameses II -Image at the Abu Simbel Temple 105
Figure 14: Bottom left-Ancient Egyptians (musicians) and Nubians (dancers) depicted in the Tombs of the Nobles with the same hue and features. Bottom right- Nubian King Taharka and the Queen offering to Amun (blue) and Mut (colored in yellow) depicted as a red Egyptians. 7th cent BCE 105
Figure 15: Below-left, Egyptian man and woman-(tomb of Payry) 18th Dynasty displaying the naturalistic style (as people really appeared in ancient times). Below right- Egyptian man and woman-Theban tomb – depicted in the colors red and yellow, respectively. 106
Figure 16: Below-left, Stele of Niptah - end of Middle Kingdom (man in red, woman in white with breasts exposed). 106
Figure 17: Nubians (three figures prostrating) and Egyptians (standing figures) are depicted with the same colors of their skin of alternating black and brown -Tomb of Huy 107
Figure 18: Nubians and Egyptians are depicted with the same colors of alternating black and brown -Tomb of Huy (Full Scene) 107
Figure 19: above right - Nubian depictions from Akhnaton period (1352 B.C.E-1347 B.C.E) Brooklyn Museum (Photo by M. Ashby) 107
Figure 20: Above left, the God Amun-Ra from Ancient Egypt as a man. Above right- the god Amun-Ra from Ancient Egypt as a ram. 128
Figure 21- Above: left -Heru as a Divine child, master of nature, controller of beasts (evil, unrighteousness, the lower self), wearing mask of Basu. Above right – Basu as the dwarf with the characteristic Nubian plumes as headdress. 129
Figure 22- Above left: Kamitan depictions of the Kamitan/Nubian God Bas as the Harpist. Above right: The Kamitan/Nubian god Bas in the form of the all-encompassing divinity, Neberdjer. 130
Figure 23: Above far-left The god Asar. Middle- is Ptah-Seker-Asar as an average sized man. Far right- The god Ptah of Memphis. 132
Figure 24: Goddess Mut, the Mother of Asar and Aset and Blackness as a Metaphor of Consciousness and as a Description of the gods and goddesses 134
Figure 25: Trading Vessel in the 18th Dynasty (1580 B.C.E) 139
Figure 26: Pre-Dynastic Ancient Egyptian Temple 144
Figure 27: Ancient Egyptian New Kingdom Temple Design (Temple of Hatshepsut to Amun) 146
Figure 28: Below left - Image of the boat of Ptah-Sokar-Asar (Dynastic Periods) 150
Figure 29 Above: Map of Ancient Egypt (A) and Kush (B) showing the locations of the cataracts along the Nile River (numbers 1-6) from southern Egypt into northern Nubia (present day Sudan). 151
Figure 30: Above- The Land of Ancient Egypt-Nile Valley - The cities wherein the theology of the Trinity of Amun-Ra-Ptah was developed were: A- Sais (temple of Net), B- Anu (Heliopolis- temple of Ra), C-Men-nefer or Hetkaptah (Memphis, temple of Ptah), and D- Sakkara (Pyramid Texts), E- Akhet-Aton (City of Akhnaton, temple of Aton), F- Abdu (temple of Asar), G- Denderah (temple of Hetheru), H- Waset (Thebes, temple of Amun), I- Edfu (temple of Heru), J- Philae (temple of Aset). The cities wherein the theology of the Trinity of Asar-Aset-Heru was developed were Anu, Abydos, Philae, Edfu, Denderah and Edfu. 152

Figure 31: The Kamitan Zodiac and the Precession of the Equinoxes and the History of Ancient Egypt.......... 171
Figure 32: The Per-Aah (Pharaoh) Djehutimes IIII (Thutmosis) makes offerings to the Great Heru m Akhet (Sphinx) 175
Figure 33: Above- The Heru-m-akhet (Sphinx) Pharaonic headdress. 177
Figure 34: Below- Drawing of the Sphinx from a sculpture in Egypt 177
Figure 35: Below- The Ancient Egyptian zodiacal signs for the ages of the Ram, Bull and Lion 179
Figure 36: The Great Pyramid of Egypt with the Mystical Constellations (view from the East) and the Perishable and Imperishable stars. 180
Figure 37: The Great Pyramid of Egypt with the Mystical Constellations (view from the South). 180
Figure 38: Below left- Hieroglyph for the Chepesh (foreleg). Center-The Chepesh with constellation. Right- The Chepesh as part of the Hetep offering in the *Pert M Heru* Texts and temple inscriptions. 181
Figure 39: The Hetep Offering Slab with the foreleg symbol. 181
Figure 40: Vignettes from the Opening of the Mouth Ceremonies from the Ancient Egyptian texts. Left- with Chepesh (Chpsh-foreleg), Right with the Seba (Sba) ur instruments. 181
Figure 41: Above-left Pyramid tomb of the Old Kingdom Period. 201
Figure 42: Above-right Mastaba tomb of Giza area. 201
Figure 43: Human Origins- Modern Human Beings Originate in Africa – 150,000 – 100,000 B.C.E. 227
Figure 44: Human Cultural Development -Cultures develop throughout Africa – 36.000-10,000 B.C.E. 228
Figure 45: African High Culture- Kamitan Culture Influences African Cultures. 229
Figure 46: Kamitan Civilization Influences Cultures Outside of Africa 4,000 B.C.E.-500 A.C.E. 229
Figure 47: Above left- Kamitan Temple. 232
Figure 48: Above right- Dogon Temple 232
Figure 49: Above Left: Ankh-Ancient Egyptian Symbol and instrument of life. Right: Ahsanti Fertility doll from West African 233
Figure 50: Above-Left- The God Montju of Ancient Egypt. Above-Right Heru-Behded, The Warrior 234
Figure 51: Above- (A-B) North-east Africa , Asia Minor, (C-D) South Asia (India) and the Egyptian-Indian trade routes in the Hellenistic (Greek) and Roman times. 235
Figure 52: The map above shows the documented influence of Ancient Egyptian Culture on world religions. 246
Figure 53: Priestesses in Ancient Egypt playing the Drum 247
Figure 54: Below-left, Stele of Niptah - end of Middle Kingdom (Kamitan man in red, Kamitan woman in white with breasts exposed). Below right- Minoan man in red and Minoan woman in white with breasts exposed. (1,400 B.C.E.). 260
Figure 55: Winged Sphinx and Griffin from Ancient Egypt 273
Figure 56: Below from left to right- Goddess Net, Goddess Antat and Goddess Athena............................. 289
Figure 57: Map of Northern Canaan (Modern - Lebanon) *Ancient city: Byblos (Modern- Jubayl) See asterisk(*) 290
Figure 58: Map showing the rivers mentioned in the Book of Genesis 298
Figure 59: The Descendants of Noah-From the Judeo-Christian Biblical System. 300
Figure 60: Below left- Map of Southern Canaan (Modern - Israel) * city Beth-Shan 305
Figure 61: Below right-Goddess Anat (Anath) of Ancient Egypt 305
Figure 62: A- The Ancient Egyptian Tree of Life of the Goddess, B- Christian Tree of Life. C Buddhist Tree of Life, D- Christian Christmas tree. E- The Caduceus of Djehuti (Hermes), F- The Psycho-spiritual Energy Centers of Serpent Power Yoga in Ancient Egypt and India. 316
Figure 63: Below- The Divine Tree grows from the coffin of Asar (A), The tree is cut down to make a pillar (B), Examples of the Asarian Djed (C), the Tree of Life which is the body of Asar Himself (D). 317
Figure 64: Map of Ancient India. 388
Figure 65: Above-The Indus Valley, India (in modern times-Pakistan {See Below}). 389
Figure 66: Below- Typical Late Middle and New Kingdom Temple Pylons (3,500 B.C.E.- 200 B.C.E.) 407
Figure 67: Below- Architecture of Sakkara - Ancient Egypt- Early Dynastic (5,000-4,000 B.C.E.) 408
Figure 68: Below- Sphinx and the Sphinx Temple (10,500 B.C.E.) 408
Figure 69: The "Osirion" at Abdu (Abydos) in Upper (Southern) Egypt (Pre-Dynastic 10,500-5000 B.C.E.). 409
Figure 70: The Eyes of Heru, the Solar Hawk... 411
Figure 71: The parts of the Left Eye of Heru Divided Into Fractions (A) 411
Figure 72: The parts of the Left Eye of Heru Divided Into Fractions (B) 411
Figure 73: Eye of Heru Fractions From *The Book Mathematics in the Time of the Pharaohs* 412
Figure 74: Left- The Ancient Egyptian God Djehuti Presents the Eye to the Goddess Hetheru, the Female Counterpart of Heru. 413
Figure 75: Left- The Ancient Egyptian God Djehuti Presents the Eye to Heru After Making it Whole Again. 413

AFRICAN ORIGINS Of Civilization, Religion, Yoga Mystical Spirituality And Ethics Philosophy

Figure 76: Map of Migration Out of Africa From the Book *The History and Geography of Human Genes* 417
Figure 77: The Travels of Asar (Osiris) in Ancient Times 420
Figure 78: The Spread of Humanity. 424
Figure 79: Left: A drawing of a Human DNA strand. 425
Figure 80: Map of North-east Africa, and Southern Asia, showing (A) Sakkara in Ancient Egypt, (B) Tepe Hissar in Persia (Iran) and (C) Harappa in India. 426
Figure 81: Above, the *Djozer Pyramid Complex* with the *Step Pyramid of Imhotep* located in Sakkara, Egypt– From the Old Kingdom Period – Third Dynasty 427
Figure 82: Above-(A) The God Montu of Ancient Egypt. (B) Heru-Behded, The Warrior, (C) Karttikeya on his peacock son of Shiva, also known as Skanda Gray (800-900 A.C.E.), (D) The God Warrior Subrahmania of India. 434
Figure 83: Above-North-east Africa, Asia Minor, South Asia (India) and the Egyptian-Indian trade routes in the Hellenistic (Greek) and Roman times. 435
Figure 84: Below left- Pottery Black and Red - from north and south India- c. 500 B.C.E. tomb at Manla Ali, Hyderabad (British Museum) – Below right- Black and Red pottery from Pre-Dynastic Egyptian burial now at Metropolitan Museum New York. Photos by M. Ashby. 438
Figure 85: One of a handful of depictions of a person in a Yoga posture being worshipped by two others and two serpents on either side. (Indus Valley-Pre Aryan) 451
Figure 86: The God Asar (Osiris) with the goddess Aset (Isis) at the foot of the bed and goddess Nebethet (Nephthys) at the head. 452
Figure 87: Goddesses Nebethet (left) and Aset (right) –with their serpent designations (goddess) 452
Figure 88: Below- Ancient Egyptian depiction of the god Asar with the two serpent goddesses in the form of a Caduceus, symbolizing the Serpent Power (Kundalini Yoga). 453
Figure 89: Above: Sema (Smai) Heru-Set, ... 455
Figure 90: The image of goddess Aset (Isis) suckling the young king. 461
Figure 91: The Dua Pose- Upraised arms with palms facing out towards the Divine Image 463
Figure 92: Kamitan Meditation Posture-Sitting With Hands on Thighs 464
Figure 59: Above left: The Kamitan goddess Nut and god Geb and the higher planes of existence. Above center and right: The goddess Nut performs the forward bend posture. 476
Figure 60: The varied postures found in the Kamitan papyruses and temple inscriptions 477
Figure 61: The practice of the postures is shown in the sequence below. 477
Figure 62: Below- the Goddess Parvati from India, practicing the Tree Pose – modern rendition. 478
Figure 63: Some of the postures as they developed in the Hindu Hatha Yoga system compared to the Ancient Egyptian Postures 479
Figure 98: Above- The Kamitan God Geb and the Kamitan Goddess Nut separate after the sexual union that gave birth to the gods and goddesses and Creation. Figure 99: Below: Three depictions of the god Asar in tantric union with Aset. 481
Figure 100: Above-(A) and (B) Reliefs from Ancient Egyptian Temples of the virgin birth of Heru (Horus) - The resurrection of Asar (Osiris) - Higher Self, Heru consciousness). Isis in the winged form hovers over the reconstructed penis of the dead Asar. 481
Figure 101: Drawing found in an Ancient Egyptian Building of The Conception of Heru-*From a Stele at the British Museum 1372. 13th Dyn.* 481
Figure 102: Above- the god Shiva and his consort Shakti 482
Figure 103: Above- Buddha and his consort. Tibetan Buddhist representation of The Dharmakaya, the cosmic father-mother, expressing the idea of the Supreme Being as a union of both male and female principals. 482
Figure 104: Below left- The Triune ithyphallic form of Asar. 483
Figure 105: Below right- the Trilinga (Triune ithyphallic form) of Shiva. 483
Figure 106: The Winged Sundisk of Heru – Kamitan. 483
Figure 107: Below - the multi-armed (all-pervasive) dancing Shiva-whose dance sustains the Creation. 483
Figure 108: Below- left Ashokan pillar with lion capital-Kamitan pillar with lion capitals. Center: Ancient Egyptian pillar with lion capitals. Far right: the Ethiopian divinity Apedemak, displaying the same leonine trinity concept and the multi-armed motif. 484
Figure 109: Below: a diagram of the Temple of Amun-Ra at Karnak, Egypt, showing the Pylons (A), the Court (B), the Hypostyle Hall (C), the Chapel of Amun (Holy of Holies - D), the Chapel of Mut (E), the Chapel of Chons (F). 486
Figure 110: Left (A), the East Indian rendition of the Life Force energy centers (chakras) in the subtle spine of the individual 488

AFRICAN ORIGINS Of Civilization, Religion, Yoga Mystical Spirituality And Ethics Philosophy

Figure 111: Center (B 1-2), Ptah-Asar-Ancient Egyptian rendition of the Life Force energy centers in the subtle spine of the individual. The god Asar displays the four upper centers as centers of higher consciousness. ... 488

Figure 112: The figure at right (C) shows the scale of Maat displaying the seven spheres or energy centers called the *"seven souls of Ra"* and *"the seven arms of the balance (Maat)."* ... 488

Figure 113: Left-An East Indian depiction of the Chakras with the Sushumna (central) and Ida and Pingala (intertwining conduits). ... 489

Figure 114: Two Center images- left - the Hermetic Caduceus with the central Shaft (Asar), and the intertwining serpents (Uadjit and Nekhebit, also known as Aset and Nebethet); right-Ancient caduceus motif: Asar with the serpent goddesses. ... 489

Figure 115: Far Right- The Kamitan Energy Consciousness Centers (depicted as Spheres-Chakras or serpentine chains) ... 489

Figure 116: Above left: the Arat Serpent of Ancient Egyptian mysticism (Basket of Isis) showing the classic 3 ½ turns of the Serpent Power. Above right: the Kundalini Serpent of Indian mysticism showing the classic 3 ½ turns of the Serpent Power. ... 489

Figure 117: Below -Stele of *Paneb*. Dyn. 19. From Dier el-Medina (Waset Egypt) He worships the serpent goddess *Mertseger* (She who loves silence) in order to propitiate her favor in the development of Transcendental awareness. ... 490

Figure 118: Below –An Indian yoga practitioner touches his body in the areas corresponding to the Chakras in order to focus the mantras (words of power) and develop the Kundalini (Serpent Power) while worshipping the Kundalini Serpent. From Rajasthan, 1858, gauche on paper. ... 490

Figure 119: Below- Deity with worshipers and Serpents Indus Valley, Ancient India. Recognized as possibly the oldest known depiction of Yoga in India, this image incorporates the philosophy later known as Kundalini Yoga. ... 491

Figure 120 Below: The Serpent goddesses Aset (Isis) and Nebethet (Nephthys) worship Asar (Osiris), Ancient Egypt, Africa. The Hawk above symbolizes raising consciousness. The two goddesses represent the Serpent Power in Kamitan mysticism from the earliest period of Ancient Egyptian history. ... 491

Figure 121: Below- The Serpent goddesses Aset (Isis) and Nebethet (Nephthys) depicted as the dual serpents with are in reality manifestations of the one singular essence. ... 491

Figure 122: Below- Left-The Ancient Egyptian Papyrus Greenfield (British Museum) displaying the rings signifying the serpentine path of the Life Force, and the levels of spiritual consciousness (the Chakras or Psycho-spiritual consciousness centers). ... 492

Figure 123 Below: Papyrus Qenna (Leyden Museum), displaying the spheres signifying the serpentine path of the Life Force from the Spirit above to the heart below, and the levels of spiritual consciousness (the Chakras or Psycho-spiritual consciousness centers). ... 492

Figure 124: Above: The Ancient Egyptian God Khepri ... 501
Figure 125: Above: The Indian God Vishnu ... 501
Figure 126: Below - Two Ancient Egyptian Soul-Offering Houses ... 502
Figure 127: Below- Ancient Indian Soul-Offering House ... 502
Figure 128: Harpocrates (Heru-papkhart, Heru the child)-Egypt First-Third Century A.C.E. Photograph-British Museum. ... 503
Figure 129: Above left-Mauna Vishnu depicted in the gesture of a raised finger close to the mouth. Khajuraho. Tenth Century A.C.E. ... 503
Figure 130: Above right- Risya Sringa. Second century A.C.E.. Collection: Government Museum, Mathura. Photograph: Government Museum, Mathura. ... 503
Figure 131: Above left –Depiction of the god Brahma of India. ... 504
Figure 132: Above right- The god Nefertem (Heru pakhart) of Kamit. ... 504
Figure 133: Above- The Hindu God Shiva with his bull, Nandi and the serpent wrapped around his neck. ... 504
Figure 134: Below- The God Heru (left) and the god Krishna/Brahma (right) sitting on the lotus. ... 505
Figure 135: Below- The Winged Sundisk of Ra - one serpent with two heads, from Ancient Egypt ... 507
Figure 136: Amun and Krishna and the Mysticism of Blue and Black ... 511
Figure 137: Above left- Black Amun (Luxor Museum). Above right- Black Vishnu-Krishna doll. ... 511
Figure 138: Above: Top- The Pharaoh as Heru on the chariot. Bottom- Lord Krishna on the chariot. ... 512
Figure 139: Left- Heru as a child (anthropomorphic form). Right- Krishna as a child. ... 514
Figure 140: Below Left- Pre-Vedic Male Divinity with Horn headdress-Indus Valley Civilization. ... 514
Figure 141: Below left - The god Heru from Ancient Egypt in the form of the Hawk, leading the Divine Cow Hetheru. Below right: The hawk-headed god, Heru. ... 515
Figure 142: Right- the god Krishna of India, leading the Divine Cow. ... 515

AFRICAN ORIGINS Of Civilization, Religion, Yoga Mystical Spirituality And Ethics Philosophy

Figure 143: Below left – The Ancient Egyptian Goddess Aset (Isis) in her avian aspect (all-encompassing flight of wisdom, i.e. intuitional vision) 516

Figure 144: Above right: Hindu Goddess of wisdom, truth and learning, Saraswati, in her avian aspect......... 516

Figure 145: Above left- Line art drawing of the Hindu Lingam-Yoni. Right: Picture of an actual Hindu Lingam-Yoni offering stand. 517

Figure 146: Above left- Lotus Feet of the god Vishnu in Hindu Mythology 518

Figure 147: Above right: Lotus Feet of the god Asar in Kamitan Mythology. Full picture shown below center. 518

Figure 148: Left- A- symbol of Djehuti. B- the god Djehuti. C- The Ancient Egyptian god Khonsu. B & C: The Ancient Egyptian Gods Djehuti (symbol of intellect) and Khonsu (reflection of consciousness in time and space) with their Crescent Moon symbolisms.. 519

Figure 149: Right- D- The Hindu God Shiva with his symbol, the Crescent Moon, (symbol of increasing wisdom). 519

Figure 150: Below left-Worship of the Tree Goddess. Indus Valley, pre-Vedic Ancient India. 520

Figure 151: Above-right: Worship of the life sustaining tree goddess, Papyrus of Ani, Ancient Egypt, Africa. 520

Figure 152: Below- Left- The Priest Per-aah (Pharaoh) Akhnaton worships the multi-armed divinity, Aton, with his wife Nefertiti and their daughters. At Right- Late period depiction of the multi-armed, all-encompassing Neberdjer encompasses all the attributes of the other gods and goddesses. 521

Figure 153: Below far right- The multi-armed (all-pervasive) dancing Shiva as *Nataraja*, Lord of the Cosmic Dance -whose dance sustains the Creation. 521

Figure 154: Below- Far left: The Ethiopian divinity Apedemak, displaying the same leonine trinity concept and the multi-armed motif. 521

Figure 155: Above left- The God Asar of Ancient Egypt.. 522

Figure 156: Above right- The God Vishnu of India 522

Figure 157: Left- The god Asar (Osiris) of Kamit... 523

Figure 158: Right- The God Shiva of India 523

Figure 159: Below - The Brahma Bull in Pre-Vedic India –Indus Seal 523

Figure 160: Above left- Parashakty - The Trimurti Mother. Right: Trinity of Brahma-Vishnu- Shiva. 524

Figure 161: Above right- The Ancient Egyptian Goddess Mehurt-Mother of Creation............................... 524

Figure 162: Lord Nun pushing the boat of Khepri out of the ocean to engender and sustain Creation. 527

Figure 163: Above- Lord Narayan (Vishnu-Krishna) rests on the Primeval Ocean. 527

Figure 164: The Hindu Supreme Being Brahman manifesting as the Trinity 528

Figure 165: The Kamitan Supreme Being Neberdjer manifesting as the Trinity 528

Figure 166: Above right- The Hindu symbol known as the Sri Yantra. 529

Figure 167: Above left- The Symbol of Ra, the Sundisk.. 529

Figure 168: Left- the Company of Nine Gods and Goddesses of Ra. Below- Nine sections of the Sri Yantra. 529

Figure 169: Below Left- Pre-Vedic Male Divinity with Horn headdress. 533

Figure 170: Below-right- Pre-Vedic Female Tree Divinity.. 533

Figure 171: Behdety or Ur Uadjit.. 536

Figure 172: (A) Above-left-Set protecting boat of Ra from the giant serpent of disorder-(dissolution-unrighteousness). (B) Krishna dances on the head of Kalya Naga (serpent), after defeating him. 538

Figure 173: The Vedic-Hindu God Surya (Savitri or Savitar)... 538

Figure 174: The Hindu Supreme Being Brahman 546

Figure 175: The Kamitan Supreme Being Neberdjer 546

Figure 176: Below-The Solar aspect, Nefertem, or Heru-pa-khart (Heru {Sun-god}) as the Child, i.e. Creator-morning sun. 547

Figure 177: Above- The Ancient Egyptian *Ptah-Tanen (Tem)* sitting on the primeval ocean with the sundisk (Tem, Nefertem) issuing from his head, his seat has the Sema (Sma) symbol of mystic union............... 548

Figure 178: The Ancient Egyptian divinity: Nefertem 549

Figure 179: Above- The Shabaka Stone (now with much of its text rubbed off due to mishandling).............. 553

Figure 180: Above: The God Asar embraced by the goddesses Aset and Nebethet.. 557

Figure 181: Above- The Hindu King and his two Queens. 558

Figure 182: Above: A-Left to right- Bengali Raja (King of the South of India) with the crown of the south. B-C-Ancient Egyptian King of the South of Egypt with the white crown of the south. D- Crown of the south and north together-Kamit. 563

Figure 183: Below Left- The Vedic-Hindu God Yama, "Restrainer"... 567

Figure 184: Below Right- The Ancient Egyptian God Asar, "Judge of the Dead"...................................... 567

Figure 185: Above- Vignette from Chapter 33 of Papyrus Ani: The Judgment scene from the *Pert m Heru* Text of Ancient Egypt. 569
Figure 186: Left- Meskhent seated; Right- Meskhent as birthing block.. 573
Figure 187: The Great Trinity of Ancient Egypt: Neberdjer Becomes Amun-Ra-Ptah..................... 575
Figure 188: The Images of the Divine Mother and Child from Ancient Egypt, India and Christianity and the Philosophy of Blackness in Mystical Religion... 576
Figure 189: The Forms of Goddess Aset (Isis) 583
Figure 190: (right) Another example of the Kamitan Caduceus, with Atum-Ra................................ 589
Figure 191: Akhnaton with his family, receiving Life Force from Aten through the sun's rays........ 591
Figure 192: Below left- Amunhotep, son of Hapu, Ancient Egyptian philosopher, priest and Sage at 80 years old in a meditative posture. Below right - Buddha "The Enlightened One" of India........................... 609
Figure 193: Hieroglyphic text for the Ancient Egyptian Book of Enlightenment 609
Figure 194: Samples of Ancient Egyptian Blue Lotus Panels 616
Figure 195: Below left-Indian-Buddhist -*Vandevatas* -wood spirits- giving drink from the tree. Bharhut, Sunga 2nd Cent. B.C.E. 617
Figure 196: Below- left, Nefertem/Asar emerges, resurrected, from the Divine Lotus - Ancient Egypt. Papyrus Ani. Below right- Aspirant receives sustenance from the tree. Ancient Egyptian Papyrus Nu 617
Figure 197: Above left- a Buddhist temple 619
Figure 198: Above right- a Kamitan artifact known as the Djed Pillar 619
Figure 199: Above- a map of North-east Africa and South-east Asia. 620
Figure 200: Below – The Feet of Buddha, displaying the Kamitan Ankh Symbol 620
Figure 201: Above-left- The Ancient Egyptian *Ankh* symbol. Above-right- Ancient Egyptian Sandal symbol 621
Figure 202: Figure 203: Ancient Egyptian *Swastika*. 622
Figure 204: Below-left- Modern rendition of the Tantric Hindu divinity, Ardhanari-Ishvara. 623
Figure 205: Below-right- the Ancient Egyptian god Ra, the serpent on top of his head and ankh in hand. Far right – Ra in the form of Nefertem.. 623

AFRICAN ORIGINS Of Civilization, Religion, Yoga Mystical Spirituality And Ethics Philosophy

Table of Plates

Plate 1: Ancient Egyptian Depiction of Ethnic Groups (New Kingdom Dynastic Period) (Originally in the tomb of *Ramose* – drawn by Prisse d' Avennes) 102
Plate 2: Left- Peraah (Pharaoh) Muntuhotep II (Muntuhotep) – 11th Dynasty.. 115
Plate 3: Center- Peraah Senusert I statue – 12th Dynasty... 115
Plate 4: Right- Peraah Senusert I relief – 12th Dynasty.. 115
Plate 5: Below left, Per-aah Akhnaton Statue (18 Dynasty) – Cairo Museum 116
Plate 6: Below right, Per-aah Akhnaton Relief (18 Dynasty).. 116
Plate 7: Pre-Dynastic-Ancient Egyptian Neolithic Period Grave-including black and red pottery. (British Museum-Photo by M. Ashby)... 136
Plate 8: Late Middle Kingdom-Early New Kingdom Temple of Queen Hatshepsut................................... 146
Plate 9: Left-Pre-Dynastic image of the Nile Goddess. Right- Dynastic Period image of goddess Aset. ... 149
Plate 10: Below right- Pre-Dynastic Pottery from Ancient Egypt.. 150
Plate 11: Left Per-aah (Pharaoh) Muntuhotep II (Muntuhotep) – 11th Dynasty... 154
Plate 12: The Giza Pyramid Complex-Great Pyramid, far right.. 164
Plate 13: Great Pyramid Compared to the European Cathedrals 164
Plate 14: The Great Sphinx of Ancient Egypt-showing the classical Pharaonic headdress popularized in Dynastic times. Also, the water damage can be seen in the form of vertical indentations in the sides of the monument. 168
Plate 15: Sphinx rump and Sphinx enclosure show detail of the water damage (vertical damage). 168
Plate 16: The Great Sphinx, covered in sand - Drawing by early Arab explorers 174
Plate 17: Predynastic Ancient Egyptian Boat Displaying Ibex.. 271
Plate 18: Ancient Egyptian Pottery with Boat and Ibex Painting 272
Plate 19: Pottery from Western and Northern Ancient Iran... 272
Plate 20: Greek and Mesopotamian Sphinxes 273
Plate 21: Mesopotamian versions of the Winged Sundisk and the Ritual of Smelling the Lotus. 274
Plate 22: Cylinder seal Syria I 1820-1730 BC Met Museum 274
Plate 23: Below left- Egyptian Goddess worship in Beth-Shan 13 century B.C.E.–Palestine 305
Plate 24 Below: Asiatics bringing tribute to Egypt (18th Dynasty – New Kingdom Period) 307
Plate 25: Above- A Painting of an Ancient Egyptian man-From the Tomb of Rameses III, Thebes, Egypt, Africa 423
Plate 26: Picture of a display at the Brooklyn Museum (1999-2000) showing the similarity between the headrest of Ancient Egypt (foreground) and those used in other parts of Africa (background). (Photo by M. Ashby) 432
Plate 27: Below left- Painted Pottery from Mohenjodaro –Indus Valley, India 438
Plate 28: Below right- Painted Pottery from the Pre-Dynastic Period – Egypt Africa. 438
Plate 29: Below left-The Hindu god Shiva, "the Master Yogi," sitting in meditation on the tiger skin. This iconography is thought to be a late development of the "the Indus Yogi" (above)............. 453
Plate 30: Below right- an Ancient Egyptian man in the Lotus Posture 453
Plate 31: The Offering of Maat-Symbolizing the Ultimate act of Righteousness (Temple of Seti I) The King offers to Asar (not pictured). 462
Plate 32: Basic Instructions for the Glorious Light Meditation System- Given in the Tomb of Seti I. (c. 1350 B.C.E.) 465
Plate 18: Above- The god Geb in the plough posture engraved on the ceiling of the antechamber to the Asarian Resurrection room of the Temple of Hetheru in Egypt. (photo taken by Ashby). Below: Illustration of the posture engraved on the ceiling. 475
Plate 19: Below- The Egyptian Gods and Goddesses act out the Creation through their movements: Forward bend -Nut, Spinal twist -Geb, Journey of Ra – Ra in his boat, and the squatting and standing motions of Nun and Shu.. 476
Plate 35: Frontal Close Up View of the Great Sphinx... 485
Plate 36: Cobra of the Great Sphinx now in the British Museum.. 485
Plate 37: Left-Lotus from Egypt... 505
Plate 38: Right: Indian Lotus.. 505
Plate 39: Left- The God Ra of Ancient Egypt with the serpent encircled Sundisk...................................... 507
Plate 40: Right- The God Shiva of India with the serpent encircled Sundisk - one serpent with two heads. 507
Plate 41: Above Left- The Goddess Hetheru of Ancient Egypt... 508

Plate 42: Above Center- The lioness Goddess Sekhmet of Ancient Egypt, an aspect of Hetheru 508
Plate 43: Right- from India, the goddess Durga, with her most important symbol, the lion, her expression of power. 508
Plate 44: Above left- The Ancient Egyptian lioness aspect, Goddess Sekhmet the "destroyer" in her shrine. . 509
Plate 45: Above right and below- The Ancient Hindu goddess Kali the "destroyer" in her shrine (above). 509
Plate 46: The Goddess Nut from Ancient Egypt (Tomb of Seti I), reverenced as the life giving Cow. Right- The Cow of Egypt and India. 510
Plate 47: Above-right Goddess Parvati from India – ancient rendition. 510
Plate 48: Above left- Lord Heru of Kamit. Right- Lord Krishna of India 513
Plate 49: Akhnaton as a Sphinx 544
Plate 50: Blue Lotus panel. Stupa (Buddhist) at Bharhut. 2nd Cent. BC Indian Museum Calcutta 616

List of Tables

Table 1: Categories of Cultural Expression and Factors of Cultural Expression 38
Table 2: Example of Single Event (one occurrence) Unsupported Matches in One Cultural Category Occurring in the Presence of Other Unrelated Single Event Matches in the Same Cultural Categories 71
Table 3: Example of Single Event (occurrence) Unsupported Match in One Cultural Category Occurring in the Presence of Other Unrelated Single Event Matches in Related but Separate Cultural Categories 71
Table 4: Supported Matching Cultural Factors 72
Table 5: Example-Supported Matching Cultural Factors within the Cultural Factor/Category: Myth 73
Table 6: Example-Supported Matching Cultural Factors within the wide range of Cultural Factor/Categories . 73
Table 7: Single Event Unsupported Cross Cultural Correlations 74
Table 8: Single Event Supported Cross Cultural Correlations 75
Table 9: Chronology of Nubian History 135
Table 10: Major Cultural-Theological Developments 138
Table 11: Chronology of Ancient Egypt according to Flinders Petrie 166
Table 12: List of African Religions 188
Table 13: Examples of African Religions with the System of Supreme Being and Lesser Divinities 193
Table 14: Kamitan Names of the main Gods and Goddesses of Ancient Egypt and the Greek translation in common use. 264
Table 15: Ancient Egyptian Mythology and Extrapolated Sumerian Mythology 269
Table 16: Major Religious Categories 283
Table 17: The Stages of Spiritual Evolution 284
Table 18: The Teachings of Jesus and the Teachings of Ancient Egypt 331
Table 19: Chronologies of India According to Western and Indian Indologists 396
Table 20: Chronology of Ancient Egypt based on Independently Confirmed Archeological Dating and the Chronology of India based on dates given by Indian Scholars 439
Table 21: A Timeline of the Discipline of Physical Postures in Ancient Egypt and India 474
Table 22: The Life Force: 488
Table 23: Additional Kamitan and Dravidian-Hindu Motifs, Symbols and Metaphysics Correlations 499
Table 24: The Fundamental Principles of Memphite Theology and Vaishnavism 551
Table 25: Maat Philosophy Compared with Hindu Dharma Philosophy 566
Table 26: Essential "I Am" Formulas from the Upanishads, Bible and Prt m Hru 593
Table 27: Timeline of Buddhism and Ancient Egypt 602
Table 28: Maat Philosophy Compared with Buddhist Dharma Philosophy 614

AFRICAN ORIGINS Of Civilization, Religion, Yoga Mystical Spirituality And Ethics Philosophy

About the Author

Who is Sebai Muata Abhaya Ashby D.D. Ph. D.?

Priest, Author, lecturer, poet, philosopher, musician, publisher, counselor and spiritual preceptor and founder of the Sema Institute-Temple of Aset, Muata Ashby was born in Brooklyn, New York City, and grew up in the Caribbean. His family is from Puerto Rico and Barbados. Displaying an interest in ancient civilizations and the Humanities, Sebai Maa began studies in the area of religion and philosophy and achieved doctorates in these areas while at the same time he began to collect his research into what would later become several books on the subject of the origins of Yoga Philosophy and practice in ancient Africa (Ancient Egypt) and also the origins of Christian Mysticism in Ancient Egypt.

Sebai Maa (Muata Abhaya Ashby) holds a Doctor of Philosophy Degree in Religion, and a Doctor of Divinity Degree in Holistic Health. He is also a Pastoral Counselor and Teacher of Yoga Philosophy and Discipline. Dr. Ashby received his Doctor of Divinity Degree from and is an adjunct faculty member of the American Institute of Holistic Theology. Dr. Ashby is a certified as a PREP Relationship Counselor. Dr. Ashby has been an independent researcher and practitioner of Egyptian Yoga, Indian Yoga, Chinese Yoga, Buddhism and mystical psychology as well as Christian Mysticism. Dr. Ashby has engaged in Post Graduate research in advanced Jnana, Bhakti and Kundalini Yogas at the Yoga Research Foundation. He has extensively studied mystical religious traditions from around the world and is an accomplished lecturer, musician, artist, poet, screenwriter, playwright and author of over 25 books on Kamitan yoga and spiritual philosophy. He is an Ordained Minister and Spiritual Counselor and also the founder the Sema Institute, a non-profit organization dedicated to spreading the wisdom of Yoga and the Ancient Egyptian mystical traditions. Further, he is the spiritual leader and head priest of the Per Aset or Temple of Aset, based in Miami, Florida. Thus, as a scholar, Dr. Muata Ashby is a teacher, lecturer and researcher. However, as a spiritual leader, his title is *Sebai,* which means Spiritual Preceptor.

Sebai Dr. Ashby began his research into the spiritual philosophy of Ancient Africa (Egypt) and India and noticed correlations in the culture and arts of the two countries. This was the catalyst for a successful book series on the subject called "Egyptian Yoga". Now he has created a series of musical compositions which explore this unique area of music from ancient Egypt and its connection to world music.

Who is Hemt Neter Dr. Karen Vijaya Clarke-Ashby?

Karen Clarke-Ashby (Seba Dja) is a Kamitan (Kamitan) priestess, and an independent researcher, practitioner and teacher of Sema (Smai) Tawi (Kamitan) and Indian Integral Yoga Systems, a Doctor of Veterinary Medicine, a Pastoral Spiritual Counselor, a Pastoral Health and Nutrition Counselor, and a Sema (Smai) Tawi Life-style Consultant." Dr. Ashby has engaged in post-graduate research in advanced Jnana, Bhakti, Karma, Raja and Kundalini Yogas at the Sema Institute of Yoga and Yoga Research Foundation, and has also worked extensively with her husband and spiritual partner, Dr. Muata Ashby, author of the Egyptian Yoga Book Series, editing many of these books, as well as studying, writing and lecturing in the area of Kamitan Yoga and Spirituality. She is a certified Tjef Neteru Sema Paut (Kamitan Yoga Exercise system) and Indian Hatha Yoga Exercise instructor, the Coordinator and Instructor for the Level 1 Teacher Certification Tjef Neteru Sema Training programs, and a teacher of health and stress management applications of the Yoga / Sema Tawi systems for modern society, based on the Kamitan and/or Indian yogic principles. Also, she is the co-author of "The Egyptian Yoga Exercise Workout Book," a contributing author for "The Kamitan Diet, Food for Body, Mind and Soul," author of the soon to be released, "Yoga Mystic Metaphors for Enlightenment."

Hotep -Peace be with you!
Seba Muata Ashby & Karen Ashby

NOTE on the use of encyclopedic and dictionary references.

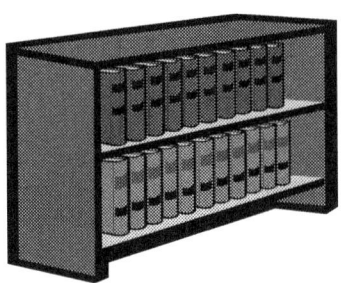

The use of encyclopedias in this book will not be for the purpose of providing proofs or to verify specific correspondences between cultures. Rather, the encyclopedia references will be provided to show the reader what the current state of established knowledge is. The sum total of modern cultural knowledge is based on the amassing of information. This information is collected into volumes. As time passes and the knowledge base changes, so too does the knowledge collection (encyclopedia). So the encyclopedic and dictionary references are provided (wherever used) to establish what the currently accepted norms of culture are, and also to provide a reference point for the reader for the study of history, culture, religion, and even philosophy. Even though a knowledge source may be faulty or incomplete, it is still necessary to begin somewhere. This reference point, tempered by our own understanding and scholarship, allows us to take on distance in our exploration and then *sankofa,* or turn back to see where we were and determine indeed where we have been and where we truly are so that we may begin to know where we are heading.

Preface

The Impetus For This Work

Over the past several years I have been asked to put together, in one volume, the most important evidences showing the ancient origins of civilization and religion in Africa, and the correlations and common teachings between Kamitan (Ancient Egyptian) culture and religion and that of India. The history of Ancient Egypt, especially in the light of the most recent archeological evidences documenting civilization and culture in Ancient Egypt and its spread to other countries, has intrigued many scholars, as well as mystics, over the years. Also, the possibility that Ancient Egyptian Priests and Priestesses and sages migrated to Greece, India and other countries to carry on the traditions of the Ancient Egyptian Mysteries has been speculated over the years as well.

In Chapter 1 of the book *Egyptian Yoga: The Philosophy of Enlightenment* (first edition 1995), I first introduced the basic comparisons between Ancient Egypt and India that had been brought forth up to that time. Now, in the year 2002, this new book, *THE AFRICAN ORIGINS of Civilization, Religion and Yoga Spirituality,* more fully explores the motifs, symbols and philosophical correlations between Ancient Egyptian and Indian mysticism and clearly shows not only that Ancient Egypt and India were connected culturally, but also spiritually. It shows that the mysteries of Ancient Egypt were essentially a yoga tradition which did not die, but rather, developed into the modern day systems of Yoga technology and mysticism of India, thus, India has a longer history and heritage than was previously understood. It further shows that African culture developed Yoga Mysticism earlier than any other civilization in history. All of this expands our understanding of the unity of culture and the deep legacy of Yoga, which stretches into the distant past, beyond the Indus Valley civilization, the earliest known high culture in India, as well as the Vedic tradition of Aryan culture. Therefore, Ancient Egyptian Yoga culture and mysticism are the oldest known traditions of spiritual development, and Indian mysticism an extension of the Ancient Egyptian tradition. By understanding the legacy which Ancient Egypt passed on to India, the mysticism of India is better understood, and also, by comprehending the heritage of Indian Yoga, rooted in Ancient Egyptian Mysticism, Ancient Egypt is also better understood. This expanded understanding allows us to prove the underlying kinship of humanity, through the common symbols, motifs and philosophies which are not disparate and confusing teachings, but in reality expressions of the same study of truth through metaphysics and mystical realization of Self. This has great importance for the Yogis and mystics who follow the philosophy of Ancient Egypt and the mysticism of India.

The origins and influences that the Ancient Egyptian religion had on world religion and philosophy is another important theme explored in this volume. We will also explore the basis of Christianity, Hinduism, Buddhism, Ancient Greek religion and Nubian religion in Ancient Egyptian religion.

The Goals of This Book and How to use This Book

This book was created to assist in the study of comparative mythology and yoga mysticism, specifically related to the Kamitan culture and spiritual systems (Neterianism) and their relationship to Indian culture and spiritual traditions coming down to modern times.

This book follows along with a 2-hour video Introduction to the Ancient Egyptian Origins of Yoga and a 12-hour video presentation entitled *African Origins of Civilization, Religion and Yoga Spirituality,* and the course *African Origins of Civilization, Religion and Philosophy* conducted at Florida International University by Dr. Muata Ashby. Since this book is fully referenced, it can also be used as a stand-alone text book for the study of the historical-cultural-spiritual connections between Ancient Egypt (Africa) and India as well the origins of Kamitan and Hindu religion, mythology and Yoga philosophy. The suggested method of study is to first become well grounded in the understanding of the purpose of religion, mythology and history, and the nature of culture and its manifestations. Then the items of comparison may be approached and their significance better understood in the context of this study. References for each item of comparison are provided in each section. In order to understand how the following scriptural, iconographic and archeological evidences discovered by myself or others demonstrate a connection between the seemingly different spiritual traditions, it is necessary to establish a basis for the study and comparison of religions and philosophies. This book is in no way complete, since the flow of more and more points of comparison continue to be discovered. However, the sheer magnitude of the present compilation should provide a good, broad picture of the interaction between Ancient Egypt and India. It is anticipated that there will be expanded versions of this volume in the coming years.

The purpose of this book is in many ways to build upon the work of other scholars in the area of Ancient African civilization and culture. However, these subjects are very relevant to us today because the heritage of a people plays an important role in directing those people in their present endeavors. Therefore, these studies are not entered into for the purpose of denigrating other cultures or to impose an Africentric ideal on people while excluding their achievements and struggles in the Diaspora as if any and all answers for today's problems could be found by, for example, reviving Ancient Egyptian Culture. Rather, it is enjoined for the purpose of providing a basis, a foundation for modern culture, because it has been determined that humanity is operating in accordance with an incorrect basis, a notion about history that has led it astray from the possibility of achieving a real harmony and prosperity for all human beings. In seeking a destination it is important to start a journey with the proper direction and this direction leads to the eventual discovery of the destination that was sought. A peoples direction comes from their culture and all of its elements. If the culture is damaged, as the Kenyan Social and Political Sciences researcher Ali Mazrui[1] would say, then that direction will be faulty. If the directive is erroneous the destination will elude the seeker. Likewise, without a proper basis, a proper foundation, people of African descent and all humanity will be forever searching and missing the path to peace, prosperity and enlightenment.

---

[1] *The Africans* by Ali Mazrui

Foreword

New Terms

This volume introduces new concepts for understanding the culture and philosophy of the civilization today known as "Ancient Egypt." In order to understand this subject most effectively a proper terminology more closely based on the language of Ancient Egypt has been adopted in order to more fully convey the feeling and essence of Ancient Egyptian society and tradition. The detailed explanation for the use of these terms and their origin based in the culture and tradition of Ancient Egypt will be explained throughout the book.

"Kamit"

Firstly, the term Kamit, as a name for Ancient Egypt, has received wide attention. This term rightly uses the consonant elements of the word (Kmt) since the Ancient Egyptians did not record the vowels in a way that is easy to discern. This term will be used interchangeably with the term "Ancient Egypt."

"Kamitan"

This volume will adopt the term Kamitan when referring to the country itself. This term will be used interchangeably with the term "Ancient Egyptian." The term "Kamitan" therefore replaces the term Kamitan.

"Neterianism"

When referring to the religion of Ancient Egypt itself the term "Neterianism" will be used. So this term will substitute for or be used interchangeably with the term "Ancient Egyptian Religion" or Kamitan Religion.

"Neterian"

When referring to anything related to the religion of Ancient Egypt, the term Neterian will be used interchangeably with the terms Shetaut Neter, as it relates to the Kamitan term for religion, "Shetaut Neter."

Introduction to The Study of African Origins of Civilization And Religion and Comparative Cultural and Mythological Studies

    My hope is that a comparative elucidation may contribute to the perhaps not-quite desperate cause of those forces that are working in the present world for unification, not in the name of some ecclesiastical or political empire, but in the sense of human mutual understanding. As we are told in the Vedas: "Truth is one, the sages speak of it by many names."

—Joseph Campbell
June 10, 1948

As one can ascend to the top of a house by means of a ladder or a tree or a staircase or a rope, so diverse is the ways and means to approach God, and every religion in the world shows one of these ways.

—Paramahamsa Ramakrishna (1836-1886)
(Indian Sage)

There is no more important knowledge to a people than their history and culture. If they do not know this they are lost in the world.

—Cicero, Roman Philosopher (106-43 BC)

The Basis for the Study of Comparative Religions and Mythologies

This first section deals with the most important questions that will shape the context as well as the manner in which we will explore the themes presented. Therefore, it is prudent to establish, as it were, a common basis for our study, and present the parameters which we will use to conduct our study and look at evidences to determine social interrelationships and the interconnectedness of certain cultures. The following questions are vital to our study. The implications of the answers will be a prominent aspect of this first section, but will also be a central theme throughout the entire book.

Question: What is Humanity and how is the origin and history of humanity classified by scholars?

Question: What is "Culture"? What are the characteristics of culture? How important is culture in studying a people, their customs and traditions?

Question: What is "Civilization"?

Question: Where did Civilization begin?

Questions: Can the common basis of cultural expressions, concepts and doctrines between cultures be determined? If so, what are the criteria or factors to be examined and compared for such a study, and what is the methodology to be applied to those criteria to reveal their similarity or disparity? Can a scientific procedure be applied to those criteria in order to systematically arrive at a conclusive determination and thereby allow a researcher to ascertain the existence or non-existence of a relationship between the cultures, and possibly also the nature of such a relationship?

Question: If it is possible to answer the questions above might it also be possible to rediscover and perhaps even reconstruct and authentic history and description of ancient African Culture so as to repair or reconstruct African civilization, Religion and Philosophy?

The Origins of Civilization and the Classifications of Human Social Evolution

The Ancient Origins of the Human Species

Generally, human beings are regarded by science as a species of beings who evolved from primitive forms to the more advanced form, known today as *Homo Sapiens*. Homo Sapiens means "the modern species of human beings, the only extant species of the primate family Hominidae."[3] Species means "a fundamental category of taxonomic classification, ranking below a genus or subgenus and consisting of related organisms capable of interbreeding."[4] Webster's encyclopedia describes the scholarly consensus on "the origins of human species" as follows:

> Evolution of humans from ancestral primates. The African apes (gorilla and chimpanzee) are shown by anatomical and molecular comparisons to be the closest living relatives of humans. Humans are distinguished from apes by the size of their brain and jaw, their bipedalism, and their elaborate culture. Molecular studies put the date of the split between the human and African ape lines at 5–10 million years ago. There are only fragmentary remains of ape and hominid (of the human group) fossils from this period. Bones of the earliest known human ancestor, a hominid named Australopithecus ramidus 1994, were found in Ethiopia and dated as 4.4 million years old.[5]

AFRICAN ORIGINS Of Civilization, Religion, Yoga Mystical Spirituality And Ethics Philosophy

The Stone Age period of history is that span of time regarded as being early in the development of human cultures. The Stone Age refers to the period before the use of metals. The artifacts used by people as tools and weapons were made of stone. In the discipline of archaeology, the Stone Age has been divided into the following main periods: Eolithic, Paleolithic, Mesolithic and Neolithic. The ages were experienced at different times in different geographical areas of the world in accordance with the particular culture's capacity for technological ingenuity or contact with other technologically advanced groups.

Following the Stone Age is the Metal Age. Three important ages follow which are marked by the use of metals. These are the Copper Age, Iron Age and the Bronze Age.

> **Copper Age**, or Chalcolithic Age, is the time period in which man discovered how to extract copper by heating its ore with charcoal. This art was known in the Middle East before 3500 BC. A subsequent important development was the alloying of copper with tin to produce bronze.[6]

> **Bronze Age,** period from the early fourth millennium BC onward, in which man learned to make bronze artifacts and to use the wheel and the ox-drawn plow which allowed agriculture to support a larger population. The resulting growth of technology and trade occasioned the rise of the first civilizations in Sumer and Egypt.[7] In the Bronze Age, copper and bronze became the first metals worked extensively and used for tools and weapons. It developed out of the Stone Age, preceded the Iron Age, and may be dated 5000–1200 BC in the Middle East and about 2000–500 BC in Europe. Recent discoveries in Thailand suggest that the Far East, rather than the Middle East, was the cradle of the Bronze Age.[8]

> **Iron Age,** period succeeding the Bronze Age in which man learned to smelt iron. The Hittites probably developed the first important iron industry in Armenia soon after 2000 BC. Iron's superior strength and the widespread availability of its ore caused it gradually to supersede bronze.[9]

The theories about the origins of humanity are not firm because much of the evidence of the evolutionary development of human beings has been swept away by the active nature of the planet. Volcanoes, storms, floods, etc., eventually wipe away all remnants of everything that happens on the surface of the earth as they recycle matter to bring forth life sustaining conditions again. For example, the city of Rome was buried in several feet of dust, ash and other natural particles, which eventually claimed the surface of the earth through the action of wind and other natural phenomena of planetary weather. The encroaching sands of North East Africa tend to erode and encroach on the monuments in Egypt. For example, the Sphinx enclosure can fill up and cover the Sphinx with sand due to winds and sandstorms in just 20 years. Complicating these factors is the modern urbanizing of archeological areas. People move in and actually live over important archeological sites, preventing their discovery. Also, there is the confirmed fact that entire cultures have been lost over time, leaving little more than a scarce trace of their existence. Further, new scientific evidence compels scientists to revise their estimates to account for the new findings. One important example in this subject relates to the Ancient Egyptian Sphinx, located in the area today known as Giza, in Egypt. The Great Sphinx was once known as *Horemakhet* or "Heru in the Horizon." It was later known by the Greeks as Harmachis. New discoveries show the Ancient Egyptian Sphinx to be much older than previously thought. The importance of this discovery is that it places advanced civilization first in northeast Africa (Ancient Egypt), at the time when Europe, Mesopotamia[10] and the rest of Asia were just coming out of the Paleolithic Age.

Thus, when Ancient Egyptians had already created the Sphinx monument, and its attendant massive temple and other structures that would have required multitudes of workers, food, organization, etc., the rest of the world was just beginning to learn how to practice farming and to use sleds, boats and other elementary instruments which were just being invented there. The new findings related to the Sphinx, which are supported by many ancient writings, are leading us to realize the true depths of human origins and the starting point for civilization.

Principles of Cultural Expression

What is Culture?

The concept of culture will be an extremely important if not the most important aspect of humanity to our study and so it will be a developing theme throughout our study. The following principles are offered as a standard for understanding what culture is, how it manifests in the world, and how that manifestation affects other cultures.

> **cul·ture** (kŭl′chər) *n.* **1.a.** The totality of socially transmitted behavior patterns, arts, beliefs, institutions, and all other products of human work and thought.
> —American Heritage Dictionary

Purpose of Culture:

- Culture is a people's window on whatever they perceive as reality (to understand the world around them) and their concept of self.

- Culture is a conditioning process, necessary for the early development of a human being.

- Culture defines the agenda of a society (government, economics, religion). Religion is the most powerful force driving culture.

The Study of Culture

Cultural Anthropology is the study concerned with depicting the character of various cultures, and the similarities and differences between them. This branch of anthropology is concerned with all cultures whether simple or complex and its methodology entails a holistic view, field work, comparative analysis (both within the society and cross-culturally), and a tendency to base theoretical models on empirical data rather than vice versa.[11]

Ethnology, is the comparative study of cultures. Using ethnographic material from two or more societies, ethnology can attempt to cover their whole cultural range or concentrate on a single cultural trait. Ethnology was originally a term covering the whole of anthropology, toward the end of the 19th century historical ethnology was developed in an attempt to trace cultural diffusion. Now ethnologists concentrate on cross-cultural studies, using statistical methods of analysis.[12]

While this work may be considered as a form of cultural anthropology and ethnology, it will also serve as an overview of the theological principles espoused by the cultures in question. The techniques used in this book to compare cultures will lay heavy emphasis on iconographical and philosophical factors as well as historical evidences, as opposed to statistical methods of analysis. It is possible to focus on the apparent differences between cultures and religious philosophies. This has been the predominant form of philosophical discourse and study of Western scholarship. The seeming differences between religions have led to innumerable conflicts between the groups throughout history, all because of the outer expression of religion. However, throughout this work I will attempt to focus on the synchretic aspects of the philosophies and religions in question because it is in the similarities wherein harmony is to be found; harmony in the form of concurrence in ideas and meaning. In light of this idea of harmony, it is possible to look at the folklore of cultural traditions throughout the world and see the same psycho-mythological message being espoused through the various cultural masks. They are all referring to the same Supreme Being. While giving commentary and adding notes, which I feel will be helpful to the understanding of the texts which I will compare, I have endeavored to use the actual texts wherever possible so that you, the reader, may see for yourself and make your own judgment.

Culture is everything a human being learns from living in a society including language, history, values and religion, etc. However, the outer learning masks an inner experience. Spirituality is that movement to transcend culture and discover the essence of humanity. This Ultimate Truth, known by many names, such as God, Goddess, Supreme Being, and their varied names in all of the world's cultures, is revered by all peoples, though culture and folk differences color the expression of that reverence. This is what is called the *folk expression of religion based on culture and local traditions.* For example, the same Ultimate Reality is expressed by Christians based on European culture and traditions, as God. The same Ultimate Reality is expressed by Muslims based on Arab culture and traditions as Allah. The same Ultimate and Transcendental Reality is worshipped by Jews based on Hebrew culture and traditions. The same Ultimate and Transcendental Reality is worshipped by the Chinese based on Chinese culture and traditions, etc. If people who practice religion stay at the outer levels (basing their religious practice and wisdom on their culture, myths and traditions), they will always see differences between faiths. Religion has three aspects, myth, ritual and mysticism. Myth and ritual relate to the folk expression of religion, whereas mysticism relates to that movement of self-discovery that transcends all worldly concepts. Mysticism allows any person in any religion to discover that the same Supreme Being is being worshipped by all under different names and forms, and by different means. It is the worship itself and the object of that worship that underlies the human movement. Therefore, the task of all true mystics (spiritual seekers) is to go beyond the veil of the outer forms of religion, including the symbols, but more importantly, the doctrines, rituals and traditions (see model below).

Figure 1: Below: The Culture-Myth Model, showing how the folk expression of religion is based on culture and local traditions.

Figure 2: Below: The Culture-Myth Models of two world spiritual systems, showing how the folk expression of each religion is based on culture and local traditions.

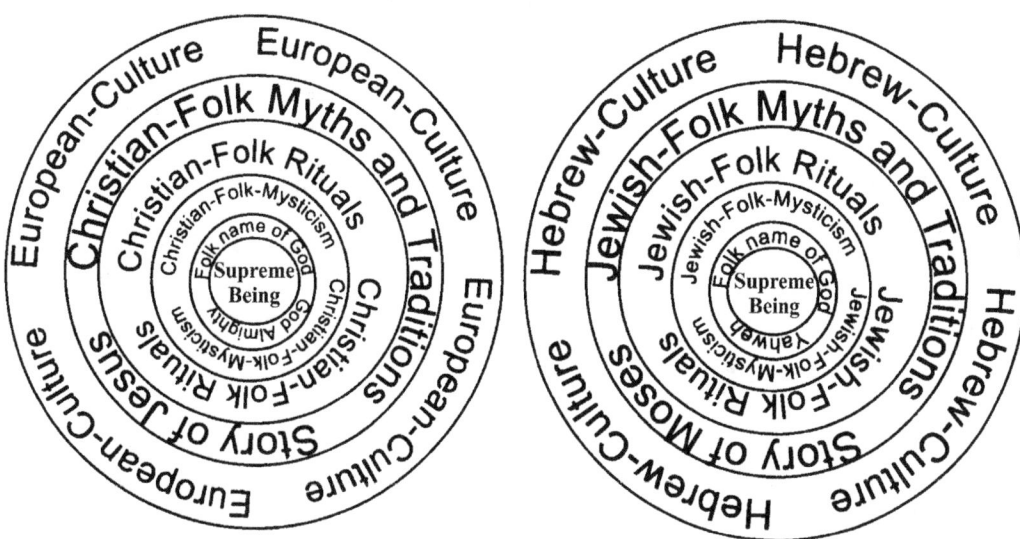

In studying and comparing diverse groups of peoples, we are essentially comparing their cultures. Culture includes all activities and manners of manifestation, which a group of peoples have developed over the period of their existence. Cultural expressions may fall under the following categories. An important theme to understand throughout this study is that the underlying principle purpose or function of culture in a given society may be equal to that of another culture, but the mode of manifestation will invariably be unique. The exception to this is when there is contact between the cultures. Some coincidental similarities may be found between two cultures that have never been in contact with each other, but the frequency and quality of those correlations belies the superficiality of the contact or random nature of the correlation. Similarities and commonalties pointing to a strong interrelationship between the cultures can be expected when comparing two apparently different cultures if the cultures in question have sustained some form of contact or emerged from a common origin. The degree of parallelism and harmony between varied cultures can be measured by the nature and frequency of synchronicity or concordance of the factors from each culture being compared.

In the study of the theology[13] of the varied religious traditions of the world (comparative religious studies), it is very possible to encounter similar general points of philosophical conceptualization in reference to the institutions for the worship of a spiritual being or divinities. In other words, religion itself is a point of commonality in all cultures and all historical periods. The basic common ideas manifested by cultures in and of themselves cannot be used as justification for concluding that there is a common origin or common cultural concept being expressed by two different religions. So just because two religions espouse the idea that there is a Supreme Being or that Supreme Being is one, a scholar cannot conclude that the religions have a common origin or that their concept in reference to the entity being worshipped is compatible. The factor of theology is there in both cultures, but the mode of expression may be different, and even if it is not different, it may have been arrived at by different means. That is, the myth-plot system of the religion may contain various episodes which are not synchronous, thus expressing a divergent theological idea even though it may ultimately lead to the same philosophical realization. The forms of iconography may show depictions of the divinities in different situations and engaged in different activities. The rituals and traditions related to the myths of the religions may be carried out in different ways and at different times. These deviating factors point to a different origin for the two cultures in question. On the other hand it is possible to have a common origin and later observe some divergence from the original expression while the theme and plot of myth within the religion stays essentially the same. This finding may not only point to a common origin, but also to a divergent practice in later times. If two traditions are shown to have been in contact, and they are found to have common elements in the basis of their espoused philosophy, as well as the manifestation of that philosophy through iconography, artifacts, rituals, traditions, myth-plots, etc., then this determination suggests a strong correlation in the origin, and or contact throughout the development of the cultures in question. In order to make such a judgment, it is

AFRICAN ORIGINS Of Civilization, Religion, Yoga Mystical Spirituality And Ethics Philosophy

necessary to identify and match several essential specific criteria or factors confirming the commonality or convergence indicating a communal[14] origin and or common cultural factor.

Table 1: Categories of Cultural Expression and Factors of Cultural Expression

Categories of Cultural Expression	Factors of Cultural Expression

1. Art: design (lay out), composition-style, and pattern
2. Artifacts - tools
3. Customs and Traditions - secular
4. Ethnicity
5. Folklore - legend
6. Form –Architecture
7. Language
8. Music and Performing arts – Theater
9. Philosophy
   a. Social
      i. Economics
      ii. Legal system
      iii. Government
10. Religion-Spirituality
   a. Myth and Mythological motif
   b. Customs and Traditions - Ritual
   c. Mystical philosophy
	These categories can be correlated by matches in the following features:
	
	Myth and Religion Related Correlation Methods
	
	1. Gender concordance[2]
	2. Iconography
	   a. Conventional
	   b. Naturalistic
	   c. Stylized
	3. Myth-
	   a. Plot
	   b. Motif[3]
	   c. Theme
	4. Rituals and or Traditions
	   a. Function
	   b. Actions performed
	5. Scriptural Synchronicity
	
	General Correlation Methods
	
	1. Evidence of Contact
	   a. <u>Concurrent</u> – cultures develop at the same time - equal exchanges relationship
	   b. <u>Dependent</u> – one culture depends on the other for technology, instruction - Donor – recipient relationship
	   c. <u>Common Origins-</u> Cultures originate from the same point with the same primary categories and then branch off and develop independently.
	   d. <u>Eye witness accounts</u>
	   e. <u>Self descriptions</u> – Their own writings acknowledge the contact.
	   f. <u>Pacts</u> – treaties, etc.
	2. Form
	   a. Architecture
	   b. Artifacts
	3. Function – usage -purpose
	   a. Architecture
	   b. Artifacts
	4. Grammar
	   a. Phonetics
	   b. Linguistics
	5. Historical Events
	   c. Common origins of the Genesis of the Cultures
	   d. Concurrent events throughout the history of the cultures
	6. Genetics
	7. Nationality

---

[2] Gender of characters in the myth
[3] Myth and Mythological motif (subject matter)

AFRICAN ORIGINS Of Civilization, Religion, Yoga Mystical Spirituality And Ethics Philosophy

Definitions of the Categories of Cultural Expression and Factors of Cultural Expression system of Cultural Anthropology

The following are general designations to describe the dominand cultures or world views being expored in this volume. These do not include all the cultures of the world.

Definition: *Western Culture* = For the purpose of this study, "Western Culture" constitutes the traditions, beliefs and productions of those people who have developed societies in the western part of the continent of Asia (Europe), and who see this part of the world as their homeland or view the world from the perspective of the traditions (including religion) and norms of that region (Eurocentric). This includes the United States of America, Canada, as well as other countries which have societies that are descendants from the European colonial rulers, and which control the governments of the former colonies (including Australia, New Zealand, etc.). Also included are countries where the political order is supported or enforced (neocolonialism or capitalistic globalism) by the Western countries. In a broad sense, Western Culture is a way of thinking that has spread far a field and now includes all who adopt the philosophies, norms and customs of that region, including secularism and religions that are predominantly Christian, followed by the Jewish and Islamic.

Definition: *Arab Culture* = For the purpose of this study, "Arab Culture" constitutes the traditions, beliefs and productions of those people who have developed societies in the south-western part of the continent of Asia (Arabia, Mesopotamia and now also north Africa), and who see this part of the world as their homeland or view the world from the perspective of the traditions (including religion) and norms of that region. In a broad sense, Arab Culture is a way of thinking that has spread far a field and now includes all who adopt the philosophies, norms and customs of that region.

Definition: *Eastern Culture* = For the purpose of this study, "Eastern Culture" constitutes the traditions, beliefs and productions of those people who have developed societies in the Eastern part of the continent of Asia (India, China) and who see this part of the world as their homeland or view the world from the perspective of the traditions (including religion) and norms of that region (Indocentric). In a broad sense, Eastern Culture is a way of thinking that includes all who adopt the philosophies, norms and customs of that region.

Definition: *African Culture* = For the purpose of this study, "African Culture" or "Southern Culture" constitutes the traditions, beliefs and productions of those people who have developed societies in the continent of Africa (Sub-Saharan countries) and who see this part of the world as their homeland or view the world from the perspective of the native traditions (including religion) and norms of that region (Africentric {Afrocentric}). In a broad sense, African Culture is a way of thinking that includes all who adopt the philosophies, norms and customs of that region.

The following definitions are the two simple keys to understanding the Categories of Cultural Expression and Factors of Cultural Expression system of Cultural Anthropology.

Definition: *Categories of Cultural Expression* = Broad areas whereby a culture expresses itself in the world. Exp. Religion is a broad category of cultural expression. All cultures may have a religion, however, those religions are not necessarily the same. What are the differences? How can these differences be classified and compared?

Definition: *Factors of Cultural Expression* = methods or means by which a culture expresses its categories. Exp. Myth is a factor of religion by which a religion is expressed in a unique way by a particular culture. In determining the common elements of different religions, there are several factors which can be used as criteria to determine whether or not cultures had common origins. If cultures are related, they will use common stories or other common factors or patterns to express the main doctrines of the religion or spiritual path, social philosophy, etc. These are listed below.

The following section introduces the categories of cultural expression as well as factors or aspects of the Categories which reflect the unique forms of manifestation within a given culture.

Linguistics

Linguistics – Spelling, grammar and script symbols
linguistics (**a.** *Of or relating to the synchronic[15] typological[16] comparison of languages*)

Phonetics – Sound of the words
phonetics (**2.** *The system of sounds of a particular language.*)[17]

In using linguistics as a factor for determining the common elements between two religions, the following should be noted. The existence or lack thereof of commonality in the use of language spelling or script symbols to describe objects, deities and or spiritual philosophy of a culture in and of itself cannot be used to conclude that there is or is not a common basis, origin or concept between the cultures in question. It is possible that these (language, spelling or script symbols to describe objects and deities) may have developed independently over a period of time after the initial contact; the meaning may be the same while the language developed independently.

The comparison of the phonetics as opposed to linguistics, for example, the names used to describe deities or philosophies is a better factor to compare since in ancient times, before the movements to standardize spellings and script symbols, script forms tended to change while name sounds remained more constant. The impetus in society to standardize and stabilize language only began in the 18th to the 19th centuries.[18] Therefore, it is possible to find name sounds and uses for the name that are alike in two different cultures, while their spellings or script forms may be different. Therefore, the requirement of the presence of a logical sequence of grammatical relationships between the languages of the two cultures need not be present in order to establish a relationship. The common basis in this case can be confirmed by the evidence of contact and the usage of the name and can be further confirmed by the form or gender related to the name.

Many people have been led to believe that the Kamitan language pronunciations are not certain. Modern Egyptological and linguistic scholarship has reconstituted hundreds of words by means of extrapolation from the last major manifestation of the Ancient Egyptian language, the Coptic language, as well as the Ancient Greek translations of Ancient Egyptian words. However, there has been a reluctance to look at other sources for comparison and extrapolation. The language could be even further reconstituted if even more comparative work was undertaken to study the Kamitan language in light of other African languages where there is documented evidence of contact, including those of the Dogon ethnic group of Mali, the Wolof[19] ethnic group of Senegal, and as we will see, also the Indian Bengali language. A few scholars have taken up this work in the past 44 years, but still to date there is no comprehensive work which takes all the factors into account, making them available to all Egyptologists and Indologists.

Further, the Kamitan language is special in many ways because it reflects many universal cosmic principles of sound. An example of this is the Ancient Egyptian word *"mut."* Mut means mother and it is reflected in "mata" of the Hindu language, "madre" of Spanish, "mother" in English, etc. The "m" sound is a universal "seed sound" principle of motherhood. However, this is not an absolute rule because other words can and are used in other languages as well. The use of names in the Kamitan language is important because they act as keys to unlocking the mysteries of life, but this is true only for those initiated into the philosophy. In Kamitan philosophy, words are seen as abstract representatives of phenomenal reality. Since the mind is the only reality, and the external world only reflects a conceptualized form based on an idea in the mind of the Supreme Being, words are a higher reality when compared to the physical world. All Kamitan words are names for objects and/or concepts. In fact, in Kamitan and other mystical philosophies, Creation is viewed as a concept given a name and not an absolute, abiding reality in and of itself.

Thus, by studying the phonetic and pictorial (Kamitan language is not only phonetic, but also illustrative) etymology (the origin and development of a linguistic form) and etiology (the study of causes or origins) of names and applying the initiatic science, it is possible to decipher the mysteries of Creation by discovering the teachings embedded in the language by the Sages of Ancient Egypt.

Moreover, in the Kamitan language as in others such as the ancient Greek, Hebrew, and Sanskrit, where the pronunciations and meanings of some words are not known with certainty or at all, the meaning of many more words and terms are known with exactness. So, while a time traveler who has studied the Kamitan language in modern times might have some difficulty speaking to an Ancient Egyptian person, they would have less trouble communicating in the written form of the language. This means that the philosophy and myth can be understood even if the pronunciation of some words is uncertain. Therefore, comparisons can be made between the philosophy of the Kamitan culture and that of others. This also means that philosophy is a legitimate and viable means to compare mythologies as a factor in determining the contact and communication between cultures and their relationship, if any.

Form

> **form** *(fôrm) n. 1.a. The shape and structure of an object. b. The body or outward appearance of a person or an animal considered separately from the face or head; figure.)* [20]

The form of an object is related to its name and function. Thus, correlations based on form will often be noted in conjunction with the other related factors. As we saw earlier, language (name) is merely a symbol of concept, which is itself a representation of truth. However, the concept of something which exists at the level of the unconscious mind will be compatible even if at the conscious level of mind of people who speak different languages. Aspects of human activity such as concept, intent, desire, etc., can be alike, while the manifestation is variable. Again, if the concepts, intents, desires, etc., are alike, but there is an absence of manifestations (language, artifacts, myths, etc.) that can be compared in order to confirm this likeness at the conscious level, the case is hard to make that there is a commonality or contact between the two cultures. The specificity of form in ritual objects, architecture, artifacts, myths, etc. makes them excellent factors to compare between cultures in order to determine their synchronism or nonconformity. However, the unconscious psychological principles being conveyed through the medium of the forms of the objects, iconographies, rituals, etc. are to be compared along with the external forms used to symbolize those principles.

Architecture

ar·chi·tec·ture (är′kĭ-tĕk′chər) *n. Abbr.* **archit.**, **arch. 1.** The art and science of designing and erecting buildings. **2.** Buildings and other large structures. **3.** A style and method of design and construction.

Architecture is the conscious creation of buildings and dwellings which the culture may use to promote its existence. The implementation of architecture signifies the existence of organized culture because architecture requires the orderly and systematic application of mathematics, geometry, the organization of labor, resources, etc. Architecture invariably reflects the philosophical and/or spiritual outlook of a culture, and thus is distinctive. Some cultures have created architecture that supports war (castles, fortresses, etc.), others have created architecture that supports commerce, while others have created architecture that seeks to reflect spiritual principles. For example, Islamic architecture reflects Islamic culture and beliefs. Modern American architecture reflects modern American culture and beliefs. In the same manner, Ancient Egyptian architecture reflects Ancient Egyptian culture and beliefs, and includes art and iconography which give insights into the values and beliefs of the Ancient Egyptians that may be compared to the values and beliefs of other cultures.

Kamitan architecture exhibits one additional aspect which is not found in most cultures. In Ancient Egypt, architecture was used to express a concretized coming into being of the spiritual myth and to reflect the nature of the cosmos. This is to say, the architecture was created in such a way as to express the religious philosophy in a concrete form. For example, the placing of a winged sundisk above the Temple entrances follows the decree given by the God Djehuti in the myth of the Asarian Resurrection to do so. This factor of mythological expression in architecture is also found in other spiritual traditions.

Function – Usage

*(**1.a.** The act, manner, or amount of using; use.)*[21]

The usage of an artifact, particularly a ritual object, is important when considering their origins. There are some important artifacts which are central to the rituals of the religions and they, therefore, constitute "mythological anchors" or focal points for the practice of the religion or spiritual tradition. These objects remain constant throughout the history of the culture while items of lesser importance may come into and out of existence over periods of time, being created with the same general form and having the same ritual function. This constitutes an important key in determining the congruence of the religious traditions in question, as it may support other forms of congruent factors such as the symmetry between the myths and or plots in religious stories being compared.

Rituals and Traditions

rit·u·al (rĭch/ōō-əl) *n.* **1.a.** The prescribed order of a religious ceremony. **b.** The body of ceremonies or rites used in a place of worship.[22]

tra·di·tion (trə-dĭsh/ən) *n.* **1.** The passing down of elements of a culture from generation to generation, especially by oral communication. **2.a.** A mode of thought or behavior followed by a people continuously from generation to generation; a custom or usage. **b.** A set of such customs and usages viewed as a coherent body of precedents influencing the present. **3.** A body of unwritten religious precepts. **4.** A time-honored practice or set of such practices.[23]

Rituals, ritual objects and traditions (implying observances, festivals, holidays, etc., related to the myths) are used as tangible symbols of the myth. Traditions, in this context, may be understood as a legacy of rituals performed at an earlier point in history and handed down to the descendants of a mythological-religious-spiritual heritage to which a particular culture adheres. As such they are instruments to facilitate the remembrance, practice and identification with the key elements of a myth. This function of rituals and traditions is more significant than just being a social link to the past generations of a culture. When the identification is advanced, the practitioner of the rituals and traditions of the myth partakes in the myth and thus becomes one with the passion of the deity of the myth and in so doing, attains a communion with that divinity. This advanced practice of rituals and traditions constitutes the third level of religion, the metaphysics or mystical level, which will be explained in the following section.

Myth and its Origins, Psychology, Spirituality, Metaphor, Language, Plot, and Theme

Since the study of myth and mythic symbolism in ancient scriptures, iconography, etc., will form an integral part of the comparison of cultures, we must first begin by gaining a deeper understanding of what myth is, and its purpose. With this understanding, we may then undertake the study of the Asarian myth, or any other mystical story, and be able to understand the psycho-spiritual implications which are being imparted.

AFRICAN ORIGINS Of Civilization, Religion, Yoga Mystical Spirituality And Ethics Philosophy

The American Heritage Dictionary defines *Myth* as follows:

1. A traditional story presenting supernatural beings, ancestors, or heroes that serve as primordial types in a primitive view of the world.
2. A fictitious or imaginary story, person, or thing.
3. A false belief.

The American Heritage Dictionary defines *Myth* as follows:

1. A body of myths about the origin and history of a people.
2. The study of myths.

The Random House Encyclopedia defines *Myth* as follows:

Myth, a body of myths or traditional stories dealing with gods and legendary heroes. The myths of a people serves to present their world view, their explanations of natural phenomena, their religious and other beliefs. Mythological literature includes the Greek *Iliad* and *Odyssey*, the Scandinavian *Edda*, the Indian *Ramayana*, and the Babylonian *Gilgamesh*, among others. Various interpretations of myth have been made by anthropologists such as Sir James Frazer and Claude Lévi-Strauss. In literature, myth has been used as the basis for poetry, stories, plays, and other writings.

Excerpted from *Compton's Interactive Encyclopedia*:

MYTHOLOGY. The origin of the universe can be explained by modern astronomers and astrophysicists, while archaeologists and historians try to clarify the origin of human societies. In the distant past, however, before any sciences existed, the beginnings of the world and of society were explained by mythology.

The word myth is often mistakenly understood to mean fiction something that never happened, a made-up story or fanciful tale. Myth is really a way of thinking about the past. Mircea Eliade, a historian of religions, once stated: "Myths tell only of that which really happened." This does not mean that myths correctly explain what literally happened. It does suggest, however, that behind the explanation there is a reality that cannot be seen and examined.

Myth-ology is the study or science (ology) of myths and their deeper implications. In relation to mythology, the term epic is also used. The American Heritage Dictionary defines an *Epic* as:

1. A long narrative poem that celebrates episodes of a people's heroic tradition.

The Encarta/Funk & Wagnall's Encyclopedia defines an Epic as:

"A long narrative poem, majestic both in theme and style. Epics deal with legendary or historical events of national or universal significance, involving action of broad sweep and grandeur. Most epics deal with the exploits of a single individual, thereby giving unity to the composition. Typically, an epic involves the introduction of supernatural forces that shape the action, conflict in the form of battles or other physical combat, and certain stylistic conventions: an invocation to the Muse, a formal statement of the theme, long lists of the protagonists involved, and set speeches couched in elevated language. Commonplace details of everyday life may appear, but they serve as background for the story, and are described in the same lofty style as the rest of the poem."

These definitions have been included here to give a reference as to what society at large, especially in the West, has accepted as the definition and purpose of mythological and epic literature. Now we will explore the initiatic-yogic-mystical meaning of *Myth*. First however, one more definition is required. We need to understand what is a *Metaphor*. The American Heritage Dictionary defines *Metaphor* as follows:

"A figure of speech in which a term that ordinarily designates an object or idea is used to designate a dissimilar object or idea in order to suggest comparison or analogy, as in the phrase *evening of life*."

The Universal Vision of Comparative Mythology

In the book *Comparative Mythology*, the author, Jaan Puhvel, traces the term "myth" to the writings of Homer (900 B.C.E.), with the usage *épos kai muthos* 'word and speech.' In the writings of Homer and the ancient Greek writers of tragic plays, Jaan Puhvel also sees that the term can mean "tale, story, narrative," and that this story or tale can be without reference to truth content.[24] Truth content here implies a historical or real relationship to time and space events or realities. In the writings of the later Greek authors such as Herodotus, Puhvel sees a different meaning in the term Mûthos, that of fictive "narrative," "tall tale," and "legend." It is felt that Herodotus spoke of Mûthos as those items he himself found incredulous, and used the term *logos* for that information which he felt was more or less based on truth or facts. Further, with the writings of Plato, a new interpretation of the terms emerge, as Mûthos takes on a different character in relation to logos. Mûthos (myth) is more of a non-rational basis for understanding existence while logos is seen as the rational basis. In Western Culture, the term logos has come to be associated with absolute knowledge and logical thinking and analysis. In terms of mysticism, it is understood as the Divine intelligence, consciousness, which permeates and enlivens matter, time and space. In later times logos came to be known as 'the Word' or inner, esoteric spiritual knowledge, and in early Christianity, Jesus became 'the word (logos) made flesh.' From these origins and many deprecating arguments from the church and western scientists, through the middle and dark ages and into the renaissance period of Western Culture, the meaning of the word, myth, in modern times, has come to be understood primarily in Western Culture as a colloquialism to refer to anything devoid of a basis in truth or reality. Saying "it's a myth" has come to be understood by most people as a reference to something that does not contain even a fragment of truth. Myth has come to be thought of in terms of being neurotic expressions of ancient religions, movie ideas spinning out of Hollywood, governments telling myths (lies) or Madison Avenue advertising (the "myth-makers"), etc., in other words, something without any truth or factual basis. In ancient times, Plato referred to the term 'mythologia' as meaning "myth-telling," as opposed to storytelling. Modern scholars refer to this term as mythology (the study of myth), which, until recently, primarily meant Greek Mythology. The body of ancient Greek narratives relating to the legends and traditions connected to the gods and goddesses of Greece are referred to as the mythological narratives.

Mythology is the study of myths. Myths (mythos) are stories which relate human consciousness to the transcendental essence of reality. This work is essentially a study in comparative mythology. It seeks to discover the common elements in two or more systems of mythos in order to understand their deeper meaning and develop the larger picture as they are fitted into the overall patchwork of traditions throughout history. In effect, this work attempts to show a connection and continuity between traditions that will enable the comprehension of them as a flow of the one primordial and recurrent theme of self-discovery. In such a study, there are always some who object, maintaining that differences are the overriding defining factors in any aspect of life. But this way of thinking is incongruous in the face of all the scientific evidence pointing to a common origin for all humanity as well as of Creation itself. Therefore, it seems that the movement to understand our common bonds as human beings should as well move into to the arena of the mythology and psychology. In this manner we may discover that what binds us is greater than that which tears us apart, for when we examine the arguments and concepts used to separate, they are inevitably derived from emotion, politics, misconception or superficialities based on ignorance. These lead to major controversies, debates, refutations and egoistic opinions founded on nothing but faith in rumors, conjectures and speculation, and not on first hand examination of the traditions from the point of view of a practitioner. Joseph Campbell summed up this issue as follows.

> "Perhaps it will be objected that in bringing out the correspondences I have overlooked the differences between the various Oriental and Occidental, modern, ancient, and primitive traditions. The same objection might be brought, however, against any textbook or chart of anatomy, where the physiological variations of race are disregarded in the interest of a basic general understanding of the human physique. There are of course differences between the numerous mythologies and religions of mankind, but this is a book about the similarities; and once these are understood the differences will be found to be much less great than is popularly (and politically) supposed. My hope is that a comparative elucidation may contribute to the perhaps not-quite desperate cause of those forces that are working in the present world for unification, not in the name of some ecclesiastical or political empire, but in the sense of human mutual understanding. As we are told in the Vedas: "Truth is one, the sages speak of it by many names."
>
> J.C.
New York City
June 10, 1948

In *Comparative Mythology,* Puhvel underscored the importance of myth and the operation of myth as an integral, organic component of human existence. It is a defining aspect of social order in which human existence is guided to discover the "sacred" and "timeless" nature of self and Creation. He also discusses how the "historical landscape" becomes "littered with the husks of desiccated myths" even as "societies pass and religious systems change," remaining submerged in the traditions and epics of modern times.

> "Myth in the technical sense is a serious object of study, because true myth is by definition deadly serious to its originating environment. In myth are expressed the thought patterns by which a group formulates self-cognition and self-realization, attains self-knowledge and self-confidence, explains its own source and being and that of its surroundings, and sometimes tries to chart its destinies. By myth man has lived, died, and-all too often-killed. Myth operates by bringing a sacred (and hence essentially and paradoxically "timeless") past to bear preemptively on the present and inferentially on the future ("as it was in the beginning, is now, and ever shall be"). Yet in the course of human events societies pass and religious systems change; the historical landscape gets littered with the husks of desiccated myths. These are valuable nonmaterial fossils of mankind's recorded history, especially if still embedded in layers of embalmed religion, as part of a stratum of tradition complete with cult, liturgy, and ritual. Yet equally important is the next level of transmission, in which the sacred narrative has already been secularized, myth has been turned into saga, sacred time into heroic past, gods into heroes, and mythical action into "historical" plot. Many genuine "national epics" constitute repositories of tradition where the mythical underpinnings have been submerged via such literary transposition. Old chronicles can turn out to be "prose epics" where the probing modem mythologist can uncover otherwise lost mythical traditions. Such survival is quite apart from, or wholly incidental to, the conscious exploitative use of myth in literature, as raw material of fiction, something that Western civilization has practiced since artful verbal creativity began."[25]

The key element in myth is its metaphorical purpose in that its stories and characters are designed to provide a reference towards an etiological, moral or spiritual message that transcends the story itself. This means that there is an exoteric meaning which refers to the events and circumstances in the story, which may or may not have a basis in fact, and also an esoteric or mystical meaning which refers to a deeper teaching or message which transcends the boundaries of the events in the story. This message is spiritual in nature when the myth is religious. Through the myth many ideas which are not easily explained in rational, logical terms can be freely explored and elucidated in imaginative and colorful ways. Mystical myths are particularly important because their purpose is to point to where the answers to the most important questions of every individual may be found. Everyone is searching for answers to questions like "Who am I really?" "Is this all that I am?" "Where do I come from?" "What is death?" and "What is my purpose in life?" Through myths, the teachings of Sages and Saints can take full flight, free of the constraints of normal grammatical or thematic boundaries. Therefore, myths are an ideal way to impart spiritual truths which transcend ordinary human experiences and ordinary human concepts of rationality.

The question of the similarities between myths, rituals and traditions has been explored in the book *"The Mythic Image,"* where the late world renowned mythologist, Joseph Campbell explained the concepts surrounding the treatment of equivalent elements and symbols that can be seen in myths from apparently separate cultures.

> One explanation that has been proposed to account for the appearance of homologous structures and often even identical motifs in the myths and rites of widely separate cultures is psychological: namely, to cite a formula of James G. Frazer in *The Golden Bough,* that such occurrences are most likely *"the effect of similar causes acting alike on the similar constitution of the human mind in different countries and under different skies."*
>
> There are, however, instances that cannot be accounted for in this way, and then suggest the need for another interpretation: for example, in India the number of years assigned to an eon[26] is 4,320,000; whereas in the Icelandic *Poetic Edda* it is declared that in Othin's warrior hall, Valhall, there are 540 doors, through each of which, on the "day of the war of the wolf,"[27] 800 battle-ready warriors will pass to engage the antigods in combat.' But 540 times 800 equals 432,000!

Moreover, a Chaldean[28] priest, Berossos, writing in Greek ca. 289 B.C., reported that according to Mesopotamian belief 432,000 years elapsed between the crowning of the first earthly king and the coming of the deluge.

No one, I should think, would wish to argue that these figures could have arisen independently in India, Iceland, and Babylon.[29]

Campbell explains that there is a view that the commonalties observed in myth, symbolism, etc., are a factor of psychological forces that are common to all human beings. One example of this concept is that every human being on earth feels the desire for happiness. Therefore, when we see people from different places ("*different countries and under different skies*"), who have never met each other, pursuing happiness in similar ways, we should not be surprised. However, Campbell makes the point that some coincidences go beyond the nature of conformity due to a primal urge. Those concurrences can only be explained by a closer relationship, because the uniformity of "structure" or configuration of the myths as well as the usage of the exact same symbols and rites could only occur when there is an intimate relationship between the cultures. In other words, the two pursuers of happiness can be explained by the theory of common urges, however, the pursuit of happiness using the same procedures (rites or rituals), the same way of defining happiness, the same philosophy of how to go about looking for happiness, idealizing happiness in the same way (myth), representing happiness the same way (symbolism), etc., are signs that the cultures have had a common origin, upbringing, socialization, indoctrination, contact, etc. This occurs when a culture "diffuses" some new technology, philosophy or cultural element to another culture. Campbell continues:

> A second approach to interpretation has therefore been proposed, based on the observation that at certain identifiable times, in identifiable places, epochal transformations of culture have occurred, the effects of which have been diffused to the quarters of the earth; and that along with these there have traveled constellations of associated mythological systems and motifs.[30]

Thus, Campbell introduces another way to understand the commonalties observed in separate cultures that cannot be explained by the theory of similar forces operating on the minds of separate individuals. There are milestones in history wherein major social events or advancements in culture affect humanity as if like a ripple of water caused by a stone being dropped into a calm lake. The resulting undulations of powerful concepts, and technologies move along the trade and communication routs, the arteries of human communication and interaction, spreading (diffusing) the advanced knowledge in waves across the cultural ocean of humanity throughout the world. Like a surfer, being carried along with the force of the wave, so too the concepts and symbols move across the human landscape being empowered by the innate human desire to achieve higher understanding and the intellectual capacity to recognize something better or a new way to express the same treasured truths. This important principle related to the transference of ideas and symbols between cultures was seminal to Campbell's groundbreaking work as a teacher of comparative mythology in the West.

Psychomythology

Mystical teaching holds that the essence of Creation and therefore, of each individual human being, is transcendental; it transcends the ordinary bounds of mental perception and understanding. However, all human experiences occur in and through the mind. Therefore, the heart of all human experiences, be they painful or pleasurable, is rooted in the mind. The purpose of myth is to bridge the gap between the limited human mind and its conscious, worldly level and that which transcends all physicality as well as the mind and senses. Thus, religious myths, which will be our primary focus in this volume, must be understood in the light of their psychological and mystical (transcending body, mind and senses) implications. We will refer to this concept by a new term: "*Psycho-Mythology.*"

So the term "*psycho,*" as it is used here, must be understood as far more than simply that which refers to the mind in the worldly sense. The term "psycho" must be understood to mean everything that constitutes human consciousness in all of its stages and states, but most importantly, the subconscious and unconscious levels of mind. "*Mythology*" here refers to the study of the codes, messages, ideas, directives, stories, culture, beliefs, etc., that affect the personality through the conscious, subconscious and unconscious aspects of the mind of an individual, specifically those effects which result in psycho-spiritual transformation, that is, a transpersonal or transcendental change in the personality of an individual which leads to the discovery of the transcendental reality behind all existence.

A myth should never be understood literally even though some of its origins may involve actual events or actions, otherwise one will miss the transcendental message being related through the metaphor. This would be like going to a theater to see a fictional movie or reading a fantasy novel, and believing it to be real. However, as a movie or novel may be based on unreal events and yet carry an important message which is imparted through the medium of actors, a plot and so on, mystical myths are not to be understood as being completely baseless nor as having been put together purely for entertainment or as "primitive mumbo-jumbo." Myths constitute a symbolic language that speaks to people in psycho-symbolic ways, satisfying their conscious need for entertainment, but also affecting the subconscious and unconscious mind and its need for spiritual evolution. This psychological language of myths can lead people to understand and experience the transcendental truths of existence, which cannot be easily expressed in words.

Myth is the first stage of religion and the reenactment of the myth constitutes the second level religion: Ritual.[31] Myths constitute the heart and soul of rituals. Myth is a mystical language for transmitting and teaching the principles of life and creation. Rituals are the medium through which the myths are practiced, lived and realized.

The study of religious mythical stories is important to gain insight into the *"Psycho-Mythology"* or psychological implications of myth for the spiritual transformation of the individual which leads to the attainment of Enlightenment. Enlightenment implies the attainment of an expanded state of consciousness, termed as *"awet ab,"* dilation (expansion) of the heart in Ancient Egyptian Mystical Philosophy, in which there is a full and perfect awareness of one's existence beyond the mind and body. Thus, when you delve into a myth, you must expect more than just entertainment. You should be equipped with the knowledge which will allow you to decipher the hidden meanings in the story so that you may also begin to experience and benefit from them on a personal level, i.e. live the myth and on a spiritual level, i.e. attain enlightenment. Only then will a person be able to engender a real transformation in their life which will lead you to true fulfillment and happiness as well as contentment. This is the third level of religious practice, the mystical or metaphysical level.

The Keys to Reading and Understanding a Myth

> *Religion without myth not only fails to work, it also fails to offer man the promise of unity with the transpersonal and eternal.*
> —C. G. Jung (1875-1961)

Key #1: Myths (Religious/Mystical) are relevant to our lives in the present.

The first and most important key to understanding a myth is comprehending that the myth is not talking about some ancient personality or story which occurred a long time ago and which has no relevance to the present. In fact, the myth is speaking about you. It is a story about human life, its origins, its destiny, its plight and the correct action, in the present, which is based on the same principles of the past, for leading a truly successful life which paves the way to Enlightenment and true happiness.

Key #2: Myth is a journey of spiritual transformation.

The second key to understanding a myth is comprehending that it is usually written in the form of a journey in which the subject must learn about himself or herself and transcend the ordinary human consciousness, thereby discovering a greater essence of self. In this movement there are experiences of happiness, sorrow, struggle and learning. It is a movement from ignorance and darkness towards light, wisdom and ultimately, to spiritual Enlightenment.

Key #3: Myths are to be lived in order to understand their true meaning.

The third key to understanding a myth is that comprehension comes from living the myth. Living a myth does not mean simply reading a myth, being able to recount the events with perfect memory or simply practicing the rituals of a myth without a deeper understanding of their implications and purpose. It means making the essence of the teaching being conveyed through the myth an integral part of your life. If this practice is not implemented, the teachings remain at the intellectual level and the deeper truths of the myth are not revealed. One lives with dry intellectualism or blind faith, the former leading to a superficial and therefore frustrated spiritual life, and the latter leading to dogmatism and emotional frustration. Therefore, you must resolve to discover the myth in every facet of your life, and in so doing, you will be triumphant as the hero(ine) of the myth.

Key #4: Myth points the way to victory in life.

Myths show us our heritage as a culture as well as the legacy we are to receive. They give human beings a place in the scheme of things as well as a purpose in life and the means to achieve the fulfillment of that purpose. The ultimate purpose is to achieve victory in the battle of life, to defeat the forces of ignorance within oneself which lead to adversity and frustration and thereby become masters of life here and hereafter, discovering undifferentiated peace, love and joy...Enlightenment.

> "God is a metaphor for a mystery that transcends all human categories of thought...It depends on how much you want to think about it, whether or not it's doing you any good, whether it's putting you in touch with the mystery which is the ground of your own being."
>
> —Joseph Campbell

Thus, when comparing the myths of different cultures for the purpose of religious studies, it is necessary to understand their respective metaphorical aspects as well as their attendant underlying philosophies along with their apparent iconographical form and artistic intent (naturalistic[4] or stylized[5]).

Other Aspects of Myth

Plot refers to the plan of events or main story in a narrative or drama.[32] The synchronicity in the situations presented in myths can be used as a factor in discerning the communal nature of two myths. This congruence must be specific, involving characters of similar age group, gender and genealogy or provenance, experiencing similar situations in the same or similar ways.

In comparing myths, there are several important concerns. The purpose of myth, the language of myth and the levels of myth must be understood prior to making a comparison. *Myth is a language*[33] by which sages and saints transmit the basic elements of culture through a "common story" for all within the culture to believe in as well as draw answers to the basic questions of life such as, Where do I come from?, To which group do I belong? What is the purpose of life? and How do I fulfill that purpose? This is all conveyed through the story, plot and theme of the myth and their inherent teachings of social order as well as their spiritual morals.

Most religions and spiritual philosophies tend to be *deistic* at the elementary levels. **Deism**, as a religious belief or form of theism (belief in the existence of a Supreme Being or gods) holds that the Supreme Being's action was restricted to an initial act of creation, after which He/She retired (separated) to contemplate the majesty of His/Her work. Deists hold that the natural creation is regulated by laws put in place by the Supreme Being at the time of creation which are inscribed with perfect moral principles. Therefore, deism is closely related to the exoteric or personal but also outer (phenomenal) and dogmatic and conventional understanding of the Divinity.

> Two approaches to myth dominate the intellectual landscape during the first half of the twentieth century: the ritualistic and the psychoanalytic. The former, epitomized by the "myth and ritual" or Cambridge school beholden to the Oxonian E. B. Tylor's *Primitive Culture* (1871) and with James G. Frazer's *Golden Bough* as its central talisman, owes its theoretical underpinnings to Jane E. Harrison's *Prolegomena to the Study of Greek Religion* (1903) and *Themis* (1912). Harrison provided a strikingly simple and exclusionary definition of myth: myth is nothing but the verbalization of ritual, "the spoken correlative of the acted rite" *(Themis,* P. 328), *ta legomena* 'what is said'

---

[4] Imitating or producing the effect or appearance of nature.
[5] To restrict or make conform to a particular style. **2.** To represent conventionally; conventionalize.

accompanying *ta dromena* 'what is being done', myth and ritual being accordingly but two sides of the same religious coin; thus in principle there can be no myth without ritual, although time may have obliterated the act and left the narrative free to survive as myth or its debased subspecies (saga, legend, folktale, etc.).[34]

An assumption adopted by many comparative mythology scholars is the idea that myth is a means of explaining ritual. This idea is often predicated upon the concept that "primitive" cultures developed myth as a means of coping with the mysteries of life and Creation due to the lack of "scientific" knowledge. In the absence of science, ritual and superstition were substituted in order to allay the fears caused by the unknown. Further, this theory therefore holds that myth developed as an emanation of the actions of the practitioners of the rituals to justify those rituals. While this point of view is accurate with respect to certain cultures whose practitioners who are ignorant as to the reason behind the rituals of their religion, it is wholly incorrect when considering cultures possessing mystical philosophy. In those cultures the sacred writings of their religions present models of rituals as expressions of myth, and myth as expressions of philosophy or mysticism. Ritual is therefore a means to understand myth, and the realization of myth is a means to attain spiritual enlightenment. The erroneous concept is evident not only in modern scholarship, but also in ancient cultures which adopted symbols and myths from other cultures without fully understanding their purpose or the philosophy behind them. The following example given by Count Goblet D' Alviella provides an insight into the process called "iconological mythology."

> Sometimes, in similar cases, the new owners of the image will endeavor to explain it by a more or less ingenious interpretation, and in this manner they will restore to it a symbolical import, though applied to a new conception.
>
> The rising sun has often been compared to a new-born child. Amongst the Egyptians, this comparison led to Horus being represented as an infant sucking its finger. The Greeks imagined that he placed his finger on his lips to enjoin secrecy on the initiated, and they made him the image of Harpocrates, the god of silence.[35]
>
> This is what M. Clermont-Ganneau has very happily termed *iconological mythology*; it is here no longer the myth which gives rise to the image, but the image which gives rise to the myth.
>
> We may further quote, as an interpretation of the same kind, the legend related by Hygin, which made the Caduceus originate in Hermes throwing his wand between two serpents fighting. It is evident that, here also, this hypothesis, soon to be transformed into a myth by the popular imagination, was due to a desire, unconscious perhaps, to explain the Caduceus.
>
> Most frequently it is a conception pre-existent in the local traditions which we think we find amongst the products of foreign imagery.[36]

Another case in point is the relationship between Ancient Egypt and Greece. The Greeks adopted what they could understand of Ancient Egyptian philosophy, but did not adopt the culture or social philosophy. The Greeks made some changes in what they learned. Therefore, Greek culture cannot be claimed as an African (Ancient Egyptian) heritage. The problem was so severe that the Sages of Ancient Egypt felt the need to reprimand and denounce the Greek distortions. They indicted Greek culture as the culprit leading to the way of speech (communication and relation) which was of a "loose," "disdainful" and "confusing" character.

> "The Greek tongue is a noise of words, a language of argument and confusion."

> "Keep this teaching from translation in order that such mighty Mysteries might not come to the Greeks and to the disdainful speech of Greece, with all its looseness and its surface beauty, taking all the strength out of the solemn and the strong - the energetic speech of Names."

> "Unto those who come across these words, their composition will seem most simple and clear; but on the contrary, as this is unclear, and has the true meaning of its words concealed, it will be still unclear, when, afterwards, the Greeks will want to turn our tongue into their own - for this will be a very great distorting and obscuring of even what has heretofore been written. Turned into our own native tongue, the teachings keepeth

clear the meaning of the words. For that its very quality of sound, the very power of Kamitan names, have in themselves the bringing into act of what is said."

Myth in Orthodox Religion

Myth → Ritual → Mysticism

As previously discussed, in its complete form, religion is composed of three aspects, *mythological, ritual* and *metaphysical* or the *mystical experience* (mysticism - mystical philosophy). Mystical philosophy is the basis of myth. It is expressed in ritual and experienced in the metaphysics (spiritual disciplines, yoga) of the given religion. While many religions contain rituals, traditions, metaphors and myths, there are few professionals trained in understanding their deeper aspects and psychological implications (metaphysics and mystical). Thus, there is disappointment, frustration and disillusionment among many followers as well as leaders within many religions, particularly in the Western Hemisphere, because it is difficult to evolve spiritually without the proper spiritual guidance. Through introspection and spiritual research, it is possible to discover mythological vistas within religion which can rekindle the light of spirituality and at the same time increase the possibility of gaining a fuller experience of life. The exoteric (outer, ritualistic) forms of religion with which most people are familiar is only the tip of an iceberg so to speak; it is only a beginning, an invitation or prompting to seek a deeper (esoteric) discovery of the transcendental truths of existence.

While on the surface it seems that there are many differences between the philosophies, upon closer reflection there is only one major division, that of belief (theist) or non-belief (atheist). Among the believers there are differences of opinion as to how to believe. This is the source of all the trouble between religions and spiritual groups. One reason for this is because ordinary religion is deistic, based on traditions and customs which are themselves based on culture. Since culture varies from place to place and from one time in history to another, there will always be some variation in spiritual traditions. These differences will occur not only between cultures but also even within the same culture. An example of this is orthodox Christianity with its myriad of denominations and fundamental changes over the period of its existence.

Doctrine	Early church doctrine	Later church doctrine
Who is Jesus Christ?	Savior	Son of God
When is Christ returning?	any day now	nobody knows for certain
What is the Christian church?	group of those who are preparing for Christs return	those receiving the message of Christianity
Who can be part of the church?	only Jews	Gentiles as well as Jews
What is the proper way of Christian worship?	in Synagogues and Jewish temple services	the Christian church and the Christian rituals

Later we will see the changes within Indian religion, which are in many ways even more startling. Therefore, those who cling to the idea that religion has to be related to a particular culture and its specific practices or rituals will always have some difference with someone else's conception. This point of view may be considered as "dogmatic" [37] or "orthodox." [38] In the three stages of religion, Myth, Ritual and Mysticism, culture belongs to the myth and ritual stages of religious practice, the most elementary levels.

An important theme, which will be developed throughout this volume, is the understanding of complete religion, that is, in its three aspects, *mythological, ritual* and *metaphysical* or the *mystical experience*. At the first level, a human being learns the stories and traditions of the religion. At the second level, rituals are learned and practiced. At the third level the practitioner, now called a spiritual aspirant, is led to actually go beyond myths and rituals and to attain the ultimate goal of religion. This is an important principle, because many religions present different aspects of philosophy at different levels, and an uninformed onlooker may label it as primitive or idolatrous, etc., without understanding what is going on.

For example, Hinduism[39] and Ancient Egyptian religion present polytheism and duality at the first two levels of religious practice. However, at the third level, mysticism, the practitioner is made to understand that all of the gods and goddesses being worshipped do not exist in fact, but are in reality aspects of the single, transcendental Supreme Self. This means that at the mystical level of religious practice the concept of religion and its attendant symbols must also be left behind, that is to say, transcended. The mystical disciplines constitute the technology or means by which the myth and ritual of religion, and the spiritual philosophy can be developed to its highest level.

In contrast, orthodox religions present images as if they are in fact mundane realities as well as transcendental reality. By definition, idolatry is the presentation of an image of the divine as if it is a reality. Therefore, orthodox traditions are the true idolaters and mystical religions, since they do not ascribe absolute or abiding qualities to their images, are not idolatrous.

Myth: The Fluid Language of the Unconscious Mind

Myth is a fluid language. It is the language of concepts, which are represented through the symbols, themes, legends, traditions, heritage and philosophy contained in the myth. Myths are representations of the higher transcendental spiritual experience. These representations are manifestations of intuitional truths that are mirrored in the unconscious mind as the transcendent spirit projects into time and space. As it relates to something otherworldly, the language of myth is necessarily free from the encumbrance of historicity, race, politics, economics, gender, or even culture. Thus, the cultural manifestation of spiritual concepts are not the meaning or essence of the myth, but rather its mode of manifestation within that particular culture. Accordingly, myth is highly interchangeable in a way that the written word is not. This is why concepts are more easily communicated between people who speak a different language than translated words; concept is closer to reality than words. The more a concept is concretized, codified, interpreted as historical events or made into dogmatic teachings and imposed on culture, their power to communicate the transcendental nature of self is subverted. Then myth becomes a whipping tool to use against political, religious or social enemies. At this level, true religion cannot be practiced. The myth degrades to the level of dogmatism which expresses as narrow-mindedness, social pride, nationalism, sexism, prejudice, intolerance, and racism. Consequently, it is important and at times, a matter of life (peace) and death (war), to understand the deeper psychological and spiritual nature and purpose of myth.

The philosophy of spiritual transcendence and Enlightenment through mythic living did not begin with the dawn of the Dynastic Period in Ancient Egyptian history. The evidence from ancient texts and the History of Manetho show that the Ancient Egyptian history which is known and written about in modern times is only the descendent of a much more ancient era of Kamitan civilization which began many thousands of years before the dynastic era. The Ancient Egyptian sages recognized that the concept of a Supreme Being cannot be circumscribed by one image or symbol and thus, many were used, but also the symbols of other peoples were recognized and respected as manifestations of that same reality.

Cultural Interactions, Their Effect on the Emergence of New Religions and The Adoption of Myths, Symbols and Traditions from one Culture to Another

How Do Cultures Interact?

How do people from different cultures interact? How do religions borrow and or adopt myths, symbols, philosophies or traditions from each other? Several examples from history will be used here to show how spirituality, as an aspect of one culture, was influenced by other cultures. The following essays relate documented historical accounts of cultural interactions of the past between two or more civilizations. They are included to illustrate how the process of cultural interaction leads to cultural exchanges, adoptions, inculturations, etc., as well as the emergence of new religions and philosophies out of teachings received from other cultures. They will also serve to provide insight into the manner in which ancient African history has diffused into present day cultures by introducing various basic principles of cultural interaction and how these interactions are to be recognized and studied.

Cultural Interactions Between Christianity and Neterian Religion and Mysticism

In the case of Christianity it has been amply shown that several factors present in Ancient Egyptian Religion were adopted directly as the Christian religion developed in Egypt and the land of Canaan (now known as Palestine). In fact the church itself admits this as the late mythologist Joseph Campbell relates in an interview with Bill Moyers.[40] (Note: Highlighted portions are by Ashby)

> M O Y E R S: If we go back into antiquity, do we find images of the Madonna as the mother of the savior child?
>
> CAMPBELL: The antique model for the Madonna, actually, is Isis with Horus at her breast.
>
> MOYERS: Isis?
>
> CAMPBELL: In Egyptian iconography, Isis represents the throne. The Pharaoh sits on the throne, which is Isis, as a child on its mother's lap.[41] And so, when you stand before the cathedral of Chartres, you will see over one of the portals of the western front an image of the Madonna as the throne upon which the child Jesus sits and blesses the world as its emperor. That is precisely the image that has come down to us from most ancient Egypt. *The early fathers and the early artists took over these images intentionally.*
>
> MOYERS: The Christian fathers took the image of Isis?
>
> CAMPBELL: Definitely. They say so themselves. Read the text where it is declared that *"those forms which were merely mythological forms in the past are now actual and incarnate in our Savior."* The mythologies here referred to were of the dead and resurrected god: Attis, Adonis, Gilgamesh, Osiris,[42] one after the other. The death and resurrection of the god is everywhere associated with the moon, which dies and is resurrected every month. It is for two nights, or three days dark, and we have Christ for two nights, or three days in the tomb.
>
> No one knows what the actual date of the birth of Jesus might have been, but it has been put on what used to be the date of the winter solstice, December 25,[43] when the nights begin to be shorter and the days longer. That is the moment of the rebirth of light. That was exactly the date of the birth of the Persian God of light, Mithra, Sol, the Sun.

Along with the iconographies, symbols and rituals mentioned above, Christianity adopted many other aspects of the Neterian Religion such as the Ankh-cross symbol, the anointing, the resurrection, the mutilation of the savior, the triune nature of the spirit (The Trinity), the Eucharist, as well as other symbols, motifs and teachings. [44] When the Roman Emperor Justinian closed the Neo-Platonic academies in 529 A.C.E. along with other spiritual and religious institutions which were considered by him to be cult or pagan systems, such as that of the Ancient Egyptian goddess Aset (Isis), Orthodox Christianity was closing its doors on the last links to the mystical philosophy of the traditions from which they had adopted so much. This led to a situation wherein the esoteric meanings of many symbols and metaphysical teachings were lost. Still, their subtle influences on Christianity persisted through medieval times and continued into the present because in order to be accepted, the Orthodox Church had to adopt many customs and symbols of other religions. The remnants of the Ancient Egyptian and other traditions of the past are still inherent in modern Orthodox Christianity as it is practiced today. The Christian church co-opted the customs and traditions of other religions in order to be able to convince the followers of the other religions that Christianity had those symbols and customs previous to their "pagan" religions, and therefore, they should abandon their religions in favor of the only "true" and "original" religion, Orthodox Christianity.

The evidence given by the Christian tradition and its documents suggests that many icons such as the images of the Madonna and child (Mary and Jesus) were taken as is during the early years of Christianity, renamed (rededicated as it were) and used in Christian worship. This practice may be described as *inculturation*,[45] also known as *co-optation*.[46] These terms relate to the process of adopting symbols, traditions and rituals from other religions and calling them Christian, which were officially confirmed and endorsed as church policy. It is a practice that continues to be a means by which the church, as well as other groups, seek to expand their beliefs internationally. This process was instituted in the time of the early development of the Christian church. A prime example of inculturation is seen in the actions of Pope St Gregory the Great, who in a letter given to priests written in 601 A.C.E. endorsed this strategy as a means to attract followers from other spiritual traditions. He writes:

> "It is said that the men of this nation are accustomed to sacrificing oxen. It is necessary that this custom be converted into a Christian rite. On the day of the dedication of the [pagan] temples thus changed into churches, and similarly for the festivals of the saints, whose relics will be placed there, you should allow them, as in the past, to build structures of foliage around these same churches. They shall bring to the churches their animals, and kill them, no longer as offerings to the devil, but for Christian banquets in name and honor of God, to whom after satiating themselves, they will give thanks. Only thus, by preserving for men some of the worldly joys, will you lead them thus more easily to relish the joys of the spirit."

When the Roman Empire took control of Egypt, the Egyptian religion spread throughout the Roman Empire. However, later on, when Christianity took hold in Rome, the Ancient Egyptian religion and other mystical religions became an obstacle to the Christian Church which had developed divergent ideas about spirituality, and also to the Roman government which sought to consolidate the empire under Rome. Also, the plagiarism of the Ancient Egyptian symbols, traditions and holidays could not be effective if there were living Ancient Egyptian Priests and Priestesses to tell and show the truth about the origins of those symbols, traditions and holidays. Further, Ancient Egyptian religion served to refer people to Egypt as well as to mystical spiritual practice. In short, Christianity could not survive as a cult among many other more ancient religions, so it was necessary to dispose of the competition. The most politically expedient way to do this was to close all mystical religious temples.

At the end of the fourth century A.C.E., the Roman emperor Theodosius decreed that all religions except Christianity were to be stopped, and that all forms of Christianity besides that of the "Byzantine throne" would also cease to exist. During this time The Temple of Isis (Aset) at Philae in Upper Egypt (deep south of Egypt) temporarily escaped the enforcement of the decree. Consequently, the hieroglyphic inscriptions of this Temple, dated at 394 A.C.E., are the last known Kamitan hieroglyphics to be recorded. Also, the last demotic inscriptions there date to 452 A.C.E. It was not until the sixth century A.C.E. that Emperor Justinian entered a second decree that effectively stopped all mystical religious practices in the Roman Empire. This means that not only were the Mystery-Yoga schools and temples to be closed, but also all forms of mystical Christianity which did not agree with the style of Christianity espoused in Rome were to be abolished. Therefore, the Gnostic Christians (Christians who practiced mystical Christianity), were persecuted and their churches rededicated to Roman Catholicism. Much of their writings were destroyed. Thus, it is evident that the Ancient Egyptian teachings were being practiced and taught well into the Christian era.

What is Civilization, What is the Difference Between Civilization and Culture and What Causes the Rise and Fall of Civilizations?

In order to continue our journey of discovery into the origins of civilization, religion and yoga philosophy, we will need a reference point. Science offers, not an absolute, but a useful reference point to understand the progress towards human civilization and human evolution. It is important to understand the classifications of ancient societies as they are used in modern scholarship in order to better understand their meaning in context.

In anthropology, civilization is defined as an advanced socio-political stage of cultural evolution, whereby a centralized government (over a city, ceremonial center, or larger region called a state) is supported by the taxation of surplus production, and rules the agricultural, and often mercantile base. Those who do not produce food become specialists who govern, lead religious ritual, impose and collect taxes, record the past and present, plan and have executed monumental public works (irrigation systems, roads, bridges, buildings, tombs), and elaborate and formalize the style and traditions of the society. These institutions are based on the use of leisure time to develop writing, mathematics, the sciences, engineering, architecture, philosophy, and the arts. Archeological remains of cities and ceremonial centers are evaluated to determine the degree of civilization of that culture, based on the trappings of both style and content.[47] The American Heritage Dictionary defines civilization as:

> civ·i·li·za·tion *n.* **1.** An advanced state of intellectual, cultural, and material development in human society, marked by progress in the arts and sciences, the extensive use of writing, and the appearance of complex political and social institutions.

Strictly speaking, civilization is defined as a highly developed human society with structured division of labor,[48] an advanced state of intellectual, cultural, and material development, marked by progress in the arts and sciences, the extensive use of writing, and the appearance of complex political and social institutions.[49] In simple terms, civilization means acting in a civil manner towards other people, which implies cooperation in the furtherance of community goals and the upliftment of the individuals within the civilization. The earliest "highly developed human societies" developed in ancient times out of Neolithic farming societies. These in turn developed out of Mesolithic societies, and these out of Paleolithic societies. Thus, civilization or the lack thereof, can be considered in many ways. Prior to the existence of farming, human beings were considered to be "hunter gatherers," primitive groups fending for food, territory and the right to mate, with little conception of what lies beyond the basic survival activities of life. Since time is constantly spent in competition for food and warding off potential danger, there is little opportunity for the higher aspects of life such as art, religion or philosophy. At most these factors will not progress beyond a primitive level under such conditions. It is thought that the development of pottery, which follows agriculture, signifies a major step towards the establishment of a civilized society. The invention of writing is regarded as a very high development of civilization. For many years it was thought to have been first invented by the Sumerians, but the recent evidence shows that the invention of Ancient Egyptian writing and Ancient Egyptian architecture predate Sumerian civilization. The following report by the British team excavating the Ancient Egyptian city of Abdu (modern Abydos) dispels the misconceptions related to the first origins of writing in history.

> "Until recently it was thought that the earliest writing system was invented by the Sumerians in Mesopotamia towards the end of the fourth millennium BC and that the idea was borrowed by the Egyptians at the beginning of the First Dynasty (c.3100 BC). However, recent discoveries at Abydos have shown that the Egyptians had an advanced system of writing even earlier than the Mesopotamians, some 150 years before Narmer. Remarkably, there is no evidence that this writing developed from a more primitive pictographic stage. Already, at the very beginning, it incorporated signs for sounds.
> Unlike Mesopotamian writing, which can be shown to have gradually evolved through a number of stages, beginning as an accounting system, Egyptian writing appears to have been deliberately invented in a more-or-less finished form, its underlying principles fully in place right from the outset. A parallel for such a process is known from more recent times: in AD 1444 the Korean script (still widely regarded as one of the world's most efficient) was invented by order of the king, who assembled a group of scholars for the purpose.

In Egypt this invention corresponds with the birth of the Egyptian state, and its growing administrative and bureaucratic needs."[50]

However, the aforementioned criteria denoting the presence or absence of "civilization" relate mostly to technological developments and increased sociopolitical complexity. Complexity in society and highly advanced technology cannot in themselves be used to determine the presence of civilization, because many cultures have had these in the past and they have fallen into oblivion (forgetfulness, unconsciousness) nevertheless. Some examples of these are the Greek Empire, the Roman Empire, the Ottoman Empire, the British Empire, etc. And yes, what happened to the Ancient Egyptian civilization? If civilization is an advancement in society, then it would follow that the advanced civilization must be doing something better, more efficient, that would promote not only prosperity, but also its own longevity. So what were these "civilizations" missing that allowed them to fall? Where did they go wrong?

Albert Schweitzer (1875-1965), the German-born theologian, philosopher, musicologist, medical missionary, and Nobel laureate, was one of the first Western scholars to examine the issue of civilization and the causes for its downfall as well as the means for its maintenance. As a missionary doctor in Africa, prior to and after the First World War, he gained valuable experiences while treating the sick there. He would doubtless have had occasion to experience the misery imposed on Africans due to the colonial system, and also he would have experienced the African concept of Ubuntu (humanity) and caring for family.

From 1917-1918 Schweitzer, who was a German national, was incarcerated in France, which was at war with Germany. During this period he wrote two volumes which became a projected philosophical study of civilization called *The Decay and the Restoration of Civilization* and *Civilization and Ethics* (both 1923). These volumes were concerned with ethical thought in history. Schweitzer maintained that modern civilization is in decay because it lacks the will to love. As a solution to this problem he suggested that society should develop a philosophy based on what he termed "reverence for life," embracing with compassion all forms of life.[6] It is interesting to note that Schweitzer's solution, a return to love, is the primary concept behind the African philosophies of *Ubuntu* (caring for humanity) and Maat (righteousness in society and caring for humanity). He was also exposed to Eastern mysticism which also exhorts the necessity to develop the capacity for compassion and love in order to attain spiritual enlightenment. He attempted to discover the mystical love upon which Christianity is founded and to raise the awareness of this aspect of Christianity, as he saw the lack of such awareness in the Western practice of the Christian religion as contributing to Western Culture's inability to love humanity. His other works include the theological studies *Indian Thought and Its Development* (1935; trans. 1936), *The Kingdom of God and Primitive Christianity* (1967; trans. 1968), *The Mysticism of Paul the Apostle* (1930; trans. 1931) and the autobiographical *Out of My Life and Thought* (1931; trans. 1933).

The problem of inability to love and care in a civilization develops when it is not managed or ceases to be managed by leaders with the capacity to care for others, to be compassionate to others. It is often not realized that the concept of the word civilization includes the term *Civility* which means 1. Courteous behavior; politeness. 2. A courteous act or utterance. -*American Heritage Dictionary*. Caring and compassion are expressions of a spiritual consciousness, an awareness of the Divinity in all. Therefore, mystical studies (spiritual perspective encompassing all humanity transcending religion) are imperative for any true leader of a society, and any society who does not have such leaders will be bent on greed, power and pleasure seeking as opposed to human and ethical issues. Such a society will be eventually doomed to self-destruction because this way of life promotes degraded culture and selfishness instead of respect for life. Consequently, under these conditions, people develop the capacity to hurt each other to achieve their own material goals, perpetuating a cycle of vice, violence, mistrust and hatred, leading to war, disease, poverty and suffering. This of course cannot be called "civilization." It is a form of culture which is struggling to discover itself, and in the process, like a child playing with matches, it burns itself and others in the process of its learning experience.

---

[6]"Schweitzer, Albert," *Microsoft® Encarta® Encyclopedia 2000*. © 1993-1999 Microsoft Corporation. All rights reserved.

AFRICAN ORIGINS Of Civilization, Religion, Yoga Mystical Spirituality And Ethics Philosophy

So civilization means the coming together of a group of people to organize themselves and promote the general good. This they do by using technology to facilitate their activities, promote health and the perpetuation of life. What sustains civilization is an ethical social conscience. The ethical social conscience comes from an underlying spiritual basis that recognizes all life a sacred. The philosophical insight which allows a human being to realize that all life is sacred is the fact that the universe promotes the continuation of life in all respects, animal, vegetable and mineral. The spiritual consciousness is predicated upon the idea that even death is not the final reality. This can be proven through the experience of spiritual enlightenment. The process of spiritual enlightenment is achieved when a human being discovers what lies beyond their physical mortal existence. As we will see, African Religion was the first to proclaim this discovery and the means for any human being to achieve its realization. This (spiritual enlightenment) is the authentic basis for civilization. Until a society achieves this general awareness so that it is promoted in its policies, inventions, technologies and activities, (its institutions) it cannot be considered to have achieved the status of "civilized." Philosophy is the most important factor influencing the development of a culture. The way of thinking (belief system) dictates whether a culture will develop civilized institutions (promote life) or institutions that promote destruction, slavery, greed and other vices (Barbarism). Thus, "Civilization" is an outgrowth of a well ordered and spiritually based culture. A culture without a philosophy that affirms universal divinity cannot develop into a "civilization." Just as a mother expresses love for a child by taking care of the child the culture that takes care of people's social needs is a loving culture. See Appendix B for full Criteria of what constitutes a "Civilization."

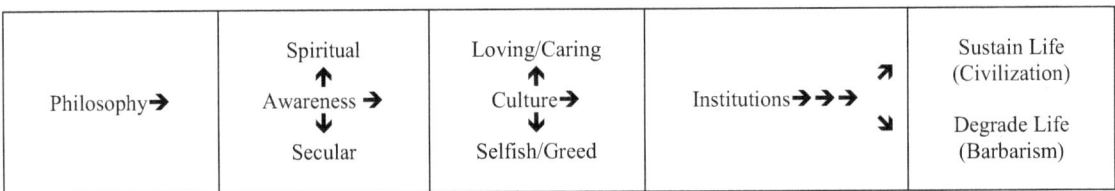

The Standard of What Constitutes Civilization

As we have seen, civilization cannot be considered just as a society possessing intellectual capacity, technology, social organization, etc. These aspects are merely the basis for civilization. Civilization is an expression of a mature culture which allows it to build social structures that perpetuate its existence. Promoting existence means promoting life. Promoting life means protecting life and the quality of life for all members of the civilization, as well as the capacity to carry on life, which means also protecting nature. Since no society or culture in the world exists in a vacuum or on an island, separate from other societies or cultures, it is erroneous to believe that a civilization can advance in the absence of the general advancement of all humanity. Therefore, a society or culture's level of civilization is judged as much by its advancement as well as its compassion and assistance to other societies or cultures. Thus, a selfish or greedy society cannot be considered by these criteria as a civilization, but rather as a degraded culture. This means that civilization is an aspect of culture. It is based on the cultural beliefs and traditions of a people and underlying this culture is a way of thinking about the world and that is based on a peoples philosophy of live, as to its meaning and purpose.

The following Standard is therefore set for the determination of a society or culture's level of civilization. In order to be considered as a civilization, the society must possess and practice the following elements of civilized culture:

1. **Mystical Philosophy** – to allow the advanced members of the society to seek for the answers to the transcendental questions of life, to Know Self.
2. **Myth** – is the means by which the ethics and spiritual consciousness are transferred from generation to generation and acts as a self-definition of culture, conveying the mythic history (folklore and legends), cultural identity and common traditions of the society.
3. **Spiritual consciousness** – religion and spirituality that affirms the universal divine essence of Creation.
4. **Ethics** – philosophy of social justice to promote equality, order, peace and harmony in the absence of which a civilization cannot function efficiently.
5. **Organization** - The society or culture must display social organization- a group of people coming together for promoting a common goal.

6. **Agriculture** - The society or culture must conduct agriculture to sustain the society and allow the members of the society to develop regular routines so as to engage in contemplative endeavors.
7. **Writing, language** or set (agreed upon) means of communication.
8. **Mathematics** – used as the foundation of distribution of resources, architecture, etc.
9. **Art** – is the means by which the ethics, spiritual consciousness and myth become visual icons for a society and through which a society views and understands the world around them. Therefore, the art of a civilization conveys its highest ethics and spiritual conscience.

The Rediscovery of Ancient Egyptian Culture, Philosophy and Religion

Many scholars and world renowned spiritual masters have recognized the strong connections between India and Ancient Africa, namely Joseph Campbell, R.A. Schwaller de Lubicz, Omraam Mikhael Aivanhov, and Swami Sivananda Radha. However, what they stated amounted to a few pieces of a larger puzzle, which until now had not been pursued in an extensive manner.

All of this comes down to the following. Mystical spiritual culture is not the exclusive property of any culture. Further, mystical philosophy operates through culture and is not culture itself. Culture relates to the mannerisms, customs, icons, language and traditions that are specific to a particular group of people. These may be related, adopted or influenced by other peoples. However, mysticism transcends cultural conventions; it is universal. Therefore, if one understands mystical philosophy, one can understand the expression of mystical philosophy through any culture. This means that if a mystic of India were to examine the mysteries of China, that mystic would understand those mysteries. Likewise, by understanding one form of mysticism, another may be recognized. Thus, by collecting the pieces of Kamitan mysticism which have survived in various cultures, the mysticism of Kamit may be fully understood and rediscovered.

Since Judaism, Christianity, Hinduism, Buddhism, Islam, Dogon and Yoruba spirituality are based on Ancient Egyptian Religion and philosophy, the basic principles of Kamitan Mysticism can be traced through those religions back to Ancient Egypt. Besides these there are other less known and less numerous groups of people who follow the Kamitan tradition and who claim to be descendants of the Ancient Egyptian living in present day Asia Minor. Their traditions also correlate with the evidences gathered from the other systems. However, in the case of Ancient Egypt and Ancient India, there is sufficient evidence to show that there was a cultural and social connection between the two cultures so close that it is possible to say that Indian spirituality is a development of Ancient Egyptian religion and mystical philosophy.

Thus, by tracing the historical connection between the two countries and tracing the evolution of culture, it is possible to see the living manifestations of Ancient Egyptian religion which are match in the major mystical principles. So even though the modern Indians may not uphold the exact disciplines or even acknowledge the Kamitan origins of their systems of spirituality, nevertheless the living Kamitan tradition can be discerned in the Indian traditions, customs and symbols.

Therefore, not only is it possible to recreate Kamitan religion and mysticism through studies based on present forms of mysticism, but it may be said that the Kamitan tradition never ceased and only transformed. So this work is more along the lines of outlining the essential elements of Kamitan religion and culture as they survive in present day cultures rather than recreating or deducing based on modern unrelated systems of spirituality. The key to the rediscovery of Ancient Egyptian spirituality was due to the understanding that is a yogic mystical system of spirituality whose goal is to promote spiritual enlightenment. This is why past attempts at reconstructing Ancient Egyptian religion were frustrated.

Thus it has been possible to understand the mysteries of Ancient Egypt as an original source for many of the most fundamental teachings surviving not just in Hinduism but also Ancient Greek Philosophy, Judaism and Christianity. So, the research that led to the Egyptian Yoga book series and the revival of Kamitan culture was like tracing back to the source, like discovering the seed from which a plant has grown. Also, in knowing the seed it is possible to know the plant (spirituality) and its branches (the religions) better and vise versa, thereby illuminating them in modern times with the depth of their own deeper history which leads back to the place where all life and civilization was born.

AFRICAN ORIGINS Of Civilization, Religion, Yoga Mystical Spirituality And Ethics Philosophy

The Methods to Rediscover and Reconstruct a Culture and its Civilization

The fundamental aspects of a culture (its categories of cultural expression) can be rediscovered through the following methods of cultural anthropology[7].

1. Studying the writings left by the ancient "extinct" culture itself (if any).
2. Studying the traditions albeit with diluted knowledge that are carried on by the descendants (if any).
3. Studying the other cultures (if any) carry on some of the customs of the "extinct" culture in the form of traditions and or legends of the "extinct" culture.
4. Studying other religions (if any) that have adopted symbols, tenets (philosophies) or rituals of the "extinct" culture.
5. Studying the other cultures (if any) that have had contact with the "extinct" culture and which have described the "extinct" culture.

Figure 3: The African Family Tree of Cultural Interactions

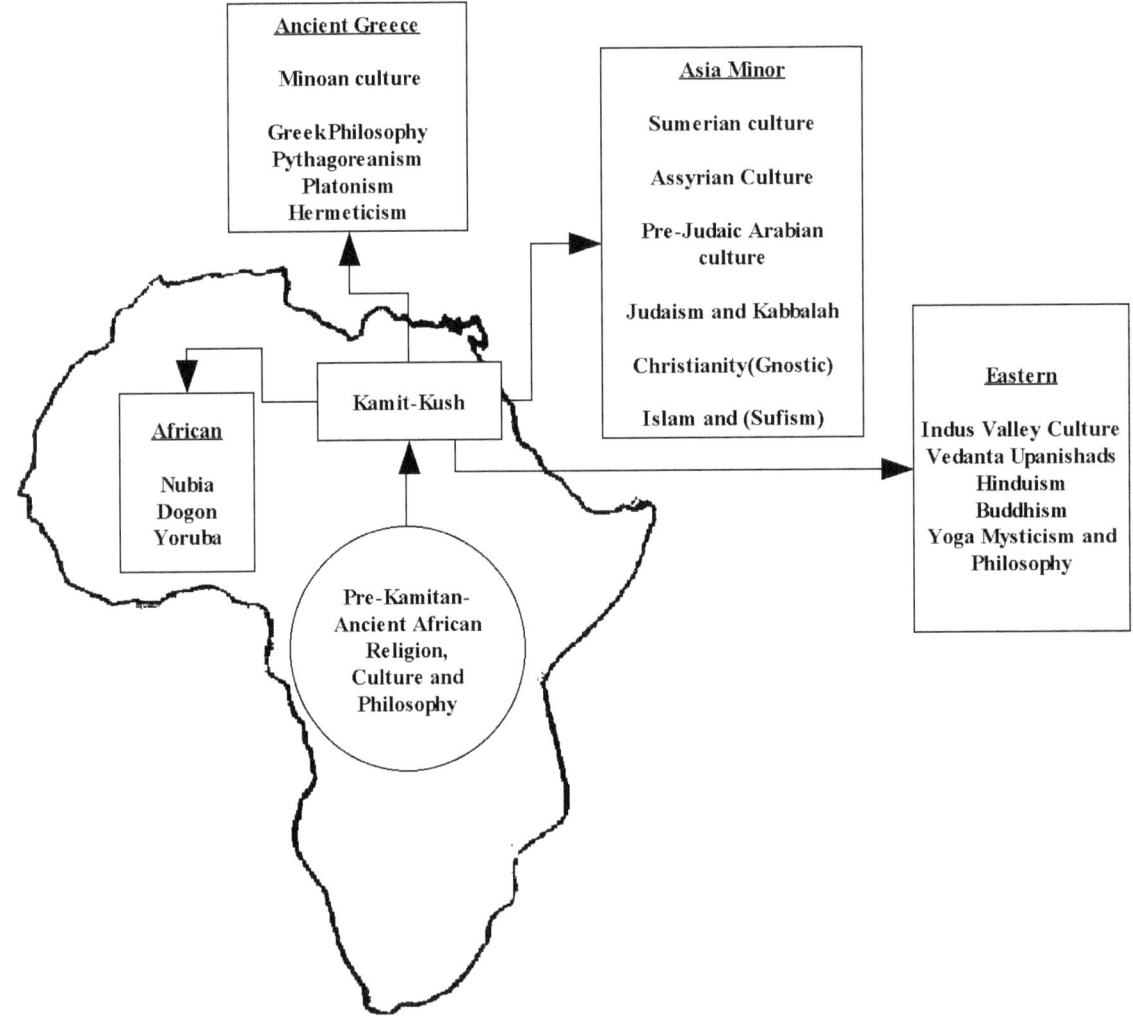

---

[7] The scientific study of the origin, the behavior, and the physical, social, and cultural development of human beings.

AFRICAN ORIGINS Of Civilization, Religion, Yoga Mystical Spirituality And Ethics Philosophy

Linguists and others who study "dead" languages are always on the look out for a "Rosetta Stone" that will allow them to decipher the language they are studying. The Rosetta Stone is a slap upon which an edict was written on behalf of the King of Egypt. The special thing about it is that it was written in three different languages, Hieroglyphic, Demotic and Greek. Since the closing of the Ancient Egyptian temples at about 450 A.C.E. had forced the hieroglyphic text into disuse it has become forgotten by the world. Even if the letters of a word are understood a language may not be understood because there is no context to understand the meaning of each world and then to relate them to each other in order to formulate rational sentences in order to derive ideas and thoughts. Such an example of the Meroitic language. Its letters have been deciphered but the language remains a mystery. Since Greek was still understood and since the texts are a translation of the same message. It was possible to discover the "context" of the images (words) upon the slab. This led to the decipherment of the Ancient Egyptian Hieroglyphic language.

In like fashion, mythologists search for "Factors of Cultural Expression" the methods in which the "Categories of Cultural Expression" such as symbols, artifacts, myths, architecture, traditions, customs, etc., are used. The Categories are the fundamental aspects of all cultures but these may have different forms of manifestation and thus may not relate to each other. If the factors match then this provides a context in which to understand the Categories of the no longer "dead" culture. Taking this a step further, when the previously "Dead" culture has left a language it is possible to verify the findings of the Cultural Anthropology studies. That is, the context that has been established can be verified by the ideas and thoughts contained in the language of the "previously dead culture." Ancient Egypt is such a case. These studies have yielded a framework through which to understand and bring back to life the culture of Ancient Africa. Having decoded the language of myth, a mythologist can understand when the fundamental principles of myth are being espoused and {she/he} can also determine the nature of those expositions in order to see if the methods used coincide with others and thereby establish relationships between myths of different peoples. Joseph Campbell and others accomplished this work successfully in their areas of study. The same success can be achieved in other Categories of Cultural Expression besides Myth. When the Factors of varied Categories are studied a quite complete picture can emerge of what the previously dead culture was all about, and this of course can lead to a revival of that culture.

So the objective of this kind of study is to discover which factors of Cultural Expression correlate (match) between the "extinct" culture and the "living" culture. Those matching Factors of Cultural Expression (aspects of culture that are proven as borrowings from one culture to another) constitute practices in common between the ancient culture and the modern culture. A partial match such as adoption of a symbol but not the meaning of a symbol denotes a possible initial adoption of the symbol and a loss of the interpretation over time due to cultural changes. Thus, an "extinct" culture whose customs, traditions, teachings and symbols have been transferred to writings, descendants, other cultures religions or philosophies cannot be said to be "dead" or "extinct" since these aspects of culture "live" on albeit in a dormant state in the present day "living" culture.

The methods of cultural anthropology outlined above are very difficult to apply in the study of most ancient cultures. This is because their impact was not felt to the degree of leaving those traces of traditions, symbols etc. with descendants of other cultures. Sometimes they have no writings about themselves for researchers to go on. The writings are the primary source material for discovering a people. Archeology is an inexact profession and cannot be relied upon completely for such determinations. There need to be language studies, cultural anthropology studies and if possible hard science evidences such as geological evidences in order to confirm the findings of archeology. Fortunately, in the case of Ancient Egypt, unlike the case of the Sumerians, we are in the position to engage in all of the methods of study outlined above and this gives us the opportunity to reconstruct Kamitan culture and thereby also discover the source of many modern cultures and religions. So in order to proceed with our study we will need to outline what the fundamental aspects of cultural expression are and how do judge cultural interactions.

Cultural Category - Factor Correlation System Application

Theoretical Methodology for the Comparison of Cultures

A myth in its pristine state is by definition specific to a given human environment. How it fares from then on (its "life;' "afterlife'" survival, transposition, revival, rediscovery, or whatever) is a matter of historical accident. It follows that the study of any specific past body of myth has to be mainly a historical discipline employing written sources, whereas contemporary myth can be pursued by the methods of field anthropology.[51]

In the book *Comparative Mythology*, (quoted above), the author introduces certain formats for the study of comparative mythology, beginning with the premise that a myth is "specific to a given human environment." If human environment is taken to mean culture, then it follows that the study of myth needs to be carried out within the context of the culture, using the parameters of the culture. In other words, the myth needs to be studied from the perspective of someone living in the culture and not as an outsider. That is, a student of myth needs to practice and live the myth, to be part of the myth. Only in this way will the myth be fully understood. Otherwise, there will be a superimposition of outside cultural bias from the researcher or student on the myth being studied. This is one of the most difficult problems for any scientist to overcome, how to fully understand the object of study. The usual logic in Western scientific methodology is to strive for "objectivity."

Modern science has now accepted that research examining or studying "physical reality" cannot exist outside of the person conducting the experiments. An older theory held that the person conducting the experiment could be considered separate and apart from the phenomena being observed. Modern science now holds that nature and all phenomena occur because of an experimenter's ability to conceptualize the phenomena and to interpret it. Therefore, the observer is inevitably part of the phenomena being observed. Consequently, modern science now uses a new term for the experimenter. The new term is <u>Participant.</u> Thus, the experimenter is really a participant in the experiment because his or her consciousness conceives, determines, perceives, interprets and understands it. No experiment or observed phenomena in nature can occur without someone to conceive that something is happening, determine that something is happening, perceive that something is happening (through instruments or the senses), and finally to interpret what has happened and to understand that interpretation.

Since everything in the universe is connected at some underlying level and since human existence and human consciousness is dependent upon relationships in order to function, then it follows that objectivity is not a realistic attitude for most human beings, including scientists. The only way to achieve objectivity is to transcend "human" consciousness. That is, one must extricate one's egoistic vision of life, which based on the limitations of the mind and senses, by discovering one's "transcendental" nature. This grants one the experience of knowing the true, unchanging and unaffected nature and essence of existence beyond the limited capacities of the mind and senses. In this capacity one can temporarily identify with the object, any object of study, and achieve a complete knowledge of the subject. This capacity has been the legacy of science and the mystical disciplines, for concentration on any subject is the key to discovering the nature of that subject. However, the mystical disciplines go a step beyond in allowing the scientists to discover their essential nature as one with the object of study. Therefore, mystical training is indispensable in the study of any subject and the acquisition of the knowledge of the essential nature of a subject or object. This form of philosophy is antithetical to the orthodox practice of the "scientific method" but until the scientific method is adjusted to incorporate the training of the mystical disciplines, the knowledge gained from the sciences will be limited to the capacities of the logical mind and senses as well as the technological instruments that may be devised to extend the range of those limited, and therefore illusory, human abilities. So the historical and field anthropology[52] disciplines of study must be guided by the mystical experience.

When comparing two given cultures, we are not only concerned with the superficial aspects of their cultural expression, but also the underlying foundations of these. The fundamental core of any culture is its outlook or philosophy on life. This underlying philosophy gives rise to the varied forms of cultural expression just as the many leaves and branches of a tree arise from a seed (common origin). The mystical philosophy of a given culture is translated by the sages and saints of that culture into an easily understandable and transmittable myth using the cultural factors available to them within that particular culture. Therefore, a sage in Kamitan culture may espouse a teaching using metaphors particular to

AFRICAN ORIGINS Of Civilization, Religion, Yoga Mystical Spirituality And Ethics Philosophy

Kamitan culture while a Christian sage may espouse the same teaching while using a different cultural metaphor which is particular to Christian culture. The myth is supported and sustained by the plots and story-lines. Next, it is supported by the rituals and traditions associated with them. The rituals and traditions are supported by the combined factors of cultural expression including: architecture, iconography, artifacts and ritual objects (amulets, etc.), spiritual scriptures, language, form and function of objects produced by the culture, etc. Thus, when there is an overwhelming number and quality of synchronicities between the factors of expression in two cultures, a commonality in their underlying philosophies will also be discovered.

How the philosophy of a culture expresses through the cultural factors of that culture:

Architecture, iconography, artifacts and ritual objects (amulets, etc.)
↑
Form and function of objects produced by the culture
↑
Ritual and Tradition
↑
Plots and story-lines of the myth
↑
Spiritual scriptures
↑
Language (linguistics-phonetics)
↑
Myth
↑
Mystical Philosophy

Through studies based on the factors and parameters listed above, it has been possible to show that there are at least four main world religions that have a strong basis in a common origin which transcends the cursory or superficial levels of similarity. These traditions are the Kamitan, Ancient Greek, Hindu, and Judeo-Christian. I have already presented and in-depth exploration of the Kamitan/Greek connection in my book *From Egypt to Greece* and the Kamitan/Judeo-Christian connection in my book *The Mystical Journey From Jesus to Christ*. Through these kinds of study, it is possible to bring unity to disparaging and conflicting points of view which lead to dissent, disagreement and misunderstanding that are based on ignorance, adherence to dogma and cultural-theological pride[53] and orthodoxy, instead of the deeper nature and purpose of culture which is to lead human beings to spiritual enlightenment. By such studies it is possible to lead open-minded people to understand the purpose of religion and to discover the value of all traditions which are ultimately seeking to accomplish the same task, to bring harmony, peace and order to the world and to allow human beings of all cultures to discover the supreme and essential nature of existence.

The Standard for Determining Whether or Not a Correlation is Present

Determining an objective standard for any critical study is an enormously difficult task since the human mind is ultimately what must be satisfied in a particular judgment. That is, when we are trying to determine some kind of rule or guideline to follow which will lead to an unbiased conclusion, the mind of the observer, with his/her preconceived notions, desires, leanings, etc., comes into play, and what one person may consider reasonable, another may regard as groundless. For example, a person may think a color is especially suited for a particular room while another person may say that that color is exactly the opposite of what should be used. Who is right? Well, in this question there is an arbitrary, aesthetic factor which draws upon a person's particular upbringing, particular experiences, particular education, etc. Another example seen often in modern culture is a situation where one person sees a business opportunity as clear as day, while others do not. That person will later capitalize on that opportunity. Was the opportunity there all along or was it a coincidence? In addition, we recognize factors in life that cannot be objectively proven, and yet we "know" they exist. There is a transcendental reality about them that we recognize. When that businessperson, with their training and intuition, spots an opportunity, they perceive it and register it as a reality. In this manner, scientists using training, data collection and intuition in order to "discern" the underlying truth of myths, can discover the correlating factors between cultures.

Nonetheless, in the study of science, one would expect the process to be more "objective," being "either right or wrong," but even in the sciences, the ego and its prejudices can impinge on reason. So what kind of standard can be used to discern between coincidences and synchronous correlations between cultures? Any standard to be used must be based on verifiable evidence and logical analysis, but also on reason. However, if unreasonable people review the evidence, no amount of evidence will suffice, because their minds are already prejudiced.

There is often much confusion and conflict in the world due to disagreements and misunderstandings. Many have cited the lack of reason as a primary cause of human conflict. But what is reason? The following dictionary and encyclopedic definitions may provide some guidance.

> **reason:** 1 to think logically about; think out systematically; analyze 2 to argue, conclude, or infer: now usually with a clause introduced by *that* as the object 3 to support, justify, etc. with reasons 4 to persuade or bring by reasoning.
>
> **reasoning:** (-i) *n.* 1 the drawing of inferences or conclusions from known or assumed facts; use of reason 2 the proofs or reasons resulting from this.
>
> **in reason**. With good sense or justification; reasonably. **Within reason**: Within the bounds of good sense or practicality.

In the context of the definitions above, reason is that faculty in human consciousness wherein two minds can arrive at a conclusion that is within the bounds of practical reality based on known or assumed facts which justify or support the conclusions drawn. But how is it possible for people to apply those standards and draw rational or reasonable conclusions? Certainly, maturity in life and qualitative experience in human interactions, (i.e. based on honesty, truth, righteousness, justice and universal love) scholarship and balance in life are prerequisites for promoting soundness of the intellect and an understanding of reality within the sphere of human interactions and social intercommunications. In order to promote social order and harmony, the ancient disciplines of righteousness, known as Maat in Kamit and Dharma in India, were devised. This shows that from ancient times, the necessity of promoting reason (ability to think and act by truth) as a mental faculty, in the philosophical disciplines as in government, was understood and appreciated.

Ancient Egyptian Hermetic Philosophy

> "Though all men suffer fated things, those led by reason (guided by the Higher Intellect), do not endure suffering with the rest; but since they've freed themselves from viciousness, not being bad, they do not suffer bad. Though having thought fornication or murder but not having committed these, the Mind-led man will suffer just as though he had committed fornication, and though he be no murderer, as though he had committed murder, because there was will to commit these things."[54]

Gita: Chapter 2: Samkhya Yogah--The Yoga of Knowledge

> "63. From anger there arises delusion, from delusion loss of memory, from loss of memory one loses the function of pure reason, and from the loss of reason one heads towards destruction."[55]

Reasoning involves objectivity and detachment. The parties must strive to pursue truth as opposed to proving a point for their own ends. The highest and best way to promote truth is to promote humility and effacement of the egoistic nature. Also, there should be a deference to evidence and reason as opposed to argument and supposition or emotion. These failings are the sources of partisanship, fanaticism and disagreement. Reasoning should follow logical thinking, and logical thinking should be based on evidence. Thereby the conclusions drawn from evidences and rational thinking about those evidences will receive the correct (reasonable) weight. In this way, the misconceived notions, misjudgments, biases and desires of the deeper aspects of the personality will not impinge on the faculty of reason. Then such a person will be able to reason with other reasonable persons and arrive at reasonable conclusions or courses of action. So while defining "reason" is an abstract endeavor, certainly mature persons can rationally understand that it is a reality in principle. Life, culture and civilization cannot exist in the absence of reason, for even when there is internal disagreement with a decision or course of action, reasonable people understand they must place their personal desires aside for the collective good, or they must simply realize that other people deserve equal consideration. That is, even in arguments where two individuals may disagree, there can be an objective resolution of the disagreement. One or both parties may choose to refrain from allowing animosity to develop and to remain patient until an answer emerges from the situation or question itself, while in the mean time assisting in the development of stronger arguments which are supportable over time until the validity or invalidity of a conclusion may no longer be avoided. The calmness of a mind unfettered by emotion and desire, a hallmark of a well-adjusted self-realized human being, allows a person to disagree with a conclusion while maintaining respect for the person advancing it. This allows people to live together and organize in order to work together.

So, for the purposes of this section, as throughout this book, the opinions of scholars will not be used in place of actual evidences or if the conclusions of scholars are used they will be supported by evidences, and "reasonable arguments" related to those evidences. In this manner, it is hoped that the discussion will be elevated to the determination of the evidences as opposed to debates over the bias of the scholars and their opinions. There are certain valid conclusions that can be drawn from the totality of evidences; these will be presented separately as summaries, conclusions or epilogues.

Methodology for the Comparisons Between Cultures in Order to Determine the Correlations Between Cultures

The methodology for understanding mythology and its purpose, which has been presented in the previous section as well as those which will follow, present myth and metaphor as abstract principles that manifest through cultural factors in the form of recurrent themes. While these are subject to some interpretation, the possibility for bias becomes reduced as the associated factors add up to support the original conjecture about the particular factor being compared. In other words, *single event proposed correlations* (correlations between cultural factors that are alleged but not yet proven or supported) between cultures can often be explained away as coincidences. However, when those correlations are supported by related factors or when those correlations are present in the framework of other correlations, then the position of bias or simple disbelief is less tenable. The basis for the objective standard will be set forth in the following logical principles which indicate congruence between the two cultures. In order to study and compare the Kamitan and Indian cultures, we will make use of the categories of cultural expression.

As explained earlier, in determining the common elements of different religions, there are several factors that can be used as criteria to determine whether or not cultures had common origins. If cultures are related, they will use common stories or other common factors or patterns to express the main doctrines of the religion or spiritual path, social philosophy, etc. These are listed below. Before proceeding to the items being compared, the criteria used to compare them must be understood. The following section introduces the categories of cultural expression factors and some subdivisions within them.

The Possible Standards for Use in Determining the Correlations Between Cultures

The Scientific Method for Studying Correlations Between Cultures

> "Scientific Method, general logic and procedures common to all the physical and social sciences, which may be outlined as a series of steps: (1) stating a problem or question; (2) forming a hypothesis (possible solution to the problem) based on a theory or rationale; (3) experimentation (gathering empirical data bearing on the hypothesis); (4) interpretation of the data and drawing conclusions; and (5) revising the theory or deriving further hypotheses for testing. Putting the hypothesis in a form that can be empirically tested is one of the chief challenges to the scientist. In addition, all of the sciences try to express their theories and conclusions in some quantitative form and to use standardized testing procedures that other scientists could repeat."[56]

Many Western scholars adhere to the "Scientific Method" of research. This concept originated in Western Culture for the study of nature, to determine the criteria for what can be accepted as truth. The definition above provides the step by step procedures accepted in the Western conception of a scientific method. It is further defined and contrasted from philosophy by the Encarta Encyclopedia as *(highlighted portions by Dr. Ashby)*:

> "Scientific Method, term denoting the principles that guide scientific research and experimentation, and also the philosophic bases of those principles. Whereas philosophy in general is concerned with the why as well as the how of things, science occupies itself with the latter question only. Definitions of scientific method use such concepts as objectivity of approach to and acceptability of the results of scientific study. Objectivity indicates the attempt to observe things as they are, without falsifying observations to accord with some preconceived worldview. Acceptability is judged in terms of the degree to which observations and experimentations can be reproduced. *Such agreement of a conclusion with an actual observation does not itself prove the correctness of the hypothesis from which the conclusion is derived.* It simply renders the premise that much more plausible. The ultimate test of the validity of a scientific hypothesis is its consistency with the totality of other aspects of the scientific framework. This inner consistency constitutes the basis for the concept of causality in science, according to which every effect is assumed to be linked with a cause."[57]

Refutation of Conclusions arrived at through the Scientific Method

Conversely, if one attempts to show that a scientific conclusion is wrong, it is necessary to:

(1) show a misconception or wrongly stated a problem or question;
(2) show that the hypothesis (possible solution to the problem) based on a theory or rationale is incorrect;
(3) show that the experimentation (gathering empirical data bearing on the hypothesis) is biased or being carried out in an incorrect way;
(4) show that the process for interpreting the data and drawing conclusions has not followed a logical procedure or is biased;
(5) show that the revising process of the theory or deriving further hypotheses for testing is needed.
(6) show that the experiment is not consistent with the totality of other aspects of the scientific framework.
(7) show evidences that contradict the conclusion.
(8) show more evidences to prove other conclusions than what have been presented to advance the other unreasonable conclusion.

The Limitations of the Scientific Method

The scientific method is an attempt to remove ambiguity from the body of human knowledge and the means by which knowledge is added to the storehouse of human learning. The problem with this method of gathering knowledge is that it necessarily receives information only from empirical evidence. However, as the great scientist Einstein and the modern day quantum physicists have proven, Creation is not absolute or empirical. Creation is composed of variables wherein some aspects operate in different ways under different circumstances. This is why the concept of cause and effect is also flawed. Ignorance of the mystical law of cause and effect known as the law of *Ari* in Kamitan philosophy and Karma in Indian philosophy, leads scientists to seek for causes or reasons for what they see in nature, somewhere within the confines of the time and space of the event in question. In reference to Yoga and mystical religion, as concerns people and their actions, mostly, what is occurring today could be a result of what happened in a previous lifetime (philosophy of reincarnation-already proven in parapsychology experiments).[58] As concerns nature, what occurs today is sustained by the Transcendental Essence, i.e. Supreme Being. Further, the observers, the scientists themselves, and the very perception of these experiments are factors in the experiments and are therefore, factors in the results. This is where the problem of skewing of the results and interpretations of results based on conscious or unconscious prejudices or misconceptions comes in, that is, the problem of "falsifying observations to accord with some preconceived worldview."

As the modern discipline of Quantum Physics has shown, nature itself is not what it appears. It is not solid and distinct but rather interrelated energies in varied forms of expression. Physics experiments have shown that matter is not solid as it appears but that it is rather, energy in different forms of manifestation. So the instruments used to discern reality, the logical conditioned mind, and the limited senses, are inadequate for discriminating between what is real and what is unreal. The fallacy of believing in the absolute authority of science is evident in the inability of science to discover anything that is absolute. Something absolute is unchangeable in the beginning, middle and end. Every decade medical science makes "new breakthroughs." This means that they are discovering something "new" which supersedes their previous knowledge. This necessarily means that the previous knowledge was conditional and imperfect and therefore, illusory. Thus, science has its value, but it is not to be considered a reliable source for truth or as a substitute for the disciplines of self-knowledge. So, only a mind that has been trained in transcendental thinking and intuitional realization can discover "truth." Yoga and mystical religion are spiritual sciences that promote the cultivation of the higher faculties of the mind. The mystics of Yoga the world over have for thousands of years proclaimed that the mystical reality which is to be discovered through the disciplines of Yoga and Mystical religion is the same Absolute essence which has always sustained Creation and all existence, including human consciousness. It is the same essence that was discovered by Imhotep and other Sages of Kamit, the Upanishadic Sages of India, Buddha, Jesus, etc., and it is the same absolute reality that can be discovered by anyone today or in the future, who applies the teachings of Yoga and Mystical religion.

So, the idea of the objective observer or that only experimental results which can bring forth repeatable results or parameters that show "consistency with the totality of other aspects of the scientific framework" are valid is sometimes contradictory with respect to nature and logic. Nature is not a machine and even if it were to be treated as such it is not a machine for which the parts are all known and understood. There is an aspect of nature that transcends empirical observation; it must be intuited. This aspect of nature is ignored by the scientific method, by its own bindings, and therefore, the ability to use science as a tool to discover truth, is limited. Since the world is variable (relative), then it follows that any "scientific" data obtained from experiments will also be relative and variable. It is useful within the framework of science, but not beyond that framework. In other words, it cannot be used to ascertain anything about realities outside of its framework. This is why philosophy is an important tool of science. It allows the intuitive faculty of the mind to be cultivated and directed towards discovering the aspects of nature that no physical testing equipment can penetrate.

The world is not to be discerned through the intellect because the intellect is also limited. It cannot comprehend the totality of Creation. However, by intuitional (knowing that transcends the thought process) reasoning through transcendence of the relativity of nature, it is possible to discover that absolute reality which is common, and therefore uniform in its *"consistency with the totality"* of human and spiritual experience. The problem is that this aspect of existence can only be approached through a scientific application of philosophical principles and disciplines that can provide results only in the mind of an individual. The Western scientific community shuns this approach, likening it to primitive and unscientific speculations. By ignoring the "why" of things, as the definition of the scientific method above suggests, the scientific method is cutting itself off from the source of knowledge, and looking only at its effect, the "what," and then accepting this as a basis to discern reality. It is like experimenting on the sunrays, neglecting to notice the sun, but extrapolating from the limited experiments and making assertions about what the sun is. In like manner, science looks at nature and notices the relativity, but does not allow itself to explore the mystical-spiritual dimensions of cause. Rather, it seeks to ascribe factors within the realm of the flawed relative field of Creation itself, as the reason behind existence. In fact, for all the knowledge that Western Culture has amassed, in reality there is perhaps no more important knowledge than that which has been recently derived from Quantum Physics, because these clearly point to a transcendental essence of Creation.[59/60/61]

Western Culture's adherence to the "Scientific Method" has turned it away from the science of self-development (myth, religion and yoga mysticism) since it (spiritual evolution) cannot be proven empirically according to its current criteria as different people are at different stages of evolution and the process may require many lifetimes to complete. Here again, even the parameters set by Western Culture as the procedure of the "Scientific Method" are not being followed. The statement that there is no science beyond the existential aspect of Creation is in effect a violation of the "scientific" rule of objectivity to *"observe things as they are, without falsifying observations to accord with some preconceived world view."* The predilection to discount the transcendent as "un-provable" is a worldview which typifies Western Culture. Thus, the objectivity in the scientific method has at least two built in flaws. First, is the insistence on determining scientific fact based on evidence that can be observable to the physical senses with or without assistance from technology, and therefore can only exist in time and space. Secondly, the necessity for human standards in determining *"conclusions"* based on the data, for it has been shown that the same data can lend itself to different interpretations based on conflicting views, even within the scientific community. A true scientific method should require an objective standard which cannot be violated by the whims of the observers or scientists. Its conclusions must be accepted and not refuted by opinions or desires to uphold particular worldviews. However, again, all of the best standards will be useless if the scientists are biased.

A further connotation, prevalent in Western Culture arising from adherence to the "scientific method" is that what is transcendent is imagined, superstition and unfounded illusion, and only what the "Scientific Method" deems as provable is correct and acceptable. Hence, since myth and mysticism are in the realm of the transcendent, then by this type of Western logic it follows that they are also un-provable and unreal. This is a very powerful argument that further develops into the most dangerous concept, that Western Culture is the determiner of what is truth and that the art, culture, science and religion, etc., of other cultures, past or present, are inferior due to their primitive and "unscientific" manner of approaching nature.

Applying the Scientific Principles and Procedures to study Mysticism

The application of scientific principles and procedures in mystical philosophy can and should be accomplished in the following manner. A theory that the Supreme Being exists, for instance, can be developed. Now the experiment is to practice certain myths, rituals and mystical exercises (technologies). Then the practitioner must insightfully look within and see if there are any changes in the personality, and if there is anything transcending the personality. The premise that observable and repeatable results can be obtained is to be understood as an intuitional realization or recognition of truth. So, while it is possible to show many illustrations and iconographical correlations in the scientific comparison of two forms of myth, the ultimate realization of the truth behind these is to be achieved in the understanding of the observer. The mystical scriptures have long held that if this procedure is followed, any person can discover the transcendental essence of Self. This is the scientific formula for Enlightened Sagehood or Sainthood, which mystical philosophy holds to be the only goal in and purpose of life. Thus, from ancient times, the Yogic and other authentic Mystical systems have defined themselves as sciences, since the proper application of the correct philosophy, disciplines and principles of living leads to the same results of spiritual awakening in all human beings who apply them.

Due to the uniqueness of each person when dealing with human beings, there are variables in the degree of understanding and practice. Thus, in evaluating students of the Yogic and other Mystical sciences (spiritual aspirants or initiates), the results of spiritual practices cannot be assessed in terms of an all or nothing equation or within a given time frame or situation, since evolution is occurring even when outwardly there appears to be a backward movement. Also, spiritual evolution occurs over a long period of time encompassing many lifetimes. So these results cannot necessarily be seen in the form of data, but other criteria may be used to evaluate them: a calmer personality, a human being who is expanding in consciousness, discovering the inner depths of consciousness and the universality of life, increasing contentment and fearlessness, a stronger will, and magnanimousness, wisdom and inner fulfillment. Some of these evidences cannot be put on paper, and yet they can be experienced just as the message of a painting or the love of a relative can be intuited and felt, but not explained or proven to others. From time immemorial, the sages and saints of all world traditions have maintained the initiatic principles and technologies, the mystical philosophy and art of spiritual culture, that has been handed down through time. It has been found that when human beings are properly instructed and when they engage in certain disciplines of Yoga and mystical culture, they develop expanded consciousness and spiritual awareness, as well as intuitional realization of the divine presence in a predictable manner.

The correct practice of myth and mystical philosophy in yoga requires a scientific approach, using the personality as the subject, and the mind as the instrument for proving the existence of the transcendent. It is necessary to apply philosophy scientifically, incorporating intuition and spiritual culture when engaging in any study of religion, myth, mysticism, etc.

The following is a standard for our exploration into comparative mythology, which will be used to discover the validity of the hypothesis that Ancient Egyptian and Ancient Indian culture and civilization were related and share common cultural manifestations. This analysis will be accomplished by establishing what culture is and what factors within it can be identified and compared. Then the procedure to be followed in comparing them will be determined.

In a scientific investigation, opinions have no place beyond the stating of the hypothesis. Also, the constraints of social propriety do not apply. It is perfectly scientific to state a theory that the Ancient Egyptians were not black Africans, but rather Asiatics, or that Indian Vedic culture and not Kamitan culture gave rise to civilization. There is nothing wrong in making those statements. However, if the person stating these ideas wants to put them forth as "facts" or "reality" or consider these ideas as "proven," then a more rigorous process of supporting those ideas must be undertaken. The evidence must be accurate, available to all investigators, and it should be primary and not second-hand conjectures. Therefore, the opinions of other scholars, no matter how reputable they may be, must be based on primary evidence, and that evidence cannot be substituted by the scholars conclusions or opinions about it. Therefore, scholarly dictums[8] are worthless if the scholar cannot or does not support them with evidence. Other terms, often used synonymously in scientific discussions are "postulate" or "axiom."

    An **axiom** is a self-evident or universally recognized truth; a maxim.

    A **dictum** is an authoritative, often formal, pronouncement.

    A **postulate** is a *statement or proposition that is to be assumed to be true without proof and that forms a framework for the derivation of theorems.*[62]

Many times scientists or others relying on them treat corollaries as proofs.

    A **corollary** is *a proposition that follows with little or no proof required from one already proven, A deduction or an inference.*[63]

So corollaries, postulates, etc., are also useless in a presentation of scientific findings. They should not even be discussed because they have no merit. Sometimes merit is placed on dictums or corollaries due to the reputation of a scientist, or for political, social or economic reasons but these have no place in a scientific discussion. Thus, if a scientist is not dispassionate, an unconscious or conscious alternative agenda will be put forth. Further, if no evidence is produced to support a contention, then a scientist might be in danger of appearing biased, promoting a political or social point of view or expressing personal beliefs and sentiments about a particular issue. Over time, they themselves begin to believe in those opinions. This is the power and danger of the human mind.

---

[8] American Heritage Dictionary

The Factors That Make Cultures Distinct and the Methodology for Comparing Them

In the book *Comparative Mythology,* the author introduces two formats or models for the study of comparative mythology, based on the concepts of abstraction and generalization.

> Comparative mythology of separately localized and attested traditions can be practiced on different levels of abstraction and generalization.
>
> "Universal mythology" is essentially reduced to explaining accordances (and, if relevant, differences or contrasts) by appeal to human universals or at least common denominators based on similarities of psychological patterning, environment, or levels of culture. Needless to say, it has to pursue the typical and usual at the expense of the specific and unique.
>
> "Diffusionary mythology" studies how traditions travel, charting the spread and transmission of myth. The trouble is precisely that myth does not "travel" very well and, when it does travel, frequently moves from its specific historical and geographical fulcrum into the international realm of legend, folktale, fairy tale, and other debased forms of originally mythical narrative.[64]

While the above author speaks primarily of mythological studies, the ideas are relevant to our study since mythology is an integral if not central aspect of culture. In our study, we will strive to raise the methodology for the comparative cultural study to a high standard that goes beyond the universalistic aspects of culture, that is, those factors that are innate to all human beings.

The author quoted above also works with the premise that mythology becomes "debased" or degrades due to the changes and additions it experiences over time. While this model occurs and may even be considered as the norm, it is also possible to see a sustained practice of myth and other aspects of culture from one group to the next. We will also strive to determine if there is a degradation that can be discerned. The criteria here is the determination of the function and metaphorical significance of the cultural factors over time. That is, if the function and metaphorical significance of the cultural factors is lost over time, the model above is correct. However, if the function and metaphorical significance of the cultural factors are sustained over time, this indicates a closer connection between the two cultures, and the model is one of initiatic continuity (culture A has taught culture B directly) as opposed to blind diffusion of ideas without their full understanding. The closer bond can be expected in the contiguous relationship of a culture with its own legacy. That is, a modern culture can be expected to exhibit a lesser degree of deterioration of indigenous fundamental cultural factors as opposed to those that have been imported. The model presented in ordinary comparative mythology studies is that myth may retain its form but degrade in content. If a sustained (un-degraded) correlation can be shown between two cultures over time (one emerging after the other), then it is possible to maintain that the cultures are not separate and disparate but actually elements of a continuous manifestation of cultural expression. In other words, the two cultures are actually part of one evolving culture. Another factor to be considered is the concept of a study that works within the framework of different levels of abstraction and generalization. The principles under which this current study of Kamitan and Indian culture will be conducted is based on the contention that when several cultural factors can be correlated or matched, then the study becomes more concrete and specific as opposed to abstract and general. This of course raises the validity of the arguments and the conclusions drawn from them.

> "The twentieth-century search for universally applicable "patterns" that so clearly marks the ritualist and psychoanalytic approaches to myth is also characteristic of the trends that remain to be mentioned, the sociological and the structuralist. Whereas ritualism had its roots in England and psychoanalysis in the German cultural orbit, the French contribution is important here, starting with the sociological school of Emile Durkheim and Marcel Mauss. Durkheim's "collective representations," Mauss's seminal studies on gift giving and sacrifice, and Bronislaw Malinowski's views on myths as social "charters" all recognized the paramount role of myths as catalysts in cementing structured human coexistence. The structural study of myth, with Claude Levi-Strauss as its most flamboyant paladin, also stresses the role of myth as a mechanism of conflict resolution and mediation between opposites in the fabric of human culture and society, not least in

the great dichotomy of nature versus culture itself. But Levi-Strauss's analytic method is one of binary oppositions influenced by structural linguistics (especially the work of Roman Jakobson) and folklore (starting with Vladimir Propp's *Morphology of the Folktale* [1928], which themselves are but manifestations of the vast structuralist movement in science and scholarship."[65]

The view that myth is a manifestation of ritual or of a psychological state is a barrier between scholarship and myth. This is because the very premise for the study is flawed. Created by sages, saints, seers, etc., mystical mythology is an "explanation" of something that is transcendental, something that exists in a form that cannot be communicated by rational thinking or linear logical conceptualizations. When mystical mythology is reduced by scholars to a support for rituals, manifestations of the psyche or a tool to "glue" or bind members of a culture to a common concept, the original intent of myth is displaced and the resulting conclusions about myths, their import and pervasiveness, will be elusive. These models may be grouped together and referred to as logical models since they neglect to take into account the transcendental aspects of myth and indeed, also the human experience. The models that take into account the mystical nature and purpose of myth along with the disciplines of anthropology, archeology, philology and historical linguistics, phonetics and phonology, may be referred to as mystic or intuitional models. In another section, the author continues to outline the previous approaches taken by other mythologists in an attempt to determine the benefits or pitfalls of their concepts and methodologies.

"While Levi-Strauss himself, after starting with the Oedipus myth, has for the most part resolutely ranged from Alaska to the Amazon, structuralist ideas have begun to seep into the study of classical myth and "historical" mythology in general. The obvious danger is that the approach is by nature generalist, universalizing, and ahistorical, thus the very opposite of text oriented, philological, and time conscious. Overlaying known data with binaristic gimmickry in the name of greater "understanding" is no substitute for a deeper probing of the records themselves as documents of a specific synchronic culture on the one hand and as outcomes of diachronic evolutionary processes on the other. In mythology, as in any other scholarly or scientific activity, it is important to recall that the datum itself is more important than any theory that may be applied to it. Hence historical and comparative mythology, as practiced in this book, is in the last resort not beholden to any one theory on the "nature" of myth or even its ultimate "function" or "purpose." But it is fully cognizant that myth operates in men's minds and societies alike, that it is involved in both self-image and worldview on an individual and a collective level (being thus tied to religion and its manifestations such as ritual and prayer, and to societal ideology as well), and that it creates potent tensions of language and history (speaking of timeless happening, narrating eternal events in the grammatical frame of tense forms for [usually]) past or [rarely] future occurrences [as in the case of prophecy], never in the generalizing present)."[66]

While there have been a wide range of scholars and writers who have taken note of and even asserted the similarities of the myths of widely varying cultures by citing simple similarities, there have been relatively few serious, rigorous, scholarly researches and documentations. Mostly, there have been many anecdotal and or unsubstantiated claims that do not reconcile history with the events that are being artificially connected. Further, there is little accounting for the discrepancies and inconsistencies that arise. While it is true that all humanity emerged from the same source, it is not necessarily correct to say that all cultures are related since people, having moved away from their original ancestral home (Africa) when humanity first appeared on earth, developed varying ways of life and cultural expression. So making the standard too tight or too loose leaves us with either biased conclusions or unsubstantiated conjecture respectively. The author ends his introduction to comparative mythology with a caveat for entering into those studies.

"Thus the twentieth-century lessons of ritualism, psychoanalysis, sociology, and structural anthropology alike deserve to be heeded by the historical and comparative student of myth and religion, but only to the extent that they offer viable insights into a study that is by definition historical, and more specifically philological, rooted in the minute and sensitive probing and comparison of primary written records."[67]

If the categories of cultural expression are found to match in several areas, the mythic principles will have survived the passage of time even as cultures interact with others and adopt new factors into their culture. The factors of cultural expression will remain embedded in the culture as layers upon which new traditions, names and idiosyncrasies[68] have been acquired. This layering of symbol, myth and metaphor is starkly evident in several examples that will be presented in this section. This pattern of diffusion was noticed early on in the study of the correlations between the myths of varied cultures. The writings of Count Goblet D' Alviella present a typical example, referring to the Sacred Tree symbolism.

> "Each race, each religion has its independent type, which it preserves and develops in accordance with the spirit of its own traditions, approximating it, however, by the addition of extraneous details and accessories, to the equivalent image adopted in the plastic art of its neighbors. Thus the current which makes the Lotus of Egypt blossom on the Paradisaic Tree of India has its counter-current which causes the *Asclepias acida* of the Hindu Kush to climb upon the Sacred Tree of Assyria. Art and mythology comply, in this respect, with the usual processes of civilization, which is not the fruit of a single tree, but has always been developed by grafts and cuttings between the most favoured branches of the human race."[69]

The models (principles) presented in this book adopt the mystic understanding of myths and cultures in the determination of their compatibility. While this study will make use of such disciplines as anthropology, archeology, philology and historical linguistics, phonetics and phonology, it will lay heavy emphasis not so much on the historicity of the factors of cultural expression, although this forms an important aspect of the evidences related to prior contact, but rather on the substance or symbolic, philosophical and metaphoric significance of the items in question. Written records do constitute an essential aspect of the study but this definition needs to be broadened to include iconography, as symbol, metaphor, and iconography are also forms of language, as we will see. The following principles will be used in this comparative cultural study.

Principle 1: Single Event (one occurrence) Match Un-supported By Matches in Other Factors

Example: If one artifact looks the same (correlation of form) in two separate cultures, *this single event proposed correlation* may be explained as a coincidence. But if the primary factor upon which the conjecture is based, for example, *form*, is supported by correlations in other factors such as usage, philosophy, myth, etc., then the argument that it is only a coincidence becomes less tenable. That is, just because the *ontology*[70] of two cultures is expressed through mythology does not suggest a correlation between the two cultures. In order to be considered as a *proposed correlation* for the purpose of determining the congruence of the two cultures, the simple correlation must be supported by at least one or more matching elements of cultural expression. So if there is no other match beyond the initial apparent match this proposed correlation will be considered as being "unsupported."

A- Example of a *Unsupported single event proposed correlation:*

Primary Category proposed as a correlation between two cultures ➔ ***Myth*** ⬅ Supported by ***Iconography***

In this example, one category, the myths of the two cultures match wholly or partially in iconography only.

Typically, the common forms of evidence used to support the theory of cultural connections is a Single Event (one occurrence) Unsupported Match in One Cultural Category which may or may not occur in the presence of other unrelated single event matches in the same or in related but separate cultural categories.

If the *single event proposed correlation* is devoid of additional supports (ex. correlation is of form only) but is found to be part of a group (occurring within the same culture) of several other *single event proposed unsupported correlations* in the same category or other cultural expression categories, then the conclusion that the correlating factors are simple coincidences is less supportable because the frequency of correlations rises beyond the threshold of chance as would be determined by statistical analysis of the normal probability of the existence of such correlations.[71] The correlations here are basic and superficial, usually of appearance, and yet they are suggestive of a deeper connection.

Table 2: Example of Single Event (one occurrence) Unsupported Matches in One Cultural Category Occurring in the Presence of Other Unrelated Single Event Matches in the Same Cultural Categories

Single Event Unsupported Match	Culture A	Culture B	Culture A	Culture B	Culture A	Culture B	Supported Matches
The primary matching Categories	*Mythic Character 1*	*Mythic Character 1*	*Mythic ritual*	*Mythic ritual*	*Mythic ritual*	*Mythic ritual*	← Matches
The primary supporting factor →	*Iconography*	*Iconography*	*Iconography*	*Iconography*	*Iconography*	*Iconography*	← Matches

Table 3: Example of Single Event (occurrence) Unsupported Match in One Cultural Category Occurring in the Presence of Other Unrelated Single Event Matches in Related but Separate Cultural Categories

Single Event Unsupported Match	Culture A	Culture B	Culture A	Culture B	Culture A	Culture B	Supported Matches
The primary matching Categories	*Mythic Character 1*	*Mythic Character 1*	*Architecture*	*Architecture*	*Ritual*	*Ritual*	← Matches
The primary supporting factors →	*Iconography*	*Iconography*	*Style*	*Style*	*Tradition*	*Tradition*	← Matches

Additional criteria for Principle 1:

Single event proposed correlations that are unsupported by other factors and unrelated to other categories require a more rigorous standard of discernment in order to be included as evidence of congruence. A *single event proposed correlation* that is unsupported by other factors and unrelated to other categories will be accepted as evidence of congruence if it occurs in the presence of at least three or more other unrelated single event matches in the same or other cultural factor categories.

B- Example of a *Supported Single event proposed correlation:*

Primary factor proposed as a correlation between two cultures ➔ ***Myth*** ⬅ Supported by
                                                                                                                                                Iconography
                                                                                                          ⬆⬆⬆

Cultural elements that may support the primary factor ➔➔➔➔   Plot,
                                                                                                               gender,
                                                                                                               theme,
                                                                                                               action,
                                                                                                               etc.

In this example, the myths of the two cultures match wholly or partially in iconography, plot, gender, theme, action, etc. Therefore, the initial correlation is supported by more than one factor (iconography).

Table 4: Supported Matching Cultural Factors

Supported Matching Cultural Factors	Culture A	Culture B	Supported Matches
The primary matching category ➔	*Myth* ⬆⬆⬆ **Supporting Factors**	*Myth* ⬆⬆⬆ **Supporting Factors**	⬅ Matches
The primary supporting factor ➔	*Iconography*	*Iconography*	⬅ Matches
Secondary supporting factor ➔	Plot,	Plot,	⬅ Matches
Tertiary supporting factor ➔	gender,	gender,	⬅ Matches
Quaternary supporting factor ➔	theme,	theme,	⬅ Matches
Quinternary supporting factor ➔	action, etc.	action, etc.	⬅ Matches

Additional criteria for Principle 1:

A *supported single event proposed correlation* between the categories being compared within the two cultures will be accepted as evidence of congruence if that *single event proposed correlation* is <u>supported</u> by at least one or more (secondary, tertiary, quaternary, etc.) cultural factors that match exactly in the two cultures (see table above).

Principle 2: Pattern-Multiple Correlations Occur Within the Same Cultural Category or Across the Landscape of Cultural Categories

Single event proposed <u>supported</u> correlations between two cultures that occur as a part of a pattern comprised of several *single event proposed supported correlations* will be accepted as evidence of congruence between the categories being compared among the two cultures. Pattern here implies consistency in the appearance of the number of correlating factors in the same or different categories.

Depth (deepness-vertical) *pattern of correlations*

If two or more independent factor matches within one category appear, they will be considered as a part of a pattern denoting congruence between the two cultures. These correlations will be considered as equivalencies within a particular category of expressions such as, art, architecture, myth, etc. This pattern is referred to as a *depth* (deepness-vertical) *pattern of correlations* and the category will be accepted as evidence in the determination of congruence between two cultures.

AFRICAN ORIGINS Of Civilization, Religion, Yoga Mystical Spirituality And Ethics Philosophy

Table 5: Example-Supported Matching Cultural Factors within the Cultural Factor/Category: Myth

Depth pattern of correlations	Culture A	Culture B	Culture A	Culture B	Culture A	Culture B	Supported Matches
The primary matching categories	*Myth*	*Myth*	*Mythic Character 1*	*Mythic Character 1*	*Mythic Theme*	*Mythic Theme*	← Matches
	↑↑↑ Supporting Factors	↑↑↑ Supporting Factors	↑↑↑ Supporting Factors	↑↑↑ Supporting Factors	↑↑↑ Supporting Factors	↑↑↑ Supporting Factors	
The primary supporting factor →	*Iconography* Plot, gender, theme, action, etc.	*Iconography* Plot, gender, theme, action, etc.	*Iconography* Plot, gender, theme, action, etc.	*Iconography* Plot, gender, theme, action, etc.	*Iconography* Plot, gender, theme, action, etc.	*Iconography* Plot, gender, theme, action, etc.	← Matches ← Matches ← Matches ← Matches ← Matches

Breadth (wideness-horizontal) *pattern of correlations*

The pattern may appear as a consistent number of single event correlations discovered in different cultural categories. For example, several correlations in a study of comparative culture may be found in any of the cultural categories discussed earlier. If two or more instances of matching factors arise then this pattern is referred to as a *breadth* (wideness-horizontal) *pattern of correlations* and the category will be accepted as evidence of congruence.

Table 6: Example-Supported Matching Cultural Factors within the wide range of Cultural Factor/Categories

Breadth pattern of correlations Factors	Culture A	Culture B	Culture A	Culture B	Culture A	Culture B	Supported Matches
The primary matching Categories	*Mythic Character 1*	*Mythic Character 1*	*Architecture*	*Architecture*	*Ritual*	*Ritual*	← Matches
	↑↑↑ Supporting Factors	↑↑↑ Supporting Factors	↑↑↑ Supporting Factors	↑↑↑ Supporting Factors	↑↑↑ Supporting Factors	↑↑↑ Supporting Factors	
The primary supporting factor →	*Iconography* Plot, gender, theme, action, etc.	*Iconography* Plot, gender, theme, action, etc.	*Iconography* Plot, gender, theme, action, etc.	*Iconography* Plot, gender, theme, action, etc.	*Iconography* Plot, gender, theme, action, etc.	*Iconography* Plot, gender, theme, action, etc.	← Matches ← Matches ← Matches ← Matches ← Matches

Principle 3: Cross-Cultural Correlations

Principle #1 represents the most common form of evidence that can be presented as proof of congruence between two cultures. Therefore, this is the principle within which most simple correlations between cultures are to be found. However, the nature and exactness of the correlations of the factors between the two cultures may be deserving of greater weight. An example of this is the correlation between the relationship of the numbers used in Indian, Icelandic and Chaldean myth, presented in this text. Cross-cultural correlations (correlations between three or more cultures) may be observed in the unsupported or supported state. They may most likely be found in the breadth pattern of distribution. This pattern of correlation suggests a *diffusion* of the expressions of the cultural factors from one original source and / or a relationship between the cultures being studied.

Table 7: Single Event Unsupported Cross Cultural Correlations

Cross-Cultural Correlations	Culture A	Culture B	Culture C	Culture D	Culture E	Culture F	Supported Matches
The primary matching category	*Mythic Character 1*	*Mythic Character 1*	*Mythic Character 1*	*Mythic Character 1*	*Mythic Character 1*	*Mythic Character 1*	← Matches
The primary supporting factor →	Iconography	Iconography	Iconography	Iconography	Iconography	Iconography	← Matches

In order for these principles to carry weight and to be considered a substantive arguments for theorizing that the given cultures are related and or that they adopted cultural factors from the other cultures, it is advisable to establish evidence of contact and a correlation of at least one additional factor of correlation. In this regard, once a factor has been preliminarily established to match, say as a mythic character appearing to possess the same iconography, if it can be determined that the mythic characters, for instance, perform the same function or if a mythic artifact or symbol carries the same usage in the mythic system, then it is possible to assert with greater confidence that there is a connection between the two cultures. The particular example used in this principle is one of the main patterns of cultural congruence discovered by mythologist Joseph Campbell, which he presented in his groundbreaking work *The Hero of A Thousand Faces*. The mythic, heroic character exhibits particular patterns in myths from various cultures which can be readily discerned. The myth of the Asarian Resurrection of Ancient Egypt, in which a prince is born, his father is killed by the uncle, the child flees into exile to be brought up by sages so that he/she may return and face the evil tyrant and reestablish order and justice, can be seen in the myth of Krishna of India, the story of Jesus, the story of Hamlet, and even in modern times with the story of the movie "Star Wars" and the even more recent "Lion King." The table gives an example of a single event supported cross-cultural correlation. Examples of multiple event supported cross-cultural correlations can be seen in the connections between Ancient Egyptian mythology, Indian mythology, Sumerian mythology, Greek mythology and Christian mythology.

Table 8: Single Event Supported Cross Cultural Correlations

Cross-Cultural Correlations	Culture A	Culture B	Culture C	Culture D	Culture E	Culture F	Supported Matches
The primary matching category	*Mythic Character 1*	*Mythic Character 1*	*Mythic Character 1*	*Mythic Character 1*	*Mythic Character 1*	*Mythic Character 1*	← Matches
The primary supporting factor →	*Iconography*	*Iconography*	*Iconography*	*Iconography*	*Iconography*	*Iconography*	← Matches
Other possible additional supporting factors →→ ↓↓↓↓	Function Actions Gender Age Metaphoric significance	Function Actions Gender Age Metaphoric significance	Function Actions Gender Age Metaphoric significance	Function Actions Gender Age Metaphoric significance	Function Actions Gender Age Metaphoric significance	Function Actions Gender Age Metaphoric significance	← Matches ← Matches ← Matches ← Matches ← Matches

Final Standard

A. CULTURAL INFLUENCE- In order to establish the influence of one culture on another it must be possible to show concordances in any categories, including Evidence of Contact, but not necessarily including Ethnicity.

   a. Each category of cultural expression match must be supported by at least one Method of Correlation –

B. COMMON CULTURAL ORIGINS- In order to establish the common origins of two given cultures it must be possible to show a pattern of concordances in any of 6 or more categories including Evidence of Contact and Ethnicity.

   a. Each category of cultural expression match must be supported by at least two Methods of Correlation – Breadth Proof

and/or

   b. Each category of cultural expression match must be supported by at least two Methods of Correlation – Depth Proof

C. CULTURAL PRIMACY- In order to demonstrate that culture has come first in history and that the later (secondary) culture has drawn cultural factors from the primary culture, it is necessary to first establish Evidence of Contact, the exchange of cultural factors from the primary to the secondary culture, and next, it is necessary to show a chronology in which the primary culture is shown to have developed previous to the secondary culture.

The Fundamental Cultural Factors

What is it that distinguishes one culture from another? What factors determine whether or not a cultural factor is borrowed by one group from another, and what criteria determines that a culture is not simply influenced, but is actually part of another culture. As stated earlier, the principles under which this current study of Kamitan and Indian culture will be conducted is based on the contention that when several cultural factors can be correlated or matched, and when these matches can be supported by varied aspects within the two cultures, then the study becomes more concrete and specific as opposed to abstract and general. This of course raises the validity of the arguments and the conclusions drawn from them. But where is the threshold wherein it becomes obvious that a group of peoples is related to another? The following cultural principles are offered as criterion for such a determination. The latter four (Ethnicity, Myth, Philosophy and Rituals and Tradition) may be considered as the basic qualities which define a culture and which it carries forth over time. These cultural factors may be thought of as the core fundamental elements of culture which makes it unique from the standpoint of the determination of its kinship to another culture. Contact is considered here because interactions with other cultures can have a profound effect on the direction of a society and its cultural development.

> **Contact** – evidence of prior contact (relationships)
> **Ethnicity** – both groups matching in their ethnic background
> **Myth synchronism**
> **Philosophical synchronism**
> **Rituals and traditions synchronism**

So under this model, even if people born in Kamit were to be found in India, if their lives and activities did not match in the other areas, they would not be considered as members of the same culture for the purposes of this study. Accordingly, it must be understood here that the term "ethnicity" does not relate to race. The word "ethnic" may have originated from the Biblical term "ethnos" meaning "of or pertaining to a group of people recognized as a class on the basis of certain distinctive characteristics, such as religion, language, ancestry, culture, or national origin."[124]

Ethnicity, Race as Culture Factors

Modern scientists and scholars say that race distinctions based on genetics is unscientific and wrong. The animosity and hatred of modern times, caused by distortion of religious scriptures when being rewritten or reinterpreted by various groups or ignorance of the true intent of the teachings of the religious holy books, has led to a situation where social problems have rendered practitioners of religion incapable of reaching a higher level of spiritual understanding. Many people in modern society are caught up in the degraded level of disputes and wars in an attempt to support ideas, which are in reality absurd and destructive in reference to the authentic doctrines of religion. Ironically, the inability of leaders in the church, synagogue or secular society to accept the truth about the origins of humanity comes from their desire to gain and maintain control and fear of losing control over their followers. Now that modern science is showing that all human beings originated from the same source, in Africa, and that racial distinctions are at least questionable and misleading and at worst, malicious lies and race baiting, it means that those who have perpetrated and sustained racism can no longer use science or religious teachings to support their iniquity and ignorant designs. They have no leg to stand on. The following excerpt was taken from Encarta Encyclopedia, and is typical of the modern scientific understanding of the question of human genetics and race issues.

> "The concept of race has often been misapplied. One of the most telling arguments against classifying people into races is that persons in various cultures have often mistakenly acted as if one race were superior to another. Although, with social disadvantages eliminated, it is possible that one human group or another might have some genetic advantages in response to such factors as climate, altitude, and specific food availability, these differences are small. There are no differences in native intelligence or mental capacity that cannot be explained by environmental circumstances. Rather than using racial classifications to study human variability, anthropologists today define geographic or social groups by geographic or social criteria. They then study the nature of the genetic attributes of these groups and seek to understand the causes of changes in their genetic makeup. Contributed by: Gabriel W. Laser "Races, Classification of," Encarta." Copyright (c) 1994

AFRICAN ORIGINS Of Civilization, Religion, Yoga Mystical Spirituality And Ethics Philosophy

It should be noted here that there is no evidence that racial classifications for the purpose of supporting racist views existed in Ancient Egypt. However, the concept of ethnicity, which is often erroneously confused with the modern concept of race, was acknowledged in ancient times. That is to say, the Ancient Egyptians recognized that some of the physical features and characteristics of the Asiatics, Europeans, and other groups were different from themselves and the Nubians. They recognized themselves as looking like the Nubians, but as possessing differences in culture. The Ancient Egyptian's depictions of themselves and their neighbors shows us beyond reasonable doubt, that they were dark skinned people like all other Africans, before the influx of Asiatics and Europeans to the country. Since genetics is increasingly being recognized as a false method of differentiating people the concept of phenotype has progressively more been used.

> **phe·no·type** (fē′nə-tīp′) *n.* **1.a.** The observable physical or biochemical characteristics of an organism, as determined by both genetic makeup and environmental influences. **b.** The expression of a specific trait, such as stature or blood type, based on genetic and environmental influences. **2.** An individual or group of organisms exhibiting a particular phenotype.[9]

It has been shown that climactic conditions, geography, solar exposure, vegetation, etc., have the effect of changing the appearance of people. This means that while people (human beings) remain equally human internally, their physiognomy and shade of skin adapt to the conditions where they live. This means that the external differences in people have little to do with their internal humanity and therefore are illusory. The concept of social typing is therefore based on ignorance about the race issue and its misconceptions, and cannot be supported by the scientific evidences. Further, an advancing society cannot hold such erroneous notions without engendering strife, and confusion, within the society. An advancing society will not be able to attain the status of "civilization" while holding on to such spurious concepts.

One of the major problems for society and non-secular groups is that the teachings and scientific evidence presented here has not been taught to the world population at large as part of the public or private education system. Even if it were, it would take time for people to adjust to their new understanding. Most people grow up accepting the ignorance of their parents who received the erroneous information from their own parents, and so on. Racism, sexism and other scourges of society are not genetically transmitted. They are transmitted by ignorant family members who pass on their ignorance, prejudices and bigotries to their children, and so on down through the generations.

The only fair and accurate standard to classify people is by means of education and ethics. Here education refers not just to trades or technical endeavors but to the origins of humanity and the contributions of all members (especially the Africans) of humanity to the evolution of world culture and the advancement towards civilization. This knowledge directly impacts a person's ethics, as once the common origins of humanity and the falseness of the race issue are understood and affirmed in a person's life, their ethics, and relations this will have an impact on how people view each other and consequently this will improve how people treat each other.

---

[9] American Heritage Dictionary

AFRICAN ORIGINS Of Civilization, Religion, Yoga Mystical Spirituality And Ethics Philosophy

Below is a listing of the world's major cultures and a timeline of their rise and fall for the purpose of comparative study.

Timeline of World Cultures

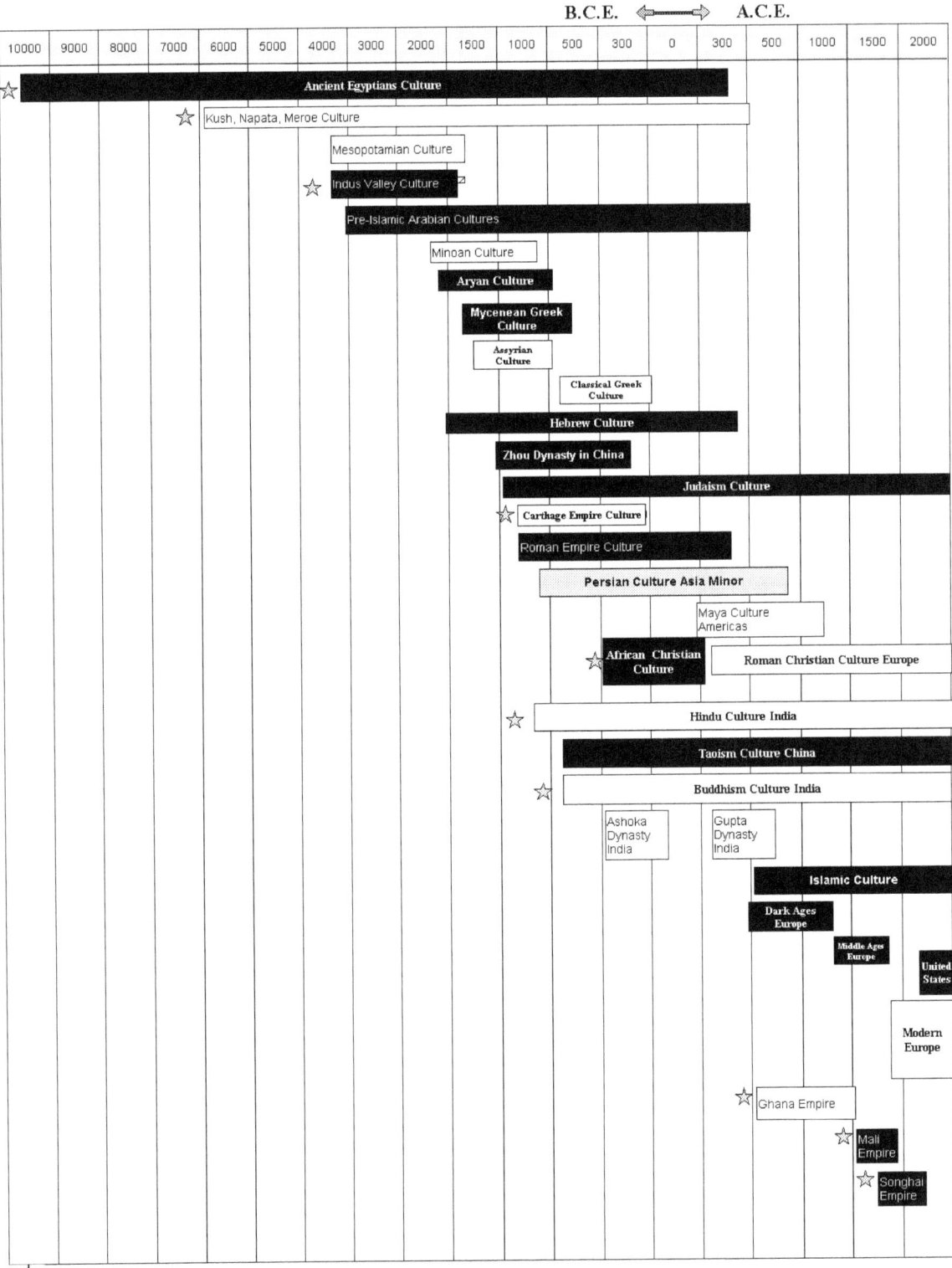

☆ = African Cultures

AFRICAN ORIGINS Of Civilization, Religion, Yoga Mystical Spirituality And Ethics Philosophy

Examples of Cultural Interactions Throughout History

The Ancient Egyptian Creation Myths and Their Relationship to Christianity and Gnosticism

Bible - Genesis 1
2 And the earth was without form, and void; and darkness [was] upon the face of the deep. And the Spirit of God moved upon the face of the waters.

The idea of the primeval waters, and the original primeval Spirit that engendered life in it, occurs in several myths from around the world. It occurs both in the Jewish Bible as well as in Hindu mythology. However, the earliest record of the idea of the primeval waters occurs in the Pre-Dynastic culture of Ancient Egyptian religion. This Pre-Dynastic (10,000-5,500 B.C.E.) myth spoke of a God who was unborn and undying, and who was the origin of all things. This Deity was described as un-namable, unfathomable, gender-less and without form, although encompassing all forms and being transcendental. This being was the *God of Light* which illumines all things, and thus was later associated (in Dynastic times) with the Sun in the form of the deities, *Ra* or *Tem, Heru* (Horus) who represents *that which is up there* and *the light*, and finally *Aton*. Tem or Temu were Ancient Egyptian names for the ocean that is full of life giving potential. This ocean is likened to the deep and boundless abyss of consciousness of the Supreme Deity from which the phenomenal universe emerged. Tem was analogous in nature to later deities such as the Babylonian *Tiamat,* the Chaldean *Thamte,* the Hebrew *Tehorn,* and the Greek *Themis*.

Cultural Interactions Between Judaism and Ancient Egypt

The next prominent example of adoption of religious culture comes from the relationship between Judaism and Ancient Egypt. Many times in the emergence of new mythologies throughout history, the founders or followers of the new system of religion will create stories to show how the new system surpasses the old. The story of Exodus is such an example. Moses went to Mount Sinai to talk to God and brought back Ten Commandments. At the time that Moses was supposed to have lived (1,200?-1,000? B.C.E.), Ancient Egypt was the most powerful culture in the ancient world. However, at the time when the bible was written (900 B.C.E.-100 B.C.E.), Egypt was on a social and cultural decline from its previous height as the foremost culture in religious practice, art, science, social order, etc. So it became necessary for the Jews, a small group of Ancient Egyptians (according to the Bible, the early Jews were ethnic Ancient Egyptians),[72] to legitimize the inception of their new theology by claiming to have triumphed over the mighty Egyptian gods with the help of their new "true god" who defeated the "weak" gods of Egypt. This triumphant story would surely bring people to convert to the new faith, since up to that time, the Ancient Egyptian gods and goddesses had been seen not only as the most powerful divinities, but also, according to the Greeks, as the source of other deities in other religions. So in effect, by saying that the Jewish God "defeated" the Ancient Egyptian God by freeing the Jews, it is the same as saying that a new, more powerful religion is to be followed. This form of commencement for a spiritual tradition is not uncommon. As an example of inculturation, the similarity between the story of Moses of the Jews and Sargon I from Assyria (reigned about 2,335-2,279 B.C.E.) is instructive. Sargon also was placed in a basket and floated down a river to be picked up by the royal household. So part of the story of Moses is borrowed from Assyrian history.

In almost the exact same expression as one of the Ancient Egyptian creation myths, the original Jewish Bible and related texts also describe the Creation in terms of an act of sexual union. *Elohim* (Ancient Hebrew for gods/goddesses) impregnates the primeval waters with *ruach,* a Hebrew word which means *spirit, wind* or the verb *to hover*. The same word means *to brood* in Syriac. Elohim, also called El, was a name used for God in some Hebrew scriptures. It was also used in the Old Testament for heathen gods. Thus, as the Book of Genesis explains, Creation began as the spirit of God "moved over the waters" and agitated those waters into a state of movement. In Western traditions the active role of Divinity has been assigned to the male gender, while the passive (receiving) role has been assigned to the female gender. This is in contrast to the Southern and Eastern philosophical views where the passive role is assigned to the male gender, and the active role to the female.

AFRICAN ORIGINS Of Civilization, Religion, Yoga Mystical Spirituality And Ethics Philosophy

Cultural Interactions Between Judaism and Babylonia

In this area of study, an important figure from Mesopotamia is Hammurabi. Hammurabi is believed to have lived around 1,792-1,750 B.C.E. He was king of Babylonia in the first dynasty. He expanded his rule over Mesopotamia and organized the empire by building wheat granaries, canals and classified the law into the famous "Code of Hammurabi." The divine origin ascribed to the Code is of particular interest to our study. Hammurabi can be seen receiving the Code in a bas-relief in which he is depicted as receiving the Code from the sun-god, Shamash, in much the same way that Moses would later receive the Ten Commandments from God, who had appeared as the burning bush (fire is a solar motif). This mode of introducing a teaching or new order, by claiming it to be divinely ordained, is in reality an attempt to impress on the masses of people the authenticity, importance and force with which the new teaching was received and must therefore be followed. Like Moses, Hammurabi created the laws himself, or in conjunction with others, wishing to institute a new order for society. Whether or not they were divinely inspired relates to the degree of communion they were able to achieve with the Divine Self, God. This they could only ascertain for themselves. Spiritually immature people tend to follow a teaching when they believe that it was inspired by God, even if they cannot know for certain intellectually. They feel they somehow "know" in their hearts as they are urged by passionate preachers to have faith. However, if people are fanatical instead of introspective and sober in their religious practice, they may follow the teachings of those who are not authentic spiritual leaders and be led blindly, even to their death.

Cultural Interactions Between Ancient Egypt and Ancient Greece

Greek Myth is a conglomeration of stories related to certain divine personalities and their interactions with each other and with human beings. The main stories about the Greek divinities (gods and goddesses) are contained in the epics, *The Iliad* and *The Odyssey,* written by Homer (900 B.C.E.). The main functions of the gods and goddesses and their mingling with human beings was outlined in these early Greek mythologies. The early Greeks also spoke of the origins of their gods and goddesses. It must be clearly understood that at the time when the early Greeks organized themselves sufficiently enough in order to take up the task of learning art, culture and civilization, they had very little in the way of culture, and what they did have was primitive by Ancient Egyptian and Indus Valley standards thousands years earlier. The force of the Ancient Egyptian culture created perhaps the strongest impression, but it was not the only impression, since the Greeks traveled to other lands and attempted to assimilate the teachings of others as well. This, coupled with their own ideas, caused a situation wherein they created a synthesis of religious philosophies. The expression of Greek culture and philosophy in later periods is reflective of this synthesis. In short, what is regarded as Greek myth was in reality a patchwork of differing ideas that had their basis in Ancient Egyptian philosophy, but which did not follow its precepts entirely as the following statement from Herodotus suggests. *(Bold portions are by Ashby)*

> 35. "Almost all the names of the gods came into Greece from Egypt. My inquiries prove that they were all derived from a foreign source, and my opinion is that Egypt furnished the greater number. For with the exception of Neptune and the Dioscuri, whom I mentioned above, and Juno, Vesta, Themis, the Graces, and the Nereids, the other gods have been known from time immemorial in Egypt. This I assert on the authority of the Egyptians themselves."
>
> — Herodotus

> "Solon, Thales, Plato, Eudoxus and Pythagoras went to Egypt and consorted with the priests. Eudoxus they say, received instruction from Chonuphis of Memphis,* Solon from Sonchis of Sais,* and Pythagoras from Oeniphis of Heliopolis."*
> —Plutarch (Greek historian c. 46-120 A.C.E.)
> *(Greek names for cities in Ancient Egypt)

Greek Philosophy has been equated with the origin of Western civilization. Ancient Greek philosophers such as Thales (c. 634-546 B.C.E.) and Pythagoras (582?-500? B.C.E.) are thought to have originated and innovated the sciences of mathematics, medicine, astronomy, philosophy of metaphysics, etc. These disciplines of the early Greek philosophers had a major impact on the development of Christianity since the version of Christianity which was practiced in the Western (Roman) and Eastern (Byzantine) empires was developed in Greece, alongside Greek culture and the Greek language.[73] However, upon closer review, the ancient writings of contemporary historians of those times (early Christianity) also point to sources other than Greek Philosophy, and hence we are led to discover similarities in philosophy by tracing their origins to a common source.

As stated earlier, there is evidence that shows how Ancient Egypt supported not only the education of the early Greek philosophers who came to study in Ancient Egypt itself, but Egypt also supported the Ancient Egyptian Mystery Temples that were established in Greece. Some Egyptian pharaohs sponsored and financed temples abroad which taught mystical philosophy as well as other disciplines. One such effort was put forth by the Ancient Egyptian king, Amasis, who financed the reconstruction of the famous Temple of Delphi in Greece, which was burnt down in 548 B.C.E.[74] This is the Temple which made the saying "Know Thyself" famous.[75] The Ancient Egyptian philosophy of self-knowledge was well known throughout the ancient world. The oracle of Zeus at Dodona was the oldest; and the one at Delphi, the most famous. Herodotus records a Greek tradition which held that Dodona was founded by the Priesthood in Egyptian Thebes. Further, he asserts that the oracle at Delos was founded by an Egyptian who became the king of Athens in 1558 B.C.E. This would be one of the earliest suggested dates for the existence of civilization in Greece, and it is being attributed to an Ancient Egyptian origin by the Greeks themselves, in their own myth and folklore. The connection to and dependence on Ancient Egypt for the creation of Greek culture is unmistakable and far-reaching. Along with this is the association between the Greek city of Athens and the Ancient Egyptian city of Sais. These two were known as "sister cities" in ancient times. The Greeks and Egyptians regarded the goddesses of those cities as being one and the same, i.e. Athena of Greece and Net (Neith) of Egypt. Also, the original rulers of Athens were Egyptians (Append. C)

Thales was the first Greek philosopher of whom there is any knowledge, and therefore he is sometimes called the "Father of Greek Philosophy." After studying in Egypt with the Sages of the Ancient Egyptian temples, he founded the Ionian school of natural philosophy which held that a single elementary matter, water, is the basis of all the transformations of nature. The similarity between this teaching, the Ancient Egyptian Primeval Waters and the creation story in Genesis may be noted here. The ancient writings of the Greeks state that Thales visited Egypt and was initiated by the Egyptian priests into the Egyptian Mystery System, and that he learned astronomy, surveying, engineering, and Egyptian Theology during his time in Egypt. This would have certainly included the theologies related to Asar, Amun and Ptah. Pythagoras was a native of Samos who traveled often to Egypt on the advice of Thales and received education there. He was introduced to each of the Egyptian priests of the major theologies which comprised the whole of the Egyptian religious system based on the Trinity principle (*Amen-Ra-Ptah*). Each of these legs of the Trinity were based in three Egyptian cities. These were Heliopolis (Priesthood of Ra), Memphis (Priesthood of Ptah) and in Thebes (Priesthood of Amen {Amun}) in Egypt.

In reference to the Ionian school that Thales founded after his studies in Egypt, a student from that school, Socrates, became one of the most famous sage-philosophers. Socrates (470? -399? B.C.E.) was regarded as one of the most important philosophers of ancient Greece. He ended up spending most of his life in Athens, however, he was known to have studied under the Ionian philosophers. This establishes a direct link between Socrates and his teaching with Ancient Egypt. Socrates had a tremendous influence on many disciples. One of the most popular of these was Plato. Plato in turn taught others, including Aristotle (384-322 B.C.E.) who was Plato's disciple for 19 years. After Plato's death, Aristotle opened a school of philosophy in Asia Minor. Aristotle educated Philip of Macedon's son, Alexander (Alexander the Great), between the years 343 and 334 B.C.E. Aristotle then returned to Athens and opened a school in the Lyceum, near Athens; here Aristotle lectured to his students. He urged Alexander onto his conquests since in the process, he, Aristotle, was able to gain in knowledge from the ancient writings of the conquered countries. After Alexander's conquest of Egypt, Aristotle became the author of over 1,000 books on philosophy. Building on Plato's *Theory of the Forms*, Aristotle developed the theory of *The Unmoved Mover*, which is a direct teaching from Memphite Theology in Ancient Egypt. Among his works are *De Anima, Nicomachean Ethics and Metaphysics*.[76]

AFRICAN ORIGINS Of Civilization, Religion, Yoga Mystical Spirituality And Ethics Philosophy

Cultural Interactions Between Greece, Rome, Egypt and Ethiopia, and the Indian, Egyptian and Ethiopian relationship.

As Rome emerged as a powerful military force in the period just prior to the birth of Christ (200 B.C.E.-30 B.C.E.), they adopted Greek customs, religion and art, seeing these as their legacy. Just as the Greeks adopted *The Illiad* and *The Odyssey*, the Romans enthusiastically embraced *The Aeneid* as their national epic. Vergil or Virgil (70-19 B.C.E.) was a Roman poet who wrote *The Aeneid* in the Latin language.[77] *The Aeneid is actually a story that was written in the same form as The Odyssey and The Illiad of the Greek writer Homer. It was widely distributed and read throughout the Roman Empire. Thus, The Aeneid is considered to be a classical Latin masterpiece of ancient world literature, which had enormous influence on later European writers.*[78] Some portions of these texts have important implications to understand the relationship between the Egyptians, the Ethiopians and the Indians in ancient times. *(italicized portions are by Ashby)*

> Mixed in the bloody battle on the plain;
> **And swarthy Memnon in his arms he knew,**
> **His pompous ensigns, and his Indian crew.**
> - *The Aeneid*, Book I, Vergil or Virgil (70-19 BC)[79]

In Greek myth, Memnon was a king from Ethiopia, and was openly referred to as being "burnt of skin", i.e. "black."[10] He was the son of Tithonus, a Troyan (Trojan) prince, and Eos, a Greek goddess of the dawn. Tithonus and Eos represent the sky and romantic love, respectively. During the Troyan war, Memnon assisted Troy[80] with his army. Even though he fought valiantly, he was killed by Achilles. In order to comfort Memnon's mother, Zeus, the king of the Greek gods and goddesses, made Memnon immortal.[81] The Greeks revered a colossal statue of the Ancient Egyptian king Amenhotep III as an image of Memnon. During the times of Greek (332 B.C.E.-30 B.C.E.) and Roman (30 B.C.E.-450 A.C.E.) conquest of Egypt, it became fashionable for Greek and Roman royalty, nobles and those of means from all over the ancient world, especially Greece, to take sightseeing trips to Egypt. The "Colossi of Memnon" were big attractions. The Colossi of Memnon are two massive statues that were built under Amenhotep III, 1,417-1,379 B.C.E.[82] The statues fronted a large temple[83] which is now in ruin, mostly depleted of its stonework by nearby Arab inhabitants who used them to build houses.

This passage is very important because it establishes a connection between Ethiopia, Egypt and India. Further, it establishes that the Indians made up the army of Memnon, that is to say, Ethiopia. Thus, in the time of Virgil, the cultural relationship between north-east Africa and India was so well known that it was mythically carried back in time to the reign of Pharaoh Amenhotep III, the father of the famous king Akhnaton. Pharaoh Amenhotep III was one of the most successful kings of Ancient Egypt. He ruled the area from northern Sudan (Nubia) to the Euphrates river. The Euphrates river is formed by the confluence of the Murat Nehri and the Kara Su Rivers. It flows from East Turkey across Syria into central modern day Iraq where it joins the Tigris River. The land referred to as Mesopotamia, along the lower Euphrates, was the birthplace of the ancient civilizations of Babylonia and Assyria, and the site of the ancient cities of Sippar, Babylon, Erech, Larsa, and Ur. The length of the river is 2,235mi (3.598km).[84] So again we have support for the writings of Herodotus and Diodorus who related the makeup of the ethnic groups in Mesopotamia as belonging to the Ancient Egyptian-Nubian culture.

At first inspection, this relationship appears to be perhaps an allusion to Virgil's times when it is well known and accepted that there was trade and cultural exchange, not only between India and Egypt, as we and other scholars have shown, but also between India and Greece.

Also, in contrast to present day society, there is no racist concept detected or being either implied or inferred, in the Greek writings. Also, there is no apparent aversion to having a personage of African descent (someone from a different ethnic group) in the Greek religion as a member of the family of Greek Gods and Goddesses. There is a remarkable feeling in reading the Greek texts that they had no compunction about admitting their association with Africa and Africans. The Greeks received much in terms of civilization and culture from Africa, in particular, Ethiopia and Ancient Egypt. This may be likened to modern college graduates who are proud to boast of their successful attendance at prestigious schools. There seems to be an eagerness to admit traveling to Egypt, as if it were a stamp of approval for

---

[10] Recall that the term Ethiopians means "land of the burnt (black) faces."

their entry into society as professionals in their fields. There are other passages of interest in *The Aeneid*, which support the cultural connection similar to the previous verse.

Figure 4: The Pharaoh Amenhotep III

Figure 5: The Colossi of Memnon- built under Amenhotep III, 1,417 B.C.E. -1,379 B.C.E. 59 feet tall

(italicized portions are by Ashby)

>   Ceasar himself, exalted in his line;
>   Augustus, promised oft, and long foretold,
>   Sent to the realm that Saturn ruled of old;
>   Born to restore a better age of gold.
>   *Africa and India shall his power obey*;
>   - The Aeneid, Book VI, Vergil or Virgil (70-19 BC)[85]
>
>   This seen, Apollo, from his Actian height,
>   Pours down his arrows; at whose winged flight
>   *The trembling Indians and Egyptians yield*,
>   - The Aeneid, Book VIII, Vergil or Virgil (70-19 BC)[86]

In the first passage above, Africa and India are being linked as two countries that will be controlled by the Roman emperors (Ceasar, Augustus). Also, this statement implies that Egypt is an African country and not an Asiatic country. The time when this text was written is the period just prior to the Roman conquest of Ancient Egypt (30 B.C.E.). Therefore, it follows that the intent of the Romans, based on this passage, was to expand their empire to encompass north-east Africa and India. This repeated reference to India in conjunction with Africa and Egypt seems to imply a connection between the two countries, relating to a vast empire with two major geographic locales (Kamit and India).

Cultural Interactions Between Hinduism and Vedic Culture In India

In India, the emergence of Hinduism saw a similar situation as with the one that occurred between the Jewish and Ancient Egyptian Religion. In a later period (c. 800 B.C.E.-600 B.C.E.), the earlier Vedic-Aryan religious teachings related to the God Indra (c. 1,000 B.C.E.) were supplanted by the teachings related to the Upanishadic and Vaishnava tradition. The Vaishnava tradition includes the worship of the god Vishnu, as well as his avatars (divine incarnations), in the form of Rama and Krishna. The Vaishnava tradition was developed by the indigenous Indian peoples to counter, surpass and evolve beyond the Vedic religious teachings. In the epic stories known as the Ramayana and the Mahabharata[87], Vishnu incarnates as Rama and Krishna, respectively, and throughout these and other stories it is related how Vishnu's incarnations are more powerful than Indra's, who is portrayed as being feeble and weak. Some of the writings of the Upanishadic Tradition,[88] the writings which succeed the Vedic tradition, contain specific verses which seem to profess that the wisdom of the Vedas is lesser than that of the Upanishads, and that they therefore supersede the Vedas. One such statement can be found in the *Mundaka Upanishad*. The following segment details the view of the two sets of scriptures in relation to each other and the two forms of knowledge. (italicized portions are by Ashby)

> Those who know Brahman (God)... say that there are two kinds of knowledge, the higher and the lower. *The lower is knowledge of the Vedas* (the Rik, the Sama, the Yajur, and the Atharva), *and also of phonetics, grammar, etymology, meter, and astronomy. The higher is the knowledge of that by which one knows the changeless reality.*

Cultural Interactions Between Hinduism and Buddhism

A similar situation that transpired with Kamitan religion with respect to Judaism, and with Hinduism with respect to Vedic religion, as discussed above, occurred between Hinduism and Buddhism with the advent of Buddhism. The story of Buddha's struggle to attain enlightenment, the inceptive and most influential work of Buddhist myth, relates how he strove to practice the austere paths of Hinduism (Upanishadic wisdom, Vedanta, Brahmanism, austerity, yoga, etc.). He practiced renunciation of the world and all sorts of penances and asceticism, even to the point of almost starving himself to death. Then he "discovered" a "new" path, "The Middle Path," and for a long time it was held to be superior to Hinduism by many. It found a great following in China and Tibet, as well as other countries of Indo-China.[89] Currently in the west, Buddhism is rarely related to its roots in Hinduism and Yoga philosophy. Upon close examination, the roots of the teaching of the middle path, along with the other major tenets of Buddhism such as the philosophy of *Karma* (action), *Maya* (cosmic illusion) and *Samsara* (philosophy of worldly suffering) can be traced to the Upanishadic Tradition,[90] especially in the Isha Upanishad. Thus, the early Buddhist teachers found it necessary to disparage the other practices in order to highlight the Buddhist faith, and yet what developed is a reworking of the same teaching that was there previously, not only in Indian mystical philosophy, but also in the mystical and yogic teachings of Ancient Egypt.

Buddha emphasized attaining salvation rather than asking so many questions. He likened people who asked too many intellectual questions to a person whose house (lifetime) is burning down while they ask, "How did the fire get started?" instead of first worrying about getting out of the house. Further, Buddha saw that renouncing attachment to worldly objects was not primarily a physical discipline, but more importantly, it was a psychological one. Therefore, he constructed a philosophical discipline, based on already existing philosophical tenets that explained the psychology behind human suffering and how to end that suffering. The Middle Path emphasized balance rather than extremes. He recognized that extremes cause mental upsets because one extreme leads to another, and the mind loses the capacity for rational thought and intuitional awareness which transcends thought itself. Therefore, mental balance is the way to achieve mental peace and serenity, which will allow the transcendental vision of the Self to emerge in the mind. The following segment from the *Isha Upanishad* shows that having a balanced approach and proceeding according to the *"middle path"* with respect to the practice of spiritual disciplines was already addressed as being desirable for spiritual growth prior to the emergence of Buddhism. Buddhism later represented an accent or emphasis on this feature of the doctrine so it is clear that Buddhism "adopted" many pre-existing philosophical principles from Hinduism.

> "To darkness are they doomed who devote themselves only to life in the world, and to a greater darkness they who devote themselves only to meditation.
> Life in the world alone leads to one result, meditation alone leads to another. So we have heard from the wise. They who devote themselves both to life in the world and to meditation, by life in the world overcome death, and by meditation achieve immortality.
> To darkness are they doomed who worship only the body, and to greater darkness they who worship only the spirit."

This Buddhist Yogic psychological discipline became known as the Noble Eight-fold Path, the disciplines of Buddhist Yoga which lead to spiritual enlightenment. The "Middle Path," is also the central feature of Maat Philosophy from Ancient Egypt. It was referred to as "Keeping the Balance."[91]

In India, five to six hundred years before Christianity, Buddhism had caused a renaissance of sorts. The Brahmanic system (based on the Vedic Tradition) of ritual, asceticism and elaborate myth began to lose favor with many aspirants who were seeking a more psychologically based approach to the pursuit of spiritual enlightenment that did not include the use of deities or elaborate symbolism. The ideas inherent in Buddhism such as *Karma*, (the law of cause and effect and reincarnation), *Maya*, (Cosmic Illusion) and *Buddhi* (Intellect) existed in the Vedantic and Yogic scriptures of India prior to the formulation of the Buddhist religion. However, the spiritual system developed in the sixth century B.C.E. by Gautama, the Buddha, represented in a way a reform as well as a refinement of the older teachings which were already widely accepted. Especially emphasized was that God, the ultimate reality, alone exists and that everyone is equally able to achieve oneness with that reality. However, the concept of God in Buddhism is that God is not to be considered as a deity, but as an abstract state of consciousness which is achieved when the mind is free of desires and consequently free of the fruits of action. Buddhism also placed important emphasis on non-violence which certainly became a central part of the Christian doctrine as well, in philosophy if not in practice. In the same sense that Buddhism proclaims everyone can have *Buddha Consciousness* (or *Buddha Nature*) and thus become a Buddha, Gnostic Christianity affirms that everyone can achieve *Christ Consciousness* and thus become a *Christ*.

As explained earlier, the Buddha or *"The Enlightened One"* developed a philosophy based on ideas that existed previously in the Upanishads. In much the same way as the term Christ refers to anyone who has attained "Christhood," the term Buddha refers to any one who has attained the "Buddha Consciousness," the state of Enlightenment. In this context there have been many male and female Christs and Buddhas throughout history, since the earliest practice of mystical spirituality in Kamit.

Prior to Buddha, other teachings such as those of the "Brahmins," (followers of the teachings related to Brahman of the Upanishads) the *Samnyasa* or renunciates, and the Jains promoted the idea that one was supposed to renounce the apparent reality of the world as an illusion by detachment, privation and austerity. The Buddhists as well as the Jains[92] deny the divine origin and authority of the Vedas. The Buddhists revere Buddha and the Jains revere certain saints who espoused the Jain philosophy in ancient times. Buddha recognized that many people took the teachings to extreme and saw this as the cause of failure in attaining progress in spirituality. Teachings such as reducing one's Karma by reducing one's worldly involvements were misunderstood by many to mean escaping the world by running away to some remote forest or mountain area. Also, the teachings of non-violence which stressed not harming any creatures were taken to the extreme by some in the Jain religion, to the point that they would not physically move so as not to step on insects, or not breathe without covering the mouth and nostrils, so as not to kill microorganisms. Others felt that they should not talk to anyone or interact with others in any way. These teachings were taken to such extremes that some aspirants would remain silent so long as to lose their capacity to speak at all. Others starved themselves while others practiced severe austerities such as meditating in the cold rivers or not sleeping. Others became deeply involved with the intellectual aspects of philosophy, endlessly questioning, "Where did I come from? Who put me here? How long will I need to do spiritual practice? Where did Brahman (God) come from?" etc. These questions were entertained ad-infinitum, without leading to answers that promote the attainment of enlightenment. Buddha saw the error of the way in which the teaching was understood and practiced. He therefore set out to reform religion.

AFRICAN ORIGINS Of Civilization, Religion, Yoga Mystical Spirituality And Ethics Philosophy

NOTES TO INTRODUCTION

[1] Photo by Gakuji Tanaka
[2] Petrie Museum, London England.
[3] American Heritage Dictionary
[4] ibid.
[5] Copyright © 1995 Helicon Publishing Ltd Encyclopedia
[6] Copyright © 1995 Helicon Publishing Ltd Encyclopedia, Random House Encyclopedia Copyright (C) 1983,1990, Microsoft (R) Encarta Encyclopedia. Copyright (c) 1994
[7] Random House Encyclopedia Copyright (C) 1983,1990
[8] Copyright © 1995 Helicon Publishing Ltd Encyclopedia
[9] Copyright © 1995 Helicon Publishing Ltd Encyclopedia, Random House Encyclopedia Copyright (C) 1983,1990, Microsoft (R) Encarta Encyclopedia. Copyright (c) 1994
[10] Mesopotamia (from a Greek term meaning "between rivers") lies between the Tigris and Euphrates rivers, a region that is part of modern Iraq.
[11] Random House Encyclopedia Copyright (C) 1983,1990
[12] ibid.
[13] **the·ol·o·gy** (thē-ŏl′ə-jē) *n., pl.* **the·ol·o·gies**. *Abbr.* **theol. 1.** The study of the nature of God and religious truth; rational inquiry into religious questions. (American Heritage Dictionary)
[14] **com·mu·nal** *(kə-myōō′nəl, kŏm′yə-) adj.* **1.** *Of or relating to a commune.* **2.** *Of or relating to a community.* **3.a.** *Of, belonging to, or shared by the people of a community; public.* **b.** *Marked by collective ownership and control of goods and property.* (American Heritage Dictionary)
[15] **syn·chro·ny** (sĭng′krə-nē, sĭn′-) *n., pl.* **syn·chro·nies**. Simultaneous occurrence; synchronism. (American Heritage Dictionary)
[16] **ty·pog·ra·phy** (tī-pŏg′rə-fē) *n., pl.* **ty·pog·ra·phies**. *Abbr.* **typ., typo.** *Printing* **2.** The arrangement and appearance of printed matter. (American Heritage Dictionary)
[17] American Heritage Dictionary
[18] Random House Encyclopedia Copyright (C) 1983,1990
[19] *The African Origin of Civilization, Civilization or Barbarism,* Cheikh Anta Diop
[20] American Heritage Dictionary
[21] American Heritage Dictionary
[22] American Heritage Dictionary
[23] American Heritage Dictionary
[24] *Comparative Mythology,* Jaan Puhvel
[25] *Comparative Mythology,* Jaan Puhvel
[26] A "Great Cycle" *(Mahayuga)* of cosmic time.
[27] i.e., at the ending of the cosmic eon, Wagner's *Götterdämmerung*.
[28] According to the Egyptians, Diodorus reports, the Chaldaens were *"a colony of their priests that Belus had transported on the Euphrates and organized on the model of the mother-caste, and this colony continues to cultivate the knowledge of the stars, knowledge that it brought from the homeland."*
[29] *The Mythic Image,* Joseph Campbell
[30] *The Mythic Image,* Joseph Campbell
[31] *Resurrecting Osiris,* Muata Ashby, 1997
[32] American Heritage Dictionary
[33] *The Power of Myth,* Joseph Campbell
[34] *Comparative Mythology,* Jaan Puhvel
[35] G. Lafaye. *Historie des divinités d'Alexandrie hors de l' Egypte.* Paris, 18984, p.259
[36] *The Migration of Symbols,* Count Goblet D' Alviella, 1894
[37] **dog·ma** (dôg′mə, dŏg′-) *n., pl.* **dog·mas** or **dog·ma·ta** (-mə-tə). **1.** *Theology.* A doctrine or a corpus of doctrines relating to matters such as morality and faith, set forth in an authoritative manner by a church.
[38] **or·tho·dox** (ôr′thə-dŏks′) *adj.* **1.** Adhering to the accepted or traditional and established faith, especially in religion.
[39] The word "Hinduism" is a Western term. The religion called Hinduism is actually referred to by the Hindus themselves as "Sanatana-Dharma," which means "the eternal law" or "the path or righteous actions or way of life." The major religion of the Indian subcontinent is Hinduism. The word derives from an ancient Sanskrit term meaning "dwellers by the Indus River," a reference to the location of India's earliest known civilization in what is now Pakistan. (*Feuerstein, Georg, The Shambhala Encyclopedia of Yoga* 1997 and *Compton's Interactive Encyclopedia.* Copyright (c) 1994, 1995 Compton's NewMedia, Inc. All Rights Reserved).
[40] *The Power of Myth,* Bill Moyers, 1989.
[41] In Ancient Egyptian mythology, the son of Isis (Aset), Heru, represents rulership and the upholding of righteousness, truth and order. Thus, the Pharaoh is Heru incarnate and when that person dies, he/she becomes Asar (Osiris), the resurrected (Enlightened) spirit.
[42] The Asar from Ancient Egypt.
[43] December 25th is also the birthday of the Ancient Egyptian god Heru.

AFRICAN ORIGINS Of Civilization, Religion, Yoga Mystical Spirituality And Ethics Philosophy

[44] For more details see the book *Christian Yoga: The Journey from Jesus to Christ* by Muata Ashby
[45] Adopting cultural expressions of other cultures and making them part of one's own culture thereby subsuming the cultural factors from other cultures within the larger one and consequently dissolving the adopted culture into the larger one. Over a period of time, the original source of the tradition becomes blurred or forgotten because the original tradition is no longer presented as such. Examples: Moslem and Christian church practice of destroying indigenous temples and placing Mosques or churches, respectively, on the same sites. Christian adoption of the Ancient Egyptian cross, eucharist, resurrection, birthday of Heru, Madonna, etc.
[46] To neutralize or win over (an independent minority, for example) through assimilation into an established group or culture. (American Heritage Dictionary)
[47] Copyright © 1995 Helicon Publishing Ltd Encyclopedia
[48] Copyright © 1995 Helicon Publishing Ltd Encyclopedia
[49] American Heritage Dictionary
[50] *Egypt Uncovered*, Vivian Davies and Renée Friedman
[51] *Comparative Mythology*, Jaan Puhvel
[52] The scientific study of the origin, the behavior, and the physical, social, and cultural development of human beings.
[53] The belief that one's own culture is primary and superior to other cultures.
[54] *Egyptian Proverbs* by Dr. Muata Ashby
[55] *Bhagavad Gita* by Swami Jyotirmayananda
[56] Random House Encyclopedia Copyright (C) 1983,1990
[57] "Scientific Method," Microsoft (R) Encarta. Copyright (c) 1994
[58] for evidences see the book *The Conscious Universe: The Scientific truth of Psychic Phenomena* By Dean Radin, Ph. D.
[59] *Memphite Theology*, Muata Ashby
[60] *The Tao of Physics*, Fritjof Capra
[61] *Dancing Wu Li Masters* by Gary Zukov
[62] American Heritage Dictionary
[63] American Heritage Dictionary
[64] *Comparative Mythology*, Jaan Puhvel
[65] Ibid
[66] Ibid
[67] Ibid
[68] A structural or behavioral characteristic peculiar to an individual or a group.
[69] *The Migration of Symbols*, Count Goblet D' Alviella, 1894
[70] Ontology, in philosophy, the branch of metaphysics that studies the basic nature of things, the essence of "being" itself.
[71] *Statistics-probability-* A number expressing the likelihood that a specific event will occur, expressed as the ratio of the number of actual occurrences to the number of possible occurrences. (American Heritage Dictionary)
[72] From more details see the book *Christian Yoga: The Journey from Jesus to Christ* by Muata Ashby
[73] ibid
[74] Stolen Legacy, George G.M. James
[75] Inscription at the Delphic Oracle. From Plutarch, Morals, *Familiar Quotations*, John Bartlett
[76] For more details on the interaction between Ancient Egypt and Greece see the book *From Egypt to Greece* by Muata Ashby.
[77] Random House Encyclopedia Copyright (C) 1983,1990
[78] "Vergil," Microsoft (R) Encarta. Copyright (c) 1994
[79] *The Aeneid By Virgil*, Translated by John Dryden
[80] Troy (Asia Minor), also Ilium (ancient Ilion), famous city of Greek legend, on the northwestern corner of Asia Minor, in present-day Turkey. "Troy (Asia Minor)," Microsoft (R) Encarta. Copyright (c) 1994
[81] "Memnon," Microsoft (R) Encarta. Copyright (c) 1994
[82] Random House Encyclopedia Copyright (C) 1983,1990
[83] *The Complete Temples of Ancient Egypt*, Richard Wilkinson, (C) 2000
[84] Random House Encyclopedia Copyright (C) 1983,1990
[85] *The Aeneid By Virgil*, Translated by John Dryden
[86] *The Aeneid By Virgil*, Translated by John Dryden
[87] **Mahabharata** (Sanskrit, *Great Story*), longer of the two great epic poems of ancient India; the other is the *Ramayana*. The *Mahabharata* was composed beginning about 300B.C.E. and received numerous additions until about 300 A.C.E.. "Mahabharata," *Microsoft® Encarta® Encyclopedia 2000*. © 1993-1999 Microsoft Corporation. All rights reserved.
[88] Any of a group of philosophical treatises contributing to the theology of ancient Hinduism-Vedanta Philosophy, elaborating on and superseding the earlier Vedas.
[89] The Indochinese peninsula includes a small part of Bangladesh, most of Myanmar (Burma), Thailand, Cambodia, and parts of Malaysia, Laos, and Vietnam.
[90] Spiritual tradition in India based on the scriptures known as the Upanishads. It is also referred to as Vedanta Philosophy, the culmination or summary of the Vedic Tradition whish is itself based on the scriptures known as the Vedas.
[91] *"The Wisdom of Maati,"* Dr. Muata Ashby. *"The Egyptian Book of the Dead,"* Dr. Muata Ashby.
[92] Religion founded by Mahavira, a contemporary of Buddha. "Jainism," Microsoft (R) Encarta. Copyright (c) 1994

PART I: THE AFRICAN ORIGINS OF AFRICAN CIVILIZATION, RELIGION, YOGA MYSTICISM AND ETHICS PHILOSOPHY

Chapter 1: The People and History of Ancient Egypt and Nubia

Rtji Ancient Egyptian

Ahsu Ancient Nubian

"From Ethiopia, he (Osiris) passed through Arabia, bordering upon the Red Sea to as far as India, and the remotest inhabited coasts; he built likewise many cities in India, one of which he called Nysa, willing to have remembrance of that (Nysa) in Egypt where he was brought up. At this Nysa in India he planted Ivy, which continues to grow there, but nowhere else in India or around it. He left likewise many other marks of his being in those parts, by which the latter inhabitants are induced, and do affirm, that this God was born in India. He likewise addicted himself to the hunting of elephants, and took care to have statues of himself in every place, as lasting monuments of his expedition."

-Recorded by Diodorus (Greek historian 100 B.C.)

Chapter 1-Section 1: Introduction

This chapter has three parts. First we will present an introduction to the Ancient Egyptians and an overview of their place in history. Secondly, we will explore the Nubian origins and history of Ancient Egypt, which will give a depth to our knowledge of the Ancient Egyptians. It is important for us to have this understanding of their origins in Nubia and their relationship to the Nubians (Ethiopians), because by doing so, we will become cognizant of and gain deeper insight into the African origins of Kamitan culture as well as the extent of its impact and influence on the rest of Africa beginning with the Nubian kingdoms, and through their influence, extending into the other countries in the interior of Africa. Then we will explore the different periods of Ancient Egyptian history in detail.

Who Were the Ancient Egyptians and why Should we Learn About Them?

The Ancient Egyptian religion (*Shetaut Neter*), language and symbols provide the first "historical" record of Mystical Philosophy and Religious literature. Egyptian Mysticism is what has been commonly referred to by Egyptologists as Egyptian "Religion" or "Myth," but to think of it as just another set of stories or allegories about a long lost civilization is to completely miss the greater teaching it has to offer. Mystical spirituality, in all of its forms and disciplines of spiritual development, was practiced in Ancient Egypt (Kamit) earlier than anywhere else in history. This unique perspective from the highest philosophical system which developed in Africa over seven thousand years ago provides a new way to look at life, religion, the discipline of psychology and the way to spiritual development leading to spiritual Enlightenment. Ancient Egyptian myth, when understood as a system of *Sema (Smai) Tawi* (Egyptian Yoga), that is, a system which promotes the union of the individual soul with the Universal Soul or Supreme Consciousness, gives every individual insight into their own divine nature, and also a deeper insight into all religions, mystical and Yoga systems.

Next, let us answer the question of "Why should we learn about the Ancient Egyptians? Of what benefit will it be to us today, in the here and now?" Ancient Egyptian culture and philosophy is crucial to the understanding of world history and spirituality. One of the misconceptions which is still promoted and prevalent in modern times is that Egypt is not a part of, or located on, the continent of Africa. Rather, it is espoused that Egypt is in the Middle East. This information is incorrect, as Egypt is where it has always been located, though in history it extended beyond its current margins, in the northeast corner of the African Continent. Further, it is widely believed by others that even though Egypt may be in Africa, that it was not an African country, and still others may agree that it was an African country, but not originally founded and populated by "black" African people (like present day Algeria, which is in Africa but populated by Middle Easterners -Arabs). These errors must be redressed in order for humanity to move forward. Truth must be promoted and in this case, it is crucial that this particular truth be brought forth into our human sphere of knowledge, as it offers a chance to humanity for achieving some level of peace and harmony as a world community. Also it will promote the redemption of African culture and thereby uplift African society and thereby the world. Africa provides a common ground, literally and figuratively, for humanity to come together, if we so choose, as both the physical origins of modern day humans is rooted in African soil, and also the spiritual roots of all religions and spiritual traditions can be traced there as well. Most of the wars that have occurred in human history after the close of Ancient Egyptian history have been due to religious differences, especially between orthodox aspects of the three major world religions, Christianity, Islam and Judaism, and the various subgroups of religions to which they each have given rise. Yet, all of these religions, and as we shall see, all spiritual traditions of the world, have their birthplace in Kamit. They are as if children and grandchildren of the Kamitan tradition. Imagine what happens in a simple human family when the children and grandchildren enter into conflicts and feuds. In the history of the U.S.A., there is a well-established example of the effects of this in the story of the Hatfields and the McCoys, a family feud that lasted for generations. Also, consider the United States' civil war. From this viewpoint, it is easy to understand why the world is in the shape it is in today. In the case of the world religions, they are not directly fighting to claim the cultural inheritance and prestige of their Kamitan ancestors, although their traditions utilize many of the symbols or concepts of the Kamitan tradition in limited ways. Rather, for the most part they have shunned their ancestry and the history of their "roots" in favor of each trying to legitimize themselves as the only "true" religion, without regards to the culture and land of origin which forms the very nucleus (core, nidus) of all current traditions. Not only have they shunned their ancestry, but in many ways also disparage it. Consequently, although they all claim to have some aspects of commonality (Muslims accept Jesus, but only as a prophet, and Jews and Christians have the Old Testament in common, etc.), they are inherently unable to unite, as ultimately, each tradition believes and espouses that it is the only one true religion and has the only one true God.

The current state of human relations in the world has been likened to a family of dysfunctional people. One of the causes cited for this disfunctionality is the misunderstanding of human origins and relationships which leads to the adoption of bogus concepts such as racism, religious sectarianism, superiority complexes, inhumanity, violence and war. The world community needs to have the knowledge of its African human and spiritual origins so that Africa can take its rightful place as the "parent" of all humanity. In this way the error by which most people live will be resolved in the understanding that we are all of one family, one "race". It is also important for people who identify themselves as being of African descent to know and understand their deepest "roots" beyond the most current history of enslavement and all the negative racist ramifications it spawned (i.e. Africans are inferior, stupid, etc.). Most people of African ancestry have had to live with, and to some degree accept, denigrating and deprecating conditions, in order to survive. Thus, those who identify themselves as being ethnically of African origins can, through espousing and accepting the truth with respect to world history, become esteemed members of the world community.

The study of Kamitan Spirituality is also of particular importance for people of Indian descent, as they too share directly in the Kamitan legacy. This knowledge will allow them to understand the depth of their own culture and spiritual tradition, as well as aid in the restoration of positive interactions with people of African descent in India, the Diaspora, and Africa itself.

Where is Egypt?

Figure 6: Egypt is located in the north-eastern corner of the African Continent.

AFRICAN ORIGINS OF CIVILIZATION, RELIGION, YOGA MYSTICAL SPIRITUALITY AND ETHICS PHILOSOPHY

Figure 7: Below left: A map of North East Africa showing the location of the land of *Ta-Meri* or *Kamit*, also known as Ancient Egypt and South of it is located the land which in modern times is called Sudan.

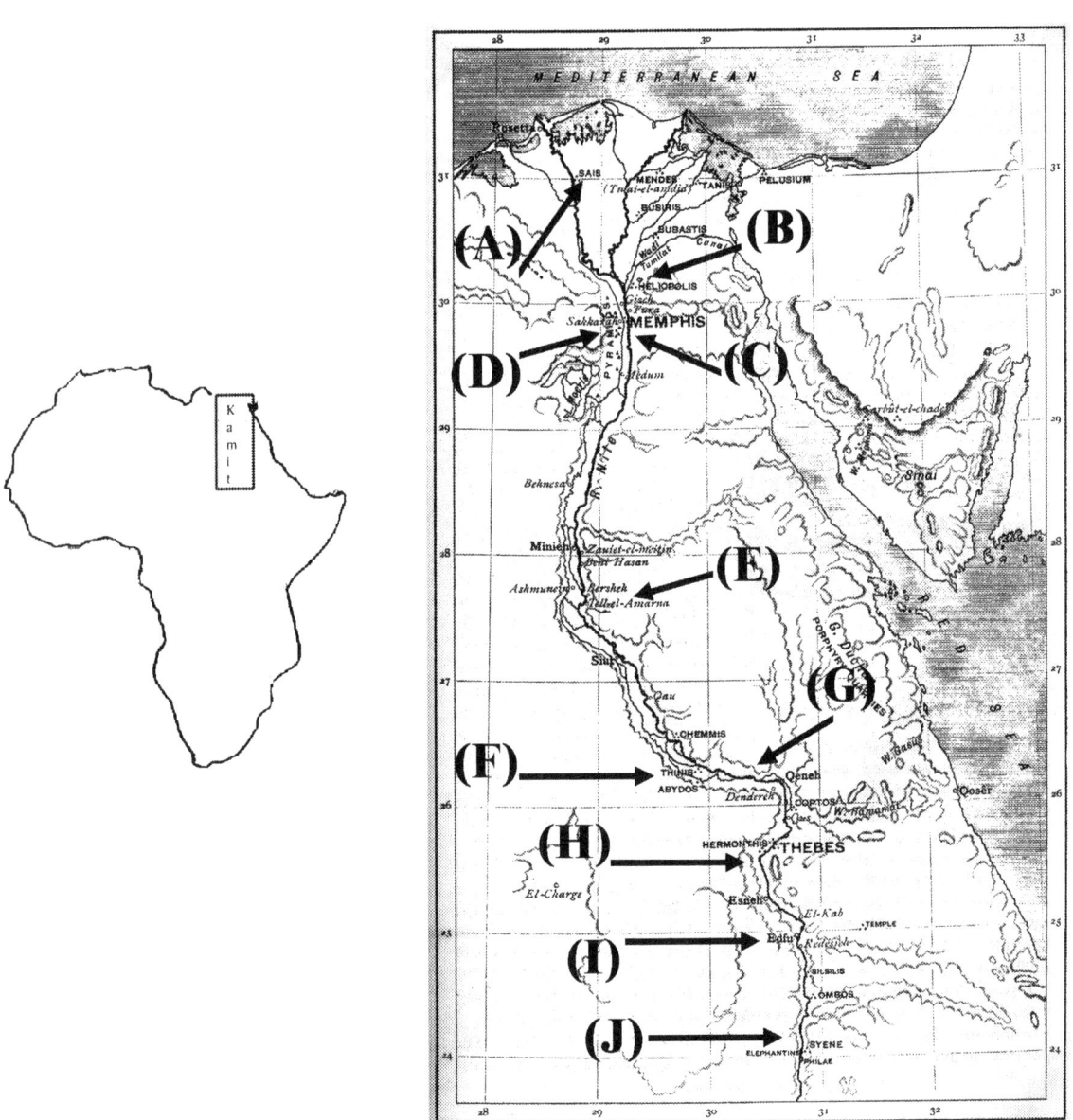

Figure 8: Above right- The Land of Ancient Egypt-Nile Valley

The cities wherein the theology of the Trinity of Amun-Ra-Ptah was developed were: A- Sais (temple of Net), B- Anu (Heliopolis- temple of Ra), C-Men-nefer or Hetkaptah (Memphis, temple of Ptah), and D- Sakkara (Pyramid Texts), E- Akhet-Aton (City of Akhnaton, temple of Aton), F- Abdu (temple of Asar), G- Denderah (temple of Hetheru), H- Waset (Thebes, temple of Amun), I- Edfu (temple of Heru), J- Philae (temple of Aset). The cities wherein the theology of the Trinity of Asar-Aset-Heru was developed were Anu, Abydos, Philae, Denderah and Edfu.

The Two Lands of Egypt

In Chapter 4[93] and Chapter 17[94] of the Ancient Egyptian mystical text, the *Prt m Hru, The Ancient Egyptian Book of Enlightenment*, more commonly known as the *Book of the Dead*, the term "Sema (Smai) Tawi" is used. It means "Union of the two lands of Egypt." The two lands refers to the two main districts of the country, North and South, and, in a mystical sense they refer to the gods Heru (the north) and Set (the south land), who are elsewhere referred to as the spiritual Higher Self and lower self of a human being, respectively. Thus, the term Sema Tawi is compatible with the Indian Sanskrit term "Yoga," which also means union of the Higher Self and lower self as well as other terms used by other systems of mystical spirituality (Enlightenment, Kingdom of Heaven, Liberation, etc.).

Diodorus Siculus (Greek Historian) writes in the time of Augustus (first century B.C.):

> "Now the Ethiopians, as historians relate, were the first of all men and the proofs of this statement, they say, are manifest. For that they did not come into their land as immigrants from abroad, but were the natives of it and so justly bear the name of autochthones (sprung from the soil itself) is, they maintain, conceded by practically all men..."

> "They also say that the Egyptians are colonists sent out by the Ethiopians, Asar having been the leader of the colony. For, speaking generally, what is now Egypt, they maintain, was not land, but sea, when in the beginning the universe was being formed; afterwards, however, as the Nile during the times of its inundation carried down the mud from Ethiopia, land was gradually built up from the deposit...And the larger parts of the customs of the Egyptians are, they hold, Ethiopian, the colonists still preserving their ancient manners. For instance, the belief that their kings are Gods, the very special attention which they pay to their burials, and many other matters of a similar nature, are Ethiopian practices, while the shapes of their statues and the forms of their letters are Ethiopian; for of the two kinds of writing which the Egyptians have, that which is known as popular (demotic) is learned by everyone, while that which is called sacred (hieratic), is understood only by the priests of the Egyptians, who learnt it from their Fathers as one of the things which are not divulged, but among the Ethiopians, everyone uses these forms of letters. Furthermore, the orders of the priests, they maintain, have much the same position among both peoples; for all are clean who are engaged in the service of the gods, keeping themselves shaven, like the Ethiopian priests, and having the same dress and form of staff, which is shaped like a plough and is carried by their kings who wear high felt hats which end in a knob in the top and are circled by the serpents which they call asps; and this symbol appears to carry the thought that it will be the lot who shall dare to attack the king to encounter death-carrying stings. Many other things are told by them concerning their own antiquity and the colony which they sent out that became the Egyptians, but about this there is no special need of our writing anything."

> The king is viewed as the incarnation of the Divine who had come to earth to carry out the will of the Divine. This is also related to the concept of priest Kingship in which kings and queens were seen as the head of the religion as well as the secular government at the same time. The priest kingship concept was a typical form of African government syste,.

Figure 9: Below- the Ancient Egyptian Hor-m-Akhet (Sphinx).

The archeological and geological evidence surrounding the great Sphinx in Giza, Egypt, Africa, shows that it was created no later than 10,000 B.C.E. to 7,000 B.C.E. This gives us the understanding that Kamit, Ancient Egypt, produced the earliest known artifacts, which denotes civilization. Thus, the Kamitan or Ancient Egyptian civilization is the oldest known civilization in our history.

How Some Western and Arab Scholars Distort Evidence Pointing to the Older Age of Ancient Egyptian Culture

After examining the writings of many Western scholars, the feeling of many Africentrists and Africologists (researchers into African culture) of African descent and some non-African Western scholars is that traditional Egyptologists, a group comprised almost entirely of people of European descent or who have been trained by Western scholars, have over the years sought to bring down the estimated date for the commencement of the Dynastic Period in Egypt in order to show that Ancient Egyptian culture emerged after Mesopotamian culture. Presumably, this was done because Mesopotamia is held by many Western scholars to be their (Western Culture's) own, if not genetic, cultural ancestral homeland. The reader should understand the context of this issue that goes to the heart of cultural relations between Western Culture and Eastern and African cultures. From the perspective of many people of non-European descent, Western Culture has sought to establish its socio-economic supremacy by suppressing and undermining the capacity of indigenous peoples worldwide, to govern themselves and control their own resources. This is verified by the documented evidence of the African slave trade,[95] military and covert intervention to destabilize governments, distortion of history,[96][97] colonial and neocolonial systems,[98] etc., either set up or supported by Western countries in the past 500 years. In order to perpetuate this control, the image of superiority demands that Western Culture should be able to project an ancestral right, as it were, to control other countries. Therefore, twisting evidence in order to make Western Culture appear ancient, wise, beneficial, etc., necessitates a denial that there is any civilization that is older or possibly better than Western civilization, or that there could be any genetic or cultural relation with the non-Western Cultures which are being subjugated, or a common ancestry with the rest of humanity. An example of this twisting of history by Western scholars is the well known and documented deliberate misinterpretation of the Biblical story of Noah, so as to make it appear that the Bible advocated and condones the enslavement of the children (descendants) of Ham (all Hamitic peoples- people of African descent) by the children (descendants) of Japheth (all peoples of Germanic {European} descent).

Along with the natural stubbornness of ordinary human beings to accept change due to the their identification with prestige of their culture and heritage as a source of self-worth instead of truth and virtue, two methods of discrediting the early achievements of Ancient Egypt have been used.

The desire of Western Culture to envision their own history as a civilized culture stretching back into antiquity, having realized that Greek culture is too late in history to establish this claim, and not wanting to acknowledge that Ancient Greece essentially owes[99] its civilization to Ancient Egypt,[100] have promoted a process of downplaying the importance of Ancient Egypt in history, by means of reducing the chronology in which history took place. How could this obfuscation of the record occur?

In addition to the resistance by some in Western scholars to accept information, which they fear, will change the prestige of their culture and heritage with which they identify as a source of their self-worth, instead of defining themselves by the standards of truth and virtue, other methods of discrediting the early achievements of Ancient Egypt have been used. Two ways of invalidating Ancient Egyptian history are prominent: 1- misunderstanding or 2- supporting erroneous theories.

One method used by Western Egyptologists to contradict Kamitan history was to examine surviving[11] Ancient Egyptian mummies and apply undetermined forensic techniques in order to assign "causes of death" to the entire Ancient Egyptian culture. From this they concluded that the Ancient Egyptians had a short life span due to "primitive living conditions," and that the average life expectancy of a Pharaoh being no more than 20 years or so. However, since the cause of death can often not be determined even in modern times, how can the results derived from any technique(s) being applied to a 3,000 + years old mummified body be conclusive? When such rationales are not considered, and the erroneous pronouncements repeated over and over again, they become "accepted" as truth by scholars and lay persons for a variety of reasons, some of which we have already touched on above. The problem becomes compounded because many scholars and lay people alike do not do their own research or look at the evidence themselves and draw their own conclusions. Rather, they are comfortable accepting the information being provided, without questioning its validity. Some don't want to know, because they do not want to risk their positions by disrupting the status quo. Others may be unwilling, or unable due to blind faith and mental weakness, to examine the evidences. In addition, there are other factors to be considered such as socio-economic obstacles, physical barriers preventing access to information, training, etc.

Another method used to revise the history of the Dynastic Period in Kamit is to say that the kings or queens were ruling concurrently in certain periods as opposed to subsequently. In certain periods such as the invasion of the Hyksos and the Assyrians, Persians, etc. who conquered part of the country, Egyptian leaders ruled in their part of the country while the conquerors temporarily ruled the conquered territory that they captured. Also, this is possible in the Intermediate period when there was a partial breakdown of social order. Further, due to the destruction of records, there are many Ancient Egyptian rulers (kings and queens) mentioned whose names are no longer recorded. (See the Ancient Egyptian King and Queen List in Appendix A)

Since we have lists of the Pharaohs of the Dynastic Period, we can easily count the number of Pharaohs and use this figure to estimate what the average life span of each Pharaoh would have to be to cover the time span of the Dynastic Period, which lasted approximately 3,000 + years. Doing the math by multiplying this number by the life expectancy proposed by scholars (20 years), one arrives at a figure that is less than 3,000 years, the duration of the Dynastic period. Also, the conclusion drawn from the above methodology used to estimate the life span of the Kamitan peoples from mummified bodies (of the average life span of 20 years), even if it were accurate, does not make sense if we consider the ample documentation showing that Ancient Egypt was reputed to have the "best doctors" in the ancient world. Further, even if it were true that ordinary people existed in "primitive living conditions," does it make sense that the kings and queens would get the worst health care out of the entire population? Thus, as a scholar, is it prudent to apply this number to the royalty? Also, there is documented evidence to show that kings and queens, as well as other members of the society, lived normal healthy lives by modern standards. There are surviving records and statues, as well as illustrations, of kings, mummies and other royalty who lived well into their 80's and 90's such as Amunhotep Son of Hapu and Rameses II and others. One might also envision the wretchedness of such a life where members of a society die at such an early age. No sooner does one realize the potential of life, than one dies, as a mere child. Life would hardly be worth living. Also, since spiritual evolution requires maturity in ordinary human terms, that is, sufficient time to grow up and discover the meaning of life, a short life-span would make the vast number of extant Kamitan texts treating the subject of spiritual enlightenment impossible to create, and useless because there would not be sufficient time to take advantage of them.

Another method used to discredit the Kamitan history is to arbitrarily claim that when the Ancient Egyptians spoke of "years," they were actually referring to "months".[101] This practice is predicated on baseless supposition, and is therefore, patently false and demeaning since there is no precedent for this practice in Ancient Egyptian culture. It is an imaginary notion introduced by some Egyptologists who prefer to fantasize

---

[11] Many mummies have been destroyed throughout history by the early Christians and Muslims who wanted to eradicate all records of religions existing prior to their own, and also early European explorers who sold the mummies for experimentation as well as other Europeans who created a fad of pulverizing the mummies and using them in potions as medicinal supplements.

rather than face the magnitude of their discoveries. Thus, the corrupt nature of the historians, scholars and those who perpetuate such iniquitous misrepresentations is evident.

Still another motivation has been to try to synchronize the events such as those described in Ancient Egyptian texts or the Greek histories with those of the Bible. An example of this kind of writing can be found in a book by W. G. Waddell, called *Manetho*. Some historians feel this kind of distortion was done to establish the prestige of the Judeo-Christian tradition, the reasoning being similar to that discussed above. They believe that Judeo-Christian view was that having other traditions that are recognized as older and having more honor, heritage and prominence would undermine the perception that the Bible is ancient and infallible.

Others feel the reason was out of an effort to prove that Ancient Egyptian culture existed within the timeframe that the Bible has posed for the Creation of the world. The Creation was dated by the 17th-century[12] Irish archbishop James Ussher to have occurred in the year 4004 B.C.E.[102] If the world is approximately 6,005[13] years old, as postulated by the archbishop, this would support the teaching presented in the church and invalidate the existence of culture, philosophy, and most of all, religion, prior to the emergence of Christianity.

The work of Darwin (theory of evolution) and other scientists caused major controversies in western society. A case in point is the attempt to correlate the events of the Biblical story of Exodus with those of Ancient Egyptian Pharaoh, Rameses II. First, there are no accounts of any conflict between the Jews and the Egyptians in any Ancient Egyptian records yet discovered, beyond an inscription at the Karnak temple in Egypt stating that the Jews were one of the tribes under Egyptian rule in Palestine. Secondly, there are no corroborating records of the events chronicled in the Bible in any of the contemporary writings from countries that had contact with the Jews and the Ancient Egyptians. Thirdly, there were at least eleven kings who went by the title Rameses (Rameses I, II, III, III, etc.), spanning a period dated by traditional Egyptologists from 1,307 B.C.E. to 1,070 B.C.E. Further, some localities were also referred to as Rameses.

The oldest scholarly dating for the existence of Moses, if he did exist, is c. 1,200 B.C.E. However, most Bible scholars agree that the earliest texts of the Bible were composed around 1,000 B.C.E or later, and were developed over the next millennia. Also, most scholars are now beginning to accept the Ancient Egyptian and therefore, African ethnicity of the original Jewish peoples. An example of modern scholarship on the question of the origins of the Jews occurs in the book *Bible Myth: The African Origins of the Jewish People*. In a section entitled "Contradictory Biblical Evidence," the author, Gary Greenberg states:

> Dating the Exodus is problematic because evidence of its occurrence appears exclusively in the Bible, and what little it tells is contradictory. Exodus 12:40-41, for example, places the Exodus 430 years after the start of Israel's sojourn in Egypt (i.e., beginning with Jacob's arrival), whereas Genesis 15:13-14 indicates that four hundred years transpired from the birth of Isaac to the end of the bondage. Both claims cannot be true. Jacob was born in Isaac's 60th year,[103] and he didn't arrive in Egypt until his 130th year.[104] If the sojourn lasted 430 years, then the Exodus would have to have occurred 620 years after Isaac's birth.[105] On the other hand, if the Exodus occurred 400 years after Isaac was born, then the sojourn could only have been 210 years long.[106] Other biblical passages raise additional problems.[107]

The story of Sargon I points to another source and purpose for the Moses story, in our present context. According to the Biblical tradition, at about 1200? B.C.E., the Hebrews were in Egypt, serving as slaves. A Jewish woman placed her son in a basket and allowed it to float downstream where the Egyptian queen found it, and then adopted the child. The child was Moses, the chosen one of God, who would lead the Jews out of bondage in Egypt. Moses was taken in by the royal family and taught the wisdom related to rulership of the nation as well as to the Egyptian religion and the Egyptian Temples (Bible: Acts 7:22). He was being groomed to be king and high priest of Egypt. This is why the Bible says he was knowledgeable in the wisdom of the Egyptians (Bible: Acts 7:22 and Koran C.144: Verses 37 to 76).

A story similar to the birth of Moses, about a child being placed in a basket and put in a stream which was later found by a queen, can be found in Zoroastrian mythology as well.[58] Also, recall the Semitic ruler, Sargon I, was rescued in the same manner after he was placed in a basket and sent floating down a river. Sargon I

---

[12] 17th century refers to the time period from 1,600-1,699 A.C.E.

[13] 4,004 + 1,600 to 1,699 gives a range of time span from 4,604-5,703; this has been conservatively rounded to 6,000.

reined about 2,335-2,279 B.C.E. He was called "Sargon, The Great." He was one of the first known major Semitic conquerors in history. He was successful in conquering the entire country of Sumer, an ancient country of southwestern Asia, which corresponds approximately to the biblical land known as Babylonia (Babylon). Babylon was an ancient city of Mesopotamia, which was located on the Euphrates River about 55mi (89km) South of present-day Baghdad. Sargon I created an empire stretching from the Mediterranean to the Persian Gulf in c.2,350 B.C.E. The adoption of the child into royalty and rulership motif was apparently a popular theme in ancient times for those who wanted to legitimize their ascendancy to power by creating the perception that it was divinely ordained.[108]

Despite the myriad of ongoing excavations that have been conducted, many sponsored by Christian or Jewish groups, no substantial evidence has been unearthed that supports the historicity of the Bible. However, new discoveries have been brought forth that corroborate Herodotus' statements and the histories relating to the fact that the land that is now called Palestine, was once part of Ancient Egypt.

> An approximately 5,000-year-old settlement discovered in southern Israel was built and ruled by Egyptians during the formative period of Egyptian civilization, a team of archaeologists announced last week.
>
> The new find, which includes the first Egyptian-style tomb known to have existed in Israel at that time, suggests that ancient Egypt exerted more control over neighboring regions than investigators have often assumed, contends project director Thomas E. Levy of the University of California, San Diego.
>
> Source: Science News, Oct 5, 1996 v150 n14 p215(1).
> Title: Ancient Egyptian outpost found in Israel.
> (Halif Terrace site in southern Israel upsets previous estimates of Egyptian imperialism) Author: Bruce Bower

Speaking out against the stronghold, which modern European and American Egyptologists have created, the Egyptologist, scholar and author, John Anthony West, detailed his experiences and those of others attempting to study the Ancient Egyptian monuments and artifacts who are not part of the "accepted" Egyptological clique. He describes the situation as a kind of "Fortress Egypt." He describes the manner in which, not only are the Ancient Egyptian artifacts closely protected from the examination of anyone outside this group, but also the interpretation of them as well. It is as if there is a propaganda machine, which, like the orthodox medical establishment, has set itself up as sole purveyors of the "correct" knowledge in the field, and thereby invalidates the findings of other scholars or scientists. In discussing the way in which mistakes made by scholars are treated, Mister West says the following:

> In academia, the rules vis-à-vis mistakes change according to location. Only those within the establishment are allowed to 'make mistakes.' Everyone else is a 'crank' 'crackpot' or 'charlatan,' and entire lifetimes of work are discredited or dismissed on the basis of minor errors.

Also, the treatment of any scholar who reads metaphysical import in the teachings, literature or iconography of Ancient Egypt is generally ridiculed by orthodox Egyptologists. For instance, anyone suggesting that the Great pyramids were not used as burial chambers (mummies or remnants of mummies have never been discovered in them), but rather as temples, is openly called a "Pyramidiot,"[109] West describes the ominous power that orthodox Egyptologists have taken to themselves and the danger this power poses to humanity:

> A tacit territorial agreement prevails throughout all Academia. Biochemists steer clear of sociology; Shakespearean scholars do not disparage radio astronomy. It's taken for granted that each discipline, scientific, scholarly or humanistic, has its own valid self-policing system, and that academic credentials ensure expertise in a given field.
>
> With its jealous monopoly on the impenetrable hieroglyphs,± its closed ranks, restricted membership, landlocked philosophical vistas, empty coffers, and its lack of impact upon virtually every other academic, scientific or humanistic field, Egyptology has prepared a near-impregnable strategic position for itself - an academic Switzerland but without chocolate, cuckoo clocks, scenery or ski slopes, and cannily concealing its banks. Not only is it indescribably boring and difficult to attack, who'd want to?
>
> But if Swiss financiers suddenly decided to jam the world's banking system, Swiss neutrality and impregnability might suddenly be at risk. That is partially analogous to the situation of Egyptology. The gold is there, but its existence is denied, and no one is allowed

to inspect the vaults except those whose credentials make them privy to the conspiracy and guarantee their silence. To date, only a handful of astute but powerless outsiders have recognized that the situation poses real danger. But it's not easy to generate a widespread awareness or appreciation of that danger.

If you think of Egyptologists at all, the chances are you conjure up a bunch of harmless pedants, supervising remote desert digs or sequestered away in libraries, up to their elbows in old papyrus. You don't think of them as sinister, or dangerous. The illuminati responsible for the hydrogen bomb, nerve gas and Agent Orange are dangerous; if you reflect upon it you see that the advanced beings who have given us striped toothpaste and disposable diapers are also dangerous ... but Egyptologists?

Possibly they are the most dangerous of all; dangerous because false ideas are dangerous. At any rate *some* false ideas are dangerous. Belief in the flat earth never hurt anyone though it made navigation problematic. Belief in a geocentric universe held back advances in astronomy but otherwise had certain metaphysical advantages. Academic Egyptology is dangerous because it maintains, in spite of Schwaller de Lubicz's documented scholarly evidence, and the obvious evidence of our own eyes and hearts when we go there, that the race responsible for the pyramids and the temples of Karnak and Luxor was less, 'advanced' than ourselves. As long as academic Egyptology prevails, children will be brought up with a totally distorted view of our human past, and by extension, of our human present. And millions of tourists will continue to visit Egypt every year, and have the experience of a lifetime vitiated and subverted by a banal explanation that the greatest art and architecture in the world to superstitious primitives.

So the fabulous metaphysical gold of Egypt remains hidden; it's existence stridently denied. For orthodox Egyptology is really little more than a covert operation within the Church of Progress. Its unspoken agenda is to maintain the faith; not to study or debate the truth about Egypt.[14]

±NOTE (by West): Who will claim authority to challenge the accepted translations of the texts, even when these read as nonsense? Actually, a number of independent scholars have learned the hieroglyphs for themselves and produced alternative less insulting translations of some of the texts. But since these are either ignored or dismissed out of hand by orthodox Egyptologists, there is no way to know if these translations come closer to the real thinking of the ancients or if they are themselves no more than figments of the translators' imaginations, and in consequence no more representative and satisfactory than the standard translations.

Noting further difficulties of sustaining independent or "alternative" Egyptology studies, West remains hopeful that the pressure to revise their unsupportable findings, not just from alternative Egyptologists, but also from geologists who bring to bear an irrefutable and exacting science to the dating of Ancient Egyptian monuments as opposed to the methods which other reputable sociologists and historians have found to be unreliable. Of the major methods accepted for establishing a chronology to understand the origins of civilization and the history of the world such as Astronomical Time, Geological Time, Archaeological Time and Political or Historical Time, the use of Scriptural chronology is recognized as being "extremely uncertain because various local chronologies were used at different times by scriptural writers, and different systems were used by contemporaneous writers."[15]

An alternative Egyptology is less easily managed. Almost no one can earn a living from it. Serious research is difficult to accomplish on a spare-time basis, and research requires access to the few major Egyptological libraries scattered around the world. In Egypt itself, excavation and all work on or in the pyramids, temples and tombs are controlled by the Egyptian Antiquities Organizations. No one without academic credentials can expect to obtain permission to carry out original work[16] Infiltration from within is also peculiarly

---

[14] *Serpent in the Sky,* John Anthony West, p. 239
[15] "Chronology," Microsoft (R) Encarta Encyclopedia. Copyright (c) 1994
[16] West adds the following footnote: Prior to the development of modern day Egyptology by the western nations, native Egyptians showed little regard or respect for their distant dynastic ancestors; the temples were quarried for stone, anything movable was cheerfully sold to antiquities dealers. Islam, along with Christianity and Judaism, tended to regard ancient Egypt as pagan and idolatrous. But today, at least in private, Egyptian Egyptologists often display a much higher degree of understanding and sensitivity toward the Pharaonic achievement than their European and American colleagues. It would not surprise me to find some closet symbolists among them. Egyptian licensed tour guides (a much coveted job) must have degrees in academic Egyptology and pass an exacting test to

difficult. At least a few people I know personally have set out to acquire degrees in Egyptology, hoping to devote themselves full time to Egypt and ultimately to legitimize the symbolist interpretation. So far, none have been able to stick out the boredom or dutifully parrot the party line for the years necessary to get the diploma, knowing better from the onset.

It seems unlikely that symbolist Egypt will ever establish itself from within its own ranks. But pressure from outside Egyptology but within academia could force a change. Academics with an interest but no personal stake in the matter must sooner or later realize that the support of highly qualified geologists (of a fundamentally geological theory) must overrule either the clamor or the silence of the Egyptological/archeological establishment. At some point they must express those views.[17]

Having read the preceding excerpts published in 1993 by West, one might think that orthodox Egyptology has never been successfully challenged. African, African American and other African Egyptologists in the Diaspora faced the same problem when they brought forth evidences, which proved that the Ancient Egyptian civilization was originally created by African people, and that people of African descent played a crucial role in the development of Ancient Egyptian culture and its interactions with other world cultures. This engendered a major storm of repudiation and ridicule beginning in the 1970's. African, African American and other African scholars and Egyptologists in the Diaspora such as Chancellor Williams, George G. M. James, John H. Clarke, Yosef A. A. ben-jochannan[110] and Cheikh Anta Diop[111] were denigrated, and their struggle to be heard even in their own communities was hampered by the constant rhetoric and derision from orthodox Egyptologists. Catching orthodox Egyptology by surprise, however, Cheikh Anta Diop not only challenged their opinion about the African origins of Ancient Egyptian culture, religion and philosophy, but offered overwhelming proof to support his contentions at the 1974 Unesco conference in which he faced 18 of the (at that time) leaders of the orthodox Egyptological community. Describing the evidence presented at the Unesco conference, scholar Asa G. Hilliard, described the proceedings as recorded by a news media reporter.[18]

In a scientific forum such opinions are unlikely to be expressed, they will be unable to compete with data-based arguments for, example, Dr. Diop presented eleven categories of evidence to support his argument for a native black African KMT[19], including eye witness testimony of classical writers, melanin levels in the skin of mummies, Bible history, linguistic and cultural comparisons with the rest of Africa, Kamitan self descriptions, Kamitan historical references, physical anthropology data, blood type studies, carvings and paintings, etc.[20] That is why the reporter at the Cairo Symposium wrote the following in the minutes of the meeting:

> "Although the preparatory working paper ... sent out by UNESCO gave particulars of what was desired, not all participants had prepared communications comparable with the painstakingly researched contributions of Professors Cheikh Anta Diop and Obenga. There was consequently a real lack of balance in the discussions."[21]

At this conference, there was either expressed or implied consensus on the following points. (No objections were raised to them.)

---

qualify. Over the course of years of research and leading tours myself, at least a few dozen have approached me, eager to learn more about symbolist Egypt. But within the closed ranks of practicing, professional Egyptology, academic prestige (such as it is) is still wielded by the major European and American Universities. So even though all ancient Egyptian sites are now entirely under Egyptian control, an Egyptian Egyptologist would be as unlikely to try to break the "common front of silence" as anyone else, whatever his or her private convictions."

[17] *Serpent in the Sky,* John Anthony West, p. 241
[18] *Egypt Child of Africa* Edited by Ivan Van Sertima, *Bringing Maat, Destroying Isfet: The African and African Diasporan Presence in the Study of Ancient KMT* by Asa G. Hilliard III
[19] Kamit (Ancient Egypt)
[20] Diop, Cheikh Anta (1981) "Origin of the ancient Egyptians" In Moktar, G. *(Ed.) General history of Africa: volume II, Ancient Civilizations of Africa.* Berkeley, California: University of California Press, pp. 27-57
[21] UNESCO, (1978) *The peopling of ancient Egypt and the deciphering of Meroitic script: The general history of Africa, studies and documents I, Proceedings of the symposium held in Cairo from 28 January to 3 February, 1974.* Paris: United Nations Educational, Scientific and Cultural Organization, p. 102.

1. In ancient KMT the south and the north were always ethnically homogeneous.
2. Professor Vercoutter's suggestion that the population of KMT had been made up of "black skinned whites" was treated as trivia.
3. There were no data presented to show that Kamitan temperament and thought were related to Mesopotamia.
4. The old Kamitan tradition speaks of the Great Lakes region in inner equatorial Africa as being the home of the ancient Kamitans.
5. There was no evidence of large-scale migration between Kamit and Mesopotamia. There were no Mesopotamian loan words in Kamitan: (therefore the two cultures could have no genetic linguistic relationship or be populated by the same people.) For comparison purposes, mention was made of the fact that when documented contact with Kamit was made by Asian Hyksos around 1700 B.C.E., loan words were left in ancient Kamit.
6. No empirical data were presented at the conference to show that the ancient Kemites were white. (Generally, there is a tendency for some historians to *assume* that developed populations are white, but to require proof of blackness.)
7. Muslim Arabs conquered Kamit during the 7th century of the Common Era. Therefore, Arabic culture is not a part of Kamit during any part of the 3,000 years of dynastic Kamit.
8. Genetic linguistic relationships exist between the African languages of Kamitan, Cushitic (Ethiopian), Puanite (Punt or Somaliland), Berber, Chadic and Arabic. Arabic only covered territory off the continent of Africa, mainly in adjacent Saudi Arabia, an area in ancient times that was as much African as Asian.
9. Dr. Diop invented a melanin dosage test and applied it to royal mummies in the Museum of Man in Paris, mummies from the Marietta Excavations. All had melanin levels consistent with a "black" population. The symposium participants made a strong recommendation that all royal mummies be tested. To date there is no word that this has been done. Dr. Diop struggled for the remaining years of his life to have access to the Cairo museum for that purpose, but to no avail.

Hilliard Concludes:

> Significantly, it was at the urging of African scholars, led by Dr. Cheikh Anta Diop, that this UNESCO sponsored scientific gathering was convened. Interestingly, the reporter's comments quoted above actually used one of the aspects of MAAT, "balance," to describe Diop and Obenga's work. Truly open dialogue brings MAAT and destroys ISFET[22]. We know this but have not required the open dialogue.

---

[22] unrighteousness

Figure 10: Pictorial Evidence of the African Origins of Ancient Egyptian Culture and Civilization.

From the Tomb of Rameses III: The four branches of mankind, according to the Egyptians: A- Egyptian as seen by himself, B- Indo-European, C- Other Africans, D- Semites (Middle Easterners) (1194-1163 B.C.E.). [112]

Careful to avoid any future such exchanges which might prove to be more injurious to the orthodox Egyptological dogma, Diop was refused further access to materials or monuments for detailed research. However, by that time the injury to the orthodox Egyptological position had been done. Since that time other evidences, such as those presented in this book and by other scholars, have steadily chipped away at the orthodox Egyptological dogmas. In this sense the struggle[23] over the "guardianship," or as some might consider "ownership," over the prestige that comes with being able to consider oneself as an Ancient Egyptian Scholar will continue, because this is apparently a war of information in which western countries have taken the lead.

All kinds of information are valued, but the information on the origins of humanity and the metaphysics of spiritual evolution are both feared and awed by most ordinary human beings, and perhaps particularly the orthodox Egyptologists, because this information truly changes everything, from the concept of human origins to what is life all about. It brings the whole Western paradigm under scrutiny. Reflect on what would happen if those people in positions of authority as well as lay people in religions, governments and schools were suddenly faced with the realization that their knowledge is deficient, and ordinary people begin to understand that they are higher beings who should not be taken advantage of. This is the power of understanding the glory and truth about Ancient Egypt. All humanity, not just Africans or Europeans, can be transformed through it, for the better, to bring about a world culture based on unity camaraderie. The illusion which orthodox Egyptologists have promoted, and with which they have self-hypnotized themselves, will gradually give way to the truth, or else they will be left behind just as the Model "T" left the horse drawn buggy behind and, electricity left oil lamps behind.

The renowned Africologist, Basil Davidson, presented Dr. Diop briefly in Davidson's documentary program "Africa." He commented on this ancient ethnography and remarked that it was "rare," dismissing it as an anomaly. However, the following picture of an Ancient Egyptian "ethnography" was discovered by Dr. Muata Ashby in the book *Arts and Crafts of Ancient Egypt,* by Flinders Petrie. However, it was not ascribed as an ethnography, which included Ancient Egyptians, but rather, unknown "Abyssinians."

---

[23] over the ownership of the prestige of being a scholar of Egyptology.

Plate 1: Ancient Egyptian Depiction of Ethnic Groups (New Kingdom Dynastic Period)[113] (Originally in the tomb of *Ramose* – drawn by Prisse d' Avennes)

The picture above is an Ancient Egyptian depiction of the four ethnic groups of the ancient world. Described by Petrie as "the Four Races" the picture is one of the ethnographies that have come down to us from Ancient Egypt. It should be noted that the formal ethnographies are rare but depictions showing the Nubians and Egyptians as having the same skin coloration are indeed quite abundant. Petrie describes the face to the far left as being a "Negro" (native African man). The next, from left to right, as a "Syrian" man, the third is described as an "Abyssinian," and the last as a "Libyan." In following along with this description by Petrie without having further insight into these classes of Ancient Egyptian art, it may go unnoticed that there is supposed to be an Ancient Egyptian person present. Having assigned the other "races," (i.e. Syrian, Libyan, Abyssinian), the Egyptian person has been omitted in the description of the group. This picture is a variation of the previous picture discovered by Dr. Diop. If the picture is rendered as the original, it would mean that the first man on the left that Petrie is referring to as a "Negro" is actually an Ancient Egyptian man, and the other person of African descent, labeled as an "Abyssinian" man, would be the Nubian (Ethiopian), since the practice of scarification, common to Nubia, is rare or unknown in Ancient Egypt.

The term "Abyssinian" refers to languages often distinguished as belonging to the subgroup of Hamitic languages. The words Semitic (Asia Minor) and Hamitic (African) are derived from the names of Noah's sons, Shem and Ham (Christian Bible-Gen. 10). Ethiopia, formerly Abyssinia, is a republic in eastern Africa, currently bounded on the northeast by Eritrea and Djibouti, on the east and southeast by Somalia, on the southwest by Kenya, and on the west and northwest by Sudan. In ancient times the country was bounded in the north by Ancient Egypt. In ancient times Ethiopia and Egypt were strongly related. In fact, Ethiopia was the birthplace of the early Egyptians and also, according to Herodotus, the Indians as well. They appeared the same to him at the time of his travels through those countries. Thus, the picture shows that the Ancient Egyptians looked no different from other Africans.

> *"And upon his return to Greece, they gathered around and asked, "tell us about this great land of the Blacks called Ethiopia." And Herodotus said, "There are two great Ethiopian nations, one in Sind (India) and the other in Egypt."*
>
> —Herodotus (c. 484-425 BC)

It is unfortunate that as a result of the mishandling of the monuments due to destruction and neglect by the Arab peoples, the harsh elements and chemicals in the environment, the dams on the Nile River, and the push for tourism, many of the images that he saw can no longer be seen today in their original form, except for a limited amount of originals, like the one discovered by Dr. Diop. Very few monuments and images retain their original color so the only other means currently available to view the images in their original forms are from drawings or pictures made by the early Egyptologists during their expeditions to Egypt. However, we have sufficient images and corroborating texts to say with certainty that the ethnicity of the original peoples who created the culture and civilization of the Nile Valley (Ancient Egypt) were the same in appearance as those people living in modern day Nubia, i.e. they were indeed "black" Africans.

Ancient Egyptian Depictions of Egyptians and Nubians

One reason for the confusion about the ethnicity of the Ancient Egyptians is the misunderstanding about their depictions of themselves. The men were represented in their art in two distinct forms, the red or reddish-brown and the black, both of which are used interchangeably. This is what the early Egyptologists such as Champollion witnessed before the colors on many depictions had been damaged or lost. In recent times, Western Egyptologists have mistakenly or intentionally characterized these images as evidence of ethnic or "racial" difference between the Ancient Egyptians and Nubians. However, the images from the Tomb of Seti I provide insight into this matter.

Assyrian Descriptions of the Ancient Egyptians and Nubians

LEFT: In the year 667 B.C.E. the Assyrians invaded Kamit, pushed out the Egyptian-Nubian army and captured the capital city of Waset (Thebes). On a relief in the palace of the Assyrian king Assurbanibal (669-635), there is depicted the battle in which the Assyrians defeated the army of Kamit. The Assyrians (men with long beards and conned hats) took prisoners which included Kamitans and Nubians as well as the spoils of the victory back to their homeland. In this relief the Nubian and Kamitan soldiers are pictured equally, meaning that they did not recognize a "racial" difference, only the ethnic difference. As far as the physical appearance of the Nubians and Kamitans the Assyrians pictured them as having the same completion. Thus, here we have independent corroboration from the ancient Assyrians as to the ethnic homogeny of the Nubians and Kamitans.

RIGHT: Philip Arrhidaeus, successor of Alexander, a Greek, in depicted in Red in accordance with Ancient Egyptian Iconographical standards to denote "Egyptian." Phillip was not an Egyptian by birth but by conquest and dictatorship. So he wanted the people to think of him as an Egyptian King and the practice was to depict Egyptians as red. However, otherwise we have seen Asiatics and others depicted as pale ("white). This means that the red color is not to denote a race or the color of the actual people but to demonstrate or differentiate one group of people from another for information purposes and not for segregation in the modern sense of Western Racism. (from the Napoleonic Expedition)

AFRICAN ORIGINS OF CIVILIZATION, RELIGION, YOGA MYSTICAL SPIRITUALITY AND ETHICS PHILOSOPHY

Figure 11: Ancient Egyptians and Nubians depicted in the Tomb of Rameses III

 *Rtji* Ancient Egyptian    *Ahsu* Ancient Nubian

The Tomb of Seti I (1306-1290 B.C.E.-below) which comes earlier than that of Rameses III (above) shows a different depiction. Note that the same labels are used to describe the Egyptians and Nubians in the pictures of both tombs.

Figure 12: Ancient Egyptians and Nubians depicted in the Tomb of Seti I

 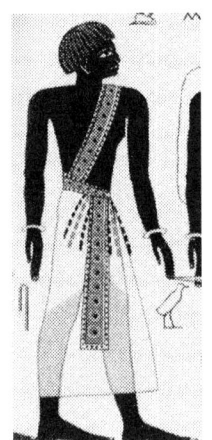

 *Rtji* Ancient Egyptian   *Ahsu* Ancient Nubian

There are two more depictions from Ancient Egypt, which shed light on the ethnological iconography of the Ancient Egyptians. First is an image from the temple of Rameses II at Abu Simbel. It provides us with the key to understanding the Kamitan depictions. At a time when Egypt and Nubia are competing with each other, Rameses symbolically brings tied up Nubian prisoners as offerings to Amun (See below).

Figure 13: Below left – late 20th century Nubian man. Below right-Nubian Prisoners of Rameses II -Image at the Abu Simbel Temple

Figure 14: Bottom left-Ancient Egyptians (musicians) and Nubians (dancers) depicted in the Tombs of the Nobles with the same hue and features. Bottom right- Nubian King Taharka and the Queen offering to Amun (blue) and Mut (colored in yellow) depicted as a red Egyptians. 7th cent BCE

Figure 15: Below-left, Egyptian man and woman-(tomb of Payry) 18th Dynasty displaying the naturalistic style (as people really appeared in ancient times). Below right- Egyptian man and woman-Theban tomb – depicted in the colors red and yellow, respectively.

Figure 16: Below-left, Stele of Niptah - end of Middle Kingdom (man in red, woman in white with breasts exposed).

Figure 17: Nubians (three figures prostrating) and Egyptians (standing figures) are depicted with the same colors of their skin of alternating black and brown -Tomb of Huy

Figure 18: Nubians and Egyptians are depicted with the same colors of alternating black and brown -Tomb of Huy (Full Scene)

The two pictures above are extremely important to our understanding of the ethnicity of the Ancient Egyptians, Nubians and Ethiopians. It is a rendition by French orientalist and architect *Prisse d' Avennes* (1807-1879 A.C.E.). It is understood by orthodox Egyptologists to be the procession of Nubians who are bringing gifts of gold to Huy, the viceroy of Kush, for the Egyptian king Tutankhamun (1333 B.C.E-1323 B.C.E). Note that the classic style of depicting Nubians with black or brown skin and the pronounced cheek line (scarification -see example right) as well as the feather on the head is maintained. In the same view, there are five figures standing behind the ones that are prostrating, who do not have the feathers or cheek lines, but do have the same skin tone and is represented in the classical style of depicting the Ancient Egyptians. Notice here that the depictions of the skin coloration of the Ancient Egyptians are the same as used for the Nubians (brown and black). While Ancient Egyptians and Nubians are depicted individually in brown and black color, the alternating pattern of brown and black is also used to more easily differentiate individuals when people are depicted in close proximity.

Figure 19: above right - Nubian depictions from Akhnaton period (1352 B.C.E-1347 B.C.E) Brooklyn Museum (Photo by M. Ashby)

The Controversy Over the "Race" of the Ancient Egyptians (Kamitans) in European Scholarship and the Move to Refute the Testimony of the Seventeenth- and Eighteenth-century European Travelers to Egypt

The move to deny the appearance of the Ancient Egyptians and promote the idea that they were not African at all has been put forth by many western writers, even in the face of the writings of the Ancient Egyptians themselves who attest that

1. They are ancestors of the Nubians, to the south, in Africa.
2. Their own depictions of themselves as dark or "black" skinned people.
3. The descriptions of them as "black" people, by the Greek classical writers.
4. The genealogies provided by the Ancient Egyptians themselves stating that their parents are Nubian (such as Amunmhat I).

Jean Franşois Champollion (1790 A.C.E.-1832 A.C.E.), the main decipherer of the hieroglyphic text in the early 19th century, who is often referred to as the "Father of Egyptology", remarked at the art he saw, which at the time was fully colored since the tombs and many other structures had been closed since the Middle Ages (Dark Ages). He described images of the Ancient Egyptians, created by them, in which they made themselves look like the Ethiopians, and concluded that they were of the same "race" as the modern day Nubians, who are "black" skinned African peoples, saying in a letter to his brother that he wrote while in Egypt examining the reliefs and studying the hieroglyphs: *"We find there Egyptians and Africans represented in the same way"*.[114] Jean Franşois Champollion later states that based on the images he saw it was clear that the Ancient Egyptians looked like the people presently living in Nubia, i.e. they were "black Africans."

In this same manner, Count Volney wrote after a trip to Egypt between 1783 and 1785:

> "Just think that this race of black men, today our slave and the object of our scorn, is the very race to which we owe our arts, sciences and even the use of speech! Just imagine, finally, that it is in the midst of people who call themselves the greatest friends of liberty and humanity that one has approved the most barbarous slavery and questioned whether black men have the same kind of intelligence as whites!"[115]

Some of the these travelers were being referred to were *Livingstone, Speke, Baker and Junker*. Documenting the observations of travelers such as Livingstone, and others J. A Rogers recorded the following statements by them in his book *Sex and Race Vol. I*:

> "Livingstone said that the Negro face as he saw it reminded him more of that on the monuments of ancient Assyria than that of the popular white fancy.[116] Sir Harry Johnston, foremost authority on the African Negro, said that "the Hamite," that Negroid stock which was the main stock of the ancient Egyptians, is best represented at the present day by the Somali, Galla, and the blood of Abyssinia and Nubia."[117] Sergi compares pictorially the features of Ramases II with that of Mtesa, noted Negro king of Uganda, and show the marked resemblance.[118] Sir M. W. Flinders Petrie, famed Egyptologist says that the Pharaohs of the Xth dynasty were of the Galla type, and the Gallas are clearly what are known in our day as Negroes. He tells further of seeing one day on a train a man whose features were "the exact living, type" of a statue of ancient Libya, and discovered that the man was a American mulatto.[119]"

The stir that the early descriptions of the Egyptians based on their own depictions, as described and reproduced by early explorers and artists, created in Europe in the early years of Egyptology after the translation of the hieroglyphic language by Champollion (1822 A.C.E.) was an unforeseen controversy that later Egyptologists tried desperately to refute. The following memoir recorded by Champollion-Figeac, the brother of Jean Franşois Champollion in 1829 denotes the "problem," which the western researchers who recognized the importance of Ancient Egyptian civilization, were facing. It was obvious that the writings were beginning to reveal religion, philosophy and evolved culture, all of which contradict the basic tenets used to justify the denigration of the "Negro" race and their enslavement in Africa, Europe and the "New World" (the Americas). Therefore, it became necessary to refute and even attempt to explain away the reason for the findings. (underlined portions by Ashby)

> The opinion that the ancient population of Egypt belonged to the Negro African race, is an error long accepted as the truth. Since the Renaissance, travelers in the East, barely capable of fully appreciating the ideas provided by Egyptian monuments on this important question, have helped to spread that false notion and geographers have not failed to reproduce it, even in our day. A serious authority declared himself in favor of this view and popularized the error. Such was the effect of what the celebrated Volney published on the various races of men that he had observed in Egypt. In his *Voyage,* which is in all libraries, he reports that the Copts are descended from the ancient Egyptians; that the Copts have a bloated face, puffed up eyes, flat nose, and thick lips, like a mulatto; that they resemble the Sphinx of the Pyramids, a distinctly Negro head. He concludes that the ancient Egyptians were true Negroes of the same species as all indigenous Africans. To support his opinion, Volney invokes that of Herodotus who, apropos the Colchians, recalls that the Egyptians had black skin and woolly hair. Yet these two physical qualities do not suffice to characterize the Negro race and Volney's conclusion as to the Negro origin of the ancient Egyptian civilization is evidently forced and inadmissible.
>
> It is recognized today that the inhabitants of Africa belong to three races, quite distinct from each other for all time: 1. Negroes proper, in Central and West Africa; 2. Kaffirs on the east coast, who have a less obtuse facial angle than Blacks and a high nose, but thick lips and woolly hair; 3. Moors, similar in stature, physiognomy and hair to the *best-formed* nations of Europe and western Asia, and differing only in skin color which is tanned by the climate. The ancient population of Egypt belonged to this latter race, that is, to the white race. To be convinced of this, we need only examine the human figures representing Egyptians on the monuments and above all the great number of mummies that have been opened. Except for the color of the skin, blackened by the hot climate, they are the same men as those of Europe and western Asia: frizzy, woolly hair is the true characteristic of the Negro race; the Egyptians, however, had long hair, identical with that of the white race of the West.[120]

Firstly, Champollion-Figeac affirms that the ancient "Egyptians had black skin and woolly hair." However, he and then goes on to say that these are not sufficient to characterize the Negro race. He thus contradicts himself later by saying "frizzy, woolly hair is the true characteristic of the Negro race." Obviously this is a contradiction in terms that is inescapable. In an attempt to formulate a thesis that the Ancient Egyptians were essentially "white people," like "the best-formed" Europeans, "except for the color of the skin, blackened by the hot climate," he stumbles on his own argument which is unreasonable at the outset. At no time previous or since has there been recognized anywhere on earth, a "race" of white-black people. This argument is based on observing the so-called "three races" of Africa of his time, as if these were representative of the ancient ethnicity of Africa and could have any baring on the question of the "race" of the Ancient Egyptians. This argument is of course contradictory and unworkable such as it is, but even more so when it is kept in mind that the Ancient Egyptians mixed with Asiatics and Europeans (Greeks) and even still the descriptions of the classical Greek writers unanimously considered them as what in the present day would be called "Negros." Also, the present day Copts, descendants of the Ancient Egyptians, of Champollion-Figeac's time were even then recognized as having "Negroid" features. By Champollion-Figeac's reasoning it would be necessary to conclude that Africans are white Europeans. The Kaffirs (Muslim word for pagans) being referred to are those people whom the Muslim Arabs found in Africa as they entered Africa from the Sinai Peninsula, which is the bridge between Asia Minor and Africa. From there they captured the countries in North Africa from Egypt, to Libya, Tunisia, Algiers and Morocco as well as Spain. Through limited genealogies left by the Moors it has been determined that they were a mixture of Arab and African blood.

Thus, the comparisons used by Champollion-Figeac are wholly useless for determining the "race" of the Ancient Egyptians, but they can however be used for comparisons to the Copts, who like the Moors, appeared to "have a bloated face, puffed up eyes, flat nose, and thick lips, like a mulatto" like the Moors, and also like the present day peoples of African descent living in the Diaspora (African Americans, African Brazilians, Africans in Jamaica, etc.). When this kind of comparison is made it is clear that the "mulatto" arises from a combination of African and Semite (Arab) or European. This of course means that the African features, (color of the skin, thick lips and woolly hair) must have been present in the past if they are present in the current population of mixed peoples, that is to say, the population goes from "black" skin to "lighter" skin color and not the other way around. Except for the effects of climactic changes on populations over a long period of time (thousands of years), which have been shown to cause changes in physical appearance, there is no record of "Black" populations arising from "white" populations. Lastly, in the time of the Ancient Egyptians, before the coming of the Greeks, there were no Europeans in Africa at all. The only populations recognized by the Egyptians were themselves, the other Africans, the Libyans and the Asiatics, all of whom vary in skin tone from dark "black" to light "brown" coloration. So if there are any "white" people in present day Africa they are descendants of the documented influx of Greeks who came in as invading forces with Alexander the Great (330 B.C.E.) and or the documented influx of Arabs which came with the advent of the expansion of Islam (650 B.C.E.) and after. In any case, when discussing the Ancient Egyptians of the Old and Middle Kingdoms and the Pre-Dynastic Period, we are not discussing "mulattos" since the admixture with other ethnic groups had not occurred until the New Kingdom period, and even more so in the Late period, through contact with the conquering Asiatic and European forces. Therefore, to look at the images of the Egyptians during the mixture period and to say that these are representative of the Ancient Egyptian ethnic origins is the worst kind of scholarship. This is a tactic used by some Western and Arab scholars to escape the conclusion that the Ancient Egyptians were "black." How is this possible? In places such as the United States of America, the "rule" established by the "white" ruling class has always been that "one drop of black blood make one black." This means that everyone from dark black skin color to the light brown or swarthy complexion, are recognized as being descendants of the African slaves, and are subject to being segregated and discriminated against. But in this argument it is also possible to say that those mulattos are not 100% African since they are mixed with European, Arab, etc. So they are trying to say that the Ancient Egyptians were either a mixed race or better yet, an indigenous Asiatic group that developed independently of the "black Africans." In any case, even in the late period the Greek classical writers witnessed the population of Kamit as being overwhelmingly "black" (Nubian). So we are not talking about "light skinned black people" or "dark skinned white people" but "dark skinned black people," like those who can be met even today (2002 A.C.E.) in the city of Aswan (Upper (southern) Egypt – see picture above).

There were several prominent and respected Linguists and Egyptologists who affirmed that the Ancient Egyptians were "African" or "Negros." Sir Henry Rawlinson, prominent linguist and decipherer of the mideastern scripts and widely regarded as the "father of Middle-Eastern Studies," said *"Seti's face is thoroughly African, strong, fierce, prognathous, with depressed nose, thick lips and a heavy chin..."*[121] Showing that certain foremost Egyptologists accept the "Negro" composition of the Ancient Egyptian people, J. A Rogers recorded the following statements by the famous British Egyptologist Flinders Petrie, in his book *Sex and Race Vol.I*:

> "Egyptian civilization, from its beginning to the Christian era, lasted for more than seven thousand years, that is, about four times as long as from "the birth of Christ" to the present, therefore, most of the records have been lost, and the little that remains must be pieced together. There are often great gaps. Between the Bushman period of 9000 B.C. and the First Dynasty (4477-4514 B.C.) very little is known. Some of the faces of the rulers of this dynasty are clearly Negroid. The founder of the Third Dynasty, Sa-nekht, was a full-blooded Negro, a type commonly seen in the Egyptian army today. Petrie says of him, "It will be seen how strongly Ethiopian the characters of it (the portrait) is even more so than Shabaka, most marked of the Ethiopian dynasty. The type is one with which we are very familiar among the Sudanese of the Egyptian police and army; it goes with a dark-brown skin and a very truculent character."

In the late 19th century (A.C.E.) the French director general of the Egyptian Service of Antiquities and regarded as a foremost Egyptologist, Gaston Maspero (1846-1916 A.C.E.), wrote about the controversy about the origins and descriptions of the Ancient Egyptians as it stood in his times. (underlined portions by Ashby)

> "In our day the origin and ethnographic affinities of the population have inspired lengthy debate. First, the seventeenth- and eighteenth-century travelers, misled by the appearance of certain mongrelized Copts, certified that their predecessors in the Pharaonic age had a puffed

up face, bug eyes, flat nose, fleshy lips. And that they presented certain characteristic features of the Negro race. This error, common at the start of the century, vanished once and for all as soon as the French Commission had published its great work."[122]

One of the questions that arise here is why was the unanimous reaction of the seventeenth- and eighteenth-century European travelers in Egypt so upsetting to the late eighteenth and twentieth century western scholars? They were the first Europeans in modern times to see the Ancient Egyptian reliefs and paintings and their reaction was the same as the Greek classical writers when it came to describing the peoples of Kamit and the rest of the Nile Valley. In fact, they did not base their assessment of the Ancient Egyptian ethnicity just by examining their descendants, the Copts, but on images left behind by the Kamitans, some that had been buried under the encroaching dessert sands, which for this reasons were preserved in very good condition. It is interesting to note that the appearance of the Copts was acknowledged as presenting the "mongrelized" features (puffed up face, bug eyes, flat nose, fleshy lips) and that these are understood as being generally representative of the "Negro race." This observation has been widely accepted by all who agree with the concept of ethnic differentiations among human populations. Yet, when it comes to acknowledging these features in the images of Ancient Egypt they become somehow unrepresentative or unreliable or insufficient in assisting in the determination about where those people came from and to which population they are related.

This move to obfuscate the issue gained momentum in the 20th century and became widely accepted by society in general, despite all the evidence to the contrary. Even in the late 20th century there are anthropologists and Egyptologists staunchly supporting the baseless construct of an other than "Negro" origin of the Ancient Egyptians. What has changed is the willingness to say that they were Africans. What has not changed is the reluctance to accept their "blackness." Being unable to refute the pictorial evidences or the writings by the Egyptians themselves, many present day researches who seek to prove that the Ancient Egyptians were not "black" Africans attempt to use other means to discredit the findings which do not support their contentions.

The work of a western scholar by the name of Martin Bernal, author of *Black Athena : The Afroasiatic Roots of Classical Civilization (The Fabrication of Ancient Greece 1785-1985*, (published in 1989), a scathing report on the western falsification of the evidences pointing to an African origin of Greek (i.e. Western civilization) received a storm of criticism from some researchers who propose that his treatment of the statements by the classical Greek writers as "eager credulity." Jacques Berlinerblan, the author of *Heresy in the University: The Black Athena Controversy and the Responsibilities of American Intellectuals* (1999) examines the charge against Bernal.

> "With this generous reading now rendered I would like to note that Bernal has offered no viable alternative or corrective to the approaches which he believes are responsible for the fall of the Ancient Model. Nor does he distinguish among better or worse types of exegetical and hermeneutic approaches, leaving us with the impression that he believes all are equally corrupt. His methodological credo seems to be *The Ancients could very well be telling us the truth*. While this is plausible, it is incumbent upon the author to advance a method which might help us to determine how scholars might go about distinguishing truthful accounts from untruthful ones. As Egyptologist John D. Ray asked, "Where are the final criteria to lie?" To this point, Bernal has neglected to articulate such criteria, and this leaves him vulnerable to Mary Lefkowitz's charge of "eager credulity" toward the ancient sources."[123]

There is an interesting process of selective acceptance of certain evidences from the ancient writers and overlooking or minimizing certain other evidences when it is convenient to explain a particular point. This is noticeable in the work of some western scholars of Ancient Egypt, Greece as well as India. Bernal's book drew such criticism, not because the information was new, since other writers such as Cheikh Anta Diop had presented it in his book *African Origins of Civilization, Myth or Reality*. The problem was that Bernal is a "white" European scholar, part of the establishment, and the information he presented was perceived by some of his peers as precipitating the fall of the walls of western academia's characterization of African civilization, and consequently the history of western civilization, and their prestige as western scholars with it. The objective here also seems to call into question the veracity of the ancient writers, or to say that they were gullible, or to make it appear that their Egyptian "guides" or "informants" were trying to impress the Greeks by telling them wild stories that they wanted to hear. In the third chapter of *Not Out of Africa: How Afrocentrism Became an Excuse to Teach Myth As History* (August 1997), Mary Lefkowitz reviews the texts which Bernal used in order to build his Ancient and Revised Ancient Models. "The idea that Greek religion and philosophy has Egyptian origins," she asserts, "may appear at first sight to be more plausible, because it derives, at least in part, from the writings of ancient Greek historians." The scholar Jacques Berlinerblan explains Lefkowitz's position, which he himself admittedly shares. (Underlined portions by Ashby)

> "Lefkowitz advances an unyieldingly critical appraisal of the writings of Herodotus, Diodorus, Plato, Strabo, and the Church Fathers on the subject of Egypt. These figures cannot be counted on to offer us objective accounts due to their "respect for the antiquity of Egyptian religion and civilization, and a desire somehow to be connected with it." This admiration inclined them to overemphasize their dependency on, and contacts with, the land of the Pyramids. But the presence of a pro-Egyptian bias in Greek thought is not the only drawback which Lefkowitz discovers. In true Hard Modern fashion she enumerates the failings of the ancients qua historical researchers. The Greeks were not sufficiently skeptical or critical of their informants and sources. They did not speak Egyptian, nor did they draw upon Egyptian archives. They misunderstood the very Egyptian phenomena they studied. Their linguistic surmises were predicated on simplistic and erroneous assumptions. They looked at Egypt "through cultural blinkers," producing an image that was "astigmatic and deeply Hellenized."[124] Again and again Lefkowitz pounds the point home-how poorly the Greeks performed when compared to us:
> Unlike modern anthropologists, who approach new cultures so far as possible with an open mind, and with the aid of a developed set of methodologies, Herodotus tended to construe whatever he saw by analogy with Greek practice, as if it were impossible for him to comprehend it any other way.
> Lest there exist any remaining question as to the reliability of the ancients, Lefkowitz proceeds to pulverize the final link in the chain of historical transmission. Not only were the Greeks unreliable, but so were their Egyptian informants. Jewish and Christian Egyptians supplied the gullible Greeks with self-aggrandizing information as "a way of asserting the importance of their culture, especially in a time when they had little or no political powers."[125]

We must keep in mind that scholars such as Lefkowitz are trying to discredit the ancient authors but the arguments of such scholars are not based on rationality or on evidences to prove their contentions.

1. People from different periods in time, removed in some cased by several hundreds of years, which means that they did not have an opportunity to conspire with each other to fabricate the same "fantasies".
2. They did not speak to the same people upon visiting Egypt or in such cases as Pythagoras and Plato, becoming students of the Egyptian masters for several years.
3. They had no reason to lie about their experiences as do present day western scholars, who need to uphold a view of the past that support western superiority and independence from the very people whose oppression is rationalized by saying that they had no culture, religion, philosophy or civilization.
4. The Greek classical writers (Herodotus, Plutarch, Pythagoras, Plato, Aristotle, Diodorus, Strabo, and others) did not rely simply on what they were told by their "informants." They presented evidences and described what they saw with their own eyes and when these descriptions are compared they are in agreement with their statements and with the evidences that can be examined by any person who takes the time to visit a serious museum of Egyptian antiquities or the monuments and tombs of Ancient Egypt themselves.
5. The use of the term "informants" in itself reveals the demeaning attitude and prejudicial manner of dealing with the Greek Classical writers, presumably because there is no other area that these scholars can attack in order to prove their theory.
6. There are ample forms of evidence besides the writings of the Greek classical authors upon which to investigate the ethnicity of the Ancient Egyptians and their contributions to early Greek culture. These other evidences, such as the adoption of Ancient Egyptian customs, tradition and religion by the

Greeks are irrefutable and inescapable and therefore, not to be mentioned. By creating a stir in one area, the western researchers hope to cloud the issue and taint an objective observer's view of other evidences.

In any case, such attacks can be easily dismissed since they are entirely without basis. The problem arises in the fact that they speak from a self-serving pulpit, the "western scholarly establishment" that is supported by the western media, which accepts documentaries that are made for television by these scholars or approved by the "legitimate" schools that they represent, rather than from conclusive evidence. Anyone who has worked in the western university setting knows that there is a lot of politics involved with attaining the coveted status as tenured professor. Of course, anyone who does not agree with the established opinions will have a difficult time breaking through the invisible walls of the western "ivory towers." The Western academia, which controls the scholars through the process of selectively accepting those who support the pre-established doctrines and rejecting those who do not. Scholarly criticism is one thing, but dismissing something just because it does not agree with one's views is simply unscientific and evidence of an ulterior motive or hidden agenda. Having the most powerful voice to speak with and being supported by the government, the western scholarly establishment has the capacity to put out skewed images of reality, that when repeated again and again over a period of time, attains a status of being "truth" and "real," but when examined closely, are found to be nothing more that the cries of unhappy children who cannot accept the evidences before them. A fault that was noted in Lefkowitz's work not by the Africentrists or by Bernal but by her own colleague Jacques Berlinerblan, which reveals her duplicitous manner of handling the statements of the Greek classical writers.

> In my own work on the Hebrew Bible I have argued, with no less passion, that we simply cannot believe what this text reports. Accordingly, I concur with her objections, and I find Lefkowitz's overarching skepticism justified. Yet in her haste to skewer Bernal, Lefkowitz avoids considering the drawbacks or implications of her - I should say "our"-position. At one point in Not Out of Africa she speaks of the "important," "generally accurate," and "useful information" which Herodotus makes apropos of the Nile, Egyptian monuments, and individual pharaohs. The problem is that Lefkowitz never pauses to tell us why she considers these particular observations to be "generally accurate." Further, she and other critics of Bernal often evince their own "eager credulity" toward ancient texts, especially when it permits them to criticize Bernal. Lefkowitz, for instance, is not averse to citing and accepting Herodotus's testimony if it helps her to refute *Black Athena's* historical claims.[126]

Lefkowitz's double standard sabotages her own integrity and thus invalidates her statements and motives as a scholar. When the empty attempts to impugn the statements of the Greek classical writers fails there is no recourse but to engage in attempts to discredit the scholars who advance their positions using the "unacceptable" evidences by referring to them as "wild," "flaky," etc., and refer to their positions as based on "fantasies." A western writer by the name of Steven Howe characterized the work of noted Africentric scholars in this way in his book. Without providing any evidence to refute their positions, a practice that is widely regarded as the hallmark of the western scientific process, he presented the opinions of other scholars who agree with him, they also being devoid of evidences to back up their positions. This of course is no scholarship at all, but merely the addition of one more voice to the cacophony of western scholarly discontent over the undeniable and overwhelming evidences contradicting their positions. The absence of real evidence to support their opinions is substituted with forceful opinions and emotional appeals and these cannot be accepted as science, but as disgruntled and frustrated outbursts. Mr. Howe makes the following assertions without supporting these with any evidence either in Egyptology, anthropology, genetics, geology or any other recognized science.

1. The ancient Egyptians belonged to no race, they were neither black nor white but Egyptian.
2. The white race did not evolve from the black.
3. The race concept did not exist in Ancient Egypt.
4. Arabs did not overrun or destroy north Africa.

The obvious misconceptions or misinformation or errors in Mr. Howe's arguments can be easily and concisely proven to be false, since there is no real evidence being presented:

A. The first point is bogus on its face. Even in the present day, the spurious concept of "racism" recognizes no such race as "Egyptian." All human beings have been regarded by the western race concept as either "white," meaning European, or of some "Negroid" stock, meaning descendant or affiliated with African ancestry, or fitting into some range of color between "black" and "white."

B. All the evidences from anthropology and genetic sciences point to a common origin for all modern human beings as having originated in Africa. Therefore, Mr. Howe is either misinformed or deliberately misdirecting the public. Inherent in the treatment of Egyptology is the practice of ignoring the findings of scientific disciplines which are widely regarded as being empirical as opposed to theoretical. These are ignored because they contradict the orthodox dogmatic position. These other sciences support the "black" African origins of Ancient Egyptian culture.

C. Mr. Howe proposes the idea that the Ancient Egyptians did not indeed have a concept of race in order to support the idea that there was no difference between how they saw themselves and the other peoples of the world. The Ancient Egyptians were not racists and consequently no record of race classifications, or racial practices such as those of modern Western Culture have been discovered even after 200 years of Egyptological research. However, the concept of ethnic differentiation did exist. The Ancient Egyptians did recognize and acknowledge the concept of ethnicity which includes an awareness of the differences in physical features like skin color, etc. Several examples of these "ethnographies" survive to this day. So the Ancient Egyptians saw themselves as being the same in appearance to the Nubians and other Africans and different from the Asiatics and the later Greeks (Europeans). Thus, the Greeks (Europeans) could not be Egyptians since the Egyptians depicted themselves as "black" Africans. It is interesting that some scholars try to hold on to the idea that race is not important based on the genetic evidence which shows the race concept to be bogus, when it suits the ideal of asserting that the Egyptians had no race so as not to be forced to admit that they were "black Africans," but when it comes to accepting people of non-European descent into European countries, equality in economics, social settings and government, the practice of segregation and discrimination based on racial bias, remains enforced.

D. Ample records and evidences from African peoples as well as the Assyrian, Persian, Greek and Arab conquerors attest to the fact of the movement from Europe, imposing Roman Christianity, and from Asia Minor into North Africa, imposing Islam and the destruction of "Kaffir" (pagan) monuments, temples and cultures which were seen as contradictory with the formation of a world dominated by Christianity, and later Islam.

Thus, even at the end of the 20th century the world is still contending with the agenda of some duplicitous or ignorant western scholars and writers of characterizing African culture as primitive and insignificant, and to elevate Western Culture and western scholarship without any footing in science. This is why the work of those who study Ancient Egyptian culture, religion and philosophy needs to confront the issue of history and the means to present evidences with rigorous standards that will lead to reasonable and useful conclusions, as opposed to disparaging remarks and insults calling the work of their opponents "wild", "flaky", "fantasies", opinion and innuendo.

Finally, this author (Ashby), knows of no African American Africentric scholar or African Africentric scholar who would say that Western civilization, as we know it today, is based on African civilization, it does however owe its existence to Ancient Africa since what the European countries built cannot be said to be in keeping with either the principles or philosophy of civilization enjoined by the Ancient Egyptian sages, nor the tenets that were learned by the Greek philosophers who were students of the Kamitan sages, who attempted to enlighten the early Greeks with the knowledge of the Land of the Pyramids. When asked by a western reporter what he thought about western civilization, the Indian leader Mahatma Ghandi is said to have replied: *"That is a good idea!"* He responded in this way because western civilization remains an idea yet to be realized. Technological advancement and material wealth or military power do not in themselves constitute "civilization." Western Culture cannot be considered to be a civilization since civilization means to be "civilized" in one's actions, constructions, and views towards the world. Being civilized means being civil (Civility = **1.** *Courteous behavior; politeness.* **2.** *A courteous act or utterance.* –American Heritage Dictionary) to other people. Civility is one of the most important concepts of Ancient Egyptian Maat philosophy. Being civilized does not mean just being courteous in social situations, but then taking advantage of the same people in another or promoting the welfare of one's own group, but promoting the welfare of all people in general, otherwise one's civilization is biased and therefore duplicitous and hypocritical, which disqualifies it from being regarded as a "civilization" in any stretch of the concept. Civilization benefits the world community as it sees all human beings as citizens of humanity. Being civilized cannot be equated with the denigration of women in the culture, the concept of a male god and the exclusion of women in religion, the global domination of people through economic manipulation and hoarding of resources, the enslavement of entire populations, the murder of entire populations and stealing their land, etc. These are not values of the ancient African culture, which was based on the principle of Humanism (Ubuntu/Maat) and required the provision of resources to meet the needs of all members of the population as well as the balance between male and female, etc. So Africa cannot be claimed to be the source of such acts of inhumanity, selfishness and greed. So wherever these were learned, they developed independently, perhaps due to the inability of people in Europe to heed the teachings of the Ancient Egyptian sages and their early Greek students. Thus, even though the early Greek philosophers created a spark in their home country that provided an impetus for the later development of European culture, that culture cannot yet be considered to be a civilization in the contexts of what was accomplished in Ancient Egypt (Africa).

References to the Nubian Genealogy of Kamitans in Kamitan Texts and Monuments

In the didactic treatise known as *The Prophesies of Neferti*, it is stated that Amunmhat I was the "son of a woman of Ta-Seti, a child of Upper Egypt. The term "Ta-Seti" means "Land of the Bow." This is one of the names used by the Ancient Egyptians to describe Nubia. Thus we are to understand that contrary to the assertions of orthodox Egyptologists, there are several Ancient Egyptian kings that can be recognized as "Nubian" besides those of the 25th dynasty. The late period Greeks and Romans accepted Pharaoh Amunhotep III (Memnon -18th Dyn.) as a Nubian in appearance and as Pharaoh. Yet there is a consistent effort to deny the obvious. When their histories and genealogies are examined, along with their statuary, it becomes clear that the Ancient Egyptians and their rulers were not just Africans but "black" skinned and also possessed the same physical features as other Africans.

One issue that western and Arab scholars who want to characterize the appearance of "Nubian features" in Ancient Egyptian art is that these are either rare or that they appear almost exclusively in the period of the 25th Dynasty when it is universally accepted that the Nubians from the south took over the all of Egypt. However, a cursory study of the Ancient Egyptian statues and relief provides insights into the insufficiency of any arguments pretending to suggest that there are no records besides the Greek classical writers which show that the Ancient Egyptians saw and depicted themselves as "black Africans," not just during the 25th Dynasty, but throughout the history of Ancient Egypt to the Greek and Roman periods.

Plate 2: Left- Peraah (Pharaoh) Muntuhotep II (Muntuhotep)[127] – 11th Dynasty

Plate 3: Center- Peraah Senusert I statue – 12th Dynasty

Plate 4: Right- Peraah Senusert I relief – 12th Dynasty

(A) (B) (C)

The images above are representative of the reliefs and statuaries that the Greek classical writers and the seventeenth- and eighteenth-century European travelers in Egypt saw in full color. Notice the features of the first two (A-B) faces. They clearly exhibit the characteristic traits that have been described as "Black African", including the "puffed up face." Plate (C) is actually a relief representing the same personality as plate (B). Notice that the features in the statues are more pronounced than in the reliefs. This same pattern of iconography can be observed in the statuary and reliefs of King Akhnaton. What we are witnessing is an Ancient Egyptian artistic standard practice of representing the personality in a more naturalistic form in the statuary, and a more standardized manner in the reliefs.[24] In all cases however, the features denote the "bloated face, puffed up eyes, flat nose, and thick lips, and woolly hair as well as the brown-red or black skin tone painting.

Plate 5: Below left, Per-aah Akhnaton Statue (18 Dynasty) – Cairo Museum

Plate 6: Below right, Per-aah Akhnaton Relief (18 Dynasty)

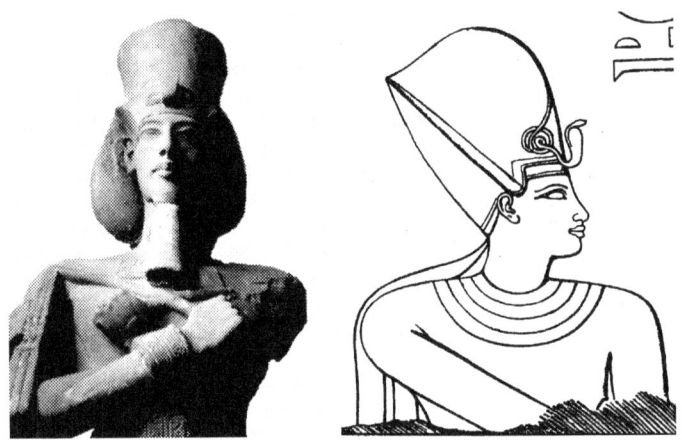

Mysticism of Color in Ancient Egyptian Art

Many Egyptologists and others have tried to put forth the idea that the reddish-brown (males) and yellow or white (for females) colors, which the Ancient Egyptians used in the artistic renditions of themselves, represented the hue of their skin. This argument is bogus since it is well known that if two people of different skin colors (pigmentation) mate, they will produce offspring displaying a mixture of the two hues, as well as a range of skin pigmentation hues which may extend even beyond the ranges represented by the parents, if the grandparents or those of even earlier generations were of different skin hues. So even if the Ancient Egyptians had consisted of a population of red men and yellow or white women, they would quickly transform themselves into pink and gold since red and yellow produces gold and red and white produces pink. Further, these mixtures would further combine until eventually only one hue would remain.

The color spectrum ranges, in order, from violet, through blue, green, yellow, and orange, to red.[128] The colors red and white hold special mystical significance, and this is why we see so many Ancient Egyptian couples represented by them, with the men painted reddish-brown and the women painted yellow or fully white. In color therapy, an art practiced in modern times as well as in Ancient Egypt,[129] the color red is understood as being an agitating or exciting (stimulating) color to the mind. White, on the other hand was considered in Ancient Egypt as soothing,[130] as the red male Hippo was considered violent, mischievous and destructive while the female was considered calm and helpful. Blue is considered as being soothing and relaxing to the mind. Mystically, red and white complement each other, as red symbolizes sexual potency or

---

[24] *The projection of figures or forms from a flat background, as in sculpture, or such a projection that is apparent only, as in painting.* – American Heritage Dictionary

virility, and white, having the capacity to reflect all colors,[131] symbolizes pregnancy and potential. This is why the Kamitan Peraahs (Pharaohs)[25] wears the double crown, consisting of red and white elements. Note that when considering the colors from a scientific standpoint, and their effect on the human mind we obtain meanings that is not to be acribed to the modern concept of race and racism. The colors do not refer to races but to energies and behavior patterns.

Mystically, the color gold symbolizes the sun and the spirit, as well as eternity and immortality. The color black symbolizes "the source" of all things, as it represents the capacity to absorb all colors."[132] Everything in Creation has color, in order to be seen. Black does not reflect any color due to its subtlety, thus it is "colorless," that is, uncolored by time and space, the realm (of Creation, duality and conditioning) where color exists. Another way to understand this is that black absorbs all colors, and does not let their light escape and white is opaque and thereby reflects all colors off itself, which is why movies use a white screen instead of black. This is why in mystical mythological philosophies of Kamit and India, the gods Asar and Amun in Ancient Egypt and the gods Vishnu and Krishna in India are referred to as the "black" ones. Amun and Krishna are also represented as dark blue. They represent the transcendent, beyond ordinary consciousness. Asar also symbolizes "nothingness." This is an allusion to the mind when it is void of concepts or thoughts. This spiritual idea is akin to the term "Shunya" used to describe the void that an aspirant strives to achieve in Buddhism.

<u>Red + White thus means: Spirit + Matter = Creation</u>. Thus these colors lead to productions (creations) in time and space as well as perfection in the physical plane.

<u>Red + Yellow = Orange-Gold thus means: Spirit + Sublimated Matter = Eternity</u>. Therefore these colors make each other whole and transcendental, i.e. symbolizing the movement from duality to non-duality.

<u>Gold = Spirit and Eternity</u>

<u>Blue → moving towards Violet → leads to Black</u>

<u>Black = Transcendent</u>

The Mystical Symbolism of Nothingness

In mystical traditions, the root of human spiritual obstruction is said to be the sense of individualism. From this individualism emerges egoistic desire. Upon reflection, you will discover that everything you are or believe yourself to be is related to your mental ideas which all reference you to a specific time and place, your body, your relatives, your society, your country, etc. Mystical traditions such as Kamitan and Eastern philosophy and Gnostic Christianity view these elements as superficial garments of the soul, which the soul clings to, due to ignorance. When these elements are given up, the practitioner of mystical spiritual discipline goes beyond them and discovers the "nothingness" out of which the universe arises. This nothingness was erroneously assumed by some to be a kind of non-existence.

At another level of understanding, this nothingness is a state of consciousness wherein there is no mental movement caused by thoughts. In reality the void refers to the absence of concepts in the mind. This state renders the mind undifferentiated, uncolored and free, that is, "black."

The Philosophy of "Nothingness" was extensively espoused by the Buddhist philosophers of India. Their attempt to explain what the phenomenal universe is began with an attempt to explain how the universe developed. It was assumed that there was a source that produced the universe. This philosophy led to the belief that the entire universe came from a primeval, ultimate void called *Shunya*.[133] Therefore, Buddhist disciplines are directed toward emptying the human mind of that which prevents the perception of that ultimate reality which according to their system of mysticism, is the source of all creation. This Buddhist discipline is directed towards the eradication of the superficial elements of the human mind, which they maintain, block {her/his} perception of ultimate existence. In effect, the mind can be trained to let go of thinking and classifying objects. When this occurs there are no more concepts in the mind and therefore, it is said to be void of concepts. When all of the concepts, which have been learned by the mind over many lifetimes, and the egoistic desires based on

---

[25] The term "Pharaoh" is a biblical (Hebrew-Jewish) translation oh the original Ancient Egyptian word "Per-aah".

those concepts, are dropped, then there arises the awareness of the Absolute. There is supreme calm and peace. Since thoughts are created by desires, the main aim of Buddhist philosophy is to end desires so that the human being may be able to discover his/her true Self as being one with the source of creation. Further, all the planets, matter, living beings, and even the individual human ego is discovered to be an emanation from that source. Hence the term *Nirvana* (Nir-vana), *without-desire* (craving), is used to denote this ultimate state of oneness with the source of creation. (See Chapter on African Origins of Buddhism)

The Mystical Symbolism of Darkness in Kamitan Philosophy and Mythology.

In Kamitan mysticism, one of the philosophies of "nothingness" is expressed in the concept of the Duat. The Duat is the netherworld of Kamitan philosophy and within it is to be found the *nrutf* region, the place of darkness, and within that region is Asar, the lord of the Perfect Black."

This notion of nothingness (*nrutf*) is akin to the Buddhist notion of *Shunya* or the "void," which refers to the area of consciousness, which is devoid of mental concepts and thoughts. When there are no thoughts or forms in the mind, it is calm, expansive and peaceful. When there are thoughts in the mind, the mental awareness is narrowed and defined in terms of concepts. If the mind is confined to these concepts and narrow forms of thought, then it is confined to that which is limited and temporal. If it eradicates its desires, cravings and illusions, then it becomes aware of the innermost reality and it realizes its connection to the entire cosmos. Thus, the teaching of the Duat gives insight into the nature of the human mind and its deeper unconscious levels. It is a description of the mental landscape, its demons, gods and goddesses (fantasies, desires and everything else that is a result of or leads to ignorance and mental agitation) as well as the way to discover the abode of the innermost Self (everything that leads to peace, harmony and wisdom). Demons, gods and goddess refer to one's mental concepts of right (gods and goddesses) and wrong (demons), and not to entities such as ghosts, angels, evil spirits, etc., as is commonly understood by non-mystical traditions. Therefore, the task of a spiritual aspirant is to eradicate the concepts, agitations, desires and cravings in the mind and to discover the "hidden" innermost reality, which is Hetep (Supreme Peace), eternity and infinite expansiveness.

From a higher level of understanding, the Duat is the unconscious mind and Asar is that level which transcends the thinking processes... its deepest region. It is the level of consciousness that is experienced during deep dreamless sleep. Therefore, it is the "hidden" aspect of the human heart, and thus, it is also known as Amun, the "witnessing consciousness".

This deepest and most dark realm of the Duat (Netherworld in Kamitan spirituality) is Asar, himself, and this is why Asar is referred to as the "Lord of the Perfect Black" and is often depicted as being black or green of hue. It is also why the goddesses Nut, Aset (Isis), and Hetheru (Hathor) are also described as "dark-skinned."[26] They are emanations from this realm of blackness, which is described as a void, or "*nothingness*" in the hieroglyphic papyrus entitled *The Laments of Aset (Isis) and Nebethet (Nephthys)*.[134]

---

[26] From an inscription in the temple of Denderah, Egypt.

CONCLUSION: About the Ancient Egyptian and Nubian depictions in Ancient Egypt

Firstly, the fact that the later depictions of the Ancient Egyptians show them as having traditional African features similar to Nubians, indicates that the Ancient Egyptians were black "African" peoples even up to that time and when the Greek classical writers made their observations (450 B.C.E.-100 A.C.E). Secondly, notice that the Nubian men at the temple of Rameses are depicted as brownish red as well as black. The Nubian dancing girls, are also painted brownish red. This means that the Ancient Egyptians painted themselves and the Nubians with the same colors, but differentiated due to particular reasons not related to racism, but to cultural distinction. Thus, they used this artistic convention of alternating coloration and scarification as a means to tell the two groups (Egyptians and Nubians) apart when they were being depicted together. The use of color has mystical implications, like almost all Kamitan inscriptions do, and there can be no validity to the concept that the Ancient Egyptians were white and red in skin color. Therefore, the use of color must be understood as a mystical symbol as opposed to an ethnic depiction.

Chapter 1 Section 2: The Nubian Origins of Ancient Egypt

In order to understand the Ancient Egyptians, we must also understand their origins in Nubia and their relationship to the Nubians (Ethiopians). In this manner we will have a full grasp of the African origins of Kamitan culture as well as fathom the full impact that it had on the rest of Africa through the Nubian kingdoms, which in turn influenced other countries in the interior of Africa. So next we will explore the Nubian origins and history of Ancient Egypt, and then we will explore in detail the different periods of Ancient Egyptian history.

The Nubian Origins of Ancient Egypt

> "Our people originated at the base of the mountain of the Moon,
> at the origin of the Nile river where the god Hapi dwells."
>
> -The Ancient Egyptian tradition.

The Ancient Egyptians themselves said that their ancestors originated in the very interior of Africa, the place known as the source of the Nile. The land they were referring to is up-river, in the area of modern day Africa that is today occupied by the countries Uganda and southern Sudan. The Nile River, which flows down to the Mediterranean sea originates in a mountainous region from which several tributary rivers flow to make one main watercourse known as the Nile River. The mountains in this region have such an elevation that even though they are located close to the equator, one may experience not only extremely low temperatures, but extreme weather conditions as well. This topography is ideal for promoting rains at particular times of the year. The interaction between the mountains and the winds and the attendant atmospheric conditions which develop annually are the key to what causes the production of snow. Then the snow melts forming streams, which then coalesce into rivers, which in turn nourish the entire region. Thus it is not surprising that this region, which includes Tanzania, would have been the place where the remains of the oldest known human being were discovered.

Below: Map of Africa

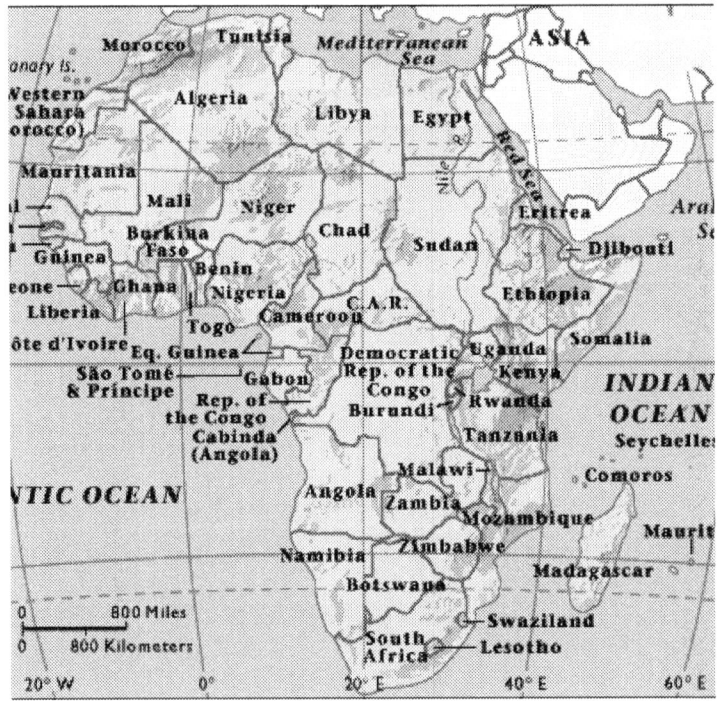

The waters that go to compose the Nile River originate in the area that is today known as southern Sudan/Uganda and Ethiopia. There are two main tributaries to the Nile. They are known as the White Nile and the Blue Nile. The White Nile originates in Southern Sudan, from waters flowing into it from the Mountain Nile, which comes from even farther south in Uganda, from other tributaries known as Albert Nile and Victoria Nile (Named after the king and queen of England at the time of the colonization[27] of the area).

Below: Map of Uganda.

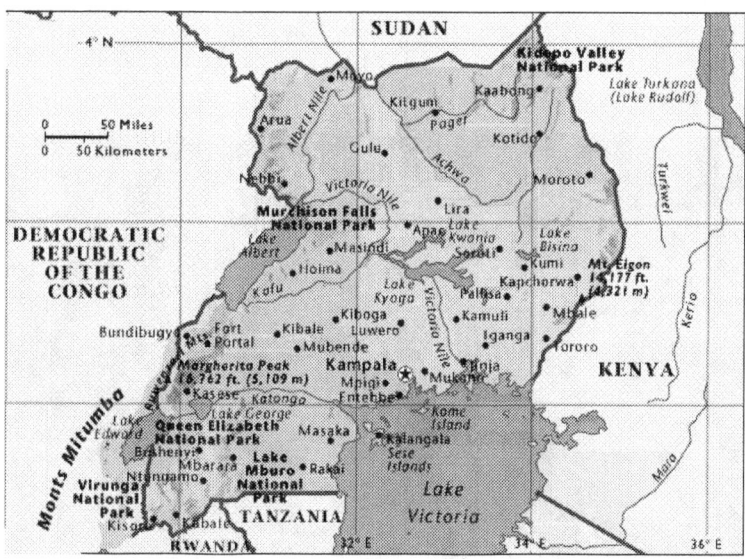

Below: Mountain Kiliminjaro – one of the mountains in the region at the source of the Nile

---

[27] Colonization, in the context of this book and as concerns the continent of Africa refers to the seizing of previously inhabited areas by force, and the enslavement of the people there, while at the same time confiscating and plundering the natural resources of the land and the wealth of the people of that land.

Images From The Early European Explorers of the Nile Valley

The following images from the early 19th century European explorers to the Nile Valley show the population that was found in Nubia and the lands to the south of Egypt as they moved in search of the sources of the Nile. Their search led them to Uganda. These images were produced to record the explorer's interactions with the Ugandans. Thus, the people who lived at the source of the Nile, the place where Ancient Egyptian legends say that the original Egyptian peoples originated, appear as with the Nubians, to be black Africans. Some of the pictures contain elements which demonstrate striking similarities with the earlier Ancient Egyptian symbolism, like the panther skin. The panther skin was a symbol of Ancient Egyptian Priests and Priestesses, teachers of the mysteries (mystical sciences).

Introducing the Bible to the native population. Note the panther skin used by the teacher. John Hanning Speke *Journal of Discovery of the Source of the Nile* (early 19th century explorations -published 1863)

Above left: Ancient Egyptian priest with the characteristic panther skin.
Above center: The King of Uganda. Above right: Nilotic dwarf man.

Descriptions of the Nubians (Ethiopians) by the Greeks

We are given to understand by the testimony of the Ancient Egyptians themselves that their ancestors came from Nubia. These were the people referred to by the Greeks as *Ethiopians*. The term Ethiopians means "land of the burnt (black) faces."

Herodotus called them *"The tallest, most beautiful and long-lived of the human races."*

Homer referred to them as *"The most just of men; the favorites of the gods."*

The Terms "Ethiopia," "Nubia," "Kush" and "Sudan"

The term "Ethiopian," "Nubian," and "Kushite" all relate to the same peoples who lived south of Egypt. In modern times, the land which was once known as Nubia ("Land of Gold"), is currently known as the Sudan, and the land even further south and east towards the coast of east Africa is referred to as Ethiopia (see map above).

Recent research has shown that the modern Nubian word *kiji* means "fertile land, dark gray mud, silt, or black land." Since the sound of this word is close to the Ancient Egyptian name Kish or Kush, referring to the land south of Egypt, it is believed that the name Kush also meant "the land of dark silt" or "the black land." Kush was the Ancient Egyptian name for Nubia. Nubia, the black land, is the Sudan of today. Sudan is an Arabic translation of *sûd* which is the plural form of *aswad*, which means "black," and *ân* which means "of the." So, Sudan means "of the blacks." In the modern Nubian language, *nugud* means "black." Also, *nuger*, *nugur*, and *nubi* mean "black" as well. All of this indicates that the words Kush, Nubia, and Sudan all mean the same thing — the "black land" and/or the "land of the blacks."[28] As we will see, the differences between the term Kush and the term Kam (Qamit, Kamit, Kemit - name for Ancient Egypt in the Ancient Egyptian language) relate more to the same meaning but different geographical locations.

The Term Kamit (Qamit, Kamit, Kamit) and Its Relation to Nubia and the term "Black"

As we have seen, the terms "Ethiopia," "Nubia," "Kush" and "Sudan" all refer to "black land" and/or the "land of the blacks." In the same manner we find that the name of Egypt which was used by the Ancient Egyptians also means "black land" and/or the "land of the blacks." The hieroglyphs below reveal the Ancient Egyptian meaning of the words related to the name of their land. It is clear that the meaning of the word Qamit is equivalent to the word Kush as far as they relate to "black land" and that they also refer to a differentiation in geographical location, i.e. Kush is the "black land of the south" and Qamit is the "black land of the north." Both terms denote the primary quality that defines Africa, "black" or "Blackness" (referring to the land and its people). The quality of blackness and the consonantal sound of K or Q as well as the reference to the land are all aspects of commonality between the Ancient Kushitic and Kamitan terms.

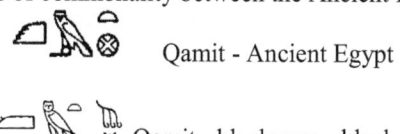

Qamit - Ancient Egypt

Qamit - blackness – black

Qamit - literature of Ancient Egypt – scriptures

Qamiu or variant - Ancient Egyptians-people of the black land.

---

[28]"Nubia," *Microsoft® Encarta® Africana.* © 1999 Microsoft Corporation. All rights reserved.

The ancient historian Stephanus of Byzantium said:

> "Ethiopia was the first established country on earth; and the Ethiopians were the first who introduced the worship of the gods, and who established laws."

The ancient historian Diodorus recorded the tradition of how the first Ethiopian/Nubian king Asar (Osiris) led a group of colonists up the Nile River and settled the area of the north-eastern corner of Africa which would later be known as "Kamit (Egypt)."

> *"From Ethiopia, he (Osiris) passed through Arabia, bordering upon the Red Sea to as far as India, and the remotest inhabited coasts; he built likewise many cities in India, one of which he called Nysa, willing to have remembrance of that (Nysa) in Egypt where he was brought up. At this Nysa in India he planted Ivy, which continues to grow there, but nowhere else in India or around it. He left likewise many other marks of his being in those parts, by which the latter inhabitants are induced, and do affirm, that this God was born in India. He likewise addicted himself to the hunting of elephants, and took care to have statues of himself in every place, as lasting monuments of his expedition."*
> —Recorded by *Diodorus* (Greek historian 100 B.C.)

Thus we are to understand that the ancient Nubians colonized (settled) the area north of the sources of the Nile River as they followed its flow, looking for more fertile lands. Further, we learn, from the legend of Asar[135], that after establishing civilization in Egypt, he proceeded to travel the ancient world and assisted those people in establishing civilizations outside of Africa, namely Asia Minor, India, China and southern Europe. Modern archeology has revealed that Asarian artifacts have been found in areas south of Uganda, specifically Zaire. Also, the Dogon peoples of West Africa hold that they are direct descendants of the Ancient Egyptians. So the influence of Asar (Ancient Egyptian civilization) was felt not only on the African continent, but far and wide. This is again supported by the ancient Greek and Roman historians.

> *"And upon his return to Greece, they gathered around and asked, "tell us about this great land of the Blacks called Ethiopia." And Herodotus said, "There are two great Ethiopian nations, one in Sind (India) and the other in Egypt."*
> —Diodorus quoting Herodotus (c. 484-425 B.C.E.)

> *"India taken as a whole, beginning from the north and embracing what of it is subject to Persia, is a continuation of Egypt and the Ethiopians."*
> -The Itinerarium Alexandri (A.C.E. 345)

Following the tradition as outlined above and taking into account the findings by geneticists and anthropologists which all show that human beings emerged from Africa through the Arabian desert and populated Asia, we are to understand that the Nubians gave rise to the Ancient Egyptians and the Ancient Egyptians gave rise to the peoples of Asia Minor and India.

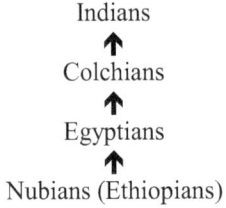

Indians
↑
Colchians
↑
Egyptians
↑
Nubians (Ethiopians)

The Ancient History of Nubia

Modern Western archeologists believe that the evidence shows that Nubian culture emerged by the year 3,800 B.C.E.,[29] with a monarchic system in place. They also consider that this monarchy emerged some generations prior to the Ancient Egyptian Pharaonic system. However, in light of the new evidence of the Sphinx, it is perhaps better to understand the monarchy of Nubia as an outgrowth of the flowering of its own child (Egypt). The Great Sphinx bears witness to the existence of the Pharaonic system as early as 10,000 B.C.E. So, the Nubians who moved to Egypt prior to 10,000 B.C.E. (now called the Kamitan people) were able to flourish there, and that prosperity affected Nubia, and there too, the same system of Pharaonic rule and culture developed.

Map of Ancient Kamit and Kush

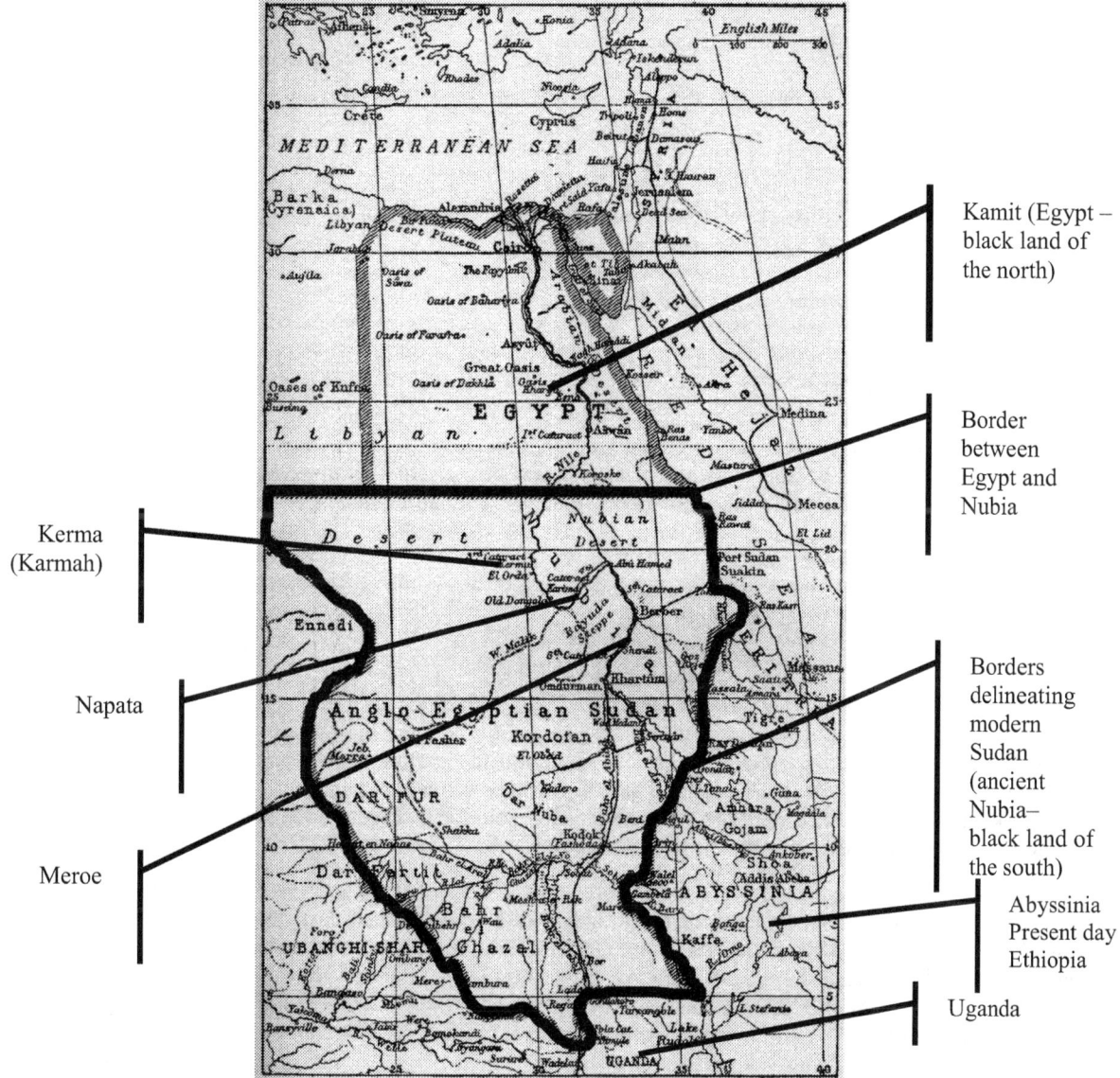

It was not until around 2000 B.C.E. that Nubia emerged from the shadow of Egypt as a strong nation, with the rise of the city-state of Kerma (see map above). Up to and during this period there was a harmonious

---

[29] Prior to that time, evidence indicates that the Nubian people had a rudimentary civilization.

relationship with Egypt, and trade boomed between the two countries. Later, during the reign of the kings Amenemhat I, Senusert I and Senusert III, Nubia was formally annexed to Egypt.

In the Late Period of Ancient Egyptian history, when it was invaded by the Assyrians, the Nubians regained control of Egypt and ruled Nubia and Egypt until the Assyrians retook Egypt and the Nubians were pushed down to Napata (see map above). Nubia defended Egypt against the Assyrians and the Libyans during their tenure. They also led a resurgence in Ancient Egyptian art and culture as well as spiritual philosophy, as evinced by the patronage of the King Shabaka towards the restoration of Memphite Theology. The Nubians did not have to undergo any conflicts with respect to whether or not they should accept the Ancient Egyptian gods and goddesses, because these were always theirs as well. An Ancient Egyptian born prince by the name of Psametichus temporarily ousted the Assyrians. The Nubians moved their capital to the south, to Napata at around 667 B.C.E., and began trading with other African states in the interior of Africa. Note that the Egyptians did not oppose the Nubians, but did oppose the Assyrians and the Libyans. The Libyans later captured Napata, and the Nubians moved their capital to Meroe (see map above) in 593 B.C.E., and a new flourishing of trade and culture emerged again in Nubia.

The Ancient Egyptians referred to Nubia as *Ta Seti* ("Land of the Bow") presumably because of the skill of the Nubian archers who served in the Egyptian armies. The Ancient Egyptians also referred to Nubia as Wawat and Yam, which were capitals or centers of power in Nubia. Thus, these names were used at different periods. The term Yam is not used after the Old Kingdom Period. The term Kush (Cush) appears at about 2000 B.C.E., and at this time Kerma was the capital of the Nubian nation.

The Relationship between Nubia and Egypt

The situation between Ancient Egypt and Nubia may be likened to that of England and the United States. Far from being a racial issue, it so happened that the child, Egypt, grew to such stature and glory, that it surpassed the parent. Due to certain cultural differences that developed between the countries, there was a vying over control of trade just as two siblings quarrel over clothing or jewelry. The true state of affairs between the two countries became evident when Egypt was besieged and occupied by foreign conquerors. The Nubians lent their support as allies, if not as family members coming to the rescue of kin in trouble, to restore Egypt to her former glory.

At around 2000 B.C.E., the Kingdom of Kerma or Karmah grew in power and ambition, and became an economic competitor with Egypt. When Egypt experienced a period of social upheaval beginning around 1700 B.C.E., when the Hyksos (Asiatics most likely from present-day Syria) conquered lower (northern) Egypt, armies of upper or southern Egypt withdrew from lower Nubia and Karmah took over this region. However, soldiers from Karmah fought on both sides in the warfare between the Egyptians and the Hyksos, pointing to the fluidity of the situation in Nubia and the ambivalence of the Nubians in this period. The Egyptians began a national war of liberation by around 1570 B.C.E. They waged war first against Karmah, because during the war conflict with the Hyksos, the Egyptian Pharaoh Kamose intercepted a message from the Hyksos ruler to the new king of Karmah. This message invited Karmah to join forces with Hyksos to conquer Egypt, and they would share its spoils between them

Egypt moved to reconquer lower Nubia to prevent such an alliance, and then the Egyptians drove the Hyksos from Egypt. The ambivalence of the Kingdom of Karmah proved costly for them since Egypt then waged a series of attacks against Karmah until around 1450 B.C.E., when Egypt destroyed the kingdom and its capital. Egypt then occupied Nubia for approximately 500 years, and the Nubians (or Kushites) absorbed Egyptian culture.[136] This period also marked the beginning of the New Kingdom era in Ancient Egyptian history, a period marked by a flowering in Egyptian culture. In the New Kingdom and Late Periods of Ancient Egyptian history, the Nubians adopted the worship of Amun, particularly in his ram form, and also the architectural style of Kamit (pyramid with attached chapel in the characteristic form with two pylons. The Nubians also adopted the art of building pyramids, but most of these were for use as tombs, somewhat like the pyramid tombs of the Ancient Egyptian Old Kingdom Period. This building boom was especially marked during the Meroitic Period of Nubian history. Thus, there is a larger total number of pyramids in Nubia than in Egypt itself.

Above-left: Pyramid temple Nubian Meroitic (last Nubian capital 4th century B.C.E. to 3rd century A.C.E.). Above right: Pyramid tomb of Nubian King and Egyptian Pharaoh Taharka- Late Period 25 Dynasty –8th century B.C.E.

Below: Nubian Meroitic Period Temple complete with pylons.

Below: Typical Egyptian New Kingdom Period Temple.

Below: left- Nubian Meroitic Period Temple complete with pylons. Below: right- Typical Egyptian New Kingdom Period Temple.

The Nubian Gods and Goddesses in the Kamitan Paut[30]

Left: The God Amun in the form of the Ram headed man.

While the divinity Amun was popular in Nubia, this popularity was exemplified in the later periods of Nubian history which began with the New Kingdom Period in Kamit. The Nubian preference was the ram-headed man while the preference in Kamit was either the ram in a completely zoomorphic (animal) form or the divinity as a man with the body and head of a man (anthropomorphic).

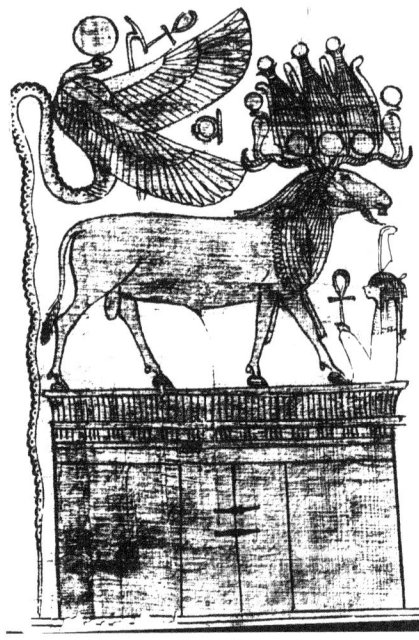

Figure 20: Above left, the God Amun-Ra from Ancient Egypt as a man. Above right- the god Amun-Ra from Ancient Egypt as a ram.

---

[30] Company of Ancient Egyptian Neteru (Gods and Goddesses) – similar in some ways to the term "Pantheon" meaning All the gods of a people. –American Heritage dictionary

If we look further back however, we will discover that the mythic association between the Kamitans and the Nubians in Pre-Dynastic times is supported by the earliest writings of Ancient Egypt. Firstly, the god Bas (Basu, Bes), who is usually referred to as a "Sudani" god, is also equated by the Ancient Egyptian scripture and iconography with the divinity Heru. The following panel shows this link most succinctly.

Figure 21- Above: left -Heru as a Divine child, master of nature, controller of beasts (evil, unrighteousness, the lower self), wearing mask of Basu. Above right – Basu as the dwarf with the characteristic Nubian plumes as headdress.

In anthropology, pigmies are known as members of any of various peoples, especially of equatorial Africa and parts of southeast Asia, having an average height less than 5 feet (127 centimeters).[138] In the ancient period, the pigmies of Nubia were renowned for knowing "the dance of the God" and for being jovial but forthright people. In this vein they were renowned musicians and lovers of play and festivity, but also leaders in wars of righteousness and protectors of children. These are all attributes of Basu. Basu also appears in the Pyramid Texts along with the other gods and goddesses of Kamit. The Pyramid Texts are the earliest known extensive writings about the myth and philosophy of Kamit (Ancient Egypt). Therefore, any divinity which is mentioned in those texts, emerges with at least the same importance of the other Kamitan gods and goddesses depending on the interrelationships provided in the text itself. The system of Neteru (gods and goddesses) of Kamit may be divided into the following groups for easy understanding.

Transcendental
Divinities: Neberdjer, Heru – beyond the cosmos, beyond time and space
⇕
Cosmic
Divinities: Ex. Asar, Amun, Ra, Net, etc.—universal worship
⇕
Natural
Divinities: Geb, Nut, Shu, Tefnut, etc.— divinities symbolizing the cosmic forces of nature
⇕
Local (worldly)
Divinities: worshipped at the particular nome (city-town) but not nationally throughout Egypt
⇕
Legendary
Divinities: – original divinities of the ancient period that gave rise to the ones worshipped in the later forms

Figure 22- Above left: Kamitan depictions of the Kamitan/Nubian God Bas as the Harpist. Above right: The Kamitan/Nubian god Bas in the form of the all-encompassing divinity, Neberdjer.[139]

Bas and a host of other Nubian divinities can be seen as the legendary divinities which appear in the early Kamitan texts, but later take on new Kamitan forms, under which their worship continues. Bas, for example, continues to be worshipped as Heru. Bas also figures prominently as a part of the Kamitan concept of the transcendental divinity, Neberdjer. The iconography of Bas in the form of Neberdjer (above) closely follows that of the representation of Heru as the Divine Child (above) in the following respects. Both are regarded as the all-encompassing Divinity, masters of the animal forces. In the picture of Heru above, this is symbolized by Heru holding and standing on the animals; his nudity is a symbol of transcendentalism (unconditioned consciousness). The Bas mask he wears is a symbol of the wonderful and magnificent nature of the Divine, who manifests as a dwarf, and at the same time as a personality overflowing with joviality and life.

Neberdjer represents all of the forces of the other divinities including Ra, Amun and Heru thus representing (see picture above) non-duality and Supreme Divinity. This being is in control of the seven eternal animal forces (seven animals encircled by the serpent with its tail in its mouth-symbolizing eternity).

Other Nubian divinities which were mentioned in the Ancient Egyptian Pyramid Texts include:

Aahs

The Nubian divinity Aahs is referred to as the "Regent of the land of the south."

Ari Hems Nefer

The Nubian divinity Ari Hems Nefer is referred to as the "beautiful womb." *Ari Hems Nefer* was a divinity of the area 15 miles south of the modern Egyptian city of Aswan, where the temple of Aset is located. In ancient times it was known as Pilak or the limit or southern border of Egypt. Today it is called Philae.

The Nubian divinity **Meril** is referred to as the "beloved lion" divinity of the city of Kalabshah (city located 35 miles south of the modern Egyptian city Aswan), where the temple of Knum is located. In ancient times it was known as Elephantine by the Greeks or the first cataract of Egypt. Today it is called Aswan.

Symbol A, Symbol B, Symbol C

The symbols above for the Nubian divinity **Dudun** show the association with one of the oldest most worshipped and most powerful divinity of Kamit, Heru, whose symbol is the falcon (hawk). Symbol A shows the characteristic Heruian icon, the hawk, perched on the divine solar boat. Symbol B shows one of the full spellings of the name including the phonetic signs and again, including the hawk, this time perched on the standard, meaning *Dudun Sa Heru:* "Dudun the son of Heru." Symbol C shows one of the full spellings of the name including the phonetic signs and this time showing the symbol of the two lands, meaning *Dudun Sa Tawi* "Dudun the son of the two lands (i.e. Nubia and Egypt)." The divinity Dudun was important in Kamitan spirituality even into the late period. The evidence of this can be found in the fact that it was Dudun who symbolically burnt the special Nubian incense through which the royalty of Kamit was to be purified for induction to the high offices, including the throne of rulership. Pharaoh Djehutimes III built temples to Dudun in Nubia at *el-Lessya* and *Uronarti*. Below we see the symbols of Heru used in Kamit. Notice the correlation to the symbols of Dudun.

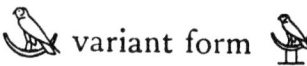 variant form

The symbols of Heru and those of Dudun are a perfect match. Therefore, Dudun was the name for the same divinity which was called Heru in Kamitan religion. Another strong correlation between Nubian and Kamitan religion is the dwarf figure. We have already been introduced to Basu. This quality of stature and Nubian features is also present in the figure of Asar in his aspect of Ptah-Seker-Asar.

Ptah-Seker-Asar (as Pigmy)

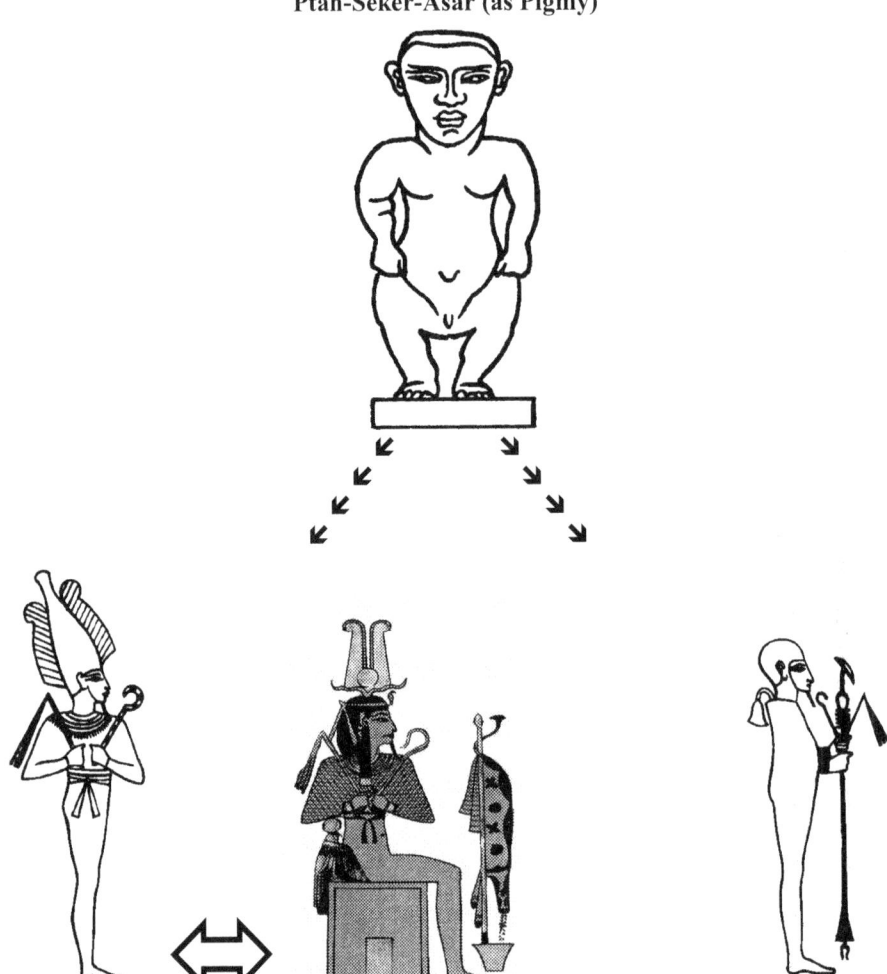

Figure 23: Above far-left The god Asar. Middle- is Ptah-Seker-Asar as an average sized man. Far right- The god Ptah of Memphis.

Ptah-Seker-Asar unites the three main spiritual traditions of the early Dynastic Period in ancient Kamit, that of Ra, Asar, and Ptah. Asar is part of Anunian theology, which is centered on the divinity Ra, and Ra is associated with the even earlier Heru as the all-encompassing Divinity. Also, Asar is associated with the divinity Heru, as Heru is Asar's son in the Asarian mystical tradition. Ptah is the central divinity in the theology of the Ancient Egyptian city of *Men-nefer* (also Het-Ka-Ptah), known as Memphis. He is associated, in his work of Creation, with the Divinity Tem, who is a form of Ra. Therefore, the dwarf figure of Ptah-Seker-Asar united the culture of Nubia with that of Kamit Also the religious iconography of Basu as the dwarf and the characteristic Nubian plumed headdress comes into the later Dynastic Period. Therefore, the impact of Nubian spirituality was felt all the way from the commencement of Kamitan religion through the late period.

Plate 2: (Below) In the upper right hand corner of the ceiling of the Peristyle Hall in the Temple of Aset a special image of the goddess Nut and the God Geb and the higher planes of existence can be seen. Nut and Geb. Below: -line drawing of the same scene. (Temple of Aset {Isis}).

The figure at left depicts another conceptualization of the Netherworld, which is at the same time the body of Nut in a forward bend posture.

The god Geb is on the ground practicing the Plough Yoga exercise posture. The goddess in the center symbolizes the lower heaven in which the moon traverses, the astral realm. The outermost goddess symbolizes the course of the sun in its astral journey and the causal plane.

Notice the characteristic Nubian headdress of Nut, which is also visible in the iconography of Bas. This iconography links the late Kamitan religion with that of the Pre-Dynastic era, and with the Nubian origins of Kamitan culture. Geb, who is in the plough posture, symbolizes the physical plane and all solid matter, while the goddesses represent the subtler levels of existence.

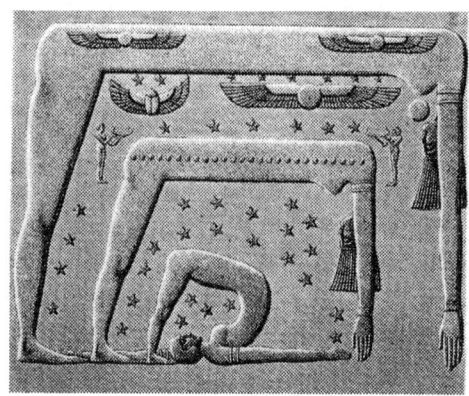

Figure 24: Goddess Mut, the Mother of Asar and Aset and Blackness as a Metaphor of Consciousness and as a Description of the gods and goddesses

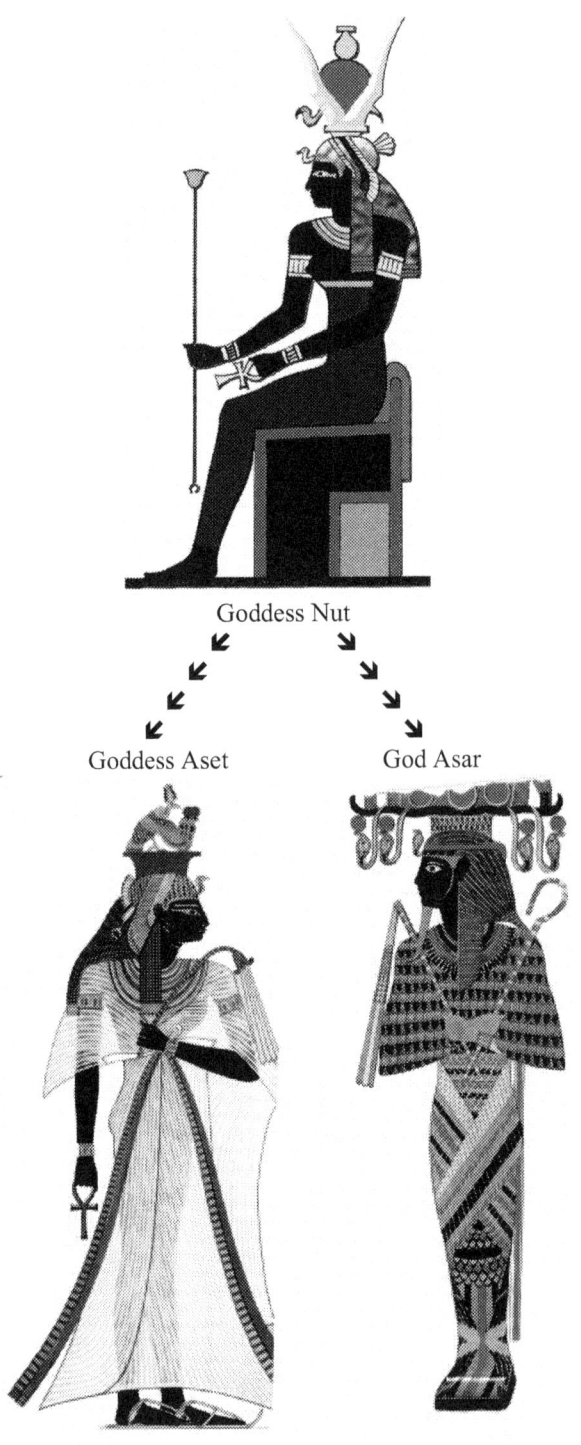

African Origins of Civilization, Religion, Yoga Mystical Spirituality and Ethics Philosophy

In Kamitan philosophy, blackness is used as a descriptive nomenclature of the people, certain of the gods and goddesses as well as the concept of the transcendental.

In the Temple of Denderah in Kamit, it is inscribed that the goddess Nut gave birth to the goddess Aset there, and that upon her birth, Nut exclaimed: *"As"* (behold), *I have become thy mother."* This was the origin of the name "Ast," (Aset) later known as Isis to the Greeks and others. It further states that *"she was a dark-skinned child and was called Khnemet-ankhet"* or "the living lady of love". Thus, Aset also symbolizes the "blackness" of the vast un-manifest regions of existence. In this capacity she is also the ultimate expression of the African ideal prototype of the Christian Madonna, especially in statues where she is depicted holding the baby Heru in the same manner Mother Mary is portrayed holding baby Jesus. Her identification is also symbolized in her aspect as *Amentet,* the Duat, itself.

Ament means "hidden." It is a specific reference to the female form of the astral plane or Netherworld known as *Amenta* (Amentet, Amentat) or the Duat. Like her husband Asar, who was known as the "Lord of the Perfect Black," Aset was the Mistress of the Netherworld (Amentet, Amentat). Thus, Aset also symbolizes the "blackness" of the vast unmanifest regions of existence (the unmanifest). Upon further reflection into the mythology it becomes obvious that since Asar is the Duat, and since the goddess Amentet is also Amentat or the realm of Asar, they are in reality one and the same (both the realms and the deities). So Aset and Asar together form the hidden recesses of Creation. In essence they are the source of Creation, and are therefore both simultaneously considered to be the source of the Life Force which courses through Creation.

Table 9: Chronology of Nubian History

8,000 B.C.E.	**Pottery and community found at Karmah**
2,000 – 1550 B.C.E.	**Karmah Period**
1549 – 850 B.C.E.	**Unification with Kamit (Ancient Egypt) Period**
850 – 270 B.C.E.	**Napata Period**
716 B.C.E.	**25th Dynasty – beginning rulership of Egypt Period**
270 B.C.E. – 350 A.C.E.	**Meroe Period Independent Nation**
1st century B.C.E.– 1st century A.C.E.	**Judaism introduced– some Kushites adopt Judaism**
3rd –6th century A.C.E.	**Christianization Period – some Kushites adopt Christianity**
1000 A.C.E.	**Islamization Period, Axum city - Kushites and Arabs Merge**

Summary

Thus, it is clear that the Ancient Egyptians, while recognizing the geographical differences (Egypt is in the north and Kush is in the south) between their land and the land of the Nubians, also recognized the similitude of the lands. In effect the name of lands of Egypt and Nubia actually mean the same thing "black land" or "land of the blacks." The different words used to identify the two cultures (Kush and Kamit) simply denote the relative geographical locations and the ethnic (tribal) differentiation of inhabitants. The ethnic differences here do not relate to race or religion as these have been shown to be the same, but of customs and traditions that developed independently due to differences in distance from each other. This is done for the purpose of showing an underlying unity while at the same time denoting the practical differences of the two lands. This of course points to the underlying ethnic homogeneity between the two peoples, and at the same time acknowledges the cultural differences which developed due to the language changes and the accelerated development of the Ancient Egyptians.

Another force, which spurred the Ancient Egyptians to develop at a faster pace, was the interaction they had with the Asiatic peoples. Since the Ancient Egyptians were geographically located closer to Asia Minor, they encountered more Asiatics and Europeans than the Ethiopians, who were in an area that afforded them a relative form of seclusion. Some of the interactions were peaceful while others were hostile and this prompted (stimulated) the Ancient Egyptians to mature and advance in the areas of building technology, warfare and social as well as spiritual philosophy.

Recent archaeological finds have revealed that the region's people were producing sophisticated ceramics by 8000 B.C.E. Indeed, it seems likely that Nubia contributed as much to Ancient Egypt's development as Egypt did to Nubia's.[140] Nubian-Egyptian pottery from the Pre-Dynastic Period is the link between the Ancient Nubian (Ethiopians), the Ancient Egyptians and the Ancient Indus Valley culture.

Plate 7: Pre-Dynastic-Ancient Egyptian Neolithic Period Grave-including black and red pottery. (British Museum-Photo by M. Ashby)

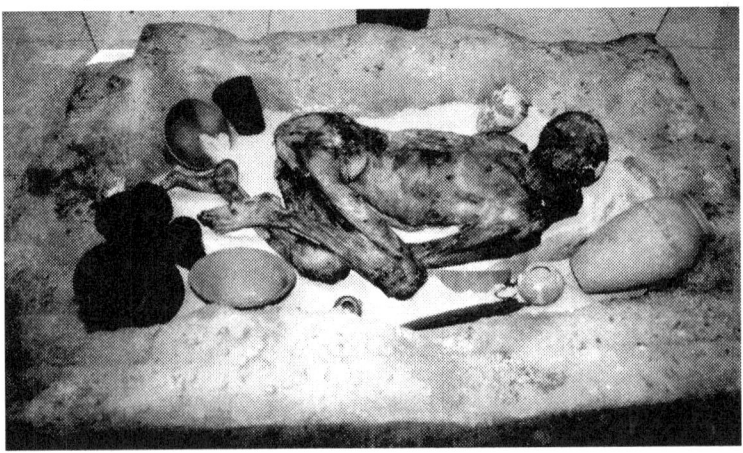

African Origins of Civilization, Religion, Yoga Mystical SPirituality and Ethics Philosophy

The foundations of Egyptian religion were evident as far back as the Pre-Dynastic era as religious amulets from that era have been found spread throughout the region (Kamit-Kush). In the early period the dead were buried in cemeteries, along with pots and other domestic implements, from Badarian times. Many of these pots found in graves show a boat with a palm branch at the bow and two cabins, over one of which, at least, is the emblem of a divinity.[141] The distinctive pottery of this period has been compared and likened to that of the later finds in the Indus Valley. On some of the pottery designs were painted. Some were first in white with a dark red background, and later in red on a light background.

There were two periods of development in the Pharaonic system of rule in northeast Africa. The first developed prior to 10,000 B.C.E. as attested by the headdress of the Great Sphinx. The second period is the late Pre-Dynastic Period (prior to 5000 B.C.E.). There is evidence that the Pharaonic system of rule (kings and queens as spiritual leaders-head of religion) emerged in the Pre-Dynastic Period in Nubia (Kush) prior to its development in Kamit. The difference between the monarchy of Ancient Nubia and the Pharaonic system of Ancient Egypt may be seen in the domain of rulership. In Egypt the Pharaonic system developed into an empire when the "two lands" (Upper and Lower Egypt) were consolidated. Egypt had 42 monarchies (referred to as nomarchs since they ruled over nomes or municipalities), but what made the Pharaonic rule different is that it was rulership that united all of the separate nomes. So the Pharaoh was not just a king, but also an emperor. When we speak of a breakdown in the Pharaonic rule in the times when Egypt was not completely overpowered, we are only speaking of the loss of Pharaonic rule and not necessarily a total crash of the society. It would be as if the President of a country lost power temporarily but the governors of the cities or states remained in power, and later conspired to bring back order by pooling resources such as personnel and material in order to rebuild the government. This is what happened during the invasions of the Hyksos as well as the Assyrians. This was the state of affairs during the "intermediate" periods between the Old and Middle Kingdom Periods and between the Middle and New Kingdoms. The Ancient Egyptians were not strong enough to overcome the second Assyrian attack, and there was never a second opportunity to overthrow them since Alexander the Great defeated them and took their place. There was still not enough strength to overcome the Greeks, but also there was lesser need, since they upheld the Egyptian culture and religion. Thus the Egyptian culture remained relatively intact under the Greeks as compared to the conditions imposed by the Hyksos and Assyrians. These conditions would not remain the same under the control by the Roman-Christians and the later Arab-Muslims who actively sought to stamp out the old religion. Nubia was the last place to practice the Ancient Egyptian religion, and thus also the last to convert to Judaism, Christianity and Islam. Today, the Nubians living in southern Egypt consider themselves ethnically as Nubian, and at the same time nationally as Egyptian, and spiritually as Muslim.

Chapter 1 Section 3: History of Predynastic and Dynastic Egypt

Summary of Major Events in Ancient Egyptian History

As stated earlier, the origins of Ancient Egyptian civilization begin in the far reaches of pre-history. Ancient Egypt or Kamit had a civilization that flourished in Northeast Africa along the Nile River from before 10,000 B.C.E. (being conservative) until 30 B.C.E. In 30 B.C.E., Octavian, who was later known as the Roman Emperor Augustus, put the last Egyptian king, Ptolemy XIV, a Greek ruler, to death. After this Egypt was formally annexed to Rome. Traditional late 20th century Egyptologists normally divide Ancient Egyptian history into the following approximate periods. Of course, these dates need to be revised in light of the new evidences.

Table 10: Major Cultural-Theological Developments

Chronology of Ancient Egypt According to Confirmed Archeological Dating of artifacts and Monuments (Based on evidences presented in this book).[142]	The dates below are based on the opinions of orthodox Egyptologists[143]
	*See Appendix A
38,000 B.C.E Beginning of the Great Year previous to the current one.	The Late Pre-Dynastic (3000-2920 B.C.E.);[144]/[145]
c. 10,500 B.C.E.-7,000 B.C.E. Creation of the Great Sphinx Modern archeological accepted dates – Sphinx means Hor-m-akhet or Heru (Horus) in the horizon. This means that the King is one with the Spirit, Ra as an enlightened person possessing an animal aspect (lion) and illuminated intellect. Anunian Theology – Ra	Early Dynastic Period (2920-2775 B.C.E.); Dynasty 1-3
c. 10,000 B.C.E.-5,500 B.C.E. The Sky GOD- Realm of Light-Day – NETER Androgynous – All-encompassing –Absolute, Nameless Being, later identified with Ra-Herakhti (Sphinx)	The Old Kingdom or Old Empire (2575-234 B.C.E.); Dynasty 4-8
>7,000 B.C.E. Kamitan Myth and Theology present in architecture	The First Intermediate Period (2134-2,040 B.C.E.); Dynasty 9-11 (Theban)
5,500-3,800 BCE EARLY DYNASTIC PERIOD – AND OLD KINGDOM PERIOD	The Middle Kingdom or Middle Empire (2040-1640 B.C.E.); Dynasty 11-14
5500+ B.C.E. to 600 A.C.E. Amun -Ra - Ptah (Horus) – Amenit - Rai – Sekhmet (male and female Trinity-Complementary Opposites)	The Second Intermediate Period (1640-1532 B.C.E.); Dynasty 15-17
5500+ B.C.E. Memphite Theology – Ptah	
5500+ B.C.E. Hermopolitan Theology- Djehuti	The New Kingdom or New Empire (1532-1070 B.C.E.); Dynasty 18-20
5500+ B.C.E. The Asarian Resurrection Theology - Asar	
5500+B.C.E. The Goddess Principle- Theology, Isis-Hathor-Net-Mut-Sekhmet-Buto	
5500 B.C.E. (Dynasty 1) Beginning of the Dynastic Period (Unification of Upper and Lower Egypt)	The third Intermediate Period (1070-712 B.C.E.); Dynasty 21-25 (Nubia and Theban Area)
5000 B.C.E. (5th Dynasty) Pyramid Texts - Egyptian Book of Coming Forth By Day - 42 Precepts of MAAT and codification of the Pre-Dynastic theologies (Pre-Dynastic Period: 10,000 B.C.E.-5,500 B.C.E.)	The Late Period (712-332 B.C.E.). Dynasty 25 (Nubia and All Egypt)-30
5000-4000 B.C.E. Construction of the Step Pyramid at Sakkara	**In the Late Period of Ancient Egyptian history the following groups controlled Egypt.**
4950 B.C.E. Neolithic – Fayum	
4241 B.C.E. The Pharaonic (royal) calendar based on the Sothic system (star Sirius) was in use.	The Nubian Dynasty (712-657 B.C.E.);
4000-3000 B.C.E CONSTRUCTION OF THE GREAT PYRAMIDS	The Persian Dynasty (525-404 B.C.E.);
3800-3500 B.C.E.- 1ST INTERMEDIATE PERIOD	The Native Revolt and re-establishment of Egyptian rule by Egyptians (404-343 B.C.E.);
3500-1730 B.C.E. MIDDLE KINGDOM	
3000 B.C.E. WISDOM TEXTS-Precepts of Ptahotep, Instructions of Any, Instructions of Amenemope, Etc.	The Second Persian Period (343-332 B.C.E.);
2040 B.C.E.-1786 B.C.E. COFFIN TEXTS	The Ptolemaic or Greek Period (Also known as the Hellenistic Period 332 B.C.E.- c. 30 B.C.E.);
1730-1580 B.C.E. 2ND INTERMEDIATE PERIOD	Roman Period (c.30 B.C.E.-395 A.C.E.);
1580-1075 B.C.E .NEW KINGDOM	The Byzantine Period (395-642 A.C.E) and
1580 B.C.E.-Theban Theology - Amun	The Arab Conquest Period includes: the Caliphate and the Mamalukes Period (642-1517 A.C.E.);
1570 B.C.E.-Books of Coming Forth By Day (Book of the Dead)	
1353 B.C.E. Non-dualist Philosophy from the Pre-Dynastic Period was redefined by Akhnaton.	Ottoman Domination Period (1082-1882 A.C.E.); British colonialism Period (1882-1952 A.C.E.);
1075-656 BCE 3RD INTERMEDIATE	Modern, Arab-Islamic Egypt (1952- present).
712-657 B.C.E. The Nubian Dynasty	
664-332 BCE LATE PERIOD	

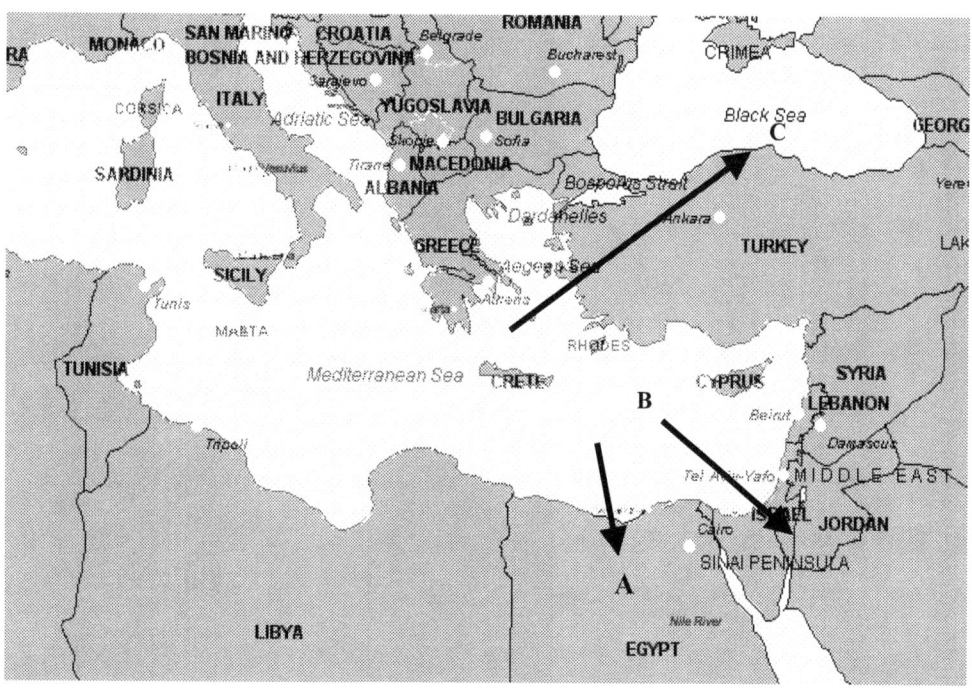

At about 2,890 B.C.E., the beginning of the IInd Dynasty, considerable trade was in progress between Egypt (A) and the Sinai (B). The Egyptians are believed to have traded as far to the north as the Black Sea (C). It is known that Pharaoh Pepi II of the VI Dynasty, ruler from c. 2,294 B.C.E.- c. 2,188 B.C.E., organized the caravan trade with Nubia, Punt and the Sudan. In the early New Kingdom period (1,580-1,075 B.C.E.), the famous Pharaoh, Queen Hatshepsut (1,473-1,458 B.C.E.) of Ancient Egypt, expanded maritime trade which is believed to have stretched as far as India[146] and the Far East.[147] It is believed that textiles, including cotton were brought back from India and used for mummy wrappings.

> In early times, the principal objects that were introduced to Egypt from Arabia and India were spices and various oriental productions. These were required either for the service of religion, or the purposes of luxury. A number of precious stones, such as lapis lazuli, and other items brought from those countries are frequently discovered in the tombs of Thebes, bearing the names of Pharaohs of the 18th[148] dynasty.[149]
>
> -Sir Garner Wilkinson

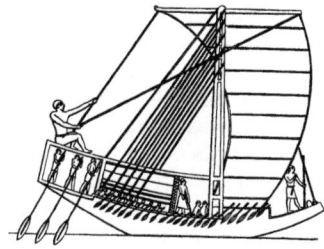

Figure 25: Trading Vessel in the 18th Dynasty (1580 B.C.E)[31]

The New Kingdom Period (1,580-1,075 B.C.E.) was a time wherein Ancient Egypt was at a peak in terms of art, philosophy, economic and political power as well as social prosperity. The period after the New Kingdom

---

[31] Revised dating based on correct evidence.

saw greatness in culture and architecture under the rulership of Rameses II. However, after his rule, Egypt saw a decline from which it would never recover. This is the period of the downfall of Ancient Egyptian culture in which the Libyans ruled after The Tanite (XXI) Dynasty. This was followed by the Nubian rulers who founded the XXII Dynasty and tried to restore Egypt to her past glory. However, having been weakened by the social and political turmoil of wars, Ancient Egypt fell to the Persians. The Persians conquered the country and were expelled briefly by native Egyptians, but they re-conquered the country until the Greeks, under Alexander, conquered them. The Romans followed the Greeks, and then the first Arab-Muslims conquered the land of Egypt in 640 A.C.E . The map below shows the areas of regular trade between the Ancient Egyptians and the other Africans living in the south. Queen Hatshepsut's trading parties and those of other Ancient Egyptian rulers commonly engaged in commerce with the land of "Punt."

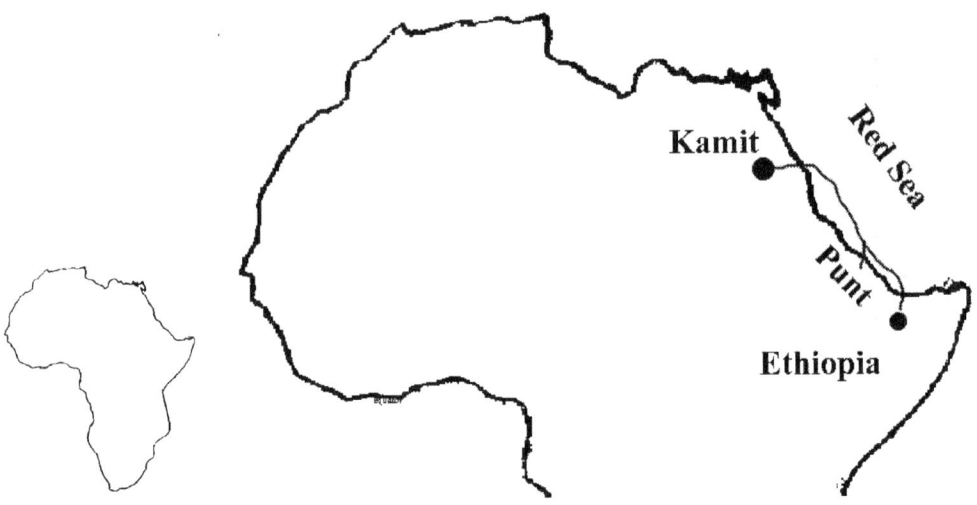

The Economy of Ancient Egypt

Ancient Egypt was a wealthy country due to its fertile lands, owing to the regular yearly Nile River deposits in the surrounding valley. It became the "grainstore" of the Roman Empire when the Romans conquered it. Corn, date-palms, vegetables and grapevines were grown, and beer and bread were the staple items of food and drink by the general population. Trade was through bartering since coinage did not exist. Royal expeditions were made to Syria, Punt, Sinai, India and other lands to obtain spices, timber, metals, and other materials through trade.

The Royal Graves and Ancient Scriptures

Much of the evidence of life in Ancient Egypt from the later periods of the 1st Dynasty derives from tombs, especially those that were found in the cemeteries at Sakkara, near Memphis, which dates up to the end of the first Dynasty. In addition, some large stone steles with the names of the Pharaohs on them survived at Abdu (Abydos). However, both sites (Abdu and Sakkara-Memphis) have suffered due to the effects of plundering in ancient and modern times, and deterioration due to the passage of time. At Sakkara, the actual burial was in a subterranean wood-lined chamber. At different periods, Mastabas and pyramids were used. These burial pyramids are not to be confused with the large Great Pyramids at Giza, Dahshur, Abusir, Maidum, the Step Pyramid at Sakkara, and other sites in which no texts or bodies or funerary implements were found. The burial pyramids contain scriptures related to the spiritual resurrection of the deceased, which were later converted to Coffin Texts, and subsequently to the Papyrus Texts. In later times these texts came to be known as "Book of the Dead" or "Book of Coming Forth by Day." The proper translation of the "Book of Coming Forth by Day," in the Kamitan language is "Rau Nu Prt M Hru," which literally translated means "Chapters of Going Into the Light," i.e. "Instructions on How to Attain Enlightenment." All of the spiritual scriptures of Ancient Egypt are based on the Pre-Dynastic myths related to the nature of the gods and goddesses. All of the scriptures are interrelated, presenting aspects of the mythic as well as mystical aspects of spirituality. The Wisdom Texts are philosophical expositions on the nature of right living, and the means to achieve harmony and spiritual enlightenment in life, which as the Kamitan sages defined it, is the only purpose and goal of life.

Phases of Ancient Egyptian Spiritual Literature

MYTHS AND BASIS OF ANCIENT EGYPTIAN RELIGION

SHEMSU HOR
The Myth of Heru and Hetheru
(Sky-Solar Theology incorporating male and female divinity) - Predynastic

SHETAUT ASAR-ASET-HERU
The Myth of Asar, Aset and Heru (Asarian Resurrection Theology) - Predynastic

SHETAUT ATUM-RA
The Myth of Creation (Anunian Theology) - Predynastic

SHETAUT PTAH
The Myth of Creation (Memphite Theology) - Predynastic and Early Dynastic

SHETAUT NET
The Myth of Creation (Saitian Theology – Goddess Spirituality) - Predynastic and Early Dynastic

PYRAMID TEXTS
(C. 5,000 B.C.E. OR PRIOR)

Pyramid of Unas
Pyramid of Teti,
Pyramid of Pepi I,
Pyramid of Mernere,
Pyramid of Pepi II

WISDOM TEXTS
(C. 3,000 B.C.E. – PTOLEMAIC PERIOD)
Precepts of Ptahotep
Instructions of Any
Instructions of Amenemope
Etc.

COFFIN TEXTS
(C. 2040 B.C.E.-1786 B.C.E.)

PAPYRUS TEXTS
(C. 1580 B.C.E.-Roman Period)[32]
Books of Coming Forth By Day
Example of famous papyruses:

Papyrus of Any
Papyrus of Hunefer
Papyrus of Kenna
Greenfield Papyrus, Etc.

Hieroglyphic Writing

Hieroglyphic Writing refers to a means "relating to, or being a system of writing, such as that of Ancient Egypt, in which pictorial symbols are used to represent meaning or sounds or a combination of meaning and sounds."[150] The term also means "carved in stone." So many cultures in history have created writings carved in stone. However, the hieroglyphs of Ancient Egypt are perhaps the most popular. Hieroglyphs have been discovered on labels and tablets from the Pre-Dynastic Period. These early hieroglyphics developed into the classical script of Egypt, however not enough have been found to render deciphering certain.[151] The decipherment of the Egyptian Hieroglyphs in the early 19th century has allowed the re-discovery of a wealth of spiritual literature and the basis for most of the modern day world religions. The *Pyramid Texts* and the *Book of Coming Forth By Day* are similar in scripture and purpose. It is correct to understand that the texts referred

---

[32] After 1570 BC they would evolve into a more unified text, the Egyptian Book of the Dead.

to as the *Book of Coming Forth By Day* evolved out of the *Pyramid Text* writings. This is because the *Pyramid Texts* are the early form of the well-known texts which have been called the *Book of Coming Forth By Day*. The *Pyramid Texts* are hieroglyphic writings contained in the pyramid tombs[33] of the kings of the early Dynastic Period. Both are collections of utterances, originally recorded in hieroglyphic, which lead the initiate (student of spiritual studies seeking to attain Enlightenment) to transform {his/her} consciousness from human to divine, by purifying the mind with wisdom about the neteru (gods and goddesses, divine forces in the universe), and through the practice of rituals which promote personality integration and thus, spiritual transformation. Each of these constitutes major treatises of Ancient Egyptian literature and philosophy, and together, as a collective, constitute an advanced, holistic system of spiritual development. All of these have, as the main purpose, to effect the union of the individual human being with the Transcendental Self. This philosophy of spiritual transcendence and enlightenment did not begin with the dawn of the Dynastic Period in Ancient Egypt.

The Writing systems used in Ancient Egypt

Hieroglyphic
(used through all periods by Priests and Priestesses)
↓
Hieratic
(shorthand hieroglyphic, used by the Priests and Priestesses - middle kingdom period to Coptic period)
↓
Demotic
(used by the general population for non-secular purposes - Late Period to Coptic period)
↓
Coptic
(still presently used by the Coptic Priesthood)

First it must be understood that ancient hieroglyphic writing is not a system like any other writing. Unlike the English language, it is not just alphabetic and literal. Rather, there are several different levels of meaning. The glyphs can have a phonetic meaning, pun meaning, literal meaning, mythological meaning, mystical meaning, etc., because they use pictures and because they are essentially mystical writings. This means that learning the technical aspects of reading the glyphs is not enough to understand the true meaning of what is being said. Any person can learn to read the glyphs; this is the exoteric (outer) practice. However, not everyone can understand their deeper esoteric (inner) meaning. A true reader of the glyphs must be well versed in the mythology behind them as well as the mystical teachings behind them.

Becoming an expert on the glyphs is an added discipline because sometimes the meaning changes in different historical periods. Also, the Ancient Egyptians made use of several variations and spellings to write one word. This means that along with having knowledge of the main words that are used, it is necessary to have knowledge of the variations for the words that may appear in any text. Further, there are over 700 main glyphs, which are considered to be most common. However, there are several hundreds of glyphs, whose meaning are not known by Egyptologists. Thus, when working with texts, a reader may often encounter new words that may not occur again, and therefore, even adept Egyptologists resort to the use of dictionaries. Otherwise a person would be required to keep thousands of obscure terms in mind, which cover a vast period of Ancient Egyptian linguistic history. The period of history encompassed by the glyph ranges from before 5,000 B.C.E to 400 A.C.E. So this is a greater expense of time and linguistic change than the difference within the English language between Chaucer and Shakespeare and between Shakespeare and modern times. People in modern times cannot easily understand Shakespeare's English and can barely understand Chaucer's. And these are only time differentials of a few hundred years. What can then be said about expanses of thousands of years that are encountered between major periods of Ancient Egyptian history (PreDynastic Period, Old Kingdom period, Middle Kingdom period and New Kingdom period)? Along with the problem of not understanding many of the glyphs at all is the problem of interpretation. A survey of the translations of Egyptologists over the last 100 years reveals that often their interpretations are completely different even for

---

[33] Not to be confused with the Pyramids in Giza.

the same exact texts. This is due to their use of their own knowledge base (from western values, myth, religion and history) instead of applying the teachings within the confines of Ancient Egyptian culture, philosophy and mythology. Ancient Egypt cannot be completely understood from a perspective of twentieth century Western Culture any more than it can be understood from Greek culture in 500 B.C.E. It must be studied from within its own context and this means living and practicing the philosophy and mythology. This is the best way to gain insight into the true meanings of the Kamitan Heiroglyphs.

On The Meaning of The Hieroglyphs:

> *"We must now speak of the Ethiopian writing which is called hieroglyphic by the Egyptians, in order that we may omit nothing in our discussion of their antiquities. Now it is found that the forms of their letters take the shape of animals of every kind, and of the members of the human body, and of implements and especially carpenter's tools; for their writing does not express the intent concept by means of syllables joined one to another, but by its figurative meaning which has been impressed upon the memory by practice. For instance, they draw the picture of a hawk, a crocodile, a snake, and all of the members of the human body-an eye, a hand, a face, and the like. Now the hawk signifies to them everything which happens swiftly, since this animal is practically the swiftest of winged creatures...And the crocodile is a symbol of all that is evil, and the eye is the warder of justice and the guardian of the entire body. And as for the members of the body, the right hand with fingers extended signifies a procuring of livelihood, and the left with the fingers closed, a keeping and guarding of property. The same way of reasoning applies to the remaining characters, which represent parts of the body and implements and all other things; for by paying close attention to the significance which is inherent in each object and by training their minds through drills and exercise of the memory over a long period, they read from habit everything which has been written."*

-*Diodorus* (Greek historian 100 B.C.)

While Diodorus speaks of **the Ethiopian writing which is called hieroglyphic,** we must remember that the Ethiopians used the same hieroglyphic writing up to the Meroitic period, when they were cut off from Egypt by the conquering forces of the Greeks. The Ancient Egyptian hieroglyphic language has many levels of complexity and therefore, the reader must be initiated into these in order to understand them. Otherwise, the understanding will remain at the superficial levels and the deeper philosophy and mysticism will be lost to the reader. The following are levels of reading in the Ancient Egyptian hieroglyphic language. Upon closer examination, the Ancient Egyptian system of writing is discovered to be an extremely sophisticated system of literature.

Phonetic (consonants and vowels) = sound of the word

Ideograms - Pictorial signs– picture of an object. Ex. Owl =

Determinatives (designate the relation of the phonetic parts to an object or concept)

       Phonetic + Pictorial + Determinative = The mundane meaning of the word.

Symbolic (quality) aspect of the phonetics or determinatives (designates symbolic meaning of the word).

Mystical meaning = The Literal meaning + Symbolic aspect of the determinative or phonetic relationship + religious philosophy teachings related to the word sounds or pictures.

So in order to understanding a word of Ancient Egyptian hieroglyphic writing it is necessary to relate the words to the symbolic aspects of the images presented in the determinative and then also the mystical philosophy.

(Ex. Owl = 🦉) = (ability to see in the dark and get through the night) = (ability to get through in a way or form.)

⇕ ⇔ ⇕ ⇔ ⇕
(mundane) (symbolic) (mystical)

There is a misconception about the Ancient Egyptian hieroglyphic language that it arrived with no development at all as if by magic to the African continent. This notion plays into the speculation that it was not produced and developed in Africa, by Africans. If the text itself is examined and if the writings from linguists who have studied it are examined, it becomes quickly obvious that there was a period of development of the language. Precisely, in relation to the developing a solution to the problem of confusion in the reading, the Ancient Egyptian scribes developed what are called determinatives, to be added to the word so as to make the meaning more accurate. However, there still remained some ambiguities, so then came the development of "alphabetic" signs. This development is recognized by linguists as being *"not derived from Mesopotamian writing, and demonstrates the total autonomy of the development of the hieroglyphic system."* The alphabetic signs are included below.

The Ancient Egyptian Hieroglyphic Alphabet:

a, A, b, a³⁴, d, dj, f, g, h, k, m, n, p, q, r, s, sh, t, tj, w, y, ch, kh

The Pyramids and Other Temples

The massive pyramid complexes at Giza, Dahshur, Abusir, Maidum, the Step Pyramid at Sakkara, and other sites denote the high order of Ancient Egyptian Religion. These structures were not used as burial chambers for the kings, but rather as Temples. It has been shown that they were astronomically aligned and refer architecturally to aspects contained in the spiritual scriptures. For example, the pyramid complex at Giza, where the Great Sphinx is located, is referred to as the "Rastau" or passageway into the Orion Star Constellation, the abode of Asar (Osiris). This may be understood literally or it may be understood mystically as a passageway into the Netherworld, which is the scriptural abode of The Supreme Being, as Asar, and therefore the destination of all enlightened souls. As such, the Pyramids at Giza are a gigantic star-map of the stars on Orion's belt, which mystically serve to direct or guide the spiritual student (initiate) to the abode of Asar. Thus, it gives the initiate insight into the means and mechanisms (disciplines) by which {he/she} may attain spiritual enlightenment.³⁵

Figure 26: Pre-Dynastic Ancient Egyptian Temple

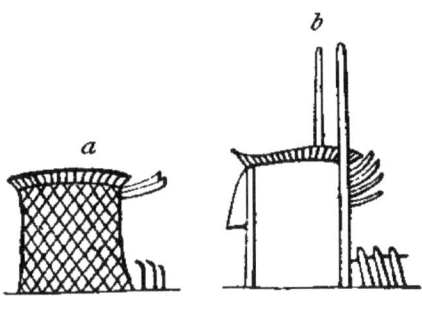

---

³⁴ Pronounced "a" in the early period and "i" in the late period.
³⁵ See the Kamitan book series by Muata Ashby

Archeological evidence has been discovered which shows that in the Pre-Dynastic era, the architecture already contained the basic elements that would be subsequently expressed in Kamitan history. The primary difference between the Pre-Dynastic architecture and the architecture in later times was that the later developments used stone instead of mud brick and wood. However in later times, houses and even royal palaces still continued to be made of mud brick and wood, a signal of the importance placed on spirituality as opposed to worldly life.

In Pre-Dynastic times, stone was mainly used for structures like the Sphinx complex in Giza, the Great Pyramids, Sun Temples, temples such as the so-called "Osirion" next to the temple of Asar (Osiris) in the Ancient Egyptian city of Abdu (Abydos), certain structures in the Saqqara (Sakkara) district, and a few other structures. Therefore, all of the elements that were present in the Pre-Dynastic architecture, including the wooden columns and palm tree elements, were faithfully reproduced in stone so that they might last "indefinitely." For example, the images above (a, b) are of the archaic temple. It shows a basic shrine with two posts (pillars) in front. The remains from such a temple have been discovered in the Ancient Egyptian city of Nekhen (Hierakonpolis), which in early Dynastic times was the capital in the south of the country.

The Anunian Temple: Cosmic Symbolism in the Solar Temple Architecture

The Benben, Tekhenu and Mer Temples

The pyramids (**Mer**) and obelisks (**Tekhenu**) are actually symbols of the primeval stone of creation upon which the spirit, in the form of the sun, first shone at the time of Creation. This stone is a metaphor of all that is solid, congealed and tangible upon which human life is based. In these sacred places, reenactments of the Mysteries of Creation that have been described in this volume were carried out.

Picture 27: Basic Ancient Egyptian Pyramid Temple Complex (Old Kingdom Period)

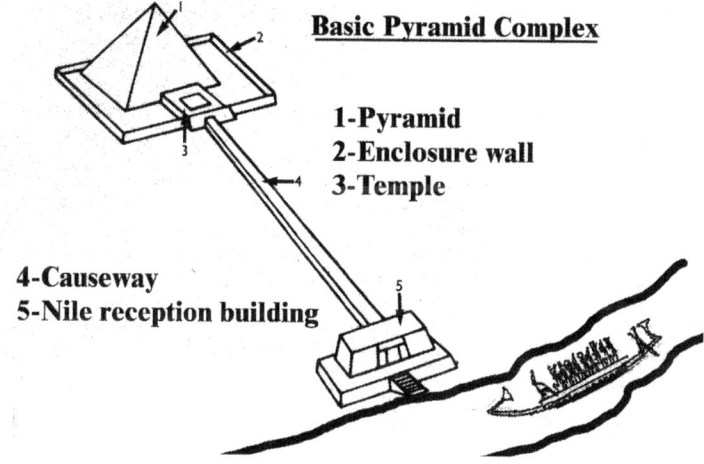

Basic Pyramid Complex

1-Pyramid
2-Enclosure wall
3-Temple
4-Causeway
5-Nile reception building

Picture 28: Basic Ancient Egyptian Obelisk Temple Complex (Old Kingdom Period)

AFRICAN ORIGINS OF CIVILIZATION, RELIGION, YOGA MYSTICAL SPIRITUALITY AND ETHICS PHILOSOPHY

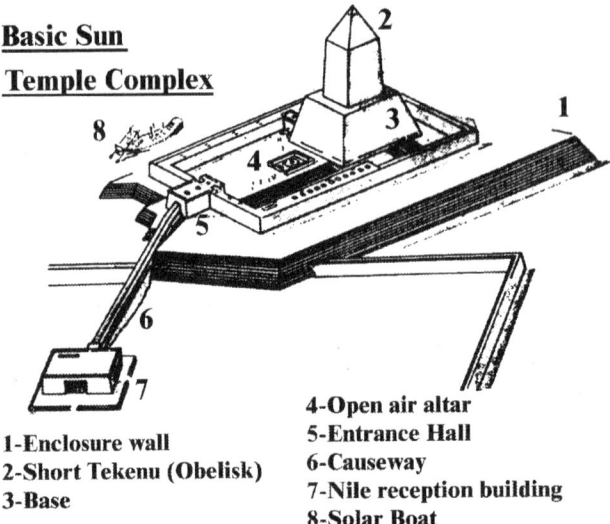

Basic Sun Temple Complex

1-Enclosure wall
2-Short Tekenu (Obelisk)
3-Base
4-Open air altar
5-Entrance Hall
6-Causeway
7-Nile reception building
8-Solar Boat

Plate 8: Late Middle Kingdom-Early New Kingdom Temple of Queen Hatshepsut

Figure 27: Ancient Egyptian New Kingdom Temple Design (Temple of Hatshepsut to Amun)

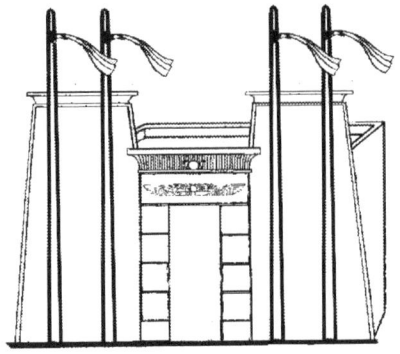

In the more ancient times (Old Kingdom and Middle-Kingdom), there were two principal temple forms, the Sun Temple (including the pyramid) and the Trinity Temple (with three main sections). There were two forms of the Sun Temples, the Ra and the Aton. In the New Kingdom period, the main Temple form used was the familiar three courts with pylon Temple design (above).

The reliefs, painted scenes and hieroglyphic texts carved on the temple complexes, tombs, and various shrines, as well as the papyrus scriptures which were buried with the deceased, give voluminous insights into the nature of the Ancient Egyptian views on life, death and the nature of the Divine. These teachings were avidly studied and recited by Priests and Priestesses of those times.

Even though, according to the mythology of the Kamitan system of the pantheon of gods and goddesses (neteru) of Ancient Egypt, the gods and goddesses are said to have come into being all at once, at various times in Kamitan history some divinities became more prominent. In the earliest periods, the mythology and mysticism of Heru and Hetheru were foremost. Next, the mythology and mysticism of Net and Ra became prominent. This was followed by the mythology and mysticism of Ptah, and subsequent to that, the mythology and mysticism of Amun became prominent. However, all throughout Ancient Egyptian history, the mythology and mysticism of the god Asar (Osiris), and the goddesses Aset (Isis), Net and Hetheru, maintained a consistent level of popularity and veneration throughout Kamit. Thus, it is clear that the Sphinx represents a high order of culture that existed prior to the Pre-Dynastic period. The pyramids represent a rejuvenation of culture, which gave rise to the Dynastic era, and this period first developed in the south, Upper Egypt, having its base in Hierakonpolis and Abdu. From there, the Per-aahs (Pharaohs) of Dynasty 1 annexed the north and established the new capital there, reestablishing Ancient Egyptian culture to its previous heights.

Egypt in the Pre-Dynastic Era: The Early History 10,000 B.C.E. (or earlier)-5,500 B.C.E.[36]

With the dating of the Sphinx we can ascertain that an advanced civilization requiring mathematics, organization of labor and religion in order to create the Sphinx complex, existed at least by 10,000 B.C.E. Remember that the Sphinx is the earliest evidence from Kamitan culture that is verifiable by archeological evidence. Using the evidences such as the Palermo Stone, the Turin Papyrus or the History of Manetho, we obtain far older dates. The oldest Egyptian paleoliths have been found in gravel sites around the river Nile. Important Mesolithic sites have been explored at Helwan, Kom Ombo, and Kharga. Neolithic sites have been studied at el-Omari, Merimda, and in the Fayum. There, barley and wheat similar to that grown today were cultivated, flax was woven into linen cloth and there is evidence of the domestication of animals, including cattle, sheep, goats, and pigs. Pottery, for the most part plain burnished, has been found, as well as stone implements, of which partly polished axes, adzes[153] (gouges) and winged arrowheads, were typical.[154] In ongoing excavations at Nekhen, Egypt (Hierakonpolis – Greek translation of the Egyptian name "city of the falcon god), several new Paleolithic sites have been discovered.

> Survey of the hill terrace on the western edge of the concession led to the discovery of at least 12 Middle Paleolithic sites, one of which was tested by limited excavation. The size and depth of deposit and the preservation and density of the artifacts at this site show it to be of immense importance for the study of this poorly understood period. Hierakonpolis just got older - by about 65,000 years![155]

The Fayum Neolithic site (of Ancient Egypt) has been dated by radiocarbon analysis to c. 4950 BC and although its age relative to the Badarian culture, the earliest prehistoric culture of Upper Egypt, has not been finally established, the Fayum appears to be earlier.[156]

Between 3800-3600 BC, black-topped polished bowls, referred to as Badarian ware and terra cotta figurines were produced in Egypt along with cosmetic articles and ivory combs. The terms Badarian, Amratian (Nagada I) and Gerzean (Nagada II) cultures are designations used to refer to the periods in the Ancient Egyptian Pre-Dynastic era. The Badarians made fine rippled pottery and used stone axes and arrowheads, which have been found to be similar to ones used in the Fayum area. While these cultures have, in the past, often been referred to as Pre-Dynastic cultures in Egypt, recent evidence has pointed to the understanding that these primitive cultures existed alongside the familiar high culture of Pharaonic Egypt. Perhaps this can be best understood by the example of differences in cultural development between people of the same culture who reside in a very isolated rural setting, as opposed to the city dwellers. In any case the evidences point to earlier human remains in the south of Egypt as opposed to the north.

---

[36] Revised dating based on most current correct evidence.

AFRICAN ORIGINS OF CIVILIZATION, RELIGION, YOGA MYSTICAL SPIRITUALITY AND ETHICS PHILOSOPHY

The Connections between the Pre-Dynastic and Dynastic culture of Ancient Egypt.

In Pre-Dynastic times (before 5,500 B.C.E.), Egyptian doctrine held that there is a realm of light (beyond our physical universe) where food, clothing and our bodies are of light, and further, that we will exist forever as beings of light along with other beings of light. This teaching is mystically related to the concept of the Pyramid texts related to "Akhus" – stars in the sky, that a human being becomes upon attaining divine status through living a life of virtue and attaining the status of divinity by reconstituting within oneself ones original cosmic forces..[37]

From the remotest times of Egypt, the Symbol of the Hawk was used to represent all-encompassing divinity (the Supreme Being, creator of all things): omnipotence, omnipresence, omniscience. The Hawk is also the symbol of the human soul. The implication is that the Supreme Being and the Human Soul are identical. Below Heru (the Hawk) is shown holding the Shen, the symbol of eternity, and the Ankh, the symbol of life. The Hawk is the symbol of Heru (Horus), the God of light, vision and speed. When looking at the Hawk symbol, we should be immediately drawn to those qualities (vision, tenacity and speed, freedom, Horus, etc.). When the hawk is enclosed within the "Het," Kamitan word for "house," it means that he is sheltered by his consort, Het-Heru. Together these two divinities compose the dynamic manifestation of the spirit in time and space, through the medium of male-female, i.e. the opposites. The universe is the Het and the spirit which inhabits it is Heru.

In Dynastic times, the doctrine of the realm of light and of a single God (Supreme Being) of whom creation is composed survived in the earliest religious texts. In chapter 64 of the *Egyptian Book of Coming Forth By Day,* the Supreme Being is referred to as *"The One Who Sees by His Own Light."* The main observable difference between the realm of light philosophy and the Pre-Dynastic and post-Dynastic philosophy of Egypt is that there were fewer deities in the Pre-Dynastic time, in the sense that the main divinity, Heru, and his counterpart, Hetheru, formed the essence of the spiritual teaching. The other divinities (beyond the central-high divinities) arise out of the central ones in the Late Pre-Dynastic and later Dynastic Periods.

Ra and Ra Herakti (Ra-Horus) are two of the symbolic forms that emerged to represent to *"Nameless One,"* the Supreme Being in later Egyptian times (Dynastic Period). In the hieroglyph to the left, below, Ra-Herakti (Ra-Horus) is shown holding the Ankh (symbol of life). The association with the sundisk gave a concrete, visual image for the purpose of public worship.

"NETER"; "Neters (Gods)"; "Ra"; "Ankh."

Before the beginning of the Dynastic Period (c 5,000 B.C.E.), the followers of Egyptian philosophy began to represent the divine forces of the Supreme Being, which operate through nature in zoomorphic forms. From the beginning of the first Dynasty until the end of Egyptian civilization (c. 600 A.C.E.), the followers of

---

[37] See also the section entitled **"The Consistent Pattern of Structure in African Religion" in Chapter 2.**

Egyptian religion that had worshipped the zoomorphic deities developed and incorporated new myths using anthropomorphic (human) forms.

One of the most popular Kamitan doctrines was that of Asar, Aset and Heru (Osiris, Isis and Horus, respectively). These Gods and Goddesses were mentioned in Pre-Dynastic times, however, the additional myths which were added to them such as the Asarian (Osirian) Resurrection myth resulted in increased popularity and gave the local priests the opportunity to add to the teachings handed down previously, and to cope with the new political and social changes throughout Egypt.

In some respects, however, the changes represented a downfall from the original teaching. For example the "realm of light" mentioned above came to be known by some as the "Land of Asar" (The West, i.e. the Netherworld) where after death, souls would go to work in the fields for Asar for all eternity. This "distasteful" prospect of working for all eternity caused some to fashion dolls (Ushabti) whose spirits would do the work for them. Some of these new doctrines and erroneous practices no doubt created new opportunities for unscrupulous priests and others with some degree of spiritual knowledge.

However, the mystical implications of the principals of the Asarian Resurrection myth and the mythology surrounding the various Gods of the Egyptian pantheon are still in accord with the Pre-Dynastic teachings. This is especially true when the teachings of the major theologies of Ancient Egypt are examined closely. For example, the Anunian Theology, Theban Theology, Memphite Theology, Zau[157] Theology (Goddess Net), Hetheru Theology, and of course Atonism and the Horemakhet (Ra-Harakti) teachings are directly related to each other, and to the solar principal, the source of all light. The realm of light theology is sometimes referred to by Western Egyptologists as the "Sky Religion."

The divinity of the realm of light was nameless and formless. Thus, a nameless "Supreme Being," *"Neter Neteru,"* *"GOD of Gods,"* was referred to as *"The Hidden One"* until later times when myths were constructed for the understanding of the common people. *"PA NETER"*, or "THE GOD" was thought of as a FATHER-MOTHER CREATOR GOD and must not be confused with the *"Neters"* or "Gods and Goddesses," which represented the cosmic forces of the Universe. From an advanced point of view however, GOD is neither male nor female, but GOD is the source from which the Gods (gods and goddesses, Neters), humans and all creation comes. Therefore, the concept of *"NETER,"* encompasses a concept that goes beyond ordinary human - mental understanding. For the "common folk" (the uninitiated), *"NETER"* was referred to as *Nebertcher (Neberdjer)*, or *Amon - Ra - Ptah* (Holy Trinity), and was represented by a Sundisk or a single flag.

Plate 9: Left-Pre-Dynastic image of the Nile Goddess. Right- Dynastic Period image of goddess Aset.

The Pre-Dynastic symbol of the female - mother - Goddess (above left) is also represented in other parts of Africa and in the Dynastic Period of Egypt in the same pose. The wings are symbolic of the Egyptian Sky God Heru. The Goddesses Aset and Maat of Egypt are also represented with wings.

Figure 28: Below left - Image of the boat of Ptah-Sokar-Asar (Dynastic Periods)

Plate 10: Below right- Pre-Dynastic Pottery from Ancient Egypt

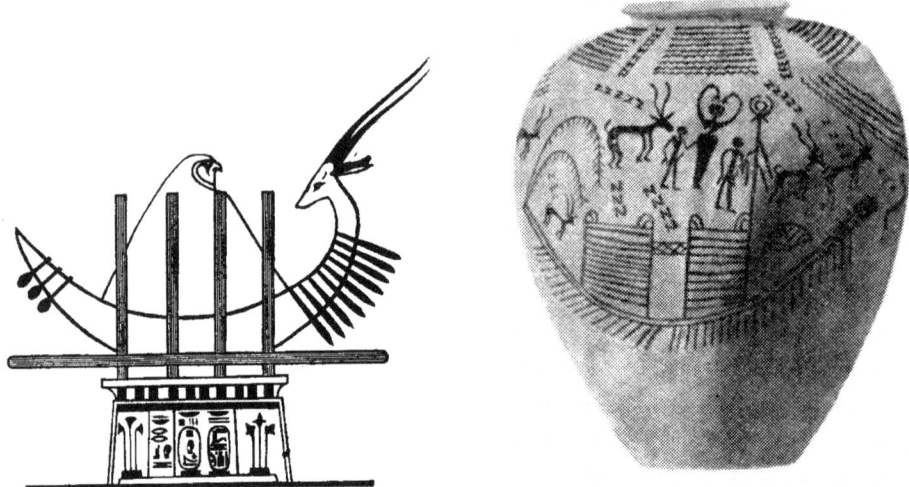

The two images above show the contiguity of the religious iconography used to depict the divine vehicle of the god "Ptah-Sokar-Asar." The image of the boat and the ritual related to its movement from one temple to another at festival times is one of the oldest and most popular rituals in Ancient Egyptian religion, so much so that it was incorporated into the religious life of the modern day Egyptians, who are Arabs, primarily practicing the religion of Islam[38]. The image includes two striking and characteristic forms, the bow shaped boat and the Ibex.

The city Neken was known to the Greeks as Hierakonpolis or the city of the Hawk. In that city and in Abdu, the city of the god Asar, have been discovered the oldest hieroglyphic writings and evidences of the existence of Ancient Egyptian religion in the predynastic era, besided the Sphinx. The Sphinx is the oldest ling between the predynastic and the dynastic eras of Ancient Egyptian culture. It denotes the existence of the philosophy of the leonine ruler and the spiritual teaching of the sun in the eastern horizon, i.e. it proves the existence of Anunian Theology and the teaching of Heru as early as 10,000 B.C.E.

Below left: The Great Heru m Akhet (Sphinx) of Ancient Egypt. (Pre-Dynastic) At right: Dynastic Pharaonic headdress (Dynastic)

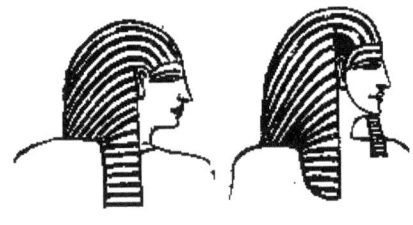

---

[38] This point will be elaborated on in more detail later in this text.

History of Dynastic Ancient Egypt

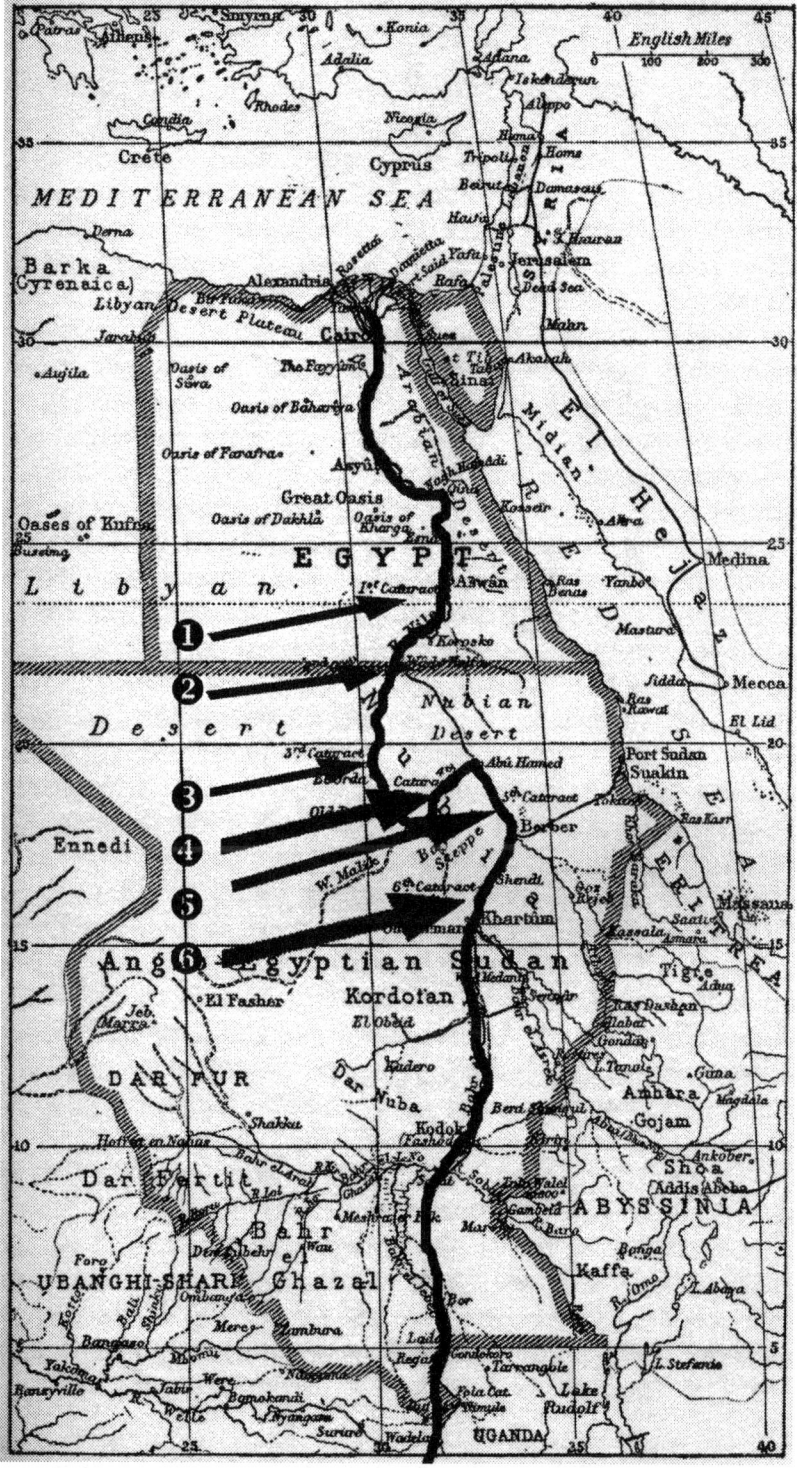

Figure 29 Above: Map of Ancient Egypt (A) and Kush (B) showing the locations of the cataracts along the Nile River (numbers 1-6) from southern Egypt into northern Nubia (present day Sudan).

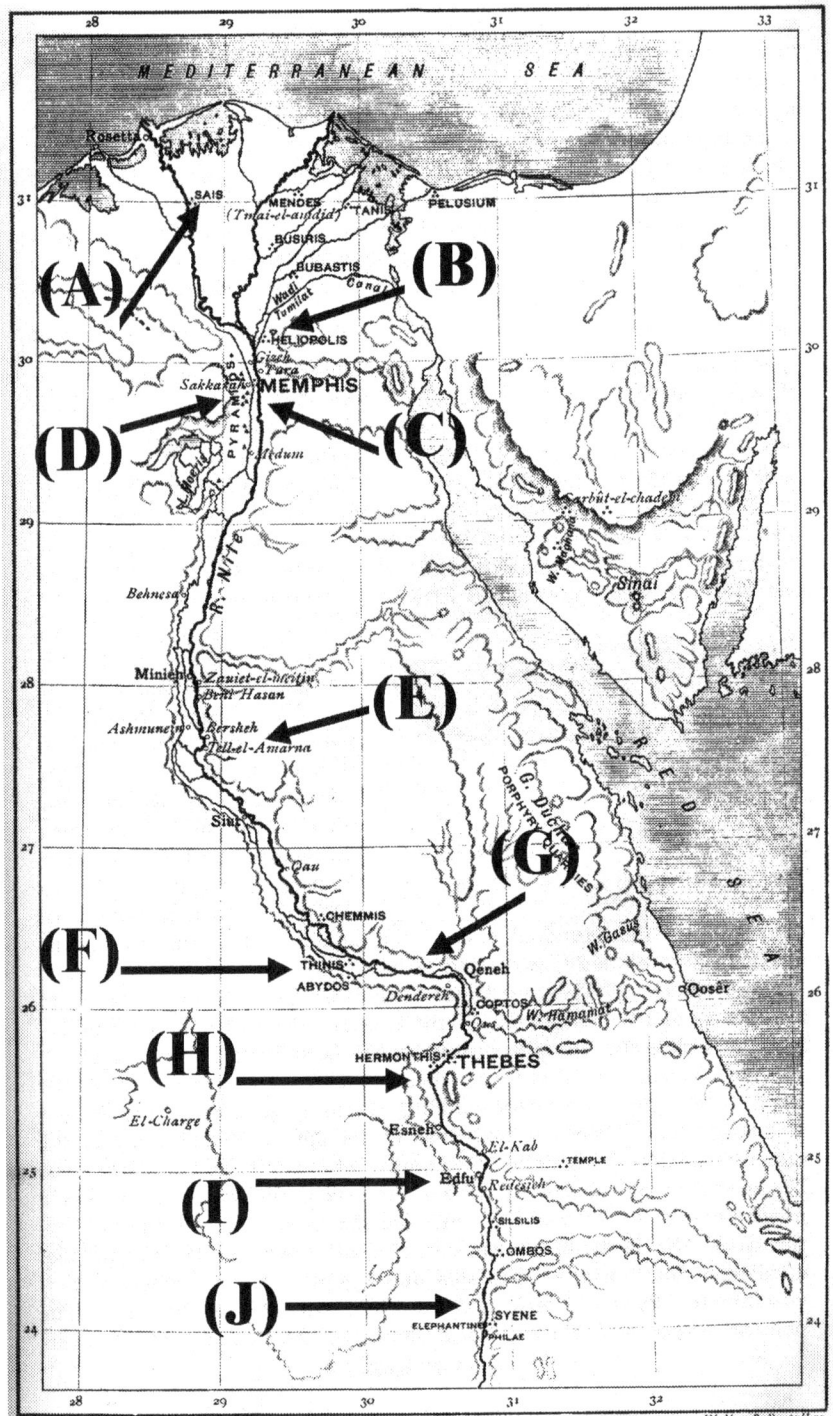

Figure 30: Above- The Land of Ancient Egypt-Nile Valley - The cities wherein the theology of the Trinity of Amun-Ra-Ptah was developed were: A- Sais (temple of Net), B- Anu (Heliopolis- temple of Ra), C-Men-nefer or Hetkaptah (Memphis, temple of Ptah), and D- Sakkara (Pyramid Texts), E- Akhet-Aton (City of Akhnaton, temple of Aton), F- Abdu (temple of Asar), G- Denderah (temple of Hetheru), H- Waset (Thebes, temple of Amun), I- Edfu (temple of Heru), J- Philae (temple of Aset). The cities wherein the theology of the Trinity of Asar-Aset-Heru was developed were Anu, Abydos, Philae, Edfu, Denderah and Edfu.

Old Kingdom Period 5,500-3,800 B.C.E.[39]

Prior to the Dynastic era, with which most people are familiar, Egypt had a long history of "nomes" (towns, governorship), ruled by kings and queens, referred to as "nomarchs" by Egyptologists and others. The Dynastic era history of Egypt begins with the unification of the two kingdoms of Upper and Lower Egypt. Actually, the unification was of several kingdoms into one Empire (one ruler over many kingdoms). This unification was achieved by king Mena (Menes) and the Shemsu Hor ("followers of Heru"). Religion began to take on the form that later became established. Evidence has been found of shrines to Heru and Hetheru, who protected the Pharaoh, and to the deities Net (Neith), Djehuti (Thoth), and Anpu (Anubis).[158] Recall that Heru is the falcon sky god, related to Ra, the Solar Divinity, whose worship is evident at the inception of the first Dynasty, but also in the Pre-Dynastic age. Mena unified the southern portion of Egypt from the base or capital at Abdu (Abydos), the ancient center of the worship of Asar (Osiris), and then the northern portion. Mena built a new capital at Men-nefer or Het-Ka-Ptah (Memphis), in the north, thereby consolidating and expanding the Ancient Egyptian religion and the foreign influence of Egyptian culture on the Asia Minor and India. With this unification, it meant that the nomes came under one ruler, the Per Aah (Pharaoh). So, in a sense Per Aah may be equated to the modern term "Emperor," however the Ancient Egyptian rulers had certain religious functions and social responsibilities that set them apart from emperors such as Alexander the Great, the Roman Emperors, the Persian Emperors, the Mesopotamian Emperors, etc.

The period of unification brought forth the first extensive books and spiritual writings in history, including the Pyramid Texts. The end of this period also elicited the greatest socio-philosophical writings from the Ancient Egyptians. These were the first "Wisdom Texts." The most famous of these was the Instructions of Ptahotep. These writings developed standards of righteous conduct much like the Confuciunist writings, and also taught about the glory of cosmic order, Maat, thereby infusing a spiritual consciousness into the social and political areas of society as they admonished rulers to rule with righteousness and by upholding truth in order to not suffer after death and to discover the Divine.

Government and Society in Ancient Egypt

The "Per-aah" or "Great House" is the institution of the seat of leadership in Ancient Egyptian civilization. The word Pharaoh is a corruption of the Ancient Egyptian word Per-Aah, and it is also erroneously translated as "king." It is more related to the status or position of being a caretaker, guardian and protector. The Per-Aah was also the High Priesthood of the country, the head of the religion and promoter and protector of the spiritual traditions, economy, safety and general welfare of the country. The Per-Aah was seen as an incarnation of Heru, the divinity of order, truth, righteousness, and redemption. Also, the Per-Aah could be a man or woman. As such the first duty of the Per-Aah was to maintain order and keep chaos (disorder, unrighteousness, famine, injustice, etc.) under control. The Per-Aah was assisted by high Priests and Priestesses (Kheri-Heb), and the day to day administration of the country was delegated to officials and educated nobility. In later times, the control of the priesthood was eroded, and the nobility as well as military leaders ruled with more autonomous control. This, along with invasions and internal corruption, weakened the Egyptian structure and led to Egypt being conquered in the Late Period by a sequence of various foreign groups (Persians, Assyrians, Libyans, Greeks, Romans and Arabs).

First intermediate Period 3,800-3,500 B.C.E.[40]

After the death of Pepi II, it is believed that Egypt was engulfed in a period of civil war and foreign infiltration, and the country began to degenerate. In Upper Egypt, the nomarchs (ruler of the individual nomes) were busy organizing their own minor kingdoms. The aristocracy was being dispossessed, cultivation of the land ceased, and famine became widespread. This period of disintegration lasted about 300 years. The kingdom was reunited when the kingdom of Thebes entered into a series of struggles due to internal instability and external pressure from attacking forces that ended with Egypt being reunited under Theban rule. The internal instability arose because Kamit reached a level of development in which the old ways and traditions which maintained order and stability were forgotten. The culture declined because of corruption and Maat

---

[39] Revised dating based on correct evidence.
[40] Revised dating based on correct evidence.

(righteousness) was not upheld. This situation is related in the didactic literature of the period which includes the writings known as the *Instructions of Merikara*. In that text and others of the period, a renewal of culture is promoted by a return to and an upholding of Maat. The next period of unification and reintegration of civilization is referred to as the *Middle Kingdom*.

The lack of strong government during this period led to an increase in tomb robbery. It is believed that the custom of burying small mummified figures with the corpse, which developed into the shabti figures and teaching of the Middle and New Kingdoms, began during this time. The shabti or ushabti is a miniature reproduction of the mummy which is supposed to serve in place of the mummified personality and endure hardships for that personality in the afterlife.

The important scripture known as the "Instruction of Merikara" emerges from this period. It details the instructions given by a king to his successor, and among the various wisdom teachings provided, it cautions against a lack of vigilance as concerns the Asiatic peoples. It gives particulars as to the psychology of the Asiatics that leads them to attack Egypt, and what must be done to uphold Egyptian culture and restore order to the land. This text shows that although Egypt was under pressure from the Asiatics, this intermediate period was not marked by total chaos.

Middle Kingdom Period 3,500-1,730 B.C.E.[41]

Plate 11: Left Per-aah (Pharaoh) Muntuhotep II (Muntuhotep)[159] – 11th Dynasty

Pharaoh Muntuhotep II completed the reunion of Egypt during the 11th Dynasty. The culture was revived, and the Pharaoh built a great temple consisting of two colonnaded terraces at Deir el-Bahri, opposite Waset (Luxor). Pharaoh Hatshepsut had a copy of this temple made alongside it several hundred years later, at an even greater scale.

The Middle Kingdom saw a return to peace and order. Egypt's borders were again expanded to include Asia Minor, central and eastern Asia and northern Nubia. Under Senusert I (Sesostris), Ancient Egyptian culture extended over a vast region. There was trade and expedition to other countries in the Mediterranean, as well as along the East Coast of Africa. Security measures including fortresses were constructed to repel future attacks.

The literature of the period consists of instructions (Wisdom Texts), prophecies and tales, such as the advice of the aged Amenemhat I to his son, as well as wisdom texts. The tales of the Shipwrecked Sailor, Sinuhe, and the Eloquent Peasant all derive from this time.[160]

---

[41] Revised dating based on correct evidence.

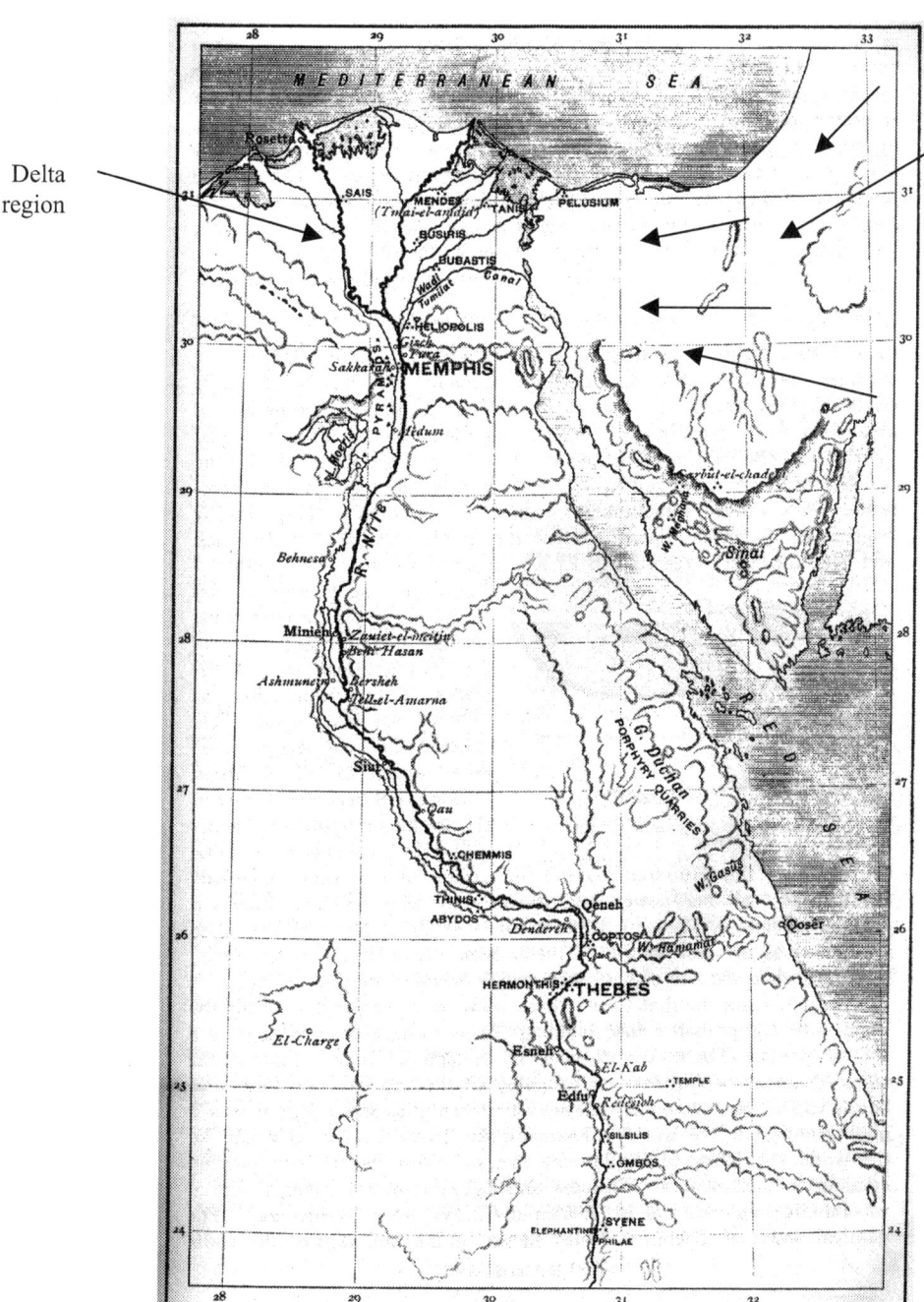

Second Intermediate Period 1,730-1,580 B.C.E.[42]

The era between the Middle Kingdom and the New Kingdom, starting with the 15th Dynasty was a degenerated age. The Hyksos were foreigners who achieved control of most of Egypt. They came into Egypt from Asia, subsequent to the emergence of the Aryans in the Near East. By the year 1730 B.C.E. they had established their capital at Avaris. In this manner they established themselves first as rulers in the Delta region, the northern part of the country. From here they easily extended their control over the chaotic and disunited parts of Egypt.

---

[42] Revised dating based on correct evidence.

The Hyksos rule was soon to end however. The 17th Dynasty was established at Waset (Thebes) at about the year 1650 B.C.E., and the Egyptians were able to gradually confine the Hyksos to north Egypt and south Palestine through a series of battles in which horse-drawn chariots were used.

New Kingdom Period 1,580 B.C.E[43]

By means of two inscriptions from the 18th Dynasty, it has been reliably established that the date for the commencement of the 18th Dynasty is 1580 B.C.E. The Pharaoh Ahmose eventually drove the Hyksos out of Egypt and pursued them into Palestine. He was the founder of the 18th Dynasty, with its capital at Thebes. Ahmose reoccupied Nubia, as far as the second cataract. His successor, Amunhotep I, extended Egyptian influence in Nubia and Syria. Thothmes I (1525–c. 1512 B.C.E.) extended the Egyptian borders even further, into Nubia, to far as Kurgus which is near the fifth cataract[44] (see map above). In Asia Minor he penetrated beyond the Euphrates river and contained a revolt in Naharein. Thothmes II, the son of Thothmes I, reigned briefly. His widow, Hatshepsut (1503–1482), became one of the most important rulers of the period.

Egypt Is The Supreme Power in Asia

Queen and Pharaoh Hatshepsut did not favor military undertakings. She instead emphasized peaceful projects such as an expedition to Punt, the construction Obelisks, and her funerary temple at Deir el-Bahri. She opened up new trade routs and bolstered the economy of Egypt.

After Hatshepsut's death, Thothmes III faced a serious threat from Asian powers, which had formed a coalition under the king of Kush. Thothmes III defeated them at Megiddo, and then mounted campaigns in Naharein and Syria. After the capture of Kush, Egypt was supreme in Asia, and there was also regular friendly contact with Crete (pre-classical Greece). During the reign of Thothmes IV, Egypt grew closer to the Mitanni (inhabitants of northern Mesopotamia-Persians) by forming an alliance with them against the Hittites. He cemented this alliance by marriage to a Mitanni princess. His successor, a weak ruler, Amunhotep III, neglected the empire in favor of lion hunts and other entertainments, even issuing large scarabs to commemorate his killing over 100 lions.[161]

The Akhnaton Period

The Hittites began expanding in Asia Minor, and won over several Asiatic princes in the reign of Amunhotep IV, later known as Akhnaton. Amunhotep IV ruled for approximately eighteen years. During his reign, he developed an overwhelming interest in religious matters, including the discipline of nonviolence, so much so that he became unwilling to issue military orders that he felt would result in the death of anyone. Thus, the Pharaoh failed to support those princes who remained loyal, and shortly thereafter Egyptian influence, even in Palestine and Syria, was diminished.

In the sixth year of his reign, Amunhotep IV proclaimed that the gods and goddesses of Egypt, including Amen-Ra, king of the gods, was at a culmination in Aton. The concept of Aton as a divinity existed as early as the concept of the other gods and goddesses (Neteru). He was born into the position as ruler under the name Amunhotep IV (peace in Amun), but he found greater fulfillment through the practices and disciplines of Aton worship, the tradition to which his mother, Queen Ti and her priest, Ai, already belonged. He changed his name to Akh-n-aton (Akhnaton, Akhenaton), which may be translated as "Spirit in the Sundisk." He simply wanted to affirm the ideal of Aton, which means face or mask of God. As Ancient Egyptian tradition always held, he affirmed that only one divinity existed, Aton, in the same manner as all the religious centers affirmed their main divinity (Amun in Thebes, Ra in Anu and Ptah in Memphis for example). In effect, Akhnaton wanted to return to a purer form of the religion, which actually leads back to Anunian theology, and the Horemakhet (Sphinx).[162]

---

[43] Revised dating based on correct evidence.
[44] Cataract: a section in a river where there are rapids, waterfalls.

Akhet-Aton: A New Capital City in The Center of the Country

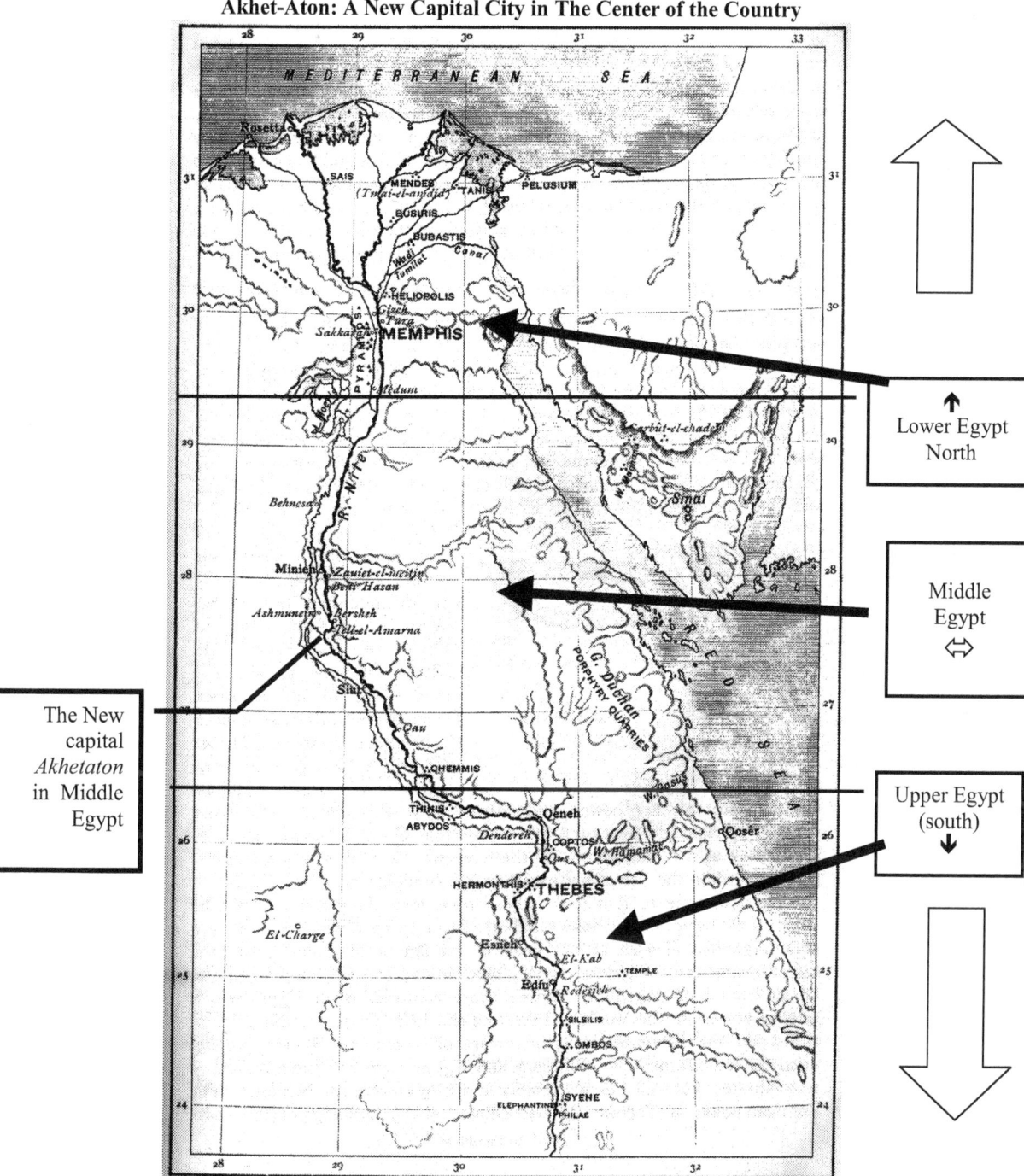

Akhnaton's move signaled a loss of power for Amun and his philosophy of the Aton was resisted, because at this time Egypt was a world Superpower and the priesthood under which this ascendancy occurred, the priests of Amun at Thebes, had become accustomed to the power and ritual of the current spiritual culture (centered around Amun), and resisted the change to Aton worship. Also, it must be noted that what Akhnaton was pushing for was a complete and utter turning away from the other symbols for the divine in favor of the Aton in the centers of Aton worship. This was perhaps an innovation not seen before in Kamitan spirituality. In previous cases where divinities rose to prominence, they did so by joining the ranks of the existing divinities, rather than by displacing them. However, Akhnaton saw that the way the other divinities were being worshipped was leading to an intensification of ritual practices as opposed to spiritual evolution. Therefore, he set out to reform Ancient Egyptian religion in the most effective manner possible. To complete the break, he founded a new capital at Akhnaton (translation "horizon of Aton" –Arab name-"Tell el-Amarna"), at a location that was exactly in the center between Upper Egypt and Lower Egypt. This signaled that he wanted to establish a tradition that was detached from the currently practicing sects. Animosity developed between Akhnaton and the Amun priesthood. Using his authority, Akhnaton had the property of Amun transferred to Aton. Akhnaton lived in a form of isolation with his court and family in the city he had created, and left control of the kingdom and preservation of the, at this time shrinking empire, to others. After his death, Tell el-Amarna was abandoned and the old religion restored by the priests of Amun.[163] Following the reign of Akhnaton came the reign of Tutankhamun. His period was short and the main interest he has drawn stems from the discovery of his tomb which was intact, and which gave much insight into the iconography and philosophy of the Ancient Egyptian religion. His name signaled the return of the dominance of religion of Amun (Tut-ankh-amun which means living image of Amun). Akhnaton was abandoned and its monuments were dismantled for constructions elsewhere.

The Akhnaton period proved to be very instructive of the extent to which the power of Waset (Thebes) and its preference for Amun (Supreme Being) and the traditional rituals of many gods and goddesses had been engrained. What Akhnaton did was not unique in Ancient Egyptian history. The elevation of Ra, Asar, Ptah and Net had all occurred in a similar way. They were all known since ancient times but were elevated by a group of Priests and Priestesses of a particular city. What Akhnaton did differently was that he tried to zealously force all the population to understand that all the gods and goddesses were "complete" in Aton, which was true in a mystical sense, but the tradition was to have a nome (city) dedicated to the newly elevated divinity and thereafter it would exist alongside the previous ones. This pragmatism that was lacking in Akhnaton's approach to elevating the Aton was not repeated in the later reign of Sage-king Seti I who elevated the god Set, while at the same time upholding the already elevated gods and goddesses by refurbishing and adding to their temples along with that of Set. So the conflict between Akhnaton and the Priests and Priestesses of Amun was not a theological one involving the rejection of a new divinity or the concept of Monotheism, but rather a rejection of what they perceived as the abandonment of thousands of years of the African religious tradition of worshipping a Supreme Being with its attendant lesser divinities, i.e. the gods and goddesses.[45]

The Ramesside Period

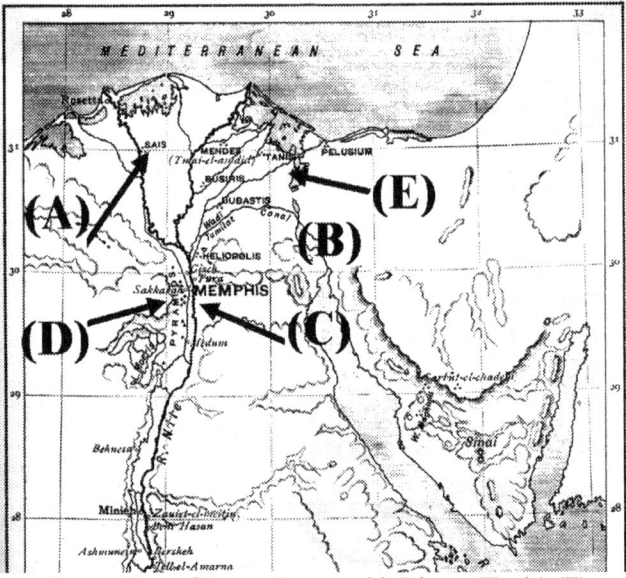

Above: Map of Lower Egypt with Djanet (Tanis) (E)

The 19th Dynasty (1290-1224 B.C.E.) was founded by Rameses I. His family came from the noble houses from the city of Tanis, which had been the seat of power of the foreign Hyksos rulers. In ancient times the worship of the god Set was popular. When the Hyksos established their capital at Tanis, they adopted Set as

---

[45] See the section entitled *The Consistent Pattern of Structure in African Religion* in Chapter 2

their tutelary symbol, and thus, the god Set became associated with invaders. During that time Set became associated with foreigners, evil, destruction and vice. Rameses' son was named Seti I (man of Set). Rameses II, who later become known as "the Great" continued on with Seti's struggle against the Hittites. This war was documented on the temple of Rameses, however other scenes proclaiming him victorious against other foes are symbolic of the king's duty to uphold righteousness (Maat) against *isfet* or n-Maat (unrighteousness), not just in war but by upholding the economy, courts, etc. In these duties Rameses proved to be most successful and his reign saw a great flowering of Kamitan culture, especially in the construction of temples. He augmented the Karnak Temple in Waset, finished his father's temple in Abdu, and built no less than three colossal temples for himself, and one for his wife, Queen Nefertari.

Rameses' 13th son, Merneptah, who by the time of Rameses' long reign was already old, succeeded him. Merneptah contended with a Palestinian revolt. The accounts of this conflict provide the first mention of Israel as one of the defeated peoples of Asia Minor under Egyptian rule. Merneptah also successfully dealt with invasions from the west of Egypt (modern day Libya). Merneptah's rule was followed by thirty years of confusion in which several Pharaohs reigned, most with uncertain claims to the throne.

The diminishing leadership of the government, as well as the increasing separation between the political leaders and the clergy and the minimization of the clergy, led to weakness in the social order of the country. In the 20th Dynasty, Rameses III was the last great Pharaoh of the New Kingdom. He reorganized the country's administration and the army, and began collecting tribute from Asia and Nubia again. His greatest victory was over the "peoples of the sea," Indo-Europeans, who, after sweeping over the Hittites, Cilicia, and Cyprus, were threatening Egypt. Advancing by land and sea along the coast of Palestine, Rameses III annihilated them and repulsed two Libyan attacks on the delta. The last 20 years of his reign were peaceful. There followed several unimportant Pharaohs, all named Rameses, most of whom were overshadowed by the High Priests of Amun. In the reign of Rameses XI, civil war broke out with Libyan involvement, and it was only suppressed due to the help of Nubian troops under the viceroy Pa-nehesi.[164] This event is one of several which show that the occasional animosity between the Nubians and Ancient Egyptians was not racially motivated, as some Western historians have suggested, but cultural and political. In the Late Period, the allegiance of the Nubians to the Ancient Egyptians would become more apparent.

In the city of Waset, during the 18th and 19th Dynasties, the Priests and Priestesses began to create a new version of *Prt M Hru*. These are usually referred to as the *Wasetian (Theban) recension* of the *Prt m Hru*. The *Wasetian Recension* adopted several texts from the older recension, but added many more new ones. This recension was produced on papyrus scrolls, and one of its principal features is the extensive use of vignettes.

Third Intermediate Period 1085 B.C.E.

The capital was moved to Tanis in 1085, signaling the end of the New Kingdom Dynastic Period. In the 21st Dynasty there were rival Pharaohs based at Tanis and at Thebes, but the two sets of rulers coexisted amicably, united by marriage ties, until the last high priest reunited Egypt as Pharaoh Psusennes II. When he died 945 B.C.E. the rule of Thebes came to an end—Sheshonq I (945–924), a member of a powerful family of Libyans based at Herakleopolis, took the throne founding the 22nd Dynasty. He asserted his authority in Upper Egypt, and it was probably then that some priests of Amun left Thebes for Napata, the future seat of the 25th Dynasty. Sheshonq (the Shishak of the Bible) attacked Palestine after the death of Solomon[46], and sacked Jerusalem, refilling his treasury and temporarily increasing the prestige of Egypt. Then followed 150 years of increasing anarchy, during which rival Libyan chieftains and the priests of Amun at Thebes vied for power.

---

[46] third king of Israel (c. 961-922 BC), son of David and Bathsheba.

Late Period

Nubian Restoration of African Rule by Africans in Egypt

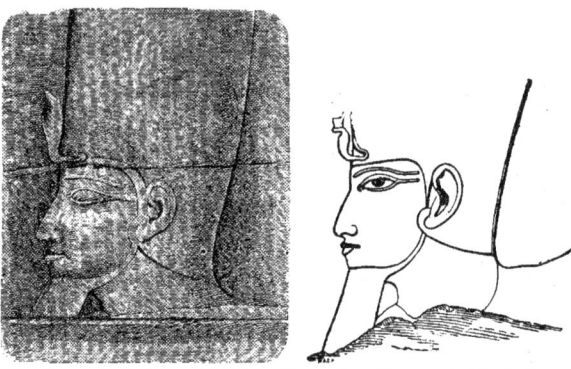

Above left- The Nubian-Egyptian Pharaoh Shabaka
Above right- The Nubian-Egyptian Pharaoh Taharka

By the year 760 B.C.E. Egypt had been debilitated, and it is believed that the Egyptian Priests and Priestesses asked the Nubians for assistance in order to repel foreign invaders. They crowned the Nubian king Kashta as Pharaoh and his daughter Amenirdas I became the wife of Amun (High Priestess). This crowning caused would be attackers to desist in their efforts. However, later on Egypt was again threatened by the Libyans at around 730 B.C.E. From around 730 B.C.E., two rival movements to reunite Egypt emerged, one led by Tefnakht of the 24th Dynasty based at Sais, the city of goddess Net, and the other was led by Pi-ankhi (747–716 B.C.E.) of the Kushite (Cushite) kingdom based at Napata in Nubia. The Kushites gradually gained the control and transferred their capital from Napata to Thebes. Pi-ankhi defeated the Libyans and took control of the entire territory. Under the successor of Pi-ankhi, King Shabaka, (716-702 B.C.E.), there was a great resurgence in Egyptian art and philosophy. He was the patron of the restoration of the city of Memphis which was the seat of the worship of the god Ptah. So with this the Nubians made Egypt part of their empire which now stretched from Libya, down the Nile into Nubia.

A Return to the Old Ways

This was a unique period in Ancient Egyptian history, the Nubian rulers supported the renaissance of culture. Directed by the Temple System (Priests and Priestesses) the government was empowered to move society towards a positive and prosperous condition as it had been in the past. For this purpose the Priests and Priestesses supervised a return to the arts of the Old Kingdom Period which included the style of writing the hieroglyphic texts, Old Kingdom artistic forms in architecture and painting as well as Old Kingdom forms in government and social order. This is the period when texts of the Old Kingdom were rediscovered, transcribed anew and the old forms of worship were practiced. An example of such a text was the "Shabaka Inscription" detailing the teachings of Memphite Theology. The leaders of society saw the solution to the decline of Egyptian culture in returning to the older forms of social organization and regulation and turning away from the practices that were perceived as contradictory to the values of the older, stable and prosperous society. This renaissance was accepted and even welcomed by the people and supported by the Temple, and this shows the harmony that existed between the Nubians and the Egyptians since they already shared the same religion and cultural values. The renaissance progressed until the Assyrians successfully attacked the country and forced the Nubian leaders to leave the country. Foreigners then ruled Egypt. The Assyrians placed Psamtik I in power as a vassal Pharaoh until the power of the Assyrians waned. Psamtik I consolidated his power and then Egypt succeeded in throwing off the Assyrian rulers and he continued the renaissance that the Nubians had begun until new foreign attackers again captured Egypt.

Then the Kushite kings came under increasing pressure from the expanding Assyrian empire. The Assyrian king Sennacherib invaded Judah[165] at the end of the 8th century B.C.E., but was forced to retire 701 B.C.E. by plague. After continual encroachments over the next thirty years the Assyrian king Ashurbanipal occupied Thebes in 666 B.C.E.

Egyptians Regain Control of Egypt

Assyrian domination ended three years later when they were driven out of Thebes by Psamtik I (Psammetichus I) who had consolidated his power to throw off the Assyrian domination and reunited Egypt under the 26th (Saite - Greek) Dynasty. Initially, the Saite Dynasty faced challenges from the remnants of the Kushites who had been driven out by Assyria, but an expedition sent by Psamtik II c. 590 B.C.E. took Napata and defeated the Kushites. There was an attempt at expansion under Necho (610–595 B.C.E.) who destroyed Josiah of Judah[166] and invaded Syria, but he was defeated at Carchemish by the Babylonians in 605 B.C.E. and driven back to Egypt. After that Egypt enjoyed a brief period of independence before the Persian invasion 525 B.C.E.

Persian Conquest Period

Persia, already supreme in Asia, began to look toward Egypt as a valuable addition to their empire and Cambyses made Egypt a Persian province in 525 B.C.E. Darius I (called "the Great" (c.558-486 BC), Achamenid king of Persia.) restored order in the Persian empire by dividing it into provinces which allowed some degree of autonomy and tolerating religious diversity. He tried to codify Egyptian laws, built a temple at Kharga, and developed Egyptian trade, reopening the canal between the Mediterranean and the Red Sea first opened by Necho.

Egyptians Regain Control of Egypt

Greek successes in the Persian Wars encouraged the Egyptians to revolt. After several unsuccessful risings, a revolt under Inaros the Libyan and Amyrtaeus of Sais[47] with Athenian backing from 460 B.C.E. succeeded in driving the Persians into Memphis, but after an 18-month siege the rebels were defeated. The Athenians then became embroiled in half a century of struggles with Sparta and were not able to help Egypt against the Persians. Eventually Amyrtaeus succeeded in freeing Egypt from the Persians 405 B.C.E., becoming sole Pharaoh of the 28th Dynasty, 404–399 B.C.E.[167]

Second Persian Conquest Period

The Second Persian Conquest Period (343-332 B.C.E.) when the Persians marshaled their forces for another attack on Egypt, which was too weakened to repel the attacks. Though successful, the Persian conquest of Egypt was brief because the Persians fell before Alexander's Greek armies.

Greek Conquest Period - Very Late Period - Saite Dynasty (332 B.C.E.- 30 B.C.E.)

The 8th century B.C.E. saw the commencement of what would later become Greek Classical civilization. The earliest Greek philosophers, such as Thales (c. 634-546 B.C.E.), were known to have gone to Egypt for instruction. There is also evidence that Ancient Egypt took on the responsibility of helping the Greeks to construct temples in Greece itself, providing both instruction as well as assistance. This explains, in part, the assistance given by the Greeks to Egypt in her time of need. During this period the Greeks saw that the Persians were a threat to them as well. However, the Greeks were known, even in ancient times, to be confrontational and argumentative people. This led to innumerable conflicts with the Spartans and others, which distracted them from the higher goals of civilized living.

In 332 B.C.E. the general, Alexander, conquered all of Greece, Asia Minor, India and Northeast Africa (including Egypt). From that time on Egypt would not have an African king or queen again. This is known as the Ptolemaic or Greek Period (also known as the Hellenistic Period). It lasted from 332 B.C.E.- c. 30 B.C.E. This is the period wherein after Alexander's death, one of his generals by the name of Ptolemy took control of

---

[47] In ancient times Sais was considered as the sister city of the Greek Athens. In fact, the Greeks considered that the Greek goddess Athena was actually the Egyptian goddess Net, also known to the Greeks as Neith. So there was a close association between the two countries in the formative period of Greek culture (1000 B.C.E-500 B.C.E.).

Egypt. Ptolemy's family and army settled in Egypt and mixed with the local population, especially in the north. This family of rulers gave rise to the famous Cleopatra. She was the last Ptolemaic ruler until the Romans took control of Egypt under the rule of Caesar.

*For more details on Ancient Egypt and the origins of civilization in Ancient Greece see Chapter 3.

Early Christian, Roman Christian Conquest Periods and the Closing of Egyptian Temples

See Chapter 4

The Coptic Church Period

The Coptic Church is the major Christian church in modern day Egypt. The name, Copt, was derived from the Greek word for "Egyptian" and the Arabic "qubt" which was westernized as "Copt." The origins of Egyptian Christianity can be found in the Gnostic mystery schools, which developed the Hermetic teachings (teachings of the Egyptian God Djehuti), in the period immediately preceding the Christian era. These schools were engendered by the early Greek philosophers who studied Egyptian philosophy and Alexander the Great who conquered Egypt and sought to establish a city of Enlightenment which would bridge the East and the West and spread the wisdom of Egypt to the world. Alexander knew, from his early instruction by Aristotle, that Egypt was the source of the most ancient knowledge and the repository of the world's greatest scholars and mystical philosophers. Thus, the Greeks under Alexander sought to appropriate and adopt the Ancient Egyptian traditions which they had been learning for the previous five centuries since the time of Thales, the first recognized Greek Philosopher (circa 700 B.C.E.), in order to carry on the mystical tradition of Egypt. These Gnostic Hellenists intermixed with the Jews living in Alexandria in northwest Lower Egypt. Four centuries after Alexander's conquest of Egypt, notable Christian philosophers would emerge out of Alexandria who would exert a strong influence on early Christianity and later cause the separation of the Egyptian Christians (Copts) from the Roman and Byzantine Christians. Some of the important Christian theologians who emerged from Alexandria included Clement of Alexandria, Origen and Arius.

The debates in the church over the true understanding of Christ (Christology) led to a separation between the Church in Egypt (Coptic Church) and the churches of Rome and Constantinople (which became the Western Empire and Eastern Empire). The majority of Egyptian Christians refused to go along with the decrees of the Council of Chalcedon in 451 A.C.E., that defined the person of Jesus the Christ as being "one in two natures." This doctrine of "two natures" seemed to imply the existence of two Christs, one being divine and the other human. These Egyptian Christians who refused the Council of Chalcedon faced charges of monophysitism. Monophysitism is the belief that Christ has only one nature rather than two. It is notable that the Council of Chalcedon was accepted both in Constantinople and in Rome, but not in Egypt. Thus, we see that the dualistic view of Christ was developed and promoted in Europe under the Roman church and in the Middle East under the church of Constantinople. It was Egypt, which sought to uphold the non-dualistic view of Christ, which viewed him as an all-encompassing Divine being. This was due to the tradition of non-dualism, which it assimilated from the Ancient Egyptian mystery schools. The Coptic Church of Egypt separated from Rome and Constantinople and set up its own Pope who is nominated by an Electoral College of clergy and laity. The Coptic Church has survived up to the present in Egypt. There are over seven million Coptic Christians there today and 22 million in total.

The sacred music of Ancient Egypt lives on in the Christian Coptic tradition of the Coptic Church mass. Anthropologists believe that the primary characteristics of modern Coptic music were adopted from the music of the Ancient Egyptians. These characteristics include the use of triangles and cymbals, and a strong vocal tradition. The Copts are regarded as the genetically purest direct descendents of the Ancient Egyptians due to their lack of intermarrying with the other Egyptians who are of Arab descent. The whole of the Coptic service is to be sung. The singing is alternated between the master chanter, the priest, and a choir of deacons. A technique of chanting and singing was also used in Ancient Egypt during the processions and recitals of the mystery rituals.

For more details on the Coptic Period see Chapter 4

Arab and Muslim Conquest Period

See Chapter 4

The Revised Chronology of Ancient Egypt Based On New Archeological Evidence and the Omitted Records

The history which has been presented in the previous section is only the history of the "Dynastic Period." It reflects the view of traditional Egyptologists who have refused to accept the evidence of a Pre-Dynastic Period in Ancient Egyptian history contained in Ancient Egyptian documents such as the *Palermo Stone, Royal Tablets at Abydos, Royal Papyrus of Turin,* and the *Dynastic List of Manetho* and also have not become aware of the new findings concerning recent excavations as well as the new dating of the Sphinx. The eye-witness accounts of Greek historians Herodotus (c. 484-425 B.C.E.) and Diodorus (Greek historian died about 20 B.C.E.) corroborate the status and makeup of Kamitan culture in the late Dynastic Period which support the earlier accounts. These sources speak clearly of a Pre-Dynastic society which stretched far into antiquity. The Dynastic Period is what most people think of whenever Ancient Egypt is mentioned. This period is when the Pharaohs (kings and queens) ruled. The latter part of the Dynastic Period is when the Biblical story of Moses, Joseph, Abraham, etc., occurs. Therefore, those with a Christian background generally only have an idea about Ancient Egypt as it is related in the Bible. Although this biblical notion is very limited in scope and portrayed in a negative light, the significant impact of Ancient Egypt on Hebrew and Christian culture is evident even from the biblical scriptures. Actually, Egypt existed much earlier than most traditional Egyptologists are prepared to admit. The new archeological evidence related to the great Sphinx monument on the Giza Plateau and the ancient writings by Manetho, one of the last High Priests of Ancient Egypt, show that Ancient Egyptian history begins earlier than 10,000 B.C.E. and dates back to as early as 30,000-50,000 B.C.E. The actual date for the construction of the great Sphinx is 10,000 B.C.E. – 15,000 B.C.E. because the erosion damage on it would have had to occur 2,000-3,000 years prior to the climate in Egypt becoming like the present desert-like conditions. This new dating should not come as a surprise in view of other new archeological evidence. The Ancient Egyptian scripture itself claims that the Ancient Egyptians originated from the south, the land of Nubia, Ta Seti, "the land of the bow," as Nubia is also referred to. A report by the Oriental Institute in Chicago, one of the important orthodox Egyptology schools, stated that Ta Seti is known to have developed a pre-Pharaonic kingdom 300 years earlier than the first Egyptian Dynasty. Thus, these and other finds show a continuous flow of culture arising from the southern portion of Africa at its heart, extending to Ethiopia and into Ancient Egypt. Therefore, the advanced Sothic calendar which has been identified as being in use at 4241 B.C.E. as well as the histories given by the Ancient Egyptian texts themselves, speaking of a history going back beyond 30,000 years are now being corroborated. Newly refined radio carbon tests on organic material found in recent years in the Great Pyramid have shown that it "was built at least 374 years earlier" than previously thought.[168] The oldest radiocarbon dating of the organic material in the Great Pyramid yielded a date of 3809 B.C.E. Further, there is evidence that the lower section of the Great Pyramid is older than the upper parts.

Plate 12: The Giza Pyramid Complex-Great Pyramid, far right.

While the date when the stone to create the Great Pyramid was originally cut apparently cannot as yet be dated with available instruments, tests performed on 16 samples of organic materials discovered in the Great Pyramid in Giza, Egypt, by a prominent orthodox Egyptologist (Mark Lehner) such as charcoal, showed that the pyramid was in use as early as 3809 B.C.E. So on this evidence alone the chronologies given for age of the Great Pyramid by traditional Egyptology as belonging to the reign of Pharaoh Khephren (Cheops) of 2551 B.C.E.- 2528 B.C.E. are simply untenable and must be revised forthwith. Therefore, while momentous, the evidence of the Sphinx fits into the larger scheme of scientific evidences which are unraveling the mysteries of history and leads us to the understanding of life in ancient Northeast Africa as a high point in human cultural achievement which was attained in Ancient Egypt and spread out to the rest of the world.

Plate 13: Great Pyramid Compared to the European Cathedrals[169]

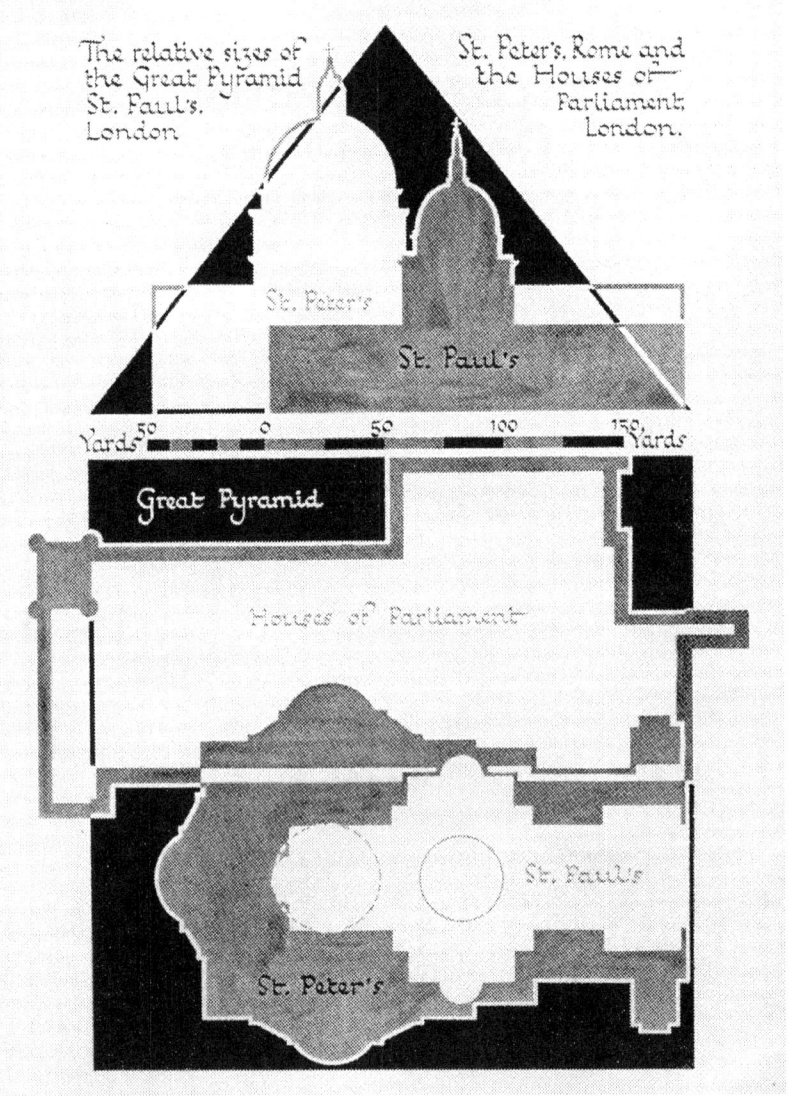

The massive size and majesty of the Great Pyramid can be discerned when compared to some of the European cathedrals, which took sometimes decades to construct. The picture above shows how these could easily fit within the volume of the pyramid with room to spear. This image also points to the organization, logistics and planning that went into the creation of the pyramids and partially explains the awe inspiring feeling that they evoke upon seeing them in person.

Also, new finds in northeastern Zaire by the Brooks and Yellen archeological team, in their dating of artifacts, arrived at refined and double-checked results confirming dates going back to 70,000 years. This means that a level of civilization had been attained in Africa 54,000 earlier than anywhere outside of Africa.[170] With this kind of evidence modern anthropology has accepted that human life began in Africa and then spread out to the rest of the world. This model has been supported by the advanced findings in the science of modern genetics, where it has been shown that all human beings have common ancestry in Africa and therefore, all humanity is of African descent. Still, the general public has received little notification except through periodic reports in journals or the occasional stories appearing in newsmagazines. Therefore, an entire reworking of the chronologies for the origins of humankind as well as the emergence of civilization must be revised. Further, the textbooks for elementary and high schools must be revised.

Many scholars have had difficulty in dating the events of Ancient Egypt. This is due to many reasons. One of these is that they have sought to date these events in terms which relate to other cultures and thereby extrapolate dates based on correlated factors which can be verified through the writings or records of other cultures. This is of course difficult because, as we will see, Ancient Egyptian history extends so far into the past that there is no other culture to compare it to except itself. Hence, the tendency has been the practice of compressing the timeline of events in Ancient Egypt so that they fit within the time frame of history that is known about other cultures. The surviving texts of Ancient Egypt have provided a chronology and timetable. The History of Manetho is only one source. However, in the last one hundred years, the traditional (orthodox) Egyptologists have rejected these records as "impossible" or "unbelievable." In the early years of Egyptology many scholars, such as Champollion, Sir Flinders Petrie and Brested gave dates of 5867 B.C.E., 5500 B.C.E. and 4241[171] respectively for the commencement of the Dynastic Period (unification of Upper and Lower Egypt under one ruler) which were more in line with the histories given by the Ancient Egyptians themselves and the revised perspective promoted by new archeological evidences. Note that the date of unification does not mean the inception of civilization or the beginning of culture, art, science, philosophy, etc., but rather the political consolidation of the country. Later Egyptologists reduced this number to 3400 B.C.E. and then 3200 B.C.E., and until recent excavations in Abydos and Hierakonpolis the consensus was c. 2900 B.C.E., which is below the date set for Mesopotamia, which was originally lower than that of the first dates set for Ancient Egypt by the early Egyptologists.

Moreover, Western renderings of the Ancient Egyptian hieroglyphic texts often promote the literal meanings of words even when there are different readings possible in accordance with the myths. The treatment is confined to the viewpoint of outsiders, looking at primitive religious superstitions. In this capacity oftentimes nonsensical translations are obtained and explained away as unintelligible or erroneous passages due to ancient scribal erratum. The inability to understand the hieroglyphic language is predicated upon the fallacy that it is a strictly literal form of language. In effect, while having performed a service to humanity by decoding the language for humanity, Western Egyptologists and linguists have *projected* their own understanding of philosophy, religion and language, and therefore cannot incorporate the mythic and mystic component of the language which constitutes its special form of *reasoning* alluded to in the following quotation. The Greek classic writer Diodorus introduces the multi-aspected nature of the hieroglyphic language.

> "We must now speak of the Ethiopian writing which is called hieroglyphic by the Egyptians, in order that we may omit nothing in our discussion of their antiquities. Now it is found that the forms of their letters take the shape of animals of every kind, and of the members of the human body, and of implements and especially carpenter's tools; for their writing does not express the intent concept by means of syllables joined one to another, but by its figurative meaning which has been impressed upon the memory by practice. For instance, they draw the picture of a hawk, a crocodile, a snake, and all of the members of the human body-an eye, a hand, a face, and the like. Now the hawk signifies to them everything which happens swiftly, since this animal is practically the swiftest of winged creatures...And the crocodile is a symbol of all that is evil, and the eye is the warder of justice and the guardian of the entire body. And as for the members of the body, the right hand with fingers extended signifies a procuring of livelihood, and the left with the fingers closed, a keeping and guarding of property. The same way of reasoning applies to the remaining characters, which represent parts of the body and implements and all other things; for by paying close attention to the

significance which is inherent in each object and by training their minds through drills and exercise of the memory over a long period, they read from habit everything which has been written."

-Recorded by Diodorus (Greek historian 100 B.C.)

Table 11: Chronology of Ancient Egypt according to Flinders Petrie[172]

Period.	Dynasty.	Names.	B.C.
Prehistoric.			8000-5500
Early kings.	I.	Narmer, Mena, Zer,	5500-5400
	II.	Khasekhem,	5000
	III.	Zeser, Senoferu,	4900-4700
Pyramid age: Old Kingdom.	IV.	Khufu, Khafra, Menkaura,	4700-4500
	V.	Noferarkara, Unas,	4400-4200
	VI.	Pepy II,	4100-4000
	IX.	Khety,	3800
	XI.	Antef V,	3500
Middle Kingdom.	XII.	Senusert I, Senusert II, Senusert III,	3400-3300
		Amenemhat III,	3300-3259
	XIII.	Hor,	3200
	XVIII.	Aahmes, Queens Aah-hotep, Aahmes,	1587-1562
		Tahutmes I, Tahutmes II, Hatshepsut,	1541-1481
New Kingdom.		Tahutmes III, Amenhotep II, Tahutmes IV,	1481-1414
		Amenhotep III, Akhenaten, Tutankhamen,	1414-1344
	XIX.	Sety I, Ramessu II, Merenptah,	1326-1214
		Sety II, Tausert,	1214-1203
	XX.	Ramessu III, IV, XII,	1202-1129
	XXI.	Isiemkheb,	1050
	XXII.	Shishak kings,	952-749
	XXIII.	Pedubast, Pefaabast,	755-725
Ethiopian.	XXV.	Amenardys, Taharqa, Tanutamen,	720-664
Saite.	XXVI.	Aahmes II,	570-526
	XXX.	Nekhthorheb (Nectanebo),	378-361
Ptolemies.		Cleopatra Cocce,	130-106
Romans.			30-A.D. 640

Ancient Egypt is in modern times populated by a culture which is classified as "Arab." The Arabs are members of an Asiatic[173] people inhabiting Arabia, whose language and Islamic religion spread widely throughout Asia Minor (the Middle East) and northern Africa from the seventh century. Having conquered Egypt since the 7th century A.C.E., the Arabs, who now refer to themselves as "Egyptians," have adopted the heritage, but not the legacy of Ancient Egypt. That is, the government and schools espouse the idea that Ancient Egyptian culture and civilization is part of the past history of the modern people. The modern Arabs admittedly care little about Ancient Egypt except to the extent that is a magnet for tourists and is therefore a tourism financial boon. The government trains "guides" to lead tourists around the temples and other sites of the country and they are taught to espouse the deficient chronology of Ancient Egypt and many distorted renditions of the myths. Further, one can hear in the speech of many guides a disdain and sometimes even disgust for the images presented in the iconography of the temples. Interviews[174] led to the discovery that the general view of those who are brought up in orthodox Islamic culture is that Ancient Egyptian religion was not religion at all, but rather feeble attempts at theorizing about spiritual matters. In fact, the underlying view, confirmed in many interviews of Arabs born in Egypt, is that they view "Islam as the only true" religion and religions such as Hinduism as "idolatry." Therefore, as Hinduism is essentially compatible with Neterianism (the religion of Shetaut Neter), one may expect the same treatment of the Ancient Egyptian religion. Consequently, the philosophy, art and spirituality of Ancient Egypt are perceived as nothing more than commodities to attract foreign dollars into the ailing economy and at another level, they are means by which some Arabs attain higher status in the society by becoming "Egyptologists." These "Egyptologists" constitute some of the most vehement opponents to any view which suggests an older chronology for Ancient Egypt and anything that might suggest that there is a form of spirituality as correct and or valid as Islam. Consequently, they are some of the most ardent supporters of the orthodox Egyptological views.

The Far Reaching Implications of the New Evidence Concerning the Sphinx and Other New Archeological Evidence in Egypt and the Rest of Africa

In the last 20 years traditional Egyptologists, archeologists and others have been taking note of recent studies performed on the Ancient Egyptian Sphinx which sits at Giza in Egypt. Beginning with such students of Ancient Egyptian culture and architecture as R. A. Schwaller de Lubicz in the 1950's, and most recently, John Anthony West, with his book *Serpent In the Sky*, many researchers have used modern technology to study the ancient monument and their discoveries have startled the world. They now understand that the erosion damage on the Sphinx could not have occurred after the period 10,000-7,000 B.C.E. because this was the last period in which there would have been enough rainfall in the area to cause such damage. This means that most of the damage which the Sphinx displays itself, which would have taken thousands of years to occur, would have happened prior to that time (10,000 B.C.E.).

Many scholars have downplayed or misunderstood the new geological evidences related to the Great Sphinx. One example are the authors of the book *In Search of the Cradle of Civilization,* Georg Feuerstein, David Frawley (prominent western Indologists), and Subhash Kak, in which the authors state the following: (highlighted text is by Ashby)

> In seeking to refute current archeological thinking about the Sphinx, West relies on a *single geological feature*. Understandably, most Egyptologists have been less than accepting of his redating of this monument, *hoping* that some other explanation can be found for the *strange* marks of erosion. P. 6

The characterization of the evidence as a "single geological feature" implies it stands alone as an anomaly that does not fit into the greater picture of Ancient Egyptian history and is completely without basis. In support of orthodox Egyptologists, the authors agree with them, stating that their attitude is understandable. Now, even if there were only a single form of evidence, does this mean that it is or should be considered suspect especially when considering the fact that Egyptology and archeology are not exact sciences and geology is an exact science? Further, the authors mention the wishful thinking of the orthodox Egyptologists as they search in vein (hoping) for some other way to explain the evidence. Yet, the authors seem to agree with the Egyptological view and thereby pass over this evidence as an inconsistency that need not be dealt with further.

> The following evidences must also be taken into account when examining the geology of the Sphinx and the Giza plateau.
>
> ➢ The surrounding Sphinx Temple architecture is similarly affected.
>
> ➢ Astronomical evidence agrees with the geological findings.
>
> ➢ Ancient Egyptian historical documents concur with the evidence.

It is important to understand that what we have in the Sphinx is not just a monument now dated as the earliest monument in history (based on irrefutable geological evidence). Its existence signifies the earliest practice not only of high-art and architecture, but it is also the first monumental statue in history dedicated to religion. This massive project including the Sphinx and its attendant Temple required intensive planning and engineering skill. Despite its deteriorated state, the Sphinx stands not only as the most ancient mystical symbol in this historical period, but also as the most ancient architectural monument, and a testament to the presence of Ancient African (Egyptian) culture in the earliest period of antiquity. Further, this means that while the two other emerging civilizations of antiquity (Sumer and Indus) were in their Neolithic period (characterized by the development of agriculture, pottery and the making of polished stone implements), Ancient Egypt had already achieved mastery over monumental art, architecture and religion as an adjunct to social order, as the Sphinx is a symbol of the Pharaoh (leader and upholder of Maat-order, justice and truth) as the god Heru. The iconography of the Sphinx is typical of that which is seen throughout Ancient Egyptian history and signals the achievement of the a culture of high morals which governs the entire civilization to the Persian and Greek conquest.

Plate 14: The Great Sphinx of Ancient Egypt-showing the classical Pharaonic headdress popularized in Dynastic times. Also, the water damage can be seen in the form of vertical indentations in the sides of the monument.

> The water erosion of the Sphinx is to history what the convertibility of matter into energy is to physics.
>
> -John Anthony West *Serpent In the Sky*

Many people have heard of the new evidence concerning the water damage on the Sphinx and how it has been shown to be much older than previously thought. However, as we saw earlier, detractors usually claim that this is only one piece of evidence that is inconclusive. This is the usual opinion of the uninformed. The findings have been confirmed by seismographic tests[175] as well as examination of the water damage on the structures related to the Sphinx and the Sphinx Temple, as compared to the rest of the structures surrounding it which display the typical decay due to wind and sand. It has been conclusively found that the Sphinx and its adjacent structures (Sphinx Temple) were built in a different era and that the surrounding structures do not display the water damage. Therefore, the wind and sand damaged structures belong to the Dynastic Era and the Sphinx belongs to the Pre-Dynastic Era. Therefore, the evidence supporting the older dating of the Sphinx is well founded and confirmed.

Plate 15: Sphinx rump and Sphinx enclosure show detail of the water damage (vertical damage).

The new evidence related to the Sphinx affects many other forms of evidence which traditional Egyptologists have also sought to dismiss. Therefore, it is a momentous discovery on the order the discernment of the Ancient Egyptian Hieroglyphic text. It requires an opening up of the closely held chronologies and timelines of ancient cultures for revision, thereby allowing the deeper study of the human experience on this earth and making the discovery of our collective past glory possible. Thus, it is clear to see that the problem in assigning dates to events in Ancient Egypt arises when there is an unwillingness to let go of closely held notions based on biased information that is accepted as truth and passed on from one generation of orthodox Egyptologists to the next generation, rather than on authentic scholarship (constant search for truth). This deficiency led to the exclusion of the ancient historical writings of Ancient Egypt (*Palermo Stone, Royal Tablets at Abydos, Royal Papyrus of Turin,* the *Dynastic List* of Manetho). However, now, with the irrefutable evidence of the antiquity of the Sphinx, and the excavations at Abydos and Hierakonpolis, the mounting archeological evidence and the loosening grip of Western scholars on the field of Egyptology, it is no longer possible to ignore the far reaching implications of the Ancient Egyptian historical documents.

The History of Manetho

The evidence concerning the new dating of the Sphinx affects the treatment of the History of Manetho. Manetho was one of the last Ancient Egyptian High Priests who retained the knowledge of the ancient history of Egypt. In 241 B.C.E. he was commissioned to compile a series of wisdom texts by King Ptolemy II, one of the Macedonian (Greek) rulers of Egypt after it was captured and controlled by the Greeks. One of Manetho's compositions included a history of Egypt. However, Manetho's original writings did not survive into the present. Therefore, the accounts of his writings by the Greeks who studied his work constitute the current remaining record of his work, and some of the accounts differ from each other in certain respects. His history has come down to us in the form of translation, part of which are missing certain portions. However, it has been ascertained that he grouped the Dynastic Rulers of Ancient Egypt into 30 Dynasties containing around 330 Pharaohs in a period of around 4,500 years (going back from his time-241 B.C.E.). According to Manetho Ancient Egyptian chronology included the following periods:

1- The Gods - This period was the genesis. It began with the emergence of the great Ennead or Company of gods and goddesses headed by Ra, the Supreme Being. According to the creation myth, the God, Ra himself, ruled over the earth.

2- The Demigods - After the Gods, the Demigods ruled the earth. Then came a descendent line of royal rulers followed by 30 rulers in the city of Memphis. These were followed by another set of royal rulers. The Heru Shemsu often mentioned in various texts referring to the ancient worship of Heru as the Supreme Spirit belong to this age. (Ra is an aspect of Heru).

3- The Spirits of the Dead - After the period of the Demigods came the Spirits of the Dead.

According to the Turin Papyrus (original Ancient Egyptian document dating to c.1440 B.C.E.), the dates of the periods are:

1- The Gods – 23,200

2- The Demigods – 13,420

3- The Spirits of the Dead – cannot be deciphered due to damage on the document.

Total: A minimum of 36,620 years before the unification (fist Dynasty).

According to Eusebius, the dates of the periods of Ancient Egypt *before* Menes, the uniter of the two lands into one empire, total: 28,927 years before the unification.

According to Diodorus of Sicily, the dates of the periods total 33,000 before the unification.

These periods were then followed by the Dynastic Period which is the only period of Ancient Egypt of which most people have knowledge (c. 5,000 B.C.E.-30 B.C.E.). Due to the deficiencies in the historical record, an exact dating for each period preceding the Dynastic is not available. However, it is reasonably certain that the total number of years outlined above goes back in history to at least 28,927 years from the time when Manetho was writing in 241 B.C.E. This gives a total of number of years around the beginning of the preceding Kamitan "Great Year" former to the commencement of our current one.

Support for this remote date comes from the writings of Herodotus. According to Herodotus, he was told by one of his Egyptian guides in 450 B.C.E. that "the sun had risen twice where it now set, and twice set where it now rises." This statement has been recognized by scholars as a reference to the processional cycles. This means that the Ancient Egyptians witnessed the beginning of the previous Great Year to our current one. Since the beginning of the current Great Year is reckoned at 10,858 B.C.E., this would mean that the beginning of Ancient Egyptian records goes back to 36,748 (10,858 + 25,890 the period of the previous great year =36,748).

> 4- Mortal Men – i.e. The Pre-Dynastic and Dynastic Periods- Rulership by Pharaohs (Kings and Queens).

This period must be divided into the Pre-Dynastic age and the Dynastic age, for the Dynastic age that is often used to represent the beginning of Ancient Egyptian civilization only refers to the time of the major unification of all the kingdoms (nomes) of the Southern ands Northern portions of the country into one single nation.

The Pharaonic (royal) calendar based on the Sothic system (star Sirius) containing cycles of 1,460 years, was in use by 4,241 B.C.E. This certainly required extensive astronomical skills and time for observation. The Sothic system is based on the *Heliacal* (i.e. appears in the sky just as the sun breaks through the eastern horizon) rising of the star Sirius in the eastern sky, signaling the New Year as well as the inundation season. Therefore, the history of Kamit (Egypt) must be reckoned to be extremely ancient. Thus, in order to grasp the antiquity of Ancient Egyptian culture, religion and philosophy, we will review the calendar systems used by the Ancient Egyptians.

The Stellar Symbolism related to the Pole Star and the Opening of the mouth and Eyes Ceremony in Ancient Egypt

As introduced earlier, Herodotus, in his book of history, quoted one of his guides as having told him that in Egyptian history had lasted for a period of time in which, "the sun had twice risen where it now set, and twice set where it now rises."[176]

> "This remark Schwaller de Lubicz interpreted as a description of the passage of one and a half precessional cycles. This would place the date of foundation around 36,000 BC, a date in broad agreement with the other sources."[177]

There are three constellations that circulate around the North Pole of the planet earth. These are Draco, Ursa Major and Ursa Minor. The Great Pyramid was discovered to have a shaft that points to the North Pole. Precession is the slow revolution of the Earth's axis of rotation (wobbling) about the poles of the ecliptic. The eclipticis a great circle inscribed on a terrestrial globe inclined at an approximate angle of 23°27' to the equator and representing the apparent motion of the sun in relation to the earth during a year. It is caused by lunar and solar perturbations acting on the Earth's equatorial bulge and causes a westward motion of the stars that takes around 25,868 years to complete.[178] During the past 5000 years the line of direction of the North Pole has moved from the star Thuban, or Alpha (a) Draconis, in the constellation Draco, to within one degree of the bright star Polaris, also known as Alpha (a) Ursae Minoris, in the constellation Ursa Minor (Little Dipper), which is now the North Star. Polaris is a binary star of second magnitude, and is located at a distance of about 300 light-years from the earth. It is easy to locate in the sky because the two stars opposite the handle in the bowl of the dipper in the constellation Ursa Major (Big Dipper), which are called the Pointers, point to the star Polaris.[179]

Figure 31: The Kamitan Zodiac and the Precession of the Equinoxes and the History of Ancient Egypt

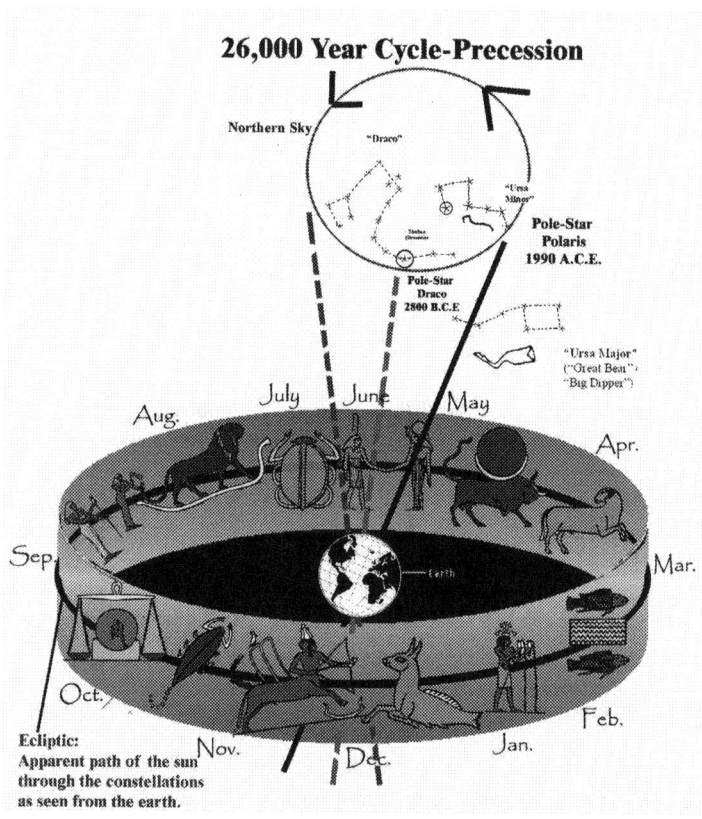

The Zodiac is an imaginary belt in the celestial sphere, extending about 8° on either side of the ecliptic. The ecliptic is a line that traces the apparent path of the Sun among the stars. It is believed that the width of the zodiac was originally determined so as to include the orbits of the Sun and Moon and of the five planets that were believed to have been known by people in ancient times (Mercury, Venus, Mars, Jupiter, and Saturn). The zodiac is divided into 12 sections of 30° each, which are called the signs of the zodiac. Because of the precession of the equinoxes about the ecliptic, a 25,920-year cycle or "Great Year" period, the first point of Aries retrogrades about 1° in 72 years, so that the sign Aries today lies in the constellation Pisces. In about 13,061 years, when the retrogression will have completed the entire circuit of 360°, the zodiacal signs and constellations will again coincide. It is believed that the zodiacal signs originated in Mesopotamia as early as 2000 B.C.E. and the Greeks adopted the symbols from the Babylonians and passed them on to the other ancient civilizations. The Chinese also adopted the 12-fold division, but called the signs rat, ox, tiger, hare, dragon, serpent, horse, sheep, monkey, hen, dog, and pig. Independently, the Aztec people devised a similar system.[180]

The calendar based on the Great Year was also used by the Ancient Egyptians. The Great Year is founded on the movement of the earth through the constellations known as the *Precession of the Equinoxes*. It is confirmed from the history given by the Ancient Egyptian Priest Manetho in the year 241 B.C.E. Each Great Year has 25,860 to 25,920 years and 12 arcs or constellations. Each passage through a constellation takes 2,155 – 2,160 years. These are known as the "Great Months" of the "Great Year." As explained earlier, the current cycle or year began at around 10,858 B.C.E. At about the year 36,766 B.C.E., according to Manetho, the Creator, Ra, ruled the earth in person from his throne in the Ancient Egyptian city of Anu (Greek-Heliopolis-city of the sun). By this reckoning our current year (2,002 A.C.E.) is actually the year 12,860 G.Y. based on the Great Year System of Ancient Egyptian reckoning.

The period of 36,525 years is also 25 times 1,460 which is the cycle of the helical rising of Sirius (when Sirius rises not only in the east but on the ecliptic, i.e. with the sun). The Sirian calendar was another time reckoning system based on the star Sirius and its relation with the sun of our solar system which contains a cycle of 1,460 years. An inscription by Censorinus informs us that the rising of Sirius occurred in 139 A.C.E. This means that the Sirian cycle also occurred in the years 1321 B.C.E, 2781 B.C.E, and 4241 B.C.E. By means of two inscriptions from the 18th Dynasty, it has been reliably established that the date for the 18th Dynasty is 1580 B.C.E.

According to the reckoning based on Manetho's history, if we take the average number of years in the Great Year and add it to the known year of the beginning of the current Great Year we get a total of 36,748 (25,890 + 10,858=36,748). If we compare this number with the history of Manetho we find a difference of 18 years, accountable by the deterioration in the translated records and the variance in the number of years in the Great Year cycle. Thus, we have match that supports the History and the practice of reckoning time by the Great Year. So we have reliable confirmations that the Sirian calendar was in use in Ancient Egypt at least as early as 4241 B.C.E.[181] and that a greater form of reckoning, the Great Year, corroborates the History of Manetho which takes Ancient Egyptian chronology and civilized use of mathematics, astronomy and time reckoning back to 36,748 B.C.E. This longer duration cycle system of time reckoning was supported by recent discoveries.

> "That the Egyptians handled astronomical cycles of even greater duration is indicated by inscriptions recently found by Soviet archeologists in newly opened graves during the period of their work on the Aswan Dam.[182] Here the cycles appear to cover periods of 35,525 years, which would be the equivalent of 25 cycles of 1461 years. The apparent discrepancy of one year in this recording of cycles is due to the sothic cycle of 1460 years being the equivalent of a civil cycle of 1461 years. According to Muck (researcher), there were three main cycles: one of 365 X 4 = 1460; another of 1460 X 25 = 36,500; and a third of 36,500 X 5 = 182,500 years."[183]

Let us recall the brilliant discovery by Joseph Campbell introduced earlier in relation to the same great age period being used in India, Iceland and Babylon and the unlikelihood of this arising by chance.

> "There are, however, instances that cannot be accounted for in this way, and then suggest the need for another interpretation: for example, in India the number of years assigned to an eon[184] is 4,320,000; whereas in the Icelandic *Poetic Edda* it is declared that in Othin's warrior hall, Valhall, there are 540 doors, through each of which, on the "day of the war of the wolf,"[185] 800 battle-ready warriors will pass to engage the antigods in combat.' But 540 times 800 equals 432,000!
>
> Moreover, a Chaldean priest, Berossos, writing in Greek ca. 289 B.C., reported that according to Mesopotamian belief 432,000 years elapsed between the crowning of the first earthly king and the coming of the deluge.
>
> No one, I should think, would wish to argue that these figures could have arisen independently in India, Iceland, and Babylon."[186]

When we compare the Indian, Icelandic and Babylonian system of Ages of time with that of Ancient Egypt some startling correlations can be observed; the same numbers appear.

Ancient Egyptian Age	Ancient Indian Age
25,920 Great Year	----------------------------------
25,920 ÷ 6 = 4320	432,000 Kali Yuga – Iron Age 4,320,000 Maha Yuga – Great Age or Cycle
25,920 ÷ 4 = 8640	864,000 Dwapar Yuga – Copper Age
25,920 ÷ 2 = 1296	1,296,000 Treta Yuga – Silver Age
25,920 ÷ 15 = 1728	1,728,000 Satya Yuga – Golden or Truth Age

The *Royal Papyrus of Turin* gives a complete list of the kings who reigned over Upper and Lower Egypt from Menes to the New Empire, including mention of the duration of each reign. Before the list comes a section devoted to the Pre-Dynastic era. This section lists the kings who reigned before Menes, and the duration of each reign, establishing that there were nine Dynasties. According to Schwaller de Lubicz, some of these were called:

> ... the (venerables) of Memphis, the venerables of the North, and finally the *Shemsu-Hor*, usually translated as the 'Companions of Horus'.

Fortunately, the last two lines have survived almost intact, as have indications regarding the number of years:

venerables Shemsu-Hor, 13,429 years
'Reigns up to Shemsu-Hor, 23,200years (total 36,620)
King Menes.[187]

The Turin Papyrus names the following neteru (gods and goddesses) as rulers in the Pre-Dynastic ages:
Ptah, Ra, Shu, Geb, Asar, Set, Heru, Djehuti, Maat

In support of the above, Diodorus of Sicily reports that several historians of his time reported Egypt was ruled by gods and heroes for a period of 18,000 years. After this Egypt was ruled by mortal kings for 15,000 years.[188] While it is true that this account differs with that of Manetho and the Turin Papyrus, the inescapable fact remains that every account refers to ages of rulers that go back beyond 30,000 B.C.E. as the earliest period of record keeping. The implications are far reaching. Consider that if we were to add the figure above for the period prior to the first king (King Menes) of our era and use the first confirmed date for the use of the calendar (4240 B.C.E.) we indeed would have a date over 40,000 B.C.E. for the beginnings of Ancient Egyptian history (36,620+4240).

Picture 26: Below right-The Great Heru m akhet (Sphinx) of Egypt-with the Panel of Djehutimes between its Paws. (19th century rendition of the Sphinx)[189]

Picture 23: Below left-The Great Heru m Akhet (Sphinx) of Ancient Egypt.

Plate 16: The Great Sphinx, covered in sand - Drawing by early Arab explorers[190]

    The Sphinx is the oldest known monument and it relates to the solar mysticism of Anu as well as to the oldest form of spiritual practice known. From it we also derive certain important knowledge in reference to the antiquity of civilization in Ancient Egypt. The picture of the Great Sphinx above-right appeared in 1876. Notice the broad nose and thick lips with which it is endowed. Any visitor to Egypt who examines the Sphinx close up will see that even with the defacement of the nose, it is clearly an African face and not an Asiatic or European personality being depicted. Many other early Egyptologists concluded the same way upon gazing at the monument and this picture is but one example of their conviction on the subject.

Figure 32: The Per-Aah (Pharaoh) Djehutimes IIII (Thutmosis) makes offerings to the Great Heru m Akhet (Sphinx)

The Heru-em-akhet (Horemacket Ra-Herakhti (Herukhuti, Heruakhuti - Great Sphinx) Stele is a panel placed directly in front of the chest of the monument in between the two front paws. It recounts the story of how the prince Djehutimes IIII (Thutmosis IV- 18th Dynasty 1401-1391 B.C.E.) fell asleep at the base of the Sphinx on a hot day and the spirit of the Sphinx came to him. The inscription that survived with the Ancient Egyptian Sphinx also has serious implications for the revision of the dating of Ancient Egyptian history. The Sphinx came to him and offered him kingship and sovereignty over the world if Djehutimes would repair him and make devout offerings and worship. Having complied with the wishes of the Divine, to maintain the great monument and sustain the worship of Ra-Herakhti, Djehutimes became king and Egypt prospered under his reign with the favor of the Divine. According to Egyptologist Maspero, this was not the first time that the Sphinx was cleared:

> The stele of the Sphinx bears, on line 13, the cartouche of Khephren in the middle of a gap .... There, I believe, is the indication of an excavation of the Sphinx carried out under this prince, and consequently the more or less certain proof that the Sphinx was already covered with sand during the time of Cheops and his predecessors.[191]

R. A. Schwaller de Lubicz reports that legends support the contention that at a very early date in Ancient Egyptian history, the Old Kingdom fourth Dynasty (Cheops {Khufu} reigned 2551-2528 B.C.E., Khephren {Ra-ka-ef} reigned 2520-2494), the Sphinx was already considered ancient and as belonging to a remote past of Ancient Egyptian Culture.

> A legend affirms that even in Cheops' day, the age of the Sphinx was already so remote that it was impossible to situate it in time. This Sphinx is a human and colossal work. There is an enigma about it that is linked with the very enigma posed by the Sphinx itself.

It has been proposed, as a support of the use of the Great Year calendar, that the Ancient Egyptians instituted the use of different symbolisms in religion and government in accordance with the current symbolism of the particular age in question.[192] Thus, during the age (great month) of Leo, the lion symbolism would be used. What is compelling about this rationale is that the new evidence in reference to the age of the Sphinx coincides with the commencement of the New Great Year and the month of Leo, which began in 10,858 B.C.E. However, when it is understood that the damage on the Sphinx would have required thousands of years to produce, and when the history of Manetho as well as the conjunction of the Sphinx with the constellation Leo when it makes its heliacal rising at the beginning of each Great Year is taken into account, it becomes possible to understand that the Sphinx was already in existence at the commencement of our current Great Year, and to envision the possibility that the Sphinx was created at the beginning of the previous Great Year anniversary (36,748 B.C.E.).

The Great Sphinx and its attendant monuments as well as other structures throughout Egypt which appear to be compatible architecturally should therefore be considered as part of a pinnacle of high culture that was reached well before the Dynastic age, i.e. previous to 5,000 B.C.E. The form of the Sphinx itself, displaying the lion body with the human head, but also with the particularly "leonine" headdress including the lion's mane, was a legacy accepted by the Pharaohs of the Dynastic Period. In the Ancient Egyptian mythological system of government, the Pharaoh is considered as a living manifestation of Heru and he or she wields the leonine power which comes from the sun, Ra, in order to rule. Thus, the Pharaohs also wore and were depicted wearing the leonine headdress. The sundisk is the conduit through which the Spirit transmits Life Force energy to the world, i.e. the Lion Power, and this force is accessed by turning towards the Divine in the form of the sun. Hence, the orientation of the Sphinx towards the east, facing the rising sun. All of this mystical philosophy and more is contained in the symbolic-metaphorical form and teaching of the Sphinx. Thus, we have a link of Ancient Egyptian culture back to the Age of Leo and the commencement of the current cycle of the Great Year in remote antiquity.

Heru-m-akhet or "Heru in the Horizon" or "manifesting" in the horizon, the "Sphinx," actually represents an ancient conjunction formed by the great Sphinx in Giza, Egypt and the heavens. This conjunction signals the beginning of the "New Great Year." It has been noted by orthodox as well as nonconformist Egyptologists alike, that the main symbolisms used in Ancient Egypt vary over time Nonconformist Egyptilogists see this as a commemoration of the zodiacal symbol pertaining to the particular Great Month in question. What is controversial to the orthodox Egyptologists is the implication that the Ancient Egyptians marked time by the Great Year, and this would mean that Ancient Egyptian civilization goes back 12 millenniums, well beyond any other civilization in history. This further signifies that all of the history books and concepts related to history and the contributions of Africa to humanity would have to be rewritten. Also, since it has been shown that the Ancient Egyptians commemorated the Zodiacal sign of Leo at the commencement of the Great Year it means that the knowledge of the precession of the equinoxes, the Great Year and the signs of the Zodiac proceeded from Ancient Egypt to Babylon and Greece and not the other way around. The twelve zodiacal signs for these constellations were named by the 2nd-century astronomer Ptolemy, as follows: Aries (ram), Taurus (bull), Gemini (twins), Cancer (crab), Leo (lion), Virgo (virgin), Libra (balance), Scorpio (scorpion), Sagittarius (archer), Capricorn (goat), Aquarius (water-bearer), and Pisces (fishes).

> That is precisely what the records reveal. Mentu the bull disappears and is superceded by the ram of Amon. The character of the architecture loses its monolithic simplicity. While still within its recognizable tradition, there is no mistaking a change of 'character'. The Pharaohs incorporate Amon in the names they assume: Amenhotep, Amenophis, Tutankhamun.
>
> Egyptologists attribute the fall of Mentu and the rise of Amon to a hypothetical priestly feud, with the priests of Amon emerging victorious. There is nothing illogical or impossible about this hypothesis, but at the same time there is no evidence whatever to support it.
>
> The evidence shows a shift of symbolism, from duality under Gemini, to the bull, to the ram. These shifts coincide with the dates of the astronomical precession.
>
> Further corroboration of Egyptian knowledge and use of the precession of the equinoxes, and of the incredible coherence and deliberation of the Egyptian tradition, was deduced by Schwaller de Lubicz from a detailed study of the famous zodiac from the Temple of Denderah. This temple was constructed by the Ptolemies in the first century BC, upon the site of an earlier temple. The hieroglyphs declare that it was constructed according to the plan laid down in the time of the 'Companions of Horus' - that is to say, prior to the beginnings of Dynastic Egypt. Egyptologists regard this statement as a ritual figure of speech, intended to express regard for the tradition of the past.[193]

One striking form of symbolism that is seen from the beginning to the end of the Ancient Egyptian history is the Sphinx/Pharaonic Leonine headdress.

Figure 33: Above- The Heru-m-akhet (Sphinx) Pharaonic headdress.[194]

Figure 34: Below- Drawing of the Sphinx from a sculpture in Egypt

Picture 24: Constellation Leo-The Lion

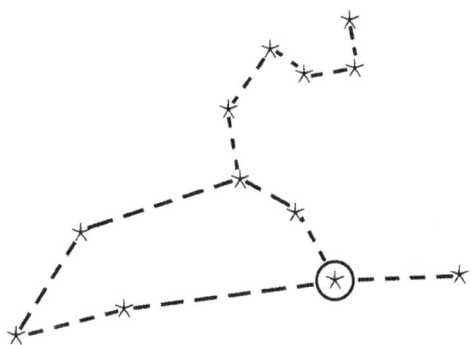

The Great Sphinx faces due east and in the year c. 10,800 B.C.E. a perfect conjunction is created as the Sphinx faces the rising sun and the constellation Leo, the lion.

Picture 25: The Sphinx faces due east at the beginning of the Great year and faces the Constellation Leo as it makes its Heliacal Rising.

Ra-Herakhti

Human Head-Lion Body
Spirit (Mind) -Matter
Subtle-Gross
Heaven-Earth
Human-Animal

Constellation Rw Ua-ti:
The Lion of the Zodiac

in conjunction with Ra, the Sun at the beginning
of the Great Year produces Her-m-akht
"Heru manifesting in the horizon."

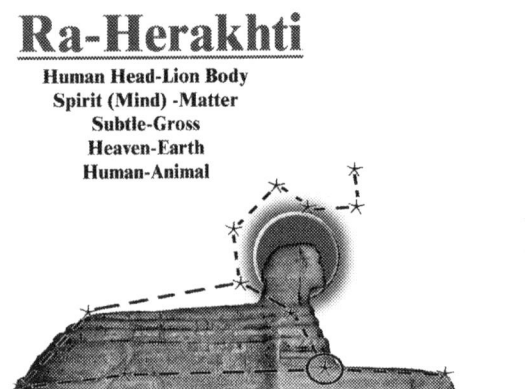

The Sphinx on Earth (Rw or Ru) as a Counterpart to the Sphinx in the Heavens.

The Sphinx on earth as a counterpart to the Sphinx in the heavens (Astral Plane), i.e. the horizon of the earth plane and the horizon of the astral plane. In this view, the Sphinx on earth and the Sphinx in heaven complement each other and form two halves of the akher-akhet symbol, but turned facing each other, looking at the sun which is between them, i.e. turning away from the earth plane and towards the Transcendental Spirit.

Conjunction between Earth and Heaven
(Physical Plane - Astral Plane)

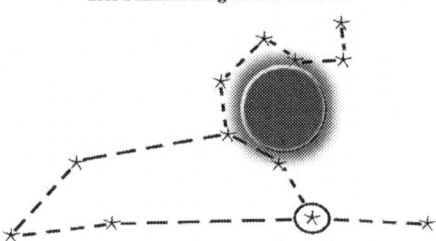

Hermakht
The Sphinx on Earth

Constellation of the Ru (lion)
Lion God Ua-ti (Lion God of the Zodiac)

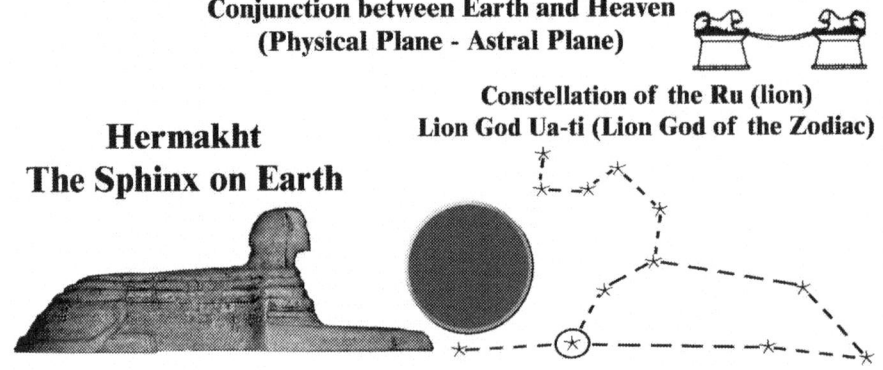

Figure 35: Below- The Ancient Egyptian zodiacal signs for the ages of the Ram, Bull and Lion

Opening of the Mouth with the Imperishable Stars

In the Hermetic Texts, which are the later development in Ancient Egyptian scripture, Hermes, the Greek name ascribed to the Ancient Egyptian god Djehuti, states to his pupil Asclepius (Egyptian Imhotep) that *"Did you know, O Asclepius, that Egypt is made in the image of heaven?"*[195] The Ancient Egyptian Pyramid Texts and the Pert M Heru (Book of Enlightenment) texts contain more references to stellar mysticism. The stellar symbolism of Ancient Egypt relates to the passage of time but also to mystical awakening and spiritual realization.

> As to these all, Maat and Djehuti, they are with Isdesba[48] Lord of Amentet. As to the divine beings behind Asar, they are again Mseti, Hapy, Duamutf, and Kebsenuf. They are behind the Chepesh[49] in the northern heavens.
>
> From Prt M Hru Chap. 4, V. 22

The Chepesh has important mystical symbolism. Mythically it represents the foreleg of the god Set which was torn out and thrown into the heavens by the god Heru during their epic battle. A similar teaching occurs in the Babylonian epic of Gilgemesh[196\197] when the "foreleg of the Bull of Heaven" is ripped out and thrown at the goddess Ishtar, who was the goddess or Queen of Heaven in Mesopotamia. It symbolizes the male generative capacity and is one of the offerings of Hetep given in Chapter 36 (usually referred to as #30B) of the Pert M Heru (Egyptian Book of the Dead). Its cosmic and mystical implications provides us with insight into Kamitan philosophy as well as ancient history.

Also, in ancient times the Chepesh symbol represented the "Northern path" of spiritual evolution. Since the constellation of the Ursa Major ("Great Bear" or "Big Dipper"), known to the Ancient Egyptians as "Meskhetiu," contains *seven* stars and occupied the location referred to as the "Pole Star." As it occupies the pole position it does not move, while all the other stars in the sky circle around it. This constellation, whose symbol is the foreleg, ⌐, was thus referred to as "the imperishables" in the earlier Pyramid Texts: "He (the king-enlightened initiate) climbs to the sky among the imperishable stars."[50]

Akhemu Seku - never setting stars – imperishable

Akhemu Urdu - never resting stars – setting

The Great Pyramid in Egypt, located in the area referred to as "The Giza Plateau" in modern times, incorporated this teaching. The main chamber in the Great Pyramid incorporates two shafts that pointed in ancient times to the Chepesh (Ursa {Bear} Major {Great} - the foreleg) in the north sky and to Orion (Sahu or Sah), the star system of Asar (Osiris) in the southern sky. The imperishable constellation refers to that which is unchanging, absolute, transcendental and perfect.

---

[48] A protector god in the Company of Gods and Goddesses of Djehuti.

[49] Big Dipper, common name applied to a conspicuous constellation in the northern celestial hemisphere, near the North Pole. It was known to the ancient Greeks as the Bear and the Wagon and to the Romans as Ursa Major (the Great Bear) and Septentriones (Seven Plowing Oxen). The seven brightest stars of the constellation form the easily identified outline of a giant dipper. To the Hindus, it represents the seven Rishis, or holy ancient Sages. "Big Dipper," Microsoft (R) Encarta. Copyright (c) 1994 Microsoft Corporation. Copyright (c) 1994 Funk & Wagnall's Corporation.

[50] Pyramid Texts 1120-23. *Egyptian Mysteries*, Lucie Lamy

Figure 36: The Great Pyramid of Egypt with the Mystical Constellations (view from the East) and the Perishable and Imperishable stars.

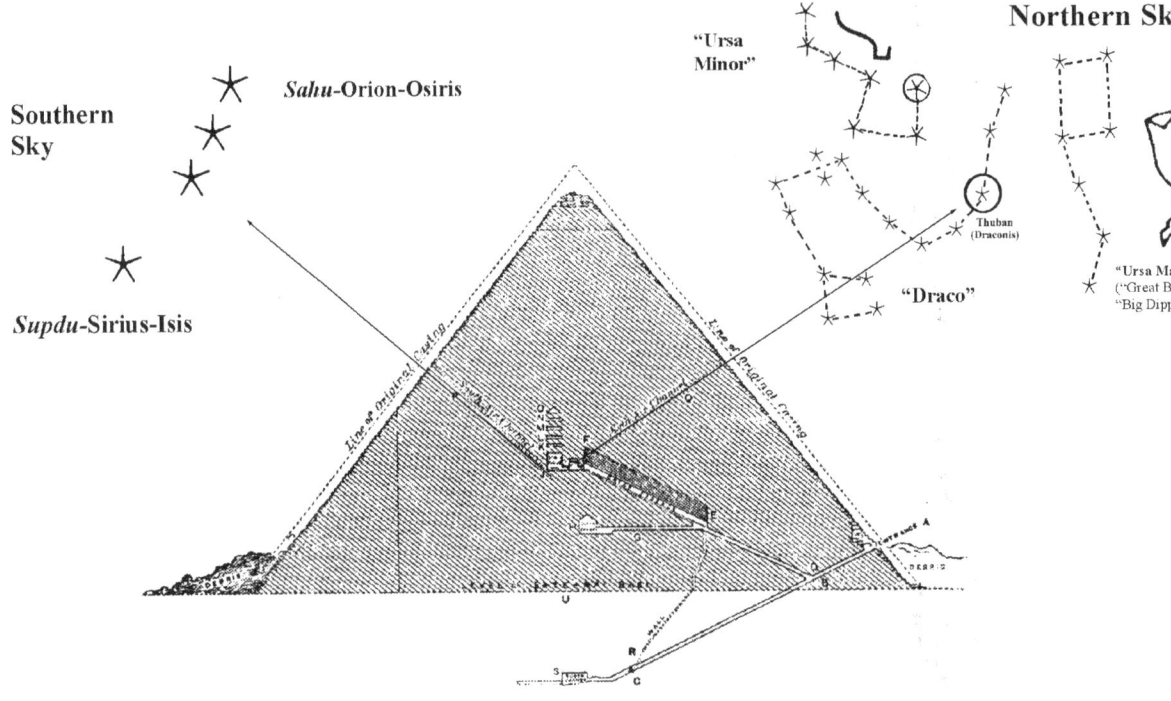

Figure 37: The Great Pyramid of Egypt with the Mystical Constellations (view from the South).

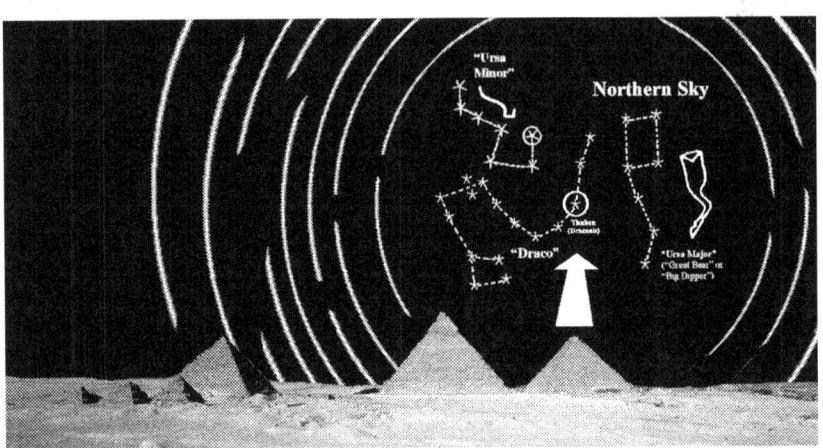

When the Great Pyramids are viewed over the course of one evening, from the south to north, the perishable stars (forming circles, moving below the horizon) can be seen moving around the the imperishable stars (those which do not set, that is go below the horizon) in the center. Time lapse photographs of this constellation (**Meskhetiu - Ursa Major ("Great Bear" or "Big Dipper")**, show it as remaining in the center and other stars moving around it. Also, it does not sink below the horizon and become "reborn" in the eastern horizon each day as do other stars. The Orion constellation refers to that which is changing, incarnating (rising in the east) and becoming. In this manner Asar is reborn through Sopdu (the star Sirius-Aset, Isis) in the form of Heru-Sopdu (Heru who is in Aset), also known as Sirius B. Therefore, mystically, the "Northern Path" is promoted as the path to immortality and enlightenment through the attainment of absolute consciousness which transcends the perishable and ever-changing nature of creation. The "Southern Path" is the process of reincarnation, renewal and repeated embodiment (*uhem ankh* {Kamitan}), for the purpose of further spiritual evolution through self-discovery by means of human experiences. This teaching is also reflected in the zodiac inscription from the temple of Hetheru at Denderah and in the "Opening of the Mouth Ceremony" where a symbol of the imperishable constellation, ⌐, is carried by the priest. The mystical intent is to open the mind, through mystical wisdom and disciplines, so as to render it *uadjit*, ⟨⟩, (universal and infinite, all-encompassing, unlimited) and beyond the fluctuations of egoism, i.e. mortal consciousness.

figure 38: Below left- Hieroglyph for the Chepesh (foreleg). Center-The Chepesh with constellation.[198] **Right- The Chepesh as part of the Hetep offering in the *Pert M Heru* Texts and temple inscriptions.**

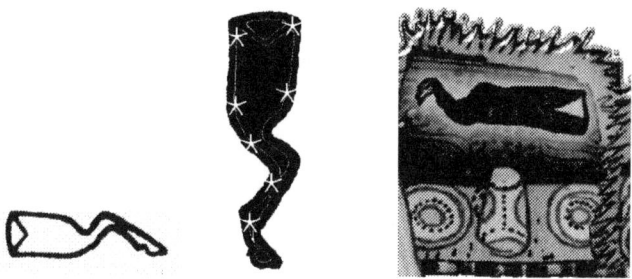

Figure 39: The Hetep Offering Slab with the foreleg symbol.

Used in the Hetep (Hotep) offering table, the leg symbolizes the male gender. The goose symbolizes the female gender. Thus, the initiate offers duality in the form of sex awareness to the divinity in exchange for the realization of non-duality, or the transcendence of gender (dual) consciousness altogether, i.e. the "imperishable" or eternal realization of the Higher Self.

Figure 40: Vignettes from the Opening of the Mouth Ceremonies from the Ancient Egyptian texts. Left- with Chepesh (Chpsh-foreleg), Right with the Seba (Sba) ur instruments.

"O Initiate, I have come in search of you, for I am Horus; I have struck your mouth for you, for I am your beloved son; I have split open your mouth for you... I have split open your eyes for you... with the Chepch (Chpsh) of the Eye of Heru- Chepesh (Foreleg). I have split open your mouth for you... I have split open your eyes for you... with the adze of Upuaut..... with the adze of iron . . . [PT 11-13]

The opening of the mouth and eyes is a mystical teaching relating to expansion in expression (mouth) and awareness (open eyes). These factors (mouth and eyes) are the signs of the existence of consciousness or its absence. From the passages above we learn that the Priests and Priestesses "open" the mouth and eyes by touching them with the ritual instruments which symbolize the eternal, the absolute, i.e. the expansion of consciousness, immortality and spiritual enlightenment. Also, we learn that the adze instrument (Ursa minor) is actually also the Eye of Heru, which is the greatest offering-eucharist of the Egyptian mysteries. The Eye symbolizes divine consciousness as it is one and the same with Heru, Asar and Ra. Therefore, being touched with these instruments means attaining god-consciousness.

AFRICAN ORIGINS OF CIVILIZATION, RELIGION, YOGA MYSTICAL SPIRITUALITY AND ETHICS PHILOSOPHY
NOTES FOR CHAPTER 1

[93] Commonly referred to as Chapter 17
[94] Commonly referred to as Chapter 176
[95] **The Middle Passage: White Ships Black Cargo** by Tom Feelings, John Henrik, Dr Clarke
[96] **Stolen Legacy**, George James
[97] *Black Athena, The Afroasiatic Origins of Classical Civilization* by Martin Bernal
[98] **Destruction of Black Civilization: Great Issues of a Race from 4500bc to 2000ad** by Chancellor Williams
[99] *Stolen Legacy*, George G.M. James
[100] *From Egypt to Greece*, M. Ashby C. M. Books 1997
[101] *Manetho*, W. G. Waddell
[102] Encarta Encyclopedia, Copyright (c) 1994
[103] Gen. 25:26
[104] Gen. 47:9
[105] 60+130+430=620.
[106] 400-130-60=210.
[107] *Bible Myth: The African Origins of the Jewish People* Gary Greenberg
[108] *The Power of Myth*, Joseph Campbell
[109] *Traveler's Key to Ancient Egypt*, John Anthony West
[110] *Black Man of The Nile and His Family* by
[111] *The African Origin of Civilization*, *Civilization or Barbarism.* Cheikh Anta Diop
[112] Photo: From Cheikh Anta Diop's "Civilisation ou Barbarie", Courtesy of Présence Africaine.
[113] *Arts and Crafts of Ancient Egypt*, Flinders Petrie
[114] Published in 1833 by the son of Champollion-Figeac, brother of Jean Fransçois Champollion.
[115] Ruins of Empires by Count Volney, (Diop, 1974, p. 28).
[116] The Zambesi and Its Tributaries, p. 526. N. Y., 1866.
[117] The Uganda Protectorate, Vol. II, p. 472. London, 1902.
[118] The Mediterranean Races, p. 243. N. Y., 1901.
[119] Royal Soc. of Arts Jour., Vol. XLIX, p. 594. 1901.
[120] *Egyptiene ancienne.*Paris: Collection l'Univers, 1839, pp 26-27
[121] Rawlinson, G. The Story of Egypt, p. 252. London. 1887.
[122] *Historie ancienne des peubles de l'Orient.*
[123] *Heresy in the University: The Black Athena Controversy and the Responsibilities of American Intellectuals* by Jacques Berlinerblan
[124] George, *Crimes of Perception*, xi (emphasis added); Peters, *Heresy and Authority*, 15, 17.
[125] P. L. Berger, Heretical Imperative, 28. Foucault, History *of* Sexuality, vol. 1, 93. On Foucault's use of this term, see James Miller, Passion *of* Michel Foucault, 108. Char, "Partage formel XXII," 0euvres completes, 160.
[126] Bernal, Black Athena 1: 2 (emphasis in original).
[127] Metropolitan Museum New York
[128] *Compton's Interactive Encyclopedia*. Copyright (c) 1994, 1995
[129] Copyright © 1995 Helicon Publishing Ltd Webster Encyclopedia
[130] *Gods and Symbols of Ancient Egypt* by Manfred Lurker
[131] *Compton's Interactive Encyclopedia*. Copyright (c) 1994, 1995
[132] *Compton's Interactive Encyclopedia*. Copyright (c) 1994, 1995
[133] Feuerstein, Georg, *The Shambhala Encyclopedia of Yoga* 1997
[134] *Aset (Isis) and Nebethet (Nephthys)* are ancient Egyptian goddesses who preside over the resurrection of Asar.
[135] See the book *Resurrecting Osiris* by Muata Ashby
[136] "Kush, Early Kingdom of," *Microsoft® Encarta® Africana*. ©&(p) 1999 Microsoft Corporation. All rights reserved.
[137] Architecture - Medinet Habu temple -New Kingdom – Waset Egypt
[138] American Heritage Dictionary
[139] Reproduced from an object in the Leyden Museum.
[140] "Kush, Early Kingdom of," *Microsoft® Encarta® Africana*. ©&(p) 1999 Microsoft Corporation. All rights reserved.
[141] Copyright © 1995 Helicon Publishing Ltd Encyclopedia
[142] Muata Ashby
[143] *Atlas of Ancient Egypt*, John Baines and Jaromir Malek, 1980
[144] *Atlas of Ancient Egypt*, John Baines and Jaromir Malek, 1980
[145] *The Complete Temples of Ancient Egypt*, Richard Wilkinson, 2000
[146] *Doshi, Saryu, Editor-Indian Council for Cultural Relations* *India and Egypt: Influences and Interactions* 1993
[147] Random House Encyclopedia.
[148] 1550 B.C.E.-1307 B.C.E. (conservative traditional Egyptology dating). 1580 B.C.E Based on 18th Dynasty inscriptions.
[149] *The Ancient Egyptians: Their Life and Customs,* Sir Garner Wilkinson

[150] American Heritage Dictionary
[151] Copyright © 1995 Helicon Publishing Ltd Encyclopedia
[152] Architecture - Medinet Habu temple -New Kingdom — Waset Egypt
[153] **adz** or **adze** (ădz) *n.* An axlike tool with a curved blade at right angles to the handle, used for dressing wood.
[154] Copyright © 1995 Helicon Publishing Ltd Encyclopedia
[155] **Nekhen News,** Expedition reports, Hierakonpolis, Petrie Museum of Egyptian Archaeology University College, London
[156] *Egypt Uncovered*, Vivian Davies and Renée Friedman
[157] Greek name *Sais*
[158] Copyright © 1995 Helicon Publishing Ltd Encyclopedia
[159] Metropolitan Museum New York
[160] Encarta Encyclopedia, Copyright (c) 1994
[161] Copyright © 1995 Helicon Publishing Ltd Encyclopedia
[162] Anunian Theology by Muata Ashby
[163] Copyright © 1995 Helicon Publishing Ltd Encyclopedia
[164] Copyright © 1995 Helicon Publishing Ltd Encyclopedia
[165] The southern kingdom when, after Solomon's death, only the tribes of Judah and Benjamin followed the house of David. There were wars between the kings of Judah and Israel for 60 years. Random House Encyclopedia Copyright (C) 1983,1990 by Random House Inc.
[166] Josiah (c. 647-609 B.C.E.) King of Judah. Grandson of Manasseh and son of Amon, he succeeded to the throne at the age of eight. The discovery of a Book of Instruction (probably Deuteronomy, a book of the Old Testament) during repairs of the Temple 621 B.C.E. stimulated thorough reform, which included the removal of all sanctuaries except that of Jerusalem. He was killed in a clash at Megiddo with Pharaoh-nechoh, king of Egypt.
Copyright © 1995 Helicon Publishing Ltd Encyclopedia
[167] Copyright © 1995 Helicon Publishing Ltd Encyclopedia
[168] *Egypt: Child of Africa,* Ivan Van Sertima 1994
[169] *Ancient Egyptian Construction and Architecture* by Somers Clarke and R. Engelbach
[170] Ibid.
[171] This is the earliest confirmed date for the use of the advanced calendar in Ancient Egypt.
[172] *Arts and Crafts of Ancient Egypt*, Flinders Petrie
[173] A group of people who originally lived in Asia Minor (Middle East), especially Arabia with mixed North (Aryan?) and East (European) Asian and African ethnicity.
[174] Conducted by Muata Ashby while traveling throughout Egypt 2000 – speaking to northern Arab-Egyptians (in Cairo) and one Nubian-Egyptian in Aswan
[175] *Traveler's Key to Ancient Egypt*, John Anthony West
[176] *Histories,* Herodotus
[177] *Serpent in the Sky,* John Anthony West, p. 97
[178] Random House Encyclopedia Copyright (C) 1983,1990
[179] "North Star," Microsoft (R) Encarta. Copyright (c) 1994 Microsoft Corporation. Copyright (c) 1994 Funk & Wagnall's Corporation.
[180] "Zodiac," Microsoft (R) Encarta. Copyright (c) 1994 Microsoft Corporation. Copyright (c) 1994 Funk & Wagnall's Corporation.
[181] *Echoes of the Old Darkland*, Charles Finch
[182] Between the years 1960-1970
[183] *Secrets of the Great Pyramid,* Peter Tompkins
[184] A "Great Cycle" *(Mahayuga)* of cosmic time.
[185] I.e., at the ending of the cosmic eon, Wagner's *Götterdämmerung*.
[186] *The Mythic Image*, Joseph Campbell
[187] Sacred Science by Schwaller de Lubicz
[188] Diodorus Book 23
[189] This illustration appeared in the book *History of Egypt*-Samuel Sharp 1876 A.C.E.
[190] *Descriptions of Egypt*
[191] G. Maspero, *The Passing of the Empires* (New York, 1900).
[192] *Echoes of the Old Darkland*, Charles Finch
[193] *Serpent in the Sky,* John Anthony West, p. 100
[194] These illustrations appeared in the book *The Ancient Egyptians: Their Life and Customs*-Sir J. Garner Wilkinson 1854 A.C.E.
[195] *Hermetica,* Asclepius III, Solos Press ed., p. 136
[196] Col. V. l, 161
[197] **Gilgamesh**, legendary king of Babylonia, hero of an epic poem written on clay tablets, found in the ruins of Nineveh; epic has affinities with Old Testament, contains story of the flood. Excerpted from *Compton's Interactive Encyclopedia*. Copyright (c) 1994, 1995
[198] Sample from various Middle Kingdom Period coffin Lids.

Chapter 2: Religion and Culture in Ancient Egypt and Other African Nations

Gue Nyame
Ghananian Adinkira symbol meaning: "God is the Supreme power"

Overview of African Religions [199,200,201,202,203]

The term "African Religions" as used in our present context relates to the forms of religions that were developed on the continent of Africa by its indigenous or native peoples from ancient times. It will refer to those forms of religions which existed prior to the introduction of religions from outside of Africa and prior to influences from other societies outside of Africa. As of 1999, about half of the people in Africa consider themselves as adherents to Islam. A lesser number are adherents to Christianity and African Religions. A smaller number are adherents to Judaism or Hinduism.[51] So despite the work of Muslim and Christian missionaries, a substantial number of Africans still practice one of the African Religions. Also there are a substantial number of people of African descent who practice one of the African Religions outside of Africa as well.

Though the colonial period in Africa was short-lived when compared to the overall view of history, it had a profound effect on the culture and also never truly ended in many parts of the continent because of the imposition of *Neocolonialism* (control of individual countries by controlling the government that is run by locals.) and the new moves in the late 20th century to impose *Globalization* (control of the world economy by Western governments) on the world community. The following excerpt from Compton's Encyclopedia concisely sums up the colonial history of European nations in Africa.

> "In what is called the "Scramble for Africa," European nations partitioned Africa at the Berlin West Africa Conference (1884-1885). The Germans got southwestern Africa, along with Tanganyika in East Africa. The Portuguese got Mozambique and Angola, in southern Africa. Belgium took the Congo, and France got Senegal, the Cameroons, and several other colonies in the western Sudan and Central Africa. The British got the rest, including Kenya and Uganda in East Africa, the Gold Coast (now Ghana) and the territory that became Nigeria in West Africa. The British already controlled Egypt, which they had occupied in 1882, as well as English-speaking Cape Colony and Natal on the southern tip of Africa. The British also dominated Southern Rhodesia (now Zimbabwe) and Northern Rhodesia (now Zambia) through the British South Africa Company under the leadership of Cecil Rhodes. The result was that almost every part of the African continent was a European colony."[204]

Another method to discern the essential elements of African religion is to study its most ancient forms, and then to correlate these with the aspects that persist into the present and compare these with the aspects that developed later. Thus, the study of Ancient Egyptian-Nubian (Cushite) religion is of extreme importance in reconstructing African religion and philosophy. As we have already seen, there are several areas of

---

[51]"African Religions: An Interpretation," *Microsoft® Encarta® Africana.* ©&(p) 1999 Microsoft Corporation. All rights reserved.

commonality between Ancient Egyptian-Nubian religion and other African religions. In this manner, Ancient Egyptian-Nubian spirituality may be seen as a centerpiece and perhaps even a pinnacle of African religious culture and philosophy.

The developments in Ancient Egypt are central to understanding African Religions and their history both before and after the rise of Kamitan civilization. This is because there was a close relationship between Neterian Religion and other African religions, as there was a relationship between Ancient Egypt and other African nations. The connection between Ancient Egypt and Nubia has been elaborated in previous chapters. Also, the fact that the Ancient Egyptians were "black" Africans and that the original Ancient Egyptians originated in the heart of Africa, the land now called Uganda, was also explained earlier. What is important to understand now is that the fundamental Ancient Egyptian Religious tenets can be found in other African religions. This means that the tenets were a common product of African spirituality. In this context, Ancient Egypt exemplified the concepts of African Spirituality in their most highly advanced form. This form, (Neterian Religion – Shetaut Neter) also led to the development of pre-Judaic and Islamic Arabian religions, Judaism, Christianity, as we will see throughout this book.

One of the problems in studying African religion is that the concepts, traditions and rituals of the varied religions were generally not committed to writing. The exception to this is the Neterian Religion, where there is extensive writing that has survived. Western researchers have tried to advance the idea that Northeast Africa and Ancient Egyptian culture and religion was part of Middle Eastern (Arabic) culture and religion, and that "Sub-Saharan Africa" is the land of "blacks" who do not have a refined notion of spirituality. From this, negative stereotyping led to the denigration of African culture and its people as backward savages who live in the jungle, ignorantly worshiping pagan gods. To those involved in initiating and perpetuation the salve trade, this made the enslavement of Africans[52] a more justifiable act during the period after the colonization of the New World (1492 A.C.E.-1800 A.C.E.) and then the colonization of Africa itself (1750 A.C.E.-1960 A.C.E.). The lack of scriptures or worship in western style churches or Mosques was used by Europeans and Arabs as an excuse to claim that they were bringing religion to Africans, and thus, according to the mandates of their scriptures (especially as will be discussed with respect to the Judeo-Christians and Muslims which sanctions the conquering of other peoples to "spread the word"), they were able to justify their actions to themselves as being Divine in nature. Another problem is that the African religious culture was and continues to be supported by language and shared history. The introduction of European languages, and the systematic prevention of the African people from speaking their own native languages or introducing tribal names has led to a situation of inter-tribal conflicts which were not previously present. This is due to the introduction of distorted *ethnonyms,* names given to the groups of villages or nations by the Europeans based on their anthropological studies and the pre-colonial African names of societies. This means that people who were at one time actually relatives might be caught in two different geographic areas, but due to colonial pressures their common language and common identity is suppressed until forgotten. Then the two begin to see one another as strangers, following the cause of the colonial ruler against the colonial ruler of the other territory. Thus, the modern interpretation for the word "tribe" as *"a group of people who are descended from common ancestors and ruled by a hereditary "chief," who share a single culture (including, in particular, language and religion), and live in a well-defined geographical region,*[53] is a misapplication as concerns many groups in present day Africa due to all of the distortion of African society in the past 200 years. In other words, people living in a present day "tribe" may not have a connection with common ancestors from other tribe members, or the tribe may have no such legacy because the disruption by colonists resulted in the tribal memory being lost or in other cases, the members of the tribe may be composed of people who lost their cultural identity (refugees, orphans, etc.) and were brought together for political or economic reasons and forced to speak a language, etc. This definition of the word "tribe" may be equated with or thought of interchangeably with the term "ethnic group."

African culture views religion as a living aspect of life which is passed on from parent to child and from elders and storytellers to the younger generations who grow up and continue the tradition by passing on the myths, culture and religious traditions to the next generation, and so on. This is called the *Sacred Oral*

---

[52] From the 1520s to the 1860s an estimated 11 to 12 million African men, women, and children were forcibly embarked on European vessels for a life of slavery in the Western Hemisphere. Many more Africans were captured or purchased in the interior of the continent but a large number died before reaching the coast. About 9 to 10 million Africans survived the Atlantic crossing to be purchased by planters and traders in the New World, where they worked principally as slave laborers in plantation economies requiring a large workforce. "Transatlantic Slave Trade," *Microsoft® Encarta® Africana.* © 1999 Microsoft Corporation. All rights reserved. Author's note: Other estimates run much higher but this one has been presented here to avoid needless arguments over the issue. Nevertheless this number pales in comparison to the deaths caused by the forced enslavement and kidnapping of Africans which estimates project at 100,000,000 (one hundred million) or more men, women and children.

[53] "Ethnicity and Identity in Africa: An Interpretation" *Microsoft® Encarta® Africana.* ©1999 Microsoft Corporation. All rights reserved.

Tradition in African religion. The *Sacred Oral Tradition* was passed on through mentorship, rituals, and intensive periods of education, including rites of passage.[54]

European travelers and missionaries later realized that the practice of religion did exist in Africa, but it was not consistent with their interpretation of what religion was supposed to be. Despite this realization, the invalidation of African spirituality continued and the missionary movements of Christianity and Islam continued, not in the spirit of sharing views on religion or having a meeting of minds on religious issues, but from a perspective of bringing a "superior" religion to people with inferior or no religion. This attitude also led to the denigration of African people as well.

Due to the transatlantic slave trade, colonization of Africa and the ensuing chaos which was perpetrated by European nations on African nations, with the special intent of preventing the continuation of the transmittance and practice of African religions and the promotion of Western religions and social concepts, the traditions of African religions have sometimes been altered, disrupted or completely lost. The lack of concrete writings prior to the time of the pre-African holocaust has led to a situation wherein much reconstruction of Ancient African traditions has been required. Some European scholars began this work, but many have been accused of distorting African religion, skewing it in light of Western cultural values and religious tenets, and in the context of European religion being superior by virtue of the fact that Europeans came to believe that monotheism is the advanced concept of religion. This means that some of the original wisdom of the practices, myths and systems of gods and goddesses has been misunderstood. The particular form of monotheism espoused by the three major Western religions (Judaism, Christianity, Islam) is actually a narrow concept which, when examined, is actually a form of intensified dogmatic idolatry. In contrast to African Religions, there are several examples of Western religions going to war against one another. The same is not the case with African religions originally. Conflicts between African groups did exist but not for the same reasons as between the Europeans; one such issue is ethnic differences as in the case of Rwanda. However, in modern times, Africans have fought each other over religion, especially those involved with Christianity and Islam. This is because the concept of African religion, while incorporating the teaching of monotheism, actually incorporates the pantheistic understanding as well. Pantheism relates to the understanding the God or the Divine, manifests as Creation and everything in it. So here we are confronted with the African concept of *Polytheistic Monotheism*, system of religion presenting a Supreme Being with many "lesser gods and goddesses" who serve the Supreme and sustain Creation and lead human beings to spiritual enlightenment and worldly prosperity. These religious principles will be discussed more in depth later on.

In this context the Western concept of monotheism has been degraded to a circumscribed idea that is expressed in a strict form of expression based on a "revelation." This is erroneous in view of the actions that Western Culture has perpetrated on other cultures and among themselves (wars, slavery, economic subjugation, etc.). The concept of revelation in the Western religions (Judaism, Christianity and Islam) holds that some absolute and perfect knowledge about the Supreme Being has been given. This is in stark contrast to the philosophy and tenet of African Religions (including Ancient Egyptian philosophy), Indian Vedanta philosophy, Buddhist philosophy, Chinese Taoism and other mystical traditions which holds that which is transcendental and unintelligible cannot be related in words, as the intellect cannot fathom the true nature of the Supreme Being. Thus, the Western religions and some orthodox religions that developed in Asia Minor such as the Zoroastrian religion, stand alone with the narrow concept of the Supreme Being that is touted as a high revelation that must be imposed on the rest of the world's societies.

As missionaries preached throughout Africa, they translated the European texts into the African languages. In the process of doing so, the missionaries realized that there was a term in African spirituality for "Supreme Being." But even then they attempted to characterize this African concept as a limited idea related to a Creator personality, and they viewed the rituals and propitiations to lesser divinities as proof of the inferiority of African religious concept. This European view of the African concept of the Supreme Being was called *deus otiotus* meaning "a remote god who is rarely invoked." The African concept of the Supreme is so lofty that it views a direct approach to the Supreme Being, an unintelligible existence, as presumptuous and irreverent. As expressed above, the African religious philosophical view is that the very naming of such a being constitutes the act of conditioning it, and this is contradictory to its essential nature. Further, the so-called reverence of Western religions which extol the glory of the Supreme Being does not cause the European practitioners of religion to be more faithful or peaceful, as history has shown. Rather, what develops is a form of lip service which denigrates the religious process since the words are expressed but the reverence, if any, does not translate to virtue or even tolerance of others. So the Western idea that reverencing a Supreme Being directly makes the people or the society more pious is unfounded. Within

---

[54] *Microsoft® Encarta® Africana.* ©1999 Microsoft Corporation. All rights reserved.

authentic Ancient African systems of Religion, the Supreme Being is to be approached not through intellectualizing (naming and classifying), but through ritual which facilitates the entering into transcendental consciousness wherein the being can be directly experienced without the encumbrances of illusory and limited mental concepts. Also, an approach through gods and goddesses was devised.

Further, Ancient African Religion does not therefore ascribe a gender to the Supreme Being. Thus it is less susceptible to male chauvinism (sexism, bigotry) unlike the patriarchal western religions. So there is more of a balance in African Religion between the roles played by men and women in the religious practices. Hence, philosophy and ritual in African Religion are highly advanced and integral aspects of religious practice and therefore, rituals are not primitive displays of superstition.

Some Western scholars have characterized African societies as resistant to change and this view has been accepted by some leading African scholars of religion such as John Mbiti. This in part explains the persistence of African religion despite the tumultuous history of Africa. In some parts of present day Africa, there is an upsurge in the revival of traditional African religion. Some Africans living in and outside of Africa feel that many social problems are due to interference from European governments, businesses and religions and a backlash of negative sentiment has begun to develop in recent years against the Western Culture and religion.

Table 12: List of African Religions

Kushite Religion	**Bambara Religion**	**Igbo Religion**
Kamitan (Ancient Egyptian) Religion	**Bambuti Religion**	**Khol Religion**
	Bandembu Religion	**Langi Religion**
	Banyakyusa Religion	**Lovedu Religion**
!Kung Religion	**Banyakyusa Religion**	**Lugbara Religion**
Acholi Religion	**Banyamwezi Religion**	**Maasai Religion**
Akamba Religion	**Banyankore Religion**	**Mende Religion**
Akhan Religion	**Banyarwanda Religion**	**Nuer Religion**
Akikuyu Religion	**Banyoro Religion**	**Nupe Religion**
Ashanti Religion	**Barundi Religion**	**San Religion**
Ateso Religion	**Basukuma Religion**	**Shilluk Religion**
Babemba Religion	**Dinka Religion**	**Shona Religion**
Bachagga Religion	**Dogon Religion**	**Sotho Religion**
Bacongo Religion	**Edo Religion**	**Swazi Religion**
Bafipa Religion	**Ewe Religion**	**Tiv Religion**
Baganda Religion	**Fang Religion**	**Tswana Religion**
Bagisu Religion	**Fanti Religion**	**Western Africa**
Bahaya Religion	**Fon Religion**	**Xhosa Religion**
Bahehe Religion	**Ga Religion**	**Yoruba Religion**
Baka Religion	**Galla Religion**	**Zulu Religion**
Baluba Religion		
Bamakonda Religion		**Unknown Past Religions**

Manifestations of African Religion in Latin America and the Caribbean

The religions of Latin America and the Caribbean are strongly rooted in African religion as a result of African peoples being brought to the Americas as slaves. These religions therefore reflect the slavery experiences (including but not limited to racism, exploitation and mistreatment) of the original African slaves and their descendants. They also reflect a mixture of traditions, including religious elements from the religions of the slave masters which were not in the original traditions brought from Africa. Some of the developments in the Americas included elements from Native American religions. One example of this is the spirituality of the African slaves who were brought to the Island of Puerto Rico in the Caribbean.

The first Africans actually arrived in Puerto Rico with Columbus in 1493 A.C.E as sailors. The African slave trade in Puerto Rico was not authorized by the Spanish government until 1510 A.C.E. The Taino Native American population were the native inhabitants of Puerto Rico and they were also enslaved by the Spaniards upon their arrival to the island. The enslavement and mistreatment of Taínos went on before and after slavery was permitted by the Spanish government. It was legally prohibited by a royal decree in 1542. However, the Spanish settlers (slave masters) continued to enslave them illegally. Since they were not physically suited for the heavy physical labor and violent clashes with European slavers as well as the rigors of European diseases, their numbers were reduced dramatically. The African slaves who were brought to the island of Puerto Rico, beginning in 1510 A.C.E., created a new culture as they mixed with the Taino Native American Population, creating an admixture of religious thought. The culture of Puerto Rico was further shaped by the amalgamation with the Spanish ruling class and the later Anglo-Americans. The Anglo-Americans who took control of the country imposed a form of racism that led to the development of a form of caste system. The almost extinct Native American population and those of (unmixed) African descent were segregated and discriminated against in favor of the mulatto population. However, even within this population, the darker skinned members were discriminated against in favor of lighter skinned members, who received the greater latitude of freedom in the general society. This policy of discrimination based on the shading of skin was instituted by the Europeans generally, but intensified when the USA took over Puerto Rico after the so called Spanish – American War.

In present day Puerto Rico, an independence movement has managed to prevent statehood. However, the majority of the population is pro-western. The society maintains an aspect of Creole[55] culture wherein the lighter skinned members of the population feel a superiority that is supported by preferential treatment from the Anglo society of the United States. It must be clear that in most, if not all of the groups brought over by slave masters, slavery destroyed traditional African secret societies and priesthoods.[205] Roman Catholicism was the only officially recognized religion in Puerto Rico as Puerto Rico was a colony of Spain and Roman Catholicism was the official religion of Spain also. However, most of the population practiced varied forms of religion which combined the African beliefs with Christian images and traditions. This situation was typical in other parts of the Caribbean and the Americas. Puerto Rico, like other Caribbean and American countries, has produced African scholars and African patriots.

Perhaps one of the best-known scholars in the field of African history and culture is Arturo Alfonso Schomburg. However, not many people know that he was born in Puerto Rico in 1874. He grew up in Puerto Rico and studied in the Dutch West Indies. When confronted by another student who challenged him by saying that peoples of African descent had not done anything significant in history, he countered with the achievements of those people of African descent on the island of Puerto Rico who had made such advances in the arts and writing that they had gained international recognition. This further spurred him on to travel the world seeking to document the achievements of Africans. He became a mentor to many 20th century Africentrists and is honored for amassing one of the largest and finest collections of books and evidences on the African contribution to humanity. By the time of his death in 1938, Arturo Alfonso Schomburg was recognized as a great scholar, humanist and African historian.

The African influence on Puerto Rican culture can be seen in such areas as the arts, food, music, dance, and language. For example, there is an African beat called *La Bomba,* that is still played especially within the circles of people of African descent and which has been recognized as an influence on latin music. The last enslaved Africans who came to the island were relatively young and came from Nigeria, Ghana, and Zaire.[206] Some African words that survive in the Puerto Rican language include:

- bembe – party
- bembas – lips
- guarapo – sugarcane juice
- mongo – limp

---

[55] **Creoles**, a name adopted by or applied to a number of ethnic groups in the New World who were descended from European colonists and/or African slaves. "Creole" can also refer to the language of such groups. Creoles," *Microsoft® Encarta® Africana.* ©&(p) 1999 Microsoft Corporation. All rights reserved.

The major African-derived religions of Latin American and Caribbean slaves include:

- Shango in Trinidad – Based on Yoruba Religion mixed with Christianity.
- Rastafarianism in Jamaica – based on Ethiopian Christianity and Judaism.
- Umbanda in Brazil – Based on Yoruba Religion mixed with Christianity
- Candomblé in Brazil – 3 Types all based on Yoruba Religion (Supreme Being with Orishas)
- Voodoo in Haiti – From Fon Vodun religion of Benin
- Santería in Cuba – Combination of Yoruba Religion and Christianity

The Common Fundamental Principles of African Religion

For many years, Westerners, specifically anthropologists, Christian missionaries and Muslims, did not regard African Religion as "true" religion. Muslims moving into Africa called the Africans *kaffirs*, or "unbelievers," which relates them as people who are atheistic, as opposed to having their own religion. Christians adopted the similar terms, and henceforth African religion came to be regarded as magic or superstition, fetishism or animism. If we look closely at the traditions of other African religions besides the Ancient Egyptian, we will discover that many, if not all, of the fundamental aspects of the highly evolved Kamitan religion that were later infused into the world religions can also be found in the African Religions of the past and present. Among the essential concepts common to all African religions are the following:

BLACK AFRICAN RELIGION (Sub-Saharan)	ANCIENT EGYPTIAN RELIGION (Corresponding name given to the same teaching in Kamit)
1. There is one God (Supreme Being)	1. Neter
2. That God expresses as Lesser divinities = gods and goddesses	2. Neteru
3. God and the universe are One =All objects in the universe are alive and divine	3. Neberdjer
4. Seek to discover the Menaing of Life.	4. Shetaut Neter
5. No separation between Sacred and Secular	5. Neter – Neterit, Heka - Hekat
6. Human beings have fallen from divinity due to vice	6. Isfet
7. Human beings can raise themselves up (discover the Divine) through virtue	7. Maakheru
8. Social order achieved through Ubuntu (African Spiritual Humanism)	8. Maat
9. Divine monarchy - King and Queen (A) administer secular (cultural) duties such as protecting the populace and administering equal justice for all and (B) (non-secular duties) officiate at spiritual ceremonies (as heads of the national religion)	9. Peraah (Pharaoh)
10. Men and Women can serve as priests and priestesses with equal rights and privilages.	10. Hm and Hmt
11. Highest Goal of Life = Mortal humans discover god and become godlike	11. Akhu

The Stages of African Religion

The Stages of African Religion		
Program of Religion (Universal Religion) 3-Stages	African Religion	Sema (Smai) Tawi (Egyptian Yoga) Based on the teachings of the Temple of Aset (Aswan, Egypt)
Myth	Storytelling (myths – proverbs)	Listening (to spiritual scriptures, teachings)
Ritual	Ritual (ceremony – Virtuous living)	Reflection (on & practice of the teachings)
Mysticism/Metaphysics	Ecstasy (Transcendental experience)	Meditation (on the teachings)

The complete program of religion has three steps which are necessary for the goal of religion, to discover and experience God, to be realized. Any spiritual movement that includes these steps can be called "religion" regardless of the name that it may be given by the culture that practices them. These steps include *Myth, Ritual* and *Mysticism* or *Metaphysics*. The table above shows how these three steps or stages manifest in African Religion (2nd column) and also how that same program is enjoined in the practice of Egyptian Yoga (3rd column). Egyptian Yoga (Sema Tawi)[207] may be thought of as the advanced disciplines to be practiced in order to promote the highest goal of the religious movement.

In African Religion, storytelling achieves the purpose of transmitting myths which contain the basic concepts of human identity as part of a culture, and offers insight into the nature of the universe. Myths also contain a special language of self-knowledge and also proverbs that provide moral education for an ethical society. Rituals are formal (ceremony) and informal (virtuous living) practices which allow a human being to come into harmony within themselves, the environment and the Spirit. This movement leads to an ecstatic experience which transcends time and space and allows a human being to discover and experience the Divine.

The African Definition for the Word "Religion"

Most African religions do not have a world that is correspondent to the western term *religion*. However, there are terms to describe the various activities, rituals, and traditions of the religious process. The African culture that developed in northeast Africa (Ancient Egyptian) did have a name for the practices and concepts of religion. In the Ancient Egyptian texts, a term appears which is used to describe the religious process as well as the disciplines to attain entry into knowledge of the higher aspects of spirituality, i.e. religion: *Shetaut Neter*.

Shetaut Neter
(Secrets about the Divine Self)

The term above is derived from *Sheta* (Mystery), *Sheta* (Hidden) and *Neter* (The Divinity). Thus we can now see why the Ancient Egyptian religion has come to be referred to as the "Egyptian Mysteries." Actually, this term is more closely approximated by the Chinese term "Tao." The term Tao in Taoism relates to the "Way of Nature." The Ancient Egyptian term relates to the quality of divinity which is "hidden." Thus, in Kamitan spirituality it means "the process of uncovering or discovering what is hidden or unknown about the Spirit - (Divine Self-Goddess-God)

The Concept of The Supreme Being and the Gods and Goddesses in African Religion

Pa Neter

In the Kamit religion, Pa-Neter means "The Supreme Being" and neteru, means "the gods and goddesses or cosmic forces in Creation." Also, the word "neteru" refers to creation itself. So, neter-u emanates from Neter. Creation is nothing but Supreme Being who has assumed various forms or neteru: trees, cake, bread, human beings, metal, air, fire, water, animals, planets, space, electricity, etc. The neteru are cosmic forces emanating from the Supreme Being. This is a profound teaching which should be reflected upon constantly so that the mind may become enlightened to its deeper meaning and thereby discover the Divinity in nature. The Divine Self is not only in Creation but is the very essence of every human being as well. Therefore, the substratum of every human being is in reality God as well. The task of authentic spiritual practice such as Yoga is to discover this essential nature within one's own heart. This can occur if one reflects upon this teaching and realizes its meaning by discovering its reality in the deepest recesses of one's own experience. When this occurs, the person who has attained this level of self-discovery is referred to as having become enlightened. They have discovered their true, divine nature. They have discovered their oneness with the Divine Self.

African religions recognize powers that emanate from the Supreme Being that circulate in the universe like a kind of *life force*. For example, the Dogon worship Amma, the Supreme Being, whose vital force, operates throughout the universe, and is called *Nyama*. The Igbo of southeastern Nigeria call the Supreme Being Chiukwu or Chineke, and the life force that operates in the universe is known as *Chi*[56]. Another example is to be found in Ancient Egyptian religion with the concept of Neberdjer, the Supreme Being, and Sekhem as the life force which operates throughout the universe. In this manner, the life force itself is to be understood as an intelligent cosmic energy which pervades all of Creation, sustaining it at all times and thereby also unifying it as well.

In African religion the Supreme Being is viewed as a transcendental essence which cannot be defined and therefore cannot be approached directly. One important reason given as to why the lesser spirit powers are invoked while the Supreme Being is seldom invoked or the recipient of offerings is that the Supreme Being, as the ultimate and all-pervasive power in the universe, already owns all and can therefore, receive nothing. For this reason representations of the Supreme Being do not occur in African religions, only the manifesting aspects are given form. These are used to promote the religious movement of the individual by allowing the individual to approach and understand a concrete aspect of the transcendental Spirit. This understanding of course relates to the higher, mystical aspect of religion. Thus, in African religion we see a consistent pattern of structure in the way in which the Spirit is presented across the panorama of African nations. This structure is simple, but extremely profound in conceptualization: The transcendental Supreme Being manifests as lesser or associated powers that emanate from the ultimate source (the same Supreme Being). There are also human beings that, through virtue, become higher powers, i.e. gods and goddesses. Thus, the higher concept behind the practice of ancestor worship in African religion is not of worshipping the souls of the departed relatives, but of propitiating the saints (deified forbears, i.e. canonized) and sages of the past who have elevated themselves and who have become part of the cosmic forces of the Supreme Being. This pattern holds true for African Religions including Ancient Egyptian religion. Again, this is the same course taken by the Western religions, although they do not admit nor profess to view the angels and saints in this way, in practice, many of the followers of those religions worship the angels and saints in the same fashion as within African Religion.

In most African religions, including the Ancient Egyptian, masks, headdress, costumes, the impersonation of lesser divinities are used as means to attract and propitiate the lesser spirits. Statues are also made of the

---

[56] Which is incidentally also the name for the life force in Chinese and Japanese spirituality.

lesser spirits as symbols (and not as idols in the Western sense of the concept). These are also used to attract and propitiate the lesser spirits. Again, these representations are not made of the Supreme Being.

Since the African Religious concept holds that God and the Universe are one, it follows thst there is no conflict between what is secular or sacred and the current, ongoing conflict in the West over Creation or Evolution as the cause behind the universe is inappropriate.

The Consistent Pattern of Structure in African Religion:

Supreme Being
⇕
Gods and Goddesses
↑
Deified Ancestors
↑
Mortal Human Beings

Human beings may attain the status of higher being through a life of virtue and or righteous leadership. This concept is accentuated in the religions of the peoples of East, Central, and Southern Africa, as well as the ancient Northeast (Nubia-Egypt) Africa. It is acknowledged within the philosophy that many of the lesser spirits in the religions of those areas once lived as human beings, often as kings. This is especially true of the Buganda of Uganda and the Shona in Zimbabwe.[57] Also, Ancient Egypt is to be included in this category, since there was a high teaching related to the Sheps and the Akhus. Shep means venerated ancestor and Akhu means enlightened ancestor, someone who has attained spiritual enlightenment. Also, the Pharaonic system of Ancient Egypt had as one of its main tenets that the kings and queens became divinities upon their death. So Ancient Egyptian religion and the religions of other African peoples appear to follow close parallels in many fundamental aspects of religious philosophy as well as the general program of religious movement.

Table 13: Examples of African Religions with the System of Supreme Being and Lesser Divinities[58]

African Religious System	Supreme Being	Lesser Spirits (Gods and Goddesses
Kamit (Ancient Egypt)	✓	✓
Nubia (Kush-Ethiopia)	✓	✓
Bakele	✓	✓
Bambara	✓	✓
Bantu	✓	✓
Buganda	✓	✓
Dahomey	✓	✓
Dinka	✓	✓
Dogon	✓	✓
Dokos	✓	✓
Edjou	✓	✓
Fon	✓	✓
Galla	✓	✓
Gugsa	✓	✓
Igbo	✓	✓
Jola	✓	✓
Makoosa	✓	✓
Masai	✓	✓
Nuer	✓	✓
Shekani	✓	✓
Yoruba	✓	✓

---

[57] *Microsoft® Encarta® Africana.* ©1999 Microsoft Corporation. All rights reserved.
[58] This is a partial list only since the list is quite extensive.

The "High God" and The Gods and Goddesses of Ancient Egypt

There were several "High God" systems in Ancient Egyptian religion as in other African religions. This is the next lowest position in the hierarchy of divinity after the Supreme Being. The term "High God (or Goddess)" means that the highest God or Goddess within that particular system of theology is considered to be the original deity from which all others emanated as cosmic forces. Thus, in the Asarian religion of Ancient Egypt, Asar is known as *Pa Neter* or *The God* (High God) and Creation is composed of the cosmic forces, *neters* or gods and goddesses, which originates from Asar. It is important to understand that the High Gods and Goddesses as well as the Egyptian Trinities originated from the same transcendental Supreme Being which was without name or form, but was referred to as *Neter Neteru* (Neter of Neters - Supreme Being above all gods and goddesses) and *Neb-er-tcher* (Neberdjer – All-encompassing Divinity).

In this manner, the initiate (in virtually all African religions) is to understand that all of the gods and goddesses are in reality symbols, with names and forms, which represent the Divine in the varied manifest forms of nature. This produces a two aspected format of religion in which there is a *personal* aspect and a *transpersonal* aspect of God. The personal aspect is fixed in time and space with a name and form. This form is readily understood by the masses of human beings with ordinary spiritual awareness and is used in myths and stories. The second aspect, the *transpersonal* side, points our interest towards that which lies beyond the symbolic form. This is the *unmanifest* form of the Divine as it is expressed in the mystical teachings of religious mythology. Thus, the High God is a personal symbol or representation, with a name and form, of the nameless, formless, unmanifest and transcendental Supreme Being. The High God or Goddess usually appears alone and gives rise to male and female gods and goddesses and human beings. One important reason given as to why the lesser spirit powers are invoked while the Supreme Being is seldom invoked or the recipient of offerings is that the Supreme Being, as the ultimate and all-pervasive power in the universe, already owns all and can therefore, receive nothing.

Single Supreme, Transcendental Being
(unmanifest realm beyond time and space - names and forms)
⬇
High God or Goddess
⬇
Lesser Gods and Goddesses

The Concept of God and Creation According to Ancient Egyptian Religion and Mystical Philosophy

The term *"Trinity"* was misunderstood by the Orthodox Catholic Christians and, because of this misunderstanding, some Gnostic groups even ridiculed them. However, upon closer examination it will be discovered that the Ancient Egyptian Trinity, which was later adopted by the Christians and Hindus, is nothing less than a development on the same system of polytheistic monotheism that characterizes African religion. The three in one metaphor was ancient by the time it was adopted by Catholicism. It was a term used to convey the idea of different aspects of the one reality. This same idea occurs in Egyptian as well as in Indian mythology. However, for deeper insights into the mystical meaning of the Trinity, we must look to Ancient Egypt. In Egyptian mythology, the Trinity was represented as three *metaphysical neters* or gods. They represent the manifestation of the unseen principles that support the universe and the visible aspects of God. The main Egyptian Trinity is composed of Amun, Ra and Ptah. Amun means that which is hidden and unintelligible, the underlying reality which sustains all things. Ra represents the subtle matter of creation as well as the mind. Ptah represents the visible aspect of Divinity, the phenomenal universe (gross physical matter). The Ancient Egyptian "Trinity" is also known as a manifestation of *Nebertcher* (Neberdjer*), the* "all encompassing" Divinity. Thus, the term Nebertcher is equivalent to the Vedantic Brahman, the Buddhist Dharmakaya and the Taoist Tao. The Ancient Egyptian text reads as follows:

"Nebertcher: Everything is Amun-Ra-Ptah, three in one."

The following passage from the *Hymns to Amun* (papyrus at Leyden) sums up the Ancient Egyptian understanding of the Trinity concept in creation, and that which transcends it.

He whose name is hidden is *AMUN*. *RA* belongeth to him as his face, and his body is *PTAH*.

Thus, within the mysticism of the Ancient Egyptian Trinity, the teaching of the triad of human consciousness (seer-seen-sight) is also found. Amun, the hidden aspect, is called the "eternal witness." This witness is one of the most important realizations in mystical philosophy, because it points to the existence of a transcendental awareness that lies beyond the conscious level of the mind. This mystical concept of the "witness" is also to be found in Indian philosophy under the Yoga teaching of *Sakshin* and the Buddhist teaching of *Mindfulness*. Sakshin is the "fourth" state of consciousness, beyond the waking, dream and dreamless sleep states. It is the goal of all mystics to achieve awareness with this state (Enlightenment).

The visible "gods" and "goddesses" with a name, form and other attributes are considered to be emanations of the one God, Nebertcher, meaning that which is without name, form or attributes (absolute). In the same way the Indian Trinity (Brahma, Shiva, and Vishnu) arises out of Brahman, the Absolute. They are responsible for the direction (management) of creation at every moment. In Indian mythology, each male aspect of the Trinity of Brahma - Shiva - Vishnu had his accompanying female aspect or manifesting energy: Saraswati - Kali - Lakshmi, respectively. Similarly, in the Egyptian system of gods and goddesses we have:

Male	Female
Amun	Amenit
Ra	Rai
Ptah	Sekhmet

Changes in the Way Lesser Beings (Spirits) are Viewed in African Religion Over Time

European and African historians have discovered many changes in the understanding and worship of lesser beings (gods and goddesses and deified human beings) in African Religion, over time. Some changes have been correlated to the emergence of agriculture, metal and even the slave trade. For example, the emergence of the earth goddess Ala religious sect among the Igbo people correlates to the increasing importance of agriculture. Among the Congo people of Central Africa and Jola people of Senegal, certain new religious sects related to lesser beings emerged in relation to the slave trade. They developed out of a need to explain the adversity that had befallen them, foreign conquest, enslavement, and the challenges of colonialism.[59]

Therefore, when studying specific African religions, the history of the peoples who developed the religion must be taken into account. Local variations should be evaluated as to their meaning for discerning the nature of African religion only in the context of general principles which are common to all the religions and exhibit the qualities that denote them as being ancient, preceding the historical influences from outside factors. The major outside factors influencing the development of African Religion include Judaism, Christianity, Islam, Arab slave trade, European slave trade, colonialism, and neocolonialism. So this means that when studying African culture and religion, caution must be exercised so as not to misinterpret the higher original aspects of African religion and culture with those that were engendered by disruptions, and then later on became assimilated into the culture. A superficial study would lead to the erroneous conclusion that all African Religion and its derivatives in the Diaspora are intact, correct or authentic forms of the practice of African Religion. Thus, careful studies, taking into account the disruptive factors above, must be undertaken.

It is also important to note that the practices of African religion, which constantly seek to bring a balance between the spirit and the material, seeing them as essentially the same, is still misunderstood by most Westerners. Many Africans who believe in the pantheistic view of African Religions have also accepted the Western religions, but this is not seen as a conflict since they inherently believe in one God. However, this belief of the Western traditions denies the divinity that is to be discovered in the realm of time and space, the realm of human events, due to the sharp demarcation between heaven and earth. In this philosophy there is a separation between God and humanity. So within the framework of orthodox Christianity, even if they see Jesus as an intermediary, a lesser spirit as the gods and goddesses of African religion, they do not see him as being able to fulfill all their needs in all situations. Thus, there is still a need for the variety of gods and goddesses in African religion. So while there is a commitment to God by many African converts to the Western religions, there remains a need to seek the assistance of minor deities to resolve concerns of a worldly nature. So there are many followers of religions like Islam, Christianity and Judaism who also continue to

---

[59] *Microsoft® Encarta® Africana*. ©1999 Microsoft Corporation. All rights reserved.

consult diviners and traditional healers, attend traditional rituals and participate in other aspects of African religion.

Manifestations of African Religious Expression and Transmission to the Next Generation

African religious thought expresses through oral traditions and the recitation of myth, and also through discussions between elders and the current generation. Rituals are a powerful means of transference of religious culture from generation to generation. They form an important part of African religion. Rituals are designed to attract and propitiate the spirit powers. Libations of millet beer, palm wine or water, and sometimes also foodstuffs are usually offered as part of a ritual. The libation is believed to augment the power of the spoken word. Less prevalent is the practice of animal sacrifice, which is believed to release the Life Force of the animal to augment the Life Force of the person promoting the ritual.

The concept of the divine word or *Hekau* is an extremely important part of Ancient Egyptian religion and is instructive in the study of all African religion. Some of the few differences between Ancient Egyptian religion and other African religions were the extensive development of the philosophy related to the "written word" in Ancient Egyptian religion and the expansive social infrastructure that allowed the development of advanced monumental architecture.

As explained earlier, the word religion is translated as Shetaut Neter in the Ancient African language of Kamit. These Shetaut (mysteries- rituals, wisdom, philosophy) about the Neter (Supreme Being) are related in the *Shetit* or writings related to the hidden teaching. Those writings are referred to as *Medu Neter* or "Divine Speech," the writings of the god Djehuti (Ancient Egyptian god of the Hekau or divine word), and also refers to any hieroglyphic texts or inscriptions generally. The term Medu Neter makes use of a special hieroglyph, , which means "*medu*" or "staff - walking stick-words." This means that speech is the support for the Divine, . Thus, just as the staff supports an elderly person, the hieroglyphic writing (the word) is a prop (staff) which sustains the Divine in the realm of time and space. That is, the Divine writings contain the wisdom that enlightens us about the Divine, *Shetaut Neter*.

If Medu Neter is mastered, then the spiritual aspirant becomes Maakheru or true of thought, word and deed, that is, purified in body, mind and soul. The symbol Medu is static while the symbol of Kheru is dynamic.

This term (Maakheru or Maa kheru) uses the glyph kheru which is a rudder – oar (rowing), symbol of voice, meaning that purification occurs when the righteous movement of the word occurs, that is, when it is used (rowing-movement) to promote virtue, order, peace, harmony and truth. So Medu Neter is the potential word and Maa kheru is the perfected word.

The hieroglyphic texts (Medu Neter), which are the spiritual scriptures in general, become useful in the process of religion (Maakheru) when they are used as hekau - the Ancient Egyptian "Words of Power" when the word is Hesi, chanted and Shmai- sung and thereby one performs or Dua or worship of the Divine. The divine word allows the speaker to control the gods and goddesses, i.e. the cosmic forces. This concept is really based on the idea that human beings are in reality higher order beings (neteru-gods and goddesses), and this attainment becomes possible if they learn about the nature of the universe and elevate themselves through virtue and wisdom.

Rites of Passage

"Rites of Passage" or "transition rites" are important formalized means of transferring religious information and culture. Boys and girls are put through programs that lead them to understand and discover their place in life, society and their developing spiritual consciousness. The government or other such institutions of the particular country do not charter most forms of religious instruction in traditional African religion. The rites of passage provide support for the initiates as they are socialized into the culture and at the same time are led to become productive members of the society. It engenders a sense of belonging, purpose and cultural identity to the initiate, all of which promote social harmony and a respect for tradition, as well as a reverence for the religion. Some societies remove the lower front incisors of the initiates during initiation rites. There is no evidence of this practice in Kamit. Removal of clothing and or ornaments may also be used to signify the loss or change of their previous status and the emergence into the new.

Male circumcision and female excision are also commonly practiced in some rites of passage. It should be noted that male circumcision and or female excision are not necessary or advisable practices, nor are they necessarily related to a spiritual perspective in life. Some societies engage in the practice as a ritual of practical necessity, for the purpose of hygiene, while others have attached to it, the concept of separating boys and girls from their childhood. In the case of the female, this practice has been used as a form of control over women by diminishing or eradicating their sexual capacity. This form of mutilation leaves not only emotional scars, but also a legacy that lasts for an entire lifetime including pain and sexual impotence (sexually unresponsiveness, frigidity). While it is true that the Ancient Egyptians circumcised the boys in the later period of the history, it is incorrect to say that this was an ancient tradition of Ancient Egypt. The existence of uncircumcised male mummies from the Old Kingdom proves that circumcision was not practiced generally in the early period of Ancient Egyptian history. When circumcision was performed, in some cases the procedure was merely cutting a slit on the foreskin of the penis enough to draw blood but not cutting it off completely. Also, there is no evidence of female circumcision, clitorectomy, or any excision at all in any Ancient Egyptian female mummies. Therefore, male circumcision and or female excision should not be considered as ancient or general practices of the African culture. So, male circumcision was used in Ancient Egypt at given periods, but not in the beginning, and even when it was performed, it was not generally throughout the entire society. At some points it did form part of a rites of passage, being performed close to the time of entering apprenticeship.

Rites of Passage in the Kamitan Society

In ancient Kamitan society, the formal Rites of Passage encompassed the movement from childhood into two main levels of social status leading to adulthood. These levels are related to the child's vocational training for later service to society. A child might be started in school sometime between the ages of 5 to 10 in accordance with his or her maturity. Thus, the first rite of passage is movement into primary school for 4 years. The child would learn to:
- read and write,
  - the exercises used to teach the reading and writing were the wisdom teachings of the great sages like Ptahotep, as well as the great stories with moral teachings.
- respect elders
- develop discipline in their actions (diligence was strictly imposed especially in the writing exercises that were used).

From here the child goes directly to an apprenticeship program. This might be in the Temple, the stables or other areas of society, to be trained in an occupation that would be useful to themselves and the nation. When the apprenticeship period is over, the student, now a teenager, moves into (graduates) to a full position that marks the passage from adolescence into adulthood. So the rites of passage was highly sophisticated and based on training to be a literate and productive member of society, having a valuable trade to offer by the age of 20. So clearly, in order to produce powerful young people who will some day rule the nation, it is important that the passages of early life be more than rituals or the child learning the ways of the elders. They should have moral and ethical training, as well as be taught reading, writing, and discipline and respect for righteous elders. The Temple and its ranks of clergy can be discerned from the following outline. The biography of the high priest Bekenchons, who served and died under Ramses II[208] provides an indication of the degrees as well as the years of training leading to the position of High Priest in his time.

1. 4 years in primary school
   a. beginning at age 5

2. 11 years education in one of the royal stables (apprenticeship period)

3. 4 Years as *Uab* priest of Amun,

4. 12 years as *divine father* priest.

5. 15 years served as *third* priest,

6. 12 years as *second* prophet.

7. Finally, in his fifty-ninth year, the king raised him to be "first prophet of Amun and chief of the prophets of all the gods."

General parameters of Rites of Passage

- Segregation from the ordinary events and duties of life for a period of time.
- Marks changes in stages of life (from the old to the new).
- Denotes new responsibilities in life.
- Initiates may be forcibly moved geographically, or made to strip themselves of clothing, hair, or other physical markings of their previous selves.
- Initiates may undergo physical trials.
- After the rites of passage program the initiates then reemerge, usually through formal ritual procedures, with a redefined identity and a changed social status (from death of the old to rebirth of the new) into the normal social fabric.
- The ritual of rites of passage should mark the culmination of the training of the initiate who will now assume a position of full participation in the social and economic activities of the community.

Religion and Dance

Dance was an important aspect of the religious festival-ritual in Ancient Egyptian religion and continues to be so in present day African religion. The dance may propitiate the spirits, and facilitate entry into an altered state of mind that is more sensitive to experiencing the spirit (higher consciousness). The !Kung of southern Africa use dance for prayer, healing and to elevate the inner Life Force, which is equivalent to the Ancient Egyptian practice of elevating the Arat Sekhem (Serpent Power, also known as Kundalini in India).

Evil, Suffering, Sin, and the Devil in African Religion

African religion (including Kamit) ascribes evil and suffering to disruptive spirits and unrighteous living. These are explained as beings called tricksters. In Kamit the disruptive spirits are referred to as *sebau*. Also, some humans who use special powers for harming others or to advance some personal gain are also blamed for maladies. Unrighteous conduct in life is a source for adversity, the experience of evil and suffering. Exú is a trickster of the Yoruba tradition and acts as the messenger god who causes strife by distorting messages between the human realm (prayers) and the Spirit realm, due to a dislike of a world that is too orderly. Exú was identified as the devil by missionaries. Actually, Exú, like the jackal character of Dogon religion, is actually a symbol of passion, desire, zest for life, curiosity and an adventurous nature. These qualities are not evil; they are expressions of a certain character. For the listener or observer, the dramatization of the consequences of the actions of such personalities through their myths develops the capacity of discernment between choices of righteousness and unrighteousness, and outcomes that lead to harmony and peace versus outcomes that lead to adversity and disturbance. The character Set in Ancient Egyptian religion, a symbol of the lower self, represents the energy of uncontrolled egoism and brute force. He was never considered as a devil, but many scholars and researchers of Ancient Egyptian mythology have made the error of considering him as the devil. Some even see him as the prototype for the devil in the Judeo-Christian and Islamic traditions. However, Set was never seen as the "source of evil itself" until the late Dynastic Period, which was when the Jewish people were living in Egypt. This notion of a personality who causes evil in human beings is extremely dangerous because it allows people with poor moral development to shirk responsibility for their actions. This is a fundamental difference between the African concept of evil and that of the orthodox Western religions. The African concept relates adversity to passion and a movement away from virtue while the Western religious traditions relate the problem of evil to a movement away from virtue under the influence of a demon (the devil). The African concept retains human responsibility while the Western model assigns the blame to an outside force.

In contrast to African religious belief, later Christian and Jewish theologians conceptualized the devil as being equated with "the supreme spirit of evil" who, for all time, has been ruling over a kingdom of all evil spirits, and is in constant opposition to God. The word "devil" is derived from the Latin *diabolus*, and from the Greek *diabolos,* which are adjectives that meaning *slanderous.* It is also used in ancient Greek as a noun to identify a specific person as being a slanderer. The term "diabolos" was used for the *Septuagint* or Greek translation of the Jewish Bible, not referring to human beings, but in order to translate the Hebrew word *ha-satan* (the satan). This expression was originally used as the title of one of the members of the divine court whose function was to act as a roving spy for God. Satan was supposed to have gathered intelligence about human beings during his travels on earth, much like the Hindu character Narada, a Sage who would relate information about the happenings on earth to Lord Vishnu (the Supreme Being).

At one point, Satan also meant "an opponent" and not a particular devil being with actual existence. At around the 6th century B.C.E., Satan appears in the Old Testament as an individual angel who is subordinate to God. Gradually, as Jewish and Christian tradition developed around this idea, Satan became known as a personality who was the source of all evil, and was responsible for leading human beings into sin. In later Jewish tradition, and therefore also in early Christian thought, this title became a proper name. Satan was then seen as a personified adversary, not only of human beings, but also primarily of God. The development of the devil as a personified evil adversary probably arose from the early Jewish and Christian association with the dualistic theologies of Persia as well as the dualistic philosophy of Zoroaster and the misunderstanding of the Egyptian character *Set*. In some segments of Jewish theology, the idea of Satan developed as an "evil impulse." Human beings are seen as susceptible to a force, which is outside of and separate from them. Therefore, with this view it is possible for a human being to become "possessed" by the evil force and coerced into wrongdoing. Jesus was seen as the savior who broke the power of the devil over human beings. As stated above, this view is dangerous because it negates the power of the human mind to control itself, the power of free will. It also opens the door to superstition and imagination about evil supernatural beings as being real and existing in fact, rather than understanding the symbolism behind these mythic portrayals.

It is important to note that in both the Christian and Jewish systems, the dualism concerning Satan, that is, of him being the antithesis of God, is without merit, since he is ultimately subject to God. This aspect is not emphasized in popular discourses. This view is more closely in tune with the original idea in the Ancient Egyptian teaching. Otherwise, if Satan were the true adversary of God, this would mean that God is not omnipotent, because there is a being who can limit his power. So the teaching related to Satan must be correctly understood in order to avoid error and misunderstanding in one's spiritual movement.

Evil must be understood as the actions of people who are ignorant of the higher spiritual reality within themselves. Such actions will be based on egoism, anger, hatred, greed, lust, jealousy, etc. Sin must therefore be understood as the idea of separation between one's self and God, the state of ignorance about one's own spiritual essence (egoism). Each person must take responsibility for their actions while striving to engender a sense of Divine Presence within themselves. When this occurs, the very basis of sin and ignorance is dispelled from the mind. At this stage of spiritual development there is transcendence of the notion of good and evil. Understanding all to be part of oneself, there is no need to debate about one's treatment of others. One's treatment of others becomes a spontaneous act based on love, compassion, forgiveness and magnanimity, much like there is instant forgiveness of one's teeth when they bite one's own tongue. This is the true goal of religion— to rise above ignorance (evil, egoism).

In Matthew Chapter 6, verses 9-13, Jesus instructs his followers as to how they should pray to God. The end of the prayer (verse 13) contains a peculiar statement, which seems, on the surface, to be very contradictory.

> 9. After this manner therefore pray ye: Our Father who art in heaven, Hallowed be thy name.
> 10 Thy kingdom come. Thy will be done on earth, as [it is] in heaven.
> 11 Give us this day our daily bread.
> 12 And forgive us our debts, as we forgive our debtors.
> 13 And lead us not into temptation, but deliver us from evil: For thine is the kingdom, and the power, and the glory, forever. Amen.

The ordinary Christian doctrine almost always presupposes the existence of an evil entity ordinarily referred to as the devil. However, verse 13 seems to refer to God as the source of temptation (evil). Thus, the prayer is implying that God has control over if whether or not one will fall into temptation (evil). Why should the asking of not being led into temptation be directed towards God and not the devil? The only answer, which is possible from a mystical point of view, is that God is the source of both evil and good. More accurately, God sustains Creation, and Creation is the venue where good and evil can exist. However, human beings always have a choice to follow the path of good or of evil. Then this understanding also leads to the conclusion that there is no devil as such, only evil or negative thoughts and actions. This teaching reflects the understanding and subtle exposition by the Christian Sages of the highly advanced teaching known as non-duality. This is an understanding that in reality the Supreme Being has no rivals or contenders. The Supreme Being is Absolute and Supreme, because {He/She} is the only reality behind good, as well as evil. In reality God transcends these two concepts which the mind has created for the purpose of understanding and explaining human activities. In the final analysis, an advanced spiritual aspirant must understand that there is no outside force that pushes an individual to evil actions. Evil is an expression of the level of the lack of understanding of one's true divine nature (God, Supreme Being), just as darkness is a manifestation of the degree to which the sun is absent.

A serious follower of the mystical teachings must develop a keen understanding of the true meaning of sin and its implications. Sinful acts are those acts *you* perform which carry you away from the discovery of your true being. They are characterized by pettiness, greed, anger, hard-heartedness, hatred, egoism, infatuation, etc. Virtuous acts are those acts *you* perform which move you forward towards integration of your personality and an eventual merging of your individual ego with the Cosmic Self, the Supreme Being. Virtue implies developing peace, contentment, selflessness, and finally, self-discovery. Virtuous acts are characterized by peacefulness, kindness, selflessness, sharing, giving, universal love, forgiveness, serenity and other lofty qualities.

From this mystical perspective, that which takes you away from Divine-realization is demoniac (sinful, satanic), while that which brings you closer to Divine-realization is divine. Hence, there is no Jesus-like "savior" outside of yourself, and likewise, there is no personality called *"the devil"* that exists in fact as a distinct personality outside of yourself. The thoughts and actions you choose are what you classify as either divine or demoniac. Therefore, your fate lies with the thoughts and actions by which you choose to live. Your present ego-personality is the creation of your past actions, feelings, thoughts and experiences.

Thus, the concept of the devil is not an indigenous African development. It is an infused notion that was brought in with Western religion, and which has been inherited by subsequent generations within those African communities practicing the Western religions in whole or in part. In this context, the Trickster spirit represents the forces of chaos that are unleashed by human ignorance and lack of mental discrimination between righteousness and unrighteousness. So the fate of every human being rests in their own hands and they must work to overcome the adversities and sufferings they themselves have engendered.

Ancestor Worship

Ancestor Worship may be defined as reverence that is granted to deceased relatives because they are believed to have influence on events in the world of the living or, less frequently, because they are believed to have attained the status of gods. In Kamitan Spirituality the correlate term is *uashu shepsu*. It means the honoring of venerated departed souls, souls who were virtuous. It is akin to the concept of saints such as those in the Christian tradition, who are prayed to for assistance in coping with worldly affairs. This concept is related to the cultural aspect of honoring elders and ancestors as a matter of respect. Further, it is a matter of promoting positive feeling towards the past through ritual and mental attitude, and making a bridge for prosperity in the future, for oneself in the hereafter as well as for the future on earth for the living descendants.

So there is a spiritual component, and also a cultural component, promoting harmony and continuity in society. The name of the deceased is remembered and food offerings are made to them at their tomb sites, which act as chapels. However, within the chapels, the ceremony becomes transformed into a worship of the Divine Self, since the divinity who presides over the chapel is understood to be the underlying essence of all souls, as well as the objective of all souls. Many examples of this can be seen all over Kamit, especially in the texts and images of worship of the tombs of the nobles and royalty.

Figure 41: Above-left Pyramid tomb of the Old Kingdom Period.

Figure 42: Above-right Mastaba tomb of Giza area.

The term *Pyramid Text* is used because some of the kings from the Old Kingdom period inscribed *Prt m Hru* texts on the walls of their tombs. Mastabas (an Arab name for "low, long stone buildings") were used later, to the end of the 6th Dynasty. These structures were built to contain the body of the deceased, but also as places were friends and relatives could make offerings for the Ka (soul) of the deceased and utter Hekau (spiritual words of power) for the well being of the deceased and themselves. After the Pre-Dynastic graves, wooden coffins were used. These wooden coffins were followed by the use of sarcophagi (a stone coffin, often inscribed or decorated with sculpture.)

Possession by Spirits

Spirit possession is practiced by some African religions. The Fon people of Benin and the Yoruba of Nigeria believe that a spirit enters into the body of a devotee and uses the body, making it move, act and speak according to the spirit's influence. This allows the spirit to communicate with those gathered at the ritual through the possessed person. Possession by spirits is an idea often associated with ancestor worship. It is believed to be a form of intimate contact that can occur between human beings and a divinity during a ritual of trance. In its highest sense the communion is with a divine ancestor, someone who has become godlike. However, most practices in modern times involve the veneration of departed souls. During this time a divine spirit is believed to be able to take possession of the worshiper. The trance is often induced by rhythmic chanting, drumming, dance, and other techniques such as drugs, which are sometimes used to facilitate an altered state of consciousness.

In other religions of Africa, such as the Ancient Egyptian, lesser spirits converse with the devotee through visions and dreams, but do not possess the body of the devotees. In fact, the Kamitan concept of Words of Power allows the human being to actually control the supernatural (cosmic) forces instead of being controlled by them. "Controlling" the cosmic forces means realizing that one is in touch with the Supreme Being who is the source and ultimate abode of all powers. In the Kamitan concept of the Neteru there is no idea of allowing any spirits to take possession of the worshipper. Rather, it is incumbent upon the worshipper to take control of the discarnate forces and exert authority over them and thereby take the rightful place as master over them. The following Kamitan proverbs provide insight into the philosophy of spirits in relation to human beings.

> "Salvation is the freeing of the soul from its bodily fetters; becoming a God through knowledge and wisdom; controlling the forces of the cosmos instead of being a slave to them;

subduing the lower nature and through awakening the higher self, ending the cycle of rebirth and dwelling with the Neteru who direct and control the Great Plan."

"Yield not to emotion, for there are discarnate forces around us who desire emotional existence. In the heat of passion one surrenders to the influence of these, ill health and unwise living results. Through firm instruction one can master one's emotions and these forces; in this, make them serve one. Thus the slave becomes the master."

The Pyramid texts, the oldest known extensive spiritual writings of Kamit and the world, speak of consuming the universal cosmic forces (neteru), literally consuming them. This is the concept of the Eucharist in which one is becoming the totality of what is consumed. In other words, the powers or energies of these lower beings (neteru) are to be assimilated and mastered by the worshipper (initiate). The initiate is thus transformed from the lower form of consciousness, whereby they exist as an ordinary mortal human being with disintegrated consciousness, in a state of weakness, to higher consciousness which is imbued with all the powers of the neteru. Thus, when all of these forces are brought together, they transform the initiate into a whole being, possessing all faculties, knowledge and capacity.

In modern times, these mystical practices and concepts have degraded in African religion due to many factors, namely slavery, colonization, disruption of African culture and tribal secret societies. Oftentimes, only the knowledge of the ritual remains and the original purpose, being forgotten, renders the ritual ineffective in its higher importance. In addition, they often become mixed with other elements and concepts which do not maintain the integrity and original intent of the practice. The practitioners often remain in a cycle of practicing the ritual for ritual sake and do not progress beyond that level, enjoying the emotional exuberance and tension relief that comes from physical exertion but gaining little higher consciousness integration. The temporary relief of tension causes many to imagine that they have discovered higher levels of consciousness, however, their personalities remain unchanged as they continue to live with the same foibles, fears, desires and faults. Authentic religion should improve life and lead human beings to empowerment both in the physical as well as the higher mental planes of existence, and not the reverse, to weakness, susceptibility and dependence.

Another problem that is prevalent in African religion is that many Priests and Priestesses within the African traditions have been accused of promoting rituals for profit, charging exorbitant fees for initiations and rituals. Priests and Priestesses are supposed to be facilitators for aspirants, to help them discover higher consciousness, and they should be compensated with a reasonable offering that will sustain their activities and service to the community. However, the usury fees charged by some practitioners approach the level of some Western Christian ministers who parade around in Cadillac's and Mercedes or even Rolls Royce cars, touting the benefits of being on the spiritual path, presenting themselves as success stories, having gained their wealth "through the grace of God," when actually they have duped the masses into believing fairy tales about what spirituality is and what the legitimate goal of Temple offerings is supposed to be. The offerings should benefit the community and not the egoistic designs of preachers, Western, Eastern or African. These misconceptions degrade the practice of religion and lead to frustration, dogmatism, ignorance and ultimately failure in the spiritual quest, both for the preachers and their followers.

Voodoo

Voodoo or vodun, is a religious and magical set of beliefs and practices of some Africans. It was originally brought over from Africa through the Africans who were taken as slaves to the Caribbean, the US South, and Brazil. Though originating in Benin, the practice of Voodoo outside Africa includes elements of West African cults and a supernatural pantheon of saints, borrowed largely from Catholicism. Magic, propitiatory rites and trance also play important roles in voodoo.[60] Some elements of the practice have been used by unscrupulous practitioners who wish harm on others. This has been popularized by the entertainment media of the West, and has maligned the practice of Voodoo. Voodoo is not a church but rather a cult or independent form of spiritual seeking. It has limited appeal and practice in the continent of Africa (restricted to Dahomey, now called Benin). It was popularized as its practice grew in the Caribbean.

---

[60] Random House Encyclopedia Copyright (C) 1983,1990 by Random House Inc.

MAAT-UBUNTU: Maat Philosophy of Ancient Africa and Humanism in Present Day African Religious Practice

After centuries of trying to stop the practice of African Religion and convert Africans to Christianity, the Catholic Church reversed itself and at the 1964 Vatican II conference of Bishops in Rome, officially accepted African Religion into the family of World religions as a full partner.[209] On a visit to Benin, Pope John Paul II apologized for centuries of denigration African religion by the Western Culture. African religion is universally accepted as a distinct and legitimate form of spirituality and continues to be practiced by a substantial number of people in and outside of Africa. It is practiced by many who on one hand profess to be converts to Western religions while at the same time retain the practice of some aspects of African religion in their life. One reason for its persistence is the quality of *Humanism* that characterizes it. The African term *Ubuntu* means humanism. Humanism is a fundamental concern for the human condition, a caring for fellow human beings with respect to their well being, but also it means a kind of openness, hospitality and compassion for those in need. The quality of Ubuntu has had the effect of tempering the harshness of other religions, as well as bringing to the forefront the sufferings and needs of others, and sometimes the inequities that are endured by others. Ubuntu is a kind of empathy and sympathy for others and a heartfelt desire to share with others. One important example of the effect of African religion and its quality of Ubuntu is the Aldura Church of Yoruba. In this church the Christian emphasis on salvation has given way to an approach that is more in line with the traditional needs of the people. The priests function as diviners, healers and ritual leaders. The concept of humanism may be best expressed in the following quotations:

> "African belief is basically the humanistic belief that doing good is good, while doing anything bad is bad. You are rewarded here on earth for your good deeds and punished for your iniquities. Indeed, many Africans believe that the ultimate punishment for bad or iniquitous behaviour is death."
>
> -N. Adu Kwabena-Essem is a freelance journalist, based in Accra, Ghana

> "You know when it is there, and it is obvious when it is absent. It has to do with what it means to be truly human, it refers to gentleness, to compassion, to hospitality, to openness to others, to vulnerability, to being available for others and to know that you are bound up with them in the bundle of life, for a person is only a person through other persons."
>
> -South Africa's Archbishop Desmond Tutu, winner of the Nobel Prize 1984

When compared to the concept of Ubuntu, the Kamitan concept of Ari Maat (Maatian Actions) is found to be in every way compatible with this concept of humanism or social awareness and caring. Maat is a philosophy, a spiritual symbol as well as a cosmic energy or force which pervades the entire universe. Maat is the path to promoting world order, justice, righteousness, correctness, harmony and peace. Maat is also the path that represents wisdom and spiritual awakening through balance and equanimity, as well as righteous living and selfless service to humanity. So Maat encompasses certain disciplines of right action which promote purity of heart and balance of mind. Maat is represented as a goddess with a feather held to the side of her head by a bandana and she is sometimes depicted with wings, a papyrus scepter in one hand and holding an ankh (symbol of life) in her other hand.

Forms of Goddess Maat

In Kamit, the judges were initiated into the teachings of MAAT, for only when there is justice and fairness in society can there be an abiding harmony and peace. Harmony and peace are necessary for the pursuit of true happiness and inner fulfillment in life. Thus, Kamitan spirituality includes a discipline for social order and harmony not unlike Confucianism of China or Dharma of India. Maat promotes social harmony and personal virtue which lead to spiritual enlightenment.

Many people are aware of the 42 Laws or Precepts of Maat. They are declarations of purity (also known as *negative confessions)*, found in the Kamitan Book of Enlightenment (Egyptian Book of the Dead), which a person who has lived a life of righteousness can utter at the time of the great judgment after death. All of the precepts concern moral rectitude in all aspects of life which leads to social order. Order leads to prosperity and harmony.

As an adjunct to the 42 precepts there are other injunctions given in the Wisdom Texts. These in turn are elaborated in the tomb inscriptions of Ancient Egypt. In Chapter 125 of the Book of the Dead, the person uttering the declarations states:

> "I have done God's will. I have given bread to the hungry, water to the thirsty, clothes to the clotheless and a boat to those who were shipwrecked. I made the prescribed offerings to the gods and goddesses and I also made offerings in the temple to the glorious spirits. Therefore, protect me when I go to face The God."[210]

The following tomb inscriptions were carved into the walls of those people who professed to have lived a righteous and orderly life. Central to this order and virtue are the acts of righteousness and the highest form of right action is selfless service. That is, all of the things a person can do to uphold truth, order and righteousness during their lives. The following is a summary of Ari Maat, which will be followed by a brief gloss on Maat Selfless Service.

The Actions of a Person Living by Maat Should Include:

❶

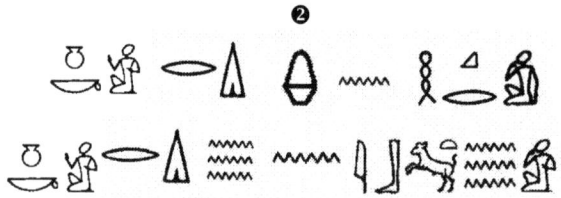

Nuk rdy maat - Give righteousness, order and truth to humanity

Maat is the ancient art of ethical conduct, righteous living (virtue) and truth. Aspirants learn to think and act with honesty, integrity, and truthfulness to promote positive self-development which will translate into the becoming reliable and responsible leaders and members of society.

❷

Nuk rdy ta n heker - Nuk rdy mu n abt
Give food to the hungry - Give water to the thirsty

Working to eradicate hunger and thirst in our community, and also world hunger, should be primary goals of a person living by Maat. Hunger prevents humanity from achieving its higher goals of peace and harmony. Hunger is a source of suffering and early death for millions of people around the world. Sharing food and drink are primary ways of showing compassion and promoting caring between human beings and societies. This promotes peace and prevents conflicts.

❸

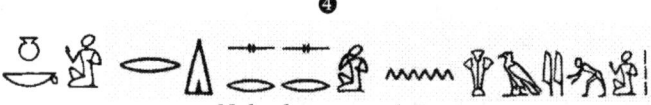

Nuk rdy het n an het
Give shelter to the homeless

Working to provide homes for the homeless and alleviating the homeless situation in society should be a priority for a person living by Maat because all human beings require a proper place to dwell so that they can live well ordered and comfortable lives. Lack of shelter gives rise to discomfort and discomfort leads to strife.

❹

Nuk rdy serser n haiu
Give comfort to the weepers (suffering-disheartened)

Pain and suffering are all too prevalent in human life. One of the concerns of a person living by Maat should be to promote compassion and consolation to people who are suffering due to any reason and to promote immediate psychological support (refuge, moral support) for those in need.

❺

Nuk rdy netu genu kher nekhtu
Give protection to the weak from the strong

One of the main concerns of a person living by Maat should be social justice, the protection of the weaker members of society who are victims of crime or who are less able to help themselves when confronted with other members of society. The goal is to assist people by standing with them to provide moral, legal or other assistance.

❻

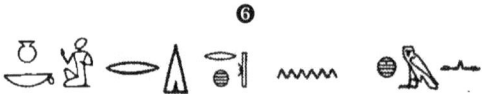

Nuk rdy rech n kheman
Give wisdom (counsel) to the ignorant

One of the main goals of a person living by Maat should be to train other human beings in the precepts of Maat and raise leaders who will study the ancient philosophy and be able to transmit it to others in society. This will promote the formation and growth of a well-informed segment of the population who will be able to promote peace, justice, understanding and spiritual enlightenment.

❼

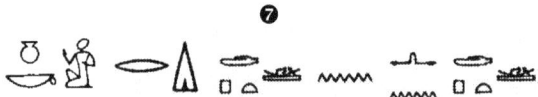

Nuk rdy dept n an dept
Give opportunity to the discouraged

Having become wise and acting with virtue, teaching the ancient Maat Philosophy and assisting others in immediate and long-term need, a person living by Maat will thereby eventually assist them to become stronger and help themselves. Every human being needs to have the opportunity to develop and discover the meaning of life so as to grow and develop to their full potential. Therefore, justice and equal opportunity are essential human concerns for all people.

Maat Selfless Service is an important aspect of Chapter 33 (125) of the Book of the Dead. Here the initiate states {his/her} qualifications to be allowed into the inner shrine to see and become one with Asar (The Supreme Being). The initiate states that {he/she} helped those in need in various ways. This is one of the greatest and most secure methods of purifying the heart (becoming virtuous), because it makes one humble and it effaces the ego. Selfless Service is a vast area of spiritual practice and it forms the major part of the Yogic Path of Right Action. Every human being needs to understand the profound implications of selfless service and how to practice selfless service effectively in order to attain spiritual enlightenment, social order and harmony.

First it must be understood that according to Maat Philosophy, the Supreme Spirit (God, Goddess) manifests as all Creation, and is also present in all human beings. This being so, one must realize that one is interacting in, with and through the Supreme Spirit in all actions, speech and thought. Since human interrelations have a most profound influence on the human mind, they are the most powerful means of effecting a change in the personality. However, if mishandled, they can be a most effective method of leading a human being to psychological attachment and suffering as well. A person should understand that Maat comes to {him/her} in the form of human beings in need, so as to give the aspirant an opportunity to grow spiritually through selfless service. To be successful in selfless service, the aspirant must be able to sublimate the ego through developing patience, dealing with difficult personalities without developing resentment, not taking attacks personally, and developing a keen understanding of human nature and human needs. Selfless Service allows a human being to discover sentiments of caring for something greater than the little "me." This leads to purity of heart from the gross fetters of anger, hatred, greed, lust, jealousy, envy, etc., and also the attachments based on blood relations and other filial relationships, for in order to serve in the highest order, one must serve all equally, without favorites. As a servant of humanity, one's family becomes all human beings and nature itself. Therefore, the cause of environmental well being is also a high concern reflected in the following injunctions of the Maat philosophy. There are two injunctions that specifically address issues of public or selfless service to the community through service to nature and the preservation of natural resources.

(15) "I have not laid waste the ploughed lands."
(36) "I have never befouled the water." Variant: I have not held back the water from flowing in its season.

—From Chapter 33 of the Ancient Egyptian Pert M Heru

When asked how she could stand to serve such severely ill people and not feel disheartened, repulsed or depressed, Mother Teresa replied "I see only Jesus coming to me through people." This reply shows the saintly attitude towards humanity, and she also displayed the highest level of spiritual practice through the path of right action, which is known as Selfless Service. When Mother Teresa was asked how she is able to do all the work she has done, she would reply, "I do nothing…God does it all." Selfishness arises when a human being sees {him/her} self as separate from Creation and develops an egoistic selfishness, typified by the attitude of "I got mine you get yours." A mature and righteous person must develop sensitivity to the fact that all Creation is inexorably linked at all levels, the material and the spiritual, and therefore, a true aspirant feels empathy and compassion for all humanity and will not rest until all human beings have the essential needs of life, those being food, shelter and opportunity to grow and thrive. All problems of the world can be traced to the selfishness and hoarding of precious basic necessities by certain segments of the population, and the subsequent development of resentments, greed, hatred and violence which lead to untold social strife.

However, a person who lives by Maat does not pursue the betterment of the world in a sentimental manner, but with deep understanding of the fact that people's ignorance of their true divine essence is the root cause that has led them to their current condition of suffering, and therefore simply sending money or aid will not resolve the issue. Where food, clothing or funds are needed, they should be given, but in addition to these, one must undertake an effort to promote mystical spiritual wisdom (which includes the complete practice of religion: myth, ritual and mysticism) in humanity. Beyond the basic necessities of life, the world needs mystical spiritual wisdom most of all. Technology, comforts of life, entertainments and other conveniences should come later. This is how a well-ordered society is structured along Maatian-Ubuntu principles: Mystical spiritual foundation which provides basic necessities (food and shelter) for its members, from which all else (development of technology, entertainment, etc.) will follow. Only in this way will the technological developments, entertainment and other aspects of society develop in a righteous (ethical), balanced and harmonious way. This can be contrasted with the current predicament of most modern day societies where the emphasis is foremost on the development of technology and entertainment, without giving much thought to spirituality (ethics, balance, harmony, truth, righteousness). Consequently, there are many people currently existing in communities all over the world who are deprived of the basic needs of life (food and shelter).

Studying the teachings of yogic mysticism and their subsequent practice through selfless service will promote the enlightenment of humanity, which will end the cycle of egoism and disharmony between peoples of differing cultures. Therefore, the act of helping others is extremely important and should be pursued. Working in service of other human beings allows a person who lives by Maat to apply the teachings and experience the results. It allows the a person who lives by Maat to develop the capacity to adapt and adjust to changing conditions of life, and to other personalities, and still maintain the detachment and poise necessary to keep equal vision and awareness of the Divine, and thereby live by truth, and not by favoritism. All of this promotes integration of the personality of the person who lives by Maat. Therefore, the results of one's selfless service actions are immediate and always good, because no matter what the results of those actions are, the service itself is the goal of a person who lives by Maat.

What are the disciplines of Selfless Service?

Service is an important ingredient in the development of spiritual life. In selfless service one adopts the attitude of seeing and serving the Divine in everyone and every creature, and one is to feel as an instrument of the Divine, working to help the less able. The following are some important points to keep in mind when practicing selfless service.

First, having controlled the body, speech and thoughts, a person who lives by Maat should see {him/her} self as an instrument of the Divine, being used to bring harmony, peace, and help to the world. All human beings and nature are expressions of the Divine. Serving human beings and nature is serving the Supreme Divine Self (God).

In Chapter 34, Verse 10 of the Pert M Hru scripture, the initiate states that {he/she} has become a spiritual doctor: *There are sick, very ill people. I go to them, I spit on the arms, I set the shoulder, and I cleanse them.* As a servant of the Divine Self, a person who lives by Maat is also a healer. Just as it would be inappropriate for a medical doctor to lose {his/her} patience with {his/her} patient because the person is complaining due to their illness, so too it is inappropriate for an initiate to lose their patience when dealing with the masses of worldly-minded people, suffering from the illness of ignorance of their true essence. So, it must be clearly and profoundly understood that in serving, you are serving the true Self, not the ego.

Secondly, as discussed above, a person who lives by Maat should not expect a particular result from their actions. In other words one does not perform actions and wait for a reward or praises, and though working to achieve success in the project, one does not develop the expectation that one's efforts will succeed, because there may be failure in what one is trying to accomplish. If a person who lives by Maat focuses on the success of the project and failure occurs, the mind will become so imbalanced that it will negate the positive developments of personality integration, expansion and concentration which occurred as the project was pursued. Therefore, one's focus should be on doing one's part by performing the service, and letting the Divine handle the results. This provides a person who lives by Maat with peace and the ability to be more qualitative in the work being performed (without the egoistic content), and more harmonious, which will lead to being more sensitive to the needs of others and of the existence of the Spirit as the very essence of one's being.

Secular Maat Selfless Service Leads to Spiritual Maat Mysticism

The highly advanced and lofty teachings from Maat Philosophy of becoming one with the Supreme Being through righteous action is further augmented by the *Hymn to Maat* contained in the scripture now referred to as the Berlin papyrus below.

Maat Ankhu Maat
Maat is the source of life
Maat neb bu ten
Maat is in everywhere you are
Cha hena Maat
Rise in the morning with Maat
Ankh hena Maat
Live with Maat
Ha sema Maat
Let every limb join with Maat (i.e. let her guide your actions)
Maat her ten
Maat is who you are deep down (i.e. your true identity is one with the Divine)
Dua Maat neb bu ten
Adorations to goddess Maat, who is in everywhere you are!

For more extensive study of the Maat-Selfless Service teaching, see the books *Wisdom of Maati, 42 Precepts of Maat* and *Ancient Egyptian Book of the Dead* by Muata Ashby.

The Fundamental Principles of Neterian Religion

NETERIANISM
(The Oldest Known Religion in History)

The term "Neterianism" is derived from the name "Shetaut Neter." Shetaut Neter means the "Hidden Divinity." It is the ancient philosophy and mythic spiritual culture that gave rise to the Ancient Egyptian civilization. Those who follow the spiritual path of Shetaut Neter are therefore referred to as "Neterians." The fundamental principles common to all denominations of Neterian Religion may be summed up as follows.

Neterian Great Truths

1. *"Pa Neter ua ua Neberdjer m Neteru"* -"The Neter, the Supreme Being, is One and alone and as Neberdjer, manifesting everywhere and in all things in the form of Gods and Goddesses."

Neberdjer means "all-encompassing divinity," the all-inclusive, all-embracing Spirit which pervades all and who is the ultimate essence of all. This first truth unifies all the expressions of Kamitan religion.

2. *"an-Maat swy Saui Set s-Khemn"* – "Lack of righteousness brings fetters to the personality and these fetters lead to ignorance of the Divine."

When a human being acts in ways that contradict the natural order of nature, negative qualities of the mind will develop within that person's personality. These are the afflictions of Set. Set is the neteru of egoism and selfishness. The afflictions of Set include: anger, hatred, greed, lust, jealousy, envy, gluttony, dishonesty, hypocrisy, etc. So to be free from the fetters of set one must be free from the afflictions of Set.

3. *"s-Uashu s-Nafu n saiu Set"* -"Devotion to the Divine leads to freedom from the fetters of Set."

To be liberated (Nafu - freedom - to breath) from the afflictions of Set, one must be devoted to the Divine. Being devoted to the Divine means living by Maat. Maat is a way of life that is purifying to the heart and beneficial for society as it promotes virtue and order. Living by Maat means practicing Shedy (spiritual practices and disciplines).

Uashu means devotion and the classic pose of adoring the Divine is called "Dua," standing or sitting with upraised hands facing outwards towards the image of the divinity.

4. *"ari Shedy Rekh ab m Maakheru"* - "The practice of the Shedy disciplines leads to knowing oneself and the Divine. This is called being True of Speech."

Doing Shedy means to study profoundly, to penetrate the mysteries (Shetaut) and discover the nature of the Divine. There have been several practices designed by the sages of Ancient Kamit to facilitate the process of self-knowledge. These are the religious (Shetaut) traditions and the Sema (Smai) Tawi (yogic) disciplines related to them that augment the spiritual practices.

All the traditions relate the teachings of the sages by means of myths related to particular gods or goddesses. It is understood that all of these neteru are related, like brothers and sisters, having all emanated from the same source, the same Supremely Divine parent, who is neither male nor female, but encompasses the totality of the two.

The Great Truths of Neterianism are realized by means of Four Spiritual Disciplines in Three Steps

The four disciples are: Rekh Shedy (Wisdom), Ari Shedy (Righteous Action and Selfless Service), Uashu (Ushet) Shedy (Devotion) and Uaa Shedy (Meditation)

The Three Steps are: Listening, Ritual, and Meditation

SEDJM REKH SHEDY

L I S T E N

- *Sedjm* **REKH** *Shedy* - <u>Listening</u> to the WISDOM of the Neterian Traditions
    - Shetaut Asar — Teachings of the Asarian Tradition
    - Shetaut Anu — Teachings of the Ra Tradition
    - Shetaut Menefer — Teachings of the Ptah Tradition
    - Shetaut Waset — Teachings of the Amun Tradition
    - Shetaut Netrit — Teachings of the Goddess Tradition
    - Shetaut Aton — Teachings of the Aton Tradition

ARI SHEDY

R I T U A L

- *Ari Maat Shedy* – **Righteous Actions** – Purifies the GROSS impurities of the Heart
    - Maat Shedy – True Study of the Ways of hidden nature of Neter
    - Maat Aakhu – True Deeds that lead to glory
    - Maat Aru – True Ritual

UASHU (USHET) SHEDY

- *Ushet Shedy* – **Devotion to the Divine** – Purifies the EMOTIONAL impurities of the Heart
    - Shmai – Divine Music
    - Sema Paut – Meditation in motion
    - Neter Arit – Divine Offerings – Selfless-Service – virtue -

UAA SHEDY

M E D I T A T E

- *Uaa m Neter Shedy* - 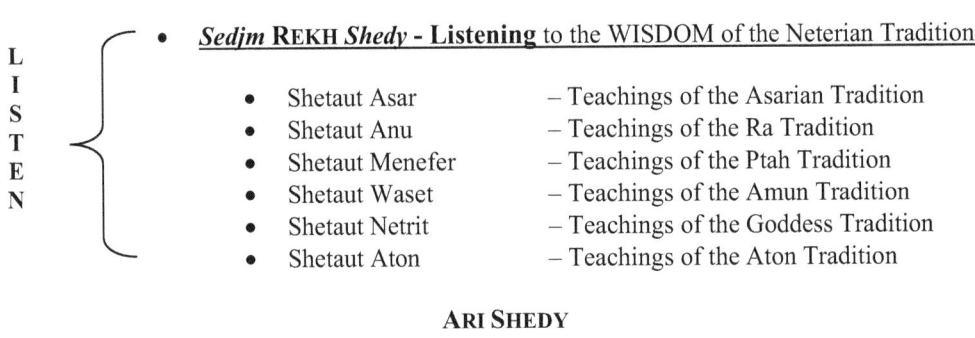 **Meditation** Experience the Transcendental Supreme Self. The five forms of Neterian Meditation discipline include.
    - Arat Sekhem, - Meditation on the Subtle Life Force
    - Ari Sma Maat, - Meditation on the Righteous action
    - Nuk Pu-Ushet, - Meditation on the I am
    - Nuk Ra Akhu, - Meditation on the Glorious Light
    - Rekh – Khemn, - Meditation on the Wisdom Teaching

Summary of The Great Truths and the Shedy Paths to their Realization

Great Truths

Shedy Disciplines

I

God is One and in all things manifesting through the Neteru

I

Listen to the Wisdom Teachings
(Become Wise)
Learn the mysteries as taught by an authentic teacher which allows this profound statement to be understood.

I I

Unrighteousness brings fetters and these cause ignorance of truth (#1)

I I

Acting (Living) by Truth
Apply the Philosophy of right action to become virtuous and purify the heart

I I I

Devotion to God allows the personality to free itself from the fetters

I I I

Devotion to the Divine
Worship, ritual and divine love allows the personality purified by truth to eradicate the subtle ignorance that binds it to mortal existence.

I I I I

The Shedy disciplines are the greatest form of worship of the Divine

I I I I

Meditation
Allows the whole person to go beyond the world of time and space and the gross and subtle ignorance of mortal human existence to discover that which transcends time and space.

Great Awakening
Occurs when all of the Great Truths have been realized by perfection of the Shedy disciplines to realize their true nature and actually experience oneness with the transcendental Supreme Being.

The Spiritual Culture and the Purpose of Life: Shetaut Neter

> "Men and women are to become God-like through a life of virtue and the cultivation of the spirit through scientific knowledge, practice and bodily discipline."
>
> -Ancient Egyptian Proverb

The highest forms of Joy, Peace and Contentment are obtained when the meaning of life is discovered. When the human being is in harmony with life, then it is possible to reflect and meditate upon the human condition and realize the limitations of worldly pursuits. When there is peace and harmony in life, a human being can practice any of the varied disciplines designated as Shetaut Neter to promote {his/her} evolution towards the ultimate goal of life, which Spiritual Enlightenment. Spiritual Enlightenment is the awakening of a human being to the awareness of the Transcendental essence which binds the universe and which is eternal and immutable. In this discovery is also the sobering and ecstatic realization that the human being is one with that Transcendental essence. With this realization comes great joy, peace and power to experience the fullness of life and to realize the purpose of life during the time on earth. The lotus is a symbol of Shetaut Neter, meaning the turning towards the light of truth, peace and transcendental harmony.

Shetaut Neter

We have established that the Ancient Egyptians were African peoples who lived in the north-eastern quadrant of the continent of Africa. They were descendants of the Nubians, who had themselves originated from farther south into the heart of Africa at the Great Lakes region, the sources of the Nile River. They created a vast civilization and culture earlier than any other society in known history and organized a nation that was based on the concepts of balance and order as well as spiritual enlightenment. These ancient African people called their land Kamit, and soon after developing a well-ordered society, they began to realize that the world is full of wonders, but also that life is fleeting, and that there must be something more to human existence. They developed spiritual systems that were designed to allow human beings to understand the nature of this secret being who is the essence of all Creation. They called this spiritual system "Shtaut Ntr (Shetaut Neter)."

Shetaut means secret.

Neter means Divinity.

Who is Neter in Kamitan Religion?

The symbol of Neter was described by an Ancient Kamitan priest as:
"That which is placed in the coffin"

The term Ntr, or Ntjr, comes from the Ancient Egyptian hieroglyphic language which did not record its vowels. However, the term survives in the Coptic language as *"Nutar."* The same Coptic meaning (divine force or sustaining power) applies in the present as it did in ancient times. It is a symbol composed of a wooden staff that was wrapped with strips of fabric, like a mummy. The strips alternate in color with yellow, green and blue. The mummy in Kamitan spirituality is understood to be the dead but resurrected Divinity. So the Nutar (Ntr) is actually every human being who does not really die, but goes to live on in a different form. Further, the resurrected spirit of every human being is that same Divinity. Phonetically, the term Nutar is related to other terms having the same meaning, such as the latin "Natura," the Spanish Naturalesa, the English "Nature" and "Nutriment", etc. In a real sense, as we will see, Natur means power manifesting as Neteru and the Neteru are the objects of creation, i.e. "nature."

Sacred Scriptures of Shetaut Neter

The following scriptures represent the foundational scriptures of Kamitan culture. They may be divided into three categories: **Mythic Scriptures**, **Mystical Philosophy** and **Ritual Scriptures**, and **Wisdom Scriptures** (Didactic Literature).

MYTHIC SCRIPTURES Literature	Mystical (Ritual) Philosophy Literature	Wisdom Texts Literature
SHETAUT ASAR-ASET-HERU The Myth of Asar, Aset and Heru (Asarian Resurrection Theology) - Predynastic **SHETAUT ATUM-RA** Anunian Theology Predynastic Shetaut Net/Aset/Hetheru Saitian Theology – Goddess Spirituality Predynastic **SHETAUT PTAH** Memphite Theology Predynastic Shetaut Amun Theban Theology Predynastic	Coffin Texts (C. 2040 B.C.E.-1786 B.C.E.) Papyrus Texts (C. 1580 B.C.E.-Roman Period)[61] Books of Coming Forth By Day Example of famous papyri: Papyrus of Any Papyrus of Hunefer Papyrus of Kenna Greenfield Papyrus, Etc.	Wisdom Texts (C. 3,000 B.C.E. – PTOLEMAIC PERIOD) Precepts of Ptahotep Instructions of Any Instructions of Amenemope Etc. Maat Declarations Literature (All Periods)

---

[61] After 1570 B.C.E they would evolve into a more unified text, the Egyptian Book of the Dead.

Neter and the Neteru

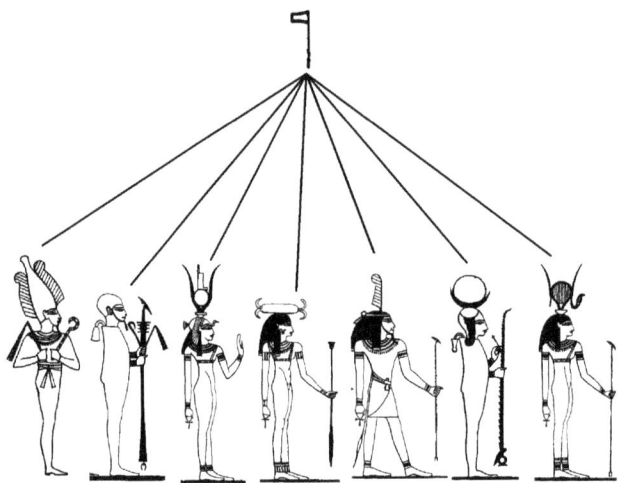

The Neteru (Gods and Goddesses) proceed from the Neter (Supreme Being)

As stated earlier, the concept of Neter and Neteru binds and ties all of the varied forms of Kamitan spirituality into one vision of the gods and goddesses all emerging from the same Supreme Being. Therefore, ultimately, Kamitan spirituality is not polytheistic, nor is it monotheistic, for it holds that the Supreme Being is more than a God or Goddess. The Supreme Being is an all-encompassing Absolute Divinity.

The Neteru

The term "Neteru" means "gods and goddesses." This means that from the ultimate and transcendental Supreme Being, "Neter," come the Neteru. There are countless Neteru. So from the one come the many. These Neteru are cosmic forces that pervade the universe. They are the means by which Neter sustains Creation and manifests through it. So Neterianism is a monotheistic polytheism. The one Supreme Being expresses as many gods and goddesses. At the end of time, after their work of sustaining Creation is finished, these gods and goddesses are again absorbed back into the Supreme Being.

All of the spiritual systems of Ancient Egypt (Kamit) have one essential aspect that is common to all; they all hold that there is a Supreme Being (Neter) who manifests in a multiplicity of ways through nature, the Neteru. Like sunrays, the Neteru emanate from the Divine; they are its manifestations. So by studying the Neteru we learn about and are led to discover their source, the Neter, and with this discovery we are enlightened. The Neteru may be depicted anthropomorphically or zoomorphically in accordance with the teaching about Neter that is being conveyed through them.

The Neteru and Their Temples

Diagram 1: The Ancient Egyptian Temple Network

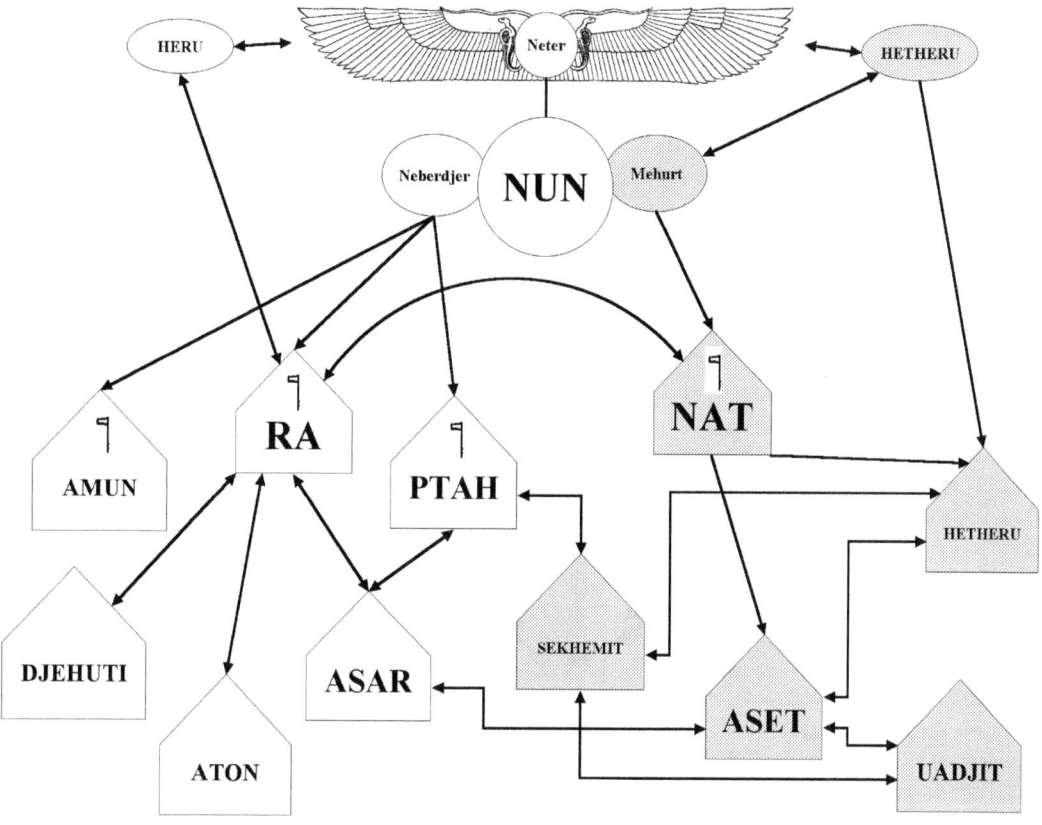

The sages of Kamit instituted a system by which the teachings of spirituality were espoused through a Temple organization. The major divinities were assigned to a particular city. That divinity or group of divinities became the "patron" divinity or divinities of that city. Also, the Priests and Priestesses of that Temple were in charge of seeing to the welfare of the people in that district as well as maintaining the traditions and disciplines of the traditions based on the particular divinity being worshipped. So the original concept of "Neter" became elaborated through the "theologies" of the various traditions. A dynamic expression of the teachings emerged, which though maintaining the integrity of the teachings, expressed nuances of variation in perspective on the teachings to suit the needs of varying kinds of personalities of the people of different locales.

In the diagram above, the primary or main divinities are denoted by the Neter symbol ( ). The house structure represents the Temple for that particular divinity. The interconnections with the other Temples are based on original scriptural statements espoused by the Temples that linked the divinities of their Temple with the other divinities. So this means that the divinities should be viewed not as separate entities operating independently, but rather as family members who are in the same "business" together, i.e. the enlightenment of society, albeit through variations in form of worship, name, form (expression of the Divinity), etc. Ultimately, all the divinities are referred to as Neteru and they are all said to be emanations from the ultimate and Supreme Being. Thus, the teaching from any of the Temples leads to an understanding of the others, and these all lead back to the source, the highest Divinity. Thus, the teaching within any of the Temple systems would lead to the attainment of spiritual enlightenment, the Great Awakening.

The Neteru and Their Interrelationships

Diagram : The Primary Kamitan Neteru and their Interrelationships

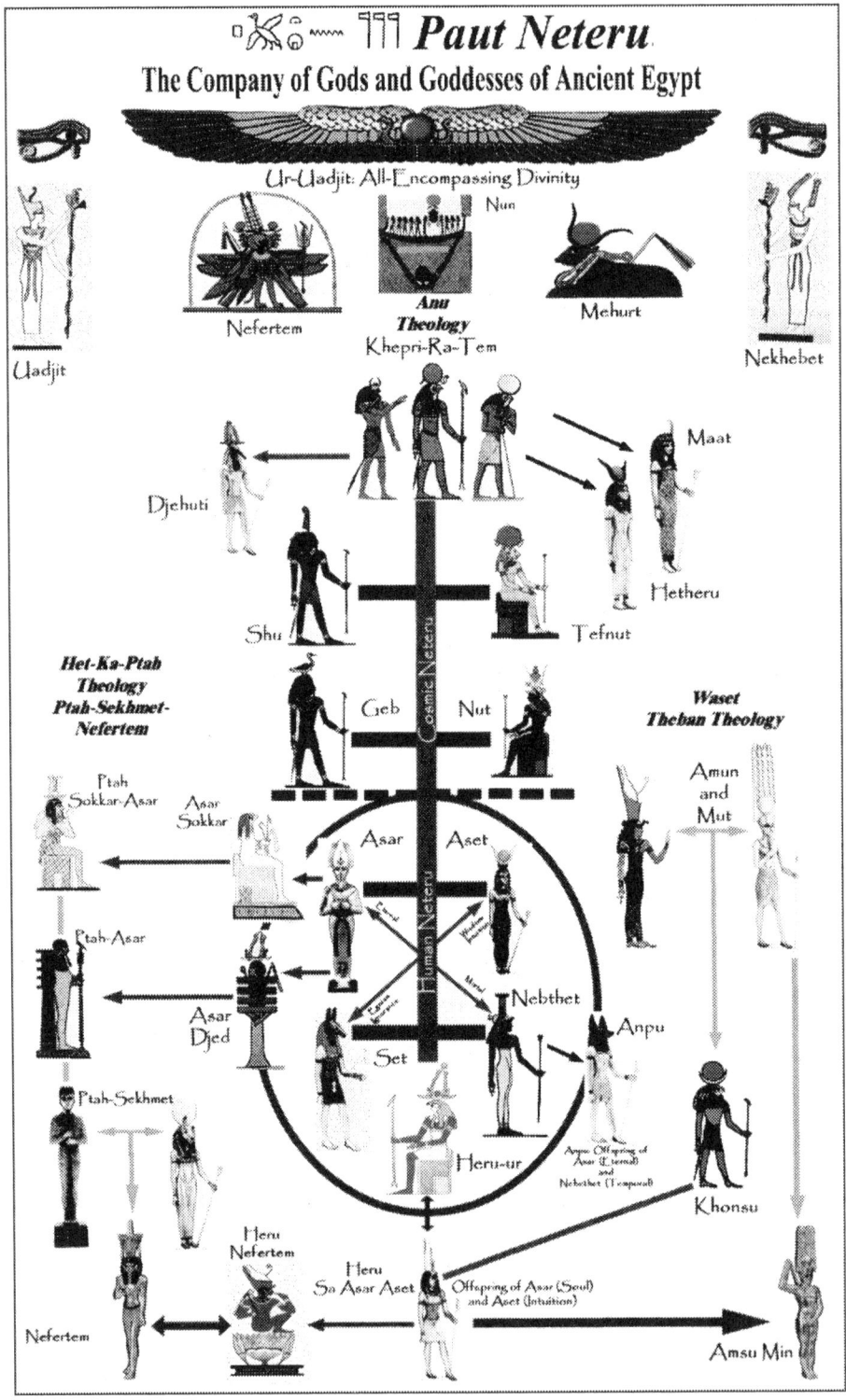

The same Supreme Being, Neter, is the winged all-encompassing transcendental Divinity, the Spirit who, in the early history, is called "Heru." The physical universe in which the Heru lives is called "Hetheru" or the "house of Heru." This divinity (Heru) is also the Nun or primeval substratum from which all matter is composed. The various divinities and the material universe are composed from this primeval substratum. Neter is actually androgynous and Heru, the Spirit, is related as a male aspect of that androgyny. However, Heru in the androgynous aspect, gives rise to the solar principle and this is seen in both the male and female divinities.

The image above provides an idea of the relationships between the divinities of the three main Neterian spiritual systems (traditions): Anunian Theology, Wasetian (Theban) Theology and Het-Ka-Ptah (Memphite) Theology. The traditions are composed of companies or groups of gods and goddesses. Their actions, teachings and interactions with each other and with human beings provide insight into their nature as well as that of human existence and Creation itself. The lines indicate direct scriptural relationships and the labels also indicate that some divinities from one system are the same in others, with only a name change. Again, this is attested to by the scriptures themselves in direct statements, like those found in the *Prt m Hru* text Chapter 4 (17).[62]

Listening to the Teachings

"*Mestchert*"

"Listening, to fill the ears, listen attentively-"

What should the ears be filled with?

The sages of Shetaut Neter enjoined that a Shemsu Neter (follower of Neter, an initiate or aspirant) should listen to the WISDOM of the Neterian Traditions. These are the myth related to the gods and goddesses containing the basic understanding of who they are, what they represent, how they relate human beings and to the Supreme Being. The myths allow us to be connected to the Divine.

An aspirant may choose any one of the 5 main Neterian Traditions.

- Shetaut Anu – Teachings of the Ra Tradition
- Shetaut Menefer – Teachings of the Ptah Tradition
- Shetaut Waset – Teachings of the Amun Tradition
- Shetaut Netrit – Teachings of the Goddess Tradition
- Shetaut Asar – Teachings of the Asarian Tradition
- Shetaut Aton – Teachings of the Aton Tradition

---

[62] See the book *The Egyptian Book of the Dead* by Muata Ashby

The Anunian Tradition

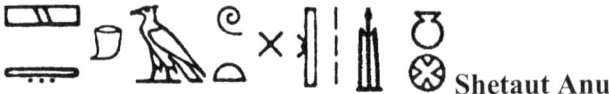 Shetaut Anu

The Mystery Teachings of the Anunian Tradition are related to the Divinity Ra and his company of Gods and Goddesses.[63] This Temple and its related Temples espouse the teachings of Creation, human origins and the path to spiritual enlightenment by means of the Supreme Being in the form of the god Ra. It tells of how Ra emerged from a primeval ocean and how human beings were created from his tears. The gods and goddesses, who are his children, go to form the elements of nature and the cosmic forces that maintain nature.

Below: The Heliopolitan Cosmogony.

The city of Anu (Amun-Ra)

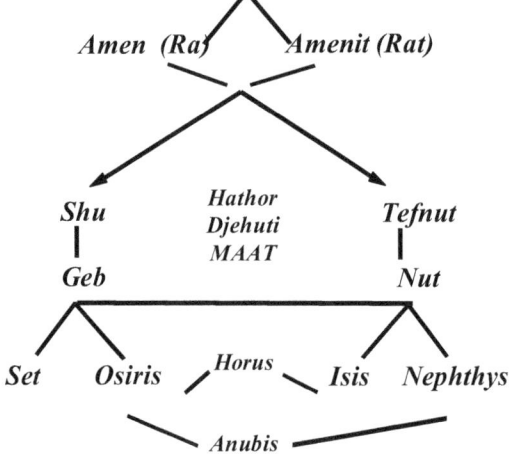

The Neters of Creation -
The Company of the Gods and Goddesses.
Neter Neteru
Nebertcher - Amun (unseen, hidden, ever present, Supreme Being, beyond duality and description)

Amen (Ra) — *Amenit (Rat)*

Shu — *Hathor Djehuti MAAT* — *Tefnut*

Geb — *Nut*

Set Osiris Horus Isis Nephthys

Anubis

Top: Ra. From left to right, starting at the bottom level- The Gods and Goddesses of Anunian Theology: Shu, Tefnut, Nut, Geb, Aset, Asar, Set, Nebthet and Heru-Ur

---

[63] See the Book Anunian Theology by Muata Ashby

The Memphite Tradition

 Shetaut Menefer

The Mystery Teachings of the Menefer (Memphite) Tradition are related to the Neterus known as Ptah, Sekhmit, Nefertem. The myths and philosophy of these divinities constitutes Memphite Theology.[64] This temple and its related temples espoused the teachings of Creation, human origins and the path to spiritual enlightenment by means of the Supreme Being in the form of the god Ptah and his family, who compose the Memphite Trinity. It tells of how Ptah emerged from a primeval ocean and how he created the universe by his will and the power of thought (mind). The gods and goddesses who are his thoughts, go to form the elements of nature and the cosmic forces that maintain nature. His spouse, Sekhmit has a powerful temple system of her own that is related to the Memphite teaching. The same is true for his son Nefertem.

Below: The Memphite Cosmogony.

The city of Hetkaptah (Ptah)

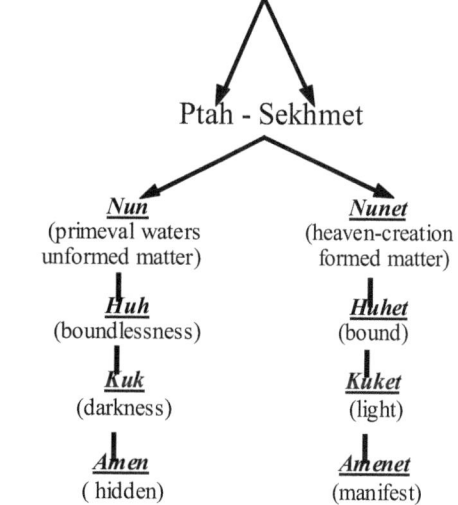

The Neters of Creation - The Company of the Gods and Goddesses.
Neter Neteru
Nebertcher - Amun (unseen, hidden, ever present, Supreme Being, beyond duality and description)

Ptah - Sekhmet

Nun (primeval waters unformed matter) — *Nunet* (heaven-creation formed matter)

Huh (boundlessness) — *Huhet* (bound)

Kuk (darkness) — *Kuket* (light)

Amen (hidden) — *Amenet* (manifest)

Ptah, Sekhmit and Nefertem

---

[64] See the Book Memphite Theology by Muata Ashby

The Theban Tradition

Shetaut Amun

The Mystery Teachings of the Wasetian Tradition are related to the Neterus known as Amun, Mut Khonsu. This temple and its related temples espoused the teachings of Creation, human origins and the path to spiritual enlightenment by means of the Supreme Being in the form of the god Amun or Amun-Ra. It tells of how Amun and his family, the Trinity of Amun, Mut and Khonsu, manage the Universe along with his Company of Gods and Goddesses. This Temple became very important in the early part of the New Kingdom Era.

Below: The Trinity of Amun and the Company of Gods and Goddesses of Amun

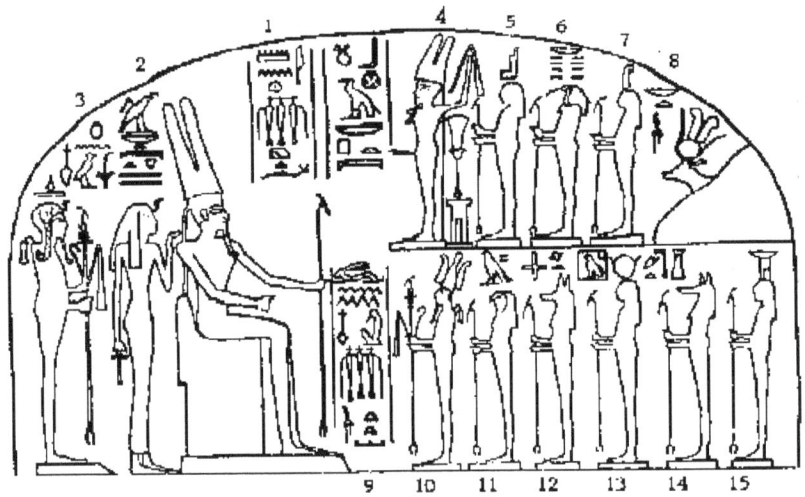

See the Book *Egyptian Yoga Vol. 2* for more on Amun, Mut and Khonsu by Muata Ashby

The Goddess Tradition

Shetaut Netrit

"Arat"

The hieroglyphic sign Arat means "Goddess." General, throughout ancient Kamit, the Mystery Teachings of the Goddess Tradition are related to the Divinity in the form of the Goddess. The Goddess was an integral part of all the Neterian traditions but special temples also developed around the worship of certain particular Goddesses who were also regarded as Supreme Beings in their own right. Thus as in other African religions, the goddess as well as the female gender were respected and elevated as the male divinities. The Goddess was also the author of Creation, giving birth to it as a great Cow. The following are the most important forms of the goddess.[65]

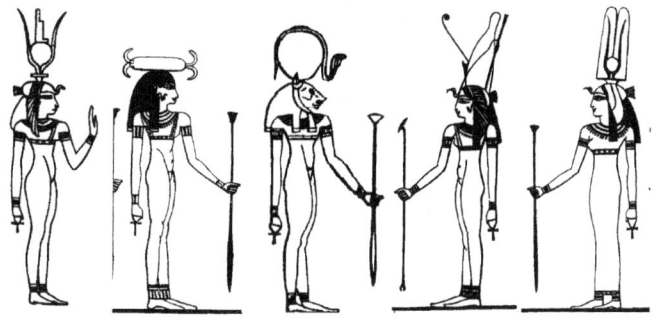

Aset, Net, Sekhmit, Mut, Hetheru

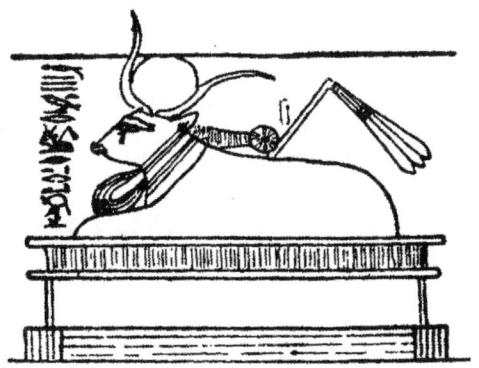

Mehurt ("The Mighty Full One")

---

[65] See the Books, *The Goddess Path, Mysteries of Isis, Glorious Light Meditation, Memphite Theology* and *Resurrecting Osiris* by Muata Ashby

The Asarian Tradition

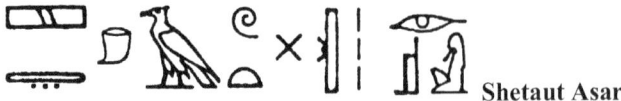 Shetaut Asar

This temple and its related temples espoused the teachings of Creation, human origins and the path to spiritual enlightenment by means of the Supreme Being in the form of the god Asar. It tells of how Asar and his family, the Trinity of Asar, Aset and Heru, manage the Universe and lead human beings to spiritual enlightenment and the resurrection of the soul. This Temple and its teaching were very important from the Pre-Dynastic era down to the Christian period. The Mystery Teachings of the Asarian Tradition are related to the Neterus known as: Asar, Aset, Heru (Osiris, Isis and Horus)

The tradition of Asar, Aset and Heru was practiced generally throughout the land of ancient Kamit. The centers of this tradition were the city of Abdu containing the Great Temple of Asar, the city of Pilak containing the Great Temple of Aset[66] and Edfu containing the Ggreat Temple of Heru.

---

[66] See the Book Resurrecting Osiris by Muata Ashby

The Aton Tradition

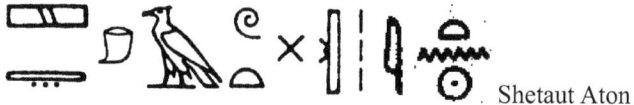 Shetaut Aton

This temple and its related temples espoused the teachings of Creation, human origins and the path to spiritual enlightenment by means of the Supreme Being in the form of the god Aton. It tells of how Aton with its dynamic life force created and sustains Creation. By recognizing Aton as the very substratum of all existence, human beings engage in devotional exercises and rituals and the study of the Hymns containing the wisdom teachings of Aton explaining that Aton manages the Universe and leads human beings to spiritual enlightenment and eternal life for the soul. This Temple and its teaching were very important in the middle New Kingdom Period. The Mystery Teachings of the Aton Tradition are related to the Neter Aton and its main exponent was the Sage King Akhnaton, who is depicted below with his family adoring the sundisk, symbol of the Aton.

Akhnaton, Nefertiti and Daughters

For more on Atonism and the Aton Theology see the Essence of Atonism Lecture Series by Sebai Muata Ashby ©2001

The General Principles of Shetaut Neter
(Teachings Presented in the Kamitan scriptures)

1. The Purpose of Life is to Attain the Great Awakening-Enlightenment-Know thyself.

2. SHETAUT NETER enjoins the Shedy (spiritual investigation) as the highest endeavor of life.

3. SHETAUT NETER enjoins that it is the responsibility of every human being to promote order and truth.

4. SHETAUT NETER enjoins the performance of Selfless Service to family, community and humanity.

5. SHETAUT NETER enjoins the Protection of nature.

6. SHETAUT NETER enjoins the Protection of the weak and oppressed.

7. SHETAUT NETER enjoins the Caring for hungry.

8. SHETAUT NETER enjoins the Caring for homeless.

9. SHETAUT NETER enjoins the equality for all people.

10. SHETAUT NETER enjoins the equality between men and women.

11. SHETAUT NETER enjoins the justice for all.

12. SHETAUT NETER enjoins the sharing of resources.

13. SHETAUT NETER enjoins the protection and proper raising of children.

14. SHETAUT NETER enjoins the movement towards balance and peace.

The Forces of Entropy

In Neterian religion, there is no concept of "evil" as is conceptualized in Western Culture. Rather, it is understood that the forces of entropy are constantly working in nature to bring that which has been constructed by human hands to their original natural state. The serpent Apep (Apophis), who daily tries to stop Ra's boat of creation, is the symbol of entropy. This concept of entropy has been referred to as "chaos" by Western Egyptologists.

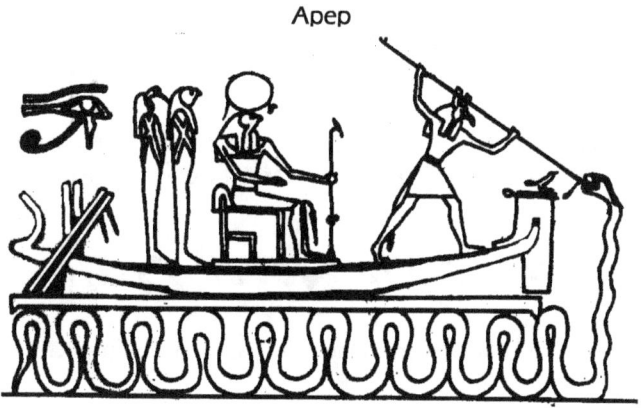

Above: Set protecting the boat of Ra from the forces of entropy (symbolized by the serpent Apep).

As expressed previously, in Neterian religion there is also no concept of a "devil" or "demon" as is conceived in the Judeo-Christian or Islamic traditions. Rather, it is understood that manifestations of detrimental situations and adversities arise as a result of unrighteous actions. These unrighteous actions are due to the "Setian" qualities in a human being. Set is the Neteru of egoism and the negative qualities which arise from egoism. Egoism is the idea of individuality based on identification with the body and mind only as being who one is. One has no deeper awareness of their deeper spiritual essence, and thus no understanding of their connectedness to all other objects (includes persons) in creation and the Divine Self. When the ego is under the control of the higher nature, it fights the forces of entropy (as above). However, when beset with ignorance, it leads to the degraded states of human existence. The vices (egoism, selfishness, extraverted ness, wonton sexuality (lust), jealousy, envy, greed, gluttony) are a result.

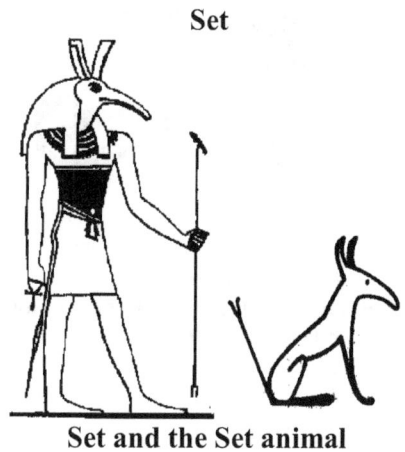

Set and the Set animal

The Great Awakening of Neterian Religion

"Nehast"

Nehast means to "wake up," to Awaken to the higher existence. In the Prt m Hru Text it is said:

Nuk pa Neter aah Neter Uah asha ren[67]

"I am that same God, the Supreme One, who has myriad of mysterious names."

The goal of all the Neterian disciplines is to discover the meaning of "Who am I?," to unravel the mysteries of life and to fathom the depths of eternity and infinity. This is the task of all human beings and it is to be accomplished in this very lifetime.

This can be done by learning the ways of the Neteru, emulating them and finally becoming like them, Akhus, (enlightened beings), walking the earth as giants and accomplishing great deeds such as the creation of the universe!

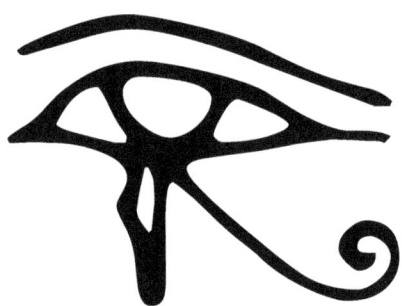

Udjat
The Eye of Heru is a quintessential symbol of awakening to Divine Consciousness, representing the concept of Nehast.

---

[67] (Prt M Hru 9:4)

Kamitan Religion as a Development of African Spirituality and the Influence of Kamitan Culture and Spirituality on African Cultures and World Cultures Over Time.

Figure 43: Human Origins- Modern Human Beings Originate in Africa – 150,000 – 100,000 B.C.E.

The history of modern humanity begins in Africa 150,000 years ago. All the human beings who are alive all over the earth today descend from an original group of human beings who lived 150,000 years ago in central-equatorial Africa. These human beings spread out from there and populated the rest of Africa over the next 50,000 years.

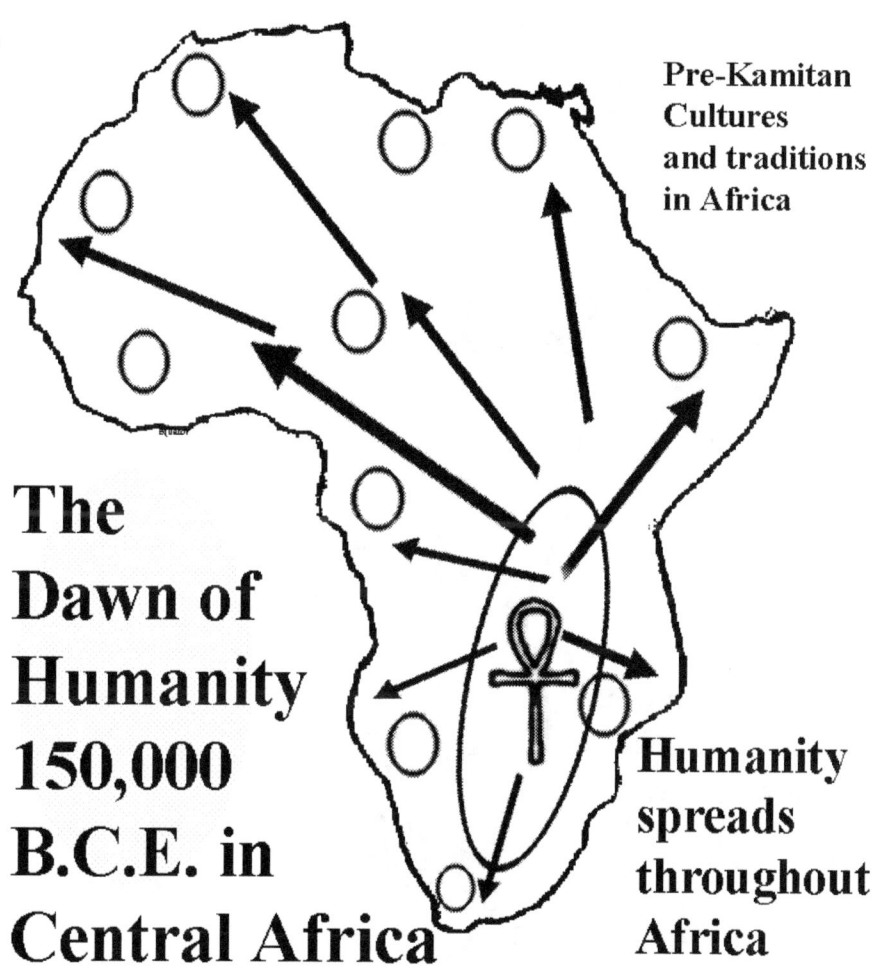

Figure 44: Human Cultural Development -Cultures develop throughout Africa – 36,000-10,000 B.C.E.

Over the next 50,000 years (150,000-100,000 B.C.E.) the people who populated Africa developed cultures that took on several unique aspects but at the same time manifested the principles that they had carried with them from the originating point to their new homes around the continent. These were a set of social (Maat-Ubuntu) and religious (Supreme Being served by lesser gods and goddesses) principles which became the basis of all African religions that would develop thereafter. Over time some of the groups lost contact and different languages developed, but the principles remained the same and became highly evolved in the Kush-Kamit region.

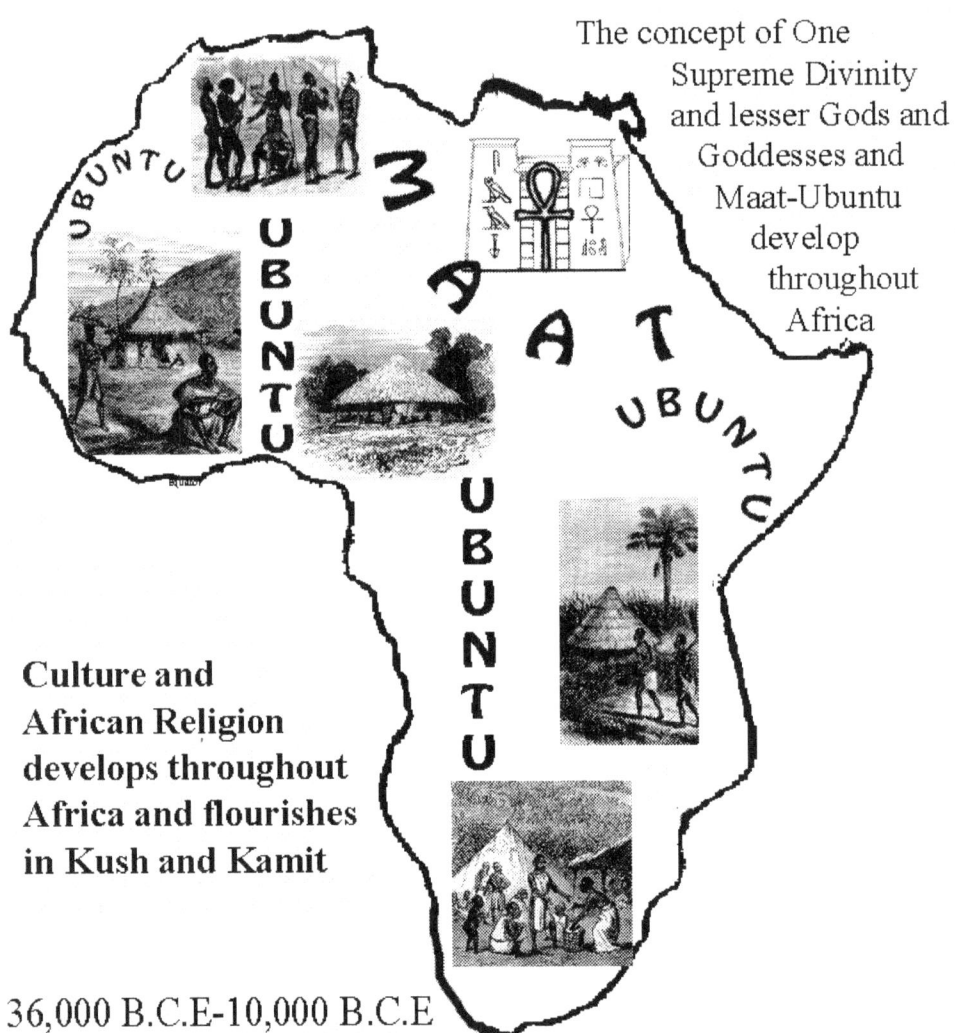

Figure 45: African High Culture- Kamitan Culture Influences African Cultures

Between 36,000 B.C.E. and 10,000 B.C.E. the peoples of the northeastern quadrant of the continent were able to develop advanced culture and civilization. This became known as the Kush-Kamit Civilization. It was based on the same essential African spiritual and social principles as all other African cultures who originated in 150,000 B.C.E. in central-equatorial Africa. At about 4,000 B.C.E. the Kamitan culture began to influence other African nations with its highly evolved African philosophy which was actually an evolution of the same principles possessed by the other African cultures.

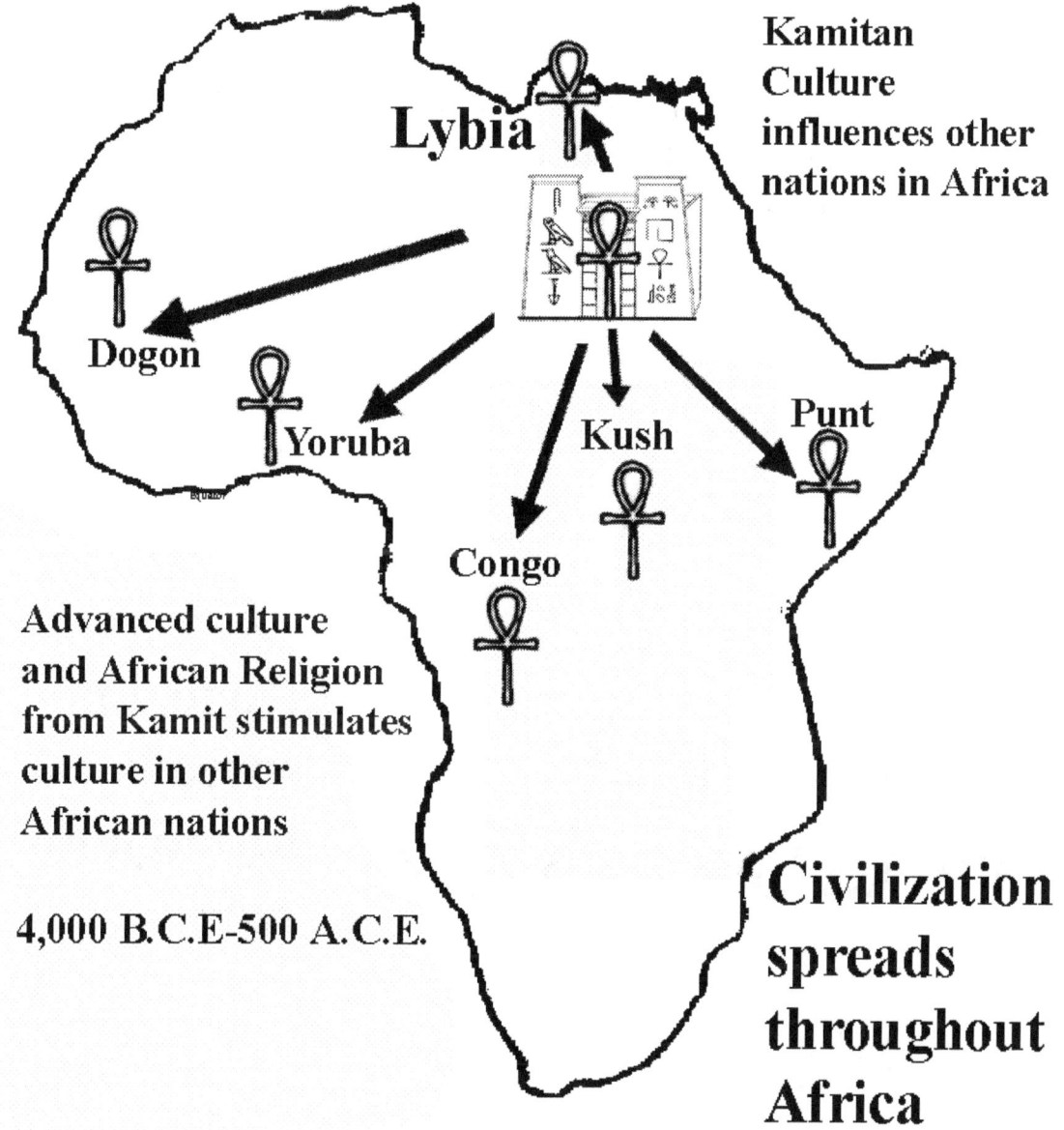

Figure 46: Kamitan Civilization Influences Cultures Outside of Africa 4,000 B.C.E.-500 A.C.E.

At about 3,500 B.C.E. or earlier, the Kamitan culture and civilization began to influence the peoples in Asia Minor (Mesopotamia) and South East Asia (India and China). At about 1,900-1,400 B.C.E. the Kamitan culture and civilization began to influence the archaic Greek culture (Minoans), thereby fomenting the development of culture and spirituality in those areas.

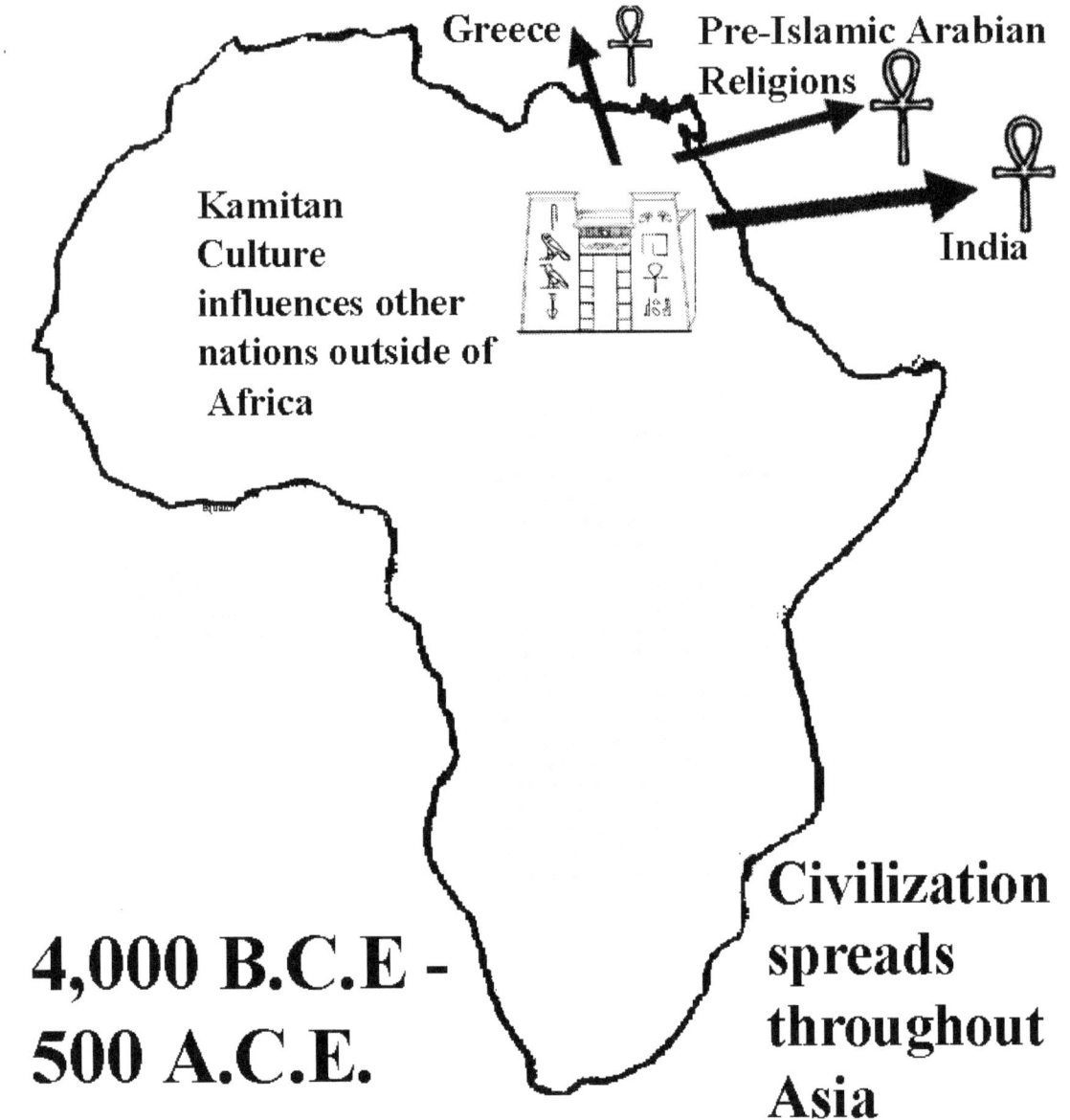

Ancient Egypt and Its Influence on Other African Religions

Plate: Picture of a display at the Brooklyn Museum (1998-2000) showing the similarity between the headrest of Ancient Egypt (foreground) and those used in other parts of Africa (background). (Photo by M. Ashby)

Foreground: Headrest and Mother nursing Child from Ancient Egypt Background: Headrest and Mother nursing Child from other parts of Africa

The display above shows the stark similarities noted widely in scholarly circles, between Ancient Egyptian artifacts and artifacts from other African nations. The headrest of Ancient Egypt in the foreground and the other African one in the background are alike in form, function, and color. The concept of the mother suckling the child depicted in the sculpture of Aset and Heru (foreground) and the West African sculpture in the background are also alike in concept, function and form. Also, Indian scholars have noted finding similar headrests in South India.[211]

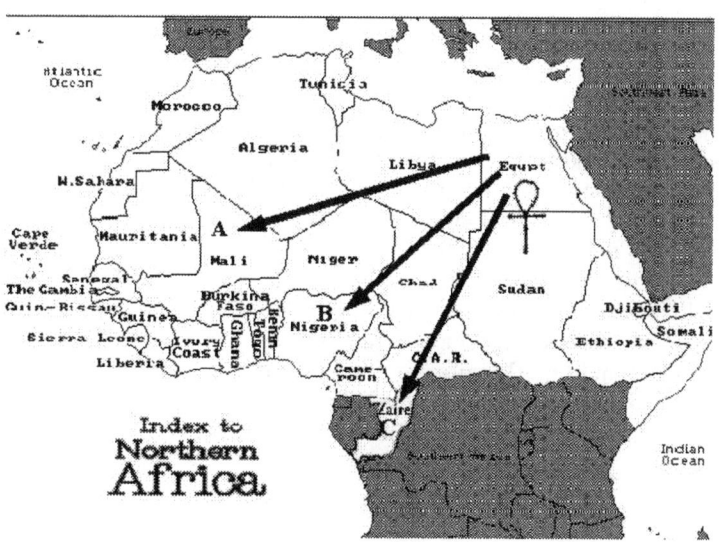

Figure-Above: A map of North-East Africa showing the location of *Ta-Meri* or *Kamit (Kamut)*, more commonly known as Ancient Egypt.

The arrows (in the map above) point to the geographical locations in Africa and Asia where the Ancient Egyptian influence spread during the height of Ancient Egyptian civilization, and also thereafter following the end of the Dynastic Period.

A- The Dogon of Mali.
B- The Yoruba of West Africa.
C- Zaire.
D- Greece and Rome.
E- India.

Ancient Egypt and the Dogon Nation

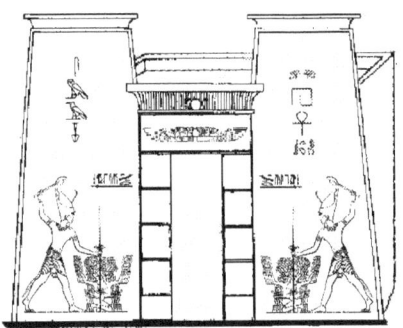 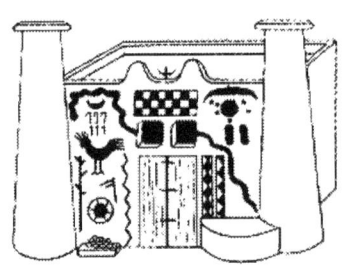

Figure 47: Above left- Kamitan Temple

The New Kingdom Period (1,900 B.C.E.-100 B.C.E.) Kamitan Temple

Figure 48: Above right- Dogon Temple

Late common era Dogon Temple (c. 1000 A.C.E.-2,000 A.C.E.)

The Dogon people of West Africa are perhaps known best for their extensive carvings of wooden figurative art and masks. The early history of the Dogon people is carried forth by oral traditions, and these claim that the Dogon came from the west bank of the Niger River during the period between the 10th to 13th centuries A.C.E. They emigrated west to northern Burkino Faso. The oral traditions also tell of their migration from north-east Africa. Thus, the Dogon claim themselves to be descendants of the Ancient Egyptians. The connection between Neterian Religion and Dogon religion is evident in several aspects of mythology including the name for the High God which is Amun in Shetaut Neter religion and Amma in Dogon religion. They share some of the Ancient Egyptian myths like the reverence for the star Sirius, but they have also incorporated elements from other religious systems over the years. In the scene above, notice the similarities of the Temples in the pylons and single entrance leading to a covered inner area of the Temples as well as the practice of placing inscriptions on the front of the Temple walls. These and other similarities, coupled with the ancestral legacy attested to by the Dogon themselves indicate that the Dogon and Kamitan cultures were at one time related, and that they have a common source in Kamit.

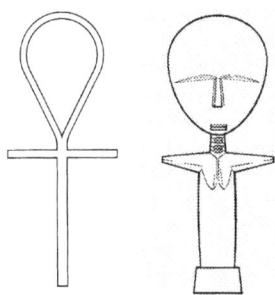

Figure 49: Above Left: Ankh-Ancient Egyptian Symbol and instrument of life. Right: Ahsanti Fertility doll from West African

Cultural Interactions Between the Ancient Egyptians and the Fon Nation

    Above: From the tomb of Pharaoh Tutankhamun, a visual exposition of the idea expressed by the God Djehuti (Thoth)-Hermes: "As above, so below," as two serpents enclose the cosmic form of man (the universe). That which is above (spirit) is eternal, that which is below (matter) is also eternal. The serpent of the earth and the serpent of the sky encircle the lower as well as the higher self. The lower self and the higher self are complementary halves of the whole if brought into harmony.
    The center area at the base of the spine is highlighted with a line and by the ram-headed hawk positioned with arms raised (in adoration "Ka") toward the sacral region of the spine - the root energy center (chakra).

The cosmic serpent went by many names in Ancient Egypt. There was the Kamutef serpent of Amun, and Mehen, the coiled serpent of the god Ra, known as the "coiled one." The Mehen serpent was known from the time of the coffin texts.[212] The serpent's body coils around the universe and stirs the primeval ocean into the varied forms of Creation as per the desire of God.

The Fon Nation of West Africa views the snake as the creator and sustainer of creation. Through its 3,500 "coils" above the earth, and 3,500 "coils" below the earth, the snake represents energy in perpetual motion, energy without which creation would immediately disintegrate. Note that the number 3,500 is a multiple of 3.5, the specific number ascribed in Kamit and India for the Serpent Power and Kundalini Yoga systems, respectively. This description recalls the Primeval Serpent of Ancient Egyptian mythology and Kundalini Yoga of India, with her "coiled up" cosmic energy which sustains all life. Another Fon story tells that a serpent carried GOD everywhere in its mouth in the making of creation. This is reminiscent of the Egyptian story of *"The Serpent in the Sky."* Also, the main character in Fon mythology, *Legba,* seeks to reconcile the rift between heaven and earth, which occurred in primeval times.

The Gods Murungu and Muntju (Monthu) of Kenya and Egypt in Africa

Murungu of Kenya

The Kikuyu people of Kenya, the tribes of Malawi, Zimbabwe, Zaire, Tanzania, Uganda and the Yao people of Mozambique worship the god Murungu (Mulungu)[213] as the supreme and transcendental divinity behind Creation. The Kikuyu's god is named "*Murungu.*" Kenya is an East-African republic in Africa, bounded on the north by Sudan and Ethiopia and on the east by Somalia and the Indian Ocean, on the south by Tanzania, and on the west by Lake Victoria and Uganda.[214] In ancient times Kenya was on the maritime trade route between Ethiopia and Egypt and India. Murungu cannot be seen, but is manifested in the sun, moon, thunder and lightning, stars, rain, the rainbow and in the great fig trees that serve as places of worship and sacrifice. These attributes of Murungu are closely related to the supreme divinity, Ra, in Ancient Kamit. Especially notable is the philosophy of understanding the Divine as supreme and transcendental and yet manifesting as Creation itself, but especially through the sun and moon. In Kamitan Anunian mysticism (based on the God Ra, whose main symbol is the sun) and Atonian (based on the divinity Aton, whose main symbol is the sundisk) mysticism, the Spirit is understood as manifesting through the sun and moon, not as being the object itself. This is an advanced understanding that there is a subtle essence beyond Creation and this conceptualization takes the religious philosophy outside the realm of idolatry.

Muntju of Ancient Egypt

In the aspect as the god of thunder and lightning, Murungu may be likened to Indra in the Vedic pantheon of Indian gods and goddesses. Indra was known to be the god of war among other attributes. Ra in Ancient Egypt has an aspect by the name of *Muntu (Montu, Monthu);* this aspect is the expression of war in Kamitan myth. The worship of Muntu was prominent in the 11th Dynasty Period. Muntu is related to Heru-Behded who is the warrior aspect of the god Heru, who is also an aspect of Ra.

Figure 50: Above-Left- The God Montju of Ancient Egypt. Above-Right Heru-Behded, The Warrior

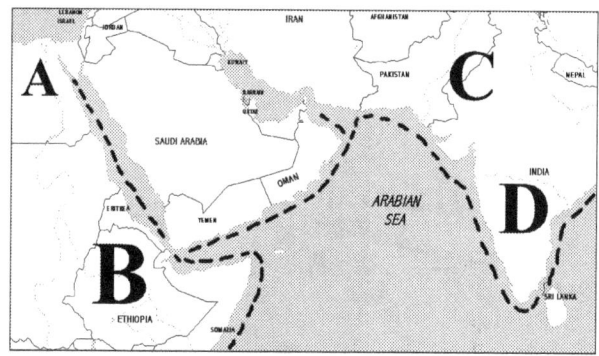

Figure 51: Above- (A-B) North-east Africa, Asia Minor, (C-D) South Asia (India) and the Egyptian-Indian trade routes in the Hellenistic (Greek) and Roman times.[215]

Evidence of Contact Between Ancient Egypt and other African Nations

Edward Wilmot Blyden (1832 - 1912) was one of the first African American theologian/scholars to recognize a connection between Ancient Egypt and the West African nations. He began to notice that the trade routs across the Sahara desert, which can be seen even today, transported goods and people, creating an inexorable connection between Northeast and West Africa. This contact existed since ancient times. The evidence of its existence can be found on the walls of the tombs of the nobles in Egypt. These are the same trade routs that were used by the Arabs to communicate, extend trade and spread the Islamic faith to West Africa, and they did so from their base in Egypt.

Ancient Traders: Painting from the "Tombs of the Nobles" in Egypt (New Kingdom) showing desert traders coming from other parts of Africa to Egypt. Note the hat of the first man from the right. This is the same type of hat used by traders in the present day region of West Sahara (Western Sudan) and it is also used by present day Dogons.

Above: The trade routs from Egypt to and from West Africa (Senegal, Mali, Nigeria, and Congo) and Kush (Nubia)

Cheikh Anta Diop presented compelling evidences to show that the Wolof language (Senegal) is derived from the Kamitan.[216] Since his time, other researchers have shown that evidences from linguistic correlations show a relationship. Also, J Olumide Lucas, in his book *The Religion of the Yorubas: Being an account of the religious beliefs and practices of the Yoruba peoples of southern Nigeria especially in relation to the religion of ancient Egypt,* presented evidences of linguistic nature as well as fundamental mythological nature to show the remnants of Ancient Egyptian religion and culture as surviving in Yoruba culture. While his work has been challenged as far as his method of classifying the evolution from the Kamitan to the Yoruba language, the mythological correlations are undeniable and powerful. What follows is a brief introduction to the mythological correlations between Kamitan and Yoruba religion. A more detailed discussion of this connection will be presented in a future volume.

Regional Correlations Between Kamitan Religion and other African Religions

Item of Correlation	Description	African Country or Culture where the Tradition was observed
Pigmies in the Royal Court	It was a tradition of the Pharaonic system in Kamit from the earliest period to have pigmies in the royal court.	Kamit, Kush, Unyoro, Mañbatto
The King Performs the ceremonial dance	The king performs a ceremonial dance for worship and renewal of the rulership and prosperity of the country.	Kamit, Unyoro, Mañbatto, Fon
Song of merriment and dispassion	At festivities the king and the people take part in a song whose statements are almost identical in two cultures.	Fon, Kamit (Song of the Harper)
Childbirth in the bush	The custom of women going into the bush to give birth.	Kamit, Kush (Sudan)
Injunctions of innocence	Statements proclaiming one's virtue, close similarity.	Kamit, Calabar

Interactions Between the Ancient Egyptians and the Yoruba Nation

Yoruba is a term that refers to a people (Oyo, Ife, Ilesha, Egbe, and Ijebu), a culture and a language originally based in Africa, as well as a religion. There are many parallels between Ancient Egyptian religion and the Yoruba religion. Both incorporate a system of divinities which represent cosmic forces, and many direct correlations can be observed between them. The Yoruba people reside in Western Africa (Nigeria). While many scholars of Yoruba openly state that there is little or no connection between these systems of spirituality, others have attempted to show linguistic correlations and contact in ancient times. As in the Dogon culture, some practitioners of Yoruba religion openly acknowledge their lineage to Ancient Egypt. The Asarian artifacts that have been discovered elsewhere in Africa[217] show that there was contact between Ancient Egypt and other countries in the interior of Africa. The Kamitan clergy carried with them certain aspects of spiritual knowledge which became incorporated in other cultures, through the influence of the clergy. Therefore, by looking at the mythology of Yoruba and Shetaut Neter, direct correlations in the fundamental theological principles of the religions are found which establish a relationship between the two.

The Yoruba religion has many similarities with the cosmogony, Gods and divination systems of Egypt. For example, one Yoruba creation story is almost identical to the Kamitan story described in the Shabaka Stone, later referred to as Memphite Theology. The Shabaka Stone describes the beginning as being a "watery and marshy place," and that the "Supreme Being" created the "Great God" whom he directed to create the world. The idea of a "Judgment after death" is also held by the Yorubas. It is similar to Kamitan idea of judgment as presented in the *Egyptian Book of the Dead* (*Egyptian Book of Coming Forth By Day*). In the Yoruba tradition, it is believed that after death, the spirit or soul of the person goes in front of God in order to give account of her or his life on earth. As in Ancient Kamit, the Yorubas believe that some will go to live with relatives in a good place, while others will end up in a bad place. Thus it is said in the Yoruba tradition:

> *All of the things we do when on earth,*
> *We will give account for in heaven.....*
> *We will state our case at the feet of GOD.*

The Yoruba and Kamitan System of Divinities

The next two images show the main divinities of Yoruba religion and those of Ancient Egyptian religion along with their mythological functions. Both systems have the same fundamental principles in relation to the nature of the Divine and the process in which that divine essence expresses in nature. From the Supreme and Transcendental Being (Olorun {Yoruba} or Neberdjer {Kamit}), the gods and goddesses emanate and thereby service Creation. Beyond matching in their manner of provenance, the correlations are homologous, matching even to the extent of the functions of the divinities. Both systems make use of an oracular scheme in which the Divinity communicates through the gods and goddesses, which represent natural (cosmic) forces in both systems, and also through direct means.

There have been many detractors within the ranks of followers of the Yoruba religion who have tried to assert that Yoruba spirituality is separate from other African religions, and some have alluded to the possibility that it emerged earlier than the Kamitan religion. While it is known and documented that Kamitan culture and spirituality go as far back as 10,000 B.C.E., Yoruba culture can only be documented to as far back as the 6th century A.C.E.[218] with the formation of Ife, the town in West Nigeria which is traditionally regarded as the oldest of the Yoruba kingdoms in the region. While Yoruba culture goes further back than the historical documentation suggests, the documentary evidences are used as a means to objectively compare historical relationships throughout history. The striking fact is that when the myths and philosophy of Yoruba spirituality are compared with the Kamitan, we begin to see a series of correlations that are inescapably well matched. Some of these include:

- Correlation of mythic characters and divinities in order and function.
- Correlation of cosmogony structure.
- Correlation of metaphysical intent of ritual.
- Correlation of oracular system.
- Correlation of metaphorical system of representing cosmic forces as divinities.
- Correlation of the function of the divinities in their mythic relationship to humanity and individual spiritual evolution.

There have been several scholars who have attempted to show a connection between Yoruba and Kamit based on linguistic correlations. However, this form of criteria is based on a mechanical interpretation of human interaction and evolutionary interaction. In other words, the idea that there needs to be a direct linguistic connection between two cultures in order to show a cultural, social or ethnic relationship is based on linear thinking rather than a scientific study of the manner in which human beings interact and influence each other. While a linguistic correlation (direct word borrowings or evolutions from one language to another) may be present, the absence of such factors should not preclude research into other forms of connection. For example, Dr. Cheikh Anta Diop discovered many connections between the Kamitan language and the Wolof language of West Africa.[219] As introduced earlier, while a linguistic correlations (direct word borrowings or evolutions from one language to another) may be present, the absence of such factors should not preclude research into other forms of connection. Therefore, phonetic connections may or be not present and in and of themselves offer only a superficial or theoretical basis to establish a connection, but if present along with correlations in other related factors (qualities-method of expression) such as meaning (definition), grammar, or etymology, then this kind of linguistic evidence carries more weight. This is what Diop has shown. What is remarkable in these numerous cited examples is that we have not only grammatical and phonetic correlations, but also meaning (sense-connotation) correlations as well.

Left: Goddess Aset of Kamit suckling the child

Right: Goddess Oya of Yoruba, suckling the child.

Examples (partial list) of Some of the Correlations Presented by Cheikh Anta Diop[220]

Kamitan Words	Wolof Words
Ta = earth	*Ta* = inundated earth, the very image of Egypt, of the Nile Valley
Ta tenen = The earth that rises, the first mound that appeared within the *Nun*, from the primordial water, in order to serve as the place where the god Ra appeared in the sensible world.	*Ten* = a formed mound (in clay), as God made to create Adam; emergence, earth mound.
Kematef - mysterious initial snake that encircles the earth and eats its own tail (?)	*Kemtef, Kematef* = the limit of something, could apply to the mythical snake encircling the world and feeding each day off its own tail.
Elbo = the "floater" = the emergent mound where the sun appeared at the beginning of time = the town of Edfu.[221]	*Temb* = to float (a parasitic "m" before "b").
Erme = Ra's tears through which he created humanity, hence the name of the Egyptians. *Erme* = men par excellence	*Erem - yeram* = mercy; the feeling of compassion often accompanied by tears.
Aar, aaru = Paradise, Elysian Fields	*Aar* = divine protection *Aaru* = protected by the divinity
Khem-min(t) = the god Min's sanctuary. = *kemmis* in Greek	*Ham "Min"* = to know Min; can also be applied to the prophet of Min, meaning, his first priest.
Anu = Osiris's ethnic group; word designated by a pillar	*Enou - yenou* = to carry on the head *K-enou* = pillar

Thus, if we look at the myth and culture of the Yoruba nation, we can then go beyond the limited standards set by mainstream European scholarship in order to discover the connection between the Yoruba and the Kamitans.

The correlations between the Yoruba and Neterian Divinities may be viewed thusly:

Kamitan Divinities	Yoruba Divinities
Olorun	Neberdjer (Temu)
Elegba	Djehuti
Obatala	Asar
Ogun	Anpu
Shango	Set
Oya	Maat
Osun	Hetheru
Yemoja	Mehurt
Orunmilas	Apis
Odudua	Aset
Aganju (earth)	Geb

Plate: Yoruba System of Divinities

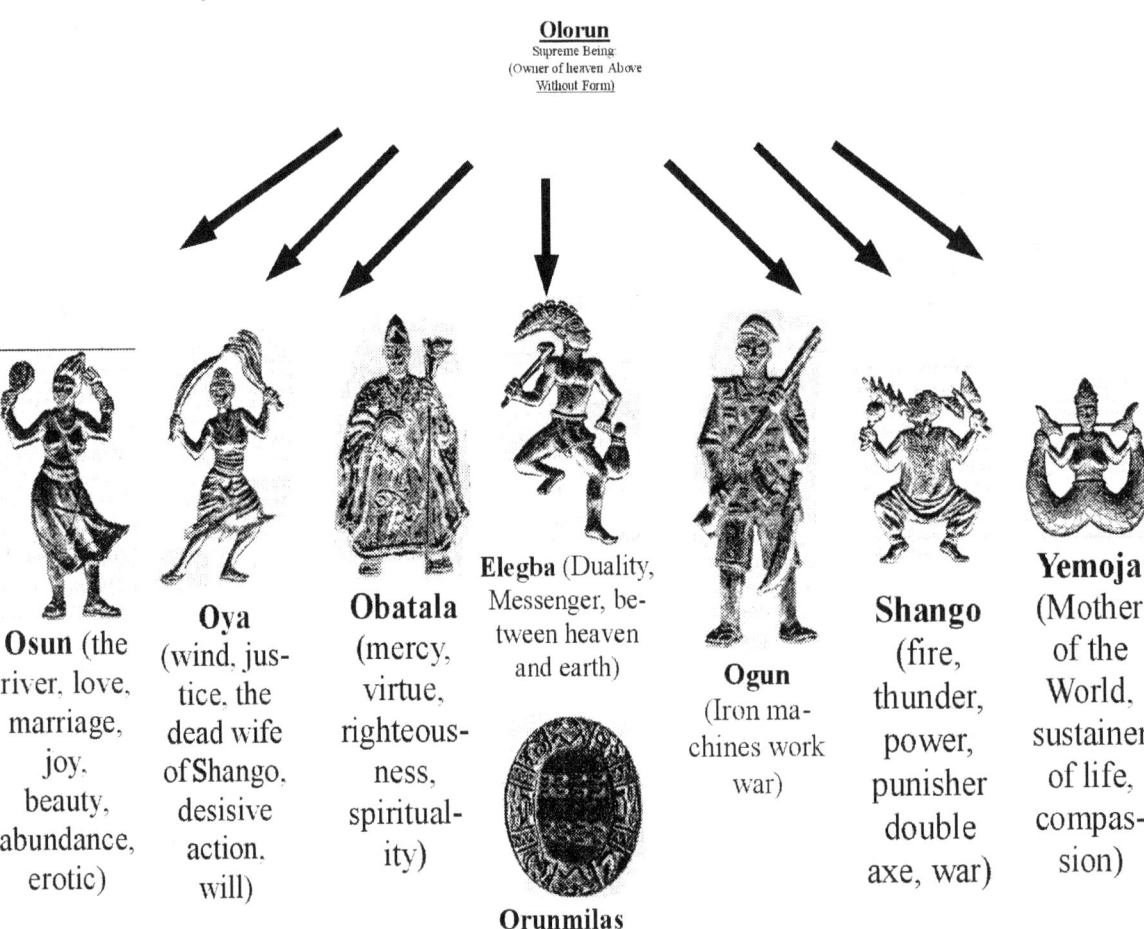

Yoruba religion holds that **Olorun** is the Supreme Divinity and that from here all other lesser divinities emanate. The lower order of divinities, the **Orishas**, control and sustain creation and interact with human beings, visiting upon them either wisdom and prosperity or retribution and adversity. Also, there is a practice of ritual trance in which the divinity is allowed to "possess" the individual and thereby guide and cleanse the individual. For some the ritual of trance and possession has degraded into a search to become the divinity. This is in contrast to the Kamitan understanding of the idea which is to discover that one already has that divinity within, and only needs to discover and express that form of consciousness. The misunderstanding also sometimes holds that the divinities exist in fact, separate from human consciousness, whereas the Kamitan philosophy shows that the cosmic forces are innate. Further, the oracular system is sometimes relied upon in Yoruba as a substitute for common sense and responsibility. Kamitan spirituality prohibits the use of oracles in ordinary situations that human beings need to face in order to grow and evolve.

"Don't rely exclusively on the oracle for guidance; sometimes it is necessary for us to live our lives for ourselves and not to lean too heavily on other minds who, after all, have their own thing to do. If the Gods in their wisdom see fit to deny us access to outer time, then it is usually because of some decision made by our own free will or spirit, maybe even prior to entering the body."

-Ancient Egyptian Proverb

Figure: Kamitan System of Divinities

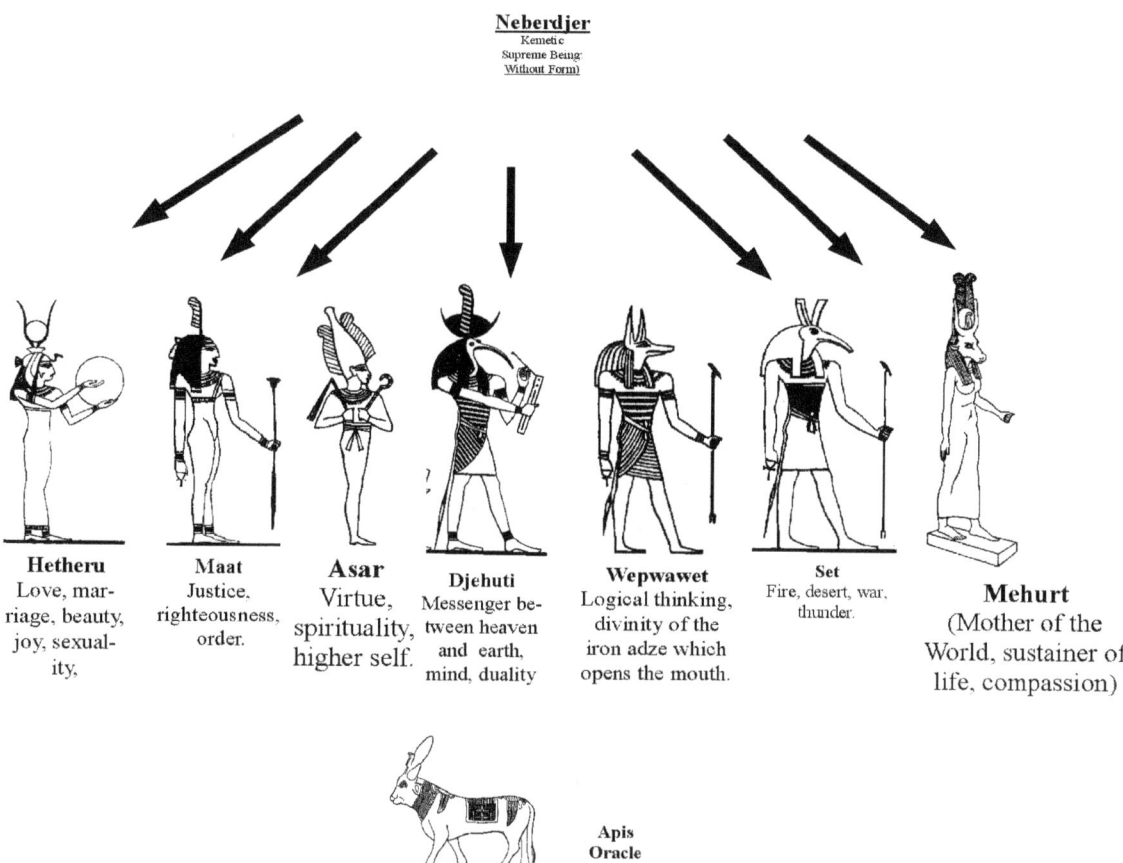

In the same manner that the Yoruba religion holds that **Olorun** is the Supreme Divinity and that from here all other lesser divinities emanate, Kamitan religion holds that **Neberdjer (Neter)** is the Supreme Divinity and that from here all other lesser divinities emanate. The lower order of divinities, the **neteru**, control and sustain creation and interact with human beings, visiting upon them either wisdom and prosperity or retribution and adversity. Further, the neteru are understood as aspects not only of Neberdjer, but also of the innermost human personality, which is essentially one with Neberdjer. Therefore, human beings are to discover their neteru nature by emulating the nature of the neteru, and opening up to the cosmic energy they represent, through ritual, but also through life discipline, i.e. living in accordance with the principles of Maat. Therefore, there is a deep mystic wisdom attached to the neteru, as they are understood to be a means by which a Kamitan initiate discovers their true nature as the Supreme Being.

The purpose of ritual identification with the neteru in Kamitan spirituality is to discover the aspects of one's innate essential nature and thereby become an enlightened being. As previously discussed, this idea is sometimes expressed as a "consumption" (eating) of the neteru since as we know, "you are what you eat."

> "Whoever has eaten the knowledge of every god (neteru), their existence is for all eternity and everlasting in their spirit body; what they willeth they doeth."

The tables which follow show more details as to the function and nature of the Yoruba gods and goddesses and the correlations with the Kamitan gods and goddesses.

Table A: General Gradations of the Main Yoruba Deities and their Mythological Significance

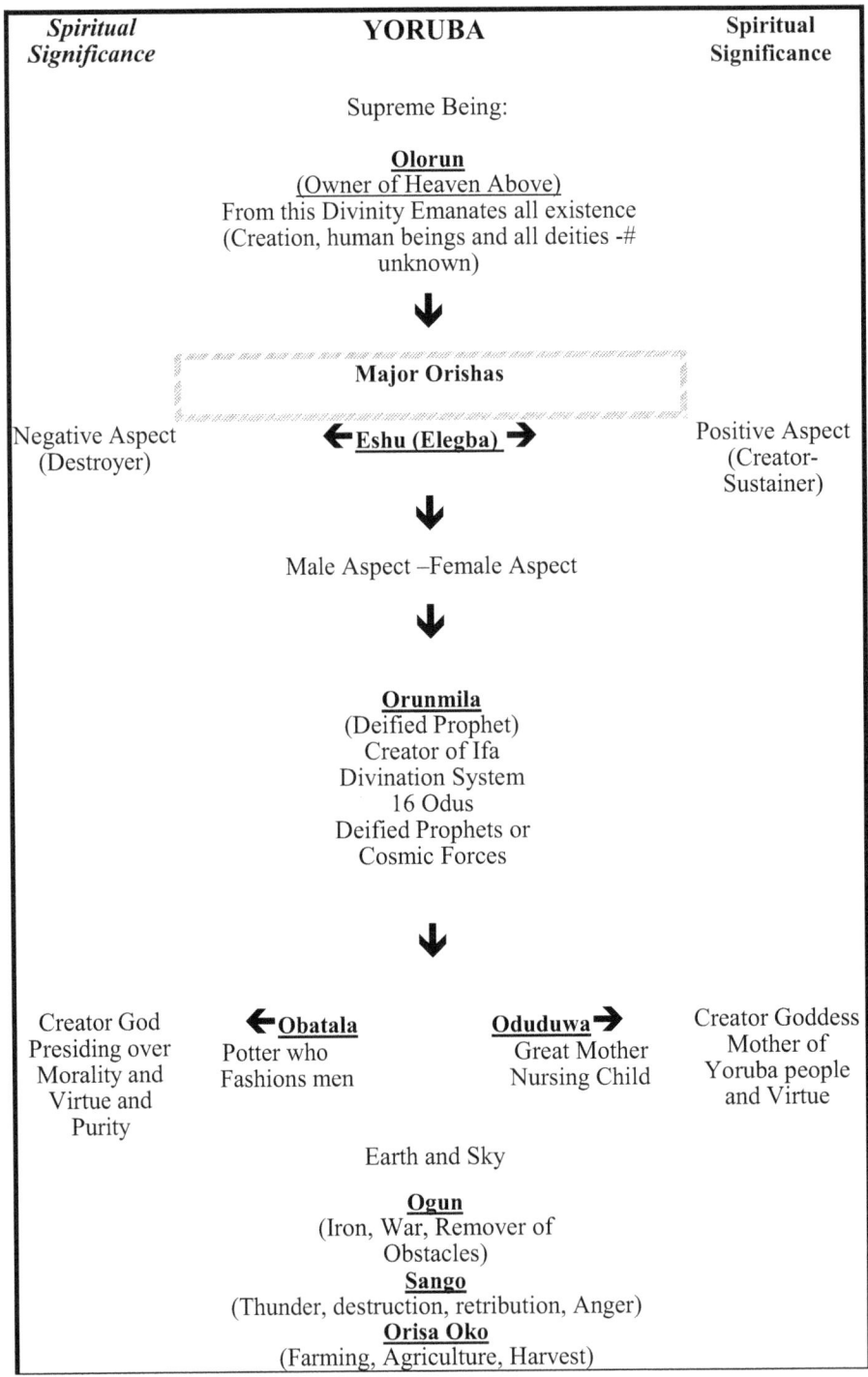

Table B: General Gradations of the Main Kamitan Deities and their Mythological Significance

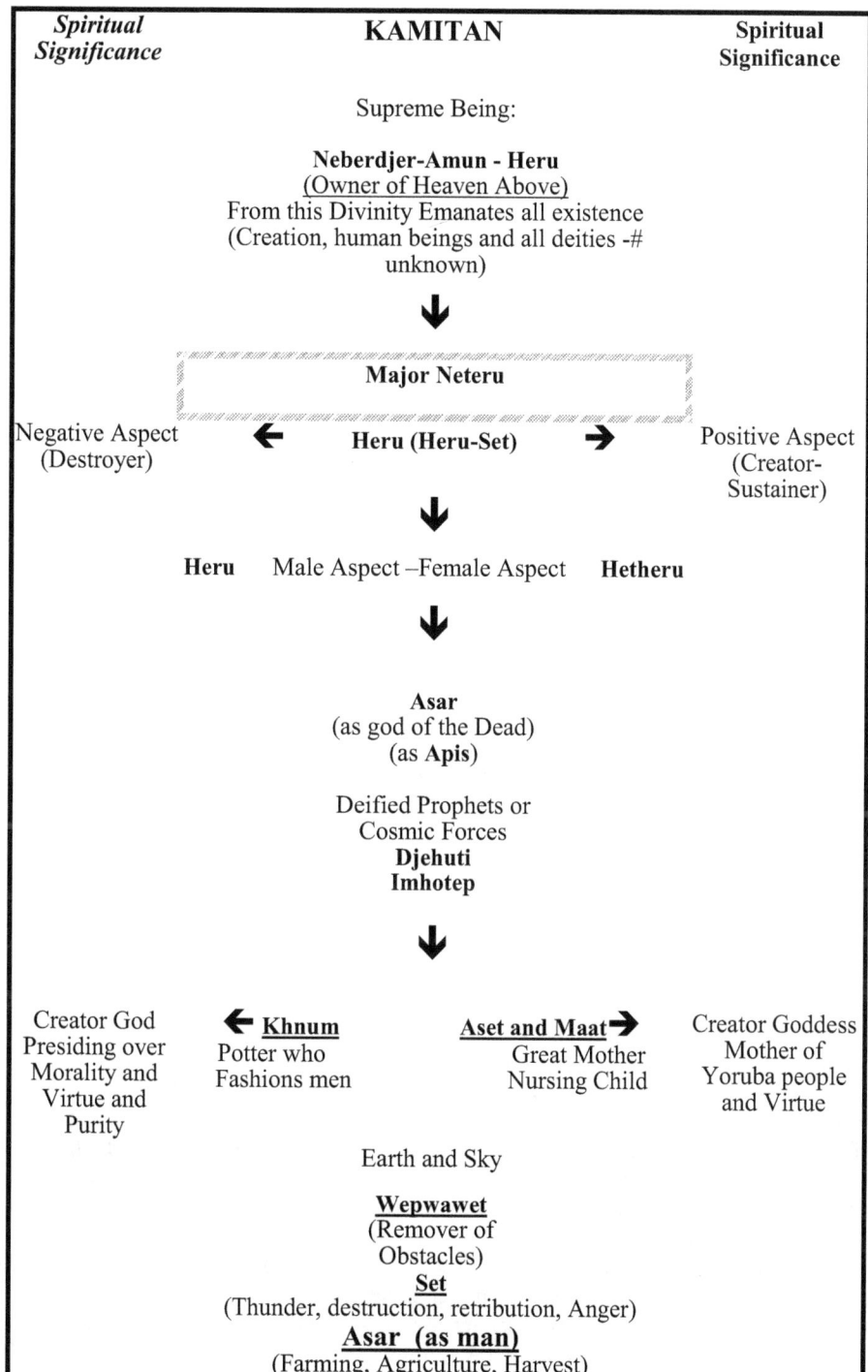

Other Correlations Between Kamitan and Yoruba Religion

Kamit	Yoruba
The Kamitans have called their temple *"Neter Het"* or "House (place) of the Divinity"	The Yoruba have called their temple *"Ile Orisha"* or "House (place) of the Divinity"
The Kamitans viewed the spirits as coming to inhabit the images upon being propitiated and the images themselves were not worshipped.	The Yoruba viewed the spirits as coming to inhabit the images upon being propitiated and the images themselves were not worshipped.
The Kamitan God Ptah Sokkar Asar is the potter who created human beings out of clay. Another potter divinity is Knum, who fashions the body out of clay (i.e. earth).	The Yoruba God Obatala created the first man and woman out of clay.
The Kamitan Goddess Aset the wife of Asar, is represented as a seated woman nursing a child.	The Yoruba Goddess Adudua, the wife of Obatala is represented as a seated woman nursing a child.
The priests in the Kamitan tradition were organized into grades.	The priests in the Yoruba tradition were organized into grades.

It should be borne in mind that prior to and during the move by European countries to colonize Africa itself (1750 A.C.E.-1960 A.C.E.), there were European explorers who visited African countries which were minimally or as yet entirely unaffected by Western Culture. Some of these travelers were Livingstone, Speke, Baker and Junker. Observations collected by researchers such as George Grenfell, Mr. Torday, Mr. Joyce of the British Museum, Sir Harry Johnston, Dr. Andrew Balfour of the Khartŭm and his colleagues, as well as the researches presented in the works of the Musée du Congo and varied other writers show the remnants of Ancient African customs and traditions prior to their disruption by the European colonization. So this form of study provides a certain perspective that may not be possible to achieve in the present day due to the social, political and economic devastations in Africa in the last 100 years.

The observations noted above have provided insights into several Kamitan rituals and traditions since the Ancient Kamitans were African, just as the study of Indian culture also provides insights, because the ancient Indians were part of the same Kushitic culture as were the Kamitans. Some examples of the traditions and rituals of other African cultures that provide insight into Kamitan traditions, have been given above. Some customs are found to have a direct correlation. On example is the Galla culture, who worship a Supreme Being which is associated with two other divinities, and so their system of religion, like the Kamitan, also contains a Trinity system. The Mpongwe believe in God who is named "Anyambia" who has both positive and negative qualities together. Anyambia is associated with two divinities, "Ombwiri" and "Onyambe," who represent good and evil, respectively, i.e. the forces of life, order, truth and righteousness (virtue) and the forces of entropy, that which is undesirable, disorder, etc. In the Ancient Egyptian Pyramid Texts and the Pert M Heru texts there are passages that speak of reestablishing the jaw bones. An ancient tradition of Uganda was to separate the jaw from the dead. A similar tradition was found among the Dahomey and Baganda. The symbolic rememberment of the body and the ability to speak again in the Netherworld is the important theme here. In Uganda, the ancient home of the Kamitans, a tradition of cutting and saving the umbilical cord and phallus of the kings were discovered.[222] These traditions can also be observed in Kamit.

These and other striking similarities between Ancient Egyptian (Kamitan) culture and traditions and those of other African cultures are not necessarily due to their having been given to African nations by the Kamitan culture. Rather, they should be thought of as indigenous developments by peoples in Africa, all of whom as we are now told by geneticist and archeologists, all emerged from the same place, the Great Lakes region and from South Africa at about 150,000 years ago. What happened in Kamit should be seen as a development from that same original common source which spread the cultural similarities throughout Africa from 150,000 B.C.E. to 100,000 B.C.E. The geography and agricultural conditions in Kamit allowed the Kamitans to develop a culture wherein the primordial customs and rituals were maintained in ritual and literary form, but not in actual literal practice. An example of this is the jaw tradition which is mentioned as an ancient tradition, but only the reconstitution part of the tradition is emphasized in Kamit and not the physical dismemberment of the king (of which there is no record or evidence of its being practiced in Kamit). This is why Kamit may be seen as the place where the flowering of African culture occurred as opposed to the sole source of culture and social advancement. However, in such cases as the correlations with the Yoruba, Nubian and Dogon cultures in Africa, Greece in Europe (western Asia), Cannanites in Asia Minor and Indians in east Asia, it is clear that there was contact and influence after the flowering in Kamit (15,000 B.C.E.-500 A.C.E.) which led to the adoption of traditions from Kamit to those other cultures. This is attested by the number and quality of correlations which rise above what could be expected as due to coincidence or simple chance. In this sense therefore, Kamitan culture can be seen as the epitome of African culture and since there are ample records to draw from, this record may be used effectively to reconstruct African culture and traditions.

African Masks

African masks are an integral part of African culture, art and spirituality. The mask tradition came to its height in Benin and Kamit. The following are examples of the Mask Art as it is used to related the earth realm to the spiritual realm through ritual.

Above left: Typical African Ritual Mask (Congo-Kinshasa) . Right Death of King Tutankhamun of Kamit

Above: Ancient Egyptian priest performs the rites of the dead while wearing a mask in the likeness of the god Anpu, the divinity of embalming.

Interactions Between the Ancient Egyptians and Cultures in the Americas

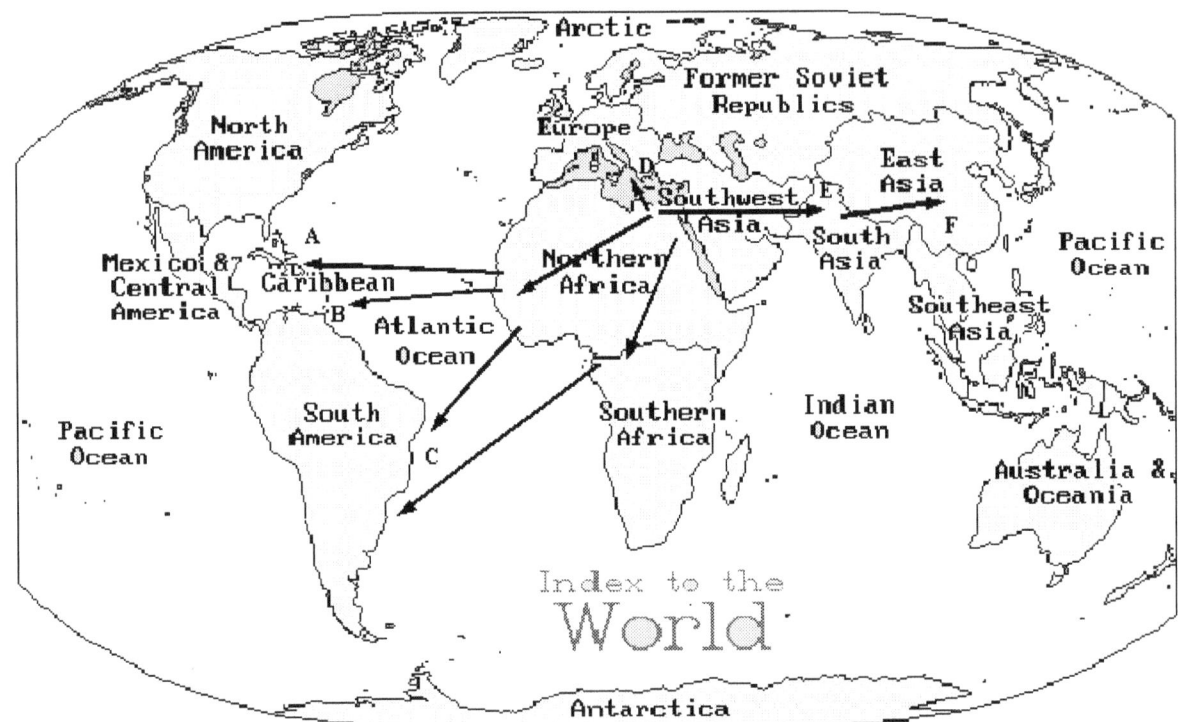

Figure 52: The map above shows the documented influence of Ancient Egyptian Culture on world religions.

A-B-C: Yoruba religion in the Caribbean was a result of the Yoruba followers in West Africa who were brought to the Western hemisphere as slaves. The influence is most visible in Cuba, Haiti and Brazil.

D-E-F: In Asia, the influence is most pronounced in Greek* mythology and philosophy, Sufism, Christian Gnosticism, Yoga and Vedanta philosophy in India, and from India, the influence was extended to Chinese Taoism.

*Here Greece is considered as part of Asia.

The map above illustrates that the traditions which passed from Ancient Egypt to other parts of Africa also influenced the Americans through the Africans who were brought there as slaves during the European slave trade period.

Brazil and the *Bumba Me Boi* – Rock the Bull

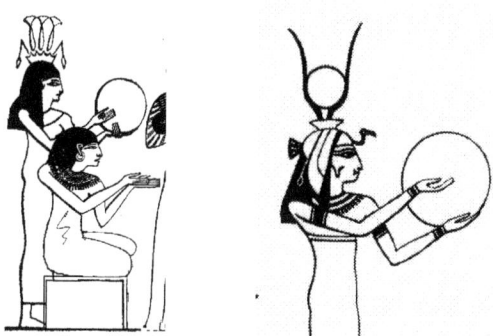

Figure 53: Priestesses in Ancient Egypt playing the Drum

There is a large population of people of African descent in South America who brought with them many of the customs and traditions of Africa as they were captured and enslaved by European peoples. Many have managed to preserve some of the traditions and at times even established cities of free people, sustaining the practice of some of their traditions without obstruction. An example of this is the culture of Bahia[68]. There is a festivity practiced by Brazilian tribes of mixed African and Native population called *Bumba Me Boi* – (Rock the Bull). It is a ritual that goes on for days in which drums (including hand drums like those played in Ancient Egypt) are used to "resurrect" a mythical bull. The hand drum is also used at births. This was also the case in Ancient Egypt; the inscriptions showing the priestesses playing the drums at the birthing houses are ample. Further, in Ancient Egypt when someone died, they were viewed as having become the god Asar, whose symbol is the bull, and the birth of a child was seen as the birth of the divinity Heru. The rituals of the *Prt M Hru* (*Ancient Egyptian Book of the Dead*) which were carried out for the deceased and the birthing house rituals were designed to effect a resurrection in consciousness of the participants. The mystic teaching is that when the drums are played a certain way, a particular tonal quality emerges that infuses the participants with life force and elevation of consciousness. In the *Bumba Me Boi* beats, this quality is called "the fifth." It is an interval of five notes played together. One drummer plays three beats and another plays two, and in so doing divide the same measure at once into three and two. After many hours and inducing a trance state, with the correct training and practice, the practitioner is supposed to be transported to higher realms of consciousness. The Brazilians practice this ritual even though it is mixed with the Christian tradition due to indoctrination during the slavery period. However, they have a tradition that their ancestors came from Egypt.[223]

Ancient Kamitans In Contact With the Americas

Another item of evidence proving the contact between Kamit and the Americas is Nicotine. Nicotine was discovered in the bowels of an Egyptian mummy. Nicotine comes from tobacco and this plant only grows in the Americas.[224]

Parapsychology and the Proofs of Ancient African Mysticism and Religion

Why should we follow or place so much importance on African religion? Why should we not consider it to be just so much superstition or primitive or childish attempts at religion, as some have called it? The basic tenets of mystical religion as put forth in such religious systems as Shetaut Neter, Yoruba, Dogon, etc. of Africa or the Hinduism, Taoism, of the East or the Native American Religions of the West cause much consternation for believers of the Western orthodox religions (Judaism, Christianity, and Islam). Yet, those Western religions believe in fantastic ideas, but these are not related as such. The idea that a man can throw a stick into a river and part the waters (Moses) is certainly supernatural. A man walking on water (Jesus) is

---

[68] **Bahia**, a state in northeastern Brazil that is considered as the cradle of Afro-Brazilian culture and is still in existence.

equally supernatural and some may even consider these ideas as superstitious or fantastic and even the rantings of a fanatic. However, since the Western Culture determines its paradigm of what is acceptable and this is reinforced through the media, these ideas are accepted and taken for granted while the beliefs of others are repudiated.

The basic tenets of mystical religions, such as reincarnation, telepathy, clairvoyance, clairaudience and premonition, which support the contention of ancient Sages that we exist in different planes and can access these to attain higher consciousness, are refuted by people without investigating deeper. Actually, experiments by Western scientists have shown these to be real and verifiable. Putting these parapsychological evidences together with the experiments of Quantum physicists takes us to another world paradigm. It takes us away from the paradigm based on an orthodox Western mentality which leads people to persist in denying the empirical evidences that have been produced to prove the existence of psychic phenomena, life after death, and the underlying unity of the material universe. It is a credit to the eminent late teacher Cheikh Anta Diop, who was an accomplished scientist, that upon examining the evidences conceded to these and included them in his book (*Civilization or Barbarism-Credit to Parapsychology*) as proofs of the validity and legitimacy of African religion and philosophy. The reader should review the following texts for more information on the proofs of psychic phenomena, reincarnation and life after death.

- *Many Lives Many Masters* – by Brian Weis
- *The Conscious Universe: The Scientific truth of Psychic Phenomena* by Dean Radin, Ph. D.
- *The Dao of Physics* by Fritjof Capra
- *Dancing Wu Li Masters* by Gary Zukav

African mystical philosophy is not merely a primitive superstition. It is based on the mystical experience of Sages and Saints throughout the history of Africa. These experiences were codified in the form of religious myths and shamanic (spiritualist) rituals that were designed to promote these experiences in others. This is the purpose for the Sema (yogic) disciplines that reached their height in Kamit. This high concept in spirituality formed the basis of the initiatic sciences of the Kamitan Temples. They constitute the highest expression of the African Spiritualist Consciousness that is common throughout the African Continent. This awareness of the underlying Supreme Being that pervades all is not a superstition, but rather an experience of the Divine and is therefore based on fact and not fiction. A religion that exhorts its followers to perpetually believe in concepts by faith alone without the prospect of attaining an actual experience of the Divine while the person is still alive is not promoting a full experience of religion and will therefore be limited, and consequently dogmatic. Therefore, faith is the beginning of religion and not its end. The end is to achieve a mystical experience of awareness and unity with the Divine, and not to simply implore the Divine or remain as an egoistic individual talking about religion and practicing its rituals, but attaining no higher experiences. That lower condition, due to the limited practice of religion, is what allows human beings to say they are practitioners of religion, while at the same time they promote war, greed and other detrimental aspects of society. That is not the advanced practice of religion. This is why it is so important to study African Religion and to bring it back to the forefront of human consciousness, so that the world will rediscover the ancient standard from which it has strayed and correct the imbalances that have characterized the practice of religion.

Challenges to African Religion in the 21st Century

Statistics:

- Currently, there are at least 730 million people in Africa, out of which 108 million practice Native African Religion.
- Most popular religion is Islam, mostly in Upper Sahara. Next is Native African Religion.
- There are fewer Christians than those practicing Native African Religion.
- There are only seven countries in Africa who have more than 50% of the population who practice Native African Religion[225]:

    - Liberia   70%
    - Togo   70%
    - Benin   70%
    - Burkina Faso   65%
    - Guinea-Bissau 65%
    - Madagascar   52%
    - Cameroon   51%

Consider that Europe is a conglomerate of countries with different languages, customs, etc., like Africa, but they follow generally the same faith. In Europe, the main religion is Christianity. Imagine what the European population would do if they were actively forced by some other country outside Europe to change their languages and their religion. This is unthinkable, and yet if the peoples ability to speak their languages, practice their rituals and customs etc. were prevented, and they were forced to practice other customs over 2-3 generations, their spirituality and concepts of social organization would be disrupted. They would end up divided, some following the new religions and norms, while others try to recapture the old ways, and still, others being frustrated, would turn towards Marxist (there is no God) or secular (worldly – movement away from spirituality) philosophies. This is what has occurred to African countries at the hands of European colonial forces.

Above: The Challenges to African Religion: *Christianity, Islam, Marxism and Secularism*

Native African Religion has been challenged by Christianity and Islam for many years, but now also it is being challenged by at least two additional pressures, Marxism and secularism. The eminent Africologist Ali A. Mazrui noted, on a visit to Ethiopia in the mid 1980's, that the country had adopted Marxism,[226] a philosophy of socialism or collectivism that requires, like its opposite extreme, capitalism – globalism (*Globalization*), the dropping of traditional customs and the adoption of a way of life that excludes spirituality, and even denies any validity to religion. Marxism repudiates religion altogether. Secularity is the turning away from religion and living with the conviction that one can direct one's life without divine guidance. Secularity is a degrading force in society, turning it towards pleasure seeking, un-tempered by the moral restraints or ethics which comes from religion. Thus, in due course of time, corruption and greed degrades the moral structure of the population. Individualism, high-living and self-gratification are facilitated by the secular viewpoint. This seduces people into engaging in capitalistic or despotic forms of government that promote certain segments of the population to become wealthy, while others languish in abject poverty. Globalism, the new term referring to opening up trade worldwide, really means giving up traditional values as well as individual rights to property and resources to be controlled by the few who become wealthy.

India is an interesting example of the failure of Secularism. Thought of by many as an exotic land of yogis and saints, after independence from British colonial rule in the late 1940's A.C.E. took a path of establishing a secular government. The mostly Hindu population protested and accused the government of turning away from Dharma (philosophy of righteousness-moral values) and also a spiritual consciousness in the upbringing of the next generation, since the turn towards secularism required the banning of Hinduism from the educational system.[227] The problem continues to this day and more conflict has ensued within the different sects of Hinduism and between Hinduism and other religions in India such as Christianity and Buddhism. A better solution, which would also apply to Africa, is to create a government that upholds the common-fundamental-traditional spiritual values of all religious traditions, leaving the minor folk differences to the local populations.

Thus, there are many challenges to African Religion in the 21st Century. One possible solution is for Africa is to create a government that upholds the common-fundamental-traditional and moral values of all Native African religions, leaving the minor folk differences to the local population. In other words, Marxism and Secularism are unnecessary since there already is an African system of philosophy designed to take care of the population. Marxism and Secularism actually disrupt that already preexisting system and substitute it with a program that is anti-spiritual and is thus doomed to failure. Africans developed and instituted long ago a program of social order that came to its height of development in Kamit and lasted for THOUSANDS of years there and this program needs to be studied and adapted for use by present day Africans. Again, this points up the importance of learning about and rediscovering Ancient Kamit as Cheikh Anta Diop admonished.

> "Ancient Egypt was a Negro civilization. The history of Black Africa will remain suspended in air and cannot be written correct until African historians dare to connect it with the history of Egypt In particular, the study of languages, institutions, and so forth, cannot be treated properly; in a word, it will be impossible to build African humanities, a body of African human sciences, so long as that relationship does not appear legitimate."
>
> -Cheikh Anta Diop July 1973
> *African Origins of Civilization: Myth or Reality*

In this manner, the government and other social institutions could be based on ancient African principles of family, righteousness, order and justice (Maat-Ubuntu) and uphold the interests of all people equally and it would be based on moral values. In this respect, a federation of African countries could join and strengthen themselves to meet the *Challenges to African Religion in the 21st Century*. Such a program for the reorganization of African Religion and government will be the subject of an upcoming volume.

Conclusion

Given the persistence of African religion, even in the face of relentless pressure from Western religions, it is remarkable that its practice has continued to this day. It follows therefore that the practice of Western religions would not have attained their status if it were not due to the disruptions in African culture (Judaism, Christianity, Islam, Arab slave trade, European slave trade, colonialism, and neocolonialism). These disruptions were imposed on Africa through coercion (compulsion, duress) and not through natural adoption. Christianity was successfully spread throughout Africa because the first missionaries indoctrinated young children and the colonial governments suppressed the practice of African religion along with any indigenous practices that might promote the movement towards freedom from colonialism. The young generation passed on the new beliefs to their children as they grew up, and gradually the new beliefs gained more adherents. The spread of Islam was also by force, by punishing many who resisted its introduction, and also by allowing its practitioners, the Muslims, to become successful members of the society (government and commerce). In addition, in the beginning, it allowed the mixing of African religion with Islam. However, later on, the African religious aspects were suppressed, allowing only the practice of Islam.

So when we examine religion in Africa, especially the Western religions, we must look with caution when assessing the level of conversion to Western religion and the true nature of African spirituality. In one important sense the Western religions are unsuccessful because they deny the essential need of the African mind to seek harmony with the here and now while at the same time discovering a harmony with the Transcendental. Western religions are too focused (fanatically) with the hereafter, and this does not serve the greater need of African Spirituality. Thus, any religion developing in Africa must be able to meet the need of the African consciousness by:

- providing a humanistic approach to spirituality,

- providing a connection between the spirit realm and the practical reality that is pantheistic,

- being ritualistically fulfilling,

- being psychologically comforting and intellectually satisfying in its ability to explain life, and able to lead its practitioners to harmony and peace through virtue.

African Spirituality has much in common with Eastern religions such as Hinduism, in seeing the spirit in the mundane, i.e. pantheism. Given this similarity, the two forms of religion will be compatible, and thus many people of African descent seeking higher mystical philosophy, unfamiliar with their Kamitan spiritual heritage, have gravitated to the mystical Eastern traditions. But still, even here, under normal conditions, there would not be mass conversion of African peoples to the more orthodox Eastern traditions such as Hinduism, because the religions at this level of practice serve not only a spiritual purpose, but also a cultural purpose of identity and social stability. Thus, most Hindus in Africa are people of Indian descent who were brought there by the British and other colonial rulers as indentured servants (slaves). They have lived side by side with Africans practicing African religions, and have not had conflicts due to religious reasons, but rather due to reasons based on issues of cultural and racial discrimination.[69]

The Importance of Neterian Religion in the Study of African Religions

Above left: Adinkra symbol- *Adinkrahene*, *"chief of adinkra symbols"* meaning charisma, greatness, leadership.
Above right: The Kamitan symbol of *"Ra"* meaning light, glory, Supreme Being.

---

[69] Due to the history of the caste system in India, suffering under British racism and colonialism, a developing self-centered national cultural ego, widespread ignorance in the Indian community about the origins of their own culture and lack of the authentic (complete) practice of their religion, there is a growing rift between Indians and Africans.

Ancient Egyptian religion is an African religion. Ancient Egyptian religion has had a significant role to play in the development of African religions, holding the place as the first African nation to create a system of writing and to commit the tenets of the spiritual philosophy to writing for posterity. These features alone are remarkable aspects of African religion. However, the study of Ancient Egyptian religion also has the added important aspect of allowing us to clearly envision the fundamental and unifying principles of African religion, as it exemplifies and intellectually expounds on these as no other African religion does. Since Ancient Egyptian religion informs not only other African religions, but also the other world religions, this allows us to gain a deeper understanding of the practice, purpose and meaning of African religion and its place among the world community of world religions.

SANKOFA

Adinkra symbol- "return and get it" meaning: learn from the past!

NOTES FOR CHAPTER 2

[199] "African Religions: An Interpretation," *Microsoft® Encarta® Africana.* © 1999 Microsoft Corporation. All rights reserved.
[200] African Religion: World Religion by Aloysius M. Lugira
[201] African Mythology by Geoffrey Parrinder
[202] African Religions and Philosophy -- by John S. Mbiti
[203] Civilization or Barbarism by Cheikh Anta Diop
[204] Colonialism and Colonies," *Microsoft® Encarta® Encyclopedia 2000.* © 1993-1999 Microsoft Corporation. All rights reserved.
[205] Religions, African, in Latin America and the Caribbean," *Microsoft® Encarta® Africana.* ©1999 Microsoft Corporation. All rights reserved.
[206] "African Religions," *Microsoft® Encarta® Encyclopedia 2000.* © 1993-1999 Microsoft Corporation. All rights reserved.
[207] See the books *Egyptian Yoga Vol. 1* for more on the disciplines of Egyptian Yoga and *Mysteries of Isis* for more on the teachings of the Temple of Aset, by Muata Ashby
[208] On his statue in the Glyptothek at Munich
[209] *African Religion: World Religion* by Aloysius M. Lugira
[210] For the full text see the *Book of the Dead* by Muata Ashby
[211] Pottery Headrests from Narsipur Sangam, F.R. Allchin, *Studies in Indian Prehistory*, D. Sen and A.K. Ghosh, eds., Calcutta, 1966, pp. 58-63
[212] A Dictionary of Egyptian Gods and Goddesses, George Hart
[213] Guide to the Gods, Marjorie Leach
[214] "Kenya," Microsoft (R) Encarta. Copyright (c) 1994 Funk & Wagnall's Corporation.
[215] Doshi, Saryu, Editor-Indian Council for Cultural Relations *India and Egypt: Influences and Interactions* 1993
[216] The African Origin of Civilization, Civilization or Barbarism, Cheikh Anta Diop
[217] The African Origin of Civilization, Cheikh Anta Diop – Civilization or Barbarism, Cheikh Anta Diop
[218] Websters Encyclopedia.
[219] *Civilization or Barbarism*
[220] Civilization or Barbarism, Cheikh Anta Diop
[221] Sauneron and Yoyotte, *La Naissance du Monde, op. cit., p. 35*
[222] See journal Ins. Anthropological Society, Vol. XXXI, p. 1117 ff.; Vol. XXXII, P. 25 ff.; and *Kibuka, the War God of the Baganda*, in *Man*, No. 95, 1907, P- 161 ff.
[223] Interview with Layne Redmond, prominent hand drummer, after attendance at a Brazilian festival.
[224] Civilization or Barbarism, Cheikh Anta Diop
[225] *African Religion: World Religion* by Aloysius M. Lugira
[226] *The Africans* by Ali A. Mazrui
[227] A Concise Encyclopedia of Hinduism, by Klaus K. Klostermaier

PART II: THE AFRICAN ORIGINS OF WESTERN CIVILIZATION, RELIGION, AND ETHICS PHILOSOPHY

Chapter 3: Atlantis, Mesopotamia, Ancient Egypt and The Origins of Civilization

Ancient Egypt and Atlantis

In conjunction with Ancient Egypt, another ancient civilization, Atlantis, must be mentioned, as there is much speculation about Atlantis and Ancient Egypt. Atlantis, in the tradition of antiquity, was a mythical land and advanced civilization. It is credited by some as having existed prior to the Ancient Egyptian civilization, and also as giving rise to the Ancient Egyptian civilization. It is evident that there is more about history that is not known than is known. This is not to say that there can be no certainties, but that there can be no certain original dates. There may be several civilizations that existed prior to Ancient Egypt, and the Ancient Egyptians may very well be their descendants, so we must keep an open mind and eye for the evidences. History, therefore, should be studied with an open mind, and never be considered as an absolute end, since the winds of time have taken all evidences of many civilizations that existed in the past. The important point here is that Ancient Egyptian civilization emerged first out of the cataclysmic flood period, and resurrected an advanced society and religious systems in the distant past, which it then spread around the world in order to civilize it for the good of all humanity. This is why scholars from all countries were accepted in the Ancient Egyptian University Temples. Some Egyptian Pharaohs even sponsored and financed temples abroad which taught mystical philosophy as well as other disciplines. One such effort was put forth by the Ancient Egyptian king, Amasis, who financed the reconstruction of the famous Temple of Delphi in Greece, which was burnt down in 548 B.C.E.

As the evidence presented in this book shows, the history of Ancient Egypt goes back farther than most historians feel comfortable admitting. So in order to make this work complete, it is necessary to review the origins and history of the legend of Atlantis. To accomplish this task, we must have a working knowledge of ancient Greek history as well as the relationship between ancient Greek culture and the Ancient Egyptian culture. Through this review we will find intriguing correlations and answers.

The civilization of Atlantis supposedly existed prior to a "flood," or natural catastrophe. The landmass itself is said to have been engulfed by the ocean as the result of an earthquake. The first recorded accounts of Atlantis appear in two dialogues by Plato, known as the *Timaeus* and *Critias*. According to the account in *Timaeus,* the island was described to the Athenian statesman Solon by an Ancient Egyptian priest, who told him that Atlantis was larger in than Libya and Asia Minor combined. The priest also said that a highly advanced civilization existed on Atlantis at about the 10th millennium B.C.E. Further, the priest related that the nation of Atlantis had conquered all the peoples of the Mediterranean, except the Athenians. Solon and other Athenians had no knowledge of this ancient land.

Overview of Ancient Greek History

Ancient Greece was a civilization that flourished on the Greek Peninsula, in western Asia Minor (modern Turkey), and on the north coast of Africa (in the Alexandrian period).

1. In 3000 B.C.E., a culture known today as the Aegean civilization developed and was centered on the island of Crete. It is also known as the Minoan civilization. It was related to the mainland population which was later know as the Mycenaean civilization at Peloponnesus. The Minoans built great palaces especially at their capital, Knossos, and developed maritime trade with African nations including the Kamitans. The name is derived from Minos, the legendary king of Crete. The civilization is divided into three main periods: early Minoan, about 3000–2200 B.C.E; middle Minoan, about 2200–1580 B.C.E; and late Minoan, about 1580–1100 B.C.E.[228]

2. This Bronze Age of Greek history is the period celebrated in the epic poems of Homer (Illiad and the Odyssey), who gives us some of the earliest records of the existence of the Minoans, besides those of the Kamitans.

3. The culture of Thera, another Aegean island Greek city-state[70], closely followed the Minoan civilization. The culture of the Mycenaeans roughly followed that of the Minoans whose civilization had deteriorated by about 1,400 B.C.E on Crete, due to a natural cataclysm (volcano eruption on Santorini), but the Mycenaeans on the mainland continued to prosper until the 12th century B.C.E.

4. About that time the Mycenaeans were conquered by the Dorians (creators of the famous dorian style architecture), who invaded from the north.

5. Hellenistic Period: The term 'Hellenism' refers to the culture of Classical Greece. It is most particularly associated with Athens during the 5th century B.C.E. This period saw the rise of Athens as the most powerful of the Greek city-states around the Aegean, epitomized by the creation of the Parthenon.

6. Macedonian Period: Philip II of Macedon (one of the Greek city-states), who ruled from 359-336 B.C.E, conquered Upper Macedon, Thrace, and Chalcidice.

7. Alexandrian Period: Philip's son, Alexander the Great, who ruled from 336-323 B.C.E, used his army to conquer the entire Greek world, Asia Minor, Western India and North East Africa (including Kamit) and placed them under his Macedonian Empire.

8. After Alexander died, the Greek city-states began infighting. This led to the deterioration of the Greek Empire. The rulership over the conquered territories fell to his generals. The general who took control of Kamit was Ptolemy. This began the Ptolemaic Pharaonic Dynasty of Kamit which lasted there from 332 B.C.E. to 30 B.C.E. In 146 B.C.E., what was left of the Greek cities fell under Roman control, and the ancient Greek world came to an end. Hellenism, as Greek culture had come to be called, retained its strength, however, and became the basis for the civilization of the Roman Empire.[229]

The Legend of Atlantis and the Minoans

Much work has been done by archeologists that reveals the Minoans as the mythical "Atlantians." This is evident in the writings of many archeologists, and it is accepted as the general view of Western historians as the following encyclopedia entry shows.

> "Atlantis"
>
> In Greek mythology, an island continent, said to have sunk following an earthquake. Although the Atlantic Ocean is probably named for it, the structure of the sea bottom rules out its ever having existed there. The Greek philosopher Plato created an imaginary early history for it and described it as a utopia.
> Legends about the disappearance of Atlantis may have some connection with the volcanic eruption that devastated Santorini in the Cyclades islands, north of Crete, about 1500 BC. The ensuing earthquakes and tidal waves are believed to have been one cause of the collapse of the empire of Minoan Crete.
>   -Copyright © 1995 Webster's Helicon Publishing Ltd

Nevertheless, many fiction writers and New Age writers have seen fit to create speculative stories related to Atlantis and even suggest that it was an ideal country with enlightened peoples. This idealized version of this culture left no records or remains in Greek history, nor are there any records in the Greek history about a civilization that was lost or destroyed by a cataclysm except those related to Solon, a Greek legislator who visited Egypt in 590 B.C.E. Solon brought the legend of Atlantis to Greece, owing to the history of the Mediterranean that was kept by the Ancient Egyptians. The priests of Zau (Sais)[71] told Solon that the island

---

[70] Ancient Greece was a confederation of cities spread over the Aegean area of the Mediterranean sea that were united by common language and culture as well as ethnicity.

[71] Ancient Egyptian city of the goddess Net- Who was known to the Greeks as Athena; recall that Sais and Athens were later considered sister cities.

city of Atlantis sunk into the ocean. In the year 395 B.C.E. Plato retold the story in his book *Timaeus and Critias.* Sometime later Plato himself consulted the Egyptian priests and was informed that there had been several great floods in history, and that the largest one had overcome Atlantis completely.

> Don't you know that in your country had lived the most beautiful and the most noble race of men that ever lived? Race of which you and your town are the descendants, or a seed that survived.... But there were violent earthquakes and floodings, and in one day and one night of rain, all of your bellicose people, as one man, were buried under the ground, and the island of Atlantis, in the same manner, disappeared under the sea.... The result is that, in comparison to what was, there remain some small islets, nothing but the skeleton of a devastated body, all of the richest and the softest parts of the soil having been swallowed up, leaving only the skeleton of the country.... And this was unknown to you, because the survivors of this destruction have been dead for several generations without leaving any traces. *(Timaeus and Critias)*

The event supposedly took place 9,000 years before Solon (in 9,590 B.C.E.), who lived in 590 B.C.E., and was reported in the Egyptian texts 1000 years later (8,590 B.C.E.). The eminent scientist and scholar Cheikh Anta Diop suggested that if the dates given were to be reduced by a factor of 10, the date falls on the devastating explosion of Santorini.[230] In most every way the known history and remains of the Minoan civilization on the island of Crete best fit the description of Atlantis. Artifacts confirming trade and contact with the Ancient Egyptians have been discovered on Crete up to the reign of Pharaoh Amenhotep III, which also confirms the date of 1400 B.C.E. (explosion at Santorini). In the Ancient Egyptian records, the Cretans are referred to as the *Keftiu*.

Above: Minoans offering tribute to the Egyptian king Djehutimes III (Thutmose 18th Dynasty). The Cretans are distinguishable by their clothing. (Norman de Garis Davies; Tomb of Rekh-mi-Ra at Thebes, vol. II, plates 19 and 18)

Above: Faience scarab from reign of Pharaoh Amenhotep III, found at Crete.

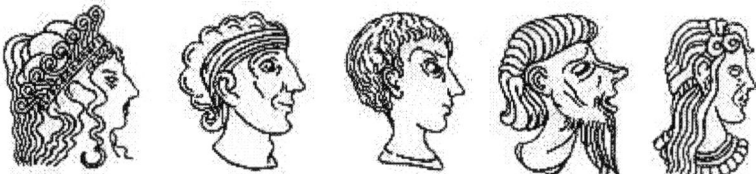

Above: The mixture of ethnic peoples in Crete is demonstrated by the different skull - types discovered in the excavations there. In general terms, however, the Minoans form part of the so - called "Mediterranean type." They were of medium height and had black curly hair and brown eyes. Essentially, they were a mixture of European (Greek), African, and Asiatic peoples, showing differences of ethnicity even from the city of Thera and Mycenae.

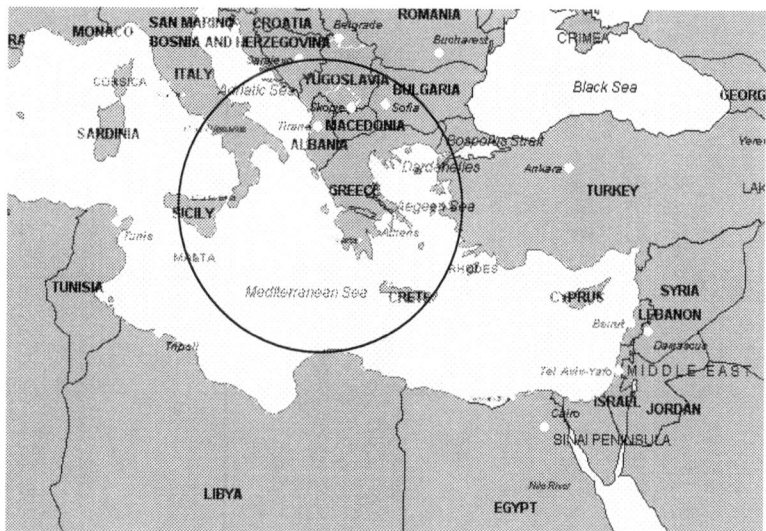

Above: Map of the Mediterranean with Crete, Greece and Egypt.

Figure 54: Below-left, Stele of Niptah - end of Middle Kingdom (Kamitan man in red, Kamitan woman in white with breasts exposed). Below right- Minoan man in red and Minoan woman in white with breasts exposed. (1,400 B.C.E.).

The fresco above shows some important aspects of Minoan society which reveal similarities to the Ancient Egyptian culture. The men and women are depicted as going about bare-breasted. Also, like the Ancient Egyptian practice, the Minoans also depicted the men with a red color and the women with the white color. As this book is mainly concerned with the earliest periods of history, before the Greek Classical period, we will explore some important correlations in the religious iconographies of the Ancient Egyptian New Kingdom period and the Greek archaic period. The images below are from goddesses of Ancient Kamit and Ancient Greece. They are included here to show the close matching in iconography, mythic symbolism and mystical philosophy. For more correlations, including the Classical Greek Period, see the book, From Ancient Egypt to Greece by Muata Ashby

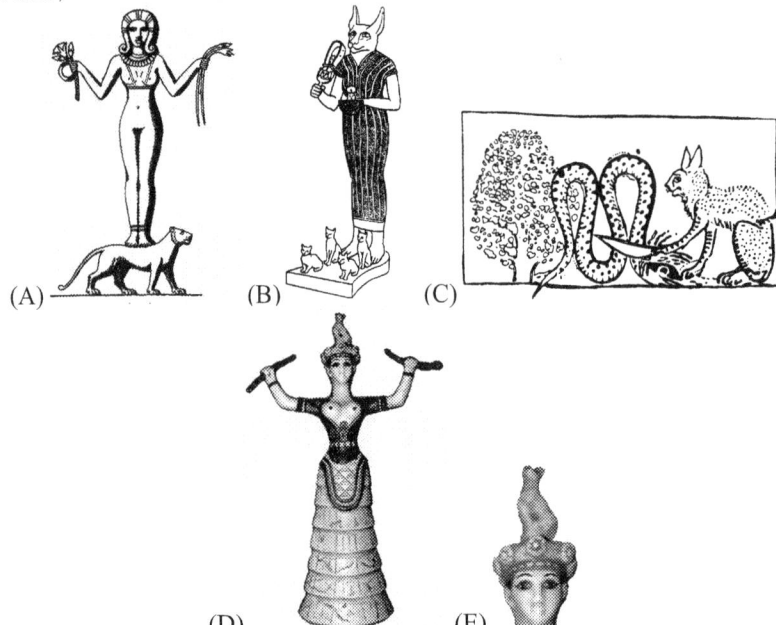

Above: Left- Goddess Qadesh (Qdesh) (A) of Ancient Egypt, standing on a lion which is a symbol of the goddess Sekhemit (F- see below - lioness goddess) who is related to the leopard-cat goddess Mafdet (C) who are a forms of goddess Hetheru (G- see below) -Old Kingdom who are also snake goddesses. Above Right: Minoan snake goddess (D) (1600-1400 B.C.E.) – Far right: closeup of the cat headdress of the Minoan goddess (E), relating her to the well known feline divinity, Bastet (B), of Ancient Egypt. Sekhmit and Bastet are related to Mafdet, the leopard goddess who kills evil snakes (the snakes the negative aspects of the personality that prevent the flow of the Serpent Power).

Qdesh is often depicted holding flowers, a mirror, or serpents. The Leopard Goddess Mafdet was associated with Sekhmet, the Eye of Ra and with Hetheru as well as the other feline forms of the Ancient Egyptian goddess. She is the embodiment of the destructive force that can be unleashed on the negative impetus, symbolized by the serpent demon Apep. Mafdet is also identified with the execution blade itself.

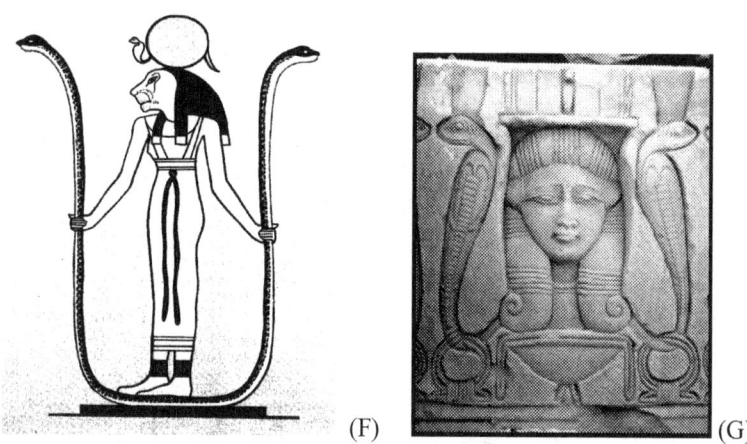

(F) (G)

Above: Left- Ancient Egyptian goddess Sekhemit (F- a form of Hetheru) with the two serpents. Right: Ancient Egyptian Goddess Hetheru (G) Temple relief with the two serpents and the upward curled hair. (New Kingdom period)

Like Hetheru of Ancient Egypt, Qadesh was also known as the "mistress of the gods and goddesses, the eye of Ra, without a second." So the Minoan snake goddess, pictured in (D) above, exhibits all of the major aspects of the Ancient Egyptian goddess including having her skin painted white in the Egyptian fashion reserved for women.

The bull figures prominently in Minoan art and spirituality. One of the Minoan myths relates that there was a great Bull who lived in the underground labyrinths beneath the great palace; king Minos defeated it. The bull was called Minator. Another myth relates that it was to be given *seven virgins*. In Ancient Egyptian mythology, the bull is the symbol of Asar, one of the most important divinities. He is given seven cows, who in turn give rise to Creation.

  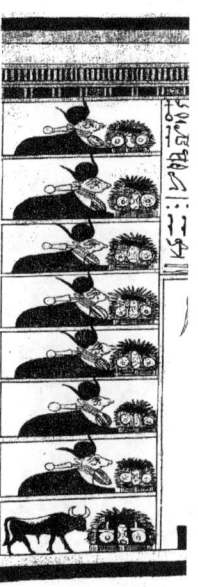

Above left: The god Asar-Hapi, also known in later times as Serapis by the Greeks and Romans, depicted as part bull and part human (mixed zoomorphic and anthropomorphic, respectively). Above center: the Asar-Hapi bull in full zoomorphic form. Above right: Asar-Hapi (bottom tier) and the seven Hetheru cows.

Above left: the Minoan bull. Above right: a late period Minoan statue of a person wearing the bull horns with upraised arms.

Above left: Ancient Egyptian *Sefer* (Griffin). Above right: Minoan Griffin (palace relief)

Above: Procession of red colored men and white colored women bringing offerings to the mummy of Any (Papyrus of Any 18th Dynasty-Ancient Egypt)

Above: Minoan sarcophagus with red colored men and white colored women bringing offerings to the dead personality.

The Ancient Egyptian Origins Of Greek Gods and Goddesses
(Greek Classical Period)

Greek Mythology is a conglomeration of stories related to certain Divine personalities (gods and goddesses) and their interactions with each other and with human beings. The main stories related to them are contained in the epics, *Iliad* and *Odyssey,* written by Homer (900 B.C.E.). The main functions of the gods and goddesses and their mingling with human beings was outlined in these stories. The early Greeks also spoke of the origins of their gods and goddesses. It must be clearly understood that at the time when the early Greeks organized themselves sufficiently enough in order to take up the task of learning art and culture, they previously had very little in the way of culture and what was there was primitive. Thus, the force of Ancient Egyptian culture created a strong impression, but it was not the only impression, since the Greeks traveled to other lands and attempted to assimilate the teachings of others as well. This coupled with their own ideas caused a situation wherein they created a synthesis. This synthesis is what should be recognized as early Greek culture and philosophy. In short, what is regarded as Greek was in reality a patchwork of differing ideas which had their basis in Ancient Egyptian philosophy, but which did not follow its precepts entirely. The following passages from the writings of Herodotus (*The Histories*) are instructive on the Ancient Egyptian origins of the Greek gods and goddesses *(highlighted portions are by Ashby).*

35. "**Almost all the names of the gods came into Greece from Egypt. My inquiries prove that they were all derived from a foreign source, and my opinion is that Egypt furnished the greater number**. For with the exception of Neptune and the Dioscuri, whom I mentioned above, and Juno, Vesta, Themis, the Graces, and the Nereids, **the other gods have been known from time immemorial in Egypt**. This I assert on the authority of the Egyptians themselves."

36. "The gods, with whose names they profess themselves unacquainted, the Greeks received, I believe, from the Pelasgi, except Neptune. Of him they got their knowledge from the Libyans, by whom he has been always honored, and who were anciently the only people that had a god of the name. **The Egyptians differ from the Greeks also in paying no divine honors to heroes.**"

37. "Besides these which have been here mentioned, there are many other practices whereof I shall speak hereafter, **which the Greeks have borrowed from Egypt. The peculiarity, however, which they observe in their statues of Mercury they did not derive from the Egyptians**, but from the Pelasgi; from them the Athenians first adopted it, and afterwards it passed from the Athenians to the other Greeks..."

38. "In early times the Pelasgi, as I know by information which I got at Dodona, offered sacrifices of all kinds, and prayed to the gods, but had no distinct names or appellations for them, since they had never heard of any. They called them gods, because they disposed and arranged all things in such a beautiful order. **After a long lapse of time the names of the gods came to Greece from Egypt**, and the Pelasgi learnt them, only as yet they knew nothing of Bacchus, of whom they first heard at a much later date."

Thus we are informed by the Greeks themselves that they derived most of their gods and goddesses from Ancient Egypt, and we are also informed that their most important spiritual philosophers studied in Egypt.

"This is also confirmed by the most learned of Greeks such as Solon, Thales, Plato, Eudoxus, Pythagoras, and as some say, even Lycurgus going to Egypt and conversing with the priests; of whom they say Euxodus was a hearer of Chonuphis of Memphis,[231] Solon of Sonchis of Sais,[232] and Pythagoras of Oenuphis of Heliopolis.[233]"

-Plutarch, Morals, 10
(c. 46-120 AD), Greek author/Initiate of Isis (Aset).

Kamitan Terms and Ancient Greek Terms

It is important to understand that the names of the Ancient Egyptian divinities which have been used widely in Western literature and by Western scholars are actually Greek interpretations of the Kamitan (Ancient Egyptian) names. In keeping with the spirit of the culture of Kamitan spirituality, in this volume we will use the Kamitan names for the divinities through which we will bring forth the Philosophy of Neterianism (Ancient Egyptian religion and myth). Therefore, the Greek name Osiris will be converted back to the Kamitan (Ancient Egyptian) Asar (Asar), the Greek Isis to Aset (Auset), the Greek Nephthys to Nebthet, Anubis to

Anpu or Apuat, Hathor to Hetheru, Thoth or Hermes to Djehuti, etc. (see the table below) Further, the term Ancient Egypt will be used interchangeably with "Kamit," or "Ta-Meri," as these were the terms used by the Ancient Egyptians to refer to their land and culture. The table below provides a listing of the corresponding names of the main Kamitan divinities.

Table 14: Kamitan Names of the main Gods and Goddesses of Ancient Egypt and the Greek translation in common use.

Kamitan (Ancient Egyptian) Names	Greek Names
Amun	Zeus
Ra	Helios
Ptah	Hephastos
Nut	Rhea
Geb	Kronos
Net	Athena
Khonsu	Heracles
Set	Ares or Typhon
Bast	Artemis
Uadjit	Leto
Asar (Asar)	Osiris or Hades
Aset (Auset)	Isis or Demeter
Nebthet	Nephthys
Anpu or Apuat	Anubis
Hetheru	Hathor (Aphrodite)
Heru	Horus or Apollo
Djehuti	Thoth or Hermes
Maat	Astraea or Themis
Sekhmit	Nemesis

The Mystic Phoenix

The Benu (A) is a bird in Ancient Egyptian mythology that lived in the desert for 500 years, and then consumed itself by fire, later to rise renewed from its ashes. It is associated with the Kamitan divinites Khepri and Ra as the eternal renewal of the sun, which after burning itself out, rises from the ashes invigorated and renewed. This image and teaching was adopted by the Greeks in the form of the Phoenix, (B), which exhibits the same mythos about the fabulous bird that dies but is renewed, and also by other peoples of the ancient world.

(A)

(B)

In the *Timaeus*, Plato confirms that the goddess Net of Ancient Egypt was the same divinity called Athena by the Greeks.

> He replied:-In the Egyptian Delta, at the head of which the river Nile divides, there is a certain district which is called the district of Sais, and the great city of the district is also called Sais, and is the city from which King Amasis came. The citizens have a deity for their foundress; she is called in the Egyptian tongue Neith, and is asserted by them to be the same whom the Hellenes call Athene; they are great lovers of the Athenians, and say that they are in some way related to them.[72]

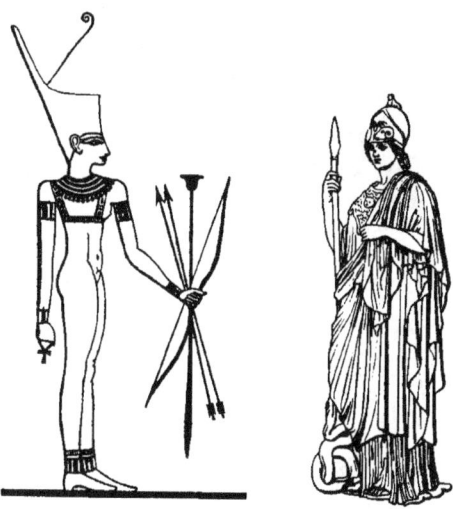

Above left: Goddess Net (Neith) of Egypt. Right- Goddess Athena of Greece

Another correlation can be found between the goddess of righteousness and justice, Maat, of Egypt and the goddess of divine justice, *Astraea* or *Themis*, of Greece.

Above left: The goddess Maat presiding over the balance scales of justice.
Above right: the goddess *Astraea* or *Themis* of Greece presiding over the balance scales of justice.

---

[72] TIMAEUS by Plato 360 BC translated by Benjamin Jowett

Below left- Goddess Baubo, linked by the Greko-Romans as a form of Isis (She lifts her skirt to show her vulva, as Hetheru (form of Isis) did in Kamitan myth. Below center- Goddess of wisdom Aset of Kamit. Below Right - Goddess of wisdom Sophia of Kamit. Both with the same avian motif and mythical function.

The Image of the Sphinx, the Quintessential Kamitan Symbol of Spiritual Enlightenment appears in Mesopotamian and Greek iconography

Left: Ancient Egyptian Winged Sphinx

Above: Left- Assyrian Winged Sphinx. Above: Right: Greek Winged Sphinx

Above: Left- Ancient Egyptian Sefer (Griffin). Above: Right: Griffin of Asian and Western myth

The Griffin is a mythical creature, originally thought to have originated in Asia Minor and Persia, the supposed guardian of hidden treasure, with the body, tail, and hind legs of a lion, and the head, forelegs, and wings of an eagle.[73] One of the most important Ancient Egyptian stories about the Sefer is the Myth of Hetheru and Djehuti.[74] The Sefer has the head of the Hawk (Falcon) because it is related to the Supreme Divinity *Heru*, whose main symbol is the Hawk.

Below: The Ancient Egyptian god Djehuti (A) holds the caduceus (from the Temple of Seti I-Abdu, Egypt). The caduceus is the symbol of the life force power wielded by the god, which sustains life and leads to spiritual enlightenment. The Greeks adopted the teaching of Djehuti and called him Hermes. (B)

(A) (B)

Summary:

The legend of Atlantis, has been romanticized since the time of Plato, and while the legend that he recorded speaks of a vast continent with an advanced civilization, the writings appear to be referring to the Ancient Greek Minoan civilization which had been forgotten by the Greeks of Plato's time. This civilization flourished between 2000 B.C.E. and 1400 B.C.E. when it was apparently disrupted by a cataclysm that caused the civilization to cease. The art and culture of the Minoan civilization shows influences in artistic forms and customs that are unmistakably Ancient Egyptian in character, and there is ample proof of contact between the two cultures. As Ancient Egypt was the older civilization (beginning around 10,000 B.C.E. or before), it is no surprise that the Ancient Egyptians retained knowledge of the Minoans after the cataclysm destroyed the Minoan civilization, especially as there was a close relationship between them. The fact that the Greeks of the Classical Period had little or no knowledge about the Minoans points to the degradation of culture which the Greeks had sustained, and the level of disconnection with their own past history, even in ancient times. These evidences, coupled with modern scientific investigation of the Atlantic Ocean and the geology of the Mediterranean which preclude the possibility of such a place (large continent) having been in those areas, leave no support for any other conclusion except that the Minoan civilization is the Atlantis to which Plato was referring. Thus, the idea that a long time ago, prior to the emergence of Ancient Egyptian civilization, there was a more advanced Greek society from which they drew culture and technology, is unfounded and unsupportable. Furthermore, while more advanced than any other society in the Mediterranean, the Minoans were not as developed as the Ancient Egyptians, either in material culture, volume of architecture, writing, etc., and also, much of what they had was drawn from Ancient Egypt.

---

[73] Copyright © 1995 Helicon Publishing Ltd
[74] See the book *The Glorious Light* by Muata Ashby

Ancient Egypt and the Origins of Mesopotamian Religion and Civilization

Many scholars have tried to advance the idea that Mesopotamia is the source of civilization, specifically referring to Sumer. Others have recently tried to promote the view that India is the source of civilization. In the case of Mesopotamia, the emergence of writing (c.3200 B.C.E.) is cited as predating the Kamitan which is said to have emerged c.3100 B.C.E. Further on the reader will discover how the dates for the estimated emergence of the Sumerian and Kamitan (Ancient Egyptian) civilizations were reset by certain scholars. The early Sumerian writings constitute simple merchant accounts and not the vast spiritual literature, such as is seen in Ancient Egypt, from the same or earlier period. Therefore, any statement about the philosophies of the religion of Sumeria will be limited due to the limited amount of literature created by the Sumerians. This problem does not occur in the study of Neterian Religion and Philosophy. As previously discussed, there are new discoveries in Hierakonpolis[234] and Abydos,[235] Egypt, which are confirming the existence of an advanced Pre-Dynastic society from which the art, architecture, language and myth of the Dynastic Period developed, prior to 3,200 B.C.E. These and other discoveries support the new dating for the construction of the great Sphinx, which is now conservatively dated at 10,000 B.C.E. to 7,000 B.C.E. This new dating now supports the era given for the reign of Asar (Osiris) by the Kamitan texts themselves. The expertise and organization required to create the Great Sphinx, and Asarian (of Osiris) era architecture, and the pyramids, constitutes proof of the existence, not of a rudimentary or emerging primitive culture, but of an advanced and powerful culture in the earliest periods of pre-history.

Many scholars have pointed to Ancient Sumer in Mesopotamia as the cradle of civilization. However, the earliest archeological remains from Sumerian settlements date to 4,000 B.C.E., and those of Egypt go back (conservatively) to at least 7,000 B.C.E. Note that this conservative estimate for Kamit does not refer to the period when Ancient Egypt entered its Neolithic age, such as with the Indians at Mehgarh, but when it was already in a state of high culture, and as we have seen, the existence of high culture in Ancient Egypt goes far back into antiquity. Also, as will be shown in the following section on the eyewitness accounts and records of the past, the borders of Ancient Egypt spanned from Ethiopia to the Ganges river in India, and beyond, in the time of Asar (PreDynastic Period) and Senusert I (Middle Kingdom Period), and from Ethiopia to the head of the Euphrates river in Southwest Asia, an area including Syria, Babylon, Mitanni, Assyria, Cyprus and Phoenicia, in the time of Pharaoh Djehutimes III (Thutmosis III) in 1,479 B.C.E. to the reign of Pharaoh Amenhotep IV (Akhnaton 1,353 B.C.E). Therefore, the Ancient Egyptian civilization encompassed Asia Minor and the Indian subcontinent. Under Rameses II, Palestine (Canaan) remained part of Egypt (c. 1200 B.C.E.), but later on it was lost to invaders under weaker rulers. Later, under the Ptolemaic[236] kings, Egypt regained control of Palestine and southern Turkey (330 B.C.E.-30 B.C.E.). Thus, Ancient Egypt controlled Mesopotamia and the Biblical lands during various periods in history, including the formative years of Judaism and Christianity. Since Sumerian culture was a later development in world civilizations, a study of the spiritual-philosophical principals which Sumer had in common with Ancient Egypt can be undertaken from this more historically accurate perspective. Recall that the early Sumerian writings do not provide extensive data on the spiritual philosophy. This comes later on with more advanced development, and interaction with the Ancient Egyptians and other cultures.

Thus, the similarities between Ancient Egyptian religion and spirituality and other religious and spiritual traditions are not likely due to the influence of the other religions and spiritual traditions on Ancient Egypt, but rather, the reverse. Sumerian religion is believed to have influenced Judaism, but it has already been shown by several scholars that Judaism was previously influenced by Neterian Religion.[237] A brief study of the limited understanding of Sumerian religion reads almost exactly like Ancient Egyptian religion in its basic respects. Sumer was known as the southern region of ancient Mesopotamia. This area was later known as the southern part of Babylonia and today it is known as south central Iraq. Like Ancient Egypt, it was an agricultural civilization. While Egyptian civilization emerged within Africa, the Sumerian culture emerged in Asia Minor. It is widely accepted that Sumerian culture emerged during the 3rd millennia B.C.E. We have already seen how archeological and geological evidences show that Ancient Egyptian civilization is much older. It must be noted that the revised history, which is based on new archeological evidences, shows that Ancient Egyptian civilization arose prior to Sumerian Civilization and the Indus Valley Civilization. The evidence of contact and correlations in the myths between Ancient Egyptian, Sumerian and the Indus Valley Civilizations again point to an influence of the Ancient Egyptian culture and its philosophy on the emerging civilizations.

The land of the Sumerians was called Sumer and was referred to as Shinar in the Bible. The Sumerians, up until recently, have been credited with forming the earliest of the ancient civilizations. However, their origins are obscured in the past. They are not believed to have been Semites like most of the peoples of the region.

They apparently spoke a language which was unrelated to other known tongues. It is believed that they may have come to southern Mesopotamia, the area of Ur, from Persia, or northeastern Mesopotamia before 4,000 B.C.E. However, this is speculation by archeologists. It has also been widely circulated that the Sumerians were the first to create writing and that they influenced Ancient Egyptian culture. As we have seen in our study of ancient history so far, that contention is implausible. In addition, the syllabic signs of Ancient Egyptian Hieroglyphic language did not indicate differences in vowel sounds, as did the Sumerian script. While the Sumerian language has been thought by some scholars to be related to the Ancient Egyptian, the similarities are only due to general correspondences which all pictographic languages have in their original forms. Thus, Ancient Egyptian, Sumerian and Mayan (Native American) scripts show several similarities, but these cannot be used to say that one originates from the other. The Sumerian language is believed to be agglutinative and unrelated to any other known language. The Ancient Egyptian language is related to the Hamitic (African) family of languages.[238]

Table 15: Ancient Egyptian Mythology and Extrapolated Sumerian Mythology

SUMERIAN RELIGION[239 / 240]	ANCIENT EGYPTIAN RELIGION
A- The Sumerians believed that the universe was ruled by a pantheon of divinities comprising a group of living beings, human in form, but immortal and possessing superhuman powers. They believed these beings to be invisible to mortal eyes, and that they controlled and guided the cosmos in accordance with well-laid plans and duly prescribed laws.	A- The Ancient Egyptian Religion was headed by a pantheon. It was comprised of Ra or Pa-Neter, the Supreme Being, and from him emanated the neteru or gods and goddesses. They were depicted with human forms, but were symbolic of unseen cosmic principles.
B- The Sumerians recognized four leading deities. They were known as gods of creation. These gods were An, the god of heaven, Ki, the goddess of earth, Enlil, the god of air, and Enki, the god of water. Thus, heaven, earth, air, and water were considered as the four major constituents of the universe. Enlil – Air Enki – Water Ki – Earth An – Heaven, Sky	B- The main gods and goddesses of the Ancient Egyptian pantheon of the city of Anu were: Shu- Air Tefnut- Moisture (water) Geb- Earth Nut- Sky, Heaven
C- It was held that the act of creation was accomplished through the utterance of the divine word. The deity doing the creating had only to make plans mentally and then pronounce the name of the thing to be created.	C- Creation was accomplished by God in the form of Neberdjer, by uttering his own name. God could create by merely thinking it into existence. The same creative word teaching was later adopted by the Greeks (logos) and the Christians (John 1:1 - *In the beginning was the Word, and the Word was with God, and the Word was God.*).
D- To maintain the universe in harmonious and continuous operation and to avoid conflict and confusion, the gods brought the "me" into being. It was a set of unchangeable and universal rules and laws that all beings were required to obey.	D- In order to maintain the universe, God instituted Maat. Maat is the principle and philosophy of cosmic order, justice, righteousness and harmony which all nature follows. All human beings were required to practice Maat in order to live in harmony with nature and each other, and to reach the eternal abode to live with God after death.
E- Each of the important deities was the patron of one or more Sumerian cities. Large temples were erected in the name of the deity, who was worshiped as the divine ruler and protector of the city. Temple rites were conducted by many priests, priestesses, singers, musicians, sacred prostitutes, and eunuchs. Sacrifices were offered daily.	E- The cities of Ancient Egypt were known as Nomes. Each had a patron deity. Many temples survive to this day. Daily rituals were performed by Priests and Priestesses.
F- The Sumerians believed that human beings were fashioned of clay.	F- The Ancient Egyptians believed that God, in the form of Knum, fashioned human beings on a potter's wheel.
G- When human beings die, it was believed that their spirits descend to the netherworld.	G- When human beings die, they go to the Duat (netherworld) where they are judged in accordance with their deeds while on earth.

The Gilgamesh Epic is an important Middle Eastern work of literature. It was written on twelve clay tablets in cuneiform about 2000 B.C.E. The Gilgamesh Epic relates the story of its hero, Gilgamesh, and includes the city of Uruk which is known in the Bible as Erech (now Warka, Iraq). The Sumerians created an advanced culture which included the development of cuneiform writing but their country soon fell to outside invasions. There was a brief Sumerian renaissance centered on Ur, which continued until c.1950 B.C.E. when Semitic Amorites overran much of Sumeria. This was the beginning of a long period of instability in Mesopotamia until the first Babylonian Dynasty was founded in 1830 B.C.E., which reached its height with Hammurabi. This date is believed to mark the end of the Sumerian state. Thereafter the Sumerian culture was then adopted almost completely by Babylonia. The dates for Abraham's departure from Ur are possibly related to this period since there were undoubtedly many migrations out of the area during that time. It is clear to see that Abraham was influenced by Sumerian culture and there is evidence that there was trade between the Sumerians and the Ancient Egyptians.

Colchis, Mesopotamia and Ancient Egypt in the First Millennium B.C.E.

The following excerpt comes from the "History" of Herodotus:

> There can be no doubt that the Colchians are an Egyptian race. Before I heard any mention of the fact from others, I had remarked it myself. After the thought had struck me, I made inquiries on the subject both in Colchis and in Egypt, and I found that the Colchians had a more distinct recollection of the Egyptians, than the Egyptians had of them. Still the Egyptians said that they believed the Colchians to be descended from the army of Sesostris. My own conjectures were founded, first, on the fact that they are black-skinned and have woolly hair, which certainly amounts to but little, since several other nations are so too; but further and more especially, on the circumstance that the Colchians, the Egyptians, and the Ethiopians, are the only nations who have practiced circumcision from the earliest times. The Phoenicians and the Syrians of Palestine themselves confess that they learnt the custom of the Egyptians; and the Syrians who dwell about the rivers Thermodon and Parthenius, as well as their neighbors the Macronians, say that they have recently adopted it from the Colchians. Now these are the only nations who use circumcision, and it is plain that they all imitate herein the Egyptians. With respect to the Ethiopians, indeed, I cannot decide whether they learnt the practice of the Egyptians, or the Egyptians of them- it is undoubtedly of very ancient date in Ethiopia- but that the others derived their knowledge of it from Egypt is clear to me from the fact that the Phoenicians, when they come to have commerce with the Greeks, cease to follow the Egyptians in this custom, and allow their children to remain uncircumcised. I will add a further proof to the identity of the Egyptians and the Colchians. These two nations weave their linen in exactly the same way, and this is a way entirely unknown to the rest of the world; they also in their whole mode of life and in their language resemble one another.

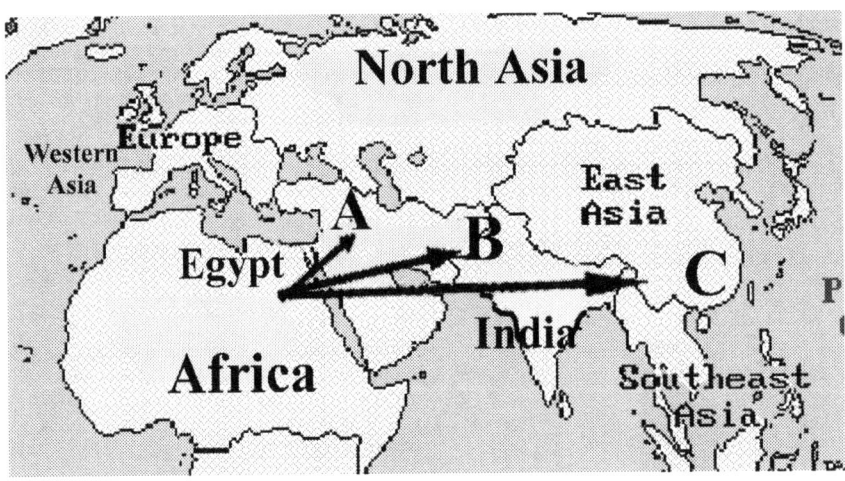

Above: Map of North Africa and Asia. A- Mesopotamia, B- Indus Valley, C- China

Colchis was an ancient country located on the eastern shore of the Black Sea. It was south of the Caucasus Mountains which are now part of the Republic of Georgia. Colchis was an independent nation until about 100 B.C.E., when it was conquered by Mithradates VI Eupator, king of Pontus. In Greek mythology, Colchis was the home of the princess Medea and the repository of the golden fleece sought by Jason and his Argonauts. The above excerpt shows that the peoples of Syria and northeastern Palestine (Caucasus – where the modern term Caucasian comes from) were originally Egyptians (dark skinned African peoples) who were strongly influenced by the culture of Egypt, not just through casual association, but by blood relation, being of the same skin color, practicing some of the same customs (including circumcision which the Jews adopted) and having similar language.

"Egyptians settled Ethiopia and Colchis."

-*Geography,* Strabo c. 64 B.C.E.,
(Greek historian and geographer)

Herodotus informed us in his writings that even the Colchians appear to be related to the Egyptians because of their customs and physical appearance, being "black skinned."

Ancient Egyptian Origin of the Chaldaens

The biblical name, "Ur of the Chaldees," refers to the Chaldaens, who settled in the area of southern Iraq about 900 B.C.E. The Book of Genesis (see 11:27-32) describes Ur as the starting point of the westward migration of the family of Abraham to Palestine about 1900-1800 B.C.E. Thus, at the time when Abraham would have lived, the Egyptian civilization was at the end of the Middle Kingdom Period (or Middle Empire 2,040-1,640 B.C.E.). Pharaoh Senusert I (Sesostris I), who reigned c. 1971-1928 B.C.E., built fortresses throughout Nubia and established trade with foreign lands; his rule stretched to the far east. He sent governors to Palestine. In more ancient times (12,000 B.C.E.), according to the Egyptian story of Asar (Osiris), the Egyptians ruled all of Asia Minor as far as India and beyond. Due to invasions and wars these lands were ceded to the conquering peoples. But during the Middle Kingdom Period, Palestine was once again controlled by Egypt as it was in ancient times.

The following are museum exhibits, which show the connection between Ancient Egypt and the peoples in Asia Minor in prehistoric times. These support the contention that Ancient Egyptian culture and religion were present in and strongly influenced Mesopotamian civilizations, including the Neo Assyrian and Sumerian.

The Ibex Period

Plate 17: Predynastic Ancient Egyptian Boat Displaying Ibex

There is a period in Ancient Egyptian Pre-Dynastic history wherein black and red pottery with *ibex* motifs begin to appear. Such pottery has also been discovered in Asia Minor (Mesopotamia), and in the Indus region of India.[75] Below are some examples. Thus, it appears that the culture of Ancient Egypt, which Herodotus reported as stretching from the Nile through Asia Minor to the Indus and beyond, is being supported by evidence based on this pottery.

---

[75] for the Indian pottery see *Part 2: Chapter 3- Section:* Black and Red Pottery

Plate 18: Ancient Egyptian Pottery with Boat and Ibex Painting

Above: Pre-Dynastic Egyptian pottery group with ibexes and boats. (Metropolitan Museum-New York)

Plate 19: Pottery from Western and Northern Ancient Iran

Above: Pottery with ibex, western and north Iran; (Metropolitan Museum A 2600BC Museum-New York)

The ibexes are several species of wild Old World goats. They are characterized by long, backward curving heavy horns measuring up to 5ft (1.5m) in males. They all have great climbing ability and long, yellow-brown hair. Height: 3ft (0.9m) at shoulder; weight: 240lb (108kg).[241] They can be found in the mountainous areas of Europe, NE Africa, and Central Asia. They are herbivorous and live in small groups.[242] At one time, these animals figured prominently in the life of the Ancient Egyptians as sources of food and also as a feature of cultural identity. The pottery and the ibex denote an agrarian lifestyle which was well established in that period.

Plate 20: Greek and Mesopotamian Sphinxes

Above left- Greek Winged Sphinx -Attica 530 BCE
Above right – North Syrian Winged Sphinx, 1100 B.C.E.

Figure 55: Winged Sphinx and Griffin from Ancient Egypt

The Greek and Syrian Winged Sphinxes appear to have been derived from the Ancient Egyptian Winged Sphinx and the Ancient Egyptian Griffin.

Above left- The Ancient Egyptian Winged Sphinx. Right- The Ancient Egyptian Sefr (Griffin).[243]

Plate 21: Mesopotamian versions of the Winged Sundisk and the Ritual of Smelling the Lotus.

Above– North Syrian Ritual of the Lotus and Winged Sundisk 1100 B.C.E.

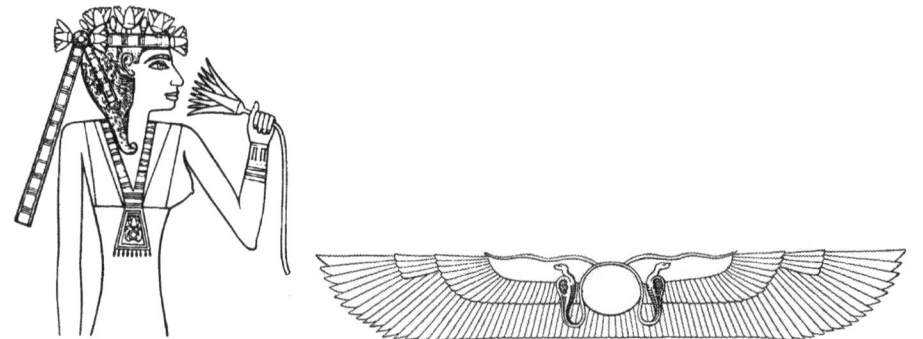

Above– Ancient Egyptian Ritual of the Lotus and Winged Sundisk, Old Kingdom Period.

Plate 22: Cylinder seal Syria I 1820-1730 BC Met Museum

Above-The cylinder seal from Syria I has been dated at 1820-1730 B.C.E. (Metropolitan Museum– New York).

The reliefs on this seal are so similar in appearance to the iconography of Ancient Egypt that the museum itself noted the similarities in its description of the displays. These reliefs show a profound impact of Ancient Egyptian culture and religion in Anatolia (Asia Minor). They depict some of the most predominant and most characteristic motifs used in Ancient Egyptian religion. Among these are the *Ibex* (top right), *winged Sphinx* (top right), *baboon* (top center) *holding the winged sundisk* (top center), *Maat positioned person with bird head and human body* (below right), *Ankh symbol* (below left), *horn headdress* (Center), and *recumbent quadruped creatures facing away from each other* (below center).

Above: Goddess Maat in her winged form (Ancient Egypt). Notice that the posture in the Mesopotamian relief is virtually identical to the Kamitan.

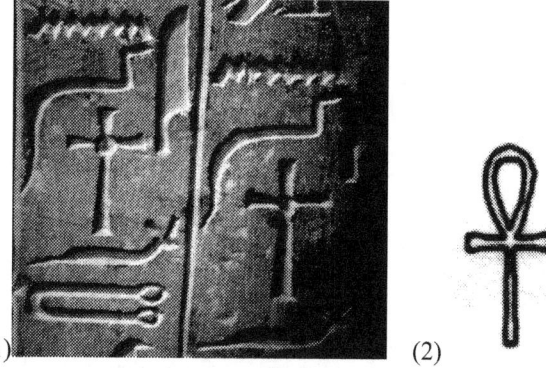

Above: A section from the pyramid of Teti in Sakkara Egypt, known as the "Pyramid Texts" (Early Dynastic Period) showing the cross (1), a symbol of protection and well being, which was later adopted by the Christians. The Ankh (2) is a form of the cross meaning life essence. It is one of the most important symbols in Ancient Egyptian religion. It can be found on the Mesopotamian relief above.

Above: The Ancient Egyptian symbol "Akher," the two lions (recumbent quadruped creatures facing away from each other) who guard the two horizons so that the sun may pass into the Netherworld (i.e. transcend the physical plane) (From Chapter 4 {17} of the Pert M Heru {Book of the Dead}).

SUMMARY

In the nineteenth century, when the deciphering of the Ancient Egyptian hieroglyphic text sparked an interest in Ancient Egypt that developed into the discipline of Egyptology, it was accepted at that time by Egyptologists that the Ancient Egyptians were originally of African (Nubian) origins. The early Greek Philosophers, Thales, Pythagoras, Plato and others acknowledged their debt to the Kamitan sages for their instruction in art, music, philosophy, etc. Several writers have demonstrated undeniably exact correlations between the religion of Ancient Egypt, Judaism and Christianity. In the 20th century there has been a concerted effort to downplay these correlations and suggest other unknown possibilities and unfounded explanations for the high culture of Ancient Egypt. Now, in the late 20th century, with the publication of the Egyptian Yoga book series as well as publications by other authors detailing archeological, anthropological and mythological evidences, it has been shown that there was contact between the peoples of Ancient Egypt and those of Ancient Greece, Mesopotamia and India. Further, there is ample evidence to show that Ancient Egyptian civilization emerged at the dawn of history and had a profound influence on the latter emerging ones.

In view of the dates now accepted for the Ancient Egyptian chronology, even by many conservative (traditionalist) scholars, Ancient Egypt must be accepted as the oldest civilization in history if the existence of language, art, agriculture, religion, myth, philosophy, architecture, mathematics, etc., are qualifying factors differentiating civilization versus the primitive Neolithic stage of evolution. The Neolithic age was characterized by the development of agriculture and the making of polished stone implements. It was a period in human evolution wherein human beings began to domesticate and breed animals, live in settled villages, practiced pottery, cultivated grain crops, practiced weaving, and flint-mining.

CONCLUSION

> "The river rises of itself, waters the fields, and then sinks back again: thereupon each man sows his field and waits for the harvest."
>
> -Herodotus

What is it that allowed the first civilizations in our history to develop in the great river valleys of the world? What promoted the development of civilization in the Nile River Valley first in history? The river valley offers a unique opportunity for people to make use of the life giving benefits of water and to conduct farming along its banks, which from time to time flood into the valley and leave deposits. These deposits create extremely fertile soil, and therefore, good conditions for farming. The great river valleys of the world are known as the Nile River Valley (Africa), the Euphrates River Valley (Mesopotamia), The Indus River Valley (India), and the Yellow River Valley (China). However, in Ancient Egypt the situation was an even more optimum than the rest. Noted by Herodotus, the regularity of the Nile flood allowed early farmers there to plan their crops and with greater ease than any other people in the world, cultivate the land. This allowed them to use the longest and most reliable river in the world as a source of sustenance, so that they might engage in other pursuits such as developing civilization in the form of art, architecture, religion, philosophy, medical science, etc.

So when can we say that civilization is present? At what point do we stop calling a society primitive and start referring to it as civilized? If we want to say the existence of farming, then how much farming qualifies as "civilized?" How much is to be considered "minimal" or "subsistence level" and how much is "substantial?" These are of course in part subjective questions, however, in general it can be said that if a family group sustains itself through farming, this qualifies as the existence of farming, and if several family groups sustain themselves through farming, we can say that a village is practicing farming. Further, if we discover farming on a scale that can sustain several hundred or thousands of people we can consider this as evidence of agriculture on a mass scale. Each level constitutes a step towards greater civilization. However, scholars usually refer to farming in the Neolithic period where it is observed that a substantial number of people are living by farming as evidence of civilization.

> Agriculture developed in the Middle East and Egypt at least 10,000 years ago. Farming communities soon became the base for society in China, India, Europe, Mexico, and Peru, then spread throughout the world.[244]

It has been discovered that farming was practiced in Ancient Egypt and Sumer early on in history. Further, when looking for evidence of civilization, we must differentiate between the origins of or first evidence of civilization and the "flourishing" or height of civilization. For instance, while it is correct to say that farming and therefore, the rudiments of civilization began in the Indus Valley Civilization in ancient India by 6500

B.C.E., it is also correct to say that civilization flourished by 3000-2500 B.C.E. In Mesopotamia, farming began by about 10,500 B.C.E., but the civilization again flourished by 5000-3100 B.C.E. In Ancient Egypt, farming existed before 10,000 B.C.E., and the civilization first flourished between 12,000-7000 B.C.E.

Writing appears in Sumeria (Sumer-Mesopotamia) in 3100 B.C.E. Writing in the form of short inscriptions was known to have existed in the Indus Valley from about 3000-2500 B.C.E. However, due to the shortness of these inscriptions it has been exceedingly difficult for scholars to achieve a satisfactory decipherment of them.[245] These writings are not long spiritual-philosophical treatises like the Pyramid texts of Kamit or the later Vedas of India. When we refer to writing we are speaking about texts longer than simple inscriptions, for these can be found in Egypt earlier, in the Pre-Dynastic era (beginning 5500-4241 B.C.E.).

Now that we have seen the implausibility that Mesopotamian civilization gave birth to Ancient Egyptian civilization, and it becomes clear that it is more likely that Ancient Egypt gave birth to Mesopotamian civilization, we move on to the important question of the other cradle of civilization which has gained much attention in recent years, the Indus Valley Civilization.

See also: **Lilith, Sumerian Religion, Judaism and the Ancient Egyptian Connection**

NOTES TO CHAPTER 3

[228] Websters Copyright © 1995 Helicon Publishing Ltd
[229] Random House Encyclopedia Copyright (C) 1983,1990 by Random House Inc.
[230] Civilization or Barbarism pp 84-85
[231] major temple and city in Ancient Egypt.
[232] See previous note.
[233] See previous note.
[234] The Hierakonpolis Expedition returned for its fourth season of renewed fieldwork under the direction of Barbara Adams (Petrie Museum of Egyptian Archaeology and Dr. Renée Friedman (University of California, Berkeley).
[235] Discovered by excavators from the German Archaeological Institute in Cairo. NEWSBRIEFS *EARLIEST EGYPTIAN GLYPHS* Volume 52 Number 2 March/April 1999
[236] Descendants of Ptolemy, a general of Alexander the Great, who took control of Egypt after Alexander died.
[237] *Christian Yoga: The Journey from Jesus to Christ,* Muata Ashby
[238] Copton's Encyclopedia
[239] "Funk and Wagnals New Encyclopedia"
[240] Random House Encyclopedia.
[241] Random House Encyclopedia Copyright (C) 1983,1990
[242] Copyright © 1995 Helicon Publishing Ltd
[243] Hieroglyphica Vol 1, Nicolas Grimal, Jochen Hallof, Dirk Van der Plas
[244] Copyright © 1995 Helicon Publishing Ltd Encyclopedia
[245] *Civilizations of the Indus Valley and Beyond*, Sir Mortimer Wheeler. *In Search of the Cradle of Civilization,* 1995, co-authored by Georg Feuerstein, David Frawley, and Subhash Kak.

Chapter 4: The Ancient Egyptian Origins of Western Religions: Judaism, Christianity and Islam and The Arabian Religions

What is Religion?

The Purpose of Religion and The Three Steps of Religion

The purpose of religion is to bring a human being closer to the Divine, which is peace, harmony, abiding happiness and self-knowledge. In broad terms, any movement which accomplishes this goal of leading the practitioner to come closer to the Divine is a form of religious movement. Religion is an organized process of accomplishing that goal. Every human being has an innate desire to discover the ultimate, the infinite, the transcendental and immortal aspect of life. This is called mysticism. Therefore, authentic religion consists of three levels: *myth, ritual and mystical experience*. If the first two levels are misunderstood or accepted literally, the spiritual movement will fail to proceed to the next higher level. In order for a religious experience to lead one to have a mystical experience, all three levels of religion must be completed. Therefore, religion and its purpose must be well understood in order that the purpose be fulfilled.

The Myth

The term religion comes from the Latin *"Relegare"* which uses the word roots *"Re"* which means *"Back"* and *"Ligon"* which means *"to hold, to link, to bind."* Therefore, the essence of true religion is the same as Yoga, that is, of linking back, specifically, linking the soul of its follower back to its original source: God. From time immemorial, human beings have devised stories and activities as well as modes of inquiry etc., to explain and understand the nature of life, its source and ultimate destiny. The stories used by sages and saints to explain the nature of Creation and our place in it are collectively called myths. Some people have come to regard the term myth as meaning "a lie" or "a fiction." Actually, the idea behind creating religious myths is that they should contain transcendental truths that cannot be conveyed rationally. They present us with insights into the nature of the divinity so that we may better understand (connect) and worship in a more profound way. Thereby, myths provide us with knowledge about ourselves, where we come from, where we are going, the purpose of life and direction in life.

The Ritual

The ritual stage of religion relates to the traditions, ceremonies and observances related to the principles presented in the myth. It is enjoined that people who believe in the myths should practice rituals related to it so that they may be drawn closer to it and thereby understand it better. If this process is successful, a human being will discover the transcendental wisdom that is at the heart of the religion.

The Mystical

Mysticism is a spiritual discipline for attaining union with the Divine through the practice of deep meditation or contemplation, and other spiritual disciplines such as austerity, detachment, renunciation, etc. In this aspect, Mysticism and Yoga are synonymous. The goal of all mysticism is to transcend the phenomenal world and all mental concepts. Ordinary religion is a part of the world and the mental concepts of people, and must too be ultimately transcended. The myth now becomes the experience of the practitioner and the journey of religion ends in a mystical experience of the divinity with the practitioner (initiate, aspirant or devotee). So a mystical teaching, while existing in an historical context, is in reality not concerned with history or ordinary human reality, since these are, in the end, transient, illusory and irrelevant to the attainment of higher consciousness. Therefore, while certain historical information is needed to set a context for spiritual studies in relation to world history, an emphasis is placed on revealing the mystical meaning contained in it, because it is this meaning alone that will lead the spiritual aspirant to attain the goal of mysticism, that of transcending ordinary human consciousness and discovering the deeper realities that lie within the heart.

The Universality of Religion

All civilizations have created a form of religion throughout history as well as practices and philosophies to aid in the advancement of its practitioners. Some religions concentrate on certain aspects of religion while others excel in other areas. Some religions are mostly philosophical, while others are mostly ritualistic, and some a more balanced mixture of ritual and philosophy. Some religions are orthodox, while others are more mystically oriented. All religions serve a purpose, to support those who need the particular type of emphasis they offer at a given point in their spiritual evolution. Ultimately, all religions should have a right to exist in an atmosphere of understanding and tolerance, just as human beings in a family, with differing desires, personalities and tendencies need to accept, cooperate, recognize, and even appreciate each other, or a florist appreciates how different flowers augment a bouquet. When the universality of the human need for religious movement is not accepted, a situation can develop in which the practice of religion is degraded to such an extent that conflict between the religions ensues.

Early Beginnings: The First Religion

The following chart, comprising the major world religions, shows the development of religion in known human history. A religion does not necessarily deserve special attention, importance or reverence because of its age, but rather for how it conveys the universal and transcendental message that is the hallmark of an authentic religious movement. Thus, how far the myth, disciplines, ritual, and mystical philosophy of a religion have evolved are the truly important criteria for determining if a religion is positive or negative for one's spiritual evolution. Also, just because a religion has many adherents or a long history or extensive rituals or traditions does not necessarily mean that it is "evolved." Many such religions promote disharmony in the world and their adherents do not grow to discover the heights of mystical experience. Therefore, religions should be judged by the standard set for its purpose and in the contexts of human spiritual evolution.

Further, learning about the history of religion will allow a religious practitioner to discover the true meaning of religion and not fall into the pitfalls of dogmatism, blind faith or dry intellectualism. In order for this to occur the spiritual seeker must be open and honest, and willing to make adjustments in the process of seeking the true religion. The aspirant must be strong enough to resist the tendency to fall for what is simple and apparently easy, for this may not be the best course for their particular needs. In general, the masses of uneducated and poor people tend to follow the religions that simplify religious tenets and espouse orthodox, dogmatic principles. These religions tend to be more sustained by fiery evangelism, patriarchy and are more easily driven to fundamentalism. They excite and agitate the personality, driving it to substantial and constant actions (rituals) in the service of the religion. There is a de-emphasis on rational thought and personal free-will. In general those who have a greater intellectual capacity and a high degree of personality integration flock to religions that are more intellectual (philosophical) and mystical. Both types of extremes can be destructive and what is necessary is to chart a balanced course which allows every aspect of the personality to become harmonized, and thus allow a situation wherein positive spiritual evolution may occur, instead of conflict, irrationality and fear. Religions which are more intellectual, meditative and philosophical tend to be more serene, ecumenical, balanced in matters of gender, supportive of free-will, and motivate through intellectual influence.

Just as there is no reason to believe that one particular religion is superior to another based solely on its age, there is also no reason to believe that one religion is inferior to another based on its age. Also, there is no intrinsic reason why one religion should usurp previously existing religions. World history shows that in parts of the world where religions are tolerant and understanding, many religions can exist together in harmony, and benefiting all people. So there is no inherent reason why one religion should seek to eradicate others and not seek to live in concert, cooperatively. The following time-line of world religions is presented so that the reader may begin to understand the relative commencement and duration of the religious systems which will be discussed in this volume, and how they relate to each other in terms of their time of prominence in history.

Ancient Egypt was the first and most ancient civilization to create a religious system that was complete with all three stages of religion, as well as an advanced spiritual philosophy of righteousness, called Maat Philosophy, that also had secular dimensions. Several Temple systems were developed in Kamit; they were all related. The pre-Judaic/Islamic religions that the later Jewish and Muslim religions drew from in order to create their religions developed out of these, ironically enough, only to later repudiate the source from whence they originated. In any case, the Great Sphinx remains the oldest known religious monument in history that denotes high culture and civilization as well. Ancient Egypt and Nubia produced the oldest religious systems and their contact with the rest of the world led to the proliferation of advanced religion and spiritual philosophy. People who were practicing simple animism, shamanism, nature based religions and witchcraft were elevated to the level of not only understanding the nature of the Supreme Being, but also attaining salvation from the miseries of life through the effective discovery of that Transcendental being, not as an untouchable aloof Spirit, but as the very essence of all that exists.

Time-line of Major World Religions

	10,000 B.C.E	5000 B.C.E.	4500 B.C.E.	4000 B.C.E.	3500 B.C.E.	3000 B.C.E.	2500 B.C.E.	2000 B.C.E.	1500 B.C.E.	1000 B.C.E.	500 B.C.E.	0	600 B.C.E.
Ancient Egyptian Religion	Pre-Dynastic Era		Old Kingdom		Middle Kingdom			New Kingdom		Nubian Period	Assyrian Period	Persian Period / Greek Period / Roman Period		Coptic Period to Present
					Indus Valley Culture				Aryan India		Hinduism India to present		
										Minoan Greek	Classical Greek to present		
											Taoism to present		
											Buddhism to present		
				Pre-Judaic Pre-Islamic	Sumerian Religion	Arabian Canaan Babylonian Syrian Religions				Pre-Islamic Allah			
									Judaism to present			
											Christianity to present	
												Islam to present

THE AFRICAN ORIGINS OF CIVILIZATION, RELIGION AND YOGA SPIRITUALITY

Selected Spiritual Categories Compared

The Sages of ancient times created philosophies through which it might be possible to explain the origins of creation, as we saw above. Then they set out to create disciplines which could lead a person to discover the spiritual truths of life for themselves, and thereby realize the higher reality which lies beyond the phenomenal world. These disciplines are referred to as religions and spiritual philosophies (mysticism-yoga). Below is a basic listing of world religious and spiritual philosophies. The following religious categories are presented so that the reader may gain a basis for comparing the varied forms of religious practice that are being discussed in this volume. The varied religions exist so that varied personalities in human beings may be able to practice religion in accordance with their current desire and or psychological inclination, based on their level of spiritual development (maturity). Some of the religions presented as examples of the varied categories contain features that are from more than one category. In these cases the number (1) besides the religious example will designate the primary category of the religion and the number (2) will signify secondary features. If the religion has more than one (1) it will signify that the religion has sects that exemplify more than one particular category. Note: while *Polytheistic Monotheism* and *Pantheistic Monotheism* contain elements of Animism, the understanding that the universe is alive with spirits or souls, it is understood that these are manifestations of the Supreme Being and not independent realities.

Table 16: Major Religious Categories

Theism	Atheism	Ethicism	Ritualism	Monism	Polytheistic Monotheism	Pantheistic Monotheism	Mysticism
Belief in a God who will punish the sinners and save the faithful.	Salvation by doing what makes you happy. There is no God, only existence, which just happened on its own without any help.	Salvation by performing the right actions.	Salvation by performing the correct rituals.	Salvation by understanding that all is the Supreme Being and nothing else exists.	Salvation by approaching the Supreme Being by {his/her} manifestations Nature, cosmic forces, mystical experience).	Salvation by devotion to Supreme Being who manifests in All Things – leads to mystical union	Salvation by disciplines that lead to union with the Supreme Being
↓	↓	↓	↓	↓	↓	↓	↓
Example	*Example*	*Example*	*Example*	*Example*	*Example*	*Example*	*Example*
Orthodox Christianity Orthodox Islam Orthodox Judaism Zoroastrianism (1) Brahmanism (1)	Epicureans Charvacas Atheists Existentialists Stoics Humanists (western)	Zoroastrianism(2) Jainism(2) Confucianism Aristotelianism Taoism(2) Gnosticism Vedanta(2) Shetaut Neter[246] Buddhism(2) Pythagoreanism(2) Humanists (African religion, Eastern religion and Native American religion) (2) Sanatana Dharma (Hinduism) (2) Yoga(2)	Brahmanism(1) Priestcraft Shetaut Neter[247] (2) Sanatana Dharma (2) (Hinduism)	Taoism(1) Gnosticism Vedanta(1) Shetaut Neter[248](2) Buddhism(1) Pythagoreanism Spinoza Cabalism Sufism(2) Idealism Pythagoreanism(2) Platonism(2) Yoga (1)[76]	African Religions (including Shetaut Neter[249])(1) Buddhism(2) Sanatana Dharma (Hinduism)(1) Sufism(1) Native American	Atonism (Akhnaton) Vaishnavites (Vishnu and Krishna) Shivaite (Shiva) Sufism(1) Jainism Goddess	Yoga Shetaut Neter Sufism Vedanta Taoism Gnosticism

---

[76] NOTE: Yoga is actually neither a religion nor a philosophy, but a way of life based on disciplines for spiritual evolution, and thus does not fit under any category. Yoga is rather, a set of disciplines that religions used to enhance the spiritual movement.

Table 17: The Stages of Spiritual Evolution

The Stages of Spiritual Evolution	Three Stages of Religion	Yoga Tradition[77]
1- **Aspiration**- Students who are being instructed on a probationary status, and have not experienced inner vision. The important factor at this level is awakening of the Spiritual Self, that is, becoming conscious of the divine presence within one's self and the universe by having faith that there is a spiritual essence beyond ordinary human understanding.	1- **Myth** Listening to the main myths of the religion which convey the story of the divinity of the religion and the cultural tradition related to the religion.	1-**Listening** to Wisdom teachings. Having achieved the qualifications of an aspirant, there is a desire to listen to the teachings from a Spiritual Preceptor.
2- **Striving**- Students who have attained inner vision and have received a glimpse of Cosmic Consciousness. The important factor at this level is purgation of the self, that is, purification of mind and body through a spiritual discipline. The aspirant tries to totally surrender "personal" identity or ego to the divine inner Self, which is the Universal Self of all Creation.	2- **Ritual** Practice of the rituals and traditions based on the myth of the religion.	2- **Reflection** on those teachings that have been listened to and living according to the disciplines enjoined by the teachings are to be practiced until the wisdom teaching is fully understood.
3- **Established**- Students who have become IDENTIFIED with or UNITED with GOD. The important factor at this level is illumination of the intellect, that is, experience and appreciation of the divine presence during reflection and meditation, Union with the Divine Self, the divine marriage of the individual with the universal.	3- **Metaphysics** (mysticism) The myth now becomes the experience of the practitioner and the journey of religion ends in a mystical experience of the Divinity with the devotee.	3- **Meditation** in Wisdom Yoga is the process of reflection that leads to a state in which the mind is continuously introspective. It means expansion of consciousness culminating in revelation of and identification with the Absolute Self.

The chart above provides insight into the nature of the religious path for spiritual evolution and how it is related to the initiatic disciplines as well as to the Yoga tradition. These are the essential aspects needed by all systems of spirituality in order to promote a positive spiritual evolution. If these steps are missing, the spiritual evolution will be limited and ineffective and will lead to strife and conflict. Thus, when studying religions, these steps can be discerned and the manner in which the varied religions provide for these can be qualified and compared in order to discover correlations and contrasts.

---

[77] Note: It is important to note here that the same teaching which was practiced in ancient Egypt of **Listening** to, **Reflecting** upon, and **Meditating** upon the teachings is the same process used in Vedanta-Jnana Yoga (from India) of today.

The Gods and Goddesses From Ancient Egypt in Pre-Judaic/Christian/Islamic Canaan and Arabia

Map of Asia Minor: A- Egypt, B- Canaan (Palestine, Israel, Lebanon, Syria, Jordan), C- Arabia, D- Persia (modern Iran), E-Indus Valley

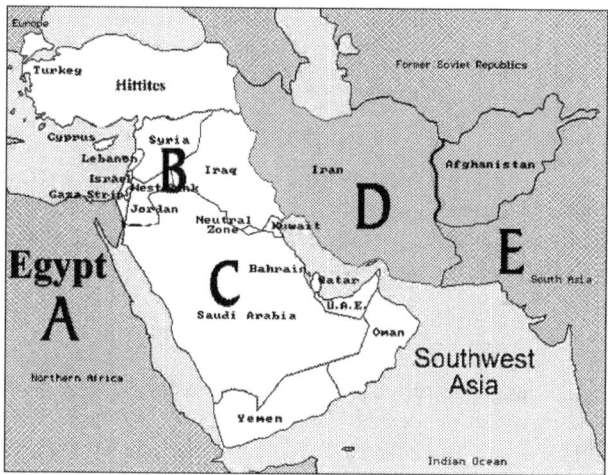

The Canaanites, or the people who lived in the area now called Palestine and Israel, worshipped many divinities prior (before 1000 B.C.E.) to and during as well as after the advent of Judaism, Christianity and Islam. One of the most important divinities was Baal. Many city gods were named Baal, which means "Lord": Baal-Berith (Lord of the Covenant), Baal-Gad (Goat Lord), Baal-Hadad (Lord of the Hunt), Baal-Hamman (Lord of the Brazier), Baal-Zebub (Lord of Flies), etc. Thus, there is an element of omnipresence in the teaching as if all (everything) is manifesting out of the same original principle. Some of these appear in the Jewish Bible (2 Kings 1:2, Matthew 12:24). In the plural, *Baalim* means idols or Baals collectively. So the same divinity was worshipped under different forms in different parts of the land. It was recognized that the same Baal energy was operating in all places. The Canaanite shrines were objects of Yahweh's wrath in the Jewish Bible (Leviticus 26:30; Psalm 78:58). Thus the Israelites were ordered to destroy them when they entered Canaanite territory (Numbers 33:52; Deuteronomy 33:29) to usurp it from the inhabitants of those times. However, the shrines were completely eliminated only under the King Hezekiah in the 7th century B.C.E.[250]

When we come to examine the iconography and some of the basic attributes of Baal we discover some remarkable correlations with Ancient Egyptian religion. Baal was recognized as a vegetation divinity and as protector against chaos. It has already been shown that Asia Minor, and especially the land of Canaan, was part of Ancient Egypt and that in fact the ancient Canaanites were descendants of the Egyptians, who were themselves descendants of the Nubians. The Ancient Egyptian God Asar (Osiris) wears the same headdress (King of Lower Egypt) as Baal, and he is also a vegetation-fertility divinity, as well as a protector from the forces of chaos.

THE AFRICAN ORIGINS OF CIVILIZATION, RELIGION AND YOGA SPIRITUALITY

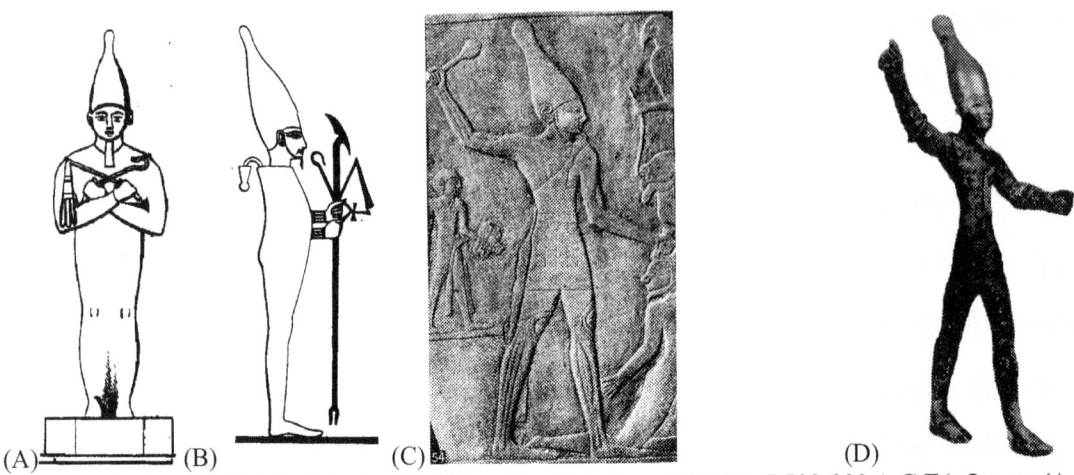

Above Left: Images (A-B) of the Ancient Egyptian God Asar (Osiris) (5,500-300 A.C.E.), Image (A-B) of the Ancient Egyptian king Narmer (founder of the 1st Dynasty 5,500-3,800 B.C.E.)
Above Right: (D) The Canaanite God Baal (2000 B.C.E.-200 B.C.E.).

Goddess Baalat was the mistress of Baal (note the consonantal "t" ending to signify "female" which is the same as the Ancient Egyptian language format). She was also a fertility goddess and was associated with and seen as a form of the Egyptian goddesses Hetheru (Hathor) and Aset (Isis) by the Canaanites. More evidences of the Ancient Egyptian influence on Pre-Judaic/Christian/Muslim religion in Arabia can be seen in the iconography and worship forms of Asia Minor.

Asar of Ancient Egypt	Baal of Arabia
A. Asar is a vegetation/fertility god. B. Represents forces of opposition to the forces of disorder in the form of the god Set, C. The bull is the second most important symbol of Asar. D. He dies and is restored through the Labors of goddess Aset. E. Aset is his sister.	A. Baal is a vegetation/fertility god. B. Represents forces of opposition to the forces of disorder in the form of the god Mot, C. Sired a bull calf to guarantee his power in his absence as he went to the netherworld to fight Mot. D. He dies and is restored through the labors of goddess Anat. E. Anat is his sister.

"There are Egyptian columns as far off as NYASA, Arabia...Isis and Osiris led an army into India, to the source of the Ganges, and as far as the Indus Ocean."

-Diodorus **(Greek historian 100 B. C.)**

The Supreme Divinity in Neterian Religion and its Manifestations in Greek Religion, Arabian Religion, Judaism, Christianity, and Islam

SUPREME DIVINITY
⬇

Encompassing both Male and Female
Differentiates into the opposites of Creation

Net-Mehurt	*Neberdjer*
Ancient Egyptian Female Aspect of Supreme Divinity	Ancient Egyptian Male Aspect of Supreme Divinity
Aset Hetheru *Sekhmit* *Qadesh*	*Amun* Ra Ptah Asar Heru
⬇	⬇
Greek Manifestations	*Greek Manifestations*
Isis Athena Aphrodite *Nemesis*	Zeus *Helios* *Hephastos* Osiris *Apollo*
⬇	⬇
Pre-Judaic/Islamic Arabian Manifestations	Pre-Judaic/Islamic Arabian Manifestations
Anat *Qadesh*	*Baal* *Asar*
⬇	⬇
Late Period Manifestations in Judaism, Christianity and Islam	Late Period Manifestations in Judaism, Christianity and Islam
Mary *Fatimah*	*Yahweh* *Allah*

More correlations between Pre-Judaic/Christian Arabian Religions and Ancient Egyptian Religion can be seen in the iconographies dedicated to the Arabian divinities.

THE AFRICAN ORIGINS OF CIVILIZATION, RELIGION AND YOGA SPIRITUALITY

Below left: Stele of the Great Sphinx in Giza, Egypt, showing one of the most typical and important Ancient Egyptian symbols, the winged sundisk with the double serpents.
Below center: The same stele style can be seen in many Ancient Egyptian monuments and panels commemorating royal evens and the spiritual virtues of specific individuals and also Heru.
Below right: King Yehawmilk (Of Asia Minor) Worships Egyptian Goddess Hetheru as "The Lady of Byblos[251]."

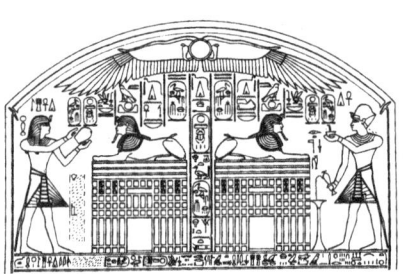  

Below: Two Panels Left- Qdesh, (1) pictured naked, with Min, (2) with worshiper and Set (New Kingdom - Cairo Museum).
(3)-Goddess Qdesh of Ancient Egypt and Syria, standing on a lion (Late Period)
(4)- Goddess Sekhmit of Ancient Egypt (Early Period)

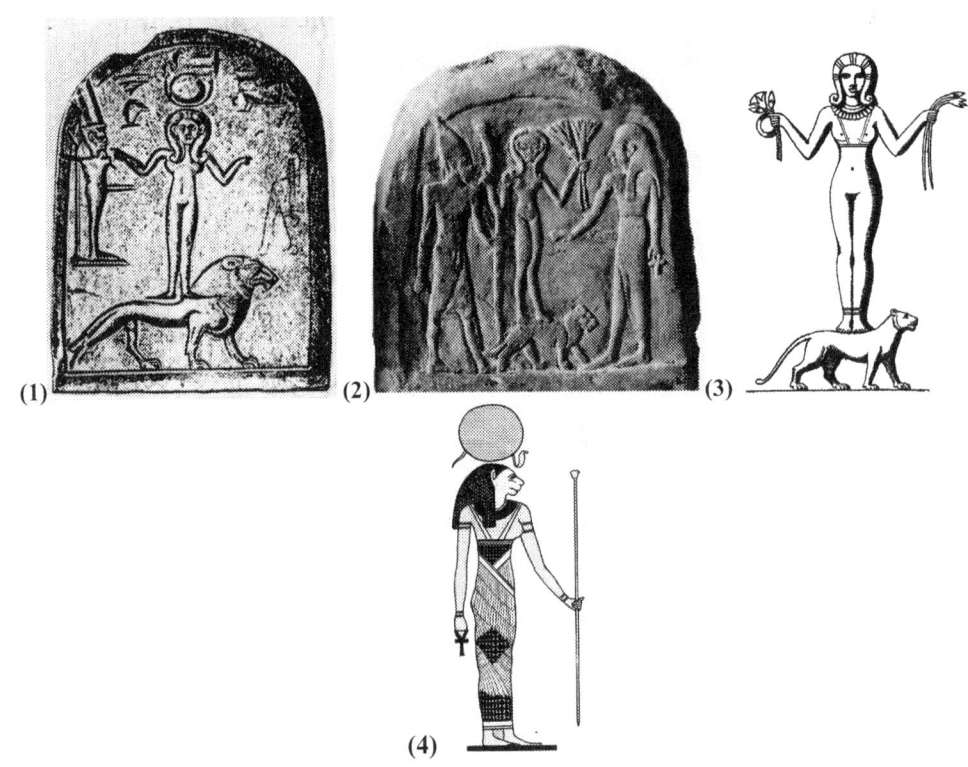

Goddess Qadshu (Qdesh, Qedesh, Qadesh Qudshu)[252] was an Ancient Egyptian fertility goddess who was also worshipped in Syria under the same name. Her name means 'holy.' Several statues have been found where she is depicted as being topless or fully disrobed. She has also been identified with (regarded as being the same divinity as) the Egyptian goddess Net, and she was also identified with the Ancient Egyptian goddesses Hetheru (curled hair is a symbol of Hetheru-Hathor) and Sekhmit (the leonine imagery is a symbol of Sekhemit who is a form of goddess Hetheru (Hathor) -Old Kingdom). One of Qadshu's forms is Athirat in Babylon.[253] She was also considered the consort of the god Min (pictured in plate #1 above), the god of virility.

Figure 56: Below from left to right- Goddess Net, Goddess Antat and Goddess Athena

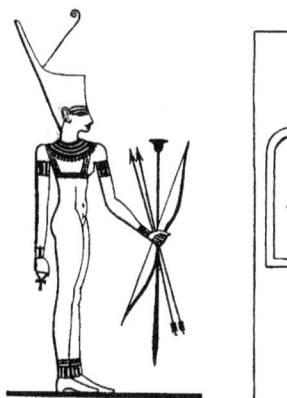

Goddess Anat[78] (Anath, Rahmay - 'the merciful') was <u>Baal</u>'s sister and the daughter of the god <u>El</u>. She is Goddess of war, the hunt, and savagery. She is also an archer and a virgin Creatoress of the universe. She was identified with Goddess Athena of Greece (above right), who was herself identified with Goddess Antat (Antit) of Ancient Egypt (above center). Goddess Antat of Kamit was herself associated with the earlier goddess Net or Anet[254]\[79] of Ancient Egypt (above left), the original prototype for the Goddess of war, the hunt, savagery, an archer and a virgin Creatoress of the universe.

Thus it is clear that the worship of the Ancient Egyptian divinities was widespread in Asia Minor, until they came under attack by the Jews, Christians and Muslims later in history. Further, with this understanding it is possible to see the worship of the Supreme Goddess of Egypt extending throughout Asia Minor and the Mediterranean. This worship of the Goddess became part of the basis for the religions that developed later, after the worship of the Ancient Egyptian goddess (and gods) was prohibited or co-opted in attempts to eradicate it.

Ishtar was the chief goddess of the Babylonians and the Assyrians and the counterpart of the Phoenician goddess, Astarte. Astarte, like the Kamitan goddess Hetheru, was represented by a crescent, symbolic of the moon and the horns of a cow.[255] The name appeared as Athtar in Arabia, Astar in Abyssinia (now Ethiopia), and Ashtart in Canaan and Israel. Like the Ancient Egyptian goddess Net, the prototype for all the Creatoress-War Goddesses of Nubia and Arabia, the sex of the divinity also varied: Athtar and Astar were male deities. Ishtar of Erech (in Babylonia) was a goddess worshiped in connection with the evening star, but Ishtar of Akkad (also in Babylonia) was a god identified with the morning star.[256] Like Net of Ancient Egypt, Ishtar was the Great Goddess, Great Mother, and the goddess of fertility and the queen of heaven. Like Net of Ancient Egypt, she was depicted as a goddess of hunting and war and was depicted with sword, bow, and quiver of arrows. Among the Babylonians, Ishtar was distinctly the Mother Goddess and was portrayed either naked and with prominent breasts, or like Aset of Ancient Egypt, as a mother with a child at her breast. She also corresponded to the Greek Aphrodite, the "Great Mother," goddess of fertility, love and war,[257] who was also known to the Greeks as Hathor (Hetheru of Kamit). So what this means is that the goddess has a creative aspect and also a destructive aspect, i.e. she brings Creation into being and she takes it back.

---

[78] For picture see the section: *The Ancient Egyptian Ancestry of The early Hebrews and Arabs*
[79] TIMAEUS by Plato 360 B.C.E. translated by Benjamin Jowett

Byblos, the home of Astarte, was an ancient city of Phoenicia, which was located on the Mediterranean Sea, near present-day Bayrut, Lebanon. It had close relations with the Ancient Egyptians. This entire region is mentioned in several Ancient Egyptian myths (Asarian Resurrection, The Story of Sinuhe and others). Archaeological investigations, begun in 1921, indicated that Byblos has remains of habitation dating from about 5,000 B.C.E. It was the capital city of Phoenicia as well as a seaport during the 2nd millennium B.C.E. The Ancient Egyptian records confirm that it exported cedar and other woods to Egypt which did not grow there due to the dessert weather conditions. The Greeks applied the name Byblos to papyrus. They imported it from Byblos, and this name is the source for the word Bible (biblia). The biblical name of the city was Gebal, in the Book of Ezekiel (see 27:9). The Phoenicians developed, based on the Kamitan script, the simplest of all the consonantal scripts, reducing the number of symbols used to represent sounds to 22.[258] It is believed by scholars that the Phoenician alphabet is a simplified form of the Ancient Egyptian Hieratic writing system, that was later adopted and changed by the Greeks. A Lebanese village called Jubayl now occupies the city of Byblos.[259] Archeological finds have revealed more evidence that there was worship of the Ancient Egyptian gods and goddesses in ancient Canaan (Palestine). In the religion of Canaan and Phoenicia, the god, *El*, was considered as the god of creation, and was represented by the bull, which is the symbol of Asar, who was the god of Creation in the Asarian religion of Ancient Egypt.[260]

Figure 57: Map of Northern Canaan (Modern - Lebanon) *Ancient city: Byblos (Modern- Jubayl) See asterisk(*)

Even earlier than Ishtar comes the goddess Inanna (Inana). Inanna is the Sumerian Creatoress and warrior goddess form. She was the most important goddess of the Sumerians, considered as the "Mother Goddess".[261] Inanna is often depicted as a woman with horned headdress, a tiered skirt, wings and weapon cases on her shoulders. These are of course the basic features of the Ancient Egyptian goddess Net and all the subsequent Creatoress-Warrior goddesses that come after. In other depictions the goddess is shown with large hips and holding her breasts in offering. These two forms can be seen in Ishtar and the Greek goddess forms as well. Like the Ancient Egyptian goddess Net /Aset, Inanna was known to be cunning and wily. She outwitted both Enki, the God of Wisdom, and also her dark sister Ereshkigal. As a powerful warrior she drove a war chariot, which was drawn by lions. While the feature of wiliness and cunning manifest in myths containing different plots, the themes and features of the personalities as well as the iconography match between the Sumerian and Ancient Egyptian goddesses.

Lilith, Sumerian Religion, Judaism and the Ancient Egyptian Connection

The goddess Lilith is another important deity that shows the connection between Ancient Egyptian Religion and Pre-Judaic Mesopotamian religion and Judaism. According to Hebrew legends, Lilith was regarded as the first wife of Adam, the first man in the Jewish Bible. However, her story was later omitted from the Bible cannon when its books were compiled. She was repudiated because of her independence and sexual freedom. Nevertheless, the images of the goddess are clearly Kamitan in origin (see below). Given the known evidence of contact between Sumerian culture and Kamitan, it is clear that she was adopted into Mesopotamian culture at a date prior to the formation of Judaism (2,000 B.C.E.-1,000 B.C.E.) According to a Hebrew legend, Adam married Lilith because he was tired of having sex relations with animals. This practice was prohibited in the Bible (Deuteronomy 27:21, proving its actual practice by ancient herdsmen in the middle east). At the time when the Old Testament was being compiled, Lilith was seen as a demoness because, according to a legend, she refused to have sexual relations while in the missionary position (male on top, female on bottom).[262] This practice of keeping women on the bottom was a product of a male oriented and patriarchal culture and it is one of the fundamental differences between the Western religions which developed out of the Western culture (Judaism, Christianity, and Islam) and African and East Asian Religions. In African and East Asian Religions mythologically the female is always seen to be on top and the male on the bottom. In African and East Asian Religions the woman is considered as the heavens and the man is earth because she does the work of Creation (movement) and he is Spirit which is the regarded as the "unmoved mover" (in nature earth is sedentary and heaven is dynamic).

Above: The Sumerio-Babylonian-Hebrew Goddess Lilith

The Muslims repudiated this kind of sexual position and so did the Christians. Muslims have expressed the opinion: "Accursed be the man who maketh woman heaven and himself earth."[263] Christians stated that any sexual position that did not maintain male dominance was sinful.[264] The contact between the early Hebrews and the Kamitan culture, which has been documented, facilitated the adoption of the Lilith iconography from the Kamitan Goddess. So Lilith was adopted by the Hebrews in pre-Judaic times[265] but was later discarded when the religion of Judaism turned away from a balance between male and female and placed more importance on the male aspect of divinity. In Judaism the concept of *Shekina* which means "female soul of God," "dwelling place" was downplayed. Note that the Jewish term in phonetically similar to the Ancient Egyptian *Shekem* (Sekhem) and the Indian *Shakti* which mean female life force energy. Also, in African and Indian tradition, the Shekhem and Shakti serve as the creative power of the Spirit which "inhabits" the force itself. In Christian religion the concept of *Holy Ghost*, which was originally the female essence of God, became a non descript "force."

Notice that Lilith is a winged goddess. She stands on two lions, she holds in her hands the symbols of the rod and ring of Sumerian royal authority (or glyph of 100,000). Lilith wears a stepped crown or turban and is accompanied by the bird of wisdom (owl). She is the master of beasts (stands on lions like the Ancient Egyptian Goddess Quadesh/Sekhmit). These are all motifs seen widely throughout Ancient Egyptian iconography, which originated much earlier that the Sumerian or Hebrew cultures. Below are some examples of the iconography of the Ancient Egyptian goddess. The image below (left) from the Temple of Hetheru (Ancient Egypt) shows the god Asar on his bed of resurrection as he ejaculates into the waiting goddess Aset who is in the form of a Kite[266]. The image on the right shows Aset in her full form with the wings and body of a woman.

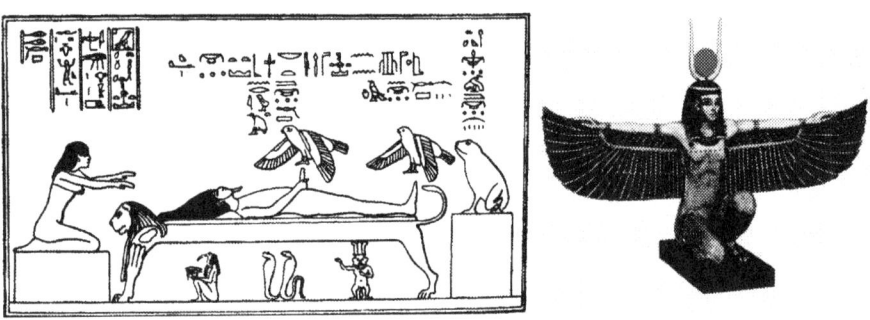

Below: The Ancient Egyptian God Geb (earth) and Nut (Heaven) who are the parents of Aset.

Aset's mother and father are known in Ancient Egyptian Religion as Geb-Male (earth) and Nut-female (heaven). In Ancient Egyptian Religion the ○ *shen* symbol is very important. It means "eternity" and this is one of the instruments that the goddess uses to bring forth the spiritual resurrection of the initiate in the Temple mysteries. The image below comes from the Ancient Egyptian *Prt m Hru* (Book of Coming Forth By Day) chapter 151.[267] It shows the goddess kneeling while holding on to the Shen symbol. The Ancient Egyptian Shen symbol is associated with the *chfnu*, tadpole symbol which, like the the rod and ring of Sumerian royalty, represents 100,000, meaning *"hundreds of thousands of infinities."*

Thus, it is clear that Judaism, Christianity and Islam are repudiating not the sexual act by itself, but also its implication as an acknowledgement of female power and equality in society and religion, and in a larger sense they also rejecting the African and Eastern religions along with other similar Mesopotamian and Canaanite related religions. In later Judaism the notion of Lilith has been lost, but the legend of her daughters, the *lilim*, persisted and disturbed Jewish men through the Dark Ages period of European history.

Summary of the Goddess Forms

The Ancient Egyptian goddesses Net or Anet (Greek Neith-Athene, Artemis), Aset (Greek Isis), Hetheru (Greek Aphrodite-Hathor), and Antat (associated with another Ancient Egyptian goddess called Astharthet) all manifest in Pre Judaic/Christian/Muslim Arabia as Creatoress and War Goddesses by the names: Ishtar (Astarte) and Qadesh, as well as Anat. In Ancient Egyptian Myth the goddess Qadesh is associated both with Hetheru and Sekhemit because they both embody the qualities of the Creatoress (Hetheru) and Destroyer (Sekhemit). She is therefore a composite of the two forms. Her descriptions as "mistress of the gods and goddesses, the eye of Ra, without a second," which are all designations of the Goddess Hetheru as Sekhmit, leave no further doubts as to the association. In Greece the goddess, Artemis,[268] like the Ancient Egyptian goddess Net (Anet), was goddess of the hunt, deity of light, associated with the moon.

Net (Anet)
Most Ancient Egyptian Goddess of Creation and War
Manifests as:

Ancient Egyptian Goddess Name	Pre Judaic/Christian/Muslim Arabian Name
Qdeshu (Hetheru/Sekhemit)	Qadesh
Antat (Antit)	Anat
Aset / Astharthet	Ishtar - Astarte
Aset	Lilith

When the Jewish religion emerged in Arabia, it began to incorporate essential aspects of preexisting religions. The Ancient Egyptian religion exerted the most influence on the Western religions both directly, through exposing the Jews and early Christians to the Ancient Egyptian religion, and indirectly through the influence exerted on Pre-Judaic/Christian Arabian religions that also had an influence on the Western religions. The Jews and early Christians adopted several aspects of Ancient Egyptian religion through co-optation. They were forced to adopt certain rituals, teachings and symbols in order to coerce the followers of the Kamitan religions to following the new religion. They were also affected indirectly as they were also exposed to the Canaanite religions, which were themselves based on Ancient Egyptian religion as we have just seen.

The Creatoress and Destroyer goddess, the dualism of Zoroastrianism and the polytheistic monotheism of Arabia were amalgamated, but not harmoniously, for it was necessary to subsume the Goddess herself as a female personality, while retaining her attributes in order to create a patriarchal religion. In like manner, the Christians further developed the concept of a Supreme Being who was a Creator and Destroyer ("wrathful" and sometimes "vengeful God"[269]) while at the same time allowing the female in the form of Mary, the mother of Jesus, and Mary Magdalene to be honored, but not worshipped as a Goddess. Islam, as we will see in the next section of this chapter, followed suit. With the same fervency and fanaticism as the Jews who set out to destroy the Canaanite religions and the Christians who set out to eradicate all non-Judeo-Christian religions (in Europe, Arabia and Africa), the Muslims set out to eradicate all non-Judeo-Christian-Islamic religions and conquer the known world for Islam.

THE AFRICAN ORIGINS OF CIVILIZATION, RELIGION AND YOGA SPIRITUALITY

Summary of the Goddess Iconography and Their Correlations

Below: The forms of the Ancient Egyptian goddess (A-1) *Net (Anet, Anat)* / (A-2) *Qdeshu* / (A-3) *Aset* (with horns and wings- form of Net) as Creatoress and Warrior (Destroyer), have diffused throughout Mesopotamia, India and Greece in the following forms:

- (B) Sumerian- Inanna (Ananna) as Warrior, As Creatoress (B-2 and B-3), and Lilith (B-4)
- (C) Babylonian and the Assyrian- Ishtar, (2000 B.C.E. Louvre Museum)
- (D) Phoenician- Astarte, (Hittite 2nd-3rd Millenium B.C.E.)
- (E) Greek- Minoan Snake Goddess / (E-1) Pre-classical Creatoress goddess (Thessaly, Greece).and (E-2) Athena / Aphrodite / Artemis, and
- (F) Indian- Durga (goddess of Creation riding on a lion) / (F-1) Kali (goddess of destruction-form of Durga).

Forms of the Ancient Egyptian Goddess:

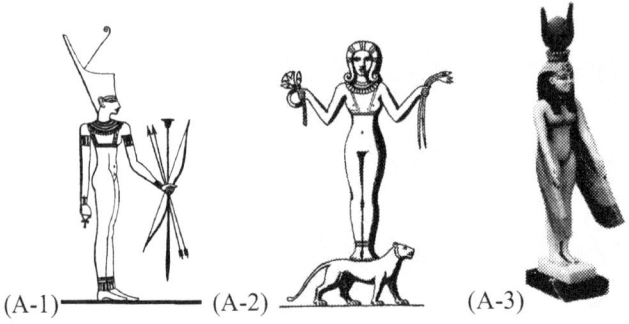

(A-1)   (A-2)   (A-3)

Forms of the Ancient Sumerian Goddess:

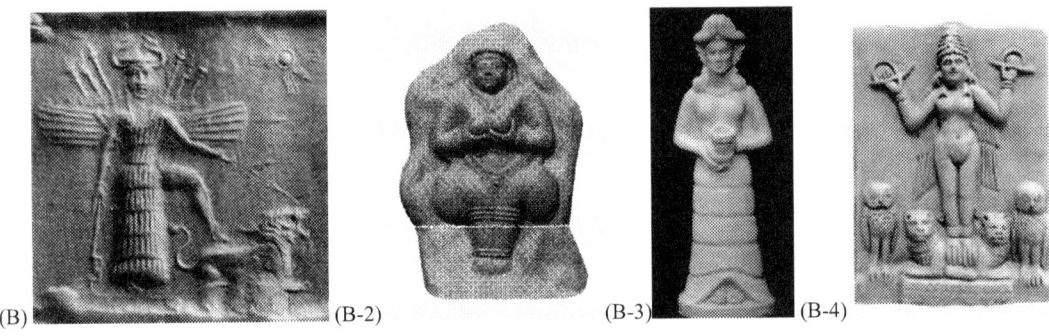

(B)   (B-2)   (B-3)   (B-4)

Forms of the Ancient Babylonian Goddess:

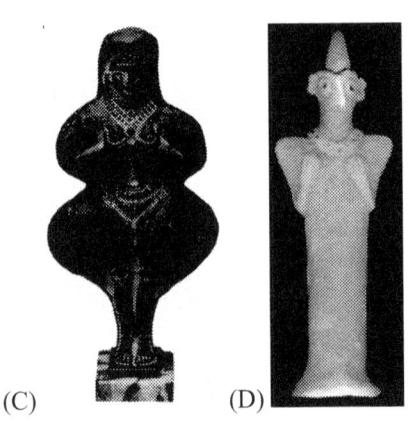

(C)   (D)

THE AFRICAN ORIGINS OF CIVILIZATION, RELIGION AND YOGA SPIRITUALITY

Forms of the Ancient and Classical Greek Goddess:

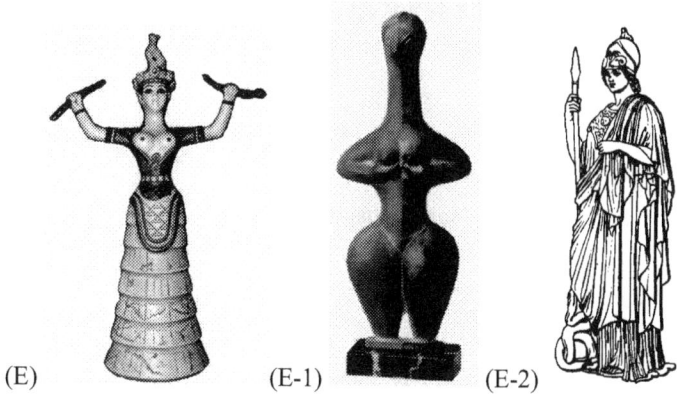

(E)   (E-1)   (E-2)

Forms of the Indian Goddess:

(F)   (F-1)

The Creatoress, warrior, lion, light/fire, Mother Goddess, wisdom, wings, horns, etc. constitute major iconographical and philosophical aspects that the goddesses share. This binds them together across the expanses of time and place, showing that they are actually manifestations of the same principles. This also parenthetically show that they have the same origin, and function. Since the oldest civilization of them all is Ancient Egypt, we are thus able to conclude that the original form and teaching emerged in Ancient Egypt and was transferred to the other countries as Ancient Egyptian influence was felt. Note that there is no record of the Ancient Egyptians imposing their religion on any peoples, rather, the virtue and compelling nature of Ancient Egyptian culture, religion and iconography elicited a desire to adopt the Ancient Egyptian religion. But even here the practice was not orthodox and rigid, so there are slight variations in the manifestations, but the religions maintain the same thrust and ecumenical relationship, even when we consider that the worship of the Ancient Egyptian gods and goddesses changed over time in a natural way after the Ancient Egyptian governments were forced out of Mesopotamia in the late period of Ancient Egyptian history. Other lioness goddesses with mythological and iconographic links to Ancient Egypt include: Bottom left- Anahita (of Canaanites and later Persia). Right- Hebat (of Hittites also as Isis, sukling the divine child).

The Ancient Egyptian Ancestry of
The early Hebrews and Arabs

Abraham Goes into Egypt

The three most prominent present day Western orthodox religions are Judaism, Christianity and Islam. Judaism is a religion which, according to the Jewish/Christian Bible, is said to have been started by a man called Abraham, who lived in a city called Ur, which is now in the area that is presently called Iraq. The city of Ur was founded in 4,000 B.C.E. by Sumerians. Abraham was said to have received revelations from God that admonished him to start a new religion. Thereby a covenant was established between Abraham and God in which God said he would raise up a people based on Abraham's family and that he would one day lead them to a promised land.

In the Book of Genesis, Abraham, whom the Jews consider to be the first Jew, lived in the city of Ur in Southern Mesopotamia. According to the Bible, Abraham migrated westward to Palestine with his family at about 1,900 B.C.E. The ruins of Ur are approximately located midway between the modern city of Baghdad, Iraq, and the Persian Gulf, on the edge of the al-Hajar Desert and south of the Euphrates River. The site of Ur is known today as Tell al-Muqayyar, Iraq. In the times of Abraham, this was the same area where Zoroastrian and Indo-Aryan beliefs were strongest. According to Jewish belief, God made a covenant with Abraham, that if he would keep God's laws and serve him above all others, that he, Abraham, would be the father of many peoples and that those peoples would be given *"the entire land of Canaan."* As previously discussed, with this statement, the idea of a *"promised land"* was born along with the sanction of God to acquire it.

> Genesis 17
> 8 And I will give to thee, and to thy seed after thee, the land in which thou art a stranger, all the land of Canaan, for an everlasting possession; and I will be their God.

Having established the covenant, Abraham and his family moved to Egypt in order to escape the famines which struck Persia and Canaan during that time.

> Genesis 12
> 10. And there was a famine in the land: and Abram (Abraham) went down into Egypt to dwell there; for the famine [was] grievous in the land.

The Bible describes the origin of humanity in a very metaphorical way. As we will see, the physical appearance of the Ancient Egyptians, Cushites, Colchians and Hebrew people can be verified by the writings of historians who lived in biblical times. The Jewish sages who were creating the Genesis text between the years 1,000 B.C.E. to 100 B.C.E. looked at the neighboring lands (Ethiopia, Egypt, Canaan and South West Asia) along with the peoples, Ethiopians, Egyptians, Canaanites (includes Hebrews) etc. Then they set about to explain how the known nations came into being and how they related to each other. This teaching is set forth in the genealogy of Noah. The word race, as referring to people according to racial classifications (black, white, red, yellow, etc.) <u>does not occur anywhere</u> in the Bible. As we saw earlier, even modern science is recognizing that race classifications are bogus forms of social analysis. They are finding that differences in appearance among people can be accounted for by environmental factors and that genetically speaking, human beings are equal in every respect.[80] However, since the usage of terms such as those used for race classifications are common, they will be used in this section for the sake of clarity in the discussion as it pertains to the understanding of who the Ancient Egyptians and Jews were. In this manner, the study of ancient history will be accurate in using modern terminology, but it should never be assumed that the author agrees with the use of the term "race" as a correct way of classifying human beings. It is crucial to understand the cultural and ethnic relationship between the

---

[80] The concept of race has often been misapplied. One of the most telling arguments against classifying people into races is that persons in various cultures have often mistakenly acted as if one race were superior to another. This has no basis in reality. Although, with social disadvantages eliminated, it is possible that one human group or another might have some genetic advantages in response to such factors as climate, altitude, and specific food availability, these differences are small and do not point to racial superiority but to a greater ability to cope with specific environmental conditions. There are no differences in native intelligence or mental capacity that cannot be explained by environmental circumstances, culture or the ability to engage in the development of the sciences or the accumulation of knowledge. Rather than using racial classifications to study human variability, anthropologists today define geographic or social groups by geographic or social criteria. They then study the nature of the genetic attributes of these groups and seek to understand the causes of changes in their genetic makeup.[75]

THE AFRICAN ORIGINS OF CIVILIZATION, RELIGION AND YOGA SPIRITUALITY

Ancient Egyptians and Jews in order to gain insight into the deeper mystical teachings that are embedded in Judaism and Christianity. Also, this study will shed light to the question of how race distinctions were adopted by the church and Western society, and how this notion of race differences came to be used, through the story of Noah, as a means to practice racism in the general society. The purpose of our study is to show that not only is racism based on ignorance, but to emphasize that the Bible scriptures themselves speak on the unity of humanity and of its common origin.

In order to discover the origins of humanity, we will examine the teachings related to the sons of Ham more closely. In the time period when the book of Genesis was written, the three basic groups of people who were observed by the Genesis writers were the Africans, Asiatics and Europeans. The Africans inhabited the area from Africa to the Caucasus mountains which includes the land now called Palestine (ancient Canaan). As discussed, the Ancient Egyptian culture at one time extended to the area covering what is now referred to as the Middle East all the way to India. Recall that the Africans and Middle Easterners were observed to have such similarity in language, customs and physical appearance that the Greek historians of 400 B.C.E. concluded that the inhabitants of that area were all one related people including the Ethiopians (Cushites), the Egyptians (descendents of Mizraim) and the Canaanites.

The biblical scriptures relating to conquering the peoples of the "Promised Land" should not be understood as the conquering of people with different ethnicity, for it has been shown through the Bible itself that the Jews were ethnically related to the Ethiopians, Egyptians and Canaanites. Rather, these passages should be understood as a group of people with one religion, trying to establish it amongst others of their own kind.

According to the Bible, the origin of humanity is described in the book of Genesis. For our present study, we will now focus on the passages found in Chapter 2, verse 8.

> 8. And the Lord God planted a garden eastward in Eden; and there he put the man whom he had formed.

In Genesis, Chapter 1, the Bible describes how God created the earth. Verse eight, above, is important because after having created the earth itself, God now created Eden upon it. Eden is defined as a place for human beings to live. This idea carries many implications. One implication is that out of the whole creation, there is a special place for human beings which is presumably most suitable for sustaining life and for providing fulfillment of a person's needs.

Genesis, Chapter 2, cont.

> 9 And out of the ground made the Lord God to grow every tree that is pleasant to the sight, and good for food[81]; the tree of life also in the midst of the garden, and the tree of knowledge of good and evil.
> 10 And a river went out of Eden to water the garden; and from there it was parted, and became into four heads.
> 11 The name of the first [is] Pison: which goest around the whole land of Havilah, where [there is] gold;
> 12 And the gold of that land [is] good: there [is] bdellium and the onyx stone.
> 13 And the name of the second river [is] Gihon: the same that goest around the whole land of Cush. {Ethiopia: Heb. Cush}
> 14 And the name of the third river [is] Hiddekel: which floweth toward the east of Assyria. And the fourth river [is] Euphrates. {toward...: or, eastward to Assyria}
> 15 And the Lord God took the man, and put him into the garden of Eden to tend it and to keep it. {the man: or, Adam}

---

[81] The Bible here advocates vegetarianism.

Figure 58: Map showing the rivers mentioned in the Book of Genesis

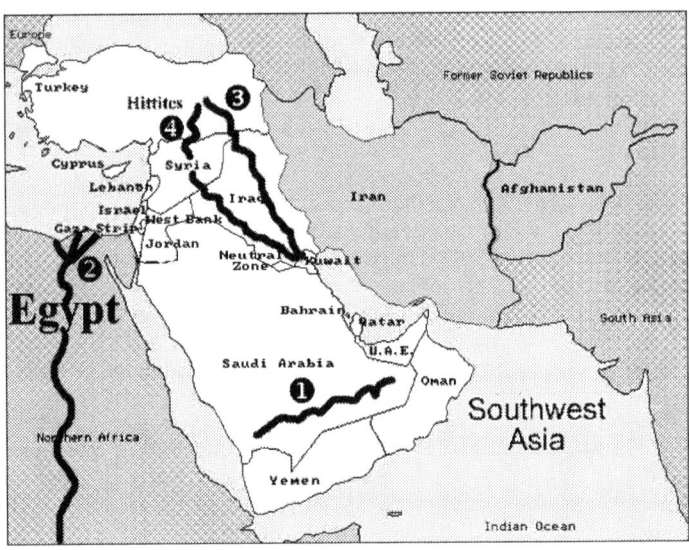

Contrary to the popular or superficial understanding of the phrase, "The Garden of Eden," it does not refer to a place called "Garden of Eden." The text is actually referring to a garden which has been created near this special location on earth called Eden. Four rivers are used to describe the location of this garden in Eden. One river went out of Eden and separated into four rivers to water the garden. The first one, Pison, means "increase."[270] ❶Pison runs through the land of Havilah, a district in Arabia named after a son of Cush (Havilah), located in the northwest part of Yemen.[271] ❷The next river is Gihon. Gihon means "bursting forth."[272] Strong's Concordance of the Bible holds that Gihon was a spring near Jerusalem where the anointing of Solomon as king took place. However, the Bible scripture says that Gihon skirts the land of Cush which is modern day Nubia/Sudan/Ethiopia. This description can only fit the Nile River[82] which originates deep in the heart of Africa with its source, the Kagera River in Burundi and runs through Cush. ❸River Hiddekel means "rapid."[273] It flowed eastward through Assyria according to the Bible (Gen. 2;14). It is now known as the Tigris river. ❹The fourth river is the Euphrates, which means "fruitfulness."[274] Its sources are in the Armenian mountains and it empties into the Persian Gulf. Keep in mind that the area being described was all connected until recently. The present separation is due to the creation of the Suez Canal. This description of the rivers clearly refers to the garden as being located in the area between Ethiopia, in northeast Africa, and the northern part of Southeast Asia at the Armenian and Caucasus mountains. This is the land of Canaan and the Arabian Peninsula which was at one time considered part of Africa. This means that the entire area including the holy land of the Jews, Muslims and Christians was said by the Bible to be the land of the descendents of Cush, the son of Ham ("black" Africans).

According to the Old Testament, Cush became the ancestor of the Ethiopians, Mizraim of the Egyptians, Canaan of the Canaanites, the pre-Israelite inhabitants of Palestine, and Phut of an African people inhabiting Libya (see Genesis 10:1, 6-20). Egypt is referred to several times as the "Land of Ham" (see Psalms 105:23, 24, 27; 106:22) in the Psalms, evidently because of the genealogy put forth in Genesis. Psalm 105:24 even confirms that the Jews increased their number by mixing with and adding to their numbers with the descendents of Ham. Philologists[83] and ethnologists recognize a distinct North African family of peoples and tongues that they term Hamito-Semitic. Canaan, in the Old Testament, is a designation of the land to the west of the Jordan River, later known as Palestine, and the name of the

---

[82] The Nile's southernmost source is the Kagera River in Burundi, which empties into Lake Victoria. From Lake Victoria the river flows through Uganda to Sudan, where the main branch is known as the Mountain Nile. It flows through the vast swamps of As Sudd in southern Sudan and then for the next 500 miles (800 kilometers) is known as the White Nile. The Blue Nile, the largest tributary, joins the White Nile near Khartoum. From Khartoum to Aswan the combined White and Blue Nile are known as the United Nile or simply as the Nile River. Its last major tributary, the Atbarah River, joins it about 200 miles (320 kilometers) north of Khartoum. Farther north the Nile flows in a broad S-bend through the arid Nubian Desert and descends in six cataracts, or waterfalls, before it enters Lake Nasser near the Egypt-Sudan border. As the Nile approaches the Mediterranean Sea north of Cairo, it fans into a broad delta and branches into two major channels, Rosetta on the west and Damietta on the east. An extensive network of irrigation canals crisscrosses the delta. Excerpted from *Compton's Interactive Encyclopedia*. Copyright (c) 1994, 1995 Compton's NewMedia, Inc.

[83] Literary studies or historical linguistics studies.

reputed ancestor of the Canaanites, the original inhabitants of that land, the Hebrew people, many of whom later adopted the Jewish religion.[275]

Israel and Jacob go Into Egypt and Ethiopia and Increased the Population with Egyptians and Ethiopians

Psalms 105
    23 Israel also came into Egypt; and Jacob sojourned in the land of Ham.
    24 And he increased his people greatly; and made them stronger than their enemies.
    27 They showed his signs among them, and wonders in the land of Ham.

Psalms 106
    22 Wondrous works in the land of Ham, [and] terrible things by the Red sea.

The ancestry of humanity and the location of Eden leads to Ethiopia and Egypt, in Africa. This is essentially the same area of the Egyptian civilization in Biblical times. Herodotus, a Greek historian who traveled the area around 484-425 B.C.E.,[276] journeyed through the ancient world, including Asia Minor, Mesopotamia, Babylon, and Egypt. He described the Ethiopians as: "The tallest, most beautiful and long-lived of the human races." Recall also some of the other statements he made in reference to the Ethiopians and the Egyptians: "There are two great Ethiopian (Black) nations, one in Sind (India) and the other in Egypt," and "The Colchians, Ethiopians and Egyptians have thick lips, broad noses, wooly hair, and they are burnt (dark) of skin color." The Christian Bible is reputed to have been written over a period of at least 1,000 years, from the time of Moses (1,200?-1,000? B.C.E.) to the end of the Roman Empire (395 A.C.E.). So if the creators of the book of Genesis observed the area described as Eden at the beginning of the creation of the Bible texts and noted the inhabitants as being of African descent, and then five hundred years later, the same is reported by independent eye witnesses (Herodotus, Diodorus, etc.), it must be concluded that the main characters of the Bible, including the Egyptians, Hebrews and Jews, were African peoples and their descendents. Further, this conclusion explains why the teachings of Judaism are so closely related to those of Ancient Egypt.

At around the time of Jesus, the Greeks and Romans had attained control of the areas which had previously encompassed the Egyptian civilization, so they would have access to every means of reproducing images of themselves. Therefore, assuming from these images that an accurate depiction of the population is being given would be an erroneous assumption. One only needs to look at the past icons and artwork of Ancient Egypt to see the presence and dominance of the African characteristics of Ancient Egyptian society. So, we have established that in early times the population of Egypt and indeed Canaan as well, were dark skinned African people. As they mixed with the Asiatics and the Europeans, the general hue of the population became lighter. However, even in the late period of the Ancient Egyptian civilization, just before the Christian era (500 B.C.E.), prominent Greek historians stated that the populations of Ethiopia, Egypt, and the areas now called Palestine and Iraq (where Abraham was born) were all populated by one ethnic group, Africans. Thus, the population in Southwest Asia (Iran, Iraq, Syria, etc.) had an African Ancestry. It was not until the Jews mixed with the Greeks, Romans and Aryans that they came to be regarded as part of the "White racial group."

According to the Bible, Ham was the progenitor of the African peoples, Shem was the progenitor of the Asians and Japheth was the progenitor of the Germanic ancient Celtic peoples. Genesis 9:27 suggests an understanding by the Bible writers that the people living in modern day Europe were related to the Asiatics where it says: "he (Japheth) shall dwell in the tents of Shem," i.e. in Asia. Europe is in reality not a continent, but a section of Asia, and therefore will be referred to as Eurasia for purposes of describing its relative geographical position in reference to the rest of Asia.

Genesis 9:26-27:

26 And he said, Blessed [be] the LORD God of Shem; and Canaan shall be his servant.
{his servant: or, servant to them}
27 God shall enlarge Japheth, and he shall dwell in the tents of Shem; and Canaan shall
be his servant. {enlarge: or, persuade}

A case often cited is the distortion of the biblical story of Ham. In the Bible itself there is an attempt to show that the main Jewish ancestors come from the bloodline of Shem (Genesis 11:10-26). This is done in an effort to follow up on the idea given in Genesis 9:26-27, that the Canaanites (descendants of Ham- i.e. Africans) should be serving the Jews. Biblical statements, like "be fruitful and multiply" (Genesis 1:28) and other "commands" of God are in reality mandates or directives written into the Bible for guiding the goals and objectives of the Jews. They are similar to political edicts, and acted to reinforce a particular agenda (manifest destiny) for the masses of people to believe in and pursue. They give a purpose and meaning to the lives of the Jews, but they are not to be understood as spiritual edicts to be followed literally. They were written for a certain time and purpose which is several thousands of years removed from the present.

Figure 59: The Descendants of Noah-From the Judeo-Christian Biblical System.

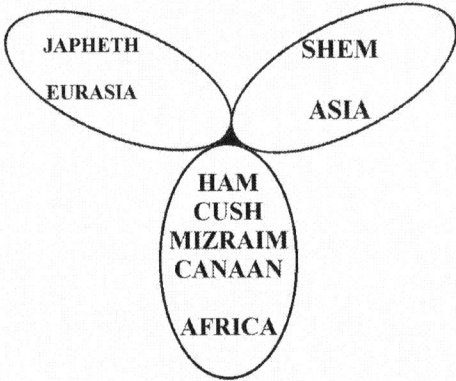

It is notable that if Noah was angry with Ham, why did he not curse Ham? Instead he cursed Canaan. This is perhaps because the land of Canaan was the place where the Hebrews had always lived as wanderers, and some of them were the writers of the Bible scriptures. They always longed to have a homeland in Canaan, and this anger offers the opportunity to vilify the current inhabitants of the land and provide an excuse to dispossess them of it. The scriptures of the Old Testament, therefore, are directed at rallying people together in a movement towards conquering the land of Canaan and its people. The early Jews wanted to live in Canaan (Palestine) and not in Ethiopia (Ham). Judging from the times (1000 B.C.E.-200 B.C.E.) that the Bible scriptures were developed, the clear implication is that the inhabitants of the land of Canaan, who were not followers of Judaism, were to be conquered by the Jews and used by them for their survival.

This theme developed into a belief system of a supposed "inferiority" of the "Hamitic" peoples (Africans and Palestinians) and superiority of the descendants of the Japhethian peoples-Eurasians. It was repeated and promoted by secular and non-secular Western scholars, and became a reality in the minds of many people. The Judeo-Christian Bible family tree of humanity may be summarized in the following diagram.

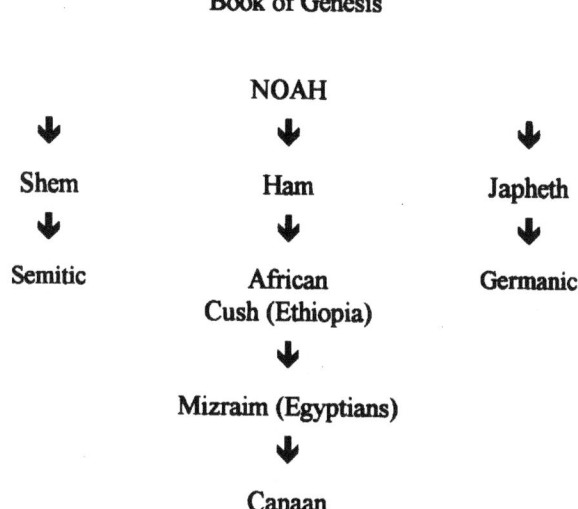

Above: The human family tree according to the Bible.

Joseph Goes Into Egypt

> Genesis 47
> 11 And Joseph placed his father and his brethren, and gave them a possession in the land of Egypt, in the best of the land, in the land of Rameses, as Pharaoh had commanded.

As Genesis 47:11 explains, the Pharaoh approved Joseph's granting of land to his family. The Jews were saved from certain death due to starvation twice. According to the Bible, the first time Jews were saved from death was when Ancient Egypt became the refuge for Abraham from the famines of the Near East. Then later, according to the story of Joseph in the Bible, the Jewish people survived the droughts and famine of Canaan by seeking refuge once again in the land of Egypt. The extension of asylum to Jesus along with his family in Egypt during the time of persecution at his birth, and his subsequent upbringing there, further explains the similarities of Jesus to the Egyptian savior character of Heru, who is also known for *walking on water,* as Jesus is said to have done in Matthew 14:26. Heru and Jesus share several titles. Like Jesus, Heru was the symbol of:

> *"The resurrection and the life," "The anointed one," "The WORD made flesh,"*
> *"The KRST (Christ)," "The WORD made TRUTH," "The one who comes to fulfill the LAW," "The destroyer of the enemies*[84] *of his father"*
> *"The one who walks upon the water of his Father"*[277]

Moses Comes Out of Egypt With 600,000 People, With a "New Religion" Said To Be More Powerful than The Neterian Religion

By the time Moses is said to have led the Jewish people out of Egypt, the small family of Abraham had become an entire community, a nation of people who had been previously living in Egypt as Egyptian. According to the Bible, when Moses is supposed to have left Egypt in the exodus, 400 years after Abraham went into Egypt with a few family members, there were 600,000 people in his group. Therefore, the people that would have left Egypt were indeed Egyptians who elected to follow Moses with his particular teaching (Judaism) which was a variation of the Ancient Egyptian religion blended with Zoroastrian ideas. They were of direct Egyptian or mixed Egyptian-Nubian and Hebrew (Canaanite) ancestry, like those who had entered Egypt previously. Therefore, they may have been religiously Jewish, but ethnically Egyptian, steeped in Egyptian culture. They are heretofore referred to as *"the people"* or *"the children of Israel"* in the Bible.

---

[84] ENEMIES: ignorance, lies, deception, too much talking, covetousness, depravity, selfishness, etc.

Exodus 13
16 And it shall be for a token upon thy hand, and for frontlets between thy eyes: for by strength of hand the LORD brought us forth out of Egypt.

Exodus 20
22. And the LORD said to Moses, Thus thou shalt say to the children of Israel, Ye have seen that I have talked with you from heaven.
23 Ye shall not make with me gods of silver, neither shall ye make to you gods of gold.
24 An altar of earth thou shalt make to me, and shalt sacrifice on it thy burnt offerings, and thy peace offerings, thy sheep, and thy oxen: in all places where I record my name I will come to thee, and I will bless thee.

We have seen how the character, Moses, played an important part in the creation of Jewish religion and how the Bible itself acknowledges that the new religion (Judaism) sprang forth out of Ancient Egypt as Moses learned the wisdom of the Egyptians (Acts 7:22), created the Pentateuch which in turn gave rise to the Jewish laws and scriptures (Torah[85]). Another correlation between Judaism and Ancient Egyptian religion is the format of daily worship which in Ancient Egypt consisted of a service at dawn, one at midday and another at sunset, commemorating the Supreme Being who manifests as the Trinity: Khepri-Ra-Tem, to sustain Creation. The Jews apparently adopted this triune format of worship and practice it to this day. The *Ten Commandments* and the other laws given by Moses can be traced to the Ancient Egyptian *Book of Coming Forth By Day* and the Wisdom Texts.[86]

Acts 7
22 And Moses was learned in all the wisdom of the Egyptians, and was mighty in words and in deeds.

So the question now arises, if Ancient Egypt had such high culture and social advancement in spiritual practice and mystical philosophy, why was it necessary for Moses to lead the people who were following Judaism out of Egypt? The following historians and writers from ancient times provide some clues to answer the previous question.

> "In the reign of Apis, the son of Pharonaeus, a portion of the Egyptian army deserted from Egypt and took up their habitation in...Palestine...These were the very men who went out with Moses."
>
> -Eusebius (260?-340? A.C.E.)[87]

> "This region (Judea[88]) lies toward the north; and it is inhabited in general, as each place in particular, by mixed stocks of people from Egyptian and Arabian and Phoenician tribes...But though the inhabitants are mixed up thus, the most prevalent of the accredited reports in regard to the temple at Jerusalem represents the ancestors of the present Judaeans, as they are called, as Egyptians.
>
> Moses, namely, was one of the Egyptian priests, and held a part of Lower Egypt, as it is called, but he went away from there to Judaea, since he was displeased with the state of affairs there, and was accompanied by many people who worshipped the Divine Being."
>
> -Strabo (63? B.C.E.- 24 A.C.E.?)[89]

> "The Jews were a tribe of Egyptians who revolted from the established religion."
>
> -Celsus, Aulus Cornelius
> (Roman writer, 1st century A.C.E.)

---

[85] The entire body of religious law and learning including both sacred literature and oral tradition.
[86] Wisdom teachings given by Ancient Egyptian Sages upon which the entire philosophy and religion of Ancient Egypt is based.
[87] (Citing the Greek philosopher, Polema) Eusebius of Caesarea (also called Pamphili) (260?-340?), Christian theologian, most learned man of his age; 'History of the Christian Church', most important ancient record of church; called Father of Church History; chief figure at Council of Nicaea (from Compton's Encyclopedia)
[88] Judea (or Judaea, or Judah), a Greek and Roman name for s. Palestine; in time of Jesus part of province of Syria and also kingdom of the Herods; in Roman times southernmost division of Palestine, Israel.[123]
[89] Greek historian and geographer who was born in Amasya, Pontus (now in Turkey). He explored the Nile with the expedition of Aelius Gallus, a Roman prefect of Egypt.

THE AFRICAN ORIGINS OF CIVILIZATION, RELIGION AND YOGA SPIRITUALITY

It must also be clearly understood that historically, the Hebrew people do not appear as anything other than a tribe or sect of Ancient Egyptians who were under the charge of the Ancient Egyptian government during the time when the Egyptian civilization encompassed southwest Asia (Syria, Palestine, Iraq, Turkey, etc.). This is not a far-fetched notion since, as we have seen, Herodotus considered the Chaldeans, a group who lived as far into the Middle East as the area that is modern day Iraq,[90] to be Egyptians as well. The term "Hebrew" means "those who pass from place to place," i.e. nomads. They were considered as an inconsequential group of wanderers. The Hebrews had no permanent place to live or permanent homeland in ancient times, as their own name attests (Hebrew = wanderer), except possibly the land of Egypt. However, Egypt was so permeated by the ancient Shetaut Neter (Neterian Religion and its gods and goddesses), that Judaism would not have survived there beyond cult status. Hence, the need for an exodus. Further, another reason arises in that from 1,000 B.C.E.-30 B.C.E. the upheavals in Egypt due to attacks by Asiatic forces caused a situation in which the country was racked with social and political turmoil and this led to other migrations both forced and voluntary, in which people left to go into the interior of Africa as well as into Asia Minor.

The Jews were enslaved by most of the great empires of the Middle East at one time or another. Many people misunderstand the word "slavery" as it is used in history. The slavery that was practiced in ancient times CANNOT be compared to that which was practiced by the European nations in reference to Africans or Native Americans. The European form of slavery was characterized by egoism, racism violence, brutality, degradation, mis-education, mistreatment and all manner of atrocities and injustices. In ancient times, people found themselves as slaves as a consequence of losing a war or incurring a debt, for example, but they were not kidnapped as part of an organized slavery business and forced to give up their religion and customs. Slaves were part of the family of the master, and might even marry into the family. Their children could be born free. This form of slavery is described in the Bible (Exodus 21:1-11). However, the European form of slavery was based on racism, the idea that one race is superior to another, and was intended to be a permanent situation. This form of slavery upheld ignorant notions of superiority, inferiority, segregation and anti-miscegenation. The perpetuators of the European slave trade were in no way sanctioned by any teaching that can be found in the Bible. Thus, though they may refer to themselves as Christians, they really cannot be considered to be Christians in the true sense of the word, and therefore, no negative judgment should fall on Christianity in its true practice, because of their actions.

Also, with respect to the enslavement of the Jews by the Ancient Egyptians, <u>there is no record of the slavery of the Jews in Egypt that is mentioned in the Bible, except in the Bible itself.</u> Yet, this biblical citation has been seen by some biblical researchers as a pretext to consider Ancient Egypt and the Ancient Egyptians as degraded, and thus as one of the reason that the Jews had to leave Egypt. They wanted to get away from the non-Hebrew people and the extensive monuments, as well as the Ancient Egyptian religion, which was still in full practice at that time.

At an early date the early Hebrews, invaded the land of Canaan (later known as Palestine), that was under the control of the Ancient Egyptians and fell to the power of the Egyptian armies.[278] These nomadic tribes moved into the Arabian Peninsula and its desert areas located southeast of the Jordan River some time between the 15th and 10th centuries B.C.E.[279] During this time they paid tribute to the Ancient Egyptian Pharaoh and were thus subjects of Egypt as were many other peoples of the time. During this time they would have been exposed to the religious traditions of Egypt (as is described in the Jewish-Christian Bible) and would have certainly known about the philosophy of Akhnaton (r.c.1379-1362 B.C.E.). In fact, many researches have speculated about this connection due to the strong similarities between the perceived form of monotheism espoused by Akhnaton (Pantheistic Monotheism) and what later became the monotheistic tradition of Judaism (Orthodox Monotheism). Indeed we have seen that the Elohim teaching of early Judaism is similar in most respects to the concept of Ancient Egyptian Polytheistic Monotheism but later was modified to its current form (Orthodox Monotheism).

Many times in the emergence of new mythologies, the founders or followers of the new system will create stories to show how the new system surpasses the old. The story of Exodus is such an example.

---

[90] Also the area where Abraham came from.

THE AFRICAN ORIGINS OF CIVILIZATION, RELIGION AND YOGA SPIRITUALITY

Moses went to Mount Sinai to talk to God and brought back Ten Commandments. At the time that Moses was supposed to have lived (1200?-1000? B.C.E.), Ancient Egypt was the most powerful culture in the ancient world. However, it was also on a social and cultural decline from its previous height as the foremost culture in religious practice, art, science, social order, etc. So it became necessary for a small group who left Egypt, that were themselves Egyptians, to legitimize the inception of the new theology by claiming to have triumphed over the mighty Egyptians with the help of their new "true God" who defeated the "weak Gods" of Egypt. This triumphant story would surely bring people to convert to the new faith since up to that time the Ancient Egyptian gods and goddesses had been seen not only as the most powerful divinities, but also as the source of all other deities in other religions. So in effect, by saying that the Jewish God "defeated" the Ancient Egyptian God by freeing the Jews, it is the same as saying that a new, more powerful religion is to be followed. This form of commencement for a spiritual tradition is not uncommon.

Other examples of this kind of emergence of "new religions" abound throughout history. Some examples are the emergence of Hinduism, while at the same time creating myths that supplant the Vedic tradition, and the emergence of Buddhism, while at the same time creating myths that supplant the Vedic and Upanishadic-Path of Renunciation.

Thus, the story of Exodus was written with the idea of justifying why the Jews needed to leave Egypt all of a sudden (recall – there is no record of any exodus except in the Bible). Recall that they took sanctuary in Egypt upon at least two occasions (story of Abraham, story of Joseph) and in neither of these times did they express fearfulness at placing themselves in the land of Kamit. If Egypt was such a degraded country of pagans and heathens why would the Bible tell of the story of Jesus and how he Mary and Joseph again take refuge there? There is actually a great dept owed to the Egyptians, without whose assistance, according to the Bible, the Jewish religion would not exist. So the Exodus story serves to give the Jews a rallying point for them to muster their energies to leave Egypt. There needed to be a strong incentive to get the people to give up their complacency and to embark on an uncertain journey to an uncertain destination, traveling through the desert. To encourage and reassure the Jewish people, they needed proof of power of their God, as it is this God into whose hands they would be placing themselves. The writers of the scriptures accomplished this by showing the powerfulness of the Jews, and thus, of the Jewish God, the only true God, over the strong Egyptians with their "idols," thus proving that the God of the Jews is the one and only God, and the true God. The story of Exodus does one more important thing. It defines the Jews as a group distinct from the Egyptians as well as all other Canaanites.[91] Further, although the Jewish religion has been erroneously linked with the idea of race or ethnicity, the term "Jew"[92] does not connote a racial, ethnic or genetic relationship. It is a religion that was developed around the Hebrew culture. The Hebrews shared the same history of wandering in ancient times with other Semitic[93] nomads, and not all Hebrews who were living in Palestine were Jews.

---

[91] Recall that the Hebrews were also considered as being Canaanites, as well as descendants of and subjects the Egyptian kingdom at the same time.
[92] **Jew** (jōō) *n.* **1.** An adherent of Judaism as a religion or culture.
[93] Of or pertaining to the Semites, especially Jewish or Arabic. 2. Pertaining to a subfamily of the Afro-Asiatic language family that includes Arabic and Hebrew.[115]

THE AFRICAN ORIGINS OF CIVILIZATION, RELIGION AND YOGA SPIRITUALITY

The Archeological Search For Proof of the Bible

Despite the myriad of ongoing excavations that have been conducted, many sponsored by Christian and Jewish groups, no substantial evidence has been unearthed that supports the historicity of the Bible. However, new discoveries have been brought forth that corroborate Herodotus' statements and the histories relating to the fact that the land that is now called Palestine was once part of Ancient Egypt.

> An approximately 5,000-year-old settlement discovered in southern Israel was built and ruled by Egyptians during the formative period of Egyptian civilization, a team of archaeologists announced last week.
>
> The new find, which includes the first Egyptian-style tomb known to have existed in Israel at that time, suggests that ancient Egypt exerted more control over neighboring regions than investigators have often assumed, contends project director Thomas E. Levy of the University of California, San Diego.

Source: Science News, Oct 5, 1996 v150 n14 p215(1).
Title: Ancient Egyptian outpost found in Israel.
(Halif Terrace site in southern Israel upsets previous estimates of Egyptian imperialism) Author: Bruce Bower

Figure 60: Below left- Map of Southern Canaan (Modern - Israel) * city Beth-Shan

Plate 23: Below left- Egyptian Goddess worship in Beth-Shan 13 century B.C.E.– Palestine

Figure 61: Below right-Goddess Anat (Anath) of Ancient Egypt

Beisan (Biblical Beth-shan, or Beth-shean, or Bet Shean), was a town in Palestine (Israel), located 50 mi (80 km) N.E. of Jerusalem. It has Egyptian and Canaanite remains and recent excavations have revealed Egyptian Temples that were built in the 13th century B.C.E. The Hebrew king, Saul, died nearby (Bible, I Sam., xxxi).[94] The early and late period Hebrews (some of whom later became Jews) were born, lived and died within the realm of Ancient Egypt, and were part of the Ancient Egyptian domain. Thus, the Ancient Egyptian presence in Canaan was strongly felt, so much so that the worship of the same Ancient Egyptian goddess under slightly different names but with the same iconography and attributes keeps on appearing again and again in Canaan and the rest of Pre-Judaic-Christian-Islamic Arabia. The archeological finds all over Canaan (modern- Palestine, Lebanon, Israel) demonstrate the extent of the presence of Ancient Egyptian culture and religion. The finds at Beth-Shan, the Halif Terrace site and other

---

[94] Excerpted from *Compton's Interactive Encyclopedia*. Copyright (c) 1994, 1995 Compton's NewMedia, Inc. All Rights Reserved

evidences show that prior to the formation of a Jewish religion and during its formation, the Ancient Egyptian religion was being followed in Asia Minor and that it was not until Egyptian military strength waned and the Assyrians, Persians, and Greeks conquered Egypt (1000 B.C.E.-100 B.C.E.) that the Hebrew-Jews set out to conquer land for themselves in the region of Canaan. This period coincides with the famous story of Exodus where the Jews are said to have raised themselves up from bondage with the help of their God who was more powerful than the gods of the Egyptians (Bible-book of Exodus).

Canaan, Palestine and Israel in Ancient and Modern Times

Jerusalem (Yerushalayim, or Al-Quds), is a city on the Israeli-Jordanian border. It is held to be a sacred city by the Christian, Jewish, and Muslim religions. It was originally a Jesubite city between 2000 B.C.E. and 1500 B.C.E., until it was captured by King David after 1000 B.C.E. Afterwards it was known as the "city of David." The Jesubites were one of the groups of Canaanites that the Jews felt compelled to oust from the land (Jerusalem), and it was there that they chose to build the first Temple, an architectural symbol of the Jewish faith. It was destroyed by Nebuchadnezzar of Babylon around c. 586 B.C.E., and rebuilt by Herod (Roman governor) around c. 35 B.C.E., but was again destroyed by Titus (Roman Emperor) in 70 A.C.E. It was then captured by the Muslim Seljuks in 1077 A.C.E., and by the Crusaders of Europe from 1094-1187 A.C.E., and the Turks from 1244-1917 A.C.E., until it became the British mandated territory of Palestine in 1917 A.C.E. The British and other Western governments, at the insistence of the Jews, partitioned the city between Israel and Jordan and created the state of Israel in 1949 A.C.E. Since then the control of the city of Jerusalem has been the source of conflict between the three Western religions (Judaism, Christianity and Islam). The controversy has spawned several wars and continuing animosity that continues to our present times, especially as Israel seized control of the city in 1967 A.C.E.

Who were the Jewish People?

As previously stated, Judaism is not a race or an ethnic group; it is a religion. In the time when Jesus would have taught, the Jewish people lived in Egypt and Palestine. They were all under the domination of the Roman Empire, especially after the destruction of the main Jewish Temple in c. 70 A.C.E. There were four main sects of Judaism. These comprised what is referred to as the "Jewish People" or followers of the Jewish religion who were, culturally speaking, Hebrews (mixed Canaanites who were previously Ancient Egyptians). The sects were: *Pharisees, Sadducees, Essenes* and the *Zealots*. Each of these groups affected the development of the Jewish scriptures and undoubtedly had members who claimed to be Messiahs.

> A- The Pharisees emphasized strict interpretation and observance of the Mosaic law (Old Testament) in both its oral and written form. In Christian times the term gained a different connotation. It came to refer to a hypocritically self-righteous person, because of Jesus' teaching given in Matthew 23:13. In Matthew 23:13, Jesus denounces the Pharisees for not practicing the teachings correctly due to greed, the desire to remain in power over the people and ignorance, adhering to the letter, rather than to the spirit, of the laws and rituals, and obstructing others from doing so also[280]. The origins of the Pharisees can be traced to the second century B.C.E.

> B- The Sadducees were a priestly, aristocratic Jewish sect, founded in the second century B.C.E. They accepted only the written Mosaic law. This group ceased to exist after the destruction of the Temple in 70 A.C.E.

> C- The early Essenes were a Jewish religious sect, which existed in Palestine from the 2nd century B.C.E. to the end of the 1st century A.C.E. The members of the sect lived in communal groups, isolated from the rest of society. Sharing all possessions in common, they stressed ritual purity and were stricter than the Pharisees in their observance. A secrecy developed about the sect, and they shunned public life as well as temple worship. The Dead Sea Scrolls were probably their work. There are groups who follow part of this tradition in modern times. They adhere to a wholistic and natural way of life, and their

teachings are presented in books outside of the Bible, that would be considered to be Gnostic in content and character.

D- The Zealots were members of a Jewish movement of the first century A.C.E. that fought against Roman rule in Palestine as incompatible with strict monotheism.

Christianity thus developed as a new independent sect of Judaism. It sought to bring forth the deeper teachings which had been lost by the other sects due to infighting, corruption and misunderstanding of the true meaning of the scriptures. The first converts to Christianity, the majority of whom were most often non-Roman peoples, the poor, slaves, the politically oppressed and women of ancient times, saw Christianity not only as a spiritual liberator, but as a philosophy which would lead them to liberation from the social oppression of the Romans as well.

Plate 24 Below: Asiatics bringing tribute to Egypt (18th Dynasty – New Kingdom Period)

In the picture above, which comes from an Ancient Egyptian tomb in Beni Hasan, the two men in the upper right hand corner are Egyptians and the rest are Asiatic (Semitic-Arab) men and women.

The Effect of Zoroastrianism on Western Religions

Zoroaster is thought to have lived in circa 630-550 B.C.E. He was a Persian religious prophet, who founded Zoroastrianism. Zoroaster (known in ancient Persian as Zarathustra) was born in the eastern Persian land of Airyana Vaejah, probably during the period preceding that of the Achaemenian kings, although earlier dates have been suggested.[281] Zoroastrianism is a religion originated by Zoroaster, a Sage who is believed to have lived in the 6th century B.C.E. Zoroastrianism became the state religion of Persia in the period from 229-652 A.C.E. Zoroastrianism viewed the world as divided between the spirits of good and evil, God and nature. The main doctrine of Zoroastrianism came to mean that there is a God who exists in fact, separate from humankind and from nature in a particular physical location. Zoroastrians worship *Ahura Mazda* as the Supreme Deity. Ahura Mazda is all light and all goodness. As soon as Ahura Mazda appeared though, another god appeared, *Angra Mainyu*, (Ahura Mazda's shadow), the Lord of Darkness. In a fit of jealousy he cast darkness upon the light. Therefore, the creation of the God of light, nature, exists in a state of mixture.

According to Zoroastrian doctrine, the human soul, which is essentially light, is also mixed with darkness by virtue of its association with the body. Thus, in order to achieve salvation, one must consciously, and with intention, reject the bad and adhere to the good. Hence, the idea emerges that we must not come into harmony with nature, the works of humanity, and the body and its desires, because these are part of the "darkness" that pull a human being away from blessedness. Instead, we must constantly fight to subdue our physical nature and our outer nature, the environment. Neither is to be respected and accepted, instead one is to despise and repudiate them for being the vehicle of darkness. The terms "Good God," "Good religion" and the "goodness of man" became central to the Zoroastrian doctrine. While there is no notion of original sin, Zoroastrians believe that every individual is responsible for {his/her} part in the cosmic struggle of good and evil. Zoroastrians also believe in a savior who will come and usher in the victory of the forces of good against the forces of evil, and then establish a golden age for the righteous as the following Zoroastrian quotation suggests:

> Powerful in immortality shall be the soul of the follower of Truth, but lasting torment shall there be for the man who cleaves to the Lie.

It must be remembered that truth, from the Zoroastrian point of view, is not to be compared with the mystical truth of the Gnostics. The Zoroastrian ideal is complete faith in a dualistic universe, which is governed by forces of light (good) and forces of darkness (evil). The mystical understanding sees duality only as a manifestation of the transcendental Self in time and space due to ignorance. However, upon transcending time and space, through enlightenment, duality is discovered to be an illusion. The Zoroastrian dualistic point of view sees and affirms only the reality of time and space. If it recognizes anything above time and space, it ascribes dualistic concepts to that as well. Thus, the dualistic concept offers no final resolution to the question of existence since one duality inevitably leads to another in an endless chain of causality. The Latin term for this kind of philosophical argument is *regresus ad infinitum* or "regressing to infinity." If there is a "good God" and a "bad God," then they both thwart each others will, but if the good one will win out one day then it must mean that the bad one is not so bad or not a god at all! The reasoning just presented points to the fallacy of dualistic thinking. Duality is an aspect of the human mind and its weak concepts about nature. When the ignorance of the mind is purged then the non-dualistic reality of the universe emerges. This is called Gnosis by the Christian Gnostic mystics.

The language and scriptures of Zoroastrianism have been found to be extremely similar to the language and scriptures of the Indo-European Aryans who invaded eastern Asia (Europe) and southern Asia (India) between 1,700 and 1,300 B.C.E. Therefore, it is likely that Zoroaster was an Aryan Sage or strongly influenced by Aryan dualistic philosophy. In much the same way as occurred in India and Europe, the Aryan views of ritualism and the worship of a God in fact who resides somewhere outside and apart from man and creation were transferred to Mesopotamia. Zoroastrian ideas contrasted with the Gnostic, Egyptian and Dravidian (pre-Aryan culture in India) understanding of God as being within nature and the human heart. The Zoroastrian ideas were introduced to the Semitic groups who lived in the Near East and became a strong religious belief which profoundly influenced other religious movements of Asia minor including Judaism with its God, Yahweh, who is all good in the writings of Moses (Torah). See Exodus 7: 13-14

Exodus 7
13. And he hardened Pharaoh's heart, that he hearkened not to them; as the LORD had said.

14. And the LORD said to Moses, Pharaoh's heart [is] hardened, he refuseth to let the people go.

In the mythology of the book of Exodus, of the Old Testament, it is related that God tells Moses to confront Pharaoh and ask him to let the Jews leave Egypt. At one point Pharaoh agreed, but then had a sudden change of heart which was prompted by God as well. So it must be asked why did God harden Pharaoh's heart if he wanted to let the Jews leave? This wonderful situation in Jewish mythology points to the universal aspect of God who is operating through the duality of human experience and through nature itself. It is a recognition that the same Supreme Being that is behind the evil people is also behind the good people as well. But how can God be good and bad at the same time? The mystical answer is that God is in reality neither good nor evil, just as the sun cannot be said to be good or evil. It sustains life on earth and makes it possible for people to act in evil ways or good ways according to their inclinations based on their ethical character, a product of their level of spiritual evolution. Thus, the mystical understanding is that God sustains Creation, and it is human beings who act in evil or righteous ways in accordance with their desires. However, God is there for all who wish to discover {Him/Her} while nature, the school of hard knocks, is there to guide wayward souls on their journey though life by means of trial and error, tribulations, frustrations and disappointments, as well as short lived successes and fleeting pleasures, until they are ready for higher guidance and self-discovery. Zoroastrian philosophy would say that good and evil are separate and distinct entities contending for control of the earth.

Zoroastrians believe that at 1,000-year intervals, a savior, born of a virgin, comes to earth, at which time the dead are raised. At this time the heavenly forces engage in a battle against the demonic or evil forces.[84] Prior to the advent of Zoroastrianism, the Ancient Egyptians held that the God Djehuti would incarnate to restore unrighteousness in the world whenever necessary. Heru exemplifies another expression of this same idea. Similarly, in Indian philosophy, the god Vishnu incarnates at regular intervals to relieve the world from evil. The stories of his incarnations are recounted in the Ramayana-Yoga Vasistha and the Mahabharata. In Buddhist scriptures, there is a story of *Kalki Avatara*, a savior who will come to earth to destroy evil and announce the end of the earth. The number 1,000 also appears in Hinduism where Indian Sages stated that a day of the god Brahma (the creator of the world) lasts 1,000 years. Likewise this same idea appeared in the Bible, Psalms 90:4. It states that *1,000 years are like a day in the sight of God*. These idea transferred to the New Testament Christian faith in the notion that Jesus would return in the year 1,000. Thus, at the end of each millennium, 1,000 years intervals after the death of Jesus Christ, Christians enter into a panic about the coming end of the world.

Zoroastrianism has important correlations to the Indo-European Vedic Aryans. The Zoroastrian god Ahura of the Seven Chapters, has wives, called Ahuranis. They are comparable to the wives of the Hindu-Vedic god, Varuna. Varuna's wives (Varunanis), are the rain clouds and waters of Creation. Ahura is possessor of Asha, as Varuna is custodian of Rta ("Truth" or "cosmic order" = Asha = Old Persian. Arta). In Zoroastrian mythology, the sun is the "eye" of both deities, and the name of Ahura is at times joined to that of the god Mithra. In a Hindu Veda, the names of Mithra and Varuna are similarly joined. The Zoroastrian Seven Chapters also revere Haoma (Hindu-Vedic, Soma), a digitized plant yielding an intoxicating juice. The worship of ancestors and nature spirits and other deities (for example, the fire god, called Agni by the Hindus) likewise have Vedic correspondences.[75] Thus, it is widely accepted that Zoroastrian mythology is an extension of Vedic Aryan mythology which entered into India, China and eastern Europe with the invading hoards of Indo-Europeans from North Asia (modern day Russia-Siberia).

Clearly, there are almost exact correlations between Zoroastrianism, early Mesopotamian mythology, Judaism of the Old Testament and Christianity in reference to the dualistic view of divinity and of spiritual life in general. So Judaism and Christianity appear to be an amalgam of Ancient Egyptian and Mesopotamian traditions. Thus, while there is a strong mystical philosophy which underlies Christianity from the African (Egyptian) and Indian influence, it is also true that much of the dualistic thinking in Christianity originated from the influences of Mesopotamian religion and the Aryan religion from north Asia. While Judaism still expects a savior, Christians accepted Jesus as the savior and Lucifer as the lord of darkness (the devil).

Ethiopia and the History of Judaism

Any discussion of Ethiopia (Kush/Nubia) should include a mention of the later religious movements and political developments of the country since the study of ancient history may shed light on modern developments there. This is because Ethiopia holds an important place in African history, as it was the only country never to be directly colonized by European countries or the United States of America. Therefore, many African peoples see Ethiopia as a symbol of African independence and strength in the face of the threat of conquest by foreign powers. First, the timeline of events needs to be established so that the emergence of Ethiopian Judaism, Christianity and Rastafarianism may be understood in the context of the beginnings of civilization, Ancient Egyptian religion and Ancient Nubian religion.

Judaism has a long history in Ethiopia which begins prior to the early period of Christianity (100-500 A.C.E.). The Falashas are a native Jewish sect of Ethiopia. The name Falasha is Amharic for "exiles" or "landless ones.[95]" This is similar to the term "Hebrews" meaning "those who pass from place to place." The Falashas themselves refer to their sect as Beta Esrael ("House of Israel"). The origin of the Falashas is unknown, but one Falasha tradition claims to trace their ancestry to Menelek (Menelik), who was the son of King Solomon[96] of Israel and the queen of Sheba.[97] Some scholars place the date of their origin before the 2nd century B.C.E. since the Falashas are unfamiliar with either the Palestinian or Babylonian Talmud (post-biblical developments of Judaism).

Southern Ancient Kamit (Egypt) Present day Nubia

Ancient Kush/Nubia/Ethiopia Present day Sudan

Present day Ethiopia

Interestingly, the Hebrew scriptures are unknown to the Falashas. The Bible of the Falashas is written in what is classified as an archaic Semitic dialect, known as Gecez. Thus, the religion of the Falashas is a modified form of Mosaic Judaism, unaffected generally by post-biblical developments. The Falashas retain animal sacrifices. They celebrate scriptural and non-scriptural feast days, although the latter are not the same as those celebrated by other Jews. One of the Falasha non-scriptural feast days, for example, is the Commemoration of Abraham. The Sabbath regulations of the Falashas are stringent. They observe biblical dietary laws, but not the post-biblical rabbinic regulations.

Among the Falashas, marriage outside the religious community is forbidden. Monogamy is practiced. Marriage at a very early age is rare, and high moral standards are maintained. The center of Falasha religious life is the Masjid, or Synagogue. The chief functionary in each village is the High Priest, who is assisted by lower Priests. Falasha monks live alone or in monasteries isolated from other Falashas. Rabbis do not exist among the Falashas.

---

[95] Recall that the original Hebrews of the Bible Old Testament tradition were nomadic wanderers.
[96] Solomon (c. 974-c. 937 B.C.E.) - In the Old Testament, third king of Israel, son of David by Bathsheba. During a peaceful reign, he was famed for his wisdom and his alliances with Egypt and Phoenicia. The much later biblical Proverbs, Ecclesiastes, and Song of Songs are attributed to him. He built the Temple in Jerusalem with the aid of heavy taxation and forced labor, resulting in the revolt of North Israel. Websters Encyclopedia
[97] Sheba: Ancient name for a kingdom which flourished in S Yemen (Sha'abijah) at around the 1st century B.C.E. It was once renowned for gold and spices. According to the Old Testament, its queen visited Solomon.

As discussed above, Ethiopia, in ancient times, had been an independent country which spawned the creation of Ancient Egypt.[98] And in those ancient times, the Ethiopians and the Egyptians recognized the same supreme Divinity under the names Asar, Amun, Ptah, etc., as well as the manifestations of God in the form of gods and goddesses. Recall that at one time Ethiopia was ruled by Egypt, and at another time (Nubian Dynasty period, 712-657 B.C.E.) it became allied with Egypt and even ruled over Egypt. However, when Egypt was finally taken over by Coptic Christianity, after the Roman edicts which outlawed all other religions except Christianity were issued, Ethiopia also converted to Coptic Christianity, but several Ethiopian groups adhered to the ancient form of Falasha Judaism, independent of other Jews in the Diaspora.

The kingdom of Aksum (Axum)[99] flourished from the 1st–10th centuries A.C.E., reaching its peak about the 4th century. Coptic Christianity from Egypt was introduced to Ethiopia around the 4th century, and began to decline in the 7th century as Islam expanded into Ethiopia. The Arab conquests isolated Aksum from the rest of the Christian world.

The experience of the Falashas in Ethiopia points to the differences between the form of Judaism that has been developed in Western countries (America, Europe and Israel) and that which existed prior to the developments of the Talmudic tradition in the last 1,700 hundred years or more. The Talmudic traditions, which form the basis of popular modern Judaism, are a product of the rabbinical tradition which has sought to explain the original teachings given in the Old Testament. Before Coptic Christianity spread to Ethiopia, Judaism was already present. Since Ethiopia was the only African nation to maintain its independence throughout history, including during the periods of the European slave trade and the African colonization, its Christians, and the Copts (Coptic Christians) in Egypt, also kept alive the oldest form of non Roman-Catholic Christianity.

During the 10th century A.C.E., a kingdom emerged in Ethiopia that formed the basis of Abyssinia (former name of Ethiopia). It was reinforced in 1270 A.C.E. with the founding of a new Dynasty. Although it remained independent throughout the period of the European colonization (enslavement) of Africa, Abyssinia suffered civil unrest and several invasions from the 16th century A.C.E. on, and was eventually reunited in 1889 A.C.E. under Menelik II, with Italian support. In 1896 A.C.E. Menelik II put down an invasion by Italy. They claimed he had agreed to make the country an Italian protectorate.[126] The next events in the history of Ethiopia led to the development of a new religious idea which traced its origins to the early followers of Judaism in Ethiopia. This new religious idea was Rastafarianism.

Since the 1930's, when Haile Selassie I came into power in Ethiopia, a few Falashas rose to positions of prominence in education and government, but reports of their persecution followed the emperor's ouster in 1974. In 1975 they were recognized by the Chief Rabbinate as Jews and allowed to settle in Israel. More than 12,000 Falashas were airlifted to Israel in late 1984 and early 1985, when the Ethiopian government halted the program. The airlifts resumed in 1989, and about 3,500 Falashas emigrated to Israel in 1990. Nearly all of the more than 14,000 Falashas remaining in Ethiopia were evacuated by the Israeli government in May 1991.[75] Since that time the Israeli government has instituted a program to assimilate the Falashas. This program has come under fire by many critics. One aspect of the program separates Falasha youths from their families and indoctrinates them into the modern religious traditions, as well as the political doctrines related to Palestine and the relations with the surrounding Arab countries.

Finally, it should be kept in mind that the "Cush" that is spoken about in the Jewish and Christian bible is not the same as the present day state of "Ethiopia." Like the present day Ghana, which adopted the name of the Ghana Empire which existed many hundreds of years earlier but is now a country that exists in a different geographical location, so too present day Ethiopia is not located in the same geographical area as the land that was referred to as "Cush" (Kush). The land that the ancient Greeks referred to as "Ethiopia" and the bible refers to as Cush is actually the present day area known as Nubia and Sudan. While there is some evidence that some of the population of the ancient Ethiopia-Cush was displaced and moved south, the present day inhabitants of Ethiopia are not directly descendant from the ancient Ethiopia-Kush-Meroitic culture that was linked to Kamit. However, many adherents to the Judeo-Christian tradition have made the association. This stems from the writings of the bible as well as the influx of Jewish and

---

[98] The Ancient Egyptian traditions says that Osiris, the first king of Egypt, was an Ethiopian who led a group of Ethiopian colonizers into northeast Africa (Egypt) and started civilization there.

[99] Aksum, Ethiopia, served as capital of ancient Kingdom of Aksum, which flourished from 1st to 10th century; extended influence over much of Arabian Peninsula; Christianized during 4th century; kingdom ended 1270 with abdication of ruling prince; city today a tourist attraction known for its 126 tall granite obelisks and other antiquities.[126]

Christian missionaries both in ancient times (300-600 A.C.E.) and in modern times, who converted many Africans who were practicing African religions up to that time, leading up to the association of present day Ethiopia with the story of Solomon and the Queen of Sheba.

Rastafarianism and the Judeo-Christian Religion

Rastafarianism is a spiritual movement based on the Judeo-Christian biblical tradition and Ethiopian culture and thus should be noted in our study of the history of the modern Judeo-Christian tradition and Ethiopian history. Rastafarianism is a philosophy that developed in the 1930's, centered in Jamaica (Caribbean). Rastafarianism is based in part on the Maroon[100] culture of Jamaica, as well as the struggle against slavery, and the Marcus Garvey Philosophy of African unity and looking to Africa as the source for the redemption of African people. Rastafarians see themselves as the true Israelites, the "chosen people" of the Bible. Ethiopia is seen as the Promised Land, while all countries outside Africa are seen as Babylon or the place of exile. As a custom, many Rastafarians do not cut their hair, citing biblical injunctions against this practice. So instead they wear it in long dreadlocks which are often covered in woolen hats displaying the Rastafarian colors, red, green, and gold. The food restrictions are very strict. No pork, shellfish, salt, milk, or coffee are allowed.

One reason why Rastafarianism is notable is that it is a religion that originated in the Caribbean. As it is partly based on some of the ideals of Marcus Garvey and on the emperor of Ethiopia, the philosophy of Rastafarianism is closely associated with the struggle of African peoples to liberate themselves from the slavery and exploitation imposed on them by European countries. The country of Ethiopia, in Africa, became a special focus since it was a symbol of African resistance. This hope also focused on one man, Haile Selassie I. Marcus Garvey had called on black people to return to Africa and set up a black-governed country there. In 1927, Garvey, the great leader, orator and founder of the Universal Negro Improvement Association (UNIA), made the statement, "look to Africa for the crowning of a king to know that your redemption is nigh." In 1930, Prince Tafari Makonnen was crowned as the Emperor of Ethiopia, with the name Haile Selassie I which means "Power of the Trinity," (this was his baptismal name). When Emperor Haile Selassie appropriated the titles "King of Kings" and "Conquering Lion of the Tribe of Judah" the prophesy of Garvey seemed to be reinforced. Many African people in Africa and the Americas saw this event as fulfilling Garvey's prophecy. The name Rastafari is taken from "Ras", meaning "prince" in the Amharic language, and "Tafari," the name of the emperor of Ethiopia.[282] Therefore, some Rastafarians acknowledged him as an incarnation of God (Jah), and others regarded him as a prophet. In Rastafarianism, the use of ganja (marijuana) is considered a sacrament. In Rastafarianism there is no church system. By 1990, there were close to one million Rastafarians in the world.

The Kebra Nagast or "Glory of Kings" is a text, originally written in the Gecez language[283] that is viewed as the Bible of Rastafarianism. It is regarded as a part of the Judeo-Christian tradition that was originally omitted from the present day versions of the Bible, like the Egyptian Gnostic Gospels and the Dead Sea Scrolls. The Kebra Nagast is also regarded by some Christian Ethiopians as a national epic. It traces the royal line of Ethiopian kings and states that they were descended from Solomon, the king of Israel. It also states that the Ark of the Covenant was brought from Jerusalem to Aksum. In a separate tradition, based on the Ethiopian Christians who are unconnected with the Catholic or Coptic churches, they believe they have the Ark carefully stored away in a secret location and none but special monks are allowed to tend to it. The text also states that the Ethiopian people are descendants from the Hebrew patriarchs and that the Jewish succession of kings passes through Solomon and Menelik, Solomon's firstborn son, to Jesus Christ and to the present day Ethiopian rulers. The Kebra Nagast asserts that the kings of Ethiopia who were descended from Menelik were of divine origin, and that their words and deeds were those of gods. The myth of the Kebra Nagast dates back to the first millennium of the common era (1000 A.C.E.), but is based on the Judeo-Christian biblical tradition such as that of the Song of Solomon.

Many people do not realize that since the tradition of the Kebra Nagast follows the Judeo-Christian model, it necessarily develops contradictions with African Culture, including the Ethiopian culture it purports to describe. The following passage is a case in point. It describes how the Ethiopian people left

---

[100] The Jamaican Maroons — African slaves, who, following the British defeat of the Spaniards in 1655, escaped to the mountains and waged guerrilla warfare against the British colonizers.

Egypt and at the same time destroyed the Egyptian "idols" while they (Ethiopians) sang and played music of Zion.

> "II Then early in the morning, the wagons rose up and resumed their journey as before; and the people sang songs of Zion, and as the people of Egypt bade them farewell, they passed before them like shadows. And the people of Ethiopia took up their flutes, horns, and drums, and the noise of their instruments smashed the idols of Egypt. These were in the forms of men, dogs, and cats. And the idols fell off their pedestals and so broke into pieces. Figures of birds made of gold and silver fell down and were broken."[284]

Historically speaking, there is no evidence to date of such occurrences as are described in the Kebra Nagast, beyond the Kebra Nagast, just as there is no evidence for what the Christian Bible describes, beyond what is contained in the Christian Bible. Historically, the Ancient Ethiopians revered the same divinities as the Ancient Egyptians and were actually the last people to practice Ancient Egyptian religion in southern Egypt and Ethiopia before the Christian zealots closed the Kamitan Temples and forced the people to worship Jesus and follow the Bible. If the Kebra Nagast means to say that the Jews who left Egypt in the Exodus were actually Ethiopians, and not Egyptians, who rejected the ancient religion, this could be true, if it occurred at all, since the Ancient Egyptians and Ethiopians were closely related (ethnically and culturally). However, it must be understood that this would represent a turning away from that which is indigenous and accepting that which is foreign because, the traditions of Judaism and Christianity, as they are known to the modern world, do not follow the pattern of African religion. Present day Christianity, which follows the Jewish tradition, but whose teachings, symbols and traditions are based on the Ancient Egyptian Asarian Resurrection religion, has strayed from its original African roots.[285] In effect, the Kebra Nagast, while seeking to elevate Ethiopians in particular and Africans in general, follows a tradition that relates its followers to the Judeo-Christian faith and away from the traditional African (Ancient Egyptian) religion. Ironically, like the Bible, the Kebra Nagast denigrates the earliest African religion and the civilization it gave rise to (Kush-Kamit), which actually gave birth to the Judeo-Christian and Islamic traditions.

Rastafarianism traces its roots to the Old Testament. The Old Testament records a visit to Ethiopia by the Queen of Sheba. Its ruling house is said to have descended from King Solomon's son. Ethiopia's nobility, had, since the Middle Ages seen themselves as being the descendants of King Solomon of Judah and the Queen of Sheba. Much of this belief was based on biblical statements, including the Song of Solomon 1:5-6, which states: "I am Black, but comely[101], O ye daughters of Jerusalem, as the tents of Kedar, as the curtains of Solomon." This verse implies that Solomon was a Black African, and his coming together with the Queen of Sheba apparently means that Ethiopians bear the distinction of the descendants of the people mentioned in the Judeo-Christian biblical tradition. Modern history dates back to Menelik II (reigned 1889-1913), whose line of succession led to Emperor Haile Selassie, who was crowned in 1930. Haile Selassie I (1892-1975), was the last emperor of Ethiopia and ruled from 1930-1974. Haile Selassie I was born near Harar on July 23, 1892. His original name was Lij Tafari Makonnen. Selassie was a grandnephew of Emperor Menelik II. In 1916 he ousted Menelik's successor, Lij Iyasu, and replaced him with Zauditu, who was the old emperor's daughter. Then he made himself the regent and heir to the throne of the country. When Zauditu died in 1930, Lij Tafari Makonnen succeeded her and took the name Haile Selassie I. His other titles included *Conquering Lion of the Tribe of Judah, Elect of God*, and *King of Kings*. His reign was interrupted by the 1936 Italian invasion, which gained control of Ethiopia. Haile Selassie fled to England and raised an army there. With the assistance of the British troops he freed the country in 1941 and ruled until 1974. Haile Selassie was seen by many as slow in dealing with issues of social injustice and economic crisis due to droughts and famine in the country as well as incompetence and corruption in the government. A military junta deposed him in 1974 due to many years of unrest (civil war and the breakdown of law and order) in the country caused by social and economic instability. He died in 1975, yet many followers of the Rastafarian movement still believe that he was the Messiah, the incarnation of God (Jah).

The Rastafarian movement still faces many problems. While Ethiopia has undergone many struggles since the death of Haile Selassie, Rastafarians still look to Ethiopia and to Africa in general, as the motherland which needs to be redeemed. The struggle of Rastafarians to maintain their identity has seen periods of persecution and outright rejection by other peoples, even others of African descent (African Americans, Africans, Jamaicans, etc.) who see them as religious rivals or as economic revolutionaries who will thwart opportunities for commerce with the governments of the dominant cultures. Also, there are

---

[101] Pleasing and wholesome in appearance; attractive.

many who don the colors of Rastafarianism but who do not follow its teachings and simply use this religion as a means to remain outside the mainstream of society and use drugs.

Recall that the "curse" upon the ancestors of Ham stems from the misinterpretation of the story of Noah and his three sons by racist slave traders and others who wanted to denigrate African peoples and establish a basis for legitimizing the practice of slavery. Rastafarianism is an effort to establish a positive connection to the Bible as well as an attempt to provide a vision for the liberation of African peoples in the Diaspora. However, as with other traditions which seek to isolate their teachings as exclusive, Rastafarianism cannot be practiced by everyone since, like Judaism, it is strongly tied in with a particular culture and tradition. While associated with the Judeo-Christian religion, Rastafarianism is actually a modern movement and therefore any search for its roots will lead to Neterian Religion since the Judeo-Christian religion derives from there as well. Therefore, it remains a minority spiritual path among the world religions. They themselves repudiate alternative forms of spirituality which do not conform to the mainstream views. It should be noted here that there is no direct connection between the terms Ras Tafari, "Lion of Judah" and the term *Rastau* of Ancient Egyptian metaphysics. The Egyptian term refers to the passageway into the astral plane (Duat), wherein the Higher Self is to be discovered.[102] Further, the idea that the Rastafarian concept of God is most ancient, as is put forth by some adherents of Rastafarianism, can only be accepted if the origins of Rastafarianism are traced to the origins in Judaism, and those origins are in turn traced back to Kamitan (Ancient Egyptian) and Nubian spirituality.

Above: Ras Tafari, "Lion of Judah" symbol from Ethiopia.

---

[102] See the book *Egyptian Book of the Dead* by Muata Ashby

Kabbalism, Ancient Egypt and the Mysticism of the Tree of Life

The *Kabbala* (also *Cabalah*) is regarded as a form of Jewish mysticism which is officially said to have originated in the 12th century. This date closely followed the crusades and it is possible that the opening up of European society, due to the foreign wars, allowed the stagnant living conditions of the Dark and Middle Ages to give way to a more mystical interpretation of the scriptures. Kabbalism is considered a way of approaching God directly as opposed to through the Temple. Through the acquisition of secret knowledge of divine revelation, an aspirant can achieve divine communion. The major text on Kabbalism of the time was the 'Book of Brightness,' which came out in the 12th century A.C.E., which contained ideas about the transmigration of souls and other ideas that were alien to orthodox Judaism. Echoing the Ancient Egyptian mystics, the Kabbalists expressed a great interest in mysticism and cosmology. Kabbalists believe that the Torah contains the knowledge of all Creation if every word is interpreted according to precise fixed principles. The meditation upon these will lead to a state of mind wherein the meditator would attain cosmic vision of the Divine Self. Kabbalism also contained elements of messianism and was later influenced by *Hasidism*.

Hasidism is a partly mystical movement within Judaism. It first appeared sometime during the 18th century A.C.E. in Poland. Partly revivalistic and partly reformist, it is considered as a reaction against the rigid and legalistic Jewish orthodoxy. It was founded by Israel ben Eliezer. Like the philosophy of the Kabbalist, he emphasized direct communion with God and awareness of His presence in all creation. In Hasidism, worship is a part of all the ordinary activities of a person's daily life. In Hasidism, the tzaddikim, or leaders of Hasidic communities are viewed as intermediaries between the people and God.

The Ancient Egyptian Hieroglyph for the tree.

The idea of having direct access to God through special knowledge was already evident in the teachings of the Ancient Egyptians, the Christian Mystics (Gnostics), the Hindus and the Buddhists who all came long before the Kabbalists. In ancient Egypt, however, the teaching of the Tree of Life took on a special meaning. In Ancient Egypt, the tree was seen as the source of life, and it was the Goddess, as the divinity being worshipped, who extended the nectar of life itself through the tree. This idea is also evident in the special Bodhi tree of Buddha and the Tree of Life in the Garden of Eden, which is also, according to some Christian traditions, known as the tree upon which Jesus was crucified. Also, the cross of Jesus is often referred to as a Tree of Life. In present day practice, the Christmas tree is supposed to be a manifestation of the same idea. The star at the top of the Christmas tree is supposed to symbolize the attainment of Cosmic Consciousness.

Figure 62: A- The Ancient Egyptian Tree of Life of the Goddess, B- Christian Tree of Life. C Buddhist Tree of Life, D- Christian Christmas tree. E- The Caduceus of Djehuti (Hermes), F- The Psycho-spiritual Energy Centers of Serpent Power Yoga in Ancient Egypt and India.

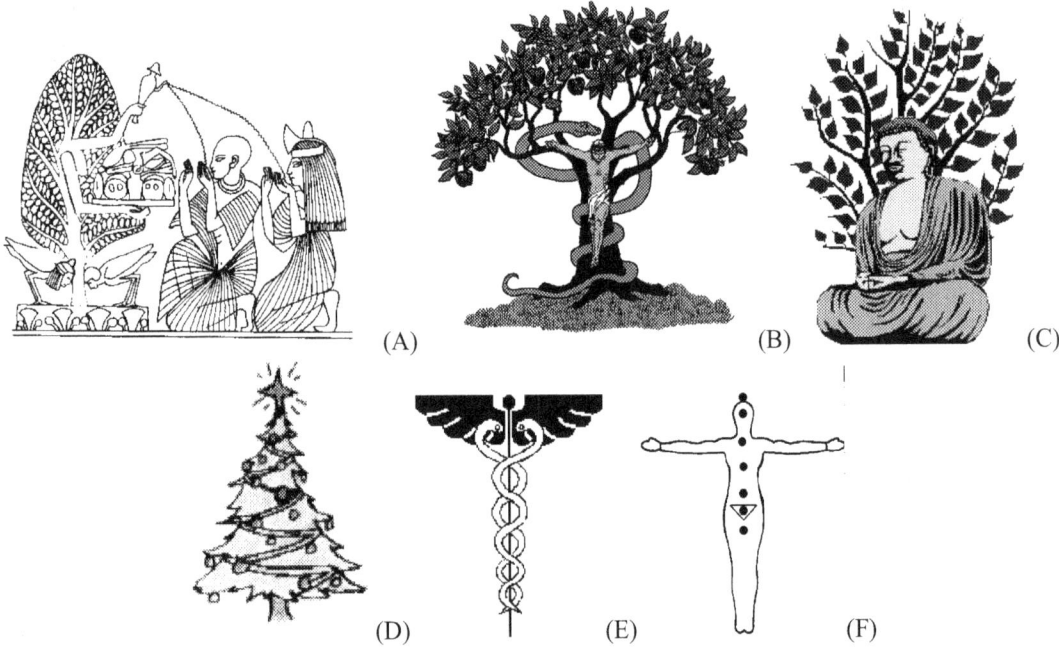

The Kabbalistic Mysticism of the Tree

As in the Ancient Egyptian Mysticism related to the Pillar of Asar (see pictures below), the discovery of the *Sefirotic Tree of Life* (see picture below) in the Kabbala is seen as the ultimate goal of life. The symbolism of the Kabbalistic Tree of Life is to be understood as a mystic code which holds the symbolism for the understanding of God and Creation, as well as a mystic map showing the path to spiritual enlightenment. The Sefirotic Tree of Life consists of ten spiritual centers or Sefirofs which emanate from the Divine Self, God. These centers represent spiritual as well as psychological principles that need to be understood and mastered by the Kabbalistic aspirant in order to attain spiritual enlightenment (at the top of the tree). It relates to the mystic symbolism of climbing up to heaven.

In the Zohar text of Kabbalism, it reads: "The Tree of Life extends from above downwards, and is the sun, which illuminates all." Similarly, in the Bhagavad Gita of India (c.500 B.C.E.), the tree is used as a metaphor symbolizing that the world is not the source of its own existence, but that indeed the Spirit is the source of Creation.

> 1. The Blessed Lord said: The scriptures speak of the imperishable Ashwattha tree (of the world-process) with its roots above and branches below; the Vedic verses constitute its leaves.
> He who knows this Tree is the knower of the essence of the Vedas.
>
> Gita: Chapter 15
> Purushottam Yogah—
> The Yoga of the Supreme Spirit

The philosophy of Kabbalism holds that the right side of the tree represents light and good and that the left side represents darkness or evil. This understanding is reminiscent of the Zoroastrian philosophy, which influenced early Judaism. Like Neberdjer of Ancient Egypt and Brahman of India, Kabbalism views God as Absolute and transcendental, *En-sof* (the infinite).

The Sefirot (spheres) are seen as attributes of God. As a human being develops these attributes they become godlike and therefore, Divine. The Spheres have been compared to Ancient Egyptian Serpent Power mysticism and the Chakras of Indian Kundalini Yoga. The meditations on these centers produce a similar mystical movement of energy (light and heat) in the subtle body of a human being which lead to greater experience of the Divine. When this form of ecstasy occurs, it is called *shefa (divine influx)*. In contrast to the Serpent Power-Kundalini Yoga system, it is seen as an energy which comes into the body rather than lying dormant in it. As a human being masters the psycho-spiritual principle of the center he or she is able to move closer to the infinite. *Malkuth* represents the physical body, *Yesod* represents the *heart*, *Hod* represents the *Glory*, *Netzach* represents the *Victory*, *Tipthereth* represents the *Intellect*, *Geburah* represents the *Force*, *Chesed* represents the *Mercy*, *Binah* represents the *Wisdom*, *Chokmah* represents the *Light*, and Kether represents the *spirit* and *humility*. The lower seven spheres have been related to the seven psycho-spiritual consciousness energy of the subtle spine (Serpent Power, Kundalini Yoga). The three upper spheres are explained as mystical steps towards unity with God. Thus, through meditation and contemplation on the tree an aspirant climbs up through the principles of life and Creation.

The *Sefer Yezirah* or Kabbalistic "Book of Creation" says that God created the universe through thirty-two paths of wisdom. These are represented by the ten Sephirot and the twenty-two letters of the Hebrew alphabet. The Sephirot originally represented numbers and later came to be interpreted as emanations from which all existence originates and has its basis.

The Mystical Tree Implications of the Pillar of Asar

The *Djed* pillar[103], , is associated with the Ancient Egyptian Gods Ptah, as well as Asar. It is part of a profound mystical teaching that encompasses the mystical Life Force energy which engenders the universe and which is the driving force that sustains all life and impels human beings to action. In the Asarian Resurrection myth, it is written that when Asar was killed by Set, his body was thrown into the Nile and it came ashore on the banks of Syria. There it grew into a tree with a fragrant aroma and the king of that land had it cut into a pillar. The pillar of Asar-Ptah refers to the human vertebrae and the Serpent Power or Life Force energy which exists in the subtle spine of every human being. It refers to the four highest states of psycho-spiritual consciousness in a human being with the uppermost tier symbolizing ultimate spiritual enlightenment. Also, the Djed refers to the special realm of the Duat (astral Plane) wherein Asar or spiritual resurrection can be discovered in much the same way as the Christian *Tree of Life* refers to resurrection in Christian mystical mythology.

Figure 63: Below- The Divine Tree grows from the coffin of Asar (A), The tree is cut down to make a pillar (B), Examples of the Asarian Djed (C), the Tree of Life which is the body of Asar Himself (D).

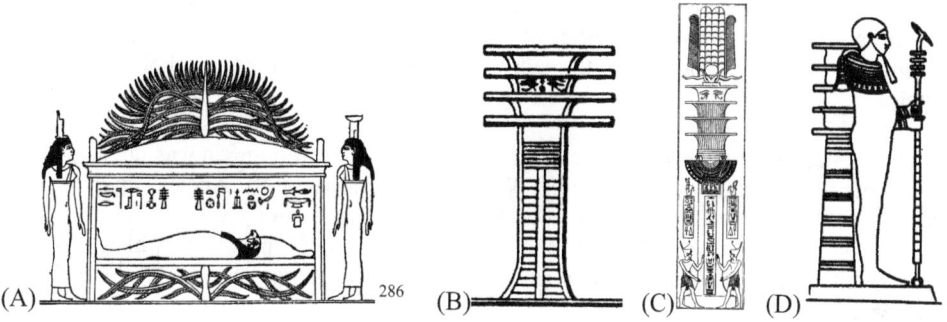

---

[103] For more on the mysticism of the Djed see the books *The Ancient Egyptian Book of the Dead* and *Serpent Power* by the author of this book.

THE AFRICAN ORIGINS OF CIVILIZATION, RELIGION AND YOGA SPIRITUALITY

The Duat or Ancient Egyptian concept of the *Netherworld* is a special place of existence. This is the abode of Asar-Ptah as well as the ultimate destination of those who become spiritually enlightened. It is the realm of Supreme Peace. It is known as *Sekhet-Aaru* or in other times *AmenDjed*. AmenDjed is a reference which unites the symbolism of Asar and Ptah with that of Amun, thus relating the deities of Ancient Egypt into a singular essence and dispelling the notion of polytheism. This underlying non-dualist monotheism is an important tantric theme. The Djed symbolizes the awakening human soul who is well "established" or "steadfast" or "stability" in the knowledge of the Self. *Djeddu*, [hieroglyphs], refers to the abode of Asar within the Duat.

In mystical terms it refers to being firmly established in the Netherworld. The Ancient Egyptian word *Djeddu* refers to "steadfastness" or "stability" as well as to the pillar of *Asar*. This is also being referred to in the following line from the *Egyptian Ru Pert Em Heru*, Rau (Chapter) I:

[hieroglyphs]

nuk Djedi, se Djedi au am-a em Djeddu Mesi - a em Djeddu
"I am Djedy (steadfast), child of Djedy (steadfast),
conceived and born in the region of *Djeddu* (steadfastness)."

The Ancient Egyptian concept of creation includes three realms. These are the TA, [hieroglyphs] (Earth), Pet, [hieroglyphs] (Heaven), and the Duat [hieroglyphs] (the Netherworld). Ta is the gross physical plane. The Duat is the abode of the gods, goddesses, spirits and souls. It is the plane of thoughts, the subtle nature devoid of gross physicality. It is the realm where those who are evil or unrighteous are punished (Hell), but it is also where the righteous live in happiness (Heaven). It is the "other world", the spirit realm. The Duat is also known as Amenta since it is the realm of Amen (Amun, The Hidden Supreme Being). The Duat is the realm where Ra, as symbolized by the sun, traverses after reaching the Western horizon, in other words, the movement of Ra between sunset and sunrise, i.e. at night. Some people thought that the Duat was under the earth since they saw Ra traverse downward and around the earth and emerged in the east, however, this interpretation is the understanding of the uninitiated masses. The esoteric wisdom about the Duat is that it is the realm of the unconscious human mind and at the same time, the realm of Cosmic Consciousness or the mind of God. Both the physical universe and the Astral plane, the Duat, are parts of that Cosmic Consciousness.

The Mysticism of the Ancient Egyptian Pautti and Its Relation to the Sefirotic Tree of Life of the Kabbala

It is clear to see that the exposition of the *Sefirotic Tree of Life* in the Kabbala expresses the understanding of Creation as an emanation from that which is subtle (the spirit) to that which is gross (the earth). A brief overview of the Ancient Egyptian Pautti or Company of Gods and Goddesses of Creation provides insights into the deeper teachings intimated in the Kabbalistic tree mysticism. The Sefer Yezirah is actually a scripture of cosmology and cosmogony which attempts to explain the nature, structure and substance of Creation. The Ancient Egyptian Creation myth also attempts to explain the nature of Creation. The extraordinary factor about the Ancient Egyptian Creation myth is that it achieves the same teaching, not through the use of spheres, but through the *Neteru*, Cosmic Forces symbolized as god and goddess principles.

Neterian Religion contained three important Creation myths. One creation myth was developed in the city of Anu, the other in Hetkaptah and the other in Waset. The Mysteries of the Ancient Egyptian city of Anu from around 5,000 B.C.E. are considered to be the oldest exposition of the teachings of Creation. They formed a foundation for the unfoldment of the teachings of mystical spirituality which followed in the mysteries of the city of *Men-nefer* through the god Ptah, and the Mysteries of *Newt (Waset or Thebes)*, through the god Amun.

The process of creation is explained in the form of a cosmological system for better understanding. Cosmology is a branch of philosophy dealing with the origin, processes, and structure of the universe. Cosmogony is the astrophysical study of the creation and evolution of the universe. Both of these disciplines are inherent facets of Egyptian philosophy through the main religious systems or Companies of the gods and goddesses. A Company of gods and goddesses is a group of deities, each of whom symbolizes a particular cosmic force or principle which emanates from the all-encompassing Supreme Being, from which they have emerged. The Self or Supreme Being manifests creation through the properties and principles represented by the *Pautti* (Company of gods and goddesses-cosmic laws of nature). The system or Company of gods and goddesses of Anu is regarded as the oldest, and forms the basis of the Asarian (Osirian) Trinity. It is expressed in the diagrams below.

It is clear that the relations between the early Jews and the Priests of Anu influenced the development of Judaism and Kabbalism. Thus it is no surprise that there would be many fundamental principles in Judaism and Kabbalism that would correlate to the Anunian doctrines of religious practice. Another such practice is the daily worship routine. Anunian Theology prescribes that there should be a three-fold worship performed daily (dawn, noon and dusk) by the initiates. This is a metaphysical discipline related to Ra, (symbolized by the sun) in his three phases (symbolized by the three phases of the sun): Creator (morning sun), Sustainer (noonday sun) and Dissolver of the world (setting sun). So too the Jewish worshiper is admonished to perform a daily three-fold worship program.

Kamitan Yoga Mysticism: The Psycho-spiritual Journey Through The Principles of Creation.

According to the teachings of Kamitan Yoga Mysticism, every human being is on a psycho-spiritual journey. They are in various ways trying to discover happiness, peace and fulfillment. Most people search in the world for these coveted goals. However, invariably they can only find limited fulfillment at best, and in the end, all of a person' achievements, no matter how grand, are relinquished by them at the time of death. Yoga philosophy shows that people are really searching for a deeper happiness and that if they were to understand how to pursue it, their worldly desires, actions and experiences would be directed towards an inner spiritual discovery. The fruit of this inner journey is the discovery that one has infinite peace and bliss within and this is the true goal of life.

In order to successfully complete the journey, everyone needs to evolve spiritually. So the characters of the myth of Creation and their various forms of interaction with each other are in reality an elaborate mystic code relating to the areas of human consciousness which need to be developed in order to grow spiritually. The first thing that is noticed, when the deities of the Ancient Egyptian Creation, based on the teachings of Anu, are placed in a hierarchical fashion based on their order of Creation by Ra (see below), is that they arise in accordance with their level of density. Density here refers to their order of subtlety of the elements in Creation. Ra is the first principle which emerges out of the Primeval Waters. He is the subtle, singular principle of Creation, the focus of oneness in time and space. The Primeval Ocean itself transcends time and space and is beyond existence and non-existence. Ra is the first principle to emerge out of the Absolute (as Ra-Tem). His emergence signifies the beginning of existence.

THE AFRICAN ORIGINS OF CIVILIZATION, RELIGION AND YOGA SPIRITUALITY

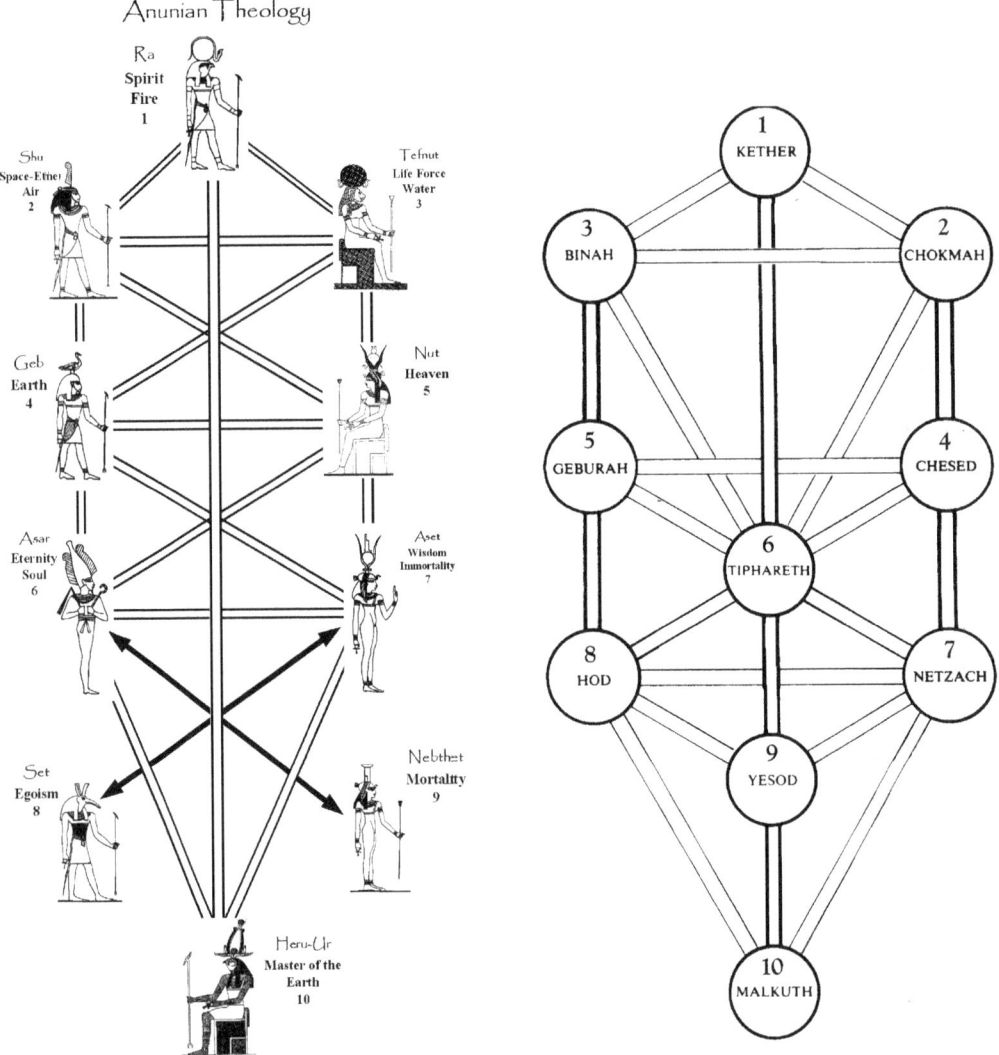

Above left: The Tree of Gods and Goddess of Anunian Theology **Above right:** The Tree of Life of the Cabalah (Kabbala), also referred to as the Caduceus of Hermes (which was the ancient Greek name for the Ancient Egyptian god Djehuti who was another son of Ra.)

    In Anunian Theology, as in the teachings of Lord Krishna and the Cabalistic Tree of Life, there is a spiritual journey of self-discovery that every human being must undertake. The journey of self-discovery refers to a coming into awareness of one's own Divine Essence. As such the mystic understanding is that the Spirit and the physical world are not separate entities. They are indeed related. Creation is rooted in the Spirit and so too is every human being. When a human being comes into this knowledge it is said that heaven has been discovered on earth. Indeed, this teaching is directly given by the Ancient Egyptian God Djehuti in the injunction "As Above, So Below." Jesus also makes this statement when he gave the prayer "Thy will be done on earth as it is in heaven." In Anunian Theology and the Cabalistic Tree of Life, it begins at the principle denoted by the number 10, and leads to the number 1, the Supreme Spirit. Each principle relates to an aspect of the personality and a cosmic aspect of Creation that must be discovered and mastered. When this occurs, the spiritual evolution of the aspirant is promoted until the ultimate destination is reached.

    The diagram of the Anunian Theology above shows that *Pautti* (Company of Gods and Goddesses), or the creative principles which are embodied in the primordial gods and goddesses of creation, emanated from the Supreme Being. Ra or Ra-Tem arose out of the *"Nu,"* the Primeval waters, the hidden essence, and began sailing the *"Boat of Millions of Years"* which included the Company of gods and goddesses. On his boat emerged the "Neteru" or cosmic principles of creation. The neters of the Pautti are Ra-Atum (Ra-Tem), Shu, Tefnut, Geb, Nut, Asar, Aset, Set, and Nebthet. Shu, Tefnut, Geb, Nut, Asar (Asar), Aset (Isis), Set, and Nebthet (Nephthys) represent the principles upon which creation manifests. "Sailing" signifies the beginning of motion in creation. Motion implies that events occur in the realm of time and space, thus, the phenomenal universe comes into existence as a mass of moving essence we call the elements. Prior to this motion, there was the primeval state of being without any form and without existence in time or space.

The Spiritual Journey To Enlightenment Based on the Pautti System of the Ancient Egyptian Anunian Theology

The Creative process comes from the top down, from the subtle to the gross, from Ra to Heru. The journey of spiritual enlightenment may be seen as a reverse of the creation process, from Heru to Ra. In the creation everything emanates from the Nun or primordial ocean and expresses in the form of elements in succeeding levels of denseness. These elements also manifest in the form of opposites which appear to be exclusive and separate from each other, but which are in reality complements to each other. Therefore, the spiritual journey is based on first discovering aspiration (Heru-Ur), sublimating the ego and its worldly desires (Set and Nebthet) which cause a person to become entrenched, as it were, in the physical realm of existence and to be oblivious to the higher planes of existence. Next it is necessary to discover intuitive wisdom (Aset), and this redeems the soul (Asar). Then it is possible for a human being to discover the mysteries of gross nature (Geb-Earth and Nut-Heavens), followed by the subtle aspect of Creation (Shu-Ether and Tefnut-Life Force energy). Having traversed this rout the aspirant discovers the force behind the Creation and Dissolution process (Ra) and the substratum from which the entire Creation and indeed human consciousness arises and is sustained (Nun).

The Process of Spiritual Enlightenment Based on the Anunian Tree of Life

Spiritual practice consists of developing the intuitional capacity, thereby discovering the true nature of Creation and Self, by understanding the illusoriness of the opposites of Creation (symbolized by the gods and goddesses) and the principles they represent. This leads a spiritual aspirant to develop spiritual aspiration and the qualities to go beyond the appearances of nature and to discover the Absolute existence which is the real basis for all that exists.

Ra-Tem
(Discovering the single essence which underlies the multiplicity of nature-Cosmic Consciousness.)
↑
Shu ⇔ Tefnut
(Discovering the more subtle aspects of nature.)
↑
Geb ⇔ Nut
(Discovering the gross aspects of nature.)
↑
Hetheru - Djehuti - Maat
(Spiritual Strength - Right Reasoning - Righteous Action
These higher spiritual qualities allow a spiritual aspirant to discover the mysteries of nature— to pierce the veil of illusion which prevents the discovery of the underlying essence of nature (Creation)—God.)
↑
Heru
(Advanced Spiritual Aspiration, having developed spiritual qualities
such as purity, truthfulness, honesty, etc., to pursue a spiritual lifestyle which will lead to success in life as well as spiritual enlightenment—self-discovery.)
↑
Asar ⇔ Aset
(Glimpses of the transcendental Divine Gory and initiation into the teachings of mystical wisdom.)
↑
Apuat
(Intellect-understanding that the world is perishable and that there is something else which is abiding. Also, understanding the real meaning of life and the real goal of life—to attain enlightenment. Understanding what is real from what is unreal, truth from untruth.)
↑
Asar ⇔ Nebthet
(Devotion to the Divine - Faith in the existence of the Divine Self
and in the idea that Enlightenment is a real possibility.)
↑
Set
(Sublimation of the ego and the lower self-control over the sex drive and the negative qualities such as anger, hatred, greed, covetousness, jealousy, etc.)

NOTE: For a more detailed study of the Pautti see the book *Anunian Theology* By Dr. Muata Ashby.

The Ancient Egyptian Origins of Christian Philosophy According to the Bible

During the reign of the Ramses' Kings, there is no record of an exodus by the Jews or by any other group. However, it would have still required divine intervention to neutralize the Ancient Egyptian forces. If this had occurred, some record would certainly have survived somewhere either in official records or in private (unofficial) writings such as the papyri or graffito, much of which survives to this day. There are many Ancient Egyptian records which have been found. They are private and graffito type records which expound on many other topics such as politics, the economy, sex, gossip, etc.

The Personality of Jesus and the Mystical Christ[287]

When studying Christianity we must differentiate the mythical Christhood figure from the Jesus of the church tradition. If we do we find that Christianity is a philosophy. But when we see it as a history, the teaching gets lost in the winds of time and conflict ensues over its origins and meaning. Christhood is a metaphor of a transcendental form of spiritual experience. Jesus is merely the human vehicle of the teaching. But this teaching is older than Jesus and older that Christianity itself.

Many Christians worship Jesus Christ as the Son of God, who lived as a man in order to bring God's message to the troubled world. They also believe he is one with God (see John 10:30), that he is at the same time truly Divine and truly human. It is believed that by his preaching and the sacrifice of his death and his resurrection, he revealed for all humankind the way to live righteously and find eternal life. The term "Son of God" was first applied to the king of Israel because he was regarded as having been chosen by God to lead the people. (2 Sm. 7, 14, Ps 2, 7). It is also used to denote the faithful Israelite. When used as a reference to Jesus, it relates his kingly nature as the Messiah as well as his faithfulness as an Israelite, but also as the actual offspring of God (Mt. 4, 1-11). In Ancient Egypt, every pharaoh (king) was referred to as the "Son of God" because they were seen as Heru, the son of Asar (Osiris) who looks after the people and protects them. The pharaoh was seen as the special chosen one of God, as stated in the following verse from the Ancient Egyptian Instructions of Meri-ka-ra:

> "From a million men God singled him (the pharaoh) out.
> A goodly office is kingship..."

While there is no direct evidence that any one person called *"Jesus"* ever existed except in the Gnostic texts and the orthodox church's New Testament. There is ample substantiation of the Christian story from a psycho-mythological perspective. Thus in the light of other evidences of how the early Christians coopted the symbols and teachings of other religions, the role ascribed to a personality called "Jesus" was a composite based on mystery religions which also included resurrection and savior themes. This idea is supported by the inclusion of various preexisting elements from ancient religions into the Christian myth. There were many sect leaders of the Jewish and non-Jewish groups who were variously called *"Teacher of Righteousness," "Master"* and so on, along with known prophets of the time who traveled widely and had also claimed to be the *"messiah"* and called themselves or were referred to by others as *"the Son of God."*

So ,there is no scholarly evidence ever produced to prove that at the time when the Roman General, Titus, conquered the city of Jerusalem (after 30 A.C.E.), there was a sect (cult) of a particular "Jesus." However, the Romans brought to an end various local Jewish customs which included human sacrifice. Therefore, while the reformers of Jewish religion, such as those who called themselves *messiah*s were pushing for changes, their teachings would have been repudiated by others whose positions in society, government and the economy would have been threatened by reform. Those who would have had the most to lose were the Roman authorities and the traditional Jewish religious leaders, both of whom would have viewed any successful sect as a threat to their authority and control over the Jewish people. The study of the period surrounding the early development of Christianity reveals one thing for certain: Jesus was not the first nor the only slain Jewish cult leader to claim to be the Messiah; there were several.

Christianity centers around the story of Jesus, an incarnation of God. It relates to his birth, life and suffering as well as the teachings that he gave to his disciples for the reformation of Jewish religion. He was therefore seen as a savior by many. After his death at the hands of the occupying Roman government that subjugated the Jewish people at the time, a following developed. His teachings were repudiated by the established Jewish leaders, but his following grew when charismatic leaders like St. Paul preached the Gospel about Jesus' life and the Roman emperors Justinian and Theodosius adopted Christianity as the state religion of Rome and outlawed all other religions. Jesus preached love, forgiveness and understanding. This teaching is commingled with the previous teachings presented in the Jewish Old Testament. The books of the Old Testament are said to have been written by Moses, however linguistic evidences indicate that they were actually written by Jewish scribes between the years 1000 B.C.E. and 100 B.C.E. The gospels recount how Jesus was born and his family persecuted. They had to flee into Egypt for safety. According to the Bible, Jesus grew up to the age of 30, and then he began to preach his message. However, the events of the years of his youth are not described. However, we are to surmise that he spent this time in Egypt because the Bible does not say he went anywhere else between the time he, Mary and Joseph went there seeking refuge and the time of his first ministry.

Jesus Goes Into Egypt

> Matthew - Chap. 2
> 13. And when they had departed, behold, the angel of the Lord appeareth to Joseph in a dream, saying, Arise, and take the young child and his mother, and flee into Egypt, and be thou there until I bring thee word: for Herod will seek the young child to destroy him.
> 14 When he arose, he took the young child and his mother by night, and departed into Egypt:
> 15 And was there until the death of Herod: that it might be fulfilled which was spoken from the Lord by the prophet, saying, Out of Egypt have I called my son.

The quote above from the Christian Bible shows that the early development of Jesus' life took place in Ancient Egypt. In reference to the journey of Jesus into Egypt, the Apocryphal Gospels[113] state that when the Virgin Mary and her son arrived in Egypt, *"there was a movement and quaking throughout all the land, and all the idols fell down from their pedestals and were broken in pieces."* It is further written that the nobles and Priests consulted with a certain Priest, *"a devil" used to speak from out of an idol."* When they asked him about the meaning of the disturbances he told them that the footsteps of the son of the *"secret and hidden God"* had fallen upon the land of Egypt. They accepted his determination and then set forth to make a figure of this God.

Jesus of Nazareth (c. 4 B.C.E. - c. 30 A.C.E.) is generally held to be the founder of Christianity. Jesus began to preach the teachings of salvation, and was thereafter referred to as Jesus Christ or Jesus the Christ. The title combines a well-known Hebrew term, Jesus, and a Greek translation of a Hebrew word for messiah, Christ. Thus, the word "Jesus," originally meaning in Hebrew: Joshua, "God is salvation," is combined with "Christ," which comes from a Greek translation for messiah, meaning "anointed one," thus rendering "the anointed savior." The messiah was a prophesied and long expected king and deliverer of Israel. Jesus was supposed to have been born around 4 B.C.E. All that is known of the life of Jesus comes from the study of the four Gospels of Matthew, Mark, Luke, and John, which are the first four books of the New Testament in the Christian Bible, along with the newly discovered texts from Egypt and Palestine. There is no other information corroborating his existence and works.

The Gospels contain little information about what Jesus looked like and what occurred in his early life prior to his initiation into the mysteries of mystical religion by John the Baptist. The Christian tradition (writings after the original Christian texts) developed several stories related to the childhood of Jesus, but these were created hundreds of years after the cited death of Jesus. However, there are three important sources which shed some light on these questions. The first is the Bible itself. In the books of Matthew and Luke, the genealogy of Jesus is presented. The story is given of Noah and his three sons: Shem, Ham and Japheth. Each son had his own wife. Noah, his wife, sons and close family relations survived the world flood due to the grace of God, and then they repopulated the earth. The Sumerian story of Gilgamesh contains a section which includes an account of the world flood that resembles the Biblical story very closely. Historians and scholars have therefore speculated that the writers of the Bible were influenced by the Sumerians. According to the Bible, in Genesis Chapter 10, the children of Ham populated ancient Africa. Ham became the father of Mizraim (Egypt), Cush (Ethiopia), Phut (Africans in Libya) and Canaan (Palestine). The Ancient Egyptian records verify that all lands from Ethiopia to the Caucasus mountains was under the control of the Egyptian government at several times through history. The entire area was populated by descendents of Ham (Ethiopians, Egyptians and Canaanites). This is the first indication of Jesus' ancestry. Since he was a Canaanite he was a descendent of the bloodline of Ham. However, the Bible is even more specific on this issue as we will see.

Determining Jesus' ancestry is important in understanding the origins and meaning of his teachings. In Matthew, Chapter 1:1-16, the genealogy of Jesus is given. You will note that we have already touched on some of the following histories in previous chapters. The genealogy presented in Matthew traces Jesus' ancestry all the way back to Abraham who is considered as the patriarch of the Jews. He lived in the ancient city known as Ur, close to the Euphrates river. Ur was situated close to southern end of the Euphrates. In ancient times this was known as the land of the Elamites. Elam[104] was a son of Shem, the son of Noah. Ur means "eternity." It was an area referred to in the Bible as a province east of Babylon and northeast of the lower Tigris.[288] While Shem was considered as the patriarch of the Semitic races of people, one should bear in mind that the appearance of the people in modern times should not be taken as a reflection of the ancient past. For instance, the people who inhabit the land of Egypt today bear little resemblance to the Ancient Egyptians. The reports from ancient historians will assist our study. Herodotus traveled the area in question. He reported that the Elamites were relatives of the Ethiopians:

> "They (Elamites) were just like the southern Ethiopians, except for their language and their hair; their hair is straight while that of the Ethiopians in Libya is the crimpest and curliest in the world."[289]

This account points to the ethnic relationship between northeast Africa and Mesopotamia. Other accounts presented earlier in this text showed how the entire area from Northeast Africa to Southern Asia was at one time, in the distant past, ethnically related. Once again, the change in hair texture, from "wooly" to "straight" can be accounted for by environmental factors. However, the presence or absence of wooly hair is not necessarily a sign which denotes all Africans because they can be either. This is one of the great misconceptions that has fostered ignorance in all peoples (white, black, brown etc.).

We learned earlier that this area (Eden) was populated by the descendents of Ham. Therefore, Jesus and all Jews of the time were Africans or Africans mixed with Asiatics, but not European as the modern iconography such as that which is promoted in movies or European art suggests. Jesus was, at least in part, a member of the dark-skinned group of Noah's ancestors. This is supported by the Bible itself. In Genesis 38 it is stated that Judah begot Perez by Tamar. Perez (Perets, Perez or Pharez {peh'-rets}) was the twin son with Zarah of Judah by Tamar and an ancestor of two families, of Judah, the Hezronites and Hamulites; from the Hezronites came the royal line of David and Christ. Among his ancestors, one in particular ties him into the line of Ham directly. Matthew 1:5 states that "And Salmon begot Boaz of Rahab." Tamar and Rahab were Canaanite women. As we learned earlier, Canaan was the son of Ham and therefore, he and all of his descendents are part of the Hamitic or African group of peoples if we use the classification system of the Bible. Thus, the blood line of the Bible indicates that Jesus is at least part African in his ancestry. This genealogy therefore supports the descriptions given in Revelation 1, Daniel 7, Ezekiel 8 and by Josephus.

Revelation 1
14 His head and [his] hairs [were] white like wool, as white as snow; and his eyes [were] as a flame of fire;
15 And his feet like fine brass, as if they burned in a furnace; and his voice as the sound of many waters.

Daniel 7
9. I beheld till the thrones were placed, and the Ancient of days did sit, whose garment [was] white as snow, and the hair of his head like the pure wool: his throne [was like] the fiery flame, [and] his wheels [as] burning fire.

Ezekiel 8

1. And it came to pass in the sixth year, in the sixth [month], in the fifth [day] of the month, [as] I sat in my house, and the elders of Judah sat before me, that the hand of the Lord God fell there upon me.

---

[104] Elam was a biblical name for an ancient Persian province of Susiana, on the northern coast of the Persian Gulf, or for the north Western part of Susiana.

2 Then I beheld, and lo a likeness as the appearance of fire: from the appearance of his loins even downward, fire; and from his loins even upward, as the appearance of brightness, as the color of amber.

The writings of one Jewish Historian, Josephus (AD 37 or 38-circa 101), of Jerusalem concur with the African ancestry of Jesus as he describes Christ as "a man of simple appearance, mature age, dark skin with little hair."

The legends of a curse upon the ancestors of Ham stem from the misinterpretation of the story of Noah and his three sons. According to the canonical Bible texts, Ham saw his father naked and drunk. Because of this, Noah cursed, not Ham, but one of Ham's sons, Canaan. The rabbinical concepts as to how the Africans became black came well after the Jews had left Egypt and had mixed with Europeans. There were many concepts which all sought to somehow show that the occupants of the "Holy Land" were not worthy of this honor. Thus, they set out to discredit the peoples of dark complexion. One such Jewish concept held that Ham had sexual relations in the Ark and violated a rule set forth by Noah. For this reason his seed was cursed with ugliness and darkness (The Midrash Rabbah, Genesis, Noah, Chapter 37.)[290]

Heru and Jesus

In the same way that the Kamitan divinity Heru was persecuted after his birth by the his uncle, Set, who came to the throne as king by murdering Heru's father (Asar, Osiris) and usurping the throne, Jesus was also persecuted after his birth because the ruling king feared that he would take the throne which was rightfully his. So, like Heru, Jesus was also viciously persecuted by the ruling king (of Egypt and Jerusalem, respectively) from the time of his birth, because he was also prophesied to be the next righteous king who would end the injustices of the existing king. Both of these characters were challenged by evil in the form of a demoniac character, Set in Ancient Egypt and Lucifer in the Canaanite Christian myth. The concept of the Eucharist as being the body and blood of the martyred savior and the concept of resurrection already existed in Ancient Egyptian religion before Jesus came into Egypt as the Bible recounts. Both Jesus (Matthew 14:26) and Heru (see below) were said to walk on water, and they are related to the same rising star (Sirius). Also, the birth of Heru and the birth of Jesus are celebrated on the same day.

> (Heru is) "the resurrection and the life," "The anointed one," "The WORD made flesh," "The KRST (Christ)," "The WORD made TRUTH," "The one who comes to fulfill the LAW," "The destroyer of the enemies[105] of his father" "The one who walks upon the water of his Father"[291]

Thus, myths surrounding these two saviors point to a special connection between Neterian Religion which worshipped Heru as the incarnation of the Supreme Being (Asar), and Christianity which worships Jesus Christ as an embodiment or incarnation of God (the word of God) on earth. The story surrounding the birth of a savior was never intended to be understood in a factual or literal sense or as referring to a single character or personality in history. There is something more important, beyond the actual facts themselves, which the ancient sages sought to convey. Heru and Jesus Christ are symbols of the Soul in each of us which is the innermost Self that is constantly engaged in a battle of opposites (duality) within our minds and physical bodies over good-evil, virtue-vice, light-dark, ying-yang, positive-negative, prosperity-adversity, etc. Principally, we are to understand that the concept of a "savior" is a metaphor for that principle within each one of us that seeks to be saved from the clutches of the ego (that aspect of human nature that promotes a sense of individuality based on the psycho-physical (mind and body) personality, of which egoism {anger, hatred, envy, jealousy, fear, anxiety, lust, insecurity, greed, etc.} is the result), and discover true peace and happiness. It is you, your deeper Self, who is the incarnating soul, and it is you who are persecuted by your ego because of your egoistic interaction with the world. But it is also you, who through your own intellect expanded by wisdom (understanding the teachings) and self-effort directed toward the Divine, can effect your own salvation and triumph over the forces of evil (the ego and egoism {selfishness, greed, hatred, lust, etc.}).

The correspondence in the birth stories of Heru and Jesus is only one correlation out of many which point to a common origin of these traditions. If these myths are understood literally (factually), then it

---

[105] ENEMIES: ignorance, lies, deception, too much talking, covetousness, depravity, selfishness, etc.

would be odd to discover exact events which match in almost every detail in different lands. The chances of this occurring are remote at best. However, if they are seen as mythological stories with deeper messages, then we are able to see that there is a common origin and that these stories refer not to an event which occurred long ago, but to an ongoing process which is occurring in the life of every human being, even now.

Savior from Ancient Egypt	Savior from Judaic/Christian Arabia	Savior from Indian Hinduism
Heru	Jesus	Krishna

Besides the adoption of Ancient Egyptian philosophies by the early Christians, there are ample evidences of co-optation and adoption of the Ancient Egyptian symbols and architecture as well. The following are some of the most commonly found in Egypt today.

Below: Stele of the Great Sphinx in Giza, Egypt, showing one of the most typical and important Ancient Egyptian symbols, the winged sundisk with the double serpents.

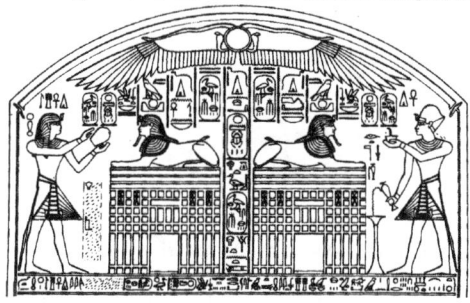

Below left: The same stele style can be seen in many Ancient Egyptian monuments and panels commemorating royal events and the spiritual virtues of specific individuals, and also Heru.
Below right: Christian stele (now at the Coptic museum in Cairo) shows the same architectural form, the winged sundisk with the double serpents and the Jesus in place of Heru.

THE AFRICAN ORIGINS OF CIVILIZATION, RELIGION AND YOGA SPIRITUALITY

Below: Front court of the Temple of Hetheru in Denderah showing one of the earliest Christian churches (center structure – see arrow) ever built (in or outside of Africa) using appropriated blocks from the main Temple and surrounding buildings.

The Christian Maltese Cross in the Temple of Aset

Below left: The Christian Maltese Cross, ✠, was carved into the walls of the Temple of Aset in Philae, Egypt, over the preexisting hieroglyphic text.
Below right: An altar was set up in the hypostyle hall of the Temple of Aset where some of the earliest Christian masses were held. Thus, the earliest Christian churches were converted Ancient Egyptian Temples.

The Christian Crosses and the Mystical Ankh Cross

THE AFRICAN ORIGINS OF CIVILIZATION, RELIGION AND YOGA SPIRITUALITY

Greeks from the early Christian times said that the Egyptian Ankh, ☥, was "common to the worship of Christ and Serapis (Greek name for Asar). In Roman times, Saint Helena (c. 255-330), the mother of Roman Emperor Constantine-I (Constantine the Great) became a Christian around the time her son became emperor of Rome. Early church historians relate many stories about Helena. One of the stories was that Helena inspired the building of the Church of the Nativity in Bethlehem. Later tradition says that she founded the true cross on which Christ died. This was the Tau Cross, T, which resembles the Druid crosses. The Maltese Cross, ✠, was related to the gods and goddesses of Malta before it was adopted by Christianity. One of the most important symbolic references of the Christian cross or "Latin Cross," ✝, is that its vertical axis symbolizes the vertical movement of spiritual discipline (self-effort) which implies true transformation in all areas (mental, spiritual, physical) of life. The vertical movement pierces the horizontal axis of the cross, a symbol of time and space (lateral movement, reincarnation, stagnation, etc.). Other important crosses used by the Christian church were: Early crosses, ⵑ ⳨ �; Anchor crosses, ⚓ ⚓ ⚓; Monograms of Christ, ☸ ✳ ✴; Greek cross, ✚; Celtic cross, ♀; Eastern cross, ☦; Craponee Swastika cross, ✛ (similar to the Indian and Persian swastika, 卐). Originally, the swastika symbol was an ancient sign used to denote the manner in which spiritual energy flows. It was not until the Nazi party of Germany adopted it in 1935 that the symbol was used for promoting hatred, racism, murder and greed. Prior to this time it was an ancient cosmic or religious symbol used by the Vedic-Aryans, Hindus and Greeks. The Swastika continues to be used today by various hate groups which seek to establish white supremacy. The Swastika is formed by a cross with the ends of the arms bent at right angles in either a clockwise or a counterclockwise direction, denoting the form of energy being manifested.

Above: The Pylons of the Temple of Isis at Agilkia Island (Aswan) in Egypt, Africa.

Below left: two styles of the Ancient Egyptian Ankh.
Below right: Coptic Cross (from the Coptic Museum).

Below: Present day Coptic-Christian church in Luxor, Egypt (picture taken in the year 2000 A.C.E.) which makes use of the classic New Kingdom archway, and the Ancient Egyptian Ankh in its ancient form, ☥ (also see above), alongside the "Latin Cross," ✞.

The following table shows the correlations between Christian philosophy and the preexisting Ancient Egyptian philosophy.

Table 18: The Teachings of Jesus and the Teachings of Ancient Egypt

The Commandments of Jesus	Teachings of Ancient Egypt
Mark 12 28. And one of the scribes came, and having heard them reasoning together, and perceiving that he had answered them well, asked him, Which is the first commandment of all?	
29 And Jesus answered him, The first of all the commandments [is], Hear, O Israel; The Lord our God is one Lord:	4. His unity is Absolute. Amun (God) is One, One [without a second].†
30 And thou shalt love the Lord thy God with all thy heart, and with all thy soul, and with all thy mind, and with all thy strength: this [is] the first commandment.	46. Thy beauties take possession of and carry away all hearts [minds], and love for Thee make all arms to relax, Thy beautiful form make the hands to tremble, and all hearts [minds] melt at the sight of Thee. †
*In the First Letter of John in the Bible it is stated that God is love: 1 John 4:8 8 He that loveth not knoweth not God; for God is love. 1 John 4:16 16 And we have known and believed the love that God hath to us. God is love; and he that dwelleth in love dwelleth in God, and God in him.	In Ancient Egypt love of God was so important that God was referred to as: "Beloved one or love itself God- *Merr*"[132] **(i.e. God is Love)**
31 And the second [is] like, [namely] this, Thou shalt love thy neighbor as thyself. There is no other commandment greater than these.	(30) Set your goodness before people, Then you are greeted by all; One welcomes the what is good, Spits upon what is bad. (31) Guard your tongue from harmful speech, Then others will love you. You will find your place in the Sanctuary, the house of God, Be kind to the poor. Get thee a seat in the sanctuary. Be strong to do the commandment of God. You will share in the offerings of your lord. ‡
Jesus on prayer	**Teachings of Sage Ani on prayer**
Matthew 6:6 But, thou, when thou prayest, enter into thy closet, and when thou hast shut thy door, pray to thy Father who is in secret; and thy Father who seeth in secret shall reward thee openly.	Do not raise your voice in the house of god, He abhors shouting; (too much talking) Pray by yourself with a loving heart, Whose every word is in secret. He will grant your needs, He will hear your words, He will accept your offerings. † Ancient Egyptian Hymns of Amun. (c. 2,500-1,500 B.C.E.) While not framed in the form of an order it promotes the same ideal but from the perspective of developing divine love in the aspirant as opposed to fear and blind obedience. ‡ Ancient Egyptian Teachings of Sage Amenemope. The concept of being good to others implies caring for them and loving them; this is a fundamental aspect of Maat philosophy within Ancient Egyptian religion.

THE AFRICAN ORIGINS OF CIVILIZATION, RELIGION AND YOGA SPIRITUALITY

Differences Between Neterian Religion and Orthodox Christianity

There is one important difference between Ancient Egyptian Mythology and Yoga and other mystical systems. The idea of God being the Father who begets the Son, who is His *Paraclete* (advocate or intercessor) and revealer, occurs first and with most primacy in Egypt in the mythology of Nebertcher and Asar. While Buddha, the founder of Buddhism and Krishna, the revered divinity of Hinduism are *Avatars*, incarnations of God, Heru in Ancient Egypt was the reincarnation of Asar, his father, who was himself an incarnation of the High God Ra who was, in this particular mythology, referred to as the Absolute Self. At the same time, Heru is the symbol of the human soul, the essential nature and the innate {hero/heroine} within every human being. In much the same way, Jesus is the revealer and Paraclete of the Father, the Lord, and the Holy Spirit. The original idea of Avatarism was that from time to time God manifests himself in order to restore virtue in the world, to reform religion in a sense.

The acceptance, adoption and transformation of religious teachings from Ancient Egypt, India and other traditions into the particular form of Christianity espoused by Rome and the Byzantine Empire fostered the development of new terms for previously existing concepts. The terms used in the New Testament and the Gnostic Gospels, *Kingdom of God* or *Kingdom of Heaven,* are new terms not found previously in Jewish texts. Most often the Kingdom is described in parable form, but if we look past the facts of the mythology itself, a mystical meaning directed towards the individual is discovered. As such these terms convey a concept which is in exact agreement with the Egyptian, Vedantic, Buddhist, and Taoist understanding that the realm of the Supreme Self is not in some far distant location which we must aspire to reach, but that it is everywhere, all around us and within us. What we must strive to do is realize this fact through virtuous living as well as growth in spiritual knowledge and wisdom.

As previously discussed, the Ancient Egyptian gods and goddesses are called *neteru,* and they emanate from *Pa Neter (Nebertcher),* the Supreme Divinity. A very important aspect of Neterian Religion and ritual can be related to Christian myth and ritual. This aspect is the consumption of the gods and goddesses or *neters* as a means of *becoming like onto them* in Ancient Egyptian mythology and ritual. However, it does not occur with the same intensity and emphasis as in the Ancient Egyptian ritual and religious thought which appear as early as the *Pyramid Texts* (5,500 B.C.E.) in the Ancient Egyptian religious scriptures. In Christianity this notion was transformed into the idea of the *Eucharist*.[292]

The use of the word *Amen (Amun)* in the Ancient Egyptian religion and later in the Christian religion requires further exploration here. The word Amen in Ancient Egyptian mythology connotes the Absolute Reality or transcendental Deity (Supreme Being). In the Hebrew religion the word Amen is usually explained or defined as an interjection meaning *so be it*. It is used at the end of a prayer or to express approval. However, in Egyptian myth and symbolism, Amen signifies an extremely sophisticated and elaborate explanation of the absolute and transcendental mystery behind all physical phenomena, in much the same way that the term *Brahman* is used in Hindu mythology and religion.

The mystical concept of Amun or Amen is the central theme of not only Ancient Egyptian religion and mystical philosophy, but also of every world religion. Having been intertwined with religious iconography and ritualism, the idea of an "eternal witness" has been mythologized by the Sages of ancient times in such a fashion that it may be possible to discover ever-increasing layers of the mystery behind it. The name *Amun (Amen)* appears in the remotest times of Egyptian history and came to prominence in the ancient city of *Waset or* "Thebes," Egypt. The mysteries of Amun represent a quintessence of Ancient Egyptian philosophy concerning the nature of the unmanifest aspect of all existence and the understanding of human consciousness. It contains within it the teachings which pre-date all other similar teachings from other cultures. These teachings speak of God as an unmanifest, nameless, formless Pure Consciousness, which supports Creation.

Thus, in Ancient Egypt, the concept of the ultimate and Absolute Reality behind all physical manifestations was called *Amn, Amun, Nebertcher, Pa Neter, Asar, Aset* and *Ptah*. In Hindu mythology it is *Brahman, Shiva, Krishna, Vishnu, Kali or Rama*; to the Taoists it is *The Tao;* in Judaism it is referred to as *Yahweh;* in Islam it is *Allah;* in Christianity it is *God* and the *Kingdom of Heaven;* and in modern physics it is *energy.* There are, however, deeper meanings to the symbolic names given to explain the Absolute. They hold formulas, which convey mystical teachings about human beings and the nature of existence. Nebertcher carries with it various additional attributes referring to the Supreme Divinity: "All-encompassing," "Utmost Limit," "All Being," "All Powerful," etc. Nebertcher, as a name for the Supreme Being, appears in the Coptic texts and the attributes associated with this name were transferred to the idea of God Almighty of Christianity.

Like the Ancient Egyptian Trinity (Asar, Aset and Heru), the Christian Trinity incorporates deep psycho-mythological implications. It is important to note that the Trinity concept is a "fundamental" concept of Ancient Egyptian religion which the Jews and Christians received through their association with the Ancient Egyptians. God the Father is the hidden creator, while the Son (Jesus) is the incarnating spirit, the body of creation. The Holy Spirit is the enlivening force, which vivifies the creation. Every human being is an aspect of this Trinity, and the universe is also an aspect of the Trinity. The human ego, mind and body are the Son who suffers and the Holy Spirit is the force by which the soul enlivens the ego and body. With this understanding, God the Father is the witnessing consciousness, which supports the existence of the Son and of the Life Force energy of Creation.

In the original understanding of the early Christian theologians, the three aspects of the Trinity (Father, Son, and the Holy Spirit) were seen as equal in power and importance and as being one in their underlying essence. However, due to the zealous destruction of competing theologies, the Orthodox Christians developed a distorted view of Divinity. Only the dualistic, male-oriented view of the Trinity was understood and promoted, although reformers such as *Arius*[106] sought to establish the non-dualistic view.

If one were to strip from the mind the mental concepts of duality which have been engendered by an elementary understanding of religion, the non-dual reality will emerge. This means that the spiritual aspirant must leave behind the understanding of the outer form of the Trinity and discover the underlying essence. When this is accomplished, the essence of the Trinity is discovered to be the same as that of every human being. When Jesus says, *I and the Father are One*, he is not referring to two individual personalities (Father and Son) which are one in a spiritual sense. Although this is certainly true, he is referring to the fact that there is only one being in existence and this being transcends the personality of Jesus and the Father. So take away the "Father" image and take away the "Son" image and what is left in the mind is the underlying basis of these concepts. That underlying basis is the ground upon which all mental concepts exist. It is this ground which is "one" with all things. This is what is referred to as the Transcendental Self or the Supreme Being, etc. This is what is eternal, while the father and Son are mere temporary manifestations of that. The mental concepts are only images of this ultimate ground, which has taken on a particular name and form. The name and form are related to time and space, but everything in time and space is temporal and illusory. In this ultimate ground there are no opposites. The opposites only seem to exist at the superficial conscious level. Therefore, in reality all names and forms have the same underlying basis and are composed of the same material: thoughts. The Self underlies all thoughts and, therefore, the Self is the goal of all spiritual movements.

Early Christian, Roman Christian Conquest Periods and the Closing of Egyptian Temples

The Roman Period in Kamit lasted from c.30 B.C.E.-395 A.C.E. when Rome disintegrated due to internal corruption and foreign wars. The early orthodox Christians (300-450 A.C.E.), who came into Egypt from Rome and the Byzantine realm were not disposed to live side by side with the native people who continued to worship the Ancient Egyptian gods and goddesses. There was a tenuous harmony with the Muslims who came into Egypt in the latter part of the 1st millennium (650-1000 A.C.E.) because they were seen to be worshipping essentially the same God. In the case of the Ancient Egyptian gods and goddesses, the already dogmatic and fanatical early orthodox Christians (not the Gnostic Christians), who had themselves been persecuted for over 300 years, now began to persecute people of all other religions and even other Christian sects that did not agree with the particular form of Christianity approved by the Roman Church. Therefore, even the Gnostic Christians, who had developed mystical Christianity in Egypt over 300 years earlier, were also persecuted. The orthodox Christian misunderstanding about the symbolism and especially the sexual imagery in Ancient Egyptian iconography and the instigation by the Roman government, coupled with the force of the Roman army were all instrumental to the development of a particular hatred and ensuing violence against the Ancient Egyptian Temples, which by now had spread across the Roman empire. The Temples of Aset (Isis) and Asar-Hapi (Serapis) were especially favored in the Roman Empire up to that time. If anyone wonders why the Ancient Egyptian Temple system persisted through the Persian conquest, the Assyrian conquest, the Greek conquest, and the Roman conquest, but came to a close during the emergence of the Roman Catholic Church, they have no further to look than the following statements by the leaders of the early church.

---

[106] Arianism, theological stance heretical to Christianity based on the teachings of Arius (c. 250-336 A.C.E.). Random House Encyclopedia Copyright (C) 1983,1990 by Random House Inc.

> "What is now called the Christian religion has existed among the Ancients and was not absent from the beginning of the human race until Christ came in the flesh from which time the true religion which was already in existence began to be called Christian."
>
> -St. Augustine

See appendix on Ancient Egyptian origin of monasticism

The reputed founder of Christian-Egyptian monasticism, Saint Anthony, led his followers in active attacks against the Ancient Egyptian Temples which practiced the ancient Egyptian religion. The ignorance, intolerance and denigration of the Kamitan Temples and their images are readily evident in the following quote by Saint Anthony.

> "Which is better, to confess the cross or to attribute adulteries and pederastys to these so called gods, beasts, reptiles and the images of men? The Christians, by their faith in God prove that the demons whom the Egyptians consider gods are no gods! The Christians trample them underfoot and drive them out for what they are, deceivers and corruptors of men. Through Jesus-Christ our lord, Amen"

Once the persecuted, in the late Roman times when the Roman emperors adopted Christianity as the state religion, the Christians murdered pagan Priests, Priestesses and leaders and led a persecution against all non-Christians, forcing new symbols on the populace. The term "Fundamentalism" is a modern interpretation of orthodox Christianity, but as we have seen its roots are deeply embedded into the fabric of the Roman Catholic Church. This was expressed later in history as the Crusades, the destruction of Native American culture, the African slave trade, African missionary movements and efforts to convert peoples around the world to Christianity and at the same time eradicate all other religions, something which has angered many nations around the world including China and the Muslim countries. Due to the persecution and wonton destruction of the Ancient Egyptian scriptures along with the murder of those who were knowledgeable about the symbolism, the initiatic (mystical) teachings were lost to the orthodox Western Culture from this time on but they remained dormant and embedded in the traditions of the church itself as well as in "pagan" religions and mystical sects that carried on the ancient traditions as best they could. The wisdom related to the Ancient Egyptian symbolism such as that displayed by Dionysus the Areopagite was misunderstood and misrepresented by the orthodox Church leaders in favor of the simple but limited symbolism of orthodox Christianity. The Gnostic Christianity followed more closely the Ancient Egyptian teachings.[107]

> "If anyone suggests that it is disgraceful to fashion base images of the Divine and most Holy orders, it is sufficient to answer that the most holy Mysteries are set forth in two modes: one by means of similar and sacred representations akin to their nature, and the other to unlike forms designed with every possible discordance ... Discordant symbols are more appropriate representations of the Divine because the human mind tends to cling to the physical form of representation believing for example that the Divine are "golden beings or shining men flashing like lightning." But lest this error befall us, the wisdom of the venerable sages leads us through disharmonious dissimilitudes, not allowing our irrational nature to become attached to those unseemly images ... Divine things may not be easily accessible to the unworthy, nor may those who earnestly contemplate the Divine symbols dwell upon the forms themselves as final truth."
>
> – Dionysus the Areopagite

Even mysticism did not escape the process of co-optation. The same Dionysus the Areopagite who wrote the statement above, which is in direct contradiction with that of Saint Anthony (above), was accepted into the Christian Church albeit in an altered form. Traditional Christian literature and scholarship have recognized St. Paul as the first great Christian mystic. The New Testament writings best known for their deeply mystical emphasis are Paul's letters and the Gospel of John (John 10:30-34). Christian mysticism, as a philosophical system, is derived from Neo-Platonism through the writings of Dionysus the Areopagite, or Pseudo-Dionysus. The original Dionysus the Areopagite, who wrote the statement above, lived in the 1st century A.C.E. He became first bishop of Athens and was martyred about 95 A.C.E. He is often confused with the Pseudo-Dionysus (c. 500 A.C.E) who created mystical writings

---

[107] See the book *The Mystical Journey From Jesus to Christ* by Muata Ashby

using the name of Dionysus the Areopagite. He (the first Dionysus) was later canonized as a Catholic Saint. Dionysus was converted to Christianity when he heard Paul preach the sermon concerning the nature of "the unknown God" on the Hill of Mars or Areopagus in Athens, as described in Acts 17:15-34. However, while some aspects of mysticism can still be found in the Christian church, they are heavily veiled and misunderstood. They are also de-emphasized by the church leadership as anomalies and thus, negated and consequently nullified in the course of Church activities.[108]

Most often the term fundamentalism is used to describe non-Christian religions, especially militant Islamic groups. However, the term fundamentalism refers to a movement within the Protestant churches in the United States of America. It attempts to maintain what its believers consider to be traditional interpretations of the Christian faith. Fundamentalism arose in reaction to what was seen as modernist or liberal trends within Protestantism, which began in the later 19th century. The conservatives began to create conferences and schools which emphasized literal interpretations of the Bible as opposed to mythological, metaphorical and mystical interpretations. The Fundamentalist movement received the name from "The Fundamentals," a series of small books produced by conservative scholars that were widely distributed in 1910-12 which supposedly contained the basic issues defining the Christian faith. The doctrines most emphasized by fundamentalists are:

1- The divinely inspired and infallible nature of the Bible.
2- The Trinity.
3- The immediate creation of Creation by the command of God.
4- Man's fall into depravity.
5- The necessity for salvation of being "Born Again" by faith in Christ.
6- Christ's deity, virgin birth, miracle-working power and substitutionary atonement for man.
7- Christ's physical resurrection, ascension, and imminent pre-millennial Second Coming.
8- The physical resurrection of man for Heaven or Hell.
9- Domestic and foreign evangelism
10- Strong opposition to evolution, Communism, and ecumenism.[293]

Thus, the oversimplified ideal of having faith and worshipping God the Father and Jesus as opposed the elaborate system of Ancient Egyptian gods and goddesses was palatable to the masses of people who had no capacity to enter into the years of training necessary to become an Egyptian Priest or Priestess. Further, the Christian exclusion of women from the Priesthood and from a primary position in the religion was agreeable to the Roman leaders whose culture, coupled with that of the Greeks, professed male dominance, unlike the Ancient Egyptian culture and religion. The fundamentalist concept of religion is necessarily in contradiction with mysticism and religions which make use of polytheistic monotheism (many deities to represent aspects of the one Supreme Being) such as the Ancient Egyptian and Hindu religions. This is because the fundamentalist model of religion is idolatrous. Orthodox religion is actually idolatrous because it espouses the belief that there is one God, one religion, one form or iconography, etc. Mystical religions do not hold this ideal. They see divinity as universal and un-circumscribable by any image or form. Therefore, while there can be many forms, they all are understood to be expressions of the same Supreme Being operating everywhere and through all religions. The Christian missionary movement has followed the Religious Conquest Pattern of:

1st -Peaceful introduction of the religion,
2nd -Where conversion is slow they begin to denigrate the other religions,
3rd -The denigration turns to hatred and statements inciting violence (hostility) and the illegitimacy of other religions,
4th -Moving actively to violently close or destroy the Temples or establishments of their religious rivals and finally,
5th -If people do not convert after their Temple or place of worship was destroyed, co-opt their symbols, rituals and traditions, forcing them to gradually believe they are worshipping the

---

[108] See the book *The Mystical Journey From Jesus to Christ* by Muata Ashby

new divinity in some of the same ways they venerated the old (ancient). The people are to be compelled to practice the new religion. This hat was done by the Portuguese missionaries and traders in Africa in the 15th century A.C.E. which began the African European African slave trade.[294] The Spanish followed this pattern in the treatment of Native Americans in the 16th century. Over a period of 1-3 generations of being deprived the opportunity to worship in the old fashion, in the old language and with the old understanding, the old religion is forgotten. Some of the rituals, symbols and traditions remain but the original meaning is forgotten, and whatever prestige was due to the old religion is now ascribed to the new.

So, where outright destruction of Temples and murdering of Priests and Priestesses failed to convert people who persisted in carrying on the ancient religious traditions even when the Priests and Priestesses had been killed or forced to leave the church, the Christian zealots had an alternative plan. The evidence given by the Christian tradition itself and its own documents suggests that images such as the cross (Ancient Egyptian Ankh), the dove (Ancient Egyptian sundisk), the Black Mary or Madonna (Ancient Egyptian Aset), and the concepts of the resurrection, the eucharist, the birthday of the savior Jesus (Ancient Egyptian Heru), and many others[109] were taken directly from Ancient Egyptian religion, renamed (rededicated as it were) and used in Christian worship. This practice was consistent with the practice of inculturation, also known as co-optation,[110] the process of adopting symbols and rituals from other religions and calling them Christian, which were officially confirmed and endorsed as church policy by Pope St Gregory the Great, in a letter given to Priests written in 601 A.C.E.:

> "It is said that the men of this nation are accustomed to sacrificing oxen. It is necessary that this custom be converted into a Christian rite. On the day of the dedication of the [pagan] Temples thus changed into churches, and similarly for the festivals of the saints, whose relics will be placed there, you should allow them, as in the past, to build structures of foliage around these same churches. They shall bring to the churches their animals, and kill them, no longer as offerings to the devil, but for Christian banquets in name and honor of God, to whom after satiating themselves, they will give thanks. Only thus, by preserving for men some of the worldly joys, will you lead them thus more easily to relish the joys of the spirit."

The Bible appears to condone the killing of people even though one of the Ten Commandments of God to Moses seems to prohibit such an act. Therefore, it is not surprising to see people of the Judeo-Christian faith fighting in wars, engaging in acts of psychological violence, criminal behavior, etc., while professing non-violence. In this the first Muslims thought they were superior, in that they exhorted a strict moral code. However, they too inflicted great pain and suffering to many people while the same time converting them to Islam. The book of Exodus in the Christian Bible, Verses 32:25-28, provide insight into one of the examples that may be found, that promote violence and even killing (murder) of those who do not submit to the religion. Moses went to commune with God and when he returned from the conference in which he received the tablets with the Ten Commandments, he found the people turning towards the idols of Ancient Egypt. He instructed that all who wanted to follow him should get on one side and others on the other and then he ordered, "on God's instruction," the children of Levi to kill the unbelievers.

Exodus 32 25:28

25 And when Moses saw that the people were naked; (for Aaron had made them naked unto their shame among their enemies:)
26 Then Moses stood in the gate of the camp, and said, Who is on the LORD'S side? let him come unto me. And all the sons of Levi gathered themselves together unto him.
27 And he said unto them, Thus saith the LORD God of Israel, Put every man his sword by his side, and go in and out from gate to gate throughout the camp, and slay every man his brother, and every man his companion, and every man his neighbour.

---

[109] See the book *The Mystical Journey From Jesus to Christ* by Muata Ashby
[110] To neutralize or win over (an independent minority, for example) through assimilation into an established group or culture.

28 And the children of Levi did according to the word of Moses: and there fell of the people that day about three thousand men.

The Byzantine Period of Christian rule over Egypt lasted from 395-642 A.C.E. This period meant Christian rulership from Constantinople in Turkey as part of the Eastern Church. The church suffered a schism when Rome disintegrated and for a time there were two popes, one in Rome and the other in Constantinople. Due to invading hoards such as that of Attila the Hun and others and also due to internal corruption and disputes over the Christian doctrine, another schism took place and Egypt separated from Constantinople and from Rome. So a third Pope was selected as head of the Coptic Church in Egypt. The Coptic churches in Egypt still, to this day, choose their own Pope.

Overview of the Judeo-Christian Manifest Destiny Philosophy

The term "Manifest Destiny" is a phrase that was coined in 1845 by John L O'Sullivan. It implied that there was a divine sanction for the United States of America *"to overspread the continent allotted by Providence for the free development of our multiplying millions."* The concept was used to justify most US territorial gains. Texas and California were shortly afterwards annexed by the US.[295] The concept has also been used to describe other similar statements or overtures preceding expansionist and or imperialist actions such as wars, annexations of lands or countries, economic control of other countries, etc. Many scholars have equated this older phrase to the more contemporary "New World Order" slogan, so often used by the leaders of the United States of America (especially the Presidents), as well as other leaders in other Western governments. It is thought to imply the ideal of Western domination of the rest of the world and is supported by the wars, economic subjugation of other countries through the actions of the World Bank and the International Monetary Fund, and destabilization and subversion of governments around the world in the last several hundred years. As we will see, the manifest destiny concept is not a new idea but has been used since ancient times by one set of people to justify their aggressions on others.

Alexandria, the city in Egypt that was founded by *Alexander the Great* upon his conquest of Egypt, became the center of scholarship and learning in the entire ancient world from 300 B.C.E. to 250 A.C.E. It was here that the doctrines of the Religion of Asar (Osiris) and Hermeticism from Ancient Egypt (5,500 B.C.E-300 B.C.E), the Buddhist missionaries from India, the cult of Christos from the Near East and the teachings of Zarathustra (Zoroaster) melded into an amalgam of several Jewish and Christian sects. *Dionysus the Areopagite* played an important role in bridging the gap between the mystical religious teachings, Judaism and Christianity. Up to this time the symbols associated with the Ancient Egyptian Religion of Asar, Hermeticism, and Gnosticism, were known to be metaphors to describe the ultimate reality of the universe and man's relationship to it. It was not until the time of the Jewish leaders who followed Yahweh,[111] Christians from the Byzantine throne and then later, the Muslims who followed Allah (the supreme being in Islam), that the symbols and metaphors of religion began to be understood literally, as facts rather than as metaphors to explain the mystery behind every individual. The idea of "God" became circumscribed by a particular doctrine, which was the exclusive property belonging to certain "chosen people." Thus, they saw all other God-forms as idols or devils. All other religions were seen as heresies. Consequently, the followers of those forms were considered as pagans who must be subdued and converted or destroyed. This point is most strongly illustrated in the Bible itself in several passages. This point is of great importance because the concept of a proprietary God is central to Western religions. (Highlighted portions by Ashby)

The Bible - Genesis 12: 1-3
> "The Lord... said to Abraham... "I will make you into a great nation and I will bless you; I will make your name great, and you will be a blessing. I will bless those who bless you, and whoever curses you I will curse; and all peoples on earth will be blessed through you."

The above statement from Genesis 12: 1-3 is especially powerful in the light of the emergence of the United States of America and the countries of Europe as world economic and military powers. The slogan "God bless America" is used with prayers, pledges of allegiance and especially at times of war, most recent examples are the Gulf War (against Iraq) and the Afghanistan War (against the Taliban). This statement brings forth the concept that the Jews and Christians are specially blessed by God with

---

[111] a name for God used by the ancient Hebrews.

prosperity. It essentially says that those who support the Jews and look out for their interests (bless them) are the only peoples on the face of the earth that will receive God's blessing. Thus, with reference to orthodox Christianity, where Jesus is said to be "the only way" to reach God, this verse presents a contradiction to those of the orthodox Christian faith, because it states in no uncertain terms that if any peoples (including Christians) wish to receive God's blessing, they can only do so through blessing (supporting) the (orthodox) Jewish faith. Recall that this statement was written before the time and movement of Jesus, and thus, by accepting the Old Testament as part of their tradition, which includes the above statement, Jesus is apparently not the sole determiner of if Christians will find their way to God. They must apparently first and foremost support the Jews, and thus their religion (orthodox Christianity) is nothing more than an extension of the orthodox Jewish faith: orthodox Christianity = orthodox Judaism + Jesus' teachings. Jesus was born into the Jewish faith, but can he and the ministry he started be considered as being Jewish? If so, there is no need to differentiate between orthodox Christianity and orthodox Judaism. Is Christianity a new teaching? If it is indeed a reformation of Judaic law (Matthew 5:17), can it be said to be in agreement with the old, unreformed Judaic law? Where is the line drawn between Judaism and Christianity? Can it be drawn in the teachings of the New Testament, and if so, then why include sections like the above from the Old Testament? What about other contradictions between the New Testament and the Old Testament, such as the Old Testament teaching (Exodus 21: 22-26), "...life for life, eye for eye, tooth for tooth, hand for hand, foot for foot, burn for burn, wound for wound, bruise for bruise" and Jesus on the other hand teaching (Matthew 5:38-42), "You have heard that it was said, "Eye for eye, tooth for tooth. But I tell you, Do not resist an evil person. If someone strikes you on the right cheek, turn to him the other also," and (Matthew 5:43-48), "You have heard that it was said, "Love your neighbor and hate your enemy. But I tell you, love your enemies and pray for those who persecute you?" The points addressed above are especially significant for Christians who subscribe not only to the contents of the New Testament which are based on the reformist teachings of Jesus, but also on the Hebrew teachings of the Old Testament. Thus, as a result, the above verses in Genesis apply to all Christians who accept the Old Testament. And thus, it follows from the literal understanding of the above verses that the success of any orthodox Christian movement and peoples, and in fact, the very destiny of Christianity as a whole, hinges on the treatment of the Jews by the Christians.

This point is crucial, perhaps to the very survival of humanity in these times of strife where some warring factions have nuclear weapons capability, as this injunction, that those who bless the Jewish nation will be blessed in turn by God, is used to rally people, consciously and unconsciously, especially predominantly Christian countries such as the USA, to the support of the orthodox Jews in their cause of Zionism[112], even when the actions of the Jewish (Israeli) governments are shown to be unrighteous and unjust.[113] This of course adds fuel to the fire of Muslims who read the verses of the Koran that speak on this issue as it manifested 1300 years ago and obviously continues to this day. Thus, the conflict appears to be religiously, as well as economically based, since the West feels that it needs the oil from the Middle East and to have strategic military bases in those areas (such as in Israel). Also, the West seeks to control and subjugate the peoples of the world, including Muslims. So there is also an ethnic struggle, but underlying this is the deep-rooted religious struggle. (Underlined portions by Ashby)

The Bible Exodus 33 1-2

> "The Lord said to Moses, Go, leave this place, you and the people whom you have brought out of the land of Egypt, and go to the land of which I swore to Abraham, Isaac, and Jacob, saying, "To your descendents I will give it. I will send an angel before you, and I will drive out the Canaanites, the Amorites, the Hittites, the Perizzites, the Hivites, and the Jesubites."

---

[112] Definition: **Zionism** is a political movement advocating the reestablishment of a Jewish homeland in Palestine, the "promised land" of the Bible, with its capital Jerusalem, the "city of Zion." **Zi·on:** The historic land of Israel as a symbol of the Jewish people. **b.** The Jewish people; Israel. **2.** A place or religious community regarded as sacredly devoted to God. **3.** An idealized, harmonious community; utopia.

[113] Many actions of the Israeli government have been found by the United Nations to be in violation of international law, such as the creation of settlements in unauthorized territories. See United Nations Resolutions.

THE AFRICAN ORIGINS OF CIVILIZATION, RELIGION AND YOGA SPIRITUALITY

The Bible 2 Kings 5.15
"Now I know that there is no God in all earth except in Israel..."

The Bible - Genesis 1.28
"Be fruitful and multiply, and fill the earth and subdue it; and have dominion over the fish of the sea and over the birds in the air and over every living thing that moves upon the earth."

Numbers 33:50-56

50 ¶ And the LORD spake unto Moses in the plains of Moab by Jordan near Jericho, saying,
51 Speak unto the children of Israel, and say unto them, When ye are passed over Jordan into the land of Canaan;
52 Then ye shall drive out all the inhabitants of the land from before you, and destroy all their pictures, and destroy all their molten images, and quite pluck down all their high places:
53 And ye shall dispossess the inhabitants of the land, and dwell therein: for I have given you the land to possess it.
54 And ye shall divide the land by lot for an inheritance among your families: and to the more ye shall give the more inheritance, and to the fewer ye shall give the less inheritance: every man's inheritance shall be in the place where his lot falleth; according to the tribes of your fathers ye shall inherit.
55 But if ye will not drive out the inhabitants of the land from before you; then it shall come to pass, that those which ye let remain of them shall be pricks in your eyes, and thorns in your sides, and shall vex you in the land wherein ye dwell.
56 Moreover it shall come to pass, that I shall do unto you, as I thought to do unto them.

The preceding statement contains a mandate and a tacit authorization to subdue the earth and control it, displace its current human inhabitants who follow other religions, and destroy the shrines and Temples of other religions. In the extreme, these statements could be interpreted as permission or consent to conquer any and all parts of the earth and its peoples, since their inhabitants are disqualified as being worthy to live or possess property, due to their pagan status, i.e., not believing in the God of the orthodox Jews, and, via extension by accepting the Old Testament teachings as part of their tradition, the orthodox Christians. An atmosphere was created in Europe wherein other peoples could be thought of and classified as "non-human," deserving less consideration and respect.[296]

Verse 55 above is especially chilling to many people because not only does it intimate that it is quite alright (righteous) for the orthodox Jews and other believers of the Old Testament to drive out the inhabitants, but in a subtle way it is also suggesting that the Bible condones genocide, as it is unlikely that peoples currently living in any land will passively give it up and move out, leaving behind their homes, and allowing their religious places of worship and other sacred places to be destroyed, etc., by some invading group. Thus, there will inevitably be war, and thus killing, and so even though the above verse does not speak of committing genocide against other peoples, but rather speaks of "dispossessing" peoples, ultimately, this action must result in genocide, as it is unlikely that the dispossessed group will quietly and peacefully leave their homeland where they have lived for generations, and which is tied to their religious beliefs. Even if they are conquered and must retreat, they will likely spend the rest of their lives, and future generations, plotting retaliation and ways to retake their homeland. The verse states that God is ordering the Jewish people, and by extension, any other religions that accept the Old Testament (i.e. Christianity), to drive people out of their land, and that even if so much as one inhabitant is left on the land, the Jews will live to regret it. This implies that the only remedy to obtain the land "free and clear" is to eradicate all people living there before, so that the people will not exert negative influences on the Jewish people but also so that the descendants will never come to claim the land as their own in the future. As you recall with respect to the history of the Hebrew people, they had seized control of the land of Canaan several times, and were also driven out several times, having not accomplishing the mandate of their Bible, exiling all non-Jewish peoples.

The usurpation of the Americas by the Western Christian countries as well as the colonial expansion into Africa, Hawaii, Polynesia, the Far East, etc., are all seen as extensions of this Biblical manifest destiny policy which can be understood by another tern, "Imperialism." It is also compared to the current situation between the Jews and the (Muslim) Palestinian people in that the Muslims have been pushed completely out of portions of their land (now called Israel) by the Jews. This is the second time in history that this situation has occurred, the first being when the Jews drove the Canaanites (early Palestinians) out of the land in the time before the birth of Jesus. The Palestinian attacks on Israel have been for the most part ineffective, while Israel's reprisals have killed many Palestinians, being highly effective due to the assistance of Western countries and successful investments by Jews abroad which finance the holding of the country (Israel) and its powerful military. The stagnation of the Palestinian nation is tantamount to a living death of sorts in which their misery, as a dispossessed people, is vented on citizens of Israel in the form of "terrorist" attacks and suicide bombings at every opportunity. Some Palestinians have charged that the behavior of the Israeli government is racist and genocidal because of the level of killing that is going on.[297] One would think the situation would be the very opposite, as the Jewish peoples themselves have experienced persecution and genocide. Thus, it would seem that they would be doing everything in their power to ensure what happened to them does not happen to another human being on the face of the earth. Yet, to the contrary, just as the abused child will likely grow up and become an abuser {him/her} self, it appears the victims of genocide have now possibly become the perpetrators. However, it would be seen, from the orthodox Biblical perspective, that the Jewish people not only have a mandate to dispossess every last peoples from their "holy" land, but also a threat that if they do not do so (follow the covenant), God will do to them (the Jewish people) what he instructed them to do to others (i.e. God will dispossess {exact genocide on} the Jewish people): "Moreover it shall come to pass, that I shall do unto you, as I thought to do unto them." Thus, whether unconsciously or consciously, the Jewish peoples have scripturally impelled themselves to, in the current war with the Palestinians, fight to completely dispossess every Palestinian person from their land, or risk, in their understanding of the scriptures, breaking their covenant with God, thus becoming the dispossessed themselves. Since the Palestinian peoples have no intention of handing over the land to the Israeli peoples, following this scriptural mandate implicitly means that the Israeli people have the right to uses whatever necessary means to accomplish this dispossession, which includes killing. Also, since the Palestinian people have made it clear that they will not leave under any circumstance, then it follows that the only way for the Israelis to rid the land of them completely, and thus be in harmony with Jewish scriptural law, is by committing genocide upon them.

Regardless of whether or not the Israeli people or for that matter, the Christians also, have designs on world domination and the mass conversion of all people, the Bible appears to support that concept. However, they are not alone in this venture of world domination, because similar messages of support for Muslim domination of the world exist within the Muslim history and scriptures. This will be presented in an upcoming section. Thus, these two[114] or three religions, depending on how they are categorized, are destined to be at odds, not only with each other, but the whole world, based on the literal interpretations of their scriptures and the historical acts that have been taken by people who follow those religions.

Moreover, the verse above means that any friendly relationships between people of the orthodox Jewish or Christian faiths and members of other faiths, religions or spiritual traditions are inevitably based on false pretenses by the Jewish or Christian person(s) because ultimately their manifest destiny states that they must usurp the lands and dispossess the current inhabitants. It is either that this is the case, or those Jews and Christians are acting impiously (in contradiction to their own edicts to destroy others), and are thus subject to punishment from God. Many Christians and Jews of the orthodox traditions would reject the above premise, that they secretly detest people of other religious or spiritual faiths or traditions that they work with or know under other circumstances, and that the relationships are phony, being based on some kind of pretext, yet, by going along and identifying themselves with the orthodox Judeo-Christian religion to any extent implies that this must be so.

With the kind of manifest destiny laid out in the Jewish-Christian Bible, where it is written that God is making a special pact with the people of Abraham and that the land that is currently occupied by the *"Canaanites, the Amorites, the Hittites, the Perizzites, the Hivites, and the Jesubites,* i.e. the Arabs, will be cleared and given to the Jews and Christians, it is no wonder that the Muslim-Arabs in the Middle East felt threatened and continue to feel that there is an impending menace from Israel and the Western countries that are supporting Israel. This feeling is expressed in the statements from the Koran itself (see below) wherein the Jews and Christians are denounced as not being content to live side by side with those of Islamic (Muslim) faith, but rather feel the need to convert them. They also feel that even if they were to befriend them, the Jews and Christians have their own agenda that does not include the Muslims.

---

[114] As discussed above, with respect to the adherence to the Old Testament, orthodox Christianity can be considered as an extension of orthodox Judaism.

2:120 <u>Never will the Jews or the Christians be satisfied with thee unless thou follow their form of religion.</u>

3:118 O ye who believe! Take not into your intimacy those outside your ranks<u>: They will not fail to corrupt you. They only desire your ruin: Rank hatred has already appeared from their mouths: What their hearts conceal is far worse.</u> We have made plain to you the Signs, if ye have wisdom.

5:54 Section 8. O ye who believe! <u>Take not the Jews and the Christians for your friends and protectors: They are but friends and protectors to each other.</u> And he amongst you that turns to them (for friendship) is of them. Verily Allah guideth not a people unjust.

We need to have a deeper understanding of the history of those who started the religion of Judaism and those who have adhered to it, in order to have a deeper understanding of why the Zionist movement has received such impetus in the mythology, ritual and secular life of Jews. Christians, Jews and Muslims will have a better understanding of Judaism and will also better understand their own position on the Zionist movement. Only correct insight and understanding will allow one to act out of truth and righteousness instead of fear and ignorance. Thus, all peoples will be benefited accordingly.

A Short History of Ancient and Modern Jewish Zionism

At the end of the Middle Ages, passages such as those in Exodus 33: 1-2 led to the idea that a particular piece of land was bequeathed to the Jews by God, and that the heathen peoples should be removed from the land and a Jewish state established there. This idea, based on the passages above, which some people took literally, was a contributing factor towards the belief that the crusades were biblically sanctioned. This doctrine was to have severe repercussions for the Native Americans who were almost completely annihilated and for the Africans who were captured and enslaved during the conquest of the New World. Thus, racism, with all its repercussions, is related to spiritual ignorance. It is estimated that over 50 million Native Americans and over 100 million Africans were killed as a result of the wars for conquest of the Americas (Native American Holocaust[115]) and the slave trade (African Holocaust) by the various European countries, respectively.[298] In modern times this feeling has led to the birth of Zionism and the State of Israel,[299] established in Palestine, which has not only displaced the Palestinian people who have lived there for centuries, but has also destabilized the entire region and fostered many wars and animosity between the Jewish and Muslim peoples.

Beginning with Abraham (c. 2,100 B.C.E?) and ending with the creation of a Jewish state in 1948 A.C.E., the events surrounding Palestine and the creation of the Jewish state of Israel shows the long struggle of the Jewish people to establish a permanent country for themselves and the conflict which ensued when the Jews were successful in taking control of the land which has been considered as the Holy Land for Jews, Christians, and Muslims. The creation of Israel had begun in ancient times, but it was not until the late 1800s that the movement took on strength due to the ability of the Jews to develop political clout and financial backing from their own sources and from the Western countries. The Balfour Declaration of 1917, which supported the idea of a Jewish state, was crucial to the plans of the Israeli leaders. In the aftermath of World War II (1945-1950 A.C.E.) when the Palestinians and other Arab Muslims were weak militarily and the Western countries were stronger, Britain took control of the area. This was the opportunity that the Jewish leaders were waiting for since 1896 when the idea of a Jewish state began to take shape. These factors, coupled with the Western interest in Middle Eastern oil and the establishment of military footholds in the Middle East, enabled the orthodox Jewish leaders to promote the partitioning of Palestine and obtain the permission and financing to start a settlement in Palestine. After World War II the establishment of a Jewish State was not officially part of the original settlement idea as authorized by the previous declarations of the United Nations or the British mandate. Having succeeded in occupying the land, the Jews then set out to establish and expand a Jewish State by military force.

---

[115] The killing of many victims, often savagely: massacre, mass murder, etc.

Many Christians support the cause of Zionism, some because they believe it is sanctioned by the Bible as a God given right of the Jews which is ordained under penalty of death and damnation for those who oppose it, as discussed above. They follow this teaching out of fear because the Old Testament in the Bible says that those who go against the chosen people (the Jews) will be destroyed by God himself. The passage below from the Bible is another one of several which espouse this idea.

1 Chronicles 17

> 9 Also I will ordain a place for my people Israel,[300] and will plant them, and they shall dwell in their place, and shall be moved no more; neither shall the children of wickedness waste them any more, as at the beginning,
> 10 And since the time that I commanded judges [to be] over my people Israel. Moreover I will subdue all thy enemies. Furthermore I tell thee that the LORD will build thee a house.

Matthew 3

> 8 Bring forth therefore fruits in keeping with repentance.

The opinion of many Arabs and many scholars of international law is that if members of the Jewish community wanted to set up a new nation or state, they should have entered into negotiations with the people living in the area (Palestinians and other Arabs). Then they could have come to a mutual agreement that might have been beneficial to both. However, this would not have been in keeping with their scriptural mandate to take this land over forcefully and dispossess its people. Having taken the land by force and expulsed the people who have been living there for several generations, and having committed atrocities on them, all with the financial backing from Jews abroad and from Western countries such as the United States, the Jews in the newly formed state of Israel have promoted a climate of mistrust, hatred and revenge. They have adopted the principle used by many Western countries, that military might (they have nuclear weapons capability) and financial power can be used to control, steal from or enslave others. In response, the Palestinians and other Arab nations have engaged in militant attacks and demonstrations against the Jews as well. Both sides have caused the deaths of children and other innocent civilians. Although the land was unjustly taken, what is needed now is justice, forgiveness and understanding. What is needed is a kind of justice that allows people an opportunity to live together and forgiveness for those who acted wrongly, out of spiritual ignorance. Also, those who have committed the wrongs, on both sides, need to forgive themselves. However, forgiveness involves making amends for one's wrongdoing. This is not necessarily to be understood as paying someone in the form of money to redress a wrong. A person can pay a fine and remain just as ignorant and harbor the same feelings which led to the past mistake until it occurs again in the future. Those who commit wrongs need to face up to them and correct their feelings, thoughts and actions so that the error will not occur again. Both the Jews and the Arabs need to reconcile their anger and forgive the attacks which both have perpetrated on each other. This is self-forgiveness and making amends. True repentance and amends for a wrongdoing means eradicating the ignorance which led to the error and, in the future, acting in ways that will promote harmony instead of strife and violence. True peace does not come from getting more guns in order to hold an opponent at bay. It comes from making an opponent into a friend. This can only occur when there is good feeling amongst people which comes from caring, sharing, trust, respect, honesty and acceptance. Ultimately, the Jews and Palestinians and other Arabs need to realize and affirm that they both have a right to exist and that both come from and are sustained by the same God. This is the only way to have true reconciliation and peace.

THE AFRICAN ORIGINS OF CIVILIZATION, RELIGION AND YOGA SPIRITUALITY

Overview of Christianity in Africa and The Missionary Movements

This vast subject cannot be fully treated in this volume of *African Origins*, since it would require a separate volume. However, it is a subject of paramount importance for understanding the history of Christianity in Africa as well as the future of Christianity in the world because Africa is fast becoming the most Christianized part of the world. As of the late 1980s (A.C.E.) the practitioners of Christianity still numbered less than those practicing native African Religion.

> While every day in the West,[116] roughly 7,500 people in effect stop being Christians every day in Africa roughly double that number become Christians…[129]

Along with the statistics above, population growth in the world has changed dramatically in the last century. While population growth has slowed to .8% in North America and 0% growth for Europe (The West) as an average, or even negative growth for some parts of Europe, it is well over 3% in Africa, even considering the problem of child mortality.

> For the less-developed world as a whole, the 1990 growth rate of 2.0 percent per year is projected to be cut in half by 2025. Africa will remain the region with the highest growth rate. In 1990 this rate was 3.1 percent; in 2025 it is projected to be about 2.2 percent. Africa's population would almost triple, from 682 million in 1990 to 1.58 billion in 2025, and then continue growing at a rate that would almost double the population size in another 35 years.[75]

If the projections above hold it is possible that Africa will at some point in the future have one of, if not, the largest population of Christians in the world. How did this come to be? As we saw earlier, Christianity originated in Ancient Egypt (which included India). From there its adherents carried the Christian teachings to Canaan/Palestine, Turkey, Greece and the rest of Europe. Rome and Byzantium became the strongholds of Christianity, which enforced it by means of military power as they set out to spread the empire abroad including North Africa and Ethiopia. When the Roman Empire adopted Christianity, it banned all other forms of religion. At the same time as it subjugated its colonies around the Empire (200-450 A.C.E.) and forced people to pay heavy taxes to support Rome, the honest followers of Christianity practiced Christian charity and developed a great reputation as a religion of the masses. This reputation drew many adherents to the Christian faith in all parts of the Roman Empire. Thus, the negative economic situations that many people found themselves in provided a fertile soil for the propagation of Christian doctrines since Jesus' teachings on promoting justice and equality are the hallmark of Christian life in society. Jesus' teachings extol the virtue of sharing and helping others regardless of their race, religion or creed. The famous story of the Good Samaritan (Luke 10:33) is an example of this. Along with helping those in distress, Christianity emphasizes the virtues of loving one's enemies (Luke 6:27) and not developing resentment towards them, but instead showing them, through love and restraint, the blessedness of peace (Matthew 5:9), and the fellowship of all human beings in Christ (Galatians 3:28) and thereby, the error of their negative actions.

Galatians 3

28 There is neither Jew nor Greek, there is neither bond nor free, there is neither male nor female: for ye are all one in Christ Jesus.

Thus, the first Christian missionaries, such as the Apostle Paul, were very welcome for many reasons. However, in modern times the Christian missionary movement has come under fire for its denigration of native cultures and its hypocrisy for not dealing with its own issues of faith. For example, the Christian churches of North America have organized several movements to end hunger or to convert peoples of foreign countries, but there are people in North America who go hungry every day. Further, the pervasive problem of racism continues in a subtle form unopposed in the churches as well as the general society. Along with these problems there are several issues of Christian doctrine, which remain unresolved.

In modern times, the missionaries sent to the Americas and to Africa by the European nations sought to convert the native populations and at the same time convince them that the religion they were following up to that time was nothing more than idol or devil worship. The church carried out the missionary role while

---

[116] **West.** The western part of the earth, especially Europe and the Western Hemisphere, controlled economically, politically and culturally by the European nations.

at the same time condoning the process of neocolonization.[117] Over the past 1,700 years since the adoption of Christianity by the Roman Empire, Christianity has experienced many low points throughout history. Some of these were the Crusades, the Inquisitions,[118] the Atlantic Slave Trade, and the Genocide of Native Americans. Consequently, many people became disillusioned with Christianity and it became an incidental part of life for many Western Christians. It was not until the emergence of the Revivalist movement that Christianity was revitalized. This was the primary force, which spurred the missionaries of the last hundred years. However, even today, the Earl of Spencer, the brother of Princess Diana of England, said publicly in an interview[119] that the death of his famous sister brought out some unexpected aspects of British life. He said that even though there is not much of an organized religion any more in the country, the outpouring of emotion took on an almost a spiritual quality as if they were expressing some "latent" feeling that had not found expression.

So, while Christianity emerged out of Africa and spread to Europe and America, it did not maintain its original form or its impact on people as an honest movement towards human fellowship and spiritual enlightenment. Thus, it is regarded by many as an inconsequential part of life even though they call themselves Christian by birth. Some people in Western countries even regard Christianity and religion in general, as a nuisance. They do not allow Christian principles to be considered in their government or business activities even though they claim that they are Christians, America is a Christian country and their motto is "in God we trust." In the eyes of many people who live in the European colonies, or who suffered slavery or military conquest at the hands of European Christians, Christianity became a symbol of European Imperialism and social injustice. Nevertheless, ironically, the missionaries that came into Africa before the independence movements[120] of the twentieth century were largely members of the revivalist Christian sects. The Reformation Movement[121] was not as interested in missionary activities as the formation of a new church doctrine in Europe. The important influence came from the followers of the Evangelical Revival Movements. In the late eighteenth century, Protestant missionary societies increased, and after that the Catholics also sent some missionaries to Africa as well. Thus, using the map of "Africa and the West," we can trace the movement of Christianity through history.

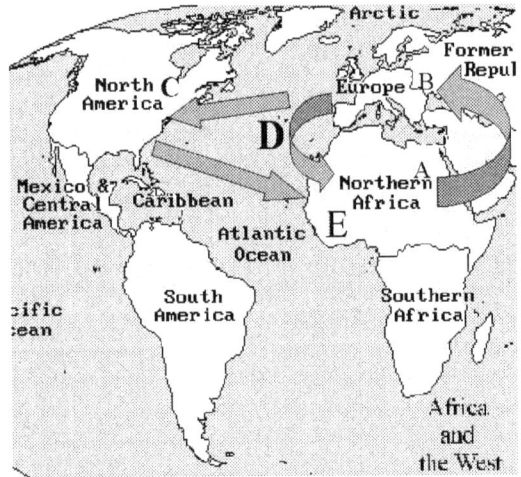

The missionary movement and the origin and return of Christianity to Africa.

A- Christianity emerges in Africa (Egypt) based on the Asarian Resurrection Religion.
B- Christianity is adopted by some of the Jews who transfer it to Europe along with some of the previous Jewish teachings (Old Testament).
C- Missionaries come to Africa from Europe trying to convert Africans to the Christianity as it was practiced in Europe based on European culture and traditions which included images of Jesus and all of the characters of the Bible as Europeans (except for those images of the Black Madonnas). Christianity adopted the Jewish traditions and folklore (not found in the Bible) related to Egypt and

---

[117] A policy whereby a major power uses military force, coercion, illegal economic and political means to perpetuate or extend its influence over underdeveloped nations or areas.

[118] A tribunal formerly held in the Roman Catholic Church and directed at the suppression of heresy but became a means to murder and eradicate any person who disagreed with the church or its wealthy followers.

[119] Interview from 1998.

[120] Independence from European colonialism.

[121] Reformation. A 16th-century movement in Western Europe that aimed at reforming some doctrines and practices of the Roman Catholic Church and resulted in the establishment of the Protestant churches.

Ethiopia as being heathens or pagans who were cursed for their blackness, thus denigrating the role of Africans in the Bible and promoting the enslavement and exploitation of African peoples during the slave trade.

D- The forms of Christianity practiced in the Britain, Anglican, Protestant, Separatist and Puritan churches, etc. were transferred to North America and were instrumental in sanctioning the colonization process which included the stealing of land from Native Americans and murdering them, the enslavement of Africans through the slave trade, as well as the Jews, the Irish and others through indentured servitude.[122]

E- Missionaries from North America come to Africa to spread the revivalist movement.

Africanized Christian Movement:

Even though Christianity is gaining adherents in Africa, they are also losing some as well. The African spiritual consciousness does in some cases come through the colonial imperative in order to project a unique and higher African vision. The movement started by Simon Kimbangu is an example of *Africanized Christianity*. Simon Kimbangu was a preacher in the Congo during the Belgian colonial period there. He founded a Christian church which deviated in fundamental respects from the established paradigms of orthodox Christianity. One such significant change was the admittance of women as Priestesses. He was ostracized by the established church and banished to prison where he died as a martyr. By the late 1980's (A.C.E.) the followers of his church numbered 4 million. Thus it is clear that Africans can have an effect on Western religions, and perhaps even alter them to better suit their needs. The acceptance of Priestesses reflects a shifting towards the reinstitution of an African paradigm. However, even with the adjustments the basis of the religious archetype remains Western, and thus renders the practice of religion not entirely African. It will, therefore, remain limited in its capacity to assist Africans in fully recovering their African consciousness.

Conclusion on the spread of Christianity in Africa

It is extremely important to understand the dynamics of the spread of Christianity in its different forms. The propagation of ignorance and distorted teachings must be understood and corrected. Like Europeans and all those who have been touched by Western missionaries, Africans need to receive the knowledge about the origins and Gnostic teachings of Christianity, which come from Africa itself, and not just the doctrines of Protestants, Orthodox Catholics or Evangelicals from Europe. For the most part, wherever Western Christian missionaries have carried Christianity, they have attempted to eradicate the preexisting religion by labeling it as a pagan cult and not a "real" religion. Then they adopt some of the symbols or traditions of that cult and call them Christian. In modern times, with the power of Tele-evangelism it is even more important to promote the message of Christian Yoga, the mystical and universal Christian philosophy which affirms the Divine in all forms of religion as well as the equality of all human beings and the necessity to love all alike. Westernized Christianity resists attempts by some Africans to Africanize Christianity just as they themselves Europeanized it. As we have seen, in Europe Christianity adopted many rituals and symbols of Ancient Egyptian religion and later the Celtic religion, as well as from others. In Africa, the move is to identify God, the Father of Christianity, with for example, the "High God" of traditional African religions such as Chukwu of Igboland or Mwari of the Shona, etc. This understanding should be encouraged and the adoption of Christianity should be seen as an advanced African expression of the universal philosophy which is already being followed instead of a new, real religion which needs to be adopted while discarding the old, ignorant, pagan, false religions. When this occurs, African peoples as well as all Christians around the world will move into a new age of real Christian faith. Christian religion cannot be practiced in a church that is contaminated with economic, political or social doctrines, which are patently unjust. Also, it cannot be correctly practiced when the traditions and doctrines are based on the ignorance of Deism, corruption and dishonesty. The Church needs to acknowledge its role in promoting economic, social and religious injustices throughout history and then reaffirm the true Christian teachings, which have yet to be practiced. The church could begin with the teachings given by Jesus at the Sermon on the Mount. While these teachings have been advocated as

---

[122] Indentured servitude and slavery were the economic factors which enabled the creation of the united States of America and its subsequent emergence as a Superpower in the mid twentieth century. A Superpower is defined in the American Heritage Dictionary as: **su·per·pow·er** (sōō'pər-pou'ər) *n.* A powerful and influential nation, especially a nuclear power that dominates its allies or client states in an international power bloc.

propaganda or doctrinal principles by the church, they have never been implemented and upheld universally in the church.

The Methodist and African Methodist Episcopal Churches

What effect have people of African descent had on the Christian church in the United States? The Methodist Church was not originally planned as a new sect of Christianity. It started in England as a trend within Protestantism, which emphasized life rather than creed. The Anglican theology was continued. Anglican refers to all groups having to do with the Church of England or any of the churches related to it in origin and communion, such as the Protestant Episcopal Church. John Wesley, an Anglican priest, was the founder of Methodism. Methodism stressed God's mercy. In 1784, the Methodist Episcopal Church in America was founded. In Methodism, the Bible is studied as a continuing form of inspired revelation.

The African Methodist Episcopal (A.M.E.) Church is the second largest Methodist group in the United States. Objecting to the church's racial discriminatory policy, a group withdrew from the Methodist Episcopal Church in 1787. The first AME church was dedicated in 1793 in Philadelphia. Richard Allen was the first bishop and formal organization followed in 1816. Its doctrines are those of traditional Methodist churches. There are approximately 1.1 million members in African Methodist Episcopal Church.

African Methodist Episcopal Zion Church was formed in 1796 by a group of black members of the John Street Church (Methodist Episcopal) in New York City who protested racial discrimination. The name was approved in 1848, and James Varick was the first bishop. The church spread rapidly throughout the northern states, and some churches developed in the South. Missionary activity and education are stressed. There are approximately 900,000 members.

Unlike the Church that was started by Simon Kimbangu, *Kimbanguism,* in Africa, the A.M.E. churches made no major changes to the religion and thus it remains a version of western Christianity that is sponsored by African Americans that espouses essentially the same message as other Christian churches in the west. It acknowledges that "black" people are of African descent but does not attempt to link the religion to African religion nor does it provide a message of African culture in the sense of reclaiming African spiritual concepts, values of paradigms. In these respects the church remains an institution that upholds western values and spiritual concepts.

Reconciliation and Peace Through Religious Reforms and The Complete Practice of Religion

Acceptance cannot come when one sees oneself as superior and others as inferior or when one sees oneself as all right and the other as all wrong. True friendship cannot come from injustice and a true coming together cannot occur if there is segregation of peoples. The idea of race and racism has become intermixed with ideas of religion in orthodox Jewish philosophy. In modern times the idea of racism, which developed out of the European kidnapping and enslaving of African peoples, also adversely affects the Jews. There are Europeans who consider themselves as "white" see the Jews as Semitic or mixed with non-white blood and discriminate against them. As we have seen, from a genetic standpoint, all peoples from the Middle East were of mixed African and Asian descent in biblical times. This was confirmed by Herodotus and other historians of ancient times as well as the writings of the Bible itself. Many people do not realize that there were no "white" or lighter skinned Jews until the latter part of the first millennium of our era (between the fifth and ninth centuries A.C.E.) when the Jews moved into Europe and began to mix with Europeans. It must be clearly understood that Judaism is supposed to be a religion and not an ethnic group or race. This idea is proven easily by the existence of the Falashas, a native Jewish sect of Ethiopia who are dark skinned African peoples, who have been followers of the Jewish faith from a time even before the Jews moved into Europe. More importantly, however, let us not forget that in the remote past, human beings originated in Africa and therefore, all human beings are African in ancestry, just as all humans are of "one blood" (Acts 17:26) and "one flesh" (1 Corinthians 15:39) in God. Therefore, this means that racial distinctions are a bogus and illusory expression of a person's level of spiritual ignorance, a feeling of separation from others which is fueled by frustration, misunderstanding, greed, anger, etc. All human beings deserve compassion, love and caring, regardless of their faith, skin color, etc. Anything less than this is inhuman and un-spiritual, and therefore, sinful. Sin brings on an effect wherein the sinner receives a punishment for the sinful behavior in the form of suffering and frustration, either in this lifetime or according to yoga and other mystical philosophies, a future one. Therefore, those who believe that might makes right or that they have gotten away with something which they know is wrong are overlooking the greater plan of cosmic order which administers absolute justice to all beings. So it is important to be fair, compassionate and forgiving, since those who you treat in this way will more easily be able to respond to you in kind. On the other hand, those whom you have treated badly will in all likelihood treat you with fear, hatred and mistrust in return.

Job 4:8
Even as I have seen, they that plow iniquity, and sow wickedness, reap the same.

Around the time of Jesus, Christianity brought in a new message to the Jews. The Kingdom of Heaven was not an exclusive place where only Jews would be able to enter. Rather, anyone would be able to enter if they did what was required, that is, practice the principles that Jesus taught, in their life. This message drew new converts from all lands. It was a principal reason why the Jewish political and religious leaders opposed Jesus, and his teaching which later came to be known as Christianity. Even though orthodox Christianity has been associated with Western civilization and with an elitist church organization based in Rome in the last 1,300 years, it was originally conceptualized as a universal religion. The following passages from Matthew in the New Testament illustrate the universal appeal of Christianity to all peoples. Furthermore, the Gnostic Gospels, Gospels that were omitted by the orthodox Bible compilers in Rome, and other omitted or altered texts[301] show a mystical and ecumenical side to Christianity that is not clearly reflected in the Bible. So this suggests that the Roman Catholics altered the true meaning of Christianity to suit their purposes.

Matthew 7:21
21. Not every one that says to me, Lord, Lord, shall enter into the kingdom of heaven; but he that doeth the will of my Father who is in heaven.

Matthew 8:11
11 And I say to you, That many shall come from the east and the west, and shall sit down with Abraham, and Isaac, and Jacob, in the kingdom of heaven.

However, the altruistic concepts of Judaism and Christianity are constantly suppressed in favor of dogmas and orthodox concepts that are deeply embedded within the Holy Scriptures themselves as *seeds of conflict*. These attitudes and the ensuing degradation of the spiritual culture gave rise to policies and practices based on the ultimate idea that Christians cannot rest until ALL human beings are Christians, to establish the "Kingdom of Heaven on Earth," but even in this there is a distinction made between the ethnic Jews, the European Christians (and there is a hierarchy within the European countries and the United States) and the non-Caucasian Christians around the world. In the United States of America, many Christian preachers have criticized and condemned the racial segregation and discrimination that continues even today within the Christian church. This order of hierarchy, which follows along "racial" lines, is denounced in the Koran as well as by non-Caucasian peoples around the world as a hypocritical use of religion to dominate the world.

Thus, these groups need to promote the complete and true practice of religion. They need to move beyond the practice of only the first two levels of religion, myth and ritual, and embrace the third step, mysticism, which will allow them to gain a more universal perspective of their religions, and thus be able to achieve true peace between their religions. Remember that religion has three steps, stages or levels. These are Myth, Ritual and Mystical. Therefore, practices of the non-mystical religions, i.e. religions that do not follow the threefold process of the practice of true religion, are only related to the lower levels of spiritual practice (myth and ritual). This is the level of practice promoted by almost all religions referred to as "orthodox." This is because, in most cases, the understanding of the religious myth is deficient. This in turn causes people to practice the religion (ritual stage) in a wrong or limited way. In Christianity, the problem is that the main doctrine of Christianity, since the time that the Roman Catholic Church, emphasized the literal interpretation of the life and teachings of Jesus. They hold that he existed as the one and only savior, a real human being who died and was bodily resurrected (literal interpretation). The mystical interpretation is that every human being's soul is Jesus, who has incarnated and been crucified by the world and its desires and distractions, turning it away from the divine vision of its own nature. The resurrection of Christ within the human heart is when the Christ Consciousness or vision of the Kingdom of God is regained. Further, the church doctrine holds that salvation, i.e. seeing the Kingdom of God, must occur through faith in Jesus and by Jesus' returning to the world and digging people out of the grave in order to resurrect them (literal interpretation). The mystical interpretation is that human beings are to grow into Christ Consciousness itself and resurrect themselves by discovering their ability to grow beyond the limiting weight of ignorance and worldly desire.

The belief in the literal interpretation of the scriptures closes the door to understanding Jesus Christ as a metaphor of our own life. With this understanding, or rather, misunderstanding, our own self-effort and responsibility for our own resurrection is negated, being dependent on Jesus alone. Thus, the last stage of religion, mysticism, is not even part of the spiritual plan of ordinary Christianity as it is understood and presented by most Christians in the world. The reason why people need constant revivals and emotional exuberance to keep them exited and interested is that the limited vision of the church will never satisfy the true yearning of the soul. This is because the worldly philosophy of the church is too limited. The soul, being Divine and infinite, will only find true peace and contentment through a mystical realization of its true nature, which is Divine and infinite. This is the higher message given by Jesus in the Bible book of John 10:34: *Jesus answered them, Is it not written in your law, I said, Ye are gods?*

So how can we unravel the intricate web of philosophies, faiths, doctrines, customs and traditions in order to discover the true meaning of spirituality in religion which transcends differences which lead to wars and strife? First we must understand what religion is and what is its purpose. Then we need to trace its origins and development. This journey will give us insights into the original intent and meaning, and show us how the forces of politics, economics and history have impacted and changed the doctrines and teachings of religion down to the present. Then we will be in a position to practice religion with an informed intellect and a pure heart which has been cleared of all diffidence.

The Ancient Egyptian Origins of Islam

Overview of Islam

In pre-Islamic Arabia, 360 gods and goddesses were worshipped.[302] They included Ancient Egyptian as well as Greek and Hindu divinities. One of these was Allah. The word *"Islam"* means to *"surrender."* In its religious application, Islam refers to *"surrendering to the will or the law of God."* Muhammad (c. 570-632 A.C.E.), the founder of Islam, said he had been given the word of God by the Angel Gabriel in a revelation. Thus, the origin of Islam is rooted in Jewish and Zoroastrian mythology. Muhammad said that Gabriel revealed to him that Allah is the Supreme Being and that the other gods and goddesses were equivalent to Angels, called *jinni*.[123] Allah was then referred to as *Allah Ta' Allah* or "The king of the gods." This concept is in every way equivalent to that of Ancient Egyptian religion, wherein the Supreme Being is referred to as *Pa Neter* or "The God." And Pa Neter is the Creator of the "Neteru" or gods and goddesses. Muhammad was convinced that he should share this revelation with others and succeeded in converting family members and friends. However, those following other religions met him with strong resistance in his hometown. When his wealthy wife Kadijah died, support from her wealthy friends was withdrawn. For a time he and his new religion lost favor in his hometown of Mecca, which up to that time worshipped the myriad of gods and goddesses, including Allah, however the worship of Allah was not in the context of Muhammad's new philosophy. Only one child of Muhammad and Kadijah, a daughter named Fatima, survived. She became a mother of many descendants of the prophet.

Mecca was a wealthy trading city and the visits by pilgrims to the already famous Kaaba shrine were very lucrative and sustaining to the city. In pre-Islamic Mecca (before 600 A.C.E.) the Kaaba was a shrine reserved from several gods and goddesses of Egyptian-Arabian origin. When Muhammad began to preach about Islam, his demands that people not only give up the other divinities, but that they also give up vices and follow a strict moral code made him and his religion unpopular. Muhammad and some close followers were forced to run away. Part of his sojourn was spent in Egypt, and later he ended up in the city of Medina. Medina had a substantial population of Christians and Jews who were familiar with the concept of monotheism, not in the original sense, as a Supreme Being, creator and source of other spirits (gods and goddesses), but rather the narrow, exclusive manner of thinking that there is only one God and no other gods and goddesses, just one entity expressing in one form and describable only through one religion, which has received a special "revelation."

The Koran and the Sonna (Sunna) texts are considered by Muslims to be the authoritative basis for the religion of Islam. The Koran is a grouping of histories, laws, and the precepts that Mohammed professed to have received directly from God or through the Angel Gabriel. Mohammed never learned to read or write. So the teachings of the Koran were written down for him. The Koran does not have any system of arrangement, and is divided into 114 chapters without a beginning, middle, or end.

When Arabs and other pilgrims of different religions traveled to Mecca to visit the Kaaba, Muhammad preached the new religion to them and told them he was God's prophet. He attacked their idolatry, and debated with followers of other religions who were opposing him. Muhammad made a few converts, but conflict escalated when his cousin Ali declared that he would do personal violence to anyone who refused to acknowledge Mohammed as the Prophet of God.

Ali's threats incurred the wrath of the people of Mecca and Mohammed was forced to leave Mecca in order to save his life in July 15, 622 A.C.E. This date marks the *Hegira* or the beginning of the Muslim calendar. In Medina he made many converts to his faith, since there were many people familiar with the Jews and Christians, and also there were many people who did not have much in the way of a financial stake in joining his faith. By contrast, the Meccans stood to lose their livelihood, just as the Pharisees stood to lose their power, wealth and prestige if they allowed Jesus to freely present his message to the

---

[123] The probable source for the lower concept of the genie, a supernatural creature who does one's bidding when summoned.

Jews. With Jesus' death, he became a martyr and the Christian faith grew. With Muhammad, he developed a political and religious power base in Medina and when he was ready, he marched on Mecca with an army of thousands, destroyed the shrines and idols to other divinities there and declared that the Kaaba was the shrine for Allah alone. From here ensued a wave of conversions throughout Arabia and the united Arab world began to produce a military expansion towards India in the east, and across North Africa in the west, and up into Spain and France in the north, where the Muslim armies were stopped by the German armies. The Muslims retreated to Spain and remained there for over 700 years until the royalty of Spain pushed the last Moors[124] out just prior to Columbus' fateful voyage in 1492 A.C.E. Thus, it is clear that Muhammad condoned war, conversion by force, and intolerance with other religions outside of the Islamic tradition. There is some measure of tolerance with Jews and Christians, but it is clear that ultimately there is a conflict, as the scriptures of each of these religions state that it is the true religion and has the right to destroy the others in order to establish the "correct" and sole worship of their Divinity. These actions (forced conversions) by the early Muslims recall to mind verses from the Bible (Exodus 32 25:28) which describe how Moses killed 3000 people who did not follow the Jewish path he had laid out, thereby opening the door to the advocacy of killing, even though God had given him the Ten Commandments, one of which stated *"Thou shalt not kill,* only minutes before.

Out of Egypt: "The Arabian People"

Through their association with Egypt from the time of Abraham, Moses, Joseph, and the early years of Jesus, the early Jews and Christians adopted many of the Ancient Egyptian ideas and rituals into the developing Jewish and Christian faiths, respectively. According to the Bible, the Jews owe their existence to Ancient Egypt, as Abraham had a son with the Egyptian slave of his wife, Sarah, who was unable to conceive a child for a period of time, as well as due to the assimilation of hundreds of Egyptians into his family which had previously been just he, his wife and children along with some close relatives. In the biblical tradition, Abraham's son, Ishmael, is held as the progenitor of the Arabian peoples. The word "Ishmael" means "God will hear."

The Koran (Quran)[125] acknowledges that Abraham was the progenitor of the Arabs. It recognizes Ismail's (Ishmael) line as well as Israel's line as originating from Abraham. It extols the virtues of Ismail and further states that Abraham, with Ismail's assistance, built the Kaaba (Temple of Mecca) and purified it, thus establishing the religion of Islam. There is no evidence to show that this actually occurred. Rather, it is a co-optation of the already existing religion present in Mecca. So now, the worship of the Kaaba continues, but under "new management" so to speak, and the new managers advertised their own propaganda about its origins and history. Over time, this new fiction came to be regarded as the real history and this idea has gained strength over the years in the absence of any challenge since none is allowed. No other religion is allowed to worship at the Kaaba and this physical prevention is in itself a means by which the myth is perpetuated that Islam is the proper religion of the Kaaba, and in fact for all Arabs and anyone else within their sphere of influence.

> The Koran
>
> 2:125 Remember We made the House a place of assembly for men and a place of safety; and take ye the Station of Abraham as a place of prayer; and We covenanted with Abraham and Ismail, that they should sanctify My house for those who compass it round, or use it as a retreat, or bow, or prostrate themselves (therein in prayer).
> 2:126 And remember Abraham said: "My Lord, make this a City of Peace, and feed its People with fruits, -- such of them as believe in Allah and the Last Day." He said: "(Yea), and such as reject Faith, -- for a while will I grant them their pleasure, but will soon drive them to the torment of Fire, -- An evil destination (indeed)!"
> 2:127 And remember Abraham and Ismail raised the foundations of the House (with this prayer): "Our Lord! Accept (this service) from us: For Thou art the All-Hearing, the All-Knowing."
> 2:128 "Our Lord! Make of us Muslims, bowing to Thy (Will), and of our progeny a people Muslim, bowing to Thy (Will); and show us our places for the celebration of (due) rites; and turn unto us (in Mercy); for Thou art the Oft-Returning, Most Merciful."

---

[124] Black African Muslims mixed with Arab Muslims from north Africa
[125] The sacred text of Islam, believed to contain the revelations made by Allah to Mohammed.

There is no historical record of proof that Ismail (Ishmael) built the Kaaba. The takeover of the Kaaba was a move to co-opt the already ongoing religious worship of the pre-Islamic Arabians and to establish Allah as the supreme power. This predicament is remindful of Matthew 23:13-16 where the scribes and Pharisees who minister to the Jewish people in Jesus' time are chastised for their worldliness and hypocrisy based on their limited understanding and practice of Judaism, and their egoistic values which limit them as well as the masses of people practicing the religion. Muhammad wanted to reform religion, but not like the Christians, who adopted the Old Testament as part of their scriptures. Muhammad was actually creating a new religion even while acknowledging a connection to the old.

> Matthew 23
> 13. But woe to you, scribes and Pharisees, hypocrites! For ye shut up the kingdom of heaven against men: for ye neither go in [yourselves], neither permit ye them that are entering to go in.
> 14 Woe to you, scribes and Pharisees, hypocrites! For ye devour widows' houses, and for a pretence make long prayer: therefore ye shall receive the greater damnation.
> 15 Woe to you, scribes and Pharisees, hypocrites! For ye travel sea and land to make one proselyte, and when he is made, ye make him twofold more the child of hell than yourselves.
> 16 Woe to you, [ye] blind guides, who say, Whoever shall swear by the temple, it is nothing; but whoever shall swear by the gold of the temple, he is a debtor!

Thus, it is clear that the people originally inhabiting Egypt were black Africans but over time the population became Arab. However, the religion of Islam has fundamental differences with the African Religion of Ancient Egypt. These differences lead to a repudiation of Ancient African Religion and its people.[303]

Muhammad Goes into Egypt

So, ironically, Muhammad, the founder of Islam, was opposed by other Arab leaders in the earlier stages of the development of his "new" religion in much the same way as Jesus was repudiated by the religious leaders of his time. Like Abraham, Josef, and Jesus, Muhammad was forced to flee into Egypt and Ethiopia where he and his followers further developed Islamic philosophy. In this manner, Muhammad gained from the Gnostic Egyptian religion and culture. He also married an Ethiopian woman.

The major tenets of Orthodox Islam are:

1- *There is only one God, unitary and omnipresent. God is separate from creation and manages it from afar.*
2- *The plurality of Gods or the extension of God's divinity to any person is strongly rejected.*
3- *God created nature through a primordial act of mercy, lest there would be only nothingness.*
4- *God governs creation. All areas of creation were given laws to follow. The following of these laws creates perfect harmony. The breaking of them creates disharmony. Since there are laws, there is no need for miracles. The Koran is the highest miracle which no man will match.*
5- *The ultimate purpose of humanity is to serve God in order to reform the earth.*
6- *God has four functions: Creation, Sustenance, Guidance, Judgment.*
7- *After death, those who lived by the laws will go to the Garden (Heaven); those who did not will go to Hell.*

The term Allah, the Muslim[126] name for the Supreme Being, provides insights into the origins of Islamic theology. It is a contraction of the Arabic word al-llah or "The God." As discussed above, the word and the idea existed in the Arabian tradition before Islam. In this (Arabian) mythology there was a limited form of monotheism which was practiced. Even though other lesser gods were recognized, the pre-Islamic Arabs also recognized Allah as their Supreme God. So the Islamic and Jewish traditions have

---
[126] A believer in or adherent of Islam - Koran 22:78

polytheistic backgrounds from which they selected one divinity to represent a Supreme Being above the others. Thus, upon closer examination, the Jewish and Islamic traditions have much in common with Ancient Egyptian religion which is composed of a Supreme Being (Pa Neter) from which the gods and goddesses (neteru) emanate. Recall also that the term Allah meaning "The God" is exactly the same as the Ancient Egyptian term Pa-Neter which means "The God," and "Supreme Being." The following statements from Ancient Egyptian mystical philosophy denote a remarkable concordance with the Islamic teachings.

> The number given in parenthesis denotes the Islamic tenet (above) to which the Ancient Egyptian philosophy corresponds.
>
> (A) Ancient Egyptian philosophy: God is "Only One Without a second." (1)
>
> (B) Plurality means: "Consisting of more than one choice." While Ancient Egyptian religion appears to consist of many gods and goddesses, in reality they are only symbols referring to the one Supreme Being. This form of religious practice was the basis of Ancient Egyptian religion and the religion of other nations, but was misunderstood over a period of time. However, before the emergence of Islam, the Arab peoples were in contact with and at one time governed by the Ancient Egyptians, and were thus exposed to their religion. The reverence of the Jews and the Muslims for a single supreme God is in agreement with Ancient Egyptian religion. However, the manner of worship and the understanding about who that Divinity is was changed by the Jews and Muslims. In Neterian Religion, God is not separate and far away from Creation. God is Creation itself, and the force which sustains all life. (2)
>
> (C) God created the universe by uttering the first thought and sound and brought order out of the preexisting void. (3)
>
> (D) Maat (cosmic principle of truth, order, righteousness and harmony {law}) is the means by which God governs the universe. (4)
>
> (E) Ancient Egyptian Proverbs: "Give thyself to The God, keep thou thyself daily for The God; and let tomorrow be as today." "What is loved by God is obedience; God hateth disobedience." (5)
>
> (F) In Ancient Egyptian Religion, God is the Creator in the form of Khepri, the Sustainer in the form of Ra and the Destroyer in the form of Tem. The first teaching related to a judgment of the soul as well as heaven and hell occurs in the Neterian Religion. However, God does not judge. Every human being is the judge of himself or herself on the day of judgment because it is each individual's own actions that lead them to experience hellish or heavenly conditions after death. The coveted goal is to go to heaven (Pet) and to meet God and become one with God. (6)

The Islamic tradition believes in a final judgment. It is believed that on the Day of Judgment, all humanity will be gathered by God. All individuals will be judged according to their deeds alone. Those who "succeed" will go to the Garden (heaven), and those who "lose" will go to hell.

The religion of Islam is in agreement with the existence of Abraham and Jesus, and there is special veneration for the Virgin Mary. While there are only seventeen references to the Virgin Mary in the Christian New Testament, she is mentioned thirty-four times in the Quran (Koran), the Islamic Holy Scripture (7th century A.C.E.). Muslims believed that she conceived miraculously, and that God had sent angels to tell her the good news. This tradition follows the New Testament closely; see the passages below from the Quran (Koran).

> "Behold!" the Angels said: 'O Mary God hath chosen thee above the women of all nations." (Quran 3:42)
>
> The Angels proceeded: "O Mary! God giveth thee glad tidings of a word from Him: his name will be Jesus, the son of Mary, held in honor in this world and the Hereafter and (of the company of) those nearest to God. He shall speak to the people in childhood and in maturity." (Quran 3:46)

Upon receiving this news, although a good piece of news, Mary in her innocence, was shocked. Mary responded: "O My Lord! How shall I have a son when no man hath touched me?" The Angel replied: "Even so: God critter what he willeth: When He decreed a Plan, He but saith to it, 'Be' and it is." (Quran 3:47-48)

Muslims believe that Jesus was a prophet of Allah. However, they believe that he was only preparing the way for Muhammad, the prophet and founder of the Islamic faith. The following passage from the Koran illustrates the Islamic view.

> 61:6 And remember, Jesus, the son of Mary, said: "O Children of Israel! I am the apostle of Allah (sent) to you, confirming the Law (which came) before me, and giving Glad Tidings of an Apostle to come after me, whose name shall be Ahmad. " But when he came to them with Clear Signs, they said, "This is evident sorcery!"

Islam and Christianity

Thus, Muhammad (also Mohammed) was an ordinary man in the sixth century A.C.E. who became a practitioner of monastic meditation. In his early life he followed the Arab religions, but broke away from these when he had a series of visions. Out of these insights he developed the teachings of Islam, and these developed into the religion of the Muslims.[127] The teachings of Islam are compiled in the *Koran* or Islamic Holy scripture. Muhammad accepted the teachings of the Old Testament in his creation of the new religion (Islam). Having originated out of the Old Testament tradition, which itself has its roots in Ancient Egyptian religion, the Islamic tradition (600 A.C.E.) picked up on the Old Testament teachings about Egypt and portrayed the same negative view, as the following verse from the Koran attests. In the same manner that the Jews denigrated Ancient Egypt for the sake of promoting Yahweh, the Muslims disparaged Egypt for the sake of promoting Allah, the Supreme Being in Islamic tradition.

It is notable that the Koran acknowledges that the God of the Jews is also the God that Islam recognizes as Allah. The following *Suras* or statements from the Koran show the similarity of ideology between Judaism, Orthodox Christianity and Islam on the question of the acceptance of Abraham (A), the idea of one God (B), and Jesus (C).

(A)
2:122 Section 15. O Children of Israel! Call to mind the special favor which I bestowed upon you, and that I preferred you to all others (for My Message).
2:123 Then guard yourselves against a day when one soul shall not avail another, nor shall compensation be accepted from her, nor shall intercession profit her, nor shall anyone be helped (from outside).
2:124 And remember that Abraham was tried by his Lord with certain Commands, which he fulfilled: He said: "I will make thee an Imam[128] to the Nations." He pleaded: "And also (Imams) from my offspring!" He answered: "But My Promise is not within the reach of evildoers."
2:125 Remember We made the House a place of assembly for men and a place of safety; and take ye the Station of Abraham as a place of prayer; and We covenanted with Abraham and Ismail, that they should sanctify My house for those who compass it round, or use it as a retreat, or bow, or Prostrate themselves (therein in prayer).

(B)
2:163 And your Allah is One God: There is no god but He, Most Gracious, Most Merciful.

(C)
4:171 O People of the Book! Commit no excesses in your religion: Nor say of Allah ought but the truth. Christ Jesus the son of Mary was (no more than) an apostle of Allah, and His Word, which He bestowed on Mary, and a Spirit proceeding from Him: So believe in Allah and His apostles. Say not "Trinity": desist: It will be better for you: For Allah is One God: Glory be to Him: (Far Exalted is He) above having a son. To Him belong all things in the heavens and on earth. And enough is Allah as a Disposer of affairs.

---

[127] A believer in or adherent of Islam.
[128] **i·mam** also **I·mam** ('-mäm") *n. Islam.* **1.a.** In law and theology, the caliph who is successor to Mohammed as the lawful supreme leader of the Islamic community.

5:76 They do blaspheme who say: Allah is one of three in a Trinity: For there is no god except One God. If they desist not from their word (of blasphemy), verily a grievous penalty will befall the blasphemers among them.

6:19 Say: "What thing is most weighty in evidence?" Say: "Allah is witness between me and you; this Koran hath been revealed to me by inspiration, that I may warn you and all whom it reaches. Can ye possibly bear witness that besides Allah there is another god?" Say: "Nay! I cannot bear witness!" Say: "But in truth He is the One God, and I truly am innocent of (your blasphemy of) joining others with Him."

9:31 They take their priests and their anchorites to be their lords in derogation of Allah, and (they take as their Lord) Christ the son of Mary; Yet they were commanded to worship but One God: There is no god but He. Praise and glory to Him: (Far is He) from having the partners they associate (with Him).

14:52 Here is a Message for mankind: Let them take warning therefrom, and let them know that He is (no other than) One God: Let men of understanding take heed.

16:51 Section 7. Allah has said: "Take not (for worship) two gods: For He is just One God: Then fear Me (and Me alone)."

21:108 Say: "What has come to me by inspiration is that your God is One God: Will ye therefore bow to His Will (in Islam)?"

Many of the statements above consist in delineating the differences between Islam, Christianity and Judaism, whereby the prophet Muhammad chastises the Christians for believing in a prophet (Jesus) as God, and as God in the form of a Trinity. Other statements are emphatic admonitions to the effect that Allah is the only God, and that he is one and alone. Further, that anyone who does not know this and who dies unbelieving will not be saved.

These statements and belief systems were adopted by honest believers and also by unscrupulous opportunists who saw a chance to wage war on other peoples. This was a driving factor which fueled the rapid expansion of Islam throughout the Middle East leading to "holy wars" which expanded the Islamic conquests to encompass North Africa, Spain, South Eastern Europe, Turkey, Persia, Arabia and Western India.

Islam's conquest of Persia around the seventh century led to the decline and near disappearance of the Zoroastrian religion in Persia. In the same manner that the Christian Church had adopted several ideas and symbols which had been previously labeled as "heretical," such as the cross, Islam adopted and accepted the teachings from the Old Testament and the worship of the *Ka'bah,* which had previously been a ritual worship center of many so called pagan gods in Mecca.

Even though the three major Western world religions (Christianity, Islam, Judaism) share several common beliefs, such as the same monotheistic and anthropomorphic belief in one God and the basic beliefs of the ancient Hebrew scriptures that are found in the Old Testament of the Christian Bible and in the Jewish Torah, the accent on *Folk* differences at the lower stage of religion (myth) has been instrumental in fueling the fires of discontent and animosity between them.[76]

Islam came to prominence at a time (c. 600 A.C.E.) when the Christian Church was in conflict due to corruption, invaders from Europe (Vikings, Vandals, Celts, Visigoths, etc.), internal disagreements and the loss of faith in church doctrine which was seen as ineffective and unfulfilling by many. The many prophecies which never came true and the disregard of the church leaders for the teachings of Jesus in favor of conquest and personal or church enrichment fostered a climate of unrest and discontent with the church.

Islam offered a new direction to those disillusioned by the Christian Church. This way was even more so grounded in the world of human activity, as it emphasized less mysticism, more action in the world, more ritualistic exercises and blind obedience rather than dogmas related to celibacy, asceticism, renunciation, humility, etc., which though espoused by Christian leaders, were misunderstood and ignored by many of them. Islam offered a polygamous lifestyle, as well as a warlike and hostile attitude towards nature. It also promoted the pursuit of fulfillment of sensual pleasures while on earth as opposed to hoping to experience heavenly enjoyments after death, a doctrine heavily promoted by the Christians. Rather than effacement of the ego self-concept, the form of Islam which developed after the passing of the Prophet Muhammad encouraged the pride of Islamic culture and the pursuit of glory through establishing supremacy over the known world. Islamic conquests would eventually encompass North Africa, Spain, Turkey, South-East Europe, the Near East and India.

Islamic Imperialism, The Fall of Rome and the Breakup of the Christian Church

The history of the early followers of Islam demonstrates the enmity that existed between the Muslims, Jews, and Christians. Also, it provides insight into the Muslim outlook on the world as a duty to spread the Islamic faith and extend Islamic authority over the world. The teachings of Islam allow for the institution of slavery, though exhorting that they should be well treated. The following teaching of Mohammed demonstrates the view reflected in his own actions as he marched on Mecca with his army, that unbelievers should be converted by force, even to their death, and that their icons should be destroyed and also that doing battle for the sake of Allah will lead to great spiritual merit: "The sword," said Mohammed, "is the key of heaven and hell; a drop of blood shed in the cause of Allah, a night spent in arms, is of more avail than two months of fasting and prayer; whosoever falls in battle, his sins are forgiven, and at the day of judgment his limbs shall be supplied by the wings of angels." This kind of ideal is a flashpoint from which many Muslims derive a divine dispensation to enter into expansionist ventures, the right to impose Islam on others and deprive them from practicing other forms of religion, and the right to engage in "holy wars" (jihad) with others. This kind of philosophy provides a basis for a form of manifest destiny among certain Islamic followers. This factor engenders consternation in the minds of many non-Muslims around the world, especially those whose countries are in close proximity to the countries of predominantly Islamic faith.

After the fall of Rome in c. 476 A.C.E., the Western Roman Empire divided into unstable "barbarian" kingdoms. There was much strife and chaos in Europe at this time and the inhabitants of Europe suffered invasions from the Vikings as well as from northern hoards of barbarians such as the Vandals[129] and others. This period is often referred to as the Dark Ages.[130] Many Europeans adopted institutions of the by then defunct Roman Empire and attempted to establish order in their own locals while at the same time fighting off outside invasions. During this time the Byzantine Empire became cut off from the West and the church in Rome. In the West Christianity became a powerful political tool among the barbarian kingdoms in the late Middle Ages.[131] Many students of history note that Christianity was almost wiped out and the kingdoms of the dark ages were almost destroyed by the invasions from outside. The Muslims were a grave threat to Western Culture, almost conquering all of Europe as they apparently intended to establish Islamic control of the known civilized world. Wherever the Muslims took over their countries, the Jews and Christians were allowed a measure of freedom to continue their form of worship, but they had little political power and were required to pay tribute (taxes) to the Muslim government. Jews and Christians were allowed a certain measure of freedom in practicing their religion because it was recognized by the Muslims that they originate from the same tradition and how would it look to make war on them on that basis. Rather, they were seen as imperfect practitioners of religion, Islam being the perfect way, and they were never allowed in leadership positions but only in subservient ones. Only Muslims could hold offices and control large businesses. The destruction of Jews and Christians would come on other pretexts such as corruption, injustice, etc. However, the segregation forced many Christians and Jews to convert to Islam if they wanted to avoid being denigrated and if they wanted to have any meaningful participation in the Arab ruled countries. Followers of any other religions were forced to convert to Islam. In this manner by 711 A.C.E. they conquered an area greater than the Roman Empire at its height, from China and central Asia in the east (including India) to Asia Minor, north Africa and Spain in the west.

In 711 A.C.E.. the Muslims crossed the Strait of Gibraltar and attacked the Visigoths, who posed little resistance, and Spain fell under Islamic rule. The Muslims crossed the Pyrenees, and overran the valley of the Rhone. They headed for the Tours, a city in NW central France, on the Loire River, 129mi (208km) SW of Paris. It was the scene of battle in which Charles Martel[132] defeated the Saracens (Arabs), in A.C.E. 732.[304] The Muslims met the army of the Germans at Tours and were defeated there. Their string

---

[129] A member of a Germanic people that overran Gaul, Spain, and northern Africa in the fourth and fifth centuries A.C.E. and sacked Rome in c. 455.
[130] The early part of the Middle Ages from about A.C.E. 500 to about A.C.E. 1000.
[131] The period in European history between antiquity and the Renaissance, regarded as dating from A.C.E. 476 to 1453.
[132] Charles Martel (688-741), Frankish ruler, natural son of Pepin of Heristal, grandfather of Charlemagne. Franks, Germanic people who settled along the Rhine in the 3rd century AD. (Random House Encyclopedia Copyright (C) 1983,1990 by Random House Inc.)

of victories in which they overran almost the entire medieval world came to an end as they were pushed back into Spain, where they and their descendants remained for over 700 years. They never again appeared north of the Pyrenees.

Charles Martel (Charles the Hammer) was a German king and the leader of the Franks at the Battle of Tours. His grandson, King Charlemagne, unified Europe and thus became the greatest figure of medieval Europe. Charlemagne was instrumental in the survival of the Western Christian church. Charlemagne (742-814 A.C.E.), was the king of the Franks,[133] (768-814 A.C.E.) and the Holy Roman emperor (sanctioned by the Roman Catholic church) from 800-814 A.C.E. He captured the Lombard throne in Italy (773 A.C.E.). Due to the Saxon raids, he waged war from 772 A.C.E. to 785 A.C.E. and conquered Saxony, thereby securing Christianity. Charlemagne also captured Bavaria and defeated the Avars of the middle Danube in 791-96 A.C.E., which added new lands to his empire. In 811 A.C.E. he strengthened Christianity in parts of northern Spain by establishing the Spanish March, a Christian refuge there. Pope Leo III in 800 A.C.E crowned him emperor. He had united the Germanic peoples for the first time, but his empire lacked strength and broke up after his death. Charlemagne was canonized[134] in 1165 A.C.E.

As time passed, various European kingdoms consolidated their power and used religion for political purposes. Christianity was used by Christian religious and political leaders as a weapon against rivals and foreigners who opposed them. In this sense the church assumed the right to persecute those who would not convert to Christianity and to suppress any dissenting religious and political views which it labeled as heresy. Thus, being in control of the government, the church was able to use religion as a way to accomplish political and economic goals as it wished.

The Byzantines considered themselves as Romans and therefore as heirs of the Roman Empire even though their society was a mixture of many social and cultural elements due to the cosmopolitan nature of the city. The Byzantines modeled their government after the Roman Empire while adopting Greek language and cultural customs in general. However, Orthodox Christianity determined their religious direction.

After the fall of Rome, the Byzantine State attempted to continue the Roman Empire. When the Roman Empire in the West had fallen into decline due to the Germanic invasions, imperial traditions were kept alive in the East. Emperor Justinian I (r.527-65) re-conquered the territory which had been held by the old Roman Empire, and codified the Roman law between the years 610 A.C.E. to 717 A.C.E. The empire defeated its Persian enemies under the Heraclian emperors. The Macedonian epoch of 867 A.C.E. to 1081 A.C.E. is referred to as the Golden Age of the Byzantine Empire. This was the time of cultural renaissance and territorial consolidation. The West was slowly emerging from the interminable wars and social crisis of the Dark and Middle ages. As the first millennium A.C.E. drew to a close, the West began to reconstruct Europe. Then the attention turned towards foreign conquests and on asserting control over all Christian churches, property and authority, which Constantinople had assumed after the fall of the Roman Empire. A struggle ensued between the Church leaders of Rome (Western Roman Empire) and Constantinople (Eastern Roman empire) due to disagreements as to the canon of the Christian doctrine and the authority of the Christian church.

The Church of Rome claimed not only the primacy of Rome, but also the doctrine of papal infallibility, which held that the Roman Pope was the final authority on Church matters. Having regained military power after defeating the barbarian groups of Europe, the Western empire promoted the crusades which would effectively expand the Western Christian Church Empire and at the same time gain control over the domain of the Eastern Empire. The crusaders gained control over Byzantium during the dominion of the Latin Empire of Constantinople (1204-61). In 1261, Michael VIII, restored the Greek Empire (Eastern Church), and founded the Palaeologan Dynasty (1261-1453). In 1453, Constantinople fell to the Turkish forces of Sultan Muhammad II and the Byzantine Empire came to a final end, never to rise again. Nevertheless, the Eastern Church subsequently broke up into two major sects, the Eastern Orthodox Church and the Coptic Church in Egypt which had, up to that time, remained in association with Constantinople.

---

[133] Germanic peoples who settled along the Rhine river in the 3rd century A.C.E.
[134] When the church declares a deceased person a saint.

Arab and Muslim Conquest of Egypt and the Schism between Judaism and Christianity and Between Judaism, Christianity and Islam

The Arab conquest periods of in Ancient Egypt includes the Caliphate and the Mamalukes[135] period (642-1517 A.C.E.). Next follows the Muslim Ottoman Turk[136] domination period (1082-1882 A.C.E.) which was interrupted by the British colonialism period (1882-1952 A.C.E.). In the developing years of Islam (7th – 10th century A.C.E.), there was a fierce conflict between the new religion (Islam) and the previously existing religious practices that existed at the time in Asia Minor, including the remnants of Ancient Egyptian religion and Christianity. The following excerpts from the Koran have been provided to give further insight into the onslaught that was experienced by the Egyptian people (descendants of the Ancient Egyptians) from the attacks of the Muslims.

In the Koran itself there is a proud, and some would even say conceited or self-important or even arrogant statement, which like those of the Judeo-Christian tradition, elevates the Muslims above other peoples, especially the Jews and Christians (3:110 Section 12), implying that the Arab culture and people are the most "evolved" form of human being because they best practice righteousness (*"enjoining what is right, forbidding what is wrong"*) when compared to other peoples.

The Muslims "Are the Best of Peoples"

> 3:110 Section 12 (Koran). <u>We are the best of Peoples, evolved for mankind, enjoining what is right, forbidding what is wrong, and believing in Allah</u>. If only the People of the Book had faith, it were best for them: Among them are some who have faith, but most of them are perverted transgressors.

In reading the Koran there is a sense that Islam is protecting itself (and also by extension, Arab culture as well) from the "unbelievers," (4:101 Section 15) who are later described as Jews and Christians, as well as polytheists, and the attempts (of the Jews and Christians) to undermine the Muslims and their way of life for their own nefarious ends (5:54 Section 8). The excerpts also show the philosophical schism between Islam and Judaism and Christianity (2:113 Section 14).

Unbelievers are the enemy

> 4:101 Section 15 (Koran). When ye travel through the earth, there is no blame on you if ye shorten your prayers, for fear the Unbelievers may attack you: For the Unbelievers are unto you open enemies.

Animosity between the Muslims and the Jews and Christians
> 2:111 (Koran) And they say: "<u>None shall enter Paradise unless he be Jew or a Christian.</u>" Those are their (vain) desires. Say: "Produce your proof if ye are truthful."
> 2:112 (Koran) Nay, -- whoever submits his whole self to Allah and is a doer of good, -- he will get his reward with his Lord; on such shall they grieve.
> 2:113 Section 14 (Koran). <u>The Jews say: "The Christians have naught (to stand) upon"; and the Christians say: "The Jews have naught (to stand) upon."</u> Yet they (profess to) study the (same) Book. Like unto their word is what those say who know not; but Allah will judge between them in their quarrel on the Day of Judgment.

In order to counteract the missionary, and expansionist designs of the Jews and Christians, the early followers of Islam, beginning with Muhammad, incorporated statements about the Christians, characterizing them as "enemies" and describing how they seek to convert the Muslims and all people to

---

[135] Originally they were Turkish and Circassian prisoners of Genghis Khan who were sold as slaves to the sultan of Egypt, who trained them as soldiers. They fought for Egypt but then seized power. (Random House Encyclopedia Copyright (C) 1983,1990 by Random House Inc)
[136] Ottoman Empire – empire by Arabs from Turkey that controlled Asia Minor for 600-years (13th century to early 20th century.)

their faith with the idea that *"None shall enter Paradise unless he be Jew or a Christian"* (2:111) and other similar tenets. The Koran contains responses that the "believers," the Muslims, should give to the "unbelievers" (Jews and Christians). The statements belie fundamental differences between the three groups and also the political necessity to resist the Jews and Christians in order to sustain the Islamic faith, to the degree that the Jews and Christians are mentioned specifically and their actions are described in detail. The Koran states emphatically that the Jews and Christians can never be satisfied with anyone who does not believe as they do (2:120), and that the Jews and Christians say that in order to "be guided" to salvation (2:135), the Muslims must "become Jews or Christians" (2:135). One of the main contentions is the belief that Jesus is the son of God. To this the Muslims are to reply to the Jews and Christians that "we believe in Allah" and the revelation given to the prophets (of the old Bible) and that "we make no difference between one and another of them (prophets): And we bow to Allah (in Islam)" (2:136)

Struggle Against the Jewish and the Christian Missionaries[137]

2:120 (Koran) <u>Never will the Jews or the Christians be satisfied with thee unless thou follow their form of religion.</u> Say: "The Guidance of Allah, -- that is the (only) Guidance." Wert thou to follow their desires after the knowledge which hath reached thee, then wouldst thou find neither Protector nor Helper against Allah.

2:121 (Koran) Those to whom We have sent the Book study it as it should be studied: They are the ones that believe therein: Those who reject faith therein, -- the loss is their own.

2:135 (Koran) <u>They say: "Become Jews or Christians if ye would be guided (to salvation)." Say thou: "Nay! (I would rather) the Religion of Abraham the True, and he joined not gods with Allah."</u>

2:136 (Koran) Say ye: "We believe in Allah, and the revelation given to us, and to Abraham, Ismail, Isaac, Jacob, and the Tribes, and that given to Moses and Jesus, and that given to (all) Prophets from their Lord: <u>We make no difference between one and another of them: And we bow to Allah (in Islam)."</u>

2:137 (Koran) So if they believe as ye believe, they are indeed on the right path; but if they turn back, it is they who are in schism; but Allah will suffice thee as against them, and He is the All-Hearing, the All-Knowing.

Verse 5:54 Section 8 is an injunction to not befriend either the Jews or the Christians or allow them to be "protectors" of the Muslims (i.e. government leaders) as they have their own interests ahead of anyone else's. Verse 3:118 goes even further, stating that the words of the "People of the Book" (i.e. Jews and Christians) are "Rank hatred" and what "their hearts conceal" is even "worse." Verse 3:119 is very telling in its implications. It states that even those Arabs who converted to the "whole of the Book" (Bible) have been mistreated by the Jews and Christians. This expresses extended dealings between the Muslims and the Jews and Christians and also implies the underlying ethnic differentiation that was made by the Jews and Christians which has been evident throughout history in the dealings between the Jews and Christians and other groups from around the world, including Native Americans, Africans, Asians, etc. Thus, a component of racism appears to be present in the concept of the early Jews and Christians, and this insincerity and duplicitous ulterior agenda further gave impetus to the rise of Islam in the Middle and Far East as well as North Africa.

5:54 Section 8 (Koran). O ye who believe! <u>Take not the Jews and the Christians for your friends and protectors</u>: They are but friends and protectors to each other. And he amongst you that turns to them (for friendship) is of them. Verily Allah guideth not a people unjust.

---

[137] One who attempts to persuade or convert others to a particular program, doctrine, or set of principles; a propagandist.

THE AFRICAN ORIGINS OF CIVILIZATION, RELIGION AND YOGA SPIRITUALITY

3:118 (Koran) O ye who believe! Take not into your intimacy those outside your ranks: <u>They will not fail to corrupt you. They only desire your ruin: Rank hatred has already appeared from their mouths: What their hearts conceal is far worse.</u> We have made plain to you the Signs, if ye have wisdom.

3:119 (Koran) <u>Ah! Ye are those who love them, but they love you not, -- though ye believe in the whole of the Book.</u> When they meet you they say, "We believe": But when they are alone, they bite off the very tips of their fingers at you in their rage. Say: "Perish in your rage; Allah knoweth well all the secrets of the heart."

Verses 3:118-9 give the impression that the early Muslims felt the pressure of the Jewish Christian movement trying to encroach on the Muslim territory and religious life. The introduction of the Jewish state into Palestine without regard to the population of Palestinians there, forcibly displacing people, and then suppressing their protests while at the same time preventing their development of their economy and infrastructure, has been likened by many Arab-Muslims in present-day Islamic countries (especially Palestine) to a form of racism[305] that is expressed in the form of Zionism[138], which is practiced by Western countries towards populations composed of non-Caucasians.

The following verse from the Koran is significant because it states in no uncertain language that the teachings brought to the world by the "holy Apostle" (Muhammad) "supercedes" that of the Jews. Verse 9:30 Section 5 specifically takes issue with the Christian idea that "Christ is the son of Allah" and that in this they *"imitate what the Unbelievers of old used to say."* This statement refers to the Ancient Egyptian religion, as Heru, the savior and prototype for the Christian Christ figure, was also stated to be the son of God (Asar, Osiris). The Muslims see this concept as a great "delusion" coming from "their mouth" i.e. not from revelation.

Thus, the Islamic faith seeks to put down and invalidate the Jewish and Christian faith just as they too seek to put down and invalidate Islam. These three religions therefore, are scripturally gridlocked in a vicious cycle of disharmony and conflict. As the seeds of dissension and disharmony are embedded in the scriptures themselves, despite the attempts to promote harmony and peace between the religions, there will ultimately be an incompatibility that will lead to conflict.

This conflict is even more pronounced when the views of these three religions, which consider themselves to be "monotheistic" are considered in so far as their relations with what they consider to be "polytheistic" religions such as the Kamitan and the Hindu religions. There is more denigration, more invalidation and hence more rejection and violence directed at those religions. So while many people claim that Islam is a religion of "peace" because the word "Islam" which means "submission to God" is related to the word for peace, in reality there can be no peace when such statements are included in the religious faith. They inevitably lead to a separation and a competition between faiths, as long as there are people who believe in the scriptures themselves. Since there is no way for these religions to continue without their "holy scriptures" and the prospect of amending them is virtually nil, then it follows that there can likely be no permanent resolution to this problem. A permanent resolution can only occur if these aspects of the scriptures are expunged, and if that were to happen, it would present a contradiction to the orthodox followers since they regard the "whole scripture" as a "divine revelation," which, to them, means that the entire scripture is "true," and "perfect," and thus must be followed in its entirety.

9:30 Section 5 (Koran). <u>The Jews call Uzair (Ezra) a son of Allah, and the Christians call Christ the Son of Allah. That is a saying from their mouth; (In this) they imitate what the Unbelievers of old used to say. Allah's curse be on them: How they are deluded away from the Truth!</u>

---

[138] An organized movement of world Jewry that arose in Europe in the late 19th century with the aim of reconstituting a Jewish state in Palestine. Modern Zionism is concerned with the development and support of the state of Israel.

Islamic Views on the Polytheists (including the Ancient Egyptian and Hindu religions)

As for the Islamic views on the followers of the Ancient Egyptian religion, they are indirectly mentioned as Polytheists and are grouped together with the Jews and Christians as well as other non-Islamic groups, i.e. any groups that do not believe "the truth." The Polytheists as well as the Jews and Christians will be "judged by Allah" (22:17) and since they have an "evil opinion of Allah" (48:6), and they "reject truth (true faith) (98:5-6) they will go to hell (48:6).

> 22:17 (Koran) Those who believe (in the Koran), those who follow the Jewish (scriptures), and the Sabians, Christians, Megians, and Polytheists, -- Allah will judge between them on the Day of Judgment: For Allah is witness of all things.

> 48:6 (Koran) And that He may punish the Hypocrites, men and women, and the Polytheists, men and women, who imagine an evil opinion of Allah. On them is a round of Evil: The Wrath of Allah is on them: He has cursed them and got Hell ready for them: and evil is it for a destination.

> 98:5 (Koran) And they have been commanded no more than this: To worship Allah, offering Him sincere devotion, being True (in faith); to establish regular Prayer; and to practice regular Charity; and that is the Religion Right and Straight.

> 98:6 (Koran) Those who reject (Truth), among the People of the Book and among the Polytheists, will be in Hellfire, to dwell therein (for aye). They are the worst of creatures.

The Spread of Islam Throughout Africa

The Conflict of Islam with African Religion

The Hierarchy of Divinity in African Religion	The Hierarchy of Divinity in Islamic Religion
Supreme Being ↓ Lesser Divinities (gods and goddesses)	No minor gods ✸✸✸
Monotheistic	Monotheistic
No separation between secular and sacred ✸	No separation between secular and sacred
Allows plural marriage (modern practice) ✸✸	Allows plural marriage
Belief in afterlife	Belief in afterlife
Belief in moral basis for living a spiritual life.	Belief in moral basis for living a spiritual life.

✸ **NOTE:** Many African countries such as Ghana have turned away from the traditional system (African model) of government, of chieftains who oversee the spiritual and secular well-being of the community. They have accepted the western model of society having secular leaders who maintain a separation between themselves and the religious leaders.

✳✳ <u>NOTE:</u> While plural marriage is a part of present day African culture this social practice is not general nor was it so in ancient times. Modern day forces such as colonialism, war, disease, etc. have promoted plural marriage to insure the continued growth of the population.

✳✳✳ <u>NOTE:</u> Islam does not officially accept the notion of lesser divinities. However, as the Christians, they do accept the concept of saints and angels which serve some of the same function of the gods and goddesses in African Religion.

The table above shows that African Religion and Islam would seem to have many aspects in common. Therefore, this similarity should tend to produce harmony between them. But why then is there enmity? The enmity comes in because the Muslims do not agree with the form or method of African worship, even if they were to agree that they are monotheists, which is the most important tenet of the religion. African monotheism is ultimately incompatible with Islam because African monotheism sees the spirit as being immanent in nature while orthodox Islam, like orthodox Christianity, sees God as separate from nature. Sufism, the mystical form of Islam, is more compatible with African religion in this regard. The facts remain that African religions do not call God by the name "Allah" or follow the rituals of Islam, or use Islamic prayers, etc. So it is not the substance of the religion that troubles Muslims but the forms of worship. This problem is a deep seeded issue that is born of the orthodox Islamic view, supported by the Koranic scriptures themselves, that "all people" should use their form of worship because it is the "true" form and God's name is "Allah" and God goes by no other name, etc. In this aspect Christianity also seeks to impose its particular format of worship on Africans and this is where the conflict is born because eventually, people will have to be forced to convert and this inevitably leads to control of social institutions, (schools, governments, etc.). Because of the similarities between African Religion and Islam, many people find it easy to convert, but later on when it is discovered that not only is the religion to change, but also the social structure and character of African culture is to be changed, many people resist such changes in their traditions and customs.

When Islam spread to Africa, it first did so by establishing or taking over settlements along trade routs. As the knowledge about the religion spread it became adopted by some people, while they at the same time incorporated the practices of previously existing religions. In this process, the practice became diluted or mixed with the practices of other religions and in time, the leaders of Islam called for a break from the older religions. Islamic reformists called for sanctions against anyone mixing Islam with other African religions or customs. These sanctions were based on the pronouncements found in Muslim scripture, law, and tradition. Sometimes reformists resorted to *jihád,* or "holy war" in order to enforce their strict concept of Islam. The systematic dismantling of the Ancient Egyptian monuments and temples is a legacy of the desire by Christians, Jews and Muslims to desecrate and denigrate Ancient Egyptian religion in favor of their practice of orthodox Western religion. Thankfully, however, the sheer massiveness of architecture, literature and artifacts that have survived, have allowed the opportunity for the Kamitan legacy to continue. This is a tribute to the power of Ancient Egyptian religion.

At other times, traveling Koranic schoolteachers or holy persons appeared in the land and offered to teach "uninitiated" children. Those children who received instruction knew more than their parents and as they grew up, the general level of practice of the rules and rituals of Islam would be increased measurably. So with successive generations, the level of knowledge and practice of Islam increased dramatically. The practice of traveling to Mecca also strengthened the practice of Islam by solidifying the common basis of the religion and focusing it in Arabia. Such a massive ritual and witnessing other Muslims coming from all over the land acted as an encouragement and an impressive impetus to continue the practice back home. The prestige of taking on such a sojourn elevated a person in the eyes of others, and this would also bestow political power. So it eventually became important to be a Muslim, and the respect that was engendered opened the way to leadership in the community and business opportunities.

The leaders of Islam, like those of Christianity, actively sought to co-opt the preexisting African religions by overlaying upon the populace the five (5) daily prayer times as well as the group meeting at the Friday Sabbath. This becomes the defining aspect in a person's weekly existence and promotes a cyclic regularity in the day-to-day and weekly lifestyle. The annual ritual of fasting and observance during Ramadan, which is based on the lunar cycle and thus changes every year, has the effect of supplanting pagan festivals that were previously dedicated to agricultural and solar cycles and their related pre-existing spiritual symbols and divinities. People in peasant communities continued to observe their festivals, but now they did so with the added Islamic impetus and terminologies. Also, they would add prayers and rituals based on the Koran and the Sunnah (Sonna) texts.[139]

These factors of assimilation, coupled with the active discouragement of other religions and the concomitant degradation in other cultures, meaning, the weakening of the traditions of other peoples, contribute to the efficacy of Islam and other Western religions as they make inroads throughout Africa. One reason for the weakening of culture is the less well-defined and outlined meaning of the practice of those religions, the corruption of leaders, laxity of teaching the youth, as well as the movement towards Western Culture and Western values, which are in contradiction with authentic spiritual life as it is practiced by Africans, Asians, or Native Americans. Thus, in this manner it is possible that eventually the older religions will be completely co-opted, that is, their wisdom, history and cultural legacy will be usurped and replaced with Islamic culture.

Akhnaton, Moses and the Concept of One God (Monotheism) in Ancient Egyptian Mythology and its effect on Judaism and Islam

Many people have come to believe that religions such as Judaism, Christianity and Islam were the first to put forth the teaching of monotheism. Upon closer review, however, we see that the monotheism of the Western religions is related to a personalized idea of God. This is true in the sense that this form of monotheism holds that there is a personality who has a particular form, a particular location of residence and a particular religion. The mysticism of Ancient Egypt and of all other mystical philosophies shows that there is a Supreme Being who manifests as all forms, gods and goddesses, animals, human beings, etc. This goes a step beyond monotheism, thereby accepting God as the reality behind all things. This form of thinking may be classified as "monism," "panentheism" or "non-dualist Divinity." This understanding is a departure from the ordinary way of thinking and it is the cornerstone of mystical philosophy, differentiating it from orthodox, logical and dualistic thinking. So we must consider that there are two forms of monotheism, the Western or Orthodox (narrow and rigid) form and the African-Asian (Pantheistic, Mystical) form.

> "God is the father of beings. God is the eternal One... and infinite and endures forever. God is hidden and no man knows God's form. No man has been able to seek out God's likeness. God is hidden to Gods and men... God's name remains hidden... It is a mystery to his children, men, women and Gods. God's names are innumerable, manifold and no one knows their number... though God can be seen in form and observation of God can be made at God's appearance, God cannot be understood... God cannot be seen with mortal eyes... God is invisible and inscrutable to Gods as well as men."
> -Portions from the Egyptian *Book of Coming forth by Day* and the papyrus of Nesi-Khensu

The statements above give the idea that God is the unfathomable mystery behind all phenomena, which cannot be discerned "even by the gods." However, God is the unfathomable mystery as well as the innermost essence of his children. This means that God is transcendental, the unmanifest, but also what is manifest as well. In order to perceive this reality it is necessary to transcend ordinary human vision. When this transcendental Self is spoken about through different names and metaphors, the idea often emerges that there are many faces to the ultimate deity or Supreme Being. Nevertheless, as has been previously discussed, it must be clear that all spiritual traditions are in reality referring to the same Supreme Being, the transcendental reality.

The many Egyptian cosmogonies and ritual systems are in reality leading toward the realization of the same Supreme Being. However, during the period of the 18th Dynasty, Egyptian religion went through a short-lived phase in which only one god symbol was worshiped. This occurred under the reign of

---

[139]"Islam and Tradition: An Interpretation," *Microsoft® Encarta® Africana.* ©1999 Microsoft Corporation. All rights reserved.

THE AFRICAN ORIGINS OF CIVILIZATION, RELIGION AND YOGA SPIRITUALITY

Akhnaton, (c.1379-1362 B.C.E.) As you recall, he suppressed the form of worship that was practiced for the other god symbols, including Amun-Ra, and instituted Aton, represented by the solar disk, as the fulfillment of them. It must be clear that what he did was not to renounce the other divinities. This is clear because in his hymn he states that Aton and Ra as well as Hrmakht (Horemakhet-Heru of the two horizons, the Sphinx) are all one and the same. Therefore, Aton symbolized the underlying essence or reality behind them, i.e. their fulfillment.

Many researchers of Egyptian religion have considered Akhnaton to be the first monotheist; however, he only wanted to return to the original idea of the Supreme Deity which had existed prior to the development in Ancient Egyptian religion that assigned primacy to the lesser gods and goddesses and to some extent de-emphasized their underlying and ultimate essential nature. This point is proven by the passages below from the Ancient Egyptian texts concerning Amun, Ra and Ptah, and the creation myths which existed prior to the reign of Akhnaton. In essence he was trying to reform the worship of God and of society in general, just as Jesus was trying to reform Judaism, Krishna and Buddha Indian religion, and Lao Tzu Chinese religion.

Sometimes religious practice becomes ritualistic and traditional, and the meaning is lost over a period of time. This is when a highly developed personality comes to reform the religion and once again emphasize the higher aspects of it in order to promote its proper function in society. The ideas of monotheism, monism, pantheism and panentheism existed in Egypt and Ethiopia prior to their emergence anywhere else in the world. Akhnaton wanted to encourage a more naturalistic style of Egyptian royal portraiture and life in general, as well as a deeper relationship with the Divine as opposed to the increasingly ritualistic development in religion, which was taking place. He saw Aten (Aton) as the benefactor of all religions and sought to establish a new order of social justice wherein all citizens would partake in the riches of society.

The corruption of some of the Egyptian priesthoods and dissatisfaction with the level of spiritual experience prompted a call for reforms. The high philosophy, which spawned the creation of the Temples and Pyramids, had degenerated to where many scribes and priests were selling religious texts to the highest bidder without imparting the true meaning of the teachings. Thus, Akhnaton attempted to make reforms in the spiritual character of Egypt. He confiscated much of the wealth of the priests of Amen and redistributed it amongst the people. He tried to foster an atmosphere of brotherhood amongst the neighboring countries by reducing appropriations for the military and thus reducing the belligerent stance of the Egyptian civilization. The priests of Amun and many people who had practiced the worship of various Egyptian deities for thousands of years rejected his efforts. Foreign countries used this opportunity to encroach upon Egyptian territories and, after Akhnaton's death; Egypt reverted to the system of gods and goddesses, which it had before.

The following passages come from the Egyptian *Book of Coming Forth By Day* (Chapter. clxxiii):

> "I praise thee, Lord of the Gods, God One, living in truth."

The following passage is taken from a hymn where princess Nesi-Khensu glorifies Amen-Ra:

> "August Soul which came into being in primeval time, the great god living in truth, the first Nine Gods who gave birth to the other two Nine Gods,[140] the being in whom every God existeth One One, the creator of the kings who appeared when the earth took form in the beginning, whose birth is hidden, whose forms are manifold, whose germination cannot be known."

UA or "One,"
UA NETER or "One God,"
"Only One",
"Only One Without a second"
"One One"

---

[140] Ancient Egyptian mythology conceives of creation as an expression of God in which there are nine primordial cosmic principles or forces in the universe. These first nine may be seen as the cause from which all other qualities of nature *(the other two Nine Gods)* or creative forces in nature arise.

THE AFRICAN ORIGINS OF CIVILIZATION, RELIGION AND YOGA SPIRITUALITY

The following excerpt from Sir Wallis Budge from *The Gods of the Egyptian* provides insight into the misconceptions by Egyptologists and the higher meaning of the Ancient Egyptian concept of monotheism within a polytheistic mythological framework. Further, the European Egyptologist makes the point that the monotheistic system of the Ancient Egyptians was in every way compatible with that of the Jews and the Muslims when the hierarchy of the various angels of the latter religions are understood in a proper context. Many times the practitioners of the Western religions as well as Western theology researchers do not like to admit the beginnings of Western religions or the fact that they are merely reworked ancient religions.

"But this contention ("that the Egyptians had no conception of a God who was One") is not well founded, because, although these attributes were ascribed to a miscellaneous number of deities, we must remember that they would not have been thus associated unless the writers recognized such gods as phases or aspects of the Great God. The fact remains that such attributes were ascribed to gods who were created by God, and that the Egyptians arrived at such ideas as those described above is a lasting proof of the exalted character of their religion and of their conception of monotheism. The main point to keep in view is that the gods of Egypt were regarded by the Egyptians generally as inferior beings to the great God who made them, and that they were not held to be equal to him in all respects. Further, we must repeat that the God referred to in the moral precepts of the Early Empire holds a position similar to that held by Yahweh among the Hebrews and Allah among the Arabs, and that the gods and goddesses who were ministers of his will and pleasure find their counterparts in the angels and archangels, and spirits of all kinds, both good and bad, whom the Hebrew and Arabic literatures are full. No surer proof of this can be given than the well-known passage in Hear, 0 Israel, Yahweh our "God (literally, gods), is Yahweh One,"[141] and the Egyptian *neter ua* "One God," as far as the application and meaning of *ua* is concerned, is identical with that of the Hebrew word אחד in the text quoted. We may note too the words, "Yahweh our gods," which show that Yahweh was identified with the gods, אֱלֹהִים, of the polytheistic period of the ancient Hebrew religion; it is, however, possible that when the verse in Deuteronomy was written the word Elohim had come to mean the great God of the Hebrews, although originally it had meant a collection of sacred or divine beings. In the Kur'ân, Sura cxii., the God of the Arabs is declared to be One, and from the commentaries on the Sura we know that this declaration was revealed to Muhammad in answer to the people of the Kurêsh, who asked him concerning the distinguishing attributes of the God he invited them to worship. If we had all the literature of the early Hebrews, and of the Arabs at the period of the propaganda of Muhammad we should probably find that many local gods in Palestine and Arabia were called One, but that only the God who had the moral aspects which were attributed to the great God of the Egyptians by the philosophers of the Early Empire succeeded in retaining it permanently."

The Underlying Concept of Supreme being and Lesser Divinities in African Religion (Ancient Egypt) and its Menifestation in the Western Religions

The Hierarchy of Divinity in African Religion	The Hierarchy of Divinity in Ancient Egyptian African Religion	The Hierarchy of Divinity in Hebrew Religion	The Hierarchy of Divinity in Islamic Religion
Supreme Being ↓ Lesser Divinities (gods and goddesses)	Pa Neter ↓ Neteru (gods and goddesses)	Yahweh ↓ Angels and Saints (Lesser Divinities)	Allah ↓ Angels and Saints (Lesser Divinities)

---

[141] Compare St. Mark XII 29

THE AFRICAN ORIGINS OF CIVILIZATION, RELIGION AND YOGA SPIRITUALITY

It would be correct to note that the Jews who entered Egypt at various times throughout its history were strongly influenced by the theology of Egypt. However, they did not carry on the ideal of universality which Akhnaton sought to foster. He viewed Aton as the Supreme Deity who is revered everywhere under different names. It must be understood that he never saw the sun itself as Aton, but as a dynamic aspect of Aton which sustains the world and all life. This is actually the same teaching, which was inherent in the teachings related to the Ancient Egyptian god Ra. Thus, he was merely transferring the same attributes that were previously held, to the form of Aton. The Jewish idea that the Jewish God is the only true god, and he belongs to them alone, is a factor of Zoroastrian influence coupled with the occidental tendency of the Jewish religion to concretize images and to exclude and segregate themselves. Nevertheless, the instruction, which the early Jews received in Egypt about the oneness of Divinity, which they transferred to the personality of *Yahweh*, cannot be overlooked.

Akhnaton was at the same time a king and mystical philosopher. He introduced not a new religion, but a form of worship, which was highly philosophical, and abstract, thus less suited for the masses and more appropriate for the monastic order. The tenets of his hymns can be found in hymns to other Ancient Egyptian gods such as Amun (Amen), Asar (Osiris), and Ra, which preceded those to Aton. However, the form of their exposition brings forth a new dimension of Ancient Egyptian philosophy, which is unsurpassed in some ways even by the Hymns of Amun[142]. However, he was not able to reconcile the worship of Aton with the pre-existing forms of worship in Ancient Egypt. Also, he was not able to balance the duties of kingship with those of his position as High Priest. While he was not able reconcile these issues, he did bring forth the most advanced exposition of Ancient Egyptian philosophy. Scholars of religious studies have classified him as the first monotheist, before Moses, but his contributions to religion go much deeper than that.

The Ancient Egyptian Pharaoh and High Priest Akhnaton with his wife, the High Priestess Nefertiti, adoring the Aton with its all pervading and life sustaining ray-hands as their children play divine sistrums.

Upon closer study, the philosophy, which Akhnaton espoused, is comparable to the most advanced spiritual philosophies developed in India, known as Vedanta philosophy. In Vedanta, two important forms of spiritual philosophy developed. They are expressions of non-dualist philosophy known as Absolute Monism. The Hymns to Aton, which also espouse Absolute Monism, were recorded at least 579 years before its exposition in India through the Hindu Upanishads which are considered to be the highest expression of Hindu mystical philosophy. Akhnaton's teachings were given less than 200 years before the supposed date for the existence of Moses. However, Moses' teaching was not understood as Absolute Monism, but rather as monotheism. Therefore, whether the Jewish Pentateuch was written by a person named Moses or by Jewish scribes much later, as most modern biblical scholars now agree, the influence of Akhnaton's teachings would have been foremost in the instruction of Moses. Remember that the Bible says Moses learned the wisdom of the Egyptians (Acts 7:22). While all of the attributes of Yahweh, the Hebrew God, are contained in the teachings related to Aton, the Hymns to Aton go farther in espousing the nature of God and God's relationship to Creation and humanity. They are based on Monism. Absolute Monism means that there is a recognition, that there is only one reality that exists: God. All else is imagination. This means that everything that is perceived with the senses, thoughts, etc., is a manifestation

---

[142] See the book "Egyptian Yoga Volume II" by Dr. Muata Ashby.

of God. Modified Monism views God as the soul of nature, just as the human body also has a soul which sustains it.

The next form of philosophy present in Akhnaton's hymns is pantheism. There are two forms of Pantheism, Absolute and Modified. Absolute Pantheism views God as being everything there is. In other words, God and Creation are one. Modified Pantheism is the view that God is the reality or principle behind nature. Panentheism is the doctrine that God is immanent in all things, but also transcendent, so that every part of the universe has its existence in God, but God is more than the sum total of the parts. God transcends physical existence. Aten or Aton was represented not as a human being, but as the sun, from which extended rays that terminated with hands which bestowed Ankhs (Life Force), to all Creation. This image was used exclusively and constituted a non-personalized form of Divine iconography pointing towards the abstract and transcendental nature of the Divine as principle, as opposed to personality. This was not a departure from Ancient Egyptian philosophy, but an attempt to reinforce elements which were already present in the very early forms of worship related to the formless, nameless *God of Light* teaching. The following excerpted verses from the Hymns to Aten, approved by Pharaoh Akhnaton exhibit the most direct exposition of the philosophies mentioned above.

THE AFRICAN ORIGINS OF CIVILIZATION, RELIGION AND YOGA SPIRITUALITY

Hymns to Aten	Philosophical Principle
A- The fish in the river swim towards thy face, thy beams are in the depths of the Great Green *(i.e., the Mediterranean and Red Seas)*. The earth becometh light, thou shootest up in the horizon, shining in the Aten in the day, thou scatterest the darkness.	A- From time immemorial the sun was worshipped as a symbol of God in Ancient Egypt. This has prompted many scholars in ancient and modern times, ignorant of the metaphorical symbolism, to refer to their worship as idolatry. This verse shows that God is seen as the principle operating through the sun and not the sun itself.
B- Thou makest offspring to take form in women, creating seed in men. Thou makest the son to live in the womb of his mother, making him to be quiet that he crieth not, thou art a nurse in the womb, giving breath to vivify that which he hath made.	B- God is not only the Creator of human life but also the very Life Force that sustains it. Worldly people would see the mother as sustaining the baby in the womb. Akhnaton affirms the higher source of sustenance i.e. God. The exact word used is "vivify." God is therefore not remote but intimately involved with Creation.
C- [When] he droppeth from the womb on the day of his birth [he] openeth his mouth in the [ordinary] manner, thou providest his sustenance…The young bird in the egg speaketh in the shell, thou givest breath to him inside it to make him to live. Thou makest for him his mature form so that he can crack the shell [being] inside the egg. He cometh forth from the egg, he chirpeth with all his might, when he hath come forth from it (the egg), he walketh on his two feet.	C- The philosophy of "breath" or breath of life has a very important teaching behind it. Breath relates to the Life Force energy, which vivifies everything. The force is subtle and thus interpenetrates all creation, thereby enlivening and sustaining it from within, much like the later Holy Spirit of the Bible. There is a recognition here that it is this same force that causes vegetation, animal and human life to grow and thrive.
D- One God, like whom there is no other. Thou didst create the earth by thy heart (or will), thou alone existing, men and women, cattle, beasts of every kind that are upon the earth, and that move upon feet (or legs), all the creatures that are in the sky and that fly with their wings, [and] the deserts of Syria and Kush (Nubia), and the Land of Egypt.	D- This important verse brings forth the understanding that there is ONE Supreme Being above all else. God caused all to come into being by his will and is not just the Creator of what exists (nature, living beings etc.) but that God and Creation are indeed one and the same, "alone existing" in the form of or manifesting as animals, people of all lands, etc.
E- Thou settest every person in his place. Thou providest their daily food, every man having the portion allotted to him; [thou] dost compute the duration of his life. Their tongues are different in speech, their characteristics (or forms), and likewise their skins (in color), giving distinguishing marks to the dwellers in foreign lands… Thou makest the life of all remote lands.	E- God has Created all peoples, all nations and countries and has appointed each person's country of residence, language and even their ethnicity and physical appearance or features. So all people, including those of foreign lands, have the same Creator and owe their continued existence to the same Divine Being.
F- Oh thou Lord of every land, thou shinest upon them…	F- In no uncertain terms, there is one God (Lord) who is the Supreme Being of all countries.
G- Thou hast made millions of creations from thy One self (viz.) towns and cities, villages, fields, roads and river. Every eye (i.e., all men) beholdeth thee confronting it. Thou art the Aton of the day at its zenith.	G- God manifests as and in countless forms, indeed, everything that exists, including life forms but also inanimate objects as well. Thus, when a person uses their senses and perceives objects, they are in reality perceiving God who is manifesting as Creation. This realization indicates the attainment of the highest goals of spiritual realization. This attainment is also known as non-dual vision, seeing God everywhere without separation between Creation and Divinity or the soul from God. This is of course the same teaching given by Jesus in the Gnostic Gospel of Thomas from Egypt where he asserts that "The Kingdom is spread upon the earth but people do not see it!"

The Original Meaning of the Hebrew Terms Elohim and Yahweh and The Difference Between Monotheism and Pantheism

In the Bible book of Genesis the first introduction we receive about the Jewish concept of God is that it is not a singular personality but a group of many. In Genesis Chapter 3:22-23 "God" refers to {him/her} self as "us."

Genesis 3

22. And the LORD God said, Behold, the man hath become as one of us, to know good and evil: and now, lest he should put forth his hand, and take also of the tree of life, and eat, and live for ever:
23 Therefore the LORD God sent him forth from the garden of Eden, to till the ground from which he was taken.

This idea of God in the plural, was prominent not just in African religion but also in the Pre-Judaic Arabian religions, which were related to the Ancient Egyptians. This is where scholars believe that the concept came from. It is not discussed and yet this is a fundamental departure from the image of presented of a single male supreme divinity presented in the Judeo/Christian/Islamic traditions. This would tend to mean that the supreme divinity is not just a single entity but rather expressing in many forms and this conceptualization has never been reconciled by the orthodox practitioners of those religious traditions.

In the present day form of the orthodox Jewish religion, it professes a non-sexual concept of the process of Creation. However, in almost the exact same manner of expression as is found in the Ancient Egyptian creation myths (Atum-Ra, Amun, Net (Neith), Neberdjer and Ptah), the original Jewish Bible scriptures and related texts describe the Creation in terms of an act of sexual union. *Elohim* (Ancient Hebrew for gods/goddesses) impregnates the primeval waters with *ruach,* a Hebrew word which means *spirit, wind* or the verb *to hover*. The same word means *to brood* in Syriac. Elohim, also called El, was a name used for God in some Hebrew scriptures. It was also used in the Old Testament for "heathen gods." Thus, as the Book of Genesis explains, Creation began as the spirit of God "moved over the waters" and agitated those waters into a state of movement. In Western traditions the active role of Divinity has been assigned to the male gender, while the passive (receiving) role has been assigned to the female gender. These waters that the spirit passes over are also to be found in the Ancient Egyptian tradition as one of the most prominent and important parts of the Ancient Egyptian Creation myth, the concept of the Nun, the Primeval Ocean.

Like the Pharaoh Akhnaton (c.1379-1362 B.C.E.), who lived earlier than the Ramases' kings, Moses was attempting to reform a religion which focused too much attention on rituals related to many gods and goddesses, and too little acknowledging the Supreme Being which is above them. While many people in modern times consider Judaism to be a monotheistic religion, it originated out of a polytheistic history or more precisely, a pantheistic tradition. Polytheism is the belief in many gods and/or goddesses who exist *independent of each other.* The key word here is "independent." Independent implies many divinities with separate powers and agendas, while pantheism is the understanding that the one Supreme Divinity manifests in multifold forms, like rays from the same sun, and therefore any form that is worshipped is in relation to all others and to the Ultimate. With this understanding, the worship of any of the divinities is proper and will lead to the same higher spiritual discovery, and also this form of worship will promote harmony amongst the worshippers of all divinities and through the system of worship (religion) of each divinity. Pantheism may therefore be viewed as a form of *"Polytheistic Monotheism."* The problem is that this high concept was forgotten or misunderstood by people in Asia Minor, and this gave rise to religions that sought to establish the worship of the one divinity by eradicating all other divinities. This is not what Pharaoh Akhnaton tried to do. He attempted to go back to the Supreme Being concept but he acknowledged that the Aton is the SAME Supreme Divinity worshipped by other peoples under different names. Akhnaton did not tear down the shrines of other divinities and replace them with the Aton or force anyone to convert to Atonism. There are no records of evidences provided by Egyptologists to such activities, which in the present day might be considered the acts of fundamentalists or fanatics. He founded a new city for the Aton and centered the worship there. The early Jews and Muslims did not understand this ecumenical[143] concept or rejected it and sought to establish the worship of one divinity and one system of worship excluding and supplanting all others.

Thus, upon closer examination, it will become clear that what most people call monotheism is in reality an extreme form of idolatry. The early polytheism of the Hebrews is evinced by the fact that *Yahweh* (*JHWH*) was originally considered to be one of the *Elohim* ("the goddesses and the gods"). The Elohim of Judaism can be equated to the *neteru* or gods and goddesses of Ancient Egypt. Thus, Moses sought to create an entirely new culture based on the same ideal as that of Ancient Egypt, but in the process of creating this new religion, the image of Ancient Egyptian culture and religion was impugned in the Torah and in the Biblical traditions. Moses and the Jewish tradition succeeded in surviving the test of time. However, this was due less to the power of the teaching than to the staunch and tenacious traditions and rituals upholding the Jewish ideas of monotheism and the covenant as exclusive, historical events instead of relating to them in a metaphorical sense. These ideas in Judaism, developed by the Priesthoods, which advocated rituals that promoted segregation and the prohibition from marrying those from other faiths has also led to racial segregation in modern times. These traditions became part of Jewish culture over time and formed the basis of the idea in many people's minds that the Jews are a racial class or a separate ethnic group. This same idea was instrumental in creating ethnic animosity against Jews. They were seen as a rival group who banded together to increase wealth amongst themselves and control the economy. They were also seen by other religious groups as spiritual elitists who consider themselves as chosen people who follow the "real" God while others are following "superstitions," or "idols worship" and "lies."

In mystical terms the name Jehovah relates to the self-existent Supreme Being which is the reality behind all things. Thus, Judaism represents an attempt to go back to that essential truth which is at the heart of all religions, which they had adopted from Ancient Egypt. As we will see, this idea was always and continues to be the central teaching of Ancient Egyptian and Indian religion and Yoga philosophy. Therefore, it cannot be said that Moses was an innovator in religious thought, but that he attempted to reinterpret some of the preexisting religious symbolism into a new system. The story of Exodus also shows the student of religion and yoga some of the pitfalls of orthodox religion. Orthodox religion uses a specific language relating to certain images and symbols which contain a particular relationship to a "special" group of people, whereas yoga and other mystical systems of philosophy are universal and apply to all forms of spirituality. This is why the Yogic-mystical aspects of religion can be easily seen and understood by a Yogi who studies any religion, but a person who is involved with orthodox religion cannot easily see the religious points in Yoga or even see points of commonality in other religions besides their own. Thus, if a person is highly advanced and has discovered that the goal of all religions and mystical philosophies is one and the same, then they will see commonality in all forms of worship. They will have a universal, inclusive point of view and not an exclusive, closed-minded point of view.

A striking example of the integration of the female principle into Ancient Egyptian mythology is to be found in Chapter 78, Line 47 of the Egyptian *Book of Coming Forth By Day*, where it is stated to the initiate:

> "To the son (initiate), the gods have given the crown of millions of years, and for millions of years it allows him to live in the Eye (Eye of Heru), which is the single eye of God who is called Neberdjer, the queen of the Gods."

The previous passage is of paramount significance since it states that the primary Trinity, *Nebertcher (Neberdjer)*, the High God of Egypt, which is elsewhere primarily associated with male names, *Amun-Ra-Ptah*, is also *"the queen of the Gods."* Therefore, the primary *"Godhead"* or Supreme Being is both male and female. The concept of the Godhead as being female in nature translated to the original Jewish theology which eventually gave birth to Christianity. Elohim is the plural of the Hebrew word Eloah which means "God." Elohim is also a general term which is used frequently in the Old Testament referring to any divine being, however it is more commonly used in reference to the God (the Father) of the Israelites. The Hebrew term *Elohim* means *"the goddesses and the gods."* However, even though this teaching is part of the scriptural writings, both the Jewish and Christian Churches emphasize the male aspect almost exclusively. This is a stark example of machismo (an exaggerated sense of masculinity), spiritual ignorance and immaturity (egoism).

This understanding of the Supreme Divinity as being androgynous, and being one entity expressing as many entities including both sexes, parallels the Ancient Egyptian and Hindu understanding. As societies

---

[143] Of worldwide scope or applicability; universal.

have changed to a male dominant structure, the translation in the Bible is usually simply "God." In the original manuscripts of the book of Genesis, Yahweh was only one of the *Elohim*. This understanding is more accurately reflected in Cabalism, the esoteric form of Judaism.[144]

The Mystery of the Kaaba Shrine and the Origins of Allah Worship in Pre-Islamic Arabian Religion

The *Ka'bah*[145] (Kaaba) (above left) is a shrine located in the city of Mecca, Saudi Arabia. It is an oblong building in the quadrangle of the "Great Mosque" which was constructed around it many hundreds of years before its use as a sacred pilgrimage center. There is a "Black Stone" placed in the NE corner of the shrine, held in place by a "mandorla" shaped opening. The Mandorla or vertical oval, 0, is related to the Madonna, Mary, the mother of Jesus. It is at once a symbol of her divinity as well as her feminine gender. The upright oval symbol is also known as the "almond." It has been regarded as a symbol of the goddess all over the world, and it has become one of the icons of Mary. It is also known as the *Vesica Piscis* or "Vessel of the Fish." The fish, ⋖, is an ancient symbol of life. It is related to Christ. It relates to transcendence of the world as well as to material and spiritual abundance.

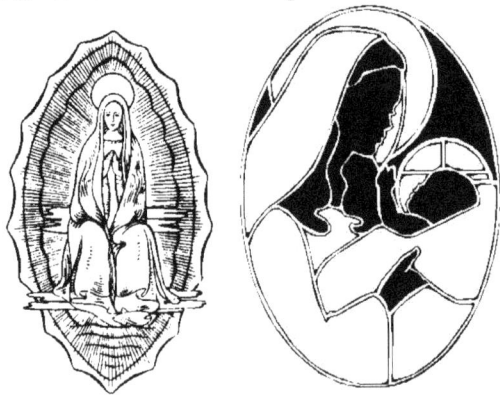

Above: Images of Mary, the mother of Jesus in the oval shaped almond enclosure.

When Muhammad and his army invaded and captured the city of Mecca where the shrine had been used as a pilgrimage center for many gods and goddesses up to that time, the stone was declared by the prophet Mohammed to have been given to Abraham by the archangel Gabriel. Henceforth it was revered

---
[144] See section entitled "Kabbalism, the Mysticism of the Tree of Life."
[145] Websters Encyclopedia

by Muslims as the most sacred Islamic shrine, and all other images of gods and goddesses were destroyed and forbidden from that time on. Today, this one time universal shrine is now used by all Muslims who must face toward the Ka'aba when they pray daily, and it is the focus of the hajj or pilgrimage that every Muslim must take in their lifetime.

The stone is thought to be a meteorite that was fixed in ancient times by the "pagan" practitioners in ancient times (prior to 300 B.C.E.). The worship of Allah was first recorded at about 300 B.C.E. at which time Allah was regarded as a Creator who was one of several Arabian divinities who were worshipped at that time. Allah was the male half of a twin divinity system. His female counterpart was Allat.[306] The female appellation "t" is used in the same fashion as in the Ancient Egyptian grammar. Allat was considered by the Greeks to be a manifestation of the Greek goddess Athena, and Athena was regarded by them as a form of the Ancient Egyptian goddess Net. Net is the Kamitan divinity of Creation who contains, within herself, the male seed. In this manner of symbolism of the Kaaba represents a Tantric form of mysticism which involves the union of the male essence, the seed (meteorite), with the female, symbolized by the shrine (the female orifice) within which the meteorite is placed.

Thus, from the perspective of Tantric mysticism, the Kaaba is therefore a symbol of androgynous (genderless) nature of the spirit which is endowed with the essence of both male and female at the same time. This concept manifests as the female in the sense that when the semen (seed-meteorite) comes into the womb (symbolized by the female orifice in the building), a birth of higher consciousness is to occur in those coming into contact with the building (shrine) or entering into the building to see the idols (hidden forms) of the divinity. Thus, mystically, they are to will be led to higher knowledge concerning these. This is the way that the mysteries of the Kaaba would have originally worked prior to the advent of Islam. This is the same concept behind the Ancient Egyptian religious system related to the male divinities Ra and Amun, but also the goddess Net (Anet). The gods expend their seed into themselves and thereby bring forth Creation through their own female nature, and the goddess brings forth Creation by engendering the seed of life within herself. So the original concept of the Creator goddess, the highest Supreme Being, occurs in Ancient Egypt and this concept has major implications for our study of pre-Islamic religion and its Ancient Egyptian influence.

As the reader has seen in this volume, the Ancient Egyptian religion strongly influenced the development of Buddhism. There is a wonderful tantric concept in Buddhism called *Om Mani Padme Hum* or *"The Jewel in the lotus."* "Om" is the name of the undivided Supreme Self. "Mani" means jewel or diamond. "Padme" means lotus. Thus this mantra means bringing the jewel of the Supreme Spirit into the lotus of the heart. This is the same philosophy originally espoused by the *"The Jewel in the lotus"* of the Kaaba. In present day Islam, neither the Tantric nor female aspect of the monument is not acknowledged. The Kaaba is seen as a symbol of the male divinity Allah.

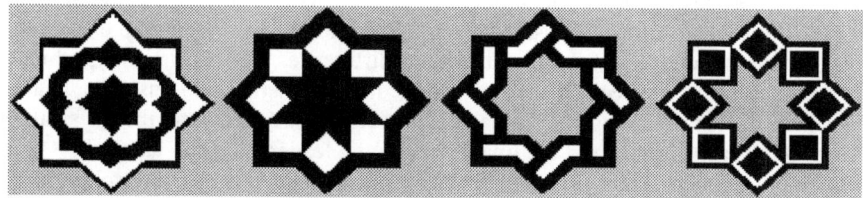

Some Geometric Designs of Islamic culture

While orthodox Islam professes a disbelief in symbols and idols, as pagan and irreligious, the actual history of Islam even up to the present day contradicts this view in practice. For many hundred of years and especially during the occupation of India, the Muslims systematically dismantled or tore down Hindu temples and on the same spot erected Mosques. The same thing was done in Kamit and elsewhere in Africa. One example which has caused much consternation to Egyptologists is the Mosque that was build on the site of the Luxor Temple to Amun in Waset (Luxor) Egypt which was constructed right on top of one of the most important temples.[307 \ 308] The picture below shows the location of the Mosque. The structure in the foreground is the Temple of Amun. The structures rising up from within the court of the temple are the minarets of the Mosque.

THE AFRICAN ORIGINS OF CIVILIZATION, RELIGION AND YOGA SPIRITUALITY

The Christians, sanctioned by the Pope in Rome, who sought to convert Native Americans when the "new world" (the Americas) were being colonized, practiced the same procedure of placing churches on Native American holy sites so that they would be forced to come to the church if they wanted to make their pilgrimage. The Mosque or Muslim place of worship is typically decorated with abstract and geometric designs. These geometric designs are said not to hold any specific meaning or symbolism, but that is not the most important issue. When one visits a mosque these symbols become immediate parts of the ambiance and feeling of the religion and provide an aesthetic, psychological quality that has intertwined art with religion. So it is not known just as art, but as "Islamic Art" and it holds an important symbolic place in the practice of the religion, comparable to Indian Yantras and Buddhist Mandalas in many respects. Islamic calligraphy, an art in itself, containing the name of God, (Allah), is a highly revered and sought after form of symbolism. The building has the mihrab, or prayer niche, and this feature shows the direction of Mecca in which the faithful are to be facing. The minaret, or tower, is the place from which the meuzzin calls the faithful to prayers, and the courtyard area is the place for the faithful to wash before their prayer. The madrasa is the school area. The first domed Mosque is called the Dome of the Rock, and it is located in Jerusalem. It was built in 691 A.C.E. Other famed Mosques are the Mosque of the Prophet, and the Mosque at Mecca, containing the Kaaba, Medina, containing Mohammed's tomb and the 3-domed Pearl Mosque in Agra.[146] Thus, it is clear that while Muslims profess to disdain the use of symbols and idols, leaders or intercessors (one of the main differences with Christianity, which accepts Jesus Christ as an intercessor between man and God), the geometric patterns, the characteristic architecture of Mosques, the Holy Scripture as well as the prayer mats that are used, the physically turning towards Mecca (with the Kaaba shrine), and the Imam or spiritual leader, all serve as symbols (objects of worship, i.e. idols) for the practitioners of Islam. For the practical practice of any religion, idols are needed. They act as objects upon which to focus the concentration and meditation, but they are not to be viewed as absolute divinities. This would be true idolatry. Therefore mystical religion accepts them as images of a higher principal to aid the focus of the mind. Practitioners of orthodox religion actually intensify their belief in the objects; this constitutes a great degradation and obstruction in the practice of religion. Many people in India have denounced the practice of destroying Hindu shrines and replacing them with Mosques as religious intolerance and bias. This is the same form of practice that was perpetrated on Native Americans during the colonization of the "New World."

---

[146] Random House Encyclopedia Copyright (C) 1983, 1990 by Random House Inc.

Islamic Calligraphy containing the name of God (Allah)

The Sects of the Islam

After the death of Muhammad in the year 632 A.C.E., it was decided by the leaders of the Muslim movement that *Abu Bakr*, the general who led Muhammad's army to conquer Arabia for Islam, should be the *khalifa* or successor. This decision was not popular with all of the Muslims and many thought that Ali, the cousin of Muhammad and husband to his daughter, *Fatimah*, should be the new leader. Dissidents broke away from Abu Bakr and followed Ali and his son. In the year 680 he was murdered along with many supporters by loyalists of Abu Bakr. The group that followed Ali came to be known as the *Shiites* (Shi'a) meaning "partisans." They are mostly based in Iran, Iraq and in some parts of India. The Shiites have since been a persecuted minority in the Muslim world. The followers of Abu Bakr came to be called the *Sunnites* meaning "sons of the tradition". In the year 641 the followers of Islam moved into Egypt and henceforth began to take over the country from the Coptic Egyptians who were there and today, the Islamic Egyptians control every aspect of the country and the Copts are a small minority with little or no say at all in the activities of the government. Therefore, not only the inception, but also the early development of Islam, like Judaism, was marked by violence, murder, and dissention.[147] So, Christianity and Islam, religions that professes forgiveness, compassion and peace, have been the greatest sources of violence and social strife. This is one of the reasons for an increase in atheism. Many people, seeing the hypocrisy, have become soured on all religions. However, it must be kept in mind that the problem itself is not religion, but rather, the opposite, a lack of practice of true (complete) religion (myth, ritual, mysticism). In a sense, even though these groups may refer to themselves or are referred to by others as being religious organizations, they cannot be considered as such until they implement all three aspects of religious practice.

There seems to be more tolerance in Western countries with having other religions in the same land, but when economic strife arises, as in the depression, scapegoating and hate crimes begin to rise, some instigated by government leaders and others instigated by religious leaders. The "other" people are viewed as the "enemy" since the end product of any association brings out the fact that there are "fundamental" differences between the religions, and therefore the minority that does not want to conform, must be the cause of the problem. Islam, the religion which professes surrender and peace is actually not a religion that allows freedom of choice or non-violence as an option. Islam is the only way in countries where the majority of the population is poor and Islamic.

The Goddess of Ancient Egypt and the Goddesses of Christianity and Islam

Another sect of Islam developed, which follows the worship of the Fatimah. Fatimah[148] was an Arabian moon goddess, the Creatoress who existed from the beginning of time. She was known as the source of the sun, moon and fate. These were all attributes ascribed to the Goddess Net of Egypt since the inception of Egyptian civilization many thousands of years earlier. When Muhammad came to power he "Mohamedanized"[309] (co-opted) the name and the previously existing spiritual tradition, and used it to attract the pre-Islamic followers of the goddess. The Shiite sect of Islam honors Ali as the rightful successor to Mohammed and also offer devotion to Fatima in a manner similar to their reverence of the

---

[147] Religions of the West Lucius Boraks C.F.X.
[148] This is not to be mistaken with the shrines and places of pilgrimage of Mary that are around the world based on alleged apparitions of Mary. One of these is Fatima, in Portugal (1917, Our Lady of Fatima). ("Mary {Virgin Mary}," *Microsoft® Encarta® Encyclopedia 2000*. © 1993-1999 Microsoft Corporation. All rights reserved.)

Virgin Mary in Roman Catholicism. Her symbol, the "hand of Fatima," is often displayed in Shiite processions, and she is accorded a place of honor in heaven.[310]

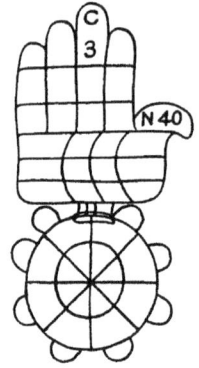

The Hand of Fatimah

Fatimah was likened to Mary of the Christian faith. However, the position of Fatimah, like that of Mary, was downgraded from goddess to mortal saint. So in reality, neither the orthodox Jewish, Christian or the Islamic faith accept or acknowledge the female aspect of the Divine or allow the possibility of worshipping the Divine in the female form due to the overbearing male dominancy that characterizes those religions and causes them to manifest a patriarchal philosophy.

Africanization of Islam

As with Christianity, even though Islam is gaining adherents in Africa, they are also losing some as well. The African spiritual consciousness does in some cases come through the colonial imperative in order to project a unique and higher African vision. The movements started by Maitatsine and Amadu Bamba are examples of the *Africanization of Islam*.[311] Amadu Bamba, like the Christian preacher in the Congo Simon Kimbangu who was accepted by Africans as a Christian prophet, , was accepted by Africans as an Islamic prophet. He never founded a sect, but a following developed around his teachings which deviated in fundamental respects from the established paradigms of orthodox Islam. His burial site is treated like that of Muhammad's, as a pilgrimage center. This is of course much to the consternation of orthodox Islamic leaders, who are afraid that this sect (that developed after his death) is developing in a way that is divergent from their concept of Islam. Orthodox Islam also repudiates Sufism. Orthodox Islam believes in the singularity of Muhammad as the last prophet that would ever come. This concept is in contradiction with African Religion, which allows the capacity to accept authentic present day leaders, and to even place them in as high a status as ancient teachers. The idea of Orthodox Islam is to keep the religion from changing through new people coming in and giving new teachings, as the authority may shift if this was to occur. Thus, the effect is to "purify" (keep it within the accepted boundaries by dropping the unauthorized practices) the religion and many are calling for such a purification to take place in the case of Bamba's sect. Again, it is clear that Africans can and do have an effect on Western religions, and can even alter them to better suit their needs. However, even with the adjustments, the basis of the religious archetype remains Western (Islamic), and thus renders the practice of religion not entirely African, and therefore will remain limited in its capacity to assist Africans in fully recovering their African consciousness.

The African-Americanization of Islam in the United States of America: Malcolm X and The Nation of Islam

In the 1950's and 60's, a movement called the Nation of Islam came to its peak in the United States of America. The Black Muslims are a United States religious movement that is officially called the Nation of Islam. The Nation of Islam is recognized as an altered version of the Islam that is practiced in the "Arab world." Malcolm X was one of the most famous practitioners to come to this realization himself, when he visited Mecca in 1964 A.C.E. Malcolm became a member of the Nation in the 1950's and turned away from a life of crime. In the Nation of Islam he was taught that white people are devils. The actions of many whites during the period of slavery and the continued practices of discrimination, lynching, etc., post-slavery, seemed to support this view. Thus, Islam, as practiced in the "Arab world" was adjusted to serve the needs of people of African descent in the United States of America who were and in many ways continue to be persecuted, abused and denigrated by the dominant culture. The Nation of Islam adhere strictly to the Koran's moral codes. They have saved the lives of many people by turning them away from a life of drug addiction, crime and lack of education. The moral codes they adhered to included abstaining from alcohol, drugs, gambling, and smoking.

The Nation of Islam was founded in Detroit in 1930 by W. D. Fard. The group's origins are founded in two Black self-improvement movements known as the Moorish Science Temple of America, which was founded in 1913 by Prophet Drew Ali, and the Universal Negro Improvement Association, which was founded in 1914 by Marcus Garvey. When Ali died, the leadership of his movement passed to Wallace D. Fard. In 1930 Fard founded a Temple in Detroit which was later known as a Mosque. This event is regarded as the actual beginning of the Nation of Islam. Mr. Fard used many names including: Walli Farad and Master Farad Muhammad. He was also called God, Allah, or the Great Mahdi by some Black Muslims. The branch of the Nation of Islam in Chicago was founded in 1933. After Mr. Fard's mysterious disappearance, the leadership of the group went to the leader of the Detroit Temple, Elijah Muhammad, who then moved to Chicago. Elijah Muhammad died in 1975 and was succeeded by his son Wallace, who called for radical changes in the movement, including the welcoming of whites into the movement and the promotion of women to leadership positions. He stressed strict Islamic beliefs and practices.

After 1975, the group was officially known as the American Muslim Mission and as the World Community of Al-Islam in the West. Its members refer to themselves as Bilalians. Its leaders advocate economic cooperation and self-sufficiency and enjoin a strict Islamic code of behavior governing such matters as diet, dress, and interpersonal relations. Members follow some Islamic religious ritual and pray five times daily. In the late 1970's a dissident faction emerged. It, led by Louis Farrakhan, assumed the original name, Nation of Islam, and reasserted the principles of black separatism.[75/115]

When Malcolm traveled abroad and discovered that there were white Muslims and other white people who were against racism, and who stood for righteousness, he began to teach that righteousness, rather than race, should be the standard for judging others. Malcolm discovered that the doctrines which formed the basis of the Nation of Islam were different from those of Orthodox Islam as practiced in the Middle East. He was suspended from the church in 1963 after which he turned away from the doctrines of hatred and racism and sought to bring forth a new vision through a purer form of Islam. He founded a new church, the Muslim Mosque in 1963, and in 1964 he converted to Islam as practiced by the Muslims in Mecca. He was assassinated in 1965 by members of the Nation of Islam due to his rift with the group, and in particular with Elijah Muhammad.

In any case the Nation of Islam is recognized as an altered version of the Islam that is practiced in the "Arab world." One of the most famous practitioners to make this realization was Malcolm X himself when he visited Mecca.[312] It was adjusted to serve the need of people of African descent in the United States of America who were and in many ways continue to be persecuted, abused and denigrated by the dominant culture. However, its ranks of followers (est. 150,000) remain in small numbers when compared to the total population of African Americans (est. 33,000,000). Further, the philosophy of the Nation of Islam, while acknowledging that African Americans are descendants of Africans does not actively advocate a return to African Religion or traditional principles and is thus based on turning their followers towards western culture and the ideal of Islamic values ultimately based on the Koran. Some critics have charged that Islam should not be the religion of Africans because it was a religion that came late in history and also it is a religion that allows slavery. During the conquest of North Africa (675 – 850 A.C.E.) many Africans were enslaved by Islamic Arabs and currently (2000 A.C.E.) the Islamic government of the Sudan permits slavery.

The Legacy of Islam in Modern Egypt

Presently, the modern Arab-Islamic control of Egypt began in 1952 and continues to the present. The Coptic Church still maintains a presence in Egypt. The Copts see themselves as the true descendants of the original Ancient Egyptians, while the Arabs are viewed as foreigners. However, the modern day Copts are combination of original Ancient Egyptian people and an admixture of Greek, European and modern day Arab peoples. According to the evidences, the Ancient Egyptians looked like the people who today live in the city of Aswan in the south and in Nubia even further south. In any case the majority of the present day population is of Arab descent, whose ancestors immigrated to Egypt from Asia Minor. They are Islamic in their spiritual tradition. This group maintains the political and economic control of the country. Currently, the dominating culture is repressive in the treatment of women's rights, and freedom of religious expression. This is typical throughout countries that are predominantly Islamic. Several fundamentalist Islamic groups have developed in the late 20th century, mostly in response to what they view as a loss of traditional Islamic values due to Western influences, and also as a reaction to oppressive or elitist governments, foreign rule or social injustices. This has led to many conflicts between Arab countries as well as between Arab groups within Arab countries. The current dispute between Israel, the United States and Palestine is a great source of strife which has led to among other things, war between the Arabs of Egypt and the Israelis (1967 and 1973). Before reaching a peace agreement with Israel in 1979, the Egyptians, under Gen. Gamal Abdal Nasser, who deposed the previous leader, opposed the formation of the Israeli state and barred them from using the Suez Canal and also invaded Israel, leading to the 1967 and the 1973 wars with Israel. Having lost both wars, the Egyptians settled their disputes, but became ostracized by the other Muslim countries. Internal unrest led to the assassination of President Sadat in 1981. Egypt thereafter became economically dependent on the Western countries and the USA in particular and tourism became a major industry. Since that time there has been an effort to eradicate domestic Islamic fundamentalist movements and to this end the Egyptian government broke off relations with Iran which it felt was financing those activities within Egypt.

Ancient Egyptian Traditions Still Practiced in Modern Egypt by The Muslim Population

The following passage illustrates many Ancient Egyptian traditions that are still practiced in Egypt, knowingly or not. Along with these there are some people who go to the Ancient Egyptian monuments to practice a kind of conglomerate of African ancestor worship, spiritualism and Islam. Of course this is not condoned or facilitated by the government or the orthodox religious leaders.

> Some ancient traditions still survive in modern Egypt. These include the Festival of Sham el-Nessim which marks the start of spring in the same way that the Festival of Khoiakh did in antiquity. Families celebrate this out-of-doors, exchanging gifts of colored eggs to reassert the renewal of the vegetation and the annual rebirth of life. Another modern festival, Awru el-Nil, takes the form of a national holiday; at this celebration of the inundation of the Nile flowers are thrown into the river. In ancient times a festival was held annually to mark the inundation, and prayers were offered to ask for a good flood (neither too high nor too low) which would ensure ample crops and general prosperity. Other modern ceremonies reflect ancient -funerary customs. Forty days after death and burial the family of the deceased will take food to the grave, and this is then distributed among the poor who have gathered there. This occasion, known as el-Arbeiyin, retains elements of the ancient service performed at the time of burial when relatives gathered at the tomb and at the conclusion of the burial rites shared the funerary meal. Another early tradition is probably preserved in the modern annual family visit to the grave when special food is brought which is then given to the poor.[313]

Another Ancient Egyptian tradition that survives in modern day Egyptian-Muslim culture is the ritual of carrying the divine boat. In Ancient Kamit the annual ritual of carrying the Divine Boat (vehicle of the god or goddess) from one Temple to another was a means to maintain the order of the cosmos, as the movement of the boat engenders and sustains Creation itself. This same act of Creation was re-enacted by the Priests and Priestesses of Ancient Egypt. This ritual is maintained by some inhabitants of modern day Egypt, albeit without the understanding of the meaning of the ritual as it relates to Ancient Egyptian religion. In Kamit, pallbearers would carry the boat while a Priest opened the way by burning incense on the path. A long procession would follow behind, some playing music and others dancing and others uttering chants. The modern ritual is very similar in many respects.

The Origins of Esoteric (Mystical) Islam: Sufism (c. 700 A.C.E)

No conversation about Islam should leave out a mention of Sufism. Sufism is a form of Islam that does not conform to the orthodox views. It is mystical, taking the best aspects of Islam and connecting them with the universal perspective of all Creation. Therefore, Sufism is compatible with other mystical religions (religions that practice all three steps) including the Ancient Egyptian, and the Hindu-Vedanta-Yoga. Therefore, the followers of orthodox Islam almost immediately repudiated Sufism after its inception. Even today, the Sufis are regarded as dangerous heretics and cannot operate freely in orthodox Muslim countries.

As stated earlier, orthodox Judaism was, in great part, an outgrowth of Ancient Egyptian Religion, Christianity an outgrowth of Judaism and Neterian Religion, and Islam an outgrowth of Judaism and Christianity. Jewish mysticism (Kabbalism or Cabalism), Christian mysticism (Gnostic Christianity) and Islamic mysticism (Sufism) can be seen as outgrowths of Shetaut Neter (Ancient Egyptian Mysticism). *Sufism* or mystical Islam emerged in the Middle East within 100 years after Islam became established there as a dominant religious doctrine. The name "*Sufi*" comes from "Suf" which means "wool." The name Sufi was adopted since the ascetic followers of this doctrine wore coarse woolen garments *(sufu)*. Sufism represented a turning away from the orthodox doctrines of Islam and Catholicism and a reaffirmation of the mystical traditions which had preceded them. In this sense, Sufism has much in common with Gnostic Christianity, Indian Vedanta and the Ancient Egyptian Asarian Mysticism.

To the followers of orthodox Islam, Sufism has almost always been regarded as heresy since its main goal is to lead the Sufi follower to have *"Mystic Knowledge of God."* Sufism is based upon the fundamental Islamic tenets of living in harmony with others but beyond these ideas, the Sufis also hold that:

A- God, as creator of the universe, transcends it.
B- God cannot be expressed in words.
C- The inner light (one's own soul-spirit) is a sufficient source of religious guidance.
D- The Universe and God are actually one.
E- Since humans are part of creation, a human being can, through mystical discipline, become one with God.

F- The Sufi mystic is described as a pilgrim on a journey following a path of seven stages:

    1- Repentance
    2- Abstinence
    3- Renunciation
    4- Poverty
    5- Patience
    6- Trust in God
    7-Acquiescence to the will of God

G- As in Ancient Egyptian Mysticism, Christian Mysticism and the Bhakti Yoga of India, some Sufis practice devotion by employing the energies of love and directing them solely towards the Divine (union with God). Through rituals such as reading, listening to poetry and other works of literature, and devotional dancing (the *Whirling Dervishes*), an ecstatic mental-emotional feeling develops which can be used to sublimate and direct psychic (spiritual) energy to becoming attuned to and attaining union with the divine forces.

The following passage from Philo of Alexandria[149] gives an impression of the worship of God in the form of Devotional Love ["heavenly love"] as he attempted to introduce it to orthodox Christianity according to his own knowledge and experience in the mystery schools of his time.

> "Now they who betake themselves to this service [of God do so], not because of any custom, or on someone's advice and appeal, but carried away with heavenly love, like those initiated into the Bacchic[150] or Corybantic[151] Mysteries, they are a-fire with God until they see the object of their love.[63]

H- Sufism incorporates teachings in reference to the subtle spiritual body which may be compared to the Egyptian teachings of the "Pillar of Asar" and the four levels of the Serpent Power (Energy Centers in the body), and the Chakras of the Indian Kundalini Yoga.

Historical evidence and Sufi Mystic literature clearly show that Sufi followers had relationships (cultural, ethnic and social ties) with Egypt, the Essenes (mystical Jewish tribe of Jesus) and the Hindus and Buddhists of the Far East. Thus, it is not surprising that the energy center system of Sufism is closely related to the Uraeus Serpent Power and Tantric Kundalini mystical yoga systems of Egypt and India, respectively.

Babism and Bahaism and Their Relation to Islam and African Religion

Babism was a religion that developed out of the Shiite sect of Islam as an offshoot. Mirza Ali Muhammad, proclaimed its principles at Shirâz, Persia (now Iran), on May 23, 1844. He later became known as "the Bab," a Persian word meaning "the Gate," because his followers considered him to be a door or the gate to spiritual truth.[314] The Bab opposed Islamic Theology in several areas. He declared that the prophets were like avatars, manifestations, incarnations of God himself and that he was not only a prophet equal to Muhammad, but that he was the predecessor of a greater "manifestation" that would arrive in nineteen years from the time of the founding of Babism. He wrote a new holy book, the *Bayán*, (meaning "revelation"), that was supposed to supercede the *Koran*. He forbade concubines and polygamy and tried to change many other Muslim customs. Also, and very important was his proclamation that one day all religions would come together under one spiritual leader. The Bab began with 17 men and 1 woman as his disciples, and the faith grew steadily until violent persecutions were initiated by Shah Nasred-Din in 1848 whose advisors were convinced that Babism's teachings were destructive to Islam and of

---

[149] Philo Judaeus, or Philo of Alexandria (c. 20 BC - c. AD 54), Jewish philosopher living in Egypt. Attempted to blend the theology of the Jewish scriptures with Egyptian-Hermetic, Gnostic, and Greek philosophy.

[150] Bacchic: pertaining to Bacchus and bacchanalia; drunken; jovial; n. drinking song. Bacchus:
In Greek and Roman mythology Bacchus is the god of fertility (related to Dionysus) and of wine. His rites (the Bacchanalia) were orgiastic.

[151] Frenzied. A corybant was a priest, votary or attendant of Cybele (Cybele- Phrygian mythology, an earth-nature goddess, identified by the Greeks with the Greek goddess Rhea and honored in Rome.). corybantic, adj. pertaining to wild and noisy rites performed by these; n. wild, frenzied dance.126

THE AFRICAN ORIGINS OF CIVILIZATION, RELIGION AND YOGA SPIRITUALITY

course, a danger to the Islamic state. After two years of revolt by the Babists, their rebellion was defeated and the Bab was imprisoned. After his death, the preaching of Babism continued in Asia Minor and Persia until 1863 when Mirza Hoseyn Ali Nuri, also known as Bahaullah, meaning "the Splendor of God," announced that he was the promised "Manifestation" spoken about by the Bab. Basing his teaching on the original tenets of Babism, Mirza Hoseyn Ali Nuri founded a new religion that was henceforth called Bahai.

While in prison, charged with blasphemy, Mirza Hoseyn Ali Nuri wrote the principal texts of the Bahai faith. The main tenets of Bahaism include:

Bahaism	Kamitanism (African Religion)	Hinduism	Orthodox Islam	Orthodox Christianity
1. Ethics and social reform	1-✓	1-✓	1-✓	1-✓
2. The unity of human kind who worship the same god through all religions	2-✓	2-✓	2-x[323]	2-x[328]
3. The equality of the sexes	3-✓	3-✓	3-x	3-x
4. All racial, religious and political prejudices are shunned.	4-✓	4-✓	4-x	4-x
5. Private prayer	5-✓[316]	5-✓	5-x	5-x
6. Annual fasting periods.	6-✓	6-✓	6-✓	6-✓
7. Pilgrimage to Bahai holy sites.	7-x[317]	7-x[320]	7-x[324]	7-x[329]
8. Monetary contributions.	8-✓	8-✓	8-✓	8-✓
9. Non-violence.	9-✓	9-✓	9-x	9-x
10. World peace through the message of equality and unity.	10-✓	10-✓	10-x[325]	10-x[330]
11. God is unknowable.	11-x[318]	11-x[321]	11-✓	11-✓
12. Immortality is assured	12-✓	12-✓	12-x	12-x
13. Ceremonial leaders are shunned.[315]	13-x[319]	13-x	13-✓	13-✓
14. Spiritual teachings given by revelation through prophets	14-x	14-x[322]	14-✓	14-✓
15. Supreme Being	15-✓	15-✓	15-✓	15-✓
16. x	16-Lesser beings (gods and goddesses)	16-✓	16-x[326]	16-x
17. x	17-Mysticism	17-✓	17-x[327]	17-x
18. x	18-Yoga philosophy	18-✓	18-x	18-x
19. x	19-Goddess Spirituality	19-✓	19-x	19-x

Table Legend: Tenet in Disagreement x, Tenet in Agreement ✓

Besides Bab and Bahaullah, the Bahai faith holds that God sent other prophets which come from the Jewish, Christian and Islamic religions (Abraham and Moses, Jesus Christ, and Mohammed, respectively). From Acre, Palestine, the spiritual center of Bahai, the Bahai followers began to spread the message of Bahai to the Americas in 1894 A.C.E. Many African Americans responded to the message of Bahaism, since like Sikhism, it has many features that are in harmony with their social needs, such as the opposition to slavery and racism. Since that time many people of African descent have joined the ranks of Bahai followers. Bahaism has added followers in India, South America and Africa, especially in the Sub-Saharan regions since the 1960's.[331] The Bahais currently have established about 17,000 local Councils called Local Spiritual Assemblies. The International Governing Body of the Bahai faith is called "The Universal House of Justice" and it meets in Haifa in Israel.

As a universal religious faith affirming human principles the Bahai faith is very compatible with the tenets of African Religion, especially the Maat-Ubuntu teachings. Therefore, Kamitans could work closely with Bahais (followers of Bahai) in relative harmony. However, many people of African descent have adopted Bahaism because of its strong stance against racism and slavery, a major problem in the African community, and the universal perspective of the unity of all religions. These tenets are integral aspects of African religions and have been so since their inception. However, as the table above shows, there are some fundamental differences. Bahaism turns the follower to a foreign land and to contribute their resources to that foreign institution. These funds need to be spent in Africa and on Africans. African religion and Indian religion have mystical disciplines that go beyond prayer and visits to pilgrimage centers that do allow an aspirant to discover the nature of God and the secrets of the universe. Moreover, it must be clearly understood that even though the Bahai faith espouses a universalist type of philosophy, it is originated from and tied to the Jewish, Christian and Islamic religions.

Slavery in Ancient Egypt, among the Hebrews, Greeks, and Muslims

The earliest record of the Hebrew people comes from an Ancient Egyptian Temple inscription (at Karnak) which describes them as a tribe of nomadic peoples in one of the subject territories of the Ancient Egyptian realm (Canaan). However, they are not referred to as slaves, but as one of the many groups which the Egyptians had conquered in the area. This misconception about the slavery of the Jews in Egypt has been promulgated throughout history based on the writings of the Bible. Yet there is no evidence that the Hebrews were ever slaves of the Ancient Egyptians, except in the writings of the Bible itself. Further, there is no evidence that the Hebrews were used as slave laborers to construct the Great Pyramids at Giza. In fact, their construction occurred long before the reputed birth date of Abraham, who is supposed to be the first Jew. While there is no factual evidence to support it, biblical scholars believe that Abraham may have lived around 2,100 B.C.E. According to the most conservative dating by modern Egyptologists, the pyramids were constructed in the Old Kingdom Period (2,575-2,134 B.C.E.). In any case, discoveries by Egyptologists in the late 20th century, such as burial tombs for the those who worked to build the Pyramids, have shown that the labor that went into the Ancient Egyptian projects came from _free_ Ancient Egyptian laborers, artisans, builders and architects. The ancient Hebrews also used slaves, but they were required by religious law to free slaves of their own nationality at certain fixed times.[152]

In Ancient Egypt and Nubia slavery did exist, but not as a dominant institution.[153] People could find themselves in the position of slavery if defeated in war, or if they had committed some violation against society. In Greek classical times, the commercial North African state of Carthage as well as the Greek states and Rome all relied on slave labor in galleys and in agriculture, and acquired some of their slaves through trade with sub-Saharan Africa. Ancient Athens (Greece) presents a sobering look at the nature of the prosperity of the Greeks in the classical period and the illusoriness of the "democracy" that was developed there. Firstly, a very large part of the population were slaves, and the historical record shows that the Athenian state was based economically on a foundation of slavery. Two fifths (some researchers say the figure was closer to four fifths) of the population was composed of slaves. As in the United States of America and the European countries that partook in the African slavery, slave labor produced most of the wealth of the country and this allowed the citizens of Athens to take time and have sufficient financial resources to pursue art and learning. When cities were conquered by the Greeks, their inhabitants were often sold as slaves. Kidnapping boys and men in "barbarian" (non-Greek) lands and even in other Greek states was also practiced by the Greeks.[154]

Furthermore, in Ancient Egypt women were full participants of the social structure. In Athens, the supposed birthplace of democracy, as in Rome, and the European governments, including the United States of America, up to the 20th century, women were not allowed to participate in any decisions of the state. Greek male citizens alone decided upon these decisions by majority vote. There was no participation by anyone else and no input or debate by anyone outside that group. So this cannot be considered a democracy or even its genesis just as the governments of the present day which advertise themselves as

---

[152] "Slavery," Microsoft (R) Encarta. Copyright (c) 1994 Microsoft Corporation. Copyright (c) 1994 Funk & Wagnall's Corporation.
[153] "Slavery in Africa," _Microsoft® Encarta® Africana._ ©1999 Microsoft Corporation. All rights reserved.
[154] Excerpted from _Compton's Interactive Encyclopedia._ Copyright (c) 1994, 1995 Compton's NewMedia, Inc. All Rights Reserved

democracies cannot be considered as such either for the same reasons. A true democracy would have decentralized power, something which is antithetical to the very concept of capitalism, the basis of Western Culture, and the chain of command structure of governments, i.e. Presidents, Vice-presidents, Prime ministers, etc.

While there are overwhelming examples of cohabitation, social interaction, trade, participating in religious rituals together and supporting each other's Temples, etc., between Ancient Egypt and Ancient Greece, one example of a statement attributed to Alexander the Great, denotes a tone which may be considered as a prototype for the modern concept of racism. Also, let us not forget that Alexander had by this time conquered India and had no doubt discovered and experienced the caste system that was at this time transforming from a system of social order to becoming a system of organized racism based on skin color. It is also possible to surmise from the tone of the letter that he despised the Nubians for having something that he did not, which also allowed them to elude his grasp. So in view of the overall relationship between Ancient Egypt and Greece, the statement may be seen as a manifestation of jealousy and frustration and not necessarily racism. However, racism can be born out of such sentiments, especially when there is an ulterior motive, i.e. the desire to conquer someone (steal their possessions, enslave them, etc.). An early biographer of Alexander the Great records that the queen of Nubia responded to an inquisitive letter from him in the following manner:

> "Do not despise us for the color of our skin. In our souls we are brighter that the whitest of your people."[332]

It should be understood that the modern concept of slavery such as is imposed in countries such as the U.S.A., Europe, Middle East and Asia, was not present in Ancient Egypt. People were imprisoned for crimes or if they were captured by Egyptian armies, but they were naturalized (incorporated into the population) and their children were made full citizens. This means that the racist, ethnic or religious segregation, or animosity of modern times was not present.

In Ancient Egyptian texts we do not find statements that are designative, demonizing, debasing or racist. Statements such as "those people are evil," "monsters," "devils," "snakes," "cowards," "animals," etc. These kinds of statements are meant to demonize and dehumanize other people, and they lead the people who do the demonizing to not think of the other group as people at all. This makes it easier to hurt them, make war against them, enslave them and set out to destroy them. These kinds of statements are still used by some modern day political leaders, much in the same manner that they were used against Africans during the African (slave trade) Holocaust, and the Jews during the World War II Holocaust, to excuse the subhuman treatment of these peoples, having now characterized them as "less than human." This is a dangerous trend and habit that continues any time other cultures act in ways that are viewed as being in contradiction to one group's policies or political desires. It is wrong, and against the philosophy of righteousness of mystical religions. The Ancient Egyptian philosophy of righteousness (Maat) would call this "evil speech."

There are however, some irritate, deploring statements expressing dissatisfaction or resentment, that can be found in Ancient Egyptian writings relating to certain foreigners –including the Nubians ('wretched,' 'the disgust of Re,' or 'the miserable enemy,' etc.). The context in which these words are used do not relate to dehumanizing others, but to understanding their desolate living conditions and consequently dull state of mind that leads to them to experience misery that causes them to go around attacking others (usually the Ancient Egyptians) due to anger, hatred, greed and lust. These vices are repugnant to the Divine, and thus all the Kamitan divinities are said to, in one way or another, repudiate such behavior because it does not allow one to enter into the Divine presence. What we see in Ancient Egyptian culture and philosophy, in such texts as the "Wisdom of Merikara," which explains the "Asiatic" mentality of violence versus the Kamitan mentality of peace, cannot be in any way compared with modern day examples of racism. At the times when Ancient Egypt and Nubia were contending with each other for supremacy in the ancient world they were doing so as competing cultures who saw each other as human beings and not as lower forms of life that are to be enslaved or derided. Just as family members have disputes, so too the Ancient Egyptians and Nubians contended.

The Sikh Religion

> "Why wilt thou go into the jungles? What do you hope to find there? Even as the scent dwells within the flower, so God within thine own heart ever abides. Seek Him with earnestness and find Him there."
>
> -Sikh Proverb

Sikhism deserves mention here because it is an evolution of Islam and Hinduism. Sikhism is a religion professed by 14 million Indians, living mainly in the Punjab region. Sikhism was founded by Guru Nanak (1469–c. 1539 A.C.E.). Sikhism melds some aspects of Islam and Hinduism but there are some fundamental differences between Sikhism and Hinduism and other similar systems of religion. One of them is the concept of Avatar or incarnation. Sikh followers believe in a single God who is the immortal creator of the universe and who has never been incarnate in any form, and in the equality of all human beings.[333] Sikhs also celebrate at the time of some of the major Hindu festivals, but their emphasis is on aspects of Sikh belief and the example of the first Sikh gurus. Sikhism is strongly opposed to caste divisions and social inequality among men and women as well as among cultures and races. Their holy book is the Guru Granth Sahib. Guru Gobind Singh (1666–1708 A.C.E.) instituted the Khanda-di-Pahul, the baptism of the sword, and established the Khalsa (meaning "pure"), the company of the faithful. As in Islam, there are specific requirements for being considered a Sikh follower. The Khalsa wear the five K's: kes - long hair, kangha - a comb, kirpan - a sword, kachh - short trousers and kara - a steel bracelet. Sikh men take the last name "Singh" ("lion") and women "Kaur" ("princess").

Sikh women take the same role as men in religious observances, for example, in reading from the Guru Granth Sahib at the gurdwara. Many Sikhs have migrated to other countries due to political strife as some of them attempt to establish a homeland. The Akali separatist movement agitates for a completely independent Sikh state, Khalistan, and a revival of fundamentalist belief. Sant Jarnail Singh Bhindranwale, a leader in the Sikh movement, was killed in the siege of the Golden Temple, Amritsar. In retaliation for this, the Indian prime minister Indira Gandhi was assassinated by her Sikh bodyguards. One thousand Sikhs were killed in heavy rioting thereafter and the struggle continues to this day. Thus, during its history, Sikhism has been involved with conflicts between themselves and either the Muslims or the Hindus.

Since Sikhism officially accepts only the original ten gurus who came since the founder of Sikhism, and no more, the reading of the scriptures, *Guru Granth Sahib*, has taken the place of a central religious leader. Guru Gobind Singh (1666–1708 A.C.E.), who instituted the Khanda-di-Pahul and established the Khalsa. Gobind Singh was assassinated by a Muslim man in 1708 A.C.E.. The militancy, (viewed by some as extremism or fundamentalism) of some Sikhs and the mandatory clothing that Sikh followers are required to wear has led to the association of many Sikh followers who are not involved with the homeland struggle directly, to be ostracized and repudiated or looked at with suspicion by some segments of the population in Western countries.

Many people have become interested in Sikhism for its religious ideals and also in part because of its strong stance on social justice and equality among the sexes as well as with leaders. There has also been an interest in the system of Kundalini Yoga instituted by Yogi Bhajan[334] which was introduced by him to the United States of America in the late 1960's A.C.E. Sikhism, as envisioned by Guru Nanak, contains many elevated teachings, though, it too, as with other religions developed outside of Africa, leads its followers to an ideal that is related to a culture and history that is not related to or in harmony with some African fundamental cultural/religious values. One example was given earlier in regard to the view on incarnations. Like Hinduism, African Religion accepts this concept. Another is the concept of Gurus. The concept of Spiritual Preceptor is a fundamental concept in African initiatic practice. The concept of monotheism is also divergent, as African religion holds the understanding of a Supreme Being that manifests in all forms of nature. The concept of accepting no more gurus is parallel to the Muslim ideal of viewing Muhammad as the last prophet. Thus, Sikhism is fundamentally more akin to Islam than Hinduism or African Religion and thus relates its followers towards an orthodox Western model or conception of the monotheism with an association to a South East Asian homeland.[335] The concepts of balance among the sexes and social justice are also to be found in African Religion and Philosophy. Also, the teaching of Arat Sekhem (Serpent Power- the Ancient African Kundalini Yoga) which has been identified as the earliest form of spiritual exercise and discipline in Kamit was practiced in Africa as early as 10,000 B.C.E. This practice can be traced from Ancient Egypt to the Indus Valley and from there further developed in the late Hindu period. So this practice is very ancient in Africa.

Conclusion

Why it is so important to study the history and philosophy of the world's religions? So that we may better understand what is needed to enter into a practice of religion that is in harmony with life, humanity and with the Spirit, and then act in accordance with that higher understanding, and pursue a course that will lead to the true practice of religion that will promote its highest ideals and prosperity for all. Otherwise, people all over the world will continue to live in fear, developing real or imagined notions about others, as potential adversaries in a race to envelop the world in their own idea of the "correct and only religion." There is no record of a pantheistic religion seeking out and destroying the peoples, shrines or idols of other peoples; why is that? Why is it that the orthodox monotheistic religions cannot live side by side with other religions that are not? Why must the other religions or spiritual traditions be eradicated? Why is it not possible for them to let others go on their way, or to try to convince them by gentle persuasion, without violence? This theme of absoluteness is a recurrent concept in orthodox monotheistic religions, that it must be their way or no way at all, so there is a choice of death or conversion.

In modern times many followers of Islam, especially in countries where the population is predominantly Muslim, feel under attack by Western Culture and especially Christian religion. Thus, they reject missionaries and suppress the practice of any form of spirituality other than Islam, and especially those forms of spirituality deemed as polytheistic, nature oriented, based on female divinity, etc. Likewise, the Jews and Christians feel besieged by the existence of people in the world who do not share their view of Judaism or Christianity, and the true religion of "Moses" or "Jesus as the savior," respectively. These feelings are spawning increasing fundamentalist movements, which of course leads to more conflict and ever more alienation.

What is needed is an abandoning of religious tenets that are based on an unenlightened view of life, in favor of those rooted and anchored in the universal principles of creation. In this manner, religion will truly serve its purpose, that of bringing forth a humanity which knows, understands and acts like the family that it is, intrinsically, leaving behind the pettiness, jealousies, suspicions and misconceptions of ignorance founded on dogmas that do not serve the goal of truth. People will be able to honestly look at the human heritage and realize that we are all children of the Divine, we are all related as descendants from the original human beings, created in Africa, and our religions are all based on the same teaching, which originated in Ancient Egypt. If the masses of people were to realize this great truth, that all religions are based on the same teaching which originated in Ancient Africa – which is also the genetic birthplace of all humanity it would be possible to renounce the concepts of orthodoxy, separateness and dogma, and see that all religions are unique expressions of the same innate human need to discover the Spirit.

NOTES FOR CHAPTER 4

[246] Ancient Egyptian religion.
[247] Ancient Egyptian religion.
[248] Ancient Egyptian religion.
[249] Ancient Egyptian religion.
[250] "Baal," Microsoft® Encarta® Online Encyclopedia 2000
[251] Byblos was an important city-states of Phoenicia, an ancient culture in the region of E Asia, along the E Mediterranean Sea coast that was associated with Ancient Egypt in trade and cultural exchange. Random House Encyclopedia Copyright (C) 1983,1990 by Random House Inc.
[252] *Encyclopedia of Gods"* by Michael Jordan
[253] *Encyclopedia of Gods"* by Michael Jordan
[254] Black Athena by Martin Bernal
[255] Random House Encyclopedia Copyright (C) 1983,1990 by Random House Inc.
[256] "Ishtar," Microsoft (R) Encarta. Copyright (c) 1994 Microsoft Corporation. Copyright (c) 1994 Funk & Wagnall's Corporation.
[257] Excerpted from *Compton's Interactive Encyclopedia*. Copyright (c) 1994, 1995 Compton's NewMedia, Inc. All Rights Reserved
[258] Random House Encyclopedia Copyright (C) 1983,1990 by Random House Inc.
[259] "Byblos," Microsoft (R) Encarta. Copyright (c) 1994 Microsoft Corporation. Copyright (c) 1994 Funk & Wagnall's Corporation.
[260] Copyright © 1995 Helicon Publishing Ltd
[261] *Encyclopedia of Gods"* by Michael Jordan
[262] *Woman's Encyclopedia of Myths and Secrets* by Barbara Walker
[263] *The Jewel in the Lotus,* Edwardes, Allen, Lancer Books, 1965, p 157
[264] *Hebrew Myths*, Robert Graves and Raphael Patai, 1964, p 67
[265] Before the formation of the Jewish religion.
[266] Any of various predatory birds of the hawk family Accipitridae, having a long, often forked tail and long pointed wings.
[267] *The Ancient Egyptian Book of the Dead,* Muata Ashby, 2000
[268] Random House Encyclopedia Copyright (C) 1983,1990 by Random House Inc.
[269] Bible – Old Testament, Jewish Christian tradition.
[270] Strong's Exhaustive Concordance of the Bible.
[271] Ibid
[272] Ibid
[273] Ibid
[274] Ibid
[275] "Funk and Wagnals New Encyclopedia"
[276] Random House Encyclopedia.
[277] "Ancient Egyptian Literature" Volume I and II, by Miriam Lichtheim
[278] "Migration," Microsoft (R) Encarta. Copyright (c) 1994 Microsoft Corporation.
[279] "Migration," Microsoft (R) Encarta. Copyright (c) 1994 Microsoft Corporation.
[280] See *The Mystical Journey From Jesus to Christ* by Muata Ashby
[281] "Zoroaster," Microsoft (R) Encarta. Copyright (c) 1994 Microsoft Corporation. Copyright (c) 1994 Funk & Wagnall's Corporation.
[282] " *Microsoft® Encarta® Africana.* ©1999 Microsoft Corporation. All rights reserved.
[283] *lessâna ge'ez* (meaning "the language of the free") or simply as Ge'ez, classical Ethiopic was used in the Aksumite royal inscriptions of the fourth century C.E. Although it ceased to be spoken by the twelfth or thirteenth century, Ge'ez remained the language of literature and religion. Like Hebrew and Arabic, it is a Semitic language. Ge'ez is written in a script developed from the South Arabian characters found in inscriptions on both sides of the Red Sea as far back as 3000 years ago (1000 B.C.E.).
[284] Kebra Nagast by Gerald Hauseman
[285] The Mystical Journey from Jesus to Christ by Muata Ashby
[286] See the book *Resurrecting Osiris* by Muata Ashby
[287] See *The Mystical Journey From Jesus to Christ* by Muata Ashby
[288] Strong's Exhaustive Concordance of the Bible.
[289] Herodotus: The Histories

[290] Sex and Race by J.A. Rogers
[291] Ancient Egyptian Literature by Miriam Lichtein
[292] See the section entitled: The Eucharist of the Ancient Egyptian Mysteries.
[293] Random House Encyclopedia.
[294] *African Religion: World Religion* by Aloysius M. Lugira
[295] Copyright © 1995 Helicon Publishing Ltd
[296] "The Isis Papers" by Dr. Frances Cress-Welsing
[297] United Nations World Conference on Racism, Durban So. Africa.
[298] *Middle Passage* Charles R. Johnson
[299] "Ferdmand's Handbook to the World's Religions"
[300] Israel, name with many biblical connotations, including the people dwelling in Palestine; the name given the North Kingdom; the name given Jacob after he wrestled with the angel; and the name taken by the returning exiles after the Babylonian captivity. (Random House Encyclopedia Copyright (C) 1983,1990 by Random House Inc.)
[301] See the books *The Mystical Journey From Jesus to Christ* by Muata Ashby, *Nag Hammadi Library*, edited by James Robinson "The Other Bible" translated by Wilhelm Schneemelcher, New Testament Apocrypha
[302] *"Encyclopedia of Gods"* by Michael Jordan
[303] *The Africans* by Ali A. Mazrui
[304] Random House Encyclopedia Copyright (C) 1983,1990 by Random House Inc.
[305] United Nations World Conference on Racism, Durban So. Africa.
[306] *"Encyclopedia of Gods"* by Michael Jordan
[307] *Traveler's Key to Ancient Egypt*, John Anthony West
[308] *The Africans* by Ali A. Mazrui
[309] Woman's Encyclopedia of Myths and Secrets by Barbara Walker
[310] Random House Encyclopedia Copyright (C) 1983,1990 by Random House Inc.
[311] *The Africans* by Ali A. Mazrui
[312] *Autobiography of Malcolm X* by Alex Haley.
[313] Handbook to Life in Ancient Egypt by Rosalie David.
[314] "Babism," Microsoft (R) Encarta. Copyright (c) 1994 Microsoft Corporation. Copyright (c) 1994 Funk & Wagnall's Corporation.
[315] Ceremonial leaders relates to an organized system of priests who lead congregations as well as pontiffs and leaders of the entire religion.
[316] Private prayer is enjoined in African religion but also ritual and mass programs as well. The same is true for Hinduism and Buddhism.
[317] Pilgrimage to Kamit and its holy sites
[318] God is unknowable to those who remain at the lower levels of human consciousness.
[319] Priests and Priestesses are necessary to lead people. In an attempt to avoid messianic leaders some religions have shunned leadership altogether. But this is only an official statement; it is not true in practice as there always needs to be someone to explain the teachings, otherwise how would the faith be transmitted? So in Islam, which also shuns leaders, there are Imams, in Sikhism, which also shuns gurus, there are revered leaders, and so too it is in Bahai. The same is true for Hinduism and Buddhism.
[320] Pilgrimage to Hindu holy sites
[321] God is unknowable to those who remain at the lower levels of human consciousness.
[322] Some orthodox sects of Hinduism believe that their tradition was started by an avatar and that this is a special revelation. However, the Hindu mystics derive insight through teachers and direct insight through spiritual disciplines.
[323] Muslims believe that the true god is the God of Islam alone and the only way to unity is through the Islamic faith.
[324] Pilgrimage to Mecca and other Islamic holy sites.
[325] The message of unity is only by accepting Muhammad and the Islamic faith, under the Islamic leadership.
[326] Even though there is a belief in angels, which is similar in most respects to the African and Indian system, these are not viewed as cosmic principles in Judaism, Christianity or Islam, but as higher order beings that do God's bidding.
[327] Neither orthodox Islam nor orthodox Judaism, or orthodox Christianity believe in mysticism; they actively oppose it in their congregations. On the other hand Jewish Kabbalists believe in mysticism, Christian Gnostics believe in mysticism, and Islamic Sufis believe in mysticism.
[328] Christians believe that the true god is the God of Israel alone and the only way to unity is through faith in Jesus.
[329] Pilgrimage to Mecca and other Islamic holy sites.
[330] The message of unity is only by accepting Jesus and the Christian faith, under the Christian leadership.
[331] "Baha'i Faith," *Microsoft® Encarta® Africana*. ©&(p) 1999 Microsoft Corporation. All rights reserved.
[332] Smithsonian Magazine issue June 1993
[333] Copyright © 1995 Helicon Publishing Ltd – Websters Encyclopedia
[334] http://www.yogatech.com/yogibhajan.html
[335] Copyright © 1995 Helicon Publishing Ltd – Websters Encyclopedia

Part III: The African Origins of Eastern Civilization, Religion, Yoga Mysticism and Ethics Philosophy

Chapter 5: The Ancient Egyptian Origins of the Indus Valley Civilization of Ancient India, Hinduism and Indian Yoga

"There are Egyptian columns as far off as NYASA, Arabia...Isis and Osiris led an army into India, to the source of the Ganges, and as far as the Indus Ocean."

-*Diodorus* (Greek historian 100 B. C.)

"Whatever information of Egyptian art and culture has come to us through the Egyptologists are mainly written in European languages and European Egyptologists generally have adopted in their popular writings all the Greek and Hebrew corruptions of Egyptian terminology which never appear to have a familiar look to any Indian scholar; therefore, he cannot imagine or feel at home with anything of Egypt.

This is why to an Indian, Egyptology on the surface seems very much foreign land unintelligible.‡ But as we learn Egyptian arts and languages through the originals, Egypt and Egyptians come nearer to us-even far closer than the so-called Aryans whom we know less but often make responsible for our languages, culture and everything."

-Sudhansu Kumar Ray
Prehistoric India and Ancient Egypt-

Where was the Indus Valley and the Indus Valley Civilization?

Figure 64: Map of Ancient India.

In order to proceed with our discovery of the origins of civilization, we must also look towards India, as new discoveries have pushed the dating of civilization there even further back than Sumerian civilization. The Indus Valley Civilization flourished at around c.2500 to about 1500 B.C.E. It was an ancient civilization of India located in the Indus River Valley, a land that is now known as present-day Pakistan. In modern times it was rediscovered by a British archaeologist named John Marshall in 1921 A.C.E. The Indus Valley Civilization is the earliest known urban culture of the Indian subcontinent. Three major cities were discovered. These were Mohenjo-daro, Harappa, and Chanhu-daro. They have been extensively excavated over the last three quarters of the 20th century. No pyramids, massive Temples or monuments have been discovered, the likes of those found in Egypt. However, it is a major achievement in its own right. All the cities thus far discovered followed the same plan. They used a grid plan to lay out the streets of the city and incorporated wide avenues which were laid out before a hill citadel. Each city had an elaborate community bath and large granaries. Agriculture was highly developed and extensive trade was carried on with Mesopotamia, by land and Egypt, by sea. In contrast to the nomadic lifestyle, the Indus Valley, being supported by the Indus River, provided the ideal location and conditions for its inhabitants to farm and create cities. The Indus culture left very little writing. It has not yet been successfully deciphered. However, there are various scholars who have advanced the idea that the script is related to the Aryan (Indo-European) family of languages, while others advance the position that it is Dravidian, belonging to the indigenous culture of India. Also, the Indus Valley Culture left interesting pictographs which give clues as to the spiritual practices of the culture before the year 1500 B.C.E., which is around the time when the Indus culture ceased to exist and when the Aryan (Vedic) culture seems to have emerged.

THE AFRICAN ORIGINS OF CIVILIZATION, RELIGION AND YOGA SPIRITUALITY

Figure 65: Above-The Indus Valley, India (in modern times-Pakistan {See Below}).

Hindu Kush is a principal Asian mountain range in India. It extends West-Southwest for a distance of 500-600mi (805-966km) from N.E. Afghanistan.[336] The Hindu Kush is also the source of many rivers including several tributaries of the Indus River on the southern slopes.[337] The correlation of the name Indus Kush with Ethiopian Kush is to be noted.

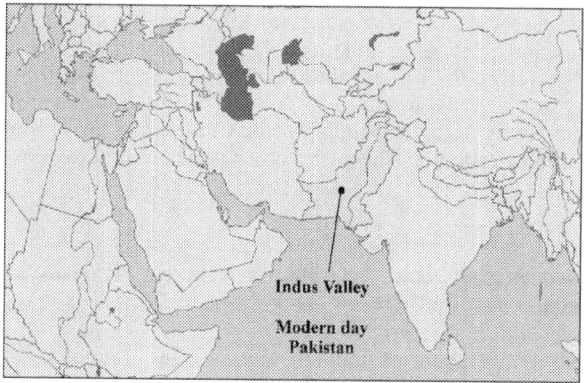

The Ethiopian Kush or Cush refers to the kingdom of Nubia[338], which according to the ancient writings of Egypt as well as the writings of the classical Greek historians is the source of both Ancient Egyptian civilization as well as Indian civilization. Both the writings as well as evidence of modern Indians reverencing north-east Africa as their ancestral home will be presented in the following sections. These relationships and others account for the startling similarities in the names, mythologies and philosophies of India and Africa (Ancient Egypt).

> "The Harappan civilization disappeared between 1750 and 1500 B.C. Disappearance was ascribed some time ago to the Aryan conquest. The word "Aryan" indicates pastoral nomads from Central Asia but is probably a misnomer; it does not seem to refer to an original population, but it means noble, from the upper castes, or even foreigner. It probably reflects the social condition of pastoral nomads after they arrived in the Indus Valley from the north and established their authority over the Harappan farming-community. There is no clear evidence of violence, however, and some suggest that the decay of the Harappan culture was due to a disaster-like a sudden major flood, or a change in the course of the Indus river (a not infrequent event)-responsible for diverting the necessary flood waters from the agricultural lands. A new explanation of the disappearance of the Harappan urban centers has been recently suggested by evidence derived from satellite photography, showing that the Saraswati River dried up when the continuing uplift of the Himalayas caused a shift of rivers, one of which the Yamuna, originally a tributary of the Indus-shifted eastward to join the Ganges. The ensuing aridity is also documented by paleobotanical information (see Gadgil and Thapar 1990 and references therein)."[339]

Inexplicably, the Indus civilization came to an end, the cities being abandoned, around the year 1500 B.C.E. and the Vedic (Aryan) culture began to flourish around the Ganges River area. It is believed by some that the cities were overrun by Aryan invaders. Others believe that there was a natural catastrophe, as the quote above suggests, that forced the people of the Indus area to move. This issue is part of the controversy surrounding the origins and fate of the Indus culture and what role, if any, was played by the Aryans, whoever they were. There are some factors pointing to the possibility of the Aryans being nomadic peoples from Northern Asia who invaded north-west India (Indus area) while other factors suggest they may have been a tribe of indigenous Indian people who came to prominence bringing their own language and spirituality to the forefront, dominating, Indian culture.

Another issue surrounding the relationship between the pre-existing peoples of the Indus and the Aryans who came onto the historical scene, is that their languages appear to be different, and the Arian language, Sanskrit, seems to be related to other languages. These languages are associated with North Asian and West Asian peoples who have been classified as "Caucasian" by those who use racial classifications. This would mean that the Aryans were of a different "race" than the original people of the Indus, who were of African descent. If so, this would also mean that the Indian philosophies of Vedanta and Yoga, which up to this time have been considered as "Indian Creations" are actually adopted from foreigners who "invaded" and conquered as well as destroyed the previous society and imposed their own. Yet others say that upon examination, the earliest Aryan texts, the Vedas, seem to be different than the later texts, referred to as "Vedanta" (meaning "essence of the Vedas" - includes Brahma sutras, the Upanishads and later epic poems such as the Mahabharata, etc.) and therefore, the discrepancies show a difference between the Vedic Culture and the pre and post Aryan (Vedic) influenced cultures of India. Still others cite this same example as evidence of the natural evolution in spiritual philosophy from the primitive to the advanced expositions. There are other scholars who say that the Aryans were of the same "race" as the Indians and that therefore the philosophies and Vedic culture are actually Indian, and there was no invasion. Rather there was a transformation in culture. All of these issues and others form the arguments surrounding the controversy of ancient India, Vedic Culture and the origins of Yoga philosophy which is referred to as "The Aryan Problem." These and other issues will be explored in the next section of this text.

Indology and Egyptology, Eurocentrism, Indocentrism, Africentrism, Racism, and the Origins of the Indus Valley Culture and Yoga

For many years, Indologists (researchers of Indian culture) have attempted to reconcile the issues related to the emergence of Aryan-Vedic culture in ancient India and to establish with certainty the role played by the Aryans and ancient indigenous Indians in the development of Yoga philosophy and Hinduism as a whole. In a book co-authored by Georg Feuerstein, David Frawley (prominent Western Indologists), and Subhash Kak, *In Search of the Cradle of Civilization,* the authors complain of facing the same problem in Indology which researchers of Ancient Egypt may also cite, that there is a tendency of Eurocentric scholars to place the origins of civilization in Greece, Rome or Mesopotamia. Also, they mention that they have noticed the inclination of Eurocentric scholars to interpret the spiritual texts in accordance with Western points of view, devoid of the understanding and sensitivity of a practitioner.

> "Twentieth-century Western scholars have seldom shown such sensitivity. They have tended to read the Vedas in the light of modern psychology, sociology, or anthropology. With few exceptions, they have failed to explore the texts from a spiritual standpoint, which is at the heart of the Vedic heritage. Nor have they looked into the mathematical and astronomical code of Vedic symbolism, which was an important part of that tradition. Their readings of the Vedas often tell more about twentieth-century trends and problems than they do about the Vedic era."

A similar sentiment to the one expressed above is felt by other scholars of Indology, such as in the following segment from *Dionysos and Kataragama: Parallel Mystery Cults,* by Patrick Harrigan, which indicate the correlations between the Dionysian (Greek) mysteries and the Kataragama mysticism of Sri Lanka[340] in India. A new generation of researcher-writer-historian-practitioners have taken up the task to recover the culture of their area of study and to bring it forth in a way that reflects the heart as well as the intellect of the ancient traditions instead of just the factual or intellectual basis of the philosophy as mere concepts or beliefs.

> "From its beginning, European Indological scholarship has tended to focus on languages, texts and traditions of Indo-European origin while overlooking indigenous and

Dravidian sources or downplaying their role in the evolution of Indian thought. As part of a general reappraisal of the history of Indian thought, the present study also aims to reapproximate the archaic worldview, alone from which archaic cults draw their soul-inspiring vision and vitality and outside of which they appear to the modern mind as mere 'belief systems' with no ontological[341] basis in what we moderns fondly cherish as 'reality'. As Walter Otto observes in his landmark study Dionysus: Myth and Cult, "It is the custom to speak only of religious concepts or religious belief. The more recent scholarship in religion is surprisingly indifferent to the ontological content of this belief. As a matter of fact, all of its methodology tacitly assumes that there could not be an essence which would justify the cults and the myths."

These arguments sounds very close to one which was made a few years earlier by Cheikh Anta Diop in his book *The African Origins of Civilization,* citing the refusal of twentieth century Egyptologists (who control the field of Egyptology and promote Eurocentrism, the prominence of European culture and contributions to civilization) to assign older dates to the emergence of civilization in Ancient Egypt. The effort here is to make Ancient Egyptian history synchronous with or younger than the Sumerian by arbitrarily setting dates of historical events, and then promoting these to the general society as a consensus based on scholarly evidence. Diop cites two Western researchers who make this point, thereby showing the important fact that not all Western Egyptologists were thus biased.

"The opinion of all the ancient writers on the Egyptian race is more or less summed up by Gaston Maspero (1846-1916): *"By the almost unanimous testimony of ancient historians, they belonged to an African race [read: Negro] which first settled in Ethiopia, on the Middle Nile; following the course of the river, they gradually reached the sea."*

In another work, published in 1934, Dr. Contenau insists: *"A general solidarity exists that must be taken into account. The historical period opens at approximately the same time in Egypt and Mesopotamia; nevertheless, Egyptologists generally refuse to fix the date of Menes, 'founder of the First Dynasty,*[342] *at later than 3200 B.C."*

From these quotations it is clear that the synchronization of Egyptian and Mesopotamian history is a necessity resulting from ideas and a particular worldview, not from facts. The motivating idea is to succeed in explaining Egypt by Mesopotamia, that is, by Western Asia, the original habitat of Indo-Europeans. The foregoing demonstrates that, if we remain within the realm of authentic facts, we are forced to view Mesopotamia as a belatedly born daughter of Egypt. The relationships of protohistory do not necessarily imply the synchronization of history in the two countries.

To conclude this section, we can ponder this passage from Lovat Dickson, quoted by Marcel Brion: *"Thirty years ago, the name Sumer meant nothing to the public. Today there is something called the Sumerian problem, a subject for controversy and constant speculation among archeologists."*

According to the Egyptians, Diodorus reports, the Chaldaens were *"a colony of their priests that Belus had transported on the Euphrates and organized on the model of the mother-caste, and this colony continues to cultivate the knowledge of the stars, knowledge that it brought from the homeland."* So it is that "Chaldean" formed the root of the Greek word for astrologer.

Referring to Persian monuments, Diodorus writes that they were built by Egyptian workers forcibly carried off by Cambyses,[343] "the Vandal." "Cambyses set fire to all the Temples in Egypt; that was when the Persians, transporting all the treasures to Asia and even kidnapping some Egyptian workmen, built the famous palaces of Persepolis, Susa, and several other cities in Media."[344]

See also Appendix C

-Cheikh Anta Diop

A similar deficiency in Western scholarship is also noted by Indologists. The authors of the book, *In Search of the Cradle of Civilization,* cite the following passage from John Anthony West's *Serpent In The Sky* to illustrate the problem of bias in Western Scholarship. Rene Guenon wrote about it in the early 20th century in the book *Introduction to the Study* of *the Hindu Doctrines.* This author referred to Western bias as a form of "classical prejudice." Mr. Guenon referred to this classical prejudice as "the predisposition to attribute the origin of all civilization to the Greeks and Romans"[345] and further went on to say:

"It seems scarcely possible to account for this attitude except by means of the following explanation: because their own civilization hardly goes any further back than the Greco-Roman period and derives for the most part from it, Westerners are led to believe that it must have been the same in every other case and they have difficulty in conceiving of the existence of entirely different and far more ancient civilizations; it might be said that they are mentally incapable of crossing the Mediterranean."[346]

Here, crossing the Mediterranean implies going to Egypt (Africa) for the source of civilization. Presumably, this difficulty in crossing the Mediterranean is due to the realization by early Egyptologists that the Greek civilization owes much to Ancient Egypt, and the discovery that Ancient Egyptian civilization was of African origin precluded the possibility of adopting that heritage and legacy, as many European scholars could not, and even today still cannot, see themselves as related to Africa, especially in the context of the racism which pervades Western Culture. Due to this issue, for a time, it was also popular among Western scholars to promote the idea that Ancient Egypt was part of the Middle East and not related to the rest of Africa, ethnically, culturally or otherwise. This fallacy became widely distributed in Western Culture through textbooks, and the news and entertainment media, etc. This idea fueled the perception of Nubians as being slaves of the Ancient Egyptians, and personalities such as Moses and the other early Hebrews of the Bible as being Middle Easterners, instead of Africans. These perceptions along with the distortion of the myth and philosophy of Ancient Egyptian religion are so widespread that even though they are not openly espoused in textbooks and encyclopedias, popular manifestations in the news entertainment media still persist.

The treatment of Ancient Egyptian history and culture is similar to the Indian situation in that there has been a move to make it appear that the spiritual culture of India is not Indian, but rather an adoption by the indigenous Indians of philosophy they received from the "Aryan Race," who are variously described as tall Caucasian (implying white skinned) peoples. In the case of both the Ancient Egyptians and Ancient Indians, the implication is that the indigenous African "Black" peoples derived their civilization, art, culture and philosophy as a result of being influenced by Caucasoid peoples, (implying Indo-European, i.e. "Whites.") Now the authors of the book, *In Search of the Cradle of Civilization,* go on to say that they have been confronted with this "classical prejudice" cited by Guenon and that it still continues. However, they also make the point that the Eurocentric frame of reference is "undermined" by the "testimony of the classical writers themselves."

> "Guenon's criticism of scholarly myopia still applies in many instances. We must also not forget that Eurocentrism is undermined by the testimony of the classical writers themselves, who made it clear that many of the Greeks' most precious ideas were inspired, if not borrowed, from the Egyptians. As Plato records in his *Timaeus,* the Egyptians looked upon the Greeks as mere children in the evolution of human civilization. Thales, Solon, and Pythagoras sat at the feet of Egyptian philosophers."[347]

While the Indologists (Feuerstein, Frawley and Kak) acknowledge the role of Ancient Egypt in the development of Ancient Greece, they turn now to as if appropriate the legacy of Ancient Egyptian culture and civilization as an Indian extraction. The authors acknowledge that there are "curious parallels" between Ancient Egyptian and Indian myth and symbolism that "deserve careful investigation," but go on nevertheless to question Egypt as being the source of culture and civilization. They turn their attention towards India as the source from which the Ancient Egyptians derived their wisdom, which they conferred upon early Greek philosophers.

> "But where did the Egyptians themselves get their wisdom? We know that they owed a great debt to the learned men and sages of India. There was a colony of Indic people in Memphis as long ago as 500 B.C. But Egypt's connection with India may go back much farther in time. Indeed, there are many curious parallels between Egyptian and Indic mythology and symbolism, which deserve careful investigation."[348]

The authors seem to acknowledge a connection between Ancient Egypt and India and even state that the possibility deserves more "careful investigation," but then seem to digress to the theory that India is the "Cradle" of world civilization, including the Mesopotamian and Ancient Egyptian civilizations. The statement seems to be used as a means to establish a connection but for the purpose of saying or implying that the connection is one in which the Ancient Egyptians drew from Indian civilization. Note that the statement is provided as a scholarly opinion without support (evidence), and yet it is used to raise the specter of dubious indigenous Ancient Egyptian origins of civilization as if the scholarship ascertaining that civilization originated in Africa, by Africans, is unfounded or questionable. The very acknowledgment that Ancient Egyptian culture and civilization can be derived from Indian culture and civilization shows that the authors recognize a connection between the two nations. Thus, if the flow of culture can be viewed in one direction, it can also be viewed in the opposite as well. This means the possibility exists that Indian culture and civilization could have been derived from Ancient Egyptian culture and civilization. However, to arrive at such a conclusion requires a thorough investigation and review of the archeological and anthropological evidence at hand. If it can be shown which culture emerged anterior, pioneered civilization, and then had contact with the other and if correlations of factors of cultural expression between the two can be shown, then it will be possible to have a basis to ascertain that there was contact and which culture derived from the other.

The authors of the book cited above, who are part of a growing segment of Indologists, may have overlooked the fact that it was the same *"classical writers themselves"* who, as the authors acknowledge, gave *"testimony,"* to the fact that the Indian tribes were actually part of the Ancient Egyptian and Ethiopian culture. Herodotus, Plutarch, Pythagoras, Plato, Aristotle, Diodorus, Strabo, and others are considered as the classical Greek writers. The authors quote Diodorus later on in their book, but only in reference to the similarities between the Dionysian mysteries of Greece and the Shivaite rites of India, and not in reference to the cultural unity between Ancient Egypt, India and Ethiopia. Here, not only the Eurocentrists, but also the Indocentrists would seem to be frustrated since the eyewitness accounts from historians such as Diodorus, Herodotus and Strabo state emphatically that the peoples of this area (Mesopotamia, India) are part of the Egyptian-Ethiopian culture and that the connection did in fact go back much further in time to an era prior to the composition of the Vedas. The specific statements by the classical writers are:

> *"Still the Egyptians said that they believed the Colchians to be descended from the army of Sesostris. My own conjectures were founded, first, on the fact that they are black-skinned and have woolly hair."*
>
> -History of Herodotus (Greek historian 484 B.C.E.)

> *"Egyptians settled Ethiopia and Colchis."*
> -*Geography,* Strabo c. 64 B.C.E., (Greek historian and geographer)

> *"I shall speak of the king who reigned next, whose name was Sesostris^{349} He, the priests said, first of all proceeded in a fleet of ships of war from the Arabian gulf along the shores of the Indian ocean, subduing the nations as he went, until he finally reached a sea which could not be navigated by reason of the shoals. Hence he returned to Egypt, where, they told me, he collected a vast armament, and made a progress by land across the continent, conquering every people which fell in his way.*
>
> *In this way he traversed the whole continent of Asia, whence he passed on into Europe, and made himself master of Scythia and of Thrace, beyond which countries I do not think that his army extended its march."*
>
> - History of Herodotus (Greek historian 484 B.C.E.)

> *"All the Indian tribes I mentioned ... their skins are all of the same color, much like the Ethiopians."*
>
> -History of Herodotus (Greek historian 484 B.C.E.)

> "And upon his return to Greece, they gathered around and asked, "tell us about this great land of the Blacks called Ethiopia." And Herodotus said, "There are two great Ethiopian nations, one in Sind (India) and the other in Egypt."
>
> -*Diodorus* (Greek historian 100 B.C.)

> "From Ethiopia, he (Osiris {Asar})^{350} passed through Arabia, bordering upon the Red Sea to as far as India, and the remotest inhabited coasts; he built likewise many cities in India, one of which he called Nysa, willing to have remembrance of that (Nysa) in Egypt where he was brought up. At this Nysa in India he planted Ivy, which continues to grow there, but nowhere else in India or around it. He left likewise many other marks of his being in those parts, by which the latter inhabitants are induced, and do affirm, that this God was born in India. He likewise addicted himself to the hunting of elephants, and took care to have statues of himself in every place, as lasting monuments of his expedition."
>
> - *Diodorus* (Greek historian 100 B.C.)

THE AFRICAN ORIGINS OF CIVILIZATION, RELIGION AND YOGA SPIRITUALITY

Many who are interested in Ancient Egypt from a cultural as well as a spiritual point of view feel that 20th century Western Egyptologists have not been reporting all of the discoveries in the ancient histories and accounts or modern Egyptian excavations, nor applying the correct dating of objects and historical events. Some scholars cite the apparent confusion in dating events in Ancient Egypt as a sufficient cause to consider Ancient Egyptian history as *"bedeviled with difficulties"* and therefore they feel justified in reaching the presumptuous conclusions such as were stated in the book *In Search of the Cradle of Civilization*: (*Highlighted text by Ashby)

> "There can be little question that the Vedas are the most impressive literary achievement of antiquity. <u>In extent</u>, they far surpass the Bible, and they dwarf Homer's epics as they do the sacred canon of the ancient Chinese civilization." p.17

> "Most of the "first time ever" claims made for the Sumerians have in recent years been exposed as exaggerated or absurd. <u>There is mounting evidence that neither Sumer nor Egypt quite deserve the pride of place among the ancient civilizations. Rather the cradle of civilization appears to lie beyond the fertile valleys of the Nile, Tigris, and Euphrates Rivers.</u>" p.xviii

The statements above have been cited by some readers as self-important, and seeming to impugn the research of scholars who have brought forth evidences of contact and cultural exchange between Ancient Egypt and India, characterizing these as spurious theories, lacking authenticity and validity in essence or origin, in favor of an "Indian Cradle of Civilization" theory. The authors seem to say that a voluminous collection of writings[155] automatically deserves a high placement on the ancient literary and civilization scale. The modern publishing industry of Western Culture puts out more books, magazines, etc., than at any other time in history. Can we automatically say that this means we live in a high culture and civilization? This argument would overlook the fringe writings, writings directed at frivolous entertainment or to prurient interests, and other negative writings which are injurious to society or have no value to society. In any case, the vast literature of Ancient Egypt, considered collectively, constitutes a staggering compilation, and is mostly dedicated to spiritual matters and philosophy. It can only be dismissed as "undeserving the pride of place among ancient civilizations" if it is approached by ignorance and languorous scholarship or biased research. In the view of the authors, early India would seem to have had no significant contact with other ancient civilizations and received little from them, or that the contact was in a one way direction with other countries receiving the benefit which led to civilization arising outside of India. Also, they seem to exclude the possibility of new information coming to light, which may in turn lead them, like so many Eurocentrists, to make statements that later need to be upheld by precluding the evidence and concepts of others. Therefore, conclusions should be based on information on hand, logical interpretation, intuition, prudence and freedom from cultural bias. Again, the *"classical writers themselves"* who gave *"testimony"* (above) seem to contradict the apparently "Indocentric" view contained in the statement of the authors.

What is Yoga?

Yoga is the practice of mental, physical and spiritual disciplines which lead to self-control and self-discovery by purifying the mind, body and spirit, so as to discover the deeper spiritual essence which lies within every human being and object in the universe. In essence, the goal of yoga practice is to unite or *yoke* one's individual consciousness with Universal or Cosmic consciousness. In a broad sense, religion, in its purest form, is also a yoga system, as it seeks to reunite the soul with its true and original source, God. In broad terms, any spiritual movement or discipline that brings one closer to self-knowledge is a "Yogic" movement. However, when speaking of yoga in terms of spiritual disciplines, a technology, designed to enhance the spiritual evolution, we are referring to specific disciplines which may or may not be part of an organized religious group. So religions can practice the yoga disciplines, but one need not be in a religion in order to practice yoga. Nevertheless, the most ancient systems of yoga, the Sema (Smai) Tawi of Ancient Egypt and the Yoga of the Upanishads and the later Bhagavad Gita developed from the teachings of Sages and Saints who were religious personalities and they initially gave their teachings through myths and religious venues, the Temples. The main recognized forms of Yoga disciplines are:

- *Yoga of Wisdom,*
- *Yoga of Devotional Love,*

---

[155] Note that in the quote above, the words "in extent" were used to refer to the literary works of the Vedas. Thus, this specific reference is to quantity, not quality or content of the works.

THE AFRICAN ORIGINS OF CIVILIZATION, RELIGION AND YOGA SPIRITUALITY

- *Yoga of Meditation,*
    - *Physical Postures Yoga*
- *Yoga of Selfless Action,*
- *Tantric Yoga*
- *Serpent Power Yoga*

Later on in the text of the book, *In Search of the Cradle of Civilization,* the authors call for a *"critical reexamination"* into the origins of Yoga. However, in view of the previous statements, the reader's first impression might be that there is a proclivity towards a point of view which suggests a contradiction with the following statements from the same book, that ignores the possibility of the origins of Yoga outside of India, and turns the attention solely towards the Vedas.

> *"The time is ripe for a critical reexamination of the question of the origin of Yoga. In looking for the roots of Yoga in the Vedas, we must first of all rid ourselves of the tendency to indulge in what scholars call arguments ex silentio; that is, to favor a particular point of view because of the absence of contrary evidence. For instance, we might argue that, because the original Pledge of Allegiance did not contain the phrase "one nation under God," the American people were irreligious prior to 1954 when the Pledge was changed by an Act of Congress. This is dearly absurd, and yet this kind of argument is frequently resorted to by scholars, especially when defending cherished positions."* p.173

While the authors honestly face the issues related to the uncertain readings of the Vedas, the uncertain "race" of the Aryan tribes, the question of the Dravidian origins and their relation to the Vedic culture and seem to have an awareness of the "archeological surprises"[351] that occur from time to time giving insight into previously unknown history, they steadfastly adhere to the Indocentric model, in effect perpetuating the same error they are cautioning in others.

There is a growing rift between Indian Indologists and Western (European) Indologists over the true nature and chronology of Ancient Indian culture and civilization. The following chronology presented in the book *A Concise Encyclopedia of Hinduism (1999),* by Klaus K. Klostermaier, shows the substantial difference between Western scholars and Indian scholars.

> "The chronology of Ancient India up to the time of Buddha is at present the focus of fierce scholarly debates. The majority of Indian scholars assume a date of 4000 B.C.E. for the Rig Veda, rejecting also the so-called 'Aryan invasion theory', whereas the majority of Western scholars maintain the invasion theory and date the Rig Veda to 1500-1200 B.C.E. The chronology offered here represents largely the traditional Indian position." P. 216

THE AFRICAN ORIGINS OF CIVILIZATION, RELIGION AND YOGA SPIRITUALITY

Table 19: Chronologies of India According to Western and Indian Indologists

Chronology of India according to Indian Scholars On the basis of the more recent research, based on archaeology and astronomy, the following chronology can be tentatively established:		Chronology of India according to Western Scholars[86]	
c. 6500 BCE (Mehrgarh)[87]	Neolithic Period	c. 2700-1500 BCE	Mature Indus civilization
c. 4000 BCE	Earliest Vedic hymns	c. 2700 BCE	Early Harappan civilization
c. 3500 BCE	Early Harappan civilization	c. 1500 BCE	Earliest Vedic hymns
c. 2700-1500 BCE	Mature Indus civilization	c. 2500-1500 BCE	Mature Indus civilization
c. 1900 BCE	Age of Ramayana	c. 700 BCE	Age of Ramayana
c. 1500-500 BCE	Major Upanishads, development of early Samkhya, early Purva Mimamsa	c. 900-700 BCE	Major Upanishads, development of early Samkhya, early Purva Mimamsa
c. 1400 BCE	Great Bharata War - Age of Krishna. Early version of Mahabharata	c. 600 BCE	Great Bharata War - Age of Krishna. Early version of Mahabharata
c. 1200 BCE	Early Sutra literature. Consolidation of Vedic civilization: Manusmrti	c. 1200 BCE	Early Sutra literature. Consolidation of Vedic civilization: Manusmrti
624-544 BCE	Life of Gautama Buddha according to traditional reckoning.	624-544 BCE	Life of Gautama Buddha according to traditional reckoning.
527 BCE	End of Mahavira's earthly life according to Jain tradition.	527 BCE	End of Mahavira's earthly life according to Jain tradition.

Klaus K. Klostermaier is not the only Indologist who has recognized the problems with the chronology of India.

> "India's Chronology is notoriously conjectural until we come to the nineteenth century."
>
> –Georg Feuerstein (Yoga Journal 12/29/2000)
> (One of the authors of "In Search Of The Cradle Of Civilization")

The Aryan Influence on India, the Caste System of the Vedas and The Laws of Manu

Since its inception in the 19th century of our era, the theory of the Aryan influence has been controversial. Due to some similarities between the Sanskrit language, the language from early Indian Aryan culture, and the Greek, Latin, German and Celtic languages, the theory emerged among Western scholars that these are part of a family of languages. As expressed above, many scholars have referred to this issue as the "Aryan Problem." However, the theories are varied since there are no direct records or historical documents outlining chronologies, except for the great Hindu epics, which are spiritual texts outlining the myth related to the Hindu gods and goddesses and their relationships to human beings. Western linguistic scholars studying the dispersion of languages in the 19th century began to claim that their studies revealed a Vedic culture which came into the Indus valley (India) and imposed themselves on the pre-existing culture. The dates given for this emergence and or invasion by the Aryans are 1500-1200 B.C.E. (according to the European Indologists). The invasion theory seemed to be supported by the evidence of human remains found in the Indus Valley, skeletons that were found in the various buildings and streets, huddled together as if killed by an attack.[352] Archeologists found the remains in the latest layers (of excavated soil) of the time period relating to the ancient human occupation of the Indus Valley. This date corresponds with the infusion of a culture with similar traits to the Aryans, into Eastern Europe, Asia Minor (Iraq, Iran, Syria, Jordan, Palestine, as well as North East Africa). The Egyptians referred to these invaders as the Hyksos, and identified them as Asians. The Aryans are believed to have come into the northwestern portion of India, settling in the Punjab area. The extent of their influence is not completely clear to many scholars.

Many scholars believe that the Aryans were Indo-Europeans, while others advance the theory that the Aryans were one of several groups of indigenous tribes of India and that the Vedas, the main spiritual texts of the Aryans, were created by the Indian people themselves without outside influence. If this is the case, then logically it must follow that the Vedic teachings and the Vedic Pantheon of gods and goddesses such as Indra, Agni and Varuna are of Indian origin. Other scholars advance the idea that the great battles described in the Hindu spiritual epics Mahabharta and Ramayana are actually relating a conflict between two racial groups, the indigenous "black" Indians and the "white" Aryan invaders. It must be kept in mind that the Hindu epics are composed mostly of metaphoric teachings and grand, sweeping stories, and therefore, provide more spiritual insight than chronological historical data.

In any case, the previous eye-witness accounts, documented above, would seem to disqualify the contention the Aryans were one of several groups of indigenous tribes of India since, even in the time of Herodotus (450 B.C.E.), the Indians were observed to have "skin like the Ethiopians" and we are told that the Aryans were light-skinned Indo-Europeans.[353] In modern times, the North-Indian peoples display a lighter hue than their southern counterparts. This may be explained by the Macedonian (Greek) armies, led by Alexander the Great, who conquered north and west India in c. 300 B.C.E. and whose population mixed with the native peoples of north-west India. Further, the subsequent conquest of India by the Mogul or Mughal Empire (founded by Babur, a Muslim 1526-1857) wherein India was controlled by Semitic peoples from the Middle East (Asia Minor), and the subsequent subjugation of India by the British Empire contributed to not only the production of mulatto[354] offspring, but also a large segment of the population with Semitic or Caucasian skin color and features. As in Ancient Egypt, the hue of skin color of the Ancient Indians was originally dark, tending towards the "blue black," like the Ancient Ethiopians (Nubians). This blue-black nature may also be the source for the *"shyam"* (swarthy, black) or blue color of divinities such as Krishna and Vishnu in India, and the "blackness" of Asar (Osiris) and the "blueness" of Amun in Ancient Egypt. The Ancient Egyptians, as late as 484 B.C.E., were considered as being "black skinned" by the accounts of visitors and by the Egyptian's own depictions of themselves. This did not change until the influx and intermarrying with other ethnic groups such as the Persians (invasion of Cambyses), Greeks (invasion of Alexander- 332 B.C.E.) and the Arabs.

The changing ethnic nature of India brings up an important theme. Many people of darker complexion recoil from the study of Yoga and Hinduism in general when they consider the question of the caste system and its racist policies which still, despite the efforts of Mahatma Ghandi, other Indian activists and the British domination period, continues to cause misery to the people of India. The philosophy of Yoga is wonderful when it speaks of universal love and all-encompassing Divinity, but what about its roots? Is this philosophy of caste a legacy of Vedic culture? Are the Vedas tainted with the vile practice of slavery and exploitation of human beings due to their skin color? The aforementioned texts in conjunction with the following article elucidate this issue.

THE AFRICAN ORIGINS OF CIVILIZATION, RELIGION AND YOGA SPIRITUALITY

"If the Caste system is part of Hinduism, then I am not a Hindu."

-Mahatma Ghandi

"The traditional caste system of India developed more than 3,000 years ago when Aryan-speaking nomadic groups migrated from the north to India about 1,500 BC. The Aryan priests, according to the ancient sacred literature of India, divided society into a basic caste system. **Sometime between 200 BC and AD 100, the Manu Smriti, or Law of Manu, was written. In it the Aryan priest-lawmakers created the four great hereditary divisions of society still surviving today, the Brahmans (priests), the Kshatriyas (warriors) Vaisyas (farmers and merchants) and the Sudras (laborers, born to be servants to the other three castes). Far lower than the Sudras were those people of no caste, the Harijans or Untouchables.** These were the Dravidians, the aboriginal inhabitants of India, to whose ranks from time to time were added the pariahs, or outcasts, people expelled for religious or social sins from the classes into which they had been born. Thus created by the priests, the caste system was made a part of Hindu religious law, rendered secure by the claim of divine revelation."

-Microsoft (R) Encarta. Copyright (c) 1994
(Highlighted portions by Ashby)

First, it must be understood that the Vedic culture (1,500 B.C.E-1,000 B.C.E.) did introduce a form of caste system. It was for the purpose of organizing the population so as to make it more productive and orderly. Again, it appears to be an outside influence or innovation in the culture, a cultural influence that is being injected into the pre-existing culture in India in order to "civilize" it. However, there does not appear to be any evidence to suggest that it instituted a philosophy of racial discrimination based on skin color at the time of its inception. The castes were instituted to allow human beings to learn the varied duties of the different aspects of society, but it was not meant to forcibly keep people rigidly in one group or one group as slaves to another particular group. In fact, there are scriptures which tell of people who rose from other castes to become Brahmans. In effect, one will find these groups or categories are a "natural" basic pattern of societies. A portion of the population are spiritual leaders, a portion are involved in government, politics and the defense of the country (warrior caste), a portion will form the business and professional segment of society, and a portion will perform service type jobs, and then there is usually a segment of the population that do not follow the so-called norms of the society, which in our day and age would include the indigent and homeless population.

During the time when the "Laws of Manu" were introduced under the aegis of "Vedic tradition," a new philosophy transformed the caste system into a form of systematic racial discrimination and slavery of women, and the darker skinned peoples whose population happened to be composed mostly of the Dravidian culture. The philosophy of the Laws of Manu included demeaning and degrading regulations for women which essentially made them the property of men, without any possibility for independent thought, ownership of property or legal recourse. The Dravidian peoples were similarly affected. Dravidian is a language and culture and not a racial type. However, the group of people who were relegated to the lowest position in the caste system were the Dravidian speaking peoples, who are recognized as being the group that was least mixed with the Greeks, Arabs, or Northern Asians and thus, closely resemble Nubians, even in modern times.

Thus, through intensive research it can be discovered that the original intent of the caste system was benign. However, it degraded into a form of social order that has led to a form of gendercide (female infanticide).[355] CNN[356] and other news services reported on this situation in the early 1990's. Female children are seen as having less value, so they are neglected, allowed to die, and sometimes even murdered. In recent years, the struggle to modernize India has promoted improvements in the system, but many injustices still continue. In the search for truth it is important to face and explain all facets of the information that may come to light. As an intelligent person, one must learn to sift out what is detrimental in any area, be it history, philosophy, religion, business, etc., and recognize what is useful. Just as the evil deeds of men who profess to be killing in the name of the Divine Self (Supreme Being, God, Goddess, etc.) cannot be taken to mean that authentic religion condones or promotes violence or murder, in the same manner the deeds of men and women based on a particular religious philosophy and its spirit or intent must be differentiated. The Vedanta and yoga philosophy and the associated disciplines of India are indeed examples of the highest tradition of spiritual philosophy as the world has ever seen, and are worthy of study and practice by those who are so inclined.

THE AFRICAN ORIGINS OF CIVILIZATION, RELIGION AND YOGA SPIRITUALITY

Gendercide and Mistreatment of Women in Modern India

Thus, through intensive research it can be discovered that the original intent of the caste system was benign. However, it degraded into a form of social order that led to a form of gendercide (female infanticide).[1] Recent reports have again surfaced that the ease of obtaining sex tests to determine the gender of unborn children has accelerated the pace of abortions of female fetuses (CNN 2001). A recent report by news services documented how young girls and women are routinely abducted, enslaved and forced to work as prostitutes. When the incumbent police chief was confronted with this issue, he defended the lack of or minimal effort of his department to protect these citizens and, in some cases, the facilitation of the perpetrators by members of his police force, saying "it is the oldest profession and a tradition to have prostitutes." The degradation of Indian society in modern times was further exposed when a report surfaced on CNN (on 8/30/01) that the problem of overpopulation in India is reaching dangerous proportions. The report stated that one of the solutions under consideration by the government was that of providing the Indian people with low cost televisions, so that they may watch television at night instead of engaging in sexual relations, since there is a reluctance among men to use contraception.

All human beings require three basic elements in order to survive and grow in a positive way, food, shelter and opportunity. If people are in constant stress due to preoccupations with survival issues, and do not have a positive outlook on life, they will resort to whatever means they perceive that they have available to them to escape the miseries of life. Sexuality is one of these perceived means, and one that is most accessible, to accomplish this temporary escape. Furthermore, producing offspring provides many people with a sense of accomplishment, a sense of having created something and therefore, for those who have little else in life to be proud of, they can at least say they produced "life." And since the more valuable gender has been assigned to the male as opposed to the female in general Indian society, the more sons produced, the more worth people (especially men) feel. In societies where people have more economic opportunities and other activities to pursue, the population growth tends to remain under control. This is even truer in societies which have altruistic pursuits and which are organized based on principles of higher philosophy. Ancient Egyptian society did not have an overpopulation problem because life was governed by the pursuits of righteousness, order and spirituality. This factor contributed to their ultimate defeat when confronted with hoards of Asiatic invaders. Thus, the population was assimilated into the populations that invaded, including the Assyrians, Greeks, Romans, Europeans, and Arabs. It is important to understand that promoting population growth is not the way to maintain the survival of a culture although this is a contributing factor. Kamitan culture did not promote celibacy except to certain orders of the Priests and Priestesses though the general population was exhorted to maintain control over their sexuality and not bring people into being who cannot be taken care of by the society. More important to maintaining a culture and its civilization is A-adopting a righteous set of moral principles to guide the culture, B-the development of technology to protect the culture from outside influences and an awareness of cultural subversion which occurs when people with other customs and traditions infiltrate the culture and thereby transform it over time, changing the values and traditions of the original culture. Therefore, the values and traditions must be upheld, through A-social, B-political and C-military policies, and if they are the culture will survive despite outside pressures.

Of course, the degradation of the Indian population and the degeneration of Kamitan society are not the fault of yoga and the righteous philosophy of Dharma or Maat, respectively, but the lack of their practice. Even the greatest philosophy cannot help a people if they do not follow it. However, the leaders in the society need to be outspoken in their opposition to such degrading policies. They must also be powerful teachers to show society a better way of living. One example of this effort comes from a prominent India spiritual leader, Swami Jyotirmayananda (see statement below). Another aspect of this issue is the failure of government leaders to follow the council of the yoga practitioners such as Ghandi and Jyotirmayananda. As long as they divorce themselves from the philosophy of righteous order even while calling themselves "Hindus," how can they be considered as authentic practitioners and leaders of the religion and its higher principles?

> "Due to limitation in understanding, people (Indians) began to give more importance to sons than to daughters. This however is a result of ignorance."
>
> -Swami Jyotirmayananda (From the book *Advice to Householders*)

THE AFRICAN ORIGINS OF CIVILIZATION, RELIGION AND YOGA SPIRITUALITY

The "Race" of the Aryans

As previously discussed, the "race" of the Aryans is a point of debate among Indologists and other scholars. More precisely, the quandary is not so much about the skin tone of the Aryans, but rather about their ethnic affiliation, namely, were they outsiders who came from northern central Asia (present day Russia) or were they a particular group of Indians that emerged to control the country and expand to other countries. In the former context, the Indo-Europeans and their languages have come to be associated with the light skinned peoples. We are told by ancient writers that the Colchians were Egyptians, and they described the Egyptians as being of the same skin coloration as the Ethiopians, and we know that ancient and present day people from Ethiopia are dark complexioned. Yet the ancient Colchians, who were dark-skinned, have given way to present day light complexioned Russians who today inhabit the land of the Colchians which is now the modern state of Georgia.. Thus by this reckoning we are able to deduce that the Indo-European peoples emerging in India in ancient times looked like the present day light complexioned Indo-Europeans, having mixed with the ancient ones mixed with the indigenous Indians living in the north of India.

While some factors point to the idea that the Aryans were Indo-Europeans, there are others that point to an indigenous Indian ancestry. Unlike the case with Ancient Egypt, there are few, if any, color pictures of the Aryans as they saw themselves, but some sculptures, if Aryan, may suggest a Semitic background. What can be discerned based on the available evidence is that the original peoples of India were of African descent. Also, the pictographs used by the original peoples of India do not seem to be related to the Vedic-Sanskrit language. Many scholars indicate that they would expect to see an Indus language influence on the Sanskrit if they had conquered the Indus culture, but such is not the case. Thus, they side with the idea of the Aryans being indigenous to India, while others say this could indicate that the Aryans wiped out the preexisting culture, which having been destroyed, would have had no opportunity to influence the invading culture. However, like the Hieroglyphic Priests and Priestesses of Ancient Egypt, the Sanskrit priests made a special effort to keep the language and grammar inviolate as a sacred idiom reserved for spiritual texts only. In the same manner that Hindi developed as a popular idiom and Sanskrit is read only by a small number of the population, including scholars, the spoken language can change while the sacred lore and its attendant scripture remains unchanged.

Cultural influences need not be accompanied by ethnic changes within the culture that is affected. That is to say, just because a culture is affected by another, it need not mean that there has been sufficient integration between the peoples of the cultures to promote a change in the appearance of the ethnic nature of a culture. For example, Buddhism[357] was introduced to Tibet from India. The Tibetans do not look like Indians, but yet they follow the Indian Buddhist culture. Christianity was introduced to the Philippines by European missionaries, but the people from the Philippines do not look like Europeans. In the same manner the Vedic culture which emerged in 2000-1500 B.C.E. may have influenced the pre-existing culture of India which was there prior to 2000-1500 B.C.E. Further, one might expect an even stronger influence between Ancient Egypt and India since there was contact in all periods of Indian history down to the Christian era. Moreover, it has been shown that Egypt and India actually shared the same ancestor culture (Ethiopia), and may thus be considered as kindred groups within the same culture.

The Aryan Culture, the Indus Culture and the Origins of Civilization

In their book *"Vedic Aryans and the Origins of Civilization,"* Navaratne S. Rajaram and David Frawley, an eminent Western Sanskrit Scholar and Vedic teacher, discuss the problems posed by the dating of ancient Indian history by means of linguistic studies. In an attempt to show the inconsistencies in the Western Indological view of the dates of ancient Indian culture, Rajaram and Frawley cite reviews and correspondences between Max Muller and other Indologists. Rajaram and Frawley show that the dating system for ancient Indian periods is inexact. This is significant because Muller had been recognized by the orthodoxy as a leading figure in Indological studies. Another important point Rajaram and Frawley bring out is the fallacy of using linguistic studies or attempting to determine the origins of proto-languages as a means to date cultures.

> "I need hardly say that I agree with almost every word of my critics. I have repeatedly dwelt on the merely hypothetical character of the dates which I ventured to assign to the first three periods of the Vedic literature." (1849-73, 4: xiii);

> "If now we ask how we can fix the date of these three periods, it is quite clear that we cannot fix a *terminus a quo*. Whether the Vedic hymns were composed [in] 1000, or 1500, or 2000, or 3,000 B.C., no power on earth will ever determine." (1891: 91).

Rajaram and Frawley explain the implications of the passages above and the dangers of using comparative linguistics in order to determine chronologies.

> "This alone should suffice to show that the prevailing chronology is little more than "conjecture supported only by other conjectures," as Aurobindo put it (1971 [1914-20]). The question becomes one of the value ascribed to linguistics (or philology) as a scholarly tool in the study of history, especially in chronology.
>
> *From the host of contradictions that bedevil this theory, misunderstanding and misapplication of the key method have continued down to the present time. It is useful to look at what modern linguists have to say, therefore, about classification and morphology.*
>
> "The comparative method," observes Leonard Bloomfield, "assumes that each branch or language bears independent witness to the forms of the parent language, and that identities or correspondences among the related languages reveal features of the parent speech. This is the same thing as assuming, firstly, that the parent community was ... uniform as to language, and, secondly, that the parent community split suddenly and sharply into two or more daughter communities, which lost all contact with each other" (1933: 310).
>
> In other words, comparative linguistics provides not a method for deriving the cause-effect relations of historical forces and events but merely a tool for studying languages (assuming rather idealized conditions)." (Rajaram and Frawley p. 62-63)

Describing the path taken by most Indologists and historians of ancient India, Rajaram and Frawley raise serious doubts about the use of the widely accepted "linguistic evidences" and translations of the Rig Veda. He charges that the linguistic evidences actually are the translations based on the literary interpretations of Vedic literature, almost exclusively, which rely on Sayana, the medieval Indian scholiast.

> "Advocates of the invasion theory have used not only "linguistic evidence" but literary interpretations of Vedic literature, notably the hymns of the *Rig Veda*. Historians who subscribe to this theory, however, are neither linguists nor Indologists. As a result, they are forced to rely on translations of these texts. The best known translations in English are those by Griffith and Muller. The former is in verse, the latter in prose. And but for this difference, there is little distinguishing the two from an interpretive point of view. Both are more than a hundred years old. Both lean heavily on Sayana, the medieval Indian scholiast. Except for a few modem interpreters such as Frawley and Kak, it can be said safely that all Western scholars of the Vedas are pupils of Sayana."

> "Herein lies the first difficulty, for Sayana belonged to the Yajur Vedic school of Brahmins. This heavily colored his Rig Vedic interpretations and commentary. The *Yajur Veda* is primarily a book of ritual, which led Sayana to impose a ritualistic interpretation on the *Rig Veda*. He faithfully notes, however, that other (non-ritualistic) interpretations are possible. European scholars have adopted Sayana's point of view in their translations. Following their lead, historians have assumed that they have a true sense of the *Rig Veda*."

> "To give just one example, historians accept Griffith's (and Muller's) reading that the Rig Veda describes northwestern India and Afghanistan, and that it knows nothing of the ocean. From the present vantage point, though it is clear that these translators were unable to gain mastery of the Vedas in all their fullness and struggled to render only the literal meaning of the texts. In doing so, they leaned heavily on Sayana. Lacking traditional Vedic schooling, they had no choice. Some errors of interpretation were inevitable."

The translations of Griffith and Muller are over one hundred years old and undoubtedly, some modern Indological researches have yielded more accurate interpretations of certain terms. However, this should not invalidate the translations completely. It is notable that modern Vedic culture seems to place more reverence and importance on the Vedas, especially the Rig, but seldom are translations available and seldom is Vedic literature studied in the normal course of spiritual practice. The passage above also acknowledges the division within the Vedic period itself, so how can it be possible to see the kind of contiguity between the Vedic and Upanishadic age that can allow us to say that they are reliable sources for historical dating or references to each other? Rajaram and Frawley admit that the Yajur school cannot be relied upon to reference the Rig school. So if the comparisons cannot be made between literature that is supposedly of the same era, how can it be made between those scriptures and others which are even different eras?

In contrast to the Vedas, the Upanishads are heavily disseminated and constantly studied universally throughout Vedantic circles. The term Vedanta is based on the Sanskrit words "veda" which means "knowledge" and "anta" which means "end." The Upanishadic culture refers to this body of literature (the Upanishads) as Vedanta, meaning "the end" or "concluding portion" or "summary" of the Vedic literature.[156] While the Upanishads are referred to as "Vedic Literature," it seems to be widely accepted by most Indologists and Sanskrit scholars that these two belong to different periods of Indian culture, one to the Aryan age and the other to the Upanishadic-Hindu. While the base literature for Vedanta (Brahma Sutras and Upanishads) began to appear in India just after 1000 B.C.E., there were major milestones in the post-Vedic period in the developments that led to the refinement of the philosophy, leading to the Advaita teachings, which are considered as the ultimate. The Mahabharata (c. 900 B.C.E.), Buddhism (c. 550 B.C.E.), Bhagavad Gita (c. 500 B.C.E.), Yoga Sutras (c. 200 B.C.E.), Shakta and Tantra Spirituality (c. 460-490 A.C.E.), Kundalini Yoga (Post Indus and Post-Vedic Hindu period) systems all led up to the teachings of Shankara (Shankaracarya). Sankara, and Indian sage, lived from 780 A.C.E.-820 A.C.E., and wrote commentaries on the Brahma Sutras and Upanishads[358] and emphasized Advaita (non-dualism).

Vedanta is considered as one of the six orthodox philosophies of Hinduism. It is most concerned with knowing and understanding Brahman, the absolute and transcendental Supreme being. Vedanta is based on the writings known as Upanishads and Aranyakas which are considered as part of the late Vedic literature. Some Indian traditions consider the Brahma sutras as the first Vedanta literature while other say that the Upanishads are the first. There have been many interpretations of the so called Vedanta texts because the sutras, literally meaning "suture of writing," is so concise that they can scarcely be understood without expert interpretation. Perhaps the most important school of Vedanta is the one based on the teachings of Sage Shankara, who developed the concept of Advaita, or nondualism.[359]

A similar situation occurs in the study of Ancient Egyptian Hieroglyphic literature. While all of the scriptures are written in Hieroglyphic or Hieratic script, certain differences ascribe the literature to different periods. This is not a determination for dating, but rather for determining relative periods to which they belong. In the case of Ancient Egyptian, the varied schools were not opposed to each other. Therefore, a sage from the school of Amun would be harmonious in treating the texts of the Asar school, and a sage from the Aset (Isis) school would have no problem treating the texts of the Memphite school, etc., because they are all understood as being related, presenting varied views but of the same underlying teaching. Also, Ancient Egyptian literature refers to the same gods and goddesses in all periods while the Sanskrit refers prominently to the Vedic gods and goddesses in the Vedic Age and to the Hindu gods and goddesses in the Hindu Age.

Coming back to the refutation of the ancient glosses and interpretations of ancient texts, discussed by Rajaram and Frawley, this is a problem that alternative Egyptologists and alternative Indologists alike face. It is important for them not just to refute what they contend to be errors of the ancient authors by presenting arguments addressing the error or implausibility, but also they must put forth their own corrected version of the literature so that informed and objective minds may determine for themselves the validity or invalidity of the positions. Lastly, as an Egyptologist living in the 21st century, one would not contradict the teachings, glosses or interpretations of any authentic sage who lived in ancient times, who was part of the "living" tradition when it was in full expression or who was part of the creation of the document or similar documents, as opposed to later translators. One should defer to their interpretation unless it is inconsistent with the majority of other ancient references. If this is the case in the situation with Sayana, no evidence of this has been put forth.

---

[156] Recall that there are serious questions with the contention that the Upanishads are a summary of the Vedas since the fundamental teachings of the Upanishadic tradition are absent in the Vedas. This point is acknowledged by orthodox and alternative as well as Indian Indologists alike. See the section of this book entitled: *Changes in Indian religion from Ancient to Modern Times.*

THE AFRICAN ORIGINS OF CIVILIZATION, RELIGION AND YOGA SPIRITUALITY

While admitting that the similarities in the evidences do require explanation, Rajaram and Frawley further illustrate the serious faults in the "invasion theory" related to the Aryan culture that has been proposed by mostly Western Indologists.

> "How did this invasion theory arise when so little was known of the ancient history of the regions from which these migrations were supposed to have come? It was not based originally on *archaeological* evidence; it was based on the *linguistic* theory that similarities between Indo-European languages required an original homeland, from which the language was carried various migratory waves.
>
> The similarities do require an explanation, but the invasion theory is not the only possible one. It solves a difficult problem-similarities among Indo-European language groups-but at the cost of presenting a yet more difficult problem. What would allow these people to be so successful in conquering such a large part of the globe, overwhelming the civilizations of India, Mesopotamia, Anatolia, and Greece? The imposition of their language on so many peoples would have been almost unparalleled before the advent of European colonialism. And all this is said to have been achieved by wandering groups moving by chance rather than plan.
>
> The invasion theory was promoted because it was the most convenient theory that existed at the time. It came at an early point in modern historical thought, when migration and invasion theories were used to explain all sorts of changes. For example, if a new technology appeared, a new people-a pottery people, say, or an iron people-was invented to bring in the change. This line of thinking probably reflected the colonial period, when invasions really were the basis of many cultural changes."[360]

The questions posed by Rajaram and Frawley are important because they shed light on the "assumptions" and overlooking of common sense factors, which makes the theory look less plausible. However, while debunking the Western Indologists and pointing out the flaws in their methodology, it would seem that it is only a case of Rajaram and Frawley substituting one theory for another. For even if the invasion theory were implausible, this does not automatically mean that another possibility is automatically the correct or more plausible one. And while many explanations may be offered to account for the Aryan origins, questions still remain because there is apparently no hard or irrefutable evidence on either side. This same method of argument is used again by Rajaram and Frawley in reference to the wars mentioned in Vedic text, that Western Indologist use to show that there was a struggle in ancient times between the "invading" Aryans and the local Dravidian population of India.

> The Vedas do mention wars or battles that could be taken as indicators of an invasion. But must we *assume* that these were between indigenous people and intruders? Must we *ignore* the Vedic and Puranic literature of a society indigenous to India, which spread from an original homeland on Indian rivers such as the Saraswati or the Ganga?[361]

In the statement above, Rajaram and Frawley allow the possibility for the explanation of Western Indologists but then, while stating his alternative possibility, inserts the concept that the Vedic literature is indigenous to India. This last concept has not been established and yet it is stated as a fact. Also, there is an issue of the separation between the first Veda, the Rig Veda, in time from the other Vedas. If the argument is that the three last Vedas, which Rajaram and Frawley in the Appendix admit come from a different periods suggested by him (Rig Veda 4,000 B.C.E-Early Vedic Age as opposed to the Late Vedic Age –Yajur Veda, Sama Veda and Atharva Veda 3,600 B.C.E), it seems well agreed among all Indologists that the Rig Veda is the earliest and that it was composed by different authors and at a different (earlier) time than the remaining three. If this is the case, can the remaining three Vedas be relied upon as authoritative historical documents or as references to the earlier text, being removed from the earlier age? A similar situation occurs in Christology where the creation of the Christian gospels is found to be removed by many years from the actual age in which Jesus was supposed to have lived. Further, certain gospels were written earlier and others later.[362] While they may all be regarded as part of the same body of literature or tradition, can they be used as references as to the veracity or historical authenticity of the earlier works?

Further, the purpose of the writings is an important factor to include in the deliberation. Is the scripture designed as a historical document or as a treatise on spiritual matters, i.e. as a promoter of myth for the masses, like a gospel? Clearly, a spiritual treatise speaks less on history and more on spirituality, primarily through metaphor and simile. This is why scriptural sources are recognized as poor historical documents. In the case of the Ancient Egyptian, the documents known as *The Palermo Stone, Royal Tablets at Abydos, Royal Papyrus of Turin*, the Dynastic List and the *History of Manetho*, they were designed as historical documents. The problem with them is that orthodox Egyptologists simply refuse to believe them and pass them off as mysterious or erroneous references, et cetera. Rajaram and Frawley succeed in casting doubts on the orthodox Indological view but seem to offer little more than their own suggestions, even while trying to make a distinction between *"hypothetical scenarios and established facts."*

> "The thrust of this chapter is twofold. First, it examines the linguistic evidence and theories that resulted in the current historical model. Second, it offers a chronological framework, a synthesis based on mathematics and astronomy, that will be supplemented when necessary by archaeology. At every stage of this investigation, one is forced to confront the opinions and barriers of nineteenth-century scholarship, the appearance that no further examination is warranted. These long-standing opinions are subjected to detailed scrutiny and challenged whenever they fail to withstand critical analysis. The primary aim of what might seem at first like overkill is to ensure that future investigators have a clear path so that they can go wherever the evidence leads them. In the past, promising lines of inquiry have been ignored all too often because of the failure to distinguish between hypothetical scenarios and established facts."[363]

Navaratne S. Rajaram and David Frawley attempt to show that the Vedic culture is older than previously thought. To do so they offer the archeological evidence related to the drying up of the Saraswati river and note that the Vedic literature speaks highly of this river. There is a logical assumption that can be made, therefore, that the Aryans lived near the river and flourished during the time of its existence which is older than the time ascribed by Western Indologists. (highlighted text is by Ashby)

> "The first piece of *hard evidence* that throws the old chronology into doubt concerns the course of the ancient Sarasvati River and the central place it occupies in Vedic literature. The sites of Harappa and Mohenjodaro gave the name "Indus Valley civilization" to the vast network of settlements covering in excess of a million square kilometers. Those sites can now be recognized as its outposts, not its heartland. Recent excavations in India and Pakistan have shown that the center of this civilization lay well to the east of the Indus, along the course of the Sarasvati (which is now dry). The *Rig Veda* glorifies the latter as the greatest of rivers, as the holy mother. <u>Satellite photography, archaeology, and hydrological surveys all show that the center of this civilization lay well to the east of the Indus</u>, along the course of the Saraswati (which is now dry).
> It is now known that the Sarasvati changed its course several times and finally dried up completely around 1900 B.C.E. (Kenoyer 1991). The main cause of this was the loss of its two principal tributaries, the Yamund and the Sutlej, to the Ganga and the Indus respectively. The focus of this civilization then shifted east to the Ganga, which then became the holiest of rivers. Political supremacy also passed from the Bharatas of the Sarasvati heartland to Magadha in the east. All of these developments are noted in late Vedic and post-Vedic texts such as the Brahmanas and Puranas.
> My point here is that the Aryan-invasion theory leads to an incredible conclusion: the invaders crossed six great rivers-the Indus and its five tributaries-only to establish the great majority of their settlements along the course of a river, worshipped as a holy mother, that had gone dry five hundred years earlier. The verdict of archaeology, however, seems unambiguous: the *Rig Veda* describes northern India as it was *before* the Sarasvati dried up. The Vedic people must have been in India, therefore, when the Sarasvati was still a flourishing river. The collapse of Indus (Harappan) civilization, which has been attributed by linguists to the depredations of invading Aryans, was in reality due to a gradual yet fundamental change in the hydrology of northern India, which led eventually to the desertification of the region that now forms Rajasthan."[364]

The idea that the reverence for a river can be equated with an extinct river is certainly possible, and there is some evidence to support this contention. however, even if the archeological evidence shows peopling of the Saraswati area, how exactly has it been determined and by whom was it determined that the evidence means the Saraswati area was the center of civilization as opposed to the Indus area? The geological evidence about the Saraswati river may be correct but the connection to the cultures and civilization in the area is related to archeological evidences and therefore the connection is not conclusive. The interpretations of the data by one group or the other can skew the results, as we have seen in other cases. This argument, theoretically based on presumably hard evidence, is the main archeological evidence put forth as a means to place the Vedic age in time, and its tenuousness is reflected by the authors themselves as they refer to it as a "probability." It would seem that "hard evidence" should point to a certain "hard" or "concrete" conclusion or conclusions. However, the authors proceed to make certain assumptions based on the previously established probability, namely that the Harappan civilization or the culture known as the Indus valley civilization actually comes after and not before the Vedic age.

> "The body of hard evidence now points to the probability that (Harappan) civilization in the Indus Valley (ca. 3000-1900) actually represents the declining stages of a civilization centered in the Sarasvati Valley. I will show, or at least try to show, that it corresponds to the late Brahmanic and early Sutric periods. It is therefore post-Vedic. To make it Dravidian wholly artificial divide-and place the period of the *Rig Veda* after the collapse of the Harappan (Indus or Sarasvati) civilization is to ignore evidence." [365]

Further, Rajaram and Frawley look at mathematics and its potential use as a means to derive chronological information about the provenance of mathematics in ancient times. He cites the work of Seidenberg, who wrote a book based on his researches called "The Origin of Mathematics."

> "In "The Origin of Mathematics," Seidenberg noted the existence of two quite distinct traditions in ancient mathematics: the algebraic or computational and the geometric or constructive.
>
> > If it could be shown that each of these has a single source-and there are many rather familiar facts that suggest that this is so-and if, moreover, in both cases the sources turn out to be the *same,* it would be plausible to claim that we have found the unique origin of mathematics (Seidenberg- emphasis in original).[366]
>
> "Culminating nearly twenty years of research, Seidenberg went on to trace the origin of mathematics to the knowledge in a class of commentaries on the Vedas, the Sulbasultras. <u>But though his primary interest lay in the origin of mathematics, he established indirectly that the Sutras had to precede the mathematics of both Egypt and Babylonia.</u> Seidenberg's work opens the way for <u>an alternative approach to the chronology of the ancient world, a way that is significantly more rigorous than the linguistic approaches surveyed so far.</u>"[367] (underlined text is by Ashby)

Relying on the research of Seidenberg, which Rajaram and Frawley consider to have been a rigorous, "comparative analysis," he proceeds to build an argument for the much earlier dating of the Rig Veda. (underlined text is by Ashby)

> "Of particular historical interest are some recent findings on the mathematics of Babylonia (the Old Babylonian period, ca. 1960-1600 B.C.E.) and Egypt (the Middle Kingdom, ca. 2050-1800) as well as mathematical appendices to post-Vedic texts, the Sulbasultras. A comparative analysis of these makes it possible to establish 2000 as the latest limit for the early Sutras. This line of research, pioneered by Seidenberg, is expanded here to arrive at a scientifically sound framework for the chronology of the Vedic and post-Vedic periods. By establishing a mathematically rigorous foundation, moreover, it becomes possible to make a systematic examination of astronomical and other data, leading to a more comprehensive chronology. As an immediate consequence, the widely held date for the composition of the Rig Vedic hymns, 1200, is no longer tenable. *It is late, I suggest, by some two thousand years.*"

Reviewing as a historian and philosopher and student of geometry, I have refrained from using association arguments as proofs except when there is corroborating evidence and/or direct associations can be literally shown. Association arguments, however, are sometimes all that the shreds of historical evidence leave for us to peace together. The argument which Rajaram and Frawley are trying to prove is likened to an "if-then" (if this is so, then it follows that...) proof, for example: Since the Ancient Egyptian mathematics drew from the Sulbas, and since that math in Ancient Egypt was from the Middle Kingdom Period (ca. 2050-1800), then it follows that since the Sulbas supposedly came after the Rig Veda, it must be older that the Ancient Egyptian period in question. While it is true that there is scanty scriptural evidence of mathematics in early Ancient Egyptian history, this is not a proof of the absence of its existence, just as the absence of patients in a doctor's office does not prove that there is no doctor in the office. In these cases, strong circumstantial evidence along with a knowledgeable and intuitive historian can come together in order to fill the gaps of history. Sometimes when there is no "smoking gun" type of evidence, as in this case where the direct transference of mathematical formulas is not detected, a mathematician would have to intuitively determine if the same process of thinking out the mathematical problems is present. If the work of Seidenberg is correct, and he has proven some connection between Ancient Egyptian mathematics and Ancient Indian mathematics, this would also prove a relationship between the two cultures. Further, since it has been established thus far that Ancient Egyptian civilization is earliest, being well established (10000-7000 B.C.E.)[368] at the time when Indian culture was entering its Neolithic stage as evinced by the discoveries at Mehgarh (7000 B.C.E.),[369] could this not therefore mean that the Sulbas were influenced by Ancient Egyptian mathematics?

Rajaram and Frawley state that the Sulbas' little known and studied literature were written in the early Sutric period. According to his chronology, the Sutric period followed "the final redaction of the Vedas." They contain much that is relevant to the history and chronology of ancient India. By using his own chronology, Rajaram and Frawley place the Sutric period at 3000 B.C.E-2000 B.C.E. He further used the architecture of Indus valley to suggest that mathematics were used in the very layout of the ancient cities of the Indus Valley, thus proving its existence in the culture at the time of the construction of the cities.

> "Before beginning a more detailed examination of mathematical knowledge in ancient India, I must note that the very existence of elaborate cities such as Harappa and Mohenjodaro presupposes an extensive knowledge of geometry."[370]

It is a logical approach to draw the conclusion that architecture that makes use of geometry requires the creator to have some knowledge of geometry. Further, I agree that evidence of the application, and hence the existence of mathematics and geometry, precludes the need for discovering treatises in mathematics and geometry in order to determine their existence in a particular culture. If we were to use the same argument with respect to Ancient Egypt and Ancient Egyptian architecture, we would have to conclude that they had knowledge of mathematics as well. From the Sphinx and Pyramids in the North, with their geometric construction and geographical harmony, to the "Osirion" or ancient Pre-Dynastic Temple in Abdu (Abydos), and other monuments which have been generally classified as belonging to the early age of civilization in Egypt, there is ample evidence of proportion and harmony. Also, the proportions used reflect a knowledge of astronomy. Certain Temples, such as the Temple of Hetheru at Denderah and the Temple of Heru at Edfu, which are located hundreds of miles from each other, were created with complementary architectural features which shows knowledge of surveying, that is, the practice of determining the boundaries, area, or elevations of land or structures on the earth's surface by means of measuring angles and distances, using the techniques of geometry and trigonometry.[371]

Using the previous supposition that the Ancient Egyptians drew their mathematical knowledge from the Indian Sulbas, Rajaram and Frawley proceed later in the book to present this theory as an established fact in order to build a new chronology for the Sulbas, and thus also for the Vedas, which by his reckoning, come earlier in history than the Sulbas. In this manner, the Vedas would appear to have originated at some remote period (4000 B.C.E.).

> "Because the Egyptians borrowed mathematical ideas from the Sulbas, and because their mathematics was already ancient and far removed from its source, the Sulbas can also be assigned to the Harappan-Sumerian period. The fact that the *Baudhayana Sulba* describes a commonly occurring object on Harappan seals, the spoked wheel, lends further support to this theory. As I intend to show, the Sulbas and other Sutras should now be dated long before the rise of Egypt."

Rajaram and Frawley also tend to group Egypt and Babylonia together as part of related Near Eastern cultures. This follows the approach of Western scholars, treating Egypt as a Middle Eastern country, contemporary with the Sumerians or Babylonians and drawing from them civilizing knowledge. This procedure ignores the evidence proving the African origins of Egyptian civilization. We should also note that Babylonia comes into history only in the 3rd millennium B.C.E. as a consolidated and civilized culture.[372] Even conservative orthodox Egyptologists now accept that Ancient Egyptian high culture was well established by the early 4th millennium. Given the documented history of Ancient Egypt in the land of Asia Minor as rulers, the argument that the Babylonians drew from Ancient Egypt is more plausible than the reverse. Further, given the evidences presented in this volume related to the contact between Ancient Egypt and Ancient India, it is more likely that the mathematical knowledge of the Sulbas was derived wholly or in part from Egypt, as opposed to the other way around.

Rajaram and Frawley offer the physical evidence of the Indus Valley cities as proof that geometry was known to the Indus Valley inhabitants. This of course is primary and self-evident evidence, which is acknowledged by many Indologists. Physical evidence, especially architecture, is particularly compelling because of its size and accessibility. Also, any person with the intention, may investigate and verify this for themselves. (underlined text is by Ashby)

> "Furthermore, the ruins of the Indus Valley (elaborately planned cities and geometrically laid-out streets, which existed as long ago as 2700) make it impossible for Indian mathematics to have been borrowed from the Near East of many centuries later. Misinterpretation of the Vedas and the history of ancient India was due to nineteenth-century preconceptions and political needs. It was also due, however, to the low level of scientific knowledge. But archaeological evidence alone is enough to show that Indian geometry precedes the mathematics of the Near East. The views of nineteenth-century historians of science such as Cantor and Thibaut must now be reconsidered in the light of archaeological findings that did not exist in their time."

If we may apply the same sound methodology, we soon realize that the science of geometry was well known in Ancient Egypt, so well known, in fact, that monumental sculpture and architecture were created with geometric patterns. This holds true not just for the Dynastic Period architecture, but it is particularly evident in the architecture which is universally and self evidently Pre-Dynastic. There are several periods of Ancient Egyptian architecture. Perhaps the most popular and familiar is the New Kingdom architecture.

Figure 66: Below- Typical Late Middle and New Kingdom Temple Pylons (3,500 B.C.E.- 200 B.C.E.)

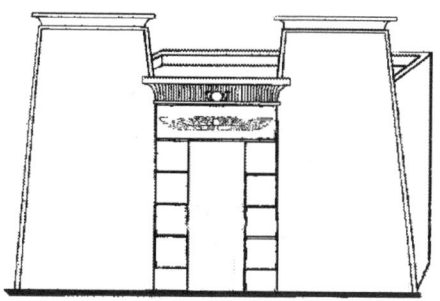

The city of Sakkara exhibited monumental architecture which the Greeks apparently called "Doric," and which became the earliest style of Greek monumental architecture. This is evinced by the fact that Doric style architecture does not appear in Greek culture prior to their association with the Ancient Egyptians.[374] The Doric style of architecture in Greece emerges between 700 and 146 B.C.E. and followed a definite system of construction based on rules of form and proportion. The best example of the Greek Doric architectural style is the Parthenon.[375] Architecture from the Sakkara era includes the reputed first pyramid, the Step Pyramid, as well as the Pyramid Text complexes. The Sakkara complex exhibits celestial orientation and geometric alignment.[376][377]

THE AFRICAN ORIGINS OF CIVILIZATION, RELIGION AND YOGA SPIRITUALITY

Figure 67: Below- Architecture of Sakkara - Ancient Egypt- Early Dynastic (5,000-4,000 B.C.E.) [378]

There is also an older form of architecture, from the Pre-Dynastic times, which will be termed as Archaic Architecture for our reference. The Sphinx complex in the north, the Osirion temple (see below) in the south, and other related architectural forms are of this era. The Sphinx Temple (foreground in the picture below) is created in a form of architecture which is considered a departure from the later Sakkara and Middle to New kingdom eras. The Sphinx Era Architecture exhibits straight lines and square column capitals as well as symmetry and attention to the rules of form and proportion.

Figure 68: Below- Sphinx and the Sphinx Temple (10,500 B.C.E.) [379]

Many lay people have come to believe, based on the limited information and misinformation they have had access to with respect to Ancient Egyptian history, that the Giza Plateau area architecture, which includes the Pyramids and the Sphinx, are the only such forms of architecture. Following this logic, it would tend to mean that this area is the oldest civilized area of the Nile valley. The next logical point would be that if this is the apparently older, civilized section in the Nile Valley, then the southern part was populated and civilized later. The next question that arises with this theoretical thought process is "Where did the people come from to populate and civilize the north (Giza area)?" The answer given by most Egyptologists was that people from Asia Minor (presumably the Sumerians or other Mesopotamians) came in and civilized northern, and later southern Egypt. Ignoring all of the eyewitness accounts, pictorial evidence from statues, etc., showing African features of the Pharaohs, this theory would mean that Ancient Egyptian culture and civilization was not of African origin, being created by Africans, but of Asiatic origin. As we have already seen previously, this theory has been discredited. Further, the Sphinx Era Architecture can be found in Southern Egypt in the Abdu area. Thus, this example shows clearly how either through ignorance or purposeful omission of evidences, the conclusions derived from those evidences can be misconstrued or used to obfuscate the truth. After some time of scholars espousing these beliefs, it becomes hard for them to let go, even when it is pointed out that the same evidence in reality leads to another conclusion. The researchers who hold on to the older opinions cast doubt on the new conclusions by making statements like "there must be another reason" or "it's a mystery and nobody knows." At other times they promote doubt by proposing many other possibilities which they cannot support with physical or other concrete (hard) evidences, so they resort to relying on scriptural evidences that support their opinions, the same criteria which has been found by the general scientific community to be unsound in principle.[380]

Figure 69: The "Osirion" at Abdu (Abydos) in Upper (Southern) Egypt (Pre-Dynastic 10,500-5000 B.C.E.)[381]

The Osirion building is located at the rear of the Temple of Asar (Osiris) in the city of Abdu (Abydos). Constructed at a time when the water table[382] was lower (as evinced by the modern day flooding), this building exhibits the same straight lines and square columns as well as symmetry and attention to the rules of form and proportion as the temple architecture. Therefore, the constructions of the north were of the same style as those of the south. With the emerging evidence from the Nekhen (Hierakonpolis) excavations, it is becoming clearer that Lower (southern) Egypt was actually older than the north. This finding is also in harmony with the legends of the Ancient Egyptians themselves which assert that they originally came from the south, from the land of Nubia.

The Temple usually referred to as the "Valley" Temple (pictured below), which is attached to the second of the Great Pyramids in Giza, Egypt and is adjacent to the Great Sphinx, exhibits the same style of architecture as the Osirion. Its imposing square lines and geometrically outlined rooms and niches reveals a mode of structural design that denotes a separate period in Ancient Egyptian history.

Above: "Valley" Temple, Giza

Rajaram and Frawley continue discussing the Indian and Egyptian mathematics, attempting to show that the use of unit fractions derived from the Indian Sulbas but apparently errs in his assessment of the use of fractions in Ancient Egypt.

"Returning to ancient mathematics: once we recognize the Sulbas as the source of Near Eastern mathematics, it becomes possible to fill several gaps that would be inexplicable otherwise. Specifically, the origins of several significant items in Egyptian and Babylonian records can now be traced to the Sulbas. Among the most interesting of these is the use of unit fractions. These are approximations to irrational numbers with terms of the form 1/n, where "n" is a whole number. The following unit fraction approximation appears frequently: $\sqrt{2} = 1 + 1/3 + 1/(3 \cdot 4) - 1/(3 \cdot 4 \cdot 34)$ (Datta 1932; see also Seidenberg 1978). The unit fractions of Egyptian and Babylonian mathematics are justly famous. They appear also in the Sulbas. Because of this, Cantor claimed that the Indians got their mathematics from the Egyptians.[12] (note see below) But the *origin* of unit fractions is nowhere to be found in Egypt. The roots are found in the Sulbas, where this unit-fraction approximation arises naturally in connection with squaring the circle. Like the theorem of Pythagoras, squaring the circle was a seminal problem of ancient mathematics. Further, the value of л (= 3.16049), used in Egypt's New Kingdom under the Pharaoh Ahmose (ca. 1540-1515 B.C.E.), is exactly the same as the one given in the relatively *late-Mdnava Sulbasutra*. What is more, it is calculated in precisely the same way: as $4 \cdot (8/9)^2$. That is to say, the *Manava Sulba* and Egyptians of the Eighteenth Dynasty used exactly the same approximation (in modern notation): $л = 3.16049 = 4 \cdot (8/9)^2$." p. 85-86

In an endnote to the passage above, the authors add the following:

"12. Others claimed that they got geometry and astronomy from the Greeks following Alexander's invasion. <u>Of course, there is no record of any Egyptian Pharaoh invading India.</u>" (Underlined text is by Ashby)

As to the theory proposed by Rajaram and Frawley that there are no know Pharaohs who "invaded" India, we have demonstrated that there were at least one Pharaohs who exercised control over all of southeast Asia. (Senusert I *c. 1971-1928 B.C.E.*) Therefore, this argument is untenable. This line of reasoning is being advanced because it is being recognized by the authors that rulers exert a considerable amount of influence over the customs of the transference of knowledge and technology from the dominant to the other culture and logically, the evidence would apparently seem to suggest that there was some possible outside connection with Egypt, but in the absence of any such evidence being considered by the authors, the logical assumption would be that Indians traveled to Egypt and influenced them instead of the other way around.

Also, the assumption in relation to the origin of unit fractions in Ancient Egypt is incorrect. The Ancient Egyptian origin of unit fractions was demonstrated by the work of Richard J. Gillings, in his book *Mathematics in the Time of the Pharaohs*. Gillings showed the use of fractions which had an ancient religious origin. The Eye of Heru (Horus) is one of the most ancient Ancient Egyptian icons. It is derived from the Pre-Dynastic era at the time of the commencement of Ancient Egyptian history. It is the main symbol of Heru, who is recognized as the first divinity worshipped in Egypt. One of his forms is the Great Sphinx at Giza, which has been extensively discussed throughout this volume. It is important to understand the mysticism of the Eye in Ancient Egyptian myth in order to appreciate the antiquity of the symbol of the Eye and how intertwined it is with Kamitan culture. The Eye of Heru represents divine consciousness embodied in a perfected (Enlightened) human being. Therefore, the Per-aah's (Pharaohs) were regarded as the embodiment of the Divine on earth. They were in effect, the Eye incarnate, and thus wielded the power of the Divine. This teaching goes back to the myth of Asar (Osiris), known as the Asarian Resurrection. This myth was the most popular, universally known religious teaching from the Pre-Dynastic age to the close of the Ancient Egyptian Dynastic Period. The Eye of Heru and the Ankh are two of the most recognizable symbols of Ancient Egypt.

THE AFRICAN ORIGINS OF CIVILIZATION, RELIGION AND YOGA SPIRITUALITY

Figure 70: The Eyes of Heru, the Solar Hawk

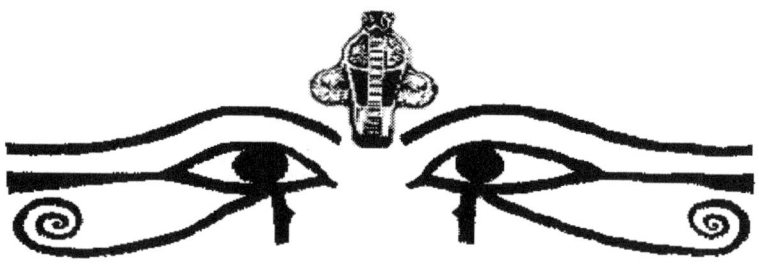

Figure 71: The parts of the Left Eye of Heru Divided Into Fractions (A)

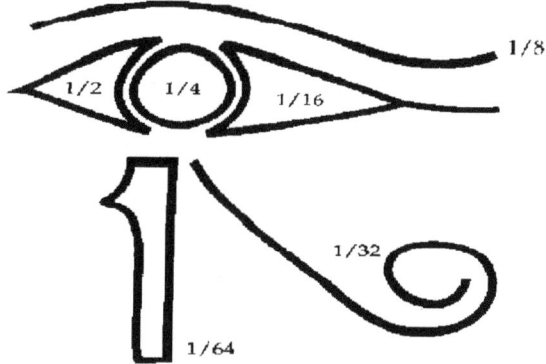

Figure 72: The parts of the Left Eye of Heru Divided Into Fractions (B)

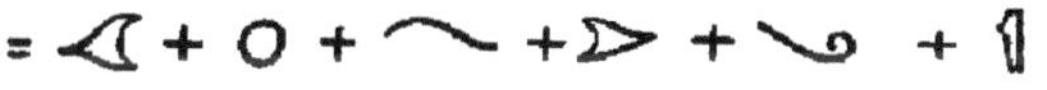

$$= \triangleleft + O + \frown + \triangleright + \backsim + \mathord{\uparrow}$$
$$= \tfrac{1}{2} + \tfrac{1}{4} + \tfrac{1}{8} + \tfrac{1}{16} + \tfrac{1}{32} + \tfrac{1}{64}$$

Figure 73: Eye of Heru Fractions From *The Book Mathematics in the Time of the Pharaohs*

Appendix Nine

TABLE A9.1
Horus-eye fractions in terms of hinu.

Line (Chace)	Fraction of a Hekat	Equivalent in Horus-eye Fractions							Equivalent in Hinu
		2	4	8	16	32	64	ro.	
a3, d3.	3̄	2		8		3̄2		3 3̄	6 3̄
c3.	2̄	2							5
a6, d4.	3̄		4̄		1̄6		6̄4	1 3̄	3 3̄
a7, c4.	4̄		4̄						2 2̄
a8, b1.	5̄			8	1̄6			4	2
a9.	6̄			8		3̄2		3 3̄	1 3̄
d5.	8̄			8					1 4̄
b2.	1̄0				1̄6	3̄2		2	1
b5.	1̄5				1̄6			1 3̄	3̄
d6.	1̄6				1̄6				2̄ 8
b3.	2̄0					3̄2	6̄4	1	2̄
c1.	3̄0					3̄2		3̄	3̄
e1.	3̄2					3̄2			4̄ 1̄6
b4.	4̄0						6̄4	3	4̄
c2.	6̄0						6̄4	3̄	6̄
e2.	6̄4						6̄4		8̄ 3̄2
c5.	2 4̄	2	4̄						7 2̄
a4, d1.	2 8̄	2		8					6 4̄
	2 1̄6	2			1̄6				5 2̄ 8
	2 3̄2	2				3̄2			5 4̄ 1̄6
	2 6̄4	2					6̄4		5 8̄ 3̄2
a5, d2.	4̄ 8		4̄	8					3 2̄ 4̄
	4̄ 1̄6		4̄		1̄6				3 8̄
	4̄ 3̄2		4̄			3̄2			2 2̄ 4̄ 1̄6
	4̄ 6̄4		4̄				6̄4		2 2̄ 8̄ 3̄2
	2 4̄ 8	2	4̄	8					8 2̄ 4̄
	2 4̄ 1̄6	2	4̄		1̄6				8 8̄
	2 4̄ 3̄2	2	4̄			3̄2			7 2̄ 4̄ 1̄6
	2 4̄ 6̄4	2	4̄				6̄4		7 2̄ 8̄ 3̄2

The author of *Mathematics in the time of the Pharaohs,* Richard J. Gillings said the following in his introduction:

> "Of course, some research still proceeds on the histories of the Hindus, the Persians, the Phoenicians, the Hebrews, the Greeks, the Romans, and the Arabic nations, all of whom come much later than the Egyptian culture with which we shall be concerned. The mathematics, astronomy, and science of these other peoples are already well authenticated; deciphered records and scholarly commentary fill many shelves. From the seventeenth century onward, many volumes came from the pens of mathematicians and historians: Moritz Cantor (4 volumes), Johannes Tropfke (7 volumes), Florian Cajori (2 volumes), David Smith (3 volumes), etc. These commentaries and histories took as their starting point the early Greeks, say Thales, about 600 B.C. But knowledge of the earlier civilizations of Egypt and Babylon was not available to these writers, and did not become generally known until the beginning of the present century.

> Well may we express our admiration of the wonderful architecture of the Egyptian Temples of Karnak and Luxor, at the grandeur and the immensity of the Pyramids and at the construction of their magnificent monuments. Well may we wonder at the government and the economics of a country extending nearly a thousand miles from north to south through which ran the longest river of the then-known world. And well may we marvel at the Egyptians' design of extensive irrigation canals, at their erection of great storage granaries, at the organization of their armies, the building of seagoing ships, the levying and collection of taxes, and at all the thought and effort concomitant with the proper organization of a civilization that existed successfully, virtually unchanged, for centuries longer than that of any other nation in recorded history."

THE AFRICAN ORIGINS OF CIVILIZATION, RELIGION AND YOGA SPIRITUALITY

Summary of The Ancient Egyptian Asarian Myth[383]

The Asarian Mystery is the most important myth of Ancient Egypt. It influenced all other centers of spirituality in Ancient Egypt and continues to have far reaching implications for modern civilization as to the origin and deeper meaning of present day religious beliefs. From Pre-Dynastic times down to 500 A.C.E., well after the dawn of Christianity, the story of Asar, Aset and the struggle of Heru was well known. It was the most popular among myths all over the ancient world, including Asia Minor, Africa, Greece and later throughout the Roman Empire.

The story of Asar is so meaningful because the principle ideas about human existence and destiny are embodied in this timeless story. These ideas were carried on in other religious systems of ancient times and their influences can be detected in present day religions as well. The myth took many forms in other religions and mystery systems which had contact with the Ancient Egyptian system. The most notable similarities are within the Christian and Hindu religions. In order to better understand the purpose and function of religion, we will need to define "religion" and its levels of practice.

The Battle of Heru (Horus) and Set

According to tradition, Asar (Osiris) and Ast (Isis) were the first King and Queen of Ancient Egypt. They taught the people agriculture, established a code of laws and taught all to worship the gods and goddesses as well as the Supreme Being, in the form of Ra. Asar traveled all over the world, including Africa, Asia (India) and Europe. He and Aset were successful and loved by the masses. Asar's brother, Set, was jealous and killed Asar. Asar's son, Heru, challenged Set for the throne. The battle between Heru and Set took many twists, sometimes one seeming to get the upper hand and sometimes the other, yet neither one gaining a clear advantage in order to decisively win. At one point Aset tried to help Heru by catching Set, but due to the pity and compassion she felt towards him she set him free. In a passionate rage Heru cut off her head and went off by himself in a frustrated state. Even Heru is susceptible to passion which leads to performing deeds that one later regrets. Set found Heru and gouged out Heru's eyes. During this time Heru was overpowered by the evil of Set. He became blinded to truth (as signified by the loss of his eyes) and thus, was unable to do battle with Set . His power of sight was later restored by Hetheru (goddess of passionate love, desire and fierce power), who also represents the left Eye of Ra. She is the fire spitting, destructive power of light that dispels the darkness (blindness) of ignorance. Heru regained the throne and unrighteousness was put down through becoming righteous. The gouging out of the eyes by Set, who represents ignorance which tears things down (disorder and unrighteousness), means that the ego has blinded Heru who represents aspiration and virtue. Virtue (Heru) redeems Asar, the Soul, by following Aset (wisdom).

Figure 74: Left- The Ancient Egyptian God Djehuti Presents the Eye to the Goddess Hetheru, the Female Counterpart of Heru.

Figure 75: Left- The Ancient Egyptian God Djehuti Presents the Eye to Heru After Making it Whole Again.

Rajaram and Frawley introduce trapezoidal shapes which he has discovered in both Ancient Egyptian and Indian culture. I (Sebai Muata Ashby) can verify that these are integral to Kamitan (Ancient Egyptian) culture.

THE AFRICAN ORIGINS OF CIVILIZATION, RELIGION AND YOGA SPIRITUALITY

"There is another connection, quite apart from unit fractions and the value of л **(pie)**. Trapezoidal figures shaped like Vedic altars are found on Egyptian monuments. Two of them, taken from Prisse d'Avennes' *Histoire de l'art egyptien d'apres les monuments* (1878-79) are reproduced in figure 2.

It is not merely [the] ... trapezoidal shapes which impress us, but their subdivisions. The subdivision of the first figure occurs in the *Sulvasutras*, and the second calls to mind the computation of the area [and its proof] in the Apastamba *Sulvasutra*. . . . If these figures occur-red on Indian monuments, we could understand the Indian interest in them: all the hopes of the Indian for health and wealth were tied up with a trapezoid (Seidenberg 1962: 519).

Figure 2

"Egyptian" figures found in the Sulbas

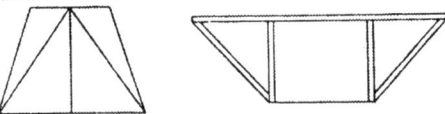

"How are we to explain the presence of trapezoidal figures on Egyptian monuments, particularly when they would have been cumbersome to construct or even to draw using the arithmetical techniques so favored by the Egyptians and Babylonians? I have argued that the Egyptians used mathematical methods derived from the Sulbas. Could the links go further back in time? One other remarkable connection suggests that the practice of building pyramids as funerary structures could have originated in the *Baudhayana Sulba*." P. 86-89[384] (underlined text is by Ashby)

"On mathematical, archaeological, and religious grounds, I consider it very likely that Egypt was in contact with post-Vedic India by 2700. It is not yet advisable, however, to establish chronological markers based on this connection." P. 88-89 [385] (underlined text is by Ashby)

It is Rajaram and Frawley's contention that these similarities and others stem from the Egyptians borrowing from the Ancient Indians. However, in view of the earlier origins of Ancient Egyptian culture and civilization it is impossible for that assertion to be correct considering the available evidence. A common sense approach dictates that if two cultures can be shown to have something in common, as Rajaram and Frawley believe they have in the case of Ancient Egypt and India, then it follows logically that if there is any dissemination of something already existing in the earlier culture, it proceeds TO the later culture and not the other way around. In this case the similarities have been shown between Ancient Egyptian and Indian mathematics and geometric figures. It has been established that these existed in the early antiquity of Ancient Egyptian civilization which predates that of India by several thousands of years. Therefore, it follows that since there was contact between the two countries, there was likely diffusion from Ancient Egyptian culture to Ancient Indian culture.

Of course the preceding statement is predicated upon the idea that the two cultures were separate and one was drawing from the other, etc. However, the evidence in this book points to an even closer relationship which goes beyond borrowing. Rather, as two family members *share* food, clothing and look out for each other's best interests, so too these two countries were part of a great family whose branches stretched from Africa to central Asia, Ancient Egypt being the older sister and India the younger. More similarities such as those alighted by Rajaram and Frawley are highlighted by another book (*Proof of Vedic Culture's Global Existence* -discussed below). Like Rajaram and Frawley's book they are used in an attempt to show that Aryan culture and civilization were first in history, preceding Ancient Egypt. However, unlike Rajaram and Frawley's attempt, this book is less scholarly and even more based on the opinions of scholars and unfounded innuendo.

In reviewing the researches of modern Indologists and historians of India, a nagging question arises. Why is there no apparent continuity in Indological studies? India is often touted as the country with the longest continuous spiritual culture, as opposed to others such as Ancient Egypt which had its culture supposedly "cut off," bringing the Ancient Egyptian religion to a close and causing the hypothetical loss of contact between the past and modern practitioners of the religion. Any person reading the writings of authors such as Frawley or Feuerstein and comparing these to the writings of more orthodox Indologists might get the impression that there is a gap somewhere in Indian history. If the Sanskrit scholars of modern times have a direct, cultural-social-historical link with the Vedic scholars and if the Rig Veda or any other Sanskrit text is an historical document, then it should be possible to determine Indian history with certainty, beyond reasonable doubts. There should be no need for using words such as "this suggests," "that points to the probability," or "I consider it very likely," etc. Especially, disconcerting are the statements made in the book "*Proof of Vedic Culture's Global Existence*" by Steven Knapp. The word "proof" means:

American Heritage Dictionary- Definition of "proof":

> "**proof** (prōof) *n. Abbr.* **prf. 1.** The evidence or argument that compels the mind to accept an assertion as true. **2.a.** The validation of a proposition by application of specified rules, as of induction or deduction, to assumptions, axioms, and sequentially derived conclusions. **b.** A statement or an argument used in such a validation. **3.a.** Convincing or persuasive demonstration."

Webster's Encyclopedia Copyright © 1995 Helicon Publishing Ltd Encyclopedia- Definition of "proof":

> "In philosophy of science, the belief that a scientific theory must be under constant scrutiny and that its merit lies only in how well it stands up to rigorous testing. It was first expounded by philosopher Karl Popper in his Logic of Scientific Discovery 1934."

While there is little in the way of "hard" evidence brought forth in the book *Proof of Vedic Culture's Global Existence* as to the influence of Vedic culture and its existence in ancient times, the author does include several opinions of scholars. Proof is not a validation of a theory by amassing scholarly opinions, treating legends as fact or citing obscure texts that may or may not relate to historical events, but rather by showing primary evidences to support the contention. Opinions of scholars, word associations without supporting corroborations, etc., cannot be accepted as proofs. Further, theories should always be stated as theories since they have a way of becoming realities in the minds of those who listen to (read) them repeatedly from those who repeat (write) them repeatedly. In this manner, sometimes the best available answer becomes accepted as truth because there is no better answer. At other times the misinformation is purposeful for the goal of furthering some agenda that is personal, political or social. Just as an unruly group can be inflamed by the wild ideas of one person and take off in a rampage, so too the unrestrained repetition of scholarly opinions eventually creates a belief system in society that what is being espoused is "truth" or "fact." In this manner later generations of scholars eventually create elite cliques in which they insulate themselves with their belief system which they support and defend as a person with blind faith supports the dogmas of his religion. Further, this book contains many errors or omissions which may mislead the reader into formulating misconceived ideas and drawing incorrect conclusions. (highlighted portions are by Ashby)

> "To explain further, Yadu was the eldest of the five sons of Yayati. Yayati was a great emperor of the world and one of the original forefathers of those of Aryan and Indo-European heritage. Yayati divided his kingdom amongst his sons, who then started their own dynasties. Yayati had two wives, Devayani and Sharmistha. Yayati had two sons from Devayani: Yadu and Turvasu. Yadu was the originator of the Yadu dynasty called the Yadavas, later known as the Lunar Dynasty. From Turvasu came the Yavana or Turk dynasty. From Sharmistha, Yayati had three sons: Druhya, who started the Bhoja dynasty; Ann, who began the Mleccha or Greek dynasty; and Puru who started the Paurava dynasty, which is said to have settled along the Ravi River and later along the Sarasvati. <u>*Some say* that this clan later went on to Egypt who became the pharaohs and rulers of the area.</u> These Aryan tribes, originating in India by King Yayati and mentioned in the *Rig-veda and Vishnu and Bhagavat Puranas,* spread all over the world.
>
> The Yadava kingdom later became divided among the four sons of Bhinia Satvata. From Vrishni, the youngest, descended Vasudeva, the father of Krishna and Balarama and their sister Pritha or Kunti. Kunti married the Yadava prince Pandu, whose descendants became the Pandavas. Kunti became the mother of Yudhisthira, Bhima and Arjuna (Partha), the three elder Pandavas. The younger Pandavas were Nakula and Saliadeva, born from Pandu's second wife Madri. After moving to the west coast of

India, they lived at Dwaraka under the protection of Lord Krishna. Near the time of Krishna's disappearance from earth, a fratricidal war broke out and most of the Pandavas were killed, who had grown to become a huge clan. **Those that survived _may have_ gone on to the Indus Valley where they joined or started another part of the advanced Vedic society. Others _may have_ continued farther into Egypt and some on to Europe, as previously explained.**"[386]

The author of this book uses simple and uncorroborated, presumed ancient names and legends[387] in order to draw a relationship between Ancient India and Egypt. Having, by his own "standards," established the earlier date of the emergence of Indian culture, the next conclusion would follow that since Egyptian culture came later, the Vedic tribes and kings supposedly that left India "may have" gone to other countries and founded civilizations there including Egypt as "some say." There is a big difference between "proven" and "maybe." The former describes reality or truth and the latter describes unproven or questionable ideas. The following example shows how the author relies on scholarly opinion in support of his theory as he cites the following passage from the book *Vedic Aryans and The Origins of Civilization*. (highlighted portions are by Ashby)

> "N. S. Rajaram so nicely explains… "To conclude: on the basis of archeology, satellite photography, metallurgy and ancient mathematics, it is now clear that there existed a great civilization--a mainly spiritual civilization **perhaps**--before the rise of Egypt, Sumeria and the Indus Valley. The heartland of this ancient world was the region from the Indus to the Ganga--the land of the Vedic Aryans."[388]

Knapp, relying on scholarly opinion and uncorroborated association of names, presumed similarities between Asian languages and religions assert that these evidences qualify as "scientific findings" and that these "corroborate" the "history" presented in the Indian Rig Veda and Puranas. Then he further ascertains that this agrees with the findings contained in the book *The History and Geography of Human Genes*. The actual entry in the book is as follows. (Highlighted portions are by Ashby)

> "This conclusion, stemming from <u>scientific findings</u> of the past three decades, demolishes the theory that nomadic Aryans from Central Asia swooped down on the plains of India in the second millennium BCE and established their civilization and composed the Rig-veda. The picture presented by science therefore is far removed from the one found in history books that place the 'Cradle of Civilization' in the river valleys of Mesopotamia. Modern science and ancient records provide us also a clue to a long standing historical puzzle: why since time immemorial, people from India and Sri Lanka, to England and Ireland have spoken languages clearly related to one another, and <u>possess mythologies and beliefs that are so strikingly similar.</u>
> "The simple answer is: they were part of a great civilization that flourished before the rise of Egypt, Sumeria and the Indus Valley. This was a civilization before the dawn of civilizations."
> **May I also say that this corroborates the history as we find it in the Vedic literature, especially the *Rig-veda* and the *Puranas*. It therefore helps prove the authenticity of the Vedic culture and our premise that it was the original ancient civilization, a spiritual society, using the knowledge as had been given by God since the time of creation, and established further by the sages that followed. According to a recent racial study *(The History and Geography of Human Genes)*, it has been confirmed that all people of Europe, the Middle East, and India belong to a single Caucasian race.** This means that they had to have come from the same source. Thus, we are all descendants of this great Vedic culture, the center of which is India. As more evidence comes forth, it will only prove how the testimony of the *Rig-veda* and the *Puranas* is confirmed, and will point to the area of northern India as the original homeland of the Vedic Aryans."[389]

Firstly, while it may be possible to draw some historical information from the Indian Rig Veda and the much later Puranas, these texts are primarily spiritual treatises and not historical documents. Thus, such information must be corroborated by secondary or even tertiary means. While it is possible to discern similarities between languages, this art is not perfect and thus draws much controversy from all quarters of the scientific community. Further, it is possible to determine similarities between cultures when they are discovered to "possess mythologies and beliefs that are so strikingly similar," as the author puts it, but no *rigorous evidences* have been presented and no *correlation of cultural factors* has been demonstrated to support these contentions by the author. No system of comparing the elements of cultures for determining

THE AFRICAN ORIGINS OF CIVILIZATION, RELIGION AND YOGA SPIRITUALITY

their correlations, if any, have been proposed by Knapp (such as the Cultural Category Factor Correlation System). The arguments that have been presented by the author (scholarly opinion and uncorroborated association of names, presumed similarities between Asian languages and religions) cannot qualify as such evidence and must therefore be disqualified. Secondly, the mammoth study contained in the book *The History and Geography of Human Genes* does not consider that "all of the people of Europe, the Middle East and India belong to a single Caucasian race." This statement by Knapp implies that the Middle Eastern and Indian people are all light skinned as modern day Europeans. This is not the case now and it was not the case in ancient times either. Recall the classical Greek writers witnessing that the ancient Indians looked like the Egyptians and Ethiopians. Also pictorial art of the Indus Valley shows people who look non-Western in appearance. The book, *The History and Geography of Human Genes,* does hold that all human beings now living (Africans, Europeans, Indians, Middle easterners and all others) come from one strain which emerged out of Africa. Further, it shows how the earlier migrations of African people moved out of Africa and into Europe, the Middle East (Asia Minor) and then into East Asia (India and China). Later, after several thousands of years, the original Africans became what we recognize today as Europeans or Caucasians with cultural and ethnic differences as well as differences of physical appearance. The European-Africans, now with lighter skin tone, having forgotten their origins and having developed a different culture and outlook on life, moved to the southern portions of Asia where they met the ancestors of Africans who migrated there as well. However, while there were some changes (minor peculiarities distinguishing Indians from Africans) in other areas such as physiognomy, the skin tone of the southern peoples remained close in appearance to the original African ancestors which was brown/black. It is only in modern times, that certain people are concerned with the preoccupation of determining which group was in Asia first and created civilization there. Much like the Encarta encyclopedia's reference on Racism, presented in this book, the book *The History and Geography of Human Genes* also mentions the problems of trying to classify a history of human genes based on modern concepts of race (racism) since these concepts are bogus.

Figure 1: Map of Migration Out of Africa From the Book *The History and Geography of Human Genes*

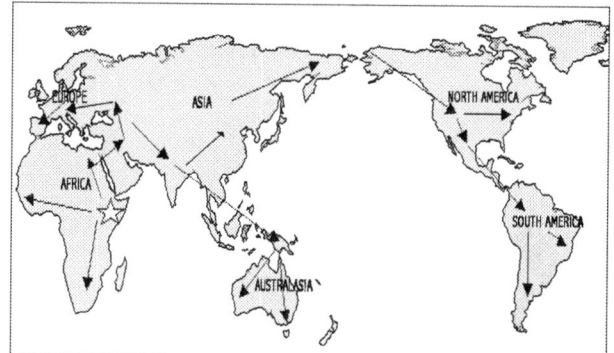

Fig. **2.2.2** The same data used in figure 2.2. 1, with the unrooted tree reconstructed with minimum path and adjusted for display on the geographic world map (after Edwards and Cavalli-Sforza 1964. modified). The branch to the Maori was moved slightly with respect to the original. (*The History and Geography of Human Genes* Luigi Luca Cavaiii-Sforza, Paolo Menozzi, Alberto Piazza. Copyright 1994 by Princeton University Press)

Image copyright Sema Institute

Further, *The History and Geography of Human Genes* treats the modern ethnic situation in India and acknowledges the Aryan, Greek and Mogul (Arabian/Muslim) infusion of physical traits. To these infusions, British colonial rule may be added. The book recognizes a difference between northern India and southern India, acknowledging that the north is more influenced by Aryan and Indo-European culture and language and the south, Dravidian. The book states that the Indo (European) peoples came into India and concentrated in the eastern and Western parts of the country. Also, the book states that there were successive waves of Indo-Europeans (Caucasians) moving into India that began in Neolithic times. It is not speaking of the ancient periods prior to the Neolithic nor is it saying that the pre-Neolithic period inhabitants of India were "Caucasians" as Knapp has suggested. (highlighted portions are by Ashby)

"It is reasonable to agree with other authors (e.g., Vidyarthi 1983) that there are at least four major components of the genetic structure of India, which we interpret in the following way:

1. The first component (Australoid or Veddoid) is an older substrate of Paleolithic occupants, perhaps represented today by a few tribals, but probably almost extinct or largely covered by successive waves and presumably leaving no linguistic relics, except perhaps for the Hunza and Nahali. There seems to be no linguistic trace of the

THE AFRICAN ORIGINS OF CIVILIZATION, RELIGION AND YOGA SPIRITUALITY

Australoid-Negrito language but Andamanese speak languages of the Indo-Pacific family. This may or may not be their original language.

2. The second is a major migration from Western Iran that began in early Neolithic times and consisted of the spread of early farmers of the eastern horn of the Fertile Crescent. These people were responsible for most of the genetic background of India; they were Caucasoid and most probably spoke proto-Dravidian languages. These languages are now confined mostly, but not exclusively, to the south because of the later arrivals of speakers of Indo European languages who imposed their domination on most of the subcontinent, especially the northern and central-Western part. But the persistence of a very large number of speakers of Dravidian languages in the center and south is an indirect indication that their genetic identity has not been profoundly altered by later events."[390]

Moreover, *The History and Geography of Human Genes* makes a distinction between modern Caucasoid and modern Asians and classifies all the people of the region as "Caucasoids" for the purpose of sampling, but later states that these Caucasoids of India originally came from Africa. So in pre-neolithic times the original migrations out of Africa gave rise to all peoples of the earth, so in effect all human beings are Africans. (highlighted portions are by Ashby)

"Ancestors of modern Caucasoids and modern East Asians (let us call them Eurasians) developed either in northeastern Africa, or in West Asia or southeastern Europe from an originally African source during the period between 100 and 50 kya. There was a wide area, difficult to locate in the absence of archaeological evidence, in which cultural maturation took place until about 50 kya. One speculates that it might have been in West Asia.[391]

There are many such discrepancies in the book *Proof of Vedic Culture's Global Existence,* so many in fact that it would take up a considerable amount of time to list. Therefore, due to the unreliability of this text, in light of the criteria for our current discussion as outlined earlier, it is unsuitable for scientific studies relating to Ancient India and the origins of civilization and will thus receive no further notice here.

Evidence of Contact Between Ancient Egypt and India

INTRODUCTION

Below: One of a handful of depictions of a person in a Yoga posture being worshipped by two others and two serpents on either side. (Indus Valley-Pre Aryan) (full description in Chapter 5)

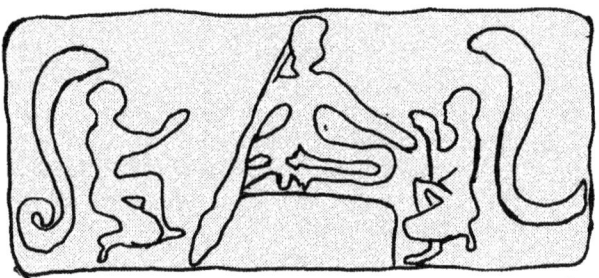

Below: The God Asar (Osiris) with the Serpent Goddesses Aset (Isis) at the foot of the bed and Nebethet (Nephthys) at the head. (full description in Chapter 5)

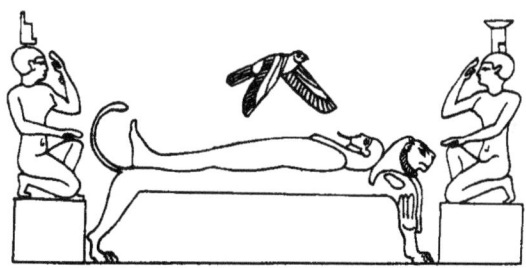

This section will show how Ancient Egypt and India were in close contact in Ancient times and how the fundamental cultural principles and Yoga Philosophy of India existed in Ancient Egypt prior to its development in India. This will be accomplished by showing direct correlations between the two societies and demonstrating that the correlations are so well matched that they rise beyond the level of chance or coincidental relationships that might be found randomly in nature. Further, this section will also show that the two cultures were related ethnically, socially, culturally and also genetically.

This section will contend with the question of the contact between Ancient Egypt and India. This section will show how Ancient Egypt and India were in close contact in Ancient times. It is possible to show many correlations between the Ancient Egyptian and Indian cultures. However, as with Minoan civilization, Sumerian civilization, Arabian cultures, Judaism, Christianity and Islam, which also show correlations, it is important to also be able to show evidence of contact. Without such evidence, the correlations, as good as they may be, will inevitably be treated as hypothetical. When there is unmistakable evidence of contact the evidences of correlation between the respective cultures being compared must be taken as serious confirmations of the interactions, and if there is a sufficient amount of such evidences they can elevate to the status of verification.

Item for Comparison 1: Evidence of Contact-Eye Witness Accounts, Anthropology, Linguistics, Mythology[392]

Asar (Osiris), the Avatar (Divine Incarnation) of Ancient Egypt, and founding King of Ancient Egypt (c. 12,000 B.C.E.) establishes civilization and religion in Asia and Europe.

"From Ethiopia, he (Osiris) passed through Arabia, bordering upon the Red Sea to as far as India, and the remotest inhabited coasts; he built likewise many cities in India, one of which he called Nysa, willing to have remembrance of that (Nysa) in Egypt where he was brought up. At this Nysa in India he planted Ivy, which continues to grow there, but nowhere else in India or around it. He left likewise many other marks of his being in those parts, by which the <u>latter inhabitants are induced, and do affirm, that this God was born in India.</u> He likewise addicted himself to the hunting of elephants, and took care to have statues of himself in every place, as lasting monuments of his expedition."

-Recorded by *Diodorus* (Greek historian 100 B.C.)

Figure 77: The Travels of Asar (Osiris) in Ancient Times

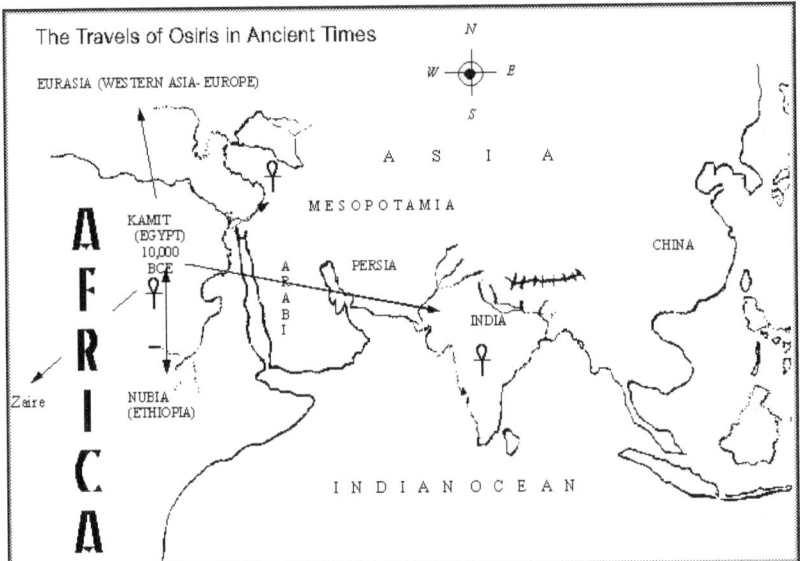

Above: A map of North-east Africa, Asia Minor and India, showing the three main locations of the use of the Ancient Egyptian Ankh symbol and also the geographic area where Asar (Osiris) traveled and spread the teachings of mystical spirituality which later became associated with Christianity in the Middle East, Rome and Greece, and Vedanta - Yoga in India.

In Support of the statements of Herodotus, Diodorus says the following:

"There are Egyptian columns as far off as NYASA, Arabia...Isis and Osiris led an army <u>into India, to the source of the Ganges, and as far as the Indus Ocean.</u>"

-*Diodorus* (Greek historian 100 B. C.)

THE AFRICAN ORIGINS OF CIVILIZATION, RELIGION AND YOGA SPIRITUALITY

King Senusert I (Greek name: Sesostris) Controls the area from India to Europe in 1,971 B.C.E.

I shall speak of the king who reigned next, whose name was Sesostris. He, the priests said, first of all proceeded in a fleet of ships of war <u>from the Arabian gulf along the shores of the Indian ocean</u>, subduing the nations as he went, until he finally reached a sea which could not be navigated by reason of the shoals. Hence he returned to Egypt, where, they told me, he collected a vast armament, and made a progress by land across the continent, conquering every people which fell in his way.

In this way he traversed the whole continent of Asia, whence he passed on into Europe, and made himself master of Scythia and of Thrace,[1] beyond which countries I do not think that his army extended its march. For thus far the pillars which he erected are still visible, but in the remoter regions they are no longer found. Returning to Egypt from Thrace, he came, on his way, to the banks of the river Phasis. Here I cannot say with any certainty what took place. Either he of his own accord detached a body of troops from his main army and left them to colonize the country, or else a certain number of his soldiers, wearied with their long wanderings, deserted, and established themselves on the banks of this stream.

- History of Herodotus (Greek historian 484 B.C.E.)[i]

The Ancient Egyptians were a colony of Ethiopians

"They also say that the Egyptians are colonists sent out by the Ethiopians, Osiris (Asar) having been the leader of the colony. For, speaking generally, what is now Egypt, they maintain, was not land, but sea, when in the beginning the universe was being formed; afterwards, however, as the Nile during the times of its inundation carried down the mud from Ethiopia, land was gradually built up from the deposit...And the larger parts of the customs of the Egyptians are, they hold, Ethiopian, the colonists still preserving their ancient manners. For instance, the belief that their kings are Gods, the very special attention which they pay to their burials, and many other matters of a similar nature, are Ethiopian practices, while the shapes of their statues and the forms of their letters are Ethiopian; for of the two kinds of writing which the Egyptians have, that which is known as popular (demotic) is learned by everyone, while that which is called sacred (hieratic), is understood only by the priests of the Egyptians, who learnt it from their Fathers as one of the things which are not divulged, but among the Ethiopians, everyone uses these forms of letters. Furthermore, the orders of the priests, they maintain, have much the same position among both peoples; for all are clean who are engaged in the service of the gods, keeping themselves shaven, like the Ethiopian priests, and having the same dress and form of staff, which is shaped like a plough and is carried by their kings who wear high felt hats which end in a knob in the top and are circled by the serpents which they call asps; and this symbol appears to carry the thought that it will be the lot of those who shall dare to attack the king to encounter death-carrying stings. Many other things are told by them concerning their own antiquity and the colony which they sent out that became the Egyptians, but about this there is no special need of our writing anything."

-Recorded by *Diodorus* (Greek historian 100 B.C.)

---

[1] **Scythia**, name given by the ancient Greeks after about 800BC to the homeland of the Scythians in the southeast part of Europe, eastward from the Carpathian Mountains to the Don River. **Thrace** (Latin *Thracia*, from Greek *Thraki*), region in southeast Europe, forming part of present-day Greece, Bulgaria, and Turkey. "Scythia," "Thrace," *Microsoft® Encarta® Encyclopedia 2000.* © 1993-1999 Microsoft Corporation. All rights reserved.

THE AFRICAN ORIGINS OF CIVILIZATION, RELIGION AND YOGA SPIRITUALITY

According to the Greek Classical Writers, The Inhabitants from the land area from Libya to Ethiopia are indigenous to the country. The Phoenicians and the Greeks are immigrants (foreigners) in the time of Herodotus.

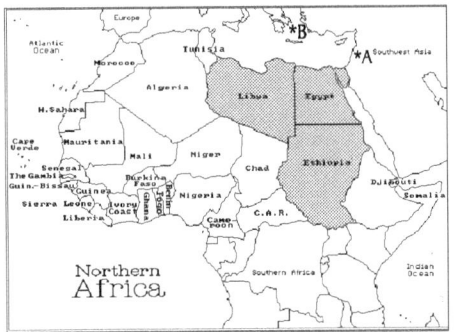

Map of northeast Africa showing Libya, Egypt and Ethiopia in the shaded area and (A) Phoenicia and (B) Greece.

The two indigenous are the Libyans and Ethiopians, who dwell respectively in the north and the south of Libya. The Phoenicians and the Greek are in-comers.
-History of Herodotus (Greek historian 484 B.C.E.)[394]

"Now the Ethiopians, as historians relate, were the first of all men and the proofs of this statement, they say, are manifest. For that they did not come into their land as immigrants from abroad but were the natives of it and so justly bear the name of autochthones (sprung from the soil itself), is, they maintain, conceded by practically all men..."
-Diodorus Siculus (Greek Historian) writes in the time of Augustus (first century B.C.)

North Africa has experienced migrations from Asia and Europe since ancient times. Anthropologists and archaeologists have traced the routes of many prehistoric migrations by the current persistence of such effects. Blond physical characteristics among some of the Berbers of North Africa are thought to be evidence of an early Nordic invasion.[395] The term "Berber" refers to a people of n. Africa which includes Kabyle, Siwans, Tibu, and Tuareg, who gave the name to the Barbary States: Algeria, Atlas Mountains, Mauritania, Middle East, Moors, Morocco, Sahara, Tunisia.[158]

On the Inhabitants of North-East Africa: The Ethiopians and Libyans look the same except the Eastern Ethiopians (South) have straight hair and the Libyan Ethiopians (Northern Ethiopians) have woolly hair.

"They differed in nothing from the other Ethiopians, save in their language, and the character of their hair. For the eastern Ethiopians have straight hair, while they of Libya are more woolly-haired than any other people in the world."
-History of Herodotus (Greek historian 484 B.C.E.)[396]

On the Ethnicity of the people of India and their relation to the Ethiopians

In the epic Greek work, *The Odyssey*, Homer writes that the Greek gods go to visit Ethiopia which is located in two locations at opposite ends of the world geographically. Based on the statements of the other Greek writers this can be interpreted to mean that there are Ethiopians in India (the east) as well as in Africa, which is west of India.

---

[158]Excerpted from *Compton's Interactive Encyclopedia.* Copyright (c) 1994, 1995 Compton's NewMedia, Inc. All Rights Reserved

THE AFRICAN ORIGINS OF CIVILIZATION, RELIGION AND YOGA SPIRITUALITY

> "Now Neptune had gone off to the Ethiopians, who are at the world's end, and lie in two halves, the one looking West and <u>the other East.</u>"
> -Homer *The Odyssey* (Book I)

> <u>All the Indian tribes</u> I mentioned ... <u>their skins are all of the same color, much like the Ethiopians.</u>
> -History of Herodotus (Greek historian 484 B.C.E.)[397]

The Statement by Herodotus in reference to the Ethiopian (Nubian) origins of the Ancient Egyptians and the relationship to India is supported by the Greek writer Diodorus.

> "And upon his return to Greece, they gathered around and asked, "tell us about this great land of the Blacks called Ethiopia." And Herodotus said, "There are two great Ethiopian nations, <u>one in Sind (India) and the other in Egypt.</u>"
> -*Diodorus* (Greek historian 100 B.C.)

The Roman Empire acknowledges India as a part of Egypt and Ethiopia in ancient times.

> "<u>India taken as a whole</u>, beginning from the north and embracing what of it is subject to Persia<u>, is a continuation of Egypt and the Ethiopians.</u>"
> -**The Itinerarium Alexandri (A.C.E. 345)**

The records above establish the ethnicity of the Ancient Ethiopians, Libyans, Egyptians and Indians. They confirm a multitude of images which can be seen in ancient sites from around Egypt as well as in the museums from around the world. They show that while Egypt was a multi-ethnic country in the latter periods, it was essentially an outgrowth of Nubian culture and civilization.

Plate 25: Above- A Painting of an Ancient Egyptian man-From the Tomb of Rameses III, Thebes, Egypt, Africa

THE AFRICAN ORIGINS OF CIVILIZATION, RELIGION AND YOGA SPIRITUALITY

The image above of an Ancient Egyptian man recalls the image of modern day Nubians as well as present day South Indians.[159] In ancient times the dark skinned inhabitants of India covered the entire country. However, due to incursions by the Greeks, Aryans, Arabs, British and others, the darker skinned population has been relegated to the south portion of the Indian subcontinent. Since we know what modern day Ethiopians look like and we have pictorial evidence of what the Ancient Egyptians (above) and Ethiopians looked like, we can extrapolate the ethnicity of the other groups. The ancient Libyans, Egyptians and Indians were all of African descent and this group included, in ancient times, dark skin peoples with either curly or straight hair. This testimony shows that even in the time of Herodotus, the Indians displayed the same skin color and different hair textures as the Africans.

The testimony of Herodotus and Diodorus as to the ethnicity of the Indians and their ethnic link to the Ethiopians and Egyptians is confirmed by the modern science of genetics, which has proven not only a common ancestor for all human beings, who, having arisen in Africa, separated at around 100,000 years ago (see map below), dispersing across the world, but also have shown a link between the Ancient Egyptians and the earliest Indian civilization, the Harappan culture. In the massive work, *The History and Geography of Human Genes*, by Luigi Luca Cavalli-Sforza, Paolo Menozzi, Alberto Piazza, 1994, containing over 14 years of genetic records for the world population, it was shown that human beings are all genetically related.

DNA and Ethnicity

DNA is an abbreviation for "Deoxyribonucleic acid." It is a complex giant molecule that contains the information needed for every cell of a living creature to create its physical features (hair, skin, bones, eyes, legs, etc., as well as their texture, coloration, their efficient functioning, etc.). All of this is contained in a chemically coded form. The Life Force of the Soul or Spirit engenders the impetus in the DNA to function. This in turn leads to the creation of the physical aspect of all living beings (human beings, animals, insects, microorganisms, etc.).

The DNA is what determines if two living beings are compatible with each other for the purpose of mating and producing offspring. If they are not compatible, then they are considered to be different species. All human beings are compatible with each other therefore, they are members of a single species, i.e. one human race.

Figure 78: The Spread of Humanity.[398]

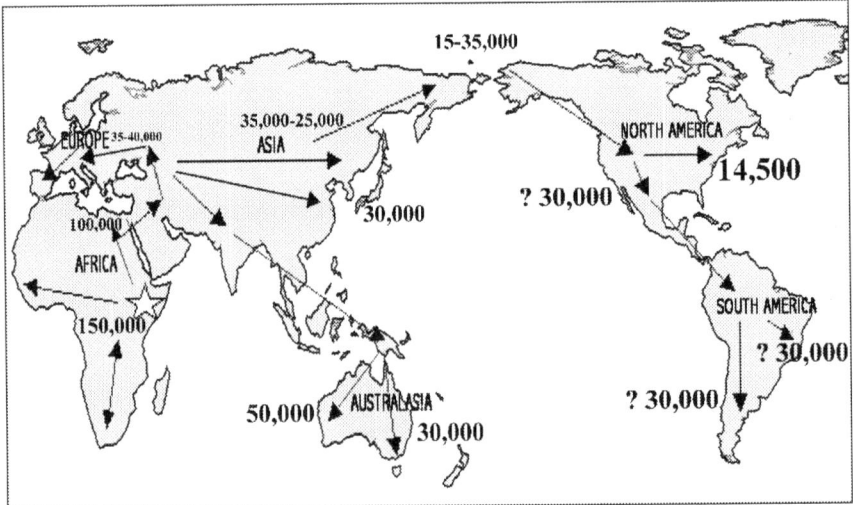

---

[159] Keep in mind that in pre-Vedic times the indigenous inhabitants of India from the south to the north were Nubian in appearance. However, due to the changes and invasions that India has endured since that time, the descendants of the people who once lived in the Indus area and north India were amalgamated with the new ethnic groups or moved to the south. So in the present, the people of darkest hue generally will be found in the south and no longer in the north. Therefore, the Dravidians who live in the present day southern part of India are in part descendants of the Ancient Indusians.

THE AFRICAN ORIGINS OF CIVILIZATION, RELIGION AND YOGA SPIRITUALITY

The map above shows the movement of humanity from its original origins in central equatorial Africa in 150,000 B.C.E. to the rest of the world. It has been demonstrated philosophically that the human body is only a vehicle of the spirit that is directed by its DNA. According to the spiritual philosophy of African Religion as well as Indian Religion, the soul has human experiences but it is not bound by them or comes into existence as a result of them. That is, DNA does not give rise to a soul. The soul associates with a body in order to have human experiences. Therefore, DNA is an instrument of the Spirit, which it uses to create the body and thereby avail itself of physical existence and experiences. According to mystical philosophy, the soul chooses the particular world, country, and family in which to incarnate in order to have the kind of experiences it wants to experience. This is all expressed in the physical plane through the miracle of DNA.[399]

Figure 79: Left: A drawing of a Human DNA strand.

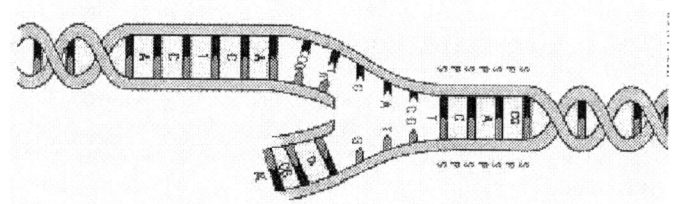

The ethnicity of the Ethiopians, Ancient Egyptians and Indians is not presented here to elevate the concept of race or one group over another, but to acknowledge ethnicity as one of the connection factors described in ancient times between these groups. When Herodotus and others wrote about the Ethiopians, Ancient Egyptians and Indians as being "black," they did not have the racial connotations that are applied in modern times in mind. In fact this term (race) is only used in this work in lieu of a better term devoid of the baggage of racism. Ethnicity is a better, though limited term that can be used. Since the concept of race, racial types and racism are false, then it follows that skin color is a cultural trait and not a racial trait. However, those of different ancestries may adopt the culture of those whose skin color trait is different and certain segments of modern society have attempted to misrepresent history, promoting the idea that people of African descent or ethnicity had little or no part in creating civilization. Thus, we must be clear when speaking about or using the skin color and clearly note that it is referenced only as a descriptive term for identifying cultural descent and ethnic genealogy. In later times (Late Period and early Christian Period), lighter skinned peoples (ethnic groups) migrated from Europe and Asia Minor to North-Eastern Africa, making it a multiethnic mixed society. It must be clearly understood that the notion of ethnicity (what in modern times some people refer to as "race") was known by the Ancient Egyptians, but the concepts of racism and racial bias were not known in ancient times. The terms race and racism are modern day misinterpretations of culture and ethnicity. The scientific community in general, and especially the science of genetics, does not recognize any such concept as it has been amply proven that all human beings belong to the same "race." Within this human race, human beings manifest variations due to geography, diet, beliefs, history and length of time (generations) removed from the original African ancestry, etc., and not due to genetics.[400] Therefore, the concept of race and its acute form, racism, are held by the ignorant. Since the concept of race is bogus, those who violently uphold the idea of race must be considered as psychologically impaired, since the belief in untruth in the face of truth must be recognized as a sign of mental illness. A primary task for all systems of spirituality is to dispel the misconceptions about race since this aspect of human interaction is a degrading force in civilization. It is a source of strife and suffering as well as misunderstanding of spiritual and religious teachings.

Finally, it was the Ancient Egyptians who first realized the underlying unity of all humanity which transcends physical manifestations. This is obvious from the following passage of the Hymns to Aton in which Sage Akhnaton recites words of adoration and praise to the Divine Self (called Aton).

> Thou settest every person in his place.
> Thou providest their daily food, every man having the portion allotted to him;
> [thou] dost compute the duration of his life.
> Their tongues are different in speech, their characteristics (or forms), and likewise their skins (in color), giving distinguishing marks to the dwellers in foreign lands…
> Thou makest the life of all remote lands.
>
> −Akhnaton

Paleoanthropology shows a connection between Ancient Egypt, Ancient Persia and Ancient India

In the book, *The People of South Asia* Edited by J. R. Lukacs, ed., Chapter 3, *Biological anthropology of Bronze Age[401] Harappans: new perspectives*, Pratap C. Dutta discusses the paleoanthropology studies of the early inhabitants of India before the Vedic period. This study is of chief importance to our present subject as its implications in the area of biological anthropology independently support the evidences presented in this volume as to the ethnic relationship between Ancient Egypt and India.

> "In South Asian paleoanthropology, however, the human osseous record I recovered from the prehistoric city site of Harappa in the Indus Basin is of paramount importance. This is indeed so, because of two pragmatic reasons that far-reaching. First, it is the only extensive prehistoric human skeletal series discovered to date from South Asia. And, second, because of its workable sample size (in the context of chance discoveries of archaeological material) and also for its well-documented record of cultural identity. The series can be programmed fruitfully for investigations seeking answers to questions relating to biocultural interrelationships and evolutionary dynamics of earlier human-population groups in South Asia. This chapter discusses some aspects of our present understanding of the biological anthropology of the Harappans who lived in Indus Valley during the third millennium B.C."

In the Culture and Society section, Dutta discusses the results of the taxonomy studies carried out, based on the comparison of the skeletal remains of the people from the ancient Harappan civilization in India with those of ancient Tepe Hissar (modern day Iran), and Sakkara (Sakhara, Saqqara) of Ancient Egypt.

> "From all these data, it becomes reasonably clear that the Harappan, Tepe Hissar, and Sakkaran series constitute a cluster of a single unit, suggesting close similarity or affinity."

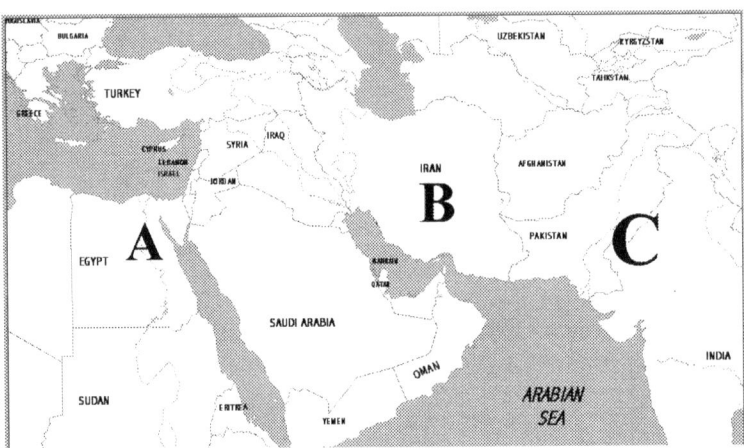

Figure 80: Map of North-east Africa, and Southern Asia, showing (A) Sakkara in Ancient Egypt, (B) Tepe Hissar in Persia (Iran) and (C) Harappa in India.

Sakkara, was one of the most important cities in the early history of Ancient Egypt, becoming a capital in the Old Kingdom Period. What is left of it is located 16 km/10 mi South of Cairo. It has 20 major pyramids, of which the oldest (third Dynasty) is the "Step Pyramid" designed by architect Imhotep.

Figure 81: Above, the *Djozer Pyramid Complex* with the *Step Pyramid of Imhotep* located in Sakkara, Egypt– From the Old Kingdom Period – Third Dynasty

Below: Statue of *Sage Imhotep,* designer/builder of the Step Pyramid

NOTE: it is sad to realize that most people learn about Africa through commercialized theme parks such as Bush Gardens and Tarzan or Cleopatra or Christian movies about the Old Testament produced in Western countries, which are based on fiction and racial stereotyping or Biblical interpretations. The "mummy" movies created by Hollywood purporting to show the mummy of Sage Imhotep as an unethical, lustful murderer and the movie and television shows such as *Stargate* showing the Ancient Egyptian gods and goddesses as evil aliens who enslave people and possess their bodies like parasites have **NO BASIS IN HISTORICAL FACT WHATSOEVER**. This shows how the repetition of untruths become facts over time in the absence of ethics in the entertainment business and scholarly silence on the issue. This practice denigrates African culture as surely as if a movie denigrating Moses or Jesus of Christianity or

Muhammad of Islam were similarly produced. Imhotep was canonized as an African saint at least 3000 years before the advent of Judaism and 4000 years before the advent of Christianity and Islam. He was a Sage, scientist and philosopher as well medical doctor. To impugn his name is to denigrate all Africans everywhere and to disparage the role of African people in the development of humanity. It is an effect of racism and cultural genocide by the western media, which is based on European fantacies about Africa that is allowed to continue by the western leaders and academia, who do not speak out against it. It is a continuation of the practice of demonizing an African personality that truly deserves the status of any great spiritual leader that has ever existed before or since, including Moses, Jesus, Buddha, Ramakrishna, Confucius, Lao Tze, etc. It is the duty of all who uphold the precepts of righteousness and truth in business to protest such erroneous and malicious, slanderous works in the arts, literature, etc.

Ancient Egyptian history provides us with the descriptions of the first men and women who served as medical doctors, some of whom were so good at their professions that they became legendary in their own time. The earliest female doctor in historical record was named *Mer-swnut – Peseshet*. Imhotep was one of the most famous doctors in Kamitan history. The name "Imhotep" means "One who comes in peace." Imhotep was perhaps the greatest Sage of Ancient Egypt. He lived in the Old Kingdom Period (c. 5,000-3,500 B.C.E.). He was a legendary figure in his own time because he was a master healer (swnu-medical doctor), royal architect, scribe, astronomer, Chief Lector Priest (Kheri-Heb), Vizier and Spiritual Philosopher. His writings have not been discovered yet, but some historical records survive that show he was revered by both Ancient Egyptians and foreigners alike. He was deified (canonized) and revered by all Ancient Egyptians. In the time when Hippocrates and other ancient Greeks went to study medical science in Ancient Egypt, they revered and worshipped Imhotep under the Greek name Aesculapius, as the god of medical science and healing.

The now ruined city of Memphis in Egypt lies beside the Nile River, approximately 19 km/12 mi South of Cairo, Egypt and Sakkara was part of its district in ancient times. Memphis was the center of the worship of the god Ptah, and the heart of Memphite Theology. Memphis was also the earliest capital of a united Egypt under King Menes about 3200 BC, but was superseded by Thebes under the new empire 1570 BC. Memphis was later used as a stone quarry, but the "cemetery city" of Sakkara survives, with the step pyramid built for King Zoser (Djozer) by Imhotep, regarded as the world's oldest stone building.[402] It should be noted here that the Step Pyramid in Sakkara is universally accepted as the oldest of all the Great Pyramids in Egypt. Its superb architecture has also been recognized as the source for the early Greek Doric forms.[403] This means that based on the now confirmed earlier date for the "Great Pyramid" (see the section "The Revised History of Ancient Egypt Based On New Archeological Evidence and the Omitted Records"), the Old Kingdom Period of Ancient Egypt must be placed in the 5th millennium B.C.E. Also, there was a community of Indians and Buddhists in Memphis in the Late Period of Ancient Egyptian history.[404]

In the discussion section of the chapter presented above, Dutta concludes with a restatement of the research, but also includes some important cautions in treating the information. Despite the compelling nature of the findings he introduces two categories for additional study, which he feels that when added to the body of knowledge in reference to the data he has gathered, will yield an even more accurate and conclusive result.

> "The investigation, using seven selected craniofacial measurements and six series, clearly brings into sharper focus the fact that the people of Harappa are biometrically close to those of the Tepe Hissar and Sakkara series. Using the result of a statistical nature, these populations from different regions, namely, the Indus Valley, Iran, and Egypt, could be fitted into a cluster of a single unit.
> It is most crucial at this stage to remember that whatever information of a statistical nature could thus be abstracted cannot be used immediately for drawing inferences about problems of biological anthropology. This is especially true in addressing questions that specifically pertain to the biological affinities of ancient human population groups inferred from skeletal samples. Rather, there is a likelihood of being in a *cul-de-sac,* if the aforementioned information is not critically read, understood, and interpreted on the basis and in the context of at least two other different categories of information. The

categories should be concerned generally with (1) historical and cultural backgrounds, and (2) geographical propinquity of the given prehistoric populations."[405]

The first category or factor is comparing the "historical and cultural backgrounds" of the peoples in question. The comparison of the cultural and philosophical basis of Ancient Egypt and India is a central concern of this present volume *The African Origins of Civilization, Religion and Yoga Spirituality*. The varied forms of cultural expression are being dealt with at length and have proven to be corroborative of the work of Mr. Dutta.

The second category that should be investigated, according to Mr. Dutta, is the "geographical propinquity"[406] of the peoples in question. It is well known that India traded with countries as far away as Greece, and Egypt is much closer to India than Greece. This factor has been found to be facilitated by the maritime trade routes. Therefore, the categories of cultural and geographic potential between Ancient Egypt and India have not only been shown to be conceivable, but they have been confirmed. As to the post-Harappan period which marked the rise of Vedic culture in India, researchers in the field of genetics and authors of the book *The History and Geography of Human Genes* concur with the Aryan takeover or migration theory of India, but also conclude that the Indus Valley culture did not die out, but rather, emerged anew in various other locations throughout in India as "regional cultures." Therefore, not only the cultural-mythological-philosophical legacy of Ancient Egypt remains alive in India, but also the ethnic legacy as well, through the modern day Indians, Africans and Mesopotamians.

> "In agreement with the indigenist trend in Anglo-American archaeology, it has been suggested that the Aryan migration is a total invention (see Shaffer 1984). However, as briefly discussed in section 4.3, events in the Neolithic cultures of Turkmenia, northwest of the Indus Valley, are well explained by assuming a migration of pastoral nomads from the north at about the same time; the end here was also not abrupt or violent. Linking the two series of events in Turkmenia and the Indus Valley, it seems very likely that both were due to the takeover of power by Aryan pastoral nomads who came from the steppes of Central Asia, spoke an Indo-European language, and used iron and horses (Masson and Sarianidi 1972). More about their origin was given in section 4.3. A possible archaeological marker of the first arrival of Aryan people is Painted Grey Ware (Thapar 1980). The events accompanying the arrival of the Aryan pastoral nomads from the oases of Central Asia are probably better described as a migration rather than a conquest or invasion, but pastoral nomads clearly introduced a social stratification and segmentation of all India based on religion and politics, in which they took the upper classes.
>
> The Harappan civilization probably did not disappear completely but is likely to have contributed to the development of modern Indian culture. Shortly after the end of the mature Harappan phase, several regional cultures arose, sometimes called post-Harappan. In any case, the Harappans were socially, culturally, and probably linguistically, different from the Aryans, who made a major contribution to the new culture. It is difficult to attribute an exact date to the Aryan takeover. Most information comes from the Vedic literature, the oldest texts written in Sanskrit, which are still the heart of modern Indian civilization. The social restructuring that took place with the Aryan invasion involved the creation of a strictly stratified society that still exists (castes) and contrasts sharply with the apparent absence of class stratification or structure in Harappan society. The Aryans of the early Vedic texts (the Rig Veda) were largely pastoral, and the horse and iron were important components of their military strength."[407]

Cultural-religious exchange between Egypt and India in the time of Emperor Ashoka in 261 B.C.E.

In the book *India and Egypt: Influences and Interactions, 1993*, Lutfi A. W. Yehya notes the archeological discoveries, in Ancient Egypt of the Ptolemaic era, which conclusively prove contact between the Ancient Egyptians and Indians of that time as well as a blending of Ancient Egyptian and Indian religion as evinced by the artifacts found in Memphis, Egypt.

> "There seems to be sufficient evidence to indicate that Indians in good number had started visiting Egypt in the Ptolemaic period and even before it-from the third century, BC onwards. Athenaeus refers to the presence of Indian women, Indian cows and camels, and Indian hunting dogs in the royal processions of Ptolemy Philadelphus in Egypt.[408] An Indian colony probably existed in Egypt even earlier at Memphis. The excavations at Memphis have yielded some terracotta fragments and figurines[409] which from their facial features and costume, appear to be Indian.[410] Some of them have been identified as the representations of Panchika, a Buddhist divinity.[411]
> Again, indicative of the close contact during Ptolemaic times is a gravestone which bears an Indian symbol of the trident and wheel, and the infant deity Horus is shown sitting in Indian attitude on a lotus."[412]

It is well known that Emperor Ashoka of India, upon becoming a Buddhist convert, was instrumental in the dissemination of the Buddhist teachings throughout the known ancient world. He sent Buddhist missionaries throughout India and to various countries. There are also several iconographical evidences, some mentioned above and others that will be presented later, that link Buddhism with Neterianism and especially with the Temple of Het-ka-Ptah (Memphis) in Egypt.

> "Asoka (c. 291-232 BC), emperor of India. He sent missionaries to countries as remote as Greece and Egypt. His reign is known from engravings on rocks and from traditions in Sanskrit literature. He was the most celebrated ruler of ancient India, known for his benevolent rule and for making Buddhism the official religion of his empire. Despite Asoka's vigorous exertions in behalf of his faith, he was tolerant of other religions, and India enjoyed marked prosperity during his reign."[413]

In the chapter of the book *India and Egypt: Influences and Interactions*, 1993, entitled "Transmission of Ideas and Imagery," the scholar M. C. Joshi reports on ancient written documents attesting to the communications and cultural exchanges between Ancient Egypt and India during the time of the Indian emperor Ashoka. This record shows not only economic exchanges but social and humanitarian exchanges, pointing to the compatibility of the two countries. Just as two people who are of opposite character cannot get along, so too countries cannot get along if their peoples are of an opposite nature.

EARLY INSCRIPTIONS AND LITERARY REFERENCES

The brightest evidence of India's direct relations with Egypt is, however, preserved in the Mauryan Emperor Asoka's thirteenth rock edict,[414] inscribed in the early decades of the third century BC. In it, Emperor Asoka refers to his contacts with Ptolemy II Philadelphus of Egypt (285-246 BC), in connection with the expansion of his policy of the propagation of the Law of Righteousness *(dharma)*. In the Asokan (Ashokan) records Ptolemy II is referred to as Turamaya. There can be little doubt that official embassies were exchanged between the Mauryan court and that of Ptolemy II. Pliny names the Egyptian Ambassador of Ptolemy II to India as Dionysus.[415]

Asoka in his second rock edict, refers to the philanthropic activities undertaken by himself. He records that he had made arrangements for the medical treatment of men and animals in the territories of his own empire as well as in the region ruled by Antiochus Theos II of Syria (260-246 BC) and its neighboring kingdoms,[416] which also included Egypt.

Interestingly, it is stated that the Egyptian ruler Ptolemy IV, Philopator, lined a part of his yacht with Indian stones. The presence of Indians in Egypt in the third century BC has been attested by Athenaeus who observes that the processions of Ptolemy II Philadelphus also included women, cows, and hunting dogs from India.[417]

THE AFRICAN ORIGINS OF CIVILIZATION, RELIGION AND YOGA SPIRITUALITY

Cultural-religious exchange between Egypt and India in the time of *Apollonius* 50 B.C.E.-50 A.C.E.

"Apollonius of Tyana[418] was another important figure who existed at the time of Jesus' proposed birth. The important factor here is that there is ample evidence in the writings of the time about Apollonius and his life. He was said to have performed miracles, healed the sick and foretold the future. He studied philosophy and the teachings of the Gnostic mystery schools of Greece and then traveled to India and Egypt where he was instructed by Sages. He returned to Rome and preached salvation and resistance against injustice."

-The Life of Apollonius of Tyana by Philostratus {220 A.C.E.}

Ethiopian Inhabitants in India

"Apollonius traveled to India in the first century A.C.E. and was told in the course of his visit that Ethiopians had lived in India when Ethiopia was a part of Ancient Egypt"

-Flavius Philostratus[419]

The writings above support the contention that there was contact between Ethiopia, Egypt and India for thousands of years in prehistory and into the Christian era. The Ancient Ethiopians, Egyptians and Indians not only shared cultural exchanges and maintained the same religious beliefs, but they also looked alike prior to their fusion with the Aryan, European and Middle Eastern peoples, who were of a lighter complexion, having lived in the northern regions of Asia for many thousands of years prior to the end of the last Ice Age. The continental ice sheets withdrew from North America and Europe about 10,000 years ago, at the end of the Pleistocene epoch.[420] The present Holocene epoch succeeded the Pleistocene around 10,000 BC.[421]

Indian Archeologists Discover Contact and Correlations Between Ancient Egypt and India

What follows is a portion of the research contributed by Indian scholars based on archeological excavations, working in India and Egypt on the question of contact and interaction between Ancient Egypt and India. The maritime trade between Ancient Egypt and India is known to have lasted longer and to have been more reliable than the over-land route through Asia Minor (Afghanistan, Iran, Iraq and Syria.). Therefore, during the periods when Egyptian rule over Asia Minor waned, due to wars and the influx of Indo-European peoples from the North of Asia, the contact between Ancient Egypt and India was maintained by sea.

"Direct contact between the two countries (India and Egypt) during this period (Pharaonic Egypt 3400-525 B.C.) is suggested by some highly specialized artifacts which are found in India as well as in Egypt but which, surprisingly, are absent in the vast West Asian region between-Afghanistan, Iran, Iraq and Syria."[422]

The material evidence of such contact includes:

"HEAD-RESTS: Indian head-rests found at some Neolithic sites such as T. Narsipur, Hemmige, and Hallur-all in Karnataka in south India-may be consigned to dates in the first half of the second millennium B.C. on the basis of radio-carbon tests. Curiously, they occur only in south India[423] and have no parallels elsewhere in tile subcontinent except for a solitary contemporaneous specimen from Chanudaro assigned to Jhukar levels[424] of circa 1800 B.C.

In Egypt, similar head-rests belonging to a period spanning the pre-Dynasty Period to Roman times have been discovered. A number of them are made of wood but in some, intended for royalty and the aristocracy, costlier materials such as ivory and lapis lazuli are employed. Egyptian headrests occur in a variety of forms. Incidentally, certain tribes of Africa[425] and India use wooden head-rests even today.[426] Strikingly identical head-rests have also been carved in rock bruisings at Piklilial in Karnataka (India), which site has, interestingly also yielded specimens in pottery belonging to the Neolithic period."

THE AFRICAN ORIGINS OF CIVILIZATION, RELIGION AND YOGA SPIRITUALITY

Plate 26: Picture of a display at the Brooklyn Museum (1999-2000) showing the similarity between the headrest of Ancient Egypt (foreground) and those used in other parts of Africa (background). (Photo by M. Ashby)

Item for Comparison 2: The Gods Murungu and Muntju of Africa and the Gods Murugan, Subrahmania and Karttikeya of India

(Note: Some of the following information has already been presented in the section on *Ancient Egypt and Its Influence of Other African Religions*. It is being repeated and expanded upon here with respect to India for the continuity and completeness of this section.)

Some modern day Hindus continue to believe Egypt is their ancestral home.

> "Some Hindus claim the Nile to be one of their sacred rivers; they also regard as sacred the Mountains of the Moon (in Uganda-Congo) and Mount Meru (in Tanzania). Both in India and in the Indianized Kingdoms, Southern Mount Meru was regarded as the mythical dwelling place of the Gods. Each of these statements reflect millennia old relationships between the blacks of Africa and South Asia. The Ethiopian Kebra Negast regarded Western India as a portion of the Ethiopian Empire. "Murugan, the God of mountains", the son of the mother Goddess is a prominent and typical deity of the Dravidian India. It is interesting to note that at least 25 tribes in East Africa worship "Murungu" as supreme God, and like the Dravidian God Murugan, the African Murungu resides in sacred mountains."
>
> -From: U.P. Upadhyaya
> "Dravidian and Negro-African International Journal of Dravidian Linguistics"
> v.5,No 1 January 1976, p 39.

The Gods Murungu and Muntju (Monthu) of Africa and the Gods Murugan, Subrahmania and Karttikeya of India, Their Origins, Mythology and Iconography

Murungu of Kenya

The Kikuyu people of Kenya, the tribes of Malawi, Zimbabwe, Zaire, Tanzania, Uganda and the Yao people of Mozambique, worship the God Murungu (Mulungu)[427] as the supreme and transcendental divinity behind Creation. The Kikuyu's God is named "*Murungu.*" Kenya is an East-African republic in Africa, bounded on the north by Sudan and Ethiopia and on the east by Somalia and the Indian Ocean, on the south by Tanzania, and on the west by Lake Victoria and Uganda.[428] In ancient times Kenya was on the maritime trade route between Ethiopia, Egypt and India.

Murungu cannot be seen, but is manifested in the sun, moon, thunder and lightning, stars, rain, the rainbow and in the great fig trees that serve as places of worship and sacrifice. These attributes of Murungu are closely related to the supreme divinity, Ra, in Ancient Kamit. Especially notable is the philosophy of understanding the Divine as supreme and transcendental, and yet manifesting as Creation itself, but especially through the sun and moon. In Kamitan Anunian mysticism (based on the God Ra, whose main symbol is the sun) and Atonian (based on the divinity Aton, whose main symbol is the sundisk) mysticism, the Spirit is understood as manifesting through the sun and moon, not as being the object itself. This is an advanced understanding that there is a subtle essence beyond Creation, and therefore this conceptualization takes the religious philosophy outside the realm of idolatry. In the aspect as the god of thunder and lightning, Murungu may be likened to Indra in the Vedic pantheon of Indian gods and goddesses. Indra was known to be the god of war among other attributes.

Muntju of Ancient Egypt

The Kamitan God Ra has a warrior aspect by the name of *Muntju (Montu, Monthu)*. The worship of Montu was prominent in the 11th Dynasty Period. Montu is related to Heru-Behded who is the warrior aspect of the god Heru, who is also an aspect of Ra.

Murugan of India

In India the worship of *Murugan*, also known as *Skanda*, was prominent among the south of the country in ancient times as a Tamil (segment of Indian Dravidian culture) God, and continues to be worshipped in modern times. The Tamil divinity, Murugan is known as : "war god," "god of victory," "Lord of the World," "god of beauty," and "god of divine freedom." Murugan was "aryanized" and renamed *Subrahmania (Subramanja, Subramanya)* in the Sangam Period (1st Century B.C.E.).[429] Thus, in the south of India Murugan is known to the Dravidians as Murugan and Subrahmania, and in the north of India Murugan is known among Hindus as *Karttikeya*. Karttikeya is also a god of war but now with the attribute of being the son of the God Shiva, one of the primary gods in the Hindu pantheon. Karttikeya is represented as having six heads, holding a bow and riding on a peacock and holding various other weapons like Heru-Behded. In addition to the common attributes just mentioned, the familiar avian attribute (the hawk in the case of Montu-the peacock in the case of Murugan-Subrahmania-Karttikeya) is also present.

THE AFRICAN ORIGINS OF CIVILIZATION, RELIGION AND YOGA SPIRITUALITY

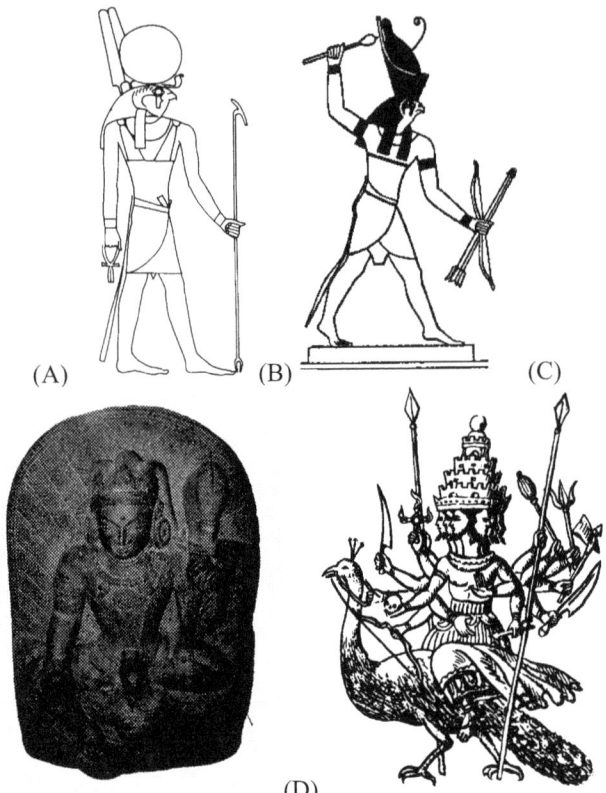

Figure 82: Above-(A) The God Montu of Ancient Egypt. (B) Heru-Behded, The Warrior, (C) Karttikeya on his peacock son of Shiva, also known as Skanda Gray (800-900 A.C.E.), (D) The God Warrior Subrahmania of India.

Conclusion

Karttikeya
(Aryan-North India)
↑
Subrahmanya
(Aryan-South India Hindu)
↑
Murugan-Skanda
(South India Dravidian)
↑
Murungu
(Kenya)
↑
Muntju
(Ancient Egypt)

This case of comparison between the warrior gods of Ancient Egypt, Kenya and India offers us the opportunity to note the process of inculturation as it progressed in India between the Aryan culture and the Dravidian culture. The specific focus here is the "aryanization" of the concept of Murugan without a noticeable or traceable linguistic trail from Murugan to Subrahmania, and then to Karttikeya. These Indian names appear to be linguistically different and yet they are accepted by Indologists as referring to the same divinity. If a traceable linguistic trail is desired, the connection to the African names is a closer possibility. However, as explained earlier, this trail need not be there in order to prove a connection. This example confirms the methodology for not requiring direct linguistic connections when determining cultural

THE AFRICAN ORIGINS OF CIVILIZATION, RELIGION AND YOGA SPIRITUALITY

relationships in the context of a comparative religious study. Such requirements are therefore more useful in determining connections between languages, but the existence or absence of connections between languages therefore also need not be present in order to ascertain cultural interrelations or affiliations. Further, it has been shown, through late 20th century photographic surveys, that the peoples of certain areas in South India dress and appear indistinguishable from each other in ethnic traits such as their hair, skin tone and physiognomy.[430] Again, this confirms the eye-witness accounts of Herodotus, who noted the similitude in the physical appearance of the Ancient Egyptians, Ethiopians and Indians.

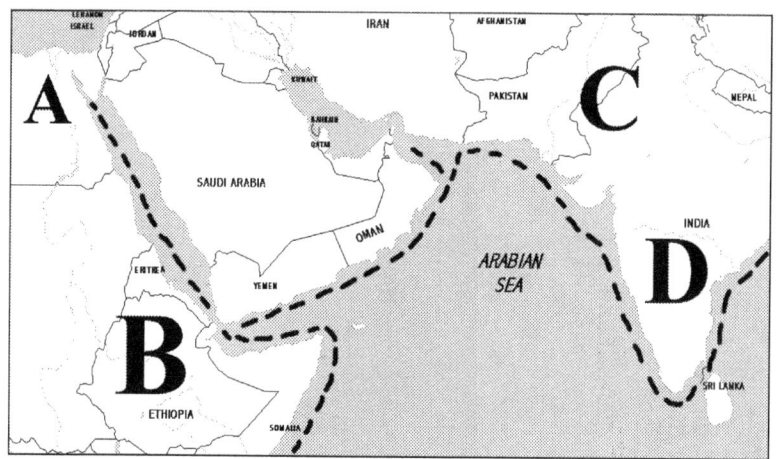

The Maritime Rout Between Ancient Egypt (A) and the Indus (C).

Figure 83: Above-North-east Africa, Asia Minor, South Asia (India) and the Egyptian-Indian trade routes in the Hellenistic (Greek) and Roman times.[431]

It is sometimes not realized how important trade routes and commerce can be to a civilization. In Ancient times the Indus Valley civilization as well as Ancient Egyptian civilization relied upon trade in order to sustain the economic prosperity of the nation. This was especially true in the time before the concept of currency and monetary exchange was invented. This view is supported by most scholars, one example is *S. M El Mansouri*, as he writes:

> "We cannot ignore the influence that trade has upon the relationship between nations. It carries the culture of one country to another. Ideas, philosophy and religions are transferred from nation to nation through trade, handicrafts, books, and artistic products go from people to people along trade routes.
>
> In many periods, India had direct relations with Egypt, Syria, and other parts of the Hellenistic West. Kings, as well as independent cities, depended to a large extent on the tributes paid by the peasantry, but a considerable portion of Egyptian - and Indian revenues came from trade in olden times.
>
> There was a considerable body of foreign residents in the ports whose affairs were looked after by a special board of municipal commissioners. These foreigners could not all, of course, have been diplomats. Some of them were, in all probability, traders.
>
> When art flourishes (this means always good relationships) it is always connected with peace, religions, traditions, and philosophy."[432]

One only has to consider how true this is in modern times with a few examples, consider the impact of Western Culture on Japan, whose government and social structure was changed by the United States of America after World War Two. The United States of America itself has been influenced by Japanese business methods as well as the infusion of Buddhism, Yoga, Henna hand art, etc., from other countries with which it trades. In fact many countries feel overwhelmed by the culture of the United States of America and have taken measures to curtail its effects on their society (Ex. China, Iran). In reference to the maritime trade in the New Kingdom Period of Ancient Egypt, Professor D. A. Mackenzie writes in his book *"Egyptian Myth and Legend"*:

> "At the time of the XVIII dynasty, the boats of the Imperial Egyptians were plying on the Mediterranean and the Indian Oceans, and far distant countries which may never have heard of Egypt, were being subjected to cultural influences that had emanated from the Nile Valley."

THE AFRICAN ORIGINS OF CIVILIZATION, RELIGION AND YOGA SPIRITUALITY

Item for Comparison 3: Body art and the use of Henna in Ancient Egypt and India

One more connection between Ancient Egypt and India showing cultural interaction is the cosmetic use of henna. It has been discovered that Ancient Egypt and India have the use of henna in common.

> "The earliest evidence of the cosmetic use of henna is from ancient Egypt. It was common practice among the Egyptians to dye their fingernails a reddish hue with henna, and it was considered ill mannered not to do so. Traces of henna have been found on the hands of Egyptian mummies up to five thousand years old.
>
> There is a great deal of evidence to suggest that the henna plant was a gift from Egypt to India. Mehndi has been practiced in India for many centuries, as can be seen in the cave paintings of Aianta and Allora, wherein a reclining princess is surrounded by women who paint her hands and feet with elaborate henna designs."
>
> - Mehndi: The Timeless Art of Henna Painting by Loretta Roome[433]

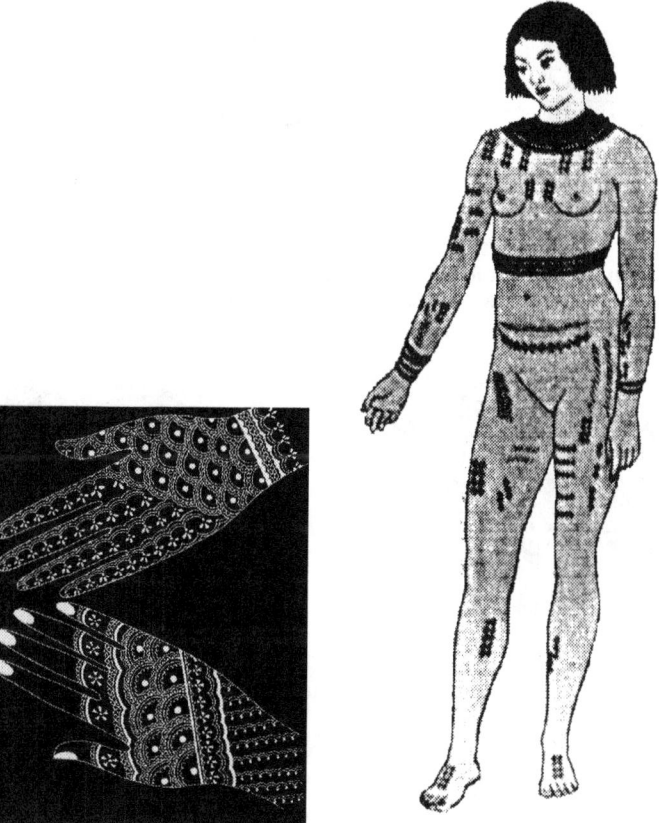

Above left- Example of Indian style Henna-Mehndi tattoo. Right Drawing of a tattooed woman based on a mummy from the tomb complex of Nebhepetra Mentuhotep II-Middle Kingdom 11th Dynasty

Discoveries by the French researchers in Aksha (Nubia) show that "tattooing" was practiced in Nubia during the time of the Kamitan 6th to the 18th Dynasties. The practice was again resumed during the Meroitic period (270 B.C.E. – 350 A.C.E.). For these reasons, some researchers feel that it is a practice that originated in Nubia and was passed on to the Ancient Egyptians.

Item for Comparison 1: Black and Red Pottery

Plate 1: Below left- Painted Pottery from Mohenjodaro –Indus Valley, India[434]
Plate 2: Below right- Painted Pottery from the Pre-Dynastic Period – Egypt Africa.[435]

The pottery of Ancient Egypt and Ancient India exhibit the following correlations.

- ❖ Color scheme
- ❖ Artistic design
- ❖ Material
- ❖ Usage – function

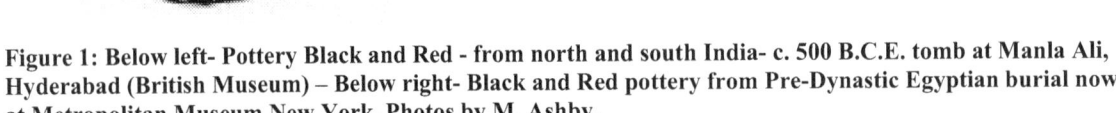

Figure 1: Below left- Pottery Black and Red - from north and south India- c. 500 B.C.E. tomb at Manla Ali, Hyderabad (British Museum) – Below right- Black and Red pottery from Pre-Dynastic Egyptian burial now at Metropolitan Museum New York. Photos by M. Ashby.

One striking correlation between Ancient Egypt (Pre-Dynastic Period) and Ancient India is the existence of the black and red pottery. This type of pottery occurs almost exclusively in these two countries and upon examination are found to be alike in appearance. This evidence supports the contention of ancient writers such as Herodotus and others, that in ancient times, the country of Kamit (Egypt) and India were culturally and ethnically related and were in actuality part of one civilization, which originated in Nubia (Africa). A team of Indian archeologist (Archeological Survey of India) report finding black and red pottery in excavations of Tumas in the Nubian Desert in Egypt dating to 1500 B.C.E., that can be easily mistaken for ancient Indian pottery of South India. The earliest recovered examples of Egyptian black and red pottery have been dated to the 5th millennium B.C.E at Tasa in the Fayum region, the Badari in Egypt and the Afyeh and Tumas in Nubia.[436]

There seems to be sufficient evidence to indicate that Indians in good number had started visiting Egypt in the Ptolemaic period and even before it-from the third century, BC onwards. Athenaeus refers to the presence of Indian women, Indian cows and camels, and Indian hunting dogs in the royal processions of Ptolemy Philadelphus in Egypt.[437] An Indian colony probably existed in Egypt even earlier at Memphis. The excavations at Memphis have yielded some terracotta fragments and figurines[438] which from their facial features and costume, appear to be Indian.[439] Some of them have been identified as the representations of Panchika, a Buddhist divinity.[440]

Table 1: Chronology of Ancient Egypt based on Independently Confirmed Archeological Dating and the Chronology of India based on dates given by Indian Scholars

Chronology of India According to Indian Scholars — The date for the Earliest Vedic hymns presented here is based on speculation by the Indian Indologists. It is presented here only to show that even when this date is used, the documented and confirmed Kamitan chronology far outstrips the Indian dates.		Confirmed and Documented Evidence of Contact Egypt-India	Chronology of Ancient Egypt According to Confirmed Archeological Dating of artifacts and Monuments (Evidences presented earlier).
Major Cultural-Theological Developments		Confirmed evidence of contact in years	**Major Cultural-Theological Developments**
		>5500 B.C.E. (Asar)	c. 65,000 B.C.E. Paleolithic – Nekhen (Hierakonpolis)
			c. 10,000 B.C.E. Neolithic – period
		Bronze Age link between Sakkara and Harappa 4,000-3,000 B.C.E.⁴⁴¹	c. 10,500 B.C.E.-7,000 B.C.E. <u>Creation of the Great Sphinx</u> Modern archeological accepted dates – Sphinx means Hor-m-akhet or Heru (Horus) in the horizon. This means that the King is one with the Spirit, Ra as an enlightened person possessing an animal aspect (lion) and illuminated intellect. <u>Anunian Theology – Ra</u>
		1,971 B.C.E. (Senusert I),	c. 10,000 B.C.E.-5,500 B.C.E. <u>The Sky GOD- Realm of Light-Day – NETER</u> Androgynous – All-encompassing –Absolute, Nameless Being, later identified with Ra-Herakhti (Sphinx)
c. 6500 BCE	Neolithic Period (Mehgarh)	500 B.C.E. Colony of Indians in Memphis⁴⁴²	>7,000 B.C.E. Kamitan Myth and Theology present in architecture
		484 B.C.E. (Herodotus),	5500+ B.C.E. to 600 A.C.E. <u>Amun -Ra - Ptah (Horus) – Amenit - Rai – Sekhmet</u> (male and female Trinity-Complementary Opposites)
		345 B.C.E. (Roman survey),	5500+ B.C.E. <u>Memphite Theology – Ptah</u>
			5500+ B.C.E. <u>Hermopolitan Theology- Djehuti</u>
			5500+ B.C.E. <u>The Asarian Resurrection Theology - Asar</u>
			5500+B.C.E. <u>The Goddess Principle- Theology</u>, Isis-Hathor-Net-Mut-Sekhmet-Buto
		261 B.C.E. (Ashoka)	5500 B.C.E. (Dynasty 1) Beginning of the Dynastic Period (Unification of Upper and Lower Egypt)
		70 B.C.E. (Virgil)	5000 B.C.E. (5ᵗʰ Dynasty) <u>Pyramid Texts - Egyptian Book of Coming Forth By Day - 42 Precepts of MAAT and codification of the Pre-Dynastic theologies</u> (Pre-Dynastic Period: 10,000 B.C.E.-5,500 B.C.E.)
c. 4000 BCE	Earliest Vedic hymns		
c. 3500 BCE	Early Harappan civilization	50 B.C.E. (Apollonius).	4950 B.C.E. Neolithic – Fayum
c. 2700-1500 BCE	Mature Indus civilization		4241 B.C.E. The Pharaonic (royal) calendar based on the Sothic system (star Sirius) was in use.
			3000 B.C.E. Wɪsᴅᴏᴍ Tᴇxᴛs-Precepts of Ptahotep, Instructions of Any, Instructions of Amenemope, Etc.
c. 1900 BCE	Age of Ramayana		2040 B.C.E.-1786 B.C.E. *Cᴏꜰꜰɪɴ Tᴇxᴛs*
c. 1500-500 BCE	Major Upanishads, development of early Samkhya, early Purva Mimamsa		1800 B.C.E.-<u>Theban Theology - Amun</u>
			1570 B.C.E.-Books of Coming Forth By Day (Book of the Dead)
c. 1400 BCE	Great Bharata War - Age of Krishna. Early version of Mahabharata		

THE AFRICAN ORIGINS OF CIVILIZATION, RELIGION AND YOGA SPIRITUALITY

c. 1200 BCE	Early Sutra literature. Consolidation of Vedic civilization: Manusmrti	1353 B.C.E. Non-dualist Philosophy from the Pre-Dynastic Period was redefined by Akhnaton.
		712-657 B.C.E. The Nubian Dynasty
624-544 BCE	Life of Gautama Buddha according to traditional reckoning.	
527 BCE	End of Mahavira's earthly life according to Jain tradition.	525-404 B.C.E. The Persian Conquest of Egypt
		404-343 B.C.E. Egyptians Regain Control
		343-332 B.C.E. The Second Persian Period
		332 B.C.E.- c. 30 B.C.E. The Ptolemaic or Greek Period Also known as the Hellenistic Period
		c.30 B.C.E.-395 A.C.E. Roman Period
		395-642 A.C.E The Byzantine Period and The Arab Conquest Period includes: the Caliphate and the 642-1517 A.C.E. Mamalukes Period
		1082-1882 A.C.E. Ottoman Domination Period
		1882-1952 A.C.E. British colonialism Period
		1952- present Modern, Arab-Islamic Egypt

🕮 Note: The dates given here are based on the work of Indian Indologists who advance the argument that the Vedic tradition came before the Indus Valley Civilization on the basis of researches into astronomy and archeology.[443] This has of course stirred up a controversy between them and the Western Indologists. The dates proposed by the Indian Indologists have been presented here for the reader to have all pertinent information related to the issue and not as an approval or disapproval of the research if the Indian Indologists. Recall that even some Indian Indologists regard the chronology of India as "notoriously conjectural"[1] and the dating beyond the time of Buddha as "the focus of fierce scholarly debates".[2] In any case, regardless of either dating system (Indian or Western) is used for dating Ancient India, the fact remains that Ancient Egyptian culture and civilization emerged prior to the Indus or Vedic.

Other Mythological Matches Between an Ancient Egyptian Myths and an Ancient Indian Myth

In the Hindu epic "Ramayana" or "Story of Rama," there is an episode where a haggardly old woman twists the mind of one of Rama's mother and caused her to have him dethroned and banished. In the same manner, in Kamitan myth called "The Story of Two Brothers," there was an old woman who twisted the mind of the virtuous man's wife, causing her to turn on him and forsake him.

In the Hindu epic, the queen beguiles the king to get promises that he cannot refuse. These she uses to force him to banish Rama. In the Kamitan, story the virtuous man's wife becomes queen and beguiles the king to get promises which he cannot refuse. She forces him to take actions that will do away with the virtuous man's (her previous husband's) way to return.

Thus, both stories contain the ideas of banishment, the old and bitter woman who influences the mind of a young woman, beguiling of the king, extracting promises from a king, who, out of lustful desire, unrighteously makes promises he will not be able to break later, etc. All of these points exhibit an uncanny similarity. Further, the theme of both of the stories is the same, which is that to be triumphant in life is to act with righteousness.

Also, it may be noted here that the epics in Ancient Egyptian myth were already in existence at beginning of Dynastic Period and into the Middle Kingdom era (5000-2500 B.C.E.). The Hindu epics are introduced with the commencement of the epic literature period in the Hindu period, which is much later (900 – 700 B.C.E.).

---

[1] "India's Chronology is notoriously conjectural until we come to the nineteenth century." –Georg Feuerstein (Yoga Journal 12/29/2000) (One of the authors of "In Search Of The Cradle Of Civilization")

[2] "The chronology of Ancient India up to the time of Buddha is at present the focus of fierce scholarly debates." (*A Concise Encyclopedia of Hinduism*, by Klaus K. Klostermaier)

THE AFRICAN ORIGINS OF CIVILIZATION, RELIGION AND YOGA SPIRITUALITY
NOTES TO CHAPTER 5

[336] Random House Encyclopedia Copyright (C) 1983,1990
[337] "Hindu Kush," Microsoft (R) Encarta. Copyright (c) 1994 Funk & Wagnall's Corporation.
[338] Random House Encyclopedia Copyright (C) 1983,1990
[339] *The History and Geography of Human Genes* Luigi Luca Cavalli-Sforza, Paolo Menozzi, Alberto Piazza. Copyright @ 1994 by Princeton University Press
[340] Sri Lanka, Republic of, formerly Ceylon; independent island-state in the Indian Ocean, 20mi (32km) off the SE coast of India. The people are of Indian origin (Sinhalese and Tamil), and the majority is Buddhist. (Random House Encyclopedia Copyright (C) 1983,1990)
[341] Ontology: the branch of metaphysics that deals with the nature of being. (Mysticism)
[342] Of Ancient Egypt.
[343] Cambyses II (d. 522 BC), son of Cyrus the Great and King of Persia (529-522 BC), his main achievement was the conquest of Egypt. His other campaigns failed and turned him from a benevolent to a harsh ruler. He died in battle in Syria. (Random House Encyclopedia Copyright (C) 1983,1990)
[344] *The African Origins of Civilization,* Cheikh Anta Diop, 1974
[345] *Mysteries of the Mexiacn Pyramids,* Peter Tompkins, 1976
[346] *In Search of the Cradle of Civilization,* 1995, p. 38, co-authored by Georg Feuerstein, David Frawley, and Subhash Kak. Quoting from *Serpent in the Sky,* John Anthony West, p. 97
[347] *In Search of the Cradle of Civilization,* 1995, co-authored by Georg Feuerstein, David Frawley, and Subhash Kak. P. 22-23
[348] Ibid.
[349] Senusert I, reigned in 1,971. B.C.E.
[350] Reigned c. 10,000 B.C.E.
[351] *In Search of the Cradle of Civilization,* 1995, p. 15, co-authored by Georg Feuerstein, David Frawley, and Subhash Kak.
[352] *Civilizations of the Indus Valley and Beyond*, Sir Mortimer Wheeler
[353] **Aryan,** one of the peoples believed to have migrated into Europe and India from central Asia; parent stock of the Hindus, Persians, Greeks, Latins, Celts, Anglo-Saxons, etc. Excerpted from *Compton's Interactive Encyclopedia.* Copyright (c) 1994, 1995 Compton's NewMedia, Inc. All Rights Reserved
[354] **Mulatto:** A person who is of part African and Eurasian descent. The child of one parent of Eurasian descent and one parent of African descent. From the Spanish and Portuguese word mulato meaning young mule. The mule is of course, one half horse and one half donkey, a hybrid.
[355] *A Concise Encyclopedia of Hinduism,* by Klaus K. Klostermaier
[356] Cable News Network – world report
[357] The word "Buddhism" is a Western term. The religion called Buddhism is actually referred to in the East as "Buddha-Dharma," which means "the teachings of the Buddha" or the path or righteous way of Buddha."
[358] Random House Encyclopedia Copyright (C) 1983,1990 by Random House Inc.
[359] "Vedanta," Microsoft (R) Encarta. Copyright (c) 1994 Microsoft Corporation. Copyright (c) 1994 Funk & Wagnall's Corporation.
[360] *Vedic Aryans and the Origins of Civilization* by David Frawley
[361] *Vedic Aryans and the Origins of Civilization* by David Frawley
[362] *Christian Yoga: The Journey from Jesus to Christ,* Muata Ashby
[363] *Vedic Aryans and the Origins of Civilization* by David Frawley
[364] *Vedic Aryans and the Origins of Civilization* by David Frawley P. 58-59
[365] *Vedic Aryans and the Origins of Civilization* by David Frawley
[366] "The Origin of Mathematics," Seidenberg (1978: 301)
[367] *Vedic Aryans and the Origins of Civilization* by David Frawley P. 72-73
[368] *Serpent in the Sky,* John Anthony West,
[369] *Vedic Aryans and the Origins of Civilization* by David Frawley, *In Search of the Cradle of Civilization,* 1995, co-authored by Georg Feuerstein, David Frawley, and Subhash Kak.
[370] *Vedic Aryans and the Origins of Civilization* by David Frawley
[371] **sur·vey-** To determine the boundaries, area, or elevations of (land or structures on the earth's surface) by means of measuring angles and distances, using the techniques of geometry and trigonometry. American Heritage Dictionary
[372] Copyright (C) 1983,1990 by Random House Inc.
[373] Architecture - Medinet Habu Temple -New Kingdom – Waset Egypt
[374] *Traveler's Key to Ancient Egypt*, John Anthony West
[375] Random House, Inc. Copyright (C) 1983,1990
[376] *Traveler's Key to Ancient Egypt*, John Anthony West
[377] *Ancient Architecture* by S. Lloyd and H.W. Müller
[378] Photo by Muata Ashby
[379] Photo by Muata Ashby
[380] "Chronology," Microsoft (R) Encarta Encyclopedia. Copyright (c) 1994
[381] Photo by Muata Ashby

[382] Water Table, the surface between an upper level, the zone of aeration, and a lower level, the zone of saturation. In the zone of aeration the open spaces are filled mainly with air. In the zone of saturation, a subsurface level, the openings are filled with water. The water table is a subdued imitation of the ground surface. Random House, Inc. Copyright (C) 1983,1990

[383] *Resurrecting Osiris: The Path of Mystical Awakening and the Keys to Immortality* by Muata Ashby

[384] *Vedic Aryans and The Origins of Civilization* by David Frawley

[385] *Vedic Aryans and The Origins of Civilization* by David Frawley

[386] *Proof of Vedic Culture's Global Existence* by Steven Knapp

[387] This kind of evidence does not pass the rigorous criteria that has been used to support the myths, legends, Ancient Egyptian literature and histories showing the Ancient Egyptian origins of Civilization, religion and Yoga Philosophy.

[388] *Vedic Aryans and The Origins of Civilization* by David Frawley (pp. 247-8), by N. S. Rajaram

[389] *Proof of Vedic Culture's Global Existence* by Steven Knapp

[390] *The History and Geography of Human Genes* Luigi Luca Cavaiii-Sforza, Paolo Menozzi, Alberto Piazza. Copyright @ 1994 by Princeton University Press

[391] *The History and Geography of Human Genes* Luigi Luca Cavaiii-Sforza, Paolo Menozzi, Alberto Piazza. Copyright @ 1994 by Princeton University Press

[392] Ashby, M. A., *"Egyptian Yoga The Philosophy of Enlightenment Vol. 1,* Sema Institute of Yoga-C.M. Book Publishing 1995

Feuerstein, Georg, *The Shambhala Encyclopedia of Yoga* 1997

Rashidi, Runoko and Van Sertima, Ivan, Editors *African Presence in Early Asia* 1985-1995

Mansouri El S. M., *Art – Culture of India and Egypt* 1959

Ray, Kumar Sudhansu, *Prehistoric India and Ancient Egypt* 1956

Doshi, Saryu, Editor-Indian Council for Cultural Relations *India and Egypt: Influences and Interactions* 1993

Kosambi, D. D., "Ancient India" a History of its Culture and Civilisation, 1965.

Macdonell, A. A., Vedic Mythology, Delhi: Motilal Banarsidass, 1974.

Mackenzie, Donald A., Indian Myth and Legend, London 1913

[393] *The Histories,* Herodotus, Translated by Aubrey de Selincourt- *The History of Herodotus By Herodotus,* Translated by George Rawlinson

[394] *The Histories,* Herodotus, Translated by Aubrey de Selincourt- *The History of Herodotus By Herodotus,* Translated by George Rawlinson

[395] "Migration," Microsoft (R) Encarta. Copyright (c) 1994 Microsoft Corporation.

[396] *The Histories,* Herodotus, Translated by Aubrey de Selincourt- *The History of Herodotus By Herodotus,* Translated by George Rawlinson

[397] *The Histories,* Herodotus, Translated by Aubrey de Selincourt- *The History of Herodotus By Herodotus,* Translated by George Rawlinson

[398] Image based on the findings contained in the books *The Great Human Diasporas,* Luigi Luca Cavalli-Sforza, Francesco Cavalli-Sforza. *The Cambridge Encyclopedia of Human Evolution,* Editor, Steve Jones

[399] Websters Encyclopedia 1996

[400] Encarta. Copyright (c) 1994Funk & Wagnall's Corporation.

[401] Bronze Age, period from the early fourth millennium BC onward, in which man learned to make bronze artifacts and to use the wheel and the ox-drawn plow. The resulting growth of technology and trade occasioned the rise of the first civilizations in Sumer and Egypt.

[402] Copyright © 1995 Helicon Publishing Ltd Encyclopedia

[403] *Travelers Guide to Ancient Egypt,* John Anthony West

[404] *In Search of the Cradle of Civilization,* 1995, co-authored by Georg Feuerstein, David Frawley, and Subhash Kak.

[405] Dutta, P. C. 1984. Biological anthropology of Bronze Ace. Harappans: new perspectives. In *The People of Soutli Asia.* J. R. Lukacs, ed., pp. 59-75. New York: Plenum.

[406] **1.** Proximity; nearness. **2.** Kinship. **3.** Similarity in nature.

[407] *The history and geography of human genes* Luigi Luca Cavalli-Sforza, Paolo Menozzi, Alberto Piazza. Copyright @ 1994 by Princeton University Press

[408] H.G. Rawlison, *Intercourse Between India and the Western World,* Cambridge, 1916, pp. 93-94

[409] Now at the Petrie Museum in London (UC nos. 8816, 8931, 8788)

[410] Flinders Petrie, *Memphis,* vol. 1, London 1909, pp. 16-17 pl. XXXIX.

[411] J.C.Harke, "The Indian Terracottas from Ancient Memphis: Are they really Indian?", *Dr. Debala Mitra Volume,* Delhi, 1991, pp. 55-61

[412] Charles Elliot, *Hinduism and Buddhism,* vol. III, London, 1954, pp. 93-94

[413] "Asoka," Microsoft (R) Encarta Copyright (c) 1994 Funk & Wagnall's Corporation. "Ashoka," Random House Encyclopedia Copyright (C) 1983,1990 by Random House Inc.

[414] K. G. Krishnan, Uttankita Sanskrit Vidya Arangnya Epigraphs, vol. II, Mysore, 1989, pp 42 ff

[415] H. G. Rawlison, *Intercourse between India and the Western World,* Cambridge, 1916, p. 92.

[416] Krishnan, op. cit., pp. 17-18

[417] Rawlison, op. cit., p. 93

[418] Tyana refers to North Turkey.

[419] *Connection of Egypt with India,* F.W.H. Migeod, Man, vol. 24, no. 118, London, 1924, p. 160

[420] "Ice Ages," Microsoft (R) Encarta. Copyright (c) 1994 Funk & Wagnall's Corporation.

[421] Random House Encyclopedia Copyright (C) 1983,1990

[422] Doshi, Saryu, Editor-Indian Council for Cultural Relations *India and Egypt: Influences and Interactions* 1993
[423] *Pottery Headrests from Narsipur Sangam,* F.R. Allchin, *Studies in Indian Prehistory*, D. Sen and A.K. Ghosh, eds., Calcutta, 1966, pp. 58-63
[424] *Chanudaro Excavations, 1935-36* E.J.H. Mackay, American Oriental Society, New Heaven, 19443, pp. 25 and 220, pl. XCII, 38
[425] Nagaraja Rao, op. Cit., p. 144; also Allchin, op. Cit.
[426] Ibid.
[427] *Guide to the Gods,* Marjorie Leach
[428] "Kenya," Microsoft (R) Encarta. Copyright (c) 1994 Funk & Wagnall's Corporation.
[429] *A Concise Encyclopedia of Hinduism,* by Klaus K. Klostermaier
[430] Rashidi, Runoko and Van Sertima, Ivan, Editors *African Presence in Early Asia 1985-1995*
[431] Doshi, Saryu, Editor-Indian Council for Cultural Relations *India and Egypt: Influences and Interactions* 1993
[432] *Mansouri El S. M., Art – Culture of India and Egypt* 1959
[433] Mehndi: The Timeless Art of Henna Painting by Loretta Roome
[434] Photo by Gakuji Tanaka
[435] Petrie Museum, London England.
[436] Doshi, Saryu, Editor-Indian Council for Cultural Relations *India and Egypt: Influences and Interactions* 1993
[437] H.G. Rawlison, *Intercourse Between India and the Western World,* Cambridge, 1916, pp. 93-94
[438] Now at the Petrie Museum in London (UC nos. 8816, 8931, 8788)
[439] Flinders Petrie, *Memphis,* vol. 1, London 1909, pp. 16-17 pl. XXXIX.
[440] J.C.Harke, "The Indian Terracottas from Ancient Memphis: Are they really Indian?, *Dr. Debala Mitra Volume,* Delhi, 1991, pp. 55-61
[441] Dutta, P. C. 1984. Biological anthropology of Bronze Ace. Harappans: new perspectives. In *The People of Soutli Asia.* J. R. Lukacs, ed., pp. 59-75. New York: Plenum.
[442] *In Search of the Cradle of Civilization,* 1995, co-authored by Georg Feuerstein, David Frawley, and Subhash Kak.p22-23
[443] *A Concise Encyclopedia of Hinduism,* by Klaus K. Klostermaier

Chapter 6: Kamitan (Ancient Egyptian) Origins of Yoga Philosophy, Yoga Disciplines And Yoga Mystic Spirituality

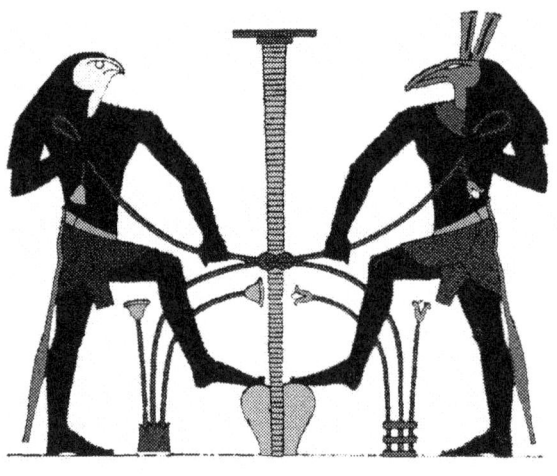

"The purpose of all human life is to achieve a state of consciousness apart from bodily concerns."

"Men and women are to become God-like through a life of virtue and the cultivation of the spirit through scientific knowledge, practice and bodily discipline."

"Salvation is the freeing of the soul from its bodily fetters; becoming a God through knowledge and wisdom; controlling the forces of the cosmos instead of being a slave to them; subduing the lower nature and through awakening the higher self, ending the cycle of rebirth and dwelling with the Neters who direct and control the Great Plan."

—Ancient Egyptian Proverb

What is Yoga?

Yoga is the practice of mental, physical and spiritual disciplines which lead to self-control and self-discovery by purifying the mind, body and spirit, so as to discover the deeper spiritual essence which lies within every human being and object in the universe. In essence, the goal of Yoga practice is to unite or *yoke* one's individual consciousness with Universal or Cosmic consciousness. Therefore, Ancient Egyptian religious practice, especially in terms of the rituals and other practices of the Ancient Egyptian Temple system known as *Shetaut Neter* (the way of the hidden Supreme Being), also known in Ancient times as *Smai Tawi* "Egyptian Yoga," should as well be considered as universal streams of self-knowledge philosophy which influenced and inspired the great religions and philosophers to this day. In this sense, religion, in its purest form, is also a Yoga system, as it seeks to reunite the soul with its true and original source, God. In broad terms, any spiritual movement or discipline that brings one closer to self-knowledge is a "Yogic" movement. The main recognized forms of Yoga disciplines are:

- *Yoga of Wisdom,*
- *Yoga of Devotional Love,*
- *Yoga of Meditation,*
    - *Physical Postures Yoga*
- *Yoga of Selfless Action,*
- *Tantric Yoga*
    - *Serpent Power Yoga*

The diagram below shows the relationship between the Yoga disciplines and the path of mystical religion (religion practiced in its three complete steps: 1st receiving the myth {knowledge}, 2nd practicing the rituals of the myth {following the teachings of the myth} and 3rd entering into a mystical experience {becoming one with the central figure of the myth}).

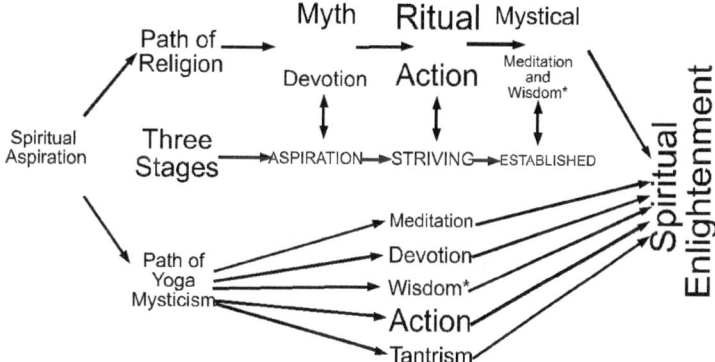

The disciplines of Yoga fall under five major categories. These are: *Yoga of Wisdom, Yoga of Devotional Love, Yoga of Meditation, Tantric Yoga* and *Yoga of Selfless Action*. When these disciplines are practiced in a harmonized manner this practice is called "Integral Yoga." Within these categories there are subsidiary forms which are part of the main disciplines. The emphasis in the Kamitan Asarian (Osirian) Myth is on the Yoga of Wisdom, Yoga of Devotional Love and Yoga of Selfless Action. The important point to remember is that all aspects of Yoga can and should be used in an integral fashion to effect an efficient and harmonized spiritual movement in the practitioner. Therefore, while there may be an area of special emphasis, other elements are bound to become part of the Yoga program as needed. For example, while a Yogin (practitioner of Yoga, aspirant, initiate) may place emphasis on the Yoga of Wisdom, they may also practice Devotional Yoga and Meditation Yoga along with the wisdom studies. So the practice of any discipline that leads to oneness with Supreme Consciousness can be called Yoga. If you study, rationalize and reflect upon the teachings, you are practicing *Yoga of Wisdom*. If you meditate upon the teachings and your Higher Self, you are practicing *Yoga of Meditation*.

Thus, whether or not you refer to it as such, if you practice rituals which identify you with your spiritual nature, you are practicing *Yoga of Ritual Identification* (which is part of the Yoga of Wisdom {Kamitan-Rekh, Indian-Jnana} and the Yoga of Devotional Love {Kamitan-Ushet, Indian-Bhakti} of the Divine). If you develop your physical nature and psychic energy centers, you are practicing *Serpent Power* (Kamitan-*Uraeus* or Indian-*Kundalini*) *Yoga* (which is part of Tantric Yoga). If you practice living according to the teachings of ethical behavior and selflessness, you are practicing *Yoga of Action* (Kamitan-Maat, Indian-Karma) in daily life. If you practice turning your attention towards the Divine by developing love for the Divine, then it is called *Devotional Yoga* or *Yoga of Divine Love*. The practitioner of Yoga is called a Yogin (male practitioner) or Yogini (female practitioner), or the term "Yogi" may be used to refer to either a female or male practitioner in general terms. One who has attained the culmination of Yoga (union with the Divine) is also called a Yogi. In this manner, Yoga has been developed into many disciplines which may be used in an integral fashion to achieve the same goal: Enlightenment. Therefore, the aspirant is to learn about all of the paths of Yoga and choose those elements which best suit {his/her} personality or practice them all in an integral, balanced way.

Enlightenment is the term used to describe the highest level of spiritual awakening. It means attaining such a level of spiritual awareness that one discovers the underlying unity of the entire universe as well as the fact that the source of all creation is the same source from which the innermost Self within every human heart arises.

> "As one can ascend to the top of a house by means of a ladder or a tree or a staircase or a rope, so diverse are the ways and means to approach God, and every religion in the world shows one of these ways."
>
> -Ramakrishna (1836-1886)

Receptivity to The Discussion About The Origins of Yoga

In a previous chapter it was introduced that the authors of the book *In Search of the Cradle of Civilization,* 1995, p. 15, co-authored by Georg Feuerstein, David Frawley, and Subhash Kak. called for a *"critical reexamination"* into the origins of Yoga. However, the point was also made that in view of the previous statements by the authors, the reader's first impression might be that there is a proclivity towards one point of view, which suggests a contradiction with the following statement from the same book that ignores the possibility of the origins of Yoga outside of India and turns the attention solely towards the Vedas.

> "The time is ripe for a critical reexamination of the question of the origin of Yoga. In looking for the roots of Yoga in the Vedas, we must first of all rid ourselves of the tendency to indulge in what scholars call arguments ex silentio; that is, to favor a particular point of view because of the absence of contrary evidence. For instance, we might argue that, because the original Pledge of Allegiance did not contain the phrase "one nation under God," the American people were irreligious prior to 1954 when the Pledge was changed by an Act of Congress. This is dearly absurd, and yet this kind of argument is frequently resorted to by scholars, especially when defending cherished positions." p.173[444]

There is a feeling among many who are interested in Yoga philosophy as it was practiced in Ancient Egypt and India that there is a refusal by many European and North Indian scholars to acknowledge the growing mountain of evidences that have been cited. Two factors have been broached to explain this apparent rebuke. It has been charged, for example, that while many practitioners and scholars of Yoga as it developed in India and later developed in the West espouse a "universalistic" perspective as to the nature of Yoga, portraying it as a phenomenon that has existed in all cultures from the beginning of civilization or as a common human need expressed by people who do not follow the Indian path, they present also in many of their statements a subtle pride in claiming the Indian origin, and Indian perfection of the art, thus relegating, by implication, other forms of spiritual practice, which might be considered "Yogically" based but not originating in India as primitive, uncivilized or meek in comparison to Indian Yoga, thereby undermining and demeaning them.

The inference is also that others claiming to practice "Yoga" outside of the Indian framework for the word and practice are actually doing something else that is alien or at least other than the Indian concepts and disciplines. Thus, by implication, the custodians of that specialty (Indian Yoga) become the purveyors as well as the sole authorities on it, and at the same time ensnaring themselves in the web of egoism spun by pride, ignorance and misunderstanding, for many such statements are a backlash against years of Western denigration of Eastern spirituality. Some have suggested the factor that many European and Indian scholars feel a sense of superiority due to their association with the Vedic-Sanskrit tradition, viewing it as the source of civilization. The pride of having a supposedly advanced literary culture gives way to narcissism and inflated egos. This understandably can lead to social castes systems placing the purveyors of the supposedly high literature at the top of the social order. It is also understandable how this conceit can lead to the great problems which follows caste systems, the attendant racism and sexism.

Others have suggested that a racist mentality has developed among some scholars, based on their association with racist Europeans and Arabs. This feeling has, in a subtle way, caused many north Indian scholars (who are of lighter complexion than their southern counterparts) to promote an "Aryan" world view as opposed to a "Dravidian" world view or the possibility of any outside influence on the Vedic tradition as opposed to an indigenous development or influence. This position remains intransigent, even after examining some of the evidences which have been presented by African and Indian scholars supporting the influence of Dravidian culture and existence of Yoga practices in Ancient Egypt as well as contact and cultural exchange between Ancient Egypt and Northern as well as Southern India both before and after the emergence of Aryan culture and Yoga philosophy in India.

Indologists on the Origins of Yoga

In reference to the origins of Yoga, the authors of the book *In Search of the Cradle of Civilization,* by Georg Feuerstein, David Frawley, and Subhash Kak assert the following on Pages 170-171. (Highlighted portions by Ashby)

> "The Hindus have traditionally *looked to* the archaic *Vedas* as the seedbed of the later Yoga tradition.* The Vedic seers are honored as illumined sages who passed down the secrets of meditation and higher consciousness to subsequent generations of spiritual practitioners. Reflecting this idea, the teachers of the school of Classical Yoga, embodied in the *Yoga-Sutra of* Patanjali and his commentators, not only employ Vedic concepts in their teachings but also speak of their tradition as thoroughly Vedic."
>
> *See, e.g., D. Frawley, *Gods, Sages and Kings: Vedic Secrets of Civilization* (Salt Lake City, UT: Passage Press, 1991), pp.203-236

> "The term *Yoga* itself first occurs in the *Rig-Veda, but* does not yet have its later technical connotation. In many instances, it simply means "application",** The word *Yoga* is one of the most flexible terms *of* the Sanskrit language and therefore has been used in many diverse contexts, in addition to its specific philosophical meaning. In the technical sense of "spiritual discipline," the term *Yoga* first made its appearance in the *Taittiriya-Upanishad,* a work belonging possibly to the era around 1000 B.C. or even earlier."
>
> **See, e.g., *Rig-Veda* 1.5.3; 1.30.11; X.114.9. The term *yogya and yojana* apparently are used as synonyms of *Yoga.*

> Many of modern India's Yoga adepts believe that the *Vedas* contain the original teachings of Yoga.

The statements above show that most practitioners of Yoga in India look to the Vedas as the source or origin of the tradition. However, even the prominent Indologists, Georg Feuerstein, David Frawley, and Subhash Kak, admit that the use of the term is just that, the use of the term and it does not relate to what we know of today as the tradition and technology of Yoga, which the authors say began with the Upanishads. Yet there is persistence in upholding the Vedic origins and the use of the word itself as synonymous with the concept is implied. We must be reminded that belief in a tradition does not mean that the tradition is real and therefore, without a direct philosophical link, the Yogic tradition of India cannot be taken further back than the Upanishadic period. It is as if the terms of the Vedas such as Yoga, Brahman, Dharma, Maya and others were taken by the Upanishadic sages and redefined to conform to the high philosophy which we have come to recognize today as Yoga.

The Kamitan (Ancient Egyptian) and Universal Origins of Yoga

> **yo·ga** (yō′gə) *n.* **1.** A Hindu discipline aimed at training the consciousness for a state of perfect spiritual insight and tranquility. **2.** A system of exercises practiced as part of this discipline to promote control of the body and mind. **–yo′gic** (-gĭk) *adj.*
> —American Heritage Dictionary

The pervasiveness of the Sanskrit term from India has become so well known that it has been added to the Western lexicons. This pervasiveness has also promoted the idea that Yoga originated or was invented in India. In the case of the origins of Indian Yoga, many scholars and world renowned spiritual masters have recognized the strong connections between India and Ancient Africa, namely Joseph Campbell, R.A. Schwaller de Lubicz, Omraam Mikhael Aivanhov, and Swami Sivananda Radha. However, what they stated amounted to a few pieces of a larger puzzle which until now had not been pursued in an extensive manner. What makes the this volume important is that attempts to put those pieces together and goes further to show that Kamitan Yoga, the Yoga practice of Ancient Africa, is a living, breathing spiritual discipline that is being followed today and which has something substantial to contribute to modern day Yogic culture and to the upliftment of humanity. Some people in the general Yogic community, who up to now, have only been aware of the Indian Yoga legacy have been surprised and delighted to discover the Kamitan Yoga legacy, while others have had their closely but sentimentally held notions about Yoga and Yoga philosophy challenged. As discussed in the previous section, some many people have come to regard Yoga is a proprietary commodity which is owned by East-Indians, since they see this as the origin. When the nature and essence of what Yoga is, is fully understood, its source as a universal human spiritual movement becomes clear.

The Debate On The Question Of The Origins Of Yoga

In reference to the question of the origins of Yoga, there has been a growing interest into exploring certain apparent correlations between the form of spirituality that was practiced in Ancient Egypt and that which is commonly referred to as Yoga mysticism of India. Again, here as well many Western Indologist as well as lay peoples ascribe the origin of Yoga to India simply because it is India where the practice expanded to the rest of the world under the name which it is known today.

The seemingly dogmatic approach to the study of Hindu history and Yoga, as expressed by many Eurocentrists and Indologists presented earlier, has led to the promotion, by some, of the idea that Yoga philosophy emerged in India simply because the word Yoga is a Sanskrit term.[445] This is like saying that a rose that grows in South America cannot be a rose because the South Americans do not use the term "rose" from the English language which is common to North America. Further, in reference to Yoga, if this view is taken, then we cannot conclude that Yoga emerged as a development of Ancient India, but was a product of outside influence since the word does not appear in India until the introduction of Sanskrit language in 1,500 B.C.E. This would mean that until it appears in the Rig Veda[446] one cannot say that Yoga "existed" at all in India since the term did not yet exist. In other words, it appeared out of nowhere or it came from outside India and it developed elsewhere. A deep philosophical discipline such as Yoga cannot appear without a long process of development and refinement unless one believes in "spontaneous generation." Moreover, when the use of the term "Yoga" in the Rig Veda is examined, it simply means to yoke, as in attaching something, an object like a cart, to something else, a horse. The great mystical philosophy which Indian Yoga has come to be known for, uniting the individual with the Universal, did not become associated with the term until the appearance of the *Taittiriya Upanishad, c.* 1,000-800 B.C.E. This argument therefore means that no Yoga was practiced anywhere (even in India) as a mystical philosophy until 1,000 B.C.E. in India at the earliest.

The problem with this argument is obvious. It would appear that in an attempt to appropriate the philosophy of Yoga as having an "Indian only" origin, many scholars as well as ignorant lay people of Indian and non-Indian origin have sought to equate the philosophy of Yoga with the appearance of the Sanskrit word. This endeavor has revealed the aforementioned inconsistency as we know that something cannot come from nothing. Yoga did not appear out of nowhere but from the early developments of sages and saints. Otherwise we would have to also conclude that gravity did not exist until Isaac Newton named the force (gravity) that holds human beings on earth and prevents them from flying off into space! Further, this would be like saying that a mystic who practices the mystical disciplines (meditation, wisdom, devotion and right action) in America could not meet a practitioner of mysticism in Africa and realize that they have the same goals and use the same techniques for attaining higher consciousness simply because they do not use the same terms to describe what they do, or that if two such individuals were to meet they could not relate to each other or would not "compare notes," that is, to consider or describe their respective systems of spirituality as similar, equal, or analogous. They would not be able to liken or examine each others systems of spirituality in order to note the similarities or differences and perhaps even merge or adopt some technique or philosophical understanding from each other that may seem useful.

Yogic philosophy and the Yogic impetus in humankind is nothing more than the innate desire to experience unbounded peace and joy and the pursuit of self-knowledge. It is a birthright of humanity and its most common and important instinct. Therefore, Yoga, regardless of the name it has been given in a particular culture, is the philosophy and technology for attaining spiritual enlightenment, the union of the Lower and Higher nature. Therefore, Yoga cannot be considered as a linguistic term but as a natural cultural expression of the desire to discover the heights of human experience. As this desire is common to all human beings, then it follows that all cultures, in all periods where civilization had reached a point where the basic necessities of life had been met, developed a form of technology and philosophy of self-discovery. Therefore, it is proper to use the term "Yoga" when describing the technology and philosophy of Yoga (main disciplines: meditation, wisdom, devotion and right action), which the word has come to be associated with in and outside of India through the popularity of the Sanskrit term. So we can now speak of the such a form or style of the technology and philosophy of meditating, understanding, worshipping and promoting virtue, as it developed in Christianity and call it "Christian Yoga," and as it developed in Ancient Egypt and call it "Egyptian or Kamitan Yoga." However, just because this technology and philosophy exists in two cultures one cannot say that they are related or that they have a common origin. Again, this is because while two separate cultures may have the same goal, their manner of pursuing that goal will usually be different due to the diverse possibilities that the world offers. Like the late great Hindu saint, Ramakrishna said, *"God is like a lake and the religions are like paths to that lake which come from all directions."* Only when we see certain correlations in various factors of cultural expression and these can be backed up by evidence of prior contact can we venture to assert that such a connection is present.

In the book *In Search of the Cradle of Civilization*, there is an admission that the Vedas do not incorporate *"technical Yoga practices"* and that they are not trying to *"communicate facts but spiritual meanings"* and that therefore, they are *"composed in a highly symbolic language."* As stated earlier, myth is a fluid language, and when two different cultures come into contact, it will be easier to exchange metaphor and symbols, which constitute the essential expressions of myth. Yoga is also a spiritual philosophy that encompasses myth, metaphor and symbol to convey the transcendental path to discover the Absolute. It accomplishes this with the use of myth, and symbolic language. While some of the disciplines of Yoga contain technical language this should not be taken to mean that there is one pathway, as there are many paths. So technical language may be used in a particular path and at the same time it does not negate others. Conversely, the language of one culture does not hamper the practice of the same religion in another. Otherwise one could only expect to see Buddhists who speak the language that Buddha spoke, or Christians who speak the language that Jesus spoke, and so on.

In recent months, the leading English language Yoga magazines in the West have run articles on *Buddhist Yoga, Chinese Yoga, Yoga of the Ancient Hebrews, Yoganics, Aikido- the Yoga of Combat, and one called The New Yoga: America is Reinventing the Practice But is it Still Yoga?*[447] And another related to an *"Egyptian Yogi"*[448] called Plotinus. For a student of Yoga literature it will be quickly apparent that these disciplines, whatever they may be, are not part of the history of the Vedas so why have they received sufficient attention to merit an article and be called Yoga? Plotinus was born in Egypt, and he followed the teachings of Plato and Pythagoras. He also taught asceticism in (70-205 A.C.E.). However, he came very late in the history of Yoga and while the article shows that these philosophies are compatible with Yoga, it stresses the possibility that there was some contact by which he might have learned some basic teachings from Indian Yogis. There is no mention of the fact that according to the Greek Classical writers, Plato and Pythagoras learned their philosophy from the Ancient Egyptian sages who received their knowledge in an unbroken line of initiation from the time thousands of years before the Indus valley civilization arose, a factor confirmed by the Greeks themselves.

> "This is also confirmed by the most learned of Greeks such as Solon, Thales, Plato, Eudoxus, Pythagoras, and as some say, even Lycurgus going to Egypt and conversing with the priests; of whom they say Euxodus was a hearer of Chonuphis of Memphis,[449] Solon of Sonchis of Sais,[450] and Pythagoras of Oenuphis of Heliopolis.[451]"
>
> -Plutarch, Morals, 10
> (c. 46-120 AD),
> Greek author/Initiate of Isis.

THE AFRICAN ORIGINS OF CIVILIZATION, RELIGION AND YOGA SPIRITUALITY

The publication of frivolous articles and the conspicuous omission of a serious treatment of Kamitan (Egyptian) Yoga as an ancient tradition denotes the incapacity to confront the issue which may possibly necessitate the rethinking of the history of Yoga and consequently the manner in which the message, heritage and legacy of Yoga is transmitted to the West. It is one thing to convince oneself that Yoga has an Indian only background, and then become an authority on that framework to focus on Mesopotamia or Egypt and espouse a rigid conservative traditionalistic view. From this standpoint it is quite comfortable to look at other traditions that may have some similar aspects and even consider these as containing some aspect of Yoga, but underlying this treatment is a "centrist" point of view which does not take these "new" traditions seriously. For someone with this notion it will be quite another thing entirely to fully and honestly consider new information that point to not only deeper roots of Yoga but also a living breathing practice of the art outside of the traditionalist view. It would be like realizing an error as well as possibly losing status and prestige as far as no longer being the only authorities on the subject of Yoga and/or its legitimate representatives. Ironically, the article itself points out that what the West has developed and called "Yoga" is actually neither what the ancients had in mind nor what authentic modern day Indian Yoga masters have in mind. The Yoga of the West is essentially an amalgam of some Yogic philosophy mixed with Western individuality, cynicism and hedonism. Further, the vast majority of Yoga practitioners in the West have nothing to do with Yoga philosophy and prefer to partake solely in the physical fitness aspects of the posture systems.[452]

It is therefore fitting that an Indian authority on the subject of Yoga should be included here. A world renowned spiritual teacher, and master of Indian Yoga, Vedanta Philosophy and Sanskrit of India, Swami Jyotirmayananda, had the following to say on the origins and universal practice of Yoga.

> "Yoga is a universal religion. It gives insight into every religion…Yoga embraces all religions of the world. It does not see the need of contradicting them. Its interest lies in giving a wider meaning to one's love for God. What is contradicted is limitation in understanding God, and a mental obstruction in developing love of God. All great mystics, saints and seers in all parts of the world proclaim the same reality, but, in different expressions, in different languages. Yogic principles are verified through all great personalities. Many practiced universal Yoga without giving it a Sanskrit name. The teachings of Jesus were inspired by the Yogic teachings that prevailed in antiquity through Buddhism. Socrates was inspired by Yogic wisdom. Directly or indirectly, all great personalities drink deep from the universal stream of wisdom which is Yoga…therefore Christianity is nothing but Yoga."
>
> —Swami Jyotirmayananda

The same sentiment, may be seen in a statement which appears in the book *Living Yoga*.[453] It is surprising to see the following statement by Mr. Georg Feuerstein in light of other statements which suggest that he advocates the idea that "Yoga" originated in India. Many advocates of the "out of India view" would like to present a universalistic perspective of Yoga philosophically or figuratively, but when it comes to discussing the origins they suddenly become fierce proponents of the idea that Yoga is a high philosophy originated by ancient Indian sages and that what other people have done through history is little more than primitive attempts at philosophy which have been influenced by contact with India.

> So, the metaphysical explanations of Yoga should not prove a stumbling block to anyone with a genuine desire to explore this ancient tradition. It is this built-in flexibility that has allowed the Yoga tradition to adapt itself so well to the conditions of the West. It can be as meaningful for nondogmatic agnostics, Christians, or Jews as it is for Hindus.
> Yoga, then, is a universal art, which flourishes wherever a person is dedicated to higher values, to a way of life that outdistances the egotistical preoccupations of the unenlightened mind: the way of inner joy and outer harmony.
>
> -Living Yoga by Georg Feuerstein, Stephan Bodian, with the staff of Yoga Journal

The Early Practice of Yoga in India and the Connection to Ancient Egypt

(Note: also see the section on Serpent Power further on in this chapter for more in depth and expanded details)

Figure 85: One of a handful of depictions of a person in a Yoga posture being worshipped by two others and two serpents on either side. (Indus Valley-Pre Aryan)

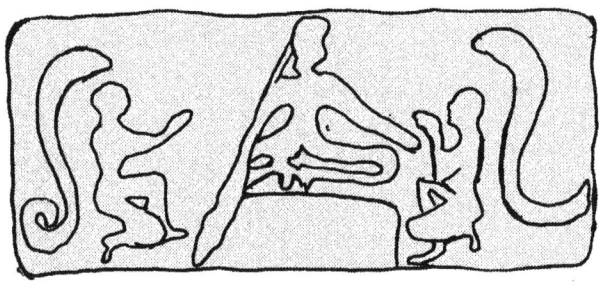

In reference to the pictograph above as well as Yoga and its origins in the Indus tradition and the possibility of Yoga practices from outside India influencing the development of Yoga in India, the mythologist Joseph Campbell explained the following:

> "The basic treatise on Yoga is the *Yoga Sutras, Thread of Yoga,* a work attributed to an ancient saint whose name, Patanjali (from pata, "falling," plus anjali, "the joined hands"), is explained by a legend of his having dropped from heaven in the shape of a small snake into the hands of the grammarian Panini, just as the latter, was bringing his palms together in prayers.[454] Its date is under debate, some assigning it to the second century B.C., others to the fifth century A.D. or later;[455] all, however, recognizing that the ideas and disciplines represented are certainly older than this writing, some perhaps dating back even to the Indus civilization, ca. 2500-1500 B.C. For the earliest known evidences of Yoga appear on a half-dozen or so of the Indus Valley seals, an example of which appears here. (see above) Two attendant serpents elevate their giant forms behind a pair of worshipers kneeling at either hand of an enthroned figure seated in what appears to be a posture of Yoga. And the fact that the elevation of the so-called Serpent Power is one of the leading motifs of Yogic symbolism suggests that we may have here an explicit pictorial reference not only to the legend of some prehistoric Yogi, but also to the concept of the unfoldment through Yoga of this subtle spiritual force.
>
> If so, the question arises whether some sort of Yoga may not have been practiced outside India at that time as well. For a number of the symbols that are interpreted in psychological terms in Yogic lore appear also in the monuments of other ancient cultures-where, however, no explanatory texts such as those that can be studied from the Hindu-Buddhist sphere are known."[456]

This extremely important passage from the eminent scholar brings up several most significant and insightful point with far reaching implications. The motif of the serpent and the raising of the "Serpent Power" can indeed be found in almost every culture which has practiced the art that is popularly known as "Kundalini Yoga" or Serpent Power Yoga. However, in Ancient Egypt we see almost an exact reproduction (see below) of the scene from the Indus Valley (above) in the Serpent Power system of Ancient Egypt.

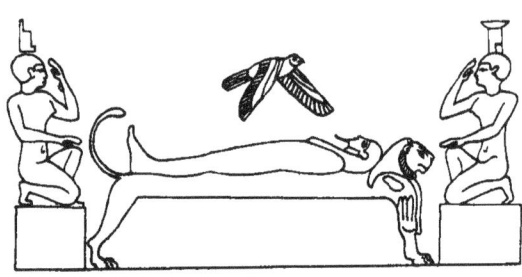

Figure 86: The God Asar (Osiris) with the goddess Aset (Isis) at the foot of the bed and goddess Nebethet (Nephthys) at the head.

The goddesses are known as the two sisters and as the *Arati,* serpents sisters. Thus, even the serpents are present in the image in a subtle way. Further, the Kamitan word "Arat" (📖), means goddess and the serpent sign is part of the names 📖 *Nebethet Arat* and 📖 *Aset Arat* of the two goddesses (see below). In the *Asarian Resurrection* Myth, one of the oldest myths of Ancient Egypt, we are informed that the goddess in her dual form, Aset and Nebethet, are the engineers of the resurrection of Asar. As we learn from the science of Kundalini Yoga as practiced in modern India, Kundalini is a goddess who manifests in a dual form, *Ida and Pingala.* They join and move up the subtle spine of the Aspirant (Yogi) and cause the raising of consciousness to cosmic levels as represented by the Chakras or psycho-spiritual energy centers. The point between the eyebrows (brow) signifies the attainment of dual vision (Cosmic consciousness {what the Indian Yoga systems refers to as *Jiva Mukti* or Buddhists Enlightenment} and phenomenal awareness). The seventh chakra signifies the attainment of transcendental consciousness. These teachings are compatible between Ancient Egypt and India. Along with this motif from Ancient Egypt, we can see not just the iconography of the Serpent Power, but also the *"technical specifications"* and *"facts"* related to the Kamitan Yoga practices and the *"concept of the unfoldment through Yoga of this subtle spiritual force."*

Figure 87: Goddesses Nebethet (left) and Aset (right) –with their serpent designations (goddess)

"The Goddess Uadjit cometh unto thee in the form of the living Uraeus, to anoint thy head with their flames. She riseth up on the left side of thy head, and she shineth from the right side of thy temples without speech; they rise up on thy head during each and every hour of the day, even as they do for their father Ra, and through them the terror which thou inspirest in the holy spirits is increased, and because Uadjit and Nekhebet rise up on thy head, and because thy brow becometh the portion of thy head whereon they establish themselves, even as they do upon the brow of Ra, and because they never leave thee, awe of thee striketh into the souls which are made perfect."

THE AFRICAN ORIGINS OF CIVILIZATION, RELIGION AND YOGA SPIRITUALITY

The preceding scripture from the Ancient Egyptian ceremonies is echoed in the *Pert M Heru* text of Ancient Egypt, *The Ancient Egyptian Book Enlightenment*. The state of enlightenment is further described in Chapters 83 and 85 where the initiate realizes that the seven Uraeus deities or bodies (immortal parts of the spirit) have been reconstituted:

"The seven Uraeuses are my body... my image is now eternal."

These seven Uraeuses are described as the *"seven souls of Ra"* and *"the seven arms of the balance (Maat)."* These designations of course refer to the seven spheres of the balance scales of Maat which correspond to the seven Chakras of the Indian Kundalini system.[457]

Figure 88: Below- Ancient Egyptian depiction of the god Asar with the two serpent goddesses in the form of a Caduceus, symbolizing the Serpent Power (Kundalini Yoga).

Plate 29: Below left-The Hindu god Shiva, "the Master Yogi," sitting in meditation on the tiger skin. This iconography is thought to be a late development of the "the Indus Yogi" (above)

Plate 30: Below right- an Ancient Egyptian man in the Lotus Posture[458]

THE AFRICAN ORIGINS OF CIVILIZATION, RELIGION AND YOGA SPIRITUALITY

In Kamitan Yogic mysticism, the "leonine bed" (feline motif) symbolizes the sleep of death from which the awakening of enlightenment will occur as the feline Life Force essence, termed *Sekhem* in Ancient Egypt, is cultivated. The avian motif symbolizes the rising of consciousness, metaphorically referred to as "resurrection." In Indian Yogic mysticism, the lotus posture on the bedding of the tiger (again a feline motif) skin has assumed the same role. Therefore, the feline motif is maintained throughout both the Kamitan and Indian systems and they are therefore compatible in class, gender, function and mythic metaphor.

The Ancient Egyptians Practiced Yoga

Most people in Western Culture have heard of Yoga as an exercise, however, Yoga is a vast science of human psychology and spiritual transformation which includes physical and mental health as the prerequisite for further progress into philosophical and meditative disciplines. Yoga, in all of its disciplines, was practiced in Ancient Egypt (Kamit, Kamut, Kamit or Ta-Meri) and is the subject of the Ancient Egyptian Mysteries. As in India, Yoga, as it was practiced in Ancient Egypt, included the disciplines of virtuous living, dietary purification, study of the wisdom teachings and their practice in daily life, psychophysical and psycho-spiritual exercises and meditation. Practitioners of Indian Yoga, Buddhist Yoga and Chinese Yoga (Taoism) today refer to all of these disciplines as Yogic disciplines. Therefore, the Ancient Egyptians were also practitioners of Yoga Philosophy. Through a process of gradually blending these disciplines in the course of ordinary life, an individual can effect miraculous changes in {{her/his}} life and thereby achieve the supreme goal of all existence, the goal of Yoga: Union with the Higher Self.

The Term "Egyptian Yoga" and The Philosophy Behind It

As previously discussed, Yoga in all of its forms was practiced in Egypt apparently earlier than anywhere else in our history. This point of view is supported by the fact that there is documented scriptural and iconographical evidence of the disciplines of virtuous living, dietary purification, study of the wisdom teachings and their practice in daily life, psychophysical and psycho-spiritual exercises and meditation being practiced in Ancient Egypt, long before the evidence of its existence is detected in India (including the Indus Valley Civilization) or any other early civilization (Sumer, Greece, China, etc.).

The teachings of Yoga are at the heart of *Prt m Hru*. As explained earlier, the word "Yoga" is a Sanskrit term meaning to unite the individual with the Cosmic. The term has been used ease of communication since the word "Yoga" has received wide popularity, especially in Western countries in recent years. The Ancient Egyptian equivalent term to the Sanskrit word Yoga is: *"Sma, Sema or Smai."* The Kamitan language did not record vowels, so there is no way to know the exact spelling or pronunciation that would have been used. It could have been *Sma, Sema, Sama, or Soma*. We will use the terms *Sema* or *Smai* (the Ancient Egyptian terms) interchangeably throughout this text to refer to Kamitan Yoga. *Sema* or *Smai* mean union, and the following determinative terms give it a spiritual significance, at once equating it with the term "Yoga" as it is used in India. When used in conjunction with the Ancient Egyptian symbol which means land, *"Ta,"* the term "union of the two lands" arises.

Sema (or *Smai*) *Tawi* (*Taui*)
(From Chapter 4 of the *Prt m Hru*)

In Chapter 4[459] and Chapter 17[460] of the *Prt m Hru*, a term "*Sma, Sema or Smai* Tawi" is used. It means "Union of the two lands of Egypt," ergo "Egyptian Yoga." The two lands refer to the two main districts of the country (North and South). In ancient times, Egypt was divided into two sections or land areas. These were known as Lower and Upper Egypt. In Ancient Egyptian mystical philosophy, the land of Upper Egypt relates to the divinity Heru (Horus), who represents the Higher Self, and the land of Lower Egypt relates to Set, the divinity of the lower self. So *Sema* (*Smai*) *Taui* means "the union of the two lands" or the "Union of the lower self with the Higher Self. The lower self relates to that which is negative and uncontrolled in the human mind including worldliness, egoism, ignorance, etc. (Set), while the Higher Self relates to that which is above temptations and is good in the human heart as well as in touch with

THE AFRICAN ORIGINS OF CIVILIZATION, RELIGION AND YOGA SPIRITUALITY

Transcendental consciousness (Heru). Thus, we also have the Ancient Egyptian term *Sema (Smai) Heru-Set*, or the union of Heru and Set. So Sema (Smai) Taui or Sema (Smai) Heru-Set are the Ancient Egyptian words which are to be translated as "Egyptian Yoga."

Above: the main symbol of Egyptian Yoga: *Sma*. The Ancient Egyptian language and symbols provide the first "historical" record of Yoga Philosophy and Religious literature. The hieroglyph Sma, ⚭ "Sema," represented by the union of two lungs and the trachea, symbolizes that the union of the duality, that is, the Higher Self and lower self, leads to Non-duality, the One, singular consciousness.

More Ancient Egyptian Symbols of Yoga

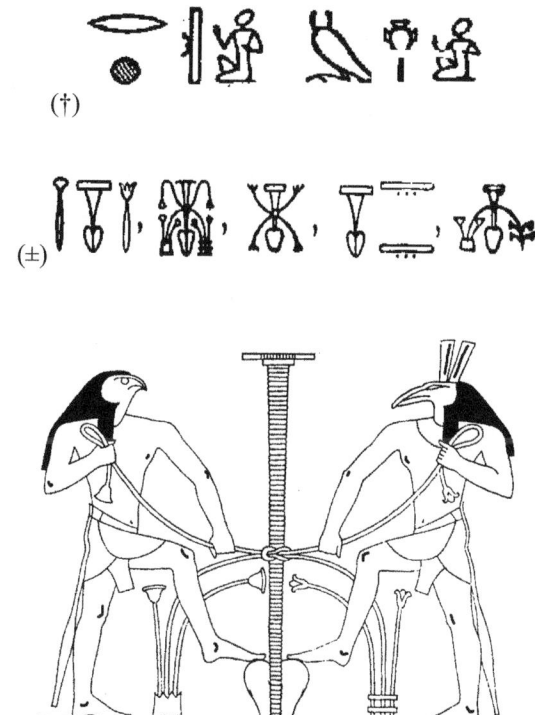

Figure 89: Above: Sema (Smai) Heru-Set,

Heru and Set join forces to tie up the symbol of Union (Sema or Sma). The Sema symbol refers to the Union of Upper Egypt (Lotus) and Lower Egypt (Papyrus) under one ruler, but also at a more subtle level, it refers to the union of one's Higher Self and lower self (Heru and Set), as well as the control of one's breath (Life Force) through the union (control) of the lungs (breathing organs). The character of Heru and Set are an integral part of the *Pert Em Heru*.

The central and most popular character within Ancient Egyptian Religion of Asar is Heru, who is an incarnation of his father, Asar. Asar was killed by his brother Set who, out of greed and demoniac (Setian) tendency, craved to be the ruler of Egypt. With the help of Djehuti, the God of purified intellect, Aset, the great mother of intuitional wisdom and Hetheru, his consort and goddess of sublimated sexual energy, Heru prevailed in the battle against Set for the rulership of Kamit (Egypt). Heru's struggle symbolizes the struggle of every human being to regain rulership of the Higher Self and to subdue the lower self.

THE AFRICAN ORIGINS OF CIVILIZATION, RELIGION AND YOGA SPIRITUALITY

The most ancient writings in our historical period are from the Ancient Egyptians. These writings are referred to as hieroglyphics. The original name given to these writings by the Ancient Egyptians is *Medu Neter*, meaning "the writing of God" or *Neter Medu* or "Divine Speech." These writings were inscribed in temples, coffins and papyruses and contained the teachings in reference to the spiritual nature of the human being and the ways to promote spiritual emancipation, awakening or resurrection. The Ancient Egyptian proverbs presented in this text are translations from the original hieroglyphic scriptures. An example of hieroglyphic text was presented above in the form of the text of Sema (Smai) Taui or "Egyptian Yoga."

Egyptian Philosophy may be summed up in the following proverbs, which clearly state that the soul is heavenly or divine and that the human being must awaken to the true reality, which is the Spirit, Self.

"Self knowledge is the basis of true knowledge."

"Soul to heaven, body to earth."

"Man is to become God-like through a life of virtue and the cultivation of the spirit through scientific knowledge, practice and bodily discipline."

*"Salvation is accomplished through the efforts of the individual.
There is no mediator between man and {{his/her}} salvation."*

*"Salvation is the freeing of the soul from its bodily fetters, becoming a God through knowledge and wisdom, controlling the forces of the cosmos instead of being a slave to them, subduing the lower nature and through awakening the Higher Self,
ending the cycle of rebirth
and dwelling with the Neters who direct and control the Great Plan."*

THE AFRICAN ORIGINS OF CIVILIZATION, RELIGION AND YOGA SPIRITUALITY

Item for Comparison 5: The Disciplines of Yoga Practiced in India and Ancient Egypt

An overview of basic Indian Yoga Philosophy will reveal important similarities and correlations with the Ancient Egyptian Neterian Philosophy.

Vedanta Yoga, and Samkhya Philosophy

Vedanta philosophy originated from the ancient spiritual scriptures of India called the *Vedas.* More specifically, Vedanta refers to the end of the Vedas or the scriptures commonly referred to as *The Upanishads* which constitute a summary or distillation of the highest philosophy of the Vedas. Vedanta philosophy, as it exists in the present, is a combination of Buddhist psychology, Hindu mythology and ancient mystical philosophy. Having its original roots in the philosophy of the oneness of GOD who manifests in a myriad of ways, Vedanta achieves a balanced blend of all the philosophies and has been adapted by the present day Sages to teach to modern day society. Vedanta, which includes the 16 Yogas (8 major, 8 minor) adapted from the Buddhist Wheel of Life, developed as an alternative to the patriarchal and racist Brahmanic system. Major Tenets:

Vedanta Philosophy is summed up in four *Mahavakyas* or *Great Utterances* to be found in the Upanishads:

1- Brahman, the Absolute is Consciousness beyond all mental concepts.
2- Thou Art That (Referring to the fact that everyone is essentially this consciousness).
3- I Am Brahman, the Absolute (To be spoken by people referring to their own essential nature).
4- The Self is Brahman (The Self is the essence of all things).

<u>Major Tenets of Vedanta</u>

1- Absolute Reality is that which is unchanging.

2- The Absolute Reality is named **Brahman.** The manifesting universe is an appearance only, an illusory modification of Brahman. Therefore, it never had a beginning and will never have an end because it is only an appearance.

3- Brahman or the Ultimate reality, GOD, Supreme Being, is ALL that exists. All the objects of the world and universe even though appearing to be different are really one entity. All physical reality is an illusory manifestation of Brahman which Brahman sustains but yet is detached from at all times just as the sun sustains life on earth and yet is detached from it.

4- Brahman is Pure consciousness. All that exists is essentially Brahman: *"Sat-Chit-Ananda"* - Existence - Knowledge - Bliss. GOD gives things existence; God is conscious of those things (therefore they exist) and GOD gives "bliss" to the experience of living.

5- The mind, body and senses of human beings are illusions. The essence of
everything in the universe, including the human soul, is pure consciousness. Even though objects appear real, tangible and permanent, it is in reality transient and illusory.

6- Brahman is the world and also assumes the role of millions of individual life forms (people, animals, insects, etc.). The Individual Soul is termed Atman.

7- Atman and Brahman are one and the same. Therefore, everyone's soul is part of the universal essence, Brahman.

8- Through a veil of mental ignorance, the individual soul (Atman) believes it is an individual entity (Jiva), separate from everything else when it is indeed part of everything. The mental veil of ignorance comes from erroneous subconscious impressions which cause the person to believe they are a body instead of a spirit and therefore, they search for happiness and fulfillment in the illusory pleasures of the world. This leads one from one unfulfilled desire to another.

9- Vedanta seeks to transform the subconscious of the individual through gradually increasing philosophical and practical discipline. Its goal is to remove the veil of ignorance by asserting that the only reality is Brahman. When this reality is "consciously realized" by intuition (through meditative experience), the veil of ignorance is lifted. Once the veil of ignorance is removed, the initiate subsists in a transformed psychological and spiritual state where they abide in the real universal, omnipresent, expansive state of consciousness termed: *"Jivan Mukta"* which means: one who is liberated while still alive. *Jivan Mukta* is an individual who has sublimated their ego-sense in favor of becoming one with the Absolute reality. No longer knowing themselves as an individual, they are one with GOD: **Brahman**. This is the state termed as *Moksha* or *Kaivalia* (liberation).

The term *"Illusory Modification"* can be better understood from a simile given by Vedanta philosophy. A person enters a dark room and steps on something which appears to feel like a snake. The person is very scared because he believes the information from his senses. The person turns the light on and finds that there is only a rope. It was due to ignorance (the darkness) that the rope was perceived to be a snake. In the same way, it is our ignorance about our true nature which allows us to perceive the multiplicity of the world as a "reality." The *"objects of the world"* are perceived as separate entities instead of what they truly are: **Brahman.** This ignorance is based on the information our brains gather from the senses rather than from that gathered through the higher intuitional capacities. The light represents intuitional wisdom of the truth whereby the questions (based on our incorrect and ignorant assumptions and ideas): Where did the snake come from?, What kind of snake is this? Who does the snake belong to?, Is the snake poisonous?, become irrelevant. In the same way questions about the origin of the world, humanity, etc., become irrelevant since time, space and physical reality are illusions, only Brahman exists. One sees oneself as Brahman therefore, one sees only oneself in existence. Relatives, people, the sun, planets are all oneself. Illusory modification made it seem like there was a multiplicity of different objects in existence.

Vedanta Philosophy holds that there are four planes of existence and that the human being is really a composite of three bodies and five sheaths or layers. In this manner, the Divine Self (Brahman) expresses itself in the form of nature and living beings.

The Planes:
- **1- Gross Plane:** Consisting of the gross elements and the senses.
- **2- Subtle Plane:** Consisting of subtle elements that may be perceived through extra-sensory perception.
- **3- Subtler Plane:** The intellect; here the ego is transcended and one experiences higher forms of being.
- **4- Subtlest Plane:** This is the level of the causal body.

The Bodies:

- **1- Physical Body.**
- **2- Astral Body.**
- **3- Causal Body.**

The Five Sheaths (coverings):

- **1- Food Sheath** (*Annamaya Kosha*).
- **2- Pranic Sheath** - Vital energy (*Pranamaya Kosha*).
- **3- Mind Sheath** (*Manomaya Kosha*).
- **4- Intellect Sheath** (*Vijnamaya Kosha*).
- **5- Bliss Sheath** ({Anandamaya Kosha} one transcends the ego and body and experiences the spirit).

The three bodies and the five sheaths may be compared to the Egyptian belief of the nine parts of the spirit including the BA or Supreme Soul. When it is considered that the Vedantic system of India proposes eight parts plus the Supreme Self or Atman - Brahman, the similarity appears almost exact in theme and number.

The practice of Yoga, as it developed in India (+1,000 B.C.E.-100 B.C.E.), is classified as a science with eight steps; their correspondence to the Egyptian system will become evident:

1- Self control (yama): Non- violence, truthfulness, chastity, avoidance of greed.

2- Practice of virtues (niyama): Actions to avoid in order to maintain yama.

3- <u>Postures (asana):</u> To condition the body and prepare the mind and body for meditation.

4- <u>Breath control (pranayama):</u> Controlling the breath is controlling the Life Force; controlling the Life Force is controlling the mind.

5- <u>Restraint (pratyahara):</u> Disciplining the sense organs to avoid overindulgence and physical temptation of the body: food, sex, drugs, etc.

6- <u>Steadying the mind (dharana):</u> Practice focusing the mind. Concentrating the mental rays on one subject over a short period of time.

7- <u>Meditation (dhyana):</u> When the object of concentration engulfs the entire mind and concentration continues spontaneously.

8- <u>Deep meditation (samadhi):</u> Personality dissolves temporarily into the object of meditation, experience of super-consciousness.

In the Yoga Sutras of Sage Patanjali (c. 200 B.C.E.), the following instruction is given for the practitioner of Yoga:

योगश्चित्तवृत्तिनिरोधः
YOGASH CHITTA VRITTI NIRODHAH.
Sutra 2: Yoga is the intentional stopping of the mind-stuff (thought waves).

This is desirable because:

वृत्तिसारूप्यमितरत्र
VRITTI SARUPYAM ITARATRA.
Sutra 4: "At times when the mind stuff flows indiscriminately, "the seer" becomes "identified" with the thought-waves."

Patanjali goes on to say that due to the identification of the seer (our true self) with the thoughts, we believe ourselves to be mortal and limited instead of immortal and immutable. He further says that there is no need to worry because through the steady practice of Yoga (dispassion, devotion, mind control exercises of meditation), even the most unruly mind can be controlled. Thus, the individual will discover their true self when the *"Chitta"* (thought waves) are controlled. It is as if one looks at oneself through colored sunglasses and believes oneself to be that color. In the same way, Yoga is the process of uncovering the eyes from the illusion of the mind's thought waves.

Kamitan Scriptural Sources of Yoga Philosophy

Most students of Yoga that are familiar with the Yogic traditions of India consider that the Indian texts such as the Bhagavad Gita, Mahabharata, Patanjali Yoga Sutras, etc., are the primary and original source of Yogic philosophy and teaching. However, upon examination, the teachings currently espoused in all of the major forms of Indian Yoga can be found in Ancient Egyptian scriptures inscribed in papyrus and on Temple walls as well as steles, statues, obelisks and other sources.

Item for Comparison 6: The Yoga of Wisdom

One discipline of Yoga requires special mention here. It is called Wisdom Yoga or the Yoga of Wisdom. In the Temple of Aset (Isis) in Ancient Egypt, the Discipline of the Yoga of Wisdom is imparted in three stages:

1-Listening to the wisdom teachings on the nature of reality (creation) and the nature of the Self.
2-Reflecting on those teachings and incorporating them into daily life.
3-Meditating on the meaning of the teachings.

Aset (Isis) was and is recognized as the goddess of wisdom, and her Temples strongly emphasized and espoused the philosophy of wisdom teaching in order to achieve higher spiritual consciousness. It is important to note here that the teaching which was practiced in the Ancient Egyptian Temple of Aset[461] of **Listening** to, **Reflecting** upon, and **Meditating** upon the teachings is the same process used in Vedanta-Jnana Yoga of India of today. **The Yoga of Wisdom** is a form of Yoga based on insight into the nature of worldly existence and the Transcendental Self, thereby transforming one's consciousness through development of the wisdom faculty. Thus, we have here a correlation between Ancient Egypt and India that matches exactly in its basic factor respects.

THE THREE-FOLD PROCESS OF WISDOM YOGA IN INDIA AND EGYPT:

Discipline of Wisdom Yoga in Ancient Egypt	Discipline of Wisdom Yoga in India
1- ***Men Mestchert:*** Listening to the wisdom teachings on the nature of reality (creation) and the nature of the Self.	1- ***Shravana:*** Listening to the wisdom teachings on the nature of reality (creation) and the nature of the Self.
2- ***Maui:*** Reflecting on those teachings and incorporating them into daily life.	2- ***Manana:*** Reflecting on those teachings and incorporating them into daily life.
3- ***Uaa:*** Meditating on the meaning of the teachings.	3- ***Niddidhyasana:*** Meditating on the meaning of the teachings.

THE AFRICAN ORIGINS OF CIVILIZATION, RELIGION AND YOGA SPIRITUALITY

Figure 90: The image of goddess Aset (Isis) suckling the young king.

This image represents the importance of the mothering, nurturing principle in the making of a human being, as well as the nurturing that must take place in order for one to give birth to one's own spirit. It is the quintessential symbol of initiation in Ancient Egypt, especially related to the Temple of Aset but also adopted by other temples within Neterian Religion.

Temple of Aset
GENERAL DISCIPLINE

Fill the ears, listen attentively- Meh mestchert.

Listening

1- Listening to Wisdom teachings. Having achieved the qualifications of an aspirant, there is a desire to listen to the teachings from a Spiritual Preceptor. There is increasing intellectual understanding of the scriptures and the meaning of truth versus untruth, real versus unreal, temporal versus eternal. The glories of God are expounded and the mystical philosophy behind the myth is given at this stage.

MAUI
"to think, to ponder, to fix attention, concentration"

Reflection

2- Reflection on those teachings that have been listened to and living according to the disciplines enjoined by the teachings is to be practiced until the wisdom teaching is fully understood. Reflection implies discovering, intellectually at first, the oneness behind the multiplicity of the world by engaging in intense inquiry into the nature of one's true Self. Chanting the hekau and divine singing, *Hesi*, are also used here.

"Devote yourself to adore God's name."
—Ancient Egyptian Proverb

uaa
"Meditation"

Meditation

3- Meditation in Wisdom Yoga is the process of reflection that leads to a state in which the mind is continuously introspective. It means expansion of consciousness culminating in revelation of and identification with the Absolute Self.

THE AFRICAN ORIGINS OF CIVILIZATION, RELIGION AND YOGA SPIRITUALITY

Item for Comparison 7: The Yoga of Righteous Action

GENERAL DISCIPLINE
In all Temples especially
The Temple of Heru and Edfu

Scripture: Prt M Hru and special scriptures including the Berlin Papyrus and other papyri.

1- Learn Ethics and Law of Cause and Effect-Practice right action (42 Precepts of Maat) to purify gross impurities of the personality *__Control Body, Speech, Thoughts.__*

2- Practice cultivation of the higher virtues (selfless-service) to purify mind and intellect from subtle impurities.

3- Devotion to the Divine - See Maatian actions as offerings to the Divine.

4- Meditation -See oneself as one with Maat, i.e. United with the cosmic order which is the Transcendental Supreme Self.

Plate 31: The Offering of Maat-Symbolizing the Ultimate act of Righteousness (Temple of Seti I) The King offers to Asar (not pictured).

One of the main duties of the king is to uphold Maat. Maat is the ethical basis for harmonious social order. It is also the duty of the king to protect Maat by opposing all who seek to destroy peace and justice. The highest expression of the king's pledge to uphold Maat is to make the "Maat Offering."

NOTE: For full description see the section entitled "The Philosophy of Social Order and Spiritual Upliftment of Humanity in Ancient Egypt and India" and also see the books Wisdom of Maati, The 42 Precepts of Maat, and The Ancient Egyptian Book of the Dead by Muata Ashby.

THE AFRICAN ORIGINS OF CIVILIZATION, RELIGION AND YOGA SPIRITUALITY

Item for Comparison 8: The Yoga of Devotion to The Divine

GENERAL DISCIPLINE
In all Temples

Scripture: Prt M Hru and Temple Inscriptions.

Discipline of Devotion

1– <u>Listening to the myth</u>
   Get to know the Divinity.
   Empathize with the divinity.
   Romantisize about the nature of the divinity.

2– <u>Ritual about the myth</u>
   Offerings to Divinity – propitiation to the divinity
   Act like the divinity
   Chant the name of the Divinity
   Sing praises of the Divinity
   COMMUNE with the Divinity

3– <u>Mysticism</u>
   Melting of the heart – effacement of the ego.
   Dissolve into Divinity
   IDENTIFY-with the Divinity

In Kamitan devotional philosophy God is termed *Merri*, "Beloved One"

Love and Be Loved
"That person is beloved by the Lord." PMH, Ch 4

Offering Oneself to God-Surrender to God- Become One with God

Figure 91: The Dua Pose- Upraised arms with palms facing out towards the Divine Image

THE AFRICAN ORIGINS OF CIVILIZATION, RELIGION AND YOGA SPIRITUALITY

Item for Comparison 9: The Discipline of Meditation

Figure 92: Kamitan Meditation Posture-Sitting With Hands on Thighs

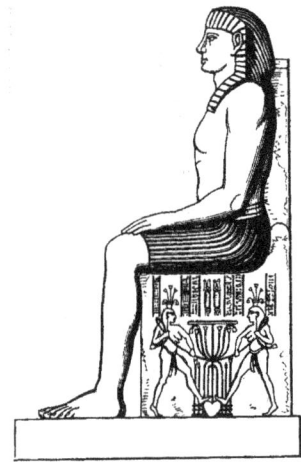

It is well known and commonly accepted that meditation has been practiced in India from ancient times, being an integral part of Vedanta and Buddhism as well as Yoga philosophy. Therefore, there is no need to site specific references to support that contention. Here we will concentrate on the evidence supporting the existence of the philosophy of meditation in Ancient Egypt.

The Paths of Meditation Practiced in Ancient Egypt	Basic Instructions for the Glorious Light Meditation System- Given in the Tomb of Seti I. (1350 B.C.E.)
System of Meditation: **Glorious Light System** Location where it was practiced in ancient times: **Temple of Seti I, City of Waset (Thebes)** [462] System of Meditation: **Wisdom System** Location where it was practiced in ancient times: **Temple of Aset – Philae Island, Aswan** System of Meditation: **Serpent Power System** Location where it was practiced in ancient times: **Temple of Asar- City of Abdu** System of Meditation: **Devotional Meditation** Location where it was practiced in ancient times: **IN ALL TEMPLES- GENERAL DISCIPLINE**	Formal meditation in Yoga consists of four basic elements: Posture, Sound (chant-words of power), Visualization, Rhythmic Breathing (calm, steady breath). The instructions, translated from the original hieroglyphic text contain the basic elements for formal meditation. (1)-**Posture and Focus of Attention** *iuf iri-f ahau maq b-phr nty hau iu* body do make stand, within the Sundisk (circle of Ra) This means that the aspirant should remain established as if in the center of a circle with a dot in the middle. (2)- **Words of power-chant**[463] *Nuk Hekau* (I am the word* itself) *Nuk Ra Akhu* (I am Ra's {God's}Glorious Shinning** Spirit) *Nuk Ba Ra* (I am the soul of Ra{God}) *Nuk Hekau* (I am the God who creates*** through sound) (3)- **Visualization** *Iuf mi Ra heru mestu-f n-shry chet* "My body is like Ra's {God's}on the day of his birth This teaching is what in Indian Vedanta Philosophy is referred to as Ahamgraha Upashama – or visualizing and meditating upon oneself as being one with God. This teaching is the main focus of the *Prt m Hru* (Book of Enlightenment) text of Ancient Egypt. It is considered as the highest form of meditation practice amongst Indian mystics.[464]

Plate 32: Basic Instructions for the Glorious Light Meditation System- Given in the Tomb of Seti I. (c. 1350 B.C.E.)

As we have seen, the practice of meditation in Ancient Egypt and its instruction to the masses, and not just to the Priests and Priestesses, can be traced to at least 800 years earlier than in India. If the instructions given by Sage Seti I and those given by Sage Patanjali are compared, many similarities appear.

DISCIPLINE OF MEDITATION IN ANCIENT EGYPT AND INDIA

Basic Instructions for the Glorious Light Meditation System- Given in the Tomb of Seti I. (c. 1350 B.C.E.)	Yoga Sutras of Patanjali (India) (200 B.C.E.)
Basic instructions given in the text: 1. **To Be Practiced by Clergy and Lay Alike** 2. **Listen to the Mystical Teaching** in the Myth of Hetheru and Djehuti 3. **Be purified physically by proper hygiene-**with Nile Flood Water (leanest); wear proper clothing. 4. **Be purified by Maat** (righteousness, truth, Non-violence, non-stealing, non-killing, etc.) 5. **Sevenfold Cleansing for three days**- Serpent Power – transcend the three forms of mental expression 6. **Posture and Focus of Attention** - Make the body still, concentrating on yourself 7. **Words of power-chant** *Nuk Hekau* (I am the word itself) *Nuk Ra Akhu* (I am Ra's Glorious Shinning Spirit – Divine Light) *Nuk Ba Ra* (I am the soul of Ra) *Nuk Hekau* (I am the God who creates through sound) 8. **Visualization-** see yourself in the center of the Sundisk (circle of Ra), see yourself as Ra (Mystic Union)	Called Raja or Royal Yoga or the Yoga of the eight steps, which may be listed as follows: 1. Restraint: nonviolence, not lying, not stealing, not lusting, and not possessing; 2. Observances: cleanliness, contentment, discipline, self-study, and surrender to the Lord; 3. Posture (seated quietly); 4. Breath control; 5. Sublimation or withdrawal from the senses; 6. Attention; 7. Concentration; 8. Meditation.

Item for Comparison 10: The Physical Yoga Postures

Contrary to popular knowledge, the practice of the discipline that was later known as "Hatha Yoga" in India began at around the year 1000 A.C.E. and not in pre-Christian (Comma Era) times as is commonly supposed. Often times the mention of the word "asana" in the Patanjali Yoga Sutras" (200 B.C.E.) is thought to represent an early practice of Hatha Yoga. However, when the statements by Patanjali are examined closely, it is clear that the meaning relates to a sitting posture for meditation and not the elaborate system of a sequence of postures designed to cultivate physical health and harmonization of the Ha (solar) and Tha (lunar) energies of the physical and astral bodies of a person.

Further, notice that the popular practices of Hatha Yoga which have come to the West are all 20th century developments. They are outgrowths of the original Hatha Yoga concept but are modern interpretations, exemplifying elaborate and in many ways intricate concepts and practices which were not enjoined by sage Goraksha. The emphasis on the physical postures as either a discipline for physical health in a limited sense or as a self-contained end of Yoga at the exclusion of the other disciplines (meditation, study of the wisdom teachings, right action, devotional worship) has prompted many Indian masters to complain about the disregard for the true meaning of Yoga and the true purpose of the exercise postures. As with so many other disciplines, Western society has taken cultural disciplines and traditions but ascribing new meanings and transforming these disciplines and traditions into something other than what they originally were. The practice of the Indian Hatha Yoga postures has been adopted by many in the western countries but the adjunct practice of meditation and the philosophy of the postures has been left aside in great measure. The postures are mostly used as a meas to promote physical health as opposed to their original intent of promoting positive spiritual evolution. The following article illustrates this point. (text emphasis by Ashby)

TAKE A SEAT by Alan Reder
If your not meditating, are you really doing Yoga?

– **Yoga Journal Feb. 2001**

THE SUCCESS OF YOGA in the West may have come at a heavy price. <u>Many teachers worry that something special has been lost in Yoga American style</u>, and that something is meditation. Meditation, not postures, is the heart of Yoga, they point out. <u>In Patanjali's India, Yoga and meditation were nearly synonymous, yet meditation plays only a minor role in many American Yoga courses. In others, it is not taught at all.</u>

<u>Some Yoga students regard meditation as boring cultural baggage</u> and appreciate learning postures without it. But what if your experience with Yoga has inspired you to go deeper, into Yogic spirituality? If your Yoga teacher doesn't offer meditation guidance, how should you begin? <u>Since Yoga comes from India</u>, should your meditation technique be Hindu or Buddhist? Is Zen Buddhist okay? Does the inner peace you already feel in Yoga class count?

Records of <u>meditation as a discipline for lay people, as opposed to priests</u>, first show up about 500 B.C. in both India and China.

Contrary to what many Yoga students believe, his (Patanjali) text said little about Hatha Yoga postures, which weren't a widespread practice at the time.

From Raja Yoga Sutras – Translated by Swami Jyotirmayananda:

Samadhi Pad Sutra 46: *seated pose for meditation*
Samadhi Pad Sutra 48-49: *perfecting the seated pose for meditation*

THE AFRICAN ORIGINS OF CIVILIZATION, RELIGION AND YOGA SPIRITUALITY

The important question arises, is Yoga *(Exercise)* in the West really being practiced correctly? In fact, can it even be said that yoga is being practiced in the west? The following excerpts from an article that appeared in the magazine Yoga Journal, explores this problem.

> "The New Yoga, America is Reinventing the Practice…But it is still Yoga?"
> *"New Light on Yoga"* – Yoga Journal – July/Aug 1999
>
> "Dr. Jayadeva Yogendra…his father, at the turn of the twentieth century, was one of the first yogic crusaders to bring hatha yoga to practices ….and begin teaching them to a lay audience. 'When I see what yoga has become I the west,'….. **'I wish my father had left it with the hermits in the caves'."**

The degradation of the practice of Yoga was typified by the comment of a well known Hollywood Actress:

> "I don't want Yoga to change my life, just my butt!"
> USA – 2000 ACE

Many teachers of the Indian Yoga postures in the western countries take pride in learning the jargon of Sanskrit words and wowing their students with difficult contortions but not including philosophy or meditation in their practice, presumably because the populations of the west are hostile to forms of spirituality other than the western religions (Christianity, Islam, and Judaism). In the current climate (late 20th century-early 21st) where the social climate is increasingly religiously intolerant, the prospects of Yoga and other mystical traditions in the west will be problematical. The following guidelines should be followed if the true Indian and Ancient Egyptian tradition of the postures is to be upheld.

Integral Practice of the Yoga postures includes physical regimen, diet, philosophy, meditation, devotional practice and virtuous living.

- **Integral Practice is not just the Postures, not just meditation, not just cultivation of the vital body, not just wisdom**
- **It must include mystical philosophy, leading to entry into higher planes of existence.**
- **It is that experiences that informs all yogic movements in all religions of history.**
- **Names, jargons, clothing, memorized texts, etc. are foundations, not attainments.**

Hatha Yoga, Buddhism and Ancient Egypt

"In Zen Buddhism, for example, students can chant a lineage of teachers stretching back for centuries, with each Zen master certified by the one preceding. No such unbroken chain of transmission exists in hatha yoga. For generations, hatha yoga was a rather obscure and occult corner of the yoga realm, viewed with disdain by mainstream practitioners, kept alive by a smattering of isolated ascetics in caves and Hindu *maths* (monasteries). It appears to have existed for centuries in seed form, lying dormant and surfacing again and again. In the twentieth century, it had almost died out in India. According to his biography, Krishnamacharya had to go all the way to Tibet to find a living master…<u>Given this lack of a clear historical lineage, how do we know what is "traditional" in hatha yoga? Where did our modern proliferation of poses and practices come from? Are they a twentieth century invention?"</u>

-July/August 1999 By Anne Cushman (Yoga Journal)

Many practitioners of Indian Hatha Yoga are fond of describing their practice as "ancient" and as being comprised of an unbroken "lineage" of teachers going back "thousands of years." Upon close examination of the practice in India we find that no such unbroken chain of transmission exists in Hatha Yoga. Actually in the early twentieth century, it had almost died out in India.

> HATHA-YOGA ("forceful Yoga"), also called hatha-vidya ("science of hatha"); the type of Yoga specific to the Kanphata sect, though this designation is also applied in general to the

vast body of doctrines and practices geared toward Self-realization by means of perfecting the body.[162]

The term Hatha Yoga is defined as "forceful union," that is forcing spiritual evolution via the cultivation of the energies of the physical body. In Ancient Egypt the program of transformation through body cultivation was described in the Pert M Heru text, more commonly known as the Egyptian Book of the Dead, as well as in other texts.

The origins of Hatha Yoga were clearly in Buddhism and not in Hinduism since we find evidence of rejection of Hatha Yoga by the Hindu sages. **Hatha Yoga is clearly rejected in the Laghu -Yoga - Vasishtha (5.6.86, 92), which maintains that it merely leads to pain. Some of criticisms, especially against the magical undercurrents.**[163]

> **GORAKSHA or GORAKSHANATHA** The most popular teacher of hathayoga, who is widely celebrated as its inventor, is Goraksha (9th or 10th cen. CE), a member of the Natha tradition, in which body cultivation played a crucial role. He is acclaimed by some as the first writer of Hindi or Punjabi prose and is credited with the authorship of numerous works, including the Goraksha-Samhit4, the Amaraugha-Prabodha, the Jnata-Amrita-Shastra, and the Siddha-SiddhantaPaddhati. Although the Tibetan sources speak of him as a Buddhist magician, the works ascribed to him and his school have a distinct leaning toward Shaivism.[164]

> The most popular teacher of hathayoga, who is widely celebrated as its inventor, is **Goraksha** (9th or 10th cen. CE), a member of the Natha tradition, in which body cultivation played a crucial role. In India it came under attack early in its development. For instance, it is clearly rejected in the Laghu -Yoga - Vasishtha (5.6.86, 92), which maintains that it merely leads to pain. The most formidable critic of hatha-yoga was Vijndna Bhiksbu, a sixteenth- century savant and Yoga practitioner. Some of his criticisms, especially against the magical undercurrents present in this yogic approach, are undoubtedly justified.[165]

Tantric philosophy figures prominently in the origins of Indian Hatha Yoga as one of its disciplines. As was discussed in the section of this book entitled "Item for Comparison 11: Tantric Philosophy," Tantrism was practiced in Ancient Egypt from the earliest times. The practice of Tantrism in Ancient Egypt was akhnowledged by Ajit Mookerjee.

> Tantric influence, however, is not limited to India alone, and there is evidence that the precepts of tantrism traveled to various parts of the world, especially Nepal, Tibet, China, Japan and parts of South-East Asia; its influence has also been evident in Mediterranean cultures such as those of Egypt and Crete.[166]
> -Ajit Mookerjee (Indian Scholar-Author –from the book *The Tantric Way*)

Specifically, Tantric Buddhism gave rise to the earliest practice of certain postures as a means to enhance spiritual evolution. Before this time, the only reference to Asana or posture was the sitting posture for meditation, mentioned in the Raja Yoga Sutras by Patanjali. Below: **Patanjali Yoga Sutras Sadhana Pad (200 B.C.E) - sutra 46: Asana – Trans. Swamiji Jyotirmayananda**

---

[162] FROM: Shambala Encyclopedia of YOGA by Georg Feuerstein
[163] ibid
[164] ibid
[165] ibid
[166] *The Tantric Way* by Ajit Mookerjee and Madhu Khanna

Sutra 46

स्थिरसुखमासनम्

STHIRA SUKHAM ASANAM.

STHIRA: Steady. SUKHAM: Comfortable. ASANAM: Pose (for meditation).

Meaning

A seated pose (for meditation) that is steady and comfortable is called *Asana*.

Explanation

To attain success in the practice of concentration, meditation and *Samadhi*, an aspirant begins by developing steadiness of a meditative pose.

There is clear evidence of the existence of the Sakkara/Memphis- School of Memphite Theology- Divinity *Ptah*. There is also clear evidence of the practice of "magi" or "Hekau" and the practice of Tjef Neteru or postures of the gods and goddesses in Egypt.

Buddhist records show that early Buddhists had visited Memphis and had set up a settlement there. Henceforth Buddhism begins to develop similar iconographies including the Divinity sitting on the lotus, and also lotus friezes[167] similar to those of Ancient Egypt appear in Buddhist art.

---

[167] 1- A plain or decorated horizontal part of an entablature between the architrave and cornice. 2-A decorative horizontal band, as along the upper part of a wall in a room.

Left: Heru on the Lotus, Right: Buddha on the Lotus

In the book Search for the Buddha by Charles Allen, the author documents the Buddhist connection to Ancient Egypt as follows. The Buddhist/Indian ruler had a practice of setting up pillars with inscriptions attesting to his following the Buddhist principles and other edicts. One was discovered that unequivocally shows that ancient Egypt and India were associated.

In March 1838 a more complete and accurate impression of the Girnar rock inscription became available to James Prinsep. On 14 'March he wrote another of those letters to Alexander Cunningham that bubble over with enthusiasm and good cheer. The Girnar inscription differed from the pillar edicts in a number of passages, and in one he had found a line that linked Piyadasi/Ashoka to Egypt and the Ptolemys:

The passage in the 14th edict is much mutilated, and I long for a more correct copy. It really becomes interesting to find Egypt and Ptolemy known to Asoka! I must give you the real text:

Yona raja paran cha tena chaptaro rajanan tulamayo
Greek king furthermore by whom the Gypta rajas Ptolemy
*cha antigina cha maga cha * * **
and Antigonus and Magus and * * *
savata devanampiya dhammanusasti anubatate yata pajati
everywhere Beloved of the God's religious precept reaches
where goes.

Hurrah for inscriptions!

Here was proof of diplomatic links between Ashoka's empire and the West, in the form of Alexander the Great's successors: the Egyptian king Ptolemy was probably Ptolemy II (ruled 285-247 BCE); Antigonus was probably Antigonos Gonatos of Macedonia[168]

TANTRIC BUDDHIST "MAGIC" YOGA begins to develop especially in Tibet – India. The following timeline indicates the early process of evolution of hatha yoga in India.

---

[168] Search for the Buddha by Charles Allen

THE AFRICAN ORIGINS OF CIVILIZATION, RELIGION AND YOGA SPIRITUALITY

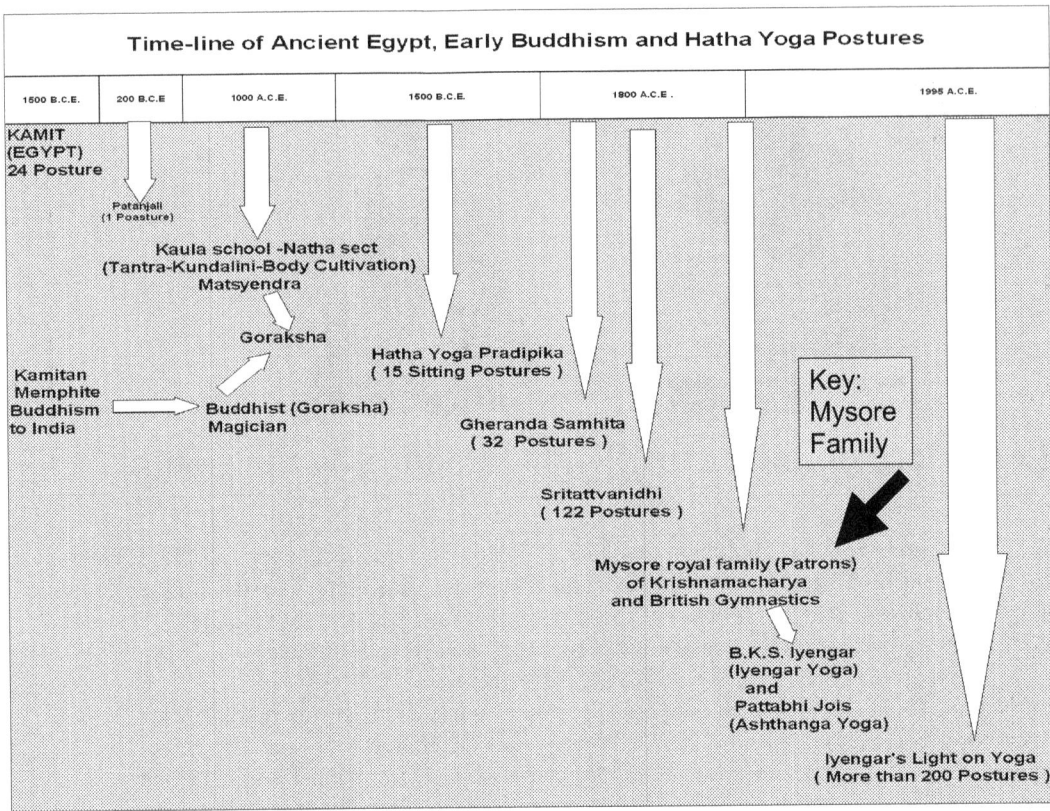

In ancient Kamit there were at least 24 postures in the spiritual practice prior to the time of Patanjali. In the practice of Kamitan Tjef Neteru (Egyptian Hatha Yoga) the "magic"[169] consists in using postures to engender certain alignments with spiritual energies and cosmic forces. This is the kind of practice repudiated by the Hindu sages and adopted by the Tantric Buddhists. Between the years 100 A.C.E. and 1000 A.C.E. the Buddhist Kaula school developed some postures. Then Goraksha developed what is regarded by present day Hatha Yoga practitioners as a practice similar to the present day. However, the number of postures only reached 15 at the time of the Hatha Yoga Pradipika scripture. The Mysore family was instrumental in the development since they were strong patrons of Hatha Yoga. Subsequent teachers developed more postures and vinyasa[170] (which was not practiced in early Indian Hatha Yoga) up to the 20th century where there are over 200. The teacher Krishnamacharya said he had learned from a yoga teacher in Tibet. Krishnamacharya's first writings, which cited the Stitattvanidhi as a source, also featured vinyasa (sequences of poses synchronized with the breath) that Krishnamacharya said he had learned from a yoga teacher in Tibet. So the practice of the postures in India does not extend to ancient times and did not begin in India with Hinduism but with Buddhism and Buddhism was associated with the Ancient Egyptian city of Memphis where postures and spiritual magic were practiced previously.

The following table (on next page) shows the dates in which the practice of spiritual postures was enjoined in Africa and Asia. The earliest recorded evidence for the practice of specific movements that lead to spiritual enlightenment occurs in Ancient Egypt (Kamit) c. 10,000 B.C.E. The earliest recorded practice in India of the yoga postures is c. 1,000 A.C.E.

---

[169] The term magic is not used in the western sense. Here it means disciplines of transformative power through sound, posture and ritual.
[170] vinyasa (sequences of poses synchronized with the breath)

THE AFRICAN ORIGINS OF CIVILIZATION, RELIGION AND YOGA SPIRITUALITY

Timeline Summary (1800 B.C.E.-1000 A.C.E.)

1800 BCE Ancient Egypt – Discipline of Sema Paut-Egyptian Yoga Postures, Arat Shetaut Neter (Goddess Mysteries), Arat Sekhem (Serpent Power), Hekau ("Magic)
Already ancient

550 BCE Cambyses invades Egypt – Buddhism, Jainism, Pythagoreaninsm, Zoroastrianism, Confucianism, Taoism - BORN

100 ACE -Tantrism – Emerges as a Distinct culture of Spirituality in Hinduism, Buddhism and Jainism Emphasizing Shaktism (Goddess female energy and Goddess as female aspect of the Absolute), Occultism, Magic, Kundalini

c. 460-490 A.C.E. Shakta and Tantra Spirituality -Writings elaborating on Tantric spirituality and mysticism of the Chakras

Goraksha – Develops Hatha Yoga to "Force" the movement of Kundalini (serpent Power)[171] # Postures ? 1000 ACE

---

[171] The practice of the Serpent Power also existed in Ancient Egypt previously.

THE AFRICAN ORIGINS OF CIVILIZATION, RELIGION AND YOGA SPIRITUALITY

Table 21: A Timeline of the Discipline of Physical Postures in Ancient Egypt and India

Time	Event
20th Century A.C.E.	1. Ananda Yoga (Swami Kriyananda) 2. Anusara Yoga (John Friend) 3. Ashtanga Yoga (K. Pattabhi) 4. Ashtanga Yoga (Pattabhi Jois) 5. Bikram Yoga (Bikram Choudhury) 6. Integral Yoga (Swami Satchidananda b. 7. Iyengar Yoga (B.K.S. Iyengar) 8. Kripalu Yoga (Amrit Desai) 9. Kundalini Yoga (Yogi Bhajan) 10. Sivananda Yoga (Swami Vishnu-devananda) 11. Svaroopa Yoga (Rama Berch) Women first admitted to Hatha Yoga practice
1893 A.C.E.	World Parliament of Religions – Vedanta Introduced to the West
1750 A.C.E.	Shiva Samhita – Hatha Yoga text – melds Vedanta with Hatha
1539 A.C.E.	Birth of Sikhism
1350 A.C.E.	Hatha Yoga Pradipika text - India
1000 A.C.E.	Goraksha – Siddha Yogis First Indian Hatha Yoga Practice
600 A.C.E.	Birth of Islam
Year 0	Birth of Jesus – Christianity
300 B.C.E.	Arat, Geb, Nut Egyptian Yoga Postures – Late Period
1,680 B.C.E.	Geb, Nut, Ra, Asar, Aset, Sobek Egyptian Yoga Postures – New Kingdom
2,000 B.C.E.	Indus Valley – Kundalini – Serpent Power-Lotus Pose
3,600 B.C.E.	Nefertem Egyptian Yoga Posture – Old-Middle Kingdom Period
10,000 B.C.E.	Serpent Power-Horemakhet Egyptian Yoga Posture – Ancient Egyptian

The Yogic Postures in Ancient Egypt and India

Since their introduction to the West, the exercise system of India known as "Hatha Yoga" has gained much popularity. The disciplines related to the yogic postures and movements were developed in India around the 10th century A.C.E. by a sage named Goraksha.[465] Up to this time, the main practice was simply to adopt the cross-legged meditation posture known as the lotus for the purpose of practicing meditation. The most popular manual on Hatha Yoga is the ***Hatha Yoga-Pradipika ("Light on the Forceful Yoga)***. It was authored by Svatmarama Yogin in mid. 14th century A.C.E.[466]

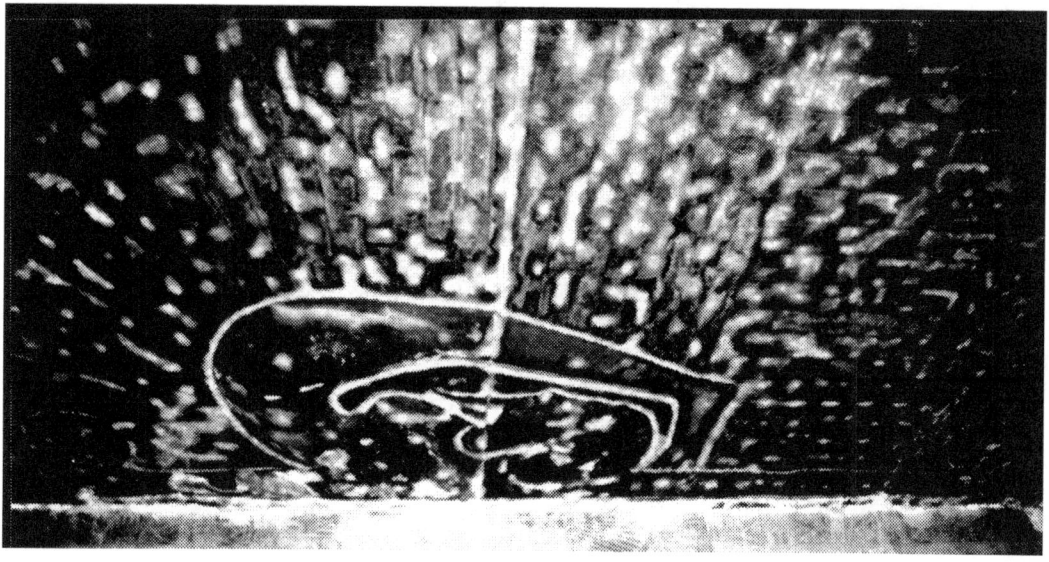

Plate 33: Above- The god Geb in the plough posture engraved on the ceiling of the antechamber to the Asarian Resurrection room of the Temple of Hetheru in Egypt. (photo taken by Ashby). Below: Illustration of the posture engraved on the ceiling.

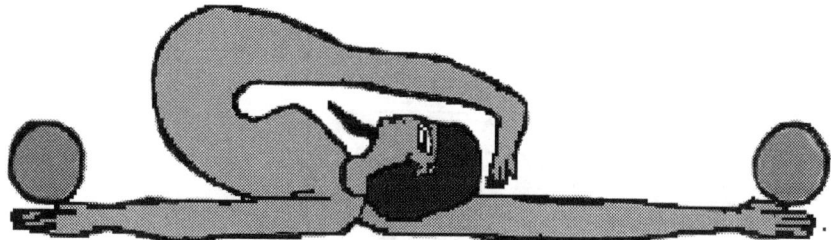

Prior to the emergence of the discipline of the physical movements in India just before 1000 A.C.E.,[467] a series of virtually identical postures to those which were practiced in India can be found in various Ancient Egyptian papyruses and inscribed on the walls and ceilings of the temples. The Ancient Egyptian practice can be dated from 10,000 B.C.E to 300 B.C.E and earlier. Examples: Temple of Hetheru (800-300 B.C.E.), Temple of Heru (800-300 B.C.E.), Tomb of Queen Nefertari (reigned 1,279-1,212 B.C.E.), and various other temples and papyruses from the New Kingdom Era (c. 1,580 B.C.E). In Ancient Egypt the practice of the postures, called *Tjef Sema Paut Neteru* which means "Movements to promote union with the gods and goddesses" or simply *Sema Paut* (Union with the gods and goddesses), were part of the ritual aspect of the spiritual myth, which when practiced, served to harmonize the energies and promote the physical health of the body and direct the mind in a meditative capacity to discover and cultivate divine consciousness. These disciplines are part of a larger process called Sema or *Smai Tawi* (Egyptian Yoga). By acting and moving like the gods and goddesses one can essentially discover their character, energy and divine agency within one's consciousness, and thereby also become one of their retinue, that is, one with the Divine Self. In modern times, most practitioners of Indian Hatha Yoga see it primarily as a means to attain physical health only. However, even the practice in India had an origin in myth and a mythic component which is today largely ignored by modern practitioners.

THE AFRICAN ORIGINS OF CIVILIZATION, RELIGION AND YOGA SPIRITUALITY

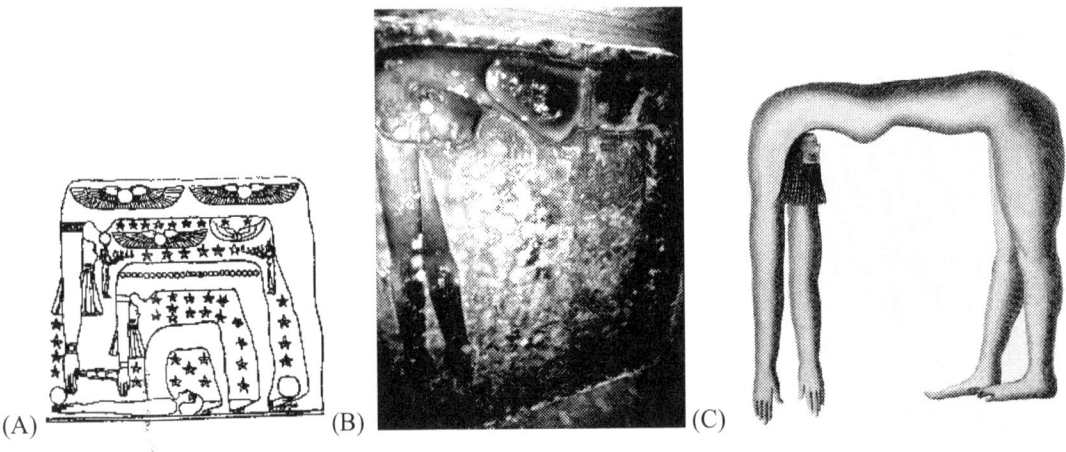

(A)   (B)   (C)

Figure 93: Above left: The Kamitan goddess Nut and god Geb and the higher planes of existence. Above center and right: The goddess Nut performs the forward bend posture.

The figure above (left) depicts another conceptualization of the Netherworld, which is at the same time the body of Nut in a forward bend yoga exercise posture. The innermost goddess symbolizes the lower heaven where the moon traverses, the physical realm. The middle one symbolizes the course of the sun in its Astral journey. This shows a differentiation between the physical heavens and the Astral plane, as well as time and physical space and Astral time and space, i.e., the concept of different dimensions and levels of consciousness. The outermost symbolizes the causal plane.

Plate 34: Below- The Egyptian Gods and Goddesses act out the Creation through their movements: Forward bend -Nut, Spinal twist -Geb, Journey of Ra – Ra in his boat, and the squatting and standing motions of Nun and Shu.

THE AFRICAN ORIGINS OF CIVILIZATION, RELIGION AND YOGA SPIRITUALITY

Figure 94: The varied postures found in the Kamitan papyruses and temple inscriptions.

Figure 95: The practice of the postures is shown in the sequence below.

Figure 96: Below- the Goddess Parvati from India, practicing the Tree Pose – modern rendition.

Many people who practice modern Indian Hatha yoga exercise do not know that when the practice of Hatha Yoga was adopted by Yoga practitioners in India in the first millennium A.C.E., it was repudiated by the established practitioners.[468] When it was opened up to the general community and ceased to be a practice of secluded yogis and was later brought to the West at the turn of the 20th century much later, it was not quickly adopted. Most people, even Indian practitioners, also do not that women were prevented from practicing the yoga postures in India until the late 19th early 20th century, pointing to the exclusive and male-oriented nature of the practice. However, in the latter part of the 20th century, due to the ardent promotion by a few Indian masters, it has gained wide notoriety. However, for the most part only the physical benefits have been adopted and acknowledged while the mythical and mystical teachings within the discipline have not been embraced generally. Beyond the misinformed and the dogmatic followers of orthodox religion, who repudiate yoga as an occult, evil practice, one comment by a famous personality in late 20th century Western Culture typifies the feeling of the vast majority of those who are involved in yoga for the "benefits" other than "spiritual" aspects of yoga (i.e. physical benefits):

"I don't want it to change my life, just my butt."
-well known actress (United States-2000 A.C.E.)[469]

Still, it must be understood that many people who are leading a worldly life are first introduced to the Science of Yoga through the discipline of the postures in ordinary sessions dedicated to promoting physical health, and later turn towards the spiritual aspects. However, there is much concern among advanced practitioners of Yoga in India and elsewhere that Western Culture has appropriated Yoga and converted it to something other than Yoga as it has been known for thousands of years. Instead of having Geb or Parvati as the role models, prominent (worldly) personalities such as actors and entertainers Julia Roberts, Madonna, Woody Haroldson and others have become the "ideal." So now, the same materialistic pursuits (physical health, beauty, sex-appeal, excitement, etc.), which are the hallmarks of Western Culture, have been projected on Yoga by Westerners who have appointed themselves as the purveyors of Yoga to the masses.

Many also distribute a myriad of products which are not necessary or desirable for the practice of yoga postures such as spandex, props, lotions, bikini yoga, etc., and conduct not spiritual yoga retreats, but yoga vacations, yoga parties and the like. Yoga originated as a non-secular spiritual discipline for transcending the world and has now been converted by many into a means to enjoy the worldly pleasures more intensely. This deviation from spiritual discipline to an instrument for enhancing worldly pleasure-seeking is perhaps most prominently visible in the discipline of Tantra Yoga. Using sexual symbolism to drive home a mystical teaching, Tantra Yoga has less to do with physical sexual intercourse between human beings than intercourse of the soul with the Divine. Yet, many so called practitioners of Tantra Yoga in the West tirelessly promote the idea that it is a form of "Sex-Yoga" designed to attain spiritual enlightenment and the heights of worldly pleasure at the same time. There are many misconceptions about the history and teachings of Yoga and this is perhaps one of the most blatant. The hedonistic[470] path of life which typifies Western Culture has been shown to be ultimately a dead end street leading to frustration and regret in later life. Yet people follow blindly the inane statements of ignorant religious and spiritual leaders, entertainers, politicians, marketers and advertisers, which lead to spiritual and worldly bankruptcy.

Many practitioners of the Hatha Yoga postures do not realize that the postures were not designed just to promote physical health. Actually, like the Kamitan system, the Hindu Yoga posture system is also designed to relate a human being to the gods and goddesses and the cosmic forces, which are symbolized by the use of animal names and visualizations using natural objects. This is accomplished by the practice of the movements, study of the mythology and philosophy behind them and meditative absorption with the principles and energies that they represent. Within the Indian system of Yoga Exercise, this aspect has been brought forth by Swami Sivananda Radha, disciple of Swami Sivananda of India, in her system called "Hatha Yoga, The Hidden Language – Symbols, Secrets and Metaphor." The promotion of health is only a means to an end, and not an end in itself. Rather, health of the body is a natural by-product of the practice of the Yoga disciplines for spiritual enlightenment. The ultimate goal of Yoga is to awaken the spiritual consciousness. Any other use of Yoga is a misuse or at least a limited use. In these respects, the Tjef Sema Paut Neteru movement systems of Kamit, Yoga from India, and Kung Fu of China are unique when compared to exercise systems. Western forms of exercise are designed to cultivate the external muscles and physical energy while the Eastern and African disciplines are designed to develop and cultivate the internal Life Force energy, which not only provides physical vitality, but also transcends physicality and the world itself.

Figure 97: Some of the postures as they developed in the Hindu Hatha Yoga system compared to the Ancient Egyptian Postures

Item for Comparison 12: Tantric Philosophy

> Tantric influence, however, is not limited to India alone, and there is evidence that the precepts of tantrism traveled to various parts of the world, especially Nepal, Tibet, China, Japan and parts of South-East Asia; its influence has also been evident in Mediterranean cultures such as those of Egypt and Crete.[471]
>
> -Ajit Mookerjee (Indian Scholar-Author –from the book *The Tantric Way*)

Tantra Yoga is purported to be the oldest system of Yoga. Tantra Yoga is a system of Yoga which seeks to promote the re-union between the individual and the Absolute Reality, through the worship of nature and ultimately the Cosmos as an expression of the Absolute. Since nature is an expression of GOD, it gives clues as to the underlying reality that sustains it and the way to achieve wisdom, i.e. transcendence of it. The most obvious and important teaching that nature holds is the idea that creation is made up of pairs of opposites: Up-down, here-there, you-me, us-them, hot-cold, male-female, Ying-Yang, etc. The interaction of these two complementary opposites we call life and movement.

Insight (wisdom) into the true nature of reality gives us a clue as to the way to realize the oneness of creation within ourselves. Tantra is a recognition of the male and female nature of Creation as a reflection of the male and female nature of the Divine which were brought together to create the universe. By re-uniting the male and female principles in our own bodies and minds, we may reach the oneness that underlies our apparent manifestation as a man or woman. Thus, the term Tantra means to create a bridge between the opposites and in so doing, the opposites dissolve, leaving unitary and transcendental consciousness. The union of the male and female principles may be effected by two individuals who worship GOD through GOD's manifestation in each other or by an individual who seeks union with GOD through uniting with his or her female or male spiritual principles, respectively, within themselves. All men and women have both female and male principles within themselves.

In the Egyptian philosophical system, all Neteru or God principles emanate from the one GOD. When these principles are created, they are depicted as having a ***male and female*** principle. All objects and life forms appear in creation as either male or female, but underlying this apparent duality, there is a unity which is rooted in the pure consciousness of oneness, the consciousness of the Transcendental Divine, which underlies and supports all things. To realize this oneness consciously deep inside is the supreme goal.

In Tantrism, sexual symbolism is used frequently because these are the most powerful images denoting the opposites of Creation and the urge to unify and become whole, for sexuality is the urge for unity and self-discovery, albeit limited to physical intercourse by most people. If this force is understood, harnessed and sublimated it will lead to unity of the highest order that is unity with the Divine Self.

THE AFRICAN ORIGINS OF CIVILIZATION, RELIGION AND YOGA SPIRITUALITY

Figure 98: Above- The Kamitan God Geb and the Kamitan Goddess Nut separate after the sexual union that gave birth to the gods and goddesses and Creation. **Figure 99:** Below: Three depictions of the god Asar in tantric union with Aset.

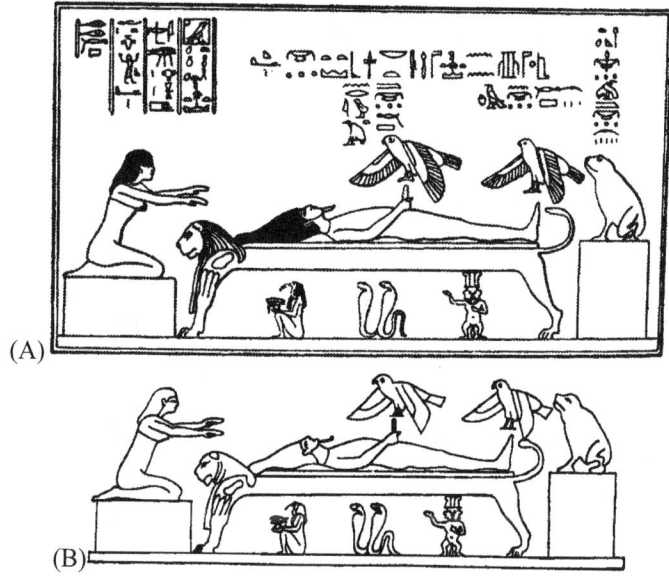

Figure 100: Above-(A) and (B) Reliefs from Ancient Egyptian Temples of the virgin birth of Heru (Horus) - The resurrection of Asar (Osiris) - Higher Self, Heru consciousness). Isis in the winged form hovers over the reconstructed penis of the dead Asar.

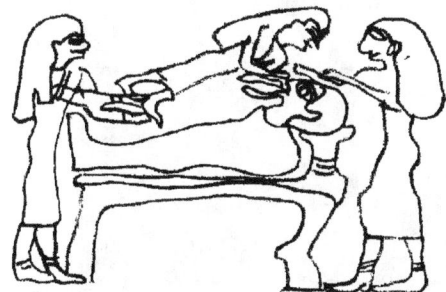

Figure 101: Drawing found in an Ancient Egyptian Building of The Conception of Heru[472]-*From a Stele at the British Museum 1372. 13th Dyn.*

Above: Isis (representing the physical body-creation) and the dead body of Asar (representing the spirit, that essence which vivifies matter) are shown in symbolic immaculate union (compare to the "Kali Position" on the following page) begetting Heru, symbolizing to the immaculate conception which takes

481

place at the birth of the spiritual life in every human: the birth of the soul (Ba) in a human is the birth of Horus.

Figure 102: Above- the god Shiva and his consort Shakti

The "Kali position" (above) features **Shiva and Shakti (Kundalini-Prakriti)** in divine union (India). As with Aset and Asar of Egypt, Shiva is the passive, male aspect who "gives" the life essence (Spirit) and creative impetus and Shakti is energy, creation, the active aspect of the Divine. Thus Creation is akin to the idea of the Divine making love with him/herself. Shiva and Shakti are the true essence of the human being, composed of spirit and matter (body). In the active aspect, the female is in the "active" position while the male is in the "passive" position. Notice in the pictures above and below that the females are in the top position and the males are on the bottom. In Kamitan philosophy, the god Geb is the earth and the goddess Nut is the sky. Just as the earth is sedentary and the sky is dynamic, so too are the divinities depicted in this way in Southern (African) and Eastern (India) iconography. Notice that the female divinities are always on the top position. This is classic in Eastern and Kamitan mysticism. It is a recognition that the spirit (male aspect) is sedentary while matter, the female aspect, is in perpetual motion, and the two complement and complete each other.

Figure 103: Above- Buddha and his consort. Tibetan Buddhist representation of The Dharmakaya, the cosmic father-mother, expressing the idea of the Supreme Being as a union of both male and female principals.

Tantric philosophy makes use of sexual imagery to convey the teaching of the principle of the opposites in creation as well as the principle of all encompassing divinity. Sexuality encompasses the entire creation and any symbol that denotes all-encompassing divinity is a tantric symbol. The phallic symbols as well as the winged disk and the multi-armed divinity all symbolize all-encompassing divinity.

Figure 104: Below left- The Triune ithyphallic form of Asar.[473]

Figure 105: Below right- the Trilinga (Triune ithyphallic form) of Shiva.[474]

Figure 106: The Winged Sundisk of Heru – Kamitan.

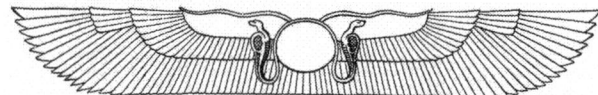

Figure 107: Below - the multi-armed (all-pervasive) dancing Shiva-whose dance sustains the Creation.

Figure 108: Below- left Ashokan[475] pillar with lion capital-Kamitan pillar with lion capitals. Center: Ancient Egyptian pillar with lion capitals. Far right: the Ethiopian divinity Apedemak, displaying the same leonine trinity concept and the multi-armed motif.

The trinity symbolically relates the nature of the Divine, who is the source and sustenance of the three worlds (physical, astral and causal), the three states of consciousness (conscious, subconscious and unconscious), the three modes of nature (dull, agitated and lucid), the three aspects of human experience (seer, seen and sight), as well as the three stages of initiation (ignorance, aspiration and enlightenment). This triad idea is common to Neterianism, Hinduism and Christianity.

The idea of the multi-armed divinity is common in Indian Iconography. However, the depiction above from Ethiopia spiritual iconography shows that it was present in Africa as well.

Item for Comparison 13: The Serpent Power Philosophy and Iconography in Ancient Egypt and India

History of the Serpent Power in Ancient Egypt

The Serpent Power teaching, known as Kundalini Yoga in India, was understood and practiced in Ancient Egypt. It is the teaching related to understanding the psychology of the human soul and personality as it relates to spiritual evolution. It is tied to the science of the Psycho-spiritual energy centers and the three main conduits of the Life Force energy, known as Sekhem in Ancient Egypt.[476]

Plate 35: Frontal Close Up View of the Great Sphinx

The origins of the Serpent Power teaching in Ancient Egypt go back to the inception of Ancient Egyptian civilization. This is proven by the fact that the oldest Ancient Egyptian monument bears the emblem of the Serpent Power tradition. The Ancient Egypt Great Sphinx once had a massive head of a cobra perched on its forehead. It is now in the British Museum. However, we know that the positioning of the serpent symbol relates to the Serpent Power teaching because a scripture describing the Serpent Power movement and how it leads a human being to spiritual evolution was discovered among various papyri related to the rituals of the Kamitan Temple. (translation by Muata Ashby)

Plate 36: Cobra of the Great Sphinx now in the British Museum

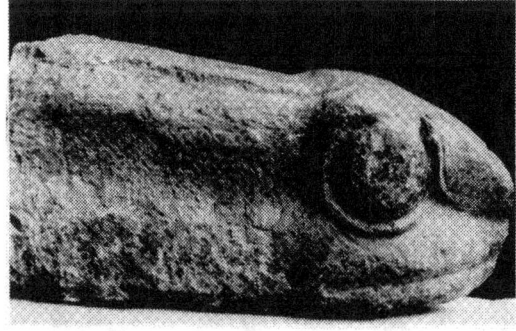

THE AFRICAN ORIGINS OF CIVILIZATION, RELIGION AND YOGA SPIRITUALITY
ORIGINAL SERPENT POWER TEXT TRANSLATION

Wadjit comes to you in the form of the Serpent Goddess to anoint you on your head.
She is the mistress of fire.
She is also the double goddess Wadjit and Nekhebit.
They rise up to your head through the left side and through the right side also and shine there on the top of your head.
Not with words (in silence, stillness) they rise to the top of your head encompassing all time, as they do for their father Ra.
They speak to you from within and illumine those becoming venerable Blessed Spirits.
It is they who give souls perfection, as they work their way, up to the brow, to their dwelling place on the brow, which is their throne.
They firmly establish themselves on your brow as they do on Ra's brow.
Not leaving, taking away the enlightenment, they stay there for you forever.

The Pharaonic headdress tradition visible in Ancient Egyptian culture from the headdress of the Sphinx in the Pre-Dynastic era to the early Christian era establishes a Serpent Power tradition and the tradition of the Pharaonic system of government in Egypt of at least 10,400 years.

Figure 109: Below: a diagram of the Temple of Amun-Ra at Karnak, Egypt, showing the Pylons (A), the Court (B), the Hypostyle Hall (C), the Chapel of Amun (Holy of Holies - D), the Chapel of Mut (E), the Chapel of Chons (F).

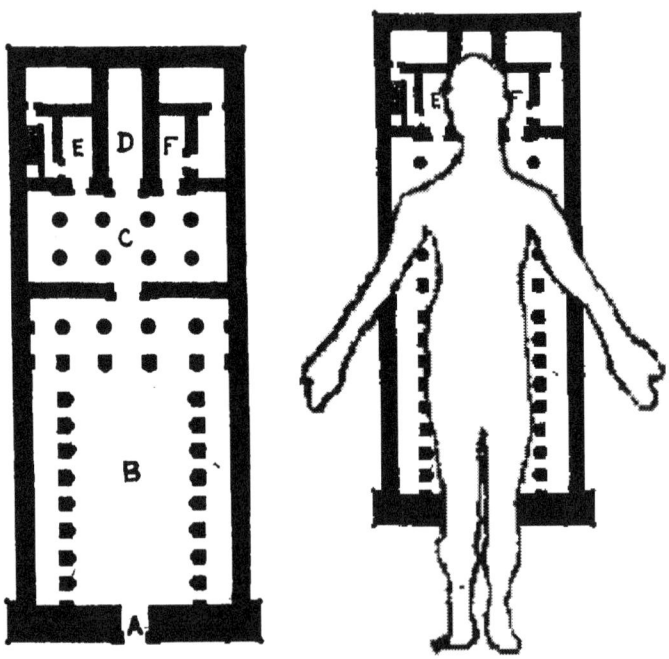

THE AFRICAN ORIGINS OF CIVILIZATION, RELIGION AND YOGA SPIRITUALITY

The typical Ancient Egyptian Temple incorporated the Serpent Power mysticism within its architecture. The Temple sections relate to the parts of the human anatomy as follows, and the serpentine movement is a precursor for the Hermetic Caduceus (Late Period Kamitan Philosophy).

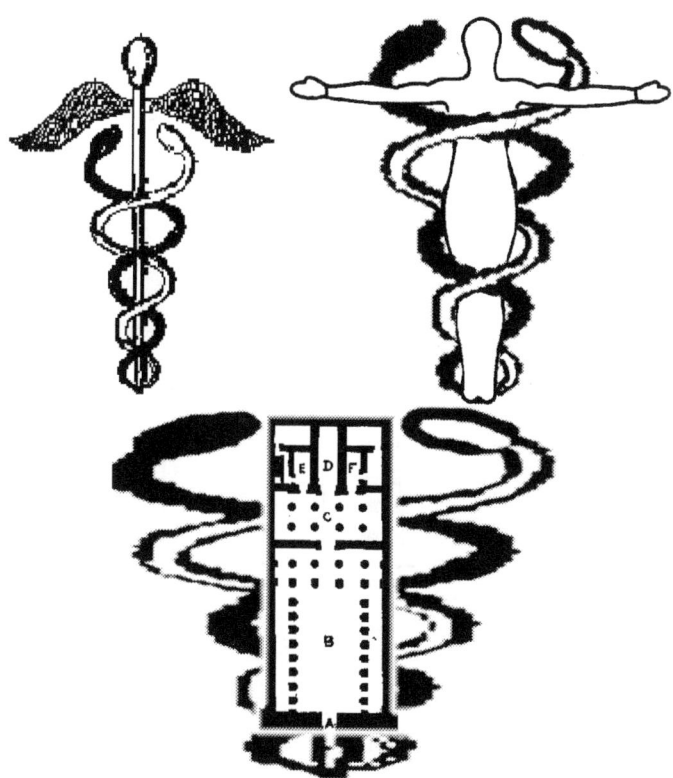

Just as it is described in the Ancient Egyptian Serpent Power scripture, the two serpents meet each other at the area of the Temple which correlates to the head of the individual human being. These sections of the Temple are known as the "great house" (left side) and the "house of fire" (right side).

Above left: Ancient Egyptian artistic representation of the yogi seated in the lotus posture displaying the three main channels of the *Arat Shekhem* (Serpent Power) and the *Sefech Ba Ra* (7 Life Force energy centers) 5th dynasty (4th millennium B.C.E.)

Above right: Indian artistic representation of the yogi seated in the lotus posture displaying the three main channels of the Kundalini Shakti (Serpent Power) and the 7 Chakras (Life Force energy centers) 19th century A.C.E.

Table 22: The Life Force:

Ancient Egypt	India	China
Sekhem	Prana (Kundalini)	Chi

The energy centers (chakras) wherein the Life Force energy is transformed from subtle to gross energy for use by the body are seven in number and are depicted as follows.

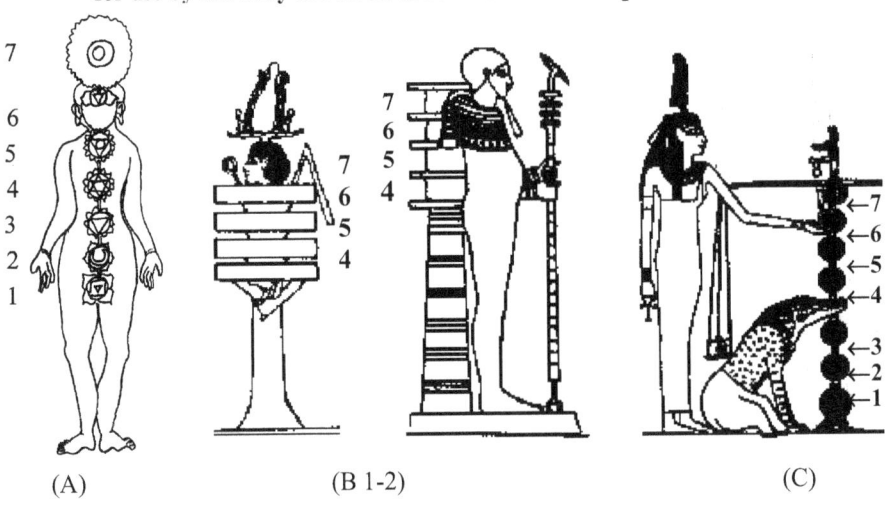

(A) (B 1-2) (C)

Figure 110: Left (A), the East Indian rendition of the Life Force energy centers (chakras) in the subtle spine of the individual.

Figure 111: Center (B 1-2), Ptah-Asar-Ancient Egyptian rendition of the Life Force energy centers in the subtle spine of the individual. The god Asar displays the four upper centers as centers of higher consciousness.

Figure 112: The figure at right (C) shows the scale of Maat displaying the seven spheres or energy centers called the *"seven souls of Ra"* and *"the seven arms of the balance (Maat)."*

Figure (C), above, includes the Ammit demon, (composite beast combining one third hippopotamus, one third lion and one third crocodile), symbolic devourer of unrighteous souls, biting between the 3rd & 4th sphere (energy center-chakra). This means that those who have not attained a consciousness level higher than the 3rd center will continue to suffer and reincarnate. The spheres represent levels of spiritual consciousness from the most ignorant (1) to the most enlightened (7). The lower three spheres are related to worldly consciousness and the upper four are related to spiritual consciousness and enlightenment, therefore, the lower must be sublimated into the higher levels. This is the project of spiritual evolution. Those who have attained higher (3rd through the 7th) will move on and attain enlightenment. This Kamitan system of energy spheres and the Caduceus with its central shaft symbolizing the subtle spine, and the two intertwining serpents, symbolizing the dual energies into which the central shaft differentiates, concurs in every detail with the later developments in East Indian Mysticism encompassed by the discipline known as Kundalini Yoga with its system of Chakras and the three main energy channels, Sushumna (central) and Ida and Pingala (intertwining conduits).

Figure 113: Left-An East Indian depiction of the Chakras with the Sushumna (central) and Ida and Pingala (intertwining conduits).

Figure 114: Two Center images- left - the Hermetic[477] Caduceus with the central Shaft (Asar), and the intertwining serpents (Uadjit and Nekhebit, also known as Aset and Nebethet); right-Ancient caduceus motif: Asar with the serpent goddesses.

Figure 115: Far Right- The Kamitan Energy Consciousness Centers (depicted as Spheres-Chakras or serpentine chains)

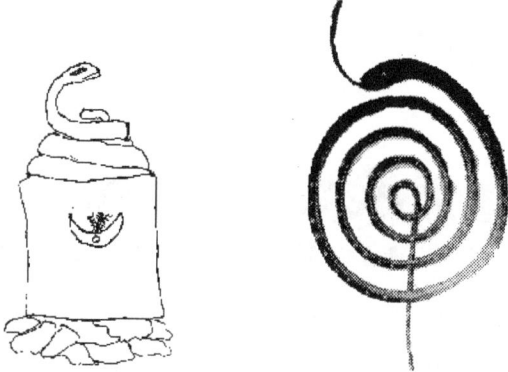

Figure 116: Above left: the Arat Serpent of Ancient Egyptian mysticism (Basket of Isis) showing the classic 3 ½ turns of the Serpent Power. Above right: the Kundalini Serpent of Indian mysticism showing the classic 3 ½ turns of the Serpent Power.

THE AFRICAN ORIGINS OF CIVILIZATION, RELIGION AND YOGA SPIRITUALITY

Figure 117: Below -Stele of *Paneb*. Dyn. 19. From Dier el-Medina (Waset Egypt) He worships the serpent goddess *Mertseger* (She who loves silence) in order to propitiate her favor in the development of Transcendental awareness.[478]

Figure 118: Below –An Indian yoga practitioner touches his body in the areas corresponding to the Chakras in order to focus the mantras (words of power) and develop the Kundalini (Serpent Power) while worshipping the Kundalini Serpent. From Rajasthan, 1858, gauche on paper.[479]

THE AFRICAN ORIGINS OF CIVILIZATION, RELIGION AND YOGA SPIRITUALITY

Note: With reference to the following three pictures, review the earlier section titled "The Early Practice of Yoga in India and the Connection to Ancient Egypt."

Figure 119: Below- Deity with worshipers and Serpents Indus Valley, Ancient India. Recognized as possibly the oldest known depiction of Yoga in India, this image incorporates the philosophy later known as Kundalini Yoga.

Figure 120 Below: The Serpent goddesses Aset (Isis) and Nebethet (Nephthys) worship Asar (Osiris), Ancient Egypt, Africa. The Hawk above symbolizes raising consciousness. The two goddesses represent the Serpent Power in Kamitan mysticism from the earliest period of Ancient Egyptian history.

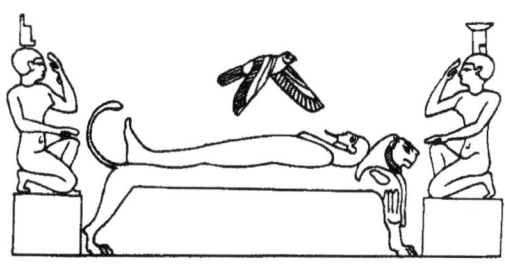

Figure 121: Below- The Serpent goddesses Aset (Isis) and Nebethet (Nephthys) depicted as the dual serpents with are in reality manifestations of the one singular essence.

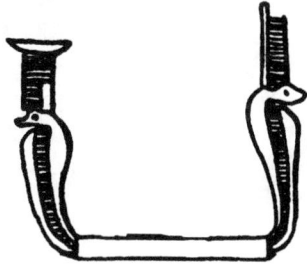

Figure 122: Below- Left-The Ancient Egyptian Papyrus Greenfield (British Museum) displaying the rings signifying the serpentine path of the Life Force, and the levels of spiritual consciousness (the Chakras or Psycho-spiritual consciousness centers).

Figure 123 Below: Papyrus Qenna (Leyden Museum), displaying the spheres signifying the serpentine path of the Life Force from the Spirit above to the heart below, and the levels of spiritual consciousness (the Chakras or Psycho-spiritual consciousness centers).

THE AFRICAN ORIGINS OF CIVILIZATION, RELIGION AND YOGA SPIRITUALITY

Summary

Thus, in the view of this researcher the evidences presented in this volume of supportable matching cultural factors and evidence of contact between Ancient Egyptian Sema Spirituality and Philosophy and Indian Yoga Spirituality and Philosophy and the nature of those contacts, show substantial borrowings from Ancient Egyptian Sema teachings and disciplines to Indian Yoga teachings and disciplines with regard to the factors of cultural expression. Therefore, it is possible to conclude that:

1. Ancient Egyptian Sema contributed substantially to the development of India Yoga.
2. The practice of Sema in Ancient Egyptian civilization was already established, thousands of years before Ancient Indian Indus and Hindu cultures, that developed yoga in India began.
3. Upon examination and comparison of the Kamitan Categories of Cultural Expression related to Sema Spirituality and Philosophy and the ancient and modern practice of Indian Yoga Categories of Cultural Expressions show clearly that the Factors (modes of expression) of the Cultural Categories of expression match closely in the two cultures.
4. Thus Ancient Indian Yoga drew from Ancient Egyptian Sema in the creation of customs and traditions as well as Yoga Spiritual Disciplines and Philosophy over a substantial period of Indian history. Indian Yoga Spirituality and Philosophy is a continuation of Nubian-Kamitan Sema culture albeit transformed through history, local folklore and customs, and influenced by outside cultures in many respects. However, the fundamental categories and principles of Indian Yoga culture match those of Sema in Ancient Egypt.

THE AFRICAN ORIGINS OF CIVILIZATION, RELIGION AND YOGA SPIRITUALITY
NOTES TO CHAPTER 6

[444] *In Search of the Cradle of Civilization,* 1995, p. 15, co-authored by Georg Feuerstein, David Frawley, and Subhash Kak.
[445] Ancient Indian scriptural written language
[446] *The RIG VEDA* Ralph T.H. Griffith, translator 1889
[447] Yoga Journal, {The New Yoga} January/February 2000
[448] Yoga International, {The Flight of the Alone to the Alone}, November 2000
[449] major temple and city in Ancient Egypt.
[450] See previous note.
[451] See previous note.
[452] Yoga Journal, {The New Yoga} January/February 2000
[453] *Living Yoga*, Georg Feuerstein, Stephan Bodian, with the staff of Yoga Journal
[454] *A Sanskrit-English Dictionary,* Monier Williams, p. 528
[455] For a summary of the argument and a bibliography on this subject see Mircea Eliade, *Yoga: Immortality and Freedom*, Bollingen Series LVI, 2nd edn. (Princeton: Princeton University Press, 1969), PP. 370-372 ("Patanjali and the Texts of Classic Yoga").
[456] *The Mythic Image*, Joseph Campbell
[457] See the section of this book entitled *The Serpent Power Philosophy and Iconography*. For more details on the Kamitan Serpent Power Yoga system see the book *The Serpent Power*, by Muata Ashby
[458] *Sports and Games of Ancient Egypt* by Wolfgang Decker
[459] Commonly referred to as Chapter 17
[460] Commonly referred to as Chapter 176
[461] See the book *The Wisdom of* Aset by Dr. Muata Ashby
[462] For More details see the book **The Glorious Light Meditation System of Ancient Egypt** by Dr. Muata Ashby.
[463] The term "Words of Power" relates to chants and or recitations given for meditation practice. They were used in a similar way to the Hindu "Mantras."
[464] Statement made by Swami Jyotirmayananda in class with his disciples.
[465] Yoga Journal, {The New Yoga} January/February 2000
[466] *Hatha-Yoga-Pradipika, The Shambhala Encyclopedia of Yoga* by Georg Feuerstein, Ph. D.
[467] *The Shambhala Encyclopedia of Yoga* by Georg Feuerstein, Ph. D.
[468] *The Shambhala Encyclopedia of Yoga* by Georg Feuerstein, Ph. D.
[469] Yoga Journal, {The New Yoga} January/February 2000
[470] **he·don·ism** (hēd'n-ĭz'əm) *n.* **1.** Pursuit of or devotion to pleasure, especially to the pleasures of the senses. **2.** *Philosophy.* The ethical doctrine holding that only what is pleasant or has pleasant consequences is intrinsically good.
[471] *The Tantric Way* by Ajit Mookerjee and Madhu Khanna
[472] *Sexual Life in Ancient Egypt* by Lise Manniche
[473] For more details see the book *Egyptian Yoga Volume 1*
[474] For more details see the book *Egyptian Yoga Volume 1*
[475] Constructed in the period of the Indian King Asoka (Ashoka) who adopted Buddhism.
[476] For a more detailed study see the book *The Serpent Power* – by Dr. Muata Ashby
[477] Late Ancient Egyptian motif.
[478] Dictionary of Ancient Egypt. Ian Shaw and Paul Nicholson
[479] Kundalini, Ajit Mookergee

Chapter 7: Comparison of Ancient Egyptian and Indian Religious Iconographical, Symbolic, and Metaphorical Cultural Factors

The Eyes of Heru, Krishna and Buddha mean the Sun and Moon

THE AFRICAN ORIGINS OF CIVILIZATION, RELIGION AND YOGA SPIRITUALITY

Item for Comparison 14: Exact Ancient Egyptian and Dravidian-Hindu and Bengali Terms and Names and Philosophical Correlations

Linguistic Studies Show Connection Between Kush (Ethiopia) and India

"Recent linguistic discovery tends to show that a Cushite or Ethiopian race did in the earliest times extend itself along the shores of the Southern ocean from Abyssinia to India. The whole peninsula of India was peopled by a race of this character before the influx of the Aryans; it extends from the Indus along the seacoast through the modern Beloochistan and Kerman, which was the proper country of Asiatic Ethiopians; the cities on the northern shores of the Persian Gulf are shown by the brick inscriptions found among their ruins to have belonged to this race; it was dormant in Susiana and Babylonia, until overpowered in the one country by Aryan, in the other by Semitic intrusion; it can be traced, both by dialect and tradition, throughout the whole south coast of the Arabian peninsula, and it still exists in Abyssinia, where the language of the principal tribe (the Galla) furnishes, it is thought, a clue to the cuneiform inscriptions (Mesopotamia) of Susiana and Elymais, which date from a period probably a thousand years before our era."

-Commentary on History of Herodotus by Henry C. Rawlinson

Kamitan Philosophy (from Ancient EGYPT)	Jain, Vedanta-Upanishads, Samkhya, Bengali Philosophies (from INDIA)
1. *Amun, Amen, Ama*- Egyptian Creator God[172]	1. *Ammaiappan* (Dravidian name of GOD).
2. *Annu (Anu)* The singular place-essence	2. *Anu* (one, atom)
3. *Buto*-Cobra Goddess.	3. *Bhujanga* (cobra), *Bhuta* (to be, become).
4. *Haari Om* – Divine name if the Supreme Being	4. *Hari Om*
5. *Maat*-cosmic order.	5. *Mahat*- cosmic mind
6. *Manu.*-	6. *Manu.*
7. *Om*- The Sound and name of the Divine Self	7. *Om*
8. *Ra - Rai* -God and goddess, spirit and matter	8. *Prana - Rai*
9. *Ra (fire)*, (sun symbol of God)	9. *Ra (fire)*, (*Surya* - sun God)
10. *Ra (sun)*.	10. *Ravi* (sun).
11. *Sahu* –glorious body	11. *Sadhu* aspirant striving for glorious consciousness.
12. *The Primeval Waters (Chaos)- Nun*	12. *The Primeval Waters (Chaos)- Nara*
13. *Sma (Sama)*	13. *Sama*
14. *Rai*	14. *Rai*
15. *Ushabti*	15. *Shabti*

---

[172] *and the Dogon Creator GOD, Amma*

The Ancient Egyptian Language and the Indian Bengali Language

As explained earlier, there has been a reluctance to look at other sources for comparison and extrapolation in order to determine the correct pronunciation for Ancient Egyptian words. The Kamitan (Ancient Egyptian) language, like the Hebrew, does not record most vowels, only consonants. The language could be even further reconstituted if there were some comparative work undertaken between the Ancient Egyptian and the Indian (Bengali). Even today, many Egyptologists and Indologists continue to work with outdated or erroneous forms of reference to the Ancient Egyptian Kamitan language just as the colleagues of Sudhansu Kumar Ray did over 40 years ago, as he relates in his book *Prehistoric India and Ancient Egypt*.

> "Indian scholars are generally well acquainted with Greek and Latin. They know much of Greek and Roman gods and goddesses, their arts and culture. But though Egypt is nearer to India than Italy and Greece and has huge literary and artistic treasures, nothing is known or discussed or has been explored yet by them. On the other hand, Egyptologists have seldom discussed or made comparative studies of Indian traditional folk-arts and culture and the Egyptian. Whatever information of Egyptian art and culture has come to us through the Egyptologists are mainly written in European languages and European Egyptologists generally have adopted in their popular writings all the Greek and Hebrew corruptions of Egyptian terminology which never appear to have a familiar look to any Indian scholar; therefore, he cannot imagine or feel at home with anything of Egypt. For example, we are told that the Pharaohs ruled Egypt. But we should know that the Egyptians never called their kings Pharaohs but knew Peros who ruled over them.†
> There was no Ramesses but a Ri'amasesu, no Bikheris but a Ba-ku-Ra, who ruled Egypt. Pyramids were not built by Cheops and Chephren but by Khufu and Khafra and they never called a Pyramid a Pyramid. They never named their country as Egypt but knew it as Ta-meri or Kem-ta. They never called their cities Elephantine, Thebes or Hermonthis, Kousai, Kynonpolis, Tanis but knew them as Yebu, Uaset, Qesi, Kasa and Thal. Egyptians never named their gods, Osiris, Thoth, Harpokrates, Horus, Socharis and goddesses, Isis, Nephthys, Neith, Thermouthis, Bouto but worshipped them as Asari, Djehuti, Har-pa-khrad, Hur, Sokan, Eset, Nebt-het, Net, Ernutet and Uadjit. This is why to an Indian, Egyptology on the surface seems very much foreign land unintelligible.‡ But as we learn Egyptian arts and languages through the originals, Egypt and Egyptians come nearer to us-even far closer than the so-called Aryans whom we know less but often make responsible for our languages, culture and everything."[480]

Notes by Sudhansu Kumar Ray
†"Pharaoh" is a Hebrew corrupt form of the Egyptian Per-O, meaning "the Great House." It was a title originally applied to the seat of the government and afterwards to the Emperor. In Bengal many historically important and old villages are still called Pero.[481]
‡"Some (Egyptologists) prefer to try to restore a name as it was probably originally pronounced: e.g., Amanhatpe. Others prefer a known Greek form (but of much later date), Amenothes. Others, disliking the first as uncertain and the second as giving an anachronistic and wrong impression, are content to use a colourless and conventional transcription, such as Amenhetep or Amenhotep (Amonhetep, Amonhotep). Sometimes erroneous forms have been used, as Amenophis, which probably is the Greek equivalent of the name Amenemope. The form "Thothmes" is a modem compound, as is also "Thutmosis": "Tuthmosis" and "Tothmosis" are late Greek renderings giving no idea of the XVIIIth dynasty pronunciation, which was probably T'hutmase, originally Djehutimase. "Rameses" is a modem compound: "Ramesses" is Greek....and so on."
Hall-GIGECBM, p. 54.[482]

Ray continues later in the book, quoting other Indian scholars, to offer some interesting aspects of early Buddhist names, which suggest a possible Ancient Egyptian origin that on their own are not conclusive but which in light of other evidences which will be shown later in this volume, deserve serious considerations in reference to their importance as a linguistic history of Kamitan embedded in the Buddhist tradition. This argument of course leads to the question of the philosophical origins of Buddhism due to its apparently close affinity with Ancient Egyptian religion.

> "Nearly half a century ago (in 1911 A.D.) Dr. Dinesh Chandra Sen observed, "The men and women in Buddhistic age had curious names, not at all pleasing to the ears ... But with the advent of the Sanskritic age, choice classical names began to be preferred. In Vijay Gupta's Padmapurana (written in 1484 A.D.) along with names which remind us of the Buddhistic period, Sanskrit names are found in large numbers...... He then quotes a. passage from the Padmapurana which contains the proper names: Rui, Saru, Kui, Ai and Sua.† A Dolly, a Dorothy, we know, who they are, we know a Radha, Kali, Kamala, Parimal, Nivanani, Malina, Kalyani, but we do not know who are Rui, Saru, Kui, Ai, Sua! Certainly, they sound Egyptian. Our household (pet)-names often include Gua, Zoti, Tepi, Khenti, Teti, Beja, Penu, Panu, Mana, Tutu, Naru, Hbu, Meni, Bhuto, Sunu, Nosi, Nofra, Buchi, Bacha, Punu, Kala, etc., which show a typical non-Sanskritic system of nomenclature again resembling Egyptian." †D.C. Sen – History of Bengali Language and Literature, pp. 391-2.

The following examples from Ray's book are included here, out of several candidates, as very strong evidence of the writer's contention of the connection between the Bengali language of India and the Kamitan language of Ancient Egypt. From the Egyptological perspective, these words have been confirmed by this author, as to their spelling, pronunciation and meaning and concur with the matching scheme proposed by Ray. Therefore, there is strong correlation here since the terms match on many levels or factors of correlation.

Example 1:

> "The 'Karonga wood-turners call their iron-ring-clip, which "unites two ends of the two pieces of wood, a "Sama." In Egyptian *Sama* means "uniter." I hope the readers will not only look to the resemblance in the words Hapor, Sama or Aske but will consider also their technological implication."[483]

Example 2:

> "A mother who is annoyed by the repeated unpleasant replies from her daughter or any younger girl of her household may stop her saying "mukh shabdi (or shapti) korishne." Don't make your mouth *"answerer (Shabti)."*"[484]

Example 2:

> "Rai means a queen in Egyptian and we know that Radha was a "Rai.""[485]

NOTE to Example 1 (by Ashby): The Ancient Egyptian word "Sma (Sema, Soma, Sama, Smai) – meaning "union," is the same symbol presented in the section of this volume entitled *"Egyptian Yoga and The Philosophy Behind It."* It represents the philosophy of uniting the lower self and the higher, i.e. what the Indians call "Yoga" and it can be found in the Ancient Egyptian Book of Enlightenment (Book of the Dead).

NOTE to Example 2 (by Ashby): The Ancient Egyptian term *Ushabti* means the images of the deceased to work for {him/her} in the afterlife, actually (literally) as a substitute for the person-does work or toils in their place.

NOTE to Example 3 (by Ashby): Rai is the consort of Ra, as well as the Queen mother in Kamitan culture. Ra is the Supreme Divinity whose main incarnation is Heru (counterpart of Krishna in Kamitan myth), and symbol is the sundisk.

THE AFRICAN ORIGINS OF CIVILIZATION, RELIGION AND YOGA SPIRITUALITY

Item for Comparison 15: Kamitan and Dravidian-Hindu Motifs, Symbols and Metaphysics Correlations

The following is a comparison of philosophical terms found in the Kamitan and Hindu philosophies of spiritual culture. They are noted here for there philosophical and or phonetic compatibility. This Comparison of Kamitan (Egyptian-Ethiopian) Philosophy and Indian (Dravidian-Hindu-Buddhist) Philosophy also shows symbolic, mythological correspondences.[486]

Table 23: Additional Kamitan and Dravidian-Hindu Motifs, Symbols and Metaphysics Correlations

Kamitan Philosophy (from Ancient EGYPT)	Jain, Vedanta Upanishads, Samkhya, Buddhist Philosophies (from INDIA)
1. Sema	1. Sama, Yoga
2. NETER, Neberdjer (transcendental absolute)	2. Brahman, Darmakaya Brahman, Darmakaya (transcendental absolute)
3. Seshen-Lotus (represents #1000)	3. Padma Lotus (represents #1000)
4. Heru	4. Krishna, Buddha
5. Asar and Aset	5. Shiva and Parvati
6. The Sacred Cow	6. The Sacred Cow
7. The Eyes of Horus	7. The Eyes of Krishna, The Eyes of Buddha.
8. Black Dot (symbol of Ra)	8. Bindu
9. Virgin Birth of Horus.	9. Virgin Birth of Krishna and Buddha.
10. The castration of Osiris.	10. The castration of Shiva.
11. In the form of Asar (Osiris), Horus is "The Lord of the Perfect Black."	11. Krishna is "The Black One."
12. Hathor Destructive aspect of Isis.	12. Kali (Durga) Destructive aspect of Parvati (Shakti).
13. The Nine Parts of the Spirit.	13. The Three Bodies, The Five Sheaths and The Supreme Self.
14. The Journey of Ra.	14. The Cosmic Dance of Shiva.
15. Cosmic Egg.	15. Cosmic Egg.
16. God abides in the body of all things.	16. God abides in the body of all things.
17. The Beautiful West.	17. The Buddha of the west.
18. Male (Geb, Osiris) passive principal and Female (Nut, Isis) active principal.	18. Male (Purusha) passive principal and Female (Prakriti) active principal.
19. The Isis Pose.	19. The Kali Pose.
20. Above as Below.	20. Above as Below.
21. Mount Meru Dwelling place of GOD.	21. Mount Meru Dwelling place of GOD.
22. Seven energy centers in the body.	22. Seven energy centers in the body.
23. The Bull of Osiris and Min.	23. The Bull of Shiva.
24. Stilling the heart Meditation from the Book of Coming Forth by Day.	24. Cessation of mind stuff Meditation from the Yoga Sutras of Patanjali.
25. Triune headed ithyphallic Osiris.	25. Trilinga of Shiva (Ithyphallic).
26. Memphite Theology and Creation Story.	26. The Creation Story from the Indian Laws of Manu.

27. "The Lord of the Perfect Black" Ithyphallic Egyptian vegetation God (Osiris).	27. "The Black One" Ithyphallic Dravidian vegetation God.
28. Mystical Nile River.	28. Mystical Ganges River.
29. Sun: GOD, Supreme Being-Moon: mind, intellect, wisdom.	29. Sun: GOD, Supreme Being-Moon: mind, intellect, wisdom.
30. Ba soul (originates from the Universal Ba-Neter Neteru, Atum).	30. Atman soul (originates from Universal Spirit. Brahman).
31. Medu Neter Sacred Speech (all Egyptian hieroglyphics are called Medu Neter).	31. Upanishads, Mahavakyas or Great Utterances.
32. Story of Horus and Set. The Uncle Who Tried to Kill The Newborn.	32. Story of The Uncle Who Tried to Kill The Newborn.
33. Hekau (words of power).	33. Mantras (words of power).
34. The Teaching of the Field and Its Knower (in Pert M Hru)	34. The Teaching of the Field and Its Knower.
35. The Veil of Isis.	35. The Veil of Maya.
36. Hetep Slab.	36. Lingam-Yoni.
37. Shu-God of Air, Supporter of Heaven.	37. Varuna God of Wind, Supporter of Heaven.
38. The World (Cosmic) Lotus rising out of Osiris.	38. The Cosmic Lotus rising out of Vishnu.
39. Seba	39. Guru
40. Mehen (Primeval Serpent)	40. Shesha Nag (Primeval Serpent)

Item for Comparison 16: The Creation Myth of The Kamitan God Khepri and the Hindu God Vishnu

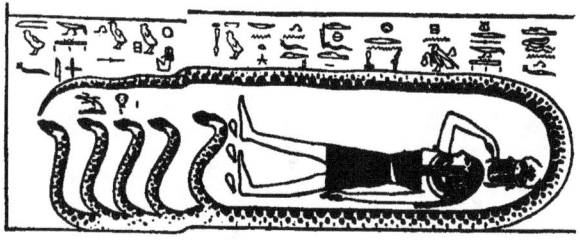

Figure 124: Above: The Ancient Egyptian God Khepri

Above: The Ancient Egyptian Supreme Being in the form of the evening sun (Tem), encircled by the serpent of "Many Faces" (symbolizing infinity and multiplicity). The Serpent symbolizes the power or Life Force through which Creation is engendered. The Serpent, "Mehen" lives in the primeval ocean out of which Creation arises. Note the symbol, " ⌒." It is an Ancient Egyptian determinative used to signify "limb," "flesh," "parts of the body." There are three symbols at the feet of Ra and next to these are the heads of the serpent. In mystical terms the meaning is that from the singular essence arise the three aspects, the Trinity, and from these arise the multiplicity of Creation. Thus, Creation is the very flesh or body of God. From his head is emerging Khepri, the Creator of the universe, who performs the actual act of creation. It is important to understand that the creation act is not something that happened once long ago. Khepri is said to create the new day every day. Thus, the implication is that creation is a continuous process, which sustains the universe at every moment just as a human being sustains their dream world at every moment during a dream. In like fashion, the Hindu god Vishnu (below) rests on the primeval serpent, *Shesha Nag*[487] who, like Mehen, is within the Primeval Ocean and sleeps over the bed of its coils during intervals of creation. As Vishnu sleeps he dreams the world which is the lotus that arises from his navel.

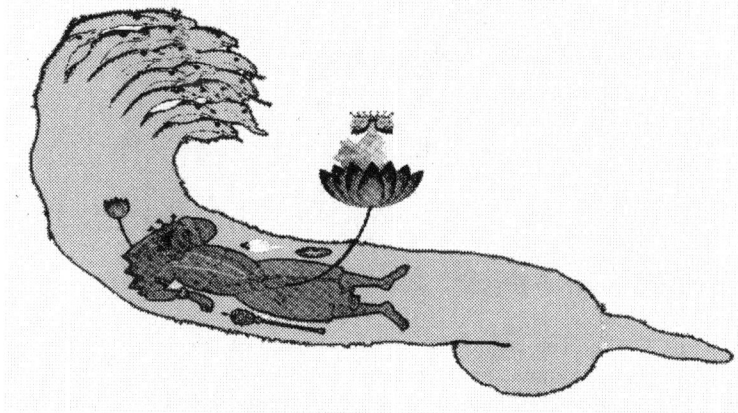

Figure 125: Above: The Indian God Vishnu

Above: The Indian god Vishnu sleeps on the thousand-headed (symbol of infinity and multiplicity) serpent who lives in the milky primeval waters of Creation. From Vishnu's navel arises Brahma, the Creator, in four-headed aspect, who causes the physical world to take shape. Thus, Creation is sustained by divine consciousness and the multiplicity of Creation is based on the multiform nature of the serpentine power as it is given form by the lotus divinity who is detached and supremely awake, but yet part of the illusion itself.

THE AFRICAN ORIGINS OF CIVILIZATION, RELIGION AND YOGA SPIRITUALITY

Item for Comparison 17: The Soul House

Figure 126: Below - Two Ancient Egyptian Soul-Offering Houses

Above: The Ancient Egyptian Soul-Offering House is a clay or mud constructed miniature house in the shape of a Hetep offering slab. It was used to place offerings for the deceased or the deity. Formed as a house, it is designed to be a model for the dwelling place of the soul of the deceased in the netherworld.

Figure 127: Below- Ancient Indian Soul-Offering House

The above Indian Soul-Offering House, made of terracotta, was found in India. Other Ancient Egyptian artifacts were also found in India. In the chapter of the book *India and Egypt: Influences and Interactions, 1993*, entitled *Transmission of Ideas and Imagery,* the scholar M. C. Joshi reports on Ancient Egyptian artifacts found in India:

> **"ART, ICONOGRAPHY, AND LEGEND**
> In the early centuries of the Christian Era, Egypt's contact with India is apparent in certain unrelated artifacts such as the solidly cast figure of the child god Harpocrates (Horus) wearing the crowns of Lower and Upper Egypt and the terracotta soul-houses, both discovered in the Saka-Parthian levels of Taxila[488] (now in Pakistan). It is, however, difficult to say whether these objects indicate just a survival of the Egyptian tradition or the presence of natives of Egypt in Taxila."

(See next page for images of child god Harpocrates)

THE AFRICAN ORIGINS OF CIVILIZATION, RELIGION AND YOGA SPIRITUALITY

Item for Comparison 18: Mysticism of Pointing to the Mouth and Name in Ancient Egypt

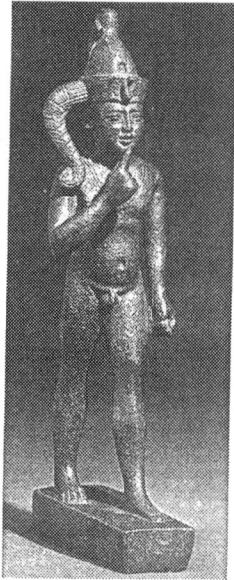
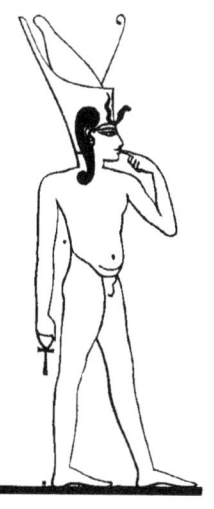

> **FROM: THE STEALE OF ABU:**
>
> "Be chief of the mysteries at festivals, know your mouth, come in Hetep (peace), enjoy life on earth but do not become attached to it; it is transitory."
>
> These words will open up the mouth of Asar _____. Oh Ptah! Open my mouth! Loosen the heavy weight of the bandages placed on my mouth by the god of my town. Come Djehuti, filled and equipped with words of power to loosen these double bandages of Set which are shielding my mouth.
>
> *Chapter of The Words For Opening the Mouth*
> Ancient Egyptian Book of Enlightenment (Book of the Dead-Ancient Egypt)

Figure 128: Harpocrates (Heru-papkhart, Heru the child)-Egypt First-Third Century A.C.E. Photograph-British Museum

Figure 129: Above left-Mauna Vishnu depicted in the gesture of a raised finger close to the mouth. Khajuraho. Tenth Century A.C.E.

Figure 130: Above right- Risya Sringa. Second century A.C.E.. Collection: Government Museum, Mathura. Photograph: Government Museum, Mathura.

Heru pointing to the mouth is one of the oldest and most important motifs in Kamitan spirituality. It relates to the concept of name and the concept of expansion in consciousness. The Ancient Egyptian word Ren means "name." The name is an essential attribute to the personification of a being. You cannot exist without a name. Everything that comes into existence receives a name. The Divinity thereby brings existence into being by "calling" its' name, which produces a vibration in the ocean of time and space and polarizes undifferentiated matter and causes it to take form as a physical object.[173]

---

[173] For a detailed examination of the principles embodied in the neteru or cosmic forces of the company of gods and goddesses, the reader is referred to the books *Memphite Theology, Resurrecting Osiris* and *Anunian Theology* by Dr. Muata Ashby.

THE AFRICAN ORIGINS OF CIVILIZATION, RELIGION AND YOGA SPIRITUALITY

Item for Comparison 19: The Gods Brahma (Prajapati, Krishna) of India and Nefertem (Heru)

Figure 131: Above left –Depiction of the god Brahma of India.

Brahma is the Creator of Creation, sitting on the lotus, which arises out of the primeval ocean, which symbolizes potential-undifferentiated, and unformed consciousness.

Figure 132: Above right- The god Nefertem (Heru pakhart) of Kamit.

Nefertem is the Creator of Creation, sitting on the lotus, which arises out of the primeval ocean, which symbolizes potential-undifferentiated, and unformed consciousness.

The Indian term "Prajapati" gives further insight into the relationship between the mythos of the Indian god Brahma and the Kamitan god Nefertem, the son of the god Ptah in Kamitan myth. Prajapati means "Lord of Creatures," i.e. the Creator.[489] In one Indian mythical account Prajapati rises on a lotus, out of the primeval waters.[490] In the book *Art – Culture of India and Egypt*, the following observation is made in reference to the Creation of human beings.

> In Egyptian cosmogony, the Sun-God Ra, we are told, shed tears of creative rays, from which all beings sprang into existence. In India, we have the counterpart of this myth in Prajapati's creative tears from which all creatures are said to have come into being. In the Chaos-Egg myth, Ra issues, like Brahma, from a golden egg.[491]

Based on the surviving iconography from the Indus culture, the serpent was revered as a sacred animal, apparently as a symbol of what in modern times has come to be known as the "Serpent Power" or "Kundalini Yoga." These images are not part of the Vedic tradition. However, they re-emerge in Hindu Iconography, such as in the image of Shiva surrounded by the bull and serpent motifs and he sits in the characteristic "lotus" sitting posture. The "Lotus Posture" relates not just to the posture, but to the idea of the divinity who is presiding over creation in the form of the lotus, and therefore sits on the lotus of creation as a king or queen sits on a throne. Therefore, the Hindu Brahma and Shiva divinities who sit on the lotus or in the lotus posture, are compatible with the divinity Nefertem of Ancient Egypt as he too sits on the lotus of creation.

Figure 133: Above- The Hindu God Shiva with his bull, Nandi and the serpent wrapped around his neck.

THE AFRICAN ORIGINS OF CIVILIZATION, RELIGION AND YOGA SPIRITUALITY

Item for Comparison 20: The Lotus Symbol of Ancient Egypt and Indian Hinduism

Plate 37: Left-Lotus from Egypt

Plate 38: Right: Indian Lotus

Figure 134: Below- The God Heru (left) and the god Krishna/Brahma (right) sitting on the lotus.

The symbolic usage of the lotus we just saw in the previous item for comparison is taken to another level when the correlations between the lotuses of Egypt and India are examined more closely. First, in both mythologies the lotus symbolizes the number 1,000 (manifold). Since the lotus opens and turns towards the light of the sun, it is a natural symbol in both Neterianism and Hinduism of turning towards the light of the Divine Spirit. Further, the lotus symbolizes dispassion in both mythologies as it grows in the muddy waters but remains untouched by the waters due to a special coating. So too a spiritual aspirant must remain detached from the world even while continuing to live and work in it, while at the same time turning away from the world and towards the Divine. In both mythologies the symbol is used to represent the creation itself, which emerges out of the murky, disordered waters of primeval potential in order to establish order and truth and make a way for life. The lotus also symbolizes the glorious fragrance of the Divine Self as well as the state of spiritual enlightenment. Thus, the symbol that was first used in Ancient Egypt was adopted in India, and though the name changes from Seshen (Kamitan - a source for the English name "Susan") to Padma (Hindu) its symbolism, number, myth and usage remained the same.

THE AFRICAN ORIGINS OF CIVILIZATION, RELIGION AND YOGA SPIRITUALITY

Item for Comparison 21: The Spiritual Eyes

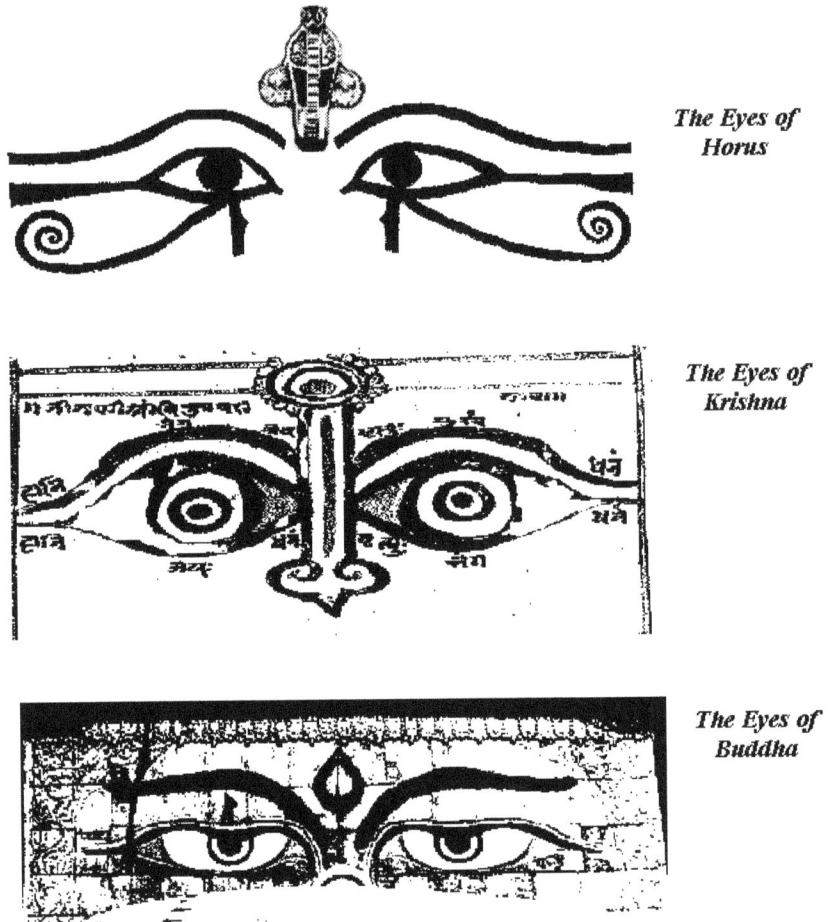

The Eyes of Horus

The Eyes of Krishna

The Eyes of Buddha

Top: The Eyes of Heru (Ancient Egypt), Center: The Eyes of Krishna, Bottom: The Eyes of Buddha. The right eye symbolizes the sun, ☉, and the left eye symbolizes the moon, ☽.

The Spiritual Eyes symbolize the attainment of divine consciousness. The left eye symbolizes inner vision or mental subtlety and enlightenment, the moon, and the right eye symbolizes the power of the spirit, the sun. Both together they represent the attainment of unitary, complete vision and power over the physical and spiritual realms. The symbolism is the same in Ancient Egypt with the eyes of Heru, and in India with the eyes of the god Krishna and the god Buddha, and also as shown in this text, the Upanishads state that the eyes of Brahman are also the "Sun and Moon."

Item for Comparison 22: The God Ra and the God Shiva and the Solar Serpentine Symbolism

Plate 39: Left- The God Ra of Ancient Egypt with the serpent encircled Sundisk

Plate 40: Right- The God Shiva of India with the serpent encircled Sundisk - one serpent with two heads.

Figure 135: Below- The Winged Sundisk of Ra - one serpent with two heads, from Ancient Egypt

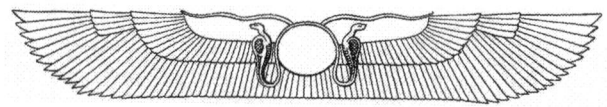

The use of the symbol of the sun on the head surrounded by the serpent first occurs in Ancient Egypt. It is characterized by the sundisk encircled by one or two serpents. The Serpent symbolism is used because its bite produces a "burning," like the scorching "fire" of the sun. This fire symbolizes the Life Force energy, which emanates from the sun, and likewise, the "fire" of consciousness which emanates from the Spirit and enlivens all as everything has a "spark" of divine consciousness to sustain its existence. This fire symbolizes the wisdom of the teaching, which upon entering the mind, "burns up" ignorance. The sun is a symbol of immortality and continuity, as it does not fluctuate like the moon. Thus it is a symbol of immortality. Also, the serpent represents rebirth, as it sheds its skin and takes on a "new" life just as the sun becomes as if reborn every morning in order to "create" a new day. This is a metaphor for the transformation that every human being must experience, from ignorance to spiritual enlightenment. Thus, the iconography of Shiva and Ra makes use of serpents and the sundisk as symbols of the movement towards enlightenment and rebirth as a spiritual being.

THE AFRICAN ORIGINS OF CIVILIZATION, RELIGION AND YOGA SPIRITUALITY

Item for Comparison 23: The Lioness Goddess and Her Destructive Aspect

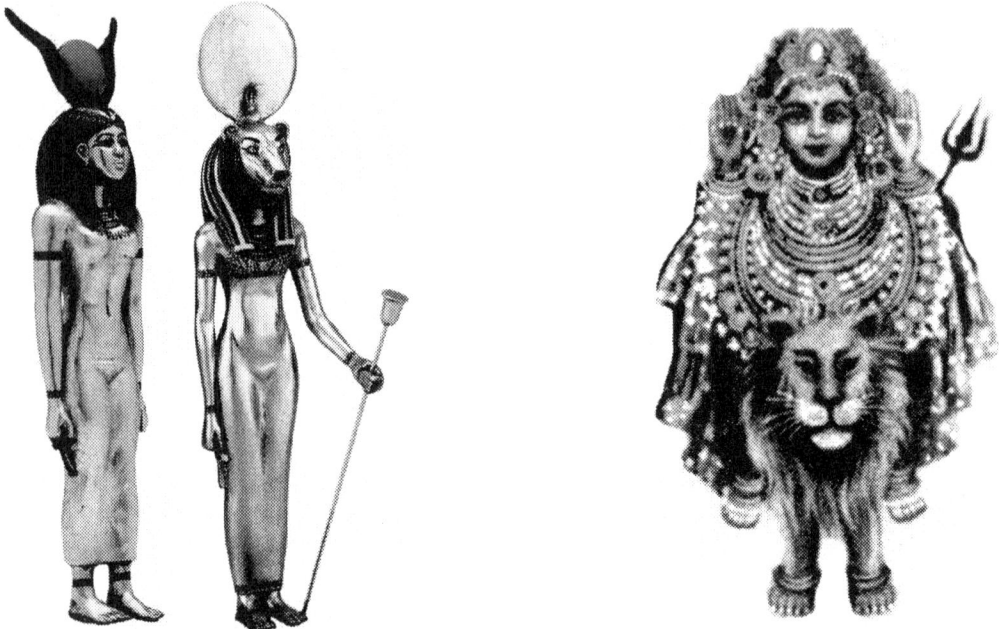

Plate 41: Above Left- The Goddess Hetheru of Ancient Egypt

Plate 42: Above Center- The lioness Goddess Sekhmet of Ancient Egypt, an aspect of Hetheru

Plate 43: Right- from India, the goddess Durga, with her most important symbol, the lion, her expression of power.[492]

The goddess Sekhmet of Kamit is actually an aspect of the goddess Hetheru, and in one myth of goddess Hetheru, represents her destructive form. In this capacity she is most closely related to the Durga aspect of the Hindu tradition. Like the goddess Hetheru, the goddess Durga also has an aspect called Kali, which is her most destructive form. As Kali, she is most closely related to the Sekhmet form of Ancient Egypt. In the ancient Kamitan mythology, Hetheru turned into Sekhmet in order to destroy the unrighteous. Similarly, goddess Durga becomes Kali, and in the Devi Mahatmia story destroyed the unrighteous.[493]

So both goddesses destroy ignorance and all of the attendant "demons" which arise in the mind of the ignorant, namely arrogance, egoism, anger, hatred, greed, lust, jealousy, envy, etc. Thus, they protect from adversities that one brings upon oneself and from the adversities that come from world. However, they also bring adversity in order to teach aspirants and the ignorant alike. When aspirants understand this, they ally with the goddesses and quickly vanquish unrighteousness, while the ignorant cry out in pain and wallow in misery. Therefore, the presence of the goddesses and the more destructiveness they display, the more auspicious it is because it means that spiritual enlightenment is close at hand. Therefore, they are propitiated with great reverence and devotion. Thus, the devotional aspects of the goddesses are Hetheru and Durga, while the Destructive aspects are Sekhmet and Kali, respectively.

Plate 44: Above left- The Ancient Egyptian lioness aspect, Goddess Sekhmet the "destroyer" in her shrine.

Plate 45: Above right and below- The Ancient Hindu goddess Kali the "destroyer" in her shrine (above).

More on Goddess Durga-Kali:

The goddess Kali-Durga has a wrathful form that transcends even the fury of Kali. In this form she is known as Chinamasta. Chinamasta is depicted as a goddess holding her head in her own hands. She is painted with yellow color and attended on by two yoginis, one on each side. In her left hand is her own head, and held in her other hand is a sword. She is nude except for some ornaments. She is depicted with her right leg out-stretched while the left is bent. In this manner the goddess destroys all enemies of the aspirant and then cuts off her own head to release the aspirant of attachment and devotion to her, so that the aspirant may attain complete and utter liberation.

In like manner, the goddess Sekhmet of Ancient Egypt destroys all people, the unrighteous as well as the righteous so that the initiate may transcend the duality of good and evil as well as attachment to virtue itself, for good as well as the bad are worldly concepts which tie consciousness down to the physical plane.

THE AFRICAN ORIGINS OF CIVILIZATION, RELIGION AND YOGA SPIRITUALITY

Item for Comparison 24: The Sacred Cow of Ancient Egypt and India

 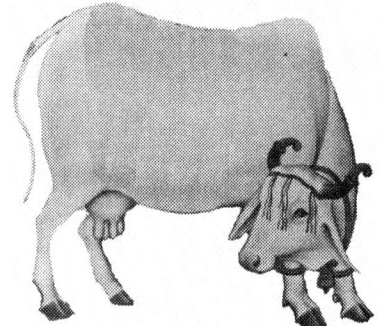

Plate 46: The Goddess Nut from Ancient Egypt (Tomb of Seti I), reverenced as the life giving Cow. Right- The Cow of Egypt and India.

The cow is revered by the religions of Ancient Egypt and India due to is association with the goddess. The Ancient Egyptian Goddess Nut is sometimes depicted as a cow, sometimes as the vast black sky, and sometimes as both. In this aspect as mother Goddess, she gives birth to the gods and goddesses which preside over and sustain Creation, as well as Creation itself. In her capacity as the cow she is an aspect of the cow goddess Mehurt, who represents the "fullness" aspect of the Primeval Ocean of Creation. Many of the Ancient Kamitan goddesses are often depicted with headdresses in the form of cow horns. The horns on the goddesses headdress, especially Aset (Isis) and Hetheru (Hathor), Nut and Mehurt, are a symbolic reference to the bovine (life-giving) nature of the female aspect of the Spirit. In Ancient Egypt goddess Nut was also known as the "Great Cow who gave birth to the sun," i.e. to the Creation and to the Divinity who presides over it.

The Yellow Goddess of India and Kamit

In India the Sanskrit root Gau (on earth), one of the sources for the word "cow," gives rise to the word Gauri (yellow, brilliant), one of the names of the goddess Parvati, who is the consort of Lord Shiva. The color yellow for the goddess constitutes another correlation with Kamitan spirituality. The ancient Egyptian goddesses and queens were depicted in yellow. She is the "Shakti" or Life Force expression of the Spirit (Shiva) which manifests as Creation. The cow is the symbol of that vehicle through which the spirit brings forth burgeoning life in the form of cattle and milk as well as all the myriad of dairy products that sustain people. The Goddess Parvathi is worshipped by several other namas (names) - Maheswari, Kaumari, Varahi, Vaishnavi, Chamundi, Durga, Kali, Bhuvaneswari, Mathangi, Lalitha, Annapurani, Rajarajeswari. The most popular forms are Durga and Kali. The god Krishna is often depicted with the sacred Cow. In this form he is known as "Gopala" or "protector of cows." He leads them to safety as he leads spiritual aspirants to enlightenment and deliverance from all evil.[494]

In the book *Art – Culture of India and Egypt,* the author S. M El Mansouri notes an interesting factor in the development of Cow worship in India:

> "Professor P. Thomas wrote in his book *Epics, Myths Legends of India* that the cow did not appear to have been particularly sacred in the Vedic times. References in the Vedas and even in the Epics indicated that beef was considered by Ancient Hindus a desirable item of food. There are passages in the epics which describe how holy sages entertained - their guests with beef and venison. The slaughter of cows was probably prohibited for the advancement of agriculture at a time when this was a difficult occupation and men had to be compelled to take to it and to leave off their ancient habit of killing. Then Professor Thomas suggested that this cow-worship had been imported to India from the banks of the Nile."

Instead of being treated as a divinity, the Shambala Encyclopedia of Yoga reports that in Vedic times, according to the Rig Veda, the cow was "Vedic people's most prized material possession."

Plate 47: Above-right Goddess Parvati from India – ancient rendition.

Item for Comparison 25: Amun and Krishna

Figure 136: Amun and Krishna and the Mysticism of Blue and Black

Above left: The Ancient Egyptian god Amun in his form as the blue divinity, meaning the deepest essence of creation. The original blue color of Amun can still be seen by visitors of the Karnak temple in the city of Luxor in Egypt. This deep blueness of Amun symbolizes his transcendental nature. Like Krishna of India, Amun is also depicted as black. (See below-left)

At right: The god Krishna of India in his blue form as the deepest essence of Creation. Both of these divinities (Amun and Krishna) as well as their alternate forms, Asar and Vishnu, are also known as being swarthy. Vishnu is also known as *shyam* which means "The Black (or blue) complexioned One." The use in this symbolic fashion occurs primarily in Kamitan and Hindu mysticism.

Figure 137: Above left- Black Amun (Luxor Museum). Above right- Black Vishnu-Krishna doll.

Item for Comparison 26: Heru and Krishna fighting Against the Forces of Evil.

Figure 138: Above: Top- The Pharaoh as Heru on the chariot. Bottom- Lord Krishna on the chariot.[495]

The Pharaoh in the form of the god Heru of Ancient Egypt, on his chariot, fights against the forces of unrighteousness to bring back Maat (order, justice, righteousness, truth) to the land. The god Krishna of India is also depicted on his chariot, fighting against the forces of unrighteousness to bring back Dharma (order, justice, righteousness, truth) to the land. The chariot symbolizes the forces of nature, the lower self, which have been controlled, sublimated and harnessed for the righteous purpose of attaining spiritual enlightenment.

Item for Comparison 27: The Mythology of Heru of Ancient Egypt and Krishna of India

The language of myth is an extremely important aspect of the comparison of two religious traditions. This example shows how mythological elements are equivalent in two apparently different cultures, using different names for the same mythological characters. While the names are different (Krishna and Heru) the forms, (as seen in the last example) and the function as well as the mythological plot and the theme of the myth are the same. In Hindu myth Lord Krishna is the incarnate avatar who is the defender of truth and righteousness against the unrighteous tyrant, his own uncle. In Kamitan myth, Lord Heru is the incarnate avatar who is the defender of truth and righteousness against the unrighteous tyrant, his own uncle.

Just as Lord Krishna was persecuted by his uncle, Kamsa, at birth, and rose to overcome this unrighteousness through Dharma (righteousness) and Vibhuti (All-encompassing transcendental nature), in the same manner, Lord Heru of Kamit was persecuted by his uncle, Set, at birth, and rose to overcome this unrighteousness through Maat (righteousness), Ur-Uadjit (All-encompassing transcendental nature), and a single-minded determination grounded firmly in the Higher Self, and not through violence, petitions or anger.

This example further shows how closely related Neterianism is to Hinduism. There are many religions, but these two match exactly in this mythological usage of the male incarnated savior who is pursued by the uncle and who will defeat him and take his rightful place on the throne to reestablish order and righteousness.

Plate **48**: Above left- Lord Heru of Kamit. Right- Lord Krishna of India

NOTE: Notice that the avian (relating to birds) principle remains constant in the symbolism of Heru and Krishna. In Heru (left) the symbolism of the hawk is a vehicle for the energy that he represents and it is also part of his body. In Krishna the peacock is also a vehicle for the energy that he represents, but here he is sitting and riding on it. This is not a difference in principle, but in iconographical style.

Heru and Krishna as The Divine Children and Masters of Nature

Figure 139: Left- Heru as a child (anthropomorphic form). Right- Krishna as a child.

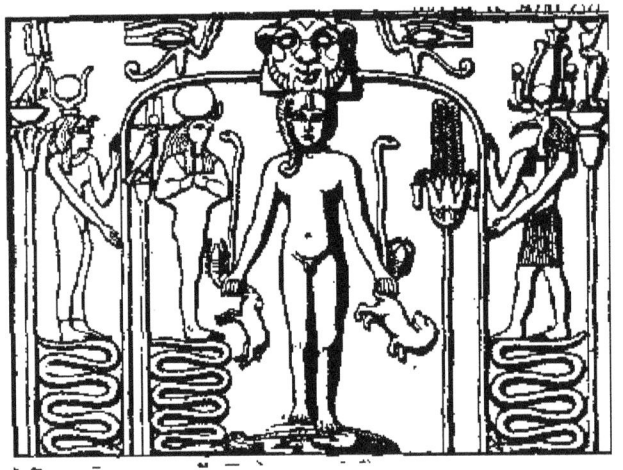 

The concept of the Divine Children is most important in Kamitan, Hindu and Christian mythologies. In each of these the divine child, who represents the birth of spiritual consciousness and redeemer of the soul which needs to be resurrected, is persecuted. Each of these personalities, Heru, Krishna and Jesus, were persecuted and put through trials which led them to becomes masters of their own lives and saviors to humanity. As the child, they are depicted as masters of nature, holding and or standing on animals, symbolizing their control over the lower nature. The images above, from Neterianism and Hinduism, recall the Indus Valley renderings of the seated personality who is among all the animals as if in reverence to that person as a deity (below). All of these images metaphorically relate to the mastery over nature, the lower self and the resultant spiritual enlightenment that arises from such an achievement.

Figure 140: Below Left- Pre-Vedic Male Divinity with Horn headdress-Indus Valley Civilization.

Heru from Ancient Egypt and Krishna of India leading the Divine Cow

Figure 141: Below left - The god Heru from Ancient Egypt in the form of the Hawk, leading the Divine Cow Hetheru. Below right: The hawk-headed god, Heru

The concepts of leading the cows can be found in the mythology of Ancient Egypt. The iconography above relates how the god Heru in the form of a Hawk leads the Divine Cow. In the same manner the god Krishna in India leads the Divine cow as well. Metaphorically, this leading process relates to how the Divine can lead the righteous spiritual aspirant on to prosperity, health and enlightenment.

Figure 142: Right- the god Krishna of India, leading the Divine Cow.

THE AFRICAN ORIGINS OF CIVILIZATION, RELIGION AND YOGA SPIRITUALITY

Item for Comparison 28: The Goddess of Wisdom- Aset (Isis) of Kamit and Saraswati of India and the Avian Principle

Figure 143: Below left – The Ancient Egyptian Goddess Aset (Isis) in her avian aspect (all-encompassing flight of wisdom, i.e. intuitional vision)

Figure 144: Above right: Hindu Goddess of wisdom, truth and learning, Saraswati, in her avian aspect.

In Kamitan (Egyptian) myth, the Goddess of Truth, Justice and Righteousness is MAAT. Her symbol is the feather. Maat is an aspect of goddess Aset. Aset assumes the winged from as a swallow or a hawk. The name "Aset" means "wisdom." She also is known as "Urt-Hekau," the "lady of words of power." In the Asarian Resurrection myth, goddess Aset outwits Set, who symbolizes egoism and vice. She gets him to admit his wrongdoing without him realizing it. This philosophical teaching embedded in the myth relates the power of wisdom to work in the unconscious mind to make a person speak truth in spite of themselves.

The image of goddess Saraswati is often shown on a white swan indicating purity of consciousness. In several epics and parables of Hindu myth, Saraswati is the goddess of wisdom and order, righteous speech. In the myths her power to "twist" the tongues of the unrighteous is legendary, as in the story of the demon Kumbakarna in the Indian *Ramayana* myth. He practiced austerity and earned a boon from the god Brahma. Kumbakarna planned to ask Brama to make him stay awake for 6 months of the year and then sleep for only night, so he would be able to indulge in his pastime of eating people. The gods, realizing he was going to ask for this went to the goddess Saraswati, the goddess of speech and intellect, and asked for her assistance so that he would not be able to make this request which would surely destroy the world. So, when Kumbakarna was about to speak, the goddess twisted his intellect so that he requested the opposite, to be asleep for 6 months of the year, and only awake for 1 day. Here we have a correlation of gender, form, function and mythological plot. The avian motif is present in both mythic characters (Aset and Saraswati).

THE AFRICAN ORIGINS OF CIVILIZATION, RELIGION AND YOGA SPIRITUALITY

Item for Comparison 29: The Ancient Egyptian Hetep (Offering) Slab and the Hindu Lingam Yoni

The "Hetep Slab" or Offering Table is another important tantric symbol and ritual artifact from Ancient Egypt. It is typically composed of a stone slab with male ⌒, thigh, and female ⇌, duck, symbols carved into the top, along with the symbol of Supreme Peace, ⌂, or Hetep, which consists of a loaf of bread, ◯, and an offering mat, ▭, which was composed of woven reeds (in Pre-Dynastic times), and two libation vessels ⋂⋂. In ancient times the actual offering mat consisted of the articles themselves (loaf, thigh, duck and libation fluids (water, wine or milk), but in Dynastic times (5,500B.C.E-400 A.C.E) the table top or slab contained the articles as engraved glyphs. The top of the table has grooves, which channel the libations around the offering toward the front and center of the table and then out through the outermost point of the protruding section. The hetep symbol, ⌂, means "rest", "peace" and "satisfaction" and when it is used in the hetep offering ritual it refers to the satisfaction of the neters (gods and goddesses) which comes from uniting the male and female principles into one Transcendental Being. The Hetep Offering Table can be seen in the innermost shrine of the Papyrus of Ani (Book of Coming Forth By Day of Ani) where the initiate Ani is shown making two offerings, one female and the other male. It can also be seen in the major museums around the world which have Ancient Egyptian collections.

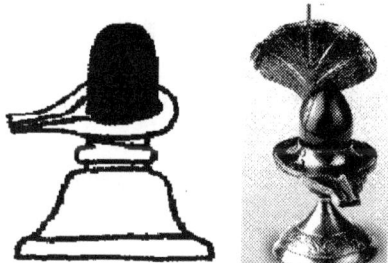

Figure 145: Above left- Line art drawing of the Hindu Lingam-Yoni. Right: Picture of an actual Hindu Lingam-Yoni offering stand.

The *Lingam-Yoni* from India is used in the same way as the Hetep Slab of Ancient Egypt. The protruding section (lingam) is a stone which symbolizes the male phallus (penis), a symbol of God (Shiva) and the oval base (yoni) which represents the female vulva as a symbol of Creation. Thus the lingam-yoni symbolizes the union of the male and female sex organs. The libation is poured over the Lingam, and it runs down to the Yoni, which surrounds the Lingam. Then it is channeled towards the front and center of the structure and then out through the outermost point of the protruding section. The libation is poured continuously and symbolizes a continuous flow of thought and feeling towards the Divine. Milk is often used in the ritual involving the Lingam-Yoni. Thus, both the Hetep Slab and Lingam-Yogi symbols of Kamit and India, respectively, specifically refers to the union of the male and female principles within the human heart, the opposites, and discovering the androgynous Supreme Spirit within.

THE AFRICAN ORIGINS OF CIVILIZATION, RELIGION AND YOGA SPIRITUALITY

Item for Comparison 30: The Lotus Feet of Vishnu and Asar

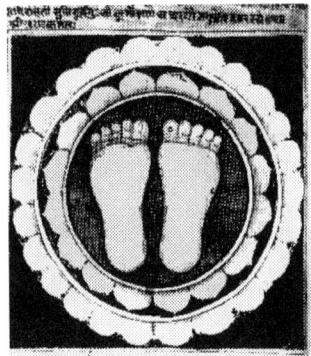

Figure 146: Above left- Lotus Feet of the god Vishnu in Hindu Mythology

From his feet came the earth. He is the innermost Self of all.

-Mundaka Upanishad[496]

The passage above from the Mundaka Upanishad denotes the reverence in Hindu culture for the feet of God. These feet stand on the sacred lotus of Creation and wherever they step there is glory and abundant life. In the same manner, in modern times the feet of gurus are adored and touched as a form of prostration and reverence for the divine consciousness that resides in that personality that gives out enlightening words to all and relieves the sorrow of life.

Figure 147: Above right: Lotus Feet of the god Asar in Kamitan Mythology. Full picture shown below center.

The teaching of the lotus feet symbolizes the understanding that the Divine is the source itself (Primeval Ocean) from which the lotus (creation) arises. Like Vishnu of India, the god Asar of Ancient Egypt is also known as the lotus footed one, the source itself from which all life arises. Like Vishnu, Asar is the "Lord of the *Black*" and from this blackness, the deepest darkness wherein no concepts apply, all Creation arises. Therefore, the lotus which symbolizes Creation is seen rising up from his feet.

Item for Comparison 31: The Crescent Moon

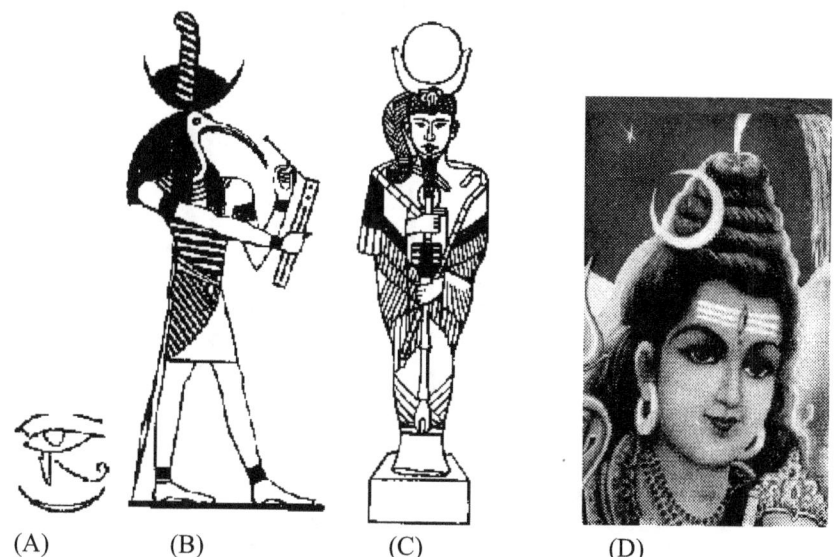

(A)　　　(B)　　　(C)　　　(D)

Figure 148: Left- A- symbol of Djehuti. B- the god Djehuti. C- The Ancient Egyptian god Khonsu. B & C: The Ancient Egyptian Gods Djehuti (symbol of intellect) and Khonsu (reflection of consciousness in time and space) with their Crescent Moon symbolisms.

Figure 149: Right- D- The Hindu God Shiva with his symbol, the Crescent Moon, (symbol of increasing wisdom).

The symbol of the crescent moon is of special importance to the Kamitans and the Hindus. As a symbol of the reflection of the sun, the moon symbolizes the reflection of Divine Consciousness which every human being can achieve as they turn towards the source of light, the Divine Self, as symbolized by the sun. The moon does not produce its own luminescence. It depends on the sun. In the same manner, the human mind, that is, human consciousness or soul, is not self-sustaining. It owes not only its existence, but also its continued survival to the presence of the sun, i.e. the Spirit.

The crescent moon symbolizes waxing or increasing spiritual knowledge, increasing purity of intellect and the development of intuitional wisdom. This is accomplished through all of the means available that the sages have prescribed for the practice of the yogic disciplines: Devotion, Study of the wisdom teachings, Right action and Meditation.

THE AFRICAN ORIGINS OF CIVILIZATION, RELIGION AND YOGA SPIRITUALITY

Item for Comparison 32: Worship of the Tree Goddess in Ancient Egypt and India

Figure 150: Below left-Worship of the Tree Goddess. Indus Valley, pre-Vedic Ancient India.

Figure 151: Above-right: Worship of the life sustaining tree goddess, Papyrus of Ani, Ancient Egypt, Africa.

The tree goddess motif is fundamental in the art of the Ancient Indus Valley tradition. In the picture above a divinity in a tree receives a worshipper. The concept of the sacred tree remains fundamental in Hindu myth and perhaps the most important example of this is the tree under which Buddha sat in order to meditate and attain enlightenment. He meditated for forty-nine days and forty-nine nights under the Bodhi Tree and attained enlightenment on the fiftieth.

Both in Kamitan and Hindu myth, the tree is a life sustaining and enlightening source. The tree goddess motif is fundamental in Ancient Egyptian iconography. It symbolizes the goddess in general, but Nut and Hetheru in particular as the compassionate, life-giving female divine essence. The goddess sustains as a mother looking after her children, and when their time is up on earth she reaches down and lifts them up to the heavens.

In Kamitan myth the tree goddess in the form of goddess Nut treats all human beings as she did her son Asar in ancient times. As she lifted him up following his resurrection, so too she treats all human beings as though all human beings are Asar, incarnated souls who will one day return to the source from whence they came.

Item for Comparison 33: The Multi-armed Divinity in Ancient Egypt and India

The "multi-armed" divinity is symbolic of the all-pervasive nature of the Transcendental essence, which supports Creation. This essence is all pervasive because it is the subtlest essence of all. Therefore, its arms stretch forth as a juggler, sustaining everything that exists. The Hymns to Aton by Akhnaton display a highly advanced understanding of the monistic nature of the Divine, even as it manifests as the myriad of forms that can be found in Creation. This is an understanding of the non-dual nature of the Divine as well as the all-encompassing character of Divine consciousness.[497]

Figure 152: Below- Left- The Priest Per-aah (Pharaoh) Akhnaton worships the multi-armed divinity, Aton, with his wife Nefertiti and their daughters. At Right- Late period depiction of the multi-armed, all-encompassing Neberdjer encompasses all the attributes of the other gods and goddesses.

Figure 153: Below far right- The multi-armed (all-pervasive) dancing Shiva as *Nataraja*, Lord of the Cosmic Dance -whose dance sustains the Creation.

Figure 154: Below- Far left: The Ethiopian divinity Apedemak, displaying the same leonine trinity concept and the multi-armed motif.

Item for Comparison 34: Asar of Kamit, Vishnu of India and the Sacred Cows

Figure 155: Above left- The God Asar of Ancient Egypt

Asar is known as the bull because he impregnates the seven cow goddesses who constitute the seven aspects of Creation. Thus, in Ancient Egypt the bull and seven cows also represent Asar as the bull or power behind the Life Force energy centers (the cows) that sustain the soul.

Figure 156: Above right- The God Vishnu of India

Vishnu, or his most popular avatar (incarnation Krishna), is known as the bull because he impregnates the cow goddesses who constitute the souls of Creation. So the Hindu divinity is the bull or power which sustains the soul.

As stated earlier, Asar and Vishnu, are also known as being swarthy and they are also known as "The Black One."

Item for Comparison 35: The Gods Asar of Kamit and Shiva of India and their Symbols.

Figure 157: Left- The god Asar (Osiris) of Kamit

Asar is understood as the source of Creation itself. He is likened to a bull because a bull has tremendous generative power. Here he is shown with his symbol, the Apis Bull.

The male divinity, symbolized as the bull, is fundamental in Ancient Egyptian iconography. In Ancient Egypt bulls were held as sacred mascots in temples, oracles and incarnations of the divinity Asar.

Figure 158: Right- The God Shiva of India

Shiva is shown here with his important symbol, the bull, Nandi. Shiva is also known to have vast generative power, and like Asar, he was mythologically castrated. Castration in mystical philosophy symbolizes the limitation or control of the spirit in the sense that the power of the spirit is to be regulated by the higher nature as opposed to the lower.

Figure 159: Below - The Brahma Bull in Pre-Vedic India –Indus Seal

It is believed by some scholars that the height of Indus culture was reached between the years 2150-1750 B.C.E.[498] This estimate is based on Carbon 14 dating of objects that were discovered there. From seals such as those above, it is clear that there was a reverence for the bull and animal nature related to the male principle and there was reverence for the tree and vegetation in general, related to the female principle.

Item for Comparison 36: The Primordial Mother of Creation in Ancient Egypt and India

Figure 160: Above left- Parashakty - The Trimurti Mother. Right: Trinity of Brahma- Vishnu- Shiva.

In the early Hindu-Brahmanic period of Indian theology, Goddess Parashakty was revered as the original source from which the Trimurti (Trinity of Brahma, Vishnu and Shiva or the three aspects of either Vishnu, Shiva or Devi)[499] arises. Devi means goddess generally. In the specific form, the term Parashakty relates to Parvati, Uma or Shakti, the wife of Shiva. In this aspect of Parashakty, the Indian goddess is equal to the Ancient Egyptian goddess Mehurt.

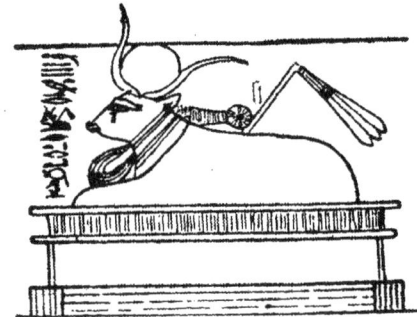

Figure 161: Above right- The Ancient Egyptian Goddess Mehurt-Mother of Creation

Ancient Egyptian Myth centered around the Creation of the universe out of a Primeval Ocean.[500] This ocean was formless and homogenous. From this original essence, the Supreme Being arose in the form of the all-encompassing Divinity known as *Neberdjer* (All-encompassing existence) or *Pa Neter* (The Supreme Being). Neberdjer is an androgynous, formless being. However, Neberdjer received many symbolic names and forms throughout the vast Ancient Egyptian history. Neberdjer was also known as *Pa Neter* or "The God," distinguishing the Supreme Divinity from the neteru, the Gods and Goddesses. The Neteru symbolize cosmic powers through which the Supreme Being manifests. Many forms were associated with the Supreme Divinity. These included both male and female forms. Thus, the Ancient Egyptian gods, Asar and Amun, who were male, were also known as Neberdjer. The Ancient Egyptian cow goddess, Mehurt, was also known as Neberdjer, the source of creation. In order to engender Creation, Neberdjer transformed into a Trinity, Amun-Ra-Ptah. This signifies that from a self-existent, singular and formless mass (Nu, the Primeval Ocean) the phenomenal universe consisting of objects with forms that have been given names, arises.[501]

Item for Comparison 37: The Divine Egg in Ancient Egypt and India

From Indian Laws of Manu (Indian):

Manu is a Sage-Creator God of Indian Hindu-Vedic tradition who recounts the process of Creation wherein the *Self-Existent Spirit* (God) felt desire. Wishing to create all things from His own body, God created the primeval waters (Nara) and threw a seed into it. From the seed came the golden cosmic egg. The Self-Existent Spirit (Narayana) developed into Brahma (Purusha) and after a year of meditation, divided into two parts (Male and Female).

Thus, Indian myth holds that Creation arose from one single Cosmic Egg. From this egg, all the universe emerged. It is said that the "golden Brahma" emerged. Brahma is the creator aspect of the Absolute Self. The primeval Egyptian creation myth is similar in many respects to the Creation story from the Indian mythology associated with the *Laws of Manu*. The Ancient Egyptian and Hindu Creation stories originate in the far reaches of antiquity (5,500 B.C.E. and 200 B.C.E. respectively). Their similarity to each other hints at their common origin.

The story related in the Ancient Egyptian *Papyrus of Nesi Amsu* is that this primeval God laid an egg in the primeval *formless* waters from which the God him/herself emerged. This primordial God who emerged out of the waters created or emanated Ra-Tem-Nefertem, the Sun or Life Force, Djehuti (Djehuti), the carrier of the **Divine Word** or creative medium, and Maat, the principle of cosmic order and regularity. The underlying emphasis was on the fact that all of these, including human beings and the phenomenal world, are in reality emanations from that same Primeval Ocean. This means that there is one primordial essence for all things, be they plants, humans, gods and goddesses, etc.

So, in Ancient Egypt the god Ra, the "Great Cakler" emerges from the Egg. Ra is the "Golden Sun" who creates the world as Khepri, the Creator. This teaching is further explained in the Hymns of Amun:

From the Ancient Egyptian Hymns of Amun:

1. He is self-created and as He fashioned Himself, none knows His forms.
2. He became in primeval time; no other being existed; there was no other god before Him; there was no other god with Him to declare His form, all the gods came into being after Him.

3. He had no mother by whom His name was made. He had no father who begat Him, saying, "It is even myself." He shaped His own *egg*. He mingled His seed with His body to make His *egg* to come into being within Himself.
4. His unity is Absolute. Amun is One - One.

In mystical philosophy God is the Self. The Self is a self-existent being which transcends concepts of creation and created. The Self emerged out of the Self and what emerged is none other than the Self. Creation and the Self are one and the same. God is the undivided principle that assumes the names and forms which human beings call objects and the varied life forms which are in existence. Although the Self is the sustaining force behind all phenomena and all life, human beings are ignorant of the existence of this force and thus see themselves as the source of their own existence. They are ignorant to the fact that their very existence is sustained by the Self. Through this process of ignorance, human consciousness is fooled into believing that its thoughts and ideas are its own and that its memories and experiences constitute its unique existence. This concept of a unique and separate existence is what constitutes egoism in the human psyche and the separation from Divine Consciousness.

Thus, the same mystical philosophy in relation to the egg can be found in the scripture of Ancient Egypt and India, including the same theme and function.

Item for Comparison 38: The Philosophy of the Primeval Ocean in Ancient Egypt and India

Figure 162: Lord Nun pushing the boat of Khepri out of the ocean to engender and sustain Creation.

In Ancient Egyptian myth there is a concept that before there was any god or goddess, even Ra or Asar and Aset, and before there was any physical matter, the planets, the sun, animals, human beings, etc., there was the Primeval Ocean, and from it emanated all that exists. The lord of the primeval waters, Nefertem or Ra, emerged from the waters and caused them to take on form (neteru) and order (Maat). There are stories of a Primeval Ocean in other cultures as well, but the oldest notion and greatest emphasis on the concept of the Primeval Ocean comes from Ancient Egypt. Nun is the name of the Primeval Ocean in Kamitan, and the lord of the Nun is also called Nun.

Hinduism also includes teachings in reference to the Primeval Ocean (Nara) and the lord of that primeval ocean is Narayan (Narayana), the Divine Self. Below, Vishnu sleeps on the primeval ocean and from his dream arises the Creator, Brahma, who brings the objects of creation into being. Thus, the primeval ocean in both the Kamitan and Hindu mythic systems serve the purpose of providing the substrate from which the physical universe comes. This substrate is transformed through the mind of the Supreme Being and thereby the varied forms of Creation come into being.

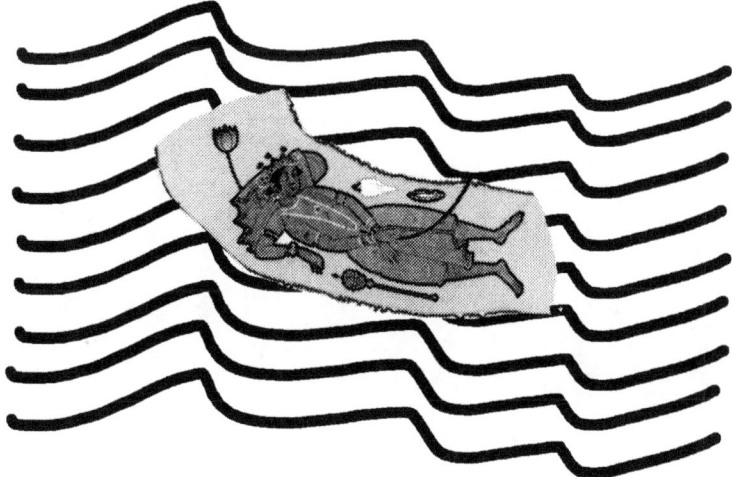

Figure 163: Above- Lord Narayan (Vishnu-Krishna) rests on the Primeval Ocean.

THE AFRICAN ORIGINS OF CIVILIZATION, RELIGION AND YOGA SPIRITUALITY

Item for Comparison 39: The Trinity Systems of Ancient Kamit (Egypt) and India

Figure 164: The Hindu Supreme Being Brahman manifesting as the Trinity

The dot symbolizes the unitary transcendental essence. The All-encompassing divinity manifests as the Hindu Trinity: Brahma, Vishnu, Shiva.

Figure 165: The Kamitan Supreme Being Neberdjer manifesting as the Trinity

The dot symbolizes the unitary transcendental essence. The All-encompassing divinity manifests as the Kamitan Trinity: Kheperi, Ra, Tem.

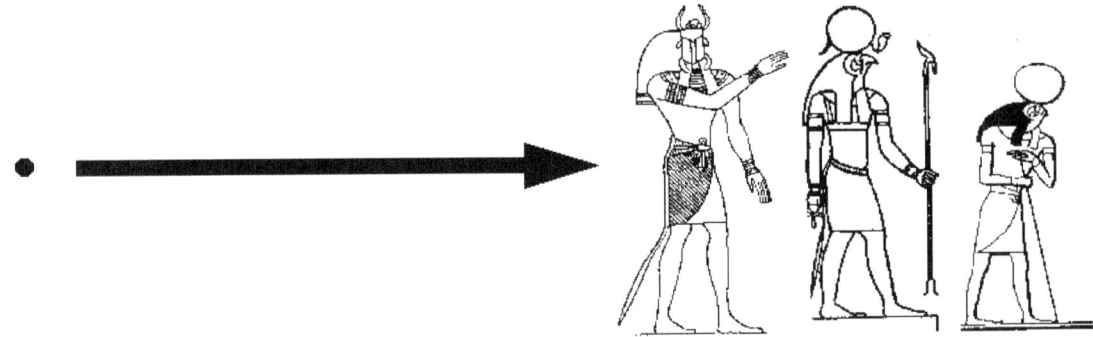

As stated earlier, the concept of the trinity in Indian culture was not formed in the Vedic tradition, but in the Hindu. The concept of three principles arising out of a single transcendental essence originates in India with the evolution of philosophical thought through religious (mythic) symbolism. Thus, in Indian Hindu myth as well as the Kamitan, the trinity signifies the divinity manifesting in three aspects: The creator (Brahma and Khepri), the sustainer (Vishnu or Ra) and the destroyer or dissolver (Shiva or Tem), respectively.

Item for Comparison 40: The Number Nine and The Indian Yantra and the Kamitan Sundisk

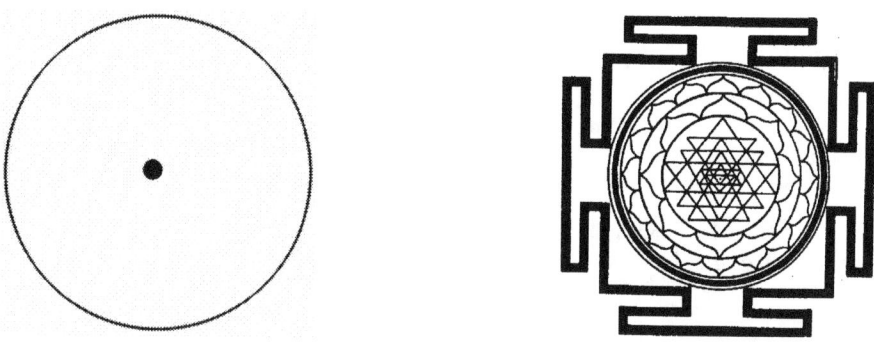

Figure 166: Above right- The Hindu symbol known as the Sri Yantra.

The Indian Sri Yantra (above right) contains the circle and "bindu" or central dot which symbolizes the one essence from which Creation arose into the manifested universe (the outer circle and successive tiers or sections). This symbol expands out from the center in nine phases (see below right), symbolizing the nine aspects (Facets-succeeding levels) of Creation. The Kamitan Sundisk (above left) shows the inner dot and outer circle, symbolizing the central point from which Creation arose and the circle which eternally encompasses all that exists. Ra created nine gods and goddesses who represent the nine "elements" of Creation. This group of divinities is known as the Company of Gods and Goddesses of Ra and the creation myth surrounding them constitutes what is referred to as Anunian Theology (see below).

Figure 167: Above left- The Symbol of Ra, the Sundisk.

Figure 168: Left- the Company of Nine Gods and Goddesses of Ra. Below- Nine sections of the Sri Yantra

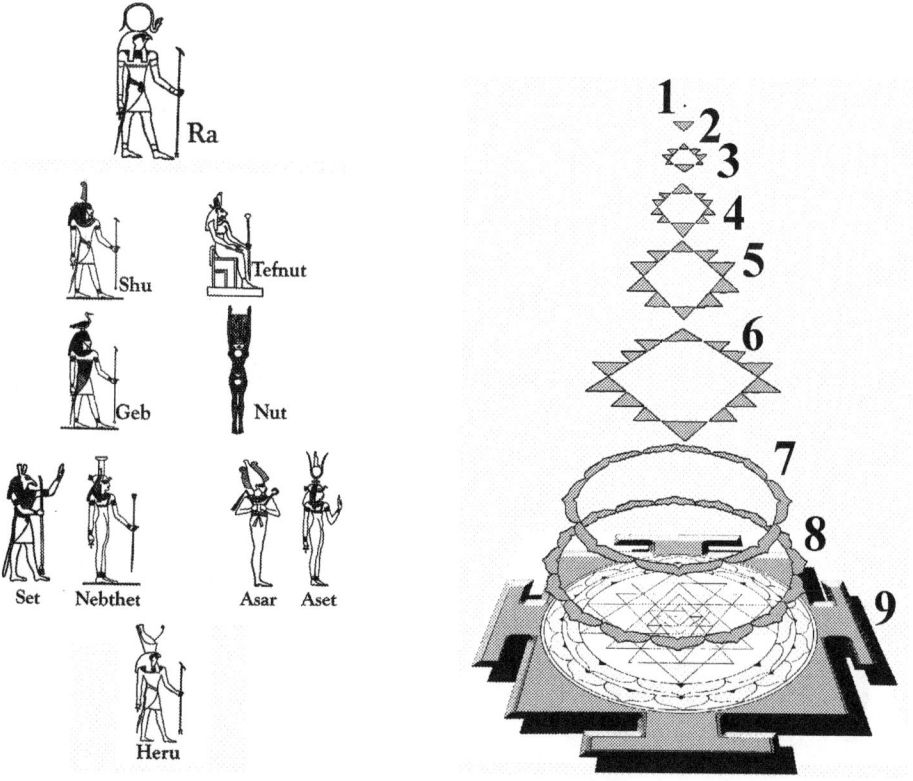

NOTES TO CHAPTER 7

[480] *"LINGUISTIC RELATIONS WITH EGYPT,"* Ray, Kumar Sudhansu, *Prehistoric India and Ancient Egypt* 1956
[481] ibid
[482] ibid
[483] *"LINGUISTIC RELATIONS WITH EGYPT,"* Ray, Kumar Sudhansu, *Prehistoric India and Ancient Egypt* 1956
[484] *"LINGUISTIC RELATIONS WITH EGYPT,"* Ray, Kumar Sudhansu, *Prehistoric India and Ancient Egypt* 1956
[485] *"LINGUISTIC RELATIONS WITH EGYPT,"* Ray, Kumar Sudhansu, *Prehistoric India and Ancient Egypt* 1956
[486] For more details see the book Egyptian Yoga Volume 1 by Dr. Muata Ashby
[487] For more details see the video presentation –Nile Valley Contributions to Civilization and the video The Ancient Egyptian Origins of Yoga Philosophy and the book Egyptian Yoga Volume 1: The Philosophy of Enlightenment – by Dr. Muata Ashby
[488] John Marshal, *Taxila,* vols, II and III, London and New York, 1951, p. 605, pl. 186(e)
[489] *The Shambhala Encyclopedia of Yoga* by Georg Feuerstein, Ph. D.
[490] *Indian Myth and Legend*, Donald A. Mckenzie
[491] *Mansouri El S. M., Art – Culture of India and Egypt* 1959
[492] *Mysticism of Hindu Gods and Goddesses* by Swami Jyotirmayananda
[493] *Mother Worship* by Swami Jyotirmayananda
[494] *A Concise Encyclopedia of Hinduism,* by Klaus K. Klostermaier
[495] International Society for Krishna Consciousness
[496] The Upanishads by Swami Prabhavananda and Frederick Manchester
[497] *Tutankhamun,* E.W. Budge
[498] *Indian Mythology,* Veronica Ions
[499] *A Concise Encyclopedia of Hinduism,* by Klaus K. Klostermaier
[500] Also referred to as the Primeval Waters.
[501] For a more detailed study of the Kamitan teachings related to the "Witnessing Self" see the book Egyptian Yoga Vol. 2.

Chapter 8: Comparison of Ancient Egyptian and Indian Yoga Philosophy

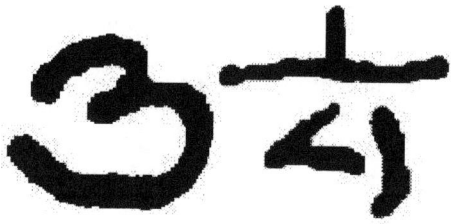

Above: The Ancient Egyptian Symbol of OM

Above The Indian Symbol of OM

The Solar Principle in Kamit

In Kamitan worship, the solar principle is of primary importance, relating to the three major theological systems: Neberdjer = Amun (basis of Theban Theology) – Ra (basis of Anunian Theology and solar principle) – Ptah (basis of Memphite Theology), as well as to Heru, Hetheru, and Aten (Aton). The sun is a perfect metaphor for the Spirit in many ways. Just as the Spirit sustains Creation, the sun sustains life on earth. Just as if the sun were to stop shining, stop sending its solar rays to the earth, the earth would cease to be, if the Spirit were to withdraw its Life Force energy from Creation, it too would cease to be. Also, the sun supports life on earth, but is unaffected by the happenings. Thus the sun can be said to be transcendental of life on earth, though supporting it and sustaining it. Likewise, in mysticism, the Spirit, though supporting and sustaining Creation, is understood to be transcendental, meaning that the Spirit is unaffected by all occurrences, whether good or bad, that occur within Creation (time and space). It is important to know about the solar worship in Kamit in our study because there are those who say that comparisons such as that of Ra of Africa and Rama of India cannot be made because the solar worship is not important at least in modern Indian theology. Upon closer examination we will discover that the solar worship was not only important in Ancient India but that it continues to be important in present day Hindu religious practices. Further, we will be able to discover correlations between the Neterian and Hindu Factors of the respective Cultural Manifestation Categories.

The Vedic Tradition and Hinduism

There are certain areas of Indology that are not often explored in reference to their far reaching implications as to the relationship between Hinduism and the Vedic Tradition. It is often assumed that Hinduism is an evolution of Vedic culture. However, upon closer inspection it is possible to see how outside influences and deep rooted internal forces promoted a shifting away from Vedicism and towards a less ritualistic and more mystical approach to spirituality which not only was more in agreement with the Indus culture, but also compatible with the Kamitan culture of the time. The Hindu concept of the Trinity is actually a development based on some elements that were in Vedic (Aryan) times which appears to be based on an even earlier teaching.[502] Hinduism is a later development which followed the Vedic tradition and the pre-Vedic spiritual culture of ancient India. In order to better understand the correlations between the philosophical and deistic principles that will be correlated to those of Ancient Egypt, it is first necessary to gain a basic understanding about some of the divinities of the Pre-Vedic Indian tradition (Indus Valley Civilization) and the Vedic pantheon.[503] Also, it will be necessary to keep the general dates and periods of the Indian religious traditions in mind as we survey their iconography.

General Timeline of Phases in Buddhist and Hindu Indian Myth and Religion

    3000 – 1500 B.C.E. Indus Valley Period
    1500 - 1000 B.C.E. Aryan Period
    1000 - 800 B.C.E. Brahmanas Period
    800 - 600 B.C.E - Upanishadic Period
    600.- 261 B.C.E. Early Hindu Period
    500 B.C.E. Buddhism founded
    261 B.C.E.- 1200 A.C.E. Buddhist prominence among conglomeration of other Indian
        belief systems.
    319-415 A.C.E. Gupta period – Dynasty of Rulers of Magadha[504] Renaissance of Hinduism –
        Puranic Age
    1500-1600 A.C.E. Sikhism - The doctrines and practices of a monotheistic religion
        founded in northern India in the 16th century and combining elements of
        Hinduism and Islam.

The Pre-Vedic Indian Divinities

Figure 169: Below Left- Pre-Vedic Male Divinity with Horn headdress.

Figure 170: Below-right- Pre-Vedic Female Tree Divinity

The Vedic Deities, the Trinity Systems and the Solar Principle

The most direct knowledge about the Vedic divinities comes from the Vedas. The Vedas are four texts encompassing Vedic mythology. They are the earliest known scriptures of the Vedic religious tradition. The first and most important Vedic text is the *Rig Veda* (Veda of hymns). There are three more Vedic texts which were added later, the *Samaveda* (Veda of melodies), the *Yayurveda* (Veda of rituals), and the *Atharvaveda* (Veda of incantations). The Rig Veda and the Ancient Egyptian Pyramid Texts have some important similarities.

- ❖ Firstly, in their respective cultural systems they are the most ancient texts that establish the mythology by which the religions are defined.
- ❖ Secondly, both provide prayers (hymns) to the divinities they serve.
- ❖ Thirdly they prescribe rituals related to the divinities they serve.
- ❖ Fourthly, they provide insight into the origins and relationships of the divinities they serve.

One of the respects in which they differ however, is that while the Ancient Egyptian texts present a pantheon of divinities at the outset that remain constant to the end of the Kamitan culture (over 5,000 years) down to the early Christian era, Indian mythology experienced additions and deletions from the pantheon. The gods Kubera, Karttikeya, Visvakarma, Dharma and Kama were added in the Early Hindu Period of Indian myth and religion. With these changes to the Indian mythic system, several fundamentally important mythological, and consequently philosophical, changes were also made over time. This phenomenon signals not only an evolutionary process in Ancient Indian religious thought, but also the infusion of new concepts, effecting a transformation of the prevailing Vedic system and creating the concepts which became known as Hinduism.

The Vedic tradition influenced northern India first for several hundreds of years, and later the southern part. The Vedic Pantheon introduced several divinities and concepts to Indian religious mythology. The Vedic deities included Varuna - Prithivi and Dyaus, Indra, The Maruts, Vayu, Tvashtri, The Ribhus, Agni, Soma, Chandra, Aditi and the Adityas, Vivasvat, Savitri, Surya, Ushas, Ratri, The Aswins, Rudra and Vishnu.[505]

Vedic-Hindu Concept of the Three Worlds and the Kamitan Concept of the Three Worlds

According to the Vedas, the earliest religious texts of Vedic mythology and philosophy in India, there were 33 divinities in all, 11 for each of the *three world categories* including the sky, air, and the earth. Some of the gods of the Vedic tradition appear in present-day Hinduism under their original names while others were transformed. The solar principle is a special characteristic in Ancient Egyptian and Indian mythologies and its correlations in the two systems can be traced from Anunian Theology in Egypt to the commencement of Hinduism in pre-Christian India, and to the practice of Indian religion in modern times. The following are important Vedic divinities that survive in Hinduism: Surya (the sun), Indra (ruler of heaven, great god of storms, thunder and lightning, regulator of the days, months, and seasons.), Varuna (the sky) and Vishnu (sustainer of Creation).

The Anunian system of mythology in Ancient Egypt held that there were three worlds. The Ancient Egyptian concept of creation recognized three realms of existence, *Ta* (Earth-Nature divinities), *Pet* (Sky-Heavens-Cosmic divinities) and the *Duat* (Astral Plane-Metaphysical divinities), as previously discussed. There are classes of Neteru (divinities) which inhabit each realm and fulfill certain functions therein to sustain Creation. The Duat is the realm where the nine primordial gods and goddesses of the Ennead were birthed, the residence of astral beings, the lower gods and goddesses as well as the demons and fiends that dwell there alongside the departed souls. It is also within this realm that Asar can be discovered. The Duat is to be understood as a parallel plane of existence in reference to the physical plane of ordinary physical human experience.

The *Metaphysical Neteru* represent the principles of the Universe. They are Ra, Amun and Ptah, the "Great Trinity," also known as *"Nebertcher: Everything is Amun-Ra-Ptah, three in one."* Amun, Ra and

Ptah are a direct creation from *Neberdjer*, i.e. The Absolute, transcendental divinity. They are responsible for the direction (management) of creation at every moment.

The *Cosmic Neteru* are fundamental expressions of the Cosmic Neteru but in time and space, sustaining Creation as the elements and principles of Creation. Examples of Cosmic Neteru are: Shu, Geb, Nut, Asar, Set, Aset and Nebethet.

The *Natural Neteru* are represented in the functioning of natural objects such as the God Hapi who is the god/goddess (androgynous) of the Nile river.

The Principle of The Creator and the Nine Divinities

Based on Anunian theology, as it is presented in the Ancient Egyptian Pyramid Texts and other Kamitan scriptures, the order, nomenclature and attributes of the Ancient Egyptian divinities of the Creation may be viewed as follows.

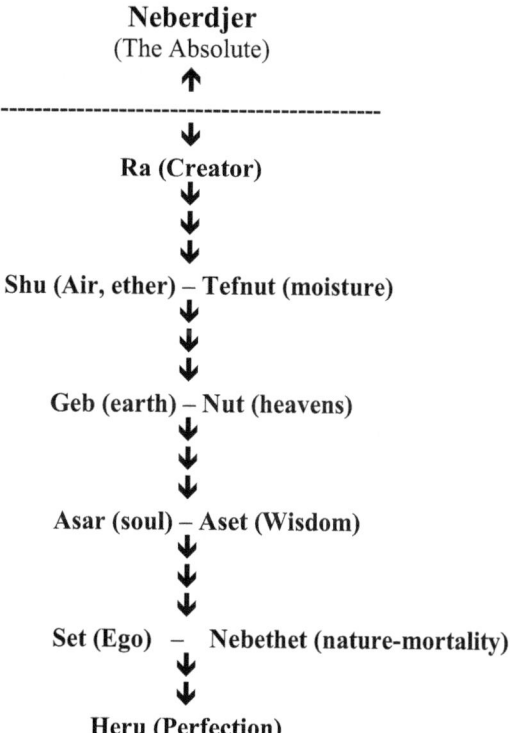

Neberdjer
(The Absolute)
↑

↓
Ra (Creator)
↓
↓
↓
Shu (Air, ether) – Tefnut (moisture)
↓
↓
↓
Geb (earth) – Nut (heavens)
↓
↓
↓
Asar (soul) – Aset (Wisdom)
↓
↓
↓
Set (Ego) – Nebethet (nature-mortality)
↓
↓
Heru (Perfection)

Varuna, the Vedic Concept of Maya and the Hindu Concept of Maya

Varuna figures prominently at the beginning of the Vedic period as the Supreme God, prime mover and sustainer of the cosmic order. He engendered Creation by his creative will (maya-creative power).[506][507] The term "maya" does not take on its mystical philosophic meaning until the Vedanta schools (Upanishadic Tradition) in the Hindu period reinterpret it as "cosmic illusion" or "hallucination."[508]

The Creation of Varuna and the Creation of Ra

The Ancient Egyptian god Ra emanated rain and waters (Tefnut), air (Shu), earth (Geb) and the heavens (Nut), all of which constitute the elements and phenomenal Creation, by his creative will[509] and watches Creation through the sundisk,[510] sustaining it with his energy. In similar fashion the god Varuna willed rain to fall, the waters (rivers) to flow, wind to blow (as his breath) and he watches Creation constantly through his eye, the sun.[511] Both divinities, Ra and Varuna, not only emanate Creation, but they "embody" it since the emanations are actually parts of divinities themselves.

Ra is the fire, Sekhem (Life Force), which sustains life, and his primary symbol is the sundisk, ⊙, and the winged sundisk (Behdety or Ur Uadjit).

Figure 171: Behdety or Ur Uadjit

The Winged Serpent, also called the Winged Sundisk, composed of a sundisk symbolizing Ra manifesting as the dual principles, symbolized by the two serpents (Uadjit -Aset and Nekhebet - Nebthet), and the wings Heru. This is an important symbol of Heru, meaning "All-Encompassing Divinity."

Varuna, the Vedic Trinity and the Solar Principle

Random House Encyclopedia Copyright (C) 1983,1990 by Random House Inc.

Surya, in Hindu mythology, the personification of the Sun, possessed of 12 names and incarnations, among them Indra, Varuna, and Mitra. As Surya he is depicted as a three-eyed, four-armed man of burnished copper, sometimes seated on a lotus or in a chariot drawn by many horses. He is prayed to as a healer and bringer of luck. His festival, the Suryapuja, occurs in the spring.

Hindu mythology, Surya, the personification of the Sun, was said to possess 12 names and incarnations. Among his names were Indra, Varuna, and Mitra.[512] At an earlier period Varuna had been referred to as Aditya (free-boundless). However, this was changed as some of Varuna's powers were distributed amongst two other divinities during the development of Aryan culture. At the close of the Vedic Period, the attributes of Varuna had been distributed between three divinities, which are often viewed by some scholars as the perhaps the earliest evidence of the concept of the Trinity in India. This Trinity system was composed of Varuna, Mitra and Aryaman. Mitra assumed the role of guardian of morality, holding humans to their sins. He became the sun and the day, while Varuna became the ruler of the night. Mitra or Mithraism spread to Persia and became a chief religion there after the 6th century B.C.E. Mitra was now also the god of both rain and sun; this spread throughout Europe. In Europe Mithraism was gradually replaced by Christianity after the 3rd century ACE.[513][514] Aryaman was associated with the heavens.

Now in India, the Trinity of these deities was called "The Asuras" and later "The Adityas," or "Celestial Beings." Together, they assumed the duties of Varuna as the sustainers and the regulators of Creation. This Trinity was joined by either three or nine divinities.[515] The Vedic god Indra became the chief of these divinities. As Hinduism developed, the functions of this Trinity became restricted to association with twelve annual phases (months) of the sun. If the number of the divinities is nine, then this follows closely the Creation Myth of the Ancient Egyptian school of the Anunian priesthood. Ra emerged as Supreme Being and emanated a total of nine divinities who constitute Creation itself. See the ***Item for Comparison: The Number Nine and The Indian Yantra and the Kamitan Sundisk***.

Agni

Agni was the son of Prithivi and Dyaus, who were earth and sky, respectively. They gave birth to three gods, Agni, Indra and Surya. Agni is the fire or Life Force of the cosmos. He feeds on the oblation fire and the food that human beings eat as he is the essence which sustains them. Agni is also in lightning and in the fire of the sun, which sustains life on earth.

Indra

The God Indra assumed the role of warrior, as he fought demons incessantly, with his bolts of lightning and other weapons. He became a celebrated divinity and was closer to the people than the transcendental Varuna. He drew his power from the alcoholic (or mind altering substance) juice beverage, *soma*, and the Vedic priests created elaborate rituals in the preparation and consumption of the beverage. The Hindu tradition repudiated the intoxicant later on in the development of religion in India. At the close of the Aryan period and the beginning of the Hindu period, Indra was replaced as the incarnations of the Hindu god Vishnu, especially Rama and Krishna, took over the duty of fighting and destroying demons in order to protect and show human beings the way to spiritual enlightenment.

Surya

Surya is the personification and essence of the sun, possessing 12 names (months). He is regarded as the vivifier of all living beings. He is subtle, and therefore pervades all. He is the source of the Soma Juice that sustains Indra's powers and Amrita "Divine Nectar" which illuminates the moon (Chandra) and enables it to wax every month. In some aspects of Hindu mythology Indra, Varuna, and Mitra are regarded as incarnations of Surya. Of golden or copper hue, Surya is sometimes depicted sitting on a lotus, at others on a chariot drawn by horses or as a three-eyed, four-armed man. He was considered to be the eye of Varuna and Mitra. Considered to be an auspicious divinity to be worshipped, the Suryapuja festival that takes place in his honor occurs in the spring. Like Ra, who has "Seven souls (Sefek Bas Ra)," Surya has "seven horses" or principles of manifestation. Recall that the "Seven souls of Ra" are actually equated in the Kamitan system to the seven spheres or psycho-spiritual consciousness centers, which the Hindu Kundalini Yoga tradition later called the "Chakras."

One of the myths surrounding Surya is that he was so brilliant that his wife (Sanjna) could not bear it, and so she left him. He brought her back and had another god, Visvakarma (engineer, master builder of the gods), the father of Sanjna, place Surya on his lathe and shave off one eighth of his brilliance so as not to overwhelm Sanjna and cause her to leave again. Having done this, Visvakarma used the one eighth of the brilliance of Surya to create a discus for Vishnu (later popularized by the incarnation, Krishna, who used it to destroy demons), a trident for Shiva (one of his most important symbols as lord of the three worlds), a lance for Karttikeya (the warrior divinity, son of Shiva and evolution {new god introduced to Hinduism} of the Murugan concept of south India), and the weapons used by all the other gods and goddesses. Thus, it is clear that while Surya does not enjoy a prominent state in Hinduism, contrary to the opinions of some Indologists, he is still revered in Hinduism and his solar principle underlies the power of the primary divinities in modern Hinduism. The correspondences between the Kamitan and Hindu solar traditions provides insight into the deeper relations between Ancient Egypt and India that continue even to this day.

THE AFRICAN ORIGINS OF CIVILIZATION, RELIGION AND YOGA SPIRITUALITY

Figure 172: (A) Above-left-Set protecting boat of Ra from the giant serpent of disorder-(dissolution-unrighteousness). (B) Krishna dances on the head of Kalya Naga (serpent), after defeating him.

There are several interesting parallels that can be found in the solar principles of Ra from Ancient Egypt and Shiva and Krishna of India. Everyday the "golden sundisk," Ra, emerges sailing on his boat across the heavens. His movement in the divine boat sustains Creation and holds back dissolution.[516] His movement is tantamount to the *Nataraja*[517] of Shiva (Lord of the Cosmic Dance-see section *The Multi-armed Divinity in Ancient Egypt and India*). At the end of an era Ra descends back into the cosmic ocean from when he emerged and Creation dissolves to give way for another Creation. In the same manner, the *Tandava* (dance of destruction-dissolution of Creation) of Shiva has the same effect. Set, who stands at the bow of the divine boat (see above), is Ra's power which he directs against the great "serpent of unrighteousness," *Apepi*.[518] In Indian mythology, Krishna makes battle in the river against *Kalya*, the serpent of unrighteousness, who symbolizes the five afflictions of human life (ignorance, egoism, attachment, aversion, and clinging to life-fear of death).[519]

Aton of Ancient Egypt and Varuna and Surya (Savitri or Savitar), The Sun Gods of India

The Hymn to the sun divinity in the Rig Veda provides insights into the similarities of Indian and Kamitan solar worship. One obvious similarity comes from the iconography itself. The Late Hindu period picture below shows the Indian sun divinity in a chariot pulled by seven horses which correlates to the Kamitan divinity Ra who has seven souls or vehicles of expression.

Figure 173: The Vedic-Hindu God Surya (Savitri or Savitar)

HYMN LIII. To Savitar[520]

1. Of Savitar the God, the sapient Asura, we crave this great gift which is worthy of our choice, Wherewith he freely grants his worshiper defense. This with his rays the Great God hath vouchsafed to us.

2 Sustainer of the heaven, Lord of the whole world's life, the Sage, he putteth on his golden-coloured mail. Clear-sighted, spreading far, filling the spacious realm, Savitar hath brought forth bliss that deserveth laud.

3 He hath filled full the regions of the heaven and earth: the God for his own strengthening waketh up the hymn. Savitar hath stretched out his arms to cherish life, producing with his rays and lulling all that moves.

4 Lighting all living creatures, neer to be deceived, Savitar, God, protects each holy ordinance. He hath stretched out his arms to all the folk of earth, and, with his laws observed, rules his own mighty course.

5 Savitar thrice surrounding with his mightiness mid-air, three regions, and the triple sphere of light, Sets the three heavens in motion and the threefold earth, and willingly protects us with his triple law.

6 Most gracious God, who brings to life and lulls to rest, he who controls the world, what moves not and what moves, May he vouchsafe us shelter, -Savitar the God,- for tranquil life, with triple bar against distress.

7 With the year's seasons hath Savitar, God, come nigh: may he prosper our home, give food and noble sons. May he invigorate us through the days and nights, and may he send us opulence with progeny.

The similarities between the Ancient Egyptian and Indian concepts of divinity using the sun motif, as expressed in the Hymn to the Indian Sun Divinity (above), have not escaped scholarly research. Many times, religions basing themselves on the sun symbol are often marginalized by modern researchers or repudiated by orthodox religions, that refer to them as "solar cults" or "idol worshippers." There is a misunderstanding as to the nature of the solar mythos and its deeper philosophical implications. The following excerpt from Ancient Egyptian scholar Sir Wallis Budge's book: *Tutankhamen, Amenism, Atenism, and Egyptian Monotheism* provides insight into these issues.

A very interesting characteristic of the hymns to Aten is the writer's insistence on the beauty and power of light, and it may be permitted to wonder if it is not due to Mitannian influence, and the penetration into Egypt of Aryan ideas concerning Mitra, Varuna, and Surya or Savitri, the Sun-god. Aten, or Horus of the Two Horizons, corresponds closely to Surya, the rising and setting sun, Ra to Savitri, the sun shining in full strength, "the golden-eyed, the golden-handed, and golden tongued." "As the Vivifier and Quickener, he raises his long arms of gold in the morning, rouses all beings from their slumber, infuses energy into them, and buries them in sleep in the evening.[521] Surya, the rising and setting sun, like Aten, was the great source of light and heat, and therefore Lord of life itself. He is like Surya was the "fountain of living Light,"[522] with the all seeing eye, whose beams revealed his presence and "gleaming like brilliant flames."[523] Went to nation after nation. Aten was not only the light of the sun, which seems to give new light to man and all creation, but the giver of light and all life in general. The bringer of light and life to-day, he is the same who brought light and life on the first of days, therefore, Aten is eternal. Light begins the day, so it was the beginning of creation; therefore Aten is the creator, neither made with hands nor begotten, and is the governor of the world. The earth was fertilized by Aten, therefore, he is the Father-Mother of all creatures. His eye saw everything and knew everything. The Hymns to Aten suggest that Amenhetep IV and his followers conceived an image of him in their minds and worshipped him inwardly. But the abstract conception of thinking was wholly inconceivable to the average Egyptian, who only understood things in a concrete form. It was probably some conception of this kind that made the cult of Aten so unpopular with the Egyptians, and caused its downfall. Aten, like Varuna, possessed a mysterious presence, a mysterious power, and a mysterious knowledge. He made the sun to shine, the winds were his breath, he made the sea, and caused the rivers to flow. He was omniscient, and though he lived remote in the heavens he was everywhere present on earth. And a passage in the Rig-Veda would form an admirable description of him.

> Light-giving Varuna! Thy piercing glance doth scan
> In quick succession all this stirring active world.
> And penetrateth, too, the broad ethereal space,
> Measuring our days and nights and spying out all creatures.[524]

But Varuna possessed one attribute, which, so far as we know, was wanting in Aten; he spied out sin and judged the sinner. The early Aryan prayed to him, saying, "Be gracious, O Mighty God, be gracious. I have sinned through want of power; be gracious. What great sin is it, Varuna, for which thou seekest in thy worshipper and friend? Tell me, O unassailable and self-dependent god; and, freed from sin, I shall speedily come to thee for adoration.[525]

It should be noted here that the Sanskrit term *"Savitri,"* means "Generator." It is a Vedic term for the Sun, to whom many hymns are dedicated. The *mysterious presence, a mysterious power, and a mysterious knowledge* that Budge speaks about as related to Varuna should not be compared to the mystical sense that is presented in the Upanishads. Varuna is referred to as a "sustainer" and as *"Lord of warrior might, Him, the far-seeing Varuna..."*[526] To the extent of this "mystery" as sustainer and all-seer, the sun itself being equated with the eye of the divinity, there is congruence with the Aton philosophy. However, the Hymn to Aton of Ancient Kamit goes further and exhorts a mystical union with the transcendental essence of the sun. So the element of mysticism and solar worship is not found in the Rig Veda. The Early Hindu Period however, brought forth such links to the solar worship. Also, in the last paragraph above, from Budge, there is a critical inaccuracy in delineating a variance between Aton (Aten) and Varuna on the principle of righteousness as a factor or prerequisite for becoming a true devotee of the Divine. In a landmark study of the correspondences between Aton and the Indian sun gods by Savitri Devi, *A Son Of God: The Life And Philosophy Of Akhnaton, King Of Egypt*, the final philosophical correspondence between Aton and Surya was confirmed as the same teaching which was inscribed in the tomb of a follower of Aton.

> The Founder of the Religion of the Disk insisted upon "life in truth." "There is in his Teaching, as it is fragmentarily preserved in his hymns and in the tomb-inscriptions of his nobles, a constant emphasis upon 'truth' such as is not found before or since," says Breasted.[527] He called himself "Ankh-em-Maat"--"the One-who-lives-in-Truth." But what is truth? "Maat," writes that learned scholar in hieroglyphics whom we have many times quoted, Sir Wallis Budge, "means what is straight, true, real, law, both physical and moral, the truth, reality, etc."[528] By "living in truth" the king, adds he, "can hardly have meant 'living in or by the law,' for he was a law to himself. But he may have meant that in Atenism he had found the truth or the 'real' thing, and that all else, in religion, was a phantom, a sham. Aten lived in maat, or in truth and reality, and the king, having the essence of Aten in him, did the same."[529]
>
> If this interpretation of maat be the right one, then it appears that a man's behaviour should be, in Akhnaton's eyes, inspired by the knowledge of the few facts and the acceptance of the few supreme values which form, as we have seen, the solid background of the Aton faith. These facts were the oneness of the ultimate essence, and the unity of all life, its manifold and ever-changing expression; the fatherhood of the Sun and, through Him, of the Power within Him--Cosmic Energy--and the subsequent brotherhood of all living creatures, not of man alone; the unity of the visible and of the invisible world, of the physical--the material and of the more subtle, as put forward in the identity of the fiery Disk with the Heat and Light within it. In other words, they were the few general truths which modern research is gradually confirming, and which would still satisfy, it seems, the thinking men of the remotest ages to come.[530]

Some authors, including Budge, have suggested that the Kingdom of Mitanni, which was dominant in north Mesopotamia until the 12th century B.C.E., might have been a source for the Ancient Egyptians coming into contact with the Vedic teachings in order to create the conceptions of Aton. This theory arises out of the idea that Egypt's trade and contacts as well as territorial control of several parts of in Asia Minor allowed them to draw from the spiritual knowledge of India through peoples such as the Mitanni, who may have had a religion similar to that of the Vedic Aryans. During the reign of Thothmes IV (1425–1417 B.C.E.) Egypt grew closer to the Mitanni in alliance against the Hittites, and he cemented this alliance by marriage to a Mitanni princess.[531] It has been speculated that Akhnaton might have been affected by the alliance since he had a harem which included wives from Middle Eastern countries, and they could have influenced him with their native religion. Archeology has not yet determined if the Mitanni had a strong relation with the Vedic Aryans of India or if they had a Solar mythos, and if so what the nature of that tradition was. Therefore, as there is no documentation for this theory it is entirely speculative and inconsistent with the evidences available. This kind of concept is one of many purporting to explain how the admittedly high philosophy of Akhnaton arose in Egypt. However, Budge himself admits that the teachings of Akhnaton are actually not different from the teachings that were espoused in Egypt from the earliest times.

> But if we examine the Hymn (to Aten), line by line, and compare it with the Hymn to Ra, Amen and other gods, we find that there is hardly an idea in it which is not borrowed from the older Egyptian religions.[532]

It is not sufficient to explain the nature of the solar concept in Neterianism and how it relates to Vedicism and Hinduism. Therefore, the actual hymns to the sun god in the Indian and Kamitan traditions have been included here with commentary so that the reader may see for {him/her} self, the nature of the correlations.

The following hymn is from the *Pert M Heru* or "Book of Enlightenment" from Ancient Egyptian Anunian Theology. Many writers have striven to show Atonism, the philosophy of Akhnaton, as a new innovation, as separate and deviant from the rest of Ancient Egyptian mythology and philosophy. However, upon closer examination, the philosophy of Atonism is quite closely related to Anunian Theology. This is because they had the same common origins and any differences are of degrees of expressing a particular aspect of theology over others at a given time. There are no fundamental differences between Atonism and other religious traditions of Ancient Egypt. The teachings presented in the Hymn to Ra will be noticeably similar to those in the Hymns to Aton (Above). Further, their similarity with the Vedic and Hindu solar conceptions will become evident.

A Hymns to Ra and Its Philosophical Principles

Hymns to Ra[533]

1. Behold Asar _____ [174] bringing divine offerings of all the gods and goddesses. Asar _____ speaks thus:

2. Homage to thee, who comes in the form of Khepri[534], Khepri the Creator of the gods and goddesses. You rise and shine, illuminating your mother, goddess Nut, the sky, crowned as king of the gods and goddesses. Your mother Nut worships you with her two arms. The western horizon receives you in peace and Maat embraces you at the double season. Give Asar _____ Glorious Spirit being[535], and spiritual strength through righteous speaking. Grant the ability to come forth as a living soul so that Asar _____ may see Heru of the two Horizons.[536] Grant this to the Ka[537] of Asar _____ who is Righteous of Speech in the presence of Asar, the Divine Self. Asar _____ says: Hail to all the gods and goddesses, weighers of the house of the soul, in heaven and on earth by means of the scales of Maat, who are givers of Life Force sustenance.

3. Tatunen,[538] One, maker of men and women as well as the company of the gods and goddesses of the south, the north, the west and the east, i.e. all the neteru[539], grant praises to Ra, the lord of heaven, sovereign of life, vitality and health, maker of the gods and goddesses. Adorations to thee in your form as all goodness, as you rise in your boat. The beings up high praise thee. Beings in the lower realms

---

[174] Spaces are left so that the initiate for whom the text was written may enter his or her name.

praise thee. Djehuti[540] and Maat[541] have written for thee, who are shining forth, every day. Your enemies are put to the fire. The fiends are put down, their arms and legs being bound securely for Ra. The children of weakness disrespect and insurrection shall not continue.

4.   The great house[542] is in festival time. The voices of the participants are in the great temple. The gods and goddesses are rejoicing. They see Ra in his glorious rising, his beams of light piercing, inundating the lands. This exalted and venerable god journeys on and unites with the land of Manu, the western horizon, illuminating the land of his birth every day and at the same time he reaches the province where he was yesterday.

5.   Be in peace with me! I see your beauties and I prosper upon the land; I smile and I defeat the ass fiend as well as the other fiends. Grant that I may defeat Apep[543] in his time of strength and to see the pilot fish of the Divine Boat of Ra, which is in its blessed pool.[544] I see Heru in the form as the guardian of the rudder. Djehuti and Maat are upon his two arms. Received am I in the prow[545] of the Mandet[546] Boat and in the stern of the Mesektet[547] Boat. Ra gives divine sight, to see the Aton[548], to view the moon god unceasingly, every day, and the ability of souls to come forth, to walk to every place they may desire. Proclaim my name! Find him in the wood board of offerings. There have been given to me offerings in the life-giving presence, like it is given to the followers of Heru[549]. It is done for me in the divine place in the boat on the day of the sailing, the journey of The God. I am received in the presence of Asar in the land of truth speaking[550] of the Ka of Asar _____.

Philosophical Principles in the Hymn to Ra[551]

The hymn to Ra is related to Aton since it was understood in Anunian Theology that Ra is the power behind the sundisk (verse 5 above). In the Hymn to Aton however, as the source of freedom from *"being [previously] restrained"* occurs through the *"movement in adoration to the Aton."* This movement in adoration allows the worshipper to be free from "worldly" restraints and allows the worshipper to attain unity with the Aton, the realization that we are all "millions of living beings within thee [the Aton] and that sustains life-breath in us." Thus, this liberating realization of the oneness which brings self-knowledge and immortality with Aton is not found in Mithraism or in the Vedic worship of Savitri or Varuna. The invocatory hymn of any scripture is an important part of the overall feeling of the spiritual tradition. Ra, of course, symbolizes the Higher Self, the Supreme Being, God. Thus, the invocation to God is a form of prayer, or devotional expression towards the Divine, but at the same time it is a form of propitiation. In essence, prayer can be understood as talking to God, but the hymn goes a step further. Most times in modern culture people pray in order to ask for something. Sometimes people want God to help them with a problem in their life. Sometimes the prayer is for good luck. Sometimes the prayer is asking for the right numbers to the lottery. At other times the prayer is for deliverance from some ordeal in life. But how often do people pray for deliverance from human life? How often do people ask God to show them the way to achieve spiritual enlightenment? This is the very objective of the Hymn to Ra. Note also, in contrast to most prayers where the devotee is asking for something from the Divine, the prayer above is primarily composed of descriptions and glorification of the beauties of the Divine.

The hymn opens with salutations and descriptive appellations of Ra, as he rises in the morning. This is not some distant God, but a familiar presence. Ra is a being who can be seen daily and who can be approached easily. He illumines all the earth and causes all life to be. Ra is the source from which all of the gods and goddesses, all life, all human beings, etc., emanate. He sustains Creation by establishing Maat (order) and Djehuti (reason) as he moves through Creation. It is especially acknowledged that Ra is not only the illuminer of the physical world, but also of the Netherworld, the Duat (kingdom of the dead). This signifies that Ra is not the sun itself. This is a very important point to understand. Recall that Ancient Egyptian mythology holds that there are three realms of existence, the Physical Plane (Ta), the Astral Plane (Duat) and the Heaven (Pet).

If a person has acted with virtue and in accordance with the voice of their conscience, their soul will experience positive conditions in the astral realm. This condition is referred to as heaven. If a person acted according to their egoistic desires, selfishness and pride, they will experience pain and sorrow in the astral realm. This condition is referred to as hell. So the hymn goes on to invoke the grace of Ra. The astral realm is a subtle universe which is in a different plane than the physical. Ra passes through the astral realm just as he also passes through the physical. He passes through the physical realm in his Andetet Boat (boat), and through the astral realm in the Sekhet night boat. However, when he passes through the Duat, there are certain ropes which hang from his boat. The desire of the spiritual aspirant reading the text is that {he/she} may be able to see and grab hold of the ropes which are hanging from the boat.

THE AFRICAN ORIGINS OF CIVILIZATION, RELIGION AND YOGA SPIRITUALITY

The ropes symbolize divine compassion and divine love. God is extending his hand, as it were, to rescue the soul from the suffering that can occur outside of the boat. The boat itself is the innermost realm of God. It is the place of contentment and peace, being closest to the Divine. All other realms are as if a separation from that divine perfection that is in the boat. They represent a distancing from God, a separation from what is Divine.

The act of reaching out to grab the ropes is the act of spiritual aspiration and it signifies the practice of all of the spiritual disciplines (of Yoga) which enable a person to move towards their Higher Self as opposed to getting more deeply involved in the relative realms which are again, a separation from the Divine.

This is a beautiful hymn dedicated to the Divine, the Supreme Being, in the form of Ra. It contains much of the same feeling and dedications as in Plate 1 of the papyrus of Ani. However, it also has several important additional teachings which are important to the study of *Pert Em Heru*.

The idea of Ra emerging and "inundating the lands" with his life giving essence has special mystical significance. This teaching refers to the original creation when the entire universe and the forms of Creation were not yet in existence. The time prior to the dawn symbolizes the undifferentiated state of the universe as well as the human mind. In the beginning the universe was like a calm ocean and there was no differentiation in it. Everything looked the same. However, when Ra emerged from the ocean he caused waves, and these waves took on many different forms. These forms are what we refer to as elements or matter. Think of the time when you fall asleep. You lose consciousness of your waking personality and you are submerged in an ocean without forms. This is like the primeval ocean of creation. From it arises your dream world in which you are a character among other characters of your own creation. Thus, you are the Creator of your dream world and God is the creator of the dream of the universe.

God created the universe by causing vibrations in that primordial ocean of his own consciousness by uttering sound. Sound is the medium by which God ordains what happens in Creation from its inception to its end. The word manifests through the power and faculty of speech. Therefore, speech is related to Cosmic Consciousness and the ability to create in the world of time and space as well as in the astral realm. In the same manner, a human being can create his or her world according to the desire of the heart.

Thus, just as a human being must breathe air in order to sustain life, this entire universe must receive the breath of life from the Divine in order to be sustained. However, ordinary human beings (ignorant masses) only know of the physical air that sustains the physical body. A spiritual aspirant seeks to breath the air which sustains the elevated states of consciousness which are above the waking state of consciousness.

The hymn goes on to show that Ani praises the Divine at dawn and at eventide. This teaching relates to the necessity for devotional exercise such as prayers, chanting and recitation of the hekau or words of power which propitiate divine grace and promote spiritual knowledge and the kindling of spiritual feeling deep within the heart leading to purity and enlightenment. A person engages constantly in the world with its illusions. Thus, spiritual practice should be daily, encompassing every aspect of life, in order to overwhelm the worldly impressions produced by distraction, ignorance and the lower desires. The process of spiritual worship leads a human being to draw divine grace to {him/her} self. This is what is referred to as being one of the "favored ones" of God. This favored status is attained by becoming "one of those who worshipped thee upon earth" meaning while they were alive and in human form.

Many people mistakenly believe that the *Pert Em Heru* is a book of rituals only for people who have passed on to the next life, but in reality it is a discipline for those who are alive. The physical body is the best place to carry out a spiritual program, the practice of Yoga and Mystical Religion. This is because it is the place where the soul can experience an extended period of waking consciousness in which to consciously work on purifying the heart. The dream and dreamless sleep states or subconscious and unconscious levels of the mind are inconstant and minimal spiritual progress can be accomplished in these states.

Akhnaton and the connection between Atonism and Anunian Theology.

The image below is a depiction of the Sage-king Akhnaton in the form of a sphinx offering Maat to the Aton. This is one of the most traditional forms of religious iconography in Ancient Egypt which can be found on several temples and scriptures. It is the highest declaration of any king or queen to say that they upheld Maat and in so doing they are worthy to attain higher consciousness. The use of the Sphinx shows that Akhnaton saw the Aton teaching as an extension of the same solar philosophy of Anunian Theology, as the Horemakhet (Sphinx) has been shown to be one, if not the most important and oldest, symbol of solar spirituality in Ancient Kamit. Therefore, Akhnaton innovated nothing. He simply expressed a teaching that was already present in Egypt, but which had become dormant until the advocacy was elevated by his mother and his mother's spiritual preceptor.

Plate 49: Akhnaton as a Sphinx

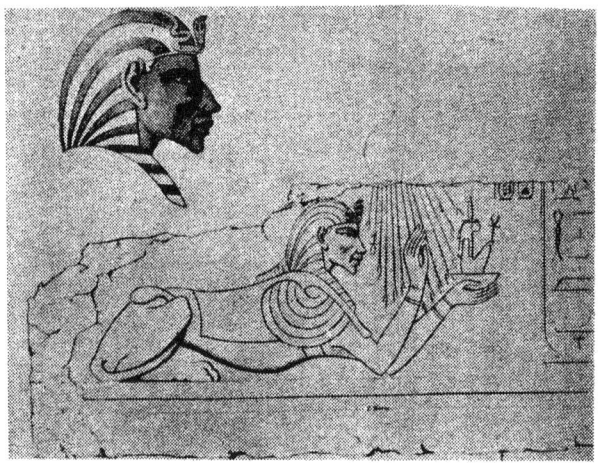

THE AFRICAN ORIGINS OF CIVILIZATION, RELIGION AND YOGA SPIRITUALITY

The opening verses of the Hymn to Aton by Akhnaton (Ahmenhotep IV {or Amenophis /Akhenaten}) provide insight into the ancient nature of Aton worship and how it is tied to the divinity Ra as well as the oldest form of worship known in Kamit, that of *Heru-Akhuti (Hormakht* - the Great Sphinx). Note that adorations are made to the *living Heru-Akhuti* (verse 1) and Akhnaton refers to being one with Ra (verse 3) through living by Maat (righteousness) – (verse 3 and 4). Thus, Aton worship is the New Kingdom Period (1580-1075 B.C.E.) renaissance of Ra worship (5,500 B.C.E.)which is a form of *Heru-Akhuti* worship that goes back to the inception of Ancient Egyptian culture and spirituality (10,000 B.C.E.).

Hymn To Aton by Akhenaton

1.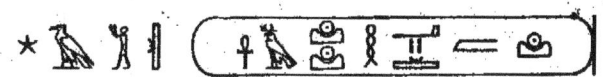

   1.1. Dua Ankh Herakhuti Hai m Akhet

   1.2. Adorations to the living Heru Akhuti whose body manifests through the sundisk (Aton)

2.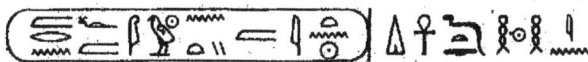

   2.1. *m ren f m shu nty m Aton rdy Ankh djeta heh in*

   2.2. through the name his through Shu who is in the Aton. Giving life forever and eternity by

3.

   3.1. *suten ankh m Maat neb tawi nefer kheperu Ra wa n Ra*

   3.2. the king living through Maat, lord of the two lands, beautiful creations of Ra, One with Ra

4.

   4.1. *sa ankh m Maat neb Kau Akhen Aton Maakheru*

   4.2. son living through Maat, lord of risings Akhu-n-Aton, true of speech

5.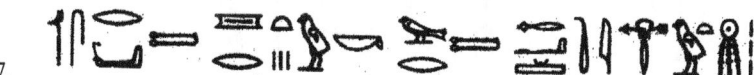

   5.1. *aha-f rdy ankh djeta heh chaa k nefer pa Aton*

   5.2. standing (raising) up living forever and eternal risings, beauteous this Aton

6.

   6.1. *ankh neb heh iu k tih n tj anti*

   6.2. living lord of eternity, it is you shining and vitalizing as you rise

7.

   7.1. *Usur tjn meritu k ur tjen aa ti shtyut*

   7.2. In power to shoot down your loving rays which are great and magnanimous

The Hindu Transformation of the Vedic Trinity and Solar Principle

Thus, in the three Vedic divinities, Agni, Indra and Surya, which are still revered in modern India, we can readily see the Trinity principle and its underlying solar mythology, which leads to the mysticism of the transcendental nature of its source. In Hindu and Buddhist texts of later Indian mythology, the remnants of the "solar mythos" remained overlaid by the newer interpretations (evolution) of Hindu thought.

The solar principle was carried on into Hinduism through the divinities Vishnu and Surya; Agni's attributes were absorbed into them. Vishnu was a deity of minor importance in the Vedic period in comparison with Varuna, Indra, Agni and Surya, being considered as an aspect of them sometimes. However, in the Early Hindu period (600 B.C.E.- 261 B.C.E.) the mythology surrounding Vishnu was changed dramatically. Firstly, he was seen as a manifestation of the rays of the sun. In the Vedas he took three steps and these measured the seven worlds. The steps are also related to the three phases of the sun, rising, zenith and setting. Vishnu welcomed the faithful to heaven and was also referred to as "the unconquerable preserver," an attribute that would be expanded in the Hindu period.

It should be clear that while the elements were there in the Vedic tradition, the concept for the Trinity was assembled in the Hindu tradition (early Period). In Hinduism the concept of the Trinity has evolved into an almost identical match to the Ancient Egyptian teaching, holding that a three-fold form of divine manifestation arises out of an inscrutable Absolute. Both in Ancient Egypt and the Hindu tradition, the Trinity serves the creative sustaining and dissolving functions.

Figure 174: The Hindu Supreme Being Brahman

The All-encompassing divinity manifests as the Hindu Trinity: Brahma, Vishnu, Shiva.

Figure 175: The Kamitan Supreme Being Neberdjer

The All-encompassing divinity manifests as the Kamitan Trinity: Kamitan Trinity: Kheperi, Ra, Tem.

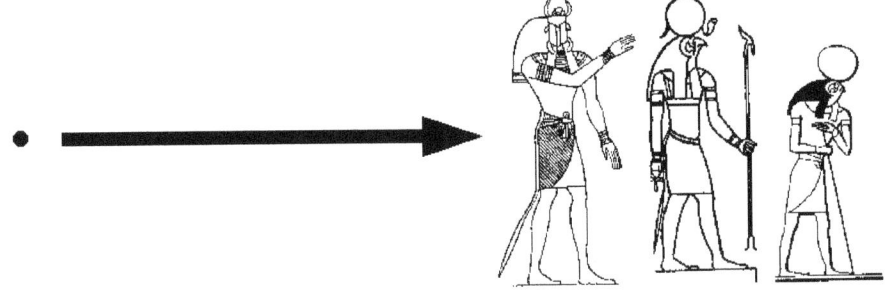

Figure 176: Below-The Solar aspect, Nefertem, or Heru-pa-khart (Heru {Sun-god}) as the Child, i.e. Creator-morning sun.

As we saw earlier, the divinities Brahma of India and Nefertem of Ancient Egypt exhibit closely matching iconographies. Both, sit on a lotus and symbolize the solar principle of Creator. In Kamitan as well as Hindu myth the trinity signifies the divinity manifesting in three aspects: The creator (Brahma or Khepri), the sustainer (Vishnu or Ra) and the destroyer or dissolver (Shiva or Tem). In the creation story involving the Asarian Mysteries[552], the divinity Asar assumes the role of the Creator, as Khepri and Tem:

> "Neb-er-tcher saith, I am the creator of what hath come into being, and I myself came into being under the form of the god Khepera, and I came into being in primeval time. I had union with my hand, and I embraced my shadow in a love embrace; I poured seed into my own mouth, and I sent forth from myself issue in the form of the gods Shu and Tefnut." "I came into being in the form of Khepera, and I was the creator of what came into being, I formed myself out of the primeval matter. My name is Ausares (Asar).
>
> I was alone, for the Gods and Goddesses were not yet born, and I had emitted from myself neither Shu nor Tefnut. I brought into my own mouth, hekau, and I forthwith came into being under the form of things which were created under the form of Khepera."

The Solar Culture in Present Day India

Some Indologists downplay the solar aspect in Hindu myth, even referring to it as a short lived cult which existed early within the panorama of the Vedic and Hindu tradition, but that passed away. However, we will see that while the solar principle plays a relatively minor role in modern Hinduism, it actually forms the underlying basis of the religion and Indian culture. There is a special reference in Hindu tradition related to the "solar race," which survives in modern times. It is possible to see that the solar myth runs through the Vedic tradition and into the Hindu, but that the particular development of the solar principle in Hinduism was not fully developed in the Vedic period. Specifically, the concept of Vishnu as the sustainer or preserver in the context of the Hindu Trinity of Brahma, Vishnu and Shiva was a new development in Indian mythology and philosophy. This development parallels the philosophy of Ancient Egypt and not the Vedic Tradition.

Rama, Krishna and Buddha are often referred to as being descended from the "solar race." The solar race was descended from one of the sons of Surya. Frequent reference to the pride of the solar race can be found in the Hindu traditions even in modern times (movies, rituals, etc.). This solar mythos is evidence of a tradition whereby worshippers are to understand that they are also descendants of the solar divinity since that divinity created all and sustains all. This form of worship is facilitated by the fact that the sun is a dynamic aspect of that solar principle whose phenomenal impact on human life can be seen and felt daily.

THE AFRICAN ORIGINS OF CIVILIZATION, RELIGION AND YOGA SPIRITUALITY

Item for Comparison 41: Ancient Egyptian Memphite Theology and Indian Vaishnavism

Another area of correlation between Ancient Egyptian religion and Indian Religion is between Memphite Theology and Vaishnavism. Vaishnavism is the worship of the divinity Vishnu and his incarnations. As explained earlier, Vishnu is a Vedic divinity that was adopted into the Early Hindu tradition of India albeit in a transformed way. His attributes were elevated above those of Indra, the king of the Vedic divinities and his incarnations were the subjects of the important Hindu epics, Ramayana and Mahabharata. The following comparison between the myth of Memphis in Ancient Egypt and the Vaishnava tradition of ancient India provides insight into the affinity of the Indians for this Ancient Egyptian tradition (Memphite Theology), to the extent of founding a settlement in Menefer (Hetkaptah - Memphis). It also gives insight into the philosophy of Memphite Theology that also appealed to the Buddhists from India who also came there. The Indian teachings of Vishnu, the Lotus, the Cosmic Serpent, The Creator Divinity sitting on the Lotus which arises out of the Primeval Ocean, etc., occur in the Ancient Egyptian Anunian-Memphite Theology. The Creator Divinity, the principle called "Brahma" in Indian myth is called "Khepri" or "Nefertem" in Ancient Egyptian myth.

Figure 177: Above- The Ancient Egyptian *Ptah-Tanen (Tem)* sitting on the primeval ocean with the sundisk (Tem, Nefertem) issuing from his head, his seat has the Sema (Sma) symbol of mystic union.

Ptah, Nefertem and the Mysticism of the Memphite Trinity

The Egyptian Trinity mythology of *Amun-Ra-Ptah* represents a major philosophical discourse on the composition of nature and the path of Kamitan spirituality. Memphite Theology, based on the god Ptah, is only a third of the entire teaching. Ptah is the Supreme Spirit and he manifests Creation through his consort Sekhmet and their child Nefertem. The Trinity of Memphis (Ptah-Sekhmet-Nefertem) relates to a profound understanding of the nature of Creation. Ptah is the hidden inner essence of creation and the essence of the human soul as well. Like Vishnu, in Hindu myth, Ptah is passive, immobile and detached. He "thinks" Creation into being by his will and has indeed become the Universe, through the actions of the Creator Nefertem. Ptah's thoughts are transformed into "word" (i.e. vibrations), and these cause the Nun (primeval Ocean) to take the varied forms of Creation which are described in detail in the foremost scripture of Memphite Theology, the "Shabaka Stone Inscription."[553] This philosophy means that just as wind and its motion are one and the same, and the ocean and its waves are one and the same, in the same way, the Supreme Self and the objects of the world are one and the same. According to Memphite Theology, the world is composed of *neteru*. These neterus are divine energy, cosmic forces that constitute all physical phenomena. These neteru have assumed the bodies (forms) of all the objects in the world which appear on the surface to be different and separate from each other, but in reality, the neteru are essentially conditioned aspects of God and therefore God has entered into all forms of existence. Memphite Theology is actually a unique form of the Kamitan religion in that it is highly philosophical and oriented towards intellectual development leading towards intuitional realization of the nature of Self. In this sense it is no surprise to find that the early Buddhists and Hindus (Upanishadic-Vedantic tradition), which were disciplines emphasizing psychology and philosophy, developed an affinity for the city of Memphis and became attached to its temple which promoted the teachings of Memphite Theology, since they all have much in common with the Buddhist and Hindu teachings. The Memphite scripture elucidates on the process of Creation and in its fundamental principles it is strikingly parallel with those of Hinduism. Ptah thinks and a Creator, Tem, on his lotus, comes into existence and Creation is brought forth.

> "2- Then, not having a place to sit Ptah causes Nun to emerge from the primeval waters as the Primeval Hill so that he may have a place to sit. Atom then emerges and sits upon Ptah."[554]

In order to understand and appreciate the word Nefertem and its relation to the Indian Brahma more fully, its definition and function will now be presented. Nefertem means "beautiful completion." In the Ancient Egyptian *Book of Coming Forth By Day* it is said that when an initiate attains resurrection, i.e. Spiritual enlightenment, they are actually becoming Nefertem. In the Creation Myth of the city of Anu (Anunian Theology), Tem is the divine aspect of the spirit as the first individuated entity to emerge from the primeval ocean. Also, in a separate but related teaching, from the myth of Ra and Aset, Tem is referred to as the third aspects of Ra as follows.

In the myth of Ra and Aset, Ra says: *"I am Kheperi in the morning, and Ra at noonday, and Temu in the evening."* Thus we have *Kheper-Ra-Tem*, ☉ ⌒ ⤳🕊 ⎟, as the Anunian Triad. In Chapter 4 of the *Prt m Hru*, the initiate identifies {him/her} self with Tem, symbolizing that {his/her} life as a human being with human consciousness is coming to an end. Instead of an awareness of individuality and human limitation, there is now a new awareness of infinity and immortality, even though the physical body continues to exist and will die in the normal course of time. The initiate will live on as a "living" soul and join with Tem (individual consciousness joins Cosmic Consciousness):

> "I am Tem in rising; I am the only One; I came into being with Nu. I am Ra who rose in the beginning."

Figure 178: The Ancient Egyptian divinity: Nefertem

The passage above is very important because it establishes the mystical transcendence of the initiate who has realized {his/her} "oneness" and union with the Divine. In other papyri, Tem is also identified with the young Herupakhart (Harmachis -young Heru, the solar child) as the early morning sun. Thus, Kheperi-Ra-Temu are forms of the same being and are the object of every initiate's spiritual goal. Being the oldest of the three theologies, the Mysteries of Anu (Anunian Theology) formed a foundation for the unfoldment of the teachings of mystical spirituality which followed in the mysteries of Hetkaptah (Memphis- Memphite Theology), through Ptah, and the Mysteries of Waset (Thebes- Theban Theology), through Amun. With each succeeding exposition, the teaching becomes more and more refined until it reaches its quintessence in the Hymns of Amun.

THE AFRICAN ORIGINS OF CIVILIZATION, RELIGION AND YOGA SPIRITUALITY

In the Ancient Egyptian Pyramid Texts there is a very important passage which provides insight into the role of Nefertem and the entire teachings behind the Trinity of Memphite Theology.

> "I become Nefertem, the lotus-bloom which is at the nostril of Ra; I will come forth from the horizon every day and the gods and goddesses will be cleansed at the sight of me."
>
> —Ancient Egyptian Pyramid Texts

Thus, we are to understand that Ptah is the source, the substratum from which all creation arises. Ptah is the will of the Spirit, giving rise to thought itself and that thought takes form as Sekhmit, Creation itself. The same spirit, Ptah, who enlivens Creation, is the very essence which rises above Creation to complete the cycle of Spirit to matter and then back to Spirit. The Lotus is the quintessential symbol of completion, perfection and glory. Thus it is used in Ancient Egyptian and Hindu mythologies as the icon par excellence of spiritual enlightenment. Therefore, smelling the lotus, and acting as the lotus means moving above the muddy waters of Creation and turning towards the sun which is the symbol of Ra, the Supreme Spirit.

In Chapter 24 of the *Pert M Heru (Book of Coming Forth By Day)*, the role of goddess Hetheru in the process of salvation is specified as the initiate speaks the words which will help {him/her} become as a lotus:

> "I am the lotus, pure, coming forth out into the day. I am the guardian of the nostril of Ra and keeper of the nose of Hetheru. I make, I come, and I seek after he, that is Heru. I am pure going out from the field."

Both the lotus and the sun have been used since ancient times to symbolize the detachment and dispassion that a spiritual aspirant must develop towards the world, that is, turning away from relating to the world from the perception of the limited senses and the conditioned mind, and rather, turning towards the underlying reality and sustainer of Creation, the illuminating transcendental Spirit, as symbolized by the sun. The lotus is a solar symbol, and as such is a wonderful metaphor for the process of spiritual evolution leading to Enlightenment. The lotus emerges everyday out of the murky waters of the pond in order to receive the rays of the sun. As it rises up through the murky waters to rise above, its leaves, which have a special coating or texture, promotes the water to run right off of them without a drop sticking or clinging to them. It then opens and blooms to the light of the sun. The spiritual aspirant, a follower of the Goddess, seeking to experience the Supreme Spirit, must rise {him/her} self up through the murky waters of egoism and negativity (anger, hatred, greed, and ignorance), eventually to rise above, leaving all remnants behind (i.e. transcending them), as {he/she} blooms to the light of the Self, i.e. attain Enlightenment. Hetheru and Heru form a composite archetype, a savior with all of the complementary qualities of the male and female principles, inseparable, complete and androgynous.

Table 24: The Fundamental Principles of Memphite Theology and Vaishnavism

Ancient Egyptian Memphite Theology	✓	Hindu Vaishnavism	Mythological and Philosophical Principles
NUN	⇔	NARA	The primeval Ocean, Nun and Nara, in both Ancient Egyptian and Indian myth, respectively, refer to the ocean of potential consciousness which can assume any form, i.e. the objects of Creation. It is this ocean which transforms itself into the objects and living beings of the universe. This ocean is the body, as it were, of the Divine (God, the Spirit).
PTAH-SOKAR	⇔	VISHNU	Both divinities, Ptah and Vishnu, hold the same mythological position. They are the "immovable" or "actionless" undivided Spirit, who emerges from the primeval ocean (Nun – Nara) and engenders a creative principle to do the work of creation. They symbolize the principle of pure individuality, the first "I am." Arising from the ocean of pure consciousness they will the "thought" of Creation. Ptah and Vishnu do not move. The creative principle performs all the action of creation and is sustained by the ocean of potential.
NEFERTEM	⇔	BRAHMA	That dynamic aspects (Nefertem – Brahma) of the individuated Spirit, the oneness, which emerge out of that first essence symbolize the principle of multiplicity, the force to produce many. From this one come the many differentiated forms of Creation. The Creator divinity arises out of the will of the Spirit.
NETERU	⇔	DEVA	The Creator brings forth creation by emanating creative energy (Neteru – Deva) or mythologically speaking, gods and goddesses, out of itself into the ocean of undifferentiated consciousness. Thereby, that part of the ocean that is moved by the creative energy assumes a particular form and quality. Thus, through the creator and the vibrations in the ocean of potential consciousness which are all aspects of the same Transcendental absolute, the Spirit transforms itself into the varied forms of Creation.

Correlations Between the Mystic Teachings of the Ancient Egyptian Coffin Texts and the Ancient Indian Upanishads

As we saw earlier, findings from the discipline of Paleoanthropology show a connection between Ancient Egypt and Ancient India. The specific evidence links the Ancient Egyptian peoples of Sakkara-Memphis with the Indus Valley Civilization (4,000 B.C.E.-3,000 B.C.E.).[555] Also, it was reported that an Indian colony existed in the city of Memphis at around 500 B.C.E.[556] Also there is documentation of the presence of Buddhist practitioners in Memphis. The deeper aspect of the mythic formats presented above, from Ancient Egypt and India, contain vast and profound schemes of cosmological and mystical teaching. The teachings of Memphite Theology, contained in the Shabaka Inscription and the attendant prayers and Hymns to Ptah are essentially a mythological interpretation of the Ancient Egyptian *Pert M Hru* or *Book of Enlightenment* texts (*Pyramid Texts, Coffin Texts and Papyrus Texts*). The myths of Hinduism are interpretations of the spiritual philosophy contained in the Upanishads, followed by the important Hindu epics (Mahabharata and the Ramayana). It is important to understand that the Upanishadic era literature is concerned with high philosophy and the gods and goddesses therefore assume a secondary role. The Later Classical epics called the Puranas, which began appearing during the Gupta period (319-415 A.C.E.)[557]

became the main source of modern Hindu mythology. By the 10th century A.C.E. the Puranas became the scriptures of the common man. Containing a great variety of legendary material, their main purpose, like all mythic scriptures such as the Asarian Resurrection of Egypt, the Gospels of Christianity, etc., was glorifying the gods and goddesses and not to prove historical events. In the case of Hinduism, the Puranas glorified Vishnu, Shiva, and Brahma for the purpose of engendering followers to the tradition, and not necessarily to provide a historical documentation. Of the eighteen principal Puranas that survive, the most popular is the Bhagavata-Purana on the early life of Krishna.[558] Therefore, it will be fruitful to compare the philosophical scriptures of Ancient Egypt and India. In doing so there are several important correlations between Ancient Egyptian and Indian spirituality.

> "After the millions of years of differentiated creation, the chaos that existed before creation will return; only the primeval god[175] and Asar will remain steadfast-no longer separated in space and time."
>
> –Ancient Egyptian *Coffin Texts*

The passage above concisely expresses the powerful teaching that all creation is perishable and that even the gods and goddesses will ultimately dissolve into the primordial state of potential consciousness. Therefore, it behooves a human being to move towards the Divine since that is the only stable truth that exists as an abiding reality. This is known as the Absolute, from which all has emanated and into which all will dissolve. *Tm* (Tem, Tum, Atum, Atum-Ra) is the Absolute, from which Creation arises and into which Creation will dissolve. The same transcendental and non-dualist philosophy evident in the passage above from the *Coffin Texts* can be found in the Indian *Upanishads*.

> "Before creation came into existence, Brahman (the Absolute) existed as the Unmanifest. From the Unmanifest was created the manifest. From himself he brought forth himself. Hence he is known as the Self-Existent."
>
> —Taittiriya Upanishad

The Ancient Egyptian concept of Nun is powerfully expressed in the following passage from the *Coffin Texts*.

> "I am Nu, The Only One, without equal and I came into being at the time of my flood...I originated in the primeval void. I brought my body into existence through my own potency. I made myself and formed myself in accordance with my own desire. That which emanated from me was under my control."
>
> –Ancient Egyptian *Coffin Texts*

Once again, the initiate is to discover that the Divine Self is the substratum of manifest creation and that {his/her} deeper essence and the deeper essence of all humanity is that same Self-existent Divinity which brought the entire creation into being by the power of her own will and desire. Nun is an aspect of Tem. In this aspect, it is to be understood as a formless potential matter which can convert itself into any form and any element (earth, water, fire, metal, etc.). This process may be likened to how temperature affects water. For example, very cold water becomes ice, and ice can have any shape. When very hot, the water evaporates and becomes so subtle (vapor) as to be "unmanifest." At room temperature, he same water is visible but formless. All matter is like the water. All matter is composed of the same essence which takes on the form of various objects, just as clay can take many forms. However, the forms are not abiding but temporary. God has assumed the forms of Creation just as an actor assumes a part in a play. When the play is over, the actor's mask is stripped away and the true essence of the actor's identity is revealed, just as ice melts to reveal water. The Divine Self is the substratum of all that is manifest. The same philosophy, and using almost the same exact language, is evident in the Indian *Upanishads*.

> "...In the beginning there was Existence alone—One only, without a second. He, the One, thought to himself: Let me be many, let me grow forth. Thus, out of himself he projected the universe; and having projected the universe out of himself he entered into every being."
>
> —Chandogya Upanishad

---

[175] Referring to the Supreme Being in the form of Atum-Ra

THE AFRICAN ORIGINS OF CIVILIZATION, RELIGION AND YOGA SPIRITUALITY

This conceptualization in the Chandogya Upanishad (c.800 B.C.E.) which states that *"out of himself he projected the universe; and having projected the universe out of himself he entered into every being,"* is exactly the same conceptualization already present in the Memphite Theology (c.5000-3000 B.C.E.). Also, the highly intellectual and philosophical nature of Memphite Theology and its consequent similarity to Buddhism become evident. *(Highlighted portions are by Ashby)*

Figure 179: Above- The Shabaka Stone (now with much of its text rubbed off due to mishandling)

The Shabaka Inscription

The nature and composition of *"matter,"* or what is termed *"physical reality,"* and the concept of *"consciousness"* were understood and clearly set down in the hieroglyphic texts which date back to 5000 B.C.E in the theological system of Memphis, Egypt, as follows:

1. *"Ptah conceived in his heart* (reasoning consciousness-mind) all that would exist and at his utterance (the word - will, power to make manifest), created Nun, the primeval waters (unformed matter-energy).

2. Then not having a place to sit Ptah causes Nun to emerge from the primeval waters as the Primeval Hill so that he may have a place to sit. Atom then emerges and sits upon Ptah. Then came out of the waters four pairs of gods and goddesses, the Ogdoad (eight Gods):

3. Nun (primeval waters) and Nunet (heaven).
4. Huh (boundlessness) and Huhet (that which has boundaries).
5. Kuk (darkness) and Kuket (light).
6. Amon (the hidden) and Amonet (that which is manifest).

7. *The Neteru (Nun, Nunet, Huh, Huhet, Kuk, Kuket, Amon, Amonet) are the lips and teeth of (God's) mouth which speaks the names of all things which come into existence . . .*

8. *. . The Heart and tongue have power over all the limbs. God is found as the heart within all bodies, and in the mouth of each neter and all humans as the tongue (will), of all things that live. . . It is God who thinks (as the Heart) and who commands (as the tongue). . .*

9. *. . . That which the nose breathes, the eyes see, the ears hear; all of these (senses) are communicated to the heart. It is the heart (mind) which makes all knowledge and awareness manifest, and then the tongue is what repeats what the heart has thought. . .*

10. *. . . All divine utterances manifested themselves through the thoughts of the heart and the commandments of the tongue. . .*

11. *. . . Justice is done to they who do what is loved, punishment to they who do what is hated. Life is given to they who are peaceful, death is given to the criminal. . .*

12. ...In truth God (Ptah) caused the neteru to be born, the creation of the cities, establishment of the nomes, the establishment of the neteru in their places of adoration. . . God made their likenesses according to their desire. Thereby, the neteru entered into their bodies, the variety of wood, all types of mineral, clay, and all things that grow from these and in which they have taken place, foods, provisions, and all good things... He (Ptah) is Heru."

13. Thus is it to be understood that Ptah is the mightiest of all Divinities.

Through the Shabaka Inscription we are to understand that Ptah created the gods and goddesses (Verse 3) through his *thought and desire* i.e. will, (verse 1-2) and they became the manifested creation which is like the body that the gods and goddesses, i.e. the spirit, exists in. In essence, since God is the innermost reality within *"each neter"* (god or goddess) and *"all humans,"* it is actually God who is thinking, perceiving and experiencing through them (Verse 5). Further, it is God who not only made the objects of creation (*the variety of wood, all types of mineral, clay, and all things that grow from these and in which they have taken place, foods, provisions, and all good things...*), but it is actually God (Ptah) who is in the objects of Creation and Creation is his body (Verse 9). In this manner, as in Buddhism, the mystic practitioner is to realize the mental nature of the universe. The mind and consequently psychology, is the key to understanding the universe and consequently also understanding God as well. The mind controls the tongue (sound-vibration – verse 7) and by righteousness (verse 8) an initiate can come to discern the mental act or will which has brought forth and sustains Creation. These are fundamental Buddhist concepts:

1. Suffering due to vices vs. peace and righteousness, Maat, which includes Truth: Maat is Right Action, Non-violence, Right Action- self-control, Right Speech, Right Worship, Selfless Service, Balance of Mind - Reason – Right Thinking, Not-stealing, Sex-Sublimation, and Maat Offering (uniting with the Divinity).
2. Creation and enlightenment by mental act,
3. Right Understanding, Ptah is the supreme Being and all objects in Creation proceed from him and are constructs of his mind.
4. Ptah "gave birth" to the gods and goddesses as the Buddhist "Dharmakaya," the cosmic father-mother gave birth to the cosmos.

In the capacities outlined above, Memphite Theology is a compatible with Buddhism and the Upanishadic tradition.

THE AFRICAN ORIGINS OF CIVILIZATION, RELIGION AND YOGA SPIRITUALITY

Memphite Theology and the Upanishadic Tradition

Again, the Hindu Upanishads contain passages that are even more closely matched to the teachings of the Shabaka Inscription, especially in relation to the concept of God creating Creation in accordance with his thought and will, and then entering into Creation and experiencing it through the mind and senses of sentient beings, who are also essentially God. This teaching may be considered one of the most important Upanishadic instructions and here we find it as the most prominent theological tenet in Memphite Theology of Sakkara-Memphis in Ancient Egypt, using almost the same language and style of writing. Also there is the teaching of the eyes of God, discussed further below. Thus, it is clear that the sages of both scriptures, though separated in time, were part of the same spiritual tradition. So Memphite Theology and the Upanishadic tradition are linked by yogic philosophy, mythic language, cosmological conception of the universe and divine consciousness, and physical contact between the practitioners of Egypt and India. Thus, the concept of Brahman (absolute)[176] of the Upanishadic tradition in India is an aspect of Ptah of Memphite Theology in Ancient Egypt.

> This Great Being has a thousand {meaning countless} heads, a thousand eyes, and a thousand feet. He envelops the universe. Though transcendent, he is to be meditated upon as residing in the lotus of the heart, at the center of the body, ten fingers above the navel.
> *He alone is all this*—what has been and what shall be. He has become the universe. Yet he remains forever changeless, and is the lord of immortality.
> -Svetasvatara Upanishad[559]

"Self-luminous is that Being (God), and formless. *He dwells within all and without all.* He is unborn, pure, greater than the greatest, without breath, without mind."
-Mundaka Upanishad[560]

> 13. *This Brahman shines forth indeed when one speaks with speech, and it dies when one does not speak.* His splendour goes to the eye alone, the life (prana) to breath (prana).
> *This Brahman shines forth indeed when one sees with the eye, and it dies when one does not see.* Its splendour goes to the ear alone, the life (prana) to breath (prana).
> *This Brahman shines forth indeed when one hears with the ear, and it dies when one does not hear.* Its splendour goes to the mind alone, the life (prana) to breath (prana).
> *This Brahman shines forth indeed when one thinks with the mind, and it dies when one does not think.* Its splendour goes to the breath (prana) alone, and the life (prana) to breath (prana).[561]
> -Kaushitaki-Upanishad. First Adhyaya.

"If Creating, I enter my Creation," the Self reflected...
-Prasna Upanishad[562]

> Self-luminous is that Being, and formless. *He dwells within all and without all.*
> He is unborn, pure, greater than the greatest, without breath, without mind.
> From him are born breath, mind, the organs of sense, ether, air, fire, water, and the earth, and he binds all these together.
> *Heaven is his head, the **sun and moon eyes**, the four quarters his ears, the revealed scriptures his voice, the air is his breath, the universe his heart. From his feet came the earth. He is the innermost Self of all.*
> From him arises the sun-illumined sky, from the sky the rain, from the rain food, and from food the seed in man which he gives to woman.
> *Thus do all creatures descend from him.*
> -Mundaka Upanishad[563]

It is notable that the description of God in the Upanishads closely matches that given in the Shabaka Inscription as the Spirit embodies the living and non-sentient Creation. The above scripture from the Mundaka Upanishad also match with the Kamitan in the description of the eyes of God being the "sun and moon." The concluding portion of the Shabaka Inscription states that Ptah is also Heru, and in Anunian

---

[176] Brahman, the Absolute, is not to be confused with Brahma, the Creator.

Theology (related to Ra and Heru) we find the exact same description for the eyes of Heru, that his eyes are the "sun and moon."

> Desiring that he should become many, that he should make himself many forms, *Brahman meditated. Meditating he created all things.*
> *Creating all things, he entered into everything.*
> -Taittiriya Upanishad[564]

> 3. *From him (when entering on creation) is born breath, mind, and all organs of sense, ether, air, light, water, and the earth*, the support of all.

> 7. *From him the many Devas (gods and goddesses) too are begotten*, the Sadhyas (genii), men, cattle, birds, the up and down breathings, rice and corn (for sacrifices), penance, faith, truth, abstinence, and law.
> -Second Mundaka. First Khanda.[565]

Thus, it has been demonstrated that Ancient Egyptian Memphite Theology and Mystical Philosophy and the Indian Upanishadic and Buddhist Theology and Mystical Philosophy correlate to each other in several fundamental as well as specific ways. These correlations, in conjunction with other factors discussed throughout this book identify a close relationship.

Item for Comparison 42: The Mystical Philosophy behind the Trinity of Enlightened Human Consciousness in Ancient Egypt and India

Figure 180: Above: The God Asar embraced by the goddesses Aset and Nebethet.

There is a very similar story to the Ancient Egyptian myth surrounding Asar, Aset and Nebethet, to be found in the Indian Vedantic text, *"Yoga Vasistha Ramayana."*[566] Asar was a king in Ancient Egypt and he had two goddesses, Aset and Nebthet. There is deep mystical symbolism in the images and teachings surrounding the Triad or Asar, Aset and Nebethet. In the Temples of *Denderah, Edfu and Philae* there are sculptured representations of the Mysteries of Asar. These show *"The Asar"* (initiate) lying on a bier and Aset and Nebethet are nearby and are referred to as the "two widows" of the dead Asar. Aset and Nebethet are represented as looking exactly alike. The only main difference being in their headdress: Aset ⌐, Nebethet ⌐ or ⌐. However, the symbols of these goddesses are in reality just inverted. The symbol of Nebethet is the symbol of Aset when inverted ⌐→⌐. Therefore, each is a reflection of the other and it may be also said that both are aspects of the same principle. Their body and facial features are exactly alike. This likeness which Aset and Nebethet share is important when they are related to Asar. In essence, Asar represents divine consciousness, which begets through Nebethet (Lady of the House-time and space) who symbolizes mortal existence, human life. Asar also gives birth to higher consciousness through Aset (Intuitional Wisdom-self-knowledge) in the form of Heru.

In the Yoga Vasistha there is a parable told to the initiate *Rama* by sage Vasistha who relates the story of *Lila*. Lila is a virtuous lady who had been practicing devotion to the Supreme Being in the form of Goddess Saraswati, the Hindu goddess of wisdom. Lila's austerities and meditations were noticed by the goddess, who then appeared to Lila and granted her the boon of wisdom and the ability to accompany her husband at the time of his death to observe his fate. The goddess led Lila to see her previous incarnations and to see the different dimensions visited by the soul at the time of death. She saw her husband in a different world system as he grew up and became a king, as he had been in the previous lifetime with Lila. In his new lifetime he had led himself, by the force of the karma (impetus in the personality due to past actions, thoughts desires and feelings), which impelled him, to experience conditions and personalities similar to those he had known in his previous lifetime with Lila. When her husband's new lifetime was coming to an end, Goddess Saraswati told Lila that he had practiced devotion to her and would become Enlightened. When he was on his deathbed, his queen came in to tend to him. To Lila's surprise, he had married another queen in that lifetime who looked exactly like her (Lila).

THE AFRICAN ORIGINS OF CIVILIZATION, RELIGION AND YOGA SPIRITUALITY

Figure 181: Above- The Hindu King and his two Queens.

Lila asked Saraswati about this and the goddess explained that the soul moves to different realms according to its karma, and this leads it to the experiences it will have. The king, at the time of his death in the previous lifetime, still had certain desires which continued to manifest themselves in the new lifetime. Therefore, his ministers and his queen looked like those of the previous lifetime. However, the queen of the second lifetime, Lila-2, was not as advanced spiritually as the first Lila. Therefore, her interests were more of a worldly nature and she asked Saraswati to allow her to go with her husband when he died since she loved him so much. Lila-1, the first Lila, had not only asked to be with her husband but also for Enlightenment. She wanted to know the secrets and mysteries of the Self. Thus, Saraswati granted them both their desires. When the king again died his soul traveled back to the original world system where he had lived with Lila-1. Through the boons given by Goddess Saraswati, Lila-2 died when the king died and awoke again to find herself in the new world system at the side of the king. Lila-1 returned also, having attained wisdom and Enlightenment, and through the force of Goddess Saraswati, the people of the kingdom forgot that the king had died and accepted the two Lilas as his queens even though there had only been one Lila originally. Now the king lived out his present lifetime with two Lilas to tend on him.

Mystically, Lila-1 represents wisdom and Enlightened consciousness. Lila-2 represents worldly or relative consciousness, the consciousness which is aware of time and space and ordinary human life. The king represents the Enlightened Sage who has double consciousness, being aware of the transcendental reality (Lila-1) while at the same time being aware of the relative or temporal (Lila-2). The power of illusion which Saraswati wielded over the kingdom is symbolic of the power which the world has to confound the human senses. In reality the physical world is not solid and yet it "appears" to be. This has been proven by modern science. When you are asleep the dream world appears to be real and solid and yet when you wake up it vanishes into thin air. This is the force of ignorance which Lila-1 and the king sought to overcome by becoming Enlightened.

In the same way, Asar sits on the throne and he is supported by the two goddesses Aset and Nebethet. Symbolically, Asar represents the Supreme Soul, the all-encompassing Divinity which transcends time and space. Aset represents wisdom and Enlightened consciousness. She is the knower of all words of power and has the power to resurrect Asar and Heru. Nebethet represents temporal consciousness or awareness of time and space. She is related to mortal life and mortal death. This symbolism is evident in the sistrums[177] which bear the likeness of Aset on one side and of Nebethet on the other. It is also apparent in the writings of Plutarch when he says that Aset represents "generation" while Nebethet represents "chaos and dissolution". Also, in the hieroglyphic texts, Aset is referred to as the "day" and Nebethet as the "night." Aset represents the things that "are" and Nebethet represents the things which will "come into being and then die." Thus, Enlightenment is being referred to here and it is this Enlightened state of mind which the initiate in the Asarian (Osirian) Mysteries (*Asar Shetaiu*) has as the goal. To become one with Asar, to become the king/queen, means to attain the consciousness of Asar, to become aware of the transcendental, infinite and immortal nature while being aware of the temporal and fleeting human nature.

In Indian myth there is another story of a king, whose name was Jarasandha. He was invulnerable since he was born of <u>two mothers</u> who had eaten of a charmed mango which fell into the lap of his father, who,

---

[177] Hand held musical instrument with the images of the goddesses carved on either side-not pictured.

being childless at that time, was undergoing penances to obtain offspring. This story correlates with the Kamitan myth related to the nature of Heru wherein the concept of two mothers is expressed (higher and lower, earthly and spiritual etc.). These are classic motifs of Aset and Nebethet. Also it correlates in the idea of the conception of such a powerful personality. In Ancient Egypt there is a story related to one of the incarnations of Heru (*Sa-Asar* which means son of Asar) who is the counterpart of Krishna in Kamitan myth. Sa-Asar also had two mothers and his earthly mother who had eaten of a charmed fruit (Note: See section "The Philosophy of Social Order and Spiritual Upliftment of Humanity in Ancient Egypt and India" for full story).

Item for Comparison 43: The Indian Philosophy of the Veil of Maya and The Kamitan Philosophy of the Veil of Aset

The Indian Philosophy of the Veil of Maya

In Indian mythos-philosophy there is a concept called *Maya*. Sometimes depicted as a goddess, Maya is a philosophical concept that means "cosmic illusion." Human beings are deluded as to the true nature of Creation. Several analogies are given to explain this concept. In the Upanishads the scripture speaks of a rope that is perceived to be a snake, creating panic in an individual when there is no danger at all. In the same way this entire world is a manifestation of the Divine, but human beings see it as an aggregate of elements in which they are subjects, separate and distinct from all other objects. This condition of ignorance leads to the sense of individuality and individuality leads to egoism and the interminable pursuit of sense pleasures that must necessarily end in frustration and suffering.

Maya is often explained as a magician who has made an audience believe they are seeing something that is actually not there. God is that magician and the world is not there as wee see it. Actually it is God but we are caught up to deeply in our delusion to make sense of it. The Indian Vedantic concept of Moksha - liberation or the Buddhist concept of Nirvana – without desire, are dedicated to freeing the mind from maya. The term "maya" does not take on its mystical philosophic meaning until the Vedanta schools (Upanishadic Tradition) reinterpret the term as "cosmic illusion" or "hallucination"[567] as described above.

The Kamitan Philosophy of the Veil of Aset

The teachings surrounding the religious tradition of Aset give important information concerning the philosophy of ignorance and the delusion or deception from which spiritually ignorant human beings suffer. The *"Veil of Aset"* is the veil of ignorance which blocks divine awareness from human perception. The following teaching reveals the nature of Aset, who in this aspect represents the all-encompassing Divine Self.

> "I Aset, am all that has been, all that is, or shall be;
> and no mortal man hath ever unveiled me."

A devotee of Aset is *One who ponders over sacred matters and seeks therein for hidden truth*. It is not enough to just hear the ancient myths or to understand them at an intellectual level. The aspirant must go deep within him/herself to discover the subtle ideas being conveyed. *Plutarch,* a Greek initiate of the Temple of Aset (Isis), describes the character of an initiate of Aset as:

> "He alone is a true servant or follower of this Goddess who, after has heard, and has been made acquainted in a proper manner (initiated into the philosophy) with the history of the actions of these gods, searches into the hidden truths which lie concealed under them, and examines the whole by the dictates of reason and philosophy. Nor indeed, ought such an examination to be looked on as unnecessary whilst there are so many ignorant of the true reason even of the most ordinary rites observed by the Egyptian priests, such as their shavings[568] and wearing linen garments. Some, indeed, there are, who never trouble themselves to think at all about these matters, whilst others rest satisfied with the most superficial accounts of them. They pay a peculiar veneration to the sheep,[569] therefore they think it their duty not only to abstain from eating flesh, but likewise from wearing its wool. They are continually mourning for their gods, therefore they shave themselves."

One particular statement in reference to the teachings, *...the hidden truths which lie concealed under them....*, begs the question: What are these "hidden truths" which are "concealed" within the "history of the actions of the gods?" The following statement from the Yoga Vasistha elucidates on this question, introducing us to the esoteric or metaphysical level of religion as opposed to the ritualistic-mythological level.

> "O Rama, Gods and Goddesses and other deities with name and form are representations created by Sages for those whose intellect is weak as a child's..."
> -Yoga Vasistha Nirvana Prakarana Section 30[570]

The elaborate system of "Gods and Goddesses" as well as the symbols representing a "Supreme Being" are merely metaphors created by the ancient Sages for those who are not spiritually mature (possessing a highly developed sense of intellectual subtlety) to understand that God transcends all thoughts, symbols and concepts of the mind. Until the intellect (**Saa**) is developed, the symbols are used, but when spiritual sensitivity dawns, the hidden or esoteric meaning of the symbols is revealed, leading the initiate to greater and greater levels of inner awareness or Enlightenment.

Aset represents the Supreme teacher (preceptor) of the mysteries. Having attained spiritual knowledge by listening to the teachings of Aset, the task of the initiate is continuously reflected upon them until the veil of ignorance (egoism) is lifted. Through the process of continued intellectual refinement (reflection on the teachings), the veil is torn away. Thus, the mortal consciousness (symbolized by the veil) is transcended and Aset is realized in her unveiled form. In order to behold her unveiled form, ordinary human perception cannot be used. This is why *no mortal man* has unveiled her. Only those who have become like Aset (divine in consciousness) can see her. This concept is echoed in the Indian *Mundaka* Upanishad, which states *"He who knows Brahman becomes Brahman."*[571] Through gradual intellectual refinement attained through the process of reflection and meditation, the mind of the initiate becomes transformed. Thus, the initiate sees with Divine eyes and not with mortal ones. He or she is now beyond birth and death (mortality). Unveiling Aset is unveiling one's true Self. One must go beyond the "mortal" waking, dream-sleep and dreamless-deep-sleep states of consciousness to discover (unveil) one's true nature.

The Garment of Nun

The Kamitan term "Weaving the garment of Nun" is an allusion to the Ancient Egyptian goddess Net, the progenitor of goddess Aset, with whom the teaching "no mortal man hath ever unveiled me" is also associated. This phrase appears as one of the descriptions of the goddess. She is known as the "weaver" who brought Ra, the light, into being. The garment of Creation is also to be understood as the patchworks, which compose the day-to-day reality of life, that in turn deludes the mind. In fact, Creation is composed of atoms and molecules, which interact and come together to compose elements. However, these atoms are in themselves composed of energy, but the limited mind and senses do not perceive this ocean of energy, which is an aspect of the Nun, the Primeval Ocean. This effect of not perceiving the most subtle essence of Creation is the veil of the goddess, and therefore, it is the goal of every aspirant to unveil her, that is, to see her true form, the pure light of consciousness devoid of the ignorance. The existence of this veil however, is not the fault of or an effect created by the Goddess. It is the fault of ignorance, which has deluded the mind of the individual. This is true because upon attaining enlightenment, a human being discovers the underlying essence of Creation, beyond the illusions they had made for themselves. This essence is there even now, but the deluded mind cannot perceive it because it is besieged by ignorance that is reinforced with desires, passions, mental agitations (anger, hatred, greed, lust, etc.) and egoism. The various paths of Yoga science act to tear asunder the veil of illusion about the world.

THE AFRICAN ORIGINS OF CIVILIZATION, RELIGION AND YOGA SPIRITUALITY

Item for Comparison 44: The terms "Hari" and "Om" in Ancient Egypt and India

While *Om* is most commonly known as a *Sanskrit* mantra (word of power from India), it also appears in the Ancient Egyptian texts and is closely related to the Kamitan *Amun* in sound and Amen of Christianity. More importantly, it has the same meaning as Amun and is therefore completely compatible with the energy pattern of the entire group. According to the Egyptian Leyden papyrus, the name of the "Hidden God," referring to Amun, may be pronounced as *Om*, or *Am*.

Below you will find the ancient glyphs of the ancient Egyptian OM symbol. Note the similarity to the Indian symbol that follows.

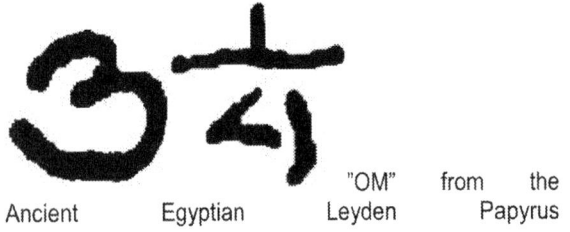

"OM" from the Ancient Egyptian Leyden Papyrus

The ancient African text containing the OM is found in the Leyden Magical Papyrus in which Supreme Being is described as follows:

> "Great is thy name, Heir is thy name, Excellent is thy name, Hidden is thy name,. Mighty one of the gods and goddesses is thy name, "He whose name is hidden from all the gods and goddesses is thy name, OM (𓏴𓏤), Mighty Am is thy name; All the gods and goddesses is thy name…"

We know that OM is the name of Amun because of the epithet "Hidden" and OM is the nameless Ancient divinity because of the epithet "name is hidden". OM is also the ancient divinity Neberdjer (All encompassing Divinity) because of the epithet "All the gods and goddesses" so OM is the name given to the most ancient divinities of Kamit (Egypt) dating to the predynastic era (prior to 5000 BCE).

Om is a powerful sound; it represents the primordial sound of creation. Thus it appears in Ancient Egypt as Om or Am, in modern day India as Om, and in Christianity as Amen, being derived from Amun. Om may also be used for engendering mental calm prior to beginning recitation of a longer set of words of power or it may be used alone as described above. One Indian Tantric scripture (*Tattva Prakash*) states that Om or AUM can be used to achieve the mental state free of physical identification and can bring union with *Brahman* (the Absolute transcendental Supreme Being - God) if it is repeated 300,000 times. In this sense, mantras such as Om, Soham, Sivoham, Aham Brahmasmi are called *Moksha Mantras* or mantras which lead to union with the Absolute Self. Their shortness promotes greater concentration and force toward the primordial level of consciousness.

The Indian Sanskrit Symbol "Aum" or "Om"

There is one more important divine name which is common to both Indian as well as Ancient Egyptian mystical philosophy. The Sanskrit mantra *Hari Om* is composed of Om preceded by the word Hari. In Hinduism, *Hari* means: "He who is Tawny." The definition of tawny is: "A light golden brown." However, Vishnu is oftentimes represented as "blue-black." This is a reference to the dark colored skin of Vishnu and Krishna. Vishnu is usually depicted with a deep blue and Krishna is depicted with a deep blue or black hue symbolizing infinity and transcendence. Hari is one of Krishna's or Vishnu's many divine names.

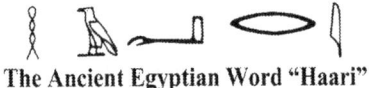

The Ancient Egyptian Word "Haari"

In the Ancient Egyptian mystical texts used to promote spiritual development (Words of Power or Heka - mantras), the word Haari also appears as one of the divine names[1] of God. Thus, the hekau-mantra Hari Om was also known and used in Ancient Egypt and constitutes a most powerful formula for mystical spiritual practice. Om or Am in Ancient Egypt was a shortened version of Amun, the divinity who like Vishnu and Krishna is depicted in Black or Blue (tawny). "Amun" also means hidden consciousness.

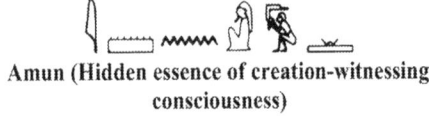

Amun (Hidden essence of creation-witnessing consciousness)

THE AFRICAN ORIGINS OF CIVILIZATION, RELIGION AND YOGA SPIRITUALITY

Item for Comparison 45: The Kingship of the Southern Land and the Northern Land

The Indian Scholar Sudhansu Kumar Ray noted a strong correlation in the following artifact from India. He noted its form, function, and mythological symbolism as areas of correlation between ancient Indian tradition and the Kamitan tradition. The white crown was worn by the Ancient Egyptian kings who represented the southern part of the country, Upper Egypt. There are several correlations to the Vedic and Hindu culture, but there are also several compelling correspondences to the southern culture of modern Egypt, which is more closely related to the Dravidian peoples. Thus, ichnographically, mythologically and also socially, this symbol has varied implications in reference to its larger context in the whole view of Ancient Egypt and India as being part of a vast culture stretching from Nubia in the south of Egypt to India.

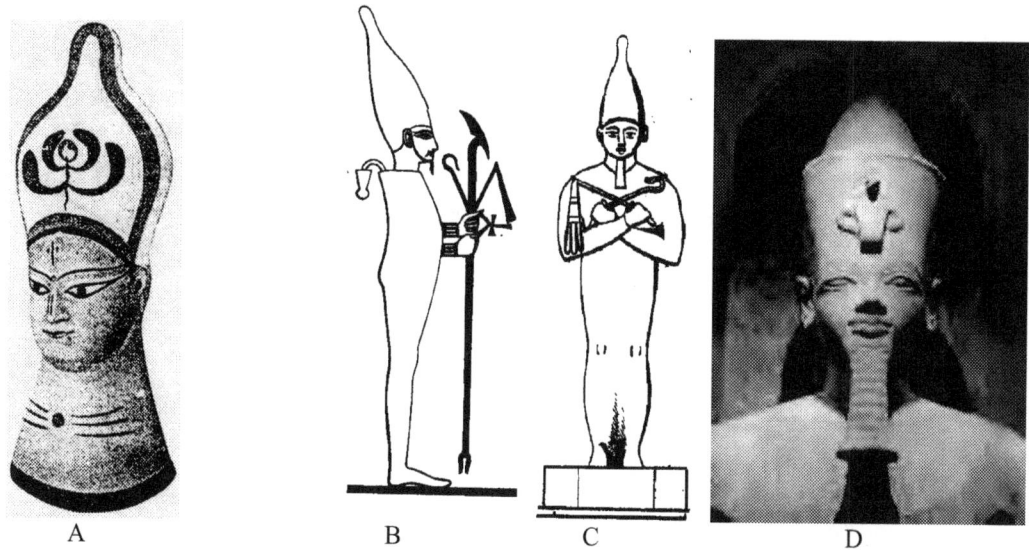

Figure 182: Above: A-Left to right- Bengali Raja (King of the South of India)[572] **with the crown of the south. B-C- Ancient Egyptian King of the South of Egypt with the white crown of the south. D- Crown of the south and north together-Kamit.**

But most important iconographical document is the "White Crown" on the head of the Bengali Door of the South, which is unusual in Indian art and archaeology but surprisingly corresponds with the tall "White Crown" (Hot) usually worn by the southern kings or Djats of Egypt.

From the above statement we can clearly ascertain the following political significances of the Bengali Door of the South:

(1) He wears a tall white crown (Hot) which signifies "South" and "Southern Government" like that in Egypt.

(2) He holds the titles "Door of the South (Dakshin-dar)" and "Great One of the Southern Eighteen (collectorates and distilleries)". He is a *Djat,* as the name of his festival denotes. He is also one of the twin-gods, (Ba-Ra), being the counterpart of the Governor of the North *(Sona-Ray).* *

(3) He is worshipped annually and occasionally only in the *south,* in the lower Gangetic delta. When a boatman passes through southern rivers, a fisherman does fishing in a tank, a wood-cutter exploits forest for his logs or a village headman repairs the old embankment, he must offer *puja* with wine to the Door of the South.

* For Sona-Ray see Modem Review for November. 1932, p. 521, and *Sonarayer* Gan (in Bengali) by A. K. Chakraberty. For Dakshin-dar see an article by Kalidas Datta, *Prabasi for* June, 1951.

It is a wonder, how and why the crown over the head of the Bengali Door of the South and the crown over the head of the Egyptian Door of the South iconographically correspond in shape and color! Why the administrative designations and titles of both the

Djats are the same? Why both the Djats are connected with the *southern* regions of the Nile and Ganges? -When we read about the office and duties of Rekhmara from the inscriptions of his tomb, who was a Djat of Southern Egypt, and held the office of the Door of the South at least about 1450 B.C., we can well understand the office and duties of our Door of the South of Bengal and the political motives which lie behind the *puja* and observance of the Zat(al) festival and can unmistakably recognize the portrait-figure of this high government officer of Egypt.**

** See Hall, AHNE, p. 280 for description about Rekhmara. in Egypt Southern Djat is 'Great One of the Southern Thirty", but in Bengal he is "Great One of the Southern Eighteen" (atharo-Bhatir-Raja). The number differs according to the number of the collectorates.[573]

NOTE: The word *"puja"* means worship or homage in the Indian language.

Mr. Ray has noted that the Indian king shown with the "White Crown" on the head of the Bengali Door of the South" follows the title format of Ancient Kamit (Crown of the south-king of the south). Also, he notes that the form of the crown in India is the same as that of Ancient Egypt (cone shaped). Furthermore, Ray notes the manner in which the king of India is described as ruler of certain collectorates or cities in the same fashion as the Ancient Egyptian king is ruler over certain "nomes" in the south or the north of Egypt.

Item for Comparison 46: The Philosophy of Righteous Action, Social Order and Spiritual Upliftment of Humanity in Ancient Egypt and India

For any society, a philosophy of righteous action, which will promote social order and harmony, is essential to the creation of a civilized community and for the survival of the population as well as the prosperity of the country. This harmony and prosperity is the basis which allows higher spiritual study and practice to take place and for the culture to endure. A society wherein discontent and unrest distract people obstructs them from attaining the higher philosophy of self-discovery. The sages and saints of Ancient Kamit introduced and perfected this philosophy; they called it Maat. This teaching influenced the creation of the regulations for righteous conduct in Greek philosophy, Hinduism, Judaism, Chinese philosophy, Christianity and Islam, as all of these peoples had contact with Ancient Egypt.

Kamitan Maat	Hindu-Buddhist Dharma	Jewish 10 Commandments	Chinese Confucianism And Taoism	Christian Beatitudes
>5,000 B.C.E.	800 B.C.E.	1,000 B.C.E.	500 B.C.E.	0 B.C.E.

Maat represents the very order which constitutes creation, that is, Cosmic Order. Therefore, it is said that Ra, the Supreme Being, created the universe by putting Maat in the place of chaos. So creation itself is Maat. Creation without order is chaos. Maat is, therefore, a profound teaching in reference to the nature of creation and the manner in which human conduct should be cultivated. It contains a cosmic as well as worldly implication. It refers to a deep understanding of Divinity and the manner in which virtuous qualities can be developed in the human heart so as to come closer to the Divine.

Maat is a philosophy, a spiritual symbol as well as a cosmic energy or force which pervades the entire universe. Maat is personified by a goddess (divinity). She is the symbolic embodiment of world order, justice, righteousness, correctness, harmony and peace. She is also known by her headdress composed of a feather, which symbolizes the qualities just mentioned. She is a form of the Goddess Aset, who represents wisdom and spiritual awakening through balance and equanimity.

In Ancient Egypt, the judges and all those connected with the judicial system were initiated into the teachings of Maat (Judges were priests of Maat). Thus, those who would discharge the laws and regulations of society were well trained in the ethical and spiritual-mystical values of life. These principles included the application of justice and the responsibility to serve and promote harmony in society as well as the possibility for spiritual development in an atmosphere of freedom and peace, for only when there is justice and fairness in society can there be an abiding harmony and peace. Harmony and peace are necessary for the pursuit of true happiness and inner fulfillment in life. The opposite of *Maat* (righteousness) is *n-Maat* (unrighteousness) or *Isfet*.

Hindu Dharma and Ancient Egyptian Maat Philosophy

In India, the term "Dharma" signifies "virtue," or "righteousness." It is contrasted with "Adharma" or "unrighteousness. While the term appears in the Rig Veda, its import and philosophical definition as a pathway to spiritual enlightenment occurs in the Upanishads and the Mahabharata epic. While the Rig Veda as a whole is cited as the source of Dharma, the concept takes shape and form as a mystical movement to act in a way, according to certain regulations for the purpose of promoting purity of heart, eradication of negative karma and attainment of enlightenment in the Hinduism period of Indian culture.[574]

> As sources of *dharma the Manusmrti* identifies the Veda in its entirety, established traditions in the heartland of Hinduism *(Aryavirta)*, the behaviour of exemplary citizens, and one's own conscience *(dtmatusti).*[575]

The Manusmriti (Manu's Law), regarded by many Hindus and Indian scholars as one of the most influential Hindu texts, is a late Hindu text dating from sometime between 200 B.C.E. and A.C.E. 100. So it is far removed even from the more generally accepted date for the creation of the Rig Veda by over 1000 years. Note that the Veda is cited, however the Veda contains no writings on Dharma nor does it explain the inner workings on Dharma and its effects on the personality. This occurs in the Upanishadic period and takes further shape in the epic literature period especially with the creation of the Mahabharata and

Ramayana texts which come much later in history than the Vedas. Therefore, Manu's assignation of the Veda in its entirety as the source for Dharma occurs because there is no specific citation in the Veda that can be made.

In Hinduism, Dharma is seen as the basis of spiritual life, the means to keep order in life so as to lead oneself to freedom from bondage to the world. As in Ancient Egypt, Dharma is represented by a deity who presides over universal (cosmic) order as well as a spiritual philosophy.

Table 25: Maat Philosophy Compared with Hindu Dharma Philosophy

Maat Principles of Ethical Conduct	Hindu Dharma Principles of Ethical Conduct (From the *Manu-Smriti*)
Truth (1), (6), (7), (9), (24) **Non-violence** (2), (3), (5), (12), (25), (26), (28), (30), (34) **Right Action- self-control (Living in accordance with the teachings of Maat)** (15), (20), (22), (36) **Right Speech** (11), (17), (23), (33), (35), (37) **Right Worship** (13), (21), (32), (38), (42) **Selfless Service** (29) **Balance of Mind - Reason – Right Thinking** (14), (16), (18), (31), (39) **Not-stealing** (4), (8), (10), (41) **Sex-Sublimation** (19), (27) The numbers within parenthesis represent the specific injunction in the 42 precepts of Maat that relate to the particular principle being expressed.	Firmness. Forgiveness, forbearance. Control of Senses. Non Stealing. Purity of body and mind. Control of mind. Purity of Intellect. Knowledge. Truthfulness. Absence of anger.

The original conception behind the idea of the *Per-ah* in Ancient Egypt was the righteous ruler concept, the ruler who is a divine minister, Heru (enlightened man or woman) on earth, upholder of truth, righteousness and order in society and leading the proper social development of civilization towards spiritual enlightenment. This is also the same concept inherent in the teaching of the Hindu scripture, *Ramayana*. After Lord Rama, an incarnation of Vishnu, succeeds in putting down the demons that have taken over the world he sits on the throne as a perfect God-man, directing society wisely, as an example for all politicians that the only way to govern is by the universal laws of God-consciousness. Rama's rule on earth is called *Rama-Raja* or Kingdom (Rulership) of Rama. This means a society of righteousness and justice as well as order and harmony, realizing that all is a Divine expression and worthy of love, compassion, fair treatment (Dharma) and wisdom so as to be led to spiritual enlightenment. Those who lead by promoting slavery, poverty, a wealthy elite, oppression, harshness, bigotry, racism, sexism, hatred, greed, lust, imprisonment for the sake of punishment rather than reform, etc., under the mantle of religion are not practicing any true religion, but a pseudo-religion of worldly desire, egoism and pride. Those who follow them will be led to adversity and frustration. When the principles of mystical religion are forgotten or put aside, it signals that humanity is in for a period of adversity and suffering. Humanity goes through repeated cycles where the forces of ignorance (unrighteousness, negativity) and Enlightenment (righteousness, good) inversely fluctuate, that is, when there are many Enlightened beings there is less ignorance, and consequently less unrighteousness in a given society, and thus in the world, and vice versa. In the Indian system, these cycles, called *Yugas* (Kali, Dwapar, Treta, Satya), are named according to the proportion of righteousness and unrighteousness that abounds. The world is always changing, and these changes are presented to lead souls, through struggles and conflicts and changes, to strive for righteousness so as to discover truth. So when a society abounds with righteousness, unrighteous souls will incarnate to challenge its ethical principles as a whole, as well as those of each individual member of that society. Likewise when unrighteousness prevails, righteous souls will incarnate to challenge it, and in so doing, attract and teach those members of society who are pure enough to recognize and desire truth.

THE AFRICAN ORIGINS OF CIVILIZATION, RELIGION AND YOGA SPIRITUALITY

In modern times, the country known as Bhutan continues this tradition. Following the Buddhist tradition, they have a king. The Bhutanese people are also guided by the spiritual leaders, the goal of the leaders being to promote the happiness of all members of the society, protecting the environment and promoting peace through order and sharing instead of egoism and greed. Consequently there are no upper and lower classes, or special allowances to the leaders or the king that are not accorded to the general populace which would ordinarily lead to animosity, strife, anger, hatred, greed, violence, etc. This is an ideal example of what was achieved in Ancient Egypt and in Ancient India, and it is therefore possible to recreate a society with such principles of high culture, even today.

kar·ma *n.* 1. *Hinduism & Buddhism.* The total effect of a person's actions and conduct during the successive phases of the person's existence, regarded as determining the person's destiny.[576]

Figure 183: Below Left- The Vedic-Hindu God Yama, "Restrainer"

Figure 184: Below Right- The Ancient Egyptian God Asar, "Judge of the Dead"

In the book *Art – Culture of India and Egypt,* the author S. M El Mansouri, discovered some important parallels in Ancient Egyptian and Indian mythology.

> "The general belief in India, was that as soon as a man died, he was conducted to "Yama", and "Chitragupta"; and in Egypt to "Osoris"[577] and "Thoth",[578] the scribe of Gods "Chitragupta" registers all the actions of man and woman, reads out a full account of their deeds, and strikes the balance, which decides whether the person deserves punishment or reward. It was so in Egypt, they had the same thing. What happened there was that, everyone had to be brought into the Hall of Double Truth, and there be judged by Osoris, God of Justice. The soul, after first confessing, before the forty-two Assessors of the Dead,[178] was conducted into the presence of God Osoris; the same balance had to be struck, in the same way as in Indian mythology. They placed on one of the scales, the heart or conscience, in the form of a small vase, and placed on the opposite scale the feather of truth; in the middle, sat the little Cynocephalus, the attendant of Thoth ... the scribe of Gods."[579]

In Indian thought, the god Yama administers the proprieties of righteousness (Dharma) on each individual and in the Kamitan system the god Asar serves the same function, administering Maat. The gods base their decisions about one's fate by means of examining one's record as a human being. This record is termed "Karma" in India and "Ari" in Ancient Egypt. In Indian history, the word "Karma" appears in the Vedic tradition with the meaning of the act of sacrifice as in a ritual. In the Upanishadic tradition the word takes on the much more expanded and profound meaning that it has come to represent in modern times, as the "residue or mental impression of any action performed by an unenlightened person."[580] This residue remains with a person even after death due to that person's desire to experience

---

[178] These 42 assessors are the same 42 judges of Maat.

pleasure from their performance of the action, because of spiritual ignorance. Since mystical philosophy maintains that happiness can only come from self-knowledge (Cosmic or Divine Consciousness) and not from worldly pursuits, all egoistic actions will inevitably lead to disappointment, if not in this lifetime, in a future one. However, this is not realized by people because when some actions are performed, they seem to give the desired result of pleasure. This then leads to the developing of craving in the personality as people become dependent on the result of their actions to experience happiness, or as it is referred to in Yoga, "the fruits" of action. The person feels that if they can engage in this action again and again, they will be a happier person or at least derive the same or more pleasure. Thus they strive to perform those actions that seem to bring them pleasure as much as possible, and strive to avoid and consequently they develop dislike for those actions or situations which they perceive as being an obstacle for their experience of pleasure. Many times, their actions to recapture the pleasure that they experienced previously in similar circumstances do not bring them the pleasure that they want due to many obstacles that develop in life, however, people simply make excuses for these times of disappointment or frustration, and continue on with their next pursuit. Another problem is that one cannot pursue that which gives pleasure on a continuous basis. Thus, this is not true happiness. True happiness is defined as an experience of the state of Enlightenment, whereby one experiences joy all the time, in all conditions and circumstances.

This means that true happiness is not a by-product of or dependent on doing some activity or acquiring some object or situation, but rather, it is a state of being. It is unaffected by any situation or circumstance in the world. It is a person's true essence. When an enlightened person performs actions, they are not doing so to become happy as a result, but because it is righteous action that they are being guided to do by their connection to the Divine…thus, in effect, they are performing divinely ordained works. Thus, karma impels a person to reincarnate in order to attempt the fulfillment of the desire left over from the previous karma, and this cycle of birth, death, birth continues until there is full self-knowledge of the illusoriness of desires, worldly attainments and actions. Thus, karma is not fate but the tendency that a person sets up, in their deep unconscious to like or dislike and desire or repudiate. This duality keeps the mind flowing from adversity to prosperity or from pleasurable to painful situations without achieving a resolution or peace, indefinitely. The same philosophy of the "residue" of action that remains in the mind of a person (deep unconscious level) may be seen in the Kamitan teachings of Meri-ka-ra.

Many people think of the philosophy of Karma as a concept that originated in India. The following text shows that it is a concept that was well understood in Kamit and is very much in harmony with what is today referred to as Karma. In Ancient Egypt the word for karma was Ari, meaning "action" which attaches to a person and leads them to their fate even beyond death. This is the same understanding in Hindu philosophy. The Kamitan teachings to Merikara and the *Pert M Hru* illuminate this teaching in detail. *(Highlighted text is by Ashby)*

Instructions of Merikara

(14) The Court that judges the wretch,
You know they are not lenient,
On the day of judging the miserable,
In the hour of doing their task.
It is painful when the accuser has knowledge,
Do not trust in length of years,
They view a lifetime in an hour!
When a man remains over after death,
His Ari (deeds, actions) are set beside him as treasure*,*
And being yonder lasts forever.
A fool is who does what they reprove!
He who reaches them without having done wrong
 Will exist there like a god,
Free-striding like the lords forever!
—Instructions of Merikara Ancient Egypt

The writings of Merikara confirm the understanding of a subtle aspect of action which follows one after death. This "residue" is judged and the destiny is administered thereby. This signifies that a person is the author of {his/her} own fate, i.e. karmic fortune. This teaching also conveys the relativity of time and space, as the "judges" exist in a different plane than the worldly, physical state and the passage of time is different for them. Thus, this passage also contains a reference which shows a comprehension of the relativity of time in different planes of existence, much like the Hindu metaphysics.[581]

Figure 185: Above- Vignette from Chapter 33 of Papyrus Ani: The Judgment scene from the *Pert m Heru* Text of Ancient Egypt.

Ani and his wife enter the judgment hall. Left to Right: Meskhenet and Rennenet, The Ba (the soul, as human-headed hawk), Shai (standing), Meskhenet (again-this time as birthing block {above Shai}), Anpu, Djehuti, Ammit.

The Judgment scene above shows how a person's own actions are judged and how this leads a person to their fate, either to move on and discover the Divine and become one with the Divine or to suffer due to negative actions of the past or to reincarnate. The Papyrus of Ani dates back to the 18th Dynasty of the Dynastic Period in Ancient Egypt (1500 B.C.E.). It denotes a philosophy related to the Asarian Resurrection theology that has been traced back to the Pre-Dynastic Age and which constitutes one of the central teachings of Ancient Egyptian religion, the Maat principle. The following detailed description of the Ancient Egyptian Judgment scene, alluded to by S. M El Mansouri (above), provides deeper insight into the workings of the Kamitan system of Ari.

> Judgment of the Soul. Text: Ani addresses his heart. At top, the gods and goddesses presiding are (right to left: Ra, Atum, Shu, Tefnut, Geb, Nut, Nebethet and Aset, Heru Ur, Hetheru, Saa and Hu (Divine Taste). Far left, Ani enters the hall of Judgment. His heart (conscience) is being weighed by Anpu (Anubis) while the Divine principals Shai, Rennenet and Meskhenet look on. Ani's soul and his destiny also look on while Anubis measures Ani's heart (unconscious mind containing the impressions or "residues") against the feather of Maat (i.e. the principles of the 42 precepts of Maat...truth, righteousness, etc.). At far right Djehuti records the result while the Ammit monster, the Devourer of the unjust, awaits the answer. The hands of Djehuti (God of Reason) are "Shai" which means "destiny" and "Rennenet" which means "Fortune and Harvest." The implication is that we reap (harvest) the result of our state of mind (heart). Our state of mind, including our subconscious feelings and desires, is weighed against cosmic order, Maat. If found to be at peace (Hetep) and therefore in accord with cosmic order (Maat) it will be allowed to join with the cosmos (Asar). Otherwise it will suffer the fate as dictated by its own contents (mental state of unrest due to lingering desires), which will lead it to Ammit who will devour the ego-personality. That soul will experience torments from demons until it learns its lessons through the process of trial and error, and then pursues an authentic process of mystical practice to become strong enough through wisdom to know itself (become Enlightened). Demons may be understood as negative cosmic energies which it has allowed itself to indulge in, in the form of mental anguish

and torments people put themselves through, due to their own ignorance. Self-torment may be regret over some action or inaction while alive or a reluctance to leave the physical realm because of a lingering desire to experience more earthly pleasure. Therefore, one controls one's own fate according to one's own level of wisdom or reasoning capacity.[582]

The Ancient Egyptian myth known as The Story of Sa-Asar succinctly and powerfully illustrates the concept of Ari (action-Karma). It describes the fate of the soul after death in accordance with the actions of the person while alive on earth.

"A man and a woman wanted to have a child, but could not conceive so the woman, named Mehusekhe, went to a temple to sleep there in the hope that a god or goddess would come to her and tell her what to do. A spirit came to her in a dream and told her to go to the place where her husband was, and to eat from a melon vine and embrace her husband in love, and that she would then conceive a child. She became pregnant and her husband, Setna, was very happy. In a dream, the spirit came to Setna and told him the child would be a boy and he is to be named "Sa-Asar," and that he will do great wonders in the land of Egypt. When the child was born Setna named him Sa-Asar, and he grew up and was always mature for his years. When Sa-Asar was a boy of 10, he was already respected as an enlightened Sage. One day he and his father were looking at two funerals. One funeral was for a rich man, who had many mourners, attendants, and offerings to the gods and goddesses. The other funeral was for a poor man, who had no one to mourn him and no offerings for the gods and goddesses to be placed in his tomb. The father exclaimed, "When my time comes, may my funeral be like the one of the rich man." Sa-Asar looked at his father, and said "Oh no father I hope you die like the poor man." Setna looked at Sa-Asar with surprise. Then Sa-Asar asked "Would you like me to show you the fate of these two souls?" Sa-Asar led his father to the Netherworld and his father saw that the rich man was judged by the gods and goddesses and was found to be unrighteous, having committed more evil deeds than virtuous deeds so his fate was to suffer. The poor man had led a virtuous life so all of the offerings of the rich man were accrued to the poor man, and the poor man was led into the presence of Asar, the Supreme Self, who was seated on his throne, with the goddesses Aset and Nebethet behind him and the gods and goddesses at his sides. Setna saw the evil rich man suffering. Others were reaching up to grasp at food that was dangling over them by a rope while under them, certain gods and goddesses were digging a pit so that they could not reach high enough. Still others were twining ropes while at the other end of the rope there were donkeys eating the rope. "Tell me Sa-Asar," Setna asked in amazement, "What is the meaning of these things I see? What happens to the people as they are judged?" Sa-Asar answered, "Those who are twining are the people who on earth labor everyday but their labors are fruitless for themselves because they do not perform the right actions, but the fruits of their actions benefit others. Those who are reaching up to get their food in vain are those who in life on earth have their life before them, but do not make use of it. Those who are found to have more misdeeds than good deeds are made to suffer. Those who have an equal amount of misdeeds and good deeds are sent to be servants of Seker-Asar.[583] Those who are found to have more virtuous deeds than misdeeds are allowed to be among the gods and goddesses as one of them, and their Ba flies up to be among the glorified spirits."[584]

The sophisticated nature of the Kamitan understanding and exposition of the philosophy of Ari (karma) incorporates the intermeshing of the myth, iconography and philosophy related to the divinities and their interactions. These yield a powerful mystical system which became the basis of Kamitan culture and civilization.[585]

THE AFRICAN ORIGINS OF CIVILIZATION, RELIGION AND YOGA SPIRITUALITY

Summary of The Philosophy of Ari (Karma) in Ancient Egypt Based on the Kamitan Text

Ari
"Action," "to do something," "things done"

Arit Maat
Work rightly, lead life of integrity, in accordance with Maatian principles.

Ari em hetep.
Work contentedly, with peace and contentment, without egoistic desire or expectations.

Maat Ab
Thus attain Purity of Heart

Maakheru
Become true of Speech, Spiritually enlightened.

Arit Heru
Receive the Eye of Heru, perfected action, the Eucharist, the act of becoming one with the Divine (the highest action).

In Kamitan Philosophy as well as the Hindu, action (Ari / Karma, respectively) is integrally related to the process of reincarnation.

THE AFRICAN ORIGINS OF CIVILIZATION, RELIGION AND YOGA SPIRITUALITY

Item for Comparison 47: The Philosophy of Reincarnation in Ancient Egypt and India

It is well known and commonly accepted that reincarnation has been practiced in India from ancient times. Therefore, there is no need to site specific references to support that contention. Here we will concentrate on the evidence supporting the existence of the philosophy of reincarnation in Ancient Egypt. Again, the term has become so pervasive that it has been added to the cultural lexicon.

> re·in·car·na·tion 1.a. Rebirth of the soul in another body. 2. A rebirth in another form; a new embodiment.[586]

Many people think of the philosophy of reincarnation as a concept that originated in India. We have shown that it is a concept that was well understood in Kamit and is very much in harmony with what is today referred to as reincarnation. In Ancient Egypt the term for reincarnation was Uhem Ankh – "to live again."

Reincarnation - *Uhem ankh*

References to Reincarnation in Kamitan texts can be found in:

A- Chapter 17 (176) An Appeal for Not Reincarnating as a Human Being Again

Disgusting is this land of Abtet (the east), the going to the dwelling. Nothing will be done to me that is considered disgusting by the gods and goddesses because I am! I pass through, pure within through the birthing place.

Neberdjer granted to me his own glory on the day that of *unity of the two lands*[587] in the presence of the Lord of Things. As to the knowledge of these words, if they are yours as a glorified spirit, a perfected soul, you will be in Neterchert.

B- From Chap. 27 (42) Pert M Hru

"eating the cakes of Asar in the eastern side of the lake of flowers."

These references relate to the understanding of life as related by the mythical journey of Ra. Every day Ra in the form of the sun-disk is metaphorically consumed by goddess Nut (sky goddess- the heavens), symbolized by the sun setting in the western horizon of the heavens (Nut), and she gives birth to him every morning, as symbolized by the sun rising in the eastern horizon of the heavens. Therefore, the east represents rebirth, the new life or the process of reincarnation. In the same fashion, those who do not attain the ability to either join Ra in his boat or join Asar (the God) in Djeddu are reborn again. Djeddu is a special location in the Duat where Asar resides, beyond time and space and thought.[588] Reincarnation implies having to once again be born in the world of time and space to suffer the limitations of youth, the trials and tribulations of adulthood, and finally the pain of disease and death once again. Therefore, human life is to be understood as a separation from Divine consciousness, a separation from the Divine. So it is not to be seen as an auspicious, desirable existence. (*Highlighted portions are by Ashby*)

C- The Hymn to Amun-Ra:

> "Amun-Ra who first was king,
> The god of earliest time,
> The vizier of the poor.
> He does not take bribes from the guilty,
> He does not speak to the witness,
> He does not look at him who promises,
> Amun judges the land with his fingers.
> He speaks to the heart,
> ***He judges the guilty,***
> ***He assigns him to the East,***
> ***The righteous to the West.***"

The hymn to Amun-Ra instructs us in the wisdom that those who are judged by God to be unrighteous will not attain the coveted goal of reaching the abode of the Supreme Divinity. Instead they will be directed towards the "East." This is a clear reference to reincarnation, the "East," as stated above, referring to the dawn and a new life for the sun in the form of Khepri, and thus, to the rebirth of the soul. In effect, it symbolizes the rebirth of the sun through Nut. Reincarnation is the continuous cycle of birth-death and rebirth into a new body, which the soul undergoes over a period of millions of years until it is purified enough to discover and return to its original source, the Supreme Divinity. In ancient times, the Greek historian, Herodotus, recorded that the Ancient Egyptians were the first to understand and teach the wisdom in reference to reincarnation. Therefore, in order to reach the West, it is necessary to be pure of heart, which implies having lived according to the principles of Maat as well as having developed reverence and devotion toward, and wisdom about, the Divine.

The following is a description of the deities in the Kamitan system who handle the mechanism of Ari (Karma) and reincarnation.

Goddess Meskhent

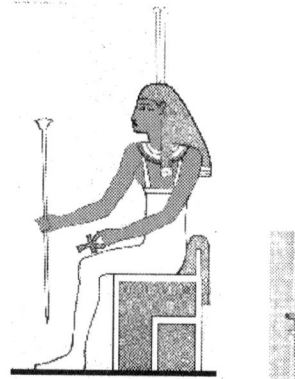

Figure 186: Left- Meskhent seated; Right- Meskhent as birthing block

Along with her associates, the goddesses *Shai*, *Rennenet* and *Meskhent*, Maat encompasses the Ancient Egyptian teachings of *Ari* (karma) and reincarnation or the destiny of every individual based on past actions, thoughts and feelings. Thus, they have important roles to play in the judgment scene of the *Prt m Hru*. Understanding their principles leads the aspirant to become free of the cycle of reincarnation and human suffering and to discover supreme bliss and immortality. If a person is ignorant about their higher essential nature, they will only have knowledge of human existence. At the time of death their soul will wander and experience either heavenly or hellish conditions in much the same way as one experiences good and bad dreams. Spiritual enlightenment means discovering your essential nature as one with the Supreme Self, and when this is achieved, there is no more hell or heaven; there is a resurrection in consciousness. This is what the goddess urges every aspirant to achieve through study, reflection and meditation on her teachings, and it is the central theme in the *Asarian Resurrection* myth.[179]

---

[179] See the Book *The Wisdom of Maati* for more on Maat philosophy.

Reincarnation in Indian Philosophy

In Indian philosophy the concept of reincarnation is called *punar-janman (janma)*.[589] The words punar and janman can be found in the Rig Veda, but like the term Yoga, they do not have the association with Karma, returning to the world as a result of ignorance, nor the mystical dimensions as they are known for today. This interpretation came later with the advent of the Upanishads. Specifically, the Chandogya Upanishad and the Brihad Aranyaka Upanishads[590] relate the term to mean rebirth of the soul into a new physical life, either through the womb of a woman in one of the different castes (human birth is considered to be auspicious), for those who lived previous lives that were in accordance with righteous principles, or into the wombs of animals and lower forms (inauspicious birth), for those who led unrighteous previous lives. Thus the new birth depends on the righteous actions (Dharma) of the person while in the previous lifetime. The lofty goal of going beyond the cycle of ignorance (Avidya), action (Karma) and reincarnation (punar-janman) by achieving liberation-spiritual enlightenment (Moksha) through the disciplines of mystical wisdom (Jnana) was introduced and prominently presented in the Upanishadic and later texts such as the Mahabharata. Thus, upon closer examination, it appears more and more that the inception of Indian mystical philosophy and Yoga, as it is known in modern times, occurs at the commencement of the Upanishadic age.

In the book *India and Egypt: Influences and Interactions,* Paul Gregorios, using the second important metaphor contained in the Asarian (Osirian) myth, relating to Asar as a regenerative force in human beings and in nature[591] notes one of the striking correlations between Ancient Egyptian religious philosophy and how it contrasts dramatically with the concept in Western religions.

> "On Analysis, the myth of Osiris can be decoded as the cycle of death and rebirth. This process is not one of resurrection, as is often cited, but of regeneration. Unlike the eschatology[592] of the Hebraic, the Christian, and the Islamic religions, the beliefs among both the Hindus and Egyptians are different in one essential sense: there is no awaiting the last Day of judgment, at the end of time, when all souls will be resurrected from their limbo-like existence, to be placed either in heaven or hell." [593]

Item for Comparison 48: The Philosophy of the Three States of Consciousness in Ancient Egypt and India

The Hindu scripture known as the *Raja Yoga Sutras*, speaks of the trinity of seer (*Drishta*), seen (*Drishya*) and sight (*Samyoga*). The single, undivided consciousness, God, refracts so as to assume the three aspects of human experience (subject, object and instrument of interaction between the two). This fragmentation of perception in consciousness constitutes duality and this duality leads to ignorance. Ignorance is defined as a lack of knowledge of Self. The purpose of Yoga is to allow an aspirant to discover the illusoriness of the triad of human consciousness so as to attain the unitary vision of existence which opens the door to spiritual enlightenment.

Figure 187: The Great Trinity of Ancient Egypt: Neberdjer Becomes Amun-Ra-Ptah

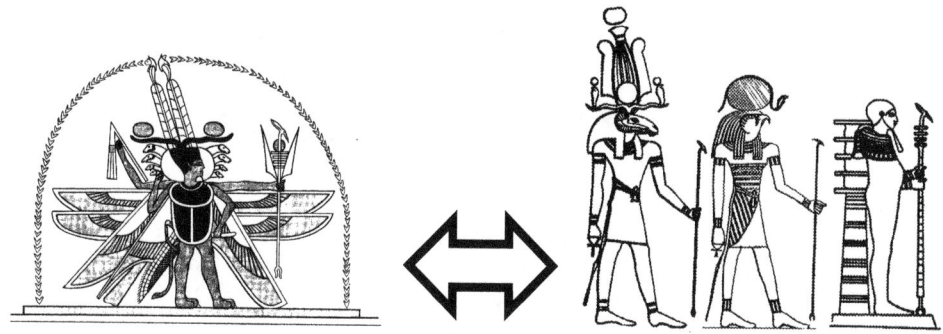

The teaching of *Neberdjer: Amun-Ra-Ptah* is a profound study of mystical philosophy which encompasses the nature of Creation, Divinity and the origins and destiny of human life. It involves a study of the very makeup of the human heart (consciousness) and the way towards realizing the greatest goal of human existence. Ancient Egyptian Religion developed over a period of tens of thousands of years. Each segment of the four-fold system of mystical philosophy (Neberdjer, Amun, Ra, Ptah) in Ancient Egyptian Theban Religion as it is known today, originates in the Ancient Egyptian city of *Anu*, known to the Ancient Greeks as Heliopolis or the city of the sun. The presiding symbol of the Supreme Divinity was known there as *Ra*. The term "Amun" means (witnessing consciousness). The term "Ra" means "Shining light or dynamic consciousness." The term "Ptah" as used in this Trinity means "Heaven and Earth." Thus we have the Kamitan interpretation of the differentiation of Neberdjer (All-encompassing, undivided Divinity), which assumes the Triad of existence and human consciousness.[594]

Creation manifests as three aspects. This teaching is expressed in the Ancient Egyptian statement:[595]

"I was One and then I became Three."

Neberdjer	Amun	Ra	Ptah
(All-encompassing divinity-eternity-the Absolute)	(Hidden essence of creation-witnessing consciousness)	(Mind and senses-Life force of creation)	(Heaven and earth-the physical universe)
Single, undivided consciousness	seer (subject)	sight (instrument of interaction between the two)	seen (object)

THE AFRICAN ORIGINS OF CIVILIZATION, RELIGION AND YOGA SPIRITUALITY

Item for Comparison 49: The Divine Mother and Child (below- left to right) of Ancient Egypt and India and the Metaphor of Blackness

Figure 188: The Images of the Divine Mother and Child from Ancient Egypt, India and Christianity and the Philosophy of Blackness in Mystical Religion

  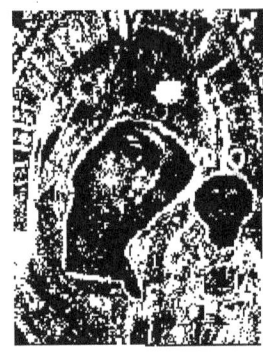

The Ancient Egyptian religion of *Aset* (Isis) which was part of the Asarian Myth that flourished until c.394 A.C.E. was so strong that it was one of the last to be overcome by the Roman Catholic religious persecutions. In giving birth to Heru as a virgin, Aset provided the prototype for Mary who gave birth to Jesus. This virgin birth is a symbol of the "second birth," the birth of the inner spiritual life that can occur in all humans. Out of a mind, which is concerned with materialism and pleasures of the body, comes a new consciousness. Aset suckling Heru (above left) is a common symbol in art and myth throughout Africa. It represents the importance of the mothering, nurturing principle in the making of a human being, as well as the nurturing that must take place in order for one to give birth to one's own spirit. This is the true meaning of the "virgin birth." Out of one's animal (lower self) existence one brings forth a higher vision and aspiration in life beyond the sensual pleasures of the physical body. This is the idealized symbolic form of the Christian Madonna (Mary) and baby Jesus (above right) and the Hindu Madonna (Yashoda) and Krishna (above center).

The Encyclopedia Britannica once reported that "Isis" was worshipped in Egypt, Greece, Rome, Gaul and almost all of the remainder of Europe and England. This was true before and during the emergence of Christianity. Thus, it is well established and accepted by most scholars that the image of the Ancient Egyptian goddess Aset sitting with the child Heru is the source of the Christian Madonna and child paintings and sculptures.[130] The noted Egyptologist A. Wallis Budge considered the mythology and iconography of Aset to be "identical with those of Mary."[23] The world-renowned psychiatrist Carl Jung also said she (the Madonna) is Isis.

As to the descriptions of the divine family, the Ancient Egyptian tradition clearly states that the divine family of Asar, Aset and Heru were black-skinned. The concept of 'blackness' is a common principle in Neterianism as well as Hinduism.

Aset is the daughter of Nut (the black night sky). In the temple of Denderah (Egypt), it is inscribed that Nut gave birth to Aset there and that upon her birth, Nut exclaimed "Ås" behold, *I have become thy mother."* This was the origin of the name "Åst," (Aset, Auset) later known as Isis to the Greeks and others. The inscription further states that she was a dark-skinned child and was called *"Khnemet-ankhet"* or the *lady of life and love.*[596] Thus, Aset also symbolizes the "blackness" of the vast un-manifest regions of existence, Asar.

Thus, the concept of blackness is here related to the depths of consciousness from which all human beings arise in the form of the "Black" mother[180] who gives birth to the black child (Heru, Krishna, Jesus) that must be protected from evil (ignorance, egoism) by being nurtured by her wisdom, so that they may some day challenge evil (ignorance and egoism) and reestablish order, truth and spiritual enlightenment.

---

[180] Mary in her form as the well known "Black Madonna."

Thus, the blackness of Heru, Krishna and Jesus correlates not only in an ethnic sense, as they have all been shown to be of African descent, but more importantly, mythically, the blackness relating to the depths of spiritual consciousness that an aspirant is to discover through the proper practice of one or all of the three respective religions.

THE AFRICAN ORIGINS OF CIVILIZATION, RELIGION AND YOGA SPIRITUALITY

Item for Comparison 50: Comparing The Indian and Kamitan Fundamental Principles

The Egyptian *Prt m Hru* is a text of wisdom about the true nature of reality and also of *Hekau* (chants, words of power, Chapters) to assist the initiate in making that reality evident. These chants are in reality wisdom affirmations which the initiate recites in order to assist him or her in changing the consciousness level of the mind. The hekau themselves may have no special power except in their assistance to the mind to change its perception through repetition with understanding and feeling in order to transform the mind into a still and centered state. Thus, the magical effect comes by their use and the force of will behind them when uttered by the purified mind. Through these affirmations, the initiate is able to change {his/her} consciousness from body consciousness ("I am a body") to Cosmic Consciousness ("I am the Divine"). Indian Gurus also recognize this form of affirmatory (using affirmation in the first person) spiritual discipline as the most intense form of spiritual discipline. However, there must be clear and profound understanding of the teachings before the affirmations can have the intended result. It is also to be found in the Bible and in the Gnostic Gospels.[597] Compare the statements in the first and second columns of the chart below from the Indian Upanishads and the following Ancient Egyptian scriptures (*Medu Neter*, Sacred Speech) taken from the *Egyptian Book of Coming Forth By Day* (*Prt M Hru*) and other hieroglyphic texts:

VEDANTA PHILOSOPHY IS SUMMED UP IN FOUR MAHAVAKYAS OR GREAT UTTERANCES TO BE FOUND IN THE UPANISHADS:	COMPARE TO THE PRT M HRU OF ANCIENT EGYPT
1- Brahman, the Absolute, is Consciousness beyond all mental concepts. (Aitareya, III, 1,13) 2- Thou Art That (referring to the fact that everyone is essentially this Consciousness). (Chandogya Up. VI, *, 7) 3- I Am Brahman, the Absolute (I am God); to be affirmed by people, referring to their own essential nature. (Brhadaranyaka Up. I, 4,) 4- The Self is Brahman (the Self is the essence of all things). (Brhadaranyaka Up. II, 5, 19)	Nuk Pu Nuk. ("I Am That I Am.") (Chapter 21 Verse 6) In reference to the relationship between God and humankind: Ntef änuk, änuk Ntef. "He is I and I am He." (Prt M Hru 31:7) I am that God, the Great one in his boat, Ra, I am. (Prt M Hru Chapter 1, Part 1, Verse 4) I am that same God, the Supreme One, who has myriad of mysterious names. (Prt M Hru 9:4)

Vedanta Philosophy In India

Vedanta philosophy is said to be based on the ancient spiritual scriptures of India called the *Vedas*, meaning "knowledge," and later developed with the creation of the Upanishads. The Vedas are related to a specific kind of knowledge, more specifically, knowledge which is heard.

Specifically, the term Vedanta refers to the end of the Vedas, referring to the scriptures commonly referred to as *the Upanishads*, which are supposed to represent a summary or distillation of the highest philosophy of the Vedas. The term *Upanishad* means "wisdom achieved by sitting close to a spiritual master." However, as we have seen throughout this text, Vedanta actually constitutes a revision, if not redaction of the Vedas.

Vedanta philosophy, as it exists in the present, is a combination of Buddhist psychology, Hindu myth relating to the gods and goddesses of India, the ancient metaphysical philosophy from the Upanishads and the mental and physical disciplines from Yoga practice. Having its original roots in the philosophy of the oneness of God who manifests in a myriad of ways, Vedanta achieves a balanced blend of all the philosophies and has been adapted by many present day Indian Sages to teach society the ancient philosophy of spiritual evolution and spiritual practice.

Vedanta philosophy has been called *The Heart of Hinduism* since it is said to represent the central teachings upon which Hindu philosophy and myth are based. Just as Ancient Egypt had many Temples dedicated to varied traditions based on different but related gods and goddesses, modern India exhibits the same process of spiritual practice. Beneath the exterior aspects of religious practice there is a deep mystical philosophy and this is what is referred to as the "heart" of religious practice. However, unlike modern day orthodox religions, the deities of India are all understood to be emanations from the same Supreme Being.[598] This is acknowledged in all of the different systems by the advanced practitioners of those systems. This feature in Hinduism is akin to the worship of the gods and goddesses of Ancient Egypt. Therefore, this system is actually leading people to the same goal, although sometimes under different names. This is why Vedanta is referred to as the end of the Vedas, "end" implying distillation or an extraction of the purest essence of the Vedas, the raw mystical philosophy which underlies all of the systems.

The Origins of the Concept of the Mahavakyas in Ancient Indian History

The concept of the Mahavakyas is often referred to by Vedantins (practitioners of Vedanta Philosophy), as originating in the Vedas. In a way this would mean that what is referred to as Vedanta literature or the Upanishads has its roots in Vedic literature and hence also in Vedic times, thereby making it more ancient. However, these utterances are to be found in the Upanishads, as listed above. While they may be attributed to notions intimated in the Vedas, they are not expressly put forth therein. This therefore, points to more verification of the innovation that the Upanishads represent in relation to the Vedic literature. In any case, the philosophies represented in the Mahavakyas was already established in Ancient Egypt well before the advent of Vedic literature, whether the date for the inception of Vedic literature is considered as 1500 B.C.E or 4000 B.C.E.

Item for Comparison 51: Vegetarianism, Asceticism and the control and Sublimation of Sexual Energy in Ancient Egypt and India

Vegetarianism and Austerity India

> **veg·e·tar·i·an·ism** *n.* The practice of subsisting on a diet composed primarily or wholly of vegetables, grains, fruits, nuts, and seeds, with or without eggs and dairy products.[599]

The practice of vegetarianism has been noted since ancient times. The Greek historian, Herodotus, reported meeting a group of people in India who practiced vegetarianism in the 5th century B.C.E. Its purpose is to augment physical health and to promote mental clarity to engender spiritual sensitivity. However, its practice is often misunderstood and maligned, especially in Western Culture, as a boring or depressing way to live. Along with vegetarianism, the practice of fasting and prayer have also been used by religions throughout history to promote spiritual transcendence.

One of the great benefits of the introduction of Hatha Yoga into Western Culture has been to promote the discipline of vegetarianism. However, when we look at the history of Yoga and the Vedas in India we find that vegetarianism was not a Vedantic tenet. The writings of the Rig Veda show that meat eating (including beef) was common in Vedic times. It was not until the emergence of Buddhism and Jainism (6th Century B.C.E.) and their protestations related to animal sacrifices and the killing of animals for commercial purposes that Hinduism began to adopt the philosophy. Vaishnavism was among the first of the Hindu traditions to adopt vegetarianism. The practice was adopted by most but not all Hindu traditions. For example, meat eating continues in the Shaiva and Shakta traditions, some Tantric traditions and some Buddhist sects. The following exerts from the *Laws of Manu* and the *Bhagavad Gita*, the premier text on Indian Yoga philosophy, provide concise descriptions as to the nature and practice of austerity, control of the senses and sexual desires as well as the consumption of food. It is remarkably similar to the Kamitan descriptions that will follow.

Laws of Manu Chapter 2

177. Let him abstain from honey, meat, perfumes, garlands, substances (used for) flavoring (food), women, all substances turned acid, and from doing injury to living creatures.

Bhagavad Gita: Chapter 2

Samkhya Yogah--The Yoga of Knowledge

54. Arjuna said: O Krishna, what are the characteristics of the Sage who is established in Samadhi? How does he of steady wisdom sit, how does he speak, how does he walk?

55. Sri Krishna said: O Arjuna, when a man thoroughly renounces all the desires of the mind and is satisfied in the Self by the Self, he is called a man of steady wisdom.

56. He who is not agitated in the midst of sorrowful conditions and who is devoid of craving in the midst of pleasant circumstances, who is free from attachment, fear, and anger, such a Sage is called a person of steady wisdom.

57. He who is without attachment in everything and while meeting with good and evil, neither rejoices nor hates, his wisdom is established.

58. When he is able to withdraw his senses from the sense-objects, even like a tortoise that withdraws its limbs from all sides, he is then established in wisdom.

Bhagavad Gita: Chapter 4 Jnan Vibhag Yogah--The Yoga of Wisdom

20. Having renounced attachment to action and its fruits, he who is eternally contented and free from dependence, even though he may be engaged in action, does nothing at all.

21. Devoid of cravings, with the body and mind under his control, having renounced all objects of pleasure, a Yogi performs actions only to maintain the body. He does not enter into the evil of the world-process.

Bhagavad Gita: Chapter 6 Adhyadma Yogah--The Yoga of Meditation

17. If one is regulated in food and entertainment, harmonized in performing actions, and balanced in sleeping and waking, then he can perfect that Yoga which leads to the cessation of pain.

Bhagavad Gita: Chapter 17 Shraddha Traya Vibhag Yogah--the Yoga of the Division of Threefold Faith

8. The foods that promote life, mental strength, vitality, health, cheerfulness, and loving nature; which are savory, nutritious, digestible and agreeable--these are dear to the Satwicas.

9. The foods that are very bitter, sour, saltish, hot, pungent, dry (tasteless), burning; which produce pain, grief and disease are dear to the Rajasicas.[600]

10. The foods that are stale, devoid of taste, foul smelling, rotten, refuse and impure are liked by those who are Tamasicas.[601]

14. Service of gods, Brahmins, Guru (spiritual preceptor) and wise men; purity, uprightness, Brahmacharya (sex-restraint), and non-violence--these are called the austerity of the body.

15. That speech which does not cause agitation in others, which is truthful, pleasant and helpful; and repeated study of scriptures--these constitute the austerity of speech.

16. Serenity of mind, gentleness, silence, control of senses, elevated feeling of the heart-- these are called the austerity of the mind.

Hindu culture developed the discipline of food in the following way. Food was classified into the system of the Gunas, *Tamasik* (Dull), *Rajasik* (agitating), and *Sattwik* (balanced-harmonious-lucid). Classifications were given as to the foods which were fit for consumption by spiritual practitioners (Sattwik), and the foods which were not conducive to the development of higher consciousness (Tamasik and Rajasik). The Samkhya philosophy[181] term Sattwik relates to foods that are lucid and this of course relates to a vegetarian diet. It is derived from the term *Sattwa,* that appears in the Bhagavad Gita,[602] meaning pure, illuminating and the like.

---

[181] Discipline of reaching enlightenment by means of a dualistic thought process for understanding the Self from not-Self. It developed contemporaneously with the Yoga – Bhagavad Gita tradition.

THE AFRICAN ORIGINS OF CIVILIZATION, RELIGION AND YOGA SPIRITUALITY

Vegetarianism and Austerity in Ancient Egypt

There are several references to the practice of vegetarianism in Ancient Egypt. The cow was revered there since ancient times, well before the emergence of Hinduism as we have seen, and the general diet of the Ancient Egyptians included a mostly vegetarian diet and fasting. The dietetic concept adopted by Hippocrates, that improper foods are the cause of disease, was espoused by the Ancient Egyptians in the early Dynastic Period. The initiates were required to keep a much more restrictive dietary regimen than the general populous, which excluded not only meats, but also alcoholic beverages and carnal indulgences. These austerities constituted an advanced form of ascetic lifestyle which allowed the Ancient Egyptian initiates to pursue the paths of spiritual development, unhindered by the proclivities of the lower nature. Ancient Egyptian Temple practices led to the development of Western Monasticism in Christianity, Judaism and Islam. The following ancient texts are instructive in these disciplines.

> "The priests (of Ancient Egypt), having renounced all other occupation and human labour, devoted their whole life to contemplation and vision of things divine. By vision they achieve honour, safety and piety, by contemplation of knowledge, and through both a discipline of lifestyle which is secret and has the dignity of antiquity. Living always with divine knowledge and inspiration puts one beyond all greed, restrains the passions, and makes life alert for understanding. They practiced simplicity, restraint, self-control, perseverance and in everything justice and absence of greed.... Their walk was disciplined, and they practiced controlling their gaze, so that if they chose they did not blink. Their laughter was rare, and if did happen, did not go beyond a smile. They kept their hands always within their clothing. . . . Their lifestyle was frugal and simple. Some tasted no wine at all, others a very little: they accused it of causing damage to the nerves and a fullness in the head which impedes research, and of producing desire for sex."[603]

Plutarch outlined the teachings of the Temple of Aset (Isis-Ancient Egypt) for the proper behavior of initiates in his writings about his experiences as an initiate of (Aset) Isis. In the following excerpts Plutarch describes the purpose and procedure of the diet observed by the initiates of Aset, and the goal to be attained through the rigorous spiritual program which is in most every equal to that which is outlined in the Bhagavad Gita (see above).

> "To desire, therefore, and covet after truth, those truths more especially which concern the divine nature, is to aspire to be partakers of that nature itself (1), and to profess that all our studies and inquiries (2) are devoted to the acquisition of holiness. This occupation is surely more truly religious than any external (3) purifications or mere service of the temple can be (4). But more especially must such a disposition of mind be highly acceptable to that goddess to whose service you are dedicated, for her special characteristics are wisdom and foresight, and her very name seems to express the peculiar relation which she bears to knowledge. For "Isis" is a Greek word, and means "knowledge or wisdom,"(5) and "Typhon," (Set) the name of her professed adversary, is also a Greek word, and means " pride and insolence."(6) This latter name is well adapted to one who, full of ignorance and error, tears in pieces (7) and conceals that holy doctrine (about Asar) which the goddess collects, compiles, and delivers to those who aspire after the most perfect participation in the divine nature. This doctrine inculcates a steady perseverance in one uniform and temperate course of life (8), and an abstinence from particular kinds of foods (9), as well as from all indulgence of the carnal appetite (10), and it restrains the intemperate and voluptuous part within due bounds, and at the same time habituates her votaries to undergo those austere and rigid ceremonies which their religion obliges them to observe. The end and aim of all these toils and labors is the attainment of the knowledge of the First and Chief Being (11), who alone is the object of the understanding of the mind; and this knowledge the goddess invites us to seek after, as being near and dwelling continually (12) with her. And this also is what the very name of her temple promiseth to us, that is to say, the knowledge and understanding of the eternal and self-existent Being - now it is called "Iseion," which suggests that if we approach the temple of the goddess rightly, we shall obtain the knowledge of that eternal and self existent Being."

THE AFRICAN ORIGINS OF CIVILIZATION, RELIGION AND YOGA SPIRITUALITY

Figure 189: The Forms of Goddess Aset (Isis)

Mystical Implications of the Discourse of Plutarch:[182]

1- It is to be understood that spiritual aspiration implies seeking the union (Sema Tawi, mystical union-Yoga) with or becoming one with the thing being sought, because this is the only way to truly "know" partake of something. You can have opinions about what it is like to be a whale, but you would never exactly know until you become one with it, enfolding all that exists, is the one being worthy of veneration and identification. "Knowing" Neter (God) is the goal of all spiritual practices. This is the supreme goal, which must be kept in mind by a spiritual aspirant.

2- In order to discover the hidden nature of God, emphasis is placed on study and inquiry into the nature of things. Who am I? What is the universe composed of? Who is God? How am I related to God? These are the questions, which when pursued, lead to the discovery of the Self (God). Those who do not engage in this form of inquiry will generate a reality for themselves according to their beliefs. Some people believe they have the answers, that the universe is atoms and electrons or energy. Others believe that the body is the soul and that there is nothing else. Still others believe that the mind is the soul or that there is no soul and no God. The first qualification for serious aspiration is that you have a serious conviction that you are greater than just a finite individual mortal body, that you are an immortal being who is somehow mixed up with a temporal form (body). If this conviction is present, then you are stepping on the road to enlightenment. The teachings will be useful to you. Those who hold other beliefs are being led by ignorance and lack of spiritual sensitivity as a result of their beliefs. Thus, their beliefs will create a reality for them based on those beliefs. They will need to travel the road of nature, which will guide them in time toward the path of spiritual aspiration.

3-4 The plan prescribed by the teachings of Mystical spirituality (Sema Tawi – Yoga) is the only true means to effective spiritual development, because it leads to a revelation of the inner meanings of the teachings; therefore it is experiential, i.e., it is based on your own personal experience and not conjecture. Otherwise, worship and religious practices remain only at the level of ritualism and do not lead to enlightenment (Pert m Heru).

5-7 The Greek name Isis means "wisdom" which bestows the knowledge of the true Self of the initiate. In the Asarian (Osirian) Mysteries, when Set killed Asar by tearing him into pieces, he was symbolically tearing up the soul. However, Aset (Isis) restores the pieces of the soul (Asar). Set symbolizes egoism: pride, anger, hatred, fear, jealousy, etc. Therefore, pride and insolence (Set-egoism) destroy the soul and

---

[182] Note: The numbers at the beginning of each paragraph below correspond to the reference numbers in the text above.

THE AFRICAN ORIGINS OF CIVILIZATION, RELIGION AND YOGA SPIRITUALITY

knowledge of the Self (Aset) restores it to its true nature. The Ancient Egyptian scriptures support the Greek name translation and meaning of the name Aset. One of the names of Aset is: *Rekhât or Rekhit* (meaning "knowledge personified"). *Rekh* is also a name of the God in the "duat" or Netherworld (astral plane) who possesses knowledge which can lead the soul to the abode of the Divine. The variation, *Rekh-t*, means Sage or learned person.

8- True spirituality cannot be pursued rashly or in a fanatical way by going to extremes. Sema Tawi, Mystical Spirituality, is a science of balance. It has been developed over a period of thousands of years with well established principles, which when followed, produce the desired effect of leading the initiate from darkness to light, ignorance to knowledge, an un-enlightened state to enlightenment.

9-10 The foods referred to are flesh foods (swine, sheep, fish, etc.), pulse,[183] and salt. Indulgence in sexual activity has two relevant aspects. First, it intensifies the physical experience of embodiment and distracts the mind by creating impressions in the subconscious and unconscious, which will produce future cravings and desires. This state of mind renders the individual incapable of concentration on significant worldly or high spiritual achievements. Secondly, control of the sexual urge leads to control of the sexual Life Force energy,[184] which can then be directed towards higher mental and spiritual achievement. Further, overindulgence in sexual activity tends to wear down the immunity as it wears down the mental capacity and one becomes a slave to sensual passions and susceptible to sexual and non-sex related diseases. The following verses from the Ancient Egyptian Book of Enlightenment show the practice of vegetarianism and celibacy.

Chapter 30B of the Ancient Egyptian mystical text *The Book of Coming Forth By Day (Book of the Dead)* states:

> *This utterance shall be recited by a person purified and washed; one who has not eaten animal flesh or fish.*

Chapter 64 of the *Book of Coming Forth By Day (Book of the Dead)* states:

> *This Chapter can be known by those who recite it and study it when they see no more, hear no more, have no more sexual intercourse and eat no meat or fish.*

Chapter 137A of the *Book of Coming Forth By Day (Book of the Dead)* states:

> *And behold, these things shall be performed by one who is clean, and is ceremonially pure, a man who hath eaten neither meat nor fish, and who hath not had intercourse with women* (applies to female initiates not having intercourse with men as well).

---

[183] **pulse** (pŭls) *n.* **1.** The edible seeds of certain pod-bearing plants, such as peas and beans. **2.** A plant yielding these seeds. (American Heritage Dictionary)
[184] The concept of the Life Force will be explained in detail later.

Item for Comparison 52: The Origins of the Philosophy of the Absolute in India and Egypt

The Philosophy of Brahman in Ancient India

For those initiated into Vedanta Philosophy, Brahman is understood as "the Absolute," transcendental Self, beyond words, thought or concept. However, when we examine the term as it appears in the Vedic age versus the Upanishadic age, we see a clear evolution in which it acquired the high philosophical interpretation. It is as if the Vedic philosophy was given and then reinterpreted to bring forth the mystical philosophy. In other words, it appears that the sages of the Upanishadic age used the prestige and high standing of the already present Vedic literature and Sanskrit language to bring forth a truly authentic mystical conception. In the Vedic literature the term Brahman has been defined by Indologists[604] as meaning "vast expanse," from the root "to grow" or "to expand" and appears as follows:

> Varuna who knows the way, as *"making the Brahman"*
> -Rig Veda (1.105.15)[605] 1,500 B.C.E.

> "He truly knows Brahman who knows him as beyond knowledge; he who thinks that he knows, knows not. The ignorant think that Brahman is known, but the wise know him to be beyond knowledge."
> -Kena Upanishad (1,000 B.C.E.- 600 B.C.E.)

The first meaning is an action and the second is a subject. In the Upanishadic age the term Brahman means Absolute Divinity beyond all others, non-dual and transcendental all-encompassing divinity. This high philosophical interpretation appears in the *Shata-Patha-Brahmana*.[185] Very often people who approach religion in a fanatical way expect religious philosophy to be perfect in its inception and this is never the case. Actually, spiritual philosophy is a refinement of concepts leading to perfect erudition, and consequently, consummate understanding as well as adept discourse of the teaching. Possibly the greatest Vedantic text ever produced is India, *The Yoga Vasistha Ramayana*.

Unlike the others, *The Yoga Vasistha* is not very well known outside of India. *The Yoga Vasistha* is a work of nearly 30,000 stanzas, containing the essence of all the Indian scriptures. It is also known as *The Maha Ramayana* or simply as *The Vasistha*. It contains the teachings which were given to Lord Rama, an incarnation of the God Vishnu, by his Guru (spiritual preceptor) Sage Vasistha, which led him to remember his divine nature and attain Enlightenment. *The Vasistha* has been revered in the circles of Yoga Philosophy as *the high Vedanta* or the most advanced mystical philosophy because it holds the purest form of the Vedantic teachings which lead to spiritual Enlightenment. It is revered as the culmination of all teachings on the paths to Enlightenment.[606] The problem with it according to orthodox Vedantins is that it is a late text, having been written between 750 A.C.E. and 1,000 A.C.E. Due to this "deficiency" (which the very first chapter of the book confronts head on) many aspirants have rebuffed it, preferring to pursue the older texts with the idea that they are more ancient and therefore more correct, enlightening or inspired.

The idea here is that just because a teaching is developed from an earlier lesser concept does not invalidate the earlier source but also the antiquity of a scripture is no guarantee as to its authenticity or capacity to provide a pathway to enlightenment. Therefore, one must rely on the guidance of spiritual masters who have discovered the clear path to understanding and making sense of the past so as to further understand the advanced teaching being received in the present time. Books cannot teach the subtle aspects of mystical philosophy; only living breathing spiritual masters and their advanced disciples can do that.

---

[185] The *Brahmanas* are texts considered alongside the *Upanishads* as the foundation of Vedantic Philosophy, though they are mostly used by scholars due to their highly intellectual and rigid character, which is a contrast to the Upanishads which are designed with a more personable character, approachable by a wider audience of aspirants. (1000 - 800 B.C.E. Brahmanas Period) (800 – 600 B.C.E. Upanishadic Period).

THE AFRICAN ORIGINS OF CIVILIZATION, RELIGION AND YOGA SPIRITUALITY

The concept of Brahman as it appears in the Brahmanas and the Upanishads (post Vedic era of Indian religion) can be found in the Kamitan teaching related to Neberdjer. The Kamitan concept of Neberdjer is of an all-encompassing, Absolute. Thus, Neberdjer also means *Absolute Divinity beyond all others and Transcendental all-encompassing divinity, and All-encompassing expansion.* As we have already seen, Neberdjer differentiates into three aspects, Khepri (creator), Ra (preserver), and Tem (dissolver) just like Brahman differentiates into three aspects: Brahma (creator), Vishnu (preserver), and Shiva (dissolver).

The Philosophy of Neberdjer in Ancient Egypt

The teaching of Neberdjer: Amun-Ra-Ptah is a profound study of mystical philosophy which encompasses the nature of Creation, Divinity and the origins and destiny of human life. It involves a study of the very makeup of the human heart (consciousness) and the way towards realizing the greatest goal of human existence. Thus, to believe that Ancient Egyptian Myth and Mystical Religion is merely a fictitious yarn about some mythical characters is to entirely miss a most important teaching about the purpose of human life and the supreme goal of human existence, Spiritual Enlightenment, the discovery of the nature of God. This pitfall was explained by the Greek classical writer and initiate of the mysteries of Aset (Isis), Plutarch.

> "When therefore, you hear the myths of the Egyptians concerning the Gods - wanderings and dismemberings and many such passions, think none of these things spoken as they really are in state and action. For they do not call Hermes "Dog" as a proper name, but they associate the watching and waking from sleep of the animal who by Knowing and not Knowing determines friend from foe with the most Logos-like of the Gods."

Each segment of the four-fold system of mystical philosophy (Neberdjer, Amun, Ra, Ptah) in Ancient Egyptian Theban Religion, as it is known today, originates in the Ancient Egyptian city of *Anu*, known to the Ancient Greeks as Heliopolis or the city of the sun. The presiding symbol of the Supreme Divinity was known there as *Heru, Amun-Ra- Tem-Ptah.*

The following passage enlightens us as to the nature of the concept of Neberdjer and also shows us that Kamitan religion is pantheistic and well as monistic, just as Hinduism is pantheistic, but in its mystical form of practice, Vedanta, it is monistic, non-dual and transcendental depending on the level of the practice. In the creation story involving the Asarian Mysteries[607], Asar assumes the role of Khepera and Tem:

> "Neb-er-tcher saith, I am the creator of what hath come into being, and I myself came into being under the form of the god Khepera, and I came into being in primeval time. I had union with my hand, and I embraced my shadow in a love embrace; I poured seed into my own mouth, and I sent forth from myself issue in the form of the gods Shu and Tefnut." "I came into being in the form of Khepera, and I was the creator of what came into being, I formed myself out of the primeval matter, and I formed myself in the primeval matter. My name is Ausares (Asar).
>
> I was alone, for the Gods and Goddesses were not yet born, and I had emitted from myself neither Shu nor Tefnut. I brought into my own mouth, *hekau*, and I forthwith came into being under the form of things which were created under the form of Khepera."

THE AFRICAN ORIGINS OF CIVILIZATION, RELIGION AND YOGA SPIRITUALITY

Item for Comparison 53: The Teaching of Non-Duality in Ancient Egypt and India

> "After the millions of years of differentiated creation, the chaos that existed before creation will return; only the primeval god[608] and Asar will remain steadfast-no longer separated in space and time."
>
> —Ancient Egyptian *Coffin Texts*

Many scholars of Buddhist, Samkhya and Vedantic philosophies have come to believe that India first developed the concept of non-duality. However, the concept was well-developed in Ancient Egyptian religion and is evident in the hieroglyphic texts and Kamitan traditions (schools) of several periods. It is explained as a Supreme Being who brought {him/her}self into being and who is "One without a second" and at the same time manifesting as the varied forms of Creation. Therefore, this concept goes beyond the ordinary Western idea of monotheism and incorporates the concepts of "monism" and "pantheism" which are usually ascribed to Hindu religions.

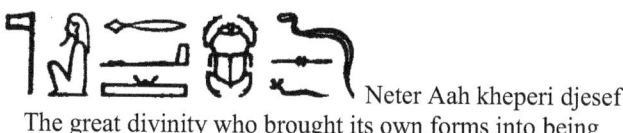 Neter Aah kheperi djesef
The great divinity who brought its own forms into being

The Supreme Being is One

> "God is the father of beings. God is the eternal One... and infinite and endures forever. God is hidden and no man knows God's form. No man has been able to seek out God's likeness. God is hidden to Gods and men... God's name remains hidden... It is a mystery to his children, men, women and Gods. God's names are innumerable, manifold and no one knows their number... though God can be seen in form and observation of God can be made at God's appearance, God cannot be understood... God cannot be seen with mortal eyes... God is invisible and inscrutable to Gods as well as men."
>
> -Portions from the Egyptian *Book of Coming forth by Day* and the papyrus of Nesi-Khensu

The statements above give the idea that God is the unfathomable mystery behind all phenomena, which cannot be discerned "even by the gods." However, God is the unfathomable mystery as well as the innermost essence of his children. This means that God is transcendental, the unmanifest, but also what is manifest as well. In order to perceive this reality it is necessary to transcend ordinary human vision. When this transcendental Self is spoken about through different names and metaphors, the idea often emerges that there are many faces to the ultimate deity or Supreme Being. Nevertheless, as has been previously discussed, it must be clear that all the Neterian spiritual traditions are in reality referring to the same Supreme Being, the transcendental reality.

UA or "One,"
UA NETER or "One God,"
"Only One",
"Only One Without a second"
"One One"

The following passages come from the Egyptian *Book of Coming Forth By Day* (Chapter. clxxiii):

> "I praise thee, Lord of the Gods, God One, living in truth."

THE AFRICAN ORIGINS OF CIVILIZATION, RELIGION AND YOGA SPIRITUALITY

The following passage is taken from a hymn where princess Nesi-Khensu glorifies Amen-Ra:

> "August Soul which came into being in primeval time, the great god living in truth, the first Nine Gods who gave birth to the other two Nine Gods,[186] the being in whom every God existeth One One, the creator of the kings who appeared when the earth took form in the beginning, whose birth is hidden, whose forms are manifold, whose germination cannot be known."

The Kamitan sages wanted to leave no doubt as to the way in which the philosophy of Neter was to be understood. We have already seen designations for the Supreme Being as "God One" and "Only One" but the sages went further and gave the following:

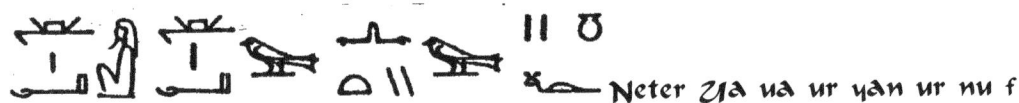

Only one the greatest -nothing greater i.e., without a second

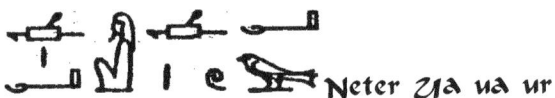

Only one the ultimate

Something holy or divine.

The following Ancient Egyptian proverbs further illustrate the concept of non-dual divinity:

> "I am the Double Lion (i.e. eternal), older than Atum."

> "I am Ra, who is exalted forever, I am Atum, more of a spirit (i.e. subtler) than the other spirits.
> I am the Lord of Eternity."

> "I am the Only One, who journeys over the Primeval Void.
> I am the One whose name is not known by human beings."

–Ancient Egyptian *Coffin Texts*

---

[186] Ancient Egyptian mythology conceives of creation as an expression of God in which there are nine primordial cosmic principles or forces in the universe. These first nine may be seen as the cause from which all other qualities of nature *(the other two Nine Gods)* or creative forces in nature arise.

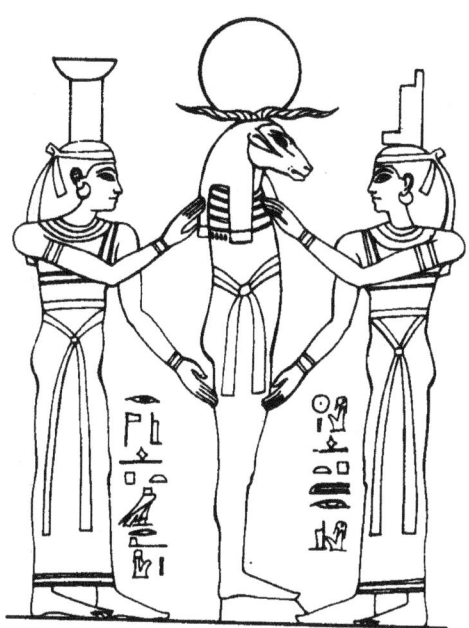

Figure 190: (right) Another example[187] of the Kamitan Caduceus, with Atum-Ra

The underlying theme of non-duality occurs across the panorama of the Neterian theologies and as the image and scripture above shows, there is an understanding of the essential nature of all divinities as being expressions of the same single and transcendental, primary divinity. In the above figure, the two great goddesses Nebethet and Aset attend on Atum-Ra as he stands on the pedestal of Maat. Once again, the image of the Trinity is given with one male aspect and two female aspects, symbolizing non-duality (one God, one Spirit) and duality (two goddesses), respectively. Further, this image essentially links three High Gods (Asar, Ra and Atum) into One. This presentation points to the highly advanced philosophical view that the Ancient Egyptian Sages were putting forth, that the gods and goddesses (Neteru) are merely images for worship, and are not to be seen as ultimate or absolute realities in and of themselves. Actually they are aspects of the same transcendental reality. The main image presented in the center is of Atum, whose name means "completion," or "totality." They are to be understood as windows into the transcendent, avenues by which the energies of the mind and body may be channeled towards a higher, spiritual goal in life. Not until Vedanta philosophy emerges in India, is there another form of mysticism like it in the world.

This means that essentially, Asar and Ra are actually one being. This is most clearly demonstrated by the depiction of Asar, in a Divine Boat (Neshmet). It is said that Ra has the Moon and Sun as his eyes, and either works as a passageway to the deeper transcendental Self, just as the eyes of a human being act as a window into the inner Self. Also, it is the sun that is responsible for both daylight (sunlight) and moonlight (a reflection of sunlight). The moon is a symbol of Asar, while the sun is a symbol of Ra. So there is a being who encompasses and transcends them and it is known as Heru. This idea of the oneness of the Supreme Being is stated again directly in the image above which reads: *This[609] is Asar resting in Ra, Ra resting in Asar.*

---

[187] See other examples in the sections entitled "Kabbalism, Ancient Egypt and the Mysticism of the Tree of Life" and "The Early Practice of Yoga in India and the Connection to Ancient Egypt"

Item for Comparison 54: The Philosophy of Pantheism in Ancient Egypt and India

Hinduism has long been recognized as a Pantheistic form of philosophy. There are two forms of Pantheism, Absolute and Modified. Absolute Pantheism views God as being everything there is. In other words, God and Creation are one (cause and manifestation). Modified Pantheism is the view that God is the reality or principle behind nature. Here the cause is the force behind the manifestation, sustaining it. Panentheism is the doctrine that God is immanent in all things but also transcendent, so that every part of the universe has its existence in God, but God is more than the sum total of the parts. God transcends physical existence. Thus, in Hinduism, as in Neterianism, all divinities are in reality to be seen as manifestations of the One and also all objects are manifestations of that singular Divinity. However, in the higher aspects of the mystical philosophies of India and Egypt the Absolute philosophy can also be discerned.

In Ancient Egypt, the same philosophical views can be found from the earliest times and when the philosopher-king Akhnaton ascended the throne, he endeavored to emphasize the Pantheistic and Panentheistic aspects of the teaching which already existed in Ancient Egypt. Many historians and Egyptologists have tried to characterize his teaching as monotheism and have even implied that Moses got the idea of Monotheism from Akhnaton. While it has been shown that the early Jews derived the basis for their teachings from Ancient Egyptian religion it is obvious that they chose to apply a more limited understanding of the concepts of divinity and they modified it to the form which survives today, stripping the Pantheistic and Panentheistic aspects and leaving a monotheistic concept, a god who exists as a personality, separate from the Creation as the original cause but after the act of Creation remaining separate as a detached observer. However, this is a misunderstanding of the scriptures authorized by Akhnaton. Upon closer examination of the original hieroglyphic text the deeper meaning of the philosophy becomes evident.

The Panentheistic and Non-dualist Philosophy of Akhnaton

Akhnaton (1353 B.C.E.) was at the same time a king and mystical philosopher. He introduced not a new religion, but emphasized an aspect of worship which was highly philosophical and abstract, and thus less suited for the masses and more appropriate for the monastic order. As explained earlier the tenets of his hymns can be found in hymns to other Ancient Egyptian gods such as Amun (Amen), Asar (Osiris), and Ra, which preceded those to Aton.

Upon closer study, the philosophy which Akhnaton espoused, is comparable to the most advanced spiritual philosophies developed in India, known as Vedanta philosophy. In Vedanta, two important forms of spiritual philosophy developed called Absolute Monism and Modified Monism. They are expressions of non-dualist philosophy. Absolute Monism means that there is recognition that there is only one reality that exists: God. All else is imagination. This means that everything that is perceived with the senses, thoughts, etc., is a manifestation of God. Modified Monism views God as the soul of nature, just as the human body also has a soul, which sustains it.

The Hymns to Aton, which also espouse Absolute Monism, were recorded at least 579 years before its exposition in India through the Hindu Upanishads which are considered to be the highest expression of Hindu mystical philosophy. Akhnaton's teachings were given less than 200 years before the supposed date for the existence of Moses. However, Moses' teaching was not understood as Absolute Monism, but rather as monotheism. Therefore, whether the Jewish Pentateuch was written by a person named Moses or by Jewish scribes much later, as most modern biblical scholars now agree, the influence of Akhnaton's teachings would have been foremost in the instruction of Moses. Remember that the Bible says, that Moses learned the wisdom of the Egyptians (Acts 7:22). While all of the attributes of Yahweh, the Hebrew God, are contained in the teachings related to Aton, the Hymns to Aton, being based on Monism, go farther in espousing the nature of God and God's relationship to Creation and humanity.

The next form of philosophy present in Akhnaton' hymns is Pantheism. The following exerted verses from the Hymns to Aten approved by Pharaoh Akhnaton exhibit the most direct exposition of the philosophies mentioned above.

Figure 191: Akhnaton with his family, receiving Life Force from Aten through the sun's rays.

"One God, like whom there is no other. Thou didst create the earth by thy heart (or will), thou alone existing, men and women, cattle, beasts of every kind that are upon the earth, and that move upon feet (or legs), all the creatures that are in the sky and that fly with their wings, [and] the deserts of Syria and Kush (Nubia), and the Land of Egypt.

Thou settest every person in his place. Thou providest their daily food, every man having the portion allotted to him; [thou] dost compute the duration of his life. Their tongues are different in speech, their characteristics (or forms), and likewise their skins (in color), giving distinguishing marks to the dwellers in foreign lands… Thou makest the life of all remote lands.

Oh thou Lord of every land, thou shinest upon them…

Thou hast made millions of creations from thy One self (viz.) towns and cities, villages, fields, roads and river. Every eye (i.e., all men) beholdeth truth, it is thee through it (the Aton)."

These statements by Akhnaton in his Hymns to Aton follow the transcendental and tantric philosophy that originated in the *Pyramid* and *Coffin Texts,* and much later, in the Gnostic Gospels espoused by Jesus.[610] Nature itself and all objects including people are manifestations of the Divine. And here there is one more important Kamitan teaching. In the last line there is an understanding that the Aten is only a visible manifestation of the transcendental nature of the Spirit. It is this transcendental nature that people both in and outside (i.e. of different religions) of Egypt, can see when they look at the objects of creation and the sun itself. That is, the view that God is the reality or principle behind nature. However, an important adjunct to this statement is the realization that this applies to all human beings and not just those that practice Atonism. This means that Atonism exemplified the Philosophy of Ancient Egypt as ecumenical and universal. It is a recognition that Atonism, and with it the entirety of Neterian Religion, is a system of spirituality which is universal, manifesting in the philosophies of other religions as well. So, there is an understanding that a person worshipping Vishnu in India or Zeus in Greece are actually worshipping the same divinity by different names.

Item for Comparison 55: Mantra, Hekau and The Importance Of The "I Am" Formula in Ancient Egypt and India

The word *"mantra"* in Indian Yoga signifies any sound which steadies the mind. Its roots are: "man" which means "mind" and "tra" which means "steady," to be recited with "meaning and feeling."[611] In Ancient Egyptian terminology, "hekau" or word formulas to be *"Hessi"* or chanted to engender spiritual evolution.

There is a special teaching contained in all mystical religious systems and yogic traditions. It is the "I Am" formula. In the philosophical disciplines, a formula is a set of words or symbols which contains a representation of the composition or structure of a complex idea or philosophy. It contains a recipe as it were, describing the ingredients that are necessary to produce the desired product. In this case the desired product is spiritual enlightenment. The "I am" formula holds the key to understanding the entire philosophy, if properly understood and practiced. The practice of reciting the "I am" formula in Indian mysticism is called *"Ahamgraha Upasana,"* or the spiritual discipline of asserting one's identity with the Divine Self. In Kamitan mysticism, this teaching formed the very basis of the Asarian Tradition and indeed all other colleges in Ancient Egypt.

According to mystical philosophy, when people become deluded and feel they belong to a certain group or culture with particular customs, language and opinions, they begin to separate from others. The separation is emotional, philosophical, etc., but it is not real otherwise. This is not a desirable situation from a spiritual point of view. Culture and language should not be seen as a person's identity. A human being cannot transcend the world as long as {he/she} holds onto the idea that {he/she} is of a particular group or other ("I am German," "I am American," "I am Spanish," "I am Jewish," "I am Christian," etc.). While living in a culture, a spiritual aspirant should assert: "I am a spirit living as a German man," "I am a spirit living as an American woman," "I am a spirit living as a Spanish man," etc. Likewise, a person should not identify with a particular religion either. A spiritual aspirant should assert: "I am practicing this religion to lead me to enlightenment. I might have been born as a Christian, a Hindu or a Muslim in a previous incarnation, but now I am a practitioner of the Kamitan mystical spirituality and I will use its wisdom to lead me to God, the goal of all religions." This attitude promotes harmony, understanding and peace between religions. This atmosphere of peace will allow for the exchange of spiritual wisdom between them. This exchange will lead to greater spiritual awareness and evolution instead of strife, distraction and unrest between them.

In modern times people often confuse their identity with their job roles and get so caught up in that false identification that they cannot find happiness without it. The executive dresses up in executive clothing, works in an executive office, drives an executive car, comes home to the executive neighborhood to the executive wife to be greeted by the executive children, and so on. If {he/she} is not treated in an executive manner, {he/she} will get upset. If others do not live up to {his/her} social standing, they are chastised. There are many forms of delusion which can arise when a person begins to identify with their occupation, birthplace, ethnicity, gender, etc. A person may feel "I am an American and all other countries are primitive" or "I was born in the city and I am sophisticated and not like you country people" or "I am a man and I'm stronger, so you women are inferior." The soul, identified with the personality as a woman, may feel, "I cannot enjoy life unless I become a mother." As a result, she will proceed to get pregnant whether or not she is healthy, can financially take care of the child, or is at a stage in life where she can handle the responsibilities, etc. This happens because ignorance, lack of will, and desire have deluded the mind and the ability to reason has been impaired. Indoctrination with ideas like "life is for having babies and becoming a mother" or the pressure from society with ideas like "if you don't get pregnant you are not worth anything" hold sway in the weak and ignorant mind. When the soul is caught up in such mental delusion, one forgets that one's role (mother, father, boss, employee, etc.) in life is only a vehicle for spiritual discovery, and not an end in itself. It is not who *you* are. What would you say about an actor who gets off the stage but continues to play the role when they go home, to the market, church, etc? You would call them insane! Yet people are constantly playing roles, in their ordinary lives, based on their erroneous notions of reality, and these ignorant notions are constantly being reinforced by society at large (government, media, misguided religious people).

The predominant form of Yoga practiced in Orthodox religion is a limited form of Devotion, while the predominant form of Yoga practice in mystical religion is a combination of Gnosis or Intuitional Wisdom and Devotion. Orthodox religion is limited because it takes a person only part way in the realization of the objective of devotion in spiritual practice. Orthodoxy admonishes a person to love the image or symbol of God, as opposed to promoting an awareness of God as an internal experience. For example, Gnostic (mystical) Christianity not only admonishes a person to love Jesus and God and follow their example, but also leads a person to allow that devotion to reach full expression. This means that a true devotee unites with the beloved and thereby becomes one with the beloved. This is the true meaning of Jesus' statements "I and The Father are One" and "Know ye not that ye are gods." The Orthodox Christian Church would consider it blasphemous for a Christian to say "I am God," but Yogic mystical religions such as the Kamitan religion would consider any statement to the contrary as a misunderstanding of the higher truth and a reinforcement of spiritual ignorance.

The Egyptian *Book of Coming Forth By Day* is a text of wisdom about the true nature of reality and also of *Hekau* (chants, words of power, utterances) to assist the initiate in making that reality evident. These chants are in reality wisdom affirmations which the initiate recites in order to assist him or her in changing the consciousness level of the mind. The hekau themselves may have no special power except in their assistance to the mind to change its perception through repetition with understanding and feeling in order to transform the mind into a still and centered state. Through these affirmations, the initiate is able to change {his/her} consciousness from body consciousness ("I am a body") to Cosmic Consciousness ("I am the Divine"). This form of affirmatory (using affirmation in the first person) spiritual discipline is recognized by Indian Gurus as the most intense form of spiritual discipline. However, there must be clear and profound understanding of the teachings before the affirmations can have the intended result. It is also to be found in the Bible and in the Gnostic Gospels as we will see. Compare the preceding statements in the Indian Upanishads to the following Ancient Egyptian scriptures (*Medu Neter,* Sacred Speech) taken from the *Egyptian Book of Coming Forth By Day* (c. 10,000-5,000 B.C.E.) and other hieroglyphic texts:

Table 26: Essential "I Am" Formulas from the Upanishads, Bible and Prt m Hru

Vedanta Philosophy is summed up in four *Mahavakyas* or *Great Utterances* to be found in the Upanishads:	Compare the preceding statements in the Indian Upanishads to the following Ancient Egyptian scriptures (*Medu Neter,* Sacred Speech) taken from the *Egyptian Book of Coming Forth By Day* and other hieroglyphic texts:
1-*Brahman, the Absolute, is Consciousness beyond all mental concepts.*	***Nuk Pu Nuk.*** *("I Am That I Am.")*[612] In reference to the relationship between God and humankind:
2- ***Thou Art That*** (referring to the fact that everyone is essentially this Consciousness).	***Ntef änuk, änuk Ntef.*** *("He is I and I am He.")*[613]
3- ***I Am Brahman, the Absolute*** (I am God); to be affirmed by people, referring to their own essential nature).	***I am that God, the Great one in his boat, Ra, I am.*** (Prt M Hru Chapter 1, Part 1, Verse 4)
4- ***The Self is Brahman*** (the Self is the essence of all things).	***I am that same God, the Supreme One, who has myriad of mysterious names.*** (Prt M Hru 9:4)

Vedanta philosophy has been called *The Heart of Hinduism* since it represents the central teachings upon which Hindu philosophy is based. Just as Christianity has many denominations, there are many traditions in India which follow different gods or goddesses. However, like the gods and goddesses of Ancient Egypt, the deities of India all emanate from the same Supreme Being and this is acknowledged in the authentic teachings of all of the different systems, thus leading people to the same goal, although sometimes under different names. The Indian Vedantic text Yoga Vasistha Vol. II describes the ego as follows:

> When the Self (transcendental-Absolute consciousness) develops identification with the limited body, it assumes the form of *ahamkara* (egoism), which expresses in this manner: "I am this body. I am this mortal individual." This egoism is the true root of all evil.

THE AFRICAN ORIGINS OF CIVILIZATION, RELIGION AND YOGA SPIRITUALITY

Pride, vanity, conceit, narcissism, vainglory, superiority, insolence, presumption, arrogance, disdain, haughtiness, hauteur, loftiness, selfishness, lordliness, superciliousness, etc., represent various forms of intensification of the ego. Through the intensification of body-consciousness and through the pursuit of selfish acts in the hopes of fulfilling personal desires, the ego idea of self becomes inflated. The mind is more and more intensely turned towards the individual self, the body and the world for fulfillment, rather than towards the transcendental Self, the spirit within.

The characteristics mentioned above are considered to be demoniac or satanic forms of behavior. On the other hand, selfless service, charity, inward renunciation of possessions, etc., represent saintly or virtuous qualities, which lead to the Divine because they cause effacement of the ego. This effacement leaves the soul free of the troubles, needs, concerns and sufferings of the ego-self and gives rise to the Higher Self. It is this ego-body consciousness idea of self which produces the major obstacle to spiritual evolution.

In the following statements we are to understand that God, as represented by the deity Krishna, is himself the light.

Gita: Chapter 7 Jnana Vijnana Yogah—the Yoga of Wisdom and Realization

8. O Son of Kunti! I am the taste in the waters, I am the light in the sun and the moon; I am Pranava (Om) in the Vedas, the sound in the Ether element, and manliness in men.

9. I am the pure fragrance in earth, I am the effulgence in fire,[614] I am the life in all living beings, and I am the austerity in the ascetics.

10. O Partha, know Me to be the eternal seed of all beings. I am the intellect in the wise, the valor of those who are valiant.

11. O Best of the Bharatas! Among the strong, I am their strength that is devoid of lust and passion. Among all beings I am the desire that is not opposed to Dharma (the ethical law).

Compare the previous statements to the following Egyptian Hermetic teaching. The *I am* statement in all of them is pointing to the same mystical truth.

"I am the Mind - the Eternal Teacher. I am the begetter of the Word - the Redeemer of all humankind - and in the nature of the wise, the Word takes flesh. By means of the Word, the world is saved. I, Thought - the begetter of the Word, the Mind - come only unto they that are holy, good, pure and merciful, and that live piously and religiously, and my presence is an inspiration and a help to them, for when I come, they immediately know all things and adore the Universal Spirit. Before such wise and philosophic ones die, they learn to renounce their senses, knowing that these are the enemies of their immortal Souls.

The idea of the *Word* or *Logos* being the savior of the world existed before Christianity. The main difference in Orthodox Roman Christianity was that the *"word"* or saving wisdom became flesh in the personality of Jesus, the man. This was an idea that Gnostic Christianity and other mystery religions rejected. The more ancient idea holds that the *word* itself is not only the Divine Presence, but its power of manifestation as well. With this understanding, the entire universe, including the human personality, body and mind are all manifestations of the *"Living Word"* itself—not just Jesus. The new Christian idea that emerged sees the *word* as being embodied in the person of Jesus himself and nowhere else. This is a more egoistic view. Christian Gnosticism holds that Jesus is a symbol of the potential realization of the divine word or essence in every human being.

In relation to the term *"word,"* another Biblical term, *"Dabhar,"* is of interest. This word implies creation, deeds, actions, and accomplishments as opposed to talk. It relates to the creative power of the Divine, of which human beings partake. Biblical scholars have often confused the meanings of these terms. However, a thorough understanding of the writings of the Hellenistic period known as *"Hermetic"* and the more ancient writings of Egypt reveal the correct interpretation, of the word as being the Creative principle. The following verses come from various chapters throughout the Egyptian *Book of Coming Forth By Day*, which show the initiate's gradual realization that the gods are in reality aspects of {him/her}self. This is the earliest known form of the *"I am"* formula used in philosophy. Thus, the *I am* (God) is the source of all action and all existence. In this respect the *I am* is related to the ancient Kamitan teaching of *Un*. Un means existence or that which is, i.e., the principle of *beingness* or abiding nature behind the changing way of Creation. This is one of the main titles of the god Asar in his aspect as Un-Nefer, or Beautiful (good) Existence. Further, the initiate understands {his/her} true nature and its power:

"I am the Great God, the self created one, Nun...I am Ra...I am Geb...I am Atum...I am Asar...I am Min...I am Shu...I am Anubis...I am Aset...I am Hathor...I am Sekhmit...I am Orion...I am Saa...I am the Lion... I am the young Bull...I am Hapi who comes forth as the river Nile..."[615]

In the following segments from Chapter 23 of the Ancient Egyptian *Book of Coming Forth By Day*, the initiate, having understood his oneness, and having identified with God in the form of Asar, exclaims the following:

"I am yesterday, today and tomorrow. I have the power to be born a second time. I am the source from which the gods arise."

This is the moment of great realization to which the entire religious system of the Asarian Resurrection was directed. The aspirant or initiate was to understand his identity with the transcendental reality properly before death, but if not, then on the way through the Duat (after-death state or astral plane of mind). As with the Gnostics, the Ancient Egyptians considered those who had not had this mystical experience as *"Mortals"* while those who had it were called *"Sons of Light."*

"And I am that God, the Great one in his boat, Ra, I am."

–From Prt m Hru Chapter 1

"I am the god Tem as I am One. I became thus from Nun; I am Ra in his rising in the beginning of time, the prince."

–From Prt m Hru Chapter 4

"It has been decreed for millions of millions of years of duration. It is given to me to send the old ones. After that period of time I am going to destroy all created things. It is the earth that came forth from Nun, now coming forth into its former state."

–From Prt m Hru Chapter 8

"I am beyond your grasp because I am one with God. I am the Single One, who is in the Primeval Water of Creation... I am that same God, the Supreme One, who has myriad of mysterious names. I was born of Temu, the first divinity that came into existence. I know this! I am one possessing the knowledge of the innermost truth."

–From Prt m Hru Chapter 9

"I am Ra, coming forth from Nun, the Divine Soul, and Creator of his own body parts."

–From Prt m Hru Chapter 22

"I am the substratum of all the gods and goddesses."

–From Prt m Hru Chapter 26

"I am Ra! I am one whose name is unknown[616], Lord of Eternity..."

–From *Prt m Hru* Chapter 27

THE AFRICAN ORIGINS OF CIVILIZATION, RELIGION AND YOGA SPIRITUALITY
NOTES TO CHAPTER 8

502 *Indian Mythology,* Veronica Ions
503 All the gods and goddesses of a people.
504 *A Concise Encyclopedia of Hinduism,* by Klaus K. Klostermaier
505 *Indian Mythology,* by Veronica Ions
506 *Indian Mythology,* Veronica Ions.
507 Feuerstein, Georg, *The Shambhala Encyclopedia of Yoga* 1997
508 Feuerstein, Georg, *The Shambhala Encyclopedia of Yoga* 1997
509 See the books *Resurrecting Osiris* by Dr. Muata Ashby
510 *Mysteries of the Creation Myth,* Muata Ashby. *The Gods of the Egyptians,* E.W. Budge
511 *Indian Mythology,* Veronica Ions. *The RIG VEDA* by Ralph T.H. Griffith, Translator. (1896)
512 Random House Encyclopedia Copyright (C) 1983,1990
513 Random House Encyclopedia Copyright (C) 1983,1990
514 Encarta Encyclopedia 2000
515 Some texts use three and others speak of nine- *Indian Mythology,* Veronica Ions.
516 See the books *The Asarian Resurrection: The Ancient Egyptian Bible* and *The Mystical Teachings of The Ausarian Resurrection: Initiation Into The Third Level of Shetaut Asar,* Muata Ashby
517 *A Concise Encyclopedia of Hinduism,* by Klaus K. Klostermaier
518 *Reading Egyptian Art,* Richard H. Wilkinson
519 *The Yoga of Wisdom,* Swami Jyotirmayananda
520 *The RIG VEDA* Ralph T.H. Griffith, translator 1889
521 Wilkins, *Hindu Mythology,* p. 33.
522 See Martin, *Gods of India,* p. 35.
523 Monier-Williams, *Indian Wisdom,* p. 19.
524 Monier-Williams' translation.
525 Rig-Veda, VII, 86, 3-6.
526 Rig-Veda, HYMN XXV. Varuna.
527 J. H. Breasted: *Cambridge Ancient History* (Edit. 1924), Vol. II, p. 120.
528 Sir Wallis Budge: *Tutankhamen, Amenism, Atenism, and Egyptian Monotheism* (Edit. 1923), p. 86.
529 Sir Wallis Budge: *Tutankhamen, Amenism, Atenism, and Egyptian Monotheism* (Edit. 1923), pp. 86-87.
530 *A SON OF GOD: THE LIFE AND PHILOSOPHY OF AKHNATON, KING OF EGYPT,* Savitri Devi, [1946]
531 Copyright © 1995 Helicon Publishing Ltd Encyclopedia
532 *Tutankhamen, Amenism, Atenism, and Egyptian Monotheism,* Sir Wallis Budge
533 From *The Ancient Egyptian Book of the Dead,* Muata Ashby, 2000
534 Morning sun, solar child-Nefertem.
535 i.e. allow the initiate to become an Akhu or Glorious Spirit.
536 The All-Encompassing Divine Self in the form of Heru.
537 Spiritual essence of the personality which holds a person's desires, impulses and impetus to incarnate; the Life Force which sustains the physical being.
538 Creator -aspect of Ra, Atum, Asar, Khepri, Amun, Neberdjer, etc) who first arose on the primeval mound. Protector of the souls of Asar and Heru.
539 Gods and goddesses
540 Ibis headed deity, minister of Ra, originator of hieroglyphic writings and music.
541 Goddess of righteousness, truth, regularity, and order.
542 Royal family.
543 Leader of the fiends, second only to Set.
544 The pool or lake is the symbol of the Primeval Ocean. In ancient times the temple complexes included a lake for ritually sailing the boat of Ra as well as for keeping fish, crocodiles and other animals as temple mascots.
545 Front section of a ship's hull, the bow.
546 The name of Ra's Divine boat when it is traveling from noon to midnight, i.e. the evening boat.
547 The name of Ra's Divine boat when it is traveling from midnight to noon, i.e. the morning boat.
548 The sundisk.
549 In Kamitan Mystical Philosophy the principle of "Shemsu Heru" is very important. It may be likened to the disciples of Jesus in Christianity who were his "followers." It means living and acting like Heru, a life of truth and increasing spiritual enlightenment.
550 Maa-kheru.
551 Gloss On The Hymns to Ra: Its Meaning and Mystical Significance, *The Ancient Egyptian Book of the Dead,* Muata Ashby, 2000
552 See the books *The Asarian Resurrection: The Ancient Egyptian Bible* and *The Mystical Teachings of The Ausarian Resurrection: Initiation Into The Third Level of Shetaut Asar.*
553 *Memphite Theology: The Hidden Properties of Matter,* Muata Ashby 1997
554 ibid.
555 *The People of South Asia* Edited by J. R. Lukacs, ed., Chapter 3, *Biological anthropology of Bronze Age*[555] *Harappans: new perspectives,* Pratap C. Dutta

556 Doshi, Saryu, Editor-Indian Council for Cultural Relations *India and Egypt: Influences and Interactions* 1993
557 *A Concise Encyclopedia of Hinduism*, by Klaus K. Klostermaier
558 Compton's Interactive Encyclopedia Copyright (c) 1994, 1995
559 The Upanishads by Swami Prabhavananda and Frederick Manchester
560 The Upanishads by Swami Prabhavananda and Frederick Manchester
561 The Upanishads, Max Müller, translator
562 The Upanishads by Swami Prabhavananda and Frederick Manchester
563 The Upanishads by Swami Prabhavananda and Frederick Manchester
564 The Upanishads by Swami Prabhavananda and Frederick Manchester
565 The Upanishads, Max Müller, translator
566 *Yoga Vasistha Ramayana* translated by Swami Jyotirmayananda
567 *Feuerstein, Georg, The Shambhala Encyclopedia of Yoga* 1997
568 In the *Papyrus of Nes-Menu*, there is an order to the priestesses of Aset and Nephthys to have "the hair of their bodies shaved off." They are also ordered to wear fillets of rams wool on their heads ⎮ 𓏏𓏤 ⎯ as a form of ritual identification with the hidden (Amun) mystery. Wool was also used by the Sufis, followers of esoteric Islam. The name "*Sufi*" comes from "Suf" which means "wool." The name Sufi was adopted since the ascetic followers of this doctrine wore coarse woolen garments (sufu) (An *ascetic* is one who practices severe and austere methods of spiritual practice.).
569 sacred to the Ancient Egyptian divinity Amun.
570 *Yoga Vasistha*, Nirvana Prakarana Swami Jyotirmayananda, 1998
571 *The Upanishads: Breath of the Eternal*, Swami Prabhavananda and Frederick Manchester
572 From a terracotta bust, traditional comes from Jayanagar-Mazilpur, 24-Parganas, South Bengal.
573 Sudhansu Kumar Ray
574 The *Mahabharata* epic is cited as an early source for the word and concept. *Feuerstein, Georg, The Shambhala Encyclopedia of Yoga* 1997
575 *A Concise Encyclopedia of Hinduism*, by Klaus K. Klostermaier
576 American Heritage Dictionary
577 Asar (Osiris)
578 Djehuti
579 *Art – Culture of India and Egypt,* the author S. M El Mansouri
580 *A Concise Encyclopedia of Hinduism*, by Klaus K. Klostermaier
581 *Mysticism of the Mahabharata* by Swami Jyotirmayananda
582 *The Ancient Egyptian Book of the Dead* by Dr. Muata Ashby 2000
583 Also Sokkar
584 *The Egyptian Book of the Dead*, Muata Ashby
585 For more details on the Philosophy of Ari see the Book *Egyptian Book of the Dead,* by Muata Ashby
586 American Heritage Dictionary
587 Smai Tawi (Egyptian Yoga).
588 For the full text and explanation see the *Book of the Dead* by Muata Ashby
589 *A Concise Encyclopedia of Hinduism*, by Klaus K. Klostermaier
590 *Feuerstein, Georg, The Shambhala Encyclopedia of Yoga* 1997
591 Book: *The Egyptian Book of the Dead,* Muata Ashby. Also, Book *Osiris*, E. W. Budge
592 **Eschatology**, branch of systematic theology, the study of final, last things. The term was first used in the 19th century with the critical analysis of the New Testament. It deals not only with the study of the kingdom of God, but also with the final destiny of mankind. Random House Encyclopedia Copyright (C) 1983,1990
593 Doshi, Saryu, Editor-Indian Council for Cultural Relations *India and Egypt: Influences and Interactions* 1993
594 For a more detailed study of the Kamitan teachings related to the "Witnessing Self" see the book Egyptian Yoga Vol. 2.
595 The Creation Story related in the Papyrus of Nesi-Amsu
596 From an inscription in the temple of Denderah, Egypt.
597 For further references see the book *Mystical Journey From Jesus to Christ* by Muata Ashby
598 In general Indian religions sects hold this ideal. However, there are some sects which hold their form of worship and iconography as being the "only" "true" path. However, unlike the western religions this is not endemic of Hinduism and is relegated to a minority as opposed to a majority of the religious practitioners.
599 American Heritage Dictionary
600 This category includes fish, and eggs. (*The Sivananda Companion to Yoga*, Lucy Lidell, Narayani, Giris Rabinovitch)
601 This category includes meat, and alcohol. (The Sivananda Companion to Yoga)
602 *Bhagavad Gita* Chapter 2 Samkhya Yogah--The Yoga of Knowledge by Swami Jyotirmayananda
603 *Porphyry,* On Abstinence from Killing Animals, trans. Gillian Clark (Ithaak, 1999). (= *De abstentia,* Book IV, chap 6)
604 *Feuerstein, Georg, The Shambhala Encyclopedia of Yoga* 1997
605 *Feuerstein, Georg, The Shambhala Encyclopedia of Yoga* 1997
606 *The Vasistha* is a blessing to all who have had an opportunity to read and understand it, even more so for those who can study its teachings as they are translated by a living master. I have had the privilege to experience this blessing, thanks to my spiritual preceptor Swami Jyotirmayananda, a world renowned teacher of Indian Yoga philosophy, who in order to complete the entire text , providing the mystical insight lectures twice weekly for a period of seven years.

[607] See the books *The Asarian Resurrection: The Ancient Egyptian Bible* and The *Mystical Teachings of The Ausarian Resurrection: Initiation Into The Third Level of Shetaut Asar.*
[608] Referring to the Supreme Being in the form of Atum-Ra
[609] The Creator, *Atum-Ra*
[610] See the book *Christian Yoga* by Muata Ashby.
[611] *Raja Yoga Sutras,* Swami Jyotirmayananda
[612] (Chapter 21 Verse 6)
[613] From the Ancient Egyptian Book of Coming Forth By Day (Book of the Dead).
[614] Fire of worldly desire.
[615] Selections from various chapters of the Prt M Hru (Ancient Egyptian Book of Enlightenment.)
[616] One of the most ancient and mystical names to describe the transcendental Divinity, "Nameless One." This term also refers to the Primeval being who arose from the Primeval Ocean, bringing Creation into existence, i.e. Atum.

Chapter 9: The Neterian Religion Origins of Indian Buddhism

The Early History of Buddhism

An overview of the origins and development of Buddhism will provide further insights into its relationship with Africa and Ancient Egypt. The historical Buddha, Siddhartha Gautama (c. 563- c. 483 B.C.E.) was mythically related to have been a prince who gave up his royal life to seek after spiritual evolution. The traditional story of this life relates that he turned to the Brahmins, the Hindu Monks, and practiced austerities, but felt that he was obtaining minimal results from his efforts. The myth goes on to say that he then turned inwards and discovered a new path to attain spiritual salvation. It was called the middle way. He developed the Eight-Fold Path. A brief look at Buddhist history reveals that Buddhism developed in a similar way as Orthodox Christianity.

Right after the death of Buddha, his followers met for the first time to decide how to best preserve the teachings of the Buddha since they were never written down. When asked about who would lead the Buddhist faith, Buddha had told them they should work out their enlightenment on their own. However, the oral nature of the teachings made them subject to variation and misinterpretation. His disciples felt the need to convene a council to decide on what the "cannon" of the teachings would be. Hundreds of years later the Roman Christians held similar councils to decide on what Jesus had said and taught since nothing was written about him during the time he had supposedly lived. There were four major councils, in total, that convened to decide on the Buddhist teachings in its early development.

One hundred years later (c. 383 B.C.E.) , a second great council met at Vaishâli. In the 3rd century B.C.E., the third council was called by King Ashoka at Pâtaliputra (present-day Patna). Its purpose was to purify the *sangha* (membership) due to the large number of charlatans (false monks and heretics) who became Buddhists since it had attained royal patronage. The compilation of the Buddhist scriptures (Tipitaka) was supposed to have been completed at this time and also *abhidharma,* an adjunct philosophy to the Dharma doctrine was added along with the set monastic discipline (vinaya) that monks had recited at the first council. After this council, missionaries were sent to various countries. It is at this time that there is firm evidence of the Buddhist presence in Memphis, Egypt. This association continued for the next three centuries until the closing of the Egyptian Temples. However, there was still contact between Egypt and the Buddhists into the early Christian era, up to and after the fourth council of Buddhism. The fourth council was held about 100 A.C.E. The main goal of this council was to make peace between the sects. However, the Theravada Buddhists did not recognize authenticity of this council. So the teachings of Buddhism were not committed to writing until about the 1st century B.C.E., some 650 years after Buddha had lived.

Conflicting interpretations of the Buddhist teaching led to the development of no less than 18 schools of Buddhist philosophy. Out of these 18 or more sects of early Buddhism only the Theravada survives. All others that we see in the world today developed later in history. The more conservative monks were accused of not taking into account the needs of the general populace and so a new sect was created to serve the needs of the laity. That new sect was called Mahayana. It developed also out of conflicting Buddhist tenets. The conservative Theravadas viewed Buddha as a perfectly enlightened human teacher. However, the liberal Mahasanghikas created a concept of Buddha an omnipresent, eternal, transcendental being. They thought that the human Buddha was only a manifestation of the transcendental Buddha that was sent to the earth for the good of humankind. In this conceptualization of Buddha nature, the Mahasanghika concept was a forerunner of Mahayana Buddhism (Buddhism for the masses). Mahayana Buddhists do not limit themselves to the original teachings of the Buddha nor to a canon of Buddhist writings. Their origins, as a group with a differing interpretation of Buddhist philosophy, are not known and yet they form a major aspect of modern Buddhism, the development of which is believed to have begun sometime between the 2nd century B.C.E. and the 1st century A.C.E.

THE AFRICAN ORIGINS OF CIVILIZATION, RELIGION AND YOGA SPIRITUALITY

The Concept of The Trinity in Buddhism

The Mahayana sect developed the doctrine of Buddha's threefold nature, or triple "body" (*trikaya*) - body of essence (ultimate nature), the body of communal bliss, and the body of transformation. Beyond the body of essence there is transcendence of form. There is the realm or state of consciousness which is changeless and absolute. This transcendental Absolute is also referred to as consciousness or the void. The essential Buddha nature manifests itself as communal bliss as well as takes on human form in order to assist human beings. Siddhartha Gautama was just one example of the body of transformation form of the historical Buddha. A similar debate raged on amongst the orthodox Christians.

The debates in the church over the true understanding of Christ (Christology) led to a separation between the Church in Egypt (Coptic Church) and the churches of Rome and Constantinople (Western Empire and Eastern Empire). The majority of Egyptian Christians refused to go along with the decrees of the Council of Chalcedon in 451 A.C.E., that defined the person of Jesus the Christ as being "one in two natures." This doctrine of "two natures" seemed to imply the existence of two Christs, one being divine and the other human. These Egyptian Christians who refused the Council of Chalcedon faced charges of monophysitism. Monophysitism is the belief that Christ has only one nature rather than two. It is notable that the Council of Chalcedon was accepted both in Constantinople and in Rome, but not in Egypt. Thus, we see that the dualistic view of Christ was developed and promoted in Europe under the Roman church and in the Middle East under the church of Constantinople. It was Egypt, which sought to uphold the non-dualistic view of Christ, which viewed him as an all-encompassing Divine being. This was due to the tradition of non-dualism, which it assimilated from the Ancient Egyptian mystery schools. The Coptic Church of Egypt separated from Rome and Constantinople and set up its own Pope who, to this day, is nominated by an Electoral College of clergy and laity. The Coptic Church has survived up to the present in Egypt. There are over seven million Coptic Christians there today and 22 million in total.

The Concept of The Trinity in Christianity

In the New Testament, the triad of "Father, and of the Son, and of the Holy Spirit" is used to describe the idea of God (Matthew 28:19). The Trinity is the central teaching of Christianity. It holds that God is three personalities, the Father, the Son, and the Holy Spirit [or Holy Ghost]. The idea is that there is only one God, but that he exists as *"Three."* Christian theologians claim that the true nature of the Trinity is a mystery, which cannot be comprehended by the human mind, although they can grasp some of its meanings. The Trinity doctrine was stated in very early Christian creeds whose purpose was to counter other beliefs such as Gnosticism. However, as we saw earlier, later church authorities misunderstood it.

The Concept Trinity According to Ancient Egyptian Religion and Mystical Philosophy

The term *"Trinity"* was misunderstood by the Orthodox Catholic Christians and, because of this misunderstanding, some Gnostic groups even ridiculed them. However, the three in one metaphor was ancient by the time it was adopted by Catholicism. It was a term used to convey the idea of different aspects of the one reality. This same idea occurs in Egyptian as well as in Indian mythology. However, for deeper insights into the mystical meaning of the Trinity we must look to Ancient Egypt. In Egyptian mythology, the Trinity was represented as three *metaphysical neters* or gods. They represent the manifestation of the unseen principles, which support the universe, and the visible aspects of God. The main Egyptian Trinity is composed of Amun, Ra and Ptah. Amun means that which is hidden and unintelligible, the underlying reality which sustains all things. Ra represents the subtle matter of creation as well as the mind. Ptah represents the visible aspect of Divinity, the phenomenal universe. The Ancient Egyptian "Trinity" is also known as a manifestation of *Nebertcher* (Neberdjer). Nebertcher means "all encompassing" Divinity. Thus, the term is equivalent to the Vedantic Brahman, the Buddhist Dharmakaya and the Taoist Tao. The Ancient Egyptian text reads as follows:

"Everything is Amun-Ra-Ptah, three in one."

Further, each member of the Trinity had a particular city in Egypt where the mysticism of each individual divinity was espoused. In each city, each divinity had their own Trinity, of which each was the head. In the city of Memphis, where the early Buddhists lived and studied, the local Trinity was headed by the Ancient Egyptian divinity Ptah. This Trinity consisted of Ptah, Sekhmit and Nefertem. In this system, Ptah represents Consciousness manifesting as mind, Sekhmit represents Life Force and Nefertem represents Creation. So this teaching of the Trinity at Memphis was studied by the early Buddhists and they were also impressed by the popular quality of Memphite Theology. While Memphite Theology is highly philosophical and intellectual, it is also personable because its teaching involves myths and deities to which people can relate. Also, the Ancient Egyptians were adept at conducting rituals that involved the entire population, thereby allowing them to take part in the mysteries of the religion, and at such time when they proved their readiness, individuals were admitted to the priestly ranks to worship and be privy to the higher teachings behind the myth.[617]

The Buddha or *"The Enlightened One"*,[618] developed a philosophy based on ideas which existed previously in Jain philosophy and the Upanishads. Buddha recognized that many people took the teachings to extreme. Teachings such as that of non-violence which stressed not harming any creatures were understood by some as not moving so as not to step on insects or not breathing in without covering the mouth so as not to kill insects or microorganisms. Prior to Buddha, other teachings such as those of the "Brahmins" and "Sanyasa" (renunciation), where one was supposed to renounce the apparent reality as an illusion, were taken to extremes wherein some followers would starve themselves to the point of death in order to achieve spiritual experience. Others became deeply involved with the intellectual aspects of philosophy, endlessly questioning, "Where did I come from?, Who put me here?, How long will I need to do spiritual practice?, Where did Brahman (GOD) come from?", etc. Buddha saw the error of the way in which the teaching was understood and set out to reform religion.

Buddha emphasized attaining salvation rather than asking so many questions. He likened people who asked too many intellectual questions to a person whose house (lifetime) is burning down while they ask "How did the fire get started?" instead of first worrying about getting out. Further, Buddha saw that renouncing attachment to worldly objects was not necessarily a physical discipline but more importantly, it was a psychological one and therefore, he created a philosophical discipline which explained the psychology behind human suffering and how to end that suffering, a philosophy emphasizing "BALANCE" rather than extremes. He recognized that extremes cause mental upset-ness because **"One extreme leads to another."** Therefore, mental balance was the way to achieve mental peace. This psychological discipline became the Noble Eight-fold Path which was later adapted by the Indian Sage Patanjali and developed into the eight major Yoga disciplines of Indian Yoga.

While never formally rejecting the existence of the gods and goddesses, Buddhism does deny any special role to them. These beings may have pleasurable and long lives in the heavens but they are under the same ultimate law as human beings and other creatures. They are not considered as creators and they must ultimately die and be reborn again. Buddhism does hold that they do not control the destiny of human beings and so there is no value in praying to them.

This same philosophy, that the gods and goddesses are subject to the same ultimate law as are human beings and other creatures is reflected in the Anunian Theology based at the city of Anu, a short distance from Memphis. It held that God, in the form of Ra, the second member of the Great Trinity, emanates the gods and goddesses from himself and they constitute the elements of Creation. He periodically ("after millions and millions of years") dissolves the world back into himself including the gods and goddesses.[619] A similar teaching is contained in the Asarian Theology which is associated with Memphite Theology.[620] However, Ancient Egyptian religion, across the board, and African religion in general, hold that there is value in approaching the gods and goddesses. That lower form of worship promotes the ability to understand and approach the Supreme Being.

One important difference between Buddhism and the other Hindu religions is that Buddhism does not advocate worshipping Buddha, whereas most other Indian religions do incorporate the worshiping of a deity or other divine figure(s). However, Buddha is to be paid homage and to be emulated through the practice of Buddhist teaching. This practice leads the aspirant to discovering his/her own essential "Buddha Nature." So if a person is interested in a psychological spiritual discipline rather than a religious based system of deities, Buddhism offers less images of deities on the surface. However, many followers of the Buddhist religion develop a deep reverential devotion to the Buddha and, in essence, "deify" him. Also, the Mahayana form of Buddhism offers many "Buddhas" which can be equated to deities. They symbolize various aspects of consciousness and various aspects of Buddhist philosophy.

Evidence of Contact Between Early Buddhists and Ancient Egyptians

Table 27: Timeline of Buddhism and Ancient Egypt

10,000 B.C.E.	5000 B.C.E.	4500 B.C.E.	4000 B.C.E.	3500 B.C.E.	3000 B.C.E.	1500 B.C.E	1000 B.C.E.	500 B.C.E.	400 B.C.E.	250 B.C.E.	0	100 A.C.E.	300 A.C.E.
Ancient Egyptian Religion								Cambyses Invades Egypt Persian Period	Alexander Invades Egypt Greek Period				Coptic Period to Present
Pre-Dynastic Era	Old Kingdom		Middle Kingdom			New Kingdom							
			Indus Valley Culture			Aryan India		Hinduism in India to present					
								Council #1	Council #2	Council #3		Council #4	
						Buddhist Councils					Early Christianity	Pre-Roman	Orthodox Councils

General Timeline of Phases in Buddhist and Hindu Indian Myth and Religion

3000 – 1500 B.C.E. Indus Valley Period

1500 - 1000 B.C.E. Aryan Period

1000 - 800 B.C.E. Brahmanas period

800 – 600 Upanishadic Period

600 B.C.E.- 261 B.C.E. Early Hindu Period

500 B.C.E. Buddhism founded

261 B.C.E.- 1200 A.C.E. Buddhist prominence among conglomeration of other Indian belief systems.

319-415 A.C.E. Gupta period – Dynasty of Rulers of Magadha[621] Renaissance of Hinduism – Puranic Age

Between the years 319 A.C.E. to 1100 A.C.E., Hinduism experienced a resurgence and Buddhism began to wane in India. The older traditions of the Brahmins, Vedic students, as well as newer traditions, including Tantrism, Kundalini Yoga and several schools of Hindu mysticism emerged including Vedanta, Jainism,[622] Shaivism,[623] Vaishnavism,[624] Shaktism,[625] Tantrism,[626] Yoga,[627] Samkhya,[628] and others.[629] The Puranas, stories about glories of the Divine in human form on earth, were a rekindling force that caused people to take a new interest in Hindu myth, legend and spirituality. Much like the Christian gospels, their function was to engender a devotional feeling and to make the divinities, especially Krishna, personal as opposed to the monastic concept of Buddha which many people saw as being more rigid, intellectual and psychological. By 1,200 A.C.E. a Muslim Dynasty had come to power in India, and Buddhism virtually disappeared from the land of its origin. Many Buddhist elements still survive in Indian Hinduism.[630]

Some scholars believe that Buddhism waned in India not just because of the Muslim conquest, but also because in its purest form, Buddhism holds a view of God as consciousness as opposed to a supernatural figure (male or female) or spirit with a name and form. Some Hindus, such as the orthodox followers of Krishna[631] consider the Buddhists and Vedantins as "impersonalists" because they revere the Divine "without name and form" and see this as an incorrect practice of religion. The Muslims on the other hand, see Buddhists as "Kaffirs" or unbelievers because they do not follow Islam and because of this they are not following religion at all. A stark example of the enmity between Buddhism and Islam was the extremist actions by some Muslims of destroying ancient Buddhist monuments in Afghanistan in the mid 1990's A.C.E.

Cultural-religious exchange between Egypt and India in the time of Emperor Ashoka in 261 B.C.E.

In the book *India and Egypt: Influences and Interactions, 1993,* Lutfi A. W. Yehya notes the archeological discoveries, in Ancient Egypt of the Ptolemaic era, which conclusively prove contact between the Ancient Egyptians and Indians of that time as well as a blending of Ancient Egyptian and Indian religion as evinced by the artifacts found in Memphis, Egypt.

> "There seems to be sufficient evidence to indicate that Indians in good number had started visiting Egypt in the Ptolemaic period and even before it-from the third century, BC onwards. Athenaeus refers to the presence of Indian women, Indian cows and camels, and Indian hunting dogs in the royal processions of Ptolemy Philadelphus in Egypt.[632] An Indian colony probably existed in Egypt even earlier at Memphis. The excavations at Memphis have yielded some terracotta fragments and figurines[633] which from their facial features and costume, appear to be Indian.[634] Some of them have been identified as the representations of Panchika, a Buddhist divinity.[635]
> Again, indicative of the close contact during Ptolemaic times is a gravestone which bears an Indian symbol of the trident and wheel, and the infant deity Horus is shown sitting in Indian attitude on a lotus."[636]

It is well known that Emperor Ashoka of India, upon becoming a Buddhist convert, was instrumental in the dissemination of the Buddhist teachings throughout the known ancient world. He sent Buddhist missionaries throughout India and to various countries. There are also several iconographical evidences, some mentioned above and others that will be presented later, that link Buddhism with Neterianism, and especially with the temple of Het-ka-Ptah (Memphis) in Egypt.

> "Ashoka (c. 291-232 BC), emperor of India He sent missionaries to countries as remote as Greece and Egypt. His reign is known from engravings on rocks and from traditions in Sanskrit literature. He was the most celebrated ruler of ancient India, known for his benevolent rule and for making Buddhism the official religion of his empire. Despite Ashoka's vigorous exertions in behalf of his faith, he was tolerant of other religions, and India enjoyed marked prosperity during his reign."[637]

In the chapter of the book *India and Egypt: Influences and Interactions, 1993*, entitled *Transmission of Ideas and Imagery,* the scholar M. C. Joshi reports on ancient written documents attesting to the communications and cultural exchanges between Ancient Egypt and India during the time of the Indian emperor Ashoka. This record shows not only economic exchanges, but social and humanitarian exchanges, pointing to the compatibility of the two countries. Just as two people who are of opposite character cannot get along, so too countries cannot get along if their peoples are of an opposite nature. Thus, the fact that the Egyptian ruler allowed the contact and allowed Indian artifacts and people into the country without fear of having his power being undermined or that the social order would fail or that the ethnic character would change, etc., as is so often the case in modern government relations which are filled with mistrust, fear and racism, further attests to the compatibility, and likely similarity, of these two cultures.

THE AFRICAN ORIGINS OF CIVILIZATION, RELIGION AND YOGA SPIRITUALITY

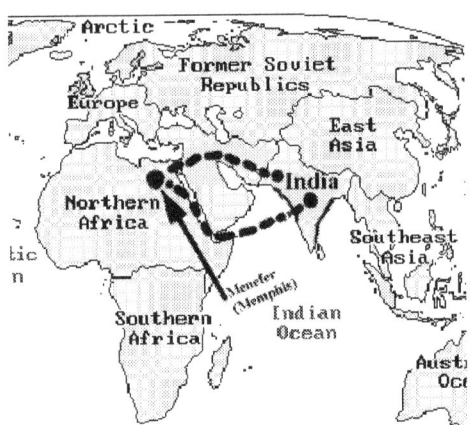

Above: Trade Routes Between Menefer (Memphis) Egypt and India

EARLY INSCRIPTIONS AND LITERARY REFERENCES

The brightest evidence of India's direct relations with Egypt is, however, preserved in the Mauryan Emperor Ashoka's thirteenth rock edict,[638] inscribed in the early decades of the third century BC. In it, Emperor Ashoka refers to his contacts with Ptolemy II Philadelphus of Egypt (285-246 BC), in connection with the expansion of his policy of the propagation of the Law of Righteousness *(dharma)*. In the Ashokan records Ptolemy II is referred to as Turamaya. There can be little doubt that official embassies were exchanged between the Mauryan court and that of Ptolemy II. Pliny names the Egyptian Ambassador of Ptolemy II to India as Dionysus.[639]

Ashoka in his second rock edict, refers to the philanthropic activities undertaken by himself. He records that he had made arrangements for the medical treatment of men and animals in the territories of his own empire as well as in the region ruled by Antiochus Theos II of Syria (260-246 BC) and its neighboring kingdoms,[640] which also included Egypt.

Interestingly, it is stated that the Egyptian ruler Ptolemy IV, Philopator, lined a part of his yacht with Indian stones. The presence of Indians in Egypt in the third century BC has been attested by Athenaeus who observes that the processions of Ptolemy II Philadelphus also included women, cows, and hunting dogs from India.[641]

Main entrance to the ancient Spiritual Center and Temple of Memphis at Sakkara, Egypt.

There was an important development in the 6th century B.C.E. that occurred in Egypt at the time when Buddhism emerged. Cambyses II (reigned 529-522 BC), the king of Persia, led an expedition to conquer Egypt, which at the time was the sole independent kingdom in the aftermath the conquests of Asia by his father. Cambyses defeated Psamtik III, king of Egypt, and succeeded in conquering Egypt as far south as Nubia, but he failed in later attacks on the Egyptian oasis of Ammonium (now Siwa) and in campaigns in Ethiopia.

The attacks and conquest of Egypt by the Persians caused an extensive displacements of the Egyptian population. It was at this time that some of the Priests and Priestesses were forced out of the Temples due to fires set by the armies of the Persians. Also, many Egyptians were forcibly taken as slave workers to Persia and other parts of Asia Minor to build monuments and Temples for the Persians in those areas.[642\643] It is during this time that the most powerful and influential philosophies of the ancient world came into being. These included:

- Buddhism   6th century B.C.E.
- Pythagoreanism   6th century B.C.E.
- Taoism   6th century B.C.E.
- Confucianism   6th century B.C.E.
- Zoroastrianism   6th century B.C.E.
- Jainism   6th century B.C.E.

The Ancient Egyptians had been attacked and the country taken over by foreigners twice before. The first time was the Hyksos invasion, which precipitated the "Second Intermediate Period," and the second time was the invasion of the Assyrians which was put down by the Nubians. However, the records indicate[644] that the viciousness of the attack and conquest by the Persians was so severe that it prompted a migration of Ancient Egyptians not only to Asia Minor, but also to India, Europe and other parts of Africa, including Nubia to the south, and West Africa also. Therefore, a causal connection can be drawn between the events in Egypt and the events in other parts of the ancient world. The surviving culture of Egypt was severely weakened after the Persian conquest, so much so that after a brief reestablishment of Egyptian rule by Egyptians, they were conquered again by the Greeks, who themselves had conquered the Persians. This period brought some stability to Egypt as the Greeks allowed the Ancient Egyptian religion to continue under their auspices, and the connection that had been established between other countries and Egypt through the Egyptians that had migrated out of Egypt 200 years earlier[645] during the invasion of Cambyses and the open relations fostered by the Ptolemaic rulers continued into a new phase. Now Egypt was fully opened to the spiritual seekers of the ancient world, and they flocked to the land of the Pyramids.

In this respect some researchers have noted the similarities between the Ancient Egyptian and Buddhist iconographies and point to these, and the evidences of philosophical correlations and evidences of contact along with the images of Buddha himself, as sufficient proof to show that Buddha was an African-Egyptian priest. Indeed, even when we consider that no images of Buddha were allowed until the 1st century B.C.E. with the advent of Mahayana Buddhism, the images that appear even at that time, and later, up to the present day, bear a resemblance to the Kamitan-Kushitic forms of imagery and human appearance. There is a resemblance especially in the depiction of the hair and certain aspects of the physiognomy, in particular the nose and eye region of the face. It is curly or in locks, a form that was originated in ancient Kamit.

THE AFRICAN ORIGINS OF CIVILIZATION, RELIGION AND YOGA SPIRITUALITY

Above left: Sculpture of an Ancient Egyptian Official from Sakkara (Old Kingdom) Brooklyn Museum
Above right: Kamitan-Kushitic sculpture, described by the Brooklyn Museum as "Black man." (**Hellenistic** period)

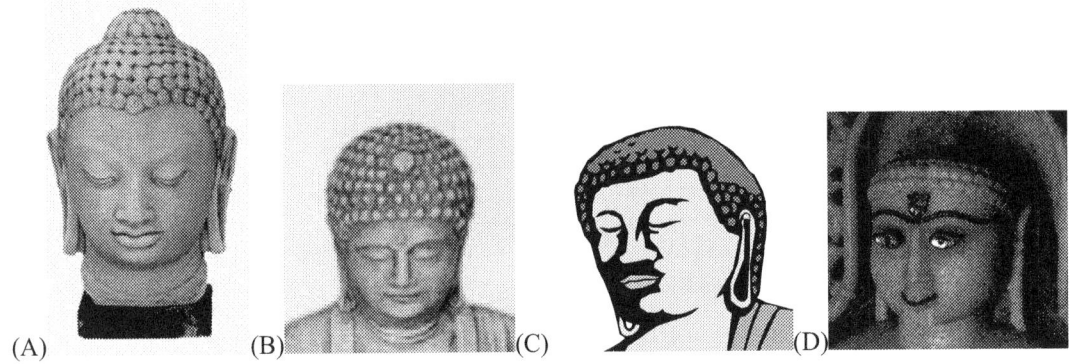

(A)   (B)   (C)   (D)

Above (A) Early Buddha sculpture now at the Sarnath Museum India 450 A.C.E., (B) and (C) Buddha of India, (D) Mahavira – from the Jain Temple at Jaiselmer, India.

Introduction to Buddhist Philosophy

An overview of Buddhist philosophy will provide insights into its relationship with Buddhism and Kamitan (Ancient Egypt) religious philosophy.

The Setting in Motion of the Wheel of the Law:

The Noble Truth of Suffering is:

The reason for all suffering is participation in the world process:

One is unhappy because one invariably expects to find happiness in worldly things.

The Noble Truth of the Cause of Suffering:

The cause of suffering is Ignorance (Avidya).
You have a fundamental misconception about reality.
I see no other single hindrance such as this hindrance of IGNORANCE, obstructed by which mankind for a long, long time runs on, round and round in circles (Ittivutaka).

The Noble Truth of the End of Suffering:

The End of Suffering is ENLIGHTENMENT (NIRVANA).
The way to Nirvana is the basis of Buddha's teaching.

The Noble Eight-fold Path:

The Noble Eight-fold Path is the practical means to disentangle the knot of ignorance and illusion.

1- Right Understanding is learning how to see the world as it truly is.
2- Right Thought is understanding that thought has great power on oneself and others and that whatever one focuses on gains more life; one becomes it.
3- Right Speech is knowing what to say, how to say it, when to say it, and when to remain silent.
4- Right Action: Guidelines for controlling one's behavior and allowing calmness of mind to pursue Enlightenment:

  1. Not intentionally taking the life of any creature.
  2. Not taking anything which is not freely given.
  3. Not indulging in irresponsible sexual behavior.
  4. Not speaking falsely, abusively or maliciously.
  5. Not consuming alcohol or drugs.

5- Right Livelihood is making a living in such a way as to benefit oneself and all other beings.
6- Right Effort is determination and perseverance in one's spiritual discipline to transcend one's lower nature.
7- Right Mindfulness is learning how to be aware of everything that one does at all times, not acting automatically, reacting to events as an animal.

8- Right Meditation is a way to transcend into higher forms of consciousness including:

> "The four stages with form" and
> "The four stages without form."

These comprise successive levels of introvertedness:

Joy, Equanimity, and Mindfulness.

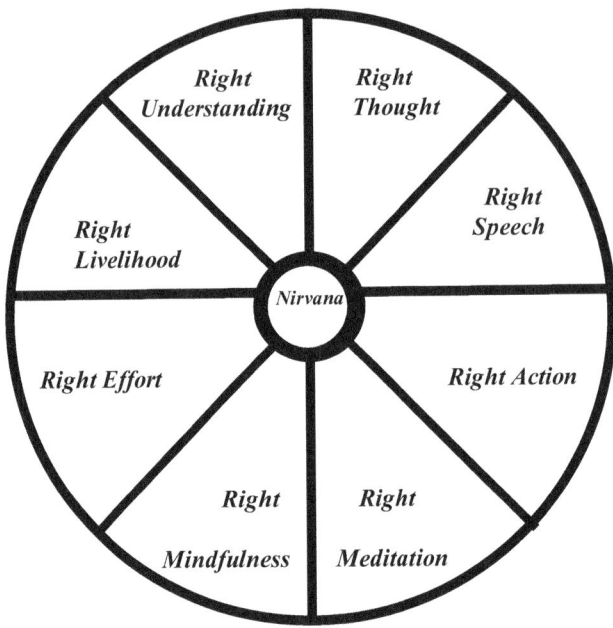

The Buddhist Wheel of Life

The Teaching of Enlightenment in India and Ancient Egypt

In light of the mounting evidence linking Buddhism with Ancient Egyptian Religion, it should be noted that the term "Buddha," meaning "enlightened one" relates to the concept that spiritual ignorance is like a form of darkness and that spiritual knowledge is like a light which illumines the mind and shines on one's innermost soul. The Buddhist term "Bodha" or "enlightenment" is synonymous with the terms "Awakening," "Self-Realization" and "Liberation." Though the use of the term "Enlightenment" was popularized by the discipline of Buddhism as a means to highlight this concept, it was also used in Ancient Egypt in the remote periods of antiquity. In Buddhism, the Transcendental consciousness is likened to a light and Buddha Consciousness is understood as wakefulness or awareness of that light. Thus, anyone who achieves that form of illumination is called a "Buddha."

Figure 192: Below left- Amunhotep, son of Hapu, Ancient Egyptian philosopher, priest and Sage at 80 years old in a meditative posture. Below right - Buddha "The Enlightened One" of India.

Ancient Egyptian Wisdom teaching:

"Passions and irrational desires are ills exceedingly great; and over these GOD hath set up the Mind to play the part of judge and executioner."

Buddhist teaching: Nirvana means

"Enlightened Consciousness, Bliss when the mind is free of all desire"

Figure 193: Hieroglyphic text for the Ancient Egyptian Book of Enlightenment

"Rau   nu   Prt   M   Hr   u"

What is The Rau nu Pert em Hru?

The scriptures commonly known as the *Egyptian Book of the Dead* contain the philosophy and technology or the *"technical yoga practices"* for attaining enlightenment. These texts span the entire history of Ancient Egypt, beginning with the *Pyramid Texts* in the early Dynastic Period. These were followed by the *Coffin Texts*, which were followed by the middle and late Dynastic texts which were recorded on a variety of different media, of which the most popularly known is papyrus.

The teachings of mystical spirituality are contained in the most ancient writings of Ancient Egypt, even those preceding the Dynastic or Pharaonic period (4,500 B.C.E.-600 A.C.E). The most extensive expositions of the philosophy may be found in the writings, which have in modern times been referred to as "The Egyptian Book of the Dead." It was originally known as "Rau nu Prt M Hru" or "Rau nu *Pert Em Heru*" or "Reu nu *Pert Em Heru*."

> ***Rau***= words, teachings, liturgy, ***nu*** = of, ***Prt*** or ***Pert*** = going out, ***em*** or ***m*** = as or through, ***Hru*** or ***Heru*** = Spiritual Light or Enlightened Being (the God Heru). This may therefore be translated as: *"The Word Utterances for Coming into the Spiritual Light (Enlightenment) or Becoming one with Heru (the light)."*

Thus, the *Rau nu Pert Em Heru* is a collection of words used to affirm spiritual wisdom and to direct a human being towards a positive spiritual movement. Each *Rau* or *Ru* contains affirmations of mystical wisdom and or practices that enable a human being to understand and experience that particular aspect of Divinity. The collection of these verses has been referred to as "Chapters," "Utterances" or "Spells" by Egyptologists. While the teachings presented in the *Rau nu Pert Em Heru* may be thought of as being presented in Chapters and referred to as such, they must also be thought of as special words which, when understood, internalized and lived, will lead a person to spiritual freedom. In this sense they are equal to the Hindu concept of "Sutras," short verses or formulas of spiritual wisdom or as "mantras," words of power. "Chapters" may be better defined as: a collection of Hekau -words of power- which impart a spiritual teaching and affirm that teaching, and by their repeated utterance make it a reality. The term "Ru" may be used as a shortened version of "Rau." It was not until after 1,500 B.C.E. that the collections of Ru were compiled in the form of papyrus scrolls and standardized to some degree. However, this process of standardization was not as rigid as the canonization of the books of the Bible, which had been separate scriptures relating to Christianity and Judaism prior to around the year 350 A.C.E.

In Egyptian myth, Hru is not only a reference to the god who is the son of Aset and Asar (Isis and Osiris), but Hru also means "Day" and "Light." In fact, Day and Light are two of the most important attributes of the god Heru who is understood as the highest potential of every human being. Therefore, the title may also be read as **"The Book of Coming Forth by (into) the Day," "The Guide for Becoming Heru,"** i.e. One with God, **"The Chapters for Coming into the Light,"** or **"The Book of Enlightenment."** The writings were named "The Egyptian Book of the Dead" by modern Egyptologists who obtained them from the modern day dwellers of the area (northeast African Arabs) who said they were found buried with the Ancient Egyptian dead.

Many people think of the philosophy of Enlightenment as a concept that originated in India, with the teachings of *Moksha* (Liberation), especially with Buddhism. We have shown that it is a concept that was well understood in ancient Kamit and is very much in harmony with what is today referred to as Enlightenment. In Ancient Egypt the terms for enlightenment were Nehast (resurrect-wake up) or Pert m Heru "coming into the light (i.e. enlightenment)"

Resurrection, spiritual Enlightenment- *Nehast*

The Kamitan term "nehast" (resurrection) is derived from the Kamitan word "Nehas" meaning "to wake up, Awaken."

Awaken - *Nehas*

Definition of Enlightenment (common to Neterianism, Hinduism {Vedanta}, Buddhism and Taoism):

Enlightenment is the term used to describe the highest level of spiritual awakening. It means attaining such a level of spiritual awareness that one discovers the underlying unity of the entire universe as well as the fact that the source of all creation is the same source from which the innermost Self within every human heart arises. It is a state of ecstasy and bliss which transcends all concepts and descriptions and which does not diminish and is not affected by the passage of time or physical conditions. It is in the state of Enlightenment that the absolute proof of the teachings of mystical spirituality are to be found and not in books, doctrines or dogmas. This is because intellectual knowledge is only the beginning of the road which leads to true knowledge. There are two forms of knowledge, intellectual (theoretical) and absolute (experiential). The teachings of Yoga and the advanced stages of religion can lead a person to experience the truth about the transcendental, immortal and eternal nature of the Soul and the existence of God. This is what differentiates Yoga from intellectual philosophies and debates, cults or religious dogma. In Yoga there is no exhortation to believe in anything other than what you can prove through your own experience. In order to do this, all that is necessary is to follow the disciplines which have been scientifically outlined since many thousands of years ago. The state of enlightenment may be summarized as follows:

THE AFRICAN ORIGINS OF CIVILIZATION, RELIGION AND YOGA SPIRITUALITY

"Enlightenment means attaining that sublime and highest goal of life which is complete Self-knowledge, to experience the state of conscious awareness of oneness with the Divine and all Creation which transcends individuality born of ego consciousness…like the river uniting with the ocean, discovering the greater essential nature of Self… that state which bestows abiding blessedness, peace, bliss, contentment, fulfillment, freedom from all limitation and supreme empowerment."

Buddhist Dharma Philosophy and Ancient Egyptian Maat Philosophy

The philosophy of the Eight-fold path has striking similarities to the concepts of Maat. This agreement is likely a product of the close relationship between India and Egypt during the time of Herodotus, and especially in the time of the Indian Emperor Ashoka. The Eight-fold path is based on the philosophy that life is suffering. The reason for all suffering is participation in the world process. One is unhappy because one invariably expects to find happiness in worldly objects and situations. Thus, one develops feelings of desire for things and fear of losing them. All life is sorrowful. Even pleasurable moments are sorrowful because they set us up for disappointment later on at some point since conditions of life always change and all attainments are ultimately ephemeral.

THE AFRICAN ORIGINS OF CIVILIZATION, RELIGION AND YOGA SPIRITUALITY

Fundamental Buddhist Philosophy 600 B.C.E.-100 A.C.E.	Neterian Religion 5,500 B.C.E-450 A.C.E
Avidya. The Noble Truth about the Cause of Suffering is Ignorance. A person has a fundamental misconception about reality. There is no other single hindrance such as this impediment of ignorance.	**On Ignorance**  *qmn* "O people of the earth, men and women born and made of the elements, but with the spirit of the Divine within you, rise from your sleep of ignorance! Be sober and thoughtful. Realize that your home is not on the earth but in the Light. Why have you delivered yourselves unto death, having power to partake of immortality? Repent, and change your minds. Depart from the dark light and forsake corruption forever. Prepare to blend your souls with the Eternal Light." (see also the proverb below)
Ittivutaka Because of ignorance a human being experiences a cycle of suffering through reincarnation for a long, long time running around and around in circles. The Noble Truth of the End of Suffering is NIRVANA ("Mind without Desires" -Contentment — Enlightenment).	**On Reincarnation** *Uhem ankh* According to the Pert M Hru text, Uhem Ankh occurs when a person has not attained Nehast or "awakening: sufficient to Pert m Hru "go into the light" due to ignorance.
Nirvana, or Nibbana Nirvana, or Nibbana, is the Buddhist term signifying the indescribable state attained by enlightened Sages and Saints. In Buddhism, Nirvana is the extinction of craving; in Hinduism, it is the home of liberated souls united with the divine and in Jainism, it is the place of liberated souls. Upon death, Enlightenment is completed in the state of Parinirvana. From a psychological perspective, Nirvana is the psychological position where one has transcended and is indifferent to elation, desire for things or the fear of their loss. The way to Nirvana is the basis of Buddha's teaching.	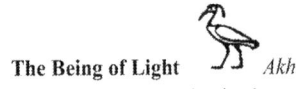 *Nehast* **Resurrection, spiritual Enlightenment** is a state attained by those who have awakened fully to the truth, that they are more than mortal, limited beings. It is the supreme victory over Set (egoism) that frees the soul to discover its oneness with the transcendental self, *Ptah-Sokkar-Asar*.
Bodha The Buddhist term "Bodha" or one who has "enlightened" intellect is synonymous with the terms "Awakening," "Self-Realization" and "Liberation."	**The Being of Light** *Akhu* The hieroglyph of the word Akhu or Khu is the "crested ibis." The ibis is representative symbol of Djehuti, the god of reason and knowledge. As such it relates to the pure spiritual essence of a human being that is purified by lucidity of mind. The Khu is the spirit, which is immortal. The Khu is also referred to as the "being of light" or "luminous being." A person who has discovered the light of spirit being, i.e. *Neberdjer* (all-encompassing transcendental consciousness) is referred to as Akhu.
Anatman Buddhism analyzes human existence as made up of five aggregates or "bundles" (*skandhas*): the material body, feelings, perceptions, predispositions or karmic tendencies, and consciousness. A person is only a temporary combination of these aggregates, which are subject to continual change.	**Ancient Egyptian Proverb on the nature of human existence:** "An infant's Soul is altogether a thing of beauty to see, not yet befouled by body's passions, still all but hanging from the Cosmic Soul! But when the body grows in bulk and draweth down the Soul into it's mass, then doth the Soul cut off itself and bring upon itself forgetfulness, and no more shareth in the Beautiful and Good (God); and this forgetfulness (ignorance) becometh vice."

THE AFRICAN ORIGINS OF CIVILIZATION, RELIGION AND YOGA SPIRITUALITY

Karma Term used in the Vedas to mean ritual act. Term used in the Upanishads and later in Buddhism to mean mysticism of actions leading to rebirth for ignorant souls.[646]	**The Concept of Ari** In Ancient Egyptian spirituality the concept of Ari held that the mysticism behind actions is their effect of causing the fate after death and possible rebirth if the soul remains ignorant.
Samsara Earlier Upanishadic meaning- the world of experience and later Buddhist meaning- rebirth leads to sorrow due to ignorance.	**Ancient Egyptian Proverb on the world of human existence and rebirth:** "Salvation is the freeing of the soul from its bodily fetters; becoming a God through knowledge and wisdom; controlling the forces of the cosmos instead of being a slave to them; subduing the lower nature and through awakening the higher self, ending the cycle of rebirth and dwelling with the Neters who direct and control the Great Plan."

Table 28: Maat Philosophy Compared with Buddhist Dharma Philosophy

Maat Principles of Ethical Conduct	Buddhist Dharma and the Noble Eight-Fold Path

The Kamitan Path of Maat 42 Precepts and the Wisdom Texts[647]
 	
 • **Truth:** Maat is Right Action-Understanding the nature of the Divine, right from wrong as well as reality from unreality.
 • **Non-violence:** This is the philosophy of Imhotep, Akhnaton, Ptahotep and other Kamitan Sages, (approaching life in peace) and Ari-m-hetep (performing actions in peace and contentment.
 • **Right Action- self-control:** Living in accordance with the teachings of Maat. (integrity, honesty)
 • **Right Speech** speaking truth and refraining from angry speech.
 • **Right Worship:** Correct practice of religion including devotional practice, chanting, meditation, donating to the temple.
 • **Selfless Service:** Service to humanity includes taking care of the homeless, clotheless, the hungry and needy.
 • **Balance of Mind - Reason – Right Thinking:** Keeping the mind in balance so as not to lose the faculty of rational cognition. This involves a close attention (mindfulness) to control, prevent and eradicate the egoistic tendencies of the mind (arrogance, conceit, self-importance, greed, etc.).
 • **Not-stealing:** Stealing is a socially disruptive practice which denotes the degraded level of human consciousness and reinforces the ignorance of worldly desire and pleasure-seeking as well as greed.
 • **Sex-Sublimation:** Sexuality is one of the primal forces of nature which must be controlled in order to allow the personality to discover the higher perspectives of life.
 • **Maat Offering:** By acting with righteousness and attaining virtue the supreme offering is made through the Maat Offering in which the person making the offering enters into a meditative awareness through the ritual and sees {him/her} self as becoming one with Maat.
	The Noble Eight-fold Path: The Noble Eight-fold Path is the practical means to disentangle the knot of ignorance and illusion in order to attain Spiritual Enlightenment.
	
	 • **Right Understanding** is learning how to see the world as it truly is.
	 • **Right Thought** is understanding that thought has great power on oneself and others, and that whatever one focuses on gains more life; one becomes it.
	 • **Right Speech** is knowing what to say, how to say it, when to say it, and when to remain silent.
	 • **Right Action:** Guidelines for controlling one's behavior and allowing calmness of mind to pursue Enlightenment:
	
	     Not intentionally taking the life of any creature. (non-violence)
	     Not taking anything which is not freely given.
	     Not indulging in irresponsible sexual behavior.
	     Not speaking falsely, abusively or maliciously.
	     Not consuming alcohol or drugs.
	
	 • **Right Livelihood** is making a living in such a way as to benefit oneself and all other beings.
	 • **Right Effort** is determination and perseverance in one's spiritual discipline to transcend one's lower nature.
	 • **Right Mindfulness** is learning how to be aware of everything that one does at all times, not acting automatically, reacting to events as an animal.
	 • **Right Meditation** is a way to transcend into higher forms of consciousness including: "The four stages with form" and "The four stages without form." These comprise successive levels of introvertedness: Joy, Equanimity, and Mindfulness.

At the level where Buddha Consciousness is reached, it is now possible to live and participate in the world though remaining completely detached from it. This concept is that of the Bodhisattva who, out of compassion, helps others on their spiritual journey to achieving Buddha Consciousness. This philosophy is known as: *"Joyful participation in the sorrows of the world."*[648] This philosophy is not unlike Jesus' compassion for the world by willingly submitting to the pain of life in order to show the path to the

Kingdom of Heaven through selfless service and humanitarianism. Also, this philosophy is not unlike Asar's (of Ancient Egypt) compassion for the world as he incarnated at the request of Ra in order to show humanity how to become civilized. He too suffered for the sake of humanity. The Yoga system of Maat from Kamit, and of Patanjali and the Philosophy of Buddha of India, represent the many paths to union with the Divine, which may be used integrally according to the psychological makeup (character) of the individual. This philosophy of service to humanity as opposed to leaving humanity and dwelling in isolation, is one of the hallmarks of Kamitan culture. Priests and Priestesses were required to serve the laity in various capacities, ministerial, medical, legal, etc., and at the same time their duties to the Temple were maintained in a balanced manner.

Thus, within the teachings of Maat can be found all of the important injunctions for living a life, which promotes righteousness, purity, harmony and sanctity akin to other great world religions and mystical philosophies. Maat philosophy of Ancient Egypt holds non-violence as one of the most important virtues. In Christianity, Jesus emphasized non-violence and in Vedantism, the discipline of *Dharma,* composed of *Yamas and Nyamas,* which are moral (righteous) observances and restraints for spiritual living, emphasizes non-violence also.

The Ancient Egyptian, Vedantic and Buddhist mystical traditions were the first to recognize the power of non-violence to heal the anger and hatred within the aggressor as well as the victim. When this spiritual force is developed, it is more formidable than any kind of physical violence. Therefore, anyone who wishes to promote peace and harmony in the world must begin by purifying every bit of negativity within themselves. This is the only way to promote true harmony and peace in others. Conversely, if there is anger within one, anger is still being promoted outside of oneself and one's efforts to encourage peace will be unsuccessful in the end.

THE AFRICAN ORIGINS OF CIVILIZATION, RELIGION AND YOGA SPIRITUALITY

The Lotus Symbol of Ancient Egypt and India

Plate 50: Blue Lotus panel. Stupa (Buddhist) at Bharhut. 2nd Cent. BC Indian Museum Calcutta

Figure 194: Samples of Ancient Egyptian Blue Lotus Panels

Figure 195: Below left-Indian-Buddhist -*Vandevatas* -wood spirits- giving drink from the tree. Bharhut, Sunga 2nd Cent. B.C.E.

Figure 196: Below- left, Nefertem/Asar emerges, resurrected, from the Divine Lotus - Ancient Egypt. Papyrus Ani. Below right- Aspirant receives sustenance from the tree. Ancient Egyptian Papyrus Nu

There are two important motifs in common here between Ancient Egyptian and Buddhist Iconographies. The first is the concept of the life-giving tree, which dispenses food and drink. The other is the blue Lotus motif.

THE AFRICAN ORIGINS OF CIVILIZATION, RELIGION AND YOGA SPIRITUALITY

Below Left: (A) The god Nefertem of Egypt, sitting on a Lotus. (B) Buddha of India, sitting on a Lotus. (C) Naga Buddha of Angkor Wat (Temple) in Cambodia, sitting on a serpent.

(A)　　　　　　　　　(B)　　　　　　　　　(C)

The images above reveal another correlation between Memphite iconography and Buddhist iconography. Nefertem (A) is the son of Ptah, the high god at Memphis. Nefertem sits on the lotus from which he speaks the world into existence (Creation). The Creation is the lotus itself upon which Nefertem sits.

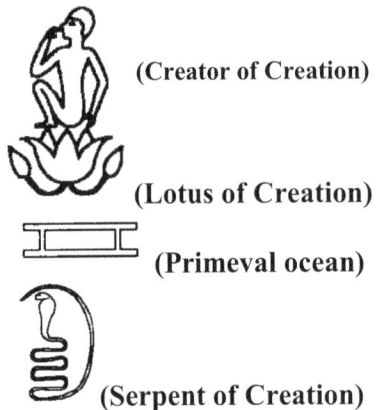

(Creator of Creation)

(Lotus of Creation)

(Primeval ocean)

(Serpent of Creation)

In Ancient Egyptian religion, the lotus of Creation emerges out of the primeval ocean which is stirred by the Mehen Serpent, a gigantic beast whose movements churn the ocean into transforming itself into the various forms of Creation as water turns to ice when it reaches a low enough temperature. In Buddhist myth the same conceptualization is given to Buddha as it is derived, like many other concepts, from Hindu theism, specifically that of Brahma, the Creator who sits on a lotus, which also comes out of the primeval ocean, in order to bring Creation into being. So the concept of the Serpent, the churning of the primeval ocean out of which a lotus emerges with a being who sits atop of it are all common to the Neterian, Hindu and Buddhist traditions.

The Ancient Egyptian God Khepri displays the same concept of "resting" on the serpent power.

Buddhism and Neterianism – the divinity Buddha and the god Asar.

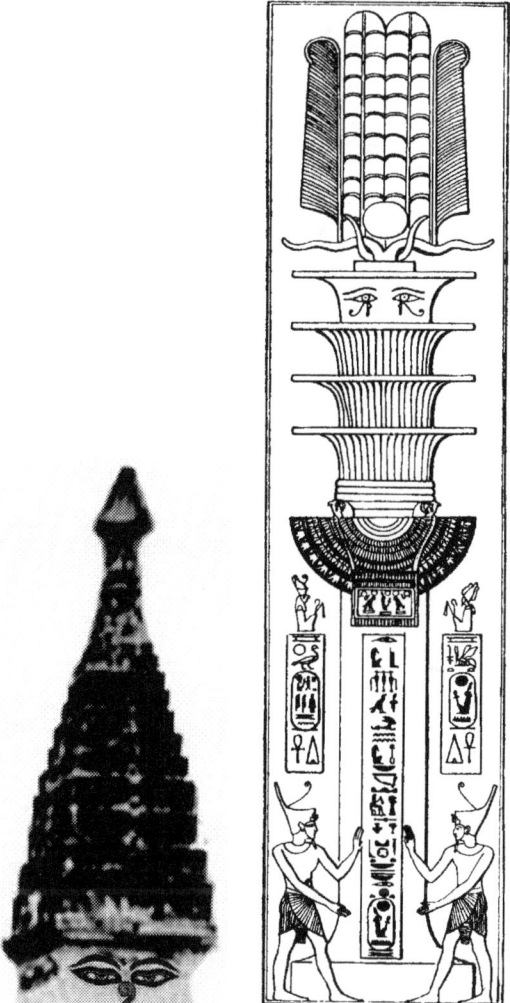

Figure 197: Above left- a Buddhist temple[649]

The Buddhist Temple displays the levels of heaven or states of spiritual consciousness, above the head of Buddha. Note the eyes of Buddha. The tiers represent levels of spiritual consciousness and these lead one to experience varied levels of experience beyond the physical realm.

Figure 198: Above right- a Kamitan artifact known as the Djed Pillar

The Djed Pillar is one of the primary symbol/artifacts of the god Asar. It displays the levels of heaven or states of spiritual consciousness, as the backbone and head of Asar. Note the eyes of Asar-Heru. In the myth when he was killed, Asar's coffin turned into a tree (tree of life). Then the tree was cut into a pillar through which Asar looked out on the world. The pillar was discovered by the goddess Aset, she cut it open and found his body in it which she resurrected. The Djed was thereafter a symbol of resurrection and glory, the raising of the four upper psycho-spiritual consciousness centers.

THE AFRICAN ORIGINS OF CIVILIZATION, RELIGION AND YOGA SPIRITUALITY

The Ankh Symbol in Ancient Egypt and India (Hinduism and Buddhism)

The Ankh, ☥, is one of the most recognizable Kamitan symbols. It signifies the life process which sustains creation and living beings. It can be seen in the earliest Kamitan reliefs, and it was adopted by the early Christians who then converted it into the present day Christian Cross. Many people do not know that it was also used by the early Indians with the same symbolism.

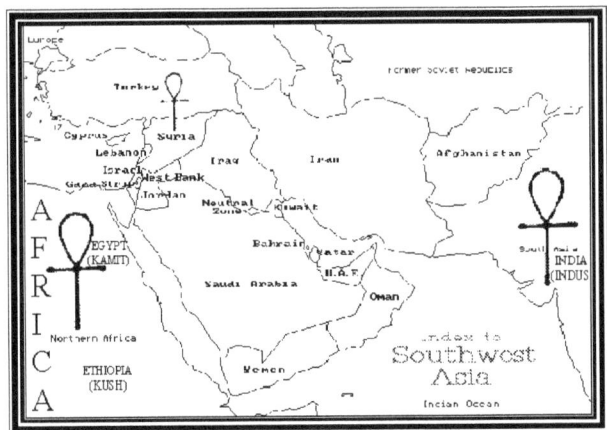

Figure 199: Above- a map of North-east Africa and South-east Asia.

This map shows the most important geographical areas where the Ankh symbol was used. It was first used in Africa by the Ancient Egyptians. In India it was used by the Indian mystics and in the Asia minor it was used by the early Christians who practiced Christian Gnosticism (Mystical Christianity).[650]

Figure 200: Below – The Feet of Buddha, displaying the Kamitan Ankh Symbol

In the book *Migration of Symbols,* Count Goblet D' Alviella, discovered the correlation of the cross symbol on the image of the "feet of Buddha" with the "Ankh" symbol of Ancient Egypt, that is more commonly known as the "Key of Life" or "Ankh Cross" or "crux ansata."

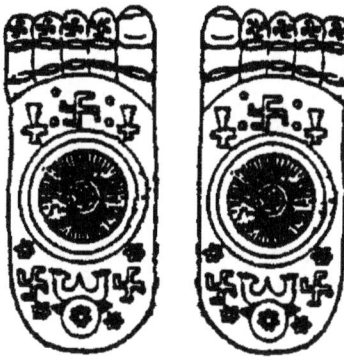

The combination of the *crux ansata* with the Sacred Cone seems to have penetrated as far as India, if this conclusion may be drawn from an enigmatical figure to be seen amongst the symbols carved, at Amaravati, on the feet of Buddha (fig. a. below).

To be sure, the Disk, or oval handle, which surmounts the Cone, is replaced, in the Buddhist symbol, by a triangular handle, or the section of a second cone inverted. But this difference is another presumption in favour of our thesis. In fact, it is precisely this substitution of a triangular for an oval handle, which characterizes the crux ansata of India, or at least the figure connected by Indian scholars with the Egyptian symbol of the Key of Life (fig. b, above- on a silver ingot (EDW. THOMAS, in *the Numismatic Chronicle,* vol. iv. (new series), pl. xi.), which reached India by way of Syria and Persia.[651]

The use of the Ancient Egyptian ankh symbol on the feet of Buddha is appropriate in view of the special relationship that has been discovered between Neterian Religion and Buddhism, especially in view of the fact that the ankh symbol is exoterically constructed from a sandal strap, implying the idea of the life giving lotus footed personality.

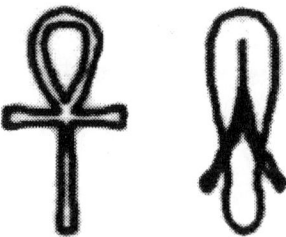

Figure 201: Above-left- The Ancient Egyptian *Ankh* symbol. Above-right- Ancient Egyptian Sandal symbol

Greeks from the early Christian times said that the Egyptian *Ankh*, ☥ , was "common to the worship of Christ and *Serapis* (Greek-Roman name for Asar). In Roman times, Saint Helena (c. 255-330), the mother of Roman Emperor Constantine-I (Constantine the Great) became a Christian around the time her son became emperor of Rome. Early church historians relate many stories about Helena. One of the stories was that Helena inspired the building of the Church of the Nativity in Bethlehem. Later tradition says that she founded the true cross on which Christ died. This was the *Tau Cross,* **T**, which resembles the Druid crosses. The *Maltese Cross,* ✠, was related to gods and goddesses of Malta before it was adopted by Christianity. One of the most important symbolic references of the Christian cross or "Latin Cross," ✝, is that its vertical axis symbolizes the vertical movement of spiritual discipline (self-effort) which implies true transformation in all areas (mental, spiritual, physical) of life. The vertical movement pierces the horizontal axis of the cross, a symbol of time and space (lateral movement, reincarnation, stagnation, etc.). Other important crosses used by the Christian church were: Early crosses, ⳨✚✱; Anchor crosses, ⚓⚓⚓; Monograms of Christ, ☧✳✸; Greek cross, ✚; Celtic cross, ✝; Eastern cross, ☦; Craponee Swastika cross, ✚ (similar to the Indian and Persian swastika, 卐).

Originally, the swastika symbol was an ancient sign used to denote the manner in which spiritual energy flows. It is also considered to be a sign of well being and auspiciousness, and can be found in the seals of the Indus Valley Civilization of Pre-Vedic India. It was thus an ancient cosmic or religious symbol used by the Pre-Vedic-Indus, Hindus and Greeks. The Swastika is formed by a cross with the ends of the arms bent at right angles in either a clockwise or a counterclockwise direction, denoting the form of energy being manifested.

Figure 202: Figure 203: Ancient Egyptian *Swastika*.

The picture above is of a fragment from a column 520- 500 B.C.E. It was found near the Temple of Aphrodite (Hetheru – Hathor) at Naucratis Egypt. (British Museum) Up to now it has been thought by many researchers that the swastika was not used in Africa. However, this evidence shows its use as well as its compatibility with Kamitan spirituality. (picture by Muata Ashby)

Figure 204: Below-left- Modern rendition of the Tantric Hindu divinity, Ardhanari-Ishvara.

Figure 205: Below-right- the Ancient Egyptian god Ra, the serpent on top of his head and ankh in hand. Far right – Ra in the form of Nefertem

The Hindu divinity, Ardhanari is the image of a half man, half woman personality, standing on the lotus of Creation, with a serpent coming out of the top of the head and an ankh symbol at the genitalia, the loop facing the female side and the cross facing the male side. The Ancient Egyptian divinity, Ra, also has a serpent on his head, symbolizing the climax of the Serpent Power, and an ankh in hand. He is also known to be androgynous, like Ardhanari, as he brought forth the company of gods and goddesses which formed Creation.[652] In the form of Nefertem, Ra emerged from the primeval ocean, sitting on his lotus.

The Philosophy of The Witnessing Inner Self in Ancient Egypt and Indian Buddhism

Wakefulness vigilant- *Snehas*

13. He the One Watcher who neither slumbers nor sleeps.
- Ancient Egyptian Hymns of Amun

Many thousands of years prior to the development of the **Sakshin Buddhi** concept in Vedanta philosophy and the **Mindfulness** concept of Buddhism, the concept of the **witnessing consciousness** was understood in Ancient Egypt. This watcher or witnessing consciousness is related to three other important utterances (33-34), which explain the relationship between the witnessing consciousness of the mind, the perceptions through the senses and the physical world. Here we will focus on understanding the watcher or witnessing consciousness, which is the innermost essence of the human mind.

The Self is the eternal and silent witness to all that goes on in the mind of every human being. It is the mind, composed of memories and desires stored in the subconscious and unconscious, which believes itself to be real and independent. But when you begin to ask "Who is this that I call me?" you begin to discover that you cannot find any "me." Is "me" the person I was at five years of age? At twenty? Or am I the person I see in the mirror today? Am I the person I will be in ten years from now or am I the person I was 500 or 1000 years ago in a different incarnation?[653] Where is "me"? Is "me" the body? Am "I" the legs, or am "I" the heart? Am "I" the brain? People have lost half their brain and continue to live, not in a vegetable state but as human beings, with consciousness. Since body parts can be lost or transplanted, these cannot be "me." What does this all mean?[654]

33. He whose name is hidden is Amun, Ra belongeth to him as His face, and the body is Ptah.
34. Their cities are established on earth forever, Waset, Anu, Hetkaptah.
-Ancient Egyptian Hymns of Amun

In Kamitan mysticism, Amun, the Self, is the "hidden" essence of all things. The Sun (Ra) is the radiant and dynamic outward appearance of the hidden made manifest, and also the light of cosmic consciousness, the cosmic mind or that through which consciousness projects. In this aspect, Ptah represents the physical world, the solidification or coagulation of the projection of consciousness (Amun) made manifest. These manifestations are reproduced symbolically on earth in the cities of *KMT* (Egypt) and Waset (Weset) or Newt (Greek - Thebes). Waset was named "Thebes" by the Greeks, who knew it also as *Diospolis* (heavenly city). They also named a sister city in Greece by the same name. Thebes is the city identified in the Old Testament of the Christian Bible as *No* (city), *No-Amon* (city of Amon), *Anu* (city of Ra) and *Hetkaptah* (city of Ptah).

THE AFRICAN ORIGINS OF CIVILIZATION, RELIGION AND YOGA SPIRITUALITY

Comparison of Religious Tenets

Basic Religious Tenets of World Religions	Neterianism (African Religion)	Buddhism	Hinduism
1- Ethics and social reform	1-✓	1-✓	1-✓
2-The unity of human kind	2-✓	2-✓	2-✓
3-The equality of the sexes	3-✓	3-✓	3-✓
4-All racial, religious and political prejudices are shunned.	4-✓	4-✓	4-✓
5-Private prayer	5-✓[655]	5-✓	5-✓
6-Annual fasting periods.	6-✓	6-✓	6-✓
7-Pilgrimage to holy sites.	7-×[656]	7-×	7-×[663]
8-Monetary contributions.	8-✓	8-✓	8-✓
9-Non-violence.	9-✓	9-✓	9-✓
10-World peace through the message of equality and unity.	10-✓	10-✓	10-✓
11-God is unknowable.	11-×[657]	11-×	11-×[664]
12-Immortality is assured	12-✓	12-✓	12-✓
13-Ceremonial leaders are shunned.	13-×[658]	13-×	13-×
14-Spiritual teachings given by revelation through prophets	14-×	14-×	14-×[665]
15-There is a Supreme Being	15-✓	15-✓	15-✓
16-Lesser beings (gods and goddesses)	16-✓	16-×[660]	16-✓
17-Mysticism	17-✓	17-✓	17-✓
18-Yoga philosophy	18-✓	18-✓	18-✓
19-Goddess Spirituality	19-✓	19-×[661]	19-✓
20- All religions worship the same god	20-✓[659]	20-×[662]	20-×[666]

Table Legend:

Tenet in Disagreement ×,

Tenet in Agreement ✓

Conclusion

We, along with some Indian researchers, have presented evidences, in addition to evidences of correlation in the iconography and philosophy, which prove that there was a strong connection between Memphite Theology and the early Buddhism, so I would say that it is reasonable to say that Buddhism and its creators were impelled by Ancient Egyptian religion just as the Confucians, the Pythagoreans, the Taoists and the other religions that emerged around the same time as the Persian invasion. However, it is not the same as saying that the modern practice of Buddhism is the same as what the Ancient Egyptians were doing. Some of the differences are obvious and others not so obvious. In order to discern the more subtle nuances a deeper study of the philosophies is required and that would follow by entering into depth studies in other volumes in this series. In any case, the close correlations and common history shared by Buddhism and Neterianism indicates that they are compatible spiritual traditions.

Summary

Thus, in the view of this researcher the evidences presented in this volume of supportable matching cultural factors and evidence of contact between Ancient Egyptian Neterianism and Indian Buddhism and the nature of those contacts, show substantial borrowings from Ancient Egyptian Neterianism to Indian Buddhism with regard to the factors of cultural expression. These are sufficient to confidently conclude that:

1. Ancient Egyptian civilization was already established, thousands of years before Ancient Indian culture began.
2. Upon examination of the Kamitan Neterian (especially Memphite Theology) Categories of Cultural Expression and the Ancient Indian Buddhist Categories of Cultural Expressions it is clear that the Factors of the categories match closely in the two cultures.
3. So it is possible to say that Indian Buddhism drew from Ancient Egyptian Neterianism in the creation of customs and traditions as well as religion and philosophy over a substantial period of the Indian Buddhist early history.
4. Indian Buddhism is a continuation of Nubian-Kamitan Memphite Neterian (religion) culture albeit transformed through history and influenced by outside cultures in many respects. However, the fundamental categories and principles of Indian Buddhist culture match those of Ancient Egyptian Neterian Religion.

THE AFRICAN ORIGINS OF CIVILIZATION, RELIGION AND YOGA SPIRITUALITY
NOTES TO CHAPTER 9

[617] See the book *Memphite Theology* by Muata Ashby
[618] *In much the same way as the term Heru refers to anyone who has attained "Heruhood" or the term Christ refers to anyone who has attained "Christhood", the term Buddha refers to any one who has attained the state of enlightenment. In this context there have been many male and female Christs and Buddhas throughout history.
[619] See the book *Glorious Light Meditation* and *Anunian Theology* by Muata Ashby
[620] See the book *Resurrecting Osiris* by Muata Ashby
[621] *A Concise Encyclopedia of Hinduism*, by Klaus K. Klostermaier
[622] Tradition founded by Mahavira – 6th century B.C.E.
[623] Worship of Shiva
[624] Worship of Vishnu and his forms.
[625] Related to the goddess, Shakti, it is the worship of the cosmic energy.
[626] Spiritual traditions which uses male and female sexual symbolism and goddess worship as metaphors for non-dual philosophy.
[627] Mystical technologies
[628] Dualistic philosophy used to discover non-dual consciousness and enlightenment.
[629] all of these taken together constitute "Hinduism" – Sanatana Dharma - in the modern interpretation of the word
[630] Excerpted from *Compton's Interactive Encyclopedia*. Copyright (c) 1994, 1995 Compton's NewMedia, Inc. All Rights Reserved
[631] Interviewed followers of the International Society For Krishna Consciousness 2000 A.C.E.
[632] H.G. Rawlinson, *Intercourse Between India and the Western World,* Cambridge, 1916, pp. 93-94
[633] Now at the Petrie Museum in London (UC nos. 8816, 8931, 8788)
[634] Flinders Petrie, *Memphis,* vol. 1, London 1909, pp. 16-17 pl. XXXIX.
[635] J.C. Harke, "The Indian Terracottas from Ancient Memphis: Are they really Indian?, *Dr. Debala Mitra Volume*, Delhi, 1991, pp. 55-61
[636] Charles Elliot, *Hinduism and Buddhism,* vol. III, London, 1954, pp. 93-94
[637] "Asoka," Microsoft (R) Encarta Copyright (c) 1994 Funk & Wagnall's Corporation. "Ashoka," Random House Encyclopedia Copyright (C) 1983,1990 by Random House Inc.
[638] K. G. Krishnan, Uttankita Sanskrit Vidya Arangnya Epigraphs, vol. II, Mysore, 1989, pp 42 ff
[639] H. G. Rawlison, *Intercourse between India and the Western World*, Cambridge, 1916, p. 92.
[640] Krishnan, op. cit., pp. 17-18
[641] Rawlison, op. cit., p 93
[642] Cambyses II (d. 522 BC), son of Cyrus the Great and King of Persia (529-522 BC), his main achievement was the conquest of Egypt. His other campaigns failed and turned him from a benevolent to a harsh ruler. He died in battle in Syria. (Random House Encyclopedia Copyright (C) 1983,1990)
[643] *The African Origins of Civilization*, Cheikh Anta Diop, 1974
[644] *History of Herodotus*, Reliefs on the palace of Ashurbanipal
[645] Review section entitled **Paleoanthropology shows a connection between Ancient Egypt, Ancient Persia and Ancient India**
[646] *A Concise Encyclopedia of Hinduism,* by Klaus K. Klostermaier
[647] For more details on the philosophy of Maat see the books *The 42 Principles of Maat and the Philosophy of Righteous Action* and *The Egyptian Book of the Dead* by Muata Ashby
[648] *The Power of Myth*, Joseph Campbell
[649] *The Mythic Image*, Joseph Campbell
[650] From more details see the book **Christian Yoga** by Dr. Muata Ashby.
[651] *The Migration of Symbols,* Count Goblet D' Alviella, 1894
[652] From more details see the book **Egyptian Yoga Vol. 1** by Dr. Muata Ashby.
[653] Reincarnation has been documented and verified by 20th century parapshychologists and past life regressionists.
[654] For a more detailed study of the Kamitan teachings related to the "Witnessing Self" see the book Egyptian Yoga Vol. 2.
[655] Private prayer is enjoined in African religion but also ritual and mass programs as well. The same is true for Hinduism and Buddhism.
[656] Pilgrimage to Kamit and its holy sites.
[657] God is unknowable to those who remain at the lower levels of human consciousness.
[658] Priests and Priestesses are necessary to lead people. In an attempt to avoid messianic leaders som religions have shunned leadership altogether but this is only an official statement but it is not true in practice as there always needs to be someone to explain the teachings, otherwise how would the faith be transmitted? So in Islam, which also shuns leaders, there are Imams, in Sikhism, which also shuns gurus, there are revered leaders, and so too it is in Bahai. The same is true for Hinduism and Buddhism.
[659] Ancient Egyptian religion contains both orthodox and mystical aspects within the same system of theology, therefore it is personal as well as impersonal and so can accommodate the needs of the masses as well as the needs of the mystics.
[660] Some sects of Buddhism believe in Buddha as a being that manifests in the form of Buddha Consciousness in all things. This is in all respects equal to the Kamitan and Hindu mystic traditions but it is not common to all Buddhist traditions.
[661] Not all Buddhist sects affirm the Goddess as an enlightener. Some Tantric sects do however.

[662] Remember that there are two main sects, not including Tantrism, Lamaism and others. The orthodox meditate on pure consciousness while the lay Buddhists see Buddha as a divinity. However, mystics in Buddhism would agree that they "worship" the same divinity as all other human beings do.

[663] Pilgrimage to Hindu holy sites

[664] God is unknowable to those who remain at the lower levels of human consciousness.

[665] Some orthodox sects of Hinduism believe that their tradition was started by an avatar and that this is a special revelation. However, the Hindu mystics derive insight through teachers and direct insight through spiritual disciplines.

[666] Some sects of Hinduism believe in an exclusive, personal god (ex. Krishna Consciousness movement). They do not believe in god as impersonal consciousness. However, mystics in Hinduism would agree that they "worship" the same divinity as all other human beings do.

Changes in Indian religion from Ancient to Modern Times, Contrasts With Ancient Egyptian Religion

Basic Differences and Similarities Between Kamitan and Ancient Indian Cultural Factors.

Before proceeding it is necessary to review the timeline of Vedic-Hindu-Buddhist culture and religion.

General Timeline of Phases in Buddhist and Hindu Indian Myth and Religion

    3000 – 1500 B.C.E. Indus Valley Period
    1500 - 1000 B.C.E. Aryan Period
    1000 - 800 B.C.E. Brahmanas Period
    800 - 600 B.C.E - Upanishadic Period - Vedanta
    600.- 261 B.C.E. Early Hindu Period
    500 B.C.E. Buddhism founded
    200 B.C.E. Patanjali Yoga Sutras
    261 B.C.E.- 1200 A.C.E. Buddhist prominence among conglomeration of other Indian belief systems.
    750 A.C.E. Sage Shankaracarya establishes Advaita (non-dualist) Vedanta based on commentaries on the major Upanishads, the Bhagavad Gita and Brahmasutras.[667]
    319-415 A.C.E. Gupta period – Dynasty of Rulers of Magadha[668] Renaissance of Hinduism – Puranic Age
    1500-1600 A.C.E. Sikhism - The doctrines and practices of a monotheistic religion founded in northern India in the 16th century and combining elements of Hinduism and Islam.
    1890 A.C.E. Modern Vedanta Movement

Summary of the Main Tenets of Hinduism and Buddhism were not Present in Vedic Culture (1500 B.C.E.) but emerged in Hindu Culture 500 years later. ✹

FUNDAMENTAL CONCEPTS OF UPANISHADIC INDIAN SPIRITUALITY NOT PRESENT IN THE VEDAS	REFERENCES
Concept of Dharma – philosophy of righteous action	1. The *Mahabharata* epic is cited as an early source for the word and concept. Feuerstein, Georg, *The Shambhala Encyclopedia of Yoga* 1997 2. *A Concise Encyclopedia of Hinduism*, by Klaus K. Klostermaier
Concept of Ahimsa – nonviolence	1. Feuerstein, Georg, *The Shambhala Encyclopedia of Yoga* 1997
Concept of Trinity	*1.* Refers to the designation of the triad of Brahma, Vishnu, Shiva or the three aspects of Vishnu, Shiva or Devi. *A Concise Encyclopedia of Hinduism,* by Klaus K. Klostermaier
Concept of Brahman as meaning "the Absolute"	1. Feuerstein, Georg, *The Shambhala Encyclopedia of Yoga* 1997
Concept of Yoga as a meaning "Union with the	1. *Taittiriya Upanishad, c.* 1,000-800 B.C.E. (*In Search of the Cradle of Civilization,* 1995, co-authored by

Divine"	Georg Feuerstein, David Frawley, and Subhash Kak.)
Concept of Reincarnation	1. First occurs in the Chandogya Upanishad and the Brihad Aranyaka Upanishads, Feuerstein, Georg, *The Shambhala Encyclopedia of Yoga* 1997 2. Doshi, Saryu, Editor-Indian Council for Cultural Relations *India and Egypt: Influences and Interactions* 1993
Concept of Maya – The Veil	1. The term "maya" does not take on its mystical philosophic meaning until the Vedanta schools (Upanishadic Tradition) reinterpret it as "cosmic illusion" or "hallucination." Feuerstein, Georg, *The Shambhala Encyclopedia of Yoga* 1997
Concept of Vegetarianism	1. *A Concise Encyclopedia of Hinduism*, by Klaus K. Klostermaier
Concept of the Sacred Cow	1. *Art – Culture of India and Egypt*, the author S. M El Mansouri Feuerstein, Georg, *The Shambhala Encyclopedia of Yoga* 1997
Concept of Hatha Yoga	1. Feuerstein, Georg, *The Shambhala Encyclopedia of Yoga* 1997
Concept of Karma – Veda – ritual act. Upanishads - mysticism	1. *A Concise Encyclopedia of Hinduism*, by Klaus K. Klostermaier
Concept of Nirvana – Appears in the Gita	1. Feuerstein, Georg, *The Shambhala Encyclopedia of Yoga* 1997
Concept of World Ages	1. Feuerstein, Georg, *The Shambhala Encyclopedia of Yoga* 1997 2. *A Concise Encyclopedia of Hinduism*, by Klaus K. Klostermaier
Concept of Samsara	1. In Hinduism and Buddhism, the cycle of repeated birth and death in the material world, which is held to be a place of suffering. The goal of yoga is release from samsara.
Concept of Avatarism	1. *Indian Mythology*, Veronica Ions
Concepts contained in the Mahavakyas or "Great Utterances"	1. *A Concise Encyclopedia of Hinduism*, by Klaus K. Klostermaier

✱All of the corresponding concepts to the Indian teachings listed above, were well developed in Kamitan Culture Prior to 4000 B.C.E.

Change of Gods and Goddesses in the Indian Pantheon

While the Ancient Egyptian texts present a pantheon of divinities at the outset that remain constant to the end of the Kamitan culture (over 5,000 years) down to the early Christian era, Indian mythology experienced additions and deletions from the pantheon. The gods Kubera, Karttikeya, Visvakarma, Dharma and Kama were added in the Hindu Period of Indian myth and religion. In Vedic times Kubera was a dwarf chief of the evil beings. In the Hindu period he was elevated to the status of a god, one of the guardians of the world. With these changes to the Indian mythic system, several fundamentally important mythological and consequently philosophical changes were made over time. This phenomenon signals not only an evolutionary process in Ancient Indian religious thought but also the infusion of new concepts, effecting a transformation of the prevailing vedic system and creating the teachingss which became known as Hinduism.

Zoomorphic and Anthropomorphic Symbols

An important change in the development from the Zoomorphic iconography of Ancient Egypt to the Anthropomorphic iconography of India is the retention of the animal symbolism but its manner use depiction is changed from being encompassed as part of the physical personality of the divinity to being the vehicle of the divinity. Still, some animal deities were retained. Among the most important of these are: Airavat (the king-god of elephants, is the mount of God Indra.) Garuda, Kamadhenu (the sacred cow deity is considered to grant all wishes and desires) Shesh Nag sleeps over the bed of its coils during intervals of creation. Also important are Hanuman (monkey god), Garuda (eagle god), Yambvawan (bear god), and Ganesha (elephant god). While the

THE AFRICAN ORIGINS OF CIVILIZATION, RELIGION AND YOGA SPIRITUALITY

combination of zoomorphic and anthropomorphic symbolism is less used in India there are some examples. (See below)

As stated earlier, there is an apparent difference between the Ancient Egyptian iconography and the Ancient Indian iconography. For example, the goddess of wisdom, Aset of Ancient Egypt is shown with wings under her arms while the goddess of wisdom in India, Saraswati, is shown sitting or riding on a swan. This apparent difference is actually a difference in expression of the same idea as opposed to a fundamental difference in concept. Therefore, it represents an evolution of the idea and not a different idea.

The Hippopotamus.
The Warrior-goddess.

The Concept of Guru and The Concept of Seba

Left: The Guru Vasistha teaches Lord Rama. Right: Lord Heru leads the initiate to the mysteries.

Guru Bhakti in India and The Seba in Ancient Egypt

The spiritual preceptor in Ancient Egypt and India have many similarities but the manifestation of their roles in their respective societies shows some fundamental differences. In Ancient Egypt the priests and priestesses were revered as enlightened councilors and spiritual leaders or sages. There are few cases where they are canonized or considered as gods and goddesses as such. Imhotep is one such example. However, in their capacity they were charged with becoming one with the divinities during rituals in order to bring forth the glory of that divinity. In India the priesthood developed into a highly revered caste of society due to the emphasis amongst spiritualists on a particular form of Yoga, the path of Bhakti as well as the discipline of upanishad (following a spiritual preceptor and revering him as possessor of god consciousness). Bhakti means "Devotion," specifically developing the capacity of divine love as a means to achieve spiritual enlightenment. In the Bhakti path one must develop love for God and it is easily directed at the Guru. The Upanishadic tradition highlighted the importance of being close and listening to the teachings of a spiritual preceptor in order to understand the mystical teachings. All of this led to a developing reverence towards spiritual seekers and the highest being the Guru. The guru is treated as God incarnate since that person is seen as a walking, talking conduit of divine awareness which can at will bestow wisdom and enlightenment directly from the source. However, the same devotion can prove to be a hinderance on the spiritual path since it can lead to stagnation instead of a movement towards God and transcendence because the object of devotion is worldly since the personality of the Guru may be a receptacle for the divine but it is nevertheless a worldly image and reminder of time and space.

This kind of reverence towards priests and priestesses was unknown in Ancient Egypt. Rather, the mysteries were kept closely amongst the initiates within the temple system and the public was only allowed to participate in the holidays, traditions and public festivals. The teaching was disseminated within the temple system and it was god and the teaching which were the primary focus and not the spiritual preceptor. It was perhaps, in their wisdom that the Kamitan priests and priestesses sought to avoid the situation which has developed in modern India, that the teachings are so proliferated that there are many charlatans throughout the country, conning the common folk. Also, there is no central authority to control the dissemination of the teachings and consequently there are many people saying many things which perhaps even they believe are correct, and yet are based on their own imaginations or fabrications. Further, one world renowned Guru remarked that the Bhagavad Gita, considered as the Hindu Bible, is revered in many homes but common people hardly ever study its text but remain only uttering mantras (verses-chants) from its text. In Ancient Egypt the Seba is a teacher of the highest mysteries and he or she leads the initiate to understand these.

For more insight into the term, Seba means star, it means an illuminating force, a shining object. Therefore the reason why preceptors are called Seba is because they illumine. Now, what do they illumine? They illumine the 'sebat' (seba with the 't' at the end of it). In Kamitan literature, those of you who have began studying the writings, when you add a 't' to a word it makes if female. What all this means is that all of you as students are females, whether you are a male or female and the preceptor is male, whether the preceptor is male or female. What that means is that the illuminator is shining on you just like the sun shines on the moon, just as the moon, a symbol of mind, receives illumination from the sun, the student receives illumination from the teacher. That illumination is a reception or being in a female capacity just as in the sexes in an ordinary sexual relationship, the male is emitting and the female is receiving. The female receives and with that takes and creates a fertilized egg and brings forth life. In the same way the student is to allow their mind to become pregnant with the teachings and through the teachings eventually give birth to enlightened consciousness. That is the deep philosophy behind the term 'Seba'.

Similarly in India, the term 'guru' symbolizes illuminator, one who illumines the cave of heart or shines a light on there to see what is in there. In the Kamitan Culture and deep mysticism you have an artifact, which is called 'Seba-ur', Ur means great, therefore, it is 'the great illuminator.'

Pralaya

Pralaya means dissolution. It is a concept that was well established in Ancient Egyptian myth and finds its counterpart in Hindu theology. It relates also to the concept of world ages wherein time courses not in a straight line but in cycles. At the end of each cycle there is a dissolution of all creation and then there is a new creation that emerges. These concepts occur in Kamitan and Hindu Myth.

Prominence of the Female Gender In Hinduism vs. Vedicism

As stated earlier, there are certain areas of Indology that are not often explored in reference to their far reaching implications as to the relationship between Hinduism and the Vedic Tradition. In the Kamitan system, the female role in the spiritual culture became more prominent in the Hindu period and with the advent of Tantrism in India, the traditions of the serpent power (Kundalini Yoga), Shaktism and the worship of Durga became important and celebrated. It should be born in mind that while the femal gender is highlighted more in Hinduism than in Vedicism this level is still far below a balanced mean. Thus, India is still to this day plagued by problems related to gender in which women are relegated to subservient positions and even abject slavery or worse, gendercide. This is of course a result of, as in Africa, the failure of the population to follow the religious ideals set forth by the righteous spiritual leaders.

Other Mythological Matches Between an Ancient Egyptian Myths and an Ancient Indian Myth

In the Hindu epic "Ramayana" or "story of Rama," there is an episode where an old hag (An old woman considered ugly or frightful.) who twisted the mind of Rama's mother and caused her to have him dethroned and banished. In the same manner, in Kamitan myth called "The Story of Two Brothers," there was an old woman. This woman twisted the mind of the virtuous man's wife, causing her to turn on him and forsake him.

In the Hindu epic the Queen beguiles the king to get promises which he cannot refuse. These she uses to force him to banish Rama. In the Kamitan story the virtuous man's wife becomes queen and beguiles the king to get promises which he cannot refuse. She forces him to take actions that will do away with the virtuous man's (her husband's) way to return.

So in the same two stories, the ideas of banishment, the old and bitter hag who twists the mind of a woman, beguiling of the king, extracting promises from a king who unrighteously makes promises he will later not be able to break, out of lustful desire, etc. all exhibit an uncanny similarity. Further, the theme of both of the stories is the same, the way to act with righteousness so as to be triumphant in life.

Also, it may be noted here that the epics in Ancient Egyptian myth were already in existence at beginning of dynastic period and into the Middle Kingdom era. The Hindu epics come it with the commencement of the epic literature period in Hindu history.

Conclusion

This study was undertaken due to an initial recognition of basic similarities between Ancient Egyptian and Indian cultural factors. This initially conjectural study transformed into a theory based on mounting evidence and later into a thesis[669] in order to discover if the evidence supported the hypothesis.[670] Also, this study was undertaken to assist in the rediscovery of Kamitan culture, philosophy and religion. The idea was that if Hindu culture is a continuation of a larger culture which once encompassed north-east Africa and southern Asia, then it might be possible to understand Ancient Egyptian mysticism and religion from the perspective of a living instead of dead culture. It would then be possible to understand the mysteries of Ancient Egypt as an original source for many of the most fundamental teachings surviving not just in Hinduism, but also Ancient Greek Philosophy, Judaism and Christianity. Thus, the research has turned out to be like tracing back to the source, like discovering the seed from which a plant has grown. In knowing the seed it is possible to know the plant (spirituality) and its branches (the religions) better and vise versa, thereby illuminating them in modern times with the depth of their own deeper history which leads back to the place where all life and civilization was born.

The work at the Sema Institute of Yoga has shown that the origins of mystical religion and Yoga run much deeper than previously understood and appear lead to Africa, but this need not be a threatening notion. It should be accepted as a wonderful example of the commonality of human consciousness which is acknowledged universally by geneticists and anthropologists as having emerged in Africa. It is a wondrous realization that Ancient Egypt did not die but still lives on in its adherents who follow the Kamitan path of spirituality, and those who follow Hinduism and Yoga as it developed in India, for these two lands are verily like mother and daughter. The mother nurtured and loved the daughter and when it came time for the mother to pass on, the daughter carried on the traditions of mystical life for generations to come. Therefore, Ancient Egypt and India may be considered to be the caretakers of the same mystical tradition and the oldest living culture, civilization and spiritual tradition, since when considered together, the span of time encompassed by Ancient Egypt and India, as one established successive culture, span well beyond the duration of any other known culture or civilization.

It must be borne in mind that cultural adoptions and adaptations are as organic in cultural relationships as in human relationships. Human beings are affected by everything they are exposed to in some degree, language difficulties not withstanding. Further, those who are at the forefront in leadership in the task of carrying on a tradition should realize that they too are in effect adopting a culture, for the teaching as it was given by the sages in Ancient Egypt or India thousands years ago related to the social needs of those times. Therefore, we too are adopting and adapting the culture of mystical spirituality, wherein time and space are ultimately discarded in favor of absolute truth. Otherwise, what remains are dates and times, concepts and histories, myths and symbols, culture and limitation. Thus, our adoption must remain true to the principles of the teaching but also realistically face the oftentimes incongruous puzzle of the world and make sense of it in a way that promotes peace and enlightenment that is in keeping with the vision or spirit of the tradition.

The fear of seeing unity is actually the fear that keeps humanity bound to the cycle of violence, war and disease as individual human beings as well as whole cultures. As a garden with many flowers produces a beautiful scenery, even with the differences, a culture must learn to see itself as one among a family of cultures that comprise the garden religions and spiritual traditions. The fragrance of the flower of spiritual traditions manifests as the myriad of human mythologies. This problem of fear is not just the province of "the ignorant masses," but it is unfortunately the mainstay among many intellectuals and "well"-educated leaders of society. This problem exists even within those ranks of yoga practitioners who find it easy to espouse the universality of yoga as long as it is said from the perspective of "yoga originated in India." The question is how can the true goals of yoga, the attainment of universal vision, be achieved by yoga practitioners and pundits with such attitudes of nationalism, pride and proprietorship over yoga? Why is the ownership of yoga so important? If Creation is infinite and God is infinite and the world, cultures and mythologies are transient, how can any society make a claim on anything but being part of a stream of spiritual consciousness which is manifest in universal myth? All human beings have built what they have, standing upon the shoulders of their forefathers and foremothers. Therefore, all culture and civilization is due to a long-standing relation to the past, going back ultimately to the beginning, and the Creator. This

THE AFRICAN ORIGINS OF CIVILIZATION, RELIGION AND YOGA SPIRITUALITY

self-evident reality denigrates no one and exalts no one, but rather shows everyone's place in time and space and history as well as the evolution of the search for self-knowledge, the coveted goal of Divine consciousness, through religious and mystical philosophy which is the single common factor uniting all human beings from the beginning of time.

We cannot live together with bias against each other, some saying that the East is best, others the West, and so on. What about the south, the very cradle of humanity itself? Africa and its pinnacle of culture in ancient times was unquestionably a major force in shaping humanity, but the nature of this force has been forgotten or misunderstood, or simply relegated to commercialism, as a vacation destination, or even a curiosity. But what about the glory, the art, the philosophy and the legacy of the spirituality of Ancient Kamit?

This book, THE AFRICAN ORIGINS OF CIVILIZATION, RELIGION, YOGA SPIRITUALITY AND ETHICS PHILOSOPHY, does not purport to give the idea that Ancient Egypt (Kamit) is the be all and end all of humanity, culture, civilization, etc., since there was certainly a deeper origin than that (from Pre-Kamitan- Ancient African Religion, Culture and Philosophy that gave rise to Kamitan Culture and Spirituality). However, what the Ancient Africans in Kamit achieved is so meritorious and of such great import in its potential contribution to the storehouse of human knowledge and understanding that its rightful place among the major factors in human development must be acknowledged and realized. If this is done it is my firm belief that the community of nations will move one giant step closer to conviviality and peace as well as collective spiritual enlightenment.

The evidences presented in this volume show that there was a strong relation between Ancient Egypt and India and that this relationship allowed the perpetuation of a mystical tradition which is today called Yoga and mysticism. Mysticism is that art of allowing oneself to be transformed, to discover one's higher identity as one with that Transcendental essence. The particular "style" of mysticism in Ancient Egypt and India has been found to match in the basic fundamentals as well as in peripheral aspects. Thus, it is in a way gratifying to see that the glory that was Ancient Egypt still lives on in India.

While it is true that yoga in its universal sense transcends communities and social structures as well as ethnic boundaries, the time and space (practical) reality of human existence requires a pragmatic approach when dealing with human beings who have not evolved into higher consciousness and who still subscribe to concepts of race or class issues. While we may transcend to higher levels of consciousness through the practice of mysticism and Yoga, we also exist on the physical plane and interact with others through the medium of physical bodies which operate and relate by means of culture. This means that our efforts towards community upliftment are ultimately related to cultural upliftment as well.

Many people have been purchasing the books from the Egyptian Yoga book series over the years but were surprised to find out that there existed disciplines of meditation and yogic postures in Ancient Africa prior to their development in India. The surprise really manifested when the workshops and lectures were held. People actually experienced for themselves the disciplines and were shown the original scriptures which provide the instruction and the point was brought home in a very powerful way. They were surprised to find that while similar, the disciplines are actually independent and more ancient and thus entirely African.

Another growing issue is that communities of African descent in the U.K., like those in other countries such as Guyana, Kenya, Trinidad and elsewhere, have developed hostility with the Indian community due to the Indian cohesiveness and systematic exclusion of people of African descent from their social, economic and political structures. Thus, due to the history of the caste system in India, suffering under British racism and colonialism, a developing self-centered national cultural ego has emerged in the Indian community, and due to widespread ignorance in the Indian community about the origins of their own culture, there is a growing rift between Indians and Africans. This point became so well-known in recent years that a major Hollywood motion picture was dedicated to the subject (*Mississippi Masalla* - {1992}). In recent years, perhaps beginning with the Apartheid and Western racist practices which conform in many respects to the caste system of India (which has been denounced by every authentic Indian spiritual leader), many Indians have become culturally conceited and openly repudiate peoples of African descent. In a sense this may be because, like an ordinary person repudiates those who remind him/her of {his/her} own degradation, Indian peoples have recently also emerged from the scourge of slavery. Although they did not suffer the decimation of their population and complete disruption of their culture, Indians do carry the scars of victimization by foreign powers including the Greeks, Arabs and British among others. When they see peoples of African descent they may be reminded of their own inadequacies and suffering as well as humiliation as they continue to observe peoples of African descent, who still even to this day find themselves caught in the mire of ignorance, disorganization and discontent. Authentic Hindu spiritual masters would never advocate racism towards any group nor would they permit their followers to engage in economic monopolies to exclude or subjugate others. Therefore, it must be understood that those people who consider themselves as Hindus but who are engaging in such negative practices are not doing so under the auspices of their authentic spiritual leaders, but rather following the instructions of community leaders who are dedicated to the ends of greed, based on the concepts of segregation and subjugation of peoples who they consider to be of a lower caste, i.e. the dark skinned South Indians and of course also the dark skinned peoples of African descent. Again, just as in every other culture, most Indians do not study the philosophy of their own heritage, but are rather content to perform rituals and praise their spiritual scriptures without studying them under the direction of qualified spiritual preceptors. This error opens the door to misinterpretation and also misunderstanding of the teachings, leading to cultural egocentricity, even to the extent of remaking the scriptures in their own image, to suit their needs or desires, or simply ignoring the injunctions of the spiritual teachings and following them in name only, for many Hindus love and accept worship services and enjoy singing and praising the Divine, but are inept and some even completely ignorant as to how to apply the teaching in their own lives within their own culture, let alone outside of it.

In the U.S., many people of African descent resent Indians and also believe Yoga originated in India, and that it is an Eastern and therefore "alien" practice. This occurs for many reasons. One is that Indian culture, generally speaking, is not in harmony with their own authentic practices within the mystical India Yoga tradition. Another may be opinions drawn from previous interactions with Indians. Another reason is that being in the West, most people follow Christianity in some form, and this system admonishes them to stay away from any "non-Christian" religions and cultures. Yet another may be that their karmic experiences dictate a different spiritual path for them in this life time and therefore, Indian Spirituality will be inherently unappealing. Karmically, they cannot approach it because it does not "belong" to their culture. Thus, the already preexisting misconceptions that "Yoga" originated or only existed in India and that Indian Culture was a separate development from the African are further compounded by the economic and political wranglings. The misconceptions on both sides need to be addressed by the spiritual leaders of each group. However, the voice of knowledge seldom finds the ear of the ego, especially when the voice is weak and lack of purity is a source of weakness. In view of the growing search for roots and self-knowledge, many people of African descent (including Yoga teachers) who have come into contact with the book *Egyptian Yoga* and the Egyptian Yoga Book Series have been pleasantly surprised and also gratified to find out about the African origins, which for many of them actually confirms much of what they already suspected based on limited research. These are perhaps some issues we may reflect upon in the light of the findings in this book.

EPILOG: What Is The Meaning Of The Correlation Between Cultures. How Should They Be Used?

What is the meaning of the Correlation between cultures? Many people have been amazed at the discoveries presented in this book and through lectures on this subject that have been presented over the years. Some people, interested in religion react with awe at the depth of Kamitan spirituality and the almost exact correlations between the eastern and western religions and Kamitan spirituality. Others, interested in the Yogic disciplines, have been amazed at the almost exact correlations between Kamitan Yoga and Indian Yoga. So what is the meaning of all of this and how should people treat these evidences?

Human beings are seldom quick to change their ways. This is because having spent much time and effort with a certain set of belief systems, a certain set of desires, the unconscious mind is forging on a particular path that is difficult to alter. This is why no matter how many evidences and facts are presented to smokers about contracting cancer, only a fraction of those people can stop and move on to better things. No matter how many evidences are presented to meat eaters about the facts linking meat eating to colon cancer, only a fraction of those people can stop and move on to better things. It is human nature to act in the way that the unconscious personality is inclined. This is why it is so important to be cognizant about what we allow to enter into our minds. The thoughts and words of others, television, advertising, our own fantasies, etc., have a strong effect on us and can lead us to great heights or great degradation.

So what is expected of a person is what can be expected of anyone who is on the path to self-discovery, to take what has been learned, reflect upon it and use it to the best ability in order to transform life and make it better. This requires not complacency, but accepting the challenges presented by this material. Some people might look at these evidences and say "well I have seen that Christianity came from Ancient Egyptian, religion and it was very interesting, so its ok if I continue practicing my Christianity." Others may say "well I see that Indian yoga originally came from Africa and the ancient Kamitans and that was fascinating, but I can continue to practice my Indian yoga anyway because there is not much difference." One can attain Enlightenment by practicing Indian style yoga or even Christianity. However, the real issue is practicing them in a limited and incorrect way as they have developed in many spiritual systems, due to generally limited understanding of what the disciplines are and are not. Also, religion serves a cultural function. Therefore, the religion needs to be matched to the culture of the person, especially for those who are not advanced practitioners of religion (most people), because they rely most on myth and ritual, the lower stages of religion, as a means to evolve. Authentic religion elevates and develops culture and this in turn promotes peace in society and peace allows spiritual aspiration to flourish in an atmosphere that is conducive to spiritual inquiry.

People who believe in the way outlined above should take care to realize that while the fundamental principles, iconographies and symbols have been shown to correlate, there are also areas of divergence between what was originally started in ancient times and what has developed since. These differences may seem to be minor variations, but they are actually crucial factors in understanding and practicing the spiritual traditions and disciplines in their proper scientific and mystical manner. So, perhaps except for those who are practicing an authentic system of spirituality or religion with proper guidance, it is not ok to go on as if no changes or adjustments are necessary. And even those who are being guided in authentic religions and mystical systems are likely to benefit from the depth and nuances of Kamitan philosophy and practice, thus enhancing their understanding and experience of the Divine. In any event, there are some general acknowledgments that must be made.

The first acknowledgment that is necessary is to give credit where it is due. Those religions and yoga systems that are advertised as originating outside of Africa must now be correctly referenced as African in origin. This being so, it is not correct to practice those disciplines without taking into account the original African roots and the original African teachings. This means that where the later tradition has deviated from the original teachings they must be modified so as to come into harmony with the original teachings, not just for the sake of harmonizing with some long ago teachings but because that deviation has led the practitioners astray from the proper practice of the teachings and also away from awareness of the underlying unity of humanity. Consider that many developments in Judaism, Christianity and Islam as well as Indian spirituality are no longer understood. Jewish, Christian and Indian scholars have admitted that not all of the Hebrew, Aramaic or Sanskrit terms are understood as they were to the ancients due to the passage of time and other intervening factors. What would happen if those faiths were to reevaluate themselves in light of Kamitan spirituality? Consider that most practitioners of western religion are not mystics who understand the higher teachings of their religions and disciplines. However, some already recognize the Kamitan roots, but most are ignorant followers of dogma, and as they intensify their practices, they believe more and more that they are following some tradition that is separate, having origins in their land, and so they develop a kind of spiritual egoism and pride that leads them off course from the teaching and astray from the family of humanity, feeling that they are some special people whom God has especially blessed among human beings, and that they have some special insight and therefore, God-given-right to act in ways that do not consider the welfare of other peoples.

The highest meaning of this work would be a world movement wherein people begin to turn towards the truth of the origins of humanity, religion and civilization in Africa and adopt a community and family approach to life on earth as opposed to greedy and selfish separatists and conceited racists and capitalists. These are the expectations of this work, lofty as they may be. For anyone who has ever climbed to the mountain top to see the promised land can see the potential of human evolution, but this is only possible if there is a basis of truth, righteousness and virtue and Enlightenment as the goal of life and the purpose of society.

NOTES TO EPILOG

[667] *A Concise Encyclopedia of Hinduism,* by Klaus K. Klostermaier
[668] *A Concise Encyclopedia of Hinduism,* by Klaus K. Klostermaier
[669] **the·sis** (thē′sĭs) *n., pl.* **the·ses** (-sēz). **1.** A proposition that is maintained by argument.
[670] **hy·poth·e·sis** (hī-pŏth′ĭ-sĭs) *n., pl.* **hy·poth·e·ses** (-sēz′). *Abbr.* **hyp., hypoth. 1.** A tentative explanation that accounts for a set of facts and can be tested by further investigation; a theory.

THE AFRICAN ORIGINS OF CIVILIZATION, RELIGION AND YOGA SPIRITUALITY

Appendix A: Timeline of the Ancient World

Pre-history and Dynasties of Ancient Egypt

Listed here are the known kings of ancient Egypt and the approximate dates of their reigns as well as important personalities in world history and the approximate dates of their existence.

Ancient Egyptian Kings and Queens and the dates of their existence	Important Personalities in World cultures and the approximate dates of their existence
10,000-5000 BCE PREDYNASTIC AND PROTODYNASTIC PERIOD 10,000 King Horemakhet (Great Sphinx) **Neolithic settlements** **5000-4000 BCE Badarian** **Naqada III** King "Scorpion" King Narmer "Baleful Catfish" **5,500-3,800 BCE EARLY DYNASTIC PERIOD – AND OLD KINGDOM PERIOD** **Neolithic settlements** **4000-3500 BCE Naqada I (Amratian)** **3500-3100 BCE Naqada II (Gerzean)** **1st Dynasty** Aha "Fighter" (Menes) Djer "Stockade" Djet "Snake" Den Anedjib Semerkhet Qaa **2nd Dynasty** Hotepsekhemwy Raneb Nynetyer(Netjeren) Wadjnas Sened Peribsen Khasekhemwy (Khasekhem) **3rd Dynasty** Sanakht Djoser (Netjerkhet) Sekhemkhet Khaba Nebka Huni	

OLD KINGDOM

4th Dynasty
Sneferu
Khufu(Cheops)
Djedefre (Redjedef)
Khafre (Chephren)
Menkaure (Mycerinus)
Wehemka
Shepseskaf

Imhotep
(Kamitan (Ancient Egypt) Sage of the Old Kingdom Period)

5th Dynasty
Userkaf
Sahure
Neferirkare Kakai
Shepseskare
Neferefre (Reneferef)
Nyuserre
Menkauhor
Djedkare Isesi
Unas

6th Dynasty
Teti
Meryre Pepy I
Merenre (Nemtyemzaf)
Neferkare Pepy II
Nitoqerty (Nitocris)

7th-8th Dynasties
Group of unknown rulers

3800-3500 B.C.E.- 1ST INTERMEDIATE PERIOD

9th-10th (Herakleopolis) Dynasties
Akhtoy I (Achthoes)
Neferkare
Akhtoy II (Achthoes)
Akhtoy III (Achthoes)
Merykare

11th (Thebes) Dynasty
Mentuhotep I ("The Ancestor")
Inyotef I
Inyotef II
Inyotef III
Nebhepetre Mentuhotep II

3500-1730 BCE MIDDLE KINGDOM

11th (Thebes) Dynasty
Sankhkare Mentuhotep III
Nebtawyre Mentuhotep IV

12th (Itj-Tawy) Dynasty
Amenemhet I (Ammenemes)
Senwosret I (Sesostris)
Amenemhet II (Ammenemes)

Yogi Meditating with Serpents
(Indus Valley 2500 B.C.E.)

Senwosret II (Sesostris)
Senwosret III (Sesostris)
Amenemhet III
Amenemhet IV
Sobekneferu

13th (Itj-Tawy) Dynasties
Many unknown kings

14th (Western Delta) Dynasties
Group of unknown kings ruling at the same time of the later part of the 13th Dynasty

1730-1580 BCE 2ND INTERMEDIATE PERIOD

15th (Avaris)("Hyksos") Dynasty
*6 Unknown Asiatic rulers
Apopi (Apophis)
Khamudi

16th Dynasties
Group of 15 Dynasty's Hyksos vassals

17th (Thebes) Dynasties
Seqenenre Tao
Kamose

1580-1075 BCE NEW KINGDOM

1539-1292 18th (Thebes) Dynasty
1539-1514 Ahmose (Amosis)
1514-1493 Ahmenhotep I (Amenophis)
1493-1482 Thutmose I (Tuthmosis)
1482-1479 Thutmose II (Tuthmosis)
1479-1425 Thutmose III (Tuthmosis)
1473-1458 Hatshepsut
1426-1400 Ahmenhotep II (Amenophis)
1400-1390 Thutmose IV (Tuthmosis)
1390-1353 Ahmenhotep III (Amenophis)
1353-1336 Ahmenhotep IV(Amenophis)/*Akhenaten*
1336-1332 Smenkhkare
1332-1322 Tutankhamun
1322-1319 Aya
1319-1292 Horemheb

1292-1190 19th (Thebes) Dynasty
1292-1290 Ramesses I (Ramses)
1290-1279 Sety I (Sethos)
1279-1213 Ramesses II (Ramses) "Ramses The Great"
1213-1204 Merneptah
1204-1198 Sety II (Sethos)
1204-1200 Amenmesse
1198-1193 Siptah
1193-1190 Tewosret

1190-1075 20th (Thebes) Dynasty
1190-1187 Sethnakhte
1187-1156 Ramesses III(Ramses)
1156-1150 Ramesses IV(Ramses)
1150-1145 Ramesses V(Ramses)

Code of Hammurabi
(fl. 1792-1750 B.C.E.).

Aryan Culture in India Emerges
(2000-1500 B.C.E.)

Abraham ?
(c. 1900-1800 B.C.E.?)

Moses ?
(1200 B.C.E.?)

THE AFRICAN ORIGINS OF CIVILIZATION, RELIGION AND YOGA SPIRITUALITY

1150-1145 Ramesses V(Ramses) 1145-1137 Ramesses VI(Ramses) 1137-1129 Ramesses VII(Ramses) 1128-1126 Ramesses VIII(Ramses) 1126-1108 Ramesses IX(Ramses) 1108-1104 Ramesses X(Ramses) 1104-1075 Ramesses XI(Ramses) **1075-656 BCE 3RD INTERMEDIATE** **1075-945 21st (Tanis) Dynasties** 1075-1049 Smendes 1049-1045 Amenemnisu 1045-997 Psusennes I 999-990 Amenemope (Amenophthis) 990-984 Osorkon the Elder (Osochor) 984-959 Siamun 959-945 Psusennes II **945-712 22nd (Bubastis) Dynasties** 945-924 Shoshenq I 924-889 Osorkon I 889-874 Takelot I 874-835 Osorkon II 830-780 Shoshenq III 780-736 Pemay 763-725 Shoshenq V **838-712 23rd Dynasties** 825-800 Takelot II 796-768 Osorkon III 773-766 Takelot III 766-747 Amunrud **727-712 24th (Sais) Dynasties** 727-719 Tefnakhte 719-712 Bakenrenef (Bocchoris) **760-656 25th ("Nubian" or "Kushite") Dynasties** 760-747 Kashta 747-716 Piye (Piankhy) 716-702 Shabaka 702-690 Shebitku 690-664 Taharqa 664-656 Tantamani **664-332 BCE LATE PERIOD** **664-525 26th (Sais) Dynasty** 664-610 Psamtik I (Psammetichus) 610-595 Necho II 595-589 Psamtik II (Psammetichus) 589-570 Apries 570-526 Amasis **525-405 27th Dynasty (Persian Conquest)** 1st Persian occupation 521-486 Darius I 486-466 Xerxes I **409-399 28th (Sais) Dynasty** 409-399 Amyrtaeos **399-380 29th (Mendes) Dynasty** 399-393 Nefaarud I (Nepherites) 393-381 Hakor (Achoris) 381 Nefaarud II(Nepherites) **381-343 30th (Sebennytos) Dynasty** 381-362 Nakhtnebef (Nectanebo I) 365-362 Djedhor (Teos) 362-343 Nakhtnebef (Nectanebo II)	 **Homer** (Greek author of Iliad and the Odyssey – 800 B.C.E.) **Lao Tzu** (Taoism - China) (c. 604- c. 531 B.C.E.) **Zoroaster, or Zarathustra** (Zoroastrianism) (c. 628- c. 551 B.C.E.) **Valmiki (Indian Sage)** (Author of the Ramayana) **Pythagoras** (Pythagoreanism) (c. 580- c. 500 B.C.E.). **Buddha, name given to Siddhartha Gautama** (Buddhism- India) **(c. 563- c. 483 B.C.E.)** **Vyasa (Indian Sage)** (Author of the Mahabharata) **Mahavira (Jainism - India)** (c. 550 B.C.E.)

THE AFRICAN ORIGINS OF CIVILIZATION, RELIGION AND YOGA SPIRITUALITY

343-332 31st Dynasty (Persian) 2nd Persian occupation **332 BCE-AD HELLENISTIC CONQUEST PERIOD** **332-305 32nd Dynasty (Alexandria)("Macedonian")** 332-323 Alexander III the Great 323-317 Philip III Arrhidaeus 323-310 Alexander IV 323-305 Ptolemy(Ptolemy I) **305-30 33rd Dynasty (Alexandria)("Ptolemaic")** 305-282 Ptolemy I Soter I 285-246 Ptolemy II Philadelphos 246-221 Ptolemy III Euergetes I 221-205 Ptolemy IV Philopator 205-180 Ptolemy V Epiphanes 180-164 Ptolemy VI Philopator 170-164 Ptolemy VIII Euergetes II 164 Ptolemy VII Neos Philopator 163-145 Ptolemy VI Philometor 145-116 Ptolemy VIII Euergetes II 116-110 Ptolemy IX Soter II 110-109 Ptolemy X Alexander I 109-107 Ptolemy IX Soter II 107-88 Ptolemy X Alexander I 88-80 Ptolemy IX Soter II 80 Ptolemy XI Alexander II 80-51 Ptolemy XII Neos Dionysos 51-30 Cleopatra VII 51-47 Ptolemy XIII 47-44 Ptolemy XIV 44-30 Ptolemy XV Caesarion **332 BCE-A.C.E. ROMAN CONQUEST PERIOD** 30 BCE-14 A.C.E. Augustus	**Socrates** (Greek Sage) (469-399 B.C.E.) **Plato** (Platonism) (427-347 B.C.E.) **Herodotus** (c. 484-425 B.C.E.) **Ashoka, emperor of India** (c. 274-136 B.C.E.) **Patanjali** –Raja Yoga Sutras (200 B.C.E.)
394 A.C.E. COPTIC CHRISTIAN CONQUEST PERIOD 394 A.C.E. Theodosius adopted Christianity as the state religion of Rome	**Apollonius** (Greek Sage) (50 B.C.E.-50 A.C.E.) **Jesus** (Christianity) (0 A.C.E.)
ARAB AND MUSLIM CONQUEST PERIOD (c. 700 A.C.E.)	Roman Catholic Christian Emperor Justinian decrees that all Egyptian temples should be closed. c. 550 century A.C.E. **Muhammad** (Islam) (c. 570-632 A.C.E.)

Appendix B: Defining Civilization

Basic Criteria of Civilization

In order to be considered a "Civilization," along with organized complex sociopolitical institutions, art, myth, agriculture, writing, and mathematics a culture must promote the following:

❶
A Civilization acknowledges the Philosophy of Universal Life

❷
A Civilization creates ethical institutions that support the Philosophy of Universal life
(Social, economic and political)

❸
A Civilization promotes transference of culture of Universal life
(traditions, rituals and ideals (ethics) in educational system (Free education-Literacy 100% Ex. Sweden)) and in government)

❹
A Civilization promotes Spiritual Conscience and Effective Spiritual Evolution
(Self-realization, spiritual evolution)

❺
A Civilization promotes health and well-being of ALL people, and nature:
protecting the rights of children, the poor, the infirm (Free healthcare), without cultural bias. Protecting animals and replenishes natural resources.

❻
A civilization manifests as
Well-ordered society with the majority of the population living in balance, truth, peace, contentment and non-violence.

Caring Culture in a Civilized Society

People (Caring) ↙ ↘ Young + Old	Nature (usage)	Government (social institutions)
<u>3 Basic Needs</u> Food Shelter Opportunity (Progeny, Career Advancement, Self-realization	Purity Replenishment	Ethics Justice (Social/Economic) Meritocracy Council of Elders Education (Writing, Math)

    A "civilization" manifests a caring culture. A caring culture is a culture that provides for its people the three basic needs of life, protects the land and replenishes it while keeping it in trust for the future generations and its government institutions are created with a basis of ethics and spiritual consciousness.

Appendix C: Ancient Egyptian Colonization of the Ancient World

(A) Ancient Egyptian Colonization of the known world:

Diodorus: History- BOOK 1. 27. 6-28. 4

28. Now the **Egyptians** say that also after these events a great number of colonies were spread from **Egypt** over all the inhabited world. To Babylon, for instance, colonists were led by Belus, who was held to be the son of Poseidon and Libya; and after establishing himself on the Euphrates river he appointed **Priests**, called Chaldaeans by the Babylonians, who were exempt from taxation and free from every kind of service to the state, as are the **Priests** of **Egypt**;1 and they also make observations of the stars, following the example of the Egyptian **Priests**, physicists, and astrologers. They say also that those who set forth with Danaus, likewise from **Egypt**, settled what is practically the oldest city of Greece, Argos, and that the nation of the Colchi in Pontus and that of the Jews, which lies between Arabia and Syria, were founded as colonies by certain emigrants from their country; and this is the reason why it is a long-established institution among these two peoples to circumcise their male children, the custom having been brought over from **Egypt**. Even, the Athenians, they say, are colonists from Sais in **Egypt** and they undertake to offer proofs of such a relationship; for the Athenians are the only Greeks who call their city " Asty," a name brought over from the city Asty in **Egypt**. Furthermore, their body politic had the same classification and division

(B) The original rulers of the city Athens were Ancient Egyptian. (Athens was originally an Egyptian colony)

Diodorus: History- BOOK 1. 29. 4-29. 1

Moreover, certain of the rulers of Athens were originally **Egyptians**, they say. Petes,4 for instance, the father of that Menestheus who took part in the expedition a against Troy, having clearly been an Egyptian, later obtained citizenship at Athens and the kingship.5 . . . He was of double form, and yet the Athenians are unable from their own point of view to give the true explanation of this nature of his, although it is patent to all that it was because of his double citizenship, Greek and barbarian, that he was held to be of double form, that is, part animal and part man.

29. In the same way, they continue, Erechtheus also, who was by birth an Egyptian, became king of Athens, and in proof of this they offer the following considerations. Once when there was a great drought, as is generally agreed, which extended over practically all the inhabited earth except **Egypt** because of the peculiar character of that country, and there followed a destruction both of crops and of men in great numbers, Erechtheus, through his racial connection with **Egypt**, brought from there to Athens a great supply of grain, and in return those who had enjoyed this aid made their benefactor king. After he had secured the throne he instituted the initiatory rites of Demeter in Eleusis and established the mysteries, transferring their ritual from **Egypt**. And the tradition that an advent of the goddess into Attica also took place at that time is reasonable, since it was then that the fruits which are named after her were brought to Athens, and this is why it was thought that the discovery of the seed had been made again, as though Demeter had bestowed the gift. And the Athenians on their part agree that it was in the reign of Erechtheus, when a lack of rain had wiped out the crops, that Demeter came to them with the gift of grain. Furthermore, the initiatory rites and mysteries of this goddess were instituted in Eleusis at that time. And their sacrifices as well as their ancient ceremonies are observed by the Athenians in the same way as by the **Egyptians**; for the Eumolpidae were derived from the **Priests** of **Egypt** and the Ceryce who swear by Isis (Aset, Demeter), and they closely resemble the **Egyptians** in both their appearance and manners. By many other statements like these, spoken more out of a love for glory than with regard for the truth, as I see the matter, they claim Athens as a colony of theirs because of the fame of that city.

Appendix D: Origins of Monasticism and Christian Monasticism in Ancient Egypt

Christian monasticism first appeared in the Eastern part of the Roman Empire a few generations before Benedict, in the Egyptian desert. Under the spiritual inspiration of Saint Anthony the Great (251-356), ascetic monks led by Saint Pachomius (286-346) formed the first Christian monastic communities under what became known as an *Abba* (Egyptian for "Father", from which the term *Abbot* originates). Within a generation, both solitary and communal monasticism became very popular and spread outside of Egypt, first to Palestine and the Judean Desert and thence to Syria and North Africa. Saint Basil of Caesarea codified the precepts for these eastern monasteries in his Ascetic Rule, or *Ascetica*, which is still used today in the Orthodox Church.

In the West in about the year 500, Benedict left the comfort of a student's life in Rome and chose the life of an ascetic monk in the pursuit of personal holiness, living as a hermit in a cave near Subiaco. In time, setting a shining example with his zeal, he began to attract disciples. After considerable initial struggles with his first community at Subiaco, he eventually founded the monastery of Monte Cassino, where he wrote his Rule in about 530.

In chapter 73 St Benedict commends the Rule of St Basil and alludes to further authorities. He was probably aware of the Rule written by (or attributed to) Pachomius; and his Rule also shows influence by the Rules of St Augustine and Saint John Cassian. Benedict's greatest debt, however, may be to the anonymous Rule of the Master, which he seems to have radically excised, expanded, revised and corrected in the light of his own considerable experience and insight.[188]

In the Ancient Egyptian Late period (c.1000-32 B.C.E.) there was a special group of ascetics that began to seek refuge at the Anicnet Egyptian temples. Unlike the previous practice of the priests and priestesses these ascetics lived a stricter discipline of abstinence and they allowed their hair to grow and they allowed their bodies to become emaciated. This class of spiritual practitioner may be likened to the Indian sadhus (ascetic aspirants) who wander around India seeking Moksha or "Liberation" for the world through privation and asceticism "like a horse's tail."

---

[188] The Rule of Saint Benedict By +Abbot Primate Jerome Theisen, OSB (*http://www.osb.org/gen/rule.html*)

General Index

1,000 year intervals, 309
Aahs, 130
Ab, 571
Abdu, 54, 92, 140, 145, 147, 152, 153, 159, 222, 267, 406, 408, 409, 464
Above as Below, 499
Abraham, 163, 270, 271, 296, 299, 301, 303, 304, 310, 325, 337, 338, 340, 341, 347, 350, 351, 352, 353, 358, 370, 379, 380, 640
Absolute, 65, 118, 138, 195, 200, 214, 284, 316, 319, 322, 331, 332, 365, 366, 439, 449, 457, 458, 461, 480, 525, 526, 535, 546, 552, 555, 575, 578, 585, 586, 590, 593, 600, 629
Absolute reality, 458
Absolute XE "Absolute" Reality, 332, 457, 480
Abstinence, 378
Abu Simbel, 104, 105
Abyssinia, 102, 108, 289, 311, 496
Abyssinian, 102
Academia, 97
Acquiescence to the will of God, 378
Acts, 96, 302, 335, 346, 365, 590
Adharma, 565
Adinkra symbols, 251, 252
Adonis, 52
Aeneid, The, 82, 83, 87, 672
Afghanistan, 337, 389, 401, 431, 603
Afghanistan War, 337
Africa, 6, 10, 27, 29, 34, 55, 57, 59, 69, 76, 82, 83, 90, 91, 92, 94, 99, 100, 101, 102, 108, 109, 110, 112, 113, 114, 120, 121, 123, 124, 126, 129, 137, 138, 144, 149, 154, 161, 163, 164, 165, 166, 167, 176, 184, 185, 186, 187, 188, 190, 191, 193, 195, 198, 201, 202, 203, 212, 227, 228, 229, 231, 232, 233, 234, 235, 237, 244, 245, 246, 247, 248, 249, 250, 251, 256, 268, 270, 272, 276, 293, 297, 298, 299, 303, 311, 312, 313, 324, 325, 328, 336, 339, 341, 343, 344, 345, 346, 350, 354, 355, 358, 360, 361, 362, 363, 371, 374, 375, 379, 380, 382, 383, 385, 389, 392, 413, 414, 417, 418, 420, 422, 423, 424, 425, 426, 431, 432, 435, 438, 448, 484, 491, 520, 532, 576, 599, 605, 620, 622, 634, 635, 637, 638, 669
African American, 99, 109, 114, 235, 313, 346, 375, 379
African Methodist Episcopal Church, 346
African Methodist Episcopal Zion Church, 346
African Religion, 56, 148, 158, 185, 186, 187, 188, 190, 191, 192, 193, 195, 198, 231, 237, 248, 249, 250, 251, 253, 283, 343, 351, 360, 361, 364, 374, 375, 378, 379, 382, 385, 425, 432, 625, 635, 676
Africanization of Islam, 374
Africanized Christianity, 345
Africentrism, 390
Agni, 309, 397, 534, 537, 546
Ahamgraha Upasana, 592
Ahsu, 7, 89, 104
Ahura Mazda, 308
Air, 269, 499, 535, 692
Aivanhov, Omraam Mikhael, 57, 448
Akhenaton, 82, 156, 157, 268, 362, 363, 365, 367, 368, 439, 521, 541, 545, 590, 591
Akhenaton, Pharaoh, 368
Akher, 275
Akhnaton, 82, 92, 107, 116, 138, 152, 156, 157, 158, 223, 268, 283, 303, 362, 363, 365, 366, 367, 368, 425, 439, 521, 540, 541, 544, 545, 590, 591, 614
Akhus, 148, 193, 226
Aksum, 311, 312
Aksum (Axum), 311, 312
Albert Schweitzer, 55
Alexander, 162
Alexander the Great, 81, 110, 137, 153, 162, 257, 278, 337, 381, 397
Alexandria, 162, 337, 378, 640
Allah, 36, 287, 332, 337, 341, 349, 350, 351, 353, 354, 355, 357, 358, 359, 360, 361, 364, 370, 371, 372, 373, 375
All-encompassing divinity, 528, 546, 575
almond, 370
Amasis, 81, 256, 640
Amen, 81, 156, 200, 318, 332, 334, 363, 365, 496, 541, 588, 590
Amenhetep IV, 539
Amenhotep III, 82, 83, 258, 259
Amenta, 135, 318, 684
Amentet, 135, 179, 686
Americas, 109, 188, 189, 246, 247, 312, 339, 341, 343, 372, 379
Amma, 192, 232, 496, 499
Ammit, 488, 569
Amun, 81, 92, 104, 105, 117, 118, 126, 128, 129, 130, 138, 146, 147, 152, 156, 157, 158, 159, 160, 194, 195, 198, 210, 213, 217, 220, 232, 233, 243, 264, 287, 311, 318, 331, 332, 363, 365, 368, 369, 371, 397, 402, 439, 486, 496, 511, 524, 525, 526, 532, 534, 548, 549, 573, 575, 586, 590, 596, 597, 600, 624, 670, 672, 681
Amunhotep, 95, 115, 156, 609
Amunmhat I, 108, 115
Amun-Ra-Ptah, 92, 152, 194, 369, 524, 534, 548, 575, 586, 600, 681
Anat, 286, 287, 289, 293, 294, 305
Ancestors, 193, 418
Ancient Egypt, 4, 7, 10, 27, 29, 30, 31, 32, 34, 40, 41, 47, 49, 51, 52, 53, 54, 55, 57, 59, 62, 65, 67, 74, 76, 77, 79, 80, 81, 82, 83, 84, 85, 86, 87, 89, 90, 92, 93, 94, 95, 96, 97, 98, 99, 101, 102, 103, 104, 105, 107, 108, 109, 110, 111, 112, 113, 114, 115, 116, 117, 119, 120, 122, 123, 124, 125, 126, 128, 129, 130, 132, 135, 136, 137, 138, 139, 140, 141, 142, 143, 144, 145, 146, 147, 148, 149, 150, 151, 152, 153, 154, 156, 158, 159, 160, 161, 162, 163, 164, 165, 166, 167, 168, 169, 170, 171, 172, 173, 174, 175, 176, 179, 181, 183, 184, 185, 186, 187, 188, 190, 191, 192, 193, 194, 195, 196, 197, 198, 199, 201, 204, 207, 208, 209,

212, 213, 214, 215, 231, 232, 233, 234, 235, 236, 237, 238, 240, 241, 244, 246, 247, 250, 252, 255, 256, 257, 258, 260, 261, 262, 263, 264, 265, 266, 267, 268, 269, 270, 271, 272, 273, 274, 275, 276, 277, 278, 279, 281, 285, 286, 287, 288, 289, 290, 291, 292, 293, 294, 295, 296, 297, 299, 301, 302, 303, 304, 305, 306, 307, 309, 310, 311, 313, 314, 315, 316, 317, 318, 319, 320, 321, 323, 324, 325, 326, 327, 328, 330, 331, 332, 333, 334, 335, 336, 337, 343, 345, 349, 350, 351, 352, 353, 357, 359, 360, 361, 362, 363, 364, 365, 366, 367, 368, 369, 371, 373, 376, 377, 378, 380, 381, 383, 384, 385, 387, 389, 390, 391, 392, 393, 394, 397, 399, 400, 402, 403, 405, 406, 407, 408, 409, 410, 413, 414, 419, 420, 421, 423, 424, 425, 426, 428, 429, 430, 431, 432, 433, 434, 435, 436, 437, 438, 439, 440, 441, 442, 444, 445, 446, 447, 448, 449, 451, 452, 453, 454, 455, 456, 457, 459, 460, 461, 462, 464, 465, 474, 475, 479, 481, 484, 485, 486, 487, 488, 489, 491, 492, 493, 494, 495, 496, 497, 498, 501, 502, 503, 504, 505, 506, 507, 508, 509, 510, 511, 512, 513, 515, 516, 517, 518, 519, 520, 521, 522, 523, 524, 525, 526, 527, 530, 531, 532, 534, 535, 536, 537, 538, 539, 541, 542, 544, 545, 546, 547, 548, 549, 550, 551, 552, 555, 556, 557, 559, 561, 562, 563, 564, 565, 566, 567, 568, 569, 570, 571, 572, 573, 574, 575, 576, 578, 579, 580, 582, 584, 585, 586, 587, 588, 589, 590, 591, 592, 593, 595, 596, 597, 598, 599, 600, 601, 602, 603, 605, 606, 607, 608, 609, 610, 611, 612, 615, 616, 617, 618, 620, 621, 622, 623, 624, 625, 626, 627, 629, 630, 631, 632, 633, 634, 635, 637, 640, 669, 670, 671, 672, 673, 675, 676, 678, 679, 681, 682, 683, 684, 685, 687, 688, 689, 690, 691

Ancient Egyptian Book of the Dead, 208, 247, 317, 384, 462, 596, 597, 669

Ancient Egyptian mystical philosophy, 352
Ancient Egyptian Mystical Philosophy, 47
Ancient Egyptian Pyramid Texts, 130, 179, 244, 534, 535, 550
Ancient Greek religion, 29
Ancient Nubian, 7, 89, 104, 136, 310
Angels, 349, 352, 364
anger, 199, 200, 615
Anger, 242, 243
Anglican, 345, 346
Angra Mainyu, 308
Ani, 331, 517, 520, 543, 569, 617, 670
Ankh, 52, 148, 208, 233, 275, 328, 329, 330, 336, 410, 420, 540, 545, 572, 612, 620, 621, 670
anointed one, 301, 326
Anu, 92, 152, 156, 171, 174, 210, 217, 218, 239, 269, 318, 319, 496, 549, 575, 586, 601, 624, 685
Anu (Greek Heliopolis), 92, 152, 156, 171, 174, 210, 217, 218, 239, 269, 318, 319, 496, 549, 575, 586, 601, 624, 685
Anubis, 153, 263, 264, 569, 595
Anunian Theology, 138, 141, 149, 184, 213, 217, 218, 319, 320, 321, 322, 439, 503, 529, 532, 534, 541, 542, 544, 549, 556, 601, 627, 669
Apedemak, 484, 521
Apep serpent, 225, 261, 542
Apocrypha, 324, 385
Apollonius, 431, 439, 640
Apophis, 225, 640
apostle, 353
Aquarian Gospel, 89, 100, 124, 139, 166, 184, 285, 286, 289, 293, 298, 305, 327, 349, 350, 354, 361, 364, 370, 373, 387, 393, 420
Arabia, 89, 100, 124, 139, 166, 184, 285, 286, 289, 293, 298, 305, 327, 349, 350, 354, 361, 364, 370, 373, 387, 393, 420
Arabs, 90, 100, 109, 110, 113, 135, 140, 150, 153, 166, 186, 235, 289, 296, 340, 342, 349, 350, 351, 355, 357, 358, 364, 375, 376, 397, 398, 399, 424, 447, 610, 636
Aramaic, 638
Arati, 452

Architecture, 38, 41, 61, 71, 73, 145, 183, 184, 407, 408, 441, 669
Ardhanari, 623
Ari, 65, 130, 203, 204, 210, 567, 568, 569, 570, 571, 573, 597, 612, 614
Ari Hems Nefer, 130
Aristotle, 81, 112, 162, 393
Arit Maat, 571
Arius, 162, 333
Arjuna, 415, 580
Ark of the Covenant, 312
Aryan, 29, 84, 184, 296, 308, 309, 388, 389, 390, 392, 395, 397, 398, 400, 402, 403, 404, 414, 415, 417, 419, 429, 431, 434, 441, 447, 451, 496, 532, 536, 537, 539, 540, 602, 629, 640, 671, 680
Aryans, 84, 155, 300, 308, 309, 329, 387, 390, 397, 400, 403, 404, 416, 424, 429, 441, 442, 496, 497, 541, 673
Asar, 65, 81, 86, 92, 93, 117, 118, 124, 129, 131, 132, 134, 135, 138, 141, 144, 145, 147, 149, 150, 152, 153, 158, 173, 179, 180, 182, 183, 194, 206, 210, 213, 217, 218, 222, 239, 243, 244, 247, 261, 262, 263, 264, 268, 271, 285, 286, 287, 290, 292, 311, 317, 318, 321, 322, 323, 326, 329, 332, 333, 337, 359, 365, 378, 393, 397, 402, 409, 410, 413, 419, 420, 421, 439, 452, 453, 455, 462, 464, 481, 482, 483, 488, 489, 491, 499, 511, 518, 520, 522, 523, 524, 527, 534, 535, 541, 542, 547, 552, 557, 558, 559, 567, 569, 570, 572, 574, 576, 582, 583, 586, 587, 589, 590, 595, 596, 597, 598, 610, 615, 617, 619, 621, 672, 687, 690
Asarian Mystery, 413
Asarian Myth, 413, 576
Asarian Resurrection, 41, 74, 138, 141, 149, 213, 290, 313, 317, 344, 410, 439, 452, 475, 516, 552, 569, 573, 595, 596, 598, 672, 687, 688
Asclepius, 179, 184, 670
Aset, 27, 53, 86, 92, 118, 130, 133, 134, 135, 141, 147, 149, 152, 180, 183, 213, 218, 221, 222, 231, 239, 243, 244, 263, 264, 286, 287, 289, 290, 292, 293, 294, 321, 322, 332, 333,

336, 402, 413, 419, 452, 455, 460, 461, 464, 481, 482, 489, 491, 494, 499, 510, 516, 527, 535, 536, 549, 557, 558, 559, 560, 561, 565, 569, 570, 576, 582, 583, 586, 589, 595, 597, 610, 619, 631, 686, 687, 690

Aset (Isis), 27, 53, 86, 92, 118, 130, 133, 134, 135, 141, 147, 149, 152, 180, 183, 213, 218, 221, 222, 231, 239, 243, 244, 263, 264, 286, 287, 289, 290, 292, 293, 294, 321, 322, 332, 333, 336, 402, 413, 419, 452, 455, 460, 461, 481, 482, 489, 491, 494, 499, 510, 516, 527, 535, 536, 549, 557, 558, 559, 560, 561, 565, 569, 570, 576, 582, 583, 586, 589, 595, 597, 610, 619, 686, 687, 690

Asha, 309

Ashoka, 161, 429, 430, 439, 442, 494, 599, 603, 604, 611, 627, 640

Asia, 34, 57, 81, 87, 97, 102, 109, 114, 124, 129, 136, 153, 154, 155, 156, 159, 161, 166, 184, 187, 230, 232, 235, 245, 246, 256, 257, 267, 268, 270, 271, 272, 274, 285, 286, 288, 289, 296, 298, 299, 300, 303, 306, 308, 309, 325, 355, 357, 368, 376, 379, 381, 384, 389, 390, 391, 393, 397, 400, 406, 408, 410, 413, 414, 416, 417, 418, 420, 421, 422, 425, 426, 429, 431, 432, 435, 441, 442, 443, 469, 480, 541, 596, 605, 620, 634, 669, 671

Asia Minor, 57, 81, 87, 102, 109, 114, 124, 136, 153, 154, 156, 159, 161, 166, 184, 187, 230, 235, 245, 256, 257, 267, 268, 271, 274, 285, 286, 288, 289, 299, 303, 306, 355, 357, 368, 376, 379, 397, 406, 408, 413, 417, 420, 425, 431, 435, 541, 605

Asians, 300, 358, 362, 397, 398, 418

Asiatic, 83, 110, 136, 154, 156, 166, 174, 259, 303, 304, 307, 381, 399, 408, 496, 640

Asoka, 430, 442, 494, 627

Aspirant, 452, 617

Assyrian, 79, 114, 137, 160, 161, 266, 271, 294, 333

Assyrians, 95, 126, 137, 153, 160, 289, 306, 399, 605

Astraea (Themis), 264, 265

Astral, 178, 318, 458, 476, 534, 542, 684

Astral Plane, 178, 318, 458, 476, 534, 542, 684

Aten, see also Aton, 363, 366, 367, 532, 539, 540, 541, 590, 591, 691

Atheists, 283

Athena, 81, 111, 161, 183, 257, 264, 265, 287, 289, 294, 371

Atlantis, 255, 256, 257, 258, 267

Atman, 457, 458, 499

Atom, 549, 553

Aton, 79, 92, 147, 152, 156, 157, 158, 210, 217, 223, 234, 363, 365, 366, 367, 368, 425, 433, 521, 532, 538, 540, 541, 542, 544, 545, 590, 591

Atonism, 149, 223, 283, 368, 541, 544, 591

Attis, 52

Augustus, 83, 93, 138, 422, 640

Ausarian religion, 377

Ausarian Resurrection, 503

Austerity, 279, 580, 582, 594

Australopithecus ramidus, 33

Avatar, 382, 420

Avidya, 574, 607, 612

Awareness, 118, 195

awet ab, 47

Axum, 135, 311

Ba (also see Soul), 464, 466, 482, 487, 497, 499, 563, 569, 570

Baal, 285, 286, 287, 289, 384

Baalat, 286

Babism, 378, 385

Babylon, 46, 82, 97, 172, 176, 268, 289, 299, 306, 312, 325, 412

Badari, 438

Badarian culture, 137, 147, 640

Bahai (see also Babism), 379, 385, 627

Balance, 85, 554, 566, 614

Balance of Mind, 554, 566, 614

Bas, 129, 130, 133, 537

Basu, 129, 131, 132

Beatitudes, 565

Being, 35, 36, 37, 48, 111, 114, 138, 148, 158, 169, 187, 192, 193, 194, 200, 209, 214, 236, 237, 238, 242, 243, 269, 293, 302, 309, 319, 332, 333, 335, 349, 351, 352, 353, 362, 367, 368, 369, 413, 439, 445, 457, 482, 496, 499, 501, 517, 524, 527, 528, 537, 542, 543, 546, 549, 552, 554, 555, 557, 561, 565, 572, 579, 582, 587, 589, 593, 598, 609, 612

Beisan (Bet-shan), 305

Benben, 145

Bengal, 497, 564, 597

Bengali, 40, 496, 497, 498, 563, 564

Benin, 10, 201, 202, 203, 249

Ben-jochannan, Yosef A. A., 99

Benu bird, 264

Bernal, Martin, 111, 183, 384, 669

Berossos, 46, 172

Bhagavad Gita, 87, 316, 394, 402, 459, 580, 581, 582, 597, 632, 672

Bhakti Yoga, 378

Bhakti Yoga See also Yoga of Divine Love, 378

Bible, 76, 79, 86, 94, 96, 97, 99, 102, 113, 122, 159, 163, 183, 199, 268, 270, 285, 290, 291, 296, 297, 298, 299, 300, 301, 302, 303, 304, 305, 307, 309, 310, 312, 313, 314, 323, 324, 325, 326, 331, 335, 336, 337, 338, 339, 340, 342, 344, 346, 347, 348, 350, 354, 358, 365, 367, 368, 370, 380, 384, 385, 392, 394, 578, 590, 593, 596, 598, 610, 624, 632, 669, 672, 687

BIBLE, 670

Big Dipper, 170, 179, 180

Bikini yoga, 478

Bindu (see also Black Dot), 499

Black, 6, 10, 110, 111, 113, 116, 117, 118, 123, 139, 183, 250, 271, 299, 313, 336, 344, 350, 370, 375, 384, 392, 438, 499, 511, 518, 576, 606, 669, 672

Black and red pottery, 136, 271, 438

Black Athena, 111, 113, 183, 384, 669

Black Dot (see also Bindu), 499

Black Madonna, 344, 576

Black Muslims, 374, 375

Blackness, 123, 134, 576

Black-skinned, 270, 393, 576

Bliss, 457, 458

Blue Nile, 121, 298

Blyden, Edward Wilmot, 235

Bodhisatva, 614

Book of Coming forth by day, 669, 670

Book of Coming forth by Day, 362, 587

Book of Coming Forth By Day, 138, 141, 142, 237, 292, 302, 363, 369, 439, 517, 549, 550, 578, 584, 587, 593, 594, 595, 598, 685

Book of Enlightenment, 93, 179, 204, 464, 498, 541, 551, 584, 598, 609, 610

Book of the Dead, see also Rau Nu Prt M Hru, 87, 93, 138, 140, 141, 179, 204, 206, 213, 217, 237, 253, 275, 314, 384, 439, 498, 584, 596, 597, 598, 609, 610, 627, 669, 670, 672, 685

Brahma, 195, 309, 390, 402, 501, 504, 505, 516, 523, 524, 525, 527, 528, 546, 547, 548, 549, 551, 552, 555, 586, 618, 629

Brahma Sutras, 402

Brahman, 84, 85, 194, 195, 284, 316, 332, 402, 447, 457, 458, 461, 499, 506, 528, 546, 547, 552, 555, 556, 561, 578, 585, 586, 593, 600, 601, 629

Brahmins, 85, 401, 581, 599, 601, 602

Brazil, 190, 202, 246, 247

Brazilians, 109, 247

Breath control, 459, 466

Brihad Aranyaka Upanishad, 574

British Empire, 55, 397

Bronze Age, 34, 256, 426, 439, 442, 596

Brooklyn Museum, 107, 231, 432, 606

Buddha, 65, 84, 85, 87, 315, 332, 363, 395, 439, 440, 441, 449, 482, 495, 499, 506, 520, 547, 599, 600, 601, 602, 605, 606, 607, 608, 609, 612, 614, 615, 618, 619, 620, 621, 627, 628, 640, 669

Buddha Consciousness, 85, 608, 614, 627

Buddhi, 85

Buddhism, 27, 29, 57, 84, 85, 117, 118, 250, 283, 304, 332, 371, 385, 400, 402, 430, 435, 441, 442, 450, 464, 494, 498, 532, 553, 554, 567, 580, 599, 600, 601, 602, 603, 605, 607, 608, 610, 612, 619, 620, 621, 624, 625, 626, 627, 628, 629, 640, 669, 676

Buddhist, 84, 85, 117, 118, 187, 194, 195, 309, 316, 332, 337, 372, 378, 400, 430, 438, 441, 449, 451, 454, 457, 467, 482, 496, 497, 499, 532, 546, 548, 551, 554, 556, 560, 565, 567, 579, 580, 587, 599, 600, 601, 602, 603, 605, 607, 608, 611, 612, 614, 615, 616, 617, 618, 619, 621, 626, 627, 629

Budge, Wallis, 364, 530, 539, 540, 541, 576, 596, 597, 670, 671, 672, 673

Bull, 179, 247, 261, 499, 523, 595

Burkina Faso, 249

Buto, 496

Byblos, 288, 290, 384

Byzantine, 53, 80, 138, 162, 332, 333, 337, 355, 356, 439

Byzantines, 356

C, 624

Caduceus, 49, 316, 320, 453, 487, 488, 489, 589

Cairo, 99, 100, 116, 184, 278, 288, 298, 327, 426, 428

Cameroon, 249

Campbell, Joseph, 11, 32, 44, 45, 48, 52, 57, 59, 74, 86, 172, 183, 184, 448, 451, 494, 627, 670, 672

Canaan, 52, 268, 285, 289, 290, 296, 297, 298, 299, 300, 301, 303, 305, 306, 324, 325, 326, 339, 343, 380

Canaanites, 298

Cannan, 296

Canonized, 335, 356

Caribbean, 27, 188, 189, 190, 202, 246, 253, 312

Carl Jung, 47, 576

Caste System, 397, 398

Categories of Cultural Expression, 38, 39, 59, 493, 626

Catholic, 194, 312, 335, 344, 347, 377, 576, 600, 686

Causal Plane, 458

Ceasar, 83, 161

Celsus, 302

Celtic, 300, 329, 345, 397, 622

Celtic cross, 329, 622

Celts, 354, 441

Chakras, 317, 378, 452, 453, 487, 488, 489, 490, 492, 537

Chakras (see energy centers of the body), 317, 378, 452, 453, 487, 488, 489, 490, 492, 537

Chaldaens, 86, 271, 391

Chaldeans, 271, 303

Champollion, Jean Franșcois, 108, 183

Champollion-Figeac, 108, 109, 183

Chandogya Upanishad, 552, 553, 574

Change, 630

Chanting, 162, 461

Chaos, 496, 504

Charlemagne, 355, 356

Cheops, see also Khufu, 164, 175, 497, 640

Chepesh, 179, 181, 182

Chi, 192, 488

Childbirth, 237

children of Israel, 301

China, 57, 84, 124, 204, 230, 270, 276, 309, 334, 355, 417, 435, 454, 467, 469, 479, 480, 488, 640

Chinamasta, 509

Chitta, 459

Chiukwu (or Chineke), 192

Christ, 52, 61, 82, 85, 87, 110, 162, 278, 301, 309, 323, 324, 325, 326, 329, 334, 335, 336, 343, 347, 348, 353, 354, 359, 370, 384, 385, 441, 597, 600, 621, 627, 669

Christ as the Son of God, 323

Christ Consciousness, 85, 347

Christhood, 85, 323, 627

Christian church, 162, 329, 354, 356, 369, 622

Christian Church, 53, 302, 334, 354, 355, 356, 369, 593

Christian cross, 329, 622

Christian Cross, 328, 620

Christian Yoga, 87, 278, 296, 343, 345, 441, 449, 598, 627, 669

Christianity, 29, 44, 50, 52, 53, 55, 57, 61, 79, 80, 85, 90, 96, 98, 114, 117, 135, 137, 162, 185, 186, 187, 195, 247, 249, 250, 251, 268, 276, 279, 283, 285, 287, 291, 292, 296, 297, 303, 306, 307, 309, 310, 311, 313, 323, 324, 326, 329, 332, 333, 334, 335, 337, 338, 339, 340, 343, 344, 345, 346, 347, 348, 353, 354, 355, 356, 357, 361, 362, 369, 372, 373, 374, 377, 378, 379, 383, 385, 400, 413, 419, 420, 449, 450, 484, 536, 552, 565, 576, 579, 582, 592, 593, 594, 596, 599, 600, 610, 615, 620, 622, 634, 636, 637, 638, 640, 669, 676, 678, 686, 687

Christology, 162, 403, 600

Chronology, 98, 135, 138, 163, 166, 396, 439, 440, 441
Church, 53, 98, 112, 162, 203, 302, 329, 333, 334, 335, 337, 344, 345, 346, 347, 354, 355, 356, 376, 593, 600, 621, 686
Church of England, 346
Cicero, 32
Civility, 55, 114
Civilization, 1, 9, 10, 29, 32, 33, 54, 55, 56, 58, 86, 88, 101, 111, 115, 167, 183, 229, 248, 250, 253, 254, 255, 268, 276, 277, 278, 386, 387, 388, 390, 391, 392, 394, 395, 396, 400, 416, 429, 440, 441, 442, 443, 446, 447, 449, 454, 494, 514, 530, 532, 551, 622, 627, 669, 670, 671, 672, 673, 675, 676
Clarke, John H., 99
Clement of Alexandria, 162
Cleopatra, 162, 640
CNN – news reports, 398, 399
Cobra Goddess, 496
Coffin Texts, 138, 140, 141, 213, 439, 551, 552, 587, 588, 591, 609
Colchians, 109, 124, 270, 271, 296, 299, 393, 400
Colchis, 270, 271, 393
colonialism, 138, 195, 251, 344, 357, 361, 403, 439, 635
Color, 116
Colossi of Memnon, 82, 83
Company of gods and goddesses, 169, 319, 321
complete religion, 50
Concentration, 466
Conception, 481
Conflict, 360
Confucianism, 204, 283, 565, 605
Confuciunist writings, 153
Congo, 10, 185, 195, 236, 244, 345, 374
Conscience, 569
Consciousness, 85, 90, 117, 134, 248, 284, 315, 318, 322, 332, 348, 445, 457, 489, 519, 526, 530, 543, 549, 557, 575, 576, 578, 593, 600, 601, 608, 614, 627, 628, 670
Constantine, 329, 621
Constantinople, 356
Contentment (see also Hetep), 212, 612
Copper Age, 34, 172

Coptic, 40, 142, 162, 213, 311, 312, 327, 330, 332, 337, 356, 373, 376, 600, 640, 684
Coptic church, 162, 600
Coptic Church, 162, 337, 356, 376, 600
Copts, 109, 110, 111, 162, 311, 373, 376
Corinthians, 346
Correlation Methods, 38
Cosmic consciousness, 394, 445, 452, 578, 593
Cosmic Egg, 499, 525
Cosmic Illusion, 85
cosmic order, 309
cosmic Self, 200
Cosmic Self, 200
Cosmogony, 318
Cosmos, 480
Council of Chalcedon, 162, 600
Council of Nicaea, 302
Count Goblet D' Alviella, 49, 70, 86, 87, 620, 627
Cow, 221, 499, 510, 515
Creation, 40, 44, 45, 46, 49, 56, 65, 66, 79, 96, 117, 132, 135, 138, 141, 145, 187, 192, 193, 194, 200, 206, 207, 212, 213, 214, 217, 218, 219, 220, 221, 222, 223, 233, 234, 238, 242, 243, 261, 269, 279, 284, 287, 289, 290, 291, 293, 294, 302, 309, 315, 316, 317, 318, 319, 320, 321, 322, 332, 333, 335, 351, 352, 365, 366, 367, 368, 371, 377, 432, 433, 439, 476, 480, 481, 482, 483, 499, 501, 504, 510, 511, 517, 518, 521, 522, 523, 524, 525, 526, 527, 529, 532, 534, 535, 536, 538, 542, 543, 548, 549, 550, 551, 552, 554, 555, 560, 561, 565, 575, 586, 587, 590, 595, 596, 597, 598, 600, 601, 611, 618, 623, 634, 671, 676, 681, 683, 685
Cretans, 258
Crete, 156, 256, 257, 258, 259, 469, 480
Cross, 74, 75, 328, 329, 330, 620, 621
Crusades, 334, 341, 344, 356
Cultural Anthropology, 35, 39, 59
Culture, 30, 33, 35, 36, 37, 44, 48, 52, 54, 57, 58, 66, 71, 72, 73, 74, 75, 76, 84, 94, 101, 175, 185, 212, 227, 229, 237, 246, 312, 388, 390, 392, 400, 414, 415, 418, 426, 442, 443, 478, 504, 510, 530, 547, 567, 592, 597, 635, 636, 640, 669, 670, 671, 676, 679, 683, 688
Culture-Myth Model, 36, 37
Cush, 126, 297, 298, 324, 389
Cushite, 160, 185, 296, 496
Cybele, 378
Cymbals, 690, 691
D, 692
Dabhar, 594
Dance, 198, 499, 521, 538
Dance of Shiva, 499
Dark Ages, 108, 292, 355
Darmakaya, 496, 499
Darwin, 96
Davidson, Basil, 101
Day of Judgment, 352
De Anima, 81
Dead Sea Scrolls, 306, 312, 672
December, 52, 86, 686
Deism, 48, 345
Delphi, 81, 256
Delta, 155, 265, 640
Demigods, 169
Demotic, 53, 59, 93, 142, 421
Denderah, 92, 118, 135, 152, 176, 181, 328, 406, 557, 576, 597, 670, 684
Detachment, 279
Deva, 551
Devi Mahatmia, 508
Devil, 198, 199
Devotional Love, 378
Dharma, 62, 86, 204, 250, 283, 399, 441, 447, 512, 513, 534, 565, 566, 567, 574, 594, 599, 611, 614, 615, 627, 629, 630
Dharmakaya, 194, 482, 554, 600
diabolus, 199
Diaspora, 30, 91, 99, 109, 195, 311, 314, 676
Diet, 27, 679
Diodorus, 82, 86, 89, 93, 112, 124, 143, 163, 165, 166, 169, 173, 184, 286, 299, 387, 391, 393, 420, 421, 422, 423, 424, 669
Dionysius, 334, 337, 430, 604
Dionysius the Areopagite, 337
Dionysius the Areopagite, 334, 337
Dionysius, Pseudo, 334
Dionysus the Areopagite, 334, 337
Diop, Cheikh Anta, 10, 11, 86, 99, 100, 101, 102, 103, 111, 183,

236, 238, 239, 248, 250, 253, 258, 391, 441, 627, 669, 672
Discipline, 27, 460, 463, 464, 474, 581
Divine Consciousness, 226, 519, 526, 568
Divine cow, 515
Djed Pillar, see also Pillar of Asar, 317
Djedu, 318
Djehuti, 41, 138, 153, 162, 173, 179, 196, 233, 239, 243, 264, 267, 309, 316, 320, 322, 413, 439, 455, 466, 497, 519, 525, 542, 569, 597, 612, 672
Djehutimes IIII, 175
DNA, 424, 425
Dogon, 40, 57, 124, 188, 192, 193, 198, 232, 237, 245, 247, 496
Dravidian, 308, 388, 391, 395, 398, 403, 405, 417, 418, 432, 433, 434, 447, 496, 499, 563
Dravidianxe "Dravidian" culture, 398, 433, 434, 447
Druid, 329, 621
Druid crosses, 329, 621
Drum, 247, 690, 691
Dualism, 162, 199, 600
Duality, 308, 333, 587
Duat, 118, 135, 269, 314, 317, 318, 534, 542, 572, 595
Dudun, 131
Durga, 294, 499, 508, 509, 510, 633
Durkheim, Emile, 68
Dynastic period, 95, 138, 142, 147, 439, 609
Dynastic Period, 6, 51, 94, 95, 102, 110, 132, 136, 137, 138, 141, 148, 149, 150, 159, 163, 165, 170, 176, 198, 232, 268, 275, 407, 410, 438, 439, 440, 569, 582, 609
E, 575, 586
Earth, 170, 178, 242, 243, 269, 318, 321, 347, 534, 575
Eastern Orthodox Church, 356
Eastern religions, 251, 292
Ecstasy, 191
Edfu, 92, 152, 222, 239, 406, 462, 557, 684
Egoism, 200, 225, 369, 593
Egyptian Antiquities Organizations, 98
Egyptian Book of Coming Forth By Day, 138, 148, 237, 302, 363, 369, 439, 549, 578, 587, 593, 594, 595, 598, 684
Egyptian Christians, 162, 600

Egyptian civilization, 51, 94, 97, 99, 109, 110, 124, 138, 148, 153, 170, 176, 232, 256, 267, 268, 271, 276, 277, 299, 303, 305, 363, 373, 389, 392, 406, 414, 435, 485
Egyptian Civilization, 299
Egyptian High Priests, 169
Egyptian Mysteries, 29, 179, 192, 385, 454, 679
Egyptian Physics, 686
Egyptian proverbs, 456, 682
Egyptian religion, 29, 51, 53, 57, 79, 90, 96, 112, 137, 144, 149, 153, 158, 166, 193, 196, 237, 252, 263, 268, 275, 285, 293, 295, 301, 302, 303, 306, 313, 326, 331, 332, 333, 334, 336, 345, 349, 351, 352, 353, 357, 361, 362, 363, 377, 392, 414, 498, 541, 548, 569, 576, 590, 605
Egyptian Yoga, 1, 9, 27, 29, 47, 57, 90, 191, 220, 253, 276, 365, 442, 445, 449, 450, 454, 455, 456, 475, 494, 498, 530, 597, 627, 635, 636, 669, 670, 671, 678, 679, 681, 683, 684, 689, 690, 691
Egyptian Yoga Book Series, 27, 636
Egyptian Yoga see also Kamitan Yoga, 1, 9, 27, 29, 57, 90, 191, 220, 253, 276, 365, 442, 445, 454, 455, 456, 475, 494, 498, 530, 597, 627, 635, 636, 669, 670, 671, 678, 679, 681, 683, 684, 689, 690, 691
Egyptians, 298
Egyptologists, 40, 90, 94, 95, 96, 97, 98, 99, 101, 103, 107, 108, 110, 111, 115, 116, 138, 142, 149, 153, 163, 165, 166, 167, 169, 174, 176, 225, 276, 364, 368, 371, 380, 387, 391, 392, 394, 402, 404, 406, 408, 497, 590, 609, 610
Elamites, 325
Elijah, 375
Elijah Muhammad, 375
Elohim, 79, 303, 364, 368, 369, 370
energy center, 378
Energy Centers, 316, 378
Enlightenment, 9, 27, 29, 47, 48, 51, 85, 90, 93, 140, 142, 162, 179, 195, 212, 224, 266, 321, 322, 442, 446, 452, 453, 464, 498, 530, 541, 550, 558, 561,

566, 568, 584, 585, 586, 607, 608, 609, 610, 611, 612, 614, 637, 638, 669, 671, 672, 679, 681, 682, 688
Ennead, 169, 534
Eos, 82
Equanimity, 607, 614
Essenes, 306, 378
eternal witness, 195, 332
Ethics, 1, 55, 56, 81, 88, 254, 379, 386, 462, 625, 635, 675
Ethiopia, 33, 82, 89, 93, 102, 121, 123, 124, 163, 193, 234, 249, 268, 270, 271, 289, 296, 297, 298, 299, 300, 310, 311, 312, 313, 314, 324, 343, 345, 346, 351, 363, 391, 393, 400, 420, 421, 422, 423, 431, 432, 484, 496, 605
Ethiopian priests, 93, 421
Ethnic, 102
Ethnicity, 38, 75, 76, 186, 422, 424, 425
Ethnographies, 102, 114
Ethnology, 35
Eucharist, 52, 202, 326, 332, 385, 571, 684
Eudoxus, 80, 263, 449, 688
Euphrates River, 97, 276, 296, 394
Eurasia, 300
Eurasians, 300, 418
Eurocentrism, 390, 391, 392
European explorers, 95, 122, 244
Eusebius, 169, 302
Evil, 198, 199, 200, 360, 512
Exercise, 27, 683
Eye of Heru, 182, 226, 369, 410, 411, 412, 571
Eye of Ra, 261, 413
Eyes of Buddha, 499, 506
Eyes of Horus, 499
Eyes of Krishna, 499, 506
Factors of Cultural Expression, 38, 39, 59
Faith, 309, 322, 333, 350, 354, 385, 581
Falashas, 310, 311, 346
Fard, W. D., 375
Fatimah, 287, 373, 374
Fayum Neolithic site, 147
Feelings, 183, 672
Female, 195, 242, 243, 287, 398, 413, 499, 525, 533, 633
Feuerstein, Georg, 86, 167, 183, 278, 390, 392, 396, 415, 440, 441, 442, 443, 446, 447, 450,

494, 530, 596, 597, 670, 671, 672
First Intermediate Period, 138
Fish, 370
Flood, 466
Folklore, 35, 56, 69, 81, 344, 493
Fon Nation, 233
forgiveness, 200
Forgiveness, 566
Form, 38, 41, 61, 692
Forty-two Assessors, 567
Frawley, David, 167, 278, 390, 392, 400, 401, 402, 403, 404, 405, 406, 409, 410, 413, 414, 415, 441, 442, 443, 446, 447, 494, 670, 673
Frazer, James G., 45, 48
Fundamentalism, 334, 335
Galla culture, 108, 188, 193, 244, 496
Ganesha, 630
Ganges River, 390, 499
Garden of Eden, 298, 315
Garment of Creation, 561
Garvey, Marcus, 312, 375
Gaul, 355, 576
Geb, 129, 133, 173, 218, 239, 264, 269, 292, 321, 322, 475, 476, 478, 481, 482, 499, 535, 536, 569, 595, 684
Gendercide, 399
Genealogy, 115
General, Roman Titus, 323
Genes, 416, 417, 418, 424, 429, 441, 442, 670
Genocide, 344
Geography, 271, 393, 416, 417, 418, 424, 429, 441, 442, 670
Ghandi, Mahatma, 114, 397, 398
Gilgamesh, 43, 52, 184, 269, 324
Giza, 34, 94, 140, 142, 144, 145, 163, 164, 167, 176, 179, 201, 288, 327, 380, 408, 409, 410
Giza Plateau, 163, 179, 408
Globalism, 249
Globalization, 185, 249
Gnosis, 308, 592
Gnostic, 53, 85, 117, 162, 194, 307, 308, 312, 323, 332, 333, 334, 345, 347, 351, 367, 377, 378, 431, 578, 591, 592, 593, 594, 600
Gnostic Christianity, 85, 117, 334, 377, 592, 594
Gnostic Christians, 53, 333
Gnostic XE "Gnostic" Gospels, 312, 347

Gnostic Gospels, 332, 578, 591, 593
Gnostics, 308, 315, 385, 595
God, 32, 36, 37, 41, 48, 51, 52, 53, 55, 65, 79, 80, 84, 85, 86, 89, 90, 96, 124, 128, 129, 130, 133, 134, 148, 149, 156, 162, 169, 175, 185, 187, 191, 192, 193, 194, 195, 199, 200, 201, 202, 204, 206, 207, 208, 211, 212, 214, 226, 233, 234, 237, 239, 242, 243, 244, 249, 253, 269, 279, 283, 285, 286, 290, 291, 292, 293, 296, 297, 300, 302, 304, 306, 308, 309, 311, 312, 313, 314, 315, 316, 317, 318, 320, 322, 323, 324, 325, 326, 331, 332, 333, 334, 335, 336, 337, 338, 339, 340, 341, 342, 344, 345, 346, 347, 349, 350, 351, 352, 353, 354, 358, 359, 361, 362, 363, 364, 365, 366, 367, 368, 369, 370, 372, 373, 375, 377, 378, 379, 382, 385, 393, 394, 395, 398, 413, 416, 419, 420, 432, 433, 434, 444, 445, 446, 449, 450, 452, 455, 456, 457, 461, 463, 464, 466, 480, 481, 496, 499, 501, 504, 505, 507, 517, 518, 519, 522, 523, 524, 525, 526, 535, 536, 537, 538, 539, 540, 542, 543, 548, 551, 552, 553, 554, 555, 557, 560, 561, 566, 567, 569, 572, 573, 575, 578, 579, 583, 584, 585, 586, 587, 588, 589, 590, 591, 592, 593, 594, 595, 597, 600, 601, 602, 609, 610, 612, 625, 627, 628, 630, 632, 634, 638, 670, 681, 685, 686, 691
God of Light, 79, 366
Goddess, 36, 134, 138, 141, 149, 192, 194, 204, 206, 208, 210, 213, 214, 217, 221, 242, 243, 244, 260, 261, 265, 275, 283, 286, 288, 289, 290, 291, 293, 294, 295, 305, 315, 316, 320, 370, 373, 379, 398, 413, 432, 439, 452, 478, 481, 486, 496, 508, 509, 510, 516, 520, 524, 550, 557, 558, 560, 561, 565, 573, 583, 596, 625, 627, 671, 686, 691
Goddesses, 82, 128, 149, 179, 192, 193, 194, 209, 214, 218, 220, 221, 253, 263, 264, 285, 289, 293, 318, 320, 373, 419, 452,

476, 524, 529, 530, 547, 560, 561, 586, 630, 671, 676, 683
Godhead, 369
Gods, 79, 82, 93, 128, 148, 149, 169, 179, 192, 193, 194, 209, 214, 218, 220, 234, 237, 240, 253, 263, 264, 285, 304, 317, 318, 320, 351, 362, 363, 369, 384, 385, 421, 432, 443, 447, 476, 504, 519, 523, 524, 529, 530, 538, 547, 553, 560, 561, 567, 586, 587, 588, 596, 630, 670, 671, 672, 676
Golden Age, 356
Good, 308, 343, 612
Good and evil, 199, 308
Good God, 308
Good religion, 308
goodness of man, 308
Gopi, 670
Gospel of John, 334
Gospels, 324, 332, 347, 552, 578, 591, 593, 600, 686
Great Months, 171
Great Pyramid, 138, 140, 145, 163, 164, 170, 179, 180, 184, 380, 409, 428, 671
Great Pyramids, 34, 138, 140, 145, 180, 380, 409, 428
Great Truths, 209, 210, 211
Great Year, 138, 170, 171, 172, 175, 176
Greece, 29, 44, 49, 61, 80, 81, 82, 87, 95, 102, 111, 124, 156, 161, 162, 176, 183, 232, 245, 246, 256, 257, 259, 260, 263, 265, 276, 289, 293, 294, 343, 380, 381, 390, 392, 393, 403, 407, 413, 420, 421, 422, 423, 429, 430, 431, 454, 497, 576, 591, 603, 624, 670, 679, 688
greed, 199, 200
Greek Classical period, 260
Greek classical writers, 108, 110, 111, 112, 113, 115, 116, 119
Greek Classical writers, 112, 449
Greek Empire, 55, 257, 356
Greek philosophers, 80, 81, 114, 161, 162, 392
Greek philosophy, 378, 565, 678
Greek Philosophy, 57, 80, 81, 634
Greeks, 34, 49, 79, 80, 81, 82, 109, 110, 111, 112, 113, 114, 115, 123, 131, 135, 137, 140, 143, 153, 161, 162, 169, 171, 179, 257, 262, 263, 264, 265,

267, 269, 270, 289, 290, 299, 306, 329, 335, 371, 378, 380, 391, 392, 397, 398, 399, 407, 410, 412, 421, 422, 424, 428, 441, 449, 575, 576, 586, 605, 621, 622, 624, 636, 688
Green, 367
Greenberg, Gary, 96, 183, 669
Greenfield papyrus, 672
Gregorios, Paul, 574
Gregory, 53, 336
Gregory the Great, 53, 336
Griffin, 262, 266, 267, 273
Gue Nyame, 185
Guinea-Bissau, 249
Gulf War, 337
Gunas, 581
Guru, 382, 499, 581, 585, 632
Haari, 496, 691
Haile Selassie, 311, 312, 313
Haile Selassie I, 311, 312, 313
Halif Terrace site, 97, 305
Ham, 94, 102, 239, 297, 298, 299, 300, 314, 324, 325, 326
Hammurabi, 80, 270, 640
Hapi, 120, 262, 333, 535, 595
Harappa, 388, 404, 406, 426, 428, 439
Harappan culture, 389, 424
Harappans, 426, 429, 442, 443, 596, 669
Hari, 496, 562
Harmachis, 34, 549
Harmony, 204, 565
Hasidism, 315
Hatha Yoga, 27, 467, 475, 478, 479, 580
Hathor, 118, 138, 153, 264, 286, 289, 293, 413, 439, 499, 510, 595, 622, 684, 686, 688
hatred, 199, 200, 615
Hatshepsut, Queen, 139, 140, 146, 154, 156, 640
Hawk, 148, 267, 411, 491, 515
Headrests, 231
Health, 27, 678
Hearing, 350, 358
Heart, 210, 308, 333, 369, 382, 553, 555, 571, 579, 593, 669, 687
Heart (also see Ab, mind, conscience), 210, 553, 571, 579, 593, 669, 687
Heaven, 93, 179, 242, 243, 269, 292, 318, 332, 335, 347, 351, 443, 499, 542, 555, 575, 615, 669
Hebrew, 36, 40, 79, 113, 117, 163, 199, 291, 296, 299, 301,

303, 304, 305, 310, 312, 317, 324, 332, 338, 339, 354, 364, 365, 368, 369, 380, 384, 387, 497, 590, 638
Hebrew religion, 332, 364
Hebrews, 96, 289, 291, 296, 299, 300, 301, 303, 304, 305, 306, 310, 337, 364, 369, 380, 392, 412, 449
Hekau, 196, 201, 464, 466, 499, 516, 578, 592, 593, 610, 691
Helena, Saint, 329, 621
Heliopolis, 80, 81, 92, 152, 171, 263, 449, 575, 586, 688
Hell, 112, 318, 335, 351, 360
Heraclian emperors, 356
Heretical, 183, 354
Hermes, 49, 179, 233, 264, 267, 316, 320, 586, 672
Hermes (see also Djehuti, Thoth), 49, 179, 233, 264, 267, 316, 320, 586, 672
Hermes (see also Tehuti, Thoth), 49, 179, 233, 264, 586, 672
Hermetic, 62, 162, 179, 378, 487, 489, 594
Hermeticism, 337
Herodotus, 44, 80, 81, 82, 97, 102, 109, 112, 113, 123, 124, 163, 170, 184, 263, 270, 271, 276, 299, 303, 305, 325, 346, 384, 393, 397, 420, 421, 422, 423, 424, 425, 435, 438, 439, 442, 496, 573, 580, 611, 627, 640, 670, 672
Heru, 34, 79, 86, 87, 92, 93, 129, 130, 131, 132, 135, 138, 141, 147, 148, 149, 152, 153, 159, 167, 169, 173, 175, 176, 177, 179, 180, 181, 182, 207, 213, 217, 218, 222, 231, 234, 243, 244, 247, 264, 267, 275, 287, 288, 301, 309, 318, 321, 322, 323, 326, 327, 332, 336, 359, 363, 369, 406, 410, 411, 412, 413, 433, 434, 439, 453, 454, 455, 462, 475, 481, 483, 495, 498, 499, 503, 504, 505, 506, 512, 513, 514, 515, 532, 535, 536, 541, 542, 543, 545, 547, 549, 550, 554, 555, 557, 558, 559, 566, 569, 571, 573, 576, 577, 583, 586, 589, 596, 609, 610, 619, 627, 632, 670, 684, 685, 686, 687, 690, 691
Heru (see Horus), 34, 79, 86, 87, 92, 93, 129, 130, 131, 132, 135, 138, 141, 147, 148, 149, 152, 153, 159, 167, 169,

173, 175, 176, 177, 179, 180, 181, 182, 207, 213, 217, 218, 222, 231, 234, 243, 244, 247, 264, 267, 275, 287, 288, 301, 309, 318, 321, 322, 323, 326, 327, 332, 336, 359, 363, 369, 406, 410, 411, 412, 413, 433, 434, 439, 453, 454, 455, 462, 475, 481, 483, 495, 498, 499, 503, 504, 505, 506, 512, 513, 514, 515, 532, 535, 536, 541, 542, 543, 545, 547, 549, 550, 554, 555, 557, 558, 559, 566, 569, 571, 573, 576, 577, 583, 586, 589, 596, 609, 610, 619, 627, 632, 670, 684, 685, 686, 687, 690, 691
Heru and Jesus, 301, 326
Heru in the Horizon, 34, 176
Heru-Akhuti, 545
Heru-Behded, 234, 433, 434
Hessi, 592
Hetep, 118, 179, 181, 499, 502, 517, 569
Hetep Slab, 499, 517
Hetheru, 92, 118, 141, 147, 148, 149, 152, 153, 181, 213, 217, 221, 239, 243, 260, 261, 262, 264, 267, 286, 287, 288, 289, 292, 293, 322, 328, 406, 413, 455, 466, 475, 508, 510, 515, 520, 532, 550, 569, 622, 688, 689
Hetheru (Hetheru, Hathor), 92, 118, 141, 147, 148, 149, 152, 153, 181, 213, 217, 221, 239, 243, 260, 261, 262, 264, 267, 286, 287, 288, 289, 292, 293, 322, 328, 406, 413, 455, 466, 475, 508, 510, 515, 520, 532, 550, 569, 622, 688, 689
Het-Ka-Ptah, see also Men-nefer, Memphis, 132, 153, 217
Hidden, 192
Hieratic, 142, 290, 402
Hieroglyphic Alphabet, 144
Hieroglyphic Writing, language, 59, 141, 142, 144, 169, 269, 400, 402, 609, 683
Hieroglyphs, 141, 143
High God, 194, 232, 332, 345, 369, 589
Hilliard, Asa G., 99
Hindu, 29, 40, 61, 70, 79, 199, 250, 309, 332, 335, 349, 359, 360, 365, 369, 371, 372, 377, 382, 385, 389, 391, 397, 398, 402, 413, 433, 434, 440, 441, 448, 449, 451, 453, 457, 467,

479, 493, 494, 496, 499, 501, 504, 505, 508, 509, 511, 513, 514, 516, 517, 518, 519, 520, 522, 524, 525, 527, 528, 529, 530, 532, 534, 536, 537, 538, 540, 541, 546, 547, 548, 550, 551, 555, 557, 558, 563, 565, 566, 567, 568, 569, 571, 575, 576, 579, 580, 581, 587, 590, 592, 593, 596, 599, 601, 602, 610, 614, 615, 618, 623, 627, 628, 629, 630, 632, 633, 634, 636, 669, 670, 671, 673

Hindu mythology, 79, 332, 457, 513, 516, 528, 536, 537, 547, 552, 579

Hindu religion, 29, 335, 359, 360, 413, 587, 601

Hinduism, 29, 51, 57, 84, 85, 86, 87, 166, 185, 247, 250, 251, 253, 283, 304, 309, 327, 332, 379, 382, 385, 387, 390, 395, 397, 398, 402, 440, 441, 442, 443, 484, 505, 513, 514, 527, 530, 532, 534, 536, 537, 541, 546, 547, 549, 551, 565, 566, 567, 576, 579, 580, 582, 586, 590, 593, 596, 597, 602, 610, 612, 620, 625, 627, 628, 629, 630, 633, 634, 639, 669, 676

Hindus, 86, 179, 194, 251, 309, 315, 329, 378, 382, 399, 412, 432, 433, 441, 447, 450, 510, 519, 548, 565, 574, 602, 622, 636

Hippocrates, 428

History of Manetho, 51, 147, 165, 169, 172, 403

Hittites, 34, 156, 159, 338, 340, 541

Holocene epoch, 431

Holy Ghost, 291, 600

Holy Land, 326, 341

Holy of Holies, 486

Holy spirit, 333

Holy Spirit, 332, 333, 367, 600

Homer, 44, 80, 82, 123, 256, 263, 394, 422, 423, 640

Homo Sapiens, 33

Horemakhet, 34, 149, 156, 363, 544, 640

Hor-m-Akhet, 94

Hormakht - the Great Sphinx, 545

Horus, 49, 52, 79, 138, 141, 148, 149, 153, 173, 176, 182, 213, 222, 264, 301, 309, 332, 369, 410, 413, 430, 439, 454, 455, 481, 497, 499, 502, 539, 558, 576, 603, 690

Howe, Steven, 113

Hyksos, 95, 100, 126, 137, 155, 156, 158, 397, 605, 640

Hymn To Aton, 545

Hymn to Ra, 541, 542

Hymns of Amun, 331, 365, 525, 549, 624, 670, 672

Hymns to Aton, 365, 425, 521, 541, 590, 591

Hymns to Ra, 541, 596

I, 547, 586, 624, 692

I and the Father are One, 333

Iam formula, 594

Iamblichus, 671

Ibex, 150, 271, 272, 275

Ibis, 596

Ice Age, 431, 442

Ida and Pingala, 452, 488, 489

Identification, 445

Igbo, 188, 192, 193, 195

Ignorance, 65, 575, 607, 612

Illusion, 85, 614

Illusory Modification, 458

Imhotep, 65, 179, 243, 426, 427, 428, 614, 640

Imperishable stars, 180

Inculturation, 53, 79, 336, 434

India, 6, 27, 29, 30, 32, 45, 46, 57, 62, 65, 70, 74, 76, 82, 83, 84, 85, 86, 87, 89, 91, 102, 111, 117, 124, 139, 140, 153, 161, 172, 183, 198, 204, 230, 231, 232, 233, 234, 235, 246, 250, 251, 253, 257, 268, 271, 276, 277, 284, 286, 294, 297, 299, 308, 309, 316, 332, 337, 343, 350, 354, 355, 365, 371, 372, 373, 378, 379, 381, 387, 388, 389, 390, 392, 393, 394, 395, 396, 397, 398, 399, 400, 401, 402, 403, 404, 406, 407, 410, 413, 414, 415, 416, 417, 418, 419, 420, 421, 422, 423, 424, 426, 429, 430, 431, 432, 433, 434, 435, 437, 438, 439, 440, 441, 442, 443, 446, 447, 448, 449, 450, 451, 452, 454, 457, 458, 459, 460, 462, 464, 465, 466, 467, 469, 474, 475, 478, 479, 480, 482, 485, 488, 491, 493, 496, 497, 498, 502, 504, 505, 506, 507, 508, 510, 511, 512, 513, 515, 516, 517, 518, 520, 521, 522, 523, 524, 525, 527, 528, 530, 532, 534, 536, 537, 538, 541, 546, 547, 548, 551, 555, 557, 559, 562, 563, 564, 565, 567, 568, 572, 574, 575, 576, 579, 580, 585, 587, 589, 590, 591, 592, 593, 596, 597, 602, 603, 604, 605, 606, 608, 609, 610, 611, 615, 616, 618, 620, 621, 622, 624, 627, 630, 631, 632, 633, 634, 635, 636, 640, 669, 670, 671, 679, 682, 691

Indian scholars, 231, 395, 431, 446, 447, 497, 565, 621, 638

Indian Yoga, 27, 29, 387, 446, 448, 450, 452, 454, 457, 459, 493, 531, 580, 592, 597, 601, 637, 676, 680, 691

Indo Europeans, 309

Indologist, 396, 403, 448

Indologists, 40, 167, 390, 391, 392, 393, 395, 396, 397, 400, 401, 402, 403, 404, 407, 414, 434, 439, 440, 447, 448, 497, 537, 547, 585

Indra, 84, 234, 397, 433, 534, 536, 537, 546, 548

Indus, 6, 29, 80, 86, 136, 137, 167, 268, 270, 271, 276, 277, 278, 285, 286, 387, 388, 389, 390, 397, 400, 402, 404, 405, 406, 407, 416, 417, 419, 420, 424, 426, 428, 429, 435, 438, 439, 440, 441, 449, 451, 453, 454, 491, 493, 496, 504, 514, 520, 523, 532, 551, 602, 622, 629, 640, 669, 680

Indus Valley, 6, 29, 80, 136, 137, 268, 270, 276, 277, 278, 285, 387, 388, 389, 390, 397, 404, 405, 406, 407, 416, 417, 419, 426, 428, 429, 435, 438, 440, 441, 451, 454, 491, 514, 520, 532, 551, 602, 622, 629, 640, 669, 680

Infanticide, 398, 399

Initiate, 182, 263, 449, 679

Intellect, 62, 85, 317, 322, 458, 566

Intellectual, 84, 85

Intercourse, 442, 443, 627, 670

Intuitional, 592

Iran, 272, 285, 300, 373, 376, 378, 397, 418, 426, 428, 431, 435

Iraq, 82, 86, 268, 270, 271, 296, 299, 303, 337, 373, 397, 431

Ireland, 416

Iron Age, 34, 172

Isfet, 99, 565

Isha Upanishad, 84

Ishmael, 350, 351

Isis, 52, 53, 86, 118, 133, 135, 138, 141, 147, 149, 180, 183, 213, 221, 222, 253, 263, 264, 286, 287, 293, 321, 333, 385, 387, 402, 413, 419, 420, 439, 449, 452, 455, 460, 461, 481, 489, 491, 497, 499, 510, 516, 527, 557, 558, 560, 565, 576, 582, 583, 586, 595, 610, 672, 684, 686, 690

ISIS, 576

Isis, See also Aset, 52, 53, 86, 118, 133, 135, 138, 147, 149, 180, 183, 221, 222, 253, 263, 264, 286, 287, 293, 321, 333, 385, 387, 402, 413, 419, 420, 439, 449, 452, 460, 461, 481, 489, 491, 497, 499, 510, 516, 560, 576, 582, 583, 586, 610, 672, 684, 686, 690

Islam, 57, 90, 98, 110, 114, 137, 150, 166, 185, 187, 195, 247, 249, 251, 279, 283, 285, 287, 291, 292, 293, 296, 306, 311, 332, 336, 337, 349, 350, 351, 352, 353, 354, 355, 357, 358, 359, 360, 361, 362, 371, 372, 373, 374, 375, 376, 377, 378, 379, 382, 383, 385, 419, 565, 582, 597, 603, 627, 638, 640, 672, 676, 678

Ismail (Ishmael), 350, 351, 353, 358

Israel, 96, 97, 159, 184, 285, 289, 299, 301, 302, 305, 306, 310, 311, 312, 315, 323, 324, 331, 336, 338, 339, 340, 341, 342, 350, 353, 359, 364, 376, 379, 385

Israelites, 369

Jacob (and Israel), 96, 299, 338, 347, 358, 385

Jah, 312, 313

Jain, 85, 439, 496, 499, 601, 606

Jainism, 85, 87, 283, 580, 602, 605, 612, 640

Jamaica, 109, 312

Jamaicans, 313

James, George G. M., 99, 672

James, George G.M., 87, 183

Japheth, 94, 300, 324

jealousy, 199

Jehovah, 369

Jerusalem, 159, 184, 298, 302, 305, 306, 310, 312, 313, 323, 326, 338, 372

Jesus, 44, 52, 53, 61, 65, 74, 87, 90, 135, 162, 195, 199, 200, 207, 247, 278, 293, 299, 301, 302, 304, 306, 309, 312, 313, 315, 320, 323, 324, 325, 326, 327, 331, 332, 333, 334, 335, 336, 338, 340, 343, 344, 345, 347, 348, 349, 350, 351, 352, 353, 354, 358, 363, 367, 370, 372, 378, 379, 383, 384, 385, 403, 431, 441, 449, 450, 514, 576, 577, 591, 592, 594, 596, 597, 599, 600, 614, 615, 640, 669, 684, 686, 687

Jesus Christ, 309, 312, 323, 324, 326, 348, 372, 379, 684

Jesus of Nazareth, 324

Jewish, 79, 84, 96, 97, 112, 117, 183, 198, 199, 281, 285, 291, 292, 293, 296, 299, 300, 301, 302, 303, 304, 305, 306, 307, 309, 310, 312, 313, 315, 319, 323, 326, 332, 337, 338, 339, 340, 341, 342, 344, 346, 347, 349, 350, 351, 352, 354, 358, 359, 360, 365, 368, 369, 374, 377, 378, 379, 384, 385, 565, 590, 592, 638, 669

Jewish Bible, 79, 199, 285, 291, 368

Jewish religion, 293, 299, 302, 304, 306, 323, 365, 368, 384

Jews, 36, 79, 90, 96, 162, 271, 289, 293, 296, 297, 298, 299, 300, 301, 302, 303, 304, 305, 306, 309, 310, 311, 313, 319, 323, 325, 326, 333, 337, 338, 339, 340, 341, 342, 344, 345, 346, 347, 349, 350, 352, 353, 355, 357, 358, 359, 360, 361, 364, 365, 368, 369, 380, 381, 383, 450, 590

JHWH, 369

Jiva, 452, 457

Jivan Mukta, 458

Jnana Yoga, 284, 460, 670

John the Baptist, 324

Joseph, 11, 32, 44, 45, 48, 52, 57, 59, 74, 86, 163, 172, 183, 184, 301, 304, 324, 350, 448, 451, 494, 627, 670, 672

Joseph Campbell, 11, 32, 44, 45, 48, 52, 57, 59, 74, 86, 172, 183, 184, 448, 451, 494, 627, 670, 672

Josephus, 326

Joshua, 324

Joy, 212, 607, 614

Judaism, 57, 79, 80, 84, 90, 98, 135, 137, 185, 186, 187, 195, 247, 251, 268, 276, 277, 279, 283, 285, 287, 291, 292, 296, 297, 299, 300, 301, 302, 303, 304, 306, 307, 308, 309, 310, 311, 313, 314, 315, 316, 319, 332, 337, 338, 340, 341, 346, 347, 351, 353, 354, 357, 362, 363, 368, 369, 370, 373, 377, 383, 385, 419, 565, 582, 610, 634, 638, 676, 678

Judeo-Christian-Islamic, 293

Justice, 379, 516, 553, 567

Justinian, Emperor I, 356

Jyotirmayananda, Swami, 87, 399, 450, 494, 530, 596, 597, 598, 670, 671, 672, 673

K, 575

Ka, 201, 233, 354, 370, 371, 541, 542

Kaaba, 349, 350, 351, 370, 371, 372

Kaba, 350

Kabah, 354

Kabbala, 315, 316, 318, 320

Kabbalah, 678

Kaffirs, 109, 603

Kaivalia, 458

Kak, Subhash, 167, 278, 390, 392, 401, 441, 442, 443, 446, 447, 494, 670

Kali, 172, 195, 294, 332, 481, 482, 498, 499, 508, 509, 510, 566

Kali XE "Kali" position, 482

Kali Position, 481

Kalki Avatara, 309

Kamit, 31, 57, 62, 65, 76, 84, 85, 90, 92, 94, 95, 99, 100, 110, 111, 117, 123, 124, 125, 126, 128, 129, 131, 132, 135, 136, 137, 138, 147, 153, 170, 192, 193, 196, 197, 198, 201, 202, 204, 209, 212, 214, 215, 221, 222, 228, 229, 232, 233, 234, 237, 238, 244, 245, 247, 248, 250, 257, 260, 264, 268, 277, 281, 289, 304, 313, 333, 371, 377, 382, 385, 433, 438, 454, 455, 479, 504, 508, 510, 513, 516, 517, 522, 523, 528, 532, 540, 544, 545, 563, 564, 565, 568, 572, 605, 610, 615, 627, 635

Kamit (Egypt), 31, 57, 62, 65, 76, 84, 85, 90, 92, 94, 95, 99, 100, 110, 111, 117, 123, 124, 125, 126, 128, 129, 131, 132, 135, 136, 137, 138, 147, 153, 170, 192, 193, 196, 197, 198, 201, 202, 204, 209, 212, 214, 215, 221, 222, 228, 229, 232,

233, 234, 237, 238, 244, 245, 247, 248, 250, 257, 260, 264, 268, 277, 281, 289, 304, 313, 333, 371, 377, 382, 385, 433, 438, 454, 455, 479, 504, 508, 510, 513, 516, 517, 522, 523, 528, 532, 540, 544, 545, 563, 564, 565, 568, 572, 605, 610, 615, 627, 635

Kamitan, 11, 27, 29, 31, 40, 41, 50, 51, 53, 57, 59, 60, 61, 63, 65, 67, 68, 76, 84, 90, 91, 94, 95, 99, 100, 104, 114, 115, 117, 118, 119, 120, 123, 125, 128, 129, 130, 131, 132, 133, 135, 138, 140, 143, 144, 145, 147, 148, 149, 157, 159, 163, 170, 171, 179, 181, 186, 188, 190, 192, 197, 200, 201, 203, 204, 209, 213, 214, 216, 224, 227, 229, 230, 232, 234, 236, 237, 238, 239, 240, 241, 242, 243, 244, 248, 251, 260, 263, 264, 266, 268, 275, 276, 289, 290, 291, 293, 313, 314, 319, 326, 334, 359, 361, 371, 381, 399, 410, 413, 428, 433, 437, 439, 440, 444, 445, 448, 449, 450, 452, 454, 459, 463, 464, 476, 477, 479, 481, 482, 483, 484, 485, 487, 488, 489, 491, 493, 494, 496, 497, 498, 499, 501, 503, 504, 505, 508, 510, 511, 513, 514, 516, 518, 520, 527, 528, 529, 530, 532, 534, 535, 537, 538, 541, 546, 547, 548, 555, 559, 560, 561, 563, 565, 567, 568, 569, 570, 571, 572, 573, 575, 578, 580, 586, 587, 588, 589, 591, 592, 593, 594, 596, 597, 605, 606, 607, 610, 614, 615, 619, 620, 622, 624, 626, 627, 634, 635, 637, 638, 640, 678, 679, 686, 688, 689, 690, 691

Karma, 27, 65, 84, 85, 446, 567, 568, 570, 571, 573, 574, 612, 630, 682

Karmah, 126, 135

Karmah Period, 126, 135

Karnak, 96, 98, 159, 380, 412, 486, 511

Karttikeya, 432, 433, 434, 534, 537

Kebra Nagast, 312, 313, 384

Kebra Negast, 432

Kemetic, 11, 27, 29, 40, 41, 60, 61, 91, 95, 99, 100, 104, 138, 157, 159, 163, 171, 179, 234, 241, 243, 256, 263, 264, 268, 275, 276, 410, 413, 428, 433, 439, 440, 444, 448, 452, 454, 459, 464, 477, 479, 481, 482, 484, 488, 489, 491, 494, 496, 497, 498, 499, 501, 503, 504, 505, 511, 513, 514, 516, 518, 520, 527, 528, 529, 530, 532, 534, 535, 537, 541, 546, 547, 548, 559, 560, 565, 567, 568, 569, 570, 571, 572, 575, 578, 580, 586, 589, 591, 592, 593, 594, 596, 597, 610, 614, 615, 619, 620, 622, 627, 630, 632, 633, 634, 689, 690, 691

Kenya, 102, 185, 234, 253, 432, 434, 443, 635

Kerma, 125, 126

Kether, 317

Khepri, 264, 302, 352, 501, 525, 527, 528, 541, 547, 548, 573, 586, 596

Kheri-Heb, 153, 428

Khu, 612

Khufu, 175, 497, 640

Khufu, see also Cheops, 175, 497, 640

Ki (see also Life Force, Ra, Buto, Kundalini), 269

Ki (see also Life ForceRaButoKundalini), 269

Kikuyu, 234, 432

Kikuyu people, 234, 432

Kiliminjaro, 121

King Amasis, 265

King David, 306

King Solomon, 310, 313

Kingdom, 55, 93, 102, 126, 138, 139, 146, 147, 153, 154, 155, 156, 159, 160, 175, 183, 184, 201, 268, 271, 274, 288, 289, 311, 332, 347, 367, 380, 385, 405, 407, 410, 426, 428, 436, 437, 440, 441, 475, 541, 542, 566, 615, 633, 671, 687

Kingdom of God, 332

Kingdom of heaven, 347

Kingdom of Heaven, 93, 332, 347, 615, 687

Kmt, 31

KMT (Ancient Egypt). See also Kamit, 99, 100, 624

Know thyself, 224

Know Thyself, 81

Knowledge, 62, 377, 457, 566, 580, 584, 597

Knum, 131, 244, 269

Koran, 96, 338, 340, 347, 349, 350, 351, 352, 353, 354, 357, 358, 359, 360, 362, 375, 378

Korean script, 54

Krishna, 74, 84, 117, 283, 309, 320, 327, 332, 363, 397, 415, 439, 495, 498, 499, 504, 505, 506, 510, 511, 512, 513, 514, 515, 522, 527, 530, 537, 538, 547, 552, 559, 576, 577, 580, 594, 602, 627, 628, 670, 687

Kundalini, 27, 198, 233, 317, 378, 382, 402, 445, 451, 452, 453, 482, 485, 487, 488, 489, 490, 491, 494, 504, 537, 602, 633, 670

Kundalini Yoga, 378

Kundalini XE "Kundalini" Yoga see also Serpent Power, 27, 233, 317, 378, 382, 402, 451, 452, 453, 485, 488, 491, 504, 537, 602

Kung Fu, 479

Kush, 70, 107, 123, 125, 126, 136, 137, 151, 156, 183, 193, 228, 229, 236, 237, 310, 313, 367, 389, 441, 496, 591

Kybalion, 672

Lake Victoria, 234, 298, 433

Lakshmi, 195

Land of Ham, 298

Lao Tzu, 363, 640

Latin, 10, 82, 188, 190, 199, 253, 279, 308, 329, 330, 356, 397, 421, 497, 622

Latin Cross, 329, 330, 622

Law of Manu, 398

Laws of Manu, 397, 398, 499, 525, 580

Lebanon, 285, 290, 305

Lefkowitz, Mary, 111, 112

Levi-Strauss, Claude, 68

Liberation, 93, 608, 610, 612

Liberia, 249

Libya, 108, 109, 159, 160, 256, 298, 324, 325, 422

Libyans, 110, 126, 140, 153, 159, 160, 263, 422, 423, 424

Life Force, 135, 176, 196, 198, 210, 317, 321, 333, 366, 367, 424, 454, 455, 459, 479, 485, 487, 488, 492, 501, 507, 510, 522, 525, 532, 536, 537, 541, 584, 591, 596, 600, 683

Light within, 540

Lila, story of, 557, 558

Lilith, 277, 291, 292, 293, 294

Lingam-Yoni, 499, 517

Linguistic Studies, 496

Linguistics, 38, 40, 420, 432

Lioness, 508
Listening, 191, 210, 217, 284, 460, 461, 463
Little Dipper, 170
Logos, 586, 594
Lord of Darkness, 308
Lord of the Perfect Black, 118, 135, 499
Lotus, 70, 274, 384, 453, 455, 499, 504, 505, 518, 548, 550, 616, 617, 618, 672
Love, 331, 338, 378, 394, 445, 463, 671, 672, 682
Lower Egypt, 137, 138, 153, 158, 162, 165, 173, 285, 302, 439, 454, 455
Lucifer, 309, 326
Luxor, 98, 154, 330, 371, 412, 511
Maakheru, 196, 209, 545, 571
Maat, 55, 62, 85, 99, 114, 149, 153, 159, 167, 173, 179, 203, 204, 205, 206, 207, 208, 209, 210, 213, 228, 239, 241, 243, 250, 264, 265, 269, 275, 281, 322, 331, 352, 381, 399, 445, 446, 453, 462, 466, 488, 496, 512, 513, 516, 525, 527, 540, 541, 542, 544, 545, 554, 565, 566, 567, 569, 571, 573, 589, 611, 614, 615, 627, 676, 682, 686, 688
MAAT, 100, 138, 203, 204, 439, 516, 565, 681, 682
Maati, 87, 208, 462, 573, 672
MAATI, 682
Maat-Ubuntu, 228, 250
Macedonian epoch, 356
Madagascar, 249
Madonna, 52, 53, 87, 135, 336, 370, 478, 576
Mafdet, leopard goddess, 260, 261
Magic, 202, 670
Mahabharata, 84, 87, 309, 390, 402, 439, 459, 548, 551, 565, 574, 597, 629, 640, 671
Mahavakyas, 457, 499, 578, 579, 593, 630
MAHAVAKYAS OR GREAT UTTERANCES, 578, 593
Mahavira, 87, 439, 606, 627, 640
Malawi, 234, 432
Malcolm X, 374, 375, 385
Male, 195, 197, 242, 243, 287, 292, 499, 514, 525, 533
Mali, 40, 232, 236
Malinowski, Bronislaw, 68
Maltese Cross, 328, 329, 622

Mandorla, 370
Manetho, 51, 96, 147, 163, 165, 169, 170, 171, 172, 173, 175, 183, 403, 671
Manetho, see also History of Manetho, 96, 163, 169, 170, 171, 172, 173, 175, 183, 671
Mantra, 592
Mantras, 494, 499
Manu, 397, 398, 496, 499, 525, 542, 565, 566, 580
Manusmriti, 565
Marcus Garvey, 312, 375
Maroon culture, 312
Mars, 171, 335
Marxism, 249, 250
Mary Magdalene, 293
Mastaba, 201
Masters, 87, 248, 514, 669
Mathematics, 57, 405, 410, 412, 441, 672
Matter, 117, 503, 596, 672, 686
Matthew, 200, 285, 301, 306, 324, 325, 326, 331, 338, 342, 343, 347, 351, 600
Mauss, Marcel, 68
Maya, 84, 85, 447, 499, 536, 560, 630
Mecca, 349, 350, 354, 355, 361, 370, 372, 374, 375, 385
medical doctors, 428
Meditating, 460
Meditation, 85, 191, 210, 211, 221, 279, 284, 395, 445, 459, 461, 462, 464, 465, 466, 467, 494, 499, 519, 581, 607, 614, 627, 671, 672, 679, 682, 683, 691
Mediterranean, 97, 120, 154, 161, 183, 256, 257, 259, 267, 289, 290, 298, 367, 384, 392, 436, 469, 480
Medu Neter, 196, 456, 499, 578, 593
Mehgarh, 268, 406, 439
Mehndi, 437, 443
Mehurt, 221, 239, 287, 510, 524
Memnon, 82, 87, 115
Memphis, 80, 81, 92, 132, 140, 152, 153, 156, 160, 161, 169, 173, 263, 392, 428, 429, 430, 438, 439, 442, 443, 449, 548, 549, 551, 553, 555, 599, 600, 601, 603, 604, 618, 627, 670, 688
Memphite Theology, 81, 87, 126, 138, 141, 149, 160, 213, 219, 221, 237, 428, 439, 499, 503, 532, 548, 549, 550, 551, 553, 554, 555, 556, 596, 600, 601, 625, 626, 627, 671
Mena, King (also Menes), 153
Menelek, 310
Menes, 153, 169, 173, 391, 428, 640
Men-nefer, see also Het-Ka-Ptah, Memphis, 92, 132, 152, 153, 318
Mer, 145, 428
Merikara, 154, 381, 568
Meri-ka-ra, 323, 568
Meril, 131
Meroe, 126, 135
Meroitic language, 59
Meroitic period, 143, 437
Meroitic Period, 126, 127, 128
Mertseger (She who loves silence), 490
Meskhenet, 569
Mesolithic, 34, 54, 147
Mesopotamia, 34, 54, 80, 82, 86, 94, 97, 100, 156, 165, 171, 179, 230, 255, 268, 269, 270, 271, 276, 277, 294, 295, 296, 299, 308, 325, 388, 390, 391, 393, 403, 416, 450, 496, 541
Mesopotamian, 309
messiah, 323, 324
messiahs, 323
Metal Age, 34
Metaphysical Neters, 194, 600
Metaphysics, 81, 191, 284, 499, 686
Methodist, 346
Metropolitan Museum, 6, 183, 184, 272, 274, 438
Metu Neter, 456, 499, 578, 593
Middle Ages, 355
Middle East, 34, 90, 101, 162, 166, 184, 186, 269, 276, 297, 303, 338, 340, 341, 346, 354, 375, 377, 381, 392, 397, 406, 416, 417, 420, 422, 431, 541, 600, 676, 678
Middle Kingdom, 106, 110, 137, 138, 142, 146, 154, 155, 184, 260, 268, 271, 405, 437, 440, 633
middle path, 84
Min, 239, 288, 289, 499, 595, 684
Mind, 27, 51, 62, 333, 458, 554, 566, 575, 594, 612, 614
mindfulness, 195
Mindfulness, 195, 607, 614, 624
Minoan, 256, 257, 258, 260, 261, 262, 267, 294, 419

Mitanni, 156, 268, 541
Mithra, 52, 309
Mizraim, 297, 298, 324
Modern science, 60, 416
Mohenjo-daro, 388
Moksha, 458, 560, 574, 610
monism, 362
Monism, 283, 365, 590
Monophysitism, 162, 600
Monotheism, 158, 187, 283, 303, 362, 364, 368, 539, 590, 596, 673
Mookerjee, Ajit, 469, 480, 494, 672
Moon, 120, 171, 432, 499, 506, 519, 589
Moors, 109, 350, 422
Morals, 87, 263, 449, 670, 688
Mortals, 595
Moses, 79, 80, 96, 163, 247, 299, 301, 302, 304, 308, 309, 324, 336, 337, 338, 339, 350, 358, 362, 365, 368, 369, 379, 383, 392, 590, 640
Mother Mary, 135
Mother Teresa, 207
Mount Meru, 432, 499
Moyers, Bill, 52, 86, 672
Mozambique, 10, 185, 234, 432
Muhammad, 349, 350, 351, 353, 354, 355, 356, 357, 359, 364, 370, 373, 374, 375, 378, 385, 640
Muhammad, Prophet, 355
Mundaka Upanishad, 84, 518, 555, 561
Muntu, 234
Muntuhotep, 115, 154
Murugan, 432, 433, 434, 537
Murungu, 234, 432, 433, 434
Music, 27, 162, 189, 276, 313, 377, 596, 690, 691
Muslim, 351
Muslims, 36, 90, 95, 137, 140, 186, 190, 251, 289, 291, 293, 298, 333, 336, 337, 338, 340, 341, 349, 350, 352, 353, 355, 357, 358, 359, 361, 364, 368, 371, 372, 373, 374, 375, 380, 382, 385, 603
Mysteries, 29, 49, 145, 179, 221, 253, 318, 334, 378, 385, 441, 454, 547, 549, 557, 558, 583, 586, 596, 671, 678, 686
Mystery religions, 323, 594
Mystery Religions, 670
Mystic Knowledge of GOD, 377

Mystical Christianity, 620
mystical experience, 279
Mystical religion, 65, 324, 335
Mysticism, 27, 29, 36, 50, 52, 55, 57, 66, 88, 90, 116, 191, 195, 208, 247, 279, 283, 315, 316, 318, 319, 334, 354, 362, 370, 377, 378, 379, 386, 441, 463, 488, 503, 511, 530, 548, 589, 597, 625, 635, 670, 671, 675, 679, 680, 684, 685, 686, 688
myth-makers, 44
Mythology, 43, 44, 45, 46, 47, 60, 68, 86, 87, 90, 118, 194, 195, 253, 263, 269, 309, 332, 349, 351, 362, 363, 369, 420, 432, 442, 513, 518, 524, 530, 576, 579, 586, 588, 596, 600, 630, 669, 670, 671, 673, 684
N, 501
Nag Hammadi, 385, 672
Napata, 126, 135, 159, 160, 161
Nara, 496, 525, 527, 551
Narayana, 525, 527
Narmer, 54, 286, 640
Nataraja, 521, 538
Nation of Islam, 374, 375
Native African Religion, 249
Native American, 188, 189, 247, 269, 283, 303, 334, 336, 341, 344, 345, 358, 362, 372
Native American Religions, 247
Native Americans, 341
Nativity, 329, 621
Nature, 65, 85, 192, 213, 283, 514, 534, 591, 601
Neberdjer, 129, 130, 149, 192, 194, 209, 238, 239, 241, 243, 269, 287, 316, 368, 369, 499, 521, 524, 528, 532, 535, 546, 572, 575, 586, 596, 600, 612, 681
Nebertcher, 149, 194, 195, 332, 369, 524, 534, 575, 586, 600
Nebertcher means, 600
Nebethet, 118, 183, 419, 452, 489, 491, 535, 557, 558, 559, 569, 570, 589, 691
Nebthet, 218, 263, 264, 321, 322, 536, 557
Nebuchadnezzar, 306
Nefer, 130, 595, 690, 691
Nefertari, Queen, 159, 475
Nefertem, 219, 504, 527, 547, 548, 549, 550, 551, 596, 600, 617, 618, 623
Negro race, 109, 111
Nehast, 226, 610, 612

Nekhen (Hierakonpolis), 145, 147, 184, 409, 439, 671
Neocolonialism, 185
Neolithic, 34, 54, 136, 138, 147, 167, 268, 276, 406, 417, 418, 429, 431, 439, 640
Neolithicxe "Neolithic" Period, 136, 439
Neo-Platonic academies, 53
Neo-Platonism, 334
Nephthys, 118, 183, 263, 264, 321, 419, 452, 491, 497, 557, 558, 597
Nesi-Khensu, 363, 588
Net, goddess, 81, 92, 129, 138, 141, 147, 149, 152, 153, 158, 160, 161, 213, 221, 257, 264, 265, 287, 289, 290, 293, 294, 368, 371, 373, 439, 497, 561, 691
Neter, 27, 31, 90, 149, 191, 192, 194, 196, 209, 210, 212, 213, 214, 215, 217, 223, 226, 241, 244, 269, 332, 349, 352, 445, 456, 499, 524, 578, 583, 587, 588, 593
Neterian, 31, 52, 186, 209, 210, 217, 221, 225, 226, 232, 239, 251, 268, 287, 301, 303, 314, 318, 326, 332, 352, 377, 457, 461, 532, 587, 589, 591, 599, 612, 618, 621, 626
Neterianism, 29, 31, 166, 209, 210, 214, 263, 430, 484, 505, 513, 514, 541, 576, 590, 603, 610, 619, 625, 626
neters, 332
Neters, 142, 148, 149, 194, 444, 456, 480, 612
Neteru, 27, 128, 129, 149, 156, 194, 201, 202, 209, 211, 213, 214, 215, 216, 225, 226, 243, 318, 321, 349, 364, 475, 479, 480, 499, 524, 534, 535, 551, 553, 589, 683, 690, 691
Netherworld, 118, 133, 135, 144, 149, 244, 275, 318, 476, 542, 570, 584
New Age, 257
New Kingdom, 102, 110, 126, 127, 128, 137, 138, 139, 142, 146, 147, 154, 155, 156, 159, 183, 184, 220, 223, 232, 235, 260, 261, 288, 307, 330, 407, 410, 436, 441, 475, 545, 671
New testament, 323
New Testament, 309, 323, 324, 332, 334, 338, 347, 352, 385, 597, 600

Nicomachean Ethics, 81
Nile River, 103, 120, 121, 124, 138, 140, 151, 212, 276, 298, 428, 499
Nile Valley, 103, 111, 122, 239, 408, 436, 530, 671, 673
Nine, 363, 499, 529, 535, 537, 588
Nirvana, 118, 560, 597, 607, 612, 630, 673
NIRVANA, 612
Noah, 94, 102, 296, 300, 314, 324, 325, 326
Noah's Ark, 296
Noble Eight-fold Path, 614
Noble Truth, 607, 612
Noble Truth of the Cause of Suffering, 612
Noble Truth of the End of Suffering, 612
Nomarchs, 137, 153
Nomes, 137, 153, 170, 269, 554, 564
non-dualism, 402
non-dualist Divinity, 362
Non-dualistic, 162, 333, 600
Non-violence, 379, 466, 554, 566, 614, 625
North Asia, 309
North East Africa . See also Egypt Ethiopia
  Cush, 34, 92
North East Africa. See also Egypt Ethiopia
  Cush, 34, 92, 257, 397
Nothingness, 117
Nrutf, 118
Nu, 320, 524, 549, 552, 617
Nubia, 10, 82, 89, 90, 102, 103, 104, 108, 115, 120, 122, 123, 125, 126, 128, 129, 131, 132, 136, 137, 138, 139, 151, 154, 156, 159, 160, 163, 186, 193, 236, 271, 281, 289, 298, 310, 367, 376, 380, 381, 389, 409, 437, 438, 563, 591, 605
Nubian, 4, 6, 7, 29, 82, 90, 102, 104, 105, 107, 108, 110, 115, 119, 120, 123, 124, 125, 126, 127, 128, 129, 130, 131, 132, 133, 135, 136, 137, 138, 140, 159, 160, 184, 185, 245, 276, 298, 301, 311, 314, 423, 424, 438, 439, 493, 626, 640
Nubian dancing girls, 119
Nubian divinity – see Dudun, Meril, Aahs, Ari Hems Nefer, 130, 131
Nubian King Taharka, 105
Nubian prisoners, 104

Nubians, 4, 6, 7, 77, 90, 102, 103, 104, 105, 107, 108, 114, 115, 119, 120, 122, 123, 124, 125, 126, 129, 136, 137, 159, 160, 212, 285, 381, 392, 397, 398, 424, 431, 605, 676
Nun, 217, 239, 321, 368, 476, 496, 527, 548, 549, 551, 552, 553, 561, 595
Nun (primeval waters-unformed matter), 217, 239, 321, 368, 476, 496, 527, 548, 549, 551, 552, 553, 561, 595
Nun (See also Nu), 217, 239, 321, 368, 476, 496, 527, 548, 549, 551, 552, 553, 561, 595
Nunet (formed matter), 553
Nut, 118, 129, 133, 134, 135, 218, 264, 269, 292, 321, 322, 476, 481, 482, 499, 510, 520, 535, 536, 541, 569, 572, 573, 576, 684
Nutrition, 27
Nyama, 192
Nysa, 89, 124, 393, 420
O, 692
Obelisk, 145
Obenga, 99, 100
Octavian, 138
Ogdoad, 553
Old Kingdom, 126, 138, 142, 145, 147, 153, 160, 175, 197, 201, 260, 274, 289, 380, 426, 427, 428, 606, 640
Old Testament, 79, 90, 184, 199, 291, 298, 300, 306, 309, 310, 311, 313, 324, 338, 339, 340, 342, 344, 351, 353, 354, 368, 369, 384, 624
Olorun, 238, 239, 240, 241, 242
Om, 371, 496, 499, 562, 594, 690, 691
One God, 353, 354, 362, 364, 367, 591
Ontology, 87, 441
Opening of the Mouth Ceremony, 179, 181
Opposites, 138, 439
Oracle, 87, 670
Oral Tradition, 187
Oriental Institute, 163
Origen, 162
Orion Star Constellation, 144, 179, 180, 595, 686
Orishas, 240, 242
Orthodox, 50, 51, 60, 90, 97, 98, 99, 101, 107, 114, 115, 138, 163, 164, 165, 166, 167, 169, 176, 187, 195, 199, 247, 248,

251, 280, 295, 296, 315, 323, 333, 334, 338, 339, 340, 341, 345, 346, 347, 359, 361, 362, 368, 369, 371, 372, 374, 376, 377, 378, 382, 383, 385, 402, 404, 406, 415, 478, 539, 579, 585, 600, 602, 627, 628
Orthodox church, 53
Orthodox Church, 53, 356, 593
Orthodox religions, 51, 187, 247, 296, 539, 579
Osiris, 52, 86, 89, 92, 118, 124, 141, 144, 145, 147, 149, 152, 153, 179, 183, 213, 221, 222, 239, 263, 264, 268, 271, 285, 286, 287, 311, 318, 323, 326, 329, 332, 337, 359, 365, 378, 384, 387, 393, 397, 409, 410, 413, 419, 420, 421, 442, 452, 455, 481, 491, 497, 499, 503, 523, 524, 527, 547, 557, 558, 559, 569, 574, 582, 583, 586, 590, 595, 596, 597, 610, 621, 627, 671, 684, 690, 691
Ottoman Empire, 55, 357
P, 118, 692
Pa Neter, 192, 194, 209, 332, 349, 352, 364, 524
pagan, 53
Pain, 205
Paleoanthropology, 426, 551, 627
Paleolithic, 34, 54, 147, 417, 439
Palermo Stone, 147, 163, 169, 403
Palestine, 52, 96, 97, 156, 159, 268, 270, 271, 285, 290, 296, 297, 298, 299, 300, 302, 303, 304, 305, 306, 307, 311, 324, 338, 341, 343, 359, 364, 376, 379, 385, 397
Palestinians, 300, 340, 341, 342, 359
panentheism, 362
Panentheism, 366, 590
Panentheistic, 590
Pantheism, 187, 366, 368, 590
Papyrus Greenfield, 492
Papyrus of Any, 141, 213, 262
Papyrus of Nesi Amsu, 525
Papyrus of Nesi-Khensu, 670
Papyrus of Turin, 163, 169, 173, 403
Papyrus Qenna, 492
Paraclete, 332
Paramahamsa Ramakrishna, 32
Parapsychology, 65, 247, 248
Parvati, 478, 499, 510, 524
Passion, 183

Patanjali, 447, 451, 459, 465, 466, 467, 494, 499, 601, 615, 640, 670, 671
Patience, 378
Paul, 55, 203, 324, 334, 343, 494, 574
Paul, St., 334
Paut, 128, 475
Pautti, 318, 319, 320, 321, 322
Peace (see also Hetep), 27, 118, 212, 318, 346, 350, 517
Pentateuch, 302, 365, 590
Pepi II, 139, 141, 153
Per-aah, 116, 117, 147, 153, 154, 410, 521
Per-Aah, 153, 175
Peristyle Hall, 133
Persia, 124, 156, 161, 199, 267, 269, 285, 296, 308, 309, 329, 354, 356, 378, 423, 426, 441, 536, 605, 621, 622, 627
Persian Gulf, 97, 296, 298, 325, 496
Persians, 95, 140, 153, 156, 161, 306, 391, 397, 412, 441, 605
Pert Em Heru, See also Book of the Dead, 318, 455, 543, 609, 670, 685
Pert em Hru, 609
Petrie, Flinders, 101, 108, 110, 165, 166, 183, 184, 442, 443, 627, 669, 670
phallus, 244, 517
Pharaonic headdress, 168, 177, 486
Pharisees, 306, 349, 351
Phenotype, 77
Philae, 53, 92, 130, 152, 328, 464, 557, 684
Philo of Alexandria, 378
Philosophy, 1, 9, 27, 29, 33, 38, 47, 56, 57, 61, 62, 76, 81, 85, 87, 88, 90, 117, 118, 138, 194, 203, 206, 208, 211, 213, 253, 254, 263, 268, 281, 312, 323, 337, 382, 386, 419, 439, 442, 444, 450, 454, 455, 456, 457, 458, 459, 462, 464, 480, 485, 487, 493, 494, 496, 498, 499, 527, 530, 531, 540, 556, 557, 559, 560, 565, 566, 571, 572, 574, 575, 576, 578, 579, 585, 586, 590, 591, 593, 596, 597, 600, 607, 611, 612, 614, 615, 624, 627, 634, 635, 669, 671, 675, 676, 679, 681, 685, 688
Philosophy of, 117
Phoenicia, 268, 290, 310, 384, 422
Phoenix, 264

Phut, 324
Physical Plane, 542
Pigmy, 132
Pillar of Asar, 316, 317, 378
Pillar of Osiris, 378
Plato, 44, 53, 80, 81, 112, 256, 257, 258, 263, 265, 267, 276, 289, 334, 392, 393, 449, 640, 688
Plutarch, 80, 87, 112, 263, 393, 449, 558, 560, 582, 583, 586, 670, 688
Poland, 315
Pole Star, 170, 179
Polytheism, 368
Poverty, 378
Prajapati, 504
Prana (also see Sekhem and Life Force), 488, 496
Pre-Dynastic Age, 569
Priests and Priestesses, 29, 53, 122, 142, 147, 153, 158, 159, 160, 182, 202, 215, 269, 336, 377, 385, 399, 400, 465, 605, 615, 627, 679
Primeval Hill, 549, 553
Primeval ocean, 618
Primeval Ocean, 319, 368, 501, 510, 518, 524, 525, 527, 548, 561, 596, 598
Primeval Waters, 81, 319, 496, 530
promised land, 296
Protestant, 335, 344, 345, 346
Protestantism, 335, 346
Protestants, 345
Psalms, 298, 299, 309
Psychology, 42, 676
Psycho-Mythology, 46, 47
Psycho-spiritual consciousness, 492
Ptah, 81, 92, 131, 132, 138, 141, 147, 149, 150, 152, 156, 158, 160, 173, 194, 195, 210, 213, 217, 219, 244, 264, 287, 311, 317, 318, 332, 363, 368, 369, 428, 430, 439, 488, 504, 524, 532, 534, 548, 549, 550, 551, 553, 554, 555, 575, 586, 600, 603, 612, 618, 624, 686
PTAH, 195, 551, 686
Ptahotep, 138, 141, 153, 197, 213, 439, 614
Ptah-Seker-Asar – see, 131, 132
Ptah-Sokkar, 612
Ptolemaic period, 430, 438, 603
Ptolemy II, 169, 430, 604, 640
Ptolemy, Greek ruler, 138, 161, 169, 176, 257, 278, 430, 438, 603, 604, 640

Puerto Rico, 27, 188, 189
Punt, 100, 139, 140, 156
Purana, 552
Puranas, 404, 415, 416, 551, 602
Pure consciousness, 332, 457
Purusha, 499, 525
Pyramid, 92, 127, 129, 138, 141, 145, 148, 152, 153, 163, 164, 170, 179, 180, 184, 201, 202, 275, 277, 332, 407, 427, 428, 439, 497, 534, 535, 550, 551, 591, 609, 670, 671
Pyramid of Unas, 141
Pyramid texts, 148, 202, 277, 670
Pyramid Texts, 92, 129, 138, 141, 142, 152, 153, 179, 275, 332, 439, 534, 535, 550, 551, 609, 670
Pyramidiot, 97
Pyramids, 109, 112, 114, 142, 144, 145, 180, 363, 380, 406, 408, 412, 441, 497, 605, 671
Pyramids at Giza, 144
Pythagoras, 80, 81, 112, 263, 276, 392, 393, 410, 449, 640, 688
Qadesh, 260, 261, 287, 289, 293
Qamit, 123
Quantum physicists, 248
Quantum Physics, 65, 66
Queen of Sheba, 313
queen of the Gods, 369
Queen Ti, 156
R, 692
Ra, 79, 81, 92, 128, 129, 130, 132, 138, 141, 147, 148, 149, 152, 153, 156, 158, 169, 171, 173, 175, 176, 182, 194, 195, 210, 213, 217, 218, 220, 225, 233, 234, 239, 251, 258, 261, 264, 269, 287, 293, 302, 318, 319, 320, 321, 322, 332, 352, 363, 365, 368, 369, 371, 413, 433, 439, 452, 453, 464, 466, 476, 486, 487, 488, 496, 497, 498, 499, 501, 504, 507, 524, 525, 527, 528, 529, 532, 534, 535, 536, 537, 538, 539, 541, 542, 543, 545, 546, 547, 548, 549, 550, 552, 556, 561, 563, 565, 569, 572, 573, 575, 578, 586, 588, 589, 590, 593, 595, 596, 598, 600, 601, 615, 623, 624, 683, 689, 691
Race, 76, 108, 110, 183, 258, 385, 392, 400, 669
racism, 341
Racism, 77, 385, 390, 417
Radha, 57, 448, 498

Rahab, 325
Ra-Harakti, 149
Raja Yoga, 575, 598, 640, 671
Raja Yoga Sutras, 575, 598, 640, 671
Rajaram, N. S., 400, 401, 402, 403, 404, 405, 406, 409, 410, 413, 414, 416, 442
Ram, 128, 179
Rama, 84, 332, 440, 532, 537, 547, 557, 560, 566, 585, 632, 633
Ramadan, 362
Ramakrishna, 32, 446, 449
Rama-Raja, 566
Ramases, 108, 368
Ramayana, 43, 84, 87, 309, 397, 439, 440, 516, 548, 551, 557, 566, 585, 597, 640, 673
Rameses II, 7, 95, 96, 101, 104, 105, 140, 159, 268, 423
Ramesside Period, see also Ramases, 158
Ramses, 323
Rastafarian, 312, 313, 314
Rastafarianism, 310, 311, 312, 313, 314
Rastau, 144, 314
Rau Nu Prt M Hru, see also Book of the Dead, 140
Rauch, 79, 368
Ray, Sudhansu Kumar, 387, 497, 563, 597
Reality, 10, 36, 111, 250, 332, 457, 480
Realization, 594, 608, 612
Realm of Light, 138, 439
Red, 6, 89, 117, 124, 161, 271, 299, 367, 384, 393, 420, 438
Red Sea, 89, 124, 161, 367, 384, 393, 420
Reflecting, 460
Reflection, 117, 191, 284, 461
reincarnation, 85, 329, 332, 622
Reincarnation, 572, 573, 574, 612, 627, 630
Relationships, 676
Relegare, 279
Religion, 1, 9, 27, 29, 31, 32, 33, 35, 36, 38, 39, 47, 48, 50, 51, 52, 57, 84, 87, 88, 90, 141, 144, 149, 153, 185, 186, 188, 191, 192, 194, 195, 198, 209, 213, 226, 227, 232, 236, 237, 244, 247, 250, 251, 253, 254, 268, 269, 277, 279, 280, 284, 287, 291, 292, 301, 303, 312, 314, 318, 326, 332, 337, 344, 346, 351, 352, 358, 360, 361,
364, 370, 377, 382, 385, 386, 425, 429, 455, 461, 532, 540, 543, 548, 575, 576, 586, 591, 599, 600, 602, 608, 612, 621, 626, 629, 635, 671, 675, 676, 684, 687, 688, 690
Ren, 503, 669, 672
Renaissance, 109, 355, 532, 602, 629
Rennenet, 569
Renunciation, 279, 304, 354, 378, 594
Repentance, 378
resurrection, 456, 573
Resurrection, 41, 74, 138, 141, 149, 213, 290, 344, 410, 439, 452, 475, 503, 516, 552, 569, 573, 595, 596, 598, 610, 612, 672, 683, 684, 686, 687
Revival Movement, 344
Rhodesia, 185
Rig Veda, 395, 401, 403, 404, 405, 415, 416, 429, 448, 510, 534, 538, 540, 565, 574, 579, 580, 585, 671
Right action, 519
Right Action, 614
Right Effort, 614
Right Livelihood, 614
Right Meditation, 614
Right Mindfulness, 614
Right Speech, 614
Right Thought, 614
Right Understanding, 614
Righteous action, 210
Righteous Action, 672
Righteousness, 323, 430, 462, 516, 604, 672
Rik, 84
Rites of Passage, 196, 197, 198
Ritual, 38, 47, 49, 50, 61, 71, 73, 191, 210, 213, 274, 279, 284, 347, 445, 463
Ritualism, 283
Rituals, 38, 42, 47, 76, 162, 191, 196, 350, 368, 369, 378, 686
River Valley, 276, 388
Roman, 32, 53, 55, 69, 80, 82, 83, 114, 115, 124, 137, 138, 140, 141, 153, 162, 189, 213, 235, 257, 299, 302, 306, 307, 311, 323, 329, 333, 334, 335, 343, 344, 347, 355, 356, 374, 378, 391, 413, 423, 431, 435, 439, 497, 576, 594, 599, 600, 621, 640
Roman Catholic, 53, 189, 333, 334, 344, 347, 356, 374, 576, 640
Roman Emperor Justinian, 53
Roman empire, 356
Roman Empire, 53, 55, 82, 140, 257, 299, 306, 333, 343, 344, 355, 356, 413, 423
Romans, 82, 83, 115, 140, 153, 162, 179, 262, 299, 307, 323, 356, 391, 399, 412
Rome, 34, 53, 82, 138, 162, 232, 324, 329, 332, 333, 337, 343, 347, 355, 356, 372, 378, 380, 390, 420, 431, 576, 600, 621, 640, 688
Rtji, 7, 89, 104
S, 624, 692
Saa (spiritual understanding faculty), 561, 569, 595
Sa-Asar, 559, 570
Sacred Cow, 499, 510, 522, 630
Sacred Tree, 70
Sadducees, 306
Sages, 40, 45, 49, 65, 81, 179, 200, 248, 283, 302, 309, 332, 394, 431, 447, 457, 560, 561, 579, 589, 612, 614, 671, 681, 684, 685, 688
Sahara, 235, 249, 422
Sahu, 179, 496
Sainthood, 66
Saints, 45, 248, 364, 394, 450, 612, 685
Sais, 80, 81, 92, 152, 160, 161, 184, 257, 263, 265, 449, 640, 688
Sakkara, 92, 138, 140, 144, 145, 152, 275, 407, 408, 426, 427, 428, 439, 551, 555, 604, 606
Sakshin, 195, 624
Salvation, 201, 283, 444, 456, 612
Salvation . See also resurrection, 283, 444, 456
Salvation, See also resurrection, 201, 283, 444, 456, 612
Samadhi (see also
Kia, Satori), 580
KiaSatori), 580
Samkhya, 62, 439, 457, 496, 499, 580, 581, 587, 597, 602
Samnyasa, 85
Sanjna, 537
Sanskrit, 40, 86, 87, 93, 390, 397, 400, 402, 415, 429, 430, 442, 446, 447, 448, 449, 450, 454, 494, 498, 510, 540, 585, 603, 627, 638, 669, 670, 671
Sanyasa, 601
Saraswati, 195, 389, 403, 404, 516, 557, 558, 631

THE AFRICAN ORIGINS OF CIVILIZATION, RELIGION AND YOGA SPIRITUALITY

Saraswati - Kali - Lakshmi, 195
Sargon I, 79, 96
Satan, 199
Sat-Chit-Ananda, 457
Savitri, 534, 538, 539, 540, 542, 596, 669
Savitri or Savitar (also see Surya), 534, 538, 539, 540, 542, 596, 669
Schwaller de Lubicz, 98, 167, 170, 173, 175, 176, 184, 671
Schwaller de Lubicz, R.A., 57, 448
Scientific Method, 64, 65, 66, 87
Sebai, 27, 223, 413
Second Intermediate Period, 138, 155, 605
Secularism, 249, 250
See also Egyptian Yoga, 11, 27, 319, 448, 449, 452, 454, 637
seer-seen-sight, 195
Sefer Yezirah, 317, 318
Sefirotic Tree of Life, 316, 318
Sekhem, 192, 198, 210, 291, 382, 454, 485, 488, 536, 640
Sekhemit, 260, 261, 289, 293
Sekhmet, 138, 195, 261, 439, 508, 509, 548, 550, 595
Self (see Ba, soul, Spirit, Universal, Ba, Neter, Heru)., 29, 38, 51, 56, 66, 80, 84, 93, 118, 142, 181, 191, 192, 200, 201, 208, 210, 225, 284, 308, 314, 315, 316, 318, 322, 326, 332, 333, 362, 371, 398, 425, 445, 446, 454, 455, 456, 457, 458, 460, 461, 462, 475, 480, 481, 496, 499, 505, 513, 518, 519, 525, 526, 527, 530, 541, 542, 543, 548, 550, 552, 555, 558, 560, 561, 570, 573, 575, 578, 580, 581, 583, 585, 587, 589, 592, 593, 594, 596, 597, 608, 610, 611, 612, 624, 627, 680, 682, 684
Self (seeBasoulSpiritUniversal BaNeterHorus)., 29, 51, 80, 84, 93, 118, 142, 181, 191, 192, 208, 210, 284, 308, 332, 333, 362, 445, 446, 454, 455, 456, 457, 458, 460, 461, 462, 475, 480, 496, 499, 505, 513, 518, 525, 526, 527, 530, 541, 542, 543, 548, 552, 555, 558, 560, 561, 570, 573, 575, 578, 580, 583, 585, 587, 589, 593, 594, 596, 597, 608, 610, 611, 612, 624, 627
Self control, 458
Selfless service, 208

Sema, 8, 27, 90, 93, 191, 209, 210, 248, 394, 442, 454, 455, 456, 475, 479, 493, 498, 499, 548, 583, 584, 634, 669, 674, 675, 692
Sema XE "Sema" Paut, see also Egyptian Yoga, 27, 210, 475, 479
Sema Tawi, 27, 93, 191, 583, 584
Semite, 110
Semitic, 96, 102, 270, 298, 304, 307, 308, 310, 325, 346, 384, 397, 400, 496
Senegal, 40, 185, 195, 236
Senses, 566
Senusert I, 115, 126, 154, 268, 271, 410, 421, 439, 441
Septuagint, 199
Serapis, 329, 621
Serpent, 98, 99, 167, 168, 184, 198, 233, 260, 316, 317, 378, 382, 391, 395, 419, 441, 445, 451, 452, 453, 464, 466, 485, 486, 487, 489, 490, 491, 494, 499, 501, 504, 507, 536, 548, 618, 623, 671, 672
Serpent in the Sky, 98, 99, 184, 233, 441, 671
Serpent Power, 198, 233, 260, 316, 317, 378, 382, 395, 445, 451, 452, 453, 464, 466, 485, 486, 487, 489, 490, 491, 494, 504, 623, 672
Serpent Power (see also Kundalini and Buto), 198, 233, 260, 316, 317, 378, 382, 395, 445, 451, 452, 453, 464, 466, 485, 486, 487, 489, 490, 491, 494, 504, 623, 672
Serpent Power see also Kundalini Yoga, 198, 233, 260, 316, 317, 378, 382, 395, 445, 451, 452, 453, 464, 466, 485, 486, 487, 489, 490, 491, 494, 504, 623, 672
Set, 93, 158, 173, 179, 198, 199, 209, 218, 225, 239, 243, 264, 286, 288, 317, 321, 322, 326, 331, 413, 454, 455, 499, 513, 516, 535, 538, 582, 583, 596, 612
Seti I, 158, 159, 267, 462, 464, 465
Seven, 156, 179, 268, 309, 499, 537, 541
Sex, 108, 110, 385, 478, 554, 566, 614, 684
Sex-Sublimation, 554, 566, 614
Sexuality, 183, 399, 482, 614
Sex XE "Sex" -Yoga, 478

Shabaka, 110, 126, 160, 237, 548, 551, 553, 554, 555, 640
Shabaka XE "Shabaka" Inscription, 160
Shabaka Inscription, 551, 553, 554, 555
Shabaka Stone, 237, 548, 553
Shabaka Stone, (Shabaka Inscription), 237, 548, 553
Shai, 569, 573
Shai XE "Shai" , Rennenet and Meskhent, 573
Shakti (see also Kundalini), 291, 482, 487, 499, 510, 524, 627
Shankaracarya, 402
Sheba, 310, 313
Shekina, 291
Shem, 102, 300, 324, 325
Shemsu Hor, 141, 153
Shen, 148, 292
Sheps, 193
Sheshonq, 159
Shetaut Neter, 31, 90, 166, 186, 191, 196, 209, 212, 213, 217, 224, 232, 237, 247, 283, 303, 377, 445, 684
Shetaut Neter See also Egyptian Religion, 31, 90, 166, 186, 191, 196, 209, 212, 213, 217, 224, 232, 237, 247, 283, 303, 377, 445, 684
Shiva, 195, 283, 332, 433, 434, 453, 482, 483, 499, 504, 507, 510, 517, 519, 521, 523, 524, 528, 537, 538, 546, 547, 552, 586, 627, 629
Shiva XE "Shiva" and Shakti, 482
Shu, 547, 586
Shu (air and space), 129, 173, 218, 269, 321, 322, 476, 499, 535, 536, 545, 547, 569, 586, 595
Shunya, 117, 118
Sikhism, 379, 382, 385, 627
Sin, 198, 199, 347
Sirius, 138, 170, 171, 180, 232, 326, 439, 686
Sivananda Radha, Swami, 11, 57, 448, 479
Sivananda, Swami, 11, 57, 448, 479, 671
Sky, 98, 99, 138, 141, 149, 167, 168, 184, 233, 242, 243, 269, 391, 439, 441, 534, 671
Slave Trade, 186, 344
Slavery, 380
Sma, 210, 454, 455, 496, 498, 548

Smai, 27, 90, 93, 191, 209, 394, 445, 454, 455, 456, 475, 498, 597
Smai Tawi, 445, 454, 475, 597
Snake, 294, 640
Snake (also see serpent), 294, 640
Society, 153, 197, 253, 426, 443, 530, 627, 669, 670
Socrates, 81, 450, 640
Solon, 80, 256, 257, 258, 263, 392, 449, 688
Somaliland, 100
son of God, 323
Sons of Light, 595
Soul, 27, 90, 148, 326, 363, 413, 424, 456, 457, 458, 502, 558, 569, 583, 588, 595, 610, 612
South India, 231, 424, 434, 435, 438, 636
South West Asia, 296
Southeast Asia, 298
Spain, 109, 189, 350, 354, 355, 356
Sphinx, 34, 94, 109, 125, 137, 138, 144, 145, 147, 156, 163, 164, 167, 168, 169, 173, 174, 175, 176, 177, 178, 266, 268, 273, 275, 281, 288, 327, 363, 406, 408, 409, 410, 439, 485, 486, 544, 640, 672
Sphinx, Winged, 266, 273
Spinal twist, 476
Spirit, 79, 117, 138, 156, 169, 176, 178, 191, 192, 198, 201, 206, 208, 209, 217, 234, 281, 291, 316, 320, 332, 333, 353, 367, 371, 383, 424, 425, 433, 439, 456, 464, 466, 482, 492, 499, 505, 507, 510, 517, 519, 525, 532, 541, 548, 550, 551, 555, 589, 591, 594, 596, 600
Spiritual discipline, 679
Spiritual Eyes, 506
spiritual sensitivity, 583
Sri Lanka, 390, 416, 441
Sri Yantra, 529
St. Augustine, 334
State of Israel, 341
Stele of Niptah, 106, 260
Stele of Niptah, Minoan, 106, 260
Stellar Symbolism, 170
Step Pyramid, 138, 140, 144, 407, 426, 427, 428
Stephanus of Byzantium, 124
Stone Age, 34
Story of Sinuhe, 290
Storytelling, 191

Strabo, 112, 271, 302, 393
Study, 32, 33, 35, 48, 99, 210, 251, 391, 519
Sublimation, 322, 466, 554, 566, 580, 614, 684
Subrahmania, 432, 433, 434
Sudan, 82, 92, 102, 120, 121, 123, 139, 151, 185, 234, 235, 237, 298, 375, 432
Suffering, 198, 554, 607, 612
Sufi, 377, 378, 597
Sufi, see also Sufism, 377, 378, 597
Sufism, 246, 283, 361, 374, 377, 378
Sufism, see also Sufi, 246, 283, 361, 374, 377, 378
Sumer, 34, 54, 59, 97, 167, 268, 269, 270, 276, 277, 290, 296, 324, 391, 394, 406, 408, 442, 454
Sumeria, 268, 270, 277, 416
Sumerian, 54, 74, 268, 269, 270, 271, 277, 290, 291, 292, 294, 324, 388, 391, 406, 419
Sumerian religion, 268
Sun, 52, 79, 145, 147, 171, 367, 495, 499, 504, 506, 525, 536, 538, 539, 540, 547, 589, 624
Sun XE "Sun" and Moon, 171, 495, 506
Sun Gods, 538
Sundisk, 149, 156, 274, 464, 466, 476, 483, 507, 529, 536, 537
Supreme being, 337
Supreme Being, 35, 36, 37, 40, 48, 51, 65, 66, 144, 148, 149, 158, 169, 187, 188, 192, 193, 194, 196, 199, 200, 201, 206, 208, 209, 211, 214, 215, 217, 218, 219, 220, 221, 222, 223, 228, 237, 241, 242, 243, 244, 248, 251, 269, 281, 283, 293, 302, 309, 318, 319, 320, 326, 332, 333, 335, 349, 351, 352, 353, 360, 362, 364, 367, 368, 369, 371, 379, 398, 413, 445, 457, 482, 496, 499, 501, 524, 527, 528, 537, 542, 543, 546, 552, 557, 561, 565, 579, 587, 588, 589, 593, 598, 601, 625, 676, 681, 686
Supreme Divinity, 130, 240, 241, 267, 287, 332, 368, 369, 498, 524, 573, 575, 586
surrender, 349
Surya, 496, 531, 534, 536, 537, 538, 539, 540, 546, 547
Sushumna, 488, 489
Svetasvatara Upanishad, 555

Swami, 11, 57, 87, 183, 399, 448, 450, 479, 494, 530, 596, 597, 598, 670, 671, 672, 673
Swami Jyotirmayananda, 87, 183, 399, 450, 494, 530, 596, 597, 598, 669, 670, 671, 672, 673
Swastika, 329, 622
Syria, 82, 126, 140, 156, 161, 268, 271, 274, 285, 288, 289, 300, 302, 303, 317, 367, 397, 430, 431, 435, 441, 591, 604, 621, 627
Ta Seti, 126, 163
Taharka, 127, 160
Talmud, 310
Ta-meri, 497
Tamil, 433, 441
Tantra, 402, 478, 480, 670, 684
Tantra Yoga, 478, 480, 494, 670, 684
Tantric Yoga, 395, 445
Tanzania, 120, 234, 432
Tao, 87, 192, 194, 332, 600, 640, 672
Tao Te Ching, 672
Taoism, 187, 192, 246, 247, 283, 454, 565, 605, 610, 640, 678
Taoist, 332
Ta-Seti, 115
Tau Cross, 329, 621
Tawi, 27, 90, 93, 131, 191, 209, 394, 454
Teacher of Righteousness, 323
Tefnut, 129, 218, 269, 321, 322, 535, 536, 547, 569, 586
Tefnut (moisture), 129, 218, 269, 321, 322, 535, 536, 547, 569, 586
Tehorn, 79
Tekhenu, 145
Tem, 79, 132, 302, 319, 320, 322, 352, 501, 525, 528, 546, 547, 548, 549, 552, 586, 595
Temple of Aset, 27, 133, 191, 222, 253, 328, 460, 461, 464, 560, 582
Temple of Delphi, 81, 256
Temu, 79, 239, 549, 595
Ten Commandments, 79, 80, 302, 304, 336, 350
Thales, 80, 81, 161, 162, 263, 276, 392, 412, 449, 688
Thamte, 79
the , Dionysius Aropagite, 334
The Absolute, 195, 457, 535, 681
The All, 528, 546, 596
The Bhagavad Gita, 672

The Black, 111, 183, 374, 499, 511, 522
The Demigods, 169
The Egyptian Book of Coming forth by Day, 362, 587
The Egyptian Book of Coming Forth By Day, 363, 369, 578, 587, 593
The Enlightened One, 85
The God, 128, 138, 149, 169, 194, 204, 218, 221, 234, 285, 349, 351, 352, 364, 373, 419, 432, 434, 439, 452, 504, 505, 507, 508, 510, 516, 522, 523, 524, 537, 542, 557, 596, 672, 683
The Gods, 138, 169, 194, 218, 234, 285, 364, 432, 439, 504, 523, 596, 672, 683
The Hero of A Thousand Faces, 74
The Hymns of Amun, 672
The Illiad and The Odyssey, 82
The Itinerarium Alexandri, 124, 423
The Pyramid Texts, 129, 141
The Self, 319, 333, 457, 525, 526, 578, 593, 624
The Spirits of the Dead, 169
The Unmoved Mover, 81
The way, 607, 612
The Word, 609
The WORD, 301, 326
The Yoga Vasistha, 585
Theban Theology, 138, 149, 213, 439, 532, 549
Thebes, 81, 92, 139, 152, 153, 156, 157, 158, 159, 160, 161, 258, 318, 332, 423, 428, 464, 497, 549, 624, 640, 681, 683
Themis, 48, 79, 80, 263, 264, 265
Theodosius, 53, 324, 640
Theory of the Forms, 81
Third Intermediate Period, 159
Thoth, 153, 233, 264, 497, 567
Thoughts (see also Mind), 462
Thrice Greatest Hermes, 672
Tiamat, 79
Tigris river, 298
Time, 98, 180, 195, 227, 410, 412, 672
Timeline, 474, 532, 602, 629
Tithonus, 82
Tobacco, 247
Togo, 249
Tomb, 7, 101, 103, 104, 107, 258, 423, 464, 465, 466, 475, 510, 683, 691
Tomb of Huy, 107

Tomb of Seti I, 7, 103, 104, 464, 465, 466, 510, 683, 691
Tombs of the Nobles, 105, 235
Torah, 302, 308, 315, 354, 369
Traders, 235
Tradition, 61, 71, 76, 84, 85, 87, 187, 210, 217, 218, 219, 220, 221, 222, 223, 237, 284, 362, 532, 536, 547, 555, 560, 592, 627
Transcendental Self, 142, 333, 460
Tree, 58, 70, 315, 316, 317, 320, 322, 370, 478, 520, 533, 589
Tree of Life, 315, 316, 317, 320, 322, 370, 589
Triad, 195, 549, 557, 575, 600, 681
Trilinga, 483, 499
Trinity, 52, 81, 92, 138, 147, 149, 152, 194, 195, 219, 220, 222, 244, 302, 312, 319, 332, 333, 335, 353, 354, 369, 439, 501, 524, 528, 532, 534, 536, 546, 547, 548, 550, 557, 575, 589, 600, 601, 629, 681, 684, 691
True happiness, 568
Trust in God, 378
Truth, 32, 36, 44, 90, 172, 211, 308, 309, 359, 360, 516, 540, 554, 566, 567, 612, 614
Turin Papyrus, 147, 169, 173, 670, 672
Turkey, 303, 354, 355, 442
Tutankhamon, 233
Tutankhamun, 107, 158, 176, 233, 530, 640
Tutankhamun, Pharaoh, 107, 158, 176, 233, 530, 640
Tutu, Desmond (Archbishop), 203
Ubuntu, 55, 115, 203, 207, 676
Uganda, 108, 120, 121, 122, 124, 183, 185, 186, 193, 234, 244, 298, 432
Unas, 141, 640
Understanding, 47, 199, 322, 554, 573, 607, 614
Unesco, 99
union, 90, 142, 455
union with GOD, 378
Union with the Divine, 284, 629
United States of America, 110, 310, 335, 337, 347, 374, 375, 380, 382, 435
Universal Ba, 499
Universal Consciousness, 684
universal love, 200
Unmoved Mover, 81

Upanishad, Svetasvatara, 555
Upanishads, 84, 85, 87, 365, 390, 394, 402, 439, 447, 457, 496, 499, 506, 530, 540, 551, 552, 555, 560, 565, 574, 578, 579, 585, 586, 590, 593, 597, 601, 612, 630, 672, 685
Upper Egypt, 53, 115, 147, 153, 158, 159, 454, 455, 502, 563
Ur, 82, 218, 269, 270, 271, 296, 321, 325, 513, 536, 569
Uraeus, 378, 445, 452, 453
Usage, 42
Vaishnava, 84, 548
Vandals, 354, 355
Varuna, 309, 397, 499, 534, 536, 537, 538, 539, 540, 542, 546, 585, 596
Vedanta, 84, 87, 187, 246, 283, 284, 365, 377, 390, 398, 402, 420, 441, 450, 457, 458, 460, 464, 496, 499, 536, 560, 578, 579, 585, 586, 589, 590, 593, 602, 610, 624, 630
Vedantic, 585
Vedantic. See also Vedanta, 85, 194, 332, 402, 458, 548, 557, 560, 580, 585, 587, 593, 600, 615
Vedas, 32, 44, 84, 85, 87, 277, 316, 390, 393, 394, 395, 397, 401, 402, 403, 405, 406, 407, 446, 447, 449, 457, 510, 534, 546, 566, 579, 580, 594, 612
Vedic, 29, 67, 84, 85, 87, 234, 304, 309, 316, 329, 388, 390, 395, 397, 398, 400, 401, 402, 403, 404, 405, 414, 415, 416, 418, 424, 426, 429, 433, 439, 440, 441, 442, 446, 447, 504, 510, 514, 520, 523, 528, 532, 533, 534, 536, 537, 538, 540, 541, 542, 546, 547, 548, 563, 567, 579, 580, 585, 586, 602, 622, 671, 673, 680
Vedic Aryan, 309
Vedic hymns, 400, 405, 439
Vedic period, 401, 402, 405, 426, 536, 546, 547
Vegetarianism, 580, 582
Veil, 499, 560, 630
Veil of Aset, 560
Veil XE "Veil" of Isis, 499
Veil of Isis (See also Veil of Maya), 499
Veil of Maya, 499, 560
Veil of Maya (see also Maya, Veil of Isis), 499, 560

THE AFRICAN ORIGINS OF CIVILIZATION, RELIGION AND YOGA SPIRITUALITY

Veil XE "Veil" of Maya XE "Veil of Maya (see also Maya, Veil of Isis)" XE "Maya" ., 499
Vesica Piscis, 370
Vessel of the Fish, 370
Vesta, 80, 263
Vikings, 354, 355
Virgil, 82, 83, 87, 439, 672
Virgin Birth, 499
Virgin Mary, 324, 352, 373, 374
Vishnu, 84, 117, 195, 199, 283, 309, 332, 397, 415, 499, 501, 503, 511, 518, 522, 524, 527, 528, 534, 537, 546, 547, 548, 551, 552, 566, 585, 586, 591, 627, 629
Visigoths, 354, 355
Visvakarma, 534, 537
Volney, Count, 108, 183
Voodoo, 190, 202
Vyasa (Indian Sage), 640
Waddel, W. G., 96, 183, 671
Waset, 92, 152, 154, 156, 158, 159, 183, 184, 210, 217, 318, 332, 371, 441, 464, 490, 549, 624, 681
Water, 269, 442, 466, 595
West Africa, 109, 124, 185, 202, 231, 232, 233, 235, 236, 238, 246, 605
West Indies, 189
West, John Anthony, 97, 98, 99, 167, 168, 183, 184, 385, 391, 441, 442, 671, 672, 673
Western civilization, 45, 80, 94, 111, 114, 347
Western Culture, 44, 55, 64, 66, 94, 114, 143, 187, 188, 203, 225, 244, 248, 334, 355, 362, 381, 383, 392, 394, 435, 454, 478, 580
Western religions, 187, 192, 195, 199, 200, 203, 247, 251, 291, 293, 306, 337, 345, 362, 364, 374, 574
Wheel of the Law, 607
Whirling Dervishes, 378
Whirling Dervishes (see also ! Kung of Africa), 378
!Kung of Afrika), 378
White, 117, 121, 183, 298, 300, 563, 564, 672
White Nile, 121, 298
Will, 350, 354, 568
Williams, Chancellor, 11, 99, 183, 669
Wisdom, 87, 138, 140, 141, 153, 154, 204, 208, 210, 211, 213, 284, 290, 302, 317, 381, 394, 439, 445, 460, 461, 462, 464, 494, 516, 535, 557, 573, 581, 592, 594, 596, 614, 671, 672, 681, 683
Wisdom (also see Djehuti), 87, 138, 140, 141, 153, 154, 213, 284, 302, 439, 445, 460, 461, 464, 494, 516, 535, 557, 573, 581, 592, 594, 596, 614, 671, 672
Wisdom (also see Djehuti, Aset), 87, 138, 140, 141, 153, 154, 204, 208, 210, 211, 213, 284, 290, 302, 317, 381, 394, 439, 445, 460, 461, 462, 464, 494, 516, 535, 557, 573, 581, 592, 594, 596, 614, 671, 672, 681, 683
Wisdom teachings, 284, 302, 460, 461
Witness, 420
Wolof, 40, 236, 238, 239
Word, Living, 594
Word, the, 594
Words of power, 464, 466
World Ba, 337
Yahweh, 285, 287, 308, 332, 337, 353, 364, 365, 368, 369, 370, 590
Yama, 567
Yamas and Nyamas (See Yoga of Righteous Action and Maat Philosophy, 615
Yantra, 529, 537
Yao, 234, 432
Yellow, 117, 276, 510
Yoga, 1, 8, 9, 11, 27, 29, 47, 51, 53, 62, 65, 67, 84, 85, 86, 87, 88, 90, 93, 133, 172, 183, 191, 192, 195, 233, 246, 253, 276, 278, 279, 283, 284, 309, 316, 317, 319, 332, 345, 369, 377, 378, 379, 386, 387, 390, 394, 395, 396, 397, 402, 419, 420, 429, 435, 440, 441, 442, 444, 445, 446, 447, 448, 449, 450, 451, 452, 454, 455, 456, 457, 458, 459, 460, 461, 462, 463, 464, 466, 467, 475, 478, 479, 480, 485, 488, 491, 493, 494, 498, 499, 504, 510, 530, 537, 543, 557, 560, 561, 568, 574, 575, 579, 580, 581, 583, 584, 585, 589, 592, 593, 594, 596, 597, 598, 601, 602, 610, 615, 625, 627, 629, 630, 632, 633, 634, 635, 636, 669, 670, 671, 672, 673, 675, 676, 678, 679, 680, 682, 683, 685, 686, 688, 689, 690, 691, 692
Yoga Exercise, 27, 479
Yoga of Action, 446
Yoga of Devotion (see Yoga of Divine Love), 394, 445, 463
Yoga of Divine Love (see Yoga of Devotion), 446
Yoga of Meditation, 395, 445, 581
Yoga of Righteous . See also Karma Yoga, 462
Yoga of Righteous. See also Karma Yoga, 462
Yoga of Selfless Action. See also Yoga of Righteous, 395, 445
Yoga of Wisdom, 460, 594
Yoga of Wisdom (see also Jnana Yoga), 394, 445, 460, 581, 594, 596, 672
Yoga Sutra, 402, 451, 459, 466, 467, 499, 575, 598, 671
Yoga Vasistha, 309, 557, 560, 585, 593, 597, 673
Yogic, 66, 85, 206, 369, 394, 445, 447, 448, 449, 450, 451, 454, 459, 467, 475, 593, 637
Yoruba, 57, 188, 193, 198, 201, 203, 232, 236, 237, 238, 239, 240, 241, 242, 243, 244, 245, 246, 247
Yoruba Divinities, 239
Yuga, 172
Yuga (Kali, Maha, Dwarpar, Treta, Satya), 172
Yugas, 566
Zaire, 124, 165, 232, 234, 432
Zambia, 185
Zealots, 306, 307
Zeus, 81, 82, 264, 287, 591
Zimbabwe, 185, 193, 234, 432
Zion, 313, 338, 346
Zionism, 338, 341, 342, 359
Zodiac, Kamitan, 171
Zohar, 316
Zoomorphic, 630
Zoroaster, 199, 308, 337, 384, 640
Zoroastrian, 354, 365
Zoroastrian religion, 187, 354
Zoroastrian, Zoroastrianism, 96, 187, 296, 301, 308, 309, 316, 349, 354, 365
Zoroastrianism, 283, 293, 308, 309, 605, 640
Zoroastrians, 308
Zulu, 188

Bibliography

A Concise Encyclopedia of Hinduism, by Klaus K. Klostermaier
A Sanskrit-English Dictionary, Monier Williams, p. 528
A SON OF GOD: THE LIFE AND PHILOSOPHY OF AKHNATON, KING OF EGYPT, Savitri Devi, [1946]
African Presence in Early Asia edited by Ivan Van Sertima and Runoko Rashidi
Am I a Hindu?: the Hinduism Primer by Ed. Viswanathan
American Heritage Dictionary.
Ancient Architecture by S. Lloyd and H.W. Miller
Ancient Egypt the Light of the World by Gerald Massey
Ancient Egyptian Literature Volume I and II, by Miriam Lichtheim
Ancient, Medieval and Modern Christianity by Charles Guignebert
Anunian Theology by Muata Ashby
Art - Culture of India and Egypt, the author S. M El Mansouri
Arts and Crafts of Ancient Egypt, Flinders Petrie
Ashby, M. A., "Egyptian Yoga The Philosophy of Enlightenment Vol. 1, Sema Institute of Yoga-C.M. Book Publishing 1995
Atlas of Ancient Egypt, John Baines and Jaromir Malek, 1980
Atlas of Ancient Egypt, John Baines and Jaromir Malek, 1980
Barbara Adams (Petrie Museum of Egyptian Archaeology and Dr. Renée Friedman (University of California, Berkeley).
Based on the new discoveries at the city of Mehrgarh - Indus Valley
Better known as The Ancient Egyptian Book of the Dead by Dr. Muata Ashby 2000
Between the years 1960-1970
Bible Myth: The African Origins of the Jewish People Gary Greenberg
Black Athena, The Afroasiatic Origins of Classical Civilization by Martin Bernal
Black Man of The Nile and His Family by
Blackwell's book of Philosophy; Zeller's History of Philosophy; Diogenes Laertius; Kendrick's Ancient Egypt.
Buddha: the Intelligent Heart by Alistair Shearer
Cable News Network - world report
Cable News Network 1990-1991
Chanudaro Excavations, 1935-36 E.J.H. Mackay, American Oriental Society, New Heaven, 19443, pp. 25 and 220, pl. XCII, 38
Chanudaro Excavations, 1935-36 E.J.H. Mackay, American Oriental Society, New
Charles Elliot, Hinduism and Buddhism, vol. III, London, 1954, pp. 93-94
Christian and Islamic Spirituality by Maria Jaoudi
Christian Yoga by Muata Ashby for more details.
Christian Yoga: The Journey from Jesus to Christ, Muata Ashby
Civilisation ou Barbarie, Courtesy of Pr,sence Africaine. Cheikh Anta Diop's
Civilization or Barbarism by Cheikh Anta Diop
Civilizations of the Indus Valley and Beyond, Sir Mortimer Wheeler.
Comparative Mythology, Jaan Puhvel
Compton's Interactive Encyclopedia Copyright (c) 1994, 1995
Connection of Egypt with India, F.W.H. Migeod, Man, vol. 24, no. 118, London, 1924, p. 160
Dancing Wu Li Masters by Gary Zukov
Destruction of Black Civilization: Great Issues of a Race from 4500bc to 2000ad by Chancellor Williams
Diodorus Book 23
Doshi, Saryu, Editor-Indian Council for Cultural Relations India and Egypt: Influences and Interactions 1993
Dutta, P. C. 1984. Biological anthropology of Bronze Ace. Harappans: new perspectives. In The People of Soutli Asia.
Echoes of the Old Darkland by Dr. Charles Finch

THE AFRICAN ORIGINS OF CIVILIZATION, RELIGION AND YOGA SPIRITUALITY

Egypt Uncovered, Vivian Davies and Ren,e Friedman
Egypt: Child of Africa, Ivan Van Sertima 1994
Egyptian Book of Coming forth by day of Anhai
Egyptian Book of Coming forth by day of Ani
Egyptian Book of Coming forth by day of Ankhwahibre
Egyptian Book of Coming forth by day of Kenna
Egyptian Book of the Dead by Gerald Massey
Egyptian Book of the Dead by Muata Ashby
Egyptian Coffin texts
Egyptian Magic by E.W. Budge
Egyptian Pyramid Texts
Egyptian Ru Pert Em Heru, Hymns of Amun and the Papyrus of Nesi-Khensu
Egyptian Tantra Yoga by Dr. Muata Ashby.
Egyptian Yoga: Volume I by Reginald Muata Ashby
Egyptian Yoga: Volume II by Reginald Muata Ashby
Eliade, Yoga: Immortality and Freedom, Bollingen Series LVI, 2nd edn. (Princeton: Princeton University Press, 1969), PP. 370-372 ("Patanjali and the Texts of Classic Yoga").
Encarta Encyclopedia. Copyright (c) 1994
Encyclopedia of Mysticism and Mystery Religions by John Ferguson
Encyclopedic Dictionary of Yoga by Georg Feurstein
Ferdmand's Handbook to the World's Religions
Feuerstein, Georg, The Shambhala Encyclopedia of Yoga 1997
Flinders Petrie, Memphis, vol. 1, London 1909, pp. 16-17 pl. XXXIX.
From an inscription in the temple of Denderah, Egypt.
From Egypt to Greece, M. Ashby C. M. Books 1997
From Fetish to God in Ancient Egypt by E.W. Budge
From the Turin Papyrus.
Funk and Wagnals New Encyclopedia
G. Lafaye. Historie des divinit,s d'Alexandrie hors de l' Egypte. Paris, 18984, p.259
G. Maspero, The Passing of the Empires (New York, 1900).
Gods of India, p. 35. Martin
Guide to the Gods, Marjorie Leach
H. G. Rawlinson, Intercourse between India and the Western World, Cambridge, 1916, p. 92.
H.G. Rawlinson, Intercourse Between India and the Western World, Cambridge, 1916, pp. 93-94
Hatha-Yoga-Pradipika, The Shambhala Encyclopedia of Yoga by Georg Feuerstein, Ph. D.
Hermetica, Asclepius III, Solos Press ed., p. 136
Hero of a Thousand Faces by Dr. Joseph Campbell
Herodotus Book III 124; Diogenes VIII 3; Pliny N. H., 36, 9; Antipho recorded by Porphyry.
Herodotus: The Histories
Hindu Myths by Wendy O'Flaherty
History and Geography of Human Genes Luigi Luca Cavaiii-Sforza, Paolo Menozzi, Alberto Piazza. Copyright @ 1994 by Princeton University Press
HOLY BIBLE- King James Version
HOLY BIBLE- New Revised Standard Version
In Search of the Cradle of Civilization, 1995, co-authored by Georg Feuerstein, David Frawley, and Subhash Kak.
Indian Myth and Legend, Donald A. Mckenzie
Indian Mythology, Veronica Ions
Initiation Into Egyptian Yoga by Dr. Muata Ashby.
Inscription at the Delphic Oracle. From Plutarch, Morals, Familiar Quotations, John Bartlett
Integral Yoga by Swami Jyotirmayananda
International Society for Krishna Consciousness
J. H. Breasted: Cambridge Ancient History (Edit. 1924), Vol. II, p. 120.
J. R. Lukacs, ed., pp. 59-75. New York: Plenum.
J.C.Harke, "The Indian Terracottas from Ancient Memphis: Are they really Indian?, Dr. Debala Mitra Volume, Delhi, 1991, pp. 55-61
Jnana Yoga by Swami Jyotirmayananda
John Marshal, Taxila, vols, II and III, London and New York, 1951, p. 605, pl. 186(e)

K. G. Krishnan, Uttankita Sanskrit Vidya Arangnya Epigraphs, vol. II, Mysore, 1989, pp 42 ff
Kosambi, D. D., Ancient India a History of its Culture and Civilisation, 1965.
Krishnan, op. cit., pp. 17-18
Kundalini by Gopi Krishna
Legends of the Egyptian Gods by E. Wallis Budge
Life in Ancient Egypt by Adolf Erman
Living Yoga, Georg Feuerstein, Stephan Bodian, with the staff of Yoga Journal
Love Lyrics of Ancient Egypt translated by Barbara Hughes Fowler
Love Songs of the New Kingdom, Translated from the Ancient Egyptian by John L. Foster.
Macdonell, A. A., Vedic Mythology, Delhi: Motilal Banarsidass, 1974.
Mackenzie, Donald A., Indian Myth and Legend, London 1913
Manetho, W. G. Waddell
Mansouri El S. M., Art - Culture of India and Egypt 1959
Meditation: The Ancient Egyptian Path to Enlightenment by Dr. Muata Ashby
Memphite Theology, Muata Ashby
Merriam-Webster Dictionary
Microsoft (R) Encarta Copyright (c) 1994 Funk & Wagnall's Corporation.
Middle Passage BET Television
Mircea Eliade, Yoga: Immortality and Freedom, Bollingen Series LVI, 2nd edn. (Princeton: Princeton University Press, 1969), PP. 370-372 (Patanjali and the Texts of Classic Yoga).
Monier-Williams, Indian Wisdom, p. 19.
Mysteries of the Creation Myth, Muata Ashby.
Mysteries of the Mexiacn Pyramids, Peter Tompkins, 1976
Mystical spirituality texts of India.
Mysticism of Hindu Gods and Goddesses by Swami Jyotirmayananda
Mysticism of the Mahabharata Swami Jyotirmayananda 1993
Mysticism of the Mahabharata by Swami Jyotirmayananda 1993
Mysticism of Ushet Reckat: Worship of the Goddess by Muata Ashby.
Myths and Symbol in Ancient Egypt by R.T. Rundle Clark
Nagaraja Rao, op. Cit., p. 144; also Allchin, op. Cit.
Nekhen News, Expedition reports, Hierakonpolis, Petrie Museum of Egyptian Archaeology
NEWSBRIEFS EARLIEST EGYPTIAN GLYPHS Volume 52 Number 2 March/April 1999
Nile Valley Contributions to Civilization and the video The Ancient Egyptian Origins of Yoga Philosophy and the book Egyptian Yoga Volume 1: The Philosophy of Enlightenment – by Dr. Muata Ashby
Of Ancient Egypt.
On the Mysteries, Iamblichus
Osiris, E. W. Budge
Pale Fox, by Marcel Griaule and Germaine Dieterlen
Petrie Museum in London (UC nos. 8816, 8931, 8788)
Porphyry, On Abstinence from Killing Animals, trans. Gillian Clark (Ithaak, 1999). (= De abstentia, Book IV, chap 6)
Pottery Headrests from Narsipur Sangam, F.R. Allchin, Studies in Indian Prehistory, D. Sen and A.K. Ghosh, eds., Calcutta, 1966, pp. 58-63
Pottery Headrests from Narsipur Sangam, F.R. Allchin, Studies in Indian Prehistory, D. Sen and A.K. Ghosh, eds., Calcutta, 1966, pp. 58-63
Prehistoric India and Ancient Egypt 1956 Ray, Kumar Sudhansu
Proof of Vedic Culture's Global Existence by Steven Knapp
Raja Yoga Sutras, Swami Jyotirmayananda
Random House Encyclopedia Copyright (C) 1983,1990
Rashidi, Runoko and Van Sertima, Ivan, Editors African Presence in Early Asia 1985-1995
Rawlinson, op. cit., p. 93
Ray, Kumar Sudhansu, Prehistoric India and Ancient Egypt 1956
Reading Egyptian Art, Richard H. Wilkinson
Resurrecting Osiris: The Path of Mystical Awakening and the Keys to Immortality by Muata Ashby
Rig Veda by Aryan and Indian Sages
Ruins of Empires by C.F. Volney
Sacred Science by Schwaller de Lubicz

THE AFRICAN ORIGINS OF CIVILIZATION, RELIGION AND YOGA SPIRITUALITY

SADHANA by Swami Sivananda
Sanskrit Keys to the Wisdom Religion, by Judith Tyberg
Secrets of the Great Pyramid, Peter Tompkins
Seidenberg (1978: 301)
Serpent in the Sky, John Anthony West,
Serpent Power by Muata Ashby.
Stele of Abu
Stele of Djehuti-nefer
Stolen Legacy" by George G. M. James
Tao Te Ching by Lao Tsu
TemTTchaas: Egyptian Proverbs by Muata Ashby
The Aeneid By Virgil, Translated by John Dryden
The African Origins of Civilization, Cheikh Anta Diop, 1974
The Ancient Egyptians: Their Life and Customs-Sir J. Garner Wilkinson 1854 A.C.E.
The Asarian Resurrection: The Ancient Egyptian Bible by Dr. Muata Ashby
The Bandlet of Righteousness: An Ethiopian Book of the Dead translated by E.A. Wallis Budge
The Bhagavad Gita translated by Antonio DE Nicolas
The Bhagavad Gita translated by Swami Jyotirmayananda
The Blooming Lotus of Divine Love by Dr. Muata Ashby
The Complete Temples of Ancient Egypt, Richard Wilkinson, (C) 2000
The Cycles of Time by Dr. Muata Ashby
The Ebers papyrus
The Egyptian Book of the Dead, Muata Ashby.
The Glorious Light Meditation System of Ancient Egypt by Dr. Muata Ashby.
The Gods of the Egyptians Vol. I, II by E. Wallis Budge
The Great Human Diasporas, Luigi Luca Cavalli-Sforza, Francesco Cavalli-Sforza. Cambridge Encyclopedia of Human Evolution, Editor, Steve Jones
The Greenfield papyrus
The Hero With A Thousand Faces, Joseph Campbell. The Power of Myth, Joseph Campbell
The Hidden Properties of Matter by Dr. Muata Ashby
The Hierakonpolis Expedition returned for its fourth season of renewed fieldwork under the direction of Barbara Adams (Petrie Museum of Egyptian Archaeology and Dr. Ren,e Friedman (University of California, Berkeley).
The Histories, Herodotus, Translated by Aubrey de Selincourt- The History of Herodotus By Herodotus, Translated by George Rawlinson
The Hymns of Amun by Dr. Muata Ashby
The Kybalion by Three Initiates (Hermes Trismegistos)
The Living Gita by Swami Satchidananda 3rd ed. 1997
The Meaning of the Dead Sea Scrolls by A. Powell Davies
The Middle Passage : White Ships Black Cargo by Tom Feelings, John Henrik, Dr Clarke
The Migration of Symbols, Count Goblet D' Alviella, 1894
The Mystery of the Sphinx on video by John Anthony West
The Mystical Teachings The Asarian Resurrection: Initiation Into The Third Level of Shetaut Asar, Muata Ashby
The Mythic Image, Joseph Campbell
The Nag Hammadi Library
The Opening of the Way by Isha Schwaller De Lubicz
The Origin of Mathematics,
The Origin of Western Barbarism by Michael Wood
The Passing of the Empires *by* G. Maspero (New York, 1900).
The Power of Myth, Bill Moyers and Joseph Campbell, 1989
The Priests of Ancient Egypt by Serge Sauneron, Grove p114
The RIG VEDA Ralph T.H. Griffith, translator 1889
The Shambhala Encyclopedia of Yoga, Feuerstein, Georg, 1997
The Sivananda Companion to Yoga, Lucy Lidell, Narayani, Giris Rabinovitch)
The Story of Islam
The Tantric Way by Ajit Mookerjee and Madhu Khanna
The Tao of Physics, Fritjof Capra
The Turin Papyrus

THE AFRICAN ORIGINS OF CIVILIZATION, RELIGION AND YOGA SPIRITUALITY

The Upanishads, Max Muller, translator
The Upanishads: Breath of the Eternal, Swami Prabhavananda and Frederick Manchester
The Wisdom of Isis by Dr. Muata Ashby
The Wisdom of Maati: Spiritual Enlightenment Through the Path of Righteous Action by Dr. Muata Ashby
The Yoga of Wisdom, Swami Jyotirmayananda
Thrice Greatest Hermes by G.R.S. Mead
Transformations of Myth Through Time by Joseph Campbell
Traveler's Key to Ancient Egypt, John Anthony West
Tutankhamen, Amenism, Atenism, and Egyptian Monotheism (Edit. 1923), p. 86. Sir Wallis Budge
Vedic Aryans and the Origins of Civilization by David Frawley
Video presentation -Nile Valley Contributions to Civilization and the video The
Websters Encyclopedia
Wilkins, Hindu Mythology, p. 33.
Yoga International, {The Flight of the Alone to the Alone}, November 2000
Yoga International, {The Flight of the Alone to the Alone}, November 2000
Yoga Journal, {The New Yoga} January/February 2000
Yoga Vasistha Ramayana translated by Swami Jyotirmayananda
Yoga Vasistha Vol. I by Sage Valmiki -Translation by Swami Jyotirmayananda
Yoga Vasistha, Nirvana Prakarana Swami Jyotirmayananda, 1998

THE AFRICAN ORIGINS OF CIVILIZATION, RELIGION AND YOGA SPIRITUALITY

This Volume Serves as the Textbook for the course given at the Florida International University. For information to obtain recorded lectures for in-depth studies contact the Sema Institute (305) 378-6253

New Course!

AFA 3993 - 3 Credits
Introduction to African Civilization, Religion and Philosophy

FLORIDA INTERNATIONAL UNIVERSITY - SOUTH CAMPUS
Term: Spring – Year 2002
January 7 – April 19 (15 weeks of class)
Tuesdays and Thursdays 12:30-1:45 PM
FOR FURTHER INFORMATION, CALL

Africa New World Studies Department
305-919-5521
Africana@ fiu.edu

Course Instructor:
Dr. Muata Ashby
Author of over 25 books on
African History, Culture, Religion and Philosophy

Through this course, you will:

♦ Discover the latest archeological evidences showing origins of civilization and culture in Ancient Egypt and its spread to other countries.
♦ Discover how the Ancient Egyptians came from Nubia to establish the greatest civilization ever known.
♦ Discover the origins of Civilization and how civilization was spread to Europe, Mesopotamia and India
♦ Discover the origins of Religion and how Africa gave birth to the present day world religions
♦ Discover the world's first university and the African philosophy of Maat, the concepts of balance, righteousness and order in society, government, and religion and how it preceded Dharma philosophy of India and Confucianism of China.
♦ Discover the worlds earliest theater and the philosophy of cosmic music
♦ Discover how the practices of Indian Yoga began in Ancient Egypt.
♦ Discover how to answer the question: What is the meaning of life? How to Know Thyself?

African History ♀ African Culture ♀ African Philosophy!

THE AFRICAN ORIGINS OF CIVILIZATION, RELIGION AND YOGA SPIRITUALITY

Syllabus for Course Title:
Introduction to Ancient Egyptian Religion and Philosophy

Term: Spring – Year 2002
January 7 – April 18   (15 weeks of class)
Tuesdays and Thursdays

Course Title:
Introduction to Ancient African Civilization, Religion and Philosophy
AFA 3993 - 3 Credits (Ref. # 6562)

Course Texts:

Main Course Texts

1. *The African Origins of Civilization, Religion and Yoga Mysticism and Ethics Philosophy* by Muata Ashby (ISBN: 1-884564-50-X) (Available through Sema Institute / C.M. Book Publishing (305) 378-6253

Instructor: Dr. Muata Ashby (305)-378-6253
Office hours: TBA / By Appointment

THE AFRICAN ORIGINS OF CIVILIZATION, RELIGION AND YOGA SPIRITUALITY

Class Schedule, Thematic Focus and Lecture Topics (Legend-T= Tuesday, R= Thursday)

Week	Class-Date	Day	Thematic Focus	Class # and Lecture Topics	Text
1	(1) Jan. 8	T	African Origins of Civilization	1. Introduction: What is Civilization, Religion, Culture and Philosophy?	
	(2) Jan. 10	R	"	2. Conceptual Basis for Comparative Cultural Studies	Book #2 pxii-xvii
2	(3) Jan. 15	T	"	3. Who were the Nubians? The Kamitans (Ancient Egyptians), Africans or Middle Easterners?	Book #2 chapter 1
	(4) Jan. 17	R	"	4. "	Book #2 Chapter 2-3
3	(5) Jan. 22	T	"	5. Ancient Egyptian civilization	Book #2 Chapter 4-5
	(6) Jan. 24	R	"	6. "	Book #2 Chapter 6-8
4	(7) Jan. 29	T	"	7. Relationships between Ancient Egypt and other African civilizations	Book #2 Chapter 9
	(8) Jan. 31	R	"	8. "	Book #2 Chapter 10-11
5	(9) Feb. 5	T	"	9. **SUMMARY AND OPEN DISCUSSION**	
	(10) Feb. 7	R	African Origins of Religion and Spiritual Philosophy	10. Introduction to African Religion	Book #1. (Preface-Chapter 1) Book #3. (Chapter 2)
6	(11) Feb. 12	T	"	11. History of Ancient Egyptian Religion Ancient Egyptian Religious philosophy and theory	"
	(12) Feb. 14	R	"	12. The Philosophy of The Supreme Being in African Religion Creation Myth and the origin of the gods and goddesses. The Philosophy of Gods and Goddesses in African Religion	Book #3 Chapter 1
7	(13) Feb. 19	T	"		
	(14) Feb. 21	R	"	13. Relationship of Ancient Egyptian Religion to Other African Religions	Book #1 Chapter 3-4 Book #3 Chapter 2
8	(15) Feb. 26	T	"	14. African Religion influences in the Diaspora	Book #1 Chapter 8 Book #3 Chapter 2
	(16) Feb. 28	R	"	15. The Ancient Egyptian origins of Greek	Book #3

				Religion and Philosophy and modern western culture.	Chapter 3
9	(17) Mar. 5	T	"	16. The Ancient Egyptian origins of Judaism, The Ancient Egyptian origins of Christianity, Christian philosophy and Ancient Egyptian Religion, The Ancient Egyptian origins of Islam.	Book #3 Chapter 6
	(18) Mar. 7	R			
			"	17. The Ancient Egyptian origins of Hinduism, and Buddhism.	Book #3 Chapter 4, 5,
10	(19) Mar. 12	T	**MIDTERM EXAM**	18. **MIDTERM EXAM**	
	(20) Mar. 14	R	Spring Break	19. Spring Break	
11	(21) Mar. 19	T	Spring Break	20. Spring Break	
	(22) Mar. 21	R	African Origins of Social Philosophy	21. African Ubuntu Philosophy and Ancient Egyptian Maat Social Philosophy	Book #3 Chapter 2
12	(23) Mar. 26	T	"	22. "	"
	(24) Mar. 28	R	"	23. The Ancient Egyptian Yoga and Yoga Psychology	Book #3 Chapter 7, 8, 9
13	(25) Apr. 2	T	"	24. "	"
	(26) Apr. 4	R	"	25. African Origins of Indian Yoga Philosophy	"
14	(27) Apr. 9	T	**Presentations based on research projects**	26. Presentations and Papers Due	
	(28) Apr. 11	R	"	27. Presentations and Papers Due	
15	(29) Apr. 16	T	Spirituality in Life, What does it mean for us today?	28. Special Open Discussion: Spirituality in Life, What does it mean for us today?	
	(30) Apr. 18	R	Student-Instructor conferences		
16	Apr. 23	T			
	Apr. 25	R			

Books by Sebai Muata Ashby
On the Kamitan Mysteries

Prices subject to change.

1. EGYPTIAN YOGA: THE PHILOSOPHY OF ENLIGHTENMENT An original, fully illustrated work, including hieroglyphs, detailing the meaning of the Egyptian mysteries, tantric yoga, psycho-spiritual and physical exercises. Egyptian Yoga is a guide to the practice of the highest spiritual philosophy which leads to absolute freedom from human misery and to immortality. It is well known by scholars that Egyptian philosophy is the basis of Western and Middle Eastern religious philosophies such as *Christianity, Islam, Judaism*, the *Kabala*, and Greek philosophy, but what about Indian philosophy, Yoga and Taoism? What were the original teachings? How can they be practiced today? What is the source of pain and suffering in the world and what is the solution? Discover the deepest mysteries of the mind and universe within and outside of your self. 8.5" X 11" ISBN: 1-884564-01-1 Soft $19.95

2. EGYPTIAN YOGA: African Religion Volume 2- Theban THeology by Dr. Muata Ashby ISBN 1-884564-39-9 $23.95 U.S. In this long awaited sequel to *Egyptian Yoga: The Philosophy of Enlightenment* you will take a fascinating and enlightening journey back in time and discover the teachings which constituted the epitome of Ancient Egyptian spiritual wisdom. What are the disciplines which lead to the fulfillment of all desires? Delve into the three states of consciousness (waking, dream and deep sleep) and the fourth state which transcends them all, Neberdjer, "The Absolute." These teachings of the city of Waset (Thebes) were the crowning achievement of the Sages of Ancient Egypt. They establish the standard mystical keys for understanding the profound mystical symbolism of the Triad of human consciousness.

3. THE KEMETIC DIET: GUIDE TO HEALTH, DIET AND FASTING Health issues have always been important to human beings since the beginning of time. The earliest records of history show that the art of healing was held in high esteem since the time of Ancient Egypt. In the early 20th century, medical doctors had almost attained the status of sainthood by the promotion of the idea that they alone were "scientists" while other healing modalities and traditional healers who did not follow the "scientific method' were nothing but superstitious, ignorant charlatans who at best would take the money of their clients and at worst kill them with the unscientific "snake oils" and "irrational theories". In the late 20th century, the failure of the modern medical establishment's ability to lead the general public to good health, promoted the move by many in society towards "alternative medicine". Alternative medicine disciplines are those healing modalities which do not adhere to the philosophy of allopathic medicine. Allopathic medicine is what medical doctors practice by an large. It is the theory that disease is caused by agencies outside the body such as bacteria, viruses or physical means which affect the body. These can therefore be treated by medicines and therapies The natural healing method began in the absence of extensive technologies with the idea that all the answers for health may be found in nature or rather, the deviation from nature. Therefore, the health of the body can be restored by correcting the aberration and thereby restoring balance. This is the area that will be covered in this volume. Allopathic techniques have their place in the art of healing. However, we should not forget that the body is a grand achievement of the spirit and built into it is the capacity to maintain itself and heal itself. Ashby, Muata ISBN: 1-884564-49-6 $28.95

4. INITIATION INTO EGYPTIAN YOGA Shedy: Spiritual discipline or program, to go deeply into the mysteries, to study the mystery teachings and literature profoundly, to penetrate the mysteries. You will learn about the mysteries of initiation into the teachings and practice of Yoga and how to become an Initiate of the mystical sciences. This insightful manual is the first in a series which introduces you to the goals of daily spiritual and yoga practices: Meditation, Diet, Words of Power and the ancient wisdom teachings. 8.5" X 11" ISBN 1-884564-02-X Soft Cover $24.95 U.S.

5. *THE AFRICAN ORIGINS OF CIVILIZATION, MYSTICAL RELIGION AND YOGA PHILOSOPHY* HARD COVER EDITION ISBN: 1-884564-50-X $80.00 U.S. 81/2" X 11" Part 1, Part 2, Part 3 in one volume 683 Pages Hard Cover First Edition Three volumes in one. Over the past several years I have been

asked to put together in one volume the most important evidences showing the correlations and common teachings between Kamitan (Ancient Egyptian) culture and religion and that of India. The questions of the history of Ancient Egypt, and the latest archeological evidences showing civilization and culture in Ancient Egypt and its spread to other countries, has intrigued many scholars as well as mystics over the years. Also, the possibility that Ancient Egyptian Priests and Priestesses migrated to Greece, India and other countries to carry on the traditions of the Ancient Egyptian Mysteries, has been speculated over the years as well. In chapter 1 of the book *Egyptian Yoga The Philosophy of Enlightenment,* 1995, I first introduced the deepest comparison between Ancient Egypt and India that had been brought forth up to that time. Now, in the year 2001 this new book, *THE AFRICAN ORIGINS OF CIVILIZATION, MYSTICAL RELIGION AND YOGA PHILOSOPHY,* more fully explores the motifs, symbols and philosophical correlations between Ancient Egyptian and Indian mysticism and clearly shows not only that Ancient Egypt and India were connected culturally but also spiritually. How does this knowledge help the spiritual aspirant? This discovery has great importance for the Yogis and mystics who follow the philosophy of Ancient Egypt and the mysticism of India. It means that India has a longer history and heritage than was previously understood. It shows that the mysteries of Ancient Egypt were essentially a yoga tradition which did not die but rather developed into the modern day systems of Yoga technology of India. It further shows that African culture developed Yoga Mysticism earlier than any other civilization in history. All of this expands our understanding of the unity of culture and the deep legacy of Yoga, which stretches into the distant past, beyond the Indus Valley civilization, the earliest known high culture in India as well as the Vedic tradition of Aryan culture. Therefore, Yoga culture and mysticism is the oldest known tradition of spiritual development and Indian mysticism is an extension of the Ancient Egyptian mysticism. By understanding the legacy which Ancient Egypt gave to India the mysticism of India is better understood and by comprehending the heritage of Indian Yoga, which is rooted in Ancient Egypt the Mysticism of Ancient Egypt is also better understood. This expanded understanding allows us to prove the underlying kinship of humanity, through the common symbols, motifs and philosophies which are not disparate and confusing teachings but in reality expressions of the same study of truth through metaphysics and mystical realization of Self. (HARD COVER)

6. AFRICAN ORIGINS BOOK 1 PART 1 African Origins of African Civilization, Religion, Yoga Mysticism and Ethics Philosophy-Soft Cover $24.95 ISBN: 1-884564-55-0

7. AFRICAN ORIGINS BOOK 2 PART 2 African Origins of Western Civilization, Religion and Philosophy(Soft) -Soft Cover $24.95 ISBN: 1-884564-56-9

8. EGYPT AND INDIA (AFRICAN ORIGINS BOOK 3 PART 3) African Origins of Eastern Civilization, Religion, Yoga Mysticism and Philosophy-Soft Cover $29.95 (Soft) ISBN: 1-884564-57-7

9. THE MYSTERIES OF ISIS: **The Ancient Egyptian Philosophy of Self-Realization** - There are several paths to discover the Divine and the mysteries of the higher Self. This volume details the mystery teachings of the goddess Aset (Isis) from Ancient Egypt- the path of wisdom. It includes the teachings of her temple and the disciplines that are enjoined for the initiates of the temple of Aset as they were given in ancient times. Also, this book includes the teachings of the main myths of Aset that lead a human being to spiritual enlightenment and immortality. Through the study of ancient myth and the illumination of initiatic understanding the idea of God is expanded from the mythological comprehension to the metaphysical. Then this metaphysical understanding is related to you, the student, so as to begin understanding your true divine nature. ISBN 1-884564-24-0 $22.99

10. EGYPTIAN PROVERBS: TEMT TCHAAS *Temt Tchaas* means: collection of ——Ancient Egyptian Proverbs How to live according to MAAT Philosophy. Beginning Meditation. All proverbs are indexed for easy searches. For the first time in one volume, ——Ancient Egyptian Proverbs, wisdom teachings and meditations, fully illustrated with hieroglyphic text and symbols. EGYPTIAN PROVERBS is a unique collection of knowledge and wisdom which you can put into practice today and transform your life. 5.5"x 8.5" $14.95 U.S   ISBN: 1-884564-00-3

11. THE PATH OF DIVINE LOVE The Process of Mystical Transformation and The Path of Divine Love This Volume focuses on the ancient wisdom teachings of "Neter Merri" –the Ancient Egyptian philosophy of Divine Love and how to use them in a scientific process for self-transformation. Love is one of the most powerful human emotions. It is also the source of Divine feeling that unifies God and the individual human being. When love is fragmented and diminished by egoism the Divine connection is lost. The Ancient tradition of Neter Merri leads human beings back to their Divine connection, allowing them to discover

THE AFRICAN ORIGINS OF CIVILIZATION, RELIGION AND YOGA SPIRITUALITY

their innate glorious self that is actually Divine and immortal. This volume will detail the process of transformation from ordinary consciousness to cosmic consciousness through the integrated practice of the teachings and the path of Devotional Love toward the Divine. 5.5"x 8.5" ISBN 1-884564-11-9 $22.99

12. INTRODUCTION TO MAAT PHILOSOPHY: Spiritual Enlightenment Through the Path of Virtue Known as Karma Yoga in India, the teachings of MAAT for living virtuously and with orderly wisdom are explained and the student is to begin practicing the precepts of Maat in daily life so as to promote the process of purification of the heart in preparation for the judgment of the soul. This judgment will be understood not as an event that will occur at the time of death but as an event that occurs continuously, at every moment in the life of the individual. The student will learn how to become allied with the forces of the Higher Self and to thereby begin cleansing the mind (heart) of impurities so as to attain a higher vision of reality. ISBN 1-884564-20-8 $22.99

13. MEDITATION The Ancient Egyptian Path to Enlightenment Many people do not know about the rich history of meditation practice in Ancient Egypt. This volume outlines the theory of meditation and presents the Ancient Egyptian Hieroglyphic text which give instruction as to the nature of the mind and its three modes of expression. It also presents the texts which give instruction on the practice of meditation for spiritual Enlightenment and unity with the Divine. This volume allows the reader to begin practicing meditation by explaining, in easy to understand terms, the simplest form of meditation and working up to the most advanced form which was practiced in ancient times and which is still practiced by yogis around the world in modern times. ISBN 1-884564-27-7 $24.99

14. THE GLORIOUS LIGHT MEDITATION TECHNIQUE OF ANCIENT EGYPT ISBN: 1-884564-15-1 $14.95 (PB) New for the year 2000. This volume is based on the earliest known instruction in history given for the practice of formal meditation. Discovered by Dr. Muata Ashby, it is inscribed on the walls of the Tomb of Seti I in Thebes Egypt. This volume details the philosophy and practice of this unique system of meditation originated in Ancient Egypt and the earliest practice of meditation known in the world which occurred in the most advanced African Culture.

15. THE SERPENT POWER: The Ancient Egyptian Mystical Wisdom of the Inner Life Force. This Volume specifically deals with the latent life Force energy of the universe and in the human body, its control and sublimation. How to develop the Life Force energy of the subtle body. This Volume will introduce the esoteric wisdom of the science of how virtuous living acts in a subtle and mysterious way to cleanse the latent psychic energy conduits and vortices of the spiritual body. ISBN 1-884564-19-4 $22.95

16. EGYPTIAN YOGA *The Postures of The Gods and Goddesses* Discover the physical postures and exercises practiced thousands of years ago in Ancient Egypt which are today known as Yoga exercises. This work is based on the pictures and teachings from the Creation story of Ra, The Asarian Resurrection Myth and the carvings and reliefs from various Temples in Ancient Egypt 8.5" X 11" ISBN 1-884564-10-0 Soft Cover $21.95   Exercise video $20

17. EGYPTIAN TANTRA YOGA: The Art of Sex Sublimation and Universal Consciousness This Volume will expand on the male and female principles within the human body and in the universe and further detail the sublimation of sexual energy into spiritual energy. The student will study the deities Min and Hathor, Asar and Aset, Geb and Nut and discover the mystical implications for a practical spiritual discipline. This Volume will also focus on the Tantric aspects of Ancient Egyptian and Indian mysticism, the purpose of sex and the mystical teachings of sexual sublimation which lead to self-knowledge and Enlightenment. 5.5"x 8.5" ISBN 1-884564-03-8 $24.95

18. AFRICAN RELIGION Volume 4: ASARIAN THEOLOGY: RESURRECTING OSIRIS The path of Mystical Awakening and the Keys to Immortality NEW REVISED AND EXPANDED EDITION! The Ancient Sages created stories based on human and superhuman beings whose struggles, aspirations, needs and desires ultimately lead them to discover their true Self. The myth of Aset, Asar and Heru is no exception in this area. While there is no one source where the entire story may be found, pieces of it are inscribed in various ancient Temples walls, tombs, steles and papyri. For the first time available, the complete myth of Asar, Aset and Heru has been compiled from original Ancient Egyptian, Greek and Coptic Texts. This epic myth has been richly illustrated with reliefs from the Temple of Heru at Edfu, the Temple of Aset at Philae, the Temple of Asar at Abydos, the Temple of Hathor at Denderah and various

THE AFRICAN ORIGINS OF CIVILIZATION, RELIGION AND YOGA SPIRITUALITY

papyri, inscriptions and reliefs. Discover the myth which inspired the teachings of the *Shetaut Neter* (Egyptian Mystery System - Egyptian Yoga) and the Egyptian Book of Coming Forth By Day. Also, discover the three levels of Ancient Egyptian Religion, how to understand the mysteries of the Duat or Astral World and how to discover the abode of the Supreme in the Amenta, *The Other World* The ancient religion of Asar, Aset and Heru, if properly understood, contains all of the elements necessary to lead the sincere aspirant to attain immortality through inner self-discovery. This volume presents the entire myth and explores the main mystical themes and rituals associated with the myth for understating human existence, creation and the way to achieve spiritual emancipation - *Resurrection.* The Asarian myth is so powerful that it influenced and is still having an effect on the major world religions. Discover the origins and mystical meaning of the Christian Trinity, the Eucharist ritual and the ancient origin of the birthday of Jesus Christ. Soft Cover ISBN: 1-884564-27-5 $24.95

19. THE EGYPTIAN BOOK OF THE DEAD MYSTICISM OF THE PERT EM HERU $28.95 ISBN# 1-884564-28-3 Size: 8½" X 11" I Know myself, I know myself, I am One With God!–From the Pert Em Heru "The Ru Pert em Heru" or "Ancient Egyptian Book of The Dead," or "Book of Coming Forth By Day" as it is more popularly known, has fascinated the world since the successful translation of Ancient Egyptian hieroglyphic scripture over 150 years ago. The astonishing writings in it reveal that the Ancient Egyptians believed in life after death and in an ultimate destiny to discover the Divine. The elegance and aesthetic beauty of the hieroglyphic text itself has inspired many see it as an art form in and of itself. But is there more to it than that? Did the Ancient Egyptian wisdom contain more than just aphorisms and hopes of eternal life beyond death? In this volume Dr. Muata Ashby, the author of over 25 books on Ancient Egyptian Yoga Philosophy has produced a new translation of the original texts which uncovers a mystical teaching underlying the sayings and rituals instituted by the Ancient Egyptian Sages and Saints. "Once the philosophy of Ancient Egypt is understood as a mystical tradition instead of as a religion or primitive mythology, it reveals its secrets which if practiced today will lead anyone to discover the glory of spiritual self-discovery. The Pert em Heru is in every way comparable to the Indian Upanishads or the Tibetan Book of the Dead." Muata Abhaya Ashby

20. AFRICAN RELIGION Volume 1: ANUNIAN THEOLOGY THE MYSTERIES OF RA The Philosophy of Anu and The Mystical Teachings of The Ancient Egyptian Creation Myth Discover the mystical teachings contained in the Creation Myth and the gods and goddesses who brought creation and human beings into existence. The Creation Myth holds the key to understanding the universe and for attaining spiritual Enlightenment. ISBN: 1-884564-38-0 40 pages $14.95

21. AFRICAN RELIGION Volume 3: THEBAN THEOLOGY-MYSTERIES OF MIND Mystical Psychology & Mental Health for Enlightenment and Immortality based on the Ancient Egyptian Philosophy of Menefer -Mysticism of Ptah, Egyptian Physics and Yoga Metaphysics and the Hidden properties of Matter. This volume uncovers the mystical psychology of the Ancient Egyptian wisdom teachings centering on the philosophy of the Ancient Egyptian city of Menefer (Memphite Theology). How to understand the mind and how to control the senses and lead the mind to health, clarity and mystical self-discovery. This Volume will also go deeper into the philosophy of God as creation and will explore the concepts of modern science and how they correlate with ancient teachings. This Volume will lay the ground work for the understanding of the philosophy of universal consciousness and the initiatic/yogic insight into who or what is God? ISBN 1-884564-07-0 $22.95

22. AFRICAN RELIGION Volume 5: THE GODDESS AND THE EGYPTIAN MYSTERIESTHE PATH OF THE GODDESS THE GODDESS PATH The Secret Forms of the Goddess and the Rituals of Resurrection The Supreme Being may be worshipped as father or as mother. *Ushet Rekhat* or *Mother Worship*, is the spiritual process of worshipping the Divine in the form of the Divine Goddess. It celebrates the most important forms of the Goddess including *Nathor, Maat, Aset, Arat, Amentet and Hathor* and explores their mystical meaning as well as the rising of *Sirius,* the star of Aset (Aset) and the new birth of Hor (Heru). The end of the year is a time of reckoning, reflection and engendering a new or renewed positive movement toward attaining spiritual Enlightenment. The Mother Worship devotional meditation ritual, performed on five days during the month of December and on New Year's Eve, is based on the Ushet Rekhit. During the ceremony, the cosmic forces, symbolized by Sirius - and the constellation of Orion ---, are harnessed through the understanding and devotional attitude of the participant. This propitiation draws the light of wisdom and health to all those who share in the ritual, leading to prosperity and wisdom. $14.95 ISBN 1-884564-18-6

THE AFRICAN ORIGINS OF CIVILIZATION, RELIGION AND YOGA SPIRITUALITY

23. *THE MYSTICAL JOURNEY FROM JESUS TO CHRIST* $24.95   ISBN# 1-884564-05-4 size: 8½" X 11" Discover the ancient Egyptian origins of Christianity before the Catholic Church and learn the mystical teachings given by Jesus to assist all humanity in becoming Christlike. Discover the secret meaning of the Gospels that were discovered in Egypt. Also discover how and why so many Christian churches came into being. Discover that the Bible still holds the keys to mystical realization even though its original writings were changed by the church. Discover how to practice the original teachings of Christianity which leads to the Kingdom of Heaven.

24. THE STORY OF ASAR, ASET AND HERU: An Ancient Egyptian Legend (For Children)   Now for the first time, the most ancient myth of Ancient Egypt comes alive for children. Inspired by the books *The Asarian Resurrection: The Ancient Egyptian Bible* and *The Mystical Teachings of The Asarian Resurrection, The Story of Asar, Aset and Heru* is an easy to understand and thrilling tale which inspired the children of Ancient Egypt to aspire to greatness and righteousness. If you and your child have enjoyed stories like *The Lion King* and *Star Wars you will love The Story of Asar, Aset and Heru*. Also, if you know the story of Jesus and Krishna you will discover than Ancient Egypt had a similar myth and that this myth carries important spiritual teachings for living a fruitful and fulfilling life. This book may be used along with *The Parents Guide To The Asarian Resurrection Myth: How to Teach Yourself and Your Child the Principles of Universal Mystical Religion*. The guide provides some background to the Asarian Resurrection myth and it also gives insight into the mystical teachings contained in it which you may introduce to your child. It is designed for parents who wish to grow spiritually with their children and it serves as an introduction for those who would like to study the Asarian Resurrection Myth in depth and to practice its teachings. 41 pages 8.5" X 11"   ISBN: 1-884564-31-3 $12.95

25. THE PARENTS GUIDE TO THE AUSARIAN RESURRECTION MYTH: How to Teach Yourself and Your Child the Principles of Universal Mystical Religion.   This insightful manual brings for the timeless wisdom of the ancient through the Ancient Egyptian myth of Asar, Aset and Heru and the mystical teachings contained in it for parents who want to guide their children to understand and practice the teachings of mystical spirituality. This manual may be used with the children's storybook *The Story of Asar, Aset and Heru* by Dr. Muata Abhaya Ashby. 5.5"x 8.5"   ISBN: 1-884564-30-5 $14.95

26. HEALING THE CRIMINAL HEART BOOK 1 Introduction to Maat Philosophy, Yoga and Spiritual Redemption Through the Path of Virtue   Who is a criminal? Is there such a thing as a criminal heart? What is the source of evil and sinfulness and is there any way to rise above it? Is there redemption for those who have committed sins, even the worst crimes?   Ancient Egyptian mystical psychology holds important answers to these questions. Over ten thousand years ago mystical psychologists, the Sages of Ancient Egypt, studied and charted the human mind and spirit and laid out a path which will lead to spiritual redemption, prosperity and Enlightenment.   This introductory volume brings forth the teachings of the Asarian Resurrection, the most important myth of Ancient Egypt, with relation to the faults of human existence: anger, hatred, greed, lust, animosity, discontent, ignorance, egoism jealousy, bitterness, and a myriad of psycho-spiritual ailments which keep a human being in a state of negativity and adversity. 5.5"x 8.5"   ISBN: 1-884564-17-8 $15.95

27. THEATER & DRAMA OF THE ANCIENT EGYPTIAN MYSTERIES: Featuring the Ancient Egyptian stage play-"The Enlightenment of Hathor' Based on an Ancient Egyptian Drama, The original Theater - Mysticism of the Temple of Hetheru $14.95   By Dr. Muata Ashby

28. GUIDE TO PRINT ON DEMAND: SELF-PUBLISH FOR PROFIT, SPIRITUAL FULFILLMENT AND SERVICE TO HUMANITY Everyone asks us how we produced so many books in such a short time. Here are the secrets to writing and producing books that uplift humanity and how to get them printed for a fraction of the regular cost. Anyone can become an author even if they have limited funds. All that is necessary is the willingness to learn how the printing and book business work and the desire to follow the special instructions given here for preparing your manuscript format. Then you take your work directly to the non-traditional companies who can produce your books for less than the traditional book printer can. ISBN: 1-884564-40-2 $16.95 U. S.

29. EGYPTIAN MYSTERIES: Vol. 1, Shetaut Neter ISBN: 1-884564-41-0 $19.99 What are the Mysteries? For thousands of years the spiritual tradition of Ancient Egypt, *Shetaut Neter,* "The Egyptian Mysteries," "The Secret Teachings," have fascinated, tantalized and amazed the world. At one time exalted and recognized as the highest culture of the world, by Africans, Europeans, Asiatics, Hindus, Buddhists and

THE AFRICAN ORIGINS OF CIVILIZATION, RELIGION AND YOGA SPIRITUALITY

other cultures of the ancient world, in time it was shunned by the emerging orthodox world religions. Its temples desecrated, its philosophy maligned, its tradition spurned, its philosophy dormant in the mystical *Medu Neter*, the mysterious hieroglyphic texts which hold the secret symbolic meaning that has scarcely been discerned up to now. What are the secrets of *Nehast* {spiritual awakening and emancipation, resurrection}. More than just a literal translation, this volume is for awakening to the secret code *Shetitu* of the teaching which was not deciphered by Egyptologists, nor could be understood by ordinary spiritualists. This book is a reinstatement of the original science made available for our times, to the reincarnated followers of Ancient Egyptian culture and the prospect of spiritual freedom to break the bonds of *Khemn*, "ignorance," and slavery to evil forces: *Såaa* .

30. EGYPTIAN MYSTERIES VOL 2: Dictionary of Gods and Goddesses ISBN: 1-884564-23-2 $21.95 This book is about the mystery of neteru, the gods and goddesses of Ancient Egypt (Kamit, Kemet). Neteru means "Gods and Goddesses." But the Neterian teaching of Neteru represents more than the usual limited modern day concept of "divinities" or "spirits." The Neteru of Kamit are also metaphors, cosmic principles and vehicles for the enlightening teachings of Shetaut Neter (Ancient Egyptian-African Religion). Actually they are the elements for one of the most advanced systems of spirituality ever conceived in human history. Understanding the concept of neteru provides a firm basis for spiritual evolution and the pathway for viable culture, peace on earth and a healthy human society. Why is it important to have gods and goddesses in our lives? In order for spiritual evolution to be possible, once a human being has accepted that there is existence after death and there is a transcendental being who exists beyond time and space knowledge, human beings need a connection to that which transcends the ordinary experience of human life in time and space and a means to understand the transcendental reality beyond the mundane reality.

31. EGYPTIAN MYSTERIES VOL. 3 The Priests and Priestesses of Ancient Egypt ISBN: 1-884564-53-4 $22.95 This volume details the path of Neterian priesthood, the joys, challenges and rewards of advanced Neterian life, the teachings that allowed the priests and priestesses to manage the most long lived civilization in human history and how that path can be adopted today; for those who want to tread the path of the Clergy of Shetaut Neter.

32. THE WAR OF HERU AND SET: The Struggle of Good and Evil for Control of the World and The Human Soul ISBN 1-8840564-44-5 $18.95 This volume contains a novelized version of the Asarian Resurrection myth that is based on the actual scriptures presented in the Book Asarian Religion (old name –Resurrecting Osiris). This volume is prepared in the form of a screenplay and can be easily adapted to be used as a stage play. Spiritual seeking is a mythic journey that has many emotional highs and lows, ecstasies and depressions, victories and frustrations. This is the War of Life that is played out in the myth as the struggle of Heru and Set and those are mythic characters that represent the human Higher and Lower self. How to understand the war and emerge victorious in the journey o life? The ultimate victory and fulfillment can be experienced, which is not changeable or lost in time. The purpose of myth is to convey the wisdom of life through the story of divinities who show the way to overcome the challenges and foibles of life. In this volume the feelings and emotions of the characters of the myth have been highlighted to show the deeply rich texture of the Ancient Egyptian myth. This myth contains deep spiritual teachings and insights into the nature of self, of God and the mysteries of life and the means to discover the true meaning of life and thereby achieve the true purpose of life. To become victorious in the battle of life means to become the King (or Queen) of Egypt.Have you seen movies like The Lion King, Hamlet, The Odyssey, or The Little Buddha? These have been some of the most popular movies in modern times. The Sema Institute of Yoga is dedicated to researching and presenting the wisdom and culture of ancient Africa. The Script is designed to be produced as a motion picture but may be addapted for the theater as well. $19.95 copyright 1998 By Dr. Muata Ashby

33. AFRICAN DIONYSUS: FROM EGYPT TO GREECE: The Kamitan Origins of Greek Culture and Religion ISBN: 1-884564-47-X $24.95 U.S. FROM EGYPT TO GREECE This insightful manual is a reference to Ancient Egyptian mythology and philosophy and its correlation to what later became known as Greek and Rome mythology and philosophy. It outlines the basic tenets of the mythologies and shoes the ancient origins of Greek culture in Ancient Egypt. This volume also documents the origins of the Greek alphabet in Egypt as well as Greek religion, myth and philosophy of the gods and goddesses from Egypt from the myth of Atlantis and archaic period with the Minoans to the Classical period. This volume also acts as a resource for Colleges students who would like to set up fraternities and sororities based on the original Ancient Egyptian principles of Sheti and Maat philosophy. ISBN: 1-884564-47-X $22.95 U.S.

34. **THE FORTY TWO PRECEPTS OF MAAT, THE PHILOSOPHY OF RIGHTEOUS ACTION AND THE ANCIENT EGYPTIAN WISDOM TEXTS <u>ADVANCED STUDIES</u>** This manual is designed for use with the 1998 Maat Philosophy Class conducted by Dr. Muata Ashby. This is a detailed study of Maat Philosophy. It contains a compilation of the 42 laws or precepts of Maat and the corresponding principles which they represent along with the teachings of the ancient Egyptian Sages relating to each. Maat philosophy was the basis of Ancient Egyptian society and government as well as the heart of Ancient Egyptian myth and spirituality. Maat is at once a goddess, a cosmic force and a living social doctrine, which promotes social harmony and thereby paves the way for spiritual evolution in all levels of society. ISBN: 1-884564-48-8 $16.95 U.S.

Music Based on the Prt M Hru and other Kemetic Texts

Available on Compact Disc $14.99 and Audio Cassette $9.99

Adorations to the Goddess

Music for Worship of the Goddess

**NEW Egyptian Yoga Music CD
by Sehu Maa
Ancient Egyptian Music CD**
Instrumental Music played on reproductions of Ancient Egyptian Instruments– Ideal for meditation and reflection on the Divine and for the practice of spiritual programs and Yoga exercise sessions.

©1999 By Muata Ashby
CD $14.99 –

**MERIT'S INSPIRATION
NEW Egyptian Yoga Music CD
by Sehu Maa
Ancient Egyptian Music CD**
Instrumental Music played on reproductions of Ancient Egyptian Instruments– Ideal for meditation and reflection on the Divine and for the practice of spiritual programs and Yoga exercise sessions.
©1999 By Muata Ashby
CD $14.99 –
UPC# 761527100429

ANORATIONS TO RA AND HETHERU
**NEW Egyptian Yoga Music CD
By Sehu Maa (Muata Ashby)
Based on the Words of Power of Ra and HetHeru**
played on reproductions of Ancient Egyptian Instruments **Ancient Egyptian Instruments used: Voice, Clapping, Nefer Lute, Tar Drum, Sistrums, Cymbals** – The Chants, Devotions, Rhythms and Festive Songs Of the Neteru – Ideal for meditation, and devotional singing and dancing.

©1999 By Muata Ashby
CD $14.99 –
UPC# 761527100221

SONGS TO ASAR ASET AND HERU
**NEW
Egyptian Yoga Music CD
By Sehu Maa**
played on reproductions of Ancient Egyptian Instruments– The Chants, Devotions, Rhythms and Festive Songs Of the Neteru - Ideal for meditation, and devotional singing and dancing.
Based on the Words of Power of Asar (Asar), Aset (Aset) and Heru (Heru) Om Asar Aset Heru is the third in a series of musical explorations of the Kemetic (Ancient Egyptian) tradition of music. Its ideas are based on the Ancient Egyptian Religion of Asar, Aset and Heru and it is

designed for listening, meditation and worship.
©1999 By Muata Ashby
CD $14.99 –
UPC# 761527100122

HAARI OM: ANCIENT EGYPT MEETS INDIA IN MUSIC
NEW Music CD
By Sehu Maa

The Chants, Devotions, Rhythms and Festive Songs Of the Ancient Egypt and India, harmonized and played on reproductions of ancient instruments along with modern instruments and beats. Ideal for meditation, and devotional singing and dancing.
Haari Om is the fourth in a series of musical explorations of the Kemetic (Ancient Egyptian) and Indian traditions of music, chanting and devotional spiritual practice. Its ideas are based on the Ancient Egyptian Yoga spirituality and Indian Yoga spirituality.
©1999 By Muata Ashby
CD $14.99 –
UPC# 761527100528

RA AKHU: THE GLORIOUS LIGHT
NEW
Egyptian Yoga Music CD
By Sehu Maa
The fifth collection of original music compositions based on the Teachings and Words of The Trinity, the God Asar and the Goddess Nebethet, the Divinity Aten, the God Heru, and the Special Meditation Hekau or Words of Power of Ra from the Ancient Egyptian Tomb of Seti I and more...
played on reproductions of Ancient Egyptian Instruments and modern instruments - **Ancient Egyptian Instruments used: Voice, Clapping, Nefer Lute, Tar Drum, Sistrums, Cymbals**
– The Chants, Devotions, Rhythms and Festive Songs Of the Neteru - Ideal for meditation, and devotional singing and dancing.
©1999 By Muata Ashby
CD $14.99 –
UPC# 761527100825

GLORIES OF THE DIVINE MOTHER
Based on the hieroglyphic text of the worship of Goddess Net.
The Glories of The Great Mother
©2000 Muata Ashby
CD $14.99 UPC# 761527101129`

THE AFRICAN ORIGINS OF CIVILIZATION, RELIGION AND YOGA SPIRITUALITY

Order Form

Telephone orders: Call 1(305) 378-6253. Have your AMEX, Optima, Visa or MasterCard ready.
Website www.Egyptianyoga.com

Fax orders: 1-(305) 378-6253

Postal Orders: Sema Institute of Yoga, P.O. Box 570459, Miami, Fl. 33257. USA.

Please send the following books and / or tapes.

ITEMS

_____ Cost $_____
_____ Cost $_____
_____ Cost $_____
_____ Cost $_____
_____ Cost $_____
_____ Cost $_____
_____ Cost $_____
Total $_____

Name:_____

Address:_____

City:_____ State:_____ Zip:_____

Sales tax: Please add 6.5% for books shipped to Florida addresses

Shipping-.
Air Mail or UPS: $4.00 for first book and $.50 for each additional_____

Total of the order: $_____

_____Payment:_____
_____Check_____
If Paying by check include your drivers license number_____

_____Credit card: _____Visa, _____MasterCard, _____Optima,
_____ AMEX.

Card number:_____

Name on card:_____ Exp. date:_____/_____

*Donations: I would like to Donate $_____ to the Inmate Education Program.
*Donations: I would like to Donate $_____ to the Yoga Center Book program.
*Tax Deductible.

Copyright 1995-2000 Dr. R. Muata Abhaya Ashby
Sema Institute of Yoga
P. O. Box 570459, Miami, Florida, 33257 Telephone (305) 378-6253

www.ingramcontent.com/pod-product-compliance
Lightning Source LLC
Chambersburg PA
CBHW060500240426
43661CB00006B/864